STRATEGIC MANAGEMENT

Concepts and Applications

Third Edition

Samuel C. Certo
Crummer Graduate School of Business at Rollins College

J. Paul Peter
University of Wisconsin—Madison

With Special Assistance of:
Edward Ottensmeyer
Clark University

AUSTEN
PRESS

IRWIN
Chicago • Bogotá • Boston • Buenos Aires • Caracas
London • Madrid • Mexico City • Sydney • Toronto

To our daughters, Sarah and Angela.
We love them dearly.
— SAMUEL C. CERTO —
— J. PAUL PETER —

Copyright © 1995 Richard D. Irwin, Inc. in a joint venture with the Austen Press.

Publisher: William Schoof
Acquisitions Editor: John R. Weimeister
Production Manager: Bob Lange
Marketing Manager: Kurt Messersmith

Development, design, and project management provided by Elm Street Publishing Services, Inc.

Compositor: G&S Typesetters, Inc.
Typeface: 10/12 New Baskerville
Printer: Von Hoffmann Press, Inc.

Library of Congress Cataloging-in-Publication Data
Certo, Samuel C.
    Strategic management; concepts and applications / Samuel C. Certo, J. Paul Peter. — 3rd ed.
        p.   cm.
    Includes index.
    ISBN 0-256-15158-X
    1. Strategic planning.   I. Peter, J. Paul.   II. Title.
HD30.28.C43   1994
658.4'012—dc20   94-40477

Printed in the United States of America
1 2 3 4 5 6 7 8 9 0 V H 9 8 7 6 5 4

Address editorial correspondence:
Austen Press
18141 Dixie Highway
Suite 105
Homewood, IL 60430

Address orders:
Richard D. Irwin, Inc.
1333 Burr Ridge Parkway
Burr Ridge, IL 60521

Austen Press
Richard D. Irwin, Inc.

Preface

The first two editions of this text were used successfully in both undergraduate and graduate strategic management or business policy courses at a variety of colleges and universities. We are gratified that many instructors found them a useful and valuable learning experience for their students and that many students reported they benefitted from their use. While we have made a number of improvements in this third edition, the major purpose of our text remains the same: to provide students with an integrative learning experience that helps them to develop strategic management knowledge and skills.

As the title implies, we believe that students need to learn strategic management *concepts* and to practice *applications* of these concepts in order to become effective strategic managers. However, we also believe that a strategic management text should do more than simply present theoretical concepts and case applications and expect students to easily relate the former to the latter. A text should also help students *bridge the gap between theoretical concepts and case applications.* To help them do so, we have included a number of special features in our text.

TEXT ORGANIZATION

Strategic Management: Concepts and Applications includes five parts devoted to concepts and nine case parts to applications, or cases. The concepts parts and chapters are organized around the strategic management model shown on page iv.

Part I: An Overview of Strategic Management

This part provides a survey of strategic management and a framework for the remainder of the textual material. After reading Chapter 1, students should have a clear understanding of the nature and scope of strategic management and the strategic management process.

Part II: Strategic Management Process

In this part we discuss the five major steps in the strategic management process. These steps include environmental analysis (Chapter 2), establishing organizational direction (Chapter 3), strategy formulation (Chapter 4), strategy implementation (Chapter 5), and strategic control (Chapter 6).

Part III: Special Issues in Strategic Management

Although the previous sections include the major topics commonly discussed in strategic management courses, we believe at least three other areas require special consideration. These areas are international operations (Chapter 7), total quality management (Chapter 8), and social responsibility and ethics

Strategic Management Model Used in Chapters 1 to 13

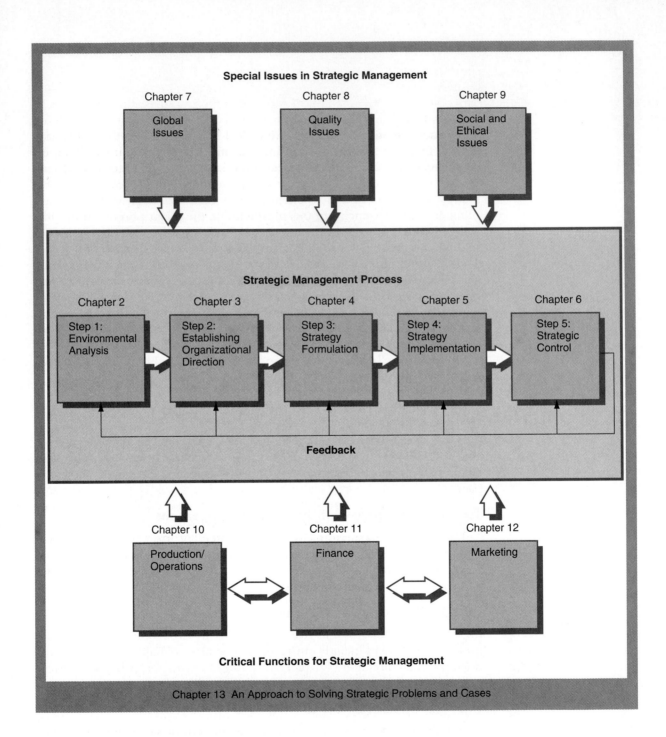

(Chapter 9). We devote an entire chapter to each of these topics because of their important influence on strategic management decision making and the need for specialized knowledge of these topics in a variety of strategic management problems and cases.

Part IV: Critical Functions for Strategic Management

Successful strategic management efforts involve the application of the major business functions both individually and collectively or cross-functionally. This part covers the fundamentals of three important business functions to help students focus on cross-functional strategic management issues. The functional issues are discussed through individual chapters on operations (Chapter 10), finance (Chapter 11), and marketing (Chapter 12). In addition, information on these and other business functions is also integrated throughout the text.

Part V: A Framework for Strategic Analysis

We recognize that no single approach can be universally applied to all strategic management cases and problems; however, we are also mindful that students often need a framework for approaching case and problem analysis. A sound framework is particularly important when students first begin analyzing major strategic management cases and problems. For this reason we have included an extended discussion of a general approach to case and problem analysis in Chapter 13. This chapter on the process of case and problem analysis is designed to provide another bridge between concepts and applications.

Case Parts I through IX: Cases in Strategic Management

The case parts have been significantly reorganized to better emphasize current strategic management problems and issues. Cases covering the foundational concepts of strategic management appear in parts introducing strategic management; environmental analysis; organizational vision, mission, and objectives; strategy formulation; and strategy implementation and control. In addition, cases covering special, contemporary issues in strategic management appear in sections on strategy formulation in service organizations, strategic management and international operations, social and ethical dimensions of strategic management, and total quality management.

The nine case parts contain thirty-six strategic management cases. These cases represent organizations in a variety of industries and time periods and deal with issues at all levels of strategic management. Overall, we believe that the cases are an outstanding collection.

SPECIAL TEXT FEATURES

Each chapter in our text contains a variety of pedagogical features designed to enhance student learning and to facilitate the transfer of concepts to applications. Each text chapter contains the following pedagogical features:

- *Company Examples* that extend text material and provide illustrations of the application of strategic management concepts to well-known organizations.
- *Skills Modules* that challenge students to apply strategic management concepts to real organizational situations. These short exercises follow selected topics in the chapters, thus affording students directed activities for increasing their understanding and ability to apply strategic management concepts.

- *Checklists* that itemize major issues to be addressed in analyzing strategic management problems and cases. These checklists are keyed to the topics covered in each chapter and offer students a starting point for applying strategic management concepts to case situations.
- *Cases* (at the end of each chapter) that provide a brief scenario focusing on one or more topics covered in the chapter. They include specific questions for analysis, thus offering students an opportunity to apply chapter material in a directed way. The cases help students reach a better understanding of strategic management concepts and their applications and prepare them for longer, more involved strategic management cases.

These pedagogical features are intended to be still another bridge between theory and application.

CHANGES IN THE THIRD EDITION

We have made several changes in the third edition to better meet the needs of strategic management educators and students:

1. Recognizing the importance of the quality movement in strategic management, we have included a new chapter on total quality management.
2. Recognizing the integrative and cross-functional nature of strategic management, we have added new material throughout the text emphasizing these issues.
3. Recognizing the importance of timeliness for enhancing student interest in text material, we have provided a variety of new examples, illustrations, activities, additional readings, and applications throughout the text.
4. Recognizing the importance of key terms and concepts, we have added a list of key terms with page references at the end of each chapter.
5. Recognizing the importance of raising student awareness of a variety of strategic management challenges, we have significantly reorganized our cases. This reorganization focuses student attention on foundations in strategic management, as well as on special, more current strategic management considerations. Cases are divided into the following parts: (1) Introduction to Strategic Management; (2) Environmental Analysis; (3) Establishing Organizational Direction: Vision, Mission, Objectives; (4) Strategy Formulation; (5) Strategy Formulation in Service Organizations; (6) Strategy Implementation and Control; (7) Strategic Management and International Operations; (8) Strategic Management—Social and Ethical Dimensions; and (9) Total Quality Management.

We have provided a variety of new cases in this edition. In fact, of the thirty-six cases in this text, thirty-one are new to this edition.

INSTRUCTOR'S RESOURCE PACKAGE

Strategic Management Concepts and Applications is supported by a comprehensive instructor's resource package. Carefully developed to meet the unique demands of strategic management educators, the package consists of the following items:

- *Instructor's Manual.* The manual covers material related to each text chapter and includes authors' overviews, chapter outlines, key concepts and issues for classroom discussion, instructor's notes for Skills Modules and Cases, a comprehensive test bank, and transparency masters.

- *Case Enrichment Portfolio.* This innovative supplement features detailed support materials for each case. The *Case Enrichment Portfolio* further reinforces the link between theory and practice with applications designed to show how specific text material relates to cases. Where appropriate, we have included transparency masters, teaching notes, financial analyses, in-class exercises, current company issues and updates, supplemental discussion questions, and a theoretical application matrix. The Case Enrichment Portfolio was prepared by Daniel G. Kopp of Southwest Missouri State University.

- *Selected Cases in Strategic Management.* For educators who prefer to use cases without extensive textual material, we have prepared *Selected Cases in Strategic Management.* This book contains 36 cases organized into case parts. A comprehensive *Instructor's Manual* is available from Austen Press. Videotapes are available to accompany some of the cases.

- *The Strategic Management Process.* For instructors who seek to use our textual material in their courses but use their own cases or other projects, we have prepared a separate paperback text. This book is titled *The Strategic Management Process* and contains thirteen chapters of text material on strategic management. A detailed *Instructor's Manual,* prepared by David Flynn of Hofstra University, is also available from Austen Press.

ACKNOWLEDGMENTS

We are indebted to many people who contributed to this project. First, we offer our sincere thanks to those dedicated individuals who contributed the strategic management cases in the case parts of the text. These educators include:

Sexton Adams
North Texas State University
A. J. Almaney
DePaul University
Anna Jakab Baane
Patricia Bilafer
Bentley College
Joanna Blattberg
University of Virginia Law School
Maria Raboczki Bordane
Gary J. Castrogiovanni
Louisiana State University
Michael Chung
University of Virginia
Angela Clontz
University of Virginia
Jeremy J. Coleman
Fort Lewis College
James G. Combs
Louisiana State University
Roy A. Cook
Fort Lewis College
Billy Deakyne
University of Virginia
Max E. Douglas
Indiana State University

Johnna Duncan
University of Virginia
Mary Fandel
Bentley College
Andras Farkas
Phil Fisher
University of Southern Indiana
Christine Forkus
Bentley College
Holly Fowler
Bentley College
Donna M. Gallo
University of Massachusetts—Amherst
Peter Gowell
University of New Hampshire
Barbara Gottfried
Bentley College
S. Green
DePaul University
Walter E. Greene
University of Texas Pan American
Adelaide Griffin
Texas Women's University
Gail Healey
Bentley College

W. Harvey Hegarty
Indiana University
Alan N. Hoffman
Bentley College
William C. House
University of Arkansas—Fayetteville
J. Jenkins
DePaul University
Shailendra Jha
Wilfrid Laurier University, Ontario, Canada
Robert Johnson
University of South Dakota
Michael J. Keeffe
Southwest Texas State University
James A. Kidney
Southern Connecticut State University
Raymond M. Kinnunen
Northeastern University
Mary Kinsell
Bentley College
Jeffrey A. Krug
The College of William & Mary
Scott Lane
Bentley College
Sharon Ungar Lane
Bentley College
K. Landauer
DePaul University
B. Logan
Texas Women's University
Franz T. Lohrke
Louisiana State University
Michael J. Merenda
University of New Hampshire
Bill J. Middlebrook
Southwest Texas State University
L. Miklichansky
North Texas State University
James F. Molloy, Jr.
Northeastern University
Jane Moreno
Bentley College
Tomasz Mroczkowski
American University
William Naumes
University of New Hampshire
Robert J. Pavan
Rutgers University

R. Pekosh
DePaul University
Jozsef Poor
*formerly of the International Management
Center, Budapest, Hungary*
Valerie J. Porciello
Bentley College
Liliana Prado
Bentley College
Ravi Ramamurti
Northeastern College
Maura Riley
Bentley College
Carolyn Rosen
Bentley College
John K. Ross III
Southwest Texas State University
D. Schacht
DePaul University
Paul J. Schlachter
Florida International University
Arthur Sharplin
McNeese State University
Jeffrey Shuman
Bentley College
S. Slotkin
DePaul University
Neil H. Snyder
University of Virginia
H. Speer
DePaul University
Melvin J. Stanford
Mankato State University
Sally Strawn
Bentley College
Paul M. Swiercz
The George Washington University
James Taylor
University of South Dakota
Eva Tihanyi
Robert P. Vichas
Texas A & M International University
Juanita Wade
Bentley College
Randall K. White
Auburn University—Montgomery
Joseph Wolfe
University of Tulsa

Second, we appreciate the helpful comments of the reviewers listed below:

Bruce Charnov
Hofstra University
V. C. Doherty
Wayne State University

James H. Donnelly, Jr.
University of Kentucky
Bruce Fisher
Northeastern Illinois University

Robert Goldberg
Northeastern University
James R. Harris
Florida State University
Alan N. Hoffman
Bentley College
Janice Jackson
Virginia State University
Calvin Kellogg
Illinois State University
Rose Knotts
North Texas State University
Daniel G. Kopp
Southwest Missouri State University
Edwin C. Leonard, Jr.
*Indiana University, Purdue University
at Fort Wayne*
William Litzinger
University of Texas at San Antonio

Martin K. Marsh
California State University, Bakersfield
Bob McGowan
University of Denver
Hugh O'Neil
University of North Carolina
Shiv Sawhney
Quinnipiac College
Marilyn Taylor
University of Kansas
Robert Vichas
Old Dominion University
Wendy Vittori
Northeastern University
Stanley Willing
St. Francis College

Over the life of this book we have engaged a Case Advisory Board as well as Case Consultants to help us develop only the best possible set of cases. We would like to extend special thanks to our colleague Alan N. Hoffman at Bentley College for his outstanding advice concerning the set of cases in this edition. Other colleagues who have helped us in the case selection process include:

Phil Fisher
University of South Dakota
C. Kendrick Gibson
Hope College
Barry Gilmore
Memphis State University
Robert Goldberg
Northeastern University
Rose Knotts
North Texas State University
Dan Kopp
Southwest Missouri State University

Charles Schilling
University of Wisconsin—Platteville
James R. Sowers
University of Houston
Irv Summers
Avila College
R. W. Swisher
Troy State University
Marilyn Taylor
University of Kansas
Charles E. Watson
Miami University

We would like to thank David Flynn and Dan Kopp for preparing the instructor's materials for this text. In addition, we extend thanks to our colleagues and students for all they have taught us, as well as the many strategic management educators who responded to our research surveys and provided other inputs into the project. In particular, we thank Ed Ottensmeyer of Clark University and Rajan Kamath of the University of Cincinnati for their insights and efforts, which greatly improved our text. We also thank Bill Schoof, John Weimeister, and the staff at Elm Street Publishing Services for their patience, understanding, and assistance throughout this project. Finally, we thank our families and friends for their encouragement and tolerance during the preparation of this text.

Samuel C. Certo
J. Paul Peter
November 1994

About The Authors

Samuel C. Certo is Professor of Management and former dean at the Roy E. Crummer Graduate School of Business, Rollins College, Winter Park, Florida. His current teaching responsibilities include an array of management courses with special emphasis on business strategy as well as a strategy-focused computer simulation course. He has been actively involved in management education at the college and university levels for over fifteen years and recently received the Charles A. Welsh Memorial Award for outstanding teaching at the Crummer School. Dr. Certo's numerous publications include articles for such journals as the *Academy of Management Review, The Journal of Experimental Learning and Simulation,* and *Training.* He has also written several successful textbooks, including *Modern Management: Diversity, Quality, Ethics, and the Global Environment; Supervision: Quality and Diversity through Leadership;* and *Human Relations Today: Concepts and Skills.* A past chairman of the Management Education and Development Division of the Academy of Management, he has been honored by that group with its Excellence of Leadership Award. Dr. Certo has also served as president of the Association for Business Simulation and Experiential Learning, as associate editor for *Simulation and Games,* and as a review board member of the *Academy of Management Review.* His consulting experience has been extensive with notable experience on boards of directors.

J. Paul Peter is James R. McManus-Bascom Professor in Marketing at the University of Wisconsin—Madison. He taught at Indiana State University, Washington University, and Ohio State University before joining the faculty at Wisconsin in 1980. He has taught a variety of courses and has won several teaching awards, including the John R. Larson School of Business Teaching Award in 1990. His articles on consumer behavior, marketing theory, and research methodology are frequently cited in the marketing literature. He was awarded the prestigious William O'Dell Award from the *Journal of Marketing Research* in 1986. Dr. Peter has coauthored several books, including *A Preface to Marketing Management, Marketing Management: Knowledge and Skills,* and *Consumer Behavior and Marketing Strategy;* he is coeditor of *Measurement Readings for Marketing Research* and *Marketing Theory and Practice.* He has served as editor of AMA Professional Publications and as editor of *JMR*'s Measurement Section. He has served on the Editorial Review Boards of the *Journal of Marketing, Journal of Marketing Research, Journal of Consumer Research,* and *Journal of Business Research* and has been a consultant and executive teacher for a variety of corporations as well as the Federal Trade Commission.

Detailed Contents

PART III   *Special Issues in Strategic Management   161*

A Collection of 36 Cases

NOTE TO THE INSTRUCTOR

Austen Press texts are marketed and distributed by Richard D. Irwin, Inc. For assistance in obtaining supplementary material for this and other Austen Press titles, please contact your Irwin sales representative or the customer service division of Richard D. Irwin at (800) 323-4560.

PART I

Overview of Strategic Management

This section provides an overview of strategic management and builds a framework for the remainder of the text. Its major purpose is to acquaint you with the nature and scope of strategic management and its development as a critical area of management education. In carefully studying this section, you should develop a basic understanding of the cross-functional process of strategic management and an appreciation for the importance of strategic management in running a successful organization.

Introduction to Strategic Management

Sega Takes Aim at Disney's World

The Profit Machine: NordicTrack Is the Muscle behind Top-Ranked CML

Losing Altitude: Once-Solid Delta Air is Burdened by Cost of European Foray

After Initial Fuzziness, AT&T Clears Up Signal to Asia

Footwear Fad Makes Nike, Reebok Run for Their Money: Doc Martens Shoes and Boots are Popular among Trend Setting Teenagers

Headlines like these from the business press capture the drama, excitement, and dynamism of strategic management in action.[1] The adventure you are about to begin with this text will help you to understand the strategies and analyses behind the headlines, and carefully selected cases will put you in the manager's chair to let you practice strategic management techniques and experience the qualities of leadership needed to translate analysis into effective action.

As in any field, a beginner must do a great deal of work, especially in the early stages, to learn the basics. The student must speak and understand a new language and view the world from a new perspective. For example, analysis of the cases in this text must extend beyond the limits of one discipline's viewpoint (marketing, finance, operations, or organizational behavior); strategic management cases address all of these topics at the same time, in the way that real managers must address them. Thus, the cases will require you to draw on what you have learned about these functions and to use the cross-functional tools of the general manager, whose responsibilities reach throughout an entire firm, or a significant part of one.

When they see that a strategic management course focuses on the general manager's perspective, some students view the course narrowly, as something they will not need for several years, or until they become general managers or high-ranking business executives themselves. We strongly encourage you to begin the study of strategic management with a wider view! Never before have business firms shown more interest in the contributions of employees and managers at all levels to the overall good of the firm. Even the smallest actions might reduce costs or improve quality—both primary focuses of strategic management. Entry-level workers may reap valuable rewards if they approach their early corporate experiences well-versed in strategic management techniques and thinking more broadly about their firms than their first specialized jobs might require. The strategic management course may not get you your first job, but it may get you promoted out of that job faster. We hope this will be your experience.

The fundamental reality is this: mastering strategic management is a career-long endeavor for the successful general manager. At its most basic, strategic management requires careful, creative thought about the future and effective action that places the organization in a better position in that future. Leaders of businesses, armies, churches, and governments have faced these challenges since humans first organized their activities.

Clearly, some strategic management efforts have been less successful than others—the Roman Empire crumbled, Napoleon lost at Waterloo, and IBM is struggling in the mid-1990s to regain its lost leadership position. Successes as well as failures dot the strategic management landscape, underscoring the dynamic and risky nature of the endeavor. However, thinking and acting strategically is vital for the modern leader who hopes to guide any enterprise to success. No one masters strategic management once and for all—it is a lifelong journey for the successful leader. We trust that this text will serve you well as a starting point and as a road map on your own journey.

Chapter 1 provides some background and an overview of the strategic management field. First, we outline the evolution of strategic management as a field of study, then we formally define the subject and describe how to apply its concepts and what benefits accrue to organizations that practice it. Next, we suggest the phases through which an organization passes in developing its strategic management process. We briefly trace the steps in the process of strategic management and consider several contemporary challenges in the field. We examine how the strategic management process relates to three major business functions, and finally we review the case analysis approach to learning the subject.

EVOLUTION OF STRATEGIC MANAGEMENT AS A FIELD OF STUDY

The study of strategic management first took shape after the Ford Foundation and the Carnegie Corporation sponsored research into the curriculum at business schools in the 1950s. A synopsis of this research, the Gordon-Howell report, recommended expanding business education to include a capstone course in an area called *business policy*.[2]

By design, the business policy course was meant to integrate other areas of study, teaching students to apply analytical techniques learned in earlier courses in marketing, finance, organizational behavior, or operations management to problems that would confront a business firm as a whole. The course would thus give students the opportunity to exercise qualities of judgment that did not arise explicitly in any earlier courses.

The Gordon-Howell report gained widespread acceptance. By the early 1970s, most schools of business included business policy courses within their curriculum requirements. As time passed, however, the focus of the course became wider. The business policy course began to consider the total organization and its environment. For example, it addressed issues such as social responsibility and ethics, as well as the potential impacts of political, legislative, and economic events on the successful operation of an organization.

In the 1980s, an impressive outpouring of research supplemented the growing literature on competitive strategy. Over time, this research effort refined a new tool kit of techniques such as industry analysis, that sharpened the traditional focus to establish the business policy course as the place in a business curriculum where students would examine the big picture of business decision making. This newer, broader emphasis prompted leaders in the field to change the name of the course from *business policy* to *strategic management*.[3]

Recent curricular innovations in business schools may affect the strategic management courses of the future. Instead of presenting a capstone course to integrate material learned earlier in function-focused courses, some business schools are now integrating functional learning from the beginning. This development reflects a conscious attempt to spread the benefits of integrative learning—long the goal of business policy and strategic management courses—across the business curriculum. It is difficult to predict the impact of such changes on strategic management courses as we have come to know them in the last decade. However, we suspect that, while some of the core material of strategic management may appear earlier in an undergraduate or MBA curriculum, students will continue to need a single, challenging, integrative experience.

This text has been carefully designed to reflect the most current research and to serve as a foundation for students to learn concepts that are both pragmatic and theoretically up to date. In addition, we expect a strong strategic management course to help students refine their communications skills through written and oral presentations. Table 1.1 presents a list of the specific skills you can expect to develop in this course.

NATURE OF STRATEGIC MANAGEMENT

Strategy and strategic management are concepts that evolve over time.[4] These ideas defy universally accepted definitions because scholars develop them and

---

TABLE 1.1

Strategic Management Course Skills

1. Identification of core problems or issues in a business situation or case
2. Wide-ranging assessment of opportunities and threats in the environment and the strengths and weaknesses of an organization and its managers
3. Analysis of strategic alternatives appropriate to a variety of situations and from the perspectives of a variety of stakeholders
4. Formulation and selection of specific courses of action to implement chosen strategies
5. Focused application of analytical skills from functional courses—production, finance, marketing, operations research, personnel, and so forth—to effectively develop, select, and implement competitive strategies
6. Oral and written communication of analyses and recommendations for action

---

managers practice them in diverse ways.[5] This lack of consensus, however, does not keep most contemporary organizations from trying to reap the benefits of strategic management by developing innovative strategies to out-maneuver their competitors.

Definition of *Strategy*

In this text, following James Brian Quinn, **strategy** will be defined as "the pattern or plan that integrates an organization's major goals, policies, and action sequences into a cohesive whole."[6] Quinn also suggests that a strategy helps a firm to allocate its resources, to capitalize on its relative strengths and mitigate its weaknesses, to exploit projected shifts in the environment, and to counter possible actions of competitors.

This definition helps students to understand and appreciate what a strategy looks like, what its key elements are, and what it is supposed to accomplish for the organization that implements it well. Thus, a firm with a well-articulated strategy should:

- Set a clear direction
- Know its strengths and weaknesses compared with its competitors
- Devote its hard-won resources to projects that employ its set of core competencies, the primary skills within the organization
- Identify factors in the political and social environment that require careful monitoring
- Recognize which competitor actions need critical attention

In short, managers in such a firm should have a rational, clear-headed notion, purged of wishful thinking, of (1) its mission, (2) its external competitive environment, and (3) its internal capabilities. Keeping this notion fresh and current, and orchestrating the changes and adaptations that updates inevitably require, is the essential task of the strategic management process. All departments and functions must contribute to complete this enormous task effectively.

We would point out, however, that a firm without a carefully articulated, written strategy statement might still have a strategy. Quinn's definition of strategy encompasses both formal plans and informal patterns of activity. This is consistent with Henry Mintzberg's notion of strategy as a "pattern in a stream of decisions."[7] Thus, even if a firm's managers cannot name or label its own strategy, the pattern of their decisions over time would define its real strategy. However, the enormous attention that corporate strategy and strategic management have received in the past 20 years, from best-selling books to regular coverage in the popular press, has increased the probability that managers in even the smallest start-up firms will discuss their competitive strategies explicitly.

Understanding a manager's comments about a firm's strategy is often tricky work. First, one must separate real strategy from competitive ploys. A firm may announce a change in its strategy or a new strategic initiative in an attempt to confuse or slow down a key competitor. The computer software industry has developed a specific term—*vaporware*—to describe a new software product that an industry competitor has announced but not yet completed. Announcements about vaporware send messages to a firm's customers (i.e., don't buy from our competitors; our product will be out soon) as well as its competitors (i.e., don't even think about trying to compete with us; we've got the new and improved version).

A manager's comments about strategy, even if a firm has a stated strategic plan, may reflect wishful thinking more than careful analysis of the competitive environment. For example, start-ups or small businesses often load strategy statements with heavy doses of wishful thinking to attract early-stage financing from banks or venture capitalists.

Answering Basic Questions to Develop Strategy

If a strategy says so much about a firm, what key questions must managers answer to develop one? Table 1.2 summarizes these questions. First, developing a strategy forces the manager to focus on the very basic question about the business in which the firm really competes, or would like to compete. *What good or service do we really sell?* What do we, as a firm, do best? For example, does an athletic shoe company sell high performance or style?

Second, *how will we produce our goods or deliver our services?* For example, in our industry at this point in time, can we succeed with an upscale entry or would a stripped-down, low-cost version be more successful? Answering these

---

TABLE 1.2

Some Key Questions in Strategy Development

1. What good or service do we really sell?
2. How will we produce our goods or deliver our services?
3. Who will buy our goods or services?
4. How will we finance the operation?
5. How much risk are we willing to take?
6. How will we implement our strategy?

first two questions forces managers to look carefully at their core competencies, which, in turn, shape product characteristics as well as manufacturing requirements.[8]

The third question asks *who will buy our goods or services?* This brings the customer and the existing industry structure squarely into the middle of the strategy equation. An answer to this question requires industry and competitor analyses, marketing research, and distribution channel and logistics analyses.

The fourth question asks *how will we finance the operation?* A new strategy can be quite costly, as the firm gears up to design new products, enter new channels, challenge competitors in new market segments, purchase new manufacturing equipment, hire new workers, etc. Finding the funds to implement a new strategy is not a trivial concern.

The fifth question is closely related to the fourth. *How much risk are we willing to take?* A new strategy may require management to bet the business on its success. If the strategy is a winner, the firm wins; if it fails, the firm collapses. These risk assessments are often among the most difficult judgments that business leaders make. Delta Airlines' expansion into the European air travel market has been unsuccessful (as the headlines at the start of this chapter hinted). This is an example of a strategic decision gone awry, with potentially serious implications for the long-term survival of the company.

The first five questions are all concerned with analysis and judgment to define a strategy for an organization. The sixth question asks *how will we implement our strategy?* How will we revise it along the way? What changes in structure, systems, or staffing will we need to make to improve an intended strategy's chance to succeed? Mintzberg and Waters remind us that intended strategies often do not survive in their initial states.[9] For example, Steve Jobs's venture, NeXT Computer, had to shift its strategy toward innovative computer software and away from new hardware because of dramatic changes in the market.[10] Thus, NeXT's intended and realized strategies differed markedly.

The six basic questions guide the analyses that underlie the firm's effort to formulate and implement a competitive strategy. From these questions flow the critical decisions that shape an organization's future. The overarching methodology or process that brings these questions into clear focus is called *strategic management.*

Definition of *Strategic Management*

Strategic management is a continuous, iterative, cross-functional process aimed at keeping an organization as a whole appropriately matched to its environment. This definition emphasizes the series of steps that a manager must take. These steps, which we will discuss individually in the following pages, include performing an environmental analysis, establishing organizational direction, formulating organizational strategy, implementing organizational strategy, and exercising strategic control. Additional information on each of these steps will appear throughout this text.

The definition also suggests that the strategic management process is continuous; the organization never finishes its strategic work. Although different strategic management activities may receive more or less emphasis and require effort of varying intensity at different times, managers should virtually always be focusing or reflecting on some aspect of strategic management.

The term *iterative* in the definition reinforces this idea. The process of strategic management starts with the first step, carries on to the last step, and then begins again with the first step. Strategic management consists of a series of steps repeated cyclically.

The term *cross-functional* signifies that the strategic management process integrates organizational human resources and expertise from critical functions such as marketing, operations, and finance in a comprehensive effort. This helps the process, and the plan it generates, to deal more effectively with potential conflicts in recommendations of individual functions operating in isolation. A cross-functional approach allows no one, not marketing nor manufacturing nor finance, to control or dominate the process; each contributes simultaneously to create a better plan and result. Working as a cross-functional team, members of the management group can more clearly visualize the overall picture of where the firm is and what it needs to do in the future to achieve a sustainable competitive advantage. This method can encourage commitment of key executives to a strategic plan.[11]

The last part of the definition of *strategic management* identifies its purpose as ensuring that an organization as a whole appropriately matches its environment, that is, its competitive surroundings. Business environments change constantly, and organizations must modify their strategies accordingly to achieve organizational goals. New legislation may affect the organization, its labor supply may change, and competitors may launch new initiatives. These are examples of changes within the organization's environment that often require the attention of top managers.

Although the definition of *strategic management* seems clear and straightforward, actually performing the task is not. Carrying out this process in an organization usually becomes a very complex job that consumes much top management time. Increasingly, the involvement of managers and employees has spread throughout organizations.

ROLES IN STRATEGIC MANAGEMENT

A firm's top management, board of directors, and planning staff tend to be most involved in and to have the most influence on its strategic management process.[12] The following sections discuss, in more detail, the roles of these participants in the strategic management process.

Top Management's Role in Strategic Management

Traditionally, top managers have made strategic decisions for organizations. The term *top management* refers to the relatively small group of people at the uppermost levels of the organization hierarchy. Titles that are generally considered to be top management positions include president, chief executive officer (CEO), chief operating officer (COO), vice president, and executive vice president.

The strategic management process of today tends to be shaped primarily by the CEO, the executive who is responsible for the performance of the organization as a whole. Although this strategic role is generally apparent in organizations of all sizes, it is most prominent in smaller organizations, where the CEO might also be an owner/entrepreneur. The CEO's central role may be somewhat diluted in medium-sized companies, and even further reduced in large companies, because CEOs of larger organizations tend to carry broader and more comprehensive duties, and the work involved in strategic management for these firms demands a larger staff.

The CEO is usually responsible and accountable for the success of the strategic management process. This does not necessarily mean, however, that the CEO carries it out alone. Instead, a successful CEO generally designs a cross-functional strategic management process that involves members from many different organizational areas and levels. For example, in addition to the CEO, organizations commonly enlist production specialists, marketing personnel, finance experts, and division managers in identifying strategic issues and making strategic decisions.

According to George Grune, chairman of the board and CEO of Reader's Digest Association, recruiting others to participate in the strategic management process generally results in more realistic goals, objectives, and strategies. In this situation, other managers often suggest to top management how to integrate their areas within the strategic management of the organization as a whole.[13] Grune maintains that such participation and involvement builds organizational commitment to achieve the goals and implement strategies that the process develops.[14]

Board of Directors' Role in Strategic Management

In a corporation, a board of directors, elected by stockholders, exercises ultimate authority and responsibility for the organization. The board guides the affairs of the corporation and protects stockholder interests.[15] Inside board members are people who already work for the organization in some other capacity; outside board members work for other organizations. Board members typically elect a chairperson to oversee board business, and they form standing committees that meet regularly to conduct their business. A list of standing committees and their responsibilities within a typical board of directors is presented in Table 1.3.

TABLE 1.3

Committees and Their Responsibilities within a Typical Board of Directors

EXECUTIVE COMMITTEE

1. To act within specified bounds for the board of directors between board meetings
2. To serve as a sounding board for the CEO's ideas before they are presented to the full board
3. To monitor extended negotiations
4. To oversee activities not specifically delegated to other committees

AUDIT COMMITTEE

1. To assure that company policies and practices remain within the bounds of accepted conduct
2. To select (or recommend) auditors and determine the scope of audits
3. To review financial reports to gain full insight into the company's current and likely future financial condition
4. To review internal accounting procedures
5. To assure the integrity of the company's operations

TABLE 1.3

Continued

COMPENSATION COMMITTEE

1. To assure that compensation (including stock options, benefits, bonuses, and salaries) attracts, holds, and motivates key personnel
2. To see that compensation and benefit plans throughout the organization are competitive, equitable, and well-executed
3. To oversee the development and implementation of human resource plans

FINANCIAL COMMITTEE

1. To review and advise the board on the financial structure and needs of the organization
2. To recommend to management and the full board the timing and types of financing that the firm needs (both long-term and short-term financing)
3. To assist top management in establishing good working relationships with the financial community
4. To provide advice about various investment, expenditure, and funding alternatives

NOMINATING COMMITTEE

1. To recommend candidates for membership on the board
2. To recommend candidates for management or officer positions in the company
3. To advise management on human resource planning

SOURCE: Adapted from J. K. Louden, *The Director* (New York: AMACOM, 1982), Chapter 7.

In general, the board of directors' time should be viewed as a scarce resource to devote to those activities in which it can uniquely and most effectively contribute to achieving organizational goals.[16] As Table 1.3 implies, board duties have historically focused on issues like financial auditing and compensation, with little or no input to the strategic management of an organization. Over the last decade, however, interest has grown in expanding the duties of the board to make it much more active in the strategic management process.[17]

Most authorities on corporate governance argue that firms should increase board involvement in the strategic management process as a way to improve the quality of strategic decisions, enabling board members to better discharge their responsibilities to represent stockholder interests.[18] One popular way to expand this involvement is by adding a strategy committee to the board's list of standing committees.[19] A strategy committee is a board committee that works with the CEO to develop corporate goals as well as strategies to reach those goals. As part of its duties, the strategy committee commonly evaluates the organization's strategic management process in order to make it more effective and efficient.

Table 1.4 shows a proposed **strategic report card** that a strategy committee might use in its evaluation of alternatives. In order to use this report card to evaluate a firm and its top management team, board members would first

TABLE 1.4

Strategic Report Card

	Key Success Attributes				Impact
	Content	**Strategic Alignment**	**Resource Allocation**	**Management Process**	
KEY SUCCESS ELEMENTS					
STRATEGY					
STRATEGIC IMPLEMENTATION PROGRAMS					
ORGANIZATION AND FUNCTIONS					
SYSTEMS					

SOURCE: Reprinted by permission of Donald K. Yee, "Pass or Fail? How to Grade Strategic Progress," *Journal of Business Strategy,* May/June, 1990.

define the Key Success Elements, shown in the far left column, and then they would evaluate each of these elements against the Key Success Attributes, shown across the top. For example, board members would grade a strategy on the basis of the adequacy of its content or scope, its match with the realities of the external environment including competition, the resources allocated to its accomplishment, the management process for developing and refining it, and its impact or results.

Overall, the board of directors should play a role in the strategic management of an organization. One barrier to this involvement, however, is the conviction of some managers and management scholars that the most effective and creative strategies emerge from interaction between the CEO and key subordinates.[20] For various reasons, some boards might handle strategic management issues more successfully than others. It seems reasonable, therefore, to conclude that most organizations benefit by some type of board involvement in the strategic management process.

Recent research in this area has found a positive relationship between board involvement in strategy making and a firm's financial performance.[21] The extent and type of involvement varies from firm to firm depending on factors such as the experience of board members in handling strategic management issues.

Planning Staff's Role in Strategic Management

The job of running the strategic management process can grow so large that the CEO must assign employees to a team, typically called a *planning staff,* specifically to help with the task. In a smaller organization, the CEO might simply appoint someone to act as a planning assistant. In a medium-sized to large organization, the CEO might establish a planning committee or even a planning department headed by its own director or vice president for organizational planning. A planning staff generally produces advisory reports by gathering and analyzing data and making recommendations to the CEO concerning various strategic management decisions.

In the past, the strategic management process has been heavily influenced by planning departments within organizations. Employees within these departments often designed and implemented strategic management systems while CEOs took a hands-off attitude, basically allowing the planners wide freedom in carrying out their duties. More recently, however, CEOs have begun taking more active roles in strategic management, especially in giving planning departments more guidance and direction. This activism of CEOs is generally seen to have reduced some of the influence of planning departments over the strategic management process.[22] Strategic management has returned to the domain of the line manager or general manager.

The role, influence, and involvement of each of the participants—CEO, board of directors, and planning staff—in the organization's strategic management process have changed significantly over the last several decades. This change will undoubtedly continue. Regardless of the specific role that each group will play in the future, they will have to work together as a team in order to best shape the strategic management process of their organization.

BENEFITS OF STRATEGIC MANAGEMENT

An organization can reap several benefits from effective strategic management. Perhaps the most important benefit is higher profit. Although past studies have concluded that strategic management does not always increase profitability, a significant number of recent investigations have suggested that a well-designed strategic management system can boost profits.[23]

In addition to financial benefits, organizations may gain other advantages by implementing strategic management programs. For example, strategic management can strengthen organization members' commitment to attaining long-term goals. Increased commitment normally accompanies participation in setting goals and strategies for reaching those goals. In addition, when strategic managers emphasize assessing the organization's environment, the organization reduces the chance of being surprised by movements within the marketplace or by actions of competitors that could put the organization at a sudden disadvantage. These potential benefits also explain the increased popularity of strategic management with not-for-profit and public sector organizations.

Of course, an organization cannot *guarantee* these benefits just by completing a strategic management exercise. As in most important areas of organizational life, success is never automatic and every effort risks failure. An organization's strategic management process may have inherent flaws (e.g., its environmental analysis may be incomplete). Even an organization with a refined, long-standing, highly regarded strategic management system may suffer disappointing results from decisions based on erroneous economic or market forecasts. Several large computer hardware firms such as IBM or Digital Equipment have learned this hard lesson.

HISTORICAL DEVELOPMENT OF STRATEGIC MANAGEMENT

Although managers may be eager to design and implement a strategic management system in their organization, accomplishing the task takes time. Most organizations develop their strategic management processes over periods of several years, adjusting and tailoring them to meet specific company needs.[24]

Figure 1.1 illustrates the developmental phases that lead firms toward their own strategic management systems. The development usually begins with a

FIGURE 1.1   Phases in the Development of a Strategic Management System

Developmental Phases

Phase 1: Basic Financial Planning	Phase 2: Forecast-based Planning	Phase 3: Externally Oriented Planning	Phase 4: Strategic Management

Increasing Effectiveness of Formal Business Planning

Phase 4: Strategic Management
- Orchestration of all resources to create competitive advantage
- Strategically chosen planning framework
- Creative, flexible planning process
- Supportive value system and climate

Phase 3: Externally Oriented Planning
- Increasing response to markets and competition
- Thorough situation analysis and competitive assessment
- Evaluation of strategic alternatives
- Dynamic allocation of resources

Phase 2: Forecast-based Planning
- More effective planning for growth
- Environmental analysis
- Multiyear plans
- Static allocation of resources

Phase 1: Basic Financial Planning
- Operational control
- Annual budget
- Functional focus

Meet Budget	Plan for the Future	Think Abstractly	Create the Future

Goals

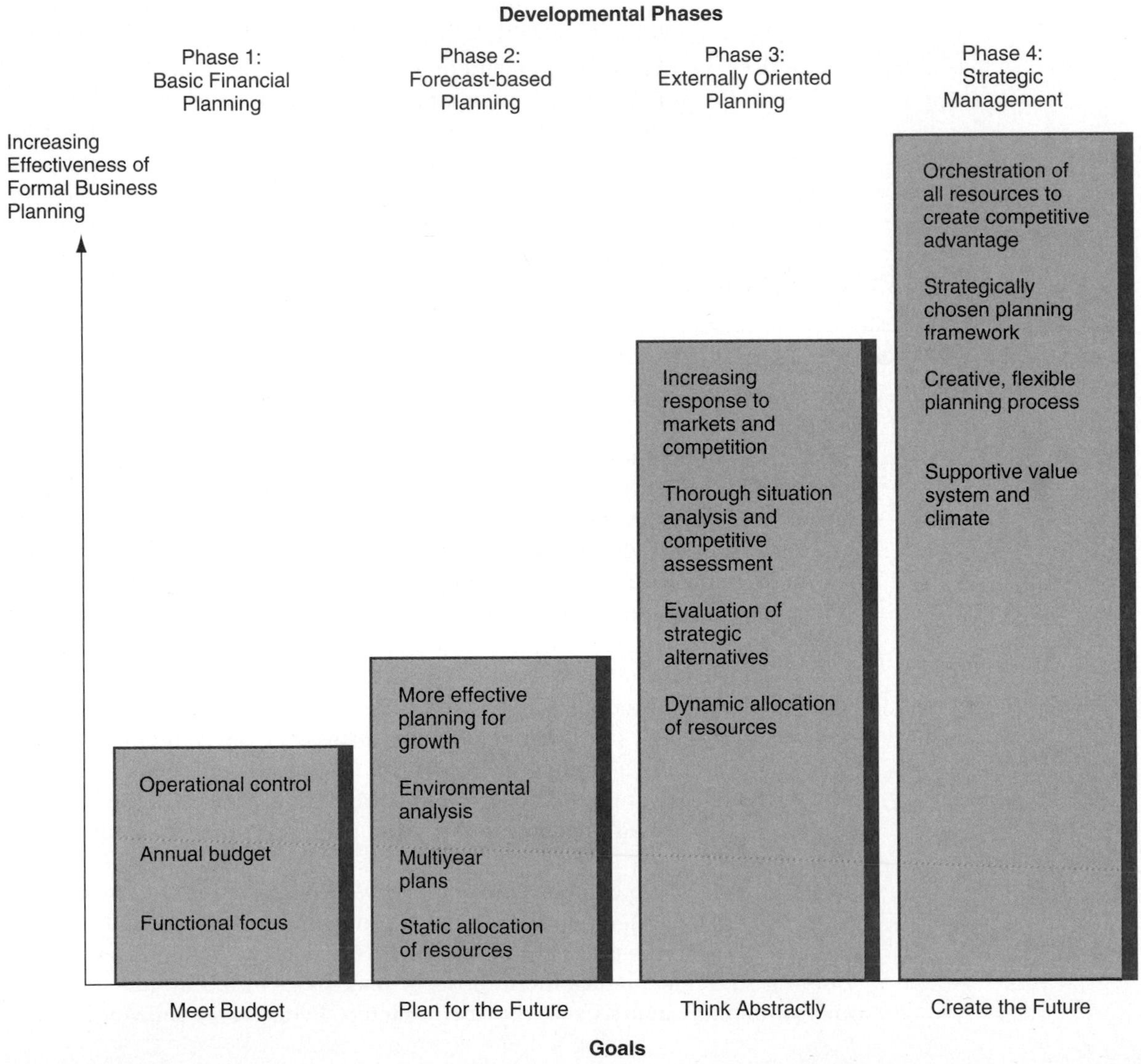

fairly simple routine of basic financial planning. During this phase, the primary concern is simply meeting budget constraints through operational control, completing the annual budgeting process, and addressing functions like operations, finance, and marketing in an isolated, nonintegrative analysis.

From these humble beginnings, the organization's perspective evolves to culminate in the process that we know as strategic management. The focus shifts over time from meeting the budget, to planning for the future, to thinking abstractly, to working to create a desired future. To create a future, decision makers orchestrate and integrate all of their organization's resources to gain a competitive advantage. Within a carefully crafted planning framework, they build flexibility into the organizational planning process, and foster a supportive, participative climate within the organization.

Managers must understand that developing an effective and efficient strategic management process in any organization can be a long and difficult task that requires sustained effort, enormous patience, and sharp political skills. In short, strategic management requires real leadership. By comparing their organizations to the system of evolutionary phases we have outlined, managers can gauge the development of strategic management in their own organizations. After realistically assessing the appropriateness of their current strategic management processes, they can begin to consider improvements and alternatives.

STRATEGIC MANAGEMENT PROCESS

We have explained strategic management as a process or series of steps. The basic steps of the strategic management process, shown in Figure 1.2, include: (1) perform an environmental analysis, (2) establish an organizational direction, (3) formulate an organizational strategy, (4) implement the organizational strategy, and (5) exert strategic control. Let's take a look at each of these steps and their places in a strategic management system.

Step 1: Perform an Environmental Analysis

The strategic management process begins with **environmental analysis,** a formal procedure to monitor the organization's environment to (a) identify present and future threats and opportunities, and (b) assess critically its own strengths and weaknesses. In this context, the organizational environment encompasses all factors both inside and outside the organization that can

FIGURE 1.2   Major Steps in the Strategic Management Process

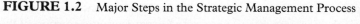

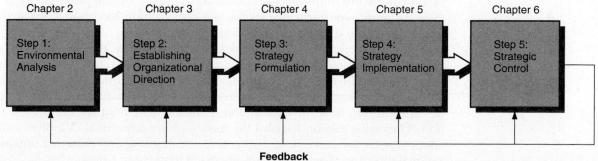

FIGURE 1.3
Sample Environmental
Factors to Monitor for
Strategic Management

Internal Characteristics
• Quality of products
• Discretionary cash flow/ gross capital investment
• Work-force morale
• Efficiency
• New product development

Market and Consumer Behavior
• Market segmentation
• Market size
• New market development
• Buyer loyalty

Supplier
• Major changes in availability or price of raw materials

Industry Structure
• Rate of technological change in products or processes
• Degree of product differentiation
• Industry price/cost structure
• Economies of scale
• Emerging international competitors

Social, Economic, and Political
• GNP trend
• Interest rates
• Energy availability
• Goverment-established and legally enforceable regulations

influence progress toward building a sustainable competitive advantage. Figure 1.3 details some examples of environmental variables that firms commonly monitor.

The Company Example, on page 17, illustrates how one firm identified and responded to significant changes in its competitive environment. Despite a historic industry downturn, Reno Air saw an opportunity to prosper. In responding to this new environment, Reno Air defined its niche and stuck to it.

Managers must grasp the purpose of environmental analysis, recognize the multiple organizational environments in which they operate, and understand the fundamental tasks of performing an environmental analysis. These issues, along with others that arise in environmental analysis, are fully discussed in Chapter 2.

Step 2: Establish an Organizational Direction

In the second step of the strategic management process, managers establish an **organizational direction** for their firm. There are three main indicators of the direction in which an organization is moving: its vision, mission statements, and objectives. An organization's vision includes its aspirations, values, and philosophies at their most general levels. Mission statements translate broad visions into more specific statements of organizational purpose. Objectives are specific performance targets the organization has chosen, through which it hopes to succeed in its mission.

A thorough environmental analysis that pinpoints the organization's strengths, weaknesses, opportunities, and threats can often help management to establish, reaffirm, or modify its organizational direction. In order to establish an appropriate organizational direction, however, management must understand how to develop a vision and a mission statement for the organization. They must also understand the nature of organizational objectives and adopt an effective and efficient process for establishing and changing organizational direction. These issues are discussed in detail in Chapter 3.

COMPANY EXAMPLE

Smooth Landing for Reno Air

Following deregulation, the airline industry hit its nadir in the early 1990s; between 1990 and 1992, the U.S. airline industry lost $10.5 billion, wiping out all of the profits earned by the industry since the Wright brothers first took off at Kitty Hawk. This environment seemed to leave little chance for a new, entrepreneurial carrier to survive, let alone make a profit. In 1993, however, Reno Air completed its first year of operations with a profit, something that only one other scheduled carrier was able to claim.

Reno's $72 million in revenues surprised the industry; no one had given its founder, Joseph A. Lorenzo, much of a chance in mid-1992 when the airline's first plane took off.

Lorenzo (no relation to Frank Lorenzo, the former chairman of Continental Airlines) saw the industry's problems as an opportunity. As these problems seemed to grow bigger and more intractable, he saw only greater potential for Reno Air.

He began by analyzing the industry, probing its soft spots and figuring out how to turn them to his advantage. Lorenzo understood the overriding lesson of the previous decade: Don't compete against the superior resources of the big carriers; define a profitable niche and stick to it.

Lorenzo knew that Reno had to steer clear of the industry's Big Three, American, Delta, and United. Together the three carried 57 percent of domestic air traffic, but their cost structures as full-service carriers—including food, computer systems, ground equipment, and maintenance expenses—made it tough to do business profitably.

Lorenzo began with one of the most basic of all strategic decisions: choosing a home base. Locating in Reno, Nevada kept his company off the radar screens of the big carriers while giving him a foothold in the midsized city where competition was thin, and potential needs were great.

Later on, Reno closely averted head-to-head competition by abandoning a route to Minneapolis that had brought it into a price war with Northwest Airlines. Lorenzo saw his mistake and cut his losses, avoiding the kind of serious error that had grounded so many other carriers.

Next, Lorenzo recognized the limits on his expertise. He hired Jeffery Erickson, president of Midway Airlines, as Reno's CEO. When Midway filed for bankruptcy, Erickson and Lorenzo snapped up some of its best assets, including personnel and equipment that lent Reno a new cohesiveness.

The most complicated decision focused on what kind of service Reno should offer. Despite high food costs, Lorenzo decided to gain a competitive advantage over other low-cost carriers by offering some food—pretzels and cookies in coach, wine and sandwiches in first class. Reno's other costs were so low that the company could add modest services, including automated ticketing through travel agents and advance seat selection, without affecting the bottom line.

Offering those services gave Reno a key boost in its effort to win the lease of American Airlines' gates in San Jose when the big carrier decided to pull out of the market. Recognizing that frequent flier programs were the only successful way to build brand loyalty in the airline industry, Lorenzo also gained a deal to offer Reno Air passengers mileage in AAdvantage, American's frequent flier program.

SOURCE: Stephen D. Solomon, "How to Start an Airline on Your Own," *Inc.*, April 1994, pp. 52–62.

Step 3: Formulate an Organizational Strategy

The third step of the strategic management process is **strategy formulation.** Earlier, we characterized a strategy as an integrative, cohesive pattern or plan that coordinates an organization's major goals, policies, and actions. Strategy formulation, then, is the process of designing a strategy that leads to a sustainable competitive advantage.[25] Once managers have analyzed the environment and set an organizational direction, they can chart alternative competitive strategies in an informed effort to improve the organization's chances of success.

In order to formulate organizational strategy properly, managers must thoroughly understand various strategy formulation tools such as industry structure analysis, value chain analysis, the Boston Consulting Group growth–share matrix, and General Electric's multifactor portfolio matrix. Chapter 4 discusses these and other tools in great detail.

Step 4: Implementing the Organizational Strategy

The fourth step of the strategic management process is implementing strategy. This step involves acting to realize the logically developed strategies that have emerged from the previous steps of the strategic management process. Without effective implementation, an organization's strategy will fail to provide the benefits of performing an environmental analysis, establishing an organizational direction, and formulating an organizational strategy.

In order to implement organizational strategy successfully, managers must have clear positions on several, diverse issues: how to handle change within the organization as it implements the new strategy, how best to deal with organization's culture in order to ensure smooth implementation of the strategy, how strategy implementation will affect organizational structures, what different implementation approaches will realize the strategy, and what skills managers need to implement the organizational strategy successfully. Chapter 5 focuses on the implementation phase of the strategic management process and explores ways to avoid or minimize the impact of strategic implementation problems.

The progress from developing a strategic plan to achieving desired performance must, however, overcome many obstacles. Table 1.5 lists eight sources of frequent breakdowns that can hinder managers' navigation through this dangerous terrain.

Step 5: Exert Strategic Control

Strategic control is a special type of organizational control that focuses on monitoring and evaluating the strategic management process in order to im-

---

TABLE 1.5

Potential Breakdowns between Planning and Implementation

1. A customer focus does not drive the planning process.
2. Planners do not organize their information to support action by those who implement the plans.
3. The strategic planning process fails to invite input from those who will implement the plan.
4. Plans are fragmented, piecemeal, or insufficient.
5. The organization does not encourage risk-takers or champions.
6. Those responsible for implementation lack the skills they need to carry out their roles.
7. The organization lacks an adequate system for measuring the results of implementation efforts.
8. The organization does not adequately recognize or reinforce the accomplishments and victories of its implementation "heroes."

SOURCE: Based on William Sandy, "Avoid the Breakdowns between Planning and Implementation," *Journal of Business Strategy*, September/October 1991, p. 30.

prove it and ensure it functions properly. To successfully perform this strategic control task, managers must understand the process of strategic control and the role of strategic audits. In addition, managers must understand the intricacies of their management information system and how such a system can complement the strategic control process. The strategic management process within any organization is only as good as the information on which it is based.[26] These and other important issues are discussed in Chapter 6.

To simplify analysis, we have presented the strategic management process as a series of discrete steps. This facilitates learning about the components of the process and how the steps commonly relate to one another. In practice, however, managers sometimes find that an organization's strategic management effort requires that they perform several steps simultaneously, or perform them in a different order from that suggested here. Managers must be creative in designing and operating strategic management systems, and they must be flexible enough to tailor their use of those systems to the organizational circumstances that confront them.

CRITICAL CHALLENGES FOR STRATEGIC MANAGEMENT

The major steps that we have outlined are fundamental to the strategic management process. In addition, three other critical challenges for strategic decision makers have received much attention in the last decade. These challenges arise from global issues, quality issues, and social/ethical issues.

Strategic Management and Global Issues

Over the last several years, businesses' activities have tended to cross international borders more frequently. Even firms with no international operations are experiencing the impact of globalization on many markets and industries. Since this trend is expected to continue, more organizations will have to consider global issues in the future in the course of their strategic management processes.

Before managers can determine how their strategic management process can most effectively accommodate international issues, they must be fully aware of critical international variables that might significantly affect their organization. Chapter 7 elaborates on the fundamental characteristics of international management and multinational corporations. In addition, this chapter devotes sections to possible international implications for each step of the strategic management model.

Strategic Management and Quality Issues

The quality movement, spearheaded by management thinkers like the late W. Edwards Deming, has had an important impact on the way organizations perform strategic management in the 1990s. Our contemporary understanding of quality has advanced far beyond the earlier reliance on postproduction procedures (called *quality control*) to weed out manufacturing mistakes. *Quality* has come to mean an organizationwide commitment to enhance the value of a good or service to the customer at every stage of bringing it to market—from design, to production, to marketing, to postsale customer service.

Managers involved in the strategic management process at all levels need to understand the history of this movement and appreciate the important role

SKILLS MODULE
Boise Cascade's Cup Runneth Over—Finally

INTRODUCTION

Issues involving quality significantly influence the strategic management process. Review the following situation and complete the related skill-development exercise. This will give you practice in confronting the kind of dilemma that often troubles managers as they seek to improve a company's quality management strategy.

SITUATION

The Southern Operations Division of Boise Cascade Corporation favors the scaled-down, focused approach to quality improvement, but without a master plan, it took the company four years to get there. The DeRidder, Louisiana, company launched its TQM program in 1986. While the program enjoyed a success story here and there, only when it became focused in 1990 did the quality mindset begin to spread like gospel throughout the mills.

This focus started with the company's Groundwood Optimization project. The project produced annual wood-cost savings of $2.2 million and defined a whole new era in quality improvement. "We picked that project because everyone in the mill could relate to it," said Richard Greer, total quality manager. "We had been talking about the high costs of wood to the mill for some time."

Those savings—and workers' move to embrace total quality—didn't come about until the company realized that it had to do more than just announce a desire for total quality. "We weren't quite sure—after you start the people talking about the process—how you actually *use* the process," admits Dave Blencke, vice president and regional manager.

The success of the Groundwood Optimization project helped the company to realize that quality initiatives cannot take shape at the corporate management level. Said Blencke, "You have to get it going at the grass roots, which is the location level. And at that level, you know specifically what the location problems are that you want to solve. People know that inherently. All the way down to the department level, they know what they want to solve. All total quality is a tool to solve [those problems]."

SKILL DEVELOPMENT EXERCISE

You are the chief executive at Boise Cascade. You decide to expand the TQM program to the company's other divisions. What main points would you emphasize in unveiling this strategy to your division managers? Explain.

SOURCE: Tracy E. Benson, "A Business Strategy Comes of Age," *Industry Week,* May 3, 1993, pp. 43–44.

---

it plays in contemporary organizational strategy. Chapter 8 traces the evolution of the quality movement and relates the search for improved quality to the cross-functional nature of strategic management. The Skills Module previews the type of strategic and quality issues we will encounter in Chapter 8.

Strategic Management and Social/Ethical Issues

Social responsibility is the managerial obligation to act, protect, and promote both organizational interests and the welfare of society as a whole. Recognition of this obligation must affect the strategic management process.

To be socially responsible, an organization's managers need to develop thorough, thoughtful answers to such questions as:

• To which societal constituencies is the organization responsible?
• What major influences within society affect business practices?
• How can an organization conduct social audits to facilitate the strategic management process?

Issues of this nature are discussed in Chapter 9.

CRITICAL FOUNDATIONS FOR STRATEGIC MANAGEMENT

To be successful, a strategic manager must mobilize and exploit the expertise of functional specialists within the organization. The importance of the relationship between business functions and the strategic management process cannot be overestimated. Strategic management is fundamentally a cross-functional undertaking; the process should draw simultaneously on functional expertise in all areas to craft a viable strategy for the whole organization, or a major part of one. Stated conversely, a strategic management process that is either dominated by one function or passed sequentially among them (i.e., from one function to the next) is likely to produce less comprehensive and less timely results than an integrated, cross-functional process.

Traditionally, three major business functions are identified within an organization: operations or production, finance, and marketing. However, these rather general categories may obscure some debate about exactly how many major business functions organizations perform. Some management theorists argue that human resource activities constitute a major business function; others maintain that research and development constitute yet another. This text discusses all important business functions and their impacts on strategic management. Separate chapters cover operations, finance, and marketing; information on human resource management activities, research and development, and other functions is integrated throughout the text.

Operations and Strategic Management

The **operations** function is performed by those people within an organization who produce the goods or services offered to its customers. Chapter 10 discusses the essential principles of operations and explains this function's contribution to the strategic management process. This chapter addresses the appropriateness of different strategies for different types of operations, characterizes operations as a vital element of strategy, presents product design as an important operations and strategy issue, and probes the nature of strategic decision making within the operations area.

Finance and Strategic Management

Financial analysis is the process of evaluating assets, liabilities, equity, and risk, and then making decisions on the basis of these evaluations.[27] Chapter 11 relates financial concepts to strategic management. These fundamental concepts underlie any serious analysis of possible strategies; the success of the strategic management process hinges on this analysis. The chapter covers the common analytical approaches, including financial ratio analysis, break-even analysis, and net present value analysis.

Marketing and Strategic Management

Marketing has been defined as, "the process of planning and executing conception, pricing, promotion, and distribution of ideas, goods, and services to create exchanges that satisfy individual and organizational objectives."[28] Chapter 12 reveals how fundamental marketing principles relate to strategic management and how they affect situational analysis, which contributes much to the strategic management process. This chapter focuses on the strategic marketing process: analysis of consumer/product relationships, selection of

FIGURE 1.4   Framework for Strategic Management: The Model for This Text

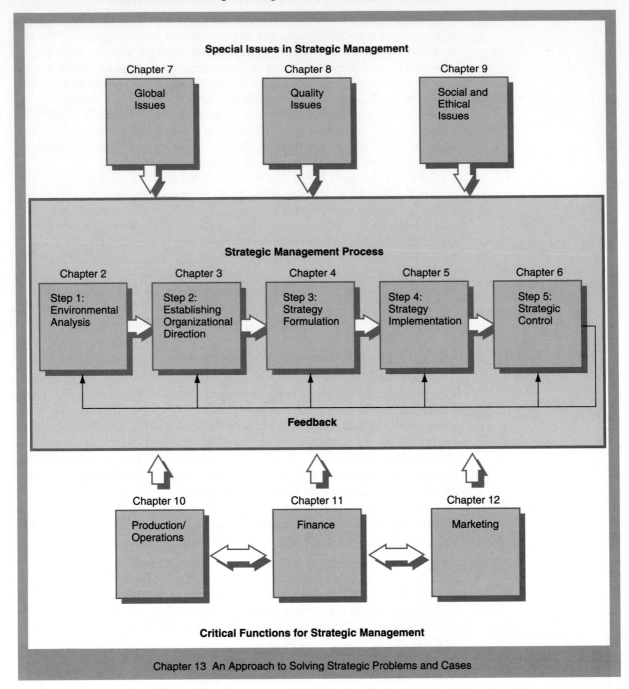

a market segmentation strategy, designing the marketing mix strategy, and implementing and controlling marketing strategy.

COMPREHENSIVE APPROACH TO ANALYZING STRATEGIC PROBLEMS AND CASES

Perhaps the most common instructional method for teaching strategic management is **case analysis.** Cases describe actual strategic management problems and invite students to analyze them critically in order to propose and defend solutions.

This text contains many cases that raise fascinating issues in strategic management. Chapter 13 details a method by which students can analyze strategic management problems and formulate recommendations. The major steps of this case analysis method are problem definition, formulation of alternative solutions to the problem, evaluation of developed alternatives, and selection and implementation of the chosen alternative. Worksheets are furnished for students to use in their analysis. The analytical method proposed in Chapter 13 is just as useful to practicing managers who face strategic management problems in real organizations.

PLAN OF THIS BOOK

Figure 1.4 outlines the overall framework for this book. It depicts all of the major topics that we have previewed in this chapter and indicates which chapter treats each one in detail. This figure will appear (with appropriate shading to highlight the relevant topic) at the beginning of each chapter to place the subject of each chapter in the context of strategic management as a whole. The figure will also serve as a review of how these diverse topics relate to one another, and it will illustrate progress in your study of strategic management.

SUMMARY

A strategy is an integrative plan or pattern of decisions that provides a road map for an organization's progress toward its goals and objectives. Strategic management is a continuous, iterative, cross-functional process aimed at keeping a strategy up to date so that the organization fits well within its environment. Typically, a firm's top management, board of directors, and planning staff contribute the most to the strategic management process. Increasingly, however, line managers, who are closer to customers and markets, and lower level employees, who must implement strategies, are playing more prominent roles.

The main steps of the process are: performing an environmental analysis establishing an organizational direction, formulating an organizational strategy, implementing that strategy, and exerting strategic control. In addition, global/international issues, social/ethical issues, and quality issues may profoundly affect an organization's strategic management process. It is critical that the strategic management process integrate input from the major business functions within the organization—operations, finance, and marketing. Each of these topics is the subject of a chapter in this text, and Chapter 13 offers guidelines for analyzing strategic management problems through case studies.

A summary checklist of questions follows the key terms. Use it to guide your analysis of problems and cases that raise fundamental strategic management issues.

KEY TERMS

strategy, p. 6	strategic control, p. 18
strategic management, p. 8	social responsibility, p. 20
strategic report card, p. 11	operations, p. 21
environmental analysis, p. 15	financial analysis, p. 21
organizational direction, p. 16	marketing, p. 21
strategy formulation, p. 17	case analysis, p. 23

CHECKLIST

Analyzing Fundamental Issues in Strategic Management

___ 1. Does the problem or case involve genuine strategic management issues?

___ 2. Are the board of directors, top management, and planning staff appropriately involved in the strategic management process?

___ 3. Are the major steps of the strategic management process appropriately ordered and integrated?

___ 4. Is organizational direction clear and well-expressed through statements of organizational mission and objectives?

___ 5. Is the strategy appropriate, given the existing organizational direction and the results of the environmental analysis?

___ 6. Has the strategy been appropriately implemented (successfully translated into action)?

___ 7. Does the focus on exerting strategic control improve the strategic management process appropriately?

___ 8. Have the impacts of global issues on the strategic management process been assessed?

___ 9. Have the impacts of quality issues on the strategic management process been considered?

___ 10. Have the impacts of social/ethical issues on the strategic management process been taken into account?

___ 11. Are the operations, finance, and marketing functions properly mobilized and utilized?

Additional Readings

Andrews, Kenneth R. *The Concept of Corporate Strategy.* Homewood, Ill.: Richard D. Irwin, 1987.

Ansoff, H. Igor, and E. McDonnell. *Implanting Strategic Management,* 2d ed. Englewood Cliffs, N.J.: Prentice-Hall, 1990.

Chakravarthy, Balaji, and Yves Doz. "Strategy Process Research: Focusing on Corporate Self-Renewal," *Strategic Management Journal,* 13 (Special Issue, Summer 1992), pp. 5–14.

Drucker, Peter. "The New Society of Organizations." *Harvard Business Review.* September/October 1992, p. 95.

Jacobson, Robert. "The 'Austrian' School of Strategy." *The Academy of Management Review,* October 1992, p. 782.

Mintzberg, Henry. "The Design School: Reconsidering the Basic Premises of Strategic Management." *Strategic Management Journal* 11, no. 3 (1990), pp. 171–195.

C A S E

STRATEGIC FACE-LIFT FOR SEARS, ROEBUCK

The February 1993 unveiling of yet another new image for Sears, Roebuck & Co. brought a collective yawn from the analysts gathered in Chicago for the announcement by the nation's third largest retailer. Over the next few months, however, the yawns turned to appreciative smiles, especially among shareholders. By the end of the year, the 800-store chain had bounced back from the previous year's record loss to a record profit, and delivered a 19 percent return on equity to its investors. Sears achieved this success, in large part, because it was able to do in one year what it had planned to do in three years: chop $328 million after taxes out of its annual costs.

Veteran observers saw one key difference between those previous, cosmetic makeovers and the most recent, substantive face-lift: its architect, Arthur C. Martinez, a Saks Fifth Avenue veteran who had joined Sears a year earlier as chairman of its merchandise group. Martinez unleashed an ambitious strategy to turn Sears into a competitive, moderately priced department store. Martinez's strategy emphasized selling apparel, which is profit-rich, while defending Sears's market share in hardware and appliances. It included a $4 billion plan to renovate stores, build more free-standing hardware stores, and move furniture into separate emporiums.

Martinez said that he began his job with three objectives: sell or close operations that were unprofitable or that diverged from Sears's new strategy, assemble a new management team, and put the new merchandising plan to work. In May 1993, step 1 closed Sears's 97-year-old catalog business, which had been losing $140 million a year.

Clearing the organizational decks was next. The 3,400 employees who accepted the company's early retirement offer included the heads of the marketing, public relations, retail, and automotive divisions. Martinez, who said that he wanted "people with a bias toward action," ended up commanding a mix of veteran Sears hands who led the home group and intimate apparel division as well as newcomers who led the advertising and women's apparel units—the two areas undergoing the most rapid changes.

Although clothing accounted for only 26 percent of Sears's annual store sales of about $28.7 billion, it brought in some 60 percent of the merchandise unit's profits. Because higher apparel sales also increased store traffic, Sears wanted to boost apparel's share to about 40 percent of store sales. Martinez's priorities included paying shoe salespeople on commission, getting more salespeople on the floor, and seeing that store racks stayed well-stocked.

To raise consumer awareness of the changes, Sears boosted its $1 billion marketing budget by 9 percent. It also began increasing the number of national brands it offered, from 40 percent to half of its merchandise mix. (The other 50 percent was private-label goods.)

Sears's new operational strategy had its costs. The big marketing push was expensive; industry analysts estimated that the company spent $60 million more on advertising in the fourth quarter of 1993 than in the year-earlier period. Shifting funds from traditional media such as newspaper inserts to newer, less-proven forms such as infomercials, and sponsoring a 30-city concert tour by singer Phil Collins also cost Sears money, and exposed the firm to risks. Yet the risks seemed to pay off. Sears's $40 million print and broadcast campaign, "Softer Side of Sears," improved the company's image among women, and apparel sales rose.

DISCUSSION QUESTIONS

1. How effectively did Martinez address the key questions in strategy development? Explain.
2. How well did Sears implement the strategy?
3. Evaluate the risks that Sears took. Do you consider them worthy ones? What are some others you would propose?
4. If you were chairman, how would a drop in profits or a surge in reorganization costs affect the various components of your overall strategic management plan at Sears?

SOURCES: Gregory A. Patterson, "'Face Lift' Gives Sears a Fresh Look and Better Results," *The Wall Street Journal*, July 20, 1993, p. B4; "Sears Earnings Signal Recovery in Retail Lines," *The Wall Street Journal*, July 21, 1993, p. A3; "Sears Funds Some New Marketing Projects," *The Wall Street Journal*, February 16, 1994, p. B3.

Notes

1. Andrew Pollack, "Sega Takes Aim at Disney's World," *New York Times*, July 4, 1993, Section 3, p. 1; Frederic M. Biddle, "The Profit Machine: NordicTrack Is the Muscle behind Top-Ranked CML," *Boston Globe*, June 8, 1993, p. 31; Bridget O'Brian, "Losing Altitude: Once-Solid Delta Air Is Burdened by Cost of European Foray," *The Wall Street Journal*, June 25, 1993, p. A1; David Hamilton, "After Initial Fuzziness, AT&T Clears Up Signal to Asia," *The Wall Street Journal*, June 30, 1993, p. B4; Joseph Pereira, "Footware Fad Makes Nike, Reebok Run for Their Money," *The Wall Street Journal*, June 24, 1993, p. B1.
2. R. A. Gordon and J. E. Howell, *Higher Education for Business* (New York: Columbia University Press, 1959).
3. M. Leontiades, "The Confusing Words of Business Policy," *Academy of Management Review*, January 1982, p. 46.
4. Mathew J. Kiernan, "The New Strategic Architecture," *The Executive*, February 1993, pp. 7–21.
5. H. Igor Ansoff, *Implanting Strategic Management* (Englewood Cliffs, N.J.: Prentice-Hall, 1984).
6. James Brian Quinn, *Strategies for Change* (Homewood, Ill.: Richard D. Irwin, 1980), p. 7.
7. Henry Mintzberg, "Patterns in Strategy Formation," *Management Science* (1978), pp. 934–948.
8. C. K. Prahalad and G. Hamel, "The Core Competence of the Corporation," *Harvard Business Review*, May/June 1990, pp. 79–91.
9. H. Mintzberg and J. Waters, "Of Strategies, Deliberate and Emergent," *Strategic Management Journal*, 1985, pp. 257–272.
10. Rich Tetzel, "Steve Jobs Leaves Hardware Behind," *Fortune*, March 8, 1993, p. 10.
11. David Nadler and Deborah Ancona, "Team-Work at the Top," in *Organizational Architecture*, ed. by D. Nadler, M. Gerstein, and R. Shaw (San Francisco: Jossey-Bass, 1992).
12. Henry Mintzberg, "Strategy-Making in Three Modes," *California Management Review*, Winter 1973, pp. 44–53.
13. Roy Forman, "Strategic Planning and the Chief Executive," *Long Range Planning* 21 (August 1988), pp. 57–64.

14. George Grune, "Strategic Planning at the Reader's Digest Association," speech given at the annual meeting of the Crummer Graduate School of Business, Corporate Council, Rollins College, 1986.

15. B. Baysinger and H. Butler, "The Composition of Boards of Directors and Strategic Control," *Academy of Management Review* (1990), pp. 72–81.

16. Ada Demb, Danielle Chouet, Tom Lossius, and Fred Neubauer, "Defining the Role of the Board," *Long Range Planning* 22 (February 1989), pp. 60–68; R. H. Rock and Marv Eisthen, "Implementing Strategic Change," in *The Management Handbook*, ed. by K. J. Albert (New York: McGraw-Hill, 1983).

17. Joseph Rosenstein, "Why Don't U.S. Boards Get More Involved in Strategy?" *Long Range Planning* 20, no. 3 (1987), pp. 30–34.

18. Kenneth R. Andrews, "Corporate Strategy as a Vital Function of the Board," *Harvard Business Review*, November/December 1981, pp. 174–184.

19. J. Richard Harrison, "The Strategic Use of Corporate Board Committees," *California Management Review* 30, no. 1 (Fall 1987), pp. 109–125.

20. Rosenstein, "Why Don't U.S. Boards."

21. W. Judge and C. Zeithaml, "Institutional and Strategic Choice Perspectives on Board Involvement in the Strategic Decision Process," *Academy of Management Journal*, October 1992, pp. 766–794.

22. "The New Breed of Strategic Planner," *Business Week*, September 17, 1984, pp. 62–66.

23. As an example of studies showing that strategic management does not always increase productivity, see R. Fulmer and L. Rue, "The Practice and Profitability of Long-Range Planning," *Managerial Planning* 22 (1974), p. 1; as an example of the opposite view, see Richard Robinson, Jr., "The Importance of Outsiders in Small Firm Strategic Planning," *Academy of Management Journal* 25, no. 1 (March 1982), p. 80.

24. Frederick W. Gluck, Stephen P. Kaufman, and A. Steven Walleck, "Strategic Management for Competitive Advantage," *Harvard Business Review*, July/August 1980, pp. 154–161.

25. Pankaj Ghemawat, *Commitment: The Dynamic of Strategy* (New York: Free Press, 1991).

26. M. D. Skipton, "Helping Managers to Develop Strategies," *Long Range Planning* 18, no. 2 (April 1985), pp. 56–68.

27. Robert Hartl, *Basics of Financial Management* (Dubuque, Ia.: William C. Brown Publishers, 1986), pp. 4–5.

28. J. Paul Peter and James H. Donnelly, Jr., *Marketing Management: Knowledge and Skills*, 4th ed. (Burr Ridge, Ill.: Richard D. Irwin, 1995), p. 7.

PART II

Strategic Management Process

Part II builds upon Part I by discussing in detail the five major steps in the strategic management process. Chapter 2 discusses the importance of environmental analysis to provide data for sound strategic management decisions. Chapter 3 concerns establishing an organization's vision, mission, and objectives to provide direction. Chapter 4 emphasizes strategy formulation, determining appropriate actions to move the organization in its chosen direction. Chapter 5 discusses strategy implementation, the process of putting formulated strategies into action. Chapter 6 focuses on strategic control to evaluate, monitor, and improve the organization's effectiveness. Careful study of this section should provide a foundation for analyzing strategic management problems and cases.

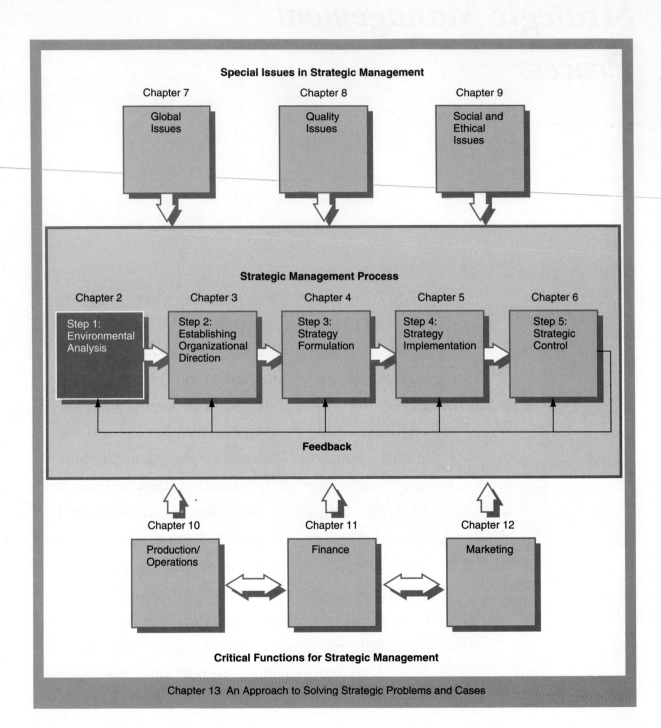

Special Issues in Strategic Management

Chapter 7 — Global Issues

Chapter 8 — Quality Issues

Chapter 9 — Social and Ethical Issues

Strategic Management Process

Chapter 2 — Step 1: Environmental Analysis

Chapter 3 — Step 2: Establishing Organizational Direction

Chapter 4 — Step 3: Strategy Formulation

Chapter 5 — Step 4: Strategy Implementation

Chapter 6 — Step 5: Strategic Control

Feedback

Chapter 10 — Production/Operations

Chapter 11 — Finance

Chapter 12 — Marketing

Critical Functions for Strategic Management

Chapter 13 An Approach to Solving Strategic Problems and Cases

CHAPTER

2

Environmental Analysis

Chapter 1 introduced the concept of strategy and described the strategic management process in very general terms. Chapter 2 focuses on the initial step of this process, environmental analysis. Companies undertake environmental analysis to ferret out information that they use in every step of the strategic management process.

We begin with the basics, describing the nature of environmental analysis and why companies devote resources to it. We then define the different levels of environments—

general, operating, and internal environments—that organizations try to understand and analyze. Next, we discuss SWOT (*S*trengths, *W*eaknesses, *O*pportunities, *T*hreats) analysis and examine the general problems top managers face in their efforts to make sense of the environments in which they operate or plan to operate. We then introduce techniques for carrying out SWOT analysis and conclude the chapter by offering ideas for evaluating the overall environmental analysis effort.

ENVIRONMENTAL ANALYSIS: DEFINITION AND RATIONALE

As we noted in Chapter 1, environmental analysis is the process of monitoring an organization's environments to identify strengths, weaknesses, opportunities, and threats that may influence the firm's ability to reach its goals. We define the **organizational environment** generally as the set of forces, both outside and inside the organization, that can affect performance.

If an organization were a closed system with no input from outside, its environment would be inconsequential; as an open system, subject to a broad range of outside inputs and influences, the organization depends for its survival on effective evaluation of its environment. An organization's success or failure depends on how accurately its top management team reads the environment, and how effectively they respond to it.[1] Accordingly, managers at various levels of the organization and in various functional departments spend a great deal of time and effort gathering and analyzing data related to what they see as important environmental factors.

Large firms often rely on outside board members for advice and counsel on long-range political or macroeconomic matters. The CEO, with help from internal functional experts from marketing, research, new product development, or production, must develop a solid grasp on the strategic issues at work in the competitive environment of the firm's industry. Internal staffers, such as planners, financial analysts, and personnel specialists, must always stay abreast of new techniques and methods that define the best practices in their respective professions in order to keep their input to the process valuable.

Clearly, many people spread throughout an organization contribute to environmental analysis. This fact underscores the importance of organizing effectively for environmental analysis. To assure themselves that they will have the information they need to make strategic decisions, top managers must think carefully about who should gather what information and how to structure the flow of that information so that they can use it most effectively.[2] Because the organization must gather and act on diverse information in a timely manner, cross-functional teams of internal specialists can often perform environmental analysis most effectively.[3]

Many companies cite valuable benefits from environmental analysis. At Connecticut General Insurance Company, for example, the overriding purpose of environmental analysis is to help management to respond to *critical issues* in the environment. Sun Oil Exploration and Production Company has stated a similar purpose for its environmental analysis: to explore *future conditions* of the organizational environment and to incorporate what it learns into organizational decision making. Sears, Roebuck has stated another main purpose in undertaking environmental analysis: to identify current *emerging issues* that are significant to the company, assign priorities to these issues, and develop a plan for handling each of them.

Upon examination, these environmental analysis efforts generally focus on identifying present and future strategic issues and planning how to deal with these issues. This overall process is sometimes termed *strategic issue management*.[4]

BASIC STRUCTURES OF ENVIRONMENTS

In order to perform an environmental analysis, a manager must understand the basic structures of organizational environments. Analysts typically divide the environment of an organization into three distinct levels: the general environment, the operating environment, and the internal environment.[5] Figure 2.1 illustrates the relationship of each of these levels with the others and with the organization at large. The figure also shows the various components that make up each level. Managers must be aware of these three environmental levels, know what factors they include, and try to understand how each factor and the relationships among the factors affect organizational performance. They can then manage organizational operations in light of this understanding.

General Environment

The **general environment** is that level of an organization's external environment with components that are broad in scope and have long-term implications for managers, firms, and strategies. What are these components?

The economic component of the general environment indicates the distribution and uses of resources within an entire society. Examples of factors within the economic component are gross national product growth, the inflation rate, productivity growth, employment rates, balance of payments issues, interest rates, tax rates, and consumer income, debt, and spending patterns.[6]

FIGURE 2.1   The Organization, the Levels of Its Environment, and the Components of Those Levels

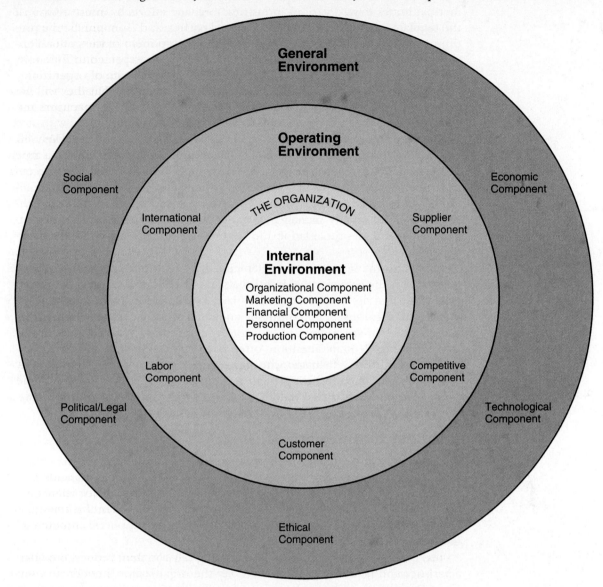

General
Environment

Operating
Environment

Social
Component

Economic
Component

THE ORGANIZATION

International
Component

Supplier
Component

**Internal
Environment**

Organizational Component
Marketing Component
Financial Component
Personnel Component
Production Component

Labor
Component

Competitive
Component

Political/Legal
Component

Technological
Component

Customer
Component

Ethical
Component

The social component of the general environment describes characteristics of the society in which the organization exists. Literacy rates, education levels, customs, beliefs, values, lifestyles, the age distribution, the geographic distribution, and the mobility of the population all contribute to the social component of the general environment. Two areas in this cluster receive special attention from corporate leaders today: the quality of public education and the aging of the Baby Boom generation of consumers. Corporate decision makers' concern with education reflects their determination to maintain the general quality of the labor force in the long term. Their attention to Baby Boomers focuses on the implications for demand for goods and services as the U.S. population ages.[7]

The political component of the general environment relates to government attitudes toward various industries, lobbying efforts by interest groups, the regulatory climate, platforms of political parties, and (sometimes) the predispositions of candidates for office. The legal component of the general environment consists of laws that members of society are expected to follow. In the United States, many legal constraints affect an organization's operations, including the Clean Air Act, the Occupational Safety and Health Act, the Consumer Product Safety Act, and the Energy Policy and Conservation Act. Naturally, over time new laws are passed and old ones rescinded.

The technological component of the general environment includes new approaches to producing goods and services: new procedures as well as new equipment. For example, the trend toward using robots to improve productivity is closely monitored by many of today's managers. The technological component of today's general environment also relates to the concepts and techniques of total quality management and continuous quality improvement. Chapter 8 examines the relationship between technology and quality in more detail.

Ethical norms of a society are elements of its culture that specify in more general ways the behavior that individuals and organizations expect of one another, but that are not prescribed by law. As the above list of laws implies, many ethical norms (e.g., consumer and worker safety and environmental protection) that are important to a society's long term future, but are seen as receiving inadequate attention, often become translated into laws. For example, in the 1950s a manager who allowed the nearby river to be polluted by run-off from a manufacturing plant was violating an ethical norm. In the 1990s, that same manager would be violating environmental protection laws. These and related issues are considered more fully in Chapter 9.

Operating Environment

The **operating environment,** sometimes termed the *competitive environment,* is that level of the organization's external environment with components that normally have relatively specific and immediate implications for managing the organization. As Figure 2.1 indicates, the major components of the operating environment are customers, competitors, labor, suppliers, and global/international issues.

The customer component of the operating environment reflects the characteristics and behavior of those who buy the organization's goods and services. Describing in detail those who buy the firm's products is a common business practice. Such profiles help management generate ideas about how to improve customer satisfaction.

The competitor component of the operating environment consists of rivals that an organization must overcome in order to reach its objectives. Understanding competitors is a key factor in developing an effective strategy, so analyzing the competition is a fundamental challenge to management. Basically, competitor analysis is intended to help management appreciate the strengths, weaknesses, and capabilities of existing and potential competitors and predict their responses to strategic initiatives.[8]

The labor component of the operating environment is made up of influences on the supply of workers available to perform needed organizational tasks. Issues such as the skill levels, union membership, wage rates, and average ages of potential workers are important to the operation of the organization. Managers often overlook another important issue: the attractiveness of working for a particular organization, as perceived by potential workers.

The supplier component of the operating environment includes the influence of providers of nonlabor resources to the organization. The firm purchases and transforms these resources during the production process into final goods and services. How many vendors offer specified resources for sale, the relative quality of materials they offer, the reliability of their deliveries, the credit terms they offer, and the potential for strategic linkages—all such issues affect managing this element in the operating environment.

The global/international component of the operating environment comprises all factors related to global issues. Though not all organizations must deal directly with international issues, the number that do is increasing dramatically. Significant aspects of the international component include the laws, political practices, cultures, and economic climates that prevail in the countries in which the firm does business.[9] Important elements in each of these categories are presented in Table 2.1. Figure 2.2 illustrates one

TABLE 2.1

International Component of the Operating Environment

Legal Forces	Cultural Forces
Legal traditions	Customs, norms, values, beliefs
Effectiveness of legal system	Language
Treaties with foreign nations	Attitudes
Patent/trademark laws	Motivations
Laws affecting business firms	Social institutions
	Status symbols
	Religious beliefs

Economic Forces	Political Forces
Level of economic development	Form of government
Population	Political ideology
Gross national product	Stability of government
Per-capita income	Strength of opposition parties and groups
Literacy level	Social unrest
Social infrastructure	Political strife and insurgency
Natural resources	Government attitude toward foreign firms
Climate	Foreign policy
Membership in regional economic blocks	
Monetary and fiscal policies	
Nature of competition	
Currency convertibility	
Inflation	
Taxation system	
Interest rates	
Wage and salary levels	

SOURCE: Reproduced from Arvind V. Phatak, *International Dimensions of Management,* 3d ed. (Boston: Kent Publishing, 1992), p. 6, with the permission of South-Western College Publishing. Copyright 1992 by South-Western College Publishing. All rights reserved.

FIGURE 2.2
World Changes in
the 1990s

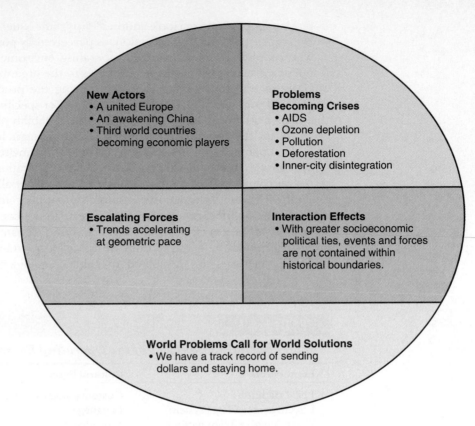

SOURCE: W. Harvey Hegarty, "The Editor's Chair/Organizational Survival Means Embracing Change,"
Business Horizons, November/December 1993, p. 2. Reprinted from *Business Horizons* (November–
December 1993). Copyright 1993 by the Foundation for the School of Business at Indiana University.
Used with permission.

observer's perspective on important forces that affect the international component of the operating environment of the 1990s. Note that while Table 2.1
provides a general list of potentially important issues from which firms can begin to analyze the international components of their operating environments,
Figure 2.2 details underlying factors critical to understanding, and managing
in, the operating environment of the 1990s. See Chapter 7 for further discussion of international issues.

Taken as a group, the five components of the operating environment
define the territory or domain in which an organization resides. The structure
of key relationships within this operating environment (or environments if a
firm operates in multiple industries) will determine the firm's profit potential, as well as its prospects for achieving a sustainable competitive advantage.[10,11] Our definition of strategic management leads us to discuss the operating environment throughout the text. In particular, Chapter 4's discussion
of strategy formulation uses environmental analysis to devise the organization's strategy.

Internal Environment

The organization's **internal environment** includes forces that operate inside
the organization with specific implications for managing organizational per-

formance. Unlike components of the general and operating environments, which act from outside the organization, components of the internal environment come from the organization itself. Table 2.2 lists a number of important components of the internal environment.

These aspects of an organization's internal environment collectively define both trouble spots that need strengthening and core competencies that the firm can nurture and build. By systematically examining its internal activities (production, marketing, etc.), a firm can better appreciate how each activity might add value or contribute significantly to shaping an effective strategy. Michael Porter has proposed a method for such an evaluation called *value chain analysis*.[12] Value chain analysis can identify internal core competencies, which, in concert with an external industry structure, are seen as the critical elements of long-term competitive advantage and profitability.[13] Chapter 4 will use the concepts of core competence and value chain analysis to enrich our discussion of the strategy formulation stage of the overall strategic management process.

The Skills Module gives you the opportunity to observe and apply environmental analysis issues in a real firm. Gerber Products has had to conduct a thorough environmental analysis in the face of a declining share of a changing market.

TABLE 2.2

Components of the Internal Environment

Organizational Component	Personnel Component
Communication network	Labor relations
Organization structure	Recruitment practices
Record of success	Training programs
Hierarchy of objectives	Performance appraisal system
Policies, procedures, rules	Incentive system
Ability of management team	Turnover and absenteeism

Marketing Component	Production Component
Market segmentation	Plant facility layout
Product strategy	Research and development
Pricing strategy	Use of technology
Promotion strategy	Purchasing of raw materials
Distribution strategy	Inventory control
	Use of subcontracting

Financial Component

Liquidity
Profitability
Activity
Investment opportunity

SKILLS MODULE
Environmental Analysis at Gerber

INTRODUCTION

We have discussed the structure of the organizational environment at some length. Review the following situation at Gerber and then complete the skill-development exercise. This will help you develop the ability to determine the impact of various environmental factors at different environmental levels on organizational success.

SITUATION

Feeding a baby isn't easy, but it's just as tough to create and sell the foods to feed a baby. The numbers are working against the big baby-food makers. Overall sales, measured in pounds, dropped 6 percent in the latest quarter, and the trend isn't likely to reverse with the Baby Boom generation graying and more women exiting their childbearing years.

Gerber Products Co., the nation's largest maker of baby food, has been losing market share to its rivals; within the most recent 12-week period, Gerber's sales declined nearly 3 percent. A 5.5 percent price increase, which rivals didn't immediately match, may have helped the competition post sales increases at Gerber's expense.

Yet the Fremont, Michigan, company maintains control of 71.2 percent of the shrinking market, selling far more peach compote and pureed beets than Beech-Nut (with 14.5 percent) and Heinz (with 11.1 percent) combined. Still, though Gerber is stocked in nearly half of the nation's supermarkets, the company has had a tough year: Its market share tumbled 1.5 percent, its new president resigned under mysterious circumstances, and it is accused, with its top rivals, of two decades of price fixing.

The changing market has led Gerber and its rivals to branch out, their growth strategies based on brand extensions. Success is mixed.

To increase overall sales, both Gerber and Beech-Nut are targeting groups with higher-than-average birth rates. For Hispanics, who buy more prepared baby food than many other ethnic groups, Gerber has unveiled a tropical line, made with fruits such as papayas and mangoes. Though successful tests in New York and Miami led to a national rollout last year, quarterly sales of the line dropped 17 percent. Beech-Nut's tropical line remains in the test marketing stage.

Angling for the toddler market, the three-year-old Gerber's Graduates line offers finger foods, snacks, and microwaved entrees. Sales of the 23-item line rose 51 percent in the most recent 12 weeks to $9.6 million, but analysts say that is short of expectations. An aggressive marketing campaign hasn't convinced people that toddler foods are anything but an unnecessary and expensive convenience item. Since a parent can easily serve macaroni and cheese, buying a six-ounce entree for $1.19 "just doesn't make sense," says Dick Landwehr, a buyer for Schultz Sav-O Stores in Milwaukee. Sales of Beech-Nut's Table Time microwaved meals rose 38 percent to $1.3 million in the same period.

Gerber has no plans to enter the hottest growth area in the marketplace—organic baby food. Although Beech-Nut discontinued its two-year effort after sales fell 44 percent, the market is healthy for Earth's Best, which saw sales climb more than 9 percent to $53.2 million for the same 12-week period.

Gerber maintains that it sets the standard for baby food, and its products show little or no traces of pesticide chemicals. Says spokesman Steve Poole, "That's as good as organic can claim to be." Analysts concur with Gerber's reluctance to enter the organic market. Says one, "It would raise the question, 'What's wrong with the other stuff?'"

SKILL DEVELOPMENT EXERCISE

Based on the situation described, list the one component from each environment—general, operating, and internal—that you think is the most critical for Gerber to deal with effectively. State your reasons for selecting this item, and make a recommendation to Gerber's top managers about what actions they should take with respect to it.

SOURCE: Carl Quintanilla, "Gerber Stumbles in a Shrinking Market," *The Wall Street Journal*, July 6, 1993, pp. B1, B5.

INTRODUCTION TO SWOT ANALYSIS

Gathering data about the general, operating, and internal environments provides the raw material from which to develop a picture of the organizational environment. **SWOT analysis** refines this body of information by applying a general framework for understanding and managing the environment in which an organization operates. (The acronym SWOT stands for Strengths, Weaknesses, Opportunities, Threats.) In many respects, the sophisticated analytical techniques discussed throughout the text are further refinements of basic SWOT analysis. In addition, students have repeatedly told us that SWOT is an excellent way to begin a case analysis. SWOT analysis attempts to assess the internal strengths and weaknesses of an organization and the opportunities and threats that its external environment presents. SWOT seeks to isolate the major issues facing an organization through careful analysis of each of these four elements. Managers can then formulate strategies to address key issues. Table 2.3 lists several key questions in each area that managers often address when performing SWOT analysis.

Although these questions may help direct a SWOT analysis, a great deal of work is required to answer them properly and to put them into perspective. For example, the analyst must assess the relative importance of each issue and the issue's potential impact on the firm and its strategy. Furthermore, the priority or relative importance of each issue may vary for strategies formulated at the corporate, business, or functional levels. We will distinguish among these levels of strategy in Chapter 4.

The case at the end of the chapter invites you to undertake a SWOT analysis for Ryka, a women's athletic shoe company. Ryka is a rapidly growing firm that generated annual revenues of $12 million in 1992. As you will see, it is also one of a handful of contemporary firms, along with Ben & Jerry's and the Body Shop, to link business strategy to social activism.

Understanding and Managing the Environment: SWOT and the Problem of Interpretation

Table 2.3 gives us some indication of the complexities of understanding and managing the environments in which managers operate. A multitude of environmental forces demand attention. Stated differently, the simplicity of SWOT analysis masks a great deal of individual and organizational complexity. For an individual manager who must complete an environmental analysis, the primary concerns are gathering and interpreting massive quantities of data about the most significant environmental forces, and then deciding what action to take in response to them. Because interpretation represents a form of judgment, interpretations, like judgments, often differ from manager to manager, even within the same firm. For example, one manager may see an environmental factor, say freer trade among nations, as an opportunity for market expansion, while another may focus on the threat of increased competition from international rivals.

This type of interpretation, often called **sensemaking,** by top managers has become the focus of a great deal of recent research by strategic management scholars.[14] This research brings the tools of psychology into the study of the strategic management process. Before it began, scholars paid little attention to sensemaking, either dismissing it as a type of mysterious black box or making some overly simple assumptions about its techniques. Mintzberg's

TABLE 2.3

Important Considerations for SWOT Analysis

Internal Analysis

Strengths	Weaknesses
A distinctive competence?	No clear strategic direction?
Adequate financial resources?	A deteriorating competitive position?
Good competitive skills?	Obsolete facilities?
Well thought of by buyers?	Subpar profitability because . . . ?
An acknowledged market leader?	Lack of managerial depth and talent?
Well-conceived functional area strategies?	Missing any key skills or competencies?
Access to economies of scale?	Poor track record in implementing strategy?
Insulated (at least somewhat) from strong competitive pressures?	Plagued with internal operating problems?
	Vulnerable to competitive pressures?
Proprietary technology?	Falling behind in R&D?
Cost advantages?	Too narrow a product line?
Competitive advantages?	Weak market image?
Product innovation abilities?	Competitive disadvantages?
Proven management?	Below-average marketing skills?
Other?	Unable to finance needed changes in strategy?
	Other?

External Analysis

Opportunities	Threats
Enter new markets or segments?	Likely entry of new competitors?
Add to product line?	Rising sales of substitute products?
Diversify into related products?	Slower market growth?
Add complementary products?	Adverse government policies?
Vertical integration?	Growing competitive pressures?
Ability to move to better strategic group?	Vulnerability to recession and business cycle?
Complacency among rival firms?	Growing bargaining power of customers or suppliers?
Faster market growth?	Changing buyer needs and tastes?
Other?	Adverse demographic changes?
	Other?

SOURCE: Adapted from Arthur A. Thompson, Jr., and A. J. Strickland III, *Strategic Management: Concepts and Cases* 7th ed. (Plano, Tex.: Business Publications, 1993), p. 88.

continuing research on how top managers really work, as opposed to the overly rational way they are often assumed to work, opened the door for renewed interest in sensemaking.[15] Herbert Simon's pioneering work on the cognitive limits inherent in managerial decision making (for which he was awarded the Nobel Prize) can be seen as the real wellspring for this research emphasis.[16]

The concept of strategic sensemaking has come to include a set of managerial activities that are basic to the task of environmental analysis—scanning, interpretation, and action-choice. In this text, we cover the first two topics in this chapter and the third in Chapter 4, in our discussion of strategy formulation.

The Aim of SWOT: Identifying and Managing Strategic Issues

SWOT analysis forces managers to better understand and respond to those factors that have the greatest importance for the firm's performance. We call these factors **strategic issues.** A strategic issue is an environmental factor, either inside or outside the organization, that is likely to have an impact on the ability of the enterprise to meet its objectives.[17]

It should be emphasized that strategic issues rarely arrive on a top manager's desk neatly labeled. Instead, data from SWOT analysis of the environment identify new technologies, market trends, new competitors, and employee morale trends. They require interpretation and translation before they are labeled *strategies.* Often, managers draw upon their experience to categorize issues as controllable or uncontrollable, as threats or opportunities. These categories then determine how an issue appears to an individual manager, how well it can be sold to other managers, and what action the firm subsequently takes.[18]

Clearly, not all issues are equally important to all organizations. Some organizations are much more sensitive to certain issues than others. Table 2.4 shows the sensitivity of a telephone equipment company and a major oil company to six different issues, or environmental factors. This example clearly supports the position that managers must carefully determine which issues have the most significant or strategic influence on organizational success. The Company Example illustrates how one top manager can look at the same situation as his predecessors, see a different set of strategic issues, and interpret them in a way that supports a different corporate strategy.

Scanning, Forecasting, and Other Data Sources for SWOT

All but the smallest organizations require cross-functional cooperation to gather data about present and future environments (sometimes termed

TABLE 2.4

Sensitivity of Two Companies to the Same Environmental Factors

Telephone Equipment	Manufacturer	Oil Company
GNP	Medium	High
Government capital spending	Very high	Low
Technical change	Very high	Medium/Low (except for electric car)
Sociological change	Very high (communication habits)	Very high (private car use)
Environmental pollution	Low	High
Middle East political risks	Low	High

SOURCE: Reprinted from *Long Range Planning,* March 1973, Basil W. Denning, "Strategic Environmental Appraisal," p. 25. Copyright 1973, with kind permission from Elsevier Science Ltd., The Boulevard, Langford Lane, Kidlington, OX5 1GB, UK.

COMPANY EXAMPLE

Kodak's Sharpshooter Surveys the Scene

Kodak, described as one of the most bureaucratic, wasteful, paternalistic, slow-moving—and beloved—companies in America, is ready to go down the path of restructuring—again. After five attempts in the past decade, the Rochester, New York, company has gotten serious. Frustrated board members, pressured by investors, fired the chairman and brought in one of American industry's best and brightest, Motorola Chairman George M. C. Fisher.

Although Fisher is too busy mapping out a strategic plan to disclose any further plans, he has already angered many analysts and investors with his initial promise: "Kodak has a great franchise, and my hope is to build on that to get exciting growth." Critics say that is impossible. They would prefer to see Kodak run as a mature cash cow, cutting costs, especially through massive layoffs, to generate as much cash flow as possible, buying in shares, and paying big dividends.

Fisher already faces competitive inroads on Kodak's highly profitable film and photographic-paper businesses, where gross margins can be as high as 80 percent. But Japan's Fuji Photo Film and private-label brands are undercutting Kodak's prices and eroding its market share, which in the past five years has fallen from about 80 percent to 70 percent. Lowering prices in 1994 helped stem the slide; next up is a film called Funtime aimed at

the low-end market and priced 20 percent below Kodak's Standard Gold brand. It will only be sold during the spring and fall, not during peak picture times of summer and Christmas.

The trend toward lowering prices could stymie any growth plans. Kodak needs a large cash flow to finance a move it must make into electronics—a small, fast-growing arena where its products have great potential—and out of chemicals, a mature, slow-growth industry. Fisher, renowned at Motorola for forming strategic alliances with other electronics companies to gain technologies or market toeholds, will likely be searching Kodak's labs for overlooked ideas to push into the market.

Margin pressures may also lead to deeper cuts. Kodak has already spun off its Eastman Chemical division. Publicly, it says that its Sterling Drug division is not for sale; that stance may simply be timing, though, for health-care reform is battering the market values of drug companies.

Still, Fisher is optimistic about Kodak and its core product. He—and analysts—think he can stem the outward flow of market share and attain big growth overseas. After all, as Kodak executives like to point out, half of the world's citizens don't take pictures yet.

SOURCE: Peter Nulty, "Kodak Grabs for Growth Again," *Fortune*, May 16, 1994, pp. 76–78.

scanning and forecasting, respectively) and to try to make sense of it all. This is a direct result of the complexity and constant change in the environments in which organizations operate, environments that one executive could never fully understand and manage.

SWOT analysis becomes a team effort performed jointly by functional specialists from marketing, production, finance, etc. These experts review the environments closest to their specialities, and bring issues they see as critical to the attention of their peers from other functions, as well as general managers who have responsibilities for overall or integrated SWOT analysis. At this stage in the SWOT analysis, the team debates issues, brings conflicts between functions to the surface, prioritizes issues, and plans actions.

In another, more formal method for assessing external environmental factors as part of a SWOT analysis, managers can gather and analyze feedback from key employees. Environmental assessment specialists for the Sun Oil Exploration and Production Company developed such a system to rate the relative importance of various external environmental factors. Key employees

---

TABLE 2.5

Some Questions to Determine the Relevance of Environmental Factors

1. If you could have perfect information about five external factors that affect our operation, what would they be? (For example, crude oil prices, GNP deflator, etc.)
2. What five external factors do you see as the major threats to our business?
3. What five factors would you like to know about our competitors' future plans?
4. If you were asked to define a company strategic direction, what five external factors would you feel would be most critical in performing this task?
5. What five external areas would be the most likely to show changes which would be most favorable to the company's future?

SOURCE: Allen H. Mesch, "Developing an Effective Environmental Assessment Function," *Managerial Planning*, March–April 1984, p. 19. Reprinted by permission of The Planning Forum, The International Society for Strategic Management and Planning.

---

from various functions at Sun were asked to respond to the questions listed in Table 2.5, and their answers were analyzed. Sun's specific objective was to guide top managers in understanding the external environment in which the firm operated and to give them some perspective on possible future events that might pose threats or offer opportunities.[19]

Managers can modify this basic data gathering method to tap other sources of information, such as customers or consultants. For example, many firms routinely conduct extensive interviews with follow-up questionnaires through their marketing departments to get feedback on customer satisfaction or dissatisfaction. This research can be viewed as assessing the customer component of the firms' environments. Likewise, a firm with an active international business might survey a small group of outside consultants (such as Kissinger and Associates, headed by former Secretary of State Henry Kissinger). By analyzing the consultants' responses, the firm could develop a better understanding of the political risks involved in expanding operations in a particular country. These two data gathering efforts have very different focuses, but both can be seen as forms of environmental scanning.

Information gathered from key employees can also help managers better understand the *internal* environment of the organization. In this situation, the questions focus on the primary components of the internal environment: the organizational component, marketing component, financial component, personnel component, and production component. Table 2.6 presents several questions that might be asked in connection with such an internal analysis. Part IV of this text examines production, finance, and marketing with emphasis on how these functions might contribute to cross-functional analysis. Studies have tried to identify the specific data sources on which managers base their environmental analyses. One study found that managers seek important information from daily newspapers such as *The New York Times,* publications of industry groups such as The Conference Board, business magazines such as *Fortune,* consultants, government publications, and seminars. These same businesspeople rated literary magazines such as *The New Yorker,* universities, professional association reports from groups such as the World Future

---

TABLE 2.6

Sample Questions for an Internal Environmental Analysis

ORGANIZATIONAL COMPONENT

Is the organizational culture well-matched to the requirements of the competitive environment?
Does the company delegate authority appropriately?
Is the organization structure of the company appropriate?
Are jobs and performance goals clearly understood by workers?

MARKETING COMPONENT

Is market research used to best advantage?
Is advertising used efficiently and effectively?
Can the product distribution system be improved?

FINANCIAL COMPONENT

Does analysis of the income statement reveal potential improvements?
Does analysis of the balance sheet reveal potential improvements?
Can break-even analysis be used to better align costs in relation to profits?

PERSONNEL COMPONENT

Are training programs adequate?
Can procedures for recruitment and selection of employees be improved?
Is the performance appraisal system fair and accurate?

PRODUCTION COMPONENT

Can the organization improve its level of technology?
Can the flow of work within the plant be made more efficient?
What form does the quality improvement system take?

Society, academic journals such as the *Harvard Business Review,* and privately published newsletters such as the Kiplinger Letter as relatively unimportant sources of external information.[20]

Figure 2.3 provides a general overview of the data sources that managers can use for environmental analysis. Several additional sources of data available to managers are cited in the Appendix to Chapter 13.

Scanning Systems   Scanning systems can take many different forms. Perhaps the most widely accepted method for categorizing these systems divides them into three types.[21]

1. Irregular scanning systems: These consist largely of ad hoc studies, often in response to environmental crises (such as an energy shortage). They focus mainly on the past in an effort to identify events that have already taken place. Emphasizing intermediate or short-run reactions to crises, irregular scanning systems pay little attention to future environmental events.
2. Regular scanning systems: These systems revolve around regular reviews of the environment or selected strategic environmental components. These reviews are often made annually. Because such a scan is perceived as decision oriented, management commonly reviews the results during decision

FIGURE 2.3   General Sources of Information for Environmental Analysis

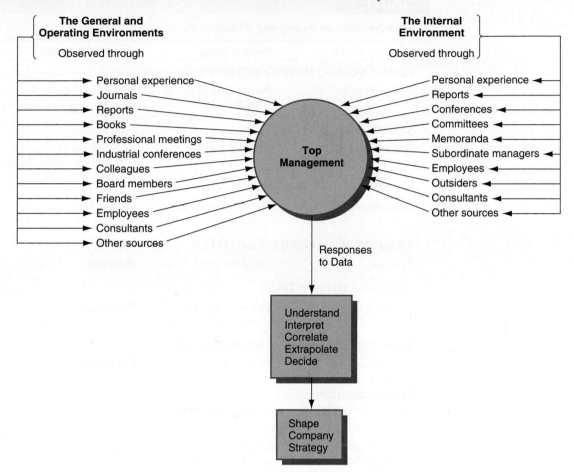

opportunities such as annual planning exercises. The focus of such a system is primarily retrospective, but some thought is given to future conditions assumed to be evolving within the environment.

3. Continuous scanning systems: These systems constantly monitor components of the organizational environment. Such scanning is an ongoing activity and is not performed by a committee set up temporarily for the sole purpose of completing a scan. Established boundary-spanning offices often coordinate this activity. Continuous scanning systems tend to be more future oriented than either irregular or regular systems.

Table 2.7 compares these three scanning systems along several dimensions. As one moves from the irregular model to the regular model to the continuous model, scanning activities generally become more sophisticated and have longer-term effects on organizational operations. A continuous scanning system generally reflects a serious, sustained commitment to environmental analysis. The first environmental analysis that many organizations conduct takes the form of some type of irregular system. Over time, this irregular scanning system can evolve into a regular and then into a continuous scanning system.

TABLE 2.7

Comparison of Scanning Models

Irregular Model	Regular Model	Continuous Model
MEDIA FOR SCANNING ACTIVITY		
Ad hoc studies	Periodically updated studies	Structured data collection and processing systems
SCOPE OF SCANNING		
Specific events	Selected events	Broad range of environmental systems
MOTIVATION FOR ACTIVITY		
Crisis initiated	Decision and issue oriented	Planning process oriented
TEMPORAL NATURE OF ACTIVITY		
Reactive	Proactive	Proactive
TIME FRAME FOR DATA		
Retrospective	Primarily current and retrospective	Prospective
TIME FRAME FOR DECISION IMPACT		
Current and near future	Near-term	Long-term
Organizational makeup		
Various staff agencies	Various staff agencies	Environmental scanning unit

SOURCE: Liam Fahey and William R. King, "Environmental Scanning for Corporate Planning," *Business Horizons,* August 1977, p. 63. Reprinted from *Business Horizons* (August 1977). Copyright 1977 by the Foundation for the School of Business at Indiana University. Used with permission.

However, regardless of the scanning approach selected, we must emphasize that the *interpretation* of the data, not the quantity or timing of the data collected, determines how the data are used in making strategic decisions.

Forecasting Systems   Environmental forecasting, a critical step in SWOT analysis, is the process of identifying strategic issues that will affect an organization's environment at some future time. Most companies find that forecasting future strategic issues is critical to organizational success.

When they perform environmental forecasts, managers try to predict the future status of strategic issues at each environmental level. An organization's environmental forecasts commonly include economic forecasts, social forecasts, political forecasts, and technological forecasts. For example, technological innovations in microelectronics and telecommunications could shift literally millions of jobs back to the home and out of the factories and offices into which the Industrial Revolution swept them.[22] Managers who judge this technological issue to be important to the future success of their organizations should already be busy planning how to cope with this trend if and when it materializes.

Naturally, the types of forecasts made by any one organization depend on the unique situation confronting that organization. Several environmental trends, however, are commonly followed by firms in very different industries. These trends are shown in Table 2.8.

TABLE 2.8

Important External and Internal Environmental Trends

EXTERNAL TRENDS

1. Trends in the global market place (protectionism versus free trade)
2. Growth of government as a customer
3. Development of the European Community
4. Business with socialist countries
5. Economic and political trends in developing countries
6. Monetary trends
7. Inflationary trends
8. Emergence of the multinational firm
9. Technology as a competitive tool
10. Bigness as a competitive tool
11. Saturation of growth
12. Emergence of new industries
13. Technological breakthroughs
14. Growth of the service sector
15. Affluent consumers
16. Changes in age distributions of customers
17. Selling to reluctant consumers
18. Social attitudes toward business
19. Government controls
20. Consumer pressures
21. Union pressures
22. Impact of society's concern with ecology
23. Impact of zero-growth advocates
24. Shrinking product life cycles
25. Intra-European nationalism
26. Conflict between multinational firms and national interests
27. Public distrust of business
28. Shrinking forecasting horizons
29. Strategic surprises
30. Competition from developing countries
31. Strategic resource shortages
32. Redistribution of power within the firm
33. Changing work attitudes
34. Pressures for employment maintenance

INTERNAL TRENDS

1. Size
2. Complexity
3. Structure
4. Systems
5. Communications
6. Power structure
7. Role definitions

Continued

TABLE 2.8

Continued

8. Centralization/decentralization
9. Values and norms
10. Management style
11. Management competence
12. Logistical competence
13. Capital intensity
14. Technological intensity
15. Product diversification
16. Market diversification
17. Technological diversification
18. Other

SOURCE: Adapted from H. Igor Ansoff, "Strategic Issues Management," *Strategic Management Journal* 1 (1980):139. Copyright 1980 by John Wiley & Sons. Reprinted by permission of John Wiley & Sons, Ltd.

TABLE 2.9

Methods of Environmental Forecasting

1. *Expert opinion.* Knowledgeable people are selected and asked to assign importance and probability ratings to various possible future developments. The most refined version, the Delphi method, puts experts through several rounds of event assessment, where they keep refining their assumptions and judgments.
2. *Trend extrapolation.* Researchers fit curves (linear, quadratic, or *S*-shaped growth curves) through past time series to serve as a basis for extrapolation. This method can be very unreliable if new developments alter the expected direction of movement.
3. *Trend correlation.* Researchers correlate various time series in the hope of identifying leading and lagging relationships that can support forecasts.
4. *Dynamic modeling.* Researchers build sets of equations to try to describe the underlying system. The coefficients in the equations are fitted through statistical means. Econometric models of more than 300 equations, for example, are used to forecast changes in the U.S. economy.
5. *Cross-impact analysis.* Researchers identify a set of key trends (those high in importance and/or probability) and ask, "If event A occurs, what will be the impact on all other trends?" The results are then used to build sets of "domino chains," with one event triggering others.
6. *Multiple scenarios.* Researchers build pictures of alternative futures, each internally consistent and with a certain probability of happening. The major purpose of the scenarios is to stimulate contingency planning.
7. *Demand/hazard forecasting.* Researchers identify major events that would greatly affect the firm. Each event is rated for its convergence with several major trends taking place in society and for its appeal to each major public group in the society. A higher convergence and appeal increases the probability that the event will occur. The highest-scoring events are then researched further.

SOURCE: Based on James R. Bright and Milton E. F. Schoeman, *A Guide to Practical Technological Forecasting* (Englewood Cliffs, N.J.: Prentice-Hall, 1973).

Many environmental forecasting techniques are available to managers. Some of these techniques (such as seeking expert opinions) can be fairly simple; others (such as trend extrapolation) can be quite complex. Some organizations may need to hire experts from outside the organization to apply these methods properly. Several forecasting techniques are presented and defined in Table 2.9.

EVALUATING THE ENVIRONMENTAL ANALYSIS PROCESS

Organizations perform environmental analysis to help them achieve their goals effectively and efficiently. Naturally, some environmental analysis efforts are better than others. Hence, it is crucial to evaluate the environmental analysis process like any other organizational activity.

Some of the important characteristics of appropriately implemented environmental analyses are discussed below. These characteristics can be used as a set of standards against which to compare a particular firm's environmental analysis activities.[23]

A Successful Environmental Analysis Is Linked Conceptually and Practically to Current Planning Operations   If the environmental analysis system is not linked to planning, the results of the analysis will contribute little toward establishing the direction the organization will take in the long run. One method commonly used to achieve this vital integration is to involve key organizational planners in some facet of environmental analysis. To ensure a strong link between planning and environmental analysis at Atlantic Richfield, for example, the manager of environmental issues is directly responsible to the director of issues and planning.[24]

A Successful Environmental Analysis Is Responsive to the Information Needs of Top Management   The client for whom environmental analysis is performed is the firm's top management team. Environmental analysts must thoroughly understand and meet the information needs of the high-level managers within their organizations. They must recognize that these information needs may change over time and adjust the environmental analysis process in accordance with such changes.

A Successful Environmental Analysis Is Continually Supported by Top Management   To be successful, any organizational effort needs the support and encouragement of top management. Environmental analysis activities are no exception. They will be perceived as important by organization members only to the extent that such support is apparent. Without this support, environmental analysis activities will be wasted.

A Successful Environmental Analysis Is Completed by Analysts Who Understand the Skills a Strategist Needs   Environmental analysts should focus on identifying existing and potential strengths, weaknesses, opportunities, and threats suggested by components of the organization's environment. Strategists must interpret the results of environmental analysis in light of their in-depth understanding of company operations. The analyst must share the strategist's skills to contribute to an effective strategy.

SUMMARY

Environmental analysis is the process of monitoring the organizational environment to identify both present and future strengths, weaknesses, opportunities, and threats that may influence the firm's ability to reach its goals. Environmental analysis is done, not by gods, but by humans; therefore we must recognize that human limitations, prior experiences, and biases will affect environmental analysis.

For purposes of analysis, a firm's environment can be divided into three main segments, or levels: the internal environment (consisting of organizational, marketing, financial, personnel, and production components), the operating environment (consisting of the supplier, competition, customer, labor, and international components), and the general environment (consisting of the economic, technological, ethical, political/legal, and social components).

Several techniques are available to help managers develop a useful environmental analysis, all of them developed from basic analysis of strengths, weaknesses, opportunities, and threats—SWOT analysis. More specifically, scanning and forecasting techniques can become parts of the SWOT analysis effort. Scanning is a technique in which the manager reviews data from various levels of the organizational environment in order to keep abreast of critical environmental issues and events. Forecasting is a technique in which the manager attempts to predict the future characteristics of the organizational environment and hence to make decisions today that will help the firm deal with the environment of tomorrow.

Having implemented an environmental analysis process, top managers should continually evaluate and improve it. The process should be linked to current planning operations, responsive to the information needs of key managers, supported by top managers, and performed by people who understand strategy.

The Checklist presents a summary of questions based on this chapter. Use it in analyzing strategic management problems and cases that focus on environmental analysis issues.

KEY TERMS

organizational environment, p. 31
general environment, p. 32
operating environment, p. 34
internal environment, p. 36
SWOT analysis, p. 39

sensemaking, p. 39
strategic issues, p. 41
scanning, p. 42
forecasting, p. 42

CHECKLIST

Analyzing Environmental Issues in Problems and Cases

___ 1. Does the strategic management problem or case raise environmental analysis issues?

___ 2. Are factors in the general environment being appropriately considered as part of the environmental analysis?

___ 3. Are factors in the operating environment being appropriately considered as part of the environmental analysis?

___ 4. Are factors in the internal environment being appropriately considered as part of the environmental analysis?

___ 5. In what way is the firm organizing its SWOT analysis?

___ 6. Does the organization have a properly functioning environmental scanning system?

___ 7. Is environmental forecasting properly employed during the environmental analysis process?

___ 8. Does the organization spend enough time evaluating and improving its environmental analysis process?

Additional Readings

Diffenbach, John, "Corporate Environmental Analysis in Large U.S. Corporations." *Long Range Planning* 16, no. 3 (1983), pp. 107–116.

Drucker, Peter F. "Managing for Tomorrow." *Industry Week,* April 14, 1980, pp. 54–64.

———. *Managing in Turbulent Times.* New York: Harper & Row, 1980.

Goss, Tracey, Richard Pascale, and Anthony Athos. "The Reinvention of the Roller Coaster: Risking the Present for a Powerful Future." *Harvard Business Review,* November/December 1993, p. 97.

Guth, William D. *Handbook of Business Strategy.* Boston: Warren, Gorham & Lamont, 1985.

Heath, Robert, and Associates. *Strategic Issue Management.* San Francisco: Jossey-Bass, 1988.

Hofstede, Geert. *Culture's Consequences: International Differences in Work Related Values.* Beverly Hills, Calif.: Sage, 1980.

Nadler, David, Marc Gerstein, and Robert Shaw. *Organizational Architecture.* San Francisco: Jossey-Bass, 1992.

Thomas, James B., Shawn M. Clark, and Dennis Gioia. "Strategic Sensemaking and Organizational Performance." *Academy of Management Journal,* April 1993, pp. 239–270.

CASE

RYKA'S SWOT ANALYSIS HELPS IT TO TAKE ON THE BIG GUYS

Finding a product niche wasn't difficult for Sheri Poe; keeping it to herself was the hard part.

When Poe came up with the idea for a women's athletic shoe, the competition was a vast wasteland—no one else had a shoe like hers—yet overwhelmingly formidable, due to competitors' brand recognition and marketing and advertising budgets. But Poe made Ryka, her Norwood, Massachusetts, company, something different: Its shoes were designed *for* a woman's foot, *based on* a woman's foot, not on a smaller version of a man's foot. "Women have different hips and pelvises and their feet strike the ground differently," said Poe. "We developed a special last (a block of foot-shaped plastic on which shoes are made) that takes that into consideration."

Poe said that retailers recognized the need for Ryka's shoes, and industry analysts agreed that Ryka was the only athletic shoemaker designing strictly for women. (Its giant competitors have since adopted special lasts more friendly to the female foot.) Like all small companies entering crowded markets, however, Ryka needed to get attention for its innovation. Also, no upstart company can compete in a market where athletic-shoe companies spend hundreds of millions of dollars on advertising.

With a smaller budget, Ryka has ventured onto smaller avenues. Its marketers discovered that the syndicated TV fitness show hosted by Jake Steinfield, a Hollywood body trainer, had a 70 percent female audience. Ryka gave the bodybuilder an undisclosed amount of stock and a small stipend to outfit his assistants in Ryka shoes.

Quality control is another problem common to small companies. Ryka confronted difficulties perfecting its patented technology—a nitrogen molding resembling clear-rubber bouncing balls that fit into the foundation of the shoe. Quality problems, including poor stitching, prompted one athletic-shoe chain to return almost its entire fall shipment to Ryka. The company corrected the molding problems and its distributors became happier. "We think their technology is excellent," said a spokesman for Jordan Marsh. "Their styling is definitely contoured for a woman's foot."

The marketing message continued to focus on shoes made by women for women. This was no accident, since the idea for Ryka arose during Poe's latent recovery from a sexual assault 21 years earlier. She wove her story into a marketing message that helped boost Ryka's sales 53 percent in 1992, to $12 million. A hard-edged print advertising campaign inspired by Poe's intimate history juxtaposed the image of a woman working out with the photo of a teary-eyed woman, with copy that read: "Sometimes the only way to work it out is to work it out."

Though the campaign received mixed reviews, it worked. The six-year-old company expected to grow another 53 percent in 1993 to more than $18 million in sales. Through a foundation that Poe established, groups helping women who have been victims of violent crimes receive 7 percent of company profits. Such moves boost Ryka's profile and further define its niche as shoes made for women, by women.

DISCUSSION QUESTIONS

1. Based on Table 2.3, what is your assessment of Ryka's strengths, weaknesses, opportunities, and threats?
2. What would you consider the most significant factor in each of these four groupings?
3. What would you recommend that Poe do about each of these four environmental factors?
4. What three environmental trends do you see as potentially critical to Ryka's future success? Explain why.
5. How should the firm prepare itself for these trends?

SOURCES: *Business Week*, June 14, 1993, pp. 82–83; Suzanne Alexander, "Tiny Ryka Seeks a Foothold with Sneakers for Women," *The Wall Street Journal*, July 31, 1989, p. B2.

Notes

1. Samuel C. Certo, *Modern Management: Diversity, Quality, Ethics, in the Global Environment*, 5th ed. (Boston: Allyn & Bacon, 1994), pp. 41–42.

2. Lawrence Rhyne, "The Relationship of Information Usage Characteristics to Planning System Sophistication," *Strategic Management Journal* 6 (1985), pp. 319–337.

3. Jon Katzenbach and Douglas Smith, *The Wisdom of Teams* (Boston: Harvard Business School Press, 1993).

4. Jane Dutton and Edward Ottensmeyer, "Strategic Issue Management Systems: Forms, Functions, and Contexts," *Academy of Management Review* 12 (1987), pp. 355–365.

5. Philip S. Thomas, "Environmental Analysis for Corporate Planning," *Business Horizons,* October 1974, pp. 27–38.

6. For more information about several of these examples, see Abraham Katz, "Evaluating the Environment: Economic and Technological Factors," in William D. Guth, ed., *Handbook of Business Strategy* (Boston: Warren, Gorham & Lamont, 1985), pp. 2–9.

7. For an illustration of how such factors can affect strategic management, see P. D. Cooper and G. Miaoulis, "Altering Corporate Strategic Criteria to Reflect the Changing Environment: The Role of Life Satisfaction and the Growing Senior Market," *California Management Review* 31 (Fall 1988), pp. 87–97; and "Saving Our Schools," *Business Week,* September 14, 1992, pp. 70–78.

8. R. S. Wilson, "Managing in the Competitive Environment," *Long Range Planning* 17, no. 1 (1984), pp. 50–63.

9. Peter Wright, "MNC—Third World Business Unit Performance: Application of Strategic Elements," *Strategic Management Journal* 5 (1984), pp. 231–240.

10. Michael Porter, *Competitive Advantage* (New York: Free Press, 1985).

11. Pankaj Ghemawat, *Commitment: The Dynamic of Strategy* (New York: Free Press, 1991).

12. Porter, *Competitive Advantage.*

13. C. K. Prahalad and G. Hamel, "The Core Competence of the Corporation," *Harvard Business Review,* May/June 1990, pp. 79–91.

14. James Thomas, Shawn Clark, and Dennis Gioia, "Strategic Sensemaking and Organizational Performance," *Academy of Management Journal* 36, no. 2 (April 1993), pp. 239–270.

15. Henry Mintzberg, *The Nature of Managerial Work* (New York: Harper & Row, 1973).

16. Herbert Simon, *Administrative Behavior,* 2d ed. (New York: Free Press, 1957).

17. Edward Ottensmeyer and Jane Dutton, "Interpreting Environments and Taking Action: Types and Characteristics of Strategic Issue Management Systems," in Charles Snow, ed., *Strategy Organization Design and Human Resource Management* (Greenwich, Conn.: JAI Press, 1989).

18. Jane Dutton and Susan Jackson, "Categorizing Strategic Issues," *Academy of Management Review* 12 (1987), pp. 76–90.

19. Allen H. Mesch, "Developing an Effective Environmental Assessment Function," *Managerial Planning* 32, no. 5 (March/April 1984), pp. 17–22.

20. Subhash C. Jain, "Environmental Scanning in U.S. Corporations," *Long Range Planning* 17, no. 2 (1984), pp. 117–128.

21. Liam Fahey and William R. King, "Environmental Scanning for Corporate Planning," *Business Horizons,* August 1977, pp. 61–71.

22. Boas Shamir and Ilan Solomon, "Work-at-Home and the Quality of Working Life," *Academy of Management Review* 10, no. 3 (1985), pp. 455–464.

23. This section is based on Engledow and Lenz, "Whatever Happened to Environmental Analysis"; Eli Segev, "Analysis of the Business Environment," *Management Review* (1979), p. 59.

24. B. Arrington, Jr., and R. N. Sawaya, "Issues Management in an Uncertain Environment," *Long Range Planning* 17, no. 6 (1984), pp. 17–24.

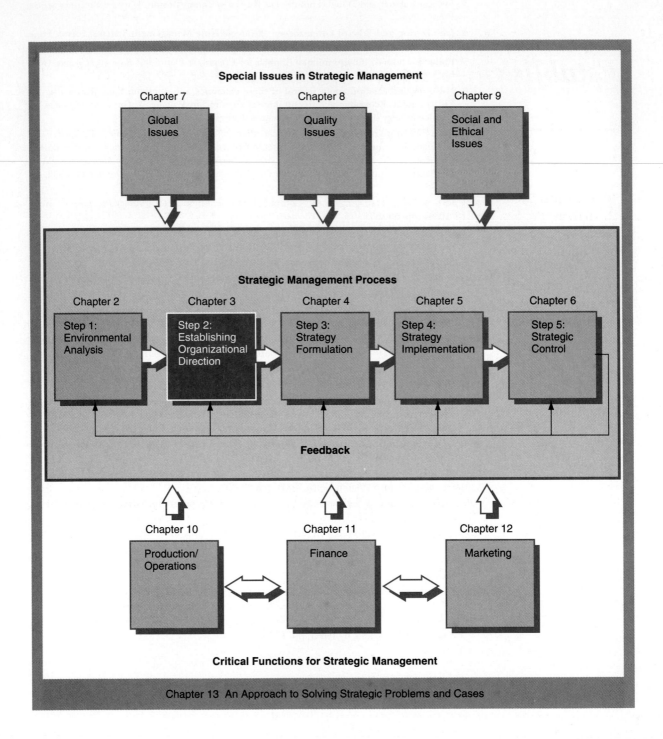

Special Issues in Strategic Management

Chapter 7

Global
Issues

Chapter 8

Quality
Issues

Chapter 9

Social and
Ethical
Issues

Strategic Management Process

Chapter 2

Step 1:
Environmental
Analysis

Chapter 3

Step 2:
Establishing
Organizational
Direction

Chapter 4

Step 3:
Strategy
Formulation

Chapter 5

Step 4:
Strategy
Implementation

Chapter 6

Step 5:
Strategic
Control

Feedback

Chapter 10

Production/
Operations

Chapter 11

Finance

Chapter 12

Marketing

Critical Functions for Strategic Management

Chapter 13 An Approach to Solving Strategic Problems and Cases

Establishing Organizational Direction

In Chapter 2, we discussed environmental analysis, the first step of the strategic management process. That chapter covered the fundamentals of environmental analysis, structures, and interpretations. This chapter focuses on establishing organizational direction, the step of the strategic management process that immediately follows environmental analysis.

Top managers commonly use three key devices to establish and document the direction in which they wish an organization to move: vision, mission, and objectives. Essentially, organizational vision and mission establish the general direction of the firm, and organizational objectives narrow the focus to define more specific targets. Only after incorporating the results of a thorough environmental analysis can managers formulate visions, develop missions, and set consistent and compatible objectives.

FUNDAMENTALS OF ORGANIZATIONAL VISION AND MISSION

Two steps are critical in establishing and maintaining direction in any organization: (1) articulating a vision of the organization's future and (2) translating that vision into a mission that defines the organization's overarching purpose. The section below on the nature of organizational objectives explains how general visions and missions become more tangible as they are translated into focused action. Chapter 4 develops this topic further.

Many successful firms see vision and mission statements as powerful shapers of effective corporate cultures. Taken together, vision and mission statements present the values, philosophies, and aspirations that guide organizational action. These statements provide motivation, and possibly inspiration, to current and future members of the organization. In the sections below, we define and discuss the importance of these potentially powerful concepts.

What Is Organizational Vision?

As part of the strategic management process, an organizational **vision** encapsulates the organization's values and aspirations in the most general terms, without specific statements about the strategies used to attain them. A corporate vision provides a point of connection for various internal and external stakeholders. In his book, *The Fifth Discipline*, Peter Senge points out that an organizational vision is the answer to the question, "What do we want to create?" [1] Senge further explains that shared visions in organizations ". . . create a sense of commonality that permeates the organization and gives coherence to diverse activities." As a result, "[w]ork becomes part of pursuing a larger purpose embodied in the organization's products and services." [2]

Colgate executive Reuben Mark emphasized this need for a vision to transform work when he said, "You're never going to get anyone to charge the machine guns only for financial objectives. It's got to make them feel better, feel part of something." [3] John Rollwagen, former CEO of Cray Research, has reported that this sense of being part of something was brought about at Cray by people seeing themselves working to make the world's fastest computers in partnership with founder and supercomputer design genius Seymour Cray, even though few employees had actually met Cray. These examples illustrate the potential power of a corporate vision to focus the collective energy of insiders and to give outsiders a better idea of what an organization really is.

However, nothing comes without a price. In order to translate the potential power of a vision into real power, organizational leaders need to recognize certain characteristics of visions and how they work. First, developing a vision that is truly shared across an organization, one that generates excitement and commitment, can be a difficult and time-consuming process. According to Senge, this is one reason why a corporate vision often represents the ideas of one or a few people at the very top of the corporate hierarchy, and why it seems to focus more on gaining compliance than on building commitment. [4] Of course, an individual, often a founder, can have a powerful impact on a corporation's vision. However, famous stories of successful visions—James Lincoln at Lincoln Electric, Edwin Land at Polaroid, Andrew Grove at Intel— involve visions that have been widely shared across entire organizations. Often these stories neglect the work that corporate leaders devote to getting others to commit to those leaders' views. [5]

Second, the methods by which a leader tries to sell a vision to others in the organization seem critical. William O'Brien of Hanover Insurance has stated that, "Being a visionary leader is not about giving speeches and inspiring the troops. How I spend my day is pretty much the same as how any executive spends [the] day. Being a visionary leader is about solving day-to-day problems with my vision in mind." [6]

Third, leaders must recognize the complexity of changing an outmoded vision to reflect new realities, possibly those uncovered during environmental analysis. News reports in the mid-1990s recount the Herculean efforts of U.S. corporations to re-create or redefine themselves in order to adapt to new competitive forces. Sears, General Motors, AT&T, and Motorola are examples of firms working to redefine themselves through updated visions of the future, and through new objectives and strategies that might flow from new visions.

The breakup of AT&T spawned seven "Baby Bell" firms (e.g., Bell Atlantic, NYNEX, US West, etc.) spread geographically around the United States. Leaders in these seven new firms have reported enormous difficulties in moving their shared visions away from taking orders from a far-off central office (i.e., AT&T) toward independent action, away from a singular focus on providing local telephone service toward greater diversification. [7] Table 3.1 shows how one firm stated its vision.

TABLE 3.1

Delta's Vision

Getting 74,000 people to agree on anything is no small task. Having spoken with people throughout the Delta system, I can assure you we not only have a shared vision, but also the shared determination to see it reflected in the service we provide.

Much has changed since Delta flew our first passengers in 1929. One thing has not: our commitment to excellence and superior customer service. That commitment is at the core of our vision for the future—one that will see Delta build on its traditional strengths to prosper in a highly competitive global marketplace.

In short, we want Delta to be the **Worldwide Airline of Choice.**

> **Worldwide,** because we are and intend to remain an innovative, aggressive, ethical, and successful competitor that offers access to the world at the highest standards of customer service. We will continue to look for opportunities to extend our reach through new routes and creative global alliances.

> **Airline,** because we intend to stay in the business we know best—air transportation and related services. We won't stray from our roots. We believe in the long-term prospects for profitable growth in the airline industry, and we will continue to focus time, attention, and investment on enhancing our place in that business environment.

> **Of Choice,** because we value the loyalty of our customers, employees, and investors. For passengers and shippers, we will continue to provide the best service and value. For our personnel, we will continue to offer an ever more challenging, rewarding, and result-oriented workplace that recognizes and appreciates their contributions. For our shareholders, we will earn a consistent, superior financial return.

That is the Delta vision. Our challenge, at one of the most critical times in our history, is to realize that vision and to build on our position as a world leader in aviation.

How? By continuing to control costs while providing excellent, high-value service. By taking steps to keep up with innovative competitors and alliances. By knowing how to operate in diverse markets and attract new customers. By recognizing that established ways of doing business that may have served us well in the past will not sustain us in the future. And by remembering at all times that people—customers, our personnel, and shareholders—are our competitive edge.

As we adapt to the new realities of a dynamic international marketplace and changing world, some of the old ways of doing business will no longer apply. But one principle remains paramount: putting people first. This airline is a "people business." Service is the cornerstone of our operation. We will work as a team to meet the needs of our customers with the quality dependable service they have come to expect. With a strong route system; a safe, dependable fleet; and uncompromising integrity, Delta will make its vision a reality and live up to a hard-earned, well-deserved reputation as the **Worldwide Airline of Choice.**

SOURCE: *SKY,* December 1993, p. 10. Delta's Vision For The Future is provided courtesy of Delta Air Lines, Inc.

Vision and Performance

Some evidence suggests that vision-driven companies outperform their competitors in the marketplace. Collins and Porras studied firms identified as visionary by other executives. They found that visionary firms, as a group, performed 55 times better than the overall stock market, and, taken individually, performed 8 times better than their nonvisionary competitors.[8]

Despite this observed link between vision-driven action and performance, some high-profile executives reject the notion that a corporate vision is important. Shortly after taking over as CEO of IBM, Louis Gerstner, Jr. stated, "There's been a lot of speculation as to when I'm going to deliver a vision of IBM. The last thing IBM needs right now is a vision."[9] Gerstner believed that what IBM needed most was a return to basic "blocking and tackling" skills, such as reducing costs and improving market focus. Chrysler's CEO, Robert Eaton, has voiced agreement: "Internally, we don't use the word *vision*. I believe in quantifiable short-term results—things we can all relate to—as opposed to some esoteric thing no one can quantify."[10]

What could account for such variation in views on the topic of vision? Noel Tichy, author and consultant, offers two answers. First, the need for and importance of a vision may differ by industry; a firm operating in a mature industry, such as an automobile component manufacturer, may need a vision less than a firm in an industry, such as biotechnology, that demands a "radically new idea to win in the marketplace."[11] Second, firms experiencing severe financial problems, as IBM was in the mid-1990s, need to focus on short-term survival before they can spare attention for longer-term matters related to vision; one source explains that, "the patient has to survive before you can [set] a workout schedule."[12]

Apart from their direct operating results, some vision-driven firms clearly behave very differently from their more traditional cousins. Consider this statement that appeared in Ben & Jerry's 1990 annual report: "Ben & Jerry's has yet to print nutritional information on packaging of its original super-premium ice cream; it has no paid parental leave policy, and it has only one minority in a senior management position. In the case of energy, due to inadequate record-keeping the company is unable to report on energy conservation actions. Relations with franchises have improved; even so, the company's communication with franchises . . . has been uneven."[13]

The type of corporate behavior reflected in this self-critical passage or in the Body Shop's decision not to advertise in an advertising-driven industry—cosmetics—has caused one observer to note a growing distinction between traditional firms, which try to position an image, and nontraditional firms that seek rather to express their true characters to realize their visions.[14] Table 3.2 shows the differences in these two approaches.

What Is Organizational Mission?

Organizational **mission** is the overarching purpose for which an organization exists. It provides an answer to the question, "Why do we exist?" Senge points out that successful organizations "have a larger sense of purpose that transcends providing for the needs of shareholders and employees. They seek to contribute to the world in some unique way, to add a distinctive source of value."[15] In general, a firm's organizational mission statement contains such

---

TABLE 3.2

Differences between Image Positioning and Character Expression

Image Positioning	Character Expression
To make company or product appealing	To build trust in business relationship
Image leads, reality may follow	Reality leads
Exaggerate trivial differences	Dramatize significant differences
Make claims, support with artificial evidence	Don't make claims, find ways to believably behave differently
Image positioning works even if it's at odds with reality	Consumers hunger for companies they trust. Images at odds with reality risk mistrust.
Communications are seen as messages to convey image	Communications are seen as behavior to express character
Depends on company-sponsored communications	Depends on news media and customer word-of-mouth
Marketing seen as separate from delivery of goods and services	Marketing seen as integral to development and delivery of goods and services

SOURCE: Peter Laundy, "Learning from the Laramie Lawyer's Letter," *Design Statements,* a journal of The American Center for Design, Fall 1992.

---

information as what types of products or services the organization produces, who its customers tend to be, and what core values it holds. **Core values** provide an answer to the question, "How do we want to act, consistent with our mission, along the path toward achieving our vision?"[16]

Many firms summarize and document their organizational missions in **mission statements.** Table 3.3 presents sample mission statements for several organizations, including: Great Scot Supermarkets, a small midwestern grocery store chain in Indiana; Federal Express, an international shipping company; and The Crummer School, a small graduate school of business at Rollins College in Winter Park, Florida.

Contents of Mission Statements

The kind of information contained in a mission statement varies from organization to organization, but most mission statements address some common themes.[17] These themes include:

- *Company product or service:* This information identifies the goods and/or services produced by the organization—what the company offers to its customers.
- *Markets:* This information describes the markets and customers that the organization intends to serve. Who these customers are and where they are located are common themes.

TABLE 3.3

Organizational Mission Statements

GREAT SCOT SUPERMARKETS

Great Scot Supermarkets is a progressive, growth-oriented company recognized as a regional leader in retail foods. We will continue to strive to improve our responsiveness to the needs and concerns of our customers, employees, suppliers, and the communities in which we serve. This will be accomplished through the development of our employees, an emphasis on volume, and profitability. We intend to expand within our existing marketing areas to both protect and improve our positions. As personnel and finances are adequate and opportunities arise, our growth will continue in other areas.

FEDERAL EXPRESS

Federal Express is committed to our People-Service-Profit philosophy. We will produce outstanding financial returns by providing totally reliable, competitively superior, global air–ground transportation of high-priority goods and documents that require rapid, time-certain delivery. Equally important, positive control of each package will be maintained utilizing real-time electronic tracking and tracing systems. A complete record of each shipment and delivery will be presented with our request for payment. We will be helpful, courteous, and professional to each other and the public. We will strive to have a completely satisfied customer at the end of each transaction.

THE CRUMMER SCHOOL

The mission of The Crummer School is to improve management through formal education programs stressing an administrative point of view, research and publication involving new knowledge and teaching materials, and relationships with businesses and the community. In fulfilling this mission the School is committed to programs that emphasize high quality, innovation, problem solving, and the application of management theory. The emphasis of The Crummer School is on the full-time MBA program. The primary target market for this core business is the national pool of applicants, with or without academic backgrounds in business, but including those who have business experience.

- *Technology:* This information generally includes such topics as the techniques and processes by which the organization produces goods and services. This discussion may consist largely of a broad description of organizational production techniques and quality-enhancing methods.
- *Company objectives:* Most mission statements refer to company objectives. For many firms, these include the general ways they propose for dealing with key stakeholders, such as shareholders, customers, or employees.
- *Company philosophy or core values:* A statement of company philosophy (sometimes called a *company creed*) commonly appears as part of the mission statement. A *company philosophy* statement reflects the basic beliefs and values that should guide organization members in conducting organizational business. Table 3.4 describes the Baxter Travenol Company and summarizes its philosophy or core values.
- *Company self-concept:* Mission statements inevitably contain or are accompanied by information on the self-concept of the company. Company self-

---

TABLE 3.4

Baxter Travenol: Description and Philosophy

Baxter Travenol is engaged in the worldwide development, manufacture, and sale of a diversified line of medical-care products and related services. These products and services are used principally by hospitals, blood centers, clinical laboratories, and dialysis centers, and by patients at home under physician supervision. Baxter Travenol products are manufactured in 17 countries and bring quality therapy to millions of patients in more than 100 countries.

FUNDAMENTAL PRINCIPLES

At Baxter Travenol, we are committed to:
Improving health care for people around the world
Meeting the highest standards in responsible corporate citizenship
Attaining a position of leadership in each of the health care markets we serve
Providing our customers with products and services of consistently high quality and value
Sustaining a strong spirit of teamwork through mutual commitment, dedication, and loyalty within our employee family
Achieving consistent, long-term financial growth and the best possible return to our stockholders

SOURCE: 1984 Baxter Travenol Annual Report. Baxter Travenol Laboratories, Inc. See also Baxter Travenol Annual Report, 1993.

---

concept is the company's own view or impression of itself. In essence, the company arrives at this self-concept by assessing its strengths, weaknesses, competition, and ability to survive in the marketplace.

- *Public image:* Mission statements generally contain some reference, either direct or indirect, to the type of impression that the organization wants to leave with its public. In the end, of course, it is not the image that top managers want to project that is important; but the image that the public actually forms. Table 3.2 provides insight into this process.

Such themes, then, as company product or service, market, technology, company goals, philosophy, self-concept, and public image are commonly addressed in a statement of organizational mission and companion statements. Table 3.5 presents a mission statement and related information prepared by Levi Strauss & Company. The Skills Module presents an opportunity for students to develop a mission statement.

TABLE 3.5

Levi Strauss & Company: Mission Statement and Related Information

MISSION STATEMENT

The mission of Levi Strauss & Co. is to sustain profitable and responsible commercial success by marketing jeans and selected casual apparel under the Levi's brand.

Continued

TABLE 3.5

Continued

We must balance goals of superior profitability and return on investment, leadership market positions, and superior products and service. We will conduct our business ethically and demonstrate leadership in satisfying our responsibilities to our communities and to society. Our work environment will be safe and productive and characterized by fair treatment, teamwork, open communications, personal accountability and opportunities for growth and development.

ASPIRATION STATEMENT

We all want a company that our people are proud of and committed to, where all employees have an opportunity to contribute, learn, grow and advance based on merit, not politics or background. We want our people to feel respected, treated fairly, listened to and involved. Above all, we want satisfaction from accomplishments and friendships, balanced personal and professional lives, and to have fun in our endeavors.

When we describe the kind of Levi Strauss & Co. we want in the future what we are talking about is building on the foundation we have inherited: affirming the best of our company's traditions, closing gaps that may exist between principles and practices and updating some of our values to reflect contemporary circumstances.

WHAT TYPE OF LEADERSHIP IS NECESSARY TO MAKE OUR ASPIRATIONS A REALITY?

New Behaviors: Leadership that exemplifies directness, openness to influence, commitment to the success of others, willingness to acknowledge our own contributions to problems, personal accountability, teamwork and trust. Not only must we model these behaviors but we must coach others to adopt them.

Diversity: Leadership that values a diverse work force (age, sex, ethnic group, etc.) at all levels of the organization, diversity in experience, and a diversity in perspectives. We have committed to taking full advantage of the rich backgrounds and abilities of all our people and to promote a greater diversity in positions of influence. Differing points of view will be sought; diversity will be valued and honesty rewarded, not suppressed.

Recognition: Leadership that provides greater recognition—both financial and psychic—for individuals and teams that contribute to our success. Recognition must be given to all who contribute: those who create and innovate and also those who continually support the day-to-day business requirements.

Ethical Management Practices: Leadership that epitomizes the stated standards of ethical behavior. We must provide clarity about our expectations and must enforce these standards through the corporation.

Communications: Leadership that is clear about company, unit, and individual goals and performance. People must know what is expected of them and receive timely, honest feedback on their performance and career aspirations.

Empowerment: Leadership that increases the authority and responsibility of those closest to our products and customers. By actively pushing responsibility, trust and recognition into the organization we can harness and release the capabilities of all our people.

SOURCE: Reprinted with permission from the Feb. 1993 issue of *Training* Magazine. Copyright 1993. Lakewood Publications, Minneapolis, MN. All rights reserved. Not for resale.

SKILLS MODULE
Wal-Mart's Growth Clouds Its Organizational Direction

INTRODUCTION

Establishing an organizational mission and direction is a critical step in the strategic management process. Review the following situation at Wal-Mart and then complete the related skill-development exercise. The exercise affords you the opportunity to review and revise Wal-Mart's organizational vision and strategy.

SITUATION

In the eyes of its detractors, Wal-Mart is the evil behemoth of retailing. The Arkansas-based chain is bigger than K mart and Sears combined, and nearly as big as the entire U.S. department store industry. It is also responsible for putting countless small-town retailers out of business and turning rural downtown areas into ghost towns. Wal-Mart's newest venture, supercenters that combine supermarkets and discount stores, are going up at the rate of more than one a week, and its buyout of a failing Canadian chain's 122 stores provides it with the means for a major thrust across the northern border.

After hearing the chorus of criticism, it would surprise many that, despite its seeming vastness, Wal-Mart controls less than 15 percent of the general merchandise business in the United States, and probably less than 3 percent of the grocery business.

The dichotomy of trying to remain a small-town, aw-shucks shopkeeper while becoming a card-carrying member of the Fortune 500 has presented mixed, albeit still rosy fortunes. In 1993, for example, Wal-Mart's routinely double-digit sales increases fell below budget and declined toward the industry's typical 5 percent. By year's end, however, sales rose 21 percent, to $67.3 billion, while profits increased 17 percent to $2.3 billion.

It was a watershed year for Wal-Mart and all of its retail operations—Sam's Club buyer's-club stores, domestic and international Wal-Mart stores and supercenters, and McLane Co., the country's leading supplier to convenience stores. The company is now so big that it risks creating diseconomies of scale. Its very size, for example, threatens its ability to restock shelves in time to catch trends. Bill Fields, president of the Wal-Mart Stores division, was taken aback recently when he asked one vendor how long it would take to stock one circle rack in each of the chain's 2,500 stores. "Eight months," he was told.

Wal-Mart's corporate culture is also threatened. The chain's late founder, Sam Walton, led from the top, but ran the company from the bottom. Growth has forced Wal-Mart to add more management layers, however, and to restructure into four divisions, themselves further divided by geographic region.

CEO David Glass, for example, now has five levels of management between him and the store manager. "Wal-Mart has achieved the size where you can't run the company," he freely admits. "Nobody can run an $80 billion retail company." His view is to simplify—run it one store at a time. The 25 to 35 Wal-Marts the company plans to build in the Northeast in 1994 will be a good test. Wal-Mart will make its first foray onto Long Island, home to 7 million people—about three times the population of Arkansas, where Wal-Mart has 77 stores—and just as far removed in regional style and taste.

The company will depend on its information infrastructure, a point-of-sale replenishment system, to customize merchandise selections for individual outlets. Already, some 40 regional buyers make sure that Portland, Oregon gets a different color palette than Portland, Maine. But there are glitches. In February, when lawns were covered with snow, stores in Maine were receiving bags of grass and fertilizer. Wal-Mart plans to customize each linear foot of space within its stores using data on purchasing variables. Figuring out the technology will help the chain market down to the household level, increasing sales per square foot and driving down operating costs.

SKILL DEVELOPMENT EXERCISE

Based on the information you have just read, write a mission statement for Wal-Mart. Keep in mind the process of establishing organizational direction.

SOURCE: Bill Saporito, "And the Winner Is Still . . . Wal-Mart," *Fortune*, May 2, 1994, pp. 62–70.

THE NATURE OF ORGANIZATIONAL OBJECTIVES

The first part of this chapter has outlined the role of vision and mission in establishing the character and general direction of the firm. This part focuses on establishing progressively more specific direction through the use of organizational objectives. We will define the term *organizational objectives,* explain their importance, describe two major types of objectives in organizations, and discuss different areas in which organizations should formulate objectives.

What Are Organizational Objectives?

An **organizational objective** is a target toward which an organization directs its efforts. The importance of establishing appropriate objectives for an organization cannot be overemphasized. Clear objectives provide the basic foundation for strategy formulation, strategy implementation, and action planning. Organizational objectives can be used much as navigators use the North Star: you "sight it on your compass and then use it as a means of getting back on track when you stray."[18]

Types of Objectives in Organizations

Organizations typically have two different sets of objectives. **Short-run objectives** identify targets that the organization wants to reach within one or two years. **Long-run objectives** are targets that the organization wants to reach within three to five years.

These two types of organizational objectives differ in significant ways. The most apparent difference, of course, is the period of time within which the organization is attempting to reach the objective. Another important difference between these objectives is how specifically they are written. In general, short-run objectives tend to give more detail about such issues as who will accomplish exactly what tasks, when they will accomplish those tasks, and in what organizational areas they fall.

Areas for Organizational Objectives

Since the early history of business and industry, most organizations have focused on one primary objective: making a profit.[19] Peter Drucker, perhaps the most influential business writer of modern times, has pointed out errors in managing an organization by focusing primarily on only one objective.[20] According to Drucker, organizations should aim at achieving several objectives. Objectives should cover all areas important to the operation of the firm. Drucker has noted eight key areas in which long-run and short-run organizational objectives should be set. Note how well these areas match up to the general themes of mission statements:

1. *Market standing:* The position of an organization—where it stands—relative to its competitors. One of the organization's objectives should indicate the position it wants to achieve relative to its competitors.
2. *Innovation:* Any change made to improve methods of conducting organizational business. Organizational objectives should indicate innovations the organization wants to implement.
3. *Productivity:* The level of goods or services produced by an organization relative to the resources used in the production process. Organizations that use fewer resources to produce specified levels of products are said to be

more productive than organizations that require more resources to produce at the same level. Objectives should set targets.

4. *Resource levels:* The relative amounts of various resources held by an organization, such as inventory, equipment, and cash. Most organizations should set objectives to indicate the relative amounts of each of these assets that they want to hold.

5. *Profitability:* The ability of an organization to earn revenue dollars beyond the expenses necessary to generate the revenue. Organizational objectives commonly indicate the levels of profitability that firms seek.

6. *Manager performance and development:* The quality of managerial performance and the rate at which managers are developing personally. Because both of these areas are critical to the long-term success of an organization, emphasizing them by establishing and striving to reach related organizational objectives is very important.

7. *Worker performance and attitude:* The quality of nonmanagement performance and such employees' feelings about their work. These areas are also crucial to long-term organizational success. The importance of these considerations should be stressed through the establishment of organizational objectives.

8. *Social responsibility:* The obligation of business to help improve the welfare of society while it strives to reach other organizational objectives. Only a few short years ago, setting organizational objectives in this area would have been somewhat controversial. Today, however, such objectives have become commonplace and are considered very important. Note the emphasis placed on this factor in the mission statements of Great Scot and Levi Strauss, shown earlier.

Note in Figure 3.1 that Rockwater, a global engineering and construction firm, has developed four clusters, or groupings, of objectives toward which it works—financial, customer, internal, and growth objectives. Note also that these four sets of objectives are united via the firm's strategy, a topic we will examine in depth in Chapter 4.

Characteristics of High-Quality Organizational Objectives

Objectives exist in some form in virtually all organizations. The quality of objectives, of course, largely determines how useful they actually are. Several guidelines have been developed over time to help managers develop high-quality organizational objectives.

Specific Objectives   Specific objectives indicate exactly what should be accomplished, who should accomplish it, and within what time frame they should accomplish it. Specific details eliminate confusion about objectives and ensure that all organization members know and understand what is expected of them. Furthermore, the step in the strategic management process that follows setting an organizational direction deals with formulating organizational strategy. In general, more specific objectives make it easier for management to develop strategies to reach them. Specific, high-quality organizational objectives provide a foundation on which managers can construct appropriate organizational strategies.

Levels of Effort   Objectives should be set high enough that employees must extend themselves somewhat to achieve them. On the other hand,

FIGURE 3.1   Rockwater's Organizational Objectives

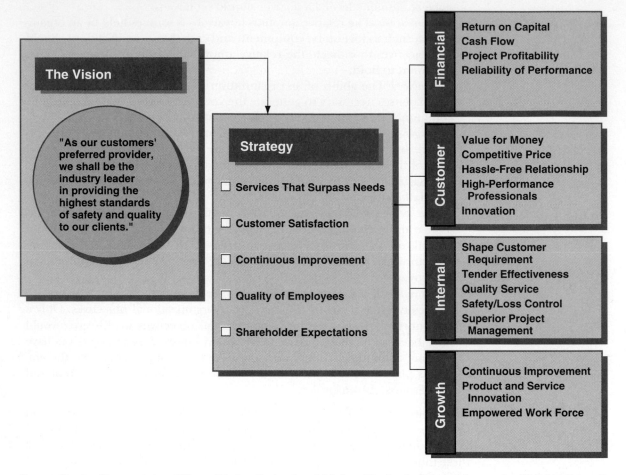

The Vision

"As our customers' preferred provider, we shall be the industry leader in providing the highest standards of safety and quality to our clients."

Strategy

☐ Services That Surpass Needs

☐ Customer Satisfaction

☐ Continuous Improvement

☐ Quality of Employees

☐ Shareholder Expectations

Financial
Return on Capital
Cash Flow
Project Profitability
Reliability of Performance

Customer
Value for Money
Competitive Price
Hassle-Free Relationship
High-Performance Professionals
Innovation

Internal
Shape Customer Requirement
Tender Effectiveness
Quality Service
Safety/Loss Control
Superior Project Management

Growth
Continuous Improvement
Product and Service Innovation
Empowered Work Force

SOURCE: Reprinted by permission of *Harvard Business Review.* An exhibit from "Putting the Balanced Scorecard to Work," by Robert S. Kaplan and David P. Norton, September–October, 1993. Copyright © 1993 by the President and Fellows of Harvard College; all rights reserved.

objectives should not be set so high that employees become frustrated and stop trying! Happily, objectives that challenge employees' abilities are generally more interesting and more motivating than easily attained objectives.[21] Managers should establish reachable organizational objectives, and all organization members should share this view. Workers who view objectives as impossible to reach may utterly ignore the objectives as an indicator of how they should apply their time and effort.

Changing Objectives   Managers must continually assess the organizational environment to recognize when organizational objectives need changes, and they must encourage all organization members to identify changes they think the firm should make.

Measurable Objectives   A measurable objective, sometimes called an **operational objective,** is an objective stated in such a way that an attempt to attain it can be compared to the objective itself to determine whether it actually has been attained. Confusion about whether an objective has been attained can result in conflict and poor relations between managers working at different levels of a firm.

Consistent Long-Run and Short-Run Objectives   Managers should establish organizational objectives that reflect a desirable mix of time frames and that support one another. Long-term objectives must be consistent with the organizational vision and mission, setting targets to be hit within a three-year to five-year period. Short-run objectives must be consistent with long-run objectives, setting targets to be reached within one or two years. As a general rule, shorter-run objectives should be derived from, and lead to the attainment of, longer-run objectives.

Figure 3.2 continues the example of Great Scot Supermarkets, which we introduced earlier. It illustrates objectives for that firm consistent with its organizational mission.

THE PROCESS OF ESTABLISHING ORGANIZATIONAL DIRECTION

The first two parts of this chapter have discussed the fundamentals of organizational visions, missions, and objectives. This section focuses on the *process* of establishing an organizational direction. This process consists of three major steps: (1) reflecting on the results of environmental analysis, (2) developing an appropriate vision and mission, and (3) establishing appropriate organizational objectives. The Company Example discusses a facet of organizational direction at Pillsbury.

Step 1: Reflecting on the Results of Environmental Analysis

Environmental analysis should provide managers with adequate information for *reflection*. It should draw data from all levels of the organizational environment—the general, operating, and internal environments. Analysis of this information, often performed by a cross-functional team, should establish the relevance of these data, and of various other issues, to the organization's performance.

Step 2: Developing an Appropriate Vision and Mission

Information derived from environmental analysis serves as a solid foundation on which to build an organizational vision and mission. Once managers understand both the internal and external organizational environments, they are better equipped to develop an appropriate vision and mission for the organization. These vision and mission statements reflect the organization's relationship to its environment and thereby increase the probability of its long-term survival. In addition, a mission statement identifies the organization's core values, which specify how it will act as it moves to fulfill its vision.

Step 3: Developing Appropriate Organizational Objectives

After developing vision and mission statements the organization needs to set organizational objectives that are consistent with its vision and mission. Because of the fundamental importance of profit in the business context, we focus our discussion on setting profit objectives. Remember that firms set objectives in many areas, as discussed earlier (market share, innovation, productivity, resource levels, manager and worker performance and development, and social responsibility) in addition to profitability. However, since

FIGURE 3.2 Consistency of Possible Mission and Objectives for Great Scot Supermarkets

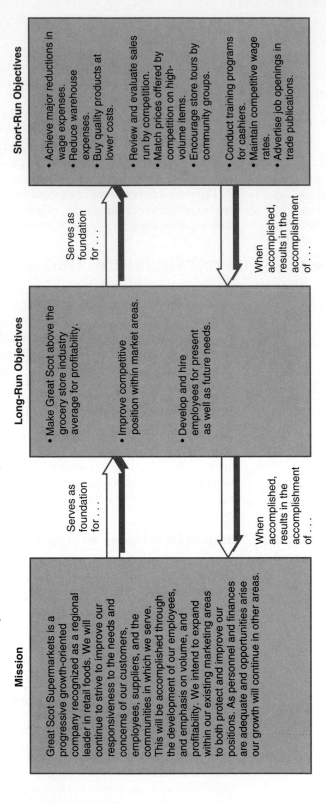

Mission

Great Scot Supermarkets is a progressive growth-oriented company recognized as a regional leader in retail foods. We will continue to strive to improve our responsiveness to the needs and concerns of our customers, employees, suppliers, and the communities in which we serve. This will be accomplished through the development of our employees, and emphasis on volume, and profitability. We intend to expand within our existing marketing areas to both protect and improve our positions. As personnel and finances are adequate and opportunities arise our growth will continue in other areas.

Serves as foundation for . . .

When accomplished, results in the accomplishment of . . .

Long-Run Objectives

• Make Great Scot above the grocery store industry average for profitability.

• Improve competitive position within market areas.

• Develop and hire employees for present as well as future needs.

Serves as foundation for . . .

When accomplished, results in the accomplishment of . . .

Short-Run Objectives

• Achieve major reductions in wage expenses.
• Reduce warehouse expenses.
• Buy quality products at lower costs.

• Review and evaluate sales run by competition.
• Match prices offered by competition on high-volume items.
• Encourage store tours by community groups.

• Conduct training programs for cashiers.
• Maintain competitive wage rates.
• Advertise job openings in trade publications.

COMPANY EXAMPLE

Communal Kitchen Charts Pillsbury's Consumer Strategy

Every weekday, more than 2,000 consumers call Pillsbury's toll-free hotline with complaints, questions, and compliments about the company's products. The phone number, printed on Pillsbury packages, promotes a service the Minneapolis manufacturer is more than happy to provide.

As the mix of packaged-foods manufacturers becomes broader and more competitive, sellers of branded goods like Pillsbury are using their toll-free consumer hotline operations to outgun the growing number of private-label products. Although the phone service costs Pillsbury, a unit of Grand Metropolitan PLC, several million dollars a year, the benefits are part of the company's mission of being responsive to its products' users and attuned to trends and changes.

Pillsbury's consumer-service center employees— mostly women, all with college degrees and backgrounds in home economics or nutrition—placate unhappy consumers and make satisfied ones even happier. The Pillsbury phone respondents are themselves satisfied; turnover is low—the last replacement was hired four years ago, pay is around $25,000 a year, and Pillsbury makes sure that these experienced workers are supplied with the best materials available. An extensive computerized database and fat technical manuals, as well as plenty of cookbooks, are close at hand.

The calls function as "a wonderful research tool" and act as a safety net, says Paul Walsh, Pillsbury's chief executive. "If we have a problem with a product, we want to be the first to hear about it."

The calls also provide Pillsbury with important information for its many operations, from product development and marketing to quality assurance and manufacturing. Susan Shlosberg, the company's vice president of consumer relations and technical services, leads an eight-person support staff to analyze data from the calls and expand on it; asking callers about product concepts was a recent idea.

Calls are taped, but each caller's privacy is protected. Shlosberg often plays recordings for product managers and plant employees, letting them hear from the source what consumers think about Pillsbury and its products.

SOURCE: Richard Gibson, "Pillsbury's Telephones Ring with Peeves, Praise," *The Wall Street Journal*, April 20, 1994, pp. B1–B4.

objectives in each of these other areas are ultimately focused on improving the firm's long-term profitability, we believe that profit objectives merit detailed discussion.

Nature of Profitability Objectives   **Profitability objectives** set targets for revenue an organization should earn beyond the expenses necessary to generate the revenue. Profitability objectives commonly state target returns on assets (ROAs), net profit margins, and returns on stockholders' equity. Table 3.6 lists these measures of profitability, defines them, and explains how to calculate them. Although the basic concept of referring to such objectives to manage organizations is not new, their role in strategic management has renewed interest in them.[22]

Guidelines for Establishing Profitability Objectives   Managers generally establish profitability objectives by collecting and analyzing information that compares specific organizational data to similar data for other organizations or groups of organizations. Gathering and analyzing this information enables managers not only to evaluate an organization's current profit performance, but also to determine how high to set profitability objectives.

TABLE 3.6

Profitability Objectives

Profitability Objectives	Description	Calculation Method[a]
Net profit margin	Organizational objective that focuses on the amount of net profit an organization earns in relation to the level of sales it attains	$\dfrac{\text{Net profit}}{\text{Sales}}$
Return on assets (ROA)	Organizational objective that focuses on the amount of net profit an organization earns in relation to its total assets	$\dfrac{\text{Net profit}}{\text{Total assets}}$
Return on stockholders' equity ROE	Organizational objective that focuses on the amount of net profit an organization earns in relation to its equity	$\dfrac{\text{Net profit}}{\text{Stockholders' equity}}$

[a] These ratios are expressed as percentages.

To illustrate how this process works, consider the task of setting objectives for net profit margin, return on assets, and return on stockholders' equity at McDonald's Corporation. Managers would normally begin by gathering past information to get a very broad view of comparable figures for business organizations in general. One source of such information is the industrial composite that appears periodically in Value Line's *Selection and Opinion*. This industrial composite averages profitability data for over 900 industrial, retail, and transportation companies that account for about 80 percent of the income earned by all U.S., nonfinancial corporations.

In addition to this industrial composite information, McDonald's Corporation managers would probably seek to evaluate the performance of companies more closely related to the fast-food business. Information about profitability performance for the restaurant industry, in general, as well as for specific competitors such as Wendy's International, would be very valuable. Information of this sort is also available periodically in Value Line's *Selection and Opinion*.

After gathering all of this information, McDonald's managers would compare it to data compiled on their own company (see Figure 3.3). Analysis of this information would probably lead McDonald's managers to conclude that their firm was performing competitively in the areas of net profit margin, return on investment, and return on stockholders' equity. Significantly unfavorable comparisons in any of these areas would have alerted McDonald's managers that improvement was possible and that profitability objectives should be revised upward. The current data indicate that perhaps the same or slightly higher profitability objectives would be appropriate for McDonald's in the next operating period.

McDonald's managers must also consider, however, that the information they gathered reflects one year only. Gathering the same information and

FIGURE 3.3   McDonald's Profitability Performance

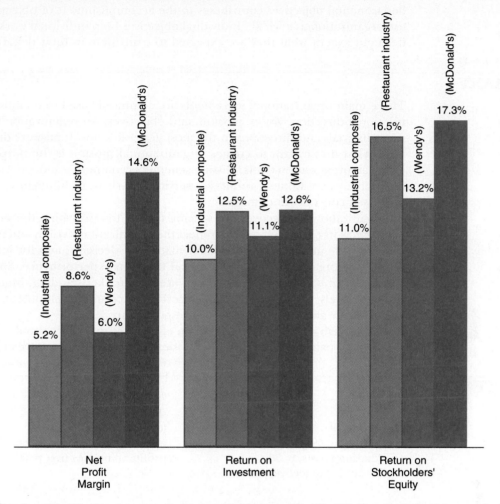

SOURCE: Data from *The Value Line Investment Survey,* June 24, 1994, pp. 294, 302, 312. Note that industrial composite figures are author estimates based on Value Line composites for individual industries.

making the same comparisons for a five-year period might reveal desirable or undesirable trends that organizational objectives should address.

The case at the end of the chapter is designed to give you some experience in spotting issues that may affect the objectives that a company establishes for itself.

DEVELOPING INDIVIDUAL OBJECTIVES

After setting overall organizational objectives, managers must continue to develop an effective and efficient pattern of objectives within an organization culminating in establishment of objectives for each individual working in significant organizational segments. **Individual objectives** are targets that specific people within an organization attempt to reach. Individual objectives are designed so that accomplishing each one contributes to the accomplishment of the broader objectives of the department. In turn, the accomplishment of departmental objectives contributes to the accomplishment of objectives for the organization as a whole. Individual objectives help individual workers understand exactly what they are expected to contribute to their departments.

SUMMARY

Three main organizational ingredients are commonly used to establish organizational direction: vision, mission, and objectives. An organization's vision states its goals and directions in the most general terms. It answers the question, What do we want to create? Organizational mission is the purpose for which an organization exists. Mission statements commonly address the topics of company core values, products or services, markets, technologies, philosophies, self-concepts, and images.

Organizational objectives are specific targets toward which the organization directs its efforts. Objectives reflect the organization's vision and mission. They provide important guidance for managers' decisions and for initiatives to increase organizational efficiency and to evaluate performance. Short-run and long-run objectives focus on such areas as market standing, innovation, resource levels, profitability, manager performance and development, worker performance and attitude, and social responsibility.

To establish organizational direction effectively, managers should develop a consistent pattern of organizational vision, mission, and objectives.

KEY TERMS

vision, p. 55
mission, p. 58
core values, p. 59
mission statements, p. 59
organizational objective, p. 64

short-run objective, p. 64
long-run objective, p. 64
operational objective, p. 66
profitability objective, p. 69

CHECKLIST Analyzing Organizational Direction in Problems and Cases

___ 1. Does the strategic problem or case involve issues related to organizational direction?

___ 2. Does the case show evidence of a clear organizational vision and mission?

___ 3. Does the organizational mission appropriately reflect the organizational environment?

___ 4. Does the situation involve organizational objectives that appropriately reflect the organizational mission?

___ 5. Are suitable types of objectives employed?

___ 6. Have objectives been established in all areas critical to organizational success?

___ 7. Are the objectives that are apparent in the case or situation high-quality objectives?

___ 8. Are individual objectives sufficiently emphasized?

___ 9. Is an acceptable process for establishing organizational direction apparent in the situation or case?

Additional Readings

Chajet, Clive. "The Making of a New Corporate Image," *Journal of Business Strategy*, May/June 1989, p. 18.

Kolesar, Peter J. "Vision, Values, and Milestones: TQM at Alcoa." *California Management Review*, Spring 1993, p. 133.

Langeler, Gerard H. "The Vision Trap." *Harvard Business Review*, March/April 1992, p. 46.

Mitroff, Ian I. *Stakeholders of the Organizational Mind*. San Francisco: Jossey-Bass, 1983.

Ruch, Richard S., and Ronald Goodman. *Image at the Top*. New York: Free Press, 1983.

Schoemaker, Paul J. H. "How to Link Strategic Vision to Core Capabilities." *Sloan Management Review*, Fall 1992, p. 67.

Smith, Patrick. "How to Present Your Firm to the World," *Journal of Business Strategy*, January/February, 1990, p. 32.

CASE

INTEL STRATEGY TAKES A CHANCE

Andy Grove is taking a big risk. The CEO of Intel, maker of microprocessor chips, is basing his business strategy on an assumption. Grove guesses that AT&T, IBM, Matsushita, Motorola, Philips, Sega, and Sony can't keep up with his firm. He's sure enough that he's gambling nearly a third of Intel's revenues, $3.5 billion in 1994, that the company will dominate a slew of businesses in which it has no experience.

Such aggressiveness has worked in the past. The so-called "Mad Hungarian" poured money into product development and factories to establish the Santa Clara, California, company as the hardware companion of Bill Gates's software champ, Microsoft. Today, Intel supplies the microprocessors in about three-quarters of all PCs sold. Its gross profit margin is 58 percent; net earnings last year were $2.3 billion on sales of $8.8 billion, making Intel the most profitable company of its size in the world. Its size is fluid, however; Intel is growing so fast, it doubles in size roughly every two years.

So, Grove might ask, what is the risk in his gamble? The firm faces growing competition from other chip makers, notably the RISC chip, an inexpensive, ultrafast microprocessor developed by IBM, Motorola, and Apple Computer and featured in Apple's PowerPC series. Also clonemakers have scored a crucial victory in a lawsuit affirming their right to copy Intel codes governing the behavior of microprocessors.

Grove thinks that his company can stay on top by flooding the market with ever faster, yet still inexpensive, chips. Its newest chip, the Pentium, is proof of how fast Intel can move. The chip crunches data at almost twice the rate of the best-selling chip today (also Intel's). The goal is simple: create chips to enable PC producers to double the performance of their machines at every price point every year. New, more powerful chips should appear every year or two.

Pushing down prices is part of the objective. Grove argues that what Intel loses in profit margins it can more than make up in volume. He says he doesn't care about margin percentages. "I want to increase dollar profits, and they are a product of margin times unit volume."

Grove anticipates that volume will grow not from corporate customers, but from the demands of consumers and home-office users for convenience and novelty. The ultimate aim: to transform the PC powered by Intel chips into an all-purpose consumer device for heading down the information superhighway, controlling the TV, VCR, telephone, answering machine, and so on.

Two lines, printed on fortune cookie slips, conveyed Grove's strategy to Intel's 29,500 employees:

1. Job 1

2. Make the PC "IT"

Grove says the first line is a reminder to strengthen Intel's No. 1 position in the microprocessor market and establish Pentium as the best-selling microprocessor faster than any before it. Line 2 refers to Grove's desire to turn the PC into the cornerstone of 21st-century information technology.

Getting there, says Grove, is easier because there is competition. If it wasn't for the threat of PowerPC, and what he calls the "megabattle," Intel would not be moving so quickly. "We are making gutsier moves investment-wise, pricing-wise, every way, because we've got a competitive threat," he says. "The net result is we'll get to advance to the next level of competition."

DISCUSSION QUESTIONS

1. What is Grove's vision for Intel? What is Intel's mission?

2. How effectively do Intel's organizational objectives define and fulfill its mission?

3. What is the purpose of the fortune cookie slips?

4. How well do Grove's objectives for Intel contribute to the objective of profitability?

SOURCE: David Kirkpatrick, "Intel Goes for Broke," *Fortune,* May 16, 1994, pp. 62–68.

Notes

1. Peter Senge, *The Fifth Discipline: The Art and Practice of the Learning Organization* (New York: Doubleday, 1990), p. 206.

2. Ibid., p. 207–208.

3. B. Dumaine, "What the Leaders of Tomorrow See," *Fortune,* July 3, 1989, pp. 49–62.

4. Senge, *Fifth Discipline,* p. 206.

5. Thomas Stewart, "GE Keeps Those Ideas Coming," *Fortune,* August 12, 1991, pp. 41–49.

6. Senge, *Fifth Discipline,* p. 217.

7. Edward Ottensmeyer and Robert McGowan, "US West: The Architecture of Corporate Transformation," *Business Horizons,* January/February 1991.

8. Reported in Chris Lee, "The Vision Thing," *Training,* February 1993, pp. 25–32.

9. Michael Miller and Laurie Hays, "Gerstner's Nonvision for IBM Raises a Management Issue," *The Wall Street Journal,* July 29, 1993, pp. B1, B6.

10. Douglas Lavin, "Robert Eaton Thinks 'Vision' Is Overrated and He's Not Alone," *The Wall Street Journal,* October 4, 1993, pp. A1, A8.

11. Ibid., p. A1.

12. Miller and Hays, "Gerstner's Nonvision," p. B6.

13. Reported in Peter Laundy, "Learning from the Laramie Lawyer's Letter," *Design Statements,* Fall 1992, pp. 3–11.

14. Ibid., p. 5.

15. Senge, *Fifth Discipline,* pp. 223–224.

16. Ibid., p. 224.

17. This discussion is based largely on John A. Pearce II, "The Company Mission as a Strategic Tool," *Sloan Management Review,* Spring 1982, pp. 15–24.

18. Marshall E. Dimock, *The Executive in Action* (New York: Harper and Brothers, 1945), p. 54. For a more recent discussion of this issue, see Samuel C. Certo, *Principles of Modern Management: Functions and Systems,* 4th ed. (Boston: Allyn & Bacon, 1989), pp. 59–60.

19. Gordon Donaldson, "Financial Goals and Strategic Consequences," *Harvard Business Review,* May/June 1985, pp. 57–66.

20. Peter F. Drucker, *The Practice of Management* (New York: Harper & Row, 1954), pp. 62–65, 126–129.

21. For more information about the effect of challenge on motivation of workers, see Frederick Herzberg, "One More Time: How Do You Motivate Employees?" *Harvard Business Review,* January/February 1968, pp. 53–62. Due to its continuing relevance for modern managers, this article has been reprinted: *Harvard Business Review,* September/October 1987, pp. 109–120.

22. John H. Quandt, "Setting Strategy Using Variable ROI Analysis," *The Journal of Business Strategy* 5, no. 1 (Summer 1984), pp. 77–79.

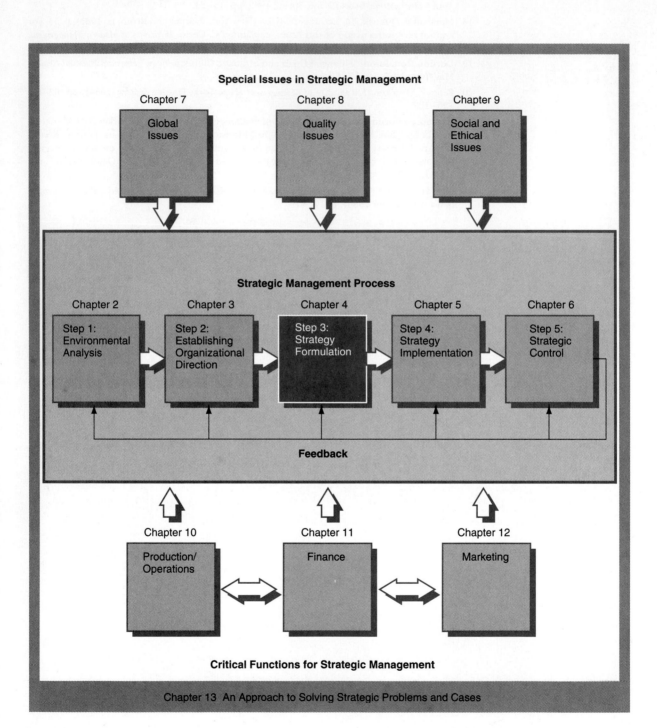

Special Issues in Strategic Management

Chapter 7

Global Issues

Chapter 8

Quality Issues

Chapter 9

Social and Ethical Issues

Strategic Management Process

Chapter 2

Step 1: Environmental Analysis

Chapter 3

Step 2: Establishing Organizational Direction

Chapter 4

Step 3: Strategy Formulation

Chapter 5

Step 4: Strategy Implementation

Chapter 6

Step 5: Strategic Control

Feedback

Chapter 10

Production/ Operations

Chapter 11

Finance

Chapter 12

Marketing

Critical Functions for Strategic Management

Chapter 13 An Approach to Solving Strategic Problems and Cases

CHAPTER 4

Strategy Formulation

Formulating a strategy for an organization involves developing a cohesive plan for achieving objectives by adapting the organization in an appropriate way to its environment. A strategy represents the embodiment of the organization's best efforts to think smart about its future—how to position its goods or services against those of competitors, how to forge tight linkages with its customers, how to build upon or develop its internal competencies, how to prepare for environmental shifts, how to diversify its portfolio of goods or services in ways that build synergy for future competitive strength.

Strategy formulation is primarily an analytical effort that relies heavily on executive judgment and creativity. It draws critical input from the environmental analysis techniques introduced in Chapter 2 in its focus on achieving an adaptive fit for the firm in its environments. Strategy, as we defined it in Chapter 1, is seen as an integrative plan that provides more specific details than the vision or mission statement discussed in Chapter 3. It further refines the general notions of what the organization wishes to create or what its overarching purposes are.

In this chapter, our discussion of strategy formulation is built around the three levels at which organizations formulate strategies. We first discuss business-level strategies, through which firms search for sustainable competitive advantage in their specific industries. We center our presentation around Michael Porter's well-known framework for analyzing the structure of an industry and its profit potential, identifying alternative business-level strategies built on foundations of either differentiation or cost leadership. In this section, we also discuss the enormous difficulties that complicate competitor analysis, and efforts to build sustainable competitive advantage in any industry.

Second, we turn our attention to functional-level strategies which govern management of internal organizational functions (e.g., finance, marketing, R&D) in order to add value to goods and services by mobilizing core competencies. Here, we draw upon Porter's work on the power of value chain analysis to ". . . disaggregate a firm into its strategically relevant activities in order to understand the behavior of costs and the existing and potential sources of differentiation."[1] We consider the ways in which internal activities both support and shape business-level strategies.

Third, we consider corporate or multibusiness strategies, defined here as strategies that seek synergy for an organization through the skillful assembly of a portfolio of businesses or business units, often stretching across several diverse industries. This section explores one fundamental question: How can diversification be managed for long-run effectiveness?

FORMULATING BUSINESS-LEVEL STRATEGIES

Shaping a **business-level strategy** involves making decisions for an entire organization that operates in a single industry. Cray Research, for example, operates only in the supercomputer industry, so its only strategy focuses on that one industry and Cray's position in it. Larger or more diversified firms formulate business-level strategy for strategic business units (SBUs) or product divisions. For example, MTV and Nickelodeon are separate units of Viacom, a diversified entertainment company. Their strategies are developed at the operating unit level, to reflect product and environmental differences. The results are then incorporated into Viacom's corporate strategy, which encompasses business-level strategies for television and radio stations, as well as cable systems.

Business-level strategy making, thus, focuses on a single industry and a few closely related industries that may affect it. Shaping a business-level strategy is a firm's answer to the question, How will we compete in this industry in a way that builds sustainable competitive advantage and, therefore, above-average profitability? As we indicated in Chapter 2, answering this basic question begins with some variation of SWOT analysis.

We begin our discussion in this section by focusing on the opportunities and threats that emerge from analysis of an industry's structure and the critical forces that shape competition and profitability within it. We then turn to the general consideration of strengths (or core competencies) and weaknesses and their effects on business-level strategy. We then use this as a jumping off point for our discussion of functional-level strategies.

Industry Structure Analysis and Competitive Positioning

Michael Porter's framework for industry analysis provides a powerful analytical device for the business strategist.[2] By assessing separately and collectively the strengths of five competitive forces, which shape all industry environments, business-level strategists are better able to position their businesses within their industries. These five forces are (1) the threat of new entrants, (2) the bargaining power of suppliers, (3) the bargaining power of buyers, (4) the threat of substitute products, and (5) the rivalry among existing competitors. Figure 4.1 shows these five forces, plus a number of factors that shape each of them. We discuss each of these critical forces in the sections below.

Threat of New Entrants   Any firm that considers entering an industry brings new capacity and a desire to gain market share and profits, but whether it actually enters the industry depends on several **barriers to entry.** (A number of these are shown in Figure 4.1.) Established firms in an industry may create barriers to entry through experience curve effects, since their cumulative experience in producing and marketing a product often reduces their per-unit costs below those of inexperienced firms. In general, higher entry barriers reduce the likelihood that outside firms will enter the industry.

Thus, a picture emerges of firms that already compete in an industry attempting to create and defend barriers that other firms must overcome to compete themselves. In effect, industry pioneers work hard to set a high price of admission for those who come later. Examples abound of industries where admission is costly (or unaffordable). The soft drink industry is dominated by a few strong competitors, notably Coca-Cola and Pepsi-Co, whose dominance

FIGURE 4.1   Elements of Industry Structure

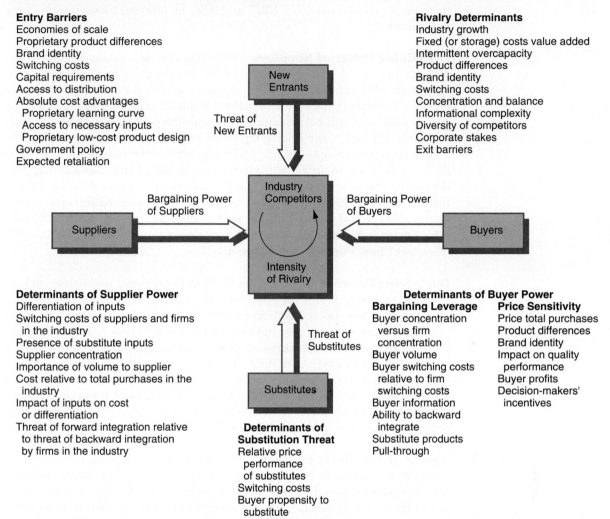

Entry Barriers
Economies of scale
Proprietary product differences
Brand identity
Switching costs
Capital requirements
Access to distribution
Absolute cost advantages
  Proprietary learning curve
  Access to necessary inputs
  Proprietary low-cost product design
Government policy
Expected retaliation

Rivalry Determinants
Industry growth
Fixed (or storage) costs value added
Intermittent overcapacity
Product differences
Brand identity
Switching costs
Concentration and balance
Informational complexity
Diversity of competitors
Corporate stakes
Exit barriers

Threat of
New Entrants

New
Entrants

Bargaining Power
of Suppliers

Bargaining Power
of Buyers

Suppliers

Industry
Competitors

Buyers

Intensity
of Rivalry

Threat of
Substitutes

Substitutes

Determinants of Supplier Power
Differentiation of inputs
Switching costs of suppliers and firms
 in the industry
Presence of substitute inputs
Supplier concentration
Importance of volume to supplier
Cost relative to total purchases in the
 industry
Impact of inputs on cost
 or differentiation
Threat of forward integration relative
 to threat of backward integration
 by firms in the industry

Determinants of
Substitution Threat
Relative price
 performance
 of substitutes
Switching costs
Buyer propensity to
 substitute

Determinants of Buyer Power

Bargaining Leverage	Price Sensitivity
Buyer concentration	Price total purchases
versus firm	Product differences
concentration	Brand identity
Buyer volume	Impact on quality
Buyer switching costs	performance
relative to firm	Buyer profits
switching costs	Decision-makers'
Buyer information	incentives
Ability to backward	
integrate	
Substitute products	
Pull-through	

SOURCE: Adapted and reprinted with the permission of The Free Press, an imprint of Simon & Schuster from COMPETITIVE AD-VANTAGE: Creating and Sustaining Superior Performance by Michael E. Porter. Copyright © 1985 by Michael E. Porter.

of distribution channels represents an especially effective barrier to entry. By one industry estimate, over 1,000 new soft drink products are developed each year; but only a few ever make it into the supermarket due to the barriers created by Coke and Pepsi. There is an important lesson here—entry barriers do not always emerge simply from the nature of an industry; they are created by competitors striving to develop their own sustainable competitive advantages.

Sometimes, of course, barriers can be overcome. A proprietary product innovation developed by a new competitor or a new product for a neglected market niche can leapfrog established competitors, and thus overcome entry barriers. Canon's small copiers gained market share in an industry previously dominated by Xerox. Reebok gained a substantial share of the athletic shoe market by catering initially to a rapidly growing niche—aerobics classes—that had been overlooked by industry leaders such as Nike. Fox Broadcasting lured a significant share of the young television viewing audience away from entrenched rivals CBS, NBC, and ABC by offering focused, innovative programming.

Bargaining Power of Suppliers   Suppliers can be a powerful force in an industry because they may be able to raise the prices of raw materials or reduce their quality. In general, when suppliers are few (i.e., the supplier industry is concentrated), when the suppliers' products are essential, or when the cost of switching suppliers is high, the bargaining **power of suppliers** is high. Suppliers, through their pricing decisions and the competitive strength that supports them, can capture some profit potential in the industry or industries they supply. Thus, in an attractive industry structure, a firm has a strong position relative to its key suppliers. Industries like breakfast cereals or baby foods feature suppliers that are highly competitive sellers of basic commodities (economists would call them *price takers*), such as farmers. Such industries offer buyers significant advantages in bargaining power. Other determinants of supplier power are listed in Figure 4.1.

Bargaining Power of Buyers   Buyers in industry structure analysis include both final consumers and key purchasers throughout the distribution process. The **power of buyers** can force an industry's prices down, bargain for higher quality or more services, play industry competitors against one another, and threaten to integrate backward (i.e., make what they need instead of buying it from another industry). All of these tactics reduce supplier industry profitability. For example, relatively small consumer-products manufacturers may sell to large retailers, such as Sears or Wal-Mart. They have little room to negotiate with such dominant buyers, and cannot expect to receive premium prices for their products. Several determinants of buyer power are shown in Figure 4.1.

Threat of Substitute Products   In a broad sense, all firms in an industry compete with firms in industries that produce substitute products. **Substitution threats** limit potential returns in an industry by placing a ceiling on the prices that firms in the industry can profitably charge. More attractive price-performance alternatives offered by substitutes place a tighter lid on industry profits. For example, the prices charged by a movie theater are affected by the prices of entertainment alternatives, such as cable television. Similarly, the prices vacation travelers pay to airlines for relatively short flights are influenced by the prices of auto or train travel. Some determinants of the degree of substitution threat are shown in Figure 4.1.

Rivalry among Existing Competitors   Porter's concept of **rivalry among competitors** comes closest to what we normally think of as competition in a business setting. Rivalry is the arena of competitive game playing, i.e., taking steps in direct or indirect opposition to those of competitors to build a more defensible position.[3] Rivalry creates exciting headlines for the business press—Coke versus Pepsi in the cola wars, AT&T versus MCI, Reebok versus Nike—the list could go on indefinitely. We are less interested in the specific actions of individual competitors to outfox one another, however, and more interested in the nature of rivalry in the industry as a whole, and the factors that cause rivalry to take a certain shape. Industry rivalry can be described with terms like *price competitive, advertising intensive, technology based,* or *service focused.* For example, technology-based rivalry would describe an industry like biotechnology, where the rivalry is based on applied research and the development of breakthrough drugs. Rivalry of this sort spurs firms to compete to attract the best scientific talent to their side, and winning these bidding wars for the best people may be the key factor in determining future competitive advantage.

Of the factors that shape rivalry in an industry, the most powerful may be industry growth or life cycle stage. Slow demand growth, due to either economic fluctuations or life cycle factors, can transform industry rivalry, for example, in the direction of brutal price competition and away from advertising wars that emphasize product differences. This is especially true when exit barriers are high for industry rivals. This scenario describes the personal computer industry in the early 1990s. As the technology became standardized, rivals could no longer sell unique products for premium prices, they had to slash prices and search for profits through low-cost manufacturing and distribution systems.

Strategy Alternatives

In Porter's framework, analysis of these five forces should guide the development of business strategy. For example, a firm has the best chance of high profitability in an industry characterized by high barriers to entry and weak competitors, weak substitutes, weak buyers, and weak suppliers. Although few industries offer all of these characteristics, the key to strategy formulation is to focus on the particular opportunities and threats in the industry. For example, in an industry with high entry barriers, competition from new entrants may be a minor concern in strategy formulation. Efforts may focus instead on changing the structure of the industry via backward integration (buying out suppliers), forward integration (buying out distribution channels), or horizontal integration (buying out existing competitors).

Typically, however, competitive analysis focuses on rivalry among existing competitors and on the formulation of strategies to outperform other firms in the industry. Porter suggests that firms can choose among three generic strategies: overall cost leadership, differentiation, and focus. The skills and resources needed and the organizational requirements of these strategies are shown in Table 4.1.

By pursuing an **overall cost leadership strategy,** a firm tries to earn above-average returns in its industry despite the presence of strong competitive forces. Cost leadership is accomplished through a consistent emphasis on efficient production of a good or service. Firms that follow cost leadership strategies are often referred to as *low-cost producers* in their industries. This strategic option is popular among firms that have high-volume production facilities and relatively high market shares in their industries. Cost leadership strategies often depend on favorable access to raw materials and the need for considerable financial resources to stay ahead of competitors in acquiring the most efficient manufacturing equipment. However, cost leaders are not always the largest producers in an industry. Southwest Airlines, a growing regional air carrier, has committed itself to a cost leadership strategy. It consistently turns a profit in the problem-plagued U.S. airline industry because its cost per available seat mile is roughly 80 percent of those of its larger rivals. The Company

TABLE 4.1

Porter's Three Generic Strategies and Their Requirements

Generic Strategy	Commonly Required Skills and Resources	Common Organizational Requirements
Overall cost leadership	Sustained capital investment and access to capital Process engineering skills Intense supervision of labor Products designed for ease in manufacture Low-cost distribution system	Tight cost control Frequent, detailed control reports Structured organization and responsibilities Incentives based on meeting strict quantitative targets
Differentiation	Strong marketing abilities Product engineering Creative flair Strong capability in basic research Corporate reputation for quality or technological leadership Long tradition in the industry or unique combination of skills drawn from other businesses Strong cooperation from channels	Strong coordination among functions in R&D, product development, and marketing Subjective measurement and incentives instead of quantitative measures Amenities to attract highly skilled labor, scientists, or creative people
Focus	Combination of the above policies directed at the particular strategic target	Combination of the above policies directed at the particular strategic target

SOURCE: Adapted and reprinted with the permission of The Free Press, an imprint of Simon & Schuster from COMPETITIVE STRATEGY: Techniques for Analyzing Industries and Competitors by Michael E. Porter. Copyright © 1980 by The Free Press.

Example illustrates a cost-leadership strategy. Kohl's Corporation, a rapidly growing department store chain, relies on a low-cost strategy to support it in the highly competitive world of retailing.

A **differentiation strategy** involves creating and marketing unique products for a mass market that command premium prices. Differentiators lead firms to work to develop unique brand images (Levi's jeans), unique technology (Intel's computer chips), unique features (Jenn-Air electric ranges), unique distribution channels (Tupperware), unique customer service (Four Seasons Hotels), or the like. Differentiation is a viable strategy for earning above-average returns in industries where customers perceive that premium prices

COMPANY EXAMPLE

Kohl's Pioneers New Retail Niche

Parquet floors and carpeting instead of linoleum; soft lighting rather than fluorescent strips; name-brand merchandise stacked on oak tables, not piled in mesh or melamine bins. The atmosphere in Kohl's Corp.'s 92 stores is markedly different from those in its competitors' outlets: discount stores and upscale department stores.

For Kohl's, it's all part of an overall strategy that industry analysts say has put the pioneering chain into a league of its own—appealing to Middle America's desire to shop in attractive stores that offer brand-name clothing at discount prices.

It's a simple concept—pleasant stores offering cutthroat prices—that has translated well to the eight states where the Wisconsin-based retailer operates. Kohl's plans to open 18 or more new stores annually for the next five years, focusing first on cities on the East and West coasts. At first glance, it may seem a tough sell; the Northeast is especially crowded with both discounters and upscale retailers. But analysts say shoppers will soon discover the difference. According to New York retail consultant Kurt Barnard, Kohl's has built a reputation for being a skillful merchandiser that frequently outflanks competitors. "They're very savvy."

Kohl's has to be savvy to afford the ambience of a department store while selling at such reduced prices. Gross margins are about 8 percent below those of other department stores, yet it generates a high return on sales—almost 11 percent in 1993.

Having better access than its competitors to popular brand names has helped Kohl's make competitive inroads, but the real key is keeping a tight rein on costs. Much of the company's initial cost savings comes from land purchases; whether for a free-standing or mall unit, it locates stores where real estate is cheap. Further, Kohl's uses only 15 percent of a store's square-footage for storage; competitors use up to 40 percent. To save labor costs, merchandise displays encourage self-selection, while checkout counters are found not in individual departments, but by store exits in discount-store-style clusters. Savings will continue with the company's expansion; Kohl's plans to keep its new locations within 400 miles of its distribution centers to speed up restocking.

Retail experts expect strong profits, due in large part to Kohl's aggressive, but down-to-earth, management style, which befits an era where level-headedness rather than glitz is paramount. The numbers are impressive: Sales at stores opened at least a year have risen at least 8 percent annually, and total sales rose 16 percent in 1993 to $1.3 billion.

SOURCE: Christina Duff, "Kohl's of the Midwest Maps an Invasion of Both Coasts," *The Wall Street Journal*, May 12, 1994, p. B4.

can bring them goods or services that are distinctly better than the lower cost versions. Differentiators (or premium product producers) define the high end of a given industry, to the extent that the industry structure and associated life cycle permit enough difference among products to allow a high end. In perishable consumer goods, for example, differentiators sell highly advertised, branded products—Perdue chickens, Heinz ketchup—rather than store labels.

A **focus strategy** seeks to segment markets and appeal to only one or a few groups of consumers or organizational buyers. A firm that limits its attention to one or a few market niches hopes to serve those niches better than firms that seek to influence the entire market. For example, products such as Rolls-Royce automobiles, Cross pens, and Hartmann luggage are designed to appeal to the upscale market and serve it well rather than trying to compete in the mass market. Not all niche players focus on upscale markets where they can command premium prices. Many combine narrow focuses with low-cost strategies to provide products to targeted customer niches. This group might include a small, regional packaging manufacturer that focuses on a small set

---

TABLE 4.2

Risks Associated with Porter's Three Generic Strategies

Risks of Cost Leadership Strategy	Risks of Differentiation Strategy	Risks of Focus Strategy
Cost leadership is not sustained • competitors imitate • technology changes • other bases for cost leadership erode	Differentiation is not sustained • competitors imitate • bases for differentiation become less important to buyers	The focus strategy is imitated The target segment becomes structurally unattractive • structure erodes • demand disappears
Proximity in differentiation is lost	Cost proximity is lost	Broadly targeted competitors overwhelm the segment • the segment's differences from other segments narrow • the advantages of a broad line increase
Cost focusers achieve even lower cost in segments	Differentiation focusers achieve even greater differentiation in segments	New focusers subsegment the industry

SOURCE: Adapted and reprinted with the permission of The Free Press, an imprint of Simon & Schuster from COMPETITIVE ADVANTAGE: Creating and Sustaining Superior Performance by Michael E. Porter. Copyright © 1985 by Michael E. Porter.

---

of customers. Manufacturing economics (which determine the smallest efficient plant size) and low overhead allow these niche players to compete effectively on the basis of low delivered cost.

By implementing one of these generic strategies a firm tries to build a competitive advantage in an industry. However, each exposes the firm to risks that threaten its sustainability over time. These risks are shown in Table 4.2. For example, a well-designed and implemented focus or niche strategy may do so well that it grows a niche market until major competitors begin to find it attractive. Pepsi's recent move into clear or colorless soft drinks follows the work of smaller firms, such as Clearly Canadian, to develop this niche market.

The Skills Module gives you an opportunity to analyze and discuss the strength and weakness of the focus strategy of one small business in the service sector.

Industry Structures and Competitive Strategies—Additional Challenges

A few additional comments can help put the Porter framework in perspective. First, there is nothing deterministic or mechanical about industry analysis. Answering the critical questions to size up the structure of an industry involves few equations and much executive judgment. The same biases and human limitations that influence efforts to interpret the environment are at work

SKILLS MODULE
KangaKab Venture Rides Twisting Road

INTRODUCTION

We have introduced three generic strategies and noted the general requirements and risks associated with each one. Translating these ideas into specific actions in specific firms is the basic challenge, however, not only to students in a strategic management course but to practicing managers in every industry. Read the short description of KangaKab and its industry and complete the skill development exercise. This should help you to understand and appreciate the challenges of developing a strategy that yields a sustainable competitive advantage.

SITUATION

It was an idea borne of exasperation. Ad executive Judith London had to leave a business meeting early to drive her kids from school to the babysitter's house. When her complaint was echoed by colleague David Parkin, the two realized that there must be thousands of working parents in the same situation. There were, and their numbers were growing: in 1993, the U.S. Census Bureau counted 8.7 million dual-income households with children under 18 and annual incomes above $50,000—24 percent more than in 1989.

Thus was born the idea for KangaKab Inc., a children's ride service that London and Parkin started in 1992. During the next six months, the partners refined their business idea by meeting with a focus group, composed mainly of employed mothers; they also raised $34,000 from family and friends to buy three vans, ran newspaper ads to recruit drivers, and solicited initially wary customers.

The Marlton, New Jersey, company's five-van fleet transports about 150 children a week at a usual per-trip rate of $6 a child. One van's midday ferrying job might generate $30 for KangaKab; Parkin's 75-minute afternoon run carrying 12 youngsters brings in practically a dollar a minute. The partners expect to turn their first profit in 1994 on projected revenue of $250,000. In an effort to accelerate growth, they began franchising the concept in several states in 1993; so far, they have sold three franchises.

KangaKab is not the only entrepreneur throwing a lifeline to working parents whose most valuable commodity has become time; recent startups include nanny referral networks and children's fitness centers. KangaKab is not alone, or even the first, to enter the business of juvenile transportation. Kid's Kab International Franchise Corp., formed in Troy, Michigan, in 1991, claims to be the nation's biggest, deriving about $500,000 in annual revenue from 32 franchisees in 14 states. Pamela Henderson, founder, president, and mother of three, says her company plans to open 28 more franchises this year and license operations in Canada and the United Kingdom.

Henderson cautions that the business is much more than buying a van and making appointments with parents. Annual liability and collision insurance coverage in suburban areas typically costs $2,500 a vehicle; various regulatory approvals and friendly, reliable drivers also are required. (KangaKab's roster includes a retired bank vice president.) Even then, making money is not easy; routes must be carefully structured to maximize the number of paying passengers per trip.

Parkin might add that the business requires one more thing: patience. He goes through two bags of sunflower seeds a day while calming himself in heavy traffic amid the din of voices chanting, "Dave has a bald spot!"

SKILL DEVELOPMENT EXERCISE

Using Porter's framework and the ideas presented in Tables 4.1 and 4.2, assess the situation at KangaKab. What type of focus strategy have they selected? Describe their strategy in as much detail as possible. Why have the owners chosen to compete this way? Could other firms develop other ways to compete in this industry? How should KangaKab attempt to protect its niche from competitors? What actions would you recommend that KangaKab take if other competitors, e.g., Kid's Kab, were to move into their market area? Why?

SOURCE: Michael Selz, "From School to the Doctor's Office to Home: Ride Service Does the Driving for Parents," *The Wall Street Journal*, May 6, 1994, pp. B1–B2.

here, and they may result in ineffective strategy formulation. To see these interpretive problems and the wrongheaded strategies they spawn at work in real companies, we need only to remember the tenacious hold of U.S. auto makers on their outmoded big-car strategies while consumers rushed toward Honda and Toyota for small cars.

Also, industry analysis quickly becomes *industries* analysis; one must understand the structures of adjacent industries in which suppliers, buyers, and potential entrants operate. In addition, industry structure is not static. It changes as the result of changes in the industry life cycle, and perhaps more importantly, as the result of the decisions and actions of key competitors. For example, if either Nike or Reebok were to adopt a cost leadership strategy in the athletic shoe industry, the structure of that industry would change dramatically from what it has been to date.

Some readers will no doubt wonder why firms cannot adopt differentiation and cost leadership strategies at the same time. Managers discover an inherent tension between what the two strategies demand of a firm. This is not to say that successful differentiators, for example, cannot also pay attention to costs or efficient production. Of course, they can. To compete effectively as differentiators, however, they must be driven by *that* imperative rather than the cost leadership imperative. A careful reading of Table 4.1, with its lists of the skills and organizational requirements associated with these two strategies, will reveal fundamental tensions between them. (The organizational requirements section also previews several issues we will review in the next chapter on strategy implementation.)

Many of today's most effective firms in advanced technology industries, for example, Intel in microprocessors, might be said to employ the two basic strategies in rapid succession or sequence. In developing and designing new products, they behave as differentiators. As soon as new products are developed firms know that many of them will be imitated in short order by competitors, i.e., their competitive advantage is not sustainable over time. Therefore, the firm shifts its strategic gears for the new product, focusing rapidly on low cost production and manufacturing efficiencies to enhance the profitability of a premium-priced product for the short period when it can still command a premium price. These enhanced profits, in turn, finance the costly development of the next differentiated product.

Finally, having identified three generic business-level strategies does not tell us how different firms with established positions in an industry will behave over time. Other typologies have been developed to explain how firms play out their chosen business strategies. One such typology, based on military strategy, is shown in Table 4.3.

The Challenge of Competitor Analysis: Sensemaking and Industry Structure

We pointed out in Chapter 2 that strategic issues do not arrive neatly packaged on the executive's desktop. Executives must interpret data from the competitive environment. Interpretation introduces biases and cognitive limitations of managers into the strategy-making equation, which may lead to flawed industry structure analyses. Making sense of competitor's actions and capabilities and judging their strategic impacts on a firm are key elements of industry structure analysis.

TABLE 4.3

Military Strategies for Industrial Warfare

Al Ries and Jack Trout argue that military strategy provides a useful perspective on competing in an industry. They identify four kinds of warfare, each appropriate for particular competitors in an industry.

DEFENSIVE WARFARE

Defensive strategies should be used only by market leaders such as General Motors and IBM. Defensive warfare involves protecting market share against competitors by introducing new products and services that render existing ones obsolete. Market leaders should block competitors' attempts at innovation by quickly copying any promising new products that they introduce.

OFFENSIVE WARFARE

Offensive strategies should be used by the second and third leading firms in the industry, firms that are large enough to mount sustained attacks on the market leader. Offensive warfare focuses on dissecting a leader's strength and finding a weakness where the leader is vulnerable to attack. The attack should be mounted on as narrow a front as possible, usually with a single product. For example, Federal Express became the market leader over Emory and Airborne by emphasizing its Priority One service and high reliability.

FLANKING WARFARE

Flanking strategies involve moving into uncontested areas where no markets exist, surprising competitors, and following up innovations relentlessly. This strategy also suits market followers rather than market leaders. For example, Miller flanked the industry with Lite beer and now dominates the light-beer market. Flanking is often a high-risk strategy, but successful flanking can be highly profitable.

GUERRILLA WARFARE

Guerilla strategies entail finding a niche in the market small enough to defend, while maintaining readiness to withdraw nimbly, if necessary. This strategy suits companies with small market shares.

SOURCE: Based on Al Ries and Jack Trout, *Marketing Warfare* (New York: McGraw-Hill, 1986).

A recent study of competitor analysis notes that "[i]t embodies both competitive intelligence to collect data on rivals and the analysis and interpretation of the data for managerial decision making."[4] This study also identified six serious blind spots often observed in competitor analysis methods. Table 4.4 lists these flaws and matches them with the actions that executives might take to remedy them.

Misjudging the boundaries of an industry, for example, is most readily observed in the business world when firms in one industry are blindsided by moves of firms from another industry that had not been identified as competitors. Classic examples include the watch industry's surprise at competition from semiconductor producers like Texas Instruments and its digital watches. More recently, IBM has entered the management consulting industry, with an as-yet-unknown impact on traditional consulting firms. In Porter's model, the

TABLE 4.4

Competitive Analysis Flaws and Managerial Actions

Flaws	Executive Actions
1. Misjudging industry boundaries	Change the view of the competition by focusing on competitors' intentions, seeing the industry from the entrant's eye, examining the reason for an entrant's failure, and performing an autopsy on failing competitors
2. Poor identification of the competition	Study competitors' response patterns and blind spots; survey customers and suppliers; focus on competitor's capabilities, not only on their forms
3. Overemphasis on competitors' visible competence	Study competitors' response patterns; analyze rivals' invisible functions
4. Overemphasis on where, not how rivals will compete	Study competitors' strategic intentions; study the industry from competitors' eyes
5. Faulty assumptions about the competition	Transform the cliché that competition is good into a living reality; study competitors' actions and response patterns; ensure representation of diverse groups in the competitive analysis process; teach employees about competitors; validate assumptions by discussing them with suppliers and customers
6. Paralysis by analysis	Pay attention to the staffing, organization, and mission of the competitive analysis unit; integrate competitive analysis with the managerial decision-making process; use nontraditional approaches to competitor analysis

SOURCE: Adapted from Shaker Zahra and Sherry Chaples, "Blind Spots in Competitive Analysis," *Academy of Management Executive*, May 1993, p. 7.

watch industry's flaw would be poor analysis of the threat of substitutes, and management consultants' failure to analyze potential entrants effectively.

Table 4.4 also suggests that managers can overcome faulty assumptions about competitors by involving diverse groups in the competitive analysis process. This observation reinforces our emphasis on a cross-functional perspective on strategic management, in this case the competitor analysis component, for firms operating in the complex environments of the 1990s.

The Challenge of Sustainability—Competitive Advantage over Time

In a competitive world, advantages are difficult to sustain. Table 4.2 confirms that the risks associated with Porter's three generic strategies mainly revolve around the sustainability issue. A strategy may yield a temporary advantage, but not one that can be sustained in the face of competitive moves by rivals.

Pankaj Ghemawat puts it this way: "For outstanding performance, a company has to beat the competition. The trouble is the competition has heard the same message."[5]

Ghemawat bolsters this assertion by pointing out the relative ease with which rivals can imitate new products, innovative production methods, and marketing approaches. Ghemawat proposes three ways to overcome the sustainability barrier—commitment to achieving size advantages in a targeted market, getting access to key resources or customers, and taking advantage of restrictions on the options of competitors. Thus, relatively large firms can hope to achieve sustainable advantage by retaining key inputs and locking in key customers (e.g., through high switching costs), when competitors find it structurally difficult to change directions.

One type of organizational skill—quick response—has received much attention lately as a possible source of sustainable competitive advantage.[6] Bower and Hout argue that quick response, if properly nurtured, can become both a critical organizational capability and a management philosophy, a new way of thinking about "how to organize and lead a company and how to gain a real advantage over competitors."[7] Fast organizations are thus better able to support their differentiation, cost leadership, of focus strategies than slower rivals.

A problem arises when a firm's commitments and key skills suit conditions less well as time passes. What a firm does to achieve sustainable advantage at Time 1 may put it into a weak position at Time 2. For example, Digital Equipment Corporation was a pioneer and a dominant player in the minicomputer industry. In Ghemawat's terms, the firm made a commitment to size, assembled the necessary talent, built strong relationships with its customers, and outflanked the larger IBM, which chose to defend its mainframe computer line instead of aggressively moving into the minicomputer market. However, Digital's very commitment to this market became one source of the troubles it experienced in later time periods, when that prior commitment cast it in the role of turf defender, and thus kept it from aggressively pursuing the personal computer or workstation markets as early as it might have. Bower and Hout might argue that Digital could have developed a quick response capability, developing new products faster and avoiding later stage problems.

One of the points underscored by the analyses of Ghemawat and others is the importance of a firm's collective know-how, or core competencies, in the search for sustainable competitive advantage.[8] In the following section, we turn our attention specifically to the analysis of a firm's internal strengths and weaknesses, and the core competencies on which it can build business-level strategies.

Core Competencies and Business-Level Strategy

In Chapter 1, we defined strategic management as a continuous process aimed at keeping an organization appropriately matched to its environment. We now consider the strengths and weaknesses of organizations, and their attempts to match core competencies to their competitive environments.

Core competency can be defined generally as "the collective learning in the organization."[9] This usually focuses on production and technology-related skills in diversified corporations. This definition challenges a corporation's managers to design an architecture in which these competencies can move flexibly and effectively across the diverse units of the firm.

Competencies can also influence the shape of business-level strategy. Once again, Michael Porter provides a conceptual framework for the systematic evaluation of a firm's internal activities to identify and refine those that are strategically important to a firm's search for competitive success through cost leadership or differentiation. Figure 4.2 shows the generic value chain of organizations, divided into primary activities and support activities. Through a detailed examination of these activities, separately and collectively, a firm can not only develop a better sense of its strengths and weaknesses, but it can also more powerfully understand the impact of, or value added by, each activity in relation to its chosen strategy.

Value chain analysis begins with the recognition that each firm or business unit is, in Porter's words, "a collection of activities that are performed to design, produce, market, deliver, and support its product."[10] By analyzing each value activity separately, and by determining each activity's cost and contributions, managers can judge the value of each activity to the firm's search for sustainable competitive advantage. By identifying and analyzing a firm's value activities, managers work with the core elements of its competitive advantage since the efficiency and effectiveness of each activity affects the firm's success in its low cost, differentiation, or focus strategy.

Porter divides value activities into two broad categories—primary and support activities. **Primary activities,** shown across the bottom of Figure 4.2, include inbound logistics, operations, outbound logistics, marketing/sales, and service. It is helpful to think of primary activities as a stream of related activities, beginning with the arrival and storage of raw materials or inputs to the firm's production processes; their transformation into final products; handling, storage, and distribution of outgoing finished products; marketing and sales activities to identify, reach, and motivate buyer groups; and service activities to provide customer and product support.

Support activities, as the name suggests, provide specialized and general support to primary activities. Support activities like procurement, technology development, human resource management, and infrastructure are shown at the top of Figure 4.2. It is useful to think of support activities as general business functions. For example, the procurement activity includes more functions than might be included in a purchasing department's activities, which normally focus narrowly on buying raw materials for use in manufacturing. Procurement includes the full range of processes or technologies that a firm might use to acquire anything from office supplies to critical raw materials, advertising services, temporary workers, or top managers.

Similarly, technology development and human resource management (HRM) can affect primary value activities in strategically important ways. For example, careful training and assignment of medical staff is critical to the profitability and service goals of a health maintenance organization. Technology development can affect new product design, selection of new materials, production processes, logistics, marketing, and services. This broad definition of *technology development* extends beyond the traditional research and develop-

FIGURE 4.2   The Generic Value Chain

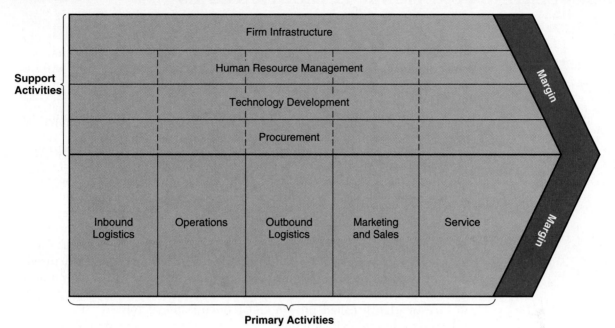

ment function to include, for example, the design of a new inventory control system and product refinements suggested by a major customer.

Firm infrastructure encompasses activities such as general management, accounting and finance, information systems, government relations, and legal affairs. Infrastructure supports primary value activities by providing both internal coordination (through systematic measurement, information flows, and strategic planning) and management of key external relationships.

As a tool for strategy formulation, value chain analysis demands not only that managers analyze each separate value activity in great detail but also that they examine the critical linkages between and among internal activities. In this way, the value chain enhances the importance of cross-functional efforts in strategy formulation. Value chain analysis calls upon managers to think creatively and broadly about how the firm goes about its activities, and about how those activities affect each other. Inevitably, such an approach draws attention to a basic reality: formulating a strategy, putting it into play, and refining it over time require the talents and energies of people from every corner of the firm. Functional strategies, then, must be analyzed and coordinated to maximize their cross-functional effects if they are to contribute optimally to a firm's overall competitive strategy.

Value chain analysis can also help firms to better understand the linkages between their value chains and those of current or potential suppliers and customers, in the interest of building a stronger competitive strategy. In the following section on functional strategies, we will look in more detail at ways to put internal activities (and the core competencies that they exploit) squarely in the middle of the strategy equation.

FORMULATING FUNCTIONAL-LEVEL STRATEGIES

Traditionally, **functional-level strategies** have been viewed as flowing harmoniously from business-level strategies. Once a business-level strategy is decided, the story goes, functional managers put together strategies that are consistent with and fully supportive of it. This may have represented wishful thinking that internal activities are always compliant, problem-free support mechanisms for the larger strategy of a business. In reality, however, this view of things as they should be may have differed significantly from things as they were.

The recent emergence of the quality movement has called attention to suboptimal operations of functions, considered separately or in combination. A growing number of firms now use benchmarking to compare their functions to those of world-class competitors. Many also aggressively employ outsourcing, deciding that an internal function can be performed more efficiently by an external supplier. These trends attest to the new ways in which firms are thinking about their functions and their functional-level strategies. Outsourcing seems to be causing a revolution in the ways organizations are structured, and the way we think about transferring functions outside the organization's traditional boundaries. *Fortune* magazine has pointed out the emerging significance of what it called the "modular organization"; *Business Week* earlier referred to the same phenomenon as creating a "hollow corporation."[11]

In the sections below, we consider several functions and appropriate functional-level strategies. For each, we focus on its ability to add value to a firm's goods or services.

Technology/Research and Development Strategies

In many industries, an organization cannot grow or even survive without generating a steady stream of new products. Research and development (R&D) specialists work to devise new products to support the business-level strategy. R&D conceives new product ideas and develops them until the products reach full production and enter the market. This process involves concept generation and screening, product planning and development, and perhaps even test marketing.

Some industry structures make R&D critical since new products can be highly profitable; still, R&D can be time consuming, expensive, and risky. For example, it is estimated that only one out of seven new product ideas ever makes it to the market. Clearly, the time and money allocated to researching and developing the other six ideas greatly increase overall R&D costs. Furthermore, an average of 30 to 35 percent of new products fail after entering the market, so *innovation strategies*—those that focus heavily on developing new products—can be very risky.[12] For this reason many organizations use *imitation* or *fast follower strategies,* rapidly copying new competitive products that do well. A number of Japanese electronics companies were quite successful in the 1970s and 1980s in copying American technology. By avoiding many R&D costs, they improved their competitive positions significantly.

In recent years, the emphasis has increased on the role of R&D in adding value through its internal linkages to manufacturing and marketing functions. We read with increasing frequency about corporate efforts to "design for manufacture" or to do "concurrent engineering"; both techniques focus on improving coordination among several functions to reduce the time a product takes to reach the market. Cross-functional communication can improve coordination and enhance the important role of the R&D function in providing the ideas and concepts needed to generate successful new product introductions or to increase the efficiency of production methods.

Operations Strategies

Specialists in this area make decisions about required plant capacity, plant layout, manufacturing and production processes, and inventory requirements. Two important aspects of operations strategy are controlling costs and improving the efficiency of plant operations. As for the technology/R&D function, manufacturing has been in the spotlight in recent years because of the total quality movement, and the tools and techniques that support this movement.

Functional-level strategies for operations in the 1990s use statistical process control, just-in-time inventory methods, continuous improvement systems, flexible manufacturing systems, and the human resource management approaches that support these quality-enhancing techniques. The work of W. Edwards Deming on quality improvement has had an increasing influence on operations strategies. Chapter 8 of this text explores the increasingly important issue of quality, and its close links to competitive strategy, while Chapter 10 offers further discussion of the operations function.

Financial Strategies

Financial specialists are responsible for forecasting and financial planning, evaluating investment proposals, securing financing for various investments, and controlling financial resources. Financial specialists contribute to strategy formulation by assessing the potential profit impacts of various strategic alternatives, using techniques such as net present value analysis, and evaluating the financial condition of the business. While much of the earlier discussion of business-level strategy emphasized product–market fit and positioning, the role of finance in strategy formulation should not be underestimated. Financial analysis answers some of the fundamental questions that drive strategy making in a firm. What will a new strategic initiative cost? What financial risk does a new strategy present versus the risk of an existing strategy? What is the lowest-cost method of financing a new initiative? Chapter 11 of this text discusses financial issues in greater detail.

Marketing Strategies

Marketing specialists determine the appropriate markets in which to offer products and they develop effective marketing mixes. (The marketing mix includes four strategic elements: price, product, promotion, and channels of distribution.) Chapter 12 of this text covers marketing strategy in greater detail, and provides insight into how the marketing function takes a product into the marketplace, and how it carries critical feedback from that marketplace back to a firm's leaders to help them fine-tune or revise a strategy.

TABLE 4.5

Effective and Ineffective Human Resource Management

Characteristics of Effective Companies	Characteristics of Ineffective Companies
Genuine concern for people; a positive view of employees as assets	Do not view employees as important assets; show little concern for work force
Good training, development, and advancement opportunities	Managed autocratically or bureaucratically; rigid and inflexible
Pay well; good compensation programs	Little or no employee development; an ineffective internal advancement process
Able to retain employees; low turnover	Poor internal communication
Good internal communication; open communication	Unclear or outdated policies; inconsistently administered and altered in difficult times
Top management committed to and supportive of HR [human resources]	High turnover
Encourage employee participation.	

SOURCE: Adapted from S. W. Alper and R. E. Mandel, "What Policies and Practices Characterize the Most Effective HR Departments, *Personnel Administrator*, vol. 29, no. 11, 1984. Copyright 1984 The American Society for Personnel Administration, 606 North Washington Street, Alexandria, Virginia 22314. Reprinted with the permission of *HRMagazine* published by the Society for Human Resource Management, Alexandria, Va.

Human Resource Strategies

In general, the human resource function is concerned with attracting, assessing, motivating, and retaining the employees the firm needs to run effectively. This function is also responsible for affirmative action planning and evaluating the safety of the work environment. Collectively, the set of decisions concerning these issues define the human resource strategy for the business.[13]

Like other strategies, human resource strategies are based on both external and internal analysis. External analysis includes tracking developments in laws and regulations that affect employment (such as equal employment opportunity laws), studying changes in labor unions and labor negotiations, and analyzing changes in the labor market. Internal analysis includes investigating specific problem areas such as low productivity, excessive turnover, or high accident rates. In addition, human resource strategies may involve analyzing and proposing changes in organizational structure and climate.

Table 4.5 lists several characteristics of effective and ineffective human resource management. Table 4.6 presents a portion of the human resource strategy for Merck and Company. As is appropriate for all functional-level strategies, it identifies goals specific to the operational level and specifies tasks that must be performed to reach these goals.

> ### TABLE 4.6
>
> ### *Excerpts from Merck and Company's Human Resource Strategy*
>
> *Develop new and more effective ways to accommodate employee participation in joint problem-solving areas and in appropriate policy/practice development.*
>
> Opinion surveys, face-to-face meetings, focus groups, quality circle groups, and labor–management committees have added channels for employees to express their concerns and suggestions. These are just the start of many avenues which will be explored to improve participation and two-way communications between employees and supervisors.
>
> There continues to be room for and need for expanding and improving employee participation. This will be achieved through improved two-way communication between employees and supervisors. Managers and supervisors need to fully understand and to put into practice the belief that the commitment of people is better assured when they are involved in the decision-making process.
>
> #### SUMMARY OF ACTION PLANS
>
> * Application of focus group techniques to develop or revise policies and procedures (successfully tested in 1980 with the Performance Appraisal Program and the Salary Administration Program).
> * Continue to measure the effectiveness of management policies, practices, and programs.
>
> #### PRIORITY 10
>
> *Develop innovative approaches to organization design, job design and scheduling, and advanced office systems to improve productivity.*
>
> Strengthen our capabilities for more effective organization planning to ensure capability of supporting business plans and objectives. It is critical that skills be broadened in long-term organization planning and in the redesign of jobs and work.
>
> Attract talented professionals who want more flexibility in the workplace.
>
> We will continue our investigation into advanced office systems and the expansion of office automation, which have significant human implications. There is a need to coordinate a stronger planning effort—on a corporatewide basis—between the three elements that are essential to make advanced office systems work effectively. These three elements include the technical (MIS), the physical office design (Engineering), and the behavioral (Human Resources). Given that Merck is office-worker intensive and will become more so in the future, this planning effort has significant implications for the Company's productivity efforts.
>
> #### SUMMARY OF ACTION PLANS
>
> * Continue to develop skills for effective organization planning and implementation of Advanced Office Systems.
> * Expand flexible working hours and test new scheduling and work pattern approaches.
> * Continue to improve consulting skills of H.R. professionals.
>
> SOURCE: G. T. Milkovich and J. D. Phillips, "Human Resource Planning at Merck & Co.," in L. Dyer, ed., *Human Resource Planning: A Case Study Reference Guide to the Tested Practices of Five Major U.S. and Canadian Companies* (New York: Random House, 1985).

FORMULATING CORPORATE-LEVEL STRATEGIES

Top managers formulate corporate-level strategies, or multibusiness strategies, to achieve sustainable synergy for an organization by assembling a portfolio of businesses or business units, which may stretch across a diverse set of industries. For example, General Electric's portfolio of businesses ranges from jet engines to financial services to a television network (NBC) to appliances to medical instruments to light bulbs. The firm's overarching plan seeks to hold together these diverse businesses to form a synergistic whole that combines individual industry structures and business-level strategies. This plan is the firm's **corporate-level strategy.**

A well-conceived corporate-level strategy guides corporate managers' efforts to manage their portfolios of businesses in much the same way that the stated objectives of a mutual fund guide the fund manager's decisions about what securities to buy, what to hold, and what to sell. Corporate strategy focuses on a portfolio of businesses, however, instead of a portfolio of stocks or bonds. A corporate strategy also guides the top managers' decision about the roles that various businesses will play in the portfolio, and thus on how resources should move from one business to another.

In this section, we first review the factors that explain most organizations' transformations from single-business firms to multibusiness firms that need corporate-level strategies. We then discuss approaches to managing for synergy across a diverse set of businesses or business units.

Diversification—Approaches to Assembling a Portfolio

What explains the emergence of multibusiness strategies? Why and how do single businesses decide to form portfolios of businesses? Answers to these basic questions may cite several motives, but we believe they center on four—growth goals, risk management, special expertise, and industry structure.

Growth Goals

An organization that operates in a single industry has chosen to concentrate its efforts and hitch its wagon to the future of that one industry. What happens if industry growth slows? The organization's leaders have a strategic choice to make. They can stay focused on that one industry and seek to strengthen their competition position within it; they may have to resign themselves to a future of slower growth, but continuing profitability. If they are not satisfied with their industry's growth picture and want better results for their shareholders (and possibly more interesting work for themselves), they may explore alternative ways to move away from a single-business strategy.

Once they decide to build a multibusiness corporate portfolio to improve their firm's growth, managers can accomplish this goal in many ways. Often, as shown below, they may seek to acquire other, existing firms in horizontal integration, vertical integration, or diversification strategies.

Horizontal Integration   In this strategy, the firm seeks to grow by acquiring competing firms in the same line of business. Such a move can quickly increase the size, sales, profits, and potential market share of an organization. Horizontal integration represents the strategic alternative that is closest to a firm's former single-business strategy. This form of integration via acquisition seeks the same result as market penetration efforts taken by a firm—that is, it results in a firm increasing its share of, and thus growth in, an industry that may be growing slowly overall.

Vertical Integration   In this strategy, the firm seeks to grow by acquiring other organizations in its channel of distribution. When an organization purchases its suppliers, it engages in *backward* vertical integration. An organization that purchases other firms that are closer to the end users of the product such as wholesalers and retailers engages in *forward* vertical integration. Vertical integration gives greater control over a line of business and increases profits through greater efficiency or better selling efforts.[14] Some vertical integration moves are carried out, not through acquisition, but by launching new manufacturing efforts. Instead of acquiring one of its key suppliers, the firm simply begins producing that supply. A soup company may acquire a metal-can maker to pursue vertical integration by acquisition. A personal computer maker may begin making its own semiconductors to pursue vertical integration by launching a new venture.

Diversification   In this strategy, a firm seeks to grow by acquiring firms in industries or lines of business that are new to it. When the acquired firm has production technology, products, channels of distribution, and/or markets similar to those of the purchasing firm, the strategy is called *related* or *concentric diversification*. This strategy is useful when shared resources can improve the organization's efficiency or market impact. H. J. Heinz, with its packaged-food related diversification, is an example of this form of diversification.

When the acquired firm is in a completely different line of business, the strategy is called *unrelated* or *conglomerate diversification*. The General Electric portfolio mentioned earlier provides an example of this form of diversification. Both related and unrelated diversification efforts often begin with the goal of achieving higher growth rates than a single industry can offer.

Risk Management

The push to expand beyond a single business, and thus the need for a multibusiness strategy, often results from a firm's desire to spread its risk across more than one industry. In much the same way that a mutual fund manager might choose a wide variety of stocks from different sectors of the economy to balance the risk of an entire portfolio, an organizational strategist might steer a firm away from the risks inherent in operating in only one industry. The risk of pinning all of their hopes on the metal container industry motivated the top managers of American Can Co. to diversify into insurance and financial services; eventually, the firm changed its name to Primerica after selling off its container operation altogether.

Special Expertise

Organizations often seek to build multibusiness portfolios to exploit some special expertise that they believe they possess that will add value to an acquired organization in a new industry. They believe they possess a core competence that is transferable into a new industry or industry segment. H. J. Heinz acquired Weight Watchers and Ore-Ida Potatoes, for example, to provide their operations with distribution clout.

Industry Structure

Before building a multibusiness portfolio, an organization needs to carefully consider the structure of the industry into which it plans to move with special emphasis on the question of how it can develop a sustainable competitive advantage there. Just because a high-growth industry is featured regularly in the business press is no justification for trying to move into it! The high entry costs of moving into a high-growth industry often consume much of the potential profit that it might generate. One of the classic stories of diversification failure is Exxon's attempted move into the office equipment business in the early 1980s, when that industry was growing rapidly. Exxon spent a great deal of money acquiring an assortment of small manufacturers and building a sales force, only to recognize that the highly visible Exxon name and vast resource base was not powerful enough to overcome the industry dominance of well-entrenched rivals like IBM, Xerox, etc.

Business Portfolio Models—Approaches to Managing a Portfolio for Sustainable Synergy

Business portfolio models are tools for analyzing (1) the relative position of each of an organization's businesses in its industry, and (2) the relationships among all of the organization's businesses. Two approaches to developing business portfolio models are the Boston Consulting Group's growth–share matrix and General Electric's multifactor portfolio matrix.

BCG Growth–Share Matrix

The Boston Consulting Group, a management consulting firm, developed and popularized an approach to multibusiness strategy making called the **growth–share matrix,** shown in Figure 4.3. The basic idea is that a firm should have a balanced portfolio of businesses in which some generate more cash than they use to help support others that need cash to develop and become profitable. The role of each business is determined on the basis of two factors: the growth rate of its market and its share of that market.

The vertical axis indicates the market growth rate, measured as the annual percentage growth of the market (current or forecasted) in which the business operates. Anything under 10 percent is typically considered a low growth rate and anything above 10 percent a high growth rate. However, depending on the industries being evaluated, other percentages are used.

The horizontal axis indicates market share dominance, or relative market share, computed by dividing the firm's market share (in units) by the market share of its largest competitor. For example, a relative market share of 0.2 means that the sales volume of the business is only 20 percent of the market leader's sales volume; a relative market share of 2.0 means that the business produces a sales volume twice that of the next largest competitor. A relative market share of 1.0 is set as the dividing line between high and low share. Each of the circles in Figure 4.3 represents the relative revenue of a single business; a larger circle represents more sales than a smaller circle.

The growth–share matrix places businesses in four cells, which reflect the four possible combinations of high and low growth with high and low market share. These cells represent particular types of businesses, each of which has a particular role to play in the overall business portfolio. The cells are labeled:

1. *Question marks* (sometimes called *problem children*): Businesses that operate in high-growth markets, but have low relative market shares. Most busi-

FIGURE 4.3
BCG's Growth–Share
Matrix

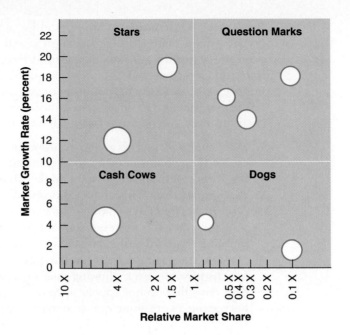

SOURCE: Adapted and reprinted with permission from *Long Range Planning,* B. Hedley, "Strategy and The Business Portfolio," February 1977, Elsevier Science Ltd., Pergamon Imprint, Oxford, England.

nesses start off as question marks either entering high-growth markets that already have market leaders, or operating as one of many small competitors in emerging industries. A question mark generally needs a lot of funds; it must keep adding plant, equipment, and personnel to keep up with a fast-growing industry that it wants to overtake or become the leader. The term *question mark* is well-chosen, because the organization has to think hard about whether to keep investing funds in the business or to get out.

2. *Stars:* Question-mark businesses that have become successful. A star is a market leader in a high-growth market, but it does not necessarily provide much cash. The organization has to spend a great deal of money keeping up with the market's rate of growth and fighting off competitors' attacks. Stars often consume cash rather than generating it. Even so, they are usually profitable in time.

3. *Cash cows:* Businesses in markets with low annual growth that have large market shares. A cash cow produces a lot of cash for the organization. The organization does not have to finance a great deal of expansion because the market's growth rate is low. Since the business is a market leader, it enjoys economies of scale and higher profit margins. The organization milks its cash-cow businesses to pay its bills and support other growing businesses.

4. *Dogs:* Businesses with weak market shares in low-growth markets. They typically generate low profits or losses, although they may bring in some cash. Such businesses frequently consume more management time than they are worth and merit elimination. However, an organization may have good reasons to hold onto a dog, such as an expected turnaround in the market growth rate or a new chance at market leadership.[15]

Strategic Alternatives   After plotting each of its businesses on the growth–share matrix, an organization's next step is to evaluate whether the portfolio is healthy and well-balanced. A balanced portfolio has a number of stars and cash cows, and not too many question marks or dogs. This balance is important because the organization needs cash, not only to maintain existing businesses, but also to develop new businesses. Depending on the position of each business, the firm can formulate one of four basic strategic goals for it:

1. *Build market share:* This goal is appropriate for question marks that must increase their shares in order to become stars. Some businesses may have to forgo short-term profits to gain market share and future, long-term profits.
2. *Hold market share:* This goal is appropriate for cash cows with strong share positions. The cash generated by mature cash cows provides critical support for other businesses and financing innovations. However, the cost of building share for cash cows is likely to be too high to be profitable.
3. *Harvest:* Harvesting involves milking as much short-term cash from a business as possible, even allowing market share to decline if necessary. Weak cash cows that do not appear to have promising futures are candidates for harvesting, as are some question marks and dogs.
4. *Divest:* Divesting involves selling or liquidating a business to invest the resources devoted to it more profitably in other businesses. Divesting is appropriate for those dogs and question marks that are not worth investments to improve their positions.

Evaluation of the Growth–Share Matrix   As an innovative approach to investigating relationships among an organization's businesses, the growth–share matrix helped stimulate interest in managing a diversified portfolio. Perhaps its main contribution came from encouraging managers to view the formulation of corporate strategy in terms of joint relationships among businesses and to take long-range views. The growth–share matrix acknowledges that businesses in different stages have different cash requirements and make different contributions to achieving organizational objectives. The growth–share matrix also provides a simple and appealing visual overview of an organization's business portfolio.

However, a variety of problems that arise with this approach suggest that it must be used cautiously in strategy formulation. Among these problems:

- The growth–share matrix focuses on balancing cash flows, whereas organizations are more likely to be interested in the returns on investment that various businesses yield.
- It is not always clear what share of what market is relevant in the analysis. For example, the analysis of Cadillac's market share would give much different results if it were determined on the basis of the overall car market rather than just the market for luxury cars.
- The growth–share matrix assumes a strong relationship between market share and return on investment. In fact, it is commonly believed that a 10 percent difference in market share is accompanied by a 5 percent difference in return on investment. However, other research has found a much weaker relationship; a 10 percent change in market share is associated with only a 1 percent change in return on investment.[16]
- Many other factors besides market share and growth rate have critical effects on strategy formulation. For example, industry structure and the core

FIGURE 4.4
GE's Multifactor
Portfolio Matrix

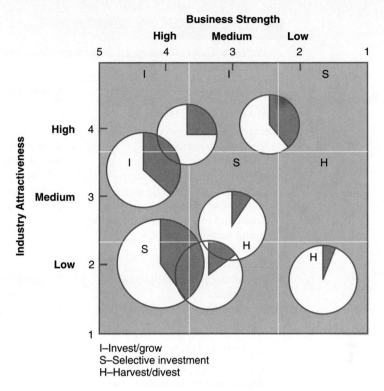

I–Invest/grow
S–Selective investment
H–Harvest/divest

competencies of the firm and its competitors are important influences that this method does not adequately consider.

• The growth–share matrix does not directly compare investment opportunities in different businesses. For example, it is not clear how to compare two question marks to decide which should be developed into a star and which should be allowed to decline.

• The approach offers only general strategy guidance without specifying how to implement such strategies.

Thus, although the growth–share matrix may provide a useful overview of a business portfolio, and it may point out some important relationships among an organization's businesses, it does not provide a complete framework for corporate strategy formulation. Several other portfolio models have been developed that overcome some of the problems inherent in the growth–share matrix. We will discuss one of them: General Electric's **multifactor portfolio matrix.**

GE's Multifactor Portfolio Matrix

This approach has a variety of names, including the *nine-cell GE matrix, GE's nine-cell business portfolio matrix,* and the *industry attractiveness–business position matrix.* It was developed at General Electric with the help of McKinsey and Company, a consulting firm. The basic matrix is shown in Figure 4.4.[17] Each circle represents an industry, and the shaded portion represents the organization's market share in that industry.

TABLE 4.7

Factors Contributing to Industry Attractiveness and Business Strength

Industry Attractiveness	Business Strength
MARKET FACTORS	
Size (dollars, units or both)	Your share (in equivalent terms)
Size of key segments	Your share of key segments
Growth rate per year:	Your annual growth rate:
Total	Total
Segments	Segments
Diversity of market	Diversity of your participation
Sensitivity to price, service features, and external factors	Your influence on the market
Cyclicality	Lags or leads in your sales
Seasonality	
Bargaining power of upstream suppliers	Bargaining power of your suppliers
Bargaining power of downstream suppliers	Bargaining power of your customers
COMPETITION	
Types of competitors	Where you fit, how you compare
Degree of concentration	in terms of products, marketing
Changes in type and mix	capability, service, production strength, financial strength, management
Entries and exits	Segments you have entered or left

SOURCE: Derek F. Abell and John S. Hammond, STRATEGIC MARKET PLANNING: Problems & Analytical Approaches, © 1979, p. 214. Reprinted by permission of Prentice-Hall, Englewood Cliffs, New Jersey.

Each of an organization's businesses is plotted in the matrix on two dimensions, industry attractiveness and business strength. Each of these two major dimensions represents a composite of a variety of factors. The two dimensions make good sense for strategy formulation, because a successful business typically operates in an attractive industry where it has the particular business strengths required to succeed. Both strengths are needed to produce outstanding performance through sustainable advantage.

To use this matrix, an organization must identify the factors that are most critical to industry attractiveness and business strength. Table 4.7 lists some of the factors that analysts commonly use to locate businesses on these dimensions.

The next step in developing this matrix is to weight each variable on the basis of its perceived importance relative to the other factors. (The weights must total 1.0.) Managers must then indicate, on a scale of 1 to 5, how low or high their business scores on that factor. Table 4.8 presents this analysis for one business. These calculations rate the business at 3.45 in industry attractiveness

TABLE 4.7

Continued

Changes in share	Your relative share change
Substitution by new technology	Your vulnerability to new technology
Degrees and types of integration	Your own level of integration

FINANCIAL AND ECONOMIC FACTORS

Contribution margins	Your margins
Leveraging factors, such as economies of scale and experience	Your scale and experience
Barriers to your entry or exit (both financial and nonfinancial)	Barriers to your entry or exit (both financial and nonfinancial)
Capacity utilization	Your capacity utilization

TECHNOLOGICAL FACTORS

Maturity and volatility	Your ability to cope with change
Complexity	Depths of your skills
Differentiation	Types of your technological skills
Patents and copyrights	Your patent protection
Manufacturing process technology required	Your manufacturing technology

SOCIOPOLITICAL FACTORS IN YOUR ENVIRONMENT

Social attitudes and trends	Your company's responsiveness and flexibility
Laws and government agency regulations	Your company's ability to cope
Influence with pressure groups and government representatives	Your company's aggressiveness
Human factors, such as unionization and community acceptance	Your company's relationships

and 4.30 in business strength. This places the business close to the high–high cell of the matrix.

Strategic Alternatives Depending on where a business plots on the matrix, the organization can formulate three basic strategies: invest/grow, invest selectively, and harvest/divest. Businesses that fall in the cells that form a diagonal from lower left to upper right are medium-strength businesses that merit only selective investment. Businesses in the cells above and to the left of this diagonal are the strongest; they deserve invest/grow strategies. Businesses in the cells below and to the right of the diagonal are weak overall; these are serious candidates for harvest/divest strategies.

Evaluation of the Multifactor Portfolio Matrix This approach has advantages over the growth–share matrix. First, it provides an explicit mechanism for matching internal strengths and weaknesses with external opportunities and threats, the fundamental task of strategic management. Second, as

TABLE 4.8

Illustration of Industry Attractiveness and Business Strength Computations

INDUSTRY ATTRACTIVENESS	Weight	Rating (1–5)	Value
Overall market size	0.20	4.00	0.80
Annual market growth rate	0.20	5.00	1.00
Historical profit margin	0.15	4.00	0.60
Competitive intensity	0.15	2.00	0.30
Technological requirements	0.15	3.00	0.45
Inflationary vulnerability	0.05	3.00	0.15
Energy requirements	0.05	2.00	0.10
Environmental impact	0.05	1.00	0.05
Social/political/legal	Must be acceptable		
	1.00		3.45

BUSINESS STRENGTH			
Market share	0.10	4.00	0.40
Share growth	0.15	4.00	0.60
Product quality	0.10	4.00	0.40
Brand reputation	0.10	5.00	0.50
Distribution network	0.05	4.00	0.20
Promotional effectiveness	0.05	5.00	0.25
Productive capacity	0.05	3.00	0.15
Productive efficiency	0.05	2.00	0.10
Unit costs	0.15	3.00	0.45
Material supplies	0.05	5.00	0.25
R&D performance	0.10	4.00	0.80
Managerial personnel	0.05	4.00	0.20
	1.00		4.30

SOURCE: Philip Kotler, MARKETING MANAGEMENT: Analysis, Planning, Implementation, and Control, 7e, © 1991, p. 45. Reprinted by permission of Prentice-Hall, Englewood Cliffs, New Jersey. Slightly modified from La Rue T. Hormer, *Strategic Management* (Englewood Cliffs, N.J.: Prentice-Hall, Inc., 1982), p. 310.

we have noted, the two dimensions of industry attractiveness and business strength are excellent criteria for rating potential business success.

However, the multifactor portfolio matrix also suffers from some of the same limitations as the growth–share matrix. For example, it does not solve the problem of determining the appropriate market, and it does not offer anything more than general strategy recommendations. In addition, the measures are subjective and can be very ambiguous, particularly when one is considering different businesses.[18]

In general, portfolio models provide graphical frameworks for analyzing relationships among the businesses of large, diversified organizations, and they can yield useful strategy recommendations. However, no model yet devised provides a universally accepted approach to dealing with these issues. Portfolio models should never be applied mechanically, and any conclusions they suggest must be carefully considered in light of sound managerial judgment and the firm's vision and goals, which no model can replace.

SUMMARY

Strategy formulation cannot begin at any level until the managers responsible for shaping strategy understand the context in which their strategies will unfold. Thus, they rely on some form of SWOT analysis to supply the information they need from the internal and external environments, filtered through the goals and values of vision and mission statements.

Strategy is formulated at three distinct levels: the business, functional, and corporate levels. Devised by top management, strategies are plans designed to ensure that the firm achieves its overall objectives.

We approached the formulation of strategy at the business, business-unit, or divisional level from the perspective of Michael Porter's analysis of five competitive forces: the threat of new entrants, the bargaining power of suppliers, the bargaining power of buyers, the threat of substitute products, and rivalry among competitors. We discussed the conditions under which the strategies of overall cost leadership, differentiation, and focus are appropriate and the risks associated with each. In addition we used Porter's value chain analysis to consider internal core competencies and their importance in achieving competitive advantage. Strategies that functional units adopt and strategies that link units in cross-functional ways ideally must support overall firm strategy. We touched on such issues as innovation versus imitation in the research and development function, controlling costs and boosting efficiency in the operations function, the planning and controlling tasks of financial specialists, the marketing function's responsibility for selecting markets and developing effective marketing mixes, and the need for the human resource function to develop and manage employees effectively.

We explored the roots of expansion from single-business to multibusiness organizations, and we examined two business portfolio models created to help top managers achieve sustainable synergy. The growth–share matrix enables managers to classify every business as a question mark, a star, a cash cow, or a dog; to ascertain whether the firm's roster of businesses is well-balanced among the four; and to determine what strategy is appropriate for each. The multifactor portfolio matrix attempts to quantify the strength of a business and the attractiveness of its industry. The placement of businesses in the matrix based on these two numbers is taken as an indication of the best strategy choice: investing aggressively, investing selectively, or refraining from further investment. Both models offer useful information in an interesting graphical format, but it is important to remember that they cannot generate goals or specific actions, and that they are not substitutes for sound managerial judgment and experience.

KEY TERMS

business-level strategy, p. 78
barriers to entry, p. 78
power of suppliers, p. 80
power of buyers, p. 80
substitution threats, p. 80
rivalry among competitors, p. 80
overall cost leadership strategy, p. 81
differentiation strategy, p. 82
focus strategy, p. 83

core competency, p. 90
value chain analysis, p. 90
primary activity, p. 90
support activity, p. 90
functional-level strategy, p. 92
corporate-level strategy, p. 96
growth–share matrix, p. 98
multifactor portfolio matrix, p. 101

CHECKLIST   **Analyzing Strategy Formulation in Situations and Cases**

___   1.   Is strategy formulation the major focus of this situation or case?

___   2.   What general strategy is the organization following, and would other strategies be more likely to achieve organizational objectives?

___   3.   What business strategies does the situation or case involve?

___   4.   Would an analysis of the five competitive forces or value chain help managers formulate a more effective business strategy?

___   5.   What functional strategies are at issue in the situation or case?

___   6.   Is this a diversified corporation for which a business portfolio analysis would be useful?

___   7.   Is enough information available for management to develop and analyze a growth–share matrix or a multifactor portfolio matrix?

Additional Readings

Adler, Paul S., D. William McDonald, and Fred MacDonald. "Strategic Management of Technical Functions." *Sloan Management Review,* Winter 1992, p. 19.

Dixit, Avinash, and Barry Nalebuff. *Thinking Strategically: The Competitive Edge in Business, Politics, and Everyday Life.* New York: W. W. Norton, 1991.

Hamel, Gary, and C. K. Prahalad. "Strategy as Stretch and Leverage." *Harvard Business Review,* March/April 1993, p. 75.

Hart, Stuart. "An Integrative Framework for Strategy-Making Processes." *The Academy of Management Review,* April 1992, p. 327.

MacMillan, Ian C., and Patricia E. Jones. *Strategy Formulation: Power and Politics.* St. Paul, Minn.: West Publishing, 1986.

Normann, Richard, and Rafael Ramirez. "From Value Chain to Value Constellation: Designing Interactive Strategy." *Harvard Business Review,* July/August 1993, p. 65.

Peteraf, Margaret. "The Cornerstones of Competitive Advantage: A Resource-Based View," *Strategic Management Journal* 14 (1993), pp. 179–191.

Schofield, Malcom, and David Arnold. "Strategies for Mature Businesses." *Long Range Planning* 21/5, no. 3 (October 1988), pp. 69–76.

Stalk, George, Philip Evans, and Lawrence Shulman. "Competing on Capabilities: The New Rules of Corporate Strategy." *Harvard Business Review,* March/April 1992, p. 57.

Williams, Jeffrey. "How Sustainable Is Your Competitive Advantage?" *California Management Review,* Spring 1992, pp. 29–51.

C A S E

FORMULATING STRATEGY FOR THE SWATCH-MOBILE

Nicolas Hayek says that a chief executive has to believe in Santa Claus. The chairman of Swatch manufacturer SMH Swiss Corp. has persuaded others, most notably automobile executives, to believe along with him. He, after all, heads a company whose product—the low-cost, Swatch timepiece with the plastic band—has sold more than 100 million units since its 1983 debut, in the process becoming a collector's item. Now, although sales of Swatch's other, larger-scale products—clothing, telephones, and sunglasses—haven't taken off, Hayek and a partner, Daimler-Benz AG's Mercedes-Benz unit, are readying the prototype of the Swatchmobile.

Observers won't be able to test-drive the car until the 1996 Olympics; it won't be available for months afterward. But the interval between the announcement and the introduction of the Swatchmobile is part of Hayek's plan to make the car known to the world. To Hayek, a car is an "emotional consumer item, like a watch. I was born to sell emotional consumer products."

The Swatchmobile, a two-seater expected to come in snappy colors, will combine what Hayek calls the three most important features of the watch: affordability, durability, and stylishness. He says the car will cost well under $10,000 and measure less than 10 feet long. Not only will it perform well, says Hayek, the Swatchmobile "will have the crash security of a Mercedes."

Some question whether the marriage of Swatch and Mercedes can work. A Swatch partnership with Volkswagen AG fell apart early last year; VW officials determined that the project wouldn't turn a sufficient profit. Hayek, however, says other top auto-industry executives came begging. Confident as he is with his product, Hayek needs Mercedes for its distribution system, if not its manufacturing facilities. (Britain's Board of Trade has already asked Hayek to consider basing production there.)

Mercedes, already planning to introduce a series of small "A-class" luxury cars in 1997, thought the collaboration with Swatch a daring bid to broaden its presence in the mass market. It hasn't disclosed many details of the partnership, including how many Swatchmobiles it would aim to produce, what price it would charge, what quality standards it would set, how much it would invest, or how closely it would tie the new car to its prestigious Mercedes name.

Hayek is not reluctant to boast that the project will aim to sell 100,000 cars in the first year, possibly 1996 or 1997, and up to 1 million annually in the fifth year. The car will succeed on low price and a with-it image, he asserts.

Others take issue with Hayek's assessment. Even one of the company's own engineers says those features alone won't do it. "There are too many small cars on the market already," says Daniel Ryhiner. He maintains that the Swatchmobile's only unique selling point will be its environmental friendliness. When operating on electricity, it will emit virtually no pollutants, and when operating on gas, it will go great distances on one gallon, thanks to an engine that weighs one-tenth as much as any existing engine with equal power. Yet he concedes that even that selling point may falter. Solar products and other "green" ideas are slow starters in the marketplace, giving Hayek "a masterful public relations and marketing challenge."

DISCUSSION QUESTIONS

1. Analyze the Swatchmobile's industry using Porter's five forces model.

2. Based on your analysis, what strategy would you recommend to Mercedes and Swatch for their new product? How would you (a) produce, (b) position, and (c) price the product?

3. Based on your analysis, what do you see as the biggest threats to the strategy you proposed above? From which competitors would you expect serious retaliation in the market?

4. From the perspectives of each of the partners in the venture, what sort of diversification move does this represent? What are the risks to Mercedes and to Swatch? Explain.

SOURCE: Audrey Choi and Margaret Studer, "Daimler-Benz's Mercedes Unit to Build a Car with Maker of Swatch Watches," *The Wall Street Journal,* February 23, 1994, p. A14; and Kevin Helliker, "Can Wristwatch Whiz Switch Swatch Cachet to an Automobile?," *The Wall Street Journal,* March 4, 1994, pp. A1–A5.

Notes

1. Michael Porter, *Competitive Advantage* (New York: Free Press, 1985), p. 33.

2. Ibid.

3. Avinash Dixit and Barry Nalebuff, *Thinking Strategically* (New York: W. W. Norton, 1991).

4. Shaker Zahra and Sherry Chaples, "Blind Spots in Competitive Analysis," *Academy of Management Executive,* May 1993, p. 7; see also, E. Zajac and M. Bazerman, "Blind Spots in Industry and Competitor Analysis," *Academy of Management Review* 16, no. 1 (1991), p. 37.

5. Pankaj Ghemawat, "Sustainable Advantage," *Harvard Business Review,* September/October 1986, p. 53.

6. Amar Bhide, "Hustle as Strategy," *Harvard Business Review,* September/October 1986, p. 59; see also Joseph Bower and Thomas Hout, "Fast-Cycle Capability for Competitive Power," *Harvard Business Review,* November/December 1988, p. 110.

7. Bower and Hout, "Fast-Cycle Capability," p. 111.

8. Jeffrey Williams, "How Sustainable Is Your Competitive Advantage?" *California Management Review,* Spring 1992, p. 29.

9. C. K. Prahalad and Gary Hamel, "The Core Competence of the Corporation," *Harvard Business Review,* May/June 1990, p. 82.

10. Porter, *Competitive Advantage,* p. 36.

11. *Fortune,* February 8, 1993; *Business Week,* March 3, 1986.

12. C. Merle Crawford, *New Product Management,* 2d ed. (Homewood, Ill.: Richard D. Irwin, 1987), p. 21.

13. For a complete discussion of human resource management and strategy, see Herbert G. Henneman III, Donald P. Schwab, Hohn A. Fossum, and Lee Dyer, *Personnel/Human Resource Management,* 4th ed. (Homewood, Ill.: Richard D. Irwin, 1989). See also Cynthia A. Lengnick-Hall and Mark L. Lengnick-Hall, "Strategic Human Resources Management: A Review of the Literature and Proposed Typology," *Academy of Management Review* 13, no. 3 (1988), pp. 454–470.

14. See Ted Kumpe and Piet T. Bolwijn, "Manufacturing: The New Case for Vertical Integration," *Harvard Business Review,* March/April 1988, pp. 75–81.

15. These descriptions are based on a discussion in Philip Kotler, *Marketing Management: Analysis, Planning, and Control,* 6th ed. (Englewood Cliffs, N.J.: Prentice-Hall, 1988), pp. 41–42.

16. See Robert Jacobson and David A. Aaker, "Is Market Share All That It's Cracked Up to Be?" *Journal of Marketing,* Fall 1985, pp. 11–22.

17. This discussion is based on Kotler, *Marketing Management,* pp. 43–46.

18. David A. Aaker, *Developing Business Strategies* (New York: John Wiley & Sons, 1984), p. 237.

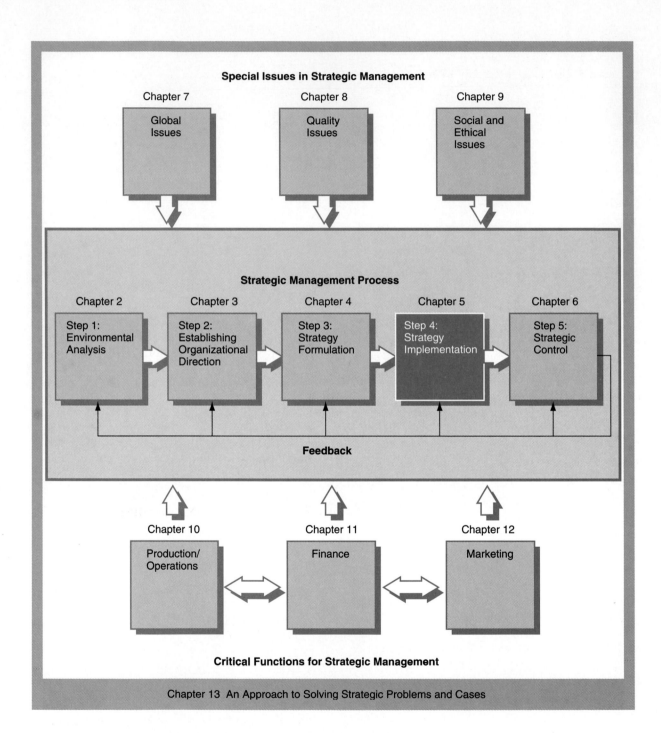

Special Issues in Strategic Management

Chapter 7

Global Issues

Chapter 8

Quality Issues

Chapter 9

Social and Ethical Issues

Strategic Management Process

Chapter 2

Step 1: Environmental Analysis

Chapter 3

Step 2: Establishing Organizational Direction

Chapter 4

Step 3: Strategy Formulation

Chapter 5

Step 4: Strategy Implementation

Chapter 6

Step 5: Strategic Control

Feedback

Chapter 10

Production/ Operations

Chapter 11

Finance

Chapter 12

Marketing

Critical Functions for Strategic Management

Chapter 13 An Approach to Solving Strategic Problems and Cases

CHAPTER 5

Strategy Implementation

In the previous chapter, we discussed a number of important issues that arise as managers formulate strategies. In this chapter, we focus on implementing those strategies—putting them into action. The success of an organization depends on how effectively it implements strategies. In fact, the first attribute listed by Thomas Peters and Robert Waterman as distinctive of excellent, innovative companies is related to the corporate view of implementation. They suggest that excellent companies have a bias for action, for getting on with the job:

> Even though these companies may be analytical in their approach to decision making, they are not paralyzed by that fact (as so many others seem to be). In many of these companies the standard operating procedure is "Do it, fix it, try it." . . . Moreover, the companies are experimenters supreme. Instead of allowing 250 engineers and marketers to work on a new product in isolation for 15 months, they form bands of 5 to 25 and test ideas out on a customer, often with inexpensive prototypes, within a matter of weeks. What is striking is the host of practical devices the excellent companies employ to maintain corporate fleetness of foot and counter the stultification that almost inevitably comes with size.[1]

As this quote suggests, effective managers often work back and forth between strategy formulation and strategy implementation. Many successful organizations do not plan every aspect of a strategy in detail and then proceed to implement it according to the predefined schedule. Rather, strategies are often partially formulated, implemented, reformulated, and extended to rapidly capitalize on strategic opportunities. Henry Mintzberg refers to this process as *crafting* a strategy: "Formulation and implementation merge into a fluid process of learning through which creative strategies evolve."[2] Thus, although this chapter focuses on implementation, remember that formulation and implementation influence each other and often evolve together.

Also, keep in mind that the managerial skills required to formulate a strategy differ significantly from those needed to implement that strategy. Formulation calls on the best analytical and technical skills that an executive or executive team can muster, while implementation draws more heavily on leadership and administrative skills of a person or team.

What forces can a top manager deploy to assist in strategy implementation? In our view, three key building blocks will, if well managed, yield effective strategy implementation—managing change, managing structure, and managing culture.

This stage of the strategic management process offers the greatest potential for wide-ranging, integrative, cross-functional methods, since strategy implementation, or acting on a strategy, involves every function and person in the organization. The top management team clearly is involved since it must assess and manage the three interrelated core elements—change, structure, and culture. Top managers depend on other managers as well as the employees of the firm, however, to translate a strategy—a plan—into a living reality. Today's business context places these managers and employees more frequently in cross-functional teams to more effectively implement strategies. Rubbermaid, Black & Decker, Ford, 3M, Microsoft, Lotus Development, General Mills, and many other U.S. firms use cross-functional teams, sometimes with self-management responsibility, to carry out implementation activities ranging from product design and development to production to sales to customer service. Firms whose strategies depend heavily on getting new products designed and manufactured efficiently and marketed quickly have achieved excellent results from cross-functional teams made up of experts from R&D, production, marketing, and finance.

We propose a five-stage model of the strategy implementation process in Figure 5.1, which is built around the three building blocks identified above. It is useful, we find, to dissect this crucial process into discrete steps of (1) determining how much the organization will have to change in order to implement the strategy under consideration and managing the change process, (2) managing the formal and informal structures of the organization, (3) managing the culture of the organization, (4) selecting an appropriate scheme to implement the strategy, and (5) evaluating implementation skills.

FIGURE 5.1
Strategic Implementation Tasks

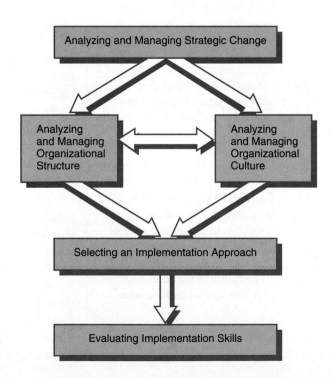

ANALYZING STRATEGIC CHANGE

A useful first step in implementing a strategy is to determine clearly how much the organization will have to change in order to succeed in the implementation. Some strategies require only minimal changes in the way a firm currently conducts its business; others require sweeping changes in its operations. For example, implementing a new pricing strategy may affect only a few people within the organization and cause very little change in day-to-day operations. However, it may require a radical change to replace a traditional organization structure based on functional boundaries with a more flexible, nontraditional structure of cross-functional teams intended to improve the firm's design-for-manufacture capabilities and its time to market.

Strategic change can be viewed as a continuum running from no variation in strategy to a complete change in an organization's mission. For analysis, it is useful to divide strategic change into the five discrete stages shown in Table 5.1. By determining the level of strategic change, managers can more accurately anticipate problems likely to arise in implementing the strategy. Typically, implementation becomes more complex with the move from a stable strategy to organizational redirection, because the number of organizational units, people, and tasks involved increases greatly. In addition, the problems involved in organizational redirection are more likely to be unique or unfamiliar. The five levels of strategic change and the implications of each for strategy implementation are discussed in the sections that follow.

Stable Strategy

A **stable strategy** essentially repeats the strategy from the previous planning period. Because this choice involves no new skills or unfamiliar tasks, successful implementation is largely a matter of monitoring activities to ensure that they are performed on schedule. At this level, experience curve effects (i.e., learning from previous experience) can help to make implementation more cost-effective and efficient.

Routine Strategy Change

A **routine strategy change** makes normal, predicted adjustments in the methods by which the firm seeks to attract customers. Firms may alter their advertising appeals, update packaging, use different pricing tactics, and change

TABLE 5.1

Levels of Strategic Change

	Industry	Organization	Products	Market Appeal
Stable strategy	same	same	same	same
Routine strategy change	same	same	same	new
Limited strategy change	same	same	new	new
Radical strategy change	same	new	new	new
Organizational redirection	new	new	new	new

distributors or distribution methods in the normal course of operations. Campbell Soup, for example, changes its radio ads with the weather. When a storm is forecasted, the commercials encourage consumers to stock up on soup before the weather worsens; after the storm has hit, the message encourages consumers to stay home and enjoy good, hot soup. Implementing such strategies requires managers to schedule and coordinate activities with ad agencies and intermediaries. In some cases, such as when the firm offers a significant price deal to intermediaries or consumers, managers must also coordinate production to ensure that enough inventory is available to handle increased demand.

An important type of routine strategy change involves positioning or repositioning a product in the minds of consumers. A classic example of this involved 7 Up, which for many years had difficulty convincing consumers that it was a soft drink and not just a mixer. By promoting 7 Up as the Uncola, the company positioned it as both a soft drink that could be consumed in the same situations as colas and an alternative to colas. This strategy proved successful, but it did not require a major change for effective implementation.

Limited Strategy Change

A **limited strategy change** involves offering new products to new markets within the same general product class. Managers must handle many variations at this level of strategic change, because products can be new in a variety of ways. For example, Extra-Strength Tylenol was a new product formulation that did not require radically different methods of production or marketing, so implementing a strategy to sell this product required no major change in Johnson & Johnson's operations. On the other hand, the creation, production, and marketing of products such as stereos, televisions, home computers, videocassette recorders, and video cameras for new or evolving markets often involve more complex implementation problems.

Radical Strategy Change

A **radical strategy change** involves a major shift for the firm. This type of change is commonly necessary to complete mergers and acquisitions between firms in the same basic industry. For example, Nestlé acquired Carnation (both of which were in the food industry), and Procter & Gamble acquired Richardson-Vicks (both in consumer products). Such acquisitions can create particularly complex problems in integrating the firms. The acquiring firm not only obtains new products and markets, but also confronts legal problems, the complexities of developing a new organizational structure, and (quite often) the need to reconcile conflicts between organizational cultures.

Radical corporate strategy change can be driven by new approaches to acquisitions and sales of businesses or business units. For example, when John F. Welch, Jr., became chairman of General Electric, the company was regarded as a "GNP company" whose growth and prosperity could never outpace those of the overall economy. Welch set out to create a company that could outpace the economy and prosper even in difficult economic times. He stripped entire levels from the corporate hierarchy and shifted resources from manufacturing businesses to fast-growing service and high-technology units. He bought NBC and automated production facilities, eliminating 100,000 employees, more than one-fourth of the work force. In his first five years as chairman, he sold 190 subsidiaries worth nearly $6 billion and spent $10 billion on 70 acquisitions. Clearly, this is a strategy of radical change, which may eventually develop into a total organizational redirection.[3]

Organizational Redirection

One form of **organizational redirection** involves mergers and acquisitions of firms in different industries. The degree of strategic change depends on how much the industries differ and on how centralized management of the new firm will be. For example, when Philip Morris, a manufacturer of cigarettes and beverages, acquired General Foods, a food products manufacturer, the redirection essentially created a single, more diversified organization operating in two similar industries. When General Motors acquired Electronic Data Systems (EDS), however, the implementation was complicated by considerable differences between the industries and between the two companies' views of appropriate business conduct. EDS personnel codes forbade employees from drinking alcohol at lunchtime or wearing tasseled shoes. GM employees who transferred to EDS were deeply dissatisfied with such rules, and over 600 of them resigned. Then Chairman Roger B. Smith had a near revolt on his hands as he attempted to reconcile the two different corporate cultures.[4]

Another form of organizational redirection occurs when a firm leaves one industry and enters a new one. For example, when one small brewery could no longer compete in the beer industry, it redirected its efforts to the trucking and packaging industries. Similarly, American Can Company redirected its business from packaging to financial services during the mid-1980s, as noted in Chapter 4.[5] This type of organizational redirection is the most complex strategy to implement. It involves changes in the firm's mission and may require development of an entirely new set of skills and technologies.

Managing Strategic Change

These broad categories can give a manager a sense of the magnitude of a newly implemented change, but they do not shed much light on how to actually manage a strategic change effort. While a fully developed discussion of managing change is outside the boundaries of this text, we do wish to present one general framework and to point the interested reader toward additional resources.

James Brian Quinn provides an outline of the steps that effective leaders often use to manage strategic change.[6] Table 5.2 shows three major sequential steps, along with the specific activities in each. Quinn's approach emphasizes the essential analytical and political roles of the executive in managing the strategic change effort and returns us to the issue of sensemaking and interpretation introduced in Chapter 2. Besides the analytical and technical skills to make sense of their environments, effective top managers also need political and leadership skills to sell those interpretations to others and to orchestrate changes that they imply.[7]

ANALYZING AND MANAGING ORGANIZATIONAL STRUCTURE

Managers must contend with two basic kinds of organizational structures. The **formal organizational structure** represents the relationships between people and functions as designed by management and conveyed in the organization

TABLE 5.2

Managing Strategic Change

INITIATING STRATEGIC CHANGE

- Build networks to sense needs
- Improve and lead the formal information system
- Amplify understanding
- Build awareness
- Change symbols
- Legitimize new viewpoints
- Develop partial solutions
- Broaden support

MOVE FROM CONCEPT TO STRATEGY

- Overcome opposition to change by finding zones of indifference and no-lose situations
- Building comfort levels; change perceived risks
- Structure flexibility
- Test trial concepts

SOLIDIFY COMMITMENT

- Create key pockets of commitment
- Keep political exposure low
- Eliminate options
- Crystallize focus and consensus; manage coalitions
- Formalize commitment; empower champions
- Design continuous strategic change process

chart. The **informal organizational structure** represents the web of social relationships based on friendships or interests shared among various members of an organization. The informal organizational structure reveals itself in the patterns of communication commonly called the *grapevine*.

When implementing a strategy, managers must consider both the formal and the informal organizational structures for three reasons. First, the existing organizational structure may or may not adequately support, or even impede, successful implementation. If the organization has so many levels of management that a strategy cannot be implemented effectively or changed rapidly to accommodate changing conditions, then successful implementation may become difficult. In some cases, effective implementation may require changes to the formal organizational structure. For example, GE shed several echelons of organizational structure under Welch and it regrouped its 15 businesses into three areas to make the company more cost-effective and responsive to change.

Second, implementation requires assigning tasks to specific management levels and personnel within the organization. A radical strategy change or organizational redirection is typically spearheaded by the chief executive officer, whereas routine strategy changes may be directed by middle management. Third, the informal organization can become a valuable tool to facilitate successful implementation. For example, if several regional managers commonly consult with each other about implementation issues, this informal network can be used to encourage rapid execution of strategic actions.

The formal organizational structure commonly displays characteristics of one of six types: the simple, functional, divisional, strategic business unit (SBU), matrix, and network structures. Schematic diagrams of these structures appear in Figure 5.2.

Simple Organizational Structure

A **simple organizational structure** has only two levels, the owner-manager and the employees. Small firms that produce only one good or service, or only a few related ones, usually exhibit this structure. A major advantage of this structure is that it allows rapid, flexible implementation of strategies and strategic changes. This advantage is a primary source of competitive advantage that can sometimes allow small firms to compete effectively with industry giants. Those independently owned and operated specialty firms we see in our communities—frozen yogurt shops, sporting goods stores—are typically structured this way, with owner and employees performing a wide range

FIGURE 5.2   Six Types of Organizational Structures

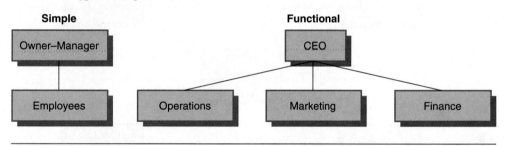

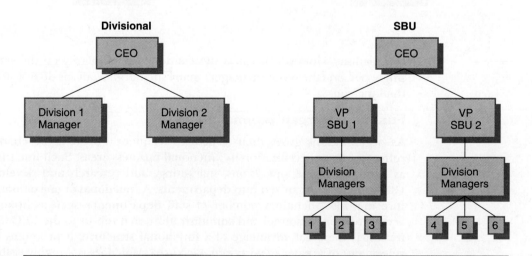

Continued

FIGURE 5.2   Continued

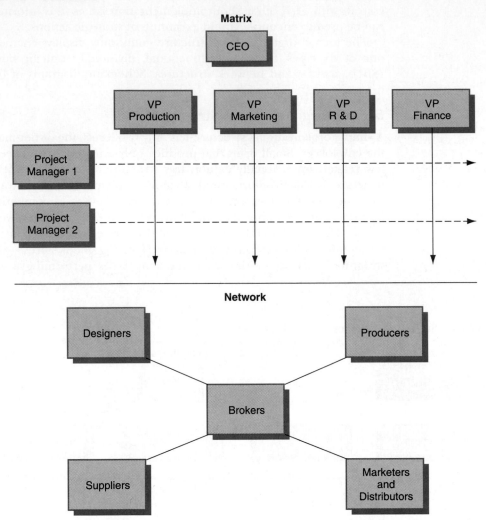

of functions. However, because success depends so heavily on the skills of a single person (the owner-manager) many such organizations do not survive in the long run.

Functional Organizational Structure

As organizations grow, their structures frequently need to be changed to reflect greater specialization in functional business areas. Such line functions as production and operations, marketing, and research and development (R&D) may be organized into departments. A **functional organizational structure** may also include a number of staff departments, such as finance and accounting or personnel and administration, that report to the CEO. Specialization is the chief advantage of a functional structure; it promotes the development of greater expertise in each area. Wal-Mart is a highly visible contemporary example of the enduring power of the functional organizational

C O M P A N Y   E X A M P L E

IBM Reorganizes Its Sales Force

Attempting to sharpen its customer focus and remain competitive, International Business Machines Corp. has undertaken the biggest reorganization of its worldwide sales and marketing force in decades. IBM intends to eliminate one or more layers of management to help transform its account executives from order-takers to business advisers.

The change reorganizes IBM's primary sales staff by industry rather than geography. Chairman Louis Gerstner had hoped to see full implementation of a less sweeping plan established by his predecessor, but he apparently decided to accelerate the effort and impose major change. The reorganization is a step that industry experts and some customers have been urging for years.

The shift to focus on industries rather than geography brings fundamental change to a company with a historic policy of promoting only from within—especially in the sales force. In setting up 14 industry areas, including banking, retail, travel, and insurance, and granting broad powers to their

chiefs, IBM will fill half of the top U.S. posts with recent hires from the consulting industry.

Today, most IBM account executives report up through an intricate network of sales branches, overseen by trading area managers, who in turn report to top managers in charge of broad regions, such as New England. The new structure has account teams that bypass branch managers and report directly to the industry group heads. The move could erode the power of IBM's geographically based sales chiefs, who previously held sway over thousands of careers, and could lead to turf wars.

The biggest impact could occur overseas, where Gerstner's team has had trouble controlling some of IBM's long-autonomous executives. These country heads could see their power diminished as the loyalties of sales executives shift to industry groups within the region.

SOURCE: Bart Ziegler, "IBM Plans to Revamp Sales Structure to Focus on Industries, Not Geography," *The Wall Street Journal*, May 6, 1994, p. A3.

structure.[8] Wal-Mart's effective profit and growth performance is supported by functional excellence in its logistics, inventory control, and distribution systems. However, functional structures may suffer from coordination problems among departments that may impede effective operations, especially when a firm's goods or services become more diverse.

Divisional Organizational Structure

As a firm acquires or develops new products in different industries and markets, it may have to adopt a **divisional organizational structure.** Each division may operate autonomously under the direction of a division manager, who reports directly to the CEO. Divisions may be based on product lines (automotive components, aircraft), markets (consumers, organizational buyers), geographic areas (north, south, international), or channels of distribution (retail stores, catalog sales). Managers in each division must handle not only their own line and staff functions, but they must also formulate and implement strategies on their own with the approval of the CEO. The overall organization has staff positions (such as vice presidents of administration and operations) to assist in coordinating activities and allocating resources. The divisional organizational structure helps large companies to remain close to their markets and responsive in their strategies, but conflict can result as the divisions compete for resources. The Company Example tells of IBM's effort to organize its sales operations along industry or customer lines rather than geographic lines. This example explores the internal political problems that corporate reorganizations often face.

Strategic Business Unit Organizational Structure

When a divisional structure becomes unwieldy, giving the CEO too many divisions to manage effectively, the organization may reorganize in the form of strategic business units (SBUs) or strategic groups. The **strategic business unit organizational structure** groups a number of divisions together on the basis of similarities in such things as product lines or markets. Vice presidents are appointed to oversee the operations of the newly formed strategic business units, and these executives report directly to the CEO. The SBU structure may be useful for coordinating divisions with similar strategic problems and opportunities. However, because it imposes another layer of management, it can also slow decision making and retard the implementation process unless authority is decentralized.

Matrix Organizational Structure

A **matrix organizational structure** facilitates the development and execution of various large programs or projects. As shown in Figure 5.2, each departmental vice president listed at the top has *functional* responsibility for all projects within the function; the project managers listed down the side have responsibility for completing and implementing strategic projects. This approach allows project managers to cut across departmental lines, and it can promote efficient implementation of strategies. In effect, project groups are cross-functional teams, that exist for the duration of a project. The matrix structure does have an important disadvantage: employees often become confused about their work responsibilities and about whether they are accountable to project managers or to their functional group managers. In their study of excellent corporations, Peters and Waterman made the following observation about matrix organization structures:

> Virtually none of the excellent companies spoke of itself as having formal matrix structures, except for project management companies like Boeing. But in a company like Boeing, where many of the matrix ideas originated, something very different is meant by matrix management. People operate in a binary way: they are either a part of a project team and responsible to that team for getting some task accomplished (most of the time), or they are part of a technical discipline, in which they spend some time making sure their technical department is keeping up with the state of the art. When they are on a project, there is no day-in, day-out confusion about whether they are really responsible to the project or not. They are.[9]

Network Organizational Structure

The sixth and most recent addition to the roster of structural types is the **network organizational structure.** Since structures do not develop independently, but as ways to more effectively implement new strategies, what factors have caused this new form to develop? In a series of seminal articles, Raymond Miles, Charles Snow, and a few co-authors have documented the emergence of a variety of network structures.[10] They argue that increased global competition and rapid technological change have caused many firms to shed traditionally internal activities, to downsize to leave only what they do best. Such a firm seeks to keep responsibility only for its core competencies, its world-class or superior skills and activities. This movement has led many firms to reduce the number of layers in their management hierarchies, and to search constantly for opportunities for out-sourcing, that is, contracting with outsiders to provide services instead of performing those functions internally. For example, instead of producing the shoes it designs, Nike contracts with a set of Asian manufacturers to produce them.

A new strategic perspective drives this movement to networks. Managers have a growing sense that value chains can be rethought and reconfigured so that a firm can achieve competitive success by building for itself, not a set of tightly controlled, internally managed activities, but a set of negotiated and cooperative relationships involving several other partner firms, *all doing what they do best.* In this way, networks can come to resemble the Japanese *keiretsu*—"organizational collectives based on cooperation and mutual shareholding among groups of manufacturers, suppliers, and trading and finance companies."[11]

Unfortunately, no hard and fast rules determine when an organization needs to change its structure to reflect new environmental and strategic realities. For example, moving from a functional to a divisional structure may help a firm to meet customer needs in the markets served by the new divisions. However, the costs of setting up each new division, with its own accounting, marketing, and R&D department, new manufacturing facilities, etc., may offset the benefits gained from increased sales. Similarly, moving from a traditional, functional structure to a network involves new ways of thinking about interfirm cooperation and trust. Miles and Snow point out, for example, that network structures may fail, because, after having shed many noncore activities, a firm might find that its expertise has become too narrow and that its role in the value chain has become more vulnerable.[12]

The 1990s have brought a great deal of experimentation in defining the core tasks and processes to include in the modern organization (e.g., network structures). In addition, innovative ways of organizing to complete tasks and processes (e.g., teams), are sometimes revolutionary. Pictures of organization structures have traditionally looked like the organization charts in Figure 5.2. However, as the tradition of vertical authority and control has faced challenges from new modes of doing work, such as cross-functional teams, new ways of picturing organization structures have emerged.[13] Figure 5.3 illustrates four examples of this new generation of organization chart.

In sum, analyzing and managing organizational structure is a necessary step in strategy implementation; it forces managers to consider a strategy in relation to the tasks that must be performed to effectively implement it. The firm's current structure and personnel are often adequate for successful implementation. In some cases, a temporary change in structure may facilitate implementation without creating undue problems. In a few cases, when a particular organizational structure is so cumbersome and inefficient that it prevents the firm from implementing a good strategy effectively, the structure may need to be completely overhauled. However, other factors must be considered before management concludes that an organization's structure must be revamped. One of the most important of these factors is the organization's culture.

FIGURE 5.3
New Models for the
Modern Organization

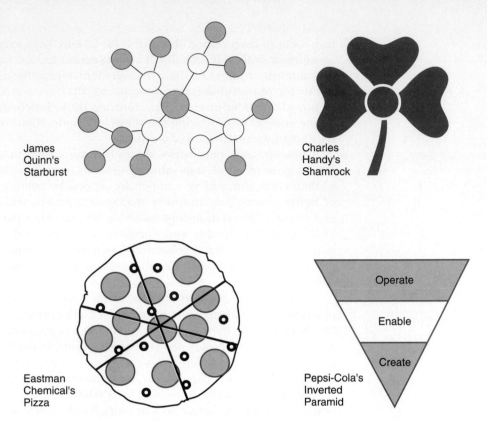

James
Quinn's
Starburst

Charles
Handy's
Shamrock

Eastman
Chemical's
Pizza

Pepsi-Cola's
Inverted
Paramid

Operate

Enable

Create

SOURCE: John Byrne, "Congratulations. You're Moving to a New Pepperoni." Reprinted from December 20, 1993 issue of *Business Week* by special permission, copyright © 1993 by McGraw-Hill, Inc.

ANALYZING AND MANAGING ORGANIZATIONAL CULTURE

Scholars have proposed many definitions of organizational or corporate culture. For the purposes of this text, we will take **organizational culture** to mean a set of shared values and beliefs that develop in an organization over time. Organizational culture affects strategy implementation by influencing the behavior of employees and, it is hoped, motivating them to achieve or surpass organizational objectives. Typically, the CEO and other present or past organization leaders exert key influence on culture. In addition, organizations often exhibit various subcultures in particular divisions or departments, which are influenced by leaders at these levels.

Organizations develop and reinforce cultures in a variety of ways. One authority identifies five primary and five secondary cultural development mechanisms.[14] The five primary mechanisms are:

1. *What leaders pay attention to, measure, and control:* Leaders can communicate their vision of the organization and what they want done very effectively by consistently emphasizing the same issues in meetings, in casual remarks and questions, and in strategy discussions. For example, if product quality is the dominant value they want to inculcate in employees, leaders may consistently inquire about the effects of any proposed changes on product quality.

2. *Leaders' reactions to critical incidents and organizational crises:* Leaders' methods for dealing with crises can create new beliefs and values and reveal underlying organizational assumptions. For example, when a firm faces a financial crisis without laying off any employees, it may broadcast the message that the organization sees itself as a family that looks out for its members.

3. *Deliberate role modeling, teaching, and coaching:* Leaders' behaviors in both formal and informal settings have important effects on employee beliefs, values, and behaviors. For example, if the CEO regularly works very long hours and on weekends, other managers may respond by spending more of their time at work, too.

4. *Criteria for allocation of rewards and status:* Leaders can quickly communicate their priorities and values by consistently linking rewards and punishments to desirable behaviors. For example, a weekly bonus for exceeding production or sales quotas may help employees to recognize the value placed on these activities and to focus their efforts appropriately.

5. *Criteria for recruitment, selection, promotion, and retirement of employees:* The types of people who are hired and who succeed in an organization are those who accept the organization's values and behave accordingly. For example, if managers who are risk takers consistently move up the organizational ladder, the organization's priorities should come through loud and clear to other managers.

The Skills Module invites you to apply these mechanisms to analyze the culture of UPS. In addition to the five primary mechanisms we've just mentioned, five secondary mechanisms contribute to the development of organizational culture:

1. *The organization's design and structure:* Designing an organization's structure offers leaders a chance to express their deeply held assumptions about the tasks and processes of the firm, the best means of accomplishing them, human nature, and the right kinds of relationships among people. For example, a highly decentralized organization suggests that leaders have confidence in the abilities of subordinate managers.

2. *Organizational systems and procedures:* Some very visible parts of organizational life influence culture, including the daily, weekly, monthly, quarterly, and annual routines, procedures, reports to file, forms to fill out, and other recurring tasks. For example, if the CEO asks for quarterly reports on all assistant managers, this requirement communicates the message that the organization values this group.

3. *Design of physical space, facades, and buildings:* Leaders who embrace a clear philosophy and management style often make that style manifest in their choices of architectural style, interior design, and decor. For example, leaders who believe in open communication may lay out office space to leave few private areas or barriers to the flow of traffic. In recent years, interior design experts have designed special work spaces for cross-functional teams.

4. *Stories, legends, myths, and parables about important events and people:* As a group develops and accumulates a history, some of this history becomes embodied in stories about events and leadership behavior.

SKILLS MODULE
UPS Reorients Its Corporate Culture

INTRODUCTION

The text outlines five primary cultural development mechanisms. Review the following situation, and then complete the related skill development exercise. This will give you an opportunity to consider some of the issues involved in creating an effective organizational culture.

SITUATION

In 1990, executives at Eastman Kodak Co. were intent on concentrating their shipping business among fewer package carriers, and United Parcel Service Inc., the nation's biggest carrier, was on the endangered list. "Every time we'd ask them about special services or discounts, I'd hear back the same thing: 'It's not in our best interest,'" said a Kodak spokesman. "Well, that's not what I was hearing from their competitors."

UPS responded to the complaints; renewed attention and volume discounts repaired the business relationship. Within three years, Kodak had increased its business with UPS by 15 percent, to 50,000 packages a week.

Kodak is only one of the many customers UPS has won over as result of what UPS insiders call the "velvet revolution." Under Chief Executive Kent Nelson, the Atlanta-based firm has discarded its we-know-what's-best-for-you imperiousness; instead, the package carrier is stressing customer satisfaction via flexible pickup and delivery times, customized shipment plans, and a $2 billion investment in technology to keep up-to-the-minute tabs on shipments. UPS has also done what many had considered unthinkable, moving away from the residential deliveries that had been its bread and butter.

Nelson says he had little choice but to change what customers saw as an aloof and rigid style: The competition had been cherry-picking many of UPS's best customers. He began the revolution in-house. In 1990, as profit margins slid toward 4 percent from nearly 7 percent two years prior, Nelson appointed four top executives to conduct an intensive review of UPS's business methods.

Key to improving customer service was beefing up the marketing staff. For years, UPS had relied on a seven-person team, too few to handle questions from both existing and potential customers. By 1992, the staff had grown to 175 and was handling 6,000 corporate inquiries annually.

The headquarters-driven overhaul of corporate culture has met little resistance from managers and supervisors in the field. Retraining helped, but executive compliance is more easily explained by UPS's compensation plan. Each year, the firm spends 15 percent of its pre-tax profit to buy company stock, which it distributes to employees from entry-level supervisors on up. "We have 25,000 owner-managers who have virtually every cent they own invested in stock of this company," says Nelson. "They knew that if we didn't change, somebody would, and there'd go your life savings."

Others within UPS are not as happy—or motivated. Relations have often been rocky between the company and the Teamsters union, which represents 165,000 drivers and package sorters. The union has long complained about how UPS treats its members; some drivers, for example, are told to make 15 deliveries or pickups an hour, no matter what the traffic conditions. Drawn-out contract negotiations and strikes loom as a long-term threat.

SKILL DEVELOPMENT EXERCISE

Kent Nelson and other UPS executives clearly recognized that they had a serious customer-service problem, but uncooperative drivers could damage corporate efforts to boost business. For each of the five primary cultural development mechanisms, suggest one thing the leaders of UPS should do to develop a more effective organizational culture that envelops all levels of UPS workers.

SOURCE: "After a U-Turn, UPS Really Delivers," *Business Week*, May 31, 1993, p. 92.

5. *Formal statements of organizational philosophy, creeds, or charters:* Explicit statements by leaders of organizations about their values are a means of shaping organizational culture.

Organizational leaders have devised a variety of methods for developing, maintaining, or changing organizational cultures. However, changing an organizational culture is a difficult task. If it is possible at all, it may require many years to complete. Continuation, routine, or limited strategy changes usually are implemented without changes to the organizational culture. Radical strategy changes and organizational redirections often require long-term changes in organizational culture.

SELECTING AN IMPLEMENTATION APPROACH

After evaluating the effect of culture on strategy implementations the manager must select an overall approach to implementing strategy based on an assessment of change, structure, and culture variables. Research on management practices at a number of companies has led David Brodwin and L. J. Bourgeois to suggest five fundamental approaches to implementing strategies.[15] These approaches range from simply telling employees to implement the strategy that has been formulated to developing employees who can formulate and implement sound strategies on their own. In each approach, the manager plays a somewhat different role and uses different methods of strategic management. Brodwin and Bourgeois call these five approaches the Commander approach, the Organizational Change approach, the Collaborative approach, the Cultural approach, and the Crescive approach. Table 5.3 presents an overview of these approaches; each is discussed below.

Commander Approach

Under this approach, the manager concentrates on formulating strategy, applying rigorous logic and analysis. The manager may either develop the strategy alone or supervise a team of strategists charged with determining the optimal course of action for the organization. Tools such as the growth–share matrix and industry and competitive analysis are commonly used by managers who employ this approach. After determining the best strategy, the manager passes it along to subordinates with instructions to execute it. The manager does not take an active role in implementing the strategy.

This approach has a serious drawback in the potential to reduce employee motivation; employees who feel that they have no say in strategy formulation are unlikely to be a very innovative group. However, the approach can work effectively in smaller companies within stable industries. It works best when the strategy to be implemented requires relatively little change.

Although the Commander approach can raise a number of problems, it is commonly advocated by certain business consultants and is used by many managers. Several factors account for its popularity. First, despite its drawbacks, it allows managers to focus their energies on strategy formulation. By dividing the strategic management task into two stages—thinking and doing—the manager reduces the number of factors that have to be considered simultaneously. Second, young managers, in particular, seem to prefer this approach because it allows them to focus on the quantitative, objective aspects of a situation rather than on qualitative, subjective behavioral interactions.

TABLE 5.3

Comparison of Five Approaches to Implementing a Strategy

	Approach				
Factor	Commander	Change	Collaborative	Cultural	Crescive
HOW ARE GOALS SET? Where in the organization (top or bottom) are the strategic goals established?	Dictated from top	Dictated from top	Negotiated among top team	Embodied in culture	Stated loosely from top, refined from bottom
WHAT SIGNIFIES SUCCESS? What signifies a successful outcome to the strategic planning/implementation process?	A good plan as judged on economic criteria	Organization and structure that fit the strategy	An acceptable plan with broad top management support	An army of busy implementers	Sound strategies with champions behind them
WHAT FACTORS ARE CONSIDERED? What kinds of factors, or types of rationality, are used in developing a strategy for resolving conflicts between alternative proposed strategies?	Economic	Economic, political	Economic, social, political	Economic, social	Economic, social, political, behavioral
WHAT TYPICAL LEVEL OF ORGANIZATION-WIDE EFFORT IS REQUIRED?					
During the planning phase	Low	Low	High	High	High
During the implementation phase	N/A	High	Low	Low	Low
HOW STRINGENT ARE THE REQUIREMENTS PLACED ON THE CEO IN ORDER FOR THE APPROACH TO SUCCEED?					
Required CEO knowledge: To what extent must the CEO be able to maintain personal awareness of all significant strategic opportunities or threats?	High	High	Moderate	Low	Low
Required CEO power: To what extent must the CEO have the power to impose a detailed implementation plan on the organization?	High	High	Moderate	Moderate	Moderate

SOURCE: David R. Brodwin and L. J. Bourgeois III, "Five Steps to Strategic Action." Copyright © 1984 by the Regents of the University of California. Reprinted from the *California Management Review,* Vol. 26, No. 3. By permission of The Regents.

(Many young managers are better trained to deal with the former than with the latter.) Finally, such an approach may make some ambitious managers feel powerful in that their thinking and decision making can affect the activities of thousands of people.

Organizational Change Approach

Whereas the manager who adopts the Commander approach avoids dealing directly with implementation, the Organizational Change approach (or simply the Change approach) focuses on how to get organization members to implement a strategy. Managers who follow the Change approach assume that they have formulated a good strategy; they view their task as getting the company moving toward new goals. The tools used to accomplish this task are largely behavioral, such as changing the organizational structure and staffing to focus attention on the organization's new priorities, revising planning and control systems, and invoking other organizational change techniques. The manager functions as an architect, designing administrative systems for effective strategy implementation.

Because the Change approach to implementation employs powerful behavioral tools, it is often more effective than the Commander approach, and it can implement more difficult strategies. However, the Change approach has several limitations that may restrict its use to smaller companies in stable industries. It doesn't deal well with politics and personal agendas that discourage objectivity among strategists. Also, because it calls for imposing strategy from the top down, it can cause the same motivational problems as the Commander approach.

Finally, this approach can backfire in uncertain or rapidly changing conditions. The manager sacrifices important strategic flexibility by manipulating the systems and structures of the organization in support of a particular strategy. Some of these systems (particularly incentive compensation) take a long time to design and install. Should a change in the environment require a new strategy, it may be very difficult to change the organization's course, which has been firmly established to support the now-obsolete strategy.

Collaborative Approach

In the Collaborative approach, the manager in charge of the strategy calls in the rest of the management team to brainstorm strategy formulation *and* implementation tactics. Managers are encouraged to contribute their points of view in order to extract group wisdom from multiple perspectives. The manager functions as a coordinator, using his or her understanding of group dynamics to ensure that all good ideas are discussed and investigated. For example, several years ago General Motors formed business teams that brought together managers from different functional areas. The teams were intended simply to bring out different points of view on strategic problems as they arose. Exxon's major strategic decisions are made by its management committee, which comprises all of Exxon's inside directors, led by the chairman of the board. Every committee member serves as a contact executive for the line managers of one or more of Exxon's 13 affiliates and subsidiaries.

The Collaborative approach overcomes two key limitations of the other two approaches we have evaluated so far. By capturing information contributed by managers closer to operations, and by offering a forum for the expression of many viewpoints, it can increase the quality and timeliness of the information incorporated in the strategy. To the degree that participation enhances commitment to the strategy, it improves the chances of efficient implementation.

Though the Collaborative approach may gain more commitment than the foregoing approaches, it has other problems. Negotiating strategy among managers with different points of view and, possibly, different goals may reduce management's chances of formulating and implementing superior strategies. For one thing, a negotiated strategy is likely to be less visionary and more conservative than one created by an individual or staff team. For another, gaming and empire building by various individual managers may skew a strategy toward a particular functional area, sacrificing an overall strategic perspective. Also, the negotiation process can take so much time that an organization misses opportunities and fails to react quickly enough to changes in the environment.

Finally, a fundamental criticism of the Collaborative approach questions whether it really amounts to collective decision making from an organizational viewpoint because upper-level managers often retain centralized control. In effect, this approach preserves the artificial distinction between thinkers and doers and fails to draw on the full human potential throughout the organization. When properly used, the Collaborative approach can increase commitment to a strategy and encourage effective implementation, yet it can also create political problems within the organization that can impede rapid and efficient strategy formulation and implementation.

Cultural Approach

The Cultural approach expands the Collaborative approach to include lower levels in the organization. In this approach, the manager guides the organization by communicating and instilling his or her vision of the overall mission for the organization and then allowing employees to design their own work activities to support this mission. Once the strategy is formulated, the manager plays the role of coach, giving general directions but encouraging individual decision making on the operating details of executing the strategy.

The implementation tools used in building a strong organizational culture range from such simple notions as publishing a company creed and singing a company song to much more complex techniques. These techniques involve what can be called *third-order control.* First-order control is direct supervision; second-order control involves using rules, procedures, and organizational structure to guide behavior. Third-order control is more subtle, and potentially more powerful. It seeks to influence behavior by shaping the norms, values, symbols, and beliefs on which managers and employees base day-to-day decisions.

The Cultural approach partially breaks down the barriers between thinkers and doers, because each member of the organization can be involved to some degree in both formulation and implementation of strategy. Hewlett-Packard is a well-known example of a company whose employees share a strong awareness of the corporate mission. They all know that the "HP way" encourages product innovation at every level. Matsushita, for its part, starts each work day with 87,000 employees singing the company song and reciting its code of values. The company creed at JCPenney is reprinted in Table 5.4.

The Cultural approach appears to work best in organizations that have sufficient resources to absorb the cost of building and maintaining suppor-

---

TABLE 5.4

JCPenney's Company Creed

JCPenney's company creed, called "The Penney Idea," was adopted in 1913. It consists of the following seven points:

1. To serve the public, as nearly as we can, to its complete satisfaction
2. To expect for the service we render a fair remuneration and not all the profit the traffic will bear
3. To do all in our power to pack the customer's dollar full of value, quality, and satisfaction
4. To continue to train ourselves and our associates so that the service we give will be more and more intelligently performed
5. To improve constantly the human factor in our business
6. To reward men and women in our organization through participation in what the business produces
7. To test our every policy, method and act in this wise: "Does it square with what is right and just?"

---

tive value systems. Often these are high-growth firms in high-technology industries.

While this approach has a number of advantages, not the least of which is dedicated, enthusiastic implementation of strategies, it also has limitations. First, it tends to work only in organizations composed primarily of informed, intelligent people. Second, its development consumes enormous amounts of time. Third, its strong sense of organizational identity can become a handicap; for example, bringing in outsiders at top management levels can be difficult because they aren't accepted by other executives. Fourth, companies with excessively strong cultures often suppress deviance, discourage attempts to change, and foster homogeneity and inbred thinking. To handle this conformist tendency, some companies (such as IBM, Xerox, and GM) have segregated their ongoing research units and their new product development efforts, sometimes placing them in physical locations far enough from other units to shield them from the corporation's dominant culture.

Crescive Approach

The manager who adopts the Crescive approach addresses strategy formulation and strategy implementation simultaneously. (*Crescive* means increasing or growing.) However, she or he does not focus on performing these tasks, but on encouraging subordinates to develop, champion, and implement sound strategies on their own. This approach differs from the others in several ways. First, instead of strategy falling downward from top management or a strategy group, it moves upward from the doers (salespeople, engineers, production workers) and lower middle-level managers and supervisors. Second, strategy becomes the sum of all the individual proposals that surface throughout the year. Third, the top-management team shapes the employees' premises, that is, the employees' notions of what would constitute supportable strategic projects. Fourth, the chief executive, or manager in charge of strategy, functions more as a judge evaluating the proposals rather than as a master strategist.

Brodwin and Bourgeois advocate the Crescive approach primarily for CEOs of large, complex, diversified organizations. In such an organization, the CEO cannot know and understand all the strategic and operating forces that affect each division. Therefore, to formulate and implement strategies effectively, the CEO must give up some control to spur opportunism and achievement. The 3M Corporation provides an example of this approach to strategy implementation. Top managers set a target for the percentage of each division's revenues that must come from new products. Division managers can then use whatever means they like to achieve these targets. One division manager, for example, restructured his divisions into cross-functional teams to bring new products to market more quickly.

This approach has several advantages. First, it encourages middle-level managers to work to formulate effective strategies and gives them opportunities to implement their own plans. This autonomy increases their motivation to make the strategy succeed. Second, strategies developed by employees and managers closer to strategic opportunities, as these are, often are operationally sound and readily implemented. However, this approach requires that the firm (1) provide funds for individuals to develop good ideas unencumbered by bureaucratic approval cycles, and (2) extend tolerance in the inevitable cases of failure despite worthy efforts. Furthermore, converting a centralized, top-down organization to the Crescive approach can be very difficult, expensive, and time consuming. Finally, the Crescive approach does not specify how managers should go about implementing the strategy. In sum, the Crescive approach is viable for complex organizations that compete in dynamic industries.

EVALUATING IMPLEMENTATION SKILLS FOR MANAGERS

By this stage, the manager has a clear idea of the level of strategic change to be implemented. In addition, analysis of the organization's structure and culture has developed an understanding of the factors within the organization that will facilitate or impede implementation. An implementation approach has been selected that promises the best job of capitalizing on the firm's strengths and overcoming, circumventing, or minimizing problems within the organization. The task at the last stage of implementation is to evaluate the implementation skills needed by managers.

Professor Thomas V. Bonoma of the Harvard Business School suggests that successful implementation of strategies requires four basic types of managerial skills.[16] These are shown in Figure 5.4 and discussed below.

Interacting skills are expressed in managing one's own and others' behavior to achieve objectives. Depending on the level of strategic change required to implement a strategy, managers may need to influence others both within and outside the organization. Bonoma suggests that, in general, managers who show empathy—the ability to understand how others feel—and have good bargaining skills are the best implementers.

Allocating skills influence managers' abilities to schedule tasks and budget time, money, and other resources efficiently. Able managers avoid putting too many resources into mature programs and recognize that new, riskier programs often demand investment of more resources.

Monitoring skills involve the efficient use of information to correct any problems that arise in the process of implementation. Good implementers have

FIGURE 5.4   Four Key Implementation Skills

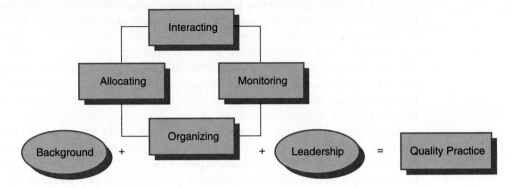

SOURCE: Adapted and reprinted with the permission of The Free Press, an imprint of Simon and Schuster from THE MARKETING EDGE: Making Strategies Work by Thomas V. Bonoma. Copyright 1985 by The Free Press.

efficient feedback systems to analyze progress toward strategy execution and any problems that occur. For example, one general manager of a company with 38 plants and 300,000 customers ran everything he considered crucial according to notations on two 3-by-5 index cards!

Organizing skills help the manager to create a new informal organization or to address each problem that occurs. Good implementers know people in every part of the organization (and outside it) who, by virtue of mutual respect, attraction, or some other tie, can and will help however they can. In other words, good implementers customize the informal organization to facilitate good execution.

Thus, implementation often depends on managers who possess particular skills tailored to overcoming obstacles and ensuring that tasks are performed efficiently. Managers must continuously evaluate how well the strategy is being executed and whether it is accomplishing organizational objectives. We focus on that topic, strategy control and evaluation, in the next chapter.

SUMMARY

In this chapter, we consider implementation as a critical part of the strategic management process that is too frequently undervalued. We develop a five-stage model of the strategy implementation process to draw attention to key facets.

First, it is important to analyze how much the firm itself will have to change in order to implement a proposed strategy successfully. Strategies can range from the no-change or stable strategy through routine strategy change, limited strategy change, and radical strategy change all the way to organizational redirection. This last step consists of sweeping transformations that a firm usually undergoes only when it enters a new industry or takes part in a merger or acquisition. We also consider the skills managers need in order to manage change effectively.

The next stage in the strategy implementation process is to analyze and manage both the formal and informal structures of the organization. A formal structure may be simple (an owner-manager and employees); the firm may be divided into functions (such as marketing, operations, and finance), divisions (handling different product lines, geographic areas, distribution channels, or the like), or groups of divisions known as *strategic business units.* In the matrix organizational structure, functional responsibility and project responsibility may overlap. In the network structure, core competencies provide the basis for reducing the number of functions held within a firm and increasing the number of functions performed by partner firms. Recognizing the linkage of structure to successful strategy implementation is always important.

Analyzing and managing organizational culture is important for implementing strategies. The organization culture consists of the values, beliefs, and attitudes toward the firm that employees share. Leader behaviors, criteria for recruiting and rewarding employees, rules and procedures, formal statements of company creeds, oft-told tales about important events and people in the history of the organization, and even the physical layout of the buildings—all of these can contribute to effective organizational cultures and help to shape employee attitudes and behavior. Once ingrained, organizational culture is persistent, and strategic changes that run counter to it are often doomed to failure.

Brodwin and Bourgeois suggested several different approaches to implement a given strategy. In the Commander approach, the manager formulates a strategy and simply instructs subordinates to implement it. The Organizational Change approach works by assuming that the strategy is good and marshaling behavioral approaches to change organizational structure to implement it. The Collaborative approach invites a management team to participate in both the formulation and the implementation of strategy. The Cultural approach democratizes the Collaborative approach to include lower levels of the organization. Finally, the Crescive approach encourages subordinates to develop, propose, and implement strategies of their own devising. We probed the merits and drawbacks of each approach and outlined the conditions under which each is most likely to be appropriate.

Finally, the implementation process hinges on managers' skills in interacting and empathizing with others, in allocating resources, in monitoring progress toward goals, and in organizing new informal networks. Managers who have such skills can oversee the implementation of strategy effectively and evaluate the implementation process as it unfolds, taking remedial action if necessary.

KEY TERMS

stable strategy, p. 113
routine strategy change, p. 113
limited strategy change, p. 114
radical strategy change, p. 114
organizational redirection, p. 115
formal organizational structure, p. 115
informal organizational structure, p. 116
simple organizational structure, p. 117

functional organizational structure, p. 118
divisional organizational structure, p. 119
strategic business unit organizational structure, p. 120
matrix organizational structure, p. 120
network organizational structure, p. 120
organizational culture, p. 122

CHECKLIST — Analyzing Strategy Implementation in Problems and Cases

___ 1. Does the situation or case involve strategy implementation issues?

___ 2. Is the strategy implementation fulfilling all of its purposes?

___ 3. Has the strategy been successfully translated into action?

___ 4. Is it clear what level of strategic change is necessary and appropriate?

___ 5. Have the organization's formal and informal structures been well-analyzed prior to strategy implementation?

___ 6. Does the situation or case focus on how a structural type can be used to implement a strategy?

___ 7. Are various levels of management appropriately involved in the strategy implementation process?

___ 8. Have the implementation skills needed by managers been evaluated?

___ 9. Have each of the primary and secondary cultural-development mechanisms been assessed?

___ 10. Does the implementation plan focus on the correct approach?

Additional Readings

Egelhoff, William G. "Great Strategy or Great Strategic Implementation—Two Ways of Competing in Global Markets." *Sloan Management Review,* Winter 1993, p. 37.

Floyd, Steven, and Bill Wooldridge. "Managing Strategic Consensus: The Foundation of Effective Implementation." *Academy of Management Executive* 6, no. 4 (November 1992), pp. 27–39.

Hatch, Mary J. "The Dynamics of Organizational Culture." *Academy of Management Review* 18, no. 4 (October 1993), pp. 657–693.

Ketchen, David J., Jr., James B. Thomas, and Charles C. Snow. "Organizational Configurations and Performance: A Comparison of Theoretical Approaches," *Strategic Management Journal* 36, no. 6 (December 1993), pp. 1,278–1,313.

Marcoulides, George, and Ronald Heck. "Organizational Culture and Performance." *Organization Science* 4, no. 2 (May 1993), pp. 209–225.

Mezias, Stephen, and Mary Ann Glynn. "The Three Faces of Corporate Renewal: Institution, Revolution, and Evolution." *Strategic Management Journal* 14, no. 2 (February 1993), pp. 77–101.

Mintzberg, Henry, and Frances Westley. "Cycles of Organizational Change." *Strategic Management Journal* 13 (Winter 1992, Special Issue), pp. 39–59.

Venkatesan, Ravi. "Strategic Sourcing: To Make or Not to Make." *Harvard Business Review,* November/December 1992, p. 98.

CASE

FORD TEAM LOOKS TO PAST FOR FUTURE STRATEGY

The Ford Mustang may be an American icon, inspiration for romance and rock songs, but in the brutal global auto industry of the 1990s, romance takes a back seat to cash flow. When Ford Motor Co. executives first looked at a Mustang overhaul in late 1989, the $1 billion development price-tag looked far too expensive.

That's when a group inside Ford known as "Team Mustang" got together. The group of about 400 people spent three years reconciling the conflicting forces of finance and feeling.

The 1989 version of the Mustang was essentially unchanged from the dumpy 1979 incarnation, one of Ford's most trouble-plagued models. It bore little resemblance to the 1964 model that swept a generation off its feet. At the model's 1966 peak, 600,000 Mustangs were sold; by 1992, sales were down to just over 86,000. Japanese cars—even the Ford Probe, built by Ford partner Mazda Motor Corp.—were literally whizzing by in sales and popularity.

In August of that year, John Coletti and a small group of managers were assigned the task of saving the Mustang. They began with a six-month global tour of auto plants, to uncover how rivals brought out new cars for hundreds of millions less than Ford had been spending. They had the backing of Alex Trotman, executive vice president of Ford's North American automotive operations.

The "skunk works" development team fleshed out a plan to bring out a new Mustang in just three years, using a new product-development approach that put everyone from engineers to stylists to financial officers under one roof. The plan would give them unprecedented freedom to make decisions without waiting for approval from headquarters or other departments. The plan for managerial autonomy cut sharply against the grain of Ford's corporate culture. It called for breaching budgetary walls and persuading department heads to cede some control to their subordinates. Dia Hothi, the program's manufacturing chief, demanded—and got—veto power over changes to the Mustang body that would threaten his plans to build the car with many of the factory tools used for the old one. Trotman signed on to the project, and in September 1990, the group began work.

Engineers were grouped into "chunk teams," with responsibility for every aspect of a particular piece, or chunk, of the car. The new process disposed of the standard bidding procedure; Mustang team leaders simply picked the best available suppliers and asked them to join the process.

Time and money were saved by testing most of the convertible's designs on computer rather than by building actual cars. Still, initial test-drives of prototypes showed the need for major structural revisions. An eight-week blitz of reengineering work, computer manipulations, and budget discussions began. Although Trotman and other senior Ford executives were aware of the crisis, they kept their promise not to interfere.

Team Mustang made its September 1993 production start date; the aerodynamically designed car, styled along the lines of the original model, went on sale December 9. Its three-year overhaul at a cost of about $700 million is about 25 percent less time and 30 percent less money than for any new car program in Ford's recent history. The automaker used the savings to price the Mustang below the $13,999 starting price of its archrival, the Chevrolet Camaro. Ford executives hope the Mustang's low-cost salvation will inspire other Ford engineers.

DISCUSSION QUESTIONS

1. What type of strategic change did the Mustang redesign effort demand at Ford?

2. What was Ford's approach to managing the Mustang project? What structure and culture challenges did Ford's top managers face in supporting the Mustang team? How did they meet these challenges?

3. What would you recommend to Mr. Trotman about overall strategy implementation at Ford, based on the results (to date) of the Mustang project?

SOURCE: Joseph B. White and Oscar Suris, "How a 'Skunk Works' Kept Mustang Alive—on a Tight Budget," *The Wall Street Journal*, September 21, 1993, p. A1.

Notes

1. Thomas J. Peters and Robert H. Waterman, Jr., *In Search of Excellence* (New York: Harper & Row, 1982), pp. 13–14.
2. Henry Mintzberg, "Crafting Strategy," *Harvard Business Review*, July/August 1987, p. 66.
3. See Peter Petre, "What Welch Has Wrought at GE," *Fortune*, July 7, 1986, pp. 43–47; Marilyn A. Harris, Zachary Schiller, Russell Mitchell, and Christopher Power, "Can Jack Welch Reinvent GE?" *Business Week*, June 30, 1986, pp. 62–67; Stratford P. Sherman, "Inside the Mind of Jack Welch," *Fortune*, March 27, 1989, pp. 38–53; and Thomas A. Stewart, "GE Keeps Those Ideas Coming," *Fortune*, August 12, 1991, pp. 41–49.
4. David E. Whiteside, "Roger Smith's Campaign to Change the GM Culture," *Business Week*, April 7, 1986, pp. 84–85; and Alex Taylor III, "The Tasks Facing General Motors," *Fortune*, March 13, 1989, pp. 52–60.
5. See Anthony Bianco, "Jerry Tsai: The Comeback Kid," *Business Week*, August 18, 1986, pp. 72–80.
6. James Brian Quinn, *Strategies for Change* (Homewood, Ill.: Richard D. Irwin, 1980).
7. Michael Beer, Russell Eisenstat, and Bert Spector, *The Critical Path to Corporate Renewal* (Boston: Harvard Business School Press, 1991); Rosabeth M. Kanter, Barry Stein, and Todd Jick, *The Challenge of Organizational Change* (New York: Free Press, 1992).
8. Raymond E. Miles and Charles C. Snow, "Causes of Failure in Network Organizations," *California Management Review*, Summer 1992, pp. 53–72.
9. Peters and Waterman, *In Search*, p. 307.
10. R. Miles and C. Snow, "Fit, Failure, and the Hall of Fame," *California Management Review*, Spring 1984, pp. 10–28; R. Miles and C. Snow, "Organizations: New Concepts for New Forms," *California Management Review*, Spring 1986, pp. 62–73; Miles and Snow, "Causes of Failure"; C. Snow, R. Miles, and H. Coleman, "Managing 21st Century Network Organizations," *Organizational Dynamics*, Winter 1992, pp. 5–20.
11. Miles and Snow, "Causes of Failure," p. 55.
12. Ibid.
13. John Byrne, "Congratulations. You're Moving to a New Pepperoni," *Business Week*, December 20, 1993, pp. 80–81.
14. Edgar H. Schein, *Organizational Culture and Leadership* (San Francisco: Jossey-Bass, 1985), pp. 223–243; the discussion that follows is based on this work. Also see Guy S. Saffold III, "Culture Traits, Strength, and Organizational Performance: Moving beyond 'Strong' Culture," *Academy of Management Review* 13, no. 4 (1988), pp. 546–558; Bernard C. Reimann and Yoash Weiner, "Corporate Culture: Avoiding the Elitist Trap," *Business Horizons*, March/April 1988, pp. 36–44; and Mary Jo Hatch, "The Dynamics of Organizational Culture," *Academy of Management Review*, October 1993, pp. 657–693.
15. The discussion that follows is based on David R. Brodwin and L. J. Bourgeois III, "Five Steps to Strategic Action," *California Management Review*, Spring 1984, pp. 176–190. Also see Paul C. Nutt, "Selecting Tactics to Implement Strategic Plans," *Strategic Management Journal* 10 (1989), pp. 145–161.
16. This discussion is based on Thomas V. Bonoma, *The Marketing Edge* (New York: Free Press, 1985), pp. 112–121. See also Thomas V. Bonoma, "Making Your Marketing Strategy Work," *Harvard Business Review*, March/April 1984, pp. 69–76; and Thomas V. Bonoma and Victoria L. Crittenden, "Managing Marketing Implementation," *Sloan Management Review*, Winter 1988, pp. 7–14.

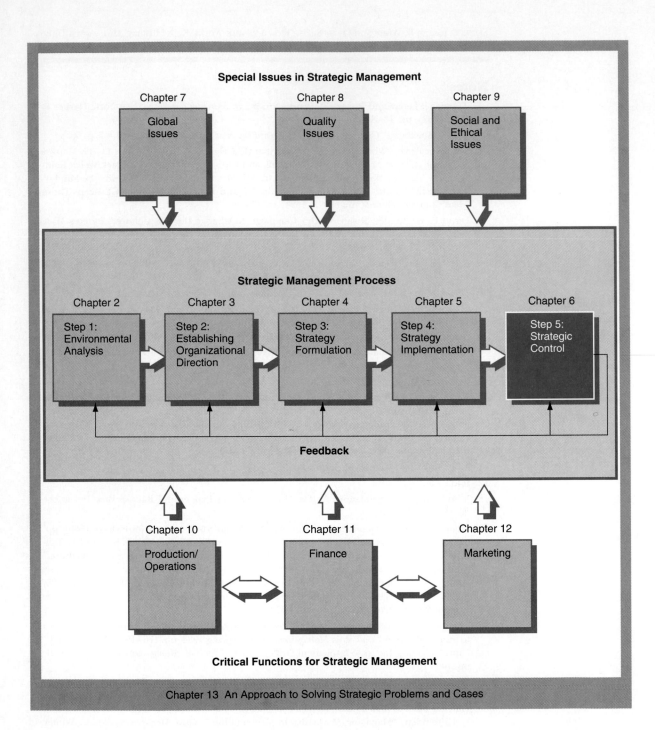

Special Issues in Strategic Management

Chapter 7 — Global Issues

Chapter 8 — Quality Issues

Chapter 9 — Social and Ethical Issues

Strategic Management Process

Chapter 2 — Step 1: Environmental Analysis

Chapter 3 — Step 2: Establishing Organizational Direction

Chapter 4 — Step 3: Strategy Formulation

Chapter 5 — Step 4: Strategy Implementation

Chapter 6 — Step 5: Strategic Control

Feedback

Chapter 10 — Production/Operations

Chapter 11 — Finance

Chapter 12 — Marketing

Critical Functions for Strategic Management

Chapter 13 An Approach to Solving Strategic Problems and Cases

Strategic Control

Previous chapters in this section have discussed the strategic management process by focusing on the interrelated steps of conducting an environmental analysis, establishing an organizational direction, formulating strategy, and implementing strategy. This chapter emphasizes the last major step in the strategic management process, exerting strategic control. This consists of making certain that strategies unfold as intended, and taking corrective action, as needed. Much like the discussion of strategy implementation, we will see that strategic control is not the domain of one functional speciality; success requires a truly cross-functional effort.

First, we briefly examine the broader topic of organizational control in order to understand the context in which more specific strategic control issues develop. We then proceed to define *strategic control* and outline the purposes of the strategic control process.

The main part of the chapter covers the process of strategic control itself. We examine at length how a strategic audit can measure organizational performance, and we differentiate between qualitative and quantitative measures. We discuss ways to compare actual organizational performance to goals and standards, and we explain how to determine whether corrective action is appropriate.

Next, we explore the link between strategic control and management information systems. Finally, we examine the role of top management in making the strategic control process successful.

ORGANIZATIONAL CONTROL AND STRATEGIC CONTROL

Without an understanding of the broader issues involved in controlling an organization, it is impossible to appreciate the special issues that arise in strategic control. For this reason, we briefly discuss the broader topic of control at the organizational level before narrowing our focus to the specific issues involved in strategic control.

Broad View of Organizational Control

Controlling an organization entails monitoring, evaluating, and improving various activities that take place within an organization. We will first define the term *control,* and then we will outline the general characteristics of the control process.

137

Definition of *Control*

Control is a major part of every manager's job. **Control** consists of making something happen the way it was planned to happen.[1] For example, if an organization plans to increase net profit by 10 percent based upon accelerating product demand, control entails monitoring organizational progress and making modifications, if necessary, to ensure that net profit does, indeed, increase by 10 percent.

Effective control requires that managers have a clear understanding of the intended results of a particular action. Only then can they ascertain whether the anticipated results are occurring and make any necessary changes to ensure that the desired results do occur. Managers control to ensure that plans become reality, so they need a clear understanding of what reality is planned.[2]

General Characteristics of the Control Process

In practice, managers actually control by following a three-step procedure: measuring performance, comparing measured performance to standards, and taking corrective action to ensure that planned events actually materialize.

Keep in mind that these steps are broad recommendations for overall organizational control. More specific types of organizational control (such as production control, inventory control, strategic control, and quality control) are based on these same three steps, tailored to the demands of the specific type of control. Figure 6.1 shows a general model of how these broad steps of the control process relate to one another. This model implies that when performance measurements differ significantly from standard or planned outcomes, managers take corrective action to ensure that expected outcomes actually occur. On the other hand, when performance does measure up to standard or planned outcomes, no corrective action is necessary and work continues without interference.

FIGURE 6.1   General Model of the Control Process

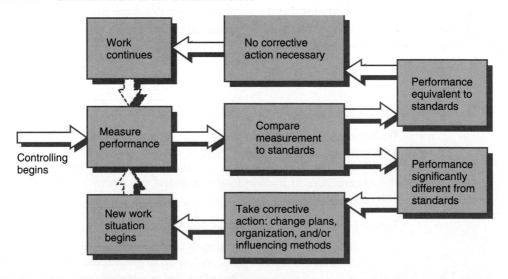

SOURCE: Samuel C. Certo, MODERN MANAGEMENT: Diversity, Quality, Ethics, and the Global Environment, 6 e., © 1994, p. 436. Reprinted by permission of Prentice Hall, Englewood Cliffs, New Jersey.

APPLICATION OF STRATEGIC CONTROL

Armed with a general understanding of control as managers apply it in organizations, we are now ready to discuss strategic control specifically. We will first define *strategic control*, then explain why strategic control is important, and finally trace the steps involved in the process of strategic control.

Definition of Strategic Control

Strategic control is a special type of organizational control that focuses on monitoring and evaluating the strategic management process to make sure that it functions properly. In essence, strategic control ensures that all outcomes planned during the strategic management process do, indeed, materialize. Although this definition oversimplifies strategic control and makes it sound somewhat mechanical, we will soon discover how challenging and intricate this process really is.

Purposes of Strategic Control

Perhaps the most fundamental purpose of strategic control is to help top managers achieve organizational goals by monitoring and evaluating the strategic management process. As we have seen, the strategic management process encompasses assessment of organizational environments (environmental analysis); establishment of organizational vision, mission, and goals (establishing organizational direction); development of ways to deal with competitors in order to reach these goals and fulfill the organization's mission (strategy formulation); and setting a plan to translate organizational strategy into action (strategy implementation). Strategic control provides feedback that is critical for determining whether all steps of the strategic management process are appropriate, compatible, and functioning properly.

PROCESS OF STRATEGIC CONTROL

Three distinct but related steps comprise the strategic control process within an organization. Because they constitute a special type of organizational control, these steps are closely related to the more general control model presented earlier. They include measuring organizational performance, comparing performance to goals and standards, and taking necessary corrective action.[3]

Step 1: Measure Organizational Performance

Before managers can plan actions to make the strategic management process more effective, they must measure current organizational performance. In order to understand performance measurements and how a manager can take such measurements, we need to introduce two important topics: strategic audits and strategic audit measurement methods.

Strategic Audit

A **strategic audit** is an examination and evaluation of organization operations affected by the strategic management process. Such an audit may be very comprehensive, emphasizing all facets of a strategic management process, or narrowly focused, emphasizing only a single part of the process, such as environmental analysis. In addition, the strategic audit can be quite formal, adhering strictly to established organizational rules and procedures, or quite informal, allowing managers wide discretion in deciding what organizational measurements to take and when. Whether it is comprehensive or focused, formal or informal, the strategic audit must work to integrate related functions. To satisfy this requirement, strategic audits are often carried out by cross-functional teams of managers.

No single method can be prescribed for performing a strategic audit, and each organization must design and implement its own audits to meet its own unique needs. Table 6.1 presents a worthwhile set of general guidelines on how to conduct a strategic audit.

Strategic Audit Measurement Methods

Managers measure organizational performance by several generally accepted methods. One way of categorizing these methods divides them into two distinct types: qualitative and quantitative methods. Although this scheme is useful for developing an understanding of strategic audit measurement methods, a few methods do not fall neatly into one or the other of these categories; instead, they combine both types.

Qualitative Organizational Measurements   These measurements give organizational assessments in the form of nonnumerical data that are subjectively summarized and organized before any conclusions are drawn on which to base strategic control action. Many managers believe that the best qualitative organizational measurements are simply answers to critical questions designed to reflect important facets of organizational operations. There is no universally endorsed list of such questions, but several that might be useful to the practicing manager appear in Table 6.2.

Seymour Tilles has written a classic article on the qualitative assessment of organizational performance.[4] This article discusses several important issues involving one small facet of organizational performance: organizational routines that result in organizational strategy. The Tilles article suggests several important questions to ask during qualitative organizational measurement that focuses on organizational procedures to develop strategy:

1. *Is organizational strategy internally consistent?* Internal consistency relates to the cumulative impact of various strategies on the organization. Do strategies serve conflicting purposes? According to Tilles, a strategy must be judged not only by its own effects, but also by its relationship to other organizational initiatives.
2. *Is the organization's strategy consistent with its environment?* Organizational strategy must make sense in light of what is happening outside the organization. Is organizational strategy consistent with pending or new government regulations, changing consumer tastes, or trends in the labor supply? Most organizational problems that arise from inconsistency between strategy and environment do not reflect extreme difficulty in matching these two variables. Rather, such problems crop up simply because organizations do not consciously work to match strategy to its environment.
3. *Is the organizational strategy appropriate, given organizational resources?* Without appropriate resources, organizations simply cannot make strategies work. Are the organization's resources sufficient to carry out a proposed strategy?

TABLE 6.1

How to Conduct a Strategic Audit

A strategic audit is conducted in three phases: diagnosis to identify how, where, and in what priority in-depth analyses need to be made; focused analysis; and generation and testing of recommendations. Objectivity and the ability to ask critical, probing questions are key requirements for conducting a strategic audit.

PHASE ONE: DIAGNOSIS

1. Review key documents such as:
   a. Strategic plan
   b. Business or operational plans
   c. Organizational arrangements
   d. Major policies governing matters such as resource allocation and performance measurement
2. Review financial, market, and operational performance against benchmarks and industry norms to identify key variances and emerging trends.
3. Gain an understanding of:
   a. Principal roles, responsibilities, and reporting relationships
   b. Decision-making processes and major decisions made
   c. Resources, including physical facilities, capital, management, and technology
   d. Interrelationships between functional staff members and businesses or operating units
4. Identify strategic implications of strategy for organization structure, behavior patterns, systems, and processes—define interrelationships and linkages to strategy.
5. Determine internal and external perspectives.
   a. Survey the attitudes and perceptions of senior and middle managers and other key employees to assess the extent to which they are consistent with the strategic direction of the firm. One way to accomplish this task is through carefully focused interviews and/or questionnaires to ask employees to identify and make trade-offs among the objectives and variables they consider most important.
   b. Interview a carefully selected sample of customers and prospective customers and other key external sources to understand their view of the company.
6. Identify aspects of the strategy that are working well. Formulate hypotheses regarding problems and opportunities for improvement based on the findings above. Define how and in what order to pursue each.

PHASE TWO: FOCUSED ANALYSIS

1. Test the hypotheses concerning problems and opportunities for improvement through analysis of specific issues. Identify interrelationships and dependencies among components of the strategic system.
2. Formulate conclusions as to weaknesses in strategy formulation, implementation deficiencies, or interactions between the two.

PHASE THREE: RECOMMENDATIONS

1. Develop alternative solutions to problems and ways of capitalizing on opportunities. Test these alternatives in light of their resource requirements, risks, rewards, priorities, and other applicable measures.
2. Develop specific recommendations to produce an integrated, measurable, and time-phased action plan to improve strategic results.

SOURCE: Adapted from A. J. Prager and M. B. Shea, "The Strategic Audit," in *The Strategic Management Handbook,* ed. K. J. Albert (New York: McGraw-Hill, 1983), pp. 8–14. Copyright © 1983. Reproduced with permission of McGraw-Hill.

TABLE 6.2

Sample Questions for Qualitative Organizational Measurement

- Are financial policies with respect to investments, dividends, and financing consistent with the opportunities likely to be available?
- Has the company defined the market segments in which it intends to operate specifically with respect to both product lines and market segments? Has it clearly defined the key capabilities it needs to succeed?
- Does the company have a viable plan for developing a significant and defensible superiority over competitors based on these capabilities?
- Will the business segments in which the company operates provide adequate opportunities for achieving corporate objectives? Do they appear attractive enough to draw an excessive amount of investment to the market from potential competitors? Is the company providing adequately for developing attractive new investment opportunities?
- Are the management, financial, technical, and other resources of the company really adequate to justify an expectation of maintaining superiority over competitors in key capabilities?
- Does the company have operations in which it cannot reasonably expect to outperform competitors? If so, can managers expect these operations to generate adequate returns on invested capital? Is there any justification for investing further in such operations, even just to maintain them?
- Has the company selected business segments that can reinforce each other by contributing jointly to the development of key capabilities? Do competitors combine operations in ways that give them superiority in the key resource areas? Can the company's scope of operations be revised to improve its chances against competitors?
- To the extent that operations are diversified, has the company recognized and provided for the special management and control systems this requires?

SOURCE: Milton Lauenstein, "Keeping Your Corporate Strategy on Track," **Journal of Business Strategy** 2, no. 1 (Summer 1981), p. 64. Reprinted by permission.

Without enough money, people, materials, or machines, it is senseless to pursue any strategy, however well-planned.

4. *Is organizational strategy too risky?* Together, strategy and resources determine the degree of risk the organization takes. Naturally, each organization must determine the amount of risk (or potential for losing resources) it wishes to incur. In this area, management must assess such issues as the total amount of resources a strategy requires, the proportion of the organization's resources that the strategy will consume, and the time commitment the strategy demands.

5. *Is the time horizon of the strategy appropriate?* Every strategy is designed to accomplish some organizational goal within a certain time period. Is the time allotted for implementing the strategy and for reaching the related organizational goals realistic and acceptable, given organizational circumstances? Managers must ensure that the time available to reach the goals and the time necessary to implement the strategy are consistent. Inconsistency between these two variables can make it impossible to reach organizational goals in a satisfactory way.

Qualitative measurement methods can be very useful, but applying them relies heavily on human judgment. Conclusions based on such methods must be drawn very carefully, because this subjective judgment, if exercised incorrectly, could easily render audit results invalid. Strategic control actions based on invalid audit results will certainly limit the effectiveness and efficiency of the strategic management process and could even become the primary reason for organizational failure.

Quantitative Organizational Measurements   These measurements give organizational assessments in the form of numerical data that are summarized and organized before conclusions are drawn on which to base strategic control action. Data gathered via such measures are generally easier to summarize and organize than data gathered through more qualitative measurements. Still interpreting or making sense of quantitative measurements and the corrective actions they signal can be very difficult and highly subjective. Quantitative measurements can evaluate the number of units produced per time period, production costs, production efficiency levels, levels of employee turnover and absenteeism, sales and sales growth, net profits earned, dividends paid, return on equity, market share, and earnings per share.

In practice, each organization uses specially designed methods to measure its overall performance quantitatively. For an extended discussion of quantitative measures of organizational performance, see Chapter 10. Here, we will briefly discuss three measurements:

1. *Return on investment (ROI):* This is the most common measure of organizational performance. It divides net income by total assets to evaluate the relationship between the amount of income the firm generates and the amount of assets needed to operate the organization. Naturally, an ROI value for one year alone may not provide the manager with much useful information. Comparing ROI values for consecutive years or consecutive quarters, or to those of similar companies or competitors, usually generates a more complete picture of organizational performance in this area.

    Managers must keep in mind several advantages and limitations of ROI as a measure of organizational performance, as presented in Table 6.3. These limitations should not discourage managers from using ROI; it is an extremely useful measure. Rather, managers must thoroughly understand these limitations and supplement ROI with such other performance measures, as needed.

2. *Weighted Performance (Z) Score:* This common quantitative measure numerically weights and sums five performance measures to arrive at an overall score.[5] The score becomes a basis for classifying firms as healthy and unlikely to go bankrupt, or as sick and likely to go bankrupt. The formula is:

$$z = 1.2\ X_1 + 1.4\ X_2 + 3.3\ X_3 + 0.6\ X_4 + 1.0\ X_5$$

Here z is defined as an index of overall financial health. All other variables in the formula (X_1, X_2, etc.) are explained in Table 6.4. The z score typically ranges from 5.0 to 10.0. According to research, a score below 1.8 signals a relatively high probability of going bankrupt. Firms that score above 3.0 have relatively low probabilities of going bankrupt. Firms that score between 1.8 and 3.0 are in a gray area. Knowing and understanding the z score for a particular firm can give top management an idea of the financial health of the firm and insights into how to improve it.

TABLE 6.3

Advantages and Limitations of ROI Performance Measures

ADVANTAGES

1. ROI is a single comprehensive figure influenced by everything that happens in a firm.
2. It measures how well the division manager uses the assets of the company to generate profits. It is also a good way to check on the accuracy of capital investment proposals.
3. It is a common denominator that can be compared among many entities.
4. It provides an incentive to use existing assets efficiently.
5. It provides an incentive to acquire new assets only when doing so would increase the firm's return.

LIMITATIONS

1. ROI is very sensitive to depreciation policy. Variances in depreciation write-offs between divisions affect their ROI performance. Accelerated depreciation techniques reduce ROI, conflicting with capital budgeting discounted cash flow analysis.
2. ROI is sensitive to book value. Older plants with more fully depreciated assets have relatively lower investment bases than newer plants, increasing ROI. (Note also that inflation can skew asset values and ROI.) Managers might be tempted to hold down asset investment or dispose of assets in order to increase ROI performance.
3. In many firms that use ROI, one division sells to another, so transfer pricing affects the measure. Expenses incurred affect profit. Since, in theory, the transfer price should be based on the total impact on firm profit, some investment center managers are bound to suffer. Equitable transfer prices are difficult to determine.
4. If one division operates in favorable industry conditions and another division operates in an industry with unfavorable conditions, the former division will automatically look better than the other.
5. ROI reflects a short time span. The performance of division managers should be measured in the long run. This is top management's time-span capacity.
6. The business cycle strongly affects ROI performance, often despite managerial performance.

SOURCE: Excerpt from ORGANIZATIONAL POLICY AND STRATEGIC MANAGEMENT: TEXT AND CASES, Second Edition, by James M. Higgins, copyright © 1983 by The Dryden Press, reprinted by permission of the publisher.

3. *Stakeholders' audit:* Stakeholders are people who are interested in a corporation's activities because they are significantly affected by accomplishment of the organization's objectives.[6] Organizational stakeholders include (a) stockholders interested in the appreciation of stock value and dividends, (b) unions interested in favorable wage rates and benefit packages, (c) creditors interested in the organization's ability to pay its debts, (d) suppliers interested in retaining the organization as a customer, (e) government units, who see organizations as taxpayers contributing to the costs of running a society, (f) social interest groups, such as consumer advocates and environmentalists, and (g) the organization's customers.

Many managers believe that one very useful measure of organizational performance is a **stakeholders' audit,** a summary of the feedback generated

TABLE 6.4

Variables for z Score

X_1 = Working capital/Total assets	Frequently found in studies of corporate problems, this is a measure of the net liquid assets of the firm relative to its total capital. Working capital is the difference between current assets and current liabilities. This variable explicitly allows for liquidity and size characteristics. Ordinarily, a firm experiencing consistent operating losses will have shrinking current assets in relation to total assets.
X_2 = Retained earnings/Total assets	This measure of cumulative profitability over time relies on balance sheet figures. It implicitly considers the age of a firm. For example, a relatively young firm will probably show a low RE/TA ratio because it has not had time to build up its cumulative profits. Therefore, this analysis may seem to discriminate against the young firm, since its chance of being classified as likely to go bankrupt is relatively higher than another, older firm. This is precisely the situation in the real world, though. Failure is much more likely in a firm's earlier years; over 50 percent of firms that fail do so in the first five years of existence. Note, however, that the retained earnings account is subject to manipulation via corporate quasi reorganizations and stock dividend declarations. A bias could be created by a substantial reorganization or stock dividend.
X_3 = Earnings before interest and taxes/Total assets	In essence, this ratio measures the true productivity of the firm's assets, abstracting from any tax or leverage factors. Since a firm's ultimate existence is based on the earning power of its assets, this ratio appears to be particularly appropriate for studies dealing with corporate failure. Furthermore, insolvency occurs when total liabilities exceed a fair valuation of the firm's assets, with value determined by the earning power of the assets.
X_4 = Market value of equity/Book value of total liabilities	Equity is measured by the combined market value of all shares of stock, preferred and common, while liabilities include both current and long-term debt. Book values of preferred and common stockholders' equity may be substituted for market values. The substitution of book values, especially for the common stock component, should be recognized as a proxy without statistical verification, however, since the model was built using market values (Price × Shares outstanding). The measure shows how much the firm's assets can decline in value (measured by market value of equity plus debt) before the liabilities exceed the assets and the firm becomes insolvent. For example, a company with equity worth $1,000 and debt worth $500 could experience a two-thirds drop in asset value before insolvency. However, the same firm with $250 in equity would be insolvent after a drop of only one-third in value.
X_5 = Sales/Total assets	This capital-turnover ratio is a standard financial ratio that illustrates the sales-generating ability of the firm's assets. It is one measure of management's capability in dealing with competitive conditions.

Note that variables X_1, X_2, X_3, and X_4 should be inserted into the model as decimal fractions; for example, a Working capital/Total assets ratio of 20 percent should be written as 0.20. The variable X_5, however, is usually a ratio greater than unity; for example, where sales are twice as large as assets, the ratio is 2.0.

SOURCE: Adapted from Edward I. Altman and James K. LaFleur, "Managing a Return to Financial Health," **Journal of Business Strategy**, 2, no. 1 (Summer 1981), pp. 31–38. Reprinted by permission.

TABLE 6.5

Stakeholder Groups and Their Impact on Organizational Performance

Stakeholder Category	Near-Term Performance Measures	Long-Term Performance Measures
Customers	Sales (value and volume) New customers Number of new customer needs met	Growth in sales Turnover in customer base Ability to control price

Suppliers	Cost of raw material
	Delivery time
	Inventory
	Availability of raw materials
		Growth rates of
		  Raw materials costs
		  Delivery time
		  Inventory
		  New ideas from suppliers

Financial community	EPS[a] Stock price Number of "buy" lists[b] ROE[c]	Ability to sell strategy to Wall Street Growth in ROE
Employees	Number of suggestions Productivity Number of grievances	Number of internal promotions Turnover

Congress	Number of new pieces of legislation
	  that affect the firm
	Access to key members and staff
		Number of new regulations that
		  affect the industry
		Ratio of cooperative to competitive
		  encounters

Consumer advocates	Number of meetings
	Number of hostile encounters
	Number of coalitions formed
	Number of legal actions
		Number of changes in policy due to
		  consumer advocates
		Number of calls for help initiated by
		  consumer advocates[d]

Environmentalists	Number of meetings
	Number of hostile encounters
	Number of coalitions formed
	Number of Environmental Protection
	  Agency complaints
	Number of legal actions
		Number of changes in policy due to
		  environmentalists
		
		Number of calls for help initiated by
		  environmentalists

[a]Earnings per share.

[b]Lists from which financial brokers recommend stock purchases for their clients.

[c]Return on equity.

[d]Calls in which consumer advocates attempt to enlist others in action against a company.

SOURCE: Adapted from Strategic Management: A Stakeholder Approach, Boston: Pitman Publishing, 1984. © R. Edward Freeman.

by stakeholder groups. The tone and content of such feedback can be an extremely valuable indicator of organizational progress toward financial and non-financial goals. Table 6.5 lists several stakeholder groups and measures to assess both the short-run and long-run impact they may have on organizational performance. The Skills Module invites you to evaluate a stakeholder analysis at Nike.

Our discussions about the variety of ways to measure strategic performance, and the variety of environments in which firms operate, suggest that strategic control systems may differ from firm to firm. Goold and Quinn propose that these systems depend on the level of environmental turbulence (high or low)

SKILLS MODULE

Assessing Stakeholder Attitudes toward Nike

INTRODUCTION

Stakeholders are groups or individuals who are interested in a corporation's activities because they are significantly affected by the organization's accomplishment of its objectives. Review the following situation at Nike, and then complete the skill development exercise that follows to analyze the reactions of various stakeholder groups to organizational strategy.

SITUATION

Philip Knight, founder and chairman of Nike Corp., has made business moves smoother than the moves of the athletes who wear—and endorse— his shoes. He capitalized on the jogging craze of the 1970s and the aerobics boom of the 1980s; by last year, his Hood River, Oregon company was the world's biggest purveyor of shoes. In the 1990s, Nike is going after the outdoor shoe market, a hot-growth area that, even for Nike, has limits.

But there are doubts about the latest twist in Nike's overall strategy. After a six-year hot streak that quadrupled annual sales to $3.9 billion and profits to $365 million, Nike has stubbed its toe. Sales of its major line, basketball shoes, have plateaued at around $600 million annually; sales of other athletic shoes have also stalled. The company's stock is down 43 percent from a high of $90.25 a share in late 1992, and Knight predicts no more than single-digit profit growth for the rest of 1994.

In 1992, Nike sold $123 million of outdoor footwear, just a small part of the company's overall U. S. sales of $2 billion. The line's growth was nearly 100 percent, though, while Nike's other sneaker lines barely registered single-digit increases. Knight predicts that his company will sell as many outdoor shoes as basketball sneakers in another couple of years.

Many retailing experts doubt that Nike's renaissance is in outdoor footwear alone; after all, the company cannot capture the market with models named after sports icons. Even if Nike does win over the outdoor windsurfing, rock-climbing, and snow-boarding crowd, retailing experts say that outdoor shoes won't generate anywhere near the multiple sales that sneakers and basketball shoes do.

But Knight is pursuing other strategies, as well, which rivals say simply reflect his desire for control. In the next year, Nike expects to open as many as 80 new boutiques within larger retailing stores that are devoted solely to Nike's products. Knight also talks of transforming Cole-Haan, the upscale shoe unit he purchased in the late 1980s, into a billion-dollar powerhouse going toe-to-toe with Timberland Inc.'s successful outdoor-style boots.

"We can see ourselves broadening out beyond shoes and clothes," he adds. Knight has been conferring with Michael Ovitz, chairman of the Hollywood talent agency Creative Artists Agency, on how to capitalize on interactive television and cable's vastly expanded channel range. Nike itself is getting involved in the talent business, taking over total management of the careers of four young professional athletes, including pro football and baseball player Deion Sanders and the NBA's Alonzo Mourning.

SKILL DEVELOPMENT EXERCISE

Nike chairman Philip Knight is busy formulating strategy while maintaining control over its implementation. Obviously, with stock prices down and long-term outlook hazy, stockholders are intensely interested in how well the various strategies will work. Some will probably respond positively to some moves, negatively to others. Analyze Nike's strategies and explain the reactions of stakeholders to its moves. Given your analysis, is Knight correct to employ so many diverse strategies, or is he overextending his ability to control the company's fortunes?

SOURCE: Bill Richards, "Nike's Management Races to Remake Company's Image," *The Wall Street Journal*, September 14, 1993, p. B4.

and a firm's ability to specify and measure precise strategic objectives. Their framework, shown in Figure 6.2, results in four strategic control types. When turbulence is low and precise goals are easy to specify and measure, strategic control systems can be described as valuable. When turbulence becomes high, however, control systems need greater flexibility to stay valuable.

When firms have difficulty specifying and measuring precise strategic objectives, low environmental turbulence calls for strategic controls that track a number of less precise indicators of performance. When turbulence is high

FIGURE 6.2
Strategic Control in
Different Sorts of
Businesses

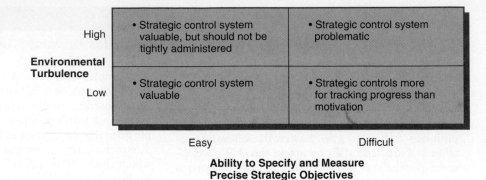

SOURCE: Michael Goold and John Quinn, "The Paradox of Strategic Controls," *Strategic Management Journal* 11, no. 1 (1990), p. 55. Reprinted by permission of John Wiley & Sons, Ltd. © 1990.

and precision difficult, strategic control, though still desirable, is problematic, due to changing external conditions that quickly make strategic control systems obsolete. For example, the biotechnology industry in the 1990s finds it difficult to specify precise objectives in a highly turbulent environment, because of both competitive conditions and the changing political climate with regard to health care.

This section has reviewed many different ways to measure organizational performance. Managers must establish and use whatever methods best suit their organization. One important guideline should govern this work, though. Organizations should measure, as best they can, performance in all critical areas targeted by goals, strategies, and plans.

Step 2: Compare Organizational Performance to Goals and Standards

After taking measurements of organizational performance, managers must compare them with two established benchmarks: goals and standards. Organizational goals are simply the output of an earlier step of the strategic management process.

Organizational standards are developed to reflect organizational goals; they are yardsticks that place organizational performance in perspective.[7] The specific standards that companies actually establish vary from firm to firm. As a rule, managers must develop standards in all performance areas that established organizational goals address. Developed many years ago at General Electric, the following standards are typical of those used by many firms in the 1990s.[8]

1. *Profitability standards:* These standards indicate how much profit General Electric would like to make in a given time period.
2. *Market position standards:* These standards indicate the percentage of a total product market that the company would like to win from its competitors.
3. *Productivity standards:* These production-oriented standards indicate various acceptable rates at which final products should be generated within the organization.

4. *Product leadership standards:* Innovation is critical for long-run organizational success. Product leadership standards indicate levels of product innovation that would make people view General Electric products as leaders in the market.
5. *Personnel development standards:* Development of organization members in all areas is critical to continued organizational success. Personnel development standards list acceptable levels of progress in this area.
6. *Employee attitude standards:* These standards indicate attitudes that General Electric employees should adopt. Not only are workers evaluated for the degree to which they project these attitudes, but managers are evaluated for the extent to which they develop them in their subordinates.
7. *Public responsibility standards:* All organizations have certain obligations to society. General Electric's standards in this area indicate acceptable levels of activity within the organization directed toward living up to social responsibilities.
8. *Standards reflecting balance between short-range and long-range goals:* General Electric, like most organizations, feels that both long-run and short-run goals are necessary to maintain a healthy and successful organization. Standards in this area indicate the acceptable long-range and short-range goals and the relationships among them.

The process of standard setting has attracted a great deal of interest in the 1990s with the popularity of the practice of **benchmarking.** In this control technique, a firm compares one of its functions, say product design, with that of another firm known for world-class excellence in that function, say 3M or Rubbermaid.

Step 3: Take Necessary Corrective Action

Once managers have collected organizational measurements and compared these measurements to established goals and standards, they should take any corrective action that is warranted. **Corrective action** is defined as a change in an organization's operations to ensure that it can more effectively and efficiently reach its goals and perform up to its established standards. Corrective action may be as simple as changing the price of a product or as complicated as a boardroom struggle, which ends in the firing of the CEO.

As the Company Example illustrates, strategic control can also result in changes as dramatic as modifying the products a company offers in the marketplace. In order to attract more customers, Radio Shack has taken corrective action to improve the design of its stores, its array of products (now to include IBM PCs), and the market appeal of its advertising campaign.

A thorough understanding of the steps of the strategic control process and their relationships to the major steps of the strategic management process should guide corrective action. Figure 6.3 summarizes the main steps of the strategic control process and illustrates its relationship with the major steps of the strategic management process.

Assume that a particular organization has failed to meet appropriate organizational goals and standards so that corrective action is necessary. As Figure 6.3 implies, this action might include attempting to improve organizational performance by focusing on one or more of the major steps of the strategic management process. Of course, this analysis could include improving the

FIGURE 6.3   Relationships between the Strategic Process and the Strategic Control Process

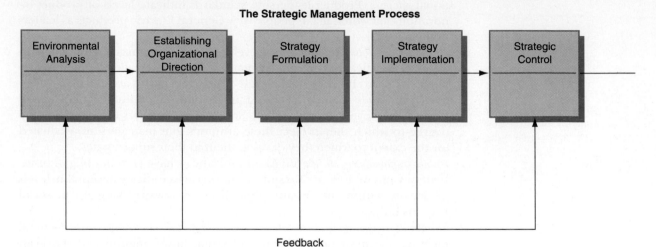

The Strategic Management Process

Environmental Analysis → Establishing Organizational Direction → Strategy Formulation → Strategy Implementation → Strategic Control

Feedback

The Strategic Control Process

Status Quo Continues

No Corrective Action Necessary

Organizational Goals and Standards Are Reached

Strategic Control Begins

Measure Organizational Performance
• Qualitative measurements (critical questions)
• Quantitative measurements (ROI, Z Score, stake-holders' audit)

Compare Organizational Performance to Goals and Standards

Organizational Goals and Standards Are *Not* Reached

Changes Go into Effect

Take Corrective Action
• Change way organization operates
• Make goals/standards more challenging
• Change functioning of strategic management process
• Change strategic control process itself

COMPANY EXAMPLE

Tandy Cedes Control and Label-Only Strategy

Change, more profound to the company's operating strategy than its new store floor plans and service offerings, more long-lasting than its new advertising campaign, was unveiled recently at Radio Shack.

Continuing its bid to revitalize the consumer-electronics store chain, parent company Tandy Corp. has abandoned its private-label-only strategy for personal computers, and says it will introduce name-brand products into its stores. In 500 Radio Shack stores that have previously recorded healthy sales of laptop computers, the chain will begin selling two IBM notebook computer models. The pilot program also includes test-marketing of IBM and AST Research Inc. desktop PCs, and possibly other brands.

Last year, the consumer-electronics giant sold its computer manufacturing business to AST, which continues to supply the Tandy label. The $175 mil-

lion sale enabled Tandy to sell PCs from competing manufacturers.

Radio Shack dealers have complained about the company's lackluster products and weak computer brand name. Tandy's chairman, John V. Roach, doesn't disagree, acknowledging that Tandy was having a tough time keeping up with technological developments and recovering development costs. "With very short product cycles, you need very fast inventory turns," said Roach. "It makes sense to supplement the line with name-brand products."

Although Roach says that Radio Shack will increase its reliance on name-brand products, he says that no decision has been made on whether to offer IBM computers at all 6,500 Radio Shack stores.

SOURCE: "Tandy's Radio Shack, Changing Strategy to Offer IBM PC's," *The Wall Street Journal*, May 5, 1994, p. B7

strategic control process itself by enhancing the validity and reliability of organizational performance measures.

In most situations, corrective action is not necessary if the organization is reaching its goals and standards. However, management must not automatically assume that this is the case. Goals and standards may have been set too low, in which case corrective action should be taken to make them more challenging.

INFORMATION FOR STRATEGIC CONTROL

Successful strategic control requires valid and reliable information about various measures of organizational performance. Without such information, strategic control action will have little chance of consistently improving organizational performance. Reliable, timely, and valid information is the lifeblood of successful strategic control.

To gather this valid, reliable, and timely information, virtually every organization develops and implements some type of formal system. The following sections discuss two such systems: management information systems (MISs) and management decision support systems (MDSSs).

Management Information System (MIS)

A **management information system** is a formal, computer-assisted organizational function designed to provide managers with information to help their decision making. Although such information has many different uses, a significant portion of it supports strategic control.

As Figure 6.4 illustrates, operating an MIS is largely a matter of performing six related steps. We interpret these steps in the context of an MIS for strategic control.

Once managers decide what information they need for strategic control, they must collect and analyze appropriate data, and disseminate the information this analysis yields to appropriate organization members, usually upper management. Next, upper management must plan and implement strategic control activities in light of this information. Finally, continuing feedback on the effect of implementing these activities, and on the functioning of the MIS system itself, must guide efforts to meet the information needs of strategic control more effectively in the future.

MIS and Management Levels   Because managers at various levels of the organization perform different kinds of activities, the MIS should be flexible enough to provide various management levels with the information they need to carry out these activities. Table 6.6 summarizes typical activities performed by top, middle, and lower-level managers. This table illustrates that strategic control and other strategic management tasks are the primary focus of top management, but all management levels have some role in the strategic management process, and the MIS should provide them the supportive information they need.

FIGURE 6.4
Major Steps in
Operating an MIS

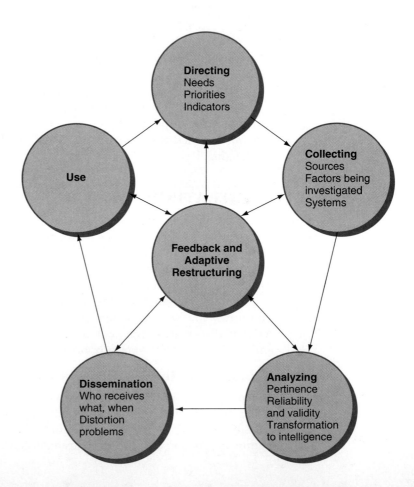

TABLE 6.6

Typical Activities of Managers at Various Organizational Levels

Organizational Level	Characteristics of Activities	Sample Activities
Top management	Future oriented Significant uncertainty Significant subjective assessment Strategic management emphasis	Establishing organizational direction Performing environmental analysis Developing organizational strategies
Middle management	Somewhat future oriented (less than top-management activities) Emphasis on implementation of strategies	Making short-term forecasts Budgeting Human resource planning
Supervisory management	Emphasis on daily production Emphasis on daily performance that reflects organizational strategy and contributes to attaining long-term goals	Assigning jobs to specific workers Managing inventory Supervising workers Handling worker complaints Maintaining organizational procedures and rules

Symptoms of an Inadequate MIS   Because the effectiveness of the strategic control process depends largely on valid and reliable organizational performance measures, managers must continually assess MIS functioning to ensure that it meets strategic control needs. Most managers agree that they must constantly watch for signals that an MIS is not operating effectively. Naturally, once such symptoms are discovered, managers must take steps to solve whatever problems plague the MIS. Once these problems are eliminated, the symptoms of trouble should disappear.

Sensing MIS-related problems can be quite difficult, or it may be as simple as listening to the comments of strategic control decision makers. These individuals may complain that they have too much information of the wrong kind and not enough of the right kind, that information is so dispersed throughout the company that they must struggle to gather simple facts, that others sometimes suppress vital information for political reasons, that vital information frequently arrives too late to be useful, or that information often defies efforts to assess its accuracy and no one can provide confirmation. Managers may bluntly worry that the information they get may be moving them in the wrong strategic direction at full speed.[9]

Bertram A. Colbert, a principal of Price Waterhouse & Company, has indicated other kinds of symptoms that can also betray malfunctions in an MIS: (1) *operational symptoms,* which are related to the way an organization functions; (2) *psychological symptoms,* which reflect the feelings of organization members; and (3) *report content symptoms,* which affect the structures of reports generated by the MIS. Table 6.7 lists several organizational symptoms that fall in each of these three categories.

As soon as they become aware of symptoms of this sort, managers should take action to solve the MIS problems. In practice, however, it may be quite difficult to determine exactly what problems within an organization are

TABLE 6.7

Symptoms of a Malfunctioning MIS

Operational Symptoms	Psychological Symptoms	Report Content Symptoms
Large physical inventory adjustments	Surprise at financial results	Excessive use of large tables of numbers
Capital expenditure overruns	Poor attitude of executives about usefulness of information	Multiple preparation and distribution of identical data
Unexplained changes from year to year in operating results	Lack of understanding of financial information by nonfinancial executives	Disagreements among information from different sources
Uncertain direction of company growth	Lack of concern for environmental changes	Lack of periodic comparative and trend information
Unexplained cost variances	Excessive homework	Late information
No order backlog awareness		Too little or excess detail
No internal discussion of reported data		Inaccurate information
Insufficient knowledge about competition		Lack of standards for comparison
Purchasing parts from outside vendors that the firm could make itself		Failure to identify variances by cause and responsibility
Failure of investments in facilities, or in programs such as R&D and advertising		Inadequate externally generated information

SOURCE: Institute for Practitioners in Work-Study, Organization, and Methods, Middlesex, England, *Management Sciences* 4, no. 5 (September–October 1967), pp. 15–24. Reprinted by kind permission of the editor—Management Services.

hampering the effectiveness of the MIS. Answering five questions may help the manager to pinpoint strategic control problems related to the MIS:

1. Where and how do managers involved in the strategic control process get information?
2. Can managers involved in strategic control make better use of their contacts to get information?
3. In what strategic control areas is the knowledge of these managers weakest, and what information might help to minimize such weaknesses?
4. Do managers involved in strategic control tend to act before receiving enough information?
5. Do managers involved in strategic control wait so long for information that opportunities pass them by and they become bottlenecks?[10]

Management Decision Support System (MDSS)[11]

An MIS that gathers data and provides information to managers electronically is invaluable. This MIS assistance has been especially useful in areas where managers must make recurring decisions; the computer repeatedly generates the information they need. An example of such a structured decision might be using the computer to track cumulative population shifts in the market a firm serves. The computer may update environmental analysis reports automatically and even remind management to consider deploying additional salespeople when the number of target customers in a specified market area increases substantially.

Closely related to the MIS is the management decision support system (MDSS), sometimes referred to as an executive information system (EIS). A **management decision support system** is an interdependent set of decision aids that helps managers make relatively unstructured, perhaps nonrecurring decisions. The computer (in conjunction with software like *Lotus* spreadsheet) is the main element of the MDSS, functioning as an analytical tool to assist in judgment decisions. The MDSS, however, does not pretend to dictate the manager's decision or impose solutions to problems. Many managers use an MDSS to help them make strategic control decisions and other types of strategic management decisions. For example, a manager may consider how best to implement strategy within an organization by determining all the different costs of various implementation alternatives. The MDSS provides and organizes the information and the manager makes the decision based on it.

Stunning technological advances in microcomputers have made MDSSs feasible and available to virtually all managers. Continuing developments in information analysis software support more subjective decision making, contributing to the popularity of the MDSS. Figure 6.5 is a recent attempt to graphically portray the information needs of executives responsible for

FIGURE 6.5 Information, Executives, and Strategic Decision Making

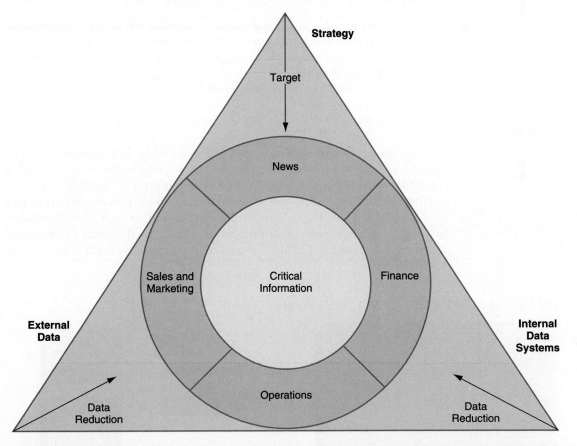

SOURCE: Reprinted with permission from *Long Range Planning* 25, no. 6 Robin Matthews and Anthony Shoebridge, "EIS—A Guide for Executives," (December 1992), p. 98, Elsevier Science Ltd., Pergamon Imprint, Oxford, England.

strategic control in their firms, and the internal functions responsible for finding, interpreting, and passing on critical information to top managers.

TOP MANAGERS AND STRATEGIC CONTROL

Because strategic management is primarily the responsibility of top managers, and because it is a critical ingredient of successful strategic management, top managers must understand strategic control and know how to take actions implied by the strategic control process. Top managers must make a solid and enduring commitment to establishing and using a strategic control system within the organization. Of course, they must commit organizational resources to support this activity.

Figure 6.6 illustrates the variables that are important to maintaining successful strategic control. According to this model, strategic control entails reaching either of two primary objectives: maintaining strategic momentum already achieved or leaping to a new strategy direction if and when it is appropriate.

According to this model, in order to reach either of these objectives, top managers must ensure that four interrelated organizational variables are consistent and complementary: (1) organizational structure, (2) reward systems, (3) information systems, and (4) organizational value systems or cultures. To maintain strategic momentum or leap to a new strategy, top management must ensure that:

1. Reward systems encourage appropriate behavior within the organization.
2. The organizational structure contributes to attainment of strategic objectives.
3. Values and norms that define the organizational culture are consistent with the firm's objectives.
4. The information support systems needed to track performance are in place.

SUMMARY

Organizational control entails monitoring, evaluating, and improving various types of activities within an organization in order to make events unfold as planned. Strategic control, a special type of organizational control, focuses on monitoring and evaluating the strategic management process to ensure that what is supposed to happen actually does happen. Although strategic control has many different purposes within an organization, the most fundamental one is to help managers achieve organizational goals via control of strategic management.

FIGURE 6.6   Variables Important to Maintaining Strategic Control

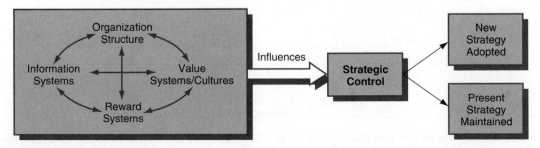

The strategic control process includes three basic steps. Step 1 measures organizational performance. Here management generally uses strategic audits to determine what is actually happening within the organization. Step 2 compares organizational performance to goals and standards. Here management builds a case to conclude whether or not what has happened as a result of the strategic management process is acceptable. Step 3 in the strategic control process is actually taking any corrective action necessary. If events are promoting organizational goals established within the strategic management process, no corrective action is necessary. If events are out of line with plans, however, some type of corrective action is usually appropriate.

Information that reflects valid and reliable measurements of organizational activities is a prerequisite for successful strategic control. Recognizing the importance of acquiring and applying such information, most organizations establish both management information systems (MISs) and management decision support systems (MDSSs). These systems typically use the computer in conjunction with specially tailored software to provide management with needed measures of organizational performance. Once established, information systems must be constantly monitored to ensure that they continue to work properly.

Top managers have an important role in making sure that strategic control is successful. Upper-level managers must design and implement the strategic control process to encourage appropriate strategic control behavior within the organization through organizational reward systems, an organizational structure consistent with strategic objectives, an organizational culture that supports strategic control, and necessary information.

KEY TERMS

control, p. 138
strategic control, p. 139
strategic audit, p. 139
stakeholders' audit, p. 144
organizational standard, p. 148
benchmarking, p. 149

corrective action, p. 149
management information system
(MIS), p. 151
management decision support system
(MDSS), p. 155

CHECKLIST   Analyzing Strategic Control in Problems and Cases

___   1.   Does the situation or case involve strategic control issues?

___   2.   Is the strategic control effort described in the case fulfilling all of its purposes?

___   3.   Does the case raise issues about the role and conduct of strategic audits?

___   4.   Have both qualitative and quantitative measures of organizational performance been appropriately employed?

___   5.   Are the interests of various stakeholder groups being considered?

___   6.   Are appropriate performance standards being set and compared to organizational performance?

___   7.   Is any necessary corrective action taken?

___   8.   Is a management information system (MIS) established and operating appropriately?

___ 9.   Is a management decision support system (MDSS) working as it should?

___ 10. Are various levels of management appropriately involved in the strategic control process?

Additional Readings

Goold, M., and J. J. Quinn. "The Paradox of Strategic Controls." *Strategic Management Journal* 11, no. 1 (1990), p. 43.

Harrison, Jeffrey S., Ernest H. Hall, Jr., and Rajendra Norgundkar. "Resource Allocation as an Outcropping of Strategic Consistency: Performance Implications." *Academy of Management Journal*, October 1993, p. 1,026.

Hinterhuber, Hans H., and Wolfgang Popp. "Are You a Strategist or Just a Manager?" *Harvard Business Review*, January/February 1992, p. 105.

Julian, Scott. "Toward a Comprehensive Framework for Strategic Control," *Academy of Management Best Paper Proceedings*, ed. by Dorothy Moore (1993), p. 17.

Kovacevic, Antonio, and Nicholás Majluf. "Six Steps of IT Strategic Management." *Sloan Management Review*, Summer 1993, p. 77.

Lorange, P., M. Scott-Morton, and S. Ghoshal. *Strategic Control Systems.* St. Paul, Minn.: West, 1986.

Preble, J. "Toward a Comprehensive System of Strategic Control." *Journal of Management Studies* 29, no. 4 (1992), p. 391.

C A S E

Benetton's Strategy for a New Era

Benetton, purveyor of brightly colored clothing in more than 7,000 shops in 110 countries, prides itself on confounding conventional wisdom. Despite the recession in its West European heartland, the Italian company's 1993 post-tax profits increased 12.6 percent on sales that were up 9.5 percent. It runs what many call tasteless advertisements—a priest kissing a nun, the bloodstained clothing of a Bosnian war victim—which offend some but bring the company a high public profile at a low cost. Benetton, still 70 percent family-owned, spends only 4 percent of sales revenue on marketing.

Now it intends to pose its greatest challenge to conventional wisdom—refuting the idea that all fashion retailers eventually go out of fashion.

Benetton has thrived through a unique organizational system and a philosophy that it is a clothing services company rather than a retailer or manufacturer. Its customers are its shops, which are owned by outsiders; unlike normal franchise systems, the shops pay no royalties and Benetton accepts no returned stock. The company's in-house responsibilities are similar; Benetton handles only those bits of manufacturing—design, cutting, dyeing, and packing—that it thinks crucial to maintain quality and cost-efficiency. The rest it contracts out to local suppliers, reducing Benetton's risk and allowing it the flexibility to respond to sales trends.

The formula has worked well; unlike most retailers, Benetton is debt-free. But there are drawbacks to the devolved structure. With little control or leverage over shop owners, Benetton has had problems encouraging them to expand and invest in larger quarters; only 5 percent have done so. Instead, the company is relying on price cuts of up to 40 percent to increase market share in Europe; volume is up 25 percent in some markets.

Luciano Benetton says that losing creativity is the biggest risk his company faces. He counters that possibility by building innovation into the corporate structure—the firm has 200 young designers and is setting up a new international design school. Nevertheless, most of Benetton's future profits depend on cut-and-dried business issues: diversification and cost-cutting. The company should soon formalize a joint venture for 300 shops in China, and it is fast expanding in Egypt, India, and South America. But progress abroad is not perfect. After breakneck expansion into the world's most competitive retail market—the United States—Benetton has only 150 stores, down from 800 in 1988.

Benetton maintains 80 percent of its clothing production in Europe; Luciano Benetton believes that the key to competing with Asia-based producers is computers, or what he calls "modern industrial production." In 1993, the company opened a 430,000-square-foot, high-tech cutting and packing plant for jeans. Plans for another plant were approved a few months later. Both will be linked by tunnels to a computerized warehouse, opened in 1986, that handles 30,000 boxes a day with a staff of 20. The company has also developed software for machine-knitted, seamless sweaters that require no hand finishing.

DISCUSSION QUESTIONS

1. How effectively has Benetton completed the three major steps in the strategic control process? Explain.

2. How can Luciano Benetton maintain strategic control within the company's structure? Will Benetton's structure be an impediment to future growth?

3. Identify the interrelationships among components of Benetton's strategic system. What are some alternative solutions to the company's problems and ways of capitalizing on opportunities?

SOURCE: *The Economist,* April 23, 1994, p. 68.

Notes

1. For a comprehensive discussion of the control function see Robert N. Anthony, *The Management Control Function* (Boston: Harvard Business School Press, 1988).

2. Robert L. Dewelt, "Control: Key to Making Financial Strategy Work," *Management Review,* March 1977, p.18. This link between planning and control is supported and illustrated in S. S. Cowen and J. K. Middaugh, "Designing an Effective Financial Planning and Control System," *Long Range Planning* 21 (December 1988), pp. 83–92. See also Robert Simons, "Strategic Orientation and Top Management Attention to Control Systems," *Strategic Management Journal* 12, no. 1 (1991), pp. 46–62.

3. For an excellent discussion of the strategic control process, see J. Preble, "Toward a Comprehensive System of Strategic Control," *Journal of Management Studies* 29, no. 4 (1992), p. 391.

4. Seymour Tilles, "How to Evaluate Corporate Strategy," *Harvard Business Review,* July/August 1963, pp. 111–121.

5. Edward I. Altman and James K. LaFleur, "Managing a Return to Financial Health," *The Journal of Business Strategy* 2, no. 1 (Summer 1981), pp. 31–38.

6. R. E. Freeman, *Strategic Management: A Stakeholder Approach* (Boston: Pitman, 1984), p. 25.

7. For insights regarding how to construct worthwhile performance indicators, see R. Kaufman, "Preparing Useful Performance Indicators," *Training and Development Journal* 42 (September 1989), pp. 80–83.

8. Robert W. Lewis, "Measuring, Reporting, and Appraising Results of Operations with Reference to Goals, Plans, and Budgets," in *Planning, Managing, and Measuring the Business: A Case Study of Management Planning and Control at General Electric Company* (New York: Controllership Foundation, 1955).

9. Daniel H. Gray, "Uses and Misuses of Strategic Planning," *Harvard Business Review,* January/February 1986, pp. 89–97.
10. Henry Mintzberg, "The Manager's Job: Folklore and Fact," *Harvard Business Review,* July/August 1975, p. 58. Some implications of this article from a strategic viewpoint are discussed in James Brian Quinn, Henry Mintzberg, and Robert M. James, *The Strategy Process: Concepts, Contexts, and Cases* (Englewood Cliffs, N. J.: Prentice-Hall, 1988), p. 21.
11. This section is based on Steven L. Mandell, *Computers and Data Processing: Concepts and Applications with BASIC* (St. Paul, Minn.: West, 1982), pp. 370–391.

PART III

Special Issues in Strategic Management

In Parts I and II of this text, we introduced and analyzed the strategic management process. The knowledge and skills you developed in your study of Chapters 1 through 6 can be successfully applied to a variety of strategic management problems and cases. However, dealing with certain situations that arise in strategic management may require additional, specialized knowledge of particular areas. In the following part, we discuss three such areas that strategic managers often need to be familiar with: international operations (Chapter 7), total quality management (Chapter 8), and social responsibility and ethics (Chapter 9). After carefully studying this part, you should understand the special problems that strategic managers confront when they deal with issues in these important areas.

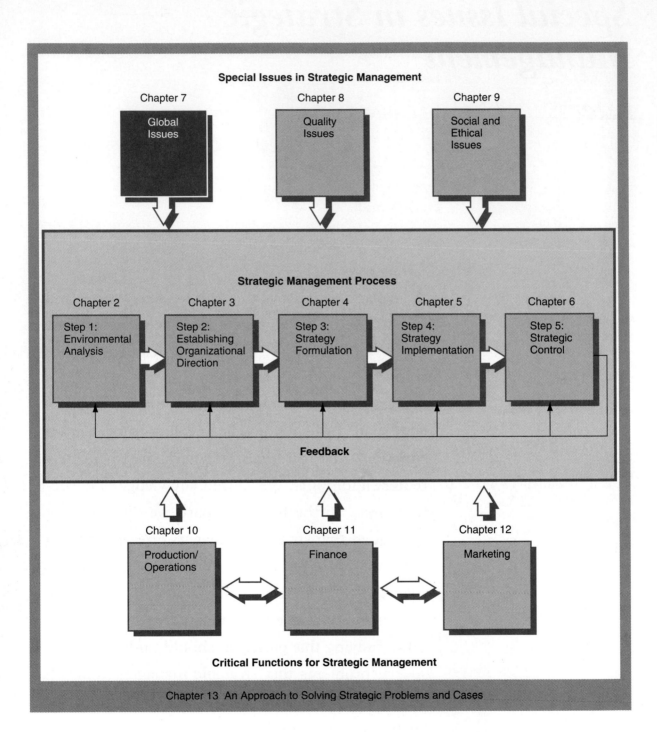

Special Issues in Strategic Management

Chapter 7

Global Issues

Chapter 8

Quality Issues

Chapter 9

Social and Ethical Issues

Strategic Management Process

Chapter 2

Step 1: Environmental Analysis

Chapter 3

Step 2: Establishing Organizational Direction

Chapter 4

Step 3: Strategy Formulation

Chapter 5

Step 4: Strategy Implementation

Chapter 6

Step 5: Strategic Control

Feedback

Chapter 10

Production/ Operations

Chapter 11

Finance

Chapter 12

Marketing

Critical Functions for Strategic Management

Chapter 13 An Approach to Solving Strategic Problems and Cases

Strategic Management of International Operations

This chapter explores the strategic management process for businesses that operate internationally. Over the last several years, businesses have increasingly crossed international borders in their operations. Since this trend is expected to continue, international issues are extremely important to the success of any effort to formulate and implement organizational strategy.

This chapter divides its discussion into four sections. First, we discuss some of the trends that drive the growth of international business in general. Second, we discuss the main international trade agreements that underlie all international business. We then discuss national industrial policies and how they facilitate or hinder an organization's progress toward its objectives. Finally, we trace the familiar steps in strategic management process, noting the special characteristics of international strategic management.

GROWING IMPORTANCE OF INTERNATIONAL MANAGEMENT

Before we can discuss the impact of international operations on the strategic management process, we must explain the meaning of the term *international management*. This leads to an overview of the growing importance of international issues in organizations.

International Management Defined

International management involves performing management activities across national borders. In other words, the organization seeks to accomplish its mission, at least partially, by conducting business in a foreign country. This could be as simple as selling a product in a foreign country or as complicated as collaborating with foreign partners to manufacture and sell products throughout the world.

Advances in transportation, technology, and communications, along with developments in the economic, political, and cultural components of the business environment, have helped organizations to cross international borders. An excerpt from the mission statement of General Motors' Asian Technical Center illustrates the extent of some U.S. firms' commitments to foreign investment:

Corporate support for further development of the market in Japan has resulted in the establishment of a technical center called the Asian Technical Center (ASTEC) in Akishima. The establishment of ASTEC is symbolic of the GM Automotive Components Group's commitment to sell automotive parts to Japanese companies. ASTEC's engineers are primarily Japanese who were trained in the United States so they can effectively communicate and provide timely responses to customers. Our sales achievement of $180 million in 1991 is an excellent base from which to move forward, and we intend to aggressively pursue a higher rate of growth. We remain committed to introducing new technology to the Japanese market as we continue to improve product quality and cost.[1]

Such strong commitments to growth and success in international markets compel managers to integrate international issues into their strategic planning and decision making. Before we examine how they do this, we must explore some important changes in the context of international business and trade.

Context of International Business

International issues are growing more important in organizations because international business is becoming more integrated around the globe. In 1993, the World Future Society sponsored its WORLD 2000 project to identify the forces that are integrating life around the earth into a coherent global order, as well as the forces that are creating disorder. This project began by reviewing research literature to identify a set of trends. A group of business executives then reviewed, evaluated, and summarized the trends. Although powerful forces drive disorder and disintegration, the overall trends seem to be leading in the direction of order, interdependence, and integration. Table 7.1 summarizes the findings of WORLD 2000.[2]

The movement toward order and interdependence shown in the table is also reflected in the growing interconnection between individuals' daily lives and events taking place around the globe. For example, two decades ago a place like Troy, a city of about 19,000 tucked away in southwestern Ohio, was considered heartland America.[3] Far removed and well-insulated from the bustle of international business and the aggravation of volatile exchange rates, the citizens of Troy could go about their daily routines without worrying about markets in China and business practices in Tokyo. Today, Troy still has the deceptive appearance of classic Americana: swings and American flags hang from inviting porches; mom-and-pop stores line Main Street; Lee's Family Restaurant promotes a $1.99 chicken gizzard dinner. Beneath this calm veneer, however, the inhabitants of Troy are plugged into a complex global network that brings events in Kuala Lumpur and Yokohama into their daily routines.

Mike Hines, a foreman in PMI Food Equipment Group in Troy, knows that at 1:30 p.m. each day, a truck picks up hand-assembled mixers from his factory to be exported to places like the United Arab Emirates, China, and Malaysia. Kay DeWeese, who farms 1,300 acres in Troy with her husband and son, regularly tracks commodity prices via a backyard satellite dish. Some of the corn and soybeans they grow are exported to Japan. "We want to see a strong enough Japanese economy to be able to buy our grain," she says. Jim Witmer, a Troy photographer, knows that the prices of Nikon cameras sold at B-K Photo Products have shot up twice during 1993. A new Nikon

TABLE 7.1	

Trends That Drive the Emerging Global Order

TRAJECTORY TOWARD INTEGRATION

Trend 1. Stable population.
Worldwide population will stabilize at 10–14 billion by the mid-21st century
Trend 2. Wiring the globe.
Advances in information technology suggest the emergence of a single, worldwide communications network.
Trend 3. International culture.
The consolidation of economic blocs and political federations, combined with new information technology, hold the promise of an emerging international culture.
Trend 4. Universal standard of freedom.
The number of nations with political systems based on freedom and the recognition of human rights continues to grow.
Trend 5. Transcendent values.
People across the globe strive for quality of life, community, and self-fulfillment—higher-order values that transcend material needs.

OBSTACLES TO INTEGRATION

Issue 1. The transition to a uniform global order requires systems that integrate the world.
Issue 2. Individual-based capitalist systems (e.g., United States) clash with collaboration-based economic systems (e.g., Japan).
Issue 3. The conflict between growth and environmental protection must be resolved.
Issue 4. We have not yet invented the new institutions needed to manage this complex new world.
Issue 5. The economic disparity between the developed countries in the North and the less-developed countries of the South continues to grow.

300-millimeter lens that cost $750 at the beginning of the year soared to more than $1,000 by December because the yen grew stronger relative to the dollar.

The dollar's decline in value helped to induce foreign corporations to manufacture in the United States. Corporations like American Matsushita Electronics Corporation employ thousands of Troy residents at plants along nearby Interstate 75. In 1993, this unit of Japan's Matsushita Electric Industrial announced that it would bolster its local work force of 600 employees, who make picture tubes for Panasonic color television sets. Honda Motor Co. and Gokoh Corp. have offices and plants nearby. More than 50 Japanese executives and their families have settled in Troy. Troy's motor vehicle bureau offers the written driver's license exam in Japanese to make it easier for the executives and their wives to take the test.

Growth of International Trade

Like the citizens of Troy, modern managers operate in an increasingly international environment. This environment has emerged from a decade of continuous growth in international trade and a steady drop in the tariffs and

166 PART THREE Special Issues in Strategic Management

duties that restrict international flows of goods and services. Tables 7.2 and 7.3 show the rates at which world trade has grown and tariffs have dropped.

As organizations scramble to stay in line with these emerging international trends, managers must evaluate and monitor the political and economic forces that drive the trends, and their influence on the strategic management process. An increasingly liberal international trade environment demands that managers evaluate threats from competitors across the globe. Lands' End hoped to pose such a threat to catalog retailers in Europe, as the Skills Module explains. Their environmental analysis must expand to encompass a number of international concerns:

- What institutional environment constrains competitors?
- What rules govern competitors' actions?

TABLE 7.2

Annual Percentage Change in International Trade

	World Merchandise Output	World Merchandise Trade
1982	−1.88%	−3.08%
1983	1.15	2.31
1984	5.77	8.08
1985	2.69	2.61
1986	2.69	4.61
1987	2.88	5.77
1988	4.92	8.84
1989	3.65	6.92
1990	1.92	5.00
1991	0.38	2.88
1992	0.96[a]	3.85[a]

[a]Figures for 1992 are preliminary estimates based on data available in March 1992.

SOURCE: Adapted from R. Scherer, "Seven Years Later: Deal Is Likely," *Christian Science Monitor,* December 10, 1993, p. 6.

TABLE 7.3

Average Tariffs on Imports to Industrial Nations

	Average Tariffs
1940	40.0%
1950	24.7
1960	16.7
1970	12.3
1980	8.0
1990	5.3
2000	2.7[a]

[a]Estimated.

SOURCE: Adapted from H. LaFranchi, "What's Next for World Trade?" *Christian Science Monitor,* December 23, 1993, p. 6.

SKILLS MODULE
Lands' End Seeks Global Future

INTRODUCTION

The impact of international operations on strategic management has become increasingly significant as trends toward domestic and bottom-line interests and global competition have become intertwined. Review the following situation at Lands' End, and then complete the skill development exercise that follows. This will help you to analyze the special considerations that affect the strategic management process on the international stage.

SITUATION

After years of growth in the United States, Lands' End Inc. decided to set sail for international markets. The Dodgeville, Wisconsin, seller of upscale apparel had enjoyed wide success with its domestic catalog sales of outdoor apparel and household goods. Like some of its U.S. competitors—including L. L. Bean, J. Crew, and Spiegel Inc.—the catalog merchant determined that its real growth opportunities lay overseas.

Although overseas sales accounted for less than 10 percent of its $870 million in overall sales, a company representative asserted that "international expansion will be a primary avenue of growth for us." William J. O'Neill, vice president, international for Lands' End, added that conditions made the environment ripe for success: two-worker families had increased, delivery service became quicker, and shopping by mail had become increasingly popular.

The U.S. mail-order industry was booming, with sales expected to increase 7 percent in 1994. In 1993, more than 8,000 catalog houses issued 12 billion catalogs in the United States. All of these small, specialty marketers competed on a level playing field; no company took more than a 6.4 percent share of the industry's $55 billion in total sales.

Still, the overseas market looked huge; in Japan alone, 1992 mail-order sales of $178 billion were more than triple U.S. sales. The situation among European catalogers was similar, and their businesses were just as dissimilar to those of their American counterparts. In Europe, huge catalog concerns published books up to 1,300 pages long to sell everything from clothing and furniture to consumer electronics and appliances. Their shares of the home-market, mail-order pie ranged from 20 percent to 35 percent.

The majority of U.S. firms that headed overseas specialized in basic work and leisure apparel—clothing that had the widest cross-cultural appeal. That's the basis of the Lands' End marketing strategy, said O'Neill. Men in Japan "wear white shirts and ties, and the women wear skirts and jackets, and we sell those things."

The Americans' skill at reproducing their marketing and distribution success overseas would decide their fate. They also had to adapt their operations to local constraints and outrun local competitors. One of France's giant catalogers had already battened down the hatches; to blunt the effect of J. Crew's arrival, it launched a new book offering clothing similar to the American company's.

Lands' End began testing the waters in 1991, mailing catalogs to customers in the United Kingdom. Two years later, it opened a distribution center there, reducing delivery time to three days from two weeks. It grew to mail 70-page versions of its standard, 160-page U.S. catalog 10 times a year in the United Kingdom. In late 1994, it planned a mass mailing to Japan.

SKILL DEVELOPMENT EXERCISE

As head of the Lands' End marketing department, outline how you can best ensure the company's success in differentiating its products and its image from both its American counterparts and its foreign competitors. Detail how you would anticipate the competition and respond to it, and trace the strategic management steps you would take to build a foundation for international success.

SOURCE: Gregory A. Patterson, "U.S. Catalogers Test International Waters," *The Wall Street Journal*, April 19, 1994, p. B1.

- What recourse is available to minimize damage from the actions of competitors?
- What government policies strengthen competitors?
- How can firms influence these government policies?
- What new markets and opportunities emerge as barriers to international trade continually shrink?

Answers to these questions are unique to specific organizations and industries. However, multilateral and regional trade agreements form a foundation for all international business operations.

INTERNATIONAL TRADE AGREEMENTS

The competitive environment varies significantly across international markets. An emerging nation like Uzbekistan may have no laws that protect the copyright of an American organization. Even when copyright protection is written into the local laws, in Thailand for example, the enforcement of the local laws may be lax. Walt Disney Co. has moved aggressively to stem the flood of pirated Disney products in Thailand. John Feenie, the head of Disney's consumer products division, hired an anticounterfeiting consultant, accumulated evidence against the pirates, staged raids to confiscate counterfeits, and burned entire consignments of counterfeit Donald Duck, Mickey Mouse, and Bambi dolls. To orchestrate his company's massive retaliation against counterfeiters in Thailand, Feenie operated within a complex web of international trade laws, economic agreements, and business regulations. This web includes broad multilateral economic agreements, as well as more narrowly focused regional arrangements. In this section we discuss the structure, intentions, and provisions of trade agreements that define the infrastructure within which managers like Feenie compete in global markets.

General Agreement on Tariffs and Trade (GATT)

The **General Agreement on Tariffs and Trade** is a broad, multilateral trade agreement designed to smooth the flow of goods between nations. Together, the 115 nations that subscribe to this treaty account for more than 90 percent of world trade. The treaty is administered by a Geneva-based bureaucracy that referees world trade. Its basic aim is to liberalize and promote world trade. Since 1948, GATT has functioned as the principal international forum for negotiating reductions in trade barriers and governing international trade relations. An abbreviated history of the GATT is provided in Table 7.4.

Although the actual GATT agreement is a long and complicated document, its provisions have emerged from a simple set of principles and aims.[4]

- Members are expected to engage in trade without discrimination. No country may give special trading advantages to another or discriminate against another. Exceptions to this rule are limited to certain special circumstances such as regional trading arrangements and trade with developing countries.
- Any protection to domestic industry must take the form of a customs tariff. This makes the extent of protection clear.
- Member nations must abide by negotiated tariff levels. This promotes stability in trade, with a provision for renegotiation of tariffs.
- When a country feels that its rights under the agreement are being denied or compromised, it may call on GATT for a fair settlement. Most of these

TABLE 7.4

History of GATT

1946–1947	The first proposal was made to form the International Trade Organization (ITO) as a special agency of the United Nations. The political climate that lingered after the protectionist trade policies of the 1920s and 1930s was not supportive. ITO was abandoned, but part of its charter was later salvaged as the General Agreement on Tariffs and Trade.
1948	GATT was established, joining 23 nations to try to liberalize world trade by eliminating tariffs. The agreement consisted of a set of articles that laid down the basic principles of trade. Member nations' trade laws had to conform with these articles.
1950–1959	The Annecy Round, the Torquay Round, and the Geneva Round, named for the cities in which the documents were signed, began seven rounds of multilateral negotiations to reduce trade barriers.
1960–1961	The Dillon Round was initiated in response to a proposal by some European nations to band together under a regional trade agreement, the European Economic Community. Steps were taken to ensure that world trade would not suffer as a result of such regional agreements.
1963–1967	The Kennedy Round was the first round to reduce tariffs comprehensively rather than product by product. Dumping—international sales of goods below cost—was recognized as a problem, and the first antidumping measures were passed.
1973–1979	The Tokyo Round was the first to recognize the importance of nontariff trade barriers such as quotas.
1986–1993	The Uruguay Round began with the goal of reducing tariffs by one-third. Additionally, it addressed the weak enforcement of GATT rules, increases in bilateral and unilateral actions, emergence of newly industrialized economies, trade in services, and protection of intellectual property rights. By this time, GATT had 115 member nations.
1994	GATT was renamed World Trade Organization.

SOURCE: Adapted from R. Scherer, "GATT's Conception and Progress," *Christian Science Monitor,* December 10, 1993, p. 6.

differences are settled directly between the countries concerned. Sometimes the GATT council appoints independent experts to facilitate the negotiations between member nations.

- A country may seek a waiver from a particular GATT obligation if special economic or trade circumstances warrant one.
- GATT generally prohibits quantitative restrictions on trade. An exception to this rule allows quantitative restrictions to deal with balance-of-payments difficulties.
- GATT permits **regional trade arrangements,** in which groups of countries agree to abolish or reduce barriers against imports from one another, as exceptions, providing they meet certain criteria. These rules are intended to ensure that the arrangements facilitate trade among the countries concerned without raising barriers to trade with the outside world.

The city of Stoke on Trent in England is the world capital of the fine tableware industry. The Dudson Group is a typical example of a local tableware manufacturer. This family-owned firm was founded in 1800 by Managing Director Ian Dudson's ancestors. In the Dudson Group's factory, workers busily mold and fire clay into fine china for customers the world over. GATT allows Ian Dudson to sell fruit bowls to a Canadian restaurant, soup dishes to roadside stalls on Italy's *autostrada*, teacups to the Belgian railway, and dinner plates to a Singapore hotel.[5]

GATT reassures Ian Dudson that his products will not suffer discrimination based on their country of origin, and it provides unambiguous information about the tariff structures and other protectionist barriers in member nations across the globe. (**Tariffs** are taxes levied on imported goods.) Italy can change its tariff on soup dishes only by renegotiating the existing tariff with all the member nations that are affected by the change. GATT gives companies like the Dudson Group a structure within which they can settle any differences that may arise out of their international trade.

Multilateral agreements such as GATT extend the economic benefits of increased world trade to all member nations. However, these economic benefits are not painless. Organizations that have thrived behind the protection of tariff barriers are usually ill-equipped to take on strong foreign competitors. Employees and organizations that face risks from more liberal world trade tend to exercise their political clout to gain protection. In fact, GATT's Uruguay Round lasted for seven years as the 115 member nations found it extremely difficult to balance these imperatives.

In summary, GATT is a multilateral trade agreement devoted to liberalizing world trade and reducing the tariffs that protect national markets from foreign competition. Although its aims are simple, finalizing the agreement is a complex political task that has required prolonged discussion and negotiation. GATT stabilizes world trade by providing a clear set of rules. Finally, when a country feels a threat to its rights, GATT provides a framework for consultation, conciliation, and settlement of differences.

Across the globe, smaller groups of nations have also tried to develop regional trade agreements to reap the benefits of liberalized regional trade. Regional agreements free nations from the horrendous complexity of appeasing the demands of hundreds of members. The North American Free Trade Agreement, the European Community, and the Asia–Pacific Economic Cooperation Forum are three of the most prominent regional trade agreements.

North American Free Trade Agreement (NAFTA)

The **North American Free Trade Agreement** (NAFTA) is designed to phase out tariffs among the United States, Canada, and Mexico over 15 years, and to liberalize investment rules in Mexico. Trade between the United States and Canada was promoted through a separate free trade agreement that predated NAFTA and was generally subsumed under NAFTA. Direct trade between Mexico and Canada is minimal, however, representing less than 3 percent of each country's exports and imports.

NAFTA will significantly affect trade between the United States and Mexico. Before NAFTA, Mexico's tariffs on U.S. goods averaged 10 percent while U.S. tariffs on Mexican goods averaged 4 percent. On January 1, 1994, the day NAFTA became effective, the United States eliminated tariffs on about half of Mexico's exports, and Mexico dropped its tariffs on about a third of U.S. exports.

Although the full text of NAFTA fills five volumes, the key provisions of the agreement can be summarized in terms of its effect on trade, investment, government spending, and two side agreements covering environmental protection and labor.[6]

Trade Provisions   U.S. and Mexican tariffs and quotas will be phased out over 15 years beginning in 1994. Goods made with material or labor from outside North America qualify for NAFTA treatment only if significant, value-added manufacturing activity takes place within the United States, Mexico, or Canada. NAFTA will reduce tariffs in different industries according to specific conditions. For example, in the automotive industry, NAFTA will eliminate a tariff after eight years only if 62.5 percent of a product's cost (50 percent for the first four years, 56 percent for the following four years) represents North American materials or labor. After 10 years, U.S. producers of automobiles need not produce in Mexico to sell there.

In the textile and apparel industries, strict rules eliminated tariffs only for goods made from North American spun yarn or from fabric made from North American fibers. In agriculture, NAFTA immediately eliminated about half of the tariffs and quotas that existed in 1993. However, tariffs on politically sensitive crops, such as U.S. corn sold to Mexico or Mexican peanuts, sugar, and orange juice sold to the United States, will be phased out over 15 years. By the end of 1999, NAFTA will lift limits on U.S. truckers driving cargo across the border. By the year 2000, U.S. companies will be allowed to buy stakes in Mexican trucking companies and by 2003 they will be allowed to own them entirely.

Investment Provisions   NAFTA places strict limits on foreign investment in Mexico's energy and railroad industries, the U.S. airlines and radio communications industries, and Canada's movie and television industries. Although Mexico will continue to restrict foreign ownership of certain land and forbid foreign investment in oil and gas exploration, it will open most petrochemical and electric-generation sectors to U.S. investment. For the first time, U.S. drilling companies will be allowed to share in the profits from oil found in Mexico. Limits on foreign investment in Mexican banks, insurers, and brokerage firms will be phased out over 7 to 15 years beginning in 1994.

Government Spending   NAFTA allows companies from all three nations to compete for government contracts. Mexico will phase out restrictions on purchases by its government-owned energy industry over 10 years beginning in 1994. The U.S. government will spend $90 million to retrain workers who lose their jobs because of NAFTA during the first 18 months of the agreement. The U.S. and Mexican governments will invest $225 million each to form a new North American Development Bank that will then borrow an additional $3 billion and lend the money to aid communities hurt by the agreement.

Side Agreements   The agreement will establish an agency in Canada to investigate environmental abuses in any of the three countries. Fines or trade sanctions could be imposed on countries that fail to enforce their own environmental laws. The U.S.–Mexico Border Environmental Commission will spend up to $8 billion on various environmental clean-up projects. An agency will be established in Washington to investigate labor abuses identified by two of the three countries. Fines or trade sanctions will be imposed if any of the countries fail to enforce worker-safety rules, child-labor laws, or minimum-wage standards.

Although it is called a *free trade agreement,* NAFTA contains special provisions designed to help specific industries or companies. These deals can make a tremendous difference in an organization's strategic management process. For example, regulations on Mexico's automotive industry will relax at a pace slow enough to block car makers from exporting there for a decade or so. This gives an advantage to companies like General Motors, Chrysler, Nissan, and Volkswagen, which were already manufacturing in Mexico before NAFTA. Similarly, Mexico is phasing out tariff controls on glass very slowly in order to benefit its big glass manufacturer, Vitro SA.

In summary, NAFTA is a regional trade agreement designed to reduce tariffs and to liberalize trade between the United States, Canada, and Mexico. Since freer trade relations between the United States and Canada predated NAFTA and direct trade between Mexico and Canada is minimal, NAFTA will affect trade relations primarily between the United States and Mexico. The agreement covers issues in trade, investment, government spending, environmental protection, and labor. NAFTA will phase out the tariffs and quotas that govern trade relations between the United States and Mexico over 15 years, beginning in 1994.

European Union (EU)

The organization that has become the **European Union** was first formed in 1951 by Belgium, France, West Germany, Italy, Luxembourg, and the Netherlands. Originally called the European Coal and Steel Community, it was designed to allow the free flow of coal, iron, steel, and scrap metal between member nations. In 1957 when the Treaty of Rome was signed, the European Economic Community was formally established and its objectives were modified. The new objectives called for the creation of a common market through elimination of internal trade barriers, creation of a common external tariff, and removal of all obstacles to the free movement of goods, services, and factors of production among member nations. Since 1957 the overall philosophy of the common market has remained the same, membership in the community has expanded, and the details of creating free trade have continued.

Original members of the European Union were Belgium, Denmark, France, Germany, Greece, Ireland, Italy, Luxembourg, the Netherlands, Portugal, Spain, and the United Kingdom. Austria, Finland, Norway, and Sweden were admitted as new members. Interest in EU membership has continued. Cyprus, Malta, Switzerland, and Turkey have applied, and applications are expected from the Czech Republic, Hungary, and Poland. The mission of the union is to weld the member states together into a single market.

The methods used to achieve the common market include:

- *Removing all frontier controls.* The elimination of passports, customs, and excise controls between member nations would eliminate border delays and reduce the size and cost of the state bureaucracy that was formerly used for these controls.

- *Establishing mutual standards.* Harmonizing the product standards of the member nations would simplify the task of competing in this market.
- *Competing for public contracts.* Companies from one member nation would be allowed to compete for the government contract from another member nation.
- *Broadening availability of financial services.* Insurance and retail banking companies in one member nation would be allowed to extend their services to other member nations.
- *Eliminating exchange controls.* All restrictions on foreign exchange transactions would be removed.
- *Relaxing freight transport regulations.* Foreign truckers could pick up and deliver goods within any member nation.

The significance of the European Union comes from its size. The population within the community totals 320 million people. Its gross domestic product is more than that of the United States. Its exports account for 33 percent of total world exports.[7]

By creating a common market, the EU's members hope to gain several benefits:

- The unified market's purchasing power would match that of the United States.
- Simplifying procedures would reduce the costs of operating within the market.
- Creating a single set of uniform standards would allow organizations to achieve economies of scale.

Whereas individual nations in Europe are relatively small, adding their markets together to form a common market would create a market with immensely attractive size and purchasing power. The complex, idiosyncratic border controls designed by individual nations waste time and raise costs for business transactions that cross national borders. Today, a French manufacturer would find that border controls make it very difficult to sell its products in Germany at cost competitive prices compared to German manufacturers. A uniform, simplified set of border controls would make it easier for manufacturers to compete effectively throughout Europe.

Also, Germany alone sets more than 20,000 product standards that govern everything from the purity of the ingredients in beer to the number of electronic scan lines on the picture tube of a color TV. France has 8,000 product standards of its own, and the French and German standards for the same product are significantly different. This makes it virtually impossible for a European manufacturer to efficiently mass produce an item; production runs have to be broken into small chunks to conform to the different product specifications in different national markets. Uniform standards would allow organizations to achieve economies of scale.

Moving beyond Maastricht   In December 1991, the European Council meeting in Maastricht marked another major step along the road to greater European unity. Concluding the work of two intergovernmental conferences on political, economic, and monetary union, the members agreed to a new Treaty on European Union.[8] They clarified old goals and attached deadlines to them. They also set some new aims with the clear intention of reinforcing the unity of the community.

However, negotiating details tends to be a complex political process. For example, the British government insisted that the word *federal* be removed from the preamble to the treaty. Plans to eliminate frontier passport checks for citizens of member nations were supposed to take effect on January 1, 1993, but they were postponed due to opposition from the United Kingdom and Denmark. Of the 219 laws called for in the blueprint for the single market, just 106 had been implemented with the necessary national legislation in all 12 original member nations by November 1993.[9] As the members of the European Union negotiate ways to make their common market work, companies across the globe are positioning themselves to benefit from the integration.

Prospecting the European Market   Some of the opportunities presented by the European Union are obvious. For example, elimination of border controls can cut the time to ship goods from Milan to London in half. Jeff Fettig, vice president for marketing at Whirlpool International BV in Comerio, Italy, considers this a boon. However, the overall success of Whirlpool Corp.'s strategy in Europe has been far from obvious.[10] In January 1989, U.S.-based Whirlpool Corp. formed a joint venture with Philips Electronics NV of Europe to manufacture white-goods when the Whirlpool name was virtually unknown in Europe. (White-goods is the term applied to washing machines, dryers, and other similar electrical appliances.) In 1991, Whirlpool bought full control of the venture and launched an aggressive campaign to court the Euroconsumer.

Several experts predicted disaster for Whirlpool's pan-European campaign. Despite all the progress toward European integration, the European nations retain fundamental differences. Not only do kitchen appliances differ from one country to another, but consumers also react differently to advertising messages. Careful market research taught Whirlpool that many of the differences in consumer products among European countries have little to do with consumer tastes. For example, experts used to argue that French consumers would not accept front-loading washing machines because they were used to the narrow, top-loading machines made by French manufacturers. Whirlpool discovered that consumers across Europe wanted an appliance that would get their clothes clean; that would be easy to use; that wouldn't use too much electricity, water, or detergent; and that had a record of trouble-free service. If it met all those criteria, other features—such as where the machine opened and its size—were less important. "We've discovered," said Alex Vente, Whirlpool's director of marketing communications, "that Europeans are a lot less set in their ways than many people believe."

Whirlpool's approach to advertising in Europe was equally meticulous. It prepared the ground with careful research and created a special team to evaluate more than 20 potential campaigns. The team agreed on a campaign that featured a cool, bluish dream world of dryers and dishwashers, emphasizing high technology and the universal desire for more free time. Apparently this campaign hit a pan-European chord. Whirlpool's polls began to show that more and more consumers had become aware of Whirlpool and had positive associations with its products. In 1991, when industrywide sales of major appliances were flat, Whirlpool increased its market share in Europe as a whole, and in Germany, France, and Britain in particular.

Asia–Pacific Economic Cooperation (APEC) Forum

On the night in 1989 when the Berlin Wall fell, Walt Rostow, an economic development expert at the University of Texas, surprised Ted Koppel on ABC's *Nightline* program by suggesting that something even more historic had happened that day: the **Asia–Pacific Economic Cooperation (APEC) forum** was founded. By the time the Berlin Wall actually fell, its collapse had become inevitable; it was a relic of the past. By contrast, East Asia's economies are gearing toward the future. They have been growing at roughly twice the rates common in western nations and are anticipated to continue to do so in the next decade.

Asia's biggest export market is America, which buys approximately one-third of the exports of Japan, Taiwan, South Korea, and China, and a quarter of Hong Kong's exports.[11] At the same time, U.S. exports to Asia are climbing steadily, creating high-wage manufacturing jobs while European markets are stagnant. Exports from the United States to developing countries and Asia's four **newly industrialized countries** (NICs)—Hong Kong, Singapore, South Korea, and Taiwan—grew 13.7 percent between 1991 and 1992 while exports to developed countries grew only 1.8 percent.[12] Businesses in the state of Washington see Asia as a booming market for Boeing jets, Microsoft computer software, Kenworth trucks, and numerous other local products.[13] In light of these trends and local successes, it is not surprising that in November 1993, President Clinton used the fifth annual meeting of the APEC forum in Seattle to bring American trade links with Asian nations into the limelight.

To boost APEC's stature, President Clinton traveled to Seattle and invited other heads of government to a meeting that is normally attended by foreign and economic ministers of the member nations. The 15-member APEC forum is not an international organization with established decision-making processes like NAFTA and GATT. Its mission is to provide a forum for discussion of economic cooperation issues among member nations. Clearly, the United States would like to see the APEC forum transformed into a body that actively promotes trade and investment liberalization within the region.

APEC's members include Australia, Brunei, Canada, China, Hong Kong, Indonesia, Japan, Malaysia, New Zealand, the Philippines, Singapore, South Korea, Taiwan, Thailand, and the United States. Mexico, Chile, and Papua New Guinea have applied for membership. Ten working groups within APEC discuss a variety of issues to promote cooperation among market-oriented Pacific Rim economies. The 15 member nations have a total population of more than 2 billion people, account for more than one-third of world trade, and have a combined gross domestic product of over $12 trillion, half the world total.[14]

With the economies of the United States, Europe, and Japan sputtering, smart American companies are moving quickly into the developing and newly industrialized nations of Asia and Latin America. Although Mexico has been the traditional focus of U.S. investment and attention, it is important to understand the emerging significance of Asian nations. Diebold Corporation is a $543 million manufacturer of banking equipment. When asked about the potential demand for his company's products in China, Diebold Chairman

Robert W. Mahoney said, "I hate to even contemplate it in strategy meetings, it gets me so excited. It's a staggering figure." In 1993, after just two weeks in China, a Diebold sales representative returned with orders for 93,000 bank safe-deposit boxes at about $1,000 a piece.[15] Since this is more than Diebold can churn out in a year, the company has had to expand its Ohio factory. In May 1993, Diebold went beyond exports in its quest to cash in on the banking boom that is taking place as Chinese citizens move savings from under their mattresses into bank accounts. It joined with Chinese partners to make automated teller machines in a new Shanghai factory.

Other Regional Trade Agreements

NAFTA, the EC, and APEC rank as critical international trading arrangements, and managers should understand them. In addition, however, other regional trade agreements have proliferated. The Association of Southeast Asian Nations (ASEAN) joined Brunei, Indonesia, Malaysia, the Philippines, Singapore, and Thailand in a cooperative organization in 1967. ASEAN has sought to foster free trade between the member nations and coordinate their industrial policies. Although some tariffs between ASEAN countries have fallen, in 1993 the intra-ASEAN trade that benefited from these reductions accounted for less than 6 percent of the total.

In 1988 Brazil and Argentina signed a free trade pact called MERCOSUR. This pact was perceived as instrumental in increasing trade between the two nations dramatically. In March 1990, it was expanded to include Paraguay and Uruguay. The long-term objective of the MERCOSUR pact is to form a free trade area by the end of 1994, and a common market soon afterward.

Since 1973 the English-speaking Caribbean nations have been trying to form a customs union called CARICOM. In 1991, these nations failed for the third time to meet a self-imposed deadline for fixing a common external tariff.

In summary, managers conduct international operations within a framework of several international trade agreements. GATT is a broad, multilateral agreement between 115 member nations aimed at worldwide reductions in tariff barriers. NAFTA is a narrowly focused regional arrangement to liberalize regional trade between three nations. Planning for international operations must include analysis of the opportunities and constraints presented by these trade agreements. For example, NAFTA allows oil companies based in the United States to bid for business from the government-owned Mexican oil companies. On the other hand, the formation of the European Union may require American beer manufacturers to meet stringent German quality standards before they can enter the vast European market.

Trade agreements can have a crucial impact on any analysis of international operations. National governments also act independently, however, to promote the success of their native firms. Usually, this action is part of a national industrial policy.

INDUSTRIAL POLICY

Industrial policy is government policy designed to promote economic growth. More detailed definitions can be either broad or narrow in scope. Broadly defined industrial policy includes a nation's macroeconomic policies, labor–

management relations, education and infrastructure, production technologies, and cultural patterns. In June 1994, Robert Reich, labor secretary in the Clinton administration, announced a nationwide program for worker training; this announcement launched a broad industrial policy initiative that was designed to spur economic growth. Training American workers to upgrade their skills would help them to work more effectively, increasing the productivity and competitiveness of American industries.

Narrowly defined, industrial policy specifies government action intended to improve a country's economic well-being by supporting particular industries. When the White House eased Cold-War era export restrictions on computers to open the door for $35 billion worth of high-tech exports each year, it launched an industrial policy initiative that focused on the computer industry.[16]

Any whisper of the term *industrial policy* used to set off alarm bells in the United States during the Reagan and Bush eras; any suggestion that government could play a key role in nurturing a worldwide economy risked charges of heresy in the Republican administrations. However, as U.S. companies compete in markets across the globe, they often encounter obstacles that can be traced to the industrial policies of other nations. For example, Boeing has found that the German government's stake in Airbus, the European aircraft manufacturing consortium, has made it almost impossible to sell U.S. aircraft in Germany. Similarly, experts suggest that companies such as AT&T have found few customers in Japan because that country's Ministry of International Trade and Industry (MITI) encourages Japanese companies to support local suppliers. Industrial policy creates opportunities or threats for organizations. By understanding how it works, managers can evaluate industrial policy as part of strategic analysis.

Effects of Industrial Policy

Industrial policy is not a recent invention. In the 19th century, the U.S. federal government backed the development of the transcontinental railroad by ceding huge tracts of land to its builders. The government has also sponsored a network of universities, extension services, and research to help U.S. farmers reap the riches of a fertile land. In today's knowledge-based economy, however, industrial policy does not require the government to pick winning and losing industries. Instead, industrial policy weaves a web of measures that support the creation and commercialization of ideas. Typical industrial policy measures have a range of effects:[17]

- *Spurring cutting-edge technology.* Sematech is one of the most prominent government–industry partnerships in the United States. The six-year-old consortium brings together a dozen of the largest U.S. makers of computer chips to conduct research in advanced fabrication technologies. Half of the $200 million annual cost is paid by the Advanced Research Projects Agency at the Department of Defense. Experts say the United States has recently caught up with Japan in worldwide sales of chips because of Sematech.
- *Diffusing new technology.* Some experts say that outdated manufacturing practices account for 85 percent of the problems of American firms. To help small companies compete, 23 state governments spend a total of $50 million a year supporting 27 technology extension centers. The Company Example illustrates one state's efforts. The federal government is pitching in several million dollars more. These amounts pale, however, in comparison

COMPANY EXAMPLE

Pennsylvania's Industrial Policy Guides Small Firm's Strategy

Not every company can be a GM, a Xerox, or a Microsoft. Industrial states are recognizing this fact as they rethink the economic importance of small, nuts-and-bolts manufacturers. After a decade spent chasing down high-tech and service jobs to replace losses from closed steel and auto plants, states are recognizing the resiliency of small industry.

In Pennsylvania, for example, steel plant closings played a big role in the 22 percent decline in factory jobs during the 1980s. The number of manufacturing jobs in the state actually increased by 5 percent during the decade, however, to more than 17,000.

Scheirer Machine Co., employer of 65, was among the companies that contributed to Pennsylvania's job growth in the 1980s. Scheirer typifies the kind of company Pennsylvania leaders had in mind in 1988 when they created a technical-assistance program for manufacturers. The state now leads the nation in developing local industrial policies geared toward preserving stable, high-paying factory jobs.

When the Pittsburgh maker of replacement parts for steel and mining equipment needed help to be-come more competitive, it turned to its local Industrial Resource Center, one of eight regional centers funded by a $9 million state outlay. For a $3,000 fee, Scheirer acquired the services of a three-person team of experts who helped the company reorganize its shop floor and raise productivity by about 15 percent in only six months. In addition, the center lent Scheirer $150,000 at 5 percent interest to buy a computerized lathe. Ongoing assistance helps the firm to further upgrade its technology.

Although some complain that funding limits focus the state's industrial policy on stable and credit-worthy firms, rather than struggling or adventurous newcomers, Pennsylvania's comprehensive program also nurtures startups, using state money under the decade-old Ben Franklin Partnership. Recently, the state started lending more low-interest money for modernization to companies that pay above-average salaries.

SOURCE: Michael Schroeder, "Small Business Has a Friend in Pennsylvania," *Business Week*, April 6, 1992, p. 75.

with the $500 million that the Japanese government spends to back 185 technology extension centers.

- *Creating a new infrastructure.* A communications infrastructure that can support information-intensive industries is a critical competitive tool for organizations in the 1990s. The U.S. government is making a massive commitment to build a communications conduit made of fiber-optic cables and high-speed digital switching equipment. This conduit, which is expected to cost billions of dollars, will make it easier to manipulate and transfer huge amounts of data at high speed.

- *Increasing free trade.* Although the U.S. government has made a tremendous effort to smooth the flow of goods and services across the globe through NAFTA and GATT, as earlier sections have described, U.S. companies routinely encounter impediments that hinder their expansion into foreign markets. Giddings & Lewis, America's largest machine tool builder and a fierce competitor, has not sold a machine in Japan since 1974. "And it's not for lack of trying," says Chairman William Fife, Jr.[18] U.S. industrial policy has long worked to open the doors of restricted markets such as Japan.

- *Investing in new technologies.* Organizations commit to new technology only when the climate for investment is correct. Research and investment tax credits can speed innovation and investment. Andrew Grove, chief executive of Intel Corp., says, "I'm not looking for a handout, but a turbocharge."[19]

STRATEGIC MANAGEMENT IN THE INTERNATIONAL ARENA

As firms position themselves to compete in the international arena, they will continue to seek external reinforcement of their efforts, such as international trade agreements and favorable national industrial policies already discussed. However, going global raises several internal issues that need to be successfully managed. The remainder of this chapter discusses multinational corporations and explores international operations from the strategic management perspective: analyzing the environment, establishing organizational direction, formulating strategy, implementing strategy, and exerting strategic control.

Multinational Corporations

Since its first appearance in 1975, the term **multinational corporation** has described an organization that has significant operations in more than one country. The organization that invests in international operations is called the *parent company;* the country in which the parent makes the investment is called the *host country*. The multinational corporation views its diverse activities as a whole and develops and implements a unified strategy to encompass all of them.

At the end of the Second World War, the United States was the most powerful industrial nation, and for the next 35 years, U.S. enterprises ranked among the biggest in the world. In 1975, 126 of the world's 260 multinational organizations were based in the United States, including 15 of the largest 25 multinationals. In the 1980s and 1990s, things began to change rapidly. Japanese, British, German, French, Dutch, Italian, and South Korean multinational organizations grew in strength and size and began challenging U.S. companies, even in the North American market.

Some organizations accomplish the transformation into multinational corporations in stages: their early foreign operations rely on exporting, and they progress gradually through licensing to direct investment. (These stages are discussed in detail in the later section on international strategy formulation.) Today, however, progress in technology and global interdependence has freed organizations that do not rank with corporations like General Electric or IBM to exploit the potential of international markets. For example, Laser Communications Inc. (LCI), based in Lancaster, Pennsylvania, found a way to replace telephone lines and ground cables with nonstop streams of airborne laser beams. LCI's technology zaps audio, video, and data transmissions through the air over distances up to one mile. Founded in 1983, LCI posts annual revenues of about $2.5 million and employs only 13, yet its technology is in more than 1,000 installations in 35 countries.[20] Organizations as small as LCI and as big as IBM all must perform the main steps of the strategic management process.

International Environmental Analysis

Recall that environmental analysis is the process of monitoring the conditions in which an organization operates to identify present and future strengths, weaknesses, opportunities, and threats (SWOT) that affect its progress toward its goals. This complicated process involves analyzing:

1. The general environment—social, economic, technological, ethical, and political/legal conditions

2. The operating environment—suppliers, competitors, customers, and labor conditions
3. The internal environment—conditions within the organization

Charles J. Fombrun and Stefan Wally suggest that the multinational corporation's operating environment is more complex than that of a purely domestic firm, due largely to changes in three forces:[21]

1. Worldwide infrastructure
2. Worldwide sociostructure
3. Worldwide superstructure

Figure 7.1 illustrates some of the relationships between the forces of change, emerging trends, and the issues that affect environmental analysis of international operations. For example, changes in sociostructure may lead to the emergence of regional trading blocs. In turn, each bloc implies a unique set of market changes, competitive changes, and regulatory changes that guide the organization's environmental analysis. This demands that the multinational organization acquire additional skills and expertise that the purely

FIGURE 7.1   Forces That Influence International Environmental Analysis

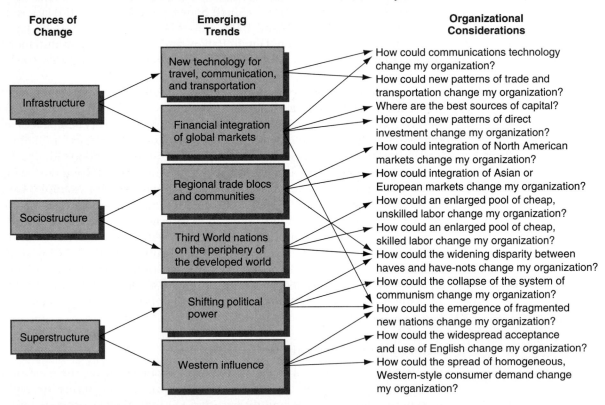

SOURCE: Adapted from C. J. Fombrun and S. Wally, "Global Entanglements: The Structure of Corporate Transnationalism," in V. Pucik, N. M. Tichy, and C. K. Barnett, eds., *Globalizing Management: Creating and Leading the Competitive Organization* (New York: John Wiley & Sons, 1993).

domestic organization does not need because it does not encounter these environmental complexities.

Within the general model for the links between the forces of change and emerging trends in Figure 7.1, several specific trends affect all multinational organizations' environmental analysis efforts. Michael Porter's analysis identifies several of these trends:[22]

- *Fewer differences among countries.* Differences in such areas as income, energy costs, marketing practices, and channels of distribution seem to be narrowing. In many industries, it is no longer meaningful to separate the German market from the American market or the Japanese market. Consumers are becoming increasingly alike. In a dark blue suit and Regal shoes, carrying a Casio pocket calculator in a Mark Cross wallet, frequenting a nearby sushi bar for lunch, and commuting in a Celica, the typical New York businessperson would not draw a second glance on the streets of Düsseldorf or Tokyo.[23]
- *More aggressive industrial policies.* The governments of such countries as Japan, Germany, and Taiwan have developed fiercely competitive attitudes toward international business. The future policies of these governments will probably make the international environment more and more competitive. For example, aggressive planning has moved Taiwan from an agricultural economy in the 1960s to worldwide economic power in the 1990s. This planning has brought so much success that in 1992, Taiwan had tangible assets worth $3.5 billion on the Chinese mainland; $5 billion in Malaysia; $3.4 billion in Thailand; $2.8 billion in Indonesia; and, as a good clue to the next century's star performer in the region, at least $500 million in Vietnam. In other words, pick any Asian country with cheap land and labor from the Philippines to Sri Lanka, and a Taiwanese business is probably putting up a factory there to make umbrellas, toys, wigs, or textiles for sale in markets across the globe.[24]
- *More vigorous protection for distinctive assets.* More and more countries seem to be focusing on determining their own unique assets and exploiting this uniqueness to best advantage. Perhaps the most obvious example is the formation of the oil cartel, the Organization of Oil Exporting Countries (OPEC). Although the effectiveness of this cartel has varied over time, its primary purpose is still clear: to protect the return its members can generate on a scarce natural resource, oil.
- *Emerging, large-scale markets.* New access to markets in countries such as India and Vietnam is establishing high-volume sales potential for successful products. For example, India is in the midst of a massive transition from a planned economy to a free-market economy. Some 40 million Indians—the "super-haves," as the local media call them—live in households with annual incomes of over 900,000 rupees, or $30,000; their purchasing power approximates a yearly income of $600,000 in the United States. These families travel and educate their children abroad and drink Coke, and they will storm the gates of McDonald's when it opens its first outlets in India within the next few years.[25] In line with this trend, a multinational corporation's environmental analysts should always watch for new markets to emerge.
- *Competition from developing countries.* Now more than ever before, smaller, developing countries are becoming competitors in international markets. Malaysia is the largest exporter of semiconductor chips in the world.

Environmental analysts for multinational corporations cannot stop after evaluating the larger, more established competitors; they must consider threats from developing countries, as well.

International Organizational Direction

The complexity of the international environment, magnified by several significant trends, affects the multinational firm's analysis of its environment. Based on this environmental analysis, managers must establish a direction for the organization that operates internationally.

Like the purely domestic organization, the multinational organization must carefully evaluate the results of environmental analysis and then develop an organizational vision and mission. Managers must decide on the type and extent of international involvement they want to pursue, because this decision guides the establishment of appropriate organizational goals.

The Mazda Motor Corp. provides an example of how an international emphasis can color a company's mission statement:

> Mazda is dedicated to developing vehicles for the world's motoring public that are distinctive and innovative. Mazda also seeks to meet the needs and values of motorists the world over with Mazda's latest and future technology. To accomplish this, Mazda has a global network of research and development bases: in Yokohama, Japan; Irvine, California and Ann Arbor, Michigan, U.S.A.; and Oberursel, near Frankfort, Germany.[26]

The goal of establishing and maintaining expensive research facilities in Europe and the United States emphasizes the significance of these markets to Mazda.

After clarifying a vision and defining a mission, managers provide further direction for a multinational organization by developing long-term and short-term goals. Naturally, these goals reflect the type and extent of international involvement outlined in the company mission statement. However, host countries often impose constraints that affect the goals of multinational organizations. These constraints can take many forms:

- A host country may require that a local person or firm maintain a major or controlling interest.
- Host countries commonly demand that their own citizens hold certain management and technology positions.
- Host countries normally require some level of training for all of their citizens employed by a foreign multinational.
- Host countries seek technology-based businesses and strive to raise the technology levels of multinational organizations within their borders.

International Strategy Formulation

Following the general model of the strategic management process, managers formulate a strategy that reflects organizational goals, which in turn reflect the organization's mission, the result of environmental analysis. Whether the organization limits itself to domestic operations or enters into international operations, the purpose of strategy is the same. Over the years many different companies have formulated and successfully implemented numerous international strategies. All of these specific strategies fall into three broad categories: exporting, licensing, and direct investment.

FIGURE 7.2
Strategies for Entering
Foreign Markets

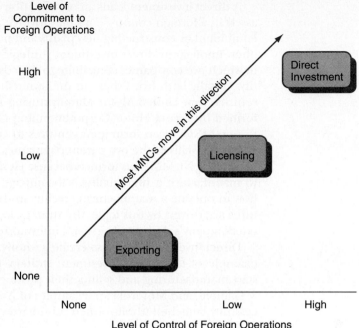

These strategies require different commitments from parent companies to foreign markets and offer parent companies varying levels of control over foreign operations (see Figure 7.2). Sometimes multinational organizations' first foreign operations involve exporting, and they progress gradually through licensing to direct investment. Regardless of the stage and the direction of a multinational corporation's progress, strategy formulation should involve an assessment of the level of commitment to and control of foreign operations that the organization's mission demands.

Exporting is selling goods or services to customers in a foreign country. This strategy leaves an organization's production facilities at home, from which it transfers products abroad. This strategy minimizes foreign investment, since the firm usually hires a foreign agent to act on its behalf, and products are often shipped directly to customers' warehouses. This strategy exposes the exporter to high transportation costs, however, and it must deal with government regulations and other operational and strategic issues from a distance.

A **licensing agreement** grants one company's right to its brand name, product specifications, and the like to another company, which sells the goods or services. The purchaser of the license hopes to profit from selling the products, whereas the seller of the license profits from the fee it charges for the license. At the international level, the purchaser and the seller of a license are from different countries, or the purchaser will sell the products in a country other than the one where it bought them. For example, all of the South Korean automobile manufacturers license technology from Japanese companies like Nissan and Toyota.

Franchising is a form of licensing that usually covers access to a wider range of rights and resources, perhaps including production equipment, managerial systems, operating procedures, advertising and trademarks. McDonald's is a good example of an MNC that sells franchises around the world.

A **direct investment** leads an organization to acquire and employ operating assets in a foreign country. This may involve purchasing existing factories and equipment or constructing new plants and purchasing new equipment. MNCs often implement direct investment strategies by entering into **joint ventures,** in which two companies contribute to the costs of creating a third business entity. Usually both firms share in the ownership of the joint venture and in its returns. New United Motor Manufacturing Inc. (NUMMI) is a joint venture formed by Toyota Motor Corporation and General Motors in Fremont, California. MNCs often form joint ventures to create synergy between the different sets of skills of the two parent companies. For example, it is commonly believed that NUMMI was formed because General Motors wanted to learn how to manufacture a high-quality, subcompact car and Toyota wanted to learn how to operate a manufacturing facility in the United States. When joint ventures are driven by this logic, the strategy formulation is guided by each parent company's desire to learn and internalize the skills of the other.[27]

Direct investment can also create a wholly owned subsidiary. An interesting example of this direct investment strategy has led American companies to start manufacturing and selling their products in Japan. Kodak, IBM, Procter & Gamble, and Motorola are examples of American companies that have successfully launched wholly owned subsidiaries in Japan.

International Strategy Implementation

After conducting an environmental analysis, establishing an appropriate organizational direction, and carefully formulating a strategy to take the firm in that direction, managers of international operations must implement the strategy they have devised. Implementing an international strategy is generally considered a much greater challenge than implementing a purely domestic strategy. Managers in multinational organizations have to design administrative systems for their employees across the globe.

The design of an administrative system is driven by two imperatives: the need to align the systems with the overall strategy of the organization, and the need to accommodate the cultural characteristics of each host country. Table 7.5 illustrates some inherent difficulties in trying to satisfy these imperatives. Although the table describes the cultural characteristics of only Japanese, North American, and Latin American managers, it demonstrates the complexities of designing systems to suit multiple host countries.

International Strategic Control

Controlling an international strategy must follow its implementation. Control ensures that the strategy is effective, given organizational conditions. Comparing this effectiveness to some predetermined standard and making any necessary changes are both part of strategic control.

Managers refer to the same financial standards at the international level to establish the appropriateness of performance as at the domestic level. Business people often mention return on investment as the most important financial measurement by which to evaluate the performance of foreign operations.

Applying such financial measurement is complicated, however, for operations in different countries. The comparison must take into account different currencies, different rates of inflation, and different tax laws, all of which contribute to this complexity. In the final analysis, comparing the financial

TABLE 7.5

Cultural Barriers to International Strategy Implementation

Japanese Values	North American Values	Latin American Values
Emotional sensitivity highly valued	Emotional sensitivity not highly valued	Emotional sensitivity valued
Restrained emotions	Straightforward or impersonal relations	Emotional passion
Subtle power plays; conciliation	Litigation; not as much conciliation	Overt power plays; exploitation of weakness
Loyalty to employer; employer taking care of employees	Lack of commitment to employer; breaking of ties by either, if necessary	Loyalty to employer (who is often family)
Group decision-making by consensus	Teamwork provides input to a single decision maker	Decisions handed down from one individual
Face-saving crucial; decisions often made simply to save someone from embarrassment	Decisions made on a cost–benefit basis; face-saving may not always matter	Face-saving crucial in decision making to preserve honor, dignity
Open special interest influence	Decision makers influenced by special interests, but often not considered ethical	Satisfying special interests expected, condoned
Nonargumentative stance; quiet when right	Argumentative when right or wrong, but impersonal	Argumentative when right or wrong; passionate
What is down in writing must be accurate, valid	Reliance on documentation as evidential proof	Impatient with documentation, seen as obstacle to understanding general principles
Step-by-step approach to decision making	Methodically organized decision making	Impulsive, spontaneous decision making
Good of group as ultimate aim	Profit motive or good of individual as ultimate aim	Good for group is good for the individual
Cultivate a good emotional social setting for decision making; get to know decision makers	Decision making impersonal; avoid involvements, conflicts of interest	Personalism necessary for good decision making

SOURCE: Courtesy of Pierre Casse, *Training for the Multicultural Manager: A Practical and Cross-Cultural Approach to the Management of People,* Washington, D.C., Copyright 1982, Society for Intercultural Education, Training and Research (SIETAR International).

performance of operations in different countries is very difficult and commonly somewhat subjective.

SUMMARY

Any organization that operates internationally must adjust the strategic management process to account for the complexities of cross-border transactions. International business has grown in importance in recent years, and this trend will only accelerate as national markets become more integrated and trade between them increases.

International trade agreements define much of the structural background for this trade. The General Agreement on Tariffs and Trade is a broad, multilateral system for negotiating reductions in tariffs and removal of other barriers to the smooth flow of products across national borders. Regional trade agreements function within the guidelines defined by GATT to promote trade between neighboring countries without excluding products from outside the region. The North American Free Trade Agreement, the European Union, and the Asia–Pacific Economic Cooperation forum are prominent regional trade agreements.

Within the provisions of these agreements, national governments develop and implement industrial policies to promote the competitive success of native organizations. These policies can seek to achieve broad, nationwide objectives or target specific industries for special attention.

Multinational corporations react to the pressures of international operations by adjusting their procedures for completing the strategic management process. Environmental analysis for such an organization must expand its scope to evaluate conditions and trends in distant, often idiosyncratic markets. Its vision and mission statements must guide later decisions about the appropriate type and extent of international involvement, given the results of the environmental analysis.

Managers then formulate strategies designed to move the firm in this chosen organizational direction, often following the traditional progression from exporting through licensing to direct investment in foreign operations. Implementing a previously formulated strategy becomes vastly more complex when it leads the firm across international borders; cultural differences can demand changes to the most successful strategy. Finally, strategic control of international operations faces problems to adjust familiar financial standards, especially return on investment, for differences in currencies, inflation levels, and tax laws, among other factors.

KEY TERMS

international management, p. 163
General Agreement on Tariffs and Trade (GATT), p. 168
regional trade agreement, p. 169
tariff, p. 170
North American Free Trade Agreement (NAFTA), p. 170
European Union (EU), p. 172
Asia–Pacific Economic Cooperation (APEC) forum, p. 175

newly industrialized countries (NICs), p. 175
industrial policy, p. 176
multinational corporation, p. 179
exporting, p. 183
license agreement, p. 183
franchising, p. 183
direct investment, p. 184
joint ventures, p. 184

CHECKLIST   ## Analyzing International Operations in Problems and Cases

___ 1. Does the case involve strategic management of international operations?

___ 2. Have decision makers assessed the impact of global/international issues on the strategic management process?

___ 3. Are the major steps of the strategic management process appropriately ordered and integrated?

___ 4. Have decision makers assessed the effects of industrial policy on the strategic management process?

___ 5. Is the strategy aimed at anticipating competitors' actions and responding to them?

___ 6. Does the strategy reflect organizational goals?

___ 7. Is the strategy appropriate, given the results of the international environmental analysis?

___ 8. Have decision makers evaluated future markets and opportunities created by lower trade barriers?

___ 9. Have decision makers considered the threat of global competition?

___ 10. Is the organizational mission clear to top managers in the various countries of operation?

Additional Readings

C. A. Bartlett and S. Ghoshal. *Managing across Borders.* Boston, Mass.: Harvard Business School Press, 1989.

J. Garland, R. N. Farmer, and M. Taylor. *International Dimensions of Business Policy and Strategy,* 2d ed. Boston, Mass.: PWS-Kent, 1990.

C. W. L. Hill. *International Business: Competing in the Global Marketplace.* Burr Ridge, Ill.: Richard D. Irwin, 1994.

C A S E

Lever Revamps Strategy to Standardize Products for the EU

Almost every large company operating in Europe has been affected by the effort to unite Europe politically and create one huge common market. As internal EU barriers fall, companies are trying to sell the same products in the same way across the continent, creating economies of scale to help them survive increasingly brutal marketing wars. Unfortunately, creating or selling a "Europroduct" is more than just difficult; the nuances of established markets, local consumer tastes, and decades-old marketing strategies are complicating standardization.

As Europe's borders began to blur in the late 1980s, Lever Europe, a subsidiary of Anglo-Dutch food and detergent maker Unilever, recognized the need to adjust its strategy. Its American arch-rival, Procter & Gamble, was introducing single products with single names across Europe.

Lever, despite being more established in Europe, has faced large-scale adjustment problems, both within its organization and among consumers. It sells hundreds of products under various brand names in different countries. Its fabric softener, for example, is known within Lever under two different brand names—Snuggle and Teddy Bear. The brand is sold in ten European countries under seven different names, often with different bottles, different marketing strategies, and sometimes even different formulas. The brands share only one thing: a picture of a teddy bear on the label.

The wide diversity of brand images is the legacy of what once seemed a shrewd strategy for many European consumer-product companies. Heavily decentralized, Lever left most product, manufacturing, and marketing decisions to powerful country managers. They, in turn, chose names that sounded appealing in the local language, designed packages to fit local tastes, manufactured the products in local factories, and sometimes tinkered with the formulas.

Lever began its attempts at unifying product lines in 1986, appointing a few European brand managers for its pan-European brands. It also began centralizing production, which required some painful plant closings. Today, Lever products like fabric softener, dishwasher soap, and skin cream are overseen across much of the continent by individual managers based in various European capitals. To stay close to local markets, though, Lever still distributes through its national marketing people. Other things have stayed the same, as well: To avoid tampering with success, the company has kept many of its established local brand names—and even some of the formula variations.

Changing those local formulas is a difficult step—one that Lever is taking gradually. Lever's strategy calls for introducing an environmentally friendly formula across the continent, which delights Lever workers in Sweden, where such a change is required by law, and in Germany, where consumers will pay premium prices for products that are gentle on lakes and rivers. But it creates problems in cost-conscious Spain; Lever's fabric softener has a quarter of the fast-growing market there, and the new strategy means higher costs for a price-sensitive product.

Lever figures that it will lose profits in the short run because of the switch, but managers remain convinced that its uniform, more advanced products will ultimately maximize profits across Europe.

Complexities continue to mount, however. For historical reasons, Lever sells its Teddy Bear and Snuggle fabric softeners in ten European countries, while it sells a creamier, more expensive product, Comfort, in seven others. To cut production costs and unify marketing, it is taking a first step toward merging the two, introducing identical bottles. To avoid alienating any loyal consumers, however, it will keep producing Comfort as a thicker liquid with a mother and child on its label while Teddy Bear features a bear. Selling fabric softener with a catalog of different brand names and at least two formulas ensures a worse cost position than P&G, which has one formula, one brand name, and one package.

DISCUSSION QUESTIONS

1. Do you agree with Lever's decisions about the pace of strategy implementation?

2. Is the strategy cost-effective? Explain.

3. How well-justified is Lever's decision to maintain dual production of Comfort and Teddy Bear?

4. How well does Lever's strategy reflect a thorough environmental analysis?

5. How can Lever maintain market share while more effectively centralizing its operations?

SOURCE: E. S. Browning, "In Pursuit of the Elusive Euroconsumer," *The Wall Street Journal*, April 23, 1992, p. B1.

Notes

1. "GM Asian Technical Center," General Motors brochure, 1992.
2. W. E. Halal, "Global Strategic Management in a New World Order," *Business Horizons*, November/December 1993, pp. 5–10.
3. V. Reitman, "Global Money Trends Rattle Shop Windows in Heartland America." *The Wall Street Journal*, November 26, 1993, p. A1.
4. "GATT: What It Is, What It Does," GATT Information Service Center brochure, 1991.
5. L. Ingrassia and A. Q. Nomani, "Firms Far and Wide Are Looking to GATT for Competitive Edge," *The Wall Street Journal*, December 7, 1993, p. A1.
6. "The Agreement's Key Provisions," *The Wall Street Journal*, November 18, 1993, p. A14.
7. "One Europe, One Economy," *The Economist*, November 30, 1991, pp. 53–54; and "A Touch of Eastern Promise," *The Economist*, March 26, 1994, p. 58.
8. M. Wise and R. Gibb, *Single Market to Social Europe: The European Community in the 1990s* (New York: Longman Scientific & Technical, 1993).
9. B. Javetski and P. Oster, "The Single Market Itself Is in Question," *Business Week*, November 1, 1993, p. 52.
10. M. M. Nelson, "Whirlpool Gives Pan-European Approach a Spin," *The Wall Street Journal*, April 23, 1992, p. B1.
11. "Balancing Act," *The Economist*, January 4, 1992, p. 30.
12. V. Reitman, "U.S. Firms Turn to the Developing World," *The Wall Street Journal*, August 4, 1993, p. A2.
13. M. Trumbull, "After the Vote: Clinton's Next Stop Is Seattle." *Christian Science Monitor*, November 16, 1993, p. 1.
14. M. Trumbull, "APEC at a Glance," *Christian Science Monitor*, November 16, 1993, p. 4.
15. Reitman, "U.S. Firms Turn."
16. J. Impoco, "President Clinton's Other Foreign Policy," *U.S. News & World Report*, November 1, 1993.
17. S. Pendleton, "Federal Labs Open Doors to Industry," *Christian Science Monitor*, May 11, 1993.
18. C. Farrell and M. S. Mandel, "Industrial Policy," *Business Week*, April 6, 1992, pp. 70–74.
19. Ibid.
20. B. W. Fraser, "Cost-Effective Laser Technology Makes Strides in Foreign Markets," *Christian Science Monitor*, June 7, 1994, p. 9.
21. C. J. Fombrun and S. Wally, "Global Entanglements: The Structure of Corporate Transnationalism," in V. Pucik, N. M. Tichy and C. K. Barnett, eds., *Globalizing Management: Creating and Leading the Competitive Organization* (New York: John Wiley & Sons, 1993).
22. M. E. Porter, "Changing Patterns of International Competition," in H. Vernon-Wortzel and L. H. Wortzel, eds., *Global Strategic Management: The Essentials* (New York: John Wiley & Sons, 1991).
23. K. Ohmae, "Becoming a Triad Power: The New Global Corporation," in H. Vernon-Wortzel and L. H. Wortzel, eds., *Global Strategic Management: The Essentials* (New York: John Wiley & Sons, 1991).
24. "A Survey of Taiwan," *The Economist*, October 10, 1992.
25. P. Fuhrman and M. Schuman, "Now We Are Our Own Masters," *Forbes*, May 23, 1994, pp. 128–138.
26. "Mazda in Brief," Mazda Motor Corp. brochure, 1992.
27. G. Hamel, "Competition for Competence and Interpartner Learning within International Strategic Alliances," *Strategic Management Journal* 12 (1991), pp. 83–103.

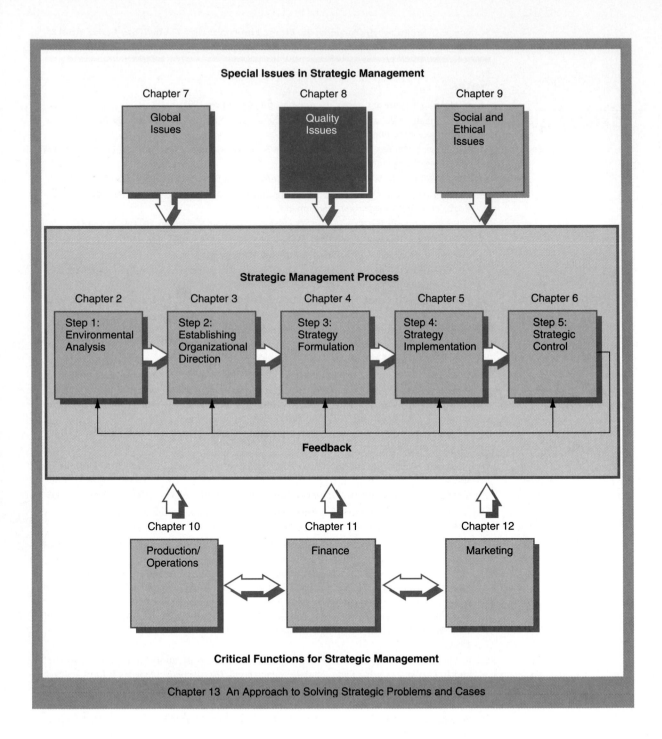

Special Issues in Strategic Management

Chapter 7	Chapter 8	Chapter 9
Global Issues	Quality Issues	Social and Ethical Issues

Strategic Management Process

Chapter 2	Chapter 3	Chapter 4	Chapter 5	Chapter 6
Step 1: Environmental Analysis	Step 2: Establishing Organizational Direction	Step 3: Strategy Formulation	Step 4: Strategy Implementation	Step 5: Strategic Control

Feedback

Chapter 10	Chapter 11	Chapter 12
Production/ Operations	Finance	Marketing

Critical Functions for Strategic Management

Chapter 13 An Approach to Solving Strategic Problems and Cases

Strategic Management and Total Quality Management

A rmed with total quality management methods, Japanese organizations have won a long string of battles for market share throughout the world's markets. American and European firms have seen the power of this new competitive weapon, and they are scrambling to learn to use it themselves.

TQM offers powerful new insight into customers' needs and a firm's own operations. By making a thorough, committed, and vigorous effort to implement TQM, a firm can build a solid foundation for sustained competitive advantage.

Adopting a quality approach requires profound changes in organizations that practice it, though. Successful implementation of TQM affects every step of the organization's strategic management process, and it diffuses a consciousness of continuous improvement throughout the organization. Quality becomes the focus of every activity of the firm, rather than an isolated concern of a few specialists, as in early systems of quality control.

HISTORICAL DEVELOPMENT OF TOTAL QUALITY MANAGEMENT

The development of the quality movement began with a focus on inspection and post-production repairs to defective products. In a search for more proactive methods, several leaders shaped the **Total Quality Management (TQM)** movement. The impact of TQM becomes clear when one compares the competitive positions of organizations that have implemented TQM with varying degrees of success. The discussion of the basic characteristics of TQM and its impact on organizations has important implications for strategic management, as the last part of the chapter explains.

Quality in the 1960s and 1970s

Product quality has always been an important part of an organization's competitive success. In the 1960s and 1970s, however, few firms viewed quality as a responsibility of every employee. U.S. companies had developed a tradition of specialization, assigning **quality control** departments the narrow task of ensuring quality through a combination of final inspection and post-production rework and repair.[1] To ensure perfection in every product seemed impossible, so they could prevent defective products from reaching consumers only by inspecting them and repairing defective units.

This approach to quality management had three flaws. First, inspections themselves are not perfect: no human inspector can catch every flaw. Second, inspection can only correct the symptoms, rather than the cause, of the problem. For example, defects could be caused by low quality input, a poor design, adverse working conditions, badly maintained equipment, haphazard handling, or faulty storage. Inspection and repair leave these underlying causes to continue to create defects. Finally, inspection and repair separate the quality control function from such areas as planning, design, production, and distribution, which actually create the defects. This separation of quality control from the other functions of the organization allows most of the people in the organization to ignore their roles in ensuring the quality of the product.

In the three decades following the end of World War II, the U.S. economy produced unparalleled wealth and technological might. A tremendous worldwide demand clamored for American-made goods. Inspect-and-repair quality control served U.S. companies well in this era when competitors could not hope to challenge their technological superiority. In this environment, most U.S. companies spent the 1960s and the 1970s straining to meet the demand for their goods and services. Quality was important, but production output targets reigned supreme and inspect-and-repair techniques yielded products of adequate quality.

The environment of the 1980s and 1990s made the flaws of this approach painfully apparent. The quality levels achieved by U.S. companies began to compare unfavorably with those of their Japanese competitors. As managers and scholars studied how Japanese firms managed quality, they discovered the legacies of American leaders like Deming, Juran, and Crosby. The next section introduces these three individuals, who developed the basic concepts at the heart of the modern quality management method known as TQM.

In the last decade TQM has emerged as a coherent management system that focuses intensely on serving the needs of the customer quickly, efficiently, and effectively. To do this, the TQM method measures customers' needs, measures and evaluates customer satisfaction delivered by the product or service, and engages the organization in continuous improvement to stay tuned-in to changes in customers' needs.

Quality Gurus

The message of TQM spread across the globe, driven by the work of the "Big Three" of the quality management movement—W. Edwards Deming, Joseph M. Juran, and Philip B. Crosby. This section summarizes the contributions of these individuals and highlights the similarities and differences in their interpretations of quality management.

Deming   W. Edwards Deming, born in Sioux City, Iowa in 1900, earned his bachelor's degree in physics from the University of Wyoming and his doctorate in mathematical physics from Yale University. From 1928 to 1939, Deming worked as a mathematical physicist for the U.S. Department of Agriculture. This work first exposed Deming to the theories and practices of statistical control. From 1939 to 1945, Deming worked extensively with the Bureau of the Census and the U.S. weapons industry. During this period, he developed his basic quality management system. Table 8.1 summarizes Deming's views on the relationship between quality and management.

Deming recommended that every organization should promote continuous quality improvement by implementing his 14 steps. This requires breaking down all quality-related activities into four interlinked steps: **Plan-Do-Check-Act.** Repetitive completion of this cycle keeps the organization constantly moving on the path of continuous quality improvement, according to Deming.

By the end of World War II, the United States was one of the few developed countries in the world whose industrial capacity had not suffered devastation

---

TABLE 8.1

Deming's 14 Points for Management

1. **Create constancy of purpose for improvement of product and service.**[a] The shift from short-term thinking to planning for the long term requires dedication to innovation in all areas to most effectively meet the needs of the customer.
2. **Adopt a new philosophy in which defects are unacceptable.** Anything that can lead to a defect—shoddy materials, poor workmanship, defective parts, careless handling, and lax service—should be clearly identified as unacceptable.
3. **Cease dependence on mass inspection.** Focus on improving the process to eliminate defects. Inspection is too late, ineffective, and costly for effective quality management.
4. **End the practice of awarding business on price tag alone.** Price has no meaning without a measure of product quality. An organization's purchasing function and suppliers must understand specifications, but they must also know what the part does for production and final customers.
5. **Constantly and forever improve the system of production and service.** Reduce waste in every activity. Improvement comes from studying the production process. Most of the responsibility for process improvement rests with management.
6. **Institute modern methods of training on the job.** Restructure training around clearly defined criteria for acceptable work.
7. **Institute modern methods of supervising.** Supervisors must have the authority to inform top management about conditions that need correction.
8. **Drive out fear.** Workers must not be afraid to ask questions, report problems, or express ideas.
9. **Break down barriers between departments.** Individuals from research, design, purchasing, sales, production, and assembly must work together as a team to ensure the success of the organization as a whole.
10. **Eliminate numerical goals for the work force.** Instead of encouraging workers to meet numerical goals for productivity improvement, the organization as a whole must share a single goal: never-ending improvement.
11. **Eliminate work standards and numerical quotas.** Since quotas focus on quantity of production, not quality, work standards practically guarantee poor quality and high costs.
12. **Remove barriers that hinder the hourly workers.** Any barriers that hinder pride in work degrade quality. For example, a poor idea of the criteria for good work, supervisors motivated by quotas, off-gauge input parts, and out-of-order machines prevent hourly workers from identifying with their work and taking pride in it.

Continued

TABLE 8.1

Continued

13. **Institute a vigorous program of education and training.** Continuous improvement leads to continuous change in the number of people required in the different parts of the organization and their duties. People should be continually trained and retrained. All training must include basic statistical techniques.

14. **Create a structure in top management that will push everyday on the above 13 points.** The ultimate responsibility for implementing these principles lies with the top management of the organization. Top management should create a system that moves the organization to engage in continuous, daily improvement.

[a]Deming's words are in boldface type. The rest of each paragraph paraphrases Deming's discussions.

SOURCE: Adapted from A. March, "A Note on Quality: The Views of Deming, Juran, and Crosby," in Harry Costin, ed., *Readings in Total Quality Management* (New York: Harcourt Brace College Publishers, 1994), p. 143.

in the war. During the post-war period, strong pent-up demand combined with the worldwide shortage of production capacity to allow U.S. organizations to sell everything that they could produce. Deming's message fell on deaf ears in North America.

In contrast, the devastation of the war left Japanese managers to search for new ways to manage the organizations that they were rebuilding. They were anxious to learn from people like Deming. Deming first visited Japan in 1946 as a representative of the Economic and Scientific Section of the American Department of War. In 1950, the Union of Japanese Scientists and Engineers invited Deming back to offer classes on quality control. By August 1950, the top managers of most of Japan's largest companies had attended Deming's seminars at the Tokyo Chamber of Commerce. In 1951, the Japanese recognized this contribution by institutionalizing the pursuit of quality improvement through the creation of a quality award called the *Deming Prize*. In 1960, the Emperor of Japan rewarded Deming for his impact on the quality and competitiveness of Japanese products by presenting him with the Second Order Medal of the Sacred Treasure, the highest possible decoration the Japanese nation could bestow.

Juran   Joseph M. Juran's impact on Japanese quality management techniques is considered second only to Deming's. Like Deming, Juran was among the initial lecturers invited to Japan in the early 1950s. He enjoyed a varied and distinguished career that included stints as a business executive, government administrator, lecturer, writer, and consultant. In 1979, he established the Juran Institute to serve as a base for his seminars, consulting, and conferences. His U.S. clientele has included organizations like Texas Instruments, DuPont, Monsanto, and Xerox. Like Deming, Juran was awarded the Second Order Medal of the Sacred Treasure by the Japanese government.

Juran's approach to quality management shared many features in common with Deming's. For example, he recommended that an organization engage in a continuous cycle of three stages in improvement—quality planning, quality control, and quality improvement. This cyclical approach is analogous to Deming's Plan-Do-Check-Act cycle. However, Juran did make some distinctive contributions to TQM.

Juran defined quality as *fitness for use.* This definition proposes that the users of a product or service should be able to count on it to do what they needed or expected when they bought it.[2] For example, a manufacturer should be able to process a purchased material or component to meet the demands of its customers while achieving high yields and minimal downtime in production; a retailer should receive a correctly labeled product that is free from shipping damage and easy to handle and display; a consumer should receive a product that performs as claimed without prematurely breaking down.

Juran measured fitness for use in five ways:

- *Quality of design.* Every design activity that goes into building a Porsche is aimed at a different quality level than the design activities that go into building a Chevrolet. This dimension of fitness for use links the quality of the final product with the marketing, design, and engineering activities of the organization. Marketing activities affect design because design staff members depend on market research data to develop and refine the concept of the product.
- *Quality of conformance. Conformance* refers to the match between the actual product and the design intent. Conformance depends on the production process, ability to maintain tolerances, work force training, supervision, and test programs. This aspect of fitness for use links the quality of the final product with the manufacturing activities of the organization.
- *Availability.* The frequency and ease of repair affect product quality. Juran uses the term *availability* because a product that is in the process of being repaired is not available for normal use. This facet of fitness for use links the quality of the final product with the design, manufacturing, and after-sales service functions of the organization.
- *Safety.* Juran defines *safety* as the risk of injury due to product hazards. This links the quality of the product with its design features, the design of its instruction manual, and the quality of its component materials.
- *Field use.* The product's performance after it reaches the customer's hands has an important role in quality. This facet of fitness for use links the quality of the final product with its packaging, transportation, storage, and field service.

Juran saw connections between quality and every activity that the organization pursues during the product's entire life. This comprehensive approach sought to anchor quality firmly in the everyday activities of personnel throughout the organization, making a distinct departure from earlier quality control methods.

Juran's other major contribution to TQM was the concept of the cost of quality. Juran argued that the costs associated with quality fall into four categories:

- *Internal failure costs.* Quality affects costs associated with scrap, rework, downtime, and loss of efficiency when a product is identified as defective before shipment to the customer.

- *External failure costs.* Quality determines significant costs associated with complaints, returns, and warranty charges when defects become apparent after the product is shipped to the customer.
- *Appraisal costs.* Quality programs incur costs for inspection, testing, and testing equipment to evaluate the quality of raw materials and purchased components.
- *Prevention costs.* Quality programs generate costs associated with quality planning, training, gathering data, and analysis.

These concepts powerfully presented quality to top managers in a language that they understood—the language of money. No matter how complex products and processes became, no matter what esoteric demands quality management techniques placed on managers, Juran translated them into simple terms—the cost of quality is the cost of making, finding, repairing, or avoiding defective products. This helped top managers to focus on the task of minimizing the cost of quality.

Crosby Philip B. Crosby began his career as a production line inspector. He worked his way up to corporate vice president of quality at ITT. In 1979, Crosby left ITT to found Philip Crosby Associates Inc. and the Crosby Quality College. By 1990, more than 70,000 executives and managers had attended Crosby's courses. General Motors acquired more than 10 percent of Crosby's stock and set up its own Crosby school for GM personnel. Other companies followed suit, including IBM, Johnson & Johnson, and Chrysler.

Crosby's approach to quality management borrowed many features from Juran and Deming. For example, he proposed his own 14 steps for quality improvement and four absolute laws of quality management that covered the same ground as Deming's 14 steps and Juran's cost of quality. Crosby continued Juran's effort to translate quality concepts into language that top managers could understand, but he went one step further. Crosby aimed to change top managers' perceptions and attitudes about quality. He tried to convince them that improved quality does not cost money; rather it saves money. As a result, an investment in a quality program will pay for itself by generating savings. This line of reasoning led Crosby to make the most dramatic statement associated with his doctrine—"Quality is free."

While Juran's statement of the cost of quality in financial terms was a powerful way of getting the attention of top managers, Crosby helped them to justify committing resources to quality improvement. These resources included management time and attention, as well as dollar investments for test equipment and employee training. If quality investments do pay for themselves, then quality programs need not compete with other resource allocation programs such as new market entries, new product introductions, and capital equipment purchases. The philosophy of continuous improvement slowly moved into the mainstream activities of American corporate giants such as General Motors, IBM, and Motorola.

Although Deming, Juran, and Crosby, the Big Three of the quality movement made distinct intellectual contributions, the practice of quality management in modern organizations usually mixes and matches their contributions. In fact, as Mike Hall's experience in the Skills Module demonstrates, employees rarely follow the sequential path from thinking about quality to solving quality problems. Instead they prefer to jump in and attack the quality

SKILLS MODULE

T. D. Williamson Takes TQM Abroad

INTRODUCTION

We have discussed the principles that led to the development of total quality management. Review the following situation at T. D. Williamson and then complete the skill development exercise that follows. This will help you better understand the practices behind the principles of TQM.

SITUATION

T. D. Williamson Inc., an oil-field equipment and service company based in Tulsa, Oklahoma, had enjoyed success in introducing its American work force to the principles of TQM. The company faced a challenge, however, teaching an American methodology and way of thinking in its Belgian factory.

Mike Hall, senior vice president and chief financial officer, heads Williamson's quality efforts. He remembers watching European employees listen to an explanation of Crosby's 14 points and other principles. Although the employees nodded courteously, no one was interested. Says Hall, "It was a waste of time."

But Williamson couldn't let the issue rest. Its European customers, the state-run oil and gas companies, insisted on high quality standards. Competitors there, mostly smaller niche players, were tough to beat. Williamson's managers began to focus on ISO 9000, a new quality standard, as a goal. They bypassed TQM theory and principle to focus on TQM practice and implementation. "We got people to measure critical aspects of the business, decide where there were problems, and work to solve them," says Hall.

It has worked. Welders once jumped from one hot project to another to meet a daily "hot list" of factory deadlines; today, they follow a simplified, better-planned, more flexible production system that allows priorities to change without disrupting the flow of work. Costs are lower; scrap rates have fallen; deadlines are being met.

SKILL DEVELOPMENT EXERCISE

Mike Hall determined that bypassing talk about Crosby's theories to put them directly into action works better abroad. If the cyclical approach to quality, such as Deming's Plan-Do-Check-Act sequence, is the lifeblood of a TQM program, how long-lived would you expect Williamson's quality program to be?

Create a TQM strategy for Williamson using the principles and ideas of Deming, Juran, and Crosby to create a workable, universal set of principles that *all* of the company's employees can understand.

SOURCE: Elizabeth Ehrlich, "The Quality Management Checkpoint," *International Business,* May 1993, p. 62.

---

problems and are often surprised to find themselves replicating the Plan-Do-Check-Act cycle or the cost of quality analyses proposed by the quality gurus.

TQM Today

TQM can be described in several ways. One way is to describe the philosophy that unifies all activities in an organization that embraces TQM. That philosophy demands *total dedication to the customer*. This abstract definition does not, however, provide any guidance about how to conduct company business. Another way to define TQM is to describe the outcomes that organizations should strive to achieve.[3] When an organization successfully implements TQM, it develops four characteristics:

- Customers are intensely loyal. They are more than satisfied because the organization meets their needs and exceeds their expectations.
- The organization can respond to problems, needs, and opportunities with minimal delays. It also minimizes costs by eliminating or minimizing tasks that do not add value. In minimizing costs, it enhances the quality of goods and services it gives to customers and the way it treats them.

- The organization's climate supports and encourages teamwork and makes work more satisfying, motivating, and meaningful for employees.
- The organization develops and nurtures a general ethic of continuous improvement. In addition, a method that employees understand leads them toward a state of continuous improvement.

To understand how managers design systems to achieve these outcomes, the next section explains the characteristics of TQM and the methods of organizations that apply TQM. This discussion reviews the criteria for the Malcolm Baldrige National Quality Award and the ISO 9000 certification process to set the stage for consideration of effective ways to configure the organization. This approach is particularly useful for two reasons: (1) When organizations compete for the Baldrige Award or apply for ISO 9000 certification, they use these criteria to guide changes in their management routines; (2) Many organizations do not apply for the award or the certification, but still design programs for continuous improvement based on the criteria. Additionally, the Baldrige Award and ISO 9000 certification have created a new set of hurdles for organizations to clear. To do business in the European Union, for example, they should now plan to become ISO 9000 certified. Motorola expects suppliers to its operations in the United States and Canada to go through the process of applying for the Baldrige Award.

APPLYING TQM METHODS

A review of the work of the quality gurus helps present the central concepts and philosophy of TQM. Still, it is important to see how these concepts can be applied to change organizations. This section identifies the characteristics that are common to all organizations that adopt TQM. The criteria for the Malcolm Baldrige National Quality Award and ISO 9000 certification provide some detail about these characteristics. Implementing these TQM methods has helped organizations achieve some impressive results.

Characteristics of TQM

Each organization applies TQM in a unique way. However, the TQM system can be defined in terms of five characteristics that are common to all organizations that have adopted TQM (see Table 8.2). Even though TQM first proved its worth in large, manufacturing organizations, many smaller organizations have found it very useful. Small organizations often find it easier to get close to their customers. Additionally, they can more easily generate the coordination, participation, and commitment that continuous improvement demands.

Malcolm Baldrige National Quality Award

In the 1980s the U.S. government decided to heighten national awareness of the characteristics and competitive significance of TQM. On August 20, 1987, President Reagan signed Public Law 100–107, the Malcolm Baldridge National Quality Improvement Act. This law established the **Malcolm Baldrige National Quality Award,** named for a former secretary of commerce. The award was designed to recognize U.S. companies that successfully implement TQM systems.

TABLE 8.2

Characteristics of TQM Organizations

CUSTOMER-DRIVEN DEFINITION OF QUALITY

TQM assumes that quality is driven by and defined by the customer. Goods and services with attributes that indicate quality to the customer will increase customer satisfaction and, ultimately, customer demand.

STRONG QUALITY LEADERSHIP

Only a strong leadership team focused on quality improvement can overcome inevitable inertia and resistance to change. Leaders make this change by creating clear quality goals and developing the systems and methods to achieve those goals.

CONTINUOUS IMPROVEMENT

TQM is driven by the quest to improve the efficiency on all business operations and work activities. Management systems must encourage identifying and seizing opportunities to improve.

RELIANCE ON FACTS, DATA, AND ANALYSIS

TQM demands careful decision making based on reliable information and analysis. Constant measurement of quality helps managers to identify and correct conditions that cause poor quality.

EMPLOYEE PARTICIPATION

All employees are accountable for quality, and all need tools and training to fulfill this responsibility. TQM assumes that the employee who is closest to daily operating procedures is in the best position to understand and improve the quality of those procedures.

SOURCE: Adapted from *Management Practices: U.S. Companies Improve Performance through Quality Efforts* (Washington, D.C.: United States General Accounting Office, May 1991), GAO/NSIAD–91–190.

Each year as many as six companies that pass rigorous examinations receive Baldrige Awards. As many as two prizes are awarded in each of three categories: manufacturing, services, and small business. The U.S. Department of Commerce's National Institute of Standards and Technology oversees the process, leaving its administration to a consortium that includes the American Society for Quality Control and the American Productivity and Quality Center.

The Baldrige Award is intended to improve American quality and productivity by:

• Stimulating organizations to produce excellent quality
• Recognizing outstanding organizations and using their experiences to teach others about quality
• Establishing guidelines by which other organizations can assess their own quality improvement efforts

These objectives form the basis of the evaluation process. Every applicant provides information on seven areas. The top scores in all examination categories

TABLE 8.3

Baldrige Award 1993 Examination Items and Point Values

1993 Examination Categories	Point Values
1.0 Leadership	95
1.1 Senior executive leadership	45
1.2 Management for quality	25
1.3 Public responsibility and corporate citizenship	25
2.0 Information and analysis	75
2.1 Quality and performance data	15
2.2 Competitive comparisons and benchmarking	20
2.3 Analysis and uses of company-level data	40
3.0 Strategic quality planning	60
3.1 Quality and company performance planning process	35
3.2 Quality and performance plans	25
4.0 Human resource development and management	150
4.1 Human resource planning and management	20
4.2 Employee involvement	40
4.3 Employee education and training	40
4.4 Employee performance and recognition	25
4.5 Employee well-being and satisfaction	25
5.0 Management of process quality	140
5.1 Design and introduction of quality goods and services	40
5.2 Process management: Production and delivery	35
5.3 Process management: Business and support services	30
5.4 Supplier quality	20
5.5 Quality assessment	15
6.0 Quality and operational results	180
6.1 Product and service quality results	70
6.2 Company operational results	50
6.3 Business process and support service results	25
6.4 Supplier quality results	35
7.0 Customer focus and satisfaction	300
7.1 Customer expectations: Current and future	35
7.2 Customer relationship management	65
7.3 Commitment to customers	15
7.4 Customer satisfaction determination	30
7.5 Customer satisfaction results	85
7.6 Customer satisfaction comparison	70
Total points	1,000

SOURCE: Adapted from M. M. Steeples, *The Corporate Guide to the Malcolm Baldrige National Quality Award* (Homewood, Ill.: Business One-Irwin, 1993).

total 1,000 points. These categories and their assigned weights are summarized in Table 8.3.

The numerous, detailed categories illustrate that applying for and winning the Baldrige Award is no easy undertaking. Category 1.0 of the examination requires the organization to describe its top managers' leadership style, personal involvement, and visibility in maintaining an environment for quality excellence. The application must demonstrate the linkage between quality and day-to-day leadership, management, and supervision activities in all organizational units. It must also document how the organization extends itself to the external community to promote public health, safety, and environmental protection. Category 2.0 of the application examines the scope, validity, use, and management of data and information that underlie the organization's quality improvement program. Applicants must show how they gather data and information and complete analysis to support a prevention-based approach to quality management. Category 3.0 examines the organization's planning process to assess how it achieves or retains quality leadership, and how it integrates quality improvement planning into its overall business planning. Category 4.0 examines how effectively the organization develops and exploits the full potential of its work force, including managers. Category 5.0 examines its statistical and procedural techniques for designing and producing goods and services. Category 6.0 examines the applicant's record of quality improvement based upon objective measures derived from analysis of customer requirements. Category 7.0 examines the organization's knowledge of its customers, overall customer service systems, responsiveness, and ability to meet customers' requirements.

Recent winners of the Baldrige Award include AT&T Network Systems (1992), Texas Instruments (1992), and Eastman Kodak Co. (1993) in the manufacturing organizations category; Granite Rock Co. (1992) and Ames Rubber Corp. (1993) in the small business organizations category; and AT&T Universal Card Services (1992) and The Ritz-Carlton Hotel Co. (1993) in the service organizations category.

ISO 9000

As the competitive significance of TQM caught the attention of the business world in the 1980s, scholars and consultants began recommending a variety of quality improvement methods, all of which judged quality in different ways. In 1987, the International Standards Organization's Technical Committee on Quality Assurance set out to develop an internationally accepted quality standard. This effort produced a set of standards commonly known as **ISO 9000.** ISO 9000 is not one standard, but a set of five documents (ISO 9000 to ISO 9004). The most commonly used standards appear in ISO 9001 to ISO 9003, divided by topic:

- ISO 9001 contains standards for engineering-based or construction-oriented organizations that design, develop, produce, install, and service products.
- ISO 9002 contains standards that are particularly relevant to chemical, process, and other related industries.
- ISO 9003 (the least frequently applied set of standards) concerns small shops and divisions within an organization (laboratories, for example).

ISO 9000 and ISO 9004 contain specialized standards for specific industrial applications.

Although ISO 9000 is often compared to the criteria for the Malcolm Baldrige National Quality Award, many important distinctions separate the two:[4]

1. Unlike the Baldrige Award, none of the ISO standard systems award points.

2. ISO standards do not pay much attention to human resource utilization and customer satisfaction.
3. When an organization applies for ISO 9000 certification, it requests that a team from an accredited registrar audit its overall quality system. At each stage, the auditors must determine whether or not the organization's quality management system conforms to ISO guidelines. The audit focuses on 20 features of this system, as summarized in Table 8.4.

Table 8.4 clearly shows that preparing for an ISO 9000 certification audit involves carefully examining every organizational activity that has an influence on the quality of the final product. The audit promotes continuous improvement by verifying that any organization that has an ISO 9000 certified quality management system in place has implemented all the organizational processes that TQM requires. The next section examines some of the obstacles and benefits associated with TQM.

Impact of TQM

None of the individual components of TQM is novel or revolutionary. Yet, implementing the entire system consistently over an extended period of time can yield startling results. One way to understand the benefits of TQM is to examine studies of organizations that have implemented it.

The most influential study of the impact of TQM reports on improvements in market share, profitability, customer satisfaction, quality, costs, and employee relations in 22 organizations.[5] These companies report that they have enjoyed an average annual market share increase of 13.7 percent after implementing TQM. Customer satisfaction has showed an average annual increase of 2.5 percent. Product reliability has improved by an annual average of 11.3 percent and the annual reduction in errors has averaged 10.3 percent. Employee relations, measured by the total number of suggestions for improvement submitted by employees, has showed an annual percentage increase of 16.6 percent.

Another way to understand the impact of TQM is to compare the characteristics of organizations in different areas where the system has been at

---

TABLE 8.4

Criteria for ISO 9000 Audit

1. *Management responsibility.* Someone in the top management of the organization must be responsible for ensuring effective management of the entire quality management system and that all goods and services delivered to customers meet or exceed their expectations.
2. *Quality system.* The organization must have a formal quality management system in place to ensure that it delivers all goods and services to customers' specifications.
3. *Contract review.* All contracts and orders accepted by the organization must go through a formal review process to verify agreement between what the marketing department sells and what the production system delivers.
4. *Design control.* All product designs must pass a formal, documented review process to verify that the design fulfills its intended use. The documentation tracks changes in the design of the product.

TABLE 8.4

Continued

5. *Document control.* The applicant must document unambiguously every bit of information needed to build, service, and maintain the product so that it is available for review.

6. *Purchasing.* The applicant must submit to a formal review of all systems that control the timing, quality, quantity, and types of purchases made by the organization. The review matches the purchases with the needs of the organization.

7. *Purchasing of supplied product.* Another review evaluates all systems for storage and maintenance of purchased components to ensure that the standards for identifying and correcting problems with purchased components are clearly articulated.

8. *Product identification and traceability.* All processes that identify, trace, and monitor parts within the production system are reviewed to determine how the organization ensures that its input components are identical to those in the design drawings.

9. *Process control.* The application process evaluates all methods to measure, control, and maintain quality in the production process to ensure valid uses of process control tools such as control charts, Pareto analysis, and cause and effect diagrams.

10. *Inspection and testing.* The process reviews all procedures designed to make sure that the product works as it should.

11. *Inspection, measuring, and testing equipment.* The application reviews all methods designed to maintain and test the accuracy of testing and inspection equipment.

12. *Inspection and test status.* Another review covers all the documentation that informs the customer that the product was tested.

13. *Control of nonconforming products.* Procedures that identify and test defective products must be reviewed.

14. *Corrective action.* Procedures used to correct identified defects must be reviewed.

15. *Handling, storage, packaging, and delivery.* Another evaluation focuses on procedures to handle, store, package, and deliver the product from the end of the manufacturing line to the hands of the customer. This review evaluates the firm's efforts to ensure that no product is damaged when it gets to the customer.

16. *Quality records.* All procedures to document the quality of products must also be reviewed. The records reviewed in this step span all activities from the raw material to the final product.

17. *Internal quality audits.* A review assesses all internal systems that help the organization to determine whether its production process is in control.

18. *Training.* An evaluation of all systems aimed at properly training employees focuses on both training methods and measures to determine whether or not a specific employee is properly trained.

19. *Servicing.* All systems to service a product after its release for use in the field must be reviewed.

20. *Statistical techniques.* All statistical techniques by which the firm maintains and controls quality must be reviewed. In addition to evaluating the proper use of these techniques, this review evaluates the training of the work force to use these techniques appropriately.

SOURCE: Adapted from M. Breen, R. Jud, and P. E. Pareja, *An Introduction to ISO 9000* (Dearborn, Mich.: Society of Manufacturing Engineers, 1993).

work for different periods of time. Since continuous improvement programs yield their benefits over the long term, experts argue that organizations with longer track records applying TQM should enjoy higher benefits. The benefits of TQM extend beyond improved product quality to improve efficiency as measured by inventory and productivity levels. Accordingly, Japanese organizations should lead American and European organizations on measures of quality, inventory levels, and productivity levels because the Japanese have almost three decades of experience in applying TQM, whereas American and European organizations began applying these techniques in the mid-1980s.

Such an analysis can meaningfully compare organizations only if they operate in the same industry. Unfortunately, many of the organizational characteristics (for example defect rates and productivity) that would provide the most interesting insight into the results of TQM are measures of competitive strength of individual organizations. It is virtually impossible to obtain up-to-date information about such sensitive, proprietary issues. Table 8.5 presents some dated information (which is easier to obtain since it is no longer sensitive) to examine the impact of TQM in the automobile industry.

The two direct measures of quality in Table 8.5 are the number of assembly defects per 100 vehicles and the percentage of total assembly space devoted to post-production repair. Japanese organizations operating in Japan lead on both of these measures. American and European organizations lag significantly behind, while Japanese plants in America fall between the two extremes, at levels close to those of the Japanese organizations. Japanese firms' plants in America are usually headed by seasoned TQM veterans from Japan. These managers have raised the quality levels of their American operations to approximately the levels of their native Japanese counterparts. This

TABLE 8.5

TQM at Automobile Assembly Plants[a]

	Japanese Firms in Japan	Japanese Firms in America	American Firms	European Firms
Assembly defects per 100 vehicles	60	65	82	97
Repair area as percentage of assembly space	4.1	4.9	12.9	14.4
Inventory (days)[b]	0.2	1.6	2.9	2.0
Percentage of work force in TQM teams	69.3	71.3	17.3	0.6
Training of new workers (hours)	380	370	46	173
Productivity (hours per vehicle)	16.8	21.2	25.1	36.2

[a]Figures in this table are averages for plants in each region.
[b]For eight sample parts.
SOURCE: Adapted from "When GM's Robots Ran Amok," *The Economist*, August 10, 1991, pp. 64–65.

demonstrates that there is nothing peculiarly Japanese about the values, work ethic and teamwork required to apply TQM; the American workers in these plants have adopted TQM very successfully. Additionally, statistics on team organization and new worker training seem to indicate that American and European managers could profit from studying the methods of their Japanese counterparts.

In summary, Japanese-managed plants in Japan have reaped the most benefits from TQM. American and European plants seem to have gained significantly less because they have less experience in implementing the system. Japanese-managed plants in the United States seem to fall between these two extremes, indicating that even if top managers have intellectually grasped the TQM system, it takes time to move their organizations to positions to reap the complete benefits of TQM.

TQM IN THE STRATEGIC MANAGEMENT PROCESS

An understanding of the basic concepts of TQM and a review of some of the results that it can deliver lead to questions about how to introduce it to the strategic management process. This section discusses some of the issues managers face when they implement or maintain a TQM program in a company. The main steps of the strategic management process include environmental analysis, establishing an organizational direction, formulating strategy, implementing strategy, and exerting strategic control. This section returns to each step to highlight the kinds of issues that arise in implementing or maintaining a TQM program. Additionally, it examines TQM programs developed by organizations like AT&T, Corning, and Harley-Davidson, and it discusses some of the methods by which these firms have tried to generate the vision, teamwork, and cooperation that are critical components of any TQM program.

Environmental Analysis and TQM

The organizational environment includes all factors, both internal and external, that affect an organization's performance. Analysis of both internal and external environmental forces defines the context of the organization's overall strategy. A TQM program represents these factors as needs of external and internal customers. The **external customer** is well-known—the entity that buys the organization's good or service. Environmental analysis connects the specific needs of the external customer with the activities of the different parts of the organization. The concept of the **internal customer**—the next stage in the firm's internal value chain—develops specifically with the TQM system, as a later discussion will explain in detail.

External Customer   TQM usually visualizes the external customer as a collection of several dimensions of customer satisfaction. For example, the external customer may express satisfaction (or its opposite) with the availability of the product, its appearance, its safety, its reliability, and its user-friendliness. Any organization must identify specific internal activities that contribute to these dimensions of customer satisfaction. The matrix in Figure 8.1 shows how some companies choose to demonstrate how each business function relates to specific dimensions of customer satisfaction.

After charting the links between customer satisfaction and the organization's activities, managers design systems within each function to ensure

FIGURE 8.1   Departmental Contributions to External Customer Satisfaction

Dimensions of External-Customer Satisfaction

Department	Availability	Appearance	Safety	Reliability	User-friendly	Warranty
Design		+	=	+	=	+
Manufacturing	=	=	+	+		=
Marketing	=		+			
Sales	+				+	
Accounting						+

Key

(+) = Department plays a critical role in determining external customer satisfaction on this dimension.

(=) = Department plays a moderate role in determining external customer satisfaction on this dimension.

continued sensitivity to customers' needs. For example, if the sales staff plays a critical role in increasing the user-friendliness of the product, the managers may decide to tie sales people's pay and bonuses to customer survey data on user-friendliness. This sends the clear message that behavior and decisions should promote user-friendliness in the product. As a result, sales staff may pay greater attention to redesigning the instruction manual or clarifying their product demonstrations.

Organizations determine the needs of their external customers by a variety of methods. Market research firms use focus groups, customer opinion surveys, and face-to-face meetings to query customers about their perceptions of the utility of specific product features and their contributions to customer satisfaction. Many organizations use toll-free customer service phone lines to gather a wealth of information about customer concerns and product performance. The firm should channel every bit of information about the customers' needs, buying habits, preferences, and perceptions into refining the product to increase customer satisfaction.

Clearly, the customer satisfaction matrix for a product within a company is unique to that product-market at that particular point in time. The best companies measure external customer satisfaction continuously. This information helps managers plan the next set of improvements in the ceaseless Plan-Do-Check-Act sequence that is the heartbeat of a TQM program.

Internal Customer   Each organization activity must identify and work to satisfy its internal customer, the next stage in the firm's internal value chain. Within the organization, each division, department, and employee can be viewed as both a customer and a supplier to other divisions, departments, or employees. Figure 8.2 provides an example of an internal value chain in a manufacturing company. The market research department feeds the design department with information on the customer's needs. In this sense, the design department is an internal customer of the market research department;

FIGURE 8.2   Internal Value Chain of a Manufacturing Organization

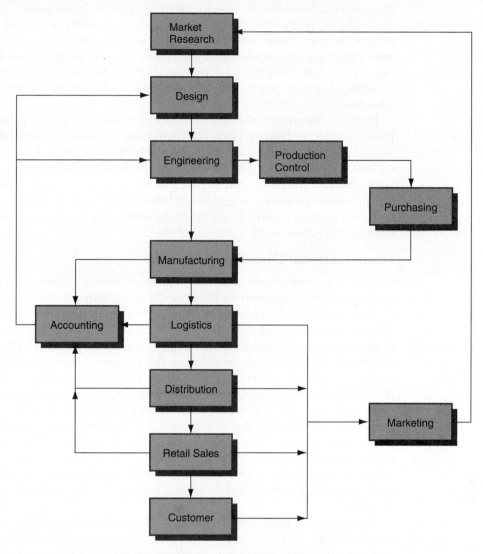

the design task cannot be completed effectively without the information from the market research department. The design department, in turn, processes the market research information and comes up with a product design, which it supplies to internal customers in the engineering department.

Each individual within the organization can identify the critical internal linkages that shape the quality of the final product by asking some simple questions: Who are my internal customers? Am I meeting their requirements? The organization can conduct an internal audit which includes a step-by-step examination of its value-adding process to identify the needs of internal customers. Experts suggest that meeting the needs of each internal customer effectively ensures that external customers will be satisfied with the product. In other words, excellent market research combines with excellence in design, which in turn combines with excellence at every stage in the internal value chain to give external customers a high-quality product.

For example, managers at AT&T believe that one of the first steps toward satisfying external customers is to get employees to focus inward and please internal customers—the people just down the assembly line or in the next office.[6] "Whatever your job is, you've got a supplier and a customer," says Edward Fuchs, director of the Quality Excellence Center at AT&T Bell Laboratories. This simple idea can have profound effects because it sets into motion a chain of quality improvement that reaches all the way to the external customer.

Internal customer satisfaction is a key element of a quality program that IBM launched in January 1990. IBM maintains a high-tech service desk at its Southeast Region headquarters in Research Triangle Park, North Carolina. Called *Solution Central,* this division guarantees a fast response to any manager or worker who is stymied by bureaucracy or needs help with a problem—any problem. To serve the region's 39,000 employees, 50 agents are on call 95 hours a week, including weekends, to reduce interference or hunt down experts that callers need.

Organizational Direction and TQM

To set an organizational direction managers evaluate their environmental analysis and craft appropriate vision and mission statements. They then specify organizational objectives to realize their vision and achieve their mission. When organizations change direction, leaders must change and renew the outmoded vision. In the early 1990s, large organizations such as Sears, IBM, Motorola, and AT&T were engaged in the mammoth task of their changing organizational directions. This involved redefining their goods or services, their technologies, their objectives, their philosophies, their self-concepts, and their public images. An organization's move toward continuous quality improvement begins with top managers shaping a new vision for the organization. A corporate vision can focus the collective energy of employees, and give external observers a better idea of where the organization is headed. Developing a vision that is truly shared across an organization is a difficult and time-consuming process, but absolutely essential to the success of any TQM initiative.

Top managers then define continuous, customer-focused improvement as a central part of the organization's mission. Quality-related themes recur throughout mission statements of organizations as diverse as Great Scot Supermarkets, Federal Express, and The Crummer School. These organizations' missions emphasize that quality and continuous improvement must drive every action of the organization.

However, crafting the mission statement does not complete top managers' role in directing the organization toward continuous improvement. Members of top management take personal responsibility for providing active, unwavering leadership over a long period of time. In this way, they keep the organization focused on meeting quality improvement objectives as part of a continuous and coherent system.

For example, James R. Houghton, chairman of Corning Inc., gives pretty much the same spiel 50 times a year at different Corning plants and offices.[7] Quality, quality, quality. World-class. Customer focus. Worker participation. At each site, he delivers a sermon for the employee ranks, then he conducts a nononsense performance review with local managers. Does Houghton get tired of this routine? Just a bit. He has been preaching this gospel since 1983, but he keeps at it. "After eight years if I stop talking about quality now, it would be a disaster," he says. The effort has paid off: Corning's operating profits are up 111 percent in five years.

Top management leadership and support is especially crucial because most organizations feel strong pressure to show financial results. TQM programs are hard to justify on the basis of short-term results; organizations have to work for a while before these programs begin to show benefits. Implementing a quality improvement program is a time-consuming process, usually prompted by severe competitive pressure. However strong the desire to demonstrate mastery of competitors, tenacious implementation over an extended time period is necessary for a successful TQM program.

For example, Modicon, a Massachusetts-based maker of industrial automation systems, threw itself into total quality management in the late 1980s. "Senior managers," says Dick Eppig, Modicon's vice president of quality, "tend to measure the firm's quality program against its short-term financial performance." They expect instant results, asking, "Has quality improved performance this quarter?" Such impatience makes doubtful positive results.[8]

Graham Sharman, a quality expert with McKinsey, reports, "Of those quality programs that have been in place in Western firms for more than two years, more than two-thirds simply grind to a halt because of their failure to produce the hoped for results." This short-term view ignores the scope and depth of TQM objectives. In the words of Glenn Eggert, vice president of operations at Allen-Bradley, "Before customers see the difference, quality must run through the company's blood."[9] Everybody from salespeople to shop-floor engineers must think about quality. Responsibility for quality has to reach down to the shop floor, organization structures have to be flattened, and barriers to cross-functional communications have to fall. This kind of change takes years.

Ron Hutchinson, head of customer service at Harley-Davidson, identifies another reason why TQM requires a long-term commitment. He says, "The continuous creeping shake-up that is needed to make quality improvements is a curious kind of goal." Human nature demands clearly defined targets, not the constantly shifting goals that lead a firm toward ever-higher quality. Maintaining the momentum of a quality program can make a manager feel like Sisyphus, the mythical laborer doomed to push a stone uphill forever. Yet, one glance at the statistics about the experience that companies have accumulated with TQM shows that a long slow effort is vital. In Japan, companies like Nippondenso, Honda, and Nissan have implemented TQM systems for more than 30 years. The Company Example presents a case of an unusually rapid implementation of a TQM program. In the United States, even exemplary practitioners like Motorola, Texas Instruments, and Xerox have implemented TQM for only 10 to 15 years. Their experience leaves them a long way from any claim to have internalized the discipline of TQM in a significant way.

Strategy Formulation and TQM

Formulating a strategy for an organization involves developing a cohesive plan to achieve objectives by adapting the organization to match its environment. Strategy formulation is primarily an analytical effort, supplemented by executive judgment and creativity. TQM injects the customer's perspective, the competitor's perspective, and the supplier's perspective into the process of formulating strategy.

COMPANY EXAMPLE

TQM at Toto

In 1984, two top officials at Toto Ltd. were converted to the cause of TQM. The change came when Toto, a maker of bathroom fixtures based on the Japanese island of Kyushu, failed to meet annual goals set out in its strategic plan.

First, Toto sent its board members to TQM seminars sponsored by the Japan Standards Association and other national organizations. It then gave five-day TQM courses to 550 of its middle managers. The structural change at Toto was supervised by the Total Quality Control Promotion Group, a task force led by a senior managing director and three board members.

To foster the TQM initiative, Toto's 8,200 employees were organized into 32 groups. The new system expected each of the 550 middle managers to uncover at least one quality problem twice a year to be solved over the next six months using the suggestions of the group. Within a period of six years, Toto had solved more than 900 quality problems ranging from missed sales quotas to misdirected deliveries.

By 1990, when Toto won its Deming Prize, the firm's culture had been transformed. The change in corporate and employee philosophy is apparent in even a quick walk through one of the company's factories. At the Kokura No. 2 plant, for example, every corridor has a quality-related name: Deming Cycle Street, Problem-Solving Street, Progressive Quality Street. The walls are covered with charts and diagrams used by the plant's 170 quality circles. In many departments, workers post their personal monthly goals, such as reducing the amount of time needed to set up a specific machine.

Toto's strategic commitment to total quality management is not confined to its factories and offices, according to Yasukazu Kitajima, general manager of the Kokura No. 2 plant. "Now, when I go out drinking with my colleagues, we spend more time talking about quality," he says.

SOURCE: R. Neff, "No. 1 and Trying Harder," *Business Week,* Special Issue on the Quality Imperative, October 25, 1991, pp. 20–24.

Strategy Formulation from the Customer's Perspective   One sees two kinds of smiles at Disneyland: the first displays the anticipation of people entering the park or boarding a ride; the second from the ride itself. The first might be a little easier to generate than the second; Disneyland consistently generates both. One secret of Disneyland's success is its consistent effort to incorporate the customer's perspective in formulating its strategy. The Disneyland handbook has the title, "We create happiness." One section reads, "Producing the Disneyland Show for our Guests requires the talents of a diverse group of people, more than 12,000 performing in more than 400 different roles. Although our individual jobs vary, we all work from the same script, speaking the same language."[10] Disneyland speaks the language of the customer.

For example, Dan Kent is manager of show quality standards for Walt Disney Imagineering. He is responsible for incorporating the customer's perspective into the design and appearance of the park and its attractions. Disneyland's commitment to customer satisfaction goes far beyond delivering safe, high-quality entertainment. The park must look right from the customer's perspective. Different attractions in the park must present a harmonious appearance. Splash Mountain, a heart-pumping water flume ride that opened in 1989, rests on a hill just north of Haunted Mansion, which opened 20 years earlier. Careful design and architectural decisions have ensured that the two attractions do not clash. "We want to make Splash Mountain look like it's been here since opening day," said Kent. "We don't want something to overshadow what's next to it."

Over time, Disneyland's commitment to satisfying customers has led it to invent a design technique called *forced perspective.* In other words, managers like Kent employ sophisticated techniques to deliver entertainment *and* to make it look just right. Sleeping Beauty Castle appears much larger than its real size because larger bricks at the base of the castle and smaller bricks at the top create an illusion. The design of buildings on Main Street is another symbol of this commitment to customer satisfaction. The distance between the Central Plaza (the hub of the park) and the Town Square (just inside the park) appears shorter from the Central Plaza end than it does from the Town Square end. That's because the Main Street buildings on the Central Plaza end are a little farther apart than the buildings on the Town Square end. This give the impression that the park is opening up to guests as they enter, and that the exit is a little closer as they leave. Disney has created a tradition of strategy formulation based on total customer satisfaction. Disney's top managers focus their analytical efforts on finding new ways to make the Disneyland experience satisfying in terms of its content and appearance. This dedication helps them identify and build the appropriate internal competencies. For example, Disney literally invented the forced perspective design technique by spending time and money to learn how to create the illusions that increase customer satisfaction.

Strategy Formulation from the Competitor's Perspective   Analysis of the effect of TQM on strategy formulation cannot ignore competitors. To think smart about an organization's future, top managers must seek sustainable advantage at the functional level, the business level, and the corporate level. The analytic effort is sharpened considerably through a systematic consideration of methods used by competitors. TQM depends on fact-based decision making aimed at continuous improvement. The facts that drive a continuous improvement strategy come from measurements of the organization's performance relative to the performance of its most successful competitor. An earlier chapter gave this analysis the name *benchmarking.* David Kearns, former president of Xerox Corporation, advocates "the continuous process of measuring products, services, and practices against the toughest competitors or those companies recognized as industry leaders."[11] The systematic search for successful methods used by other organizations can lead to valuable discoveries in the most unlikely places.

In the photocopier industry, they joke that a company can always be sure of two sales for a new model: to its own headquarters and to Xerox, which tests nearly all of its rivals' copiers. If another machine performs better, it becomes Xerox's benchmark, or goal for improvement. Xerox benchmarks more than copiers. For example, the corporation must quickly ship parts for its equipment to hundreds of thousands of customers around the world. Delays and mistakes make irate customers. To improve its logistics and distribution functions, Xerox turned to L. L. Bean. What can a copier manufacturer learn from a catalog sales firm? Xerox says plenty, since Bean may have the world's best small-item distribution system. Xerox recognized that Bean's system designed to move moccasins and tents could also move copy machine parts.

Strategy Formulation from the Supplier's Perspective   The effect of TQM on strategy formulation extends this analysis to consider maintaining and improving the quality of purchased parts, components, and raw materials. In the words of Noel Pooler, owner of Pooler Industries, "When large firms embrace TQM, it changes how everybody who deals with them does business. They reduce the number of suppliers that they have, they want long-term contracts, fewer and fewer suppliers, better and better quality."[12]

Japanese companies have pioneered supplier management methods that yield significant quality improvements. Davis Tool and Engineering Company's experience with Nissan is an example of how an organization can enrich its strategy formulation process by viewing it from the supplier's perspective.[13] Five years ago, Davis Tool bid to supply parts to the Nissan plant in Smyrna, Tennessee. Nissan sent engineers from Smyrna and Japan to examine the Davis Tool factory in Detroit before awarding the company a contract. Then, as it has done with two dozen suppliers across the United States, Nissan dispatched a pair of engineers from Smyrna for five days to help workers at Davis Tool's factory rethink their jobs. At this time five Davis employees were producing 200 oil pans per shift.

The results of Nissan's efforts astounded the managers at Davis Tool. At the end of five days, two workers were churning out 800 oil pans each shift. At Nissan's urging, Davis Tool assured its workers that efficiency gains would not cost them their jobs. Some of the changes seemed obvious, like raising parts bins to hip level so that workers no longer had to strain their backs bending over to reach the bins. The Nissan team broke down each worker's job, timing each activity to identify any waste. They then combined tasks to save time and space. Davis Tool had never before been prodded into such thorough scrutiny of its practices, explained Richard Davis II, president. The Japanese, he said, are "bringing these skills to their new supply base in America."

To help suppliers, Nissan has also created a training program in Smyrna. Managers from supplier companies visit to take courses that last about 16 days and range from problem solving to W. Edward Deming's techniques for improving quality. Nissan has divided its suppliers into regional groups. Suppliers from each region tour each other's factories to see how they have improved efficiency in everything from plant layout to lighting.

Strategy Implementation and TQM

Strategy implementation consists of managing change, organization structure, and culture to achieve strategic goals. TQM affects strategy implementation as the work force can be a source of tremendous competitive advantage, given the power to develop and implement new and better systems. For example, Exxon has two plants that make a tire ingredient in Houston and Baton Rouge, Louisiana. As part of a quality improvement program at these plants, top managers appointed Floyd, a drawling six-and-a-half footer, as an internal quality consultant in 1985. He taught himself the basics of quality management by studying Deming's books. He organized workers and managers into teams to find ways to streamline the plants. From 1988 to 1990, he says, the operation cut its working capital needs from 18 percent to 8 percent of its $400 million in yearly sales. In 1990, one of the plants won a national award for excellence in manufacturing administered by Utah State University.[14]

Strategic Control and TQM   To make certain that strategies unfold as intended, managers need yardsticks that can measure the organization's performance and provide the benchmarks for the strategic audit. After successful methods adopted by competitors and other organizations have been identified at the formulation stage, these methods have to be examined carefully and codified so that they can be used for strategic control.

To practice benchmarking, a firm continuously compares its processes with the same processes of the best competitors in the industry—including domestic and foreign firms; the comparison should also extend to the best firm outside the industry that has similar processes. The process of benchmarking consists of the following steps.[15]

- Learning how other organizations arrange their processes.
- Adapting the best-practice to the investigating organization.
- Taking action to improve the process to meet or exceed the standards of the best.

Benchmarking is a very systematic, intensive, and disciplined process that requires research about others' processes and a thorough understanding of one's own processes. This requires an investment of substantial time and resources, and it exposes the firm to a whole new world of shared experiences. Of course, competitors won't (and shouldn't) share their most important competitive secrets, but that leaves a very large number of processes about which competitors can share information.

Compaq and Apple, two highly competitive computer companies, have shared benchmarking information about certain processes with one another. IBM, Motorola, AT&T, and Xerox have benchmarked the designs of their training programs for employees. Xerox, Varian, Sun Microsystems, and Solectron have joined forces to study their methods to increase customer satisfaction. Competitors are often willing to share information (and legally they can do so under antitrust laws) provided they specify up front the areas to cover, the kind of information to exchange, and the uses of the results.

Benchmarking has become an important part of the strategic control efforts in many organizations. In 1992, the American Productivity and Quality Center released the results of a survey in which 98 percent of the respondents said they would be doing much more benchmarking over the next five years, and 80 percent agreed that companies will have to employ the technique to survive in the globally competitive world of the future.

SUMMARY

Business managers have always recognized that poor product quality could threaten customer satisfaction and perhaps even the survival of their organizations. Historically, they have tried to solve quality problems by implementing inspection and post-production repair systems. Modern organizations have developed more proactive methods of assuring quality, spurred by the teachings of W. Edwards Deming, Joseph M. Juran, and Philip B. Crosby, along with the competitive success of Japanese firms that have embraced and refined their methods.

The principles of total quality management guide unique changes in every organization's operations, but all firms that practice TQM share five characteristics: a customer-driven definition of quality; strong quality leadership; emphasis on continuous improvement; reliance on facts, data, and analysis; and encouragement of employee participation. The Malcolm Baldrige National Quality Award and ISO 9000 certification encourage organizations to embody these characteristics.

A total quality management initiative affects every step in the strategic management process. It focuses the firm's environmental analysis on the needs of external and internal customers. TQM fills the organization's vision and mission with images of continuous improvement in customer satisfaction, keeping objectives tied securely to customer's needs. TQM requires strategy formulation to develop a plan that considers customers', competitors', and suppliers' perspectives. TQM adds power to strategy implementation by tapping the potent force of employees' experience and insight into the organization's operations and to strategic control through benchmarking competitive products.

KEY TERMS

total quality management (TQM), p. 191
quality control, p. 191
Plan-Do-Check-Act, p. 193
Malcolm Baldrige National Quality Award, p. 198

ISO 9000, p. 201
external customer, p. 205
internal customer, p. 205

CHECKLIST

Analyzing Total Quality Management in Problems and Cases

___ 1. Does the problem or case involve quality issues?

___ 2. Has the organization developed a basic system or strategy for quality management?

___ 3. Has it fully explicated and adapted the principles of TQM to its own organizational characteristics?

___ 4. Are all employees appropriately involved in the TQM process and strategy?

___ 5. Does the organization's TQM philosophy focus on outcomes that the company should strive to achieve?

___ 6. Is the TQM system defined in terms of the five characteristics common to all organizations that have adopted the method?

___ 7. Does TQM improve production and quality?

___ 8. Does an internally accepted quality standard apply to the problem or case?

___ 9. Has the organization evaluated the impact of quality issues on its strategic management process?

Additional Readings

Ciampa, D. *Total Quality: A User's Guide for Implementation.* Reading, Mass.: Addison-Wesley, 1992.

Dean, J. W., Jr., and J. R. Evans. *Total Quality: Management, Organization, and Strategy.* Minneapolis, Minn.: West Publishing, 1994.

Logothetis, N. *Managing for Total Quality: From Deming to Taguchi and SPC.* Hertfordshire, U.K.: Prentice-Hall International, 1992.

Rabbit, J. T. and P. A. Bergh. *The ISO 9000 Book*. White Plains, N. Y.: Quality Resources, 1993.

The Road to Total Quality. New York: Conference Board, 1990. Research Bulletin No. 239.

Steeples, M. M., *The Corporate Guide to the Malcolm Baldrige National Quality Award*. Homewood, Ill.: Business One-Irwin, 1993.

CASE

Philips's Strategy Falls on Deaf Ears

It was supposed to be a triumphant moment at Philips Electronics' annual shareholders meeting. CEO Jan D. Timmer had done everything right; he had revived the world's third-largest consumer electronics company, coaxing healthy 1993 profits from a weakened giant that had lost $2.3 billion in 1990 and dipped into the red again in 1992.

Timmer had done it the hard way, slashing 70,000 jobs and axing businesses that were losing money. Despite a flat market, Philips had rebounded from a $486 million loss in 1992 to a profit of $1.06 billion in 1993. Still, shareholders held copies of an annual report that projected a sales increase of only 1 percent in 1993 and reported that $600 million of Philips's profit was non-recurring income from divestitures. They wanted to know why new products were selling so slowly.

Timmer acknowledged that he'd really only finished half of the job—the easy half. Keeping up with the Joneses of global electronics—Sony Corp. and Matsushita Electric Industrial Co.—meant finding new products and new industries to fuel growth. It was a theme Timmer had been pounding home to his employees for three years.

Timmer admitted that a number of obstacles complicated his plans to get Philips moving, but he asserted that the company would conquer them. He planned to unveil a new strategy in mid-June that sources said would accelerate the Dutch company's move into software, services, and multimedia, where Timmer hoped to generate 30 percent to 40 percent of revenues by 2000, compared with just 20 percent currently.

It was a bold plan, but was it fast enough? "We can't continue to restructure," said Henk Bodt, a board member in charge of consumer electronics. "We have to develop new initiatives." Philips was poised to make a major acquisition, probably a leading U.S. interactive-software company.

Many of Philips's thrusts into multimedia aren't designed to produce profits until the end of the decade, however, and Timmer grappled with a number of immediate problems, especially in the all-important consumer-electronics division.

To speed the transformation, Timmer had already shaken up the top ranks at the inward-looking company. He brought in a number of non-Dutch managers, many with strong international and marketing backgrounds. Although he sensed a change in attitude, Timmer clearly faced an uphill battle. He was stunned at a company colloquium when employees asked where Philips was headed and why. He was astonished that the company's troops had failed to comprehend the plan he had been promoting for more than three years. In a fresh attempt at communicating Philips's strategy, Timmer planned to ask all 236,000 employees about the progress they had seen under his program of renewal, dubbed Operation Centurion. "It's an invitation for people to be very critical, even about people in charge," he said. "We must encourage entrepreneurial behavior at all levels."

DISCUSSION QUESTIONS

1. In what ways could TQM help Philips achieve its manufacturing and marketing goals?
2. How effective could a TQM strategy be when the company's strategy has remained so unclear to employees?
3. Write a mission statement for Philips, focusing on potential contributions from the principles of Deming, Juran, and Crosby that could help the company achieve its sales and marketing goals.

SOURCE: "Philips Needs Laser Speed," *Business Week,* June 6, 1994, pp. 46–47.

Notes

1. *Management Practices: U.S. Companies Improve Performance through Quality Efforts* (Washington, D.C.: United States General Accounting Office, May 1991), GAO/NSIAD–91–190.
2. A. March, "A Note on Quality: The Views of Deming, Juran, and Crosby," in Harry Costin, ed., *Readings in Total Quality Management* (New York: Harcourt Brace College Publishers, 1994), p. 143.
3. D. Ciampa, *Total Quality: A User's Guide for Implementation* (Reading, Mass.: Addison-Wesley, 1992).
4. J. Lamprecht, "The ISO 9000 Certification Process: Some Important Issues to Consider," *Quality Digest,* August 1991, pp. 61–70.
5. B. Stratton, "The Value of Implementing Quality," *Quality Progress,* July 1991, p. 70.
6. O. Port and J. Carey, "Questing for the Best," *Business Week,* Special Issue on the Quality Imperative, October 25, 1991, pp. 8–16.
7. K. H. Hammonds and G. DeGeorge, "Where Did They Go Wrong?" *Business Week,* Special Issue on the Quality Imperative, October 25, 1991, pp. 34–38.
8. "The Cracks in Quality," *The Economist,* April 18, 1992, pp. 67–68.
9. Ibid.
10. B. Stratton, "How Disneyland Works," *Quality Progress,* 24, no. 7 (1991), pp. 17–31.
11. D. Wilkerson, A. Kuh, and T. Wilkerson, "A Tale of Change," *Total Quality Management,* July/August 1992, pp. 146–151.
12. M. Barrier, "Small Firms Put Quality First," *Nation's Business,* May 1992, pp. 22–30.
13. J. Bennet, "Detroit Struggles to Learn Another Lesson from Japan," *New York Times,* June 19, 1994, p. 5.
14. T. Peterson, K. Kelly, J. Weber, and N. Gross, "Top Products for Less than Top Dollar," *Business Week,* Special Issue on the Quality Imperative, October 25, 1991, pp. 66–68.
15. C. J. Grayson, Jr., "Worldwide Competition," *Total Quality Management,* July/August 1992, pp. 134–138.

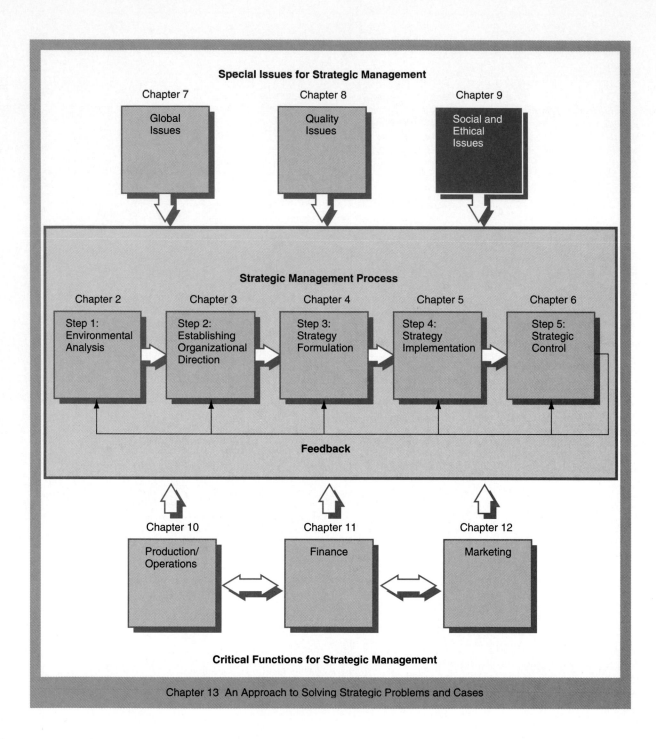

Special Issues for Strategic Management

Chapter 7

Global
Issues

Chapter 8

Quality
Issues

Chapter 9

Social and
Ethical
Issues

Strategic Management Process

Chapter 2

Step 1:
Environmental
Analysis

Chapter 3

Step 2:
Establishing
Organizational
Direction

Chapter 4

Step 3:
Strategy
Formulation

Chapter 5

Step 4:
Strategy
Implementation

Chapter 6

Step 5:
Strategic
Control

Feedback

Chapter 10

Production/
Operations

Chapter 11

Finance

Chapter 12

Marketing

Critical Functions for Strategic Management

Chapter 13 An Approach to Solving Strategic Problems and Cases

CHAPTER

9

Strategic Management: Social and Ethical Dimensions

A **stakeholder** of an organization is an individual or group who has a stake in the consequences of management decisions and can influence those decisions. The managers of a successful corporation have obligations to many different stakeholders.[1] For example, they are responsible to:

- The *stockholders* or *owners* of the corporation, to attempt to increase the value of the firm
- The *suppliers* of materials and *resellers* of products, to deal fairly with them
- *Lenders* of capital, to repay them
- *Government agencies* and society, to abide by laws
- *Interest groups*, to consider their arguments
- *Employees* and *unions*, to provide safe work environments and recognize their rights
- *Consumers*, to provide safe products and market them efficiently
- *Competitors*, to avoid practices that restrain trade
- *Local communities* and *society at large*, to avoid practices that harm the environment

Some analysts argue that one or another of these obligations is most important, but we believe that all of them must be considered. Successful business firms are powerful forces in society; because of their power, they incur certain responsibilities. For example, consider this list of the rights of businesses (sellers) relative to consumers:[2]

- Sellers have the right to introduce any products in any sizes, styles, colors, or shapes, so

long as they meet minimum health and safety requirements.
- Sellers have the right to price their products as they please so long as they avoid certain discriminatory forms of pricing that undermine competition.
- Sellers have the right to promote their products using any amount of resources, any media, and any messages so long as they commit no deception or fraud.
- Sellers have the right to introduce any buying schemes they wish so long as they avoid discriminatory practices.
- Sellers have the right to alter product offerings at any time.
- Sellers have the right to distribute products in any reasonable manner.
- Sellers have the right to limit product guarantees or post-sale services that they offer.

Although this list is not exhaustive, it does serve to illustrate the power that businesses wield. Consumers, on the other hand, are generally accorded four basic rights: the right to safety, the right to be informed, the right to choose, and the right to be heard. These rights depend on the ability and willingness of consumers to be highly involved in purchases, and many consumers are neither able or willing to become so involved. For example, young children, a number of the elderly, and many uneducated consumers lack the experience or cognitive capacity to process information well enough to protect themselves. Further, consumers' rights leave broad gray areas that require managerial judgment and interpretation. For example, how safe do consumers have a right to expect a product to be? How much information can they expect? What do consumers have a right to know about gas tank designs of the automobiles they purchase?

A singular focus on the rights of businesses in relation to those of consumers and other stakeholders may, however, cause business leaders to overlook the ever-present companions of rights—responsibilities. While legal rights and protections may serve as theoretical boundaries for business decision making and action, **ethical responsibilities** may define roles more strictly than the minimum requirements of law and industry practice. In fulfilling such roles, an organization expresses its character and managerial values, and it can also enhance its competitive advantage over rivals. Organizations as diverse as Merck, Levi-Strauss, Johnson & Johnson, The Body Shop, Tom's of Maine, Ben & Jerry's, and Herman Miller have developed reputations for ethical, responsible

actions. These firms have recognized that, in the words of one New York executive, "The only sustainable competitive advantage any business has is its reputation." [3] Of course, a good reputation requires far more than statements of good intentions and self-serving press releases. Without question, the firms named above have enhanced their competitive positions by emphasizing traditional strengths like excellent product quality and service. Part of this kind of competitive strength rests on strong, ethical organizational cultures and self-images of "doing good while doing well."

In this chapter, we investigate the responsibility of business to society. In the first part of the chapter, we review arguments against and arguments in favor of businesses performing activities that might be termed *socially responsible*. We then discuss a number of specific questions that arise about social responsibility, and we investigate four influences on the social responsibility of business: legal, political, competitive, and ethical influences. Finally, we suggest a model for analyzing social responsibility issues from a strategic management viewpoint.

SOCIAL RESPONSIBILITY DEBATE

Consensus on the meaning of the term **social responsibility,** and on obligations of businesses to society will always remain elusive. These issues defy neat, final resolutions in a dynamic society; new answers continually emerge from the ongoing dialogue about business's informal contract with the society of which it is a part.[4] For the purposes of this text, however, we define *social responsibility* as the degree to which the activities of an organization protect and improve society beyond the extent required to serve the direct legal, economic, or technical interests of the organization. In other words, social responsibility involves performing activities that may help society, even if they do not directly contribute to the firm's profits.

A major debate rages in the strategic management literature, and throughout society, over whether firms should undertake activities primarily to live up to social responsibilities. The classical view denies that businesses should seek to promote social welfare, whereas the contemporary view affirms that they should. We shall discuss and compare these two views.

Classical View of Social Responsibility

The **classical view** holds that a business should not assume any social responsibility beyond making as much money as possible for its owners. The managers of an organization are employees of the stockholders, the argument runs, and have obligations only to them. The noted economist Milton Friedman, a proponent of this view, argues that

> there is one and only one social responsibility of business—to use its resources and engage in activities designed to increase its profits so long as it stays within the rules of the game, which is to say, engages in open and free competition, without deception or fraud. . . . Few trends could so thoroughly undermine the very foundations of our free society as the acceptance by corporate officials of a social responsibility other than to make as much money for their stockholders as possible. This is a fundamentally subversive doctrine.[5]

In the classical view, the role of managers is to produce and market goods efficiently, that is, in a way that gives the owners of the firm the greatest economic profits. Any other social responsibility activity is seen as disturbing fundamental economic relationships, and eroding profits.

Contemporary View of Social Responsibility

The **contemporary view** claims that businesses, as important and influential institutions in society, have a responsibility to help maintain and improve the society's overall welfare. A strong advocate of corporate social responsibility, Keith Davis, has elaborated on this view.[6] It can be summarized in terms of the following five propositions:

- *Proposition 1: Social responsibility arises from social power.* This proposition is built on the premise that business has a significant amount of influence or power over such critical social issues as minority employment and environmental pollution. In essence, the collective action of all businesses determines the proportion of minorities employed and much of the prevailing condition of the environment. Thus, because business has power over society, society can and must hold business responsible for social conditions affected by the use of this power.
- *Proposition 2: Business shall operate as a two-way open system with open receipt of inputs from society and open disclosure of its operations to the public.* Business must be willing to listen to social representatives concerning actions to improve social welfare. Davis suggests that continuing, honest, and open communications between business and social representatives is critical to maintaining or improving the overall welfare of society.
- *Proposition 3: Both the social costs and the social benefits of an activity, good, or service shall be thoroughly calculated and considered in order to decide whether or not to proceed with it.* Technical feasibility and economic profitability are not the only factors that should influence business decision making. Business should also consider both the long-term and short-term social consequences of all business activities before undertaking them.
- *Proposition 4: Social costs related to each activity, good, or service shall be passed on to the consumer.* Business cannot be expected to finance all activities that are economically disadvantageous, but socially advantageous. The cost of maintaining socially desirable activities within business should be passed on to consumers through higher prices for the goods or services that are directly related to those socially desirable activities.
- *Proposition 5: As citizens, business institutions have the responsibility to become involved in certain social problems that are outside their normal areas of operation.* If a business possesses the expertise to solve a social problem with which it may not be directly associated, it should accept responsibility for helping society

solve the problem. Business will eventually receive increased profits from a generally improved society, so business should share in the responsibility of all citizens to improve that society.

Table 9.1 summarizes the major arguments for and against businesses accepting social responsibilities.

TABLE 9.1

Summary of Major Arguments for and against Social Responsibility for Business

FOR SOCIAL RESPONSIBILITY

1. It is in the best interest of a business to promote and improve the communities where it does business.
2. Social actions can be profitable.
3. It is the ethical thing to do.
4. It improves the public image of the firm.
5. It increases the viability of the business system. Business exists because it gives society benefits. Society can amend or take away its charter. This is the "iron law of responsibility."
6. It is necessary to avoid government regulation.
7. Sociocultural norms require it.
8. Laws cannot be passed for all circumstances. Thus, business must assume responsibility to maintain an orderly legal society.
9. It is in the stockholders' best interest. It will improve the price of stock in the long run because the stock market will view the company as less risky and open to public attack and therefore award it a higher price–earnings ratio.
10. Society should give business a chance to solve social problems that government has failed to solve.
11. Business is considered by some groups to be the institution with the financial and human resources to solve social problems.
12. Prevention of problems is better than cures—so let business solve problems before they become too great.

AGAINST SOCIAL RESPONSIBILITY

1. It might be illegal.
2. Business plus government equals monolith.
3. Social actions cannot be measured.
4. It violates profit maximization.
5. The cost of social responsibility is too great and would increase prices too much.
6. Business lacks social skills to solve societal problems.
7. It would dilute business's primary purposes.
8. It would weaken the U.S. balance of payments because price of goods will have to go up to pay for social programs.
9. Business already has too much power. Such involvement would make business too powerful.
10. Business lacks accountability to the public. Thus, the public would have no control over its social involvement.
11. Such business involvement lacks broad public support.

SOURCE: R. Joseph Monsen, Jr., "The Social Attitudes of Management," in Joseph W. McQuire, ed., *Contemporary Management* (Englewood Cliffs, N.J.: Prentice-Hall, 1974), p. 616. Reprinted by permission of R. Joseph Monsen.

Comparison of the Two Views

The classical view conceives of businesses as strictly economic entities, whereas the contemporary view conceives of businesses as members of society. Although business organizations clearly are both, recognizing this dual role does not answer the question of how much companies should incorporate social responsibility into their activities. In many cases, both views lead to the same conclusion about whether a firm should engage in a particular activity. For example, both views recognize the need to perform legally required activities. Also, in situations in which the activity enhances profits, both approaches support it.

The two views diverge when an activity (1) is not required by law *and* (2) is not profitable in the short term. Here the classical view would argue against performing the activity, but the contemporary view would argue in favor of performing the activity, if the costs were not too great.

One observer of this ongoing debate, Archie Carroll, proposes a **pyramid of corporate social responsibility,** shown in Figure 9.1, to clarify these issues. In general, economic and legal responsibilities form the base of the pyramid; the organization must fulfill these requirements to survive and continue to operate.

FIGURE 9.1
Pyramid of Corporate
Social Responsibility

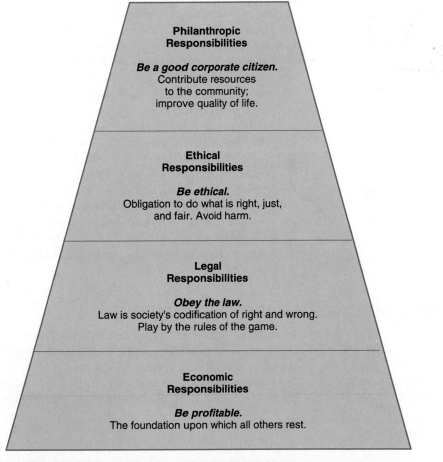

**Philanthropic
Responsibilities**

Be a good corporate citizen.
Contribute resources
to the community;
improve quality of life.

**Ethical
Responsibilities**

Be ethical.
Obligation to do what is right, just,
and fair. Avoid harm.

**Legal
Responsibilities**

Obey the law.
Law is society's codification of right and wrong.
Play by the rules of the game.

**Economic
Responsibilities**

Be profitable.
The foundation upon which all others rest.

SOURCE: Archie Carroll, "The Pyramid of Corporate Social Responsibility: Toward the Moral Management of Organizational Stakeholders." Reprinted from *Business Horizons,* July-August 1991, p. 42. Copyright 1991 by the Foundation for the School of Business at Indiana University. Used with permission.

Ethical and philanthropic responsibilities to stakeholders become critical when a firm begins to make a profit within the rules laid down by the broader society. Of course, in some industries (such as professional services, pharmaceuticals, or health care), an image of integrity and trust is critical to an organization's profitability. This forces ethical responsibilities much closer to the base of the pyramid.

Overall, we believe that the degree to which a firm seeks to advance social objectives depends on many factors, including the values of top executives, the size of the firm, its ability to invest in social programs, the structure of its industry, and the consequences of acting or not acting. Furthermore, these decisions depend on the specific problem and kind of action involved.

SPECIFIC AREAS OF SOCIAL RESPONSIBILITY

Questions have been raised about the social responsibility of business in many areas. Table 9.2 lists four of the more commonly discussed areas of concern and several specific questions related to each. As you review these questions, keep two points in mind.

First, business firms are considered socially responsible entities to the degree that they *voluntarily* act to maintain or increase social welfare without coercion by government regulations or laws. For example, a socially responsible firm would voluntarily remove a product from the market when it suspected tampering, rather than being forced to do so.

Second, managers can rely on few precise standards for socially responsible actions. In some cases, a firm's social responsibility activities can be compared with those of other firms in the same industry. However, this does not always yield a good measure. For example, consider the issue of product safety. Some might argue that only completely safe products should be allowed on the market, but imposing such a standard would be impractical. Bicycles often head the list of the most hazardous products, and every year many consumers are injured while riding them, yet few would argue that bicycles should be banned from the market. Much of the problem in resolving product safety issues involves the question of whether the harm done results from an inherent lack of product safety or from unsafe use by the consumer. Similarly, answers to many of the questions listed in Table 9.2 depend on social judgments, which differ depending on who makes the judgment, rather than on precise standards of business conduct.

INFLUENCES ON BUSINESS PRACTICES

As noted, business firms have considerable power and can powerfully influence society. However, our social system includes a number of checks and balances that guard against misuse of business power. Figure 9.2 illustrates four major influences that can inhibit the inappropriate use of business power: legal, political, competitive, and ethical influences.

Legal Influences

Legal influences consist of federal, state, and local laws and the agencies and processes by which these laws are enforced. The Company Example illustrates the threat that legal forces can pose.

TABLE 9.2

Areas of Social Responsibility Concern

CONCERN FOR CONSUMERS

1. Are products safe and well-designed?
2. Are products priced fairly?
3. Are advertisements clear and not deceptive?
4. Are customers treated fairly by salespeople?
5. Are credit terms clear?
6. Is adequate product information available?

CONCERN FOR EMPLOYEES

1. Are employees paid a fair wage?
2. Are employees provided a safe work environment?
3. Are workers hired, promoted, and treated fairly without regard to sex, race, color, or creed?
4. Are employees given special training and educational opportunities?
5. Are handicapped people given employment opportunities?
6. Does the business help rehabilitate employees with physical, mental, or emotional problems?

CONCERN FOR THE NATURAL ENVIRONMENT

1. Is the environment adequately protected from unclean air and water, excessive noise, or other types of pollution associated with manufacturing?
2. Are products and packages biodegradable or recyclable?
3. Are any by-products that pose a safety hazard to society (such as nuclear waste or commercial solvents) carefully handled and given proper treatment or disposal?

CONCERN FOR THE COMMUNITY

1. Does the firm support minority and community enterprises by purchasing from them or subcontracting to them?
2. Are donations made to help develop and support education, art, health, and community development programs?
3. Is the social impact of any plant location or relocation considered by the managers who make the decision?
4. Is appropriate information concerning business operations made public?

Table 9.3 lists several bills enacted by Congress that influence business practices. Some of this legislation is designed to control business practices in specific industries, such as toys or textiles; other laws are aimed at functional areas, such as packaging or product safety.

Units of government make laws that control business activity for a variety of reasons. Some laws reflect the collective sense of society that the business sector has not acted responsibly; these laws seek to establish tighter controls and to specify acceptable behavior (e.g., drug safety, workplace safety, and product safety laws). Such laws may result from alarming news reports such as pollution at Love Canal or accidents at unsafe factories. Other laws grow out of joint business–government efforts to equalize competitive conditions in certain industries. For example, the International Trade Commission protects U.S. firms from dumping (sales at artificially low prices) by non-U.S. competitors.

COMPANY EXAMPLE

Ethical Standards Sour at Stew Leonard's

Stew Leonard thought it important to pass along his values to his staff. With his folksiness and integrity, he became known as the Mister Rogers of food retailing.

His Norwalk, Connecticut, supermarket, Stew Leonard's, is listed by Ripley's "Believe It or Not" as the world's biggest dairy store. Leonard's animated megamarket includes dancing milk cartons, a petting zoo of live geese and goats, and employees in duck costumes waddling down the aisles. Leonard himself was often at the door, sometimes in a cow suit, greeting some of the 200,000 customers who flocked to his two stores every week.

But Stew Leonard is no longer greeting customers. The one-time milkman, called a marketing genius by Wall Street and a folk hero by his customers, is today called a criminal by the Internal Revenue Service. Leonard and executives of his $200 million business have pleaded guilty to what has been called the largest criminal tax case in Connecticut history, as well as the biggest computer-driven tax-evasion scheme in the nation.

Over the years, Leonard has been hailed for his adherence to the values of an old-fashioned family enterprise. According to the IRS, however, Leonard also had one foot in the future, pulling off "a crime of the 21st century."

Using a customized software program, Leonard was able to reduce item-by-item sales data and skim $17 million in cash, mostly during the 1980s. Computer tapes containing the real financial figures were destroyed, and the company's auditors were given the understated books. Leonard was able to divert even more money by requiring customers to pay cash for gift certificates.

Each day, say prosecutors, cash was emptied from the registers into a "money room," where it was counted, then placed in bags and dropped down a chute into the "vault room." Most of this cash was carried to the Caribbean, where Leonard owns a second home. Leonard's brother-in-law, an executive at the store, kept nearly $500,000 hidden behind a false panel in his basement.

Leonard has agreed to pay $15 million in restitution, and he faces up to five years in prison. In addition, his store is accused of short-weighing hundreds of food packages.

Yet neither the charges nor his confession of guilt has hampered business, which remains steady. "We were packed today. Our customers are extremely supportive and sympathetic," claims Stew Leonard, Jr.

SOURCE: Richard Behar, "Skimming the Cream," *Time*, August 2, 1993, p. 49.

FIGURE 9.2
Influences on Business Practices

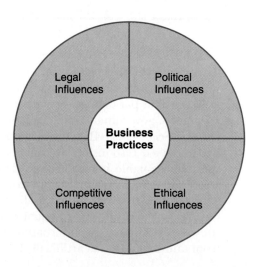

TABLE 9.3	

Examples of Federal Legislation Affecting Business Practices

Legislation	Major Provisions
Family and Medical Leave Act	Allows employees to take job-protected unpaid leaves because of family situations or their own illness
Americans with Disabilities Act	Facilitates equal access for individuals with disabilities in all major life activities, including employment
Toxic Substances Control Act Amendment	Provides adequate time for planning and implementation of school asbestos management plans
Federal Food, Drug, and Cosmetic Act Amendment	Bans reimportation of drugs produced in the United States; restricts distribution of drug samples; bans certain resales of drugs by health care facilities
Truth in Mileage Act	Amends the Motor Vehicle Information and Cost Savings Act to strengthen, for the protection of consumers, the provisions respecting disclosure of mileage when motor vehicles are transferred
Petroleum Overcharge Distribution and Restitution Act	Provides for distribution to injured consumers of escrow funds remaining from oil company settlements of alleged price allocation violations under the Emergency Petroleum Allocation Act of 1973
Superfund Amendments and Reauthorization Act	Extends and amends the Comprehensive Environmental Response Compensation and Liability Act of 1980; authorizes appropriations for and revises the EPA Hazardous Substance Response Trust Fund program for financing cleanup of uncontrolled hazardous waste sites
Anti-Drug Abuse Act	Amends the Food, Drug, and Cosmetic Act to revise provisions on regulation of infant formula manufacture
Processed Products Inspection Improvement Act	Amends the Meat Inspection Act to eliminate USDA continuous inspection requirements for meats, poultry, and egg processing plants for a six-year trial period
Emergency Response Act	Amends the Toxic Substances Control Act to require the EPA to promulgate regulations pertaining to inspections, development of asbestos management plans, and response actions
Safe Drinking Water Act Amendments	Amends the Safe Drinking Water Act; authorizes appropriations for and revises EPA safe drinking water programs, including grants to states for drinking water standards enforcement and groundwater protection programs
Drug Export Amendments Act	Amends the Food, Drug, and Cosmetic Act to remove restrictions on exports of human and veterinary drugs not yet approved by FDA or USDA for use in the United States and establishes conditions governing exports of such drugs

SOURCE: Partially based upon John R. Nevin, "Consumer Protection Legislation: Evolution, Structure and Prognosis," Working paper, University of Wisconsin–Madison, Wis., August 1989.

A variety of government agencies work to enforce these laws and investigate business practices. In addition to state and local agencies, a number of federal agencies are empowered to regulate particular areas of business activity. Table 9.4 presents a capsule summary of the activities of several federal regulatory agencies.

Table 9.4 shows clearly that federal agencies have broad and diverse powers to influence business practices, and they can impose a variety of remedies for

---

TABLE 9.4

Some Important Federal Regulatory Agencies

Agency	Responsibilities
Federal Trade Commission (FTC)	Enforces laws and develops guidelines regarding unfair business practices
Food and Drug Administration (FDA)	Enforces laws and develops regulations to prevent the distribution and sale of adulterated or misbranded foods, drugs, cosmetics, and hazardous consumer products
Consumer Product Safety Commission (CPSC)	Enforces the Consumer Product Safety Act, which covers any consumer product not assigned to other regulatory agencies
Federal Communications Commission (FCC)	Regulates interstate wire, radio, and television
Environmental Protection Agency (EPA)	Develops and enforces environmental protection standards in such areas as water, air, and noise pollution
Office of Consumer Affairs	Handles consumer complaints
Equal Employment Opportunity Commission (EEOC)	Investigates and conciliates employment discrimination complaints that are based on race, sex, or creed
Office of Federal Contract Compliance Programs	Insures that employers that hold federal contracts grant equal employment opportunities to people regardless of race or sex
Occupational Safety and Health Administration (OSHA)	Regulates safety and health conditions in nongovernment workplaces
National Highway Safety Administration (NHSA)	Attempts to reduce traffic accidents through the regulation of transportation-related manufacturers and products
Mining Enforcement and Safety Administration	Attempts to improve conditions for mine workers by enforcing mine safety and equipment standards

---

improper business conduct. For example, the Federal Trade Commission has dealt with **deceptive advertising**—advertising that misleads consumers—by requiring firms to run corrective ads to clear up any misconceptions fostered by previous ads. The FTC has identified advertising for several products as misleading; classic examples include:

- Profile Bread's advertising misled consumers to believe it was effective in weight reduction.
- Domino Sugar's advertising misled consumers to believe it was a special source of strength, energy, and stamina.
- Ocean Spray Cranberry Juice Cocktail misled consumers about food energy.
- Sugar Information, Inc. misled consumers about the benefits of eating sugar.

The FTC required these firms to run ads with text that would correct these false impressions.[7]

Profile Bread   This text had to run in 25 percent of the brand's advertising for one year:

Hi, (celebrity's name) for Profile Bread. Like all mothers, I'm concerned about nutrition and balanced meals. So, I'd like to clear up any misunderstanding you may have about Profile Bread from its advertising or even its name.

Does Profile have fewer calories than any other breads? No. Profile has about the same per ounce as other breads. To be exact, Profile has seven fewer calories per slice. That's because Profile is sliced thinner. But eating Profile will not cause you to lose weight. A reduction of seven calories is insignificant. It's total calories and balanced nutrition that count. And Profile can help you achieve a balanced meal because it provides protein and B vitamins as well as other nutrients.

How does my family feel about Profile? Well, my husband likes Profile toast, the children love Profile sandwiches, and I prefer Profile to any other bread. So you see, at our house, delicious taste makes Profile a family affair.

Amstar   This statement had to run in one of four Domino ads for one year:

Do you recall some of our past messages saying that Domino Sugar gives you strength, energy, and stamina? Actually, Domino is not a special or unique source of strength, energy, and stamina. No sugar is, because what you need is a balanced diet and plenty of rest and exercise.

Ocean Spray   This text had to appear in one of four ads for one year:

If you've wondered what some of our earlier advertising meant when we said Ocean Spray Cranberry Juice Cocktail has more food energy than orange juice or tomato juice, let us make it clear: we didn't mean vitamins and minerals. Food energy means calories. Nothing more.

Food energy is important at breakfast since many of us may not get enough calories, or food energy, to get off to a good start. Ocean Spray Cranberry Juice Cocktail helps because it contains more food energy than most other breakfast drinks.

And Ocean Spray Cranberry Juice Cocktail gives you and your family Vitamin C plus a great wake-up taste. It's . . . the other breakfast drink.

Sugar Information, Inc.   This text had to run for one insertion in each of seven magazines:

Do you recall the messages we brought you in the past about sugar? How something with sugar in it before meals could help you curb your appetite? We hope you didn't get the idea that our little diet tip was any magic formula for losing weight. Because there are no tricks or shortcuts; the whole diet subject is very complicated. Research hasn't established that consuming sugar before meals will contribute to weight reduction or even keep you from gaining weight.

Legal influences and the power of government agencies to regulate business practices grew dramatically during the 1970s. However, the 1980s and 1990s have witnessed declines in many regulatory activities. In fact, deregulation of business has become a major trend, and many government agencies have considerably reduced their control of business practices.

Political Influences

Political influences include pressure exerted by **special-interest groups** in society to control business practices. These groups use a variety of methods to influence business, such as lobbying to persuade various government agencies to enact or enforce legislation and working directly with employees or consumers. Table 9.5 lists a few organizations that are designed to serve consumer

TABLE 9.5

Political Groups Concerned with Business Practices

BROAD-BASED, NATIONAL GROUPS

Consumer Federation of America
National Wildlife Federation
Common Cause

SMALLER, MULTI-ISSUE ORGANIZATIONS

National Consumer's League
Ralph Nader's Public Citizen

SPECIAL-INTEREST GROUPS

Action for Children's Television
American Association of Retired Persons
Group against Smoking and Pollution

LOCAL GROUPS

Public-interest research groups
Local consumer protection offices
Local broadcast and newspaper consumer action lines

SOURCE: Based on Paul N. Bloom and Stephen A. Greyser, "The Maturing of Consumerism," *Harvard Business Review,* November/December 1981, pp. 130–139.

interests. One tally found over 100 national organizations and over 600 state and local groups involved in consumer advocacy.[8]

Consumerism is a movement to augment the rights of consumers in dealing with business. Paul Bloom and Stephen Greyser argue that consumerism has reached the mature stage of its life cycle and that its impact has been fragmented.[9] Still, they believe that consumerism will continue to have an impact on business, and they suggest three strategies for coping with it. First, businesses can try to accelerate the decline of consumerism by *reducing demand* for it. This could be done by improving product quality, expanding services, lowering prices, and/or toning down advertising claims.

Second, businesses can *compete* with consumer advocacy groups by offering consumer education and assistance in seeking redress of grievances through active consumer affairs departments. Alternatively, businesses can fund and coordinate activities designed to promote deregulation and other probusiness causes.

Third, businesses can *cooperate* with consumer advocacy groups by providing financial and other support. All of these strategies would likely further reduce the impact of political influences on business's approach to social responsibility. However, to the degree that following these strategies leads business firms to step up their social responsibility activities in the long run, consumers and other stakeholder groups could benefit.

Competitive Influences

Competitive influences are the actions that competing firms take to affect each other and, thus, business practices in an industry. These actions can take many forms. For example, one firm might sue another or publicly allege that it engaged in illegal activities. Johnson & Johnson has frequently gone to court to prevent competitors from showing its Tylenol brand of pain relievers in comparative ads. Burger King has publicly accused McDonald's of overstating the weight of its hamburgers. Computer software firms regularly accuse one another of copyright infringement.

Competitors also influence one another by diluting each other's political, economic, and market power. For example, in a business environment with many competitors, a single firm usually cannot dominate the flow of information to consumers. Conflicting competitive claims and price deals offered by various firms may help consumers resist the influence of a single firm.

Society may also benefit from better, safer, more efficient products and services, which are often spawned by competitive pressure. In fact, some firms focus their strategies on a receptive and growing segment of consumers who are especially interested in product safety features. Michelin tires, Volvo automobiles, and certain chainsaw manufacturers have built viable competitive positions by selling safety to consumers. Overall, then, competition may help balance business power within an industry and stimulate the development of more responsible business practices.

The Skills Module invites you to evaluate the balancing effect of the competitive influence on social responsibility.

Ethical Influences

The last type of influence on business practices that we will discuss involves ethical decision making and self-regulation of business conduct. Many businesses follow rigorous codes of ethics; some firms establish offices specifically to handle employee whistle-blowing and consumer complaints.

Efforts to evaluate the ethical influences on business practice are complicated by the lack of a single, universal standard for judging whether a particular action is ethical. Gene Laczniak summarizes five ethical standards that have been proposed:[10]

1. *The Golden Rule:* Act in the way you would expect others to act toward you.
2. *The utilitarian principle:* Act in a way that results in the greatest good for the greatest number.
3. *Kant's categorical imperative:* Act in such a way that the action you take could be a universal law or rule of behavior under the circumstances.
4. *The professional ethic:* Take actions that a disinterested panel of professional colleagues would view as proper.
5. *The TV test:* Ask, "Would I feel comfortable explaining to a national TV audience why I took this action?"

As part of top executives' leadership role, they must choose the standards for their organizations to follow. One analyst proposes that three forces shape ethical decision making in an organization. Figure 9.3 shows these forces and the separate elements of each. The personal ethical perspective of an organization depends on the personal beliefs and values of its top managers or founders, often shaped by religion and early parental influences, combined with the level of their moral development and the particular ethical framework (e.g., utilitarian principle, Golden Rule, categorical imperative, etc.) that they favor. The closely related factors of organizational culture and the systems through which this culture is sustained and transmitted throughout the firm make up the other two building blocks of ethical decision making. Culture and systems may work either to constrain or to support the top managers' ethical perspective.

SKILLS MODULE

Price Cuts Undermine Fleet Street Ethos

INTRODUCTION

This chapter's discussion of social responsibility considers competitive influences and their role in controlling the power of businesses. Review the following situation and then complete the skill development exercise that follows to develop your ability to analyze this influence.

SITUATION

The owners of Britain's two most prestigious newspapers, Rupert Murdoch of *The Times* and Conrad Black of the *Daily Telegraph,* are locked in a savage circulation battle.

Murdoch's News International launched the price war in September, just as the country was coming out of a recession and advertising revenues could be expected to rise. The initial price cut lowered the price of *The Times* to 30 pence from 45 pence (45 cents from 68 cents) and the price of the tabloid *Sun* to 20 pence from 25 pence (30 cents from 37). It was an unheard-of strategy; in the country with the world's highest newspaper readership levels, publishers tend to raise prices above the inflation rate, but declining circulation throughout the industry—and *The Times*'s long-term failure to make a profit—was the catalyst to cut prices in an effort to boost circulation and attract the advertising that would make the newspaper profitable.

The price cut was a huge and immediate success: circulation rose 88,000 in one month, climbing from an average of 354,280 a day in August 1993 to 524,270 the following June. The *Sun*'s circulation rose to 4.16 million from 3.83 million.

Judging from losses from the move, reportedly in the $60 million to $75 million range, competitors initially thought the price cut would be short-lived. The *Daily Telegraph,* whose million-papers-a-day circulation made it the leader among serious newspapers, finally became alarmed when sales fell below seven figures, reaching a 40-year low of 993,395 in May. In June, the *Telegraph* responded to the new environment and cut its prices to 30 pence (45 cents) from 48 pence (72 cents). News International shot back, slashing the price of *The Times* to 20 pence (30 cents), making it cheaper than many tabloids.

While a full-page ad in the *Telegraph* still costs more than three times as much as the same ad in *The Times,* the former's ability to charge premium rates might disappear if the challenger can reach a circulation of 600,000. Indeed, *The Times* reported an increase in ad revenue of 50 percent, or $30 million, in 1994.

Black of the *Telegraph* views the battle as a war for survival: "He is trying to kill us."

Murdoch, who has been quoted as saying that the British newspaper industry would be reduced in the next century to three titles—*The Times,* the *Sun,* and the *Daily Mail*—denies that his purpose is to kill other newspapers. Still, the price war has affected them all, knocking huge sums off the stock-market values of all major newspaper companies in Britain; it already threatens the viability of many properties. The perennially unprofitable *Guardian* has lost circulation; other casualties include the *Daily Mirror,* the *Daily Express,* and the *Daily Mail.*

Worst hit is the long-troubled *Independent,* which in the fall had raised its price to 50 pence (75 cents) from 45 pence (68 cents). Circulation plummeted by nearly 50,000, to 277,377 in June, and the paper is struggling for survival. The *Independent* has complained to the government's Office of Fair Trading about alleged predatory pricing by News International; despite a preliminary inquiry, intervention appears unlikely.

SKILL DEVELOPMENT EXERCISE

The price war initiated by News International threatens to put other newspapers out of business, while also hurting its own bottom-line performance. Prepare a detailed argument either supporting or disputing the idea that Murdoch and *The Times* are competing unfairly. Taking the point of view of a *Times* stakeholder, determine whether the paper's possible long-term gains justify the short-term costs of its strategy.

SOURCE: Ray Moseley, "London Papers' Price War Being Reported in Red Ink," *Chicago Tribune,* July 29, 1994, Sec. 3, p. 1.

FIGURE 9.3
Forces That Shape
Managerial Ethics

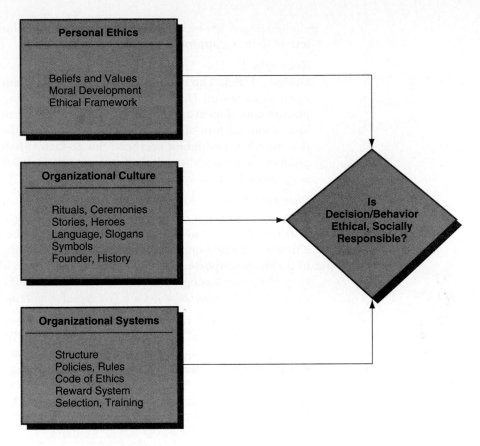

SOURCE: Reprinted by permission from p. 328 of *Organization Theory and Design,* 4th ed. by Richard Daft; Copyright © 1992 by West Publishing Company. All rights reserved.

As implied throughout this chapter, a firm best shapes its ethical standards, and its entire approach to social responsibility issues, through a cross-functional undertaking. Top managers or founders may try to set a certain climate in a firm, but managers and employees throughout the firm, by their actions and decisions, also affect that climate. In addition, different functional specialists contribute information about their functions, with their own professional ethics, codes, or standards, to the efforts of top managers. This information may help to shape the organization's internal ethical climate, as well as its externally focused approach to social responsibility. For example, managers from the marketing function may offer information about advertising codes, pricing standards and regulations, or pressures from environmentalists about product design and packaging. Accounting professionals bring a long tradition of professional ethics and accepted standards. Production managers who operate within a specific industry may have their own professional codes of conduct regarding safety, quality control, or relations with purchasing agents from supplier firms. This information, considered collectively across the several functions, can help top managers shape an organization's basic approach to social and ethical matters.

Applying diverse standards can result in different interpretations for ethical decisions or actions. Defining ethical decisions and actions in the context of international operations, with the added complexity of the diverse cultural and religious backgrounds of managers and employees, can be especially challenging. A few business scenarios may help to illustrate the practical problem of defining appropriate ethical conduct.[11]

Scenario 1   The Thrifty Supermarket Chain has 12 stores in the city of Gotham, U.S.A. The company's policy is to maintain the same prices for all items at all stores. However, the distribution manager knowingly sends the poorest cuts of meat and the lowest-quality produce to the store located in the low-income section of town. To justify this action, the manager explains that this store has the highest overhead due to factors such as employee turnover, pilferage, and vandalism. *Is the distribution manager's economic rationale sufficient justification for this allocation method?*

Scenario 2   The Independent Car Dealers of Metropolis, U.S.A. have undertaken an advertising campaign headlined by the slogan: "Is your family's life worth 45 MPG?" The ads admit that while its subcompacts are not as fuel efficient as foreign imports and cost more to maintain, they are safer according to government-sponsored crash tests. The ads implicitly ask if responsible parents, when purchasing a car, should trade off fuel efficiency for safety. *Is it ethical for the dealers association to use a fear appeal to offset an economic disadvantage?*

Scenario 3   A few recent studies have linked the presence of the artificial sweetener subsugural to cancer in laboratory rats. While the validity of these findings has been hotly debated by medical experts, the Food and Drug Administration has ordered products containing the ingredient banned from sale in the United States. The Jones Company sends all of its sugar-free J. C. Cola (which contains subsugural) to European supermarkets because the sweetener has not been banned there. *Is it acceptable for the Jones Company to send an arguably unsafe product to another market without waiting for further evidence?*

Scenario 4   The Acme Company sells industrial supplies through its own sales force, which calls on company purchasing agents. Acme has found that giving small gifts to purchasing agents helps cement cordial relationships and creates goodwill. Acme follows the policy that bigger orders justify bigger gifts to purchasing agents. The gifts range from sporting event tickets to outboard motors and snowmobiles. Acme does not give gifts to personnel at companies with known explicit policies prohibiting the acceptance of such gifts. *Assuming no laws are violated, is Acme's policy of providing gifts to purchasing agents morally proper?*

Scenario 5   The Buy American Electronics Company has been selling its highly rated System X Color TV sets (21, 19, and 12 inches) for $700, $500, and $300, respectively. These prices have been relatively uncompetitive in the market. After some study, Buy American substitutes several cheaper components (which engineering says may slightly reduce the quality of performance) and passes on the savings to the consumer in the form of a $100 price reduction on each model. Buy American institutes a price-oriented promotional campaign that neglects to mention that the second-generation System X sets are different from the first. *Is the company's competitive strategy ethical?*

MANAGING SOCIAL RESPONSIBILITY

Many managers have accepted the idea that corporate social responsibility is an integral part of a company's overall strategy. The key elements of integrating social responsibility into an organization's strategic management process are discussed below.

Environmental Analysis and Organizational Direction

Like every element of strategy development, social responsibility begins with environmental analysis. Managers analyze both problems and opportunities in the environment that affect their firm's impact on society and then decide what areas require further investigation. Organizational vision, mission, and core values guide the determination of areas of social responsibility or social involvement that raise special concerns.

Strategy Formulation

Once areas of concern about social responsibility have been identified and studied, strategy formulation for social action begins. The object is to develop appropriate responses to issues, choosing among many alternatives. For example, a firm could deal with problems associated with poor product performance by improving guarantees, installing consumer complaint hotlines, offering more detailed label information, removing products from the market, and modifying products.

Strategy Implementation

Implementation puts a formulated strategy into action, which entails assigning responsibility to individuals or groups, providing adequate information, and establishing controls to make sure the strategy is implemented efficiently. For example, Procter & Gamble developed its own consumer service department to handle consumer complaints and requests for information. In a recent year, it received over 670,000 mail and telephone contacts about its products. The consumer service department employs 75 people—30 to answer calls and the rest to answer letters and analyze data. Clearly, implementing this strategy entailed considerable expense and effort. P&G managers consider the system a very effective "distant, early warning signal" of product problems.[12]

Strategic Control

Strategic control activities help a firm to fulfill its social responsibility by measuring the results of the implemented strategy and changing it, if necessary. The specific areas in which individual companies actually take such measurements vary with their specific social objectives, but firms should probably consider four general areas:[13]

1. *Economic functional area.* A measurement should indicate whether or not the organization is producing goods and services that people need, creating jobs, paying fair wages, and ensuring worker safety. This measurement gives some indication of the organization's economic contribution to society.
2. *Quality-of-life area.* In this area, measurement should focus on determining whether the organization is improving or degrading the general quality of life in society. Producing high-quality goods, dealing fairly with employees and customers, and making an effort to preserve the natural environment could all help to assure the organization that it is upholding or improving the general quality of life. As an example, some people brand cigarette companies as socially irresponsible because they produce goods that damage the health of society overall.
3. *Social investment area.* This area deals with the degree to which the organization is investing both money and human resources to solve community social problems. The socially responsible organization might assist community organizations that promote education, charities, and the arts.

4. *Problem-solving area.* Measurements in this area should focus on the degree to which the organization deals with social problems themselves, as opposed to the symptoms of those problems. Such activities as participating in long-range community planning and conducting studies to pinpoint social problems would generally be construed as dealing with social problems rather than merely addressing their symptoms.

An organization may conduct a **social audit,** or use other reporting mechanisms, to take social responsibility measurements such as those we have listed. The basic steps in a social audit are monitoring, measuring, and appraising all aspects of an organization's social responsibility performance. The audit itself can be performed either by organization personnel or by outside consultants.

One aspect of social responsibility is public accounting on environmental issues. Table 9.6 is an excerpt from an environmental report prepared by

---

TABLE 9.6

A section of the 1994 General Motors Corporation Environmental Report (Detroit: Environmental and Energy Staff Communications 1994, p. 5).

ENVIRONMENTAL PROFESSIONALS

Currently, over 500 environmental professionals are employed at GM in the stationary source field. In addition, over 100 scientists are engaged in research and development activities. Thousands of our designers and engineers have responsibility for emissions control, fuel economy, and/or vehicle recycling as basic elements of their jobs. GM encourages professional development by offering a variety of training and educational opportunities:

- A specialized co-op program has been initiated in 1994 with four major universities for stationary source training. Mobile source environmental professionals have participated in GM's co-op programs for many years.
- GM's tuition assistance program pays eligible expenses for courses leading to most associate, undergraduate or graduate degrees from accredited institutions. Eligible expenses are also covered for course fees for job-related and certain professional development seminars.
- Corporate contracts have been established with various suppliers and learning institutions for specialized training and regulatory updates.
- GM has developed in-house training programs covering subjects such as wastewater treatment technologies, asbestos removal, chlorofluorocarbon handling, vehicle emissions, and fuel economy.

GM environmental professionals are updated on environmental initiatives and corporate policies through a variety of mechanisms:

- The first annual GM Environmental Engineers Conference was held in 1993 and included presentations regarding GM environmental initiatives and policies. Workshops were structured around pertinent environmental issues.
- Regulatory/legislative direction meetings provide in-depth updates on pertinent issues for all media including air, water, waste, remediation, and toxic substances. Summary updates are provided to environmental engineers through various internal communications. For example, GM's quarterly *Waste Watch* newsletter communicates waste minimization initiatives/projects and recommended waste management practices.

Employees are encouraged to submit suggestions for improvement in all company operations including environmental issues through the Quality Network Suggestion Program. In addition, the corporation's waste reduction program encourages the establishment of teams at each facility whereby employee suggestions for pollution prevention and waste management can be evaluated and incorporated into facility operating plans. In 1993, GM established the "GM Awareline," a 24-hour hotline that employees are encouraged to use to anonymously report actions contrary to corporate policy, possible criminal wrongdoings, and emergency or life-threatening situations.

SOURCE: Courtesy of General Motors Corporation.

General Motors Corporation. As you can see, the table focuses on company involvement with environmental professionals. Overall, the General Motors environmental report covers many other topics, including workplace hazards, pollution standards, waste management, and use of energy. The format of environmental reports vary from company to company according to management judgments regarding how best to present data and specific responsibility issues facing a company.

SUMMARY

In this chapter, we examined the social and ethical dimensions of strategic management. First, we outlined the classical view that companies should not assume any responsibility beyond their obligation to make a profit, and the contemporary view that businesses do have a responsibility to maintain and advance the welfare of society at large. We found that many businesses' activities are supported by both viewpoints and that the degree to which a firm should seek to achieve purely social objectives depends on many considerations. Then we noted several areas in which firms can exhibit social responsibility, such as concern for consumers, for employees, for the environment, and for society in general.

Next we investigated four major influences on businesses that shape their perspectives on social responsibility and curb the inappropriate use of their considerable power. These include legal influences, such as laws and government regulatory agencies; the political pressure brought to bear by various groups such as consumer advocates; the controls that competing firms exert on one another; and the ethical influences that are exhibited in many firms' self-regulation of their business conduct. We also identified three major factors—personal ethics, culture, and systems—that collectively shape the ethical climate of a firm.

Finally, we analyzed the effect of managing social and ethical issues on the strategic management process, offering examples of ways in which social responsibility can be taken into account in the course of conducting an environmental analysis, setting an organizational direction, and formulating, implementing, and controlling strategy. We examined the social audit and environmental report as effective means of appraising an organization's social responsibility performance.

KEY TERMS

stakeholder, p. 219
ethical responsibility, p. 220
social responsibility, p. 220
classical view of social responsibility, p. 220
contemporary view of social responsibility, p. 221

pyramid of corporate social responsibility, p. 223
deceptive advertising, p. 228
special-interest group, p. 229
consumerism, p. 230
social audit, p. 236

CHECKLIST   Analyzing Social Responsibility in Problems and Cases

__ 1. Does the problem or case involve social responsibility as an important concern?

—   2. Does any legislation require the organization to perform in a socially responsible manner?

—   3. Would performing social responsibility activities be economically profitable to the firm in the long run?

—   4. Can the organization afford to engage in social responsibility activities, and would they result in goodwill or other noneconomic benefits from one or more stakeholder groups?

—   5. What specific stakeholders and area(s) of social responsibility does the problem or case address?

—   6. Are any political forces attempting to change the firm's activities? If so, do they have sound arguments?

—   7. Do any competitive influences merit consideration?

—   8. Does the problem or case involve an ethical dilemma that requires a decision?

—   9. Does the organization have a well-developed program for dealing with social responsibility issues?

—   10. Would a social audit be useful for identifying problems and suggesting appropriate solutions?

Additional Readings

Dickson, Reginald. "The Business of Equal Opportunity." *Harvard Business Review,* January/February 1992, p. 46.

Nichols, Nancy A. "Profits with a Purpose: An Interview with Tom Chappell." *Harvard Business Review,* November/December 1992, p. 86.

Pearsall, A. E. "Corporate Redemption and the Seven Deadly Sins." *Harvard Business Review,* May/June 1992, p. 65.

Smith, N. Craig. *Morality and the Market: Consumer Pressure for Corporate Accountability.* London: Routledge, 1990.

Stark, Amber. "What's the Matter with Business Ethics?" *Harvard Business Review,* May/June 1993, p. 38.

Steidlmeier, Paul. *People and Profits: The Ethics of Capitalism.* Englewood Cliffs, N.J.: Prentice-Hall, 1992.

Velasquez, Manuel. *Business Ethics,* 3d ed. Englewood Cliffs, N.J.: Prentice-Hall, 1992.

CASE

ECONOMICS VERSUS SOCIAL POLICY AT STRIDE RITE

Public-service plaques line the walls of Stride Rite's Cambridge, Massachusetts, headquarters. Harvard University has honored the firm for "improving the quality of life" in its community and the nation. The shoe company has contributed 5 percent of its pre-tax profits to a charitable foundation, sent 100,000 pairs of sneakers to strife-torn Mozambique, paid Harvard graduate students to work in a Cambodian refugee camp, given scholarships to inner-city youths, permitted employees to tutor disadvantaged children on company time, and pioneered on-site facilities for day-care and elder-care.

While doing good, Stride Rite has done well. It has posted profits, usually at record levels, for the past 32 quarters. In 1993, its sales were expected to top $625 million, more than double the company's 1986 level. Its stock price has increased sixfold since then, making it a favorite of the New York Stock Exchange and socially conscious investors.

Just a few blocks away from its new headquarters, however, Stride Rite's old corporate office building sits surrounded by the empty lots and crumbling streets of Boston's tough Roxbury neighborhood. Here, 2,500 people once made Keds sneakers and Sperry Top-sider shoes; today, it houses 175 workers whose jobs will be gone by next summer. Stride Rite is closing this warehouse and one other to move its distribution operations to Kentucky. With local unemployment near 30 percent, Stride Rite's citations for good works ring hollow.

In the past decade, Stride Rite has prospered, in part, by closing 15 factories, mostly in the Northeast and several in depressed areas, and moving most of its production to various low-cost, Asian countries. The company still employs 2,500 workers in the United States, down from a peak of about 6,000.

Boston officials met frustration trying to retain Stride Rite's blue-collar jobs. They argue that good deeds are not enough; they want Stride Rite to meet the basic need of providing jobs in depressed areas, even at the expense of profits. "The most socially responsible thing a company can do is to give a person a job," says Donald Gillis, executive director of Boston's Economic Development and Industrial Corp.

"Putting jobs into places where it doesn't make economic sense is a dilution of corporate and community wealth," argues Stride Rite Chairman Ervin Shames. The company says that it could hardly avoid pulling out of Roxbury—and the rest of New England—over the past two decades to shift most of its production overseas. As much as they wish to link their corporate and social responsibilities, the company's directors concede that their primary obligation is to their stockholders. If Stride Rite cannot compete, say executives, it cannot afford its social programs, and it may not even survive. "It was a difficult decision," admits Shames. "Our hearts said, 'stay,' but our heads said, 'move.'"

Shames adds that the company will save millions by moving its distribution to the Midwest—a central location near most of its customers. The new distribution center in Louisville will eliminate 800 to 1,200 miles on some truck routes, speeding delivery by two and one-half to four days.

DISCUSSION QUESTIONS

1. Describe and evaluate Stride Rite's strategic reactions to changes in its competitive environment.

2. Does Stride Rite's dilemma and its resolution prove that the classical view of social responsibility is winning over the contemporary view?

3. Should company stakeholders demand further accountability from Stride Rite regarding its social responsibility activities?

SOURCE: Joseph Pereira, *The Wall Street Journal*, reprinted as "Split Personality," in *Utne Reader*, September/October 1993, pp. 61–66.

Notes

1. Portions of this chapter are based on Samuel C. Certo, *Modern Management: Diversity, Quality, Ethics, and the Global Environment*, 6th ed. (Boston: Allyn & Bacon, 1994), Chap. 3; and J. Paul Peter and Jerry C. Olson, *Consumer Behavior and Marketing Strategy*, 3d ed. (Homewood, Ill.: Richard D. Irwin, 1993), Chap. 21.

2. Philip Kotler, "What Consumerism Means for Marketers," *Harvard Business Review*, May/June 1972, pp. 48–57.
3. Susan Caminiti, "The Payoff from a Good Reputation," *Fortune*, February 10, 1992, p. 74.
4. Manuel Velasquez, *Business Ethics*, 3d ed. (Englewood Cliffs, N.J.: Prentice-Hall, 1992).
5. Milton Friedman, *Capitalism and Freedom* (Chicago: University of Chicago Press, 1962), p. 133, as reported in George A. Steiner and John F. Steiner, *Business, Government, and Society* (New York: Random House, 1985), p. 236.
6. Keith Davis, "Five Propositions for Social Responsibility," *Business Horizons*, June 1975, pp. 19–24. Also see Peter F. Drucker, "The New Meaning of Corporate Social Responsibility," *California Management Review*, Winter 1984, pp. 53–63; Jerry W. Anderson, "Social Responsibility and the Corporation," *Business Horizons*, July/August 1986, pp. 22–27; Jean B. McGuire, Alison Sundgren, and Thomas Schneeweis, "Corporate Social Responsibility and Firm Financial Performance," *Academy of Management Journal* 31 (December 1988), pp. 854–872; and Richard J. Klonski, "Foundational Considerations in the Corporate Social Responsibility Debate," *Business Horizons*, July/August 1991, pp. 14–28.
7. William L. Wilkie, Dennis L. McNeill, and Michael B. Mazis, "Marketing's 'Scarlet Letter': The Theory and Practice of Corrective Advertising," *Journal of Marketing*, Spring 1984, p. 13. Reprinted from *Journal of Marketing*, published by the American Marketing Association.
8. Ann P. Harvey, *Contacts in Consumerism 1980–1981* (Washington, D.C.: Fraser/Associates, 1980).
9. Paul N. Bloom and Stephen A. Greyser, "The Maturing of Consumerism," *Harvard Business Review*, November/December 1981, pp. 130–139.
10. Gene R. Laczniak, "Framework for Analyzing Marketing Ethics," *Journal of Macromarketing*, Spring 1983, pp. 7–18. Also see Harvey C. Bunke, "Should We Teach Business Ethics?" *Business Horizons*, July/August 1988, pp. 2–8; LaRue Tone Hosmer, "Adding Ethics to the Business Curriculum," *Business Horizons*, July/August 1988, pp. 9–15; Bruce H. Drake and Eileen Drake, "Ethical and Legal Aspects of Managing Corporate Cultures," *California Management Review*, Winter 1988, pp. 107–123; and R. Edward Freeman and Jeanne Liedtka, "Corporate Social Responsibility: A Critical Approach," *Business Horizons*, July/August 1991, pp. 87–99.
11. Gene R. Laczniak, "Framework for Analyzing Marketing Ethics," *Journal of Macromarketing*, Spring 1983, p. 8. Reprinted by permission of the publisher, Business Research Division, University of Colorado, Boulder.
12. "Customers: P&G's Pipeline to Product Problems," *Business Week*, June 11, 1984, p. 167. Also see Brian Dumaine, "P&G Rewrites the Marketing Rules," *Fortune*, November 6, 1989, pp. 34–48.
13. Frank H. Cassell, "The Social Cost of Doing Business," *MSU Business Topics*, Autumn 1974, pp. 19–26.

PART IV

Critical Functions for Strategic Management

We have emphasized from the start that effective strategic management is essentially a cross-functional process, relying on a variety of interdependent skills to create viable organizations by formulating and implementing innovative and defensible strategies. In this section, we explore three of those critical functions—operations (Chapter 10), finance (Chapter 11), and marketing (Chapter 12)—and the concepts and techniques that each contributes to the strategic management process. Students who have recently completed courses in these areas should approach the next three chapters as a focused review, or refresher course, on these topics.

Students should always treat strategic management, either in real time on the job or in a case analysis, as an integrative process, drawing on every skill and technique available to a manager. The concepts and tools discussed in Part IV are essential building blocks; these chapters certainly cannot cover everything a manager needs to know about the critical functions of operations, marketing, and finance.

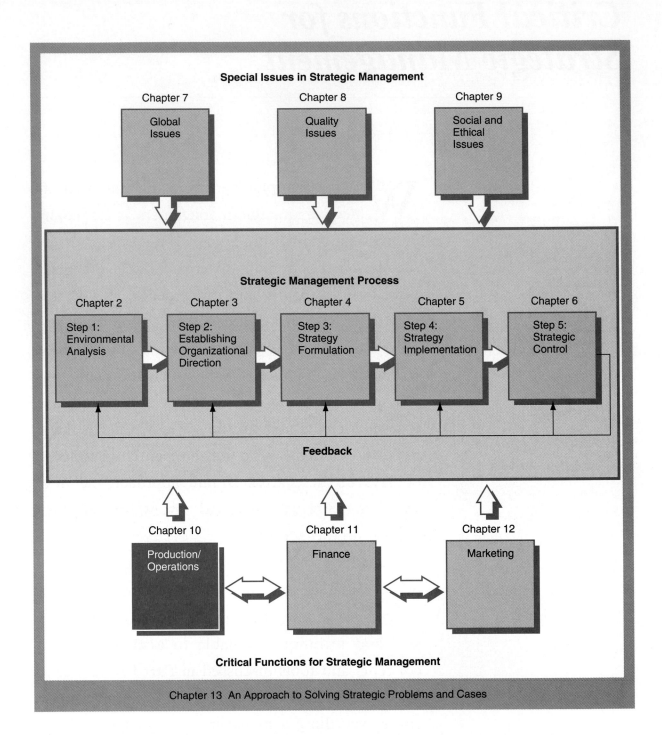

Special Issues in Strategic Management

Chapter 7

Global Issues

Chapter 8

Quality Issues

Chapter 9

Social and Ethical Issues

Strategic Management Process

Chapter 2

Step 1: Environmental Analysis

Chapter 3

Step 2: Establishing Organizational Direction

Chapter 4

Step 3: Strategy Formulation

Chapter 5

Step 4: Strategy Implementation

Chapter 6

Step 5: Strategic Control

Feedback

Chapter 10

Production/ Operations

Chapter 11

Finance

Chapter 12

Marketing

Critical Functions for Strategic Management

Chapter 13 An Approach to Solving Strategic Problems and Cases

CHAPTER 10

Operations and Strategic Management

This chapter covers the operations function, one of the major functional areas of organizations.[1] In the first part of the chapter, we explain what the operations function does. We examine its context by briefly reviewing its place among the other functions in the organization, and describe the various operations systems that have evolved to produce goods or provide services in manufacturing and non-manufacturing settings.

The second part of the chapter addresses the relationship of operations to strategic management. We note the vital association between marketing strategy and the operations function, for example, and the importance of considering the firm's operations capabilities when formulating any corporate strategy. Next we discuss strategy decisions for the operations function itself, focusing especially on the choice of which production characteristics the operations function will emphasize. Finally, we analyze the effect on operations strategy of product design.

Readers will notice the thematic relation of Chapter 10 to the discussion in Chapter 8 of quality issues. However, in Chapter 10 we extend the range of techniques and issues we consider to encompass the entire operations function.

ESSENTIALS OF ORGANIZATIONAL OPERATIONS

Operations Function

The **operations function** is performed by members of an organization who produce the goods or provide the services that it offers to the public. The operations function, also called the *production function,* is one of three primary functions within a business, the other two being finance and marketing. In a typical business, however, the operations function employs the greater number of people and uses the greatest portion of the firm's controllable assets. Clearly, operations is a very important function, and one that certainly merits detailed study. Our purpose in this chapter is to discuss the various activities within the operations function and to explore how these activities can affect strategic management.

Other Functions

The operations function is only one part of a larger system—the entire organization. It is interrelated with other functions in the organization, so its plans and actions must mesh across functions for the total organization to achieve its full potential. Before we discuss the operations function in greater detail, let us briefly review the other business functions—marketing and finance—as well as some secondary or supporting functions.

Marketing   The **marketing function** consists of organizational activities that focus on discovering or developing a need or demand for the company's goods and services. Marketing personnel seek to maintain a responsive working relationship with consumers or potential consumers. Profit-seeking companies cannot long survive without markets for their goods or services. Not-for-profit organizations, such as government agencies, may survive without genuine needs or demands for their services, but such situations represent a misapplication of a society's resources. A nonbusiness enterprise performs marketing activities when it determines the extent and location of the need for its services and when it makes the availability of its services known to the public. The marketing function is discussed in detail in Chapter 12.

Finance   The **finance function** consists primarily of organizational activities aimed at obtaining funds for planned activities and guiding the wise use of those funds. The finance function in nonbusiness enterprises may include lobbying for government support or seeking public contributions through the efforts of volunteers. The finance function includes efforts to budget and allocate funds to the various subdivisions of the firm and review of their expenditures. The finance function is discussed in detail in Chapter 11.

Supporting Functions   As explained in the discussion of value chain analysis in Chapter 4, functions other than operations, marketing, and finance exist within organizations, and they receive varying emphasis, depending on the organization's purposes, its external environment, and the persons within the organization who shape responses to the environment. If a company produces a tangible product, it must perform some research and development, design, and engineering functions. Nonmanufacturing companies must perform similar functions to decide what services to offer and how to provide them. A restaurant, for example, must decide whether to provide food for patrons through service at tables or at self-service cafeteria counters.

Because organizations require human effort, they must recruit personnel, train them, and distribute benefits to them so that they may share in the profits generated by the organization's work. The human resource function is critically important to the organization, in general, and to the operations function, in particular. Additional information on the human resource function and its relationship to strategic management is integrated throughout this text.

Interdependence of Functions   Public relations are important to all primary and secondary functions. Public attitudes can affect the success of attempts to sell stock or to borrow money. The public's attitude also affects the company's ability to sell its product and recruit competent employees to produce its goods and services.

Public relations activities illustrate some of the interrelationships among functions within businesses. Strategists may divide a company into smaller units, each with boundaries that recognize the human capacity to understand and supervise, but the parts still are only *parts*. They must work together, across functions, to make the total organization work properly.

The three major functions within a business are interdependent. Sufficient financial resources and operations to produce a product are of little value if the product finds no market. Sufficient financial resources and a market for a product are of little value if one cannot provide the product. The ability to produce a product and a market for the product are not sufficient if the organization lacks the necessary capital to employ personnel, buy raw materials, and put the other capabilities into action. All of the functions in an organization both contribute to the whole and depend on contributions from the remainder of the organization. For this reason, many firms in the 1990s are busily experimenting with new ways to integrate the work of the critical functions more efficiently. For example, they often establish cross-functional teams to develop, produce, and market new products rapidly, to improve and accelerate strategic decision making and enhance performance.

In this section, we consider each function separately as a manageable unit, but it is important to keep in mind that the other functions are necessary to, and dependent on, the function being studied. Figure 10.1 shows the interrelationships of business functions.

Today's Broader View of the Operations Function

The operations function is sometimes called the *production function,* or the *production and operations function.* In the past, the term *production* sometimes connoted only manufacturing of tangible items; later the term *operations* was added, or substituted, to include nonmanufacturing operations. Today the term *production* often has a broader meaning, referring to the production of goods or of services. Our earlier definition stated that the operations function is responsible for producing goods or providing services. In this chapter the terms *production, operations,* and *production and operations* all refer to the function in either manufacturing or nonmanufacturing settings.

Manufacturing operations perform some physical or chemical processes such as sawing, sewing, machining, welding, grinding, blending, or refining to convert some tangible raw materials into tangible products. All other operations that do not actually make goods can be called *nonmanufacturing* or **service operations.** Customers deal with some of these nonmanufacturing companies to obtain purely intangible services such as advice or instruction; they

FIGURE 10.1
Critical Functions within Organizations

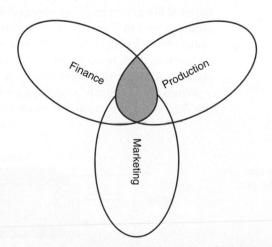

may seek help in completing tax forms, for example. Customers deal with other nonmanufacturing companies, such as wholesalers or retailers, to obtain goods, but these companies do not make the goods. These companies primarily serve their customers by transporting, packaging, storing, and the like, rather than by performing manufacturing processes. Thus, our major criterion for classifying operations depends on whether these operations manufacture goods or provide some type of service operation, even though they may provide tangible goods or some less tangible service to customers.

Operations: Providing a Product or Service   When viewed at a general or conceptual level, all types of production operations have some common characteristics. The most obvious common ground is the system's purpose or function; the production system creates the goods or services offered by the organization. The production system must transform some set of inputs into a set of outputs. All production systems share this element, illustrated schematically in Figure 10.2. The types of inputs, transformations, and outputs vary among operations.

Manufacturing operations transform or convert such inputs as raw materials, labor skills, management skills, capital, and sales revenue into some product, which the organization then sells. Other outputs are wages that flow into the economy, environmental effects, social influences, and other, even less obvious factors. The production system is a part of a larger system—the company. The company is a part of a larger system—the community. As the system boundaries expand, it becomes more difficult to determine all of the inputs, outputs, and transformations.

Service operations also transform a set of inputs into a set of outputs. A restaurant uses such inputs as meat, potatoes, lettuce, the chef's skills, servers' skills, and many others. Some of the transformation processes involve storing supplies, blending ingredients into desirable combinations, and altering the form of the inputs by cooking, freezing, heating, and transporting them to the proper tables at the proper times. Less tangible operations involve providing a pleasant atmosphere, perhaps even including entertainment. The organization hopes that its outputs include satisfied patrons. Other outputs include wages and purchase payments sent into the economy and refuse sent into the refuse collection system (which is yet another service system).

Educational institutions use such inputs as books, students, and instructional skills to produce knowledgeable and skilled individuals as output. Hospitals use scientific equipment, professional skills, and tender loving care to transform sick people into well ones. Repair shops use repair parts, equipment, and worker skills to transform malfunctioning inputs into properly functioning outputs. All types of operations, then, transform inputs into outputs.

When the output is a tangible product, the transformations performed by the operations function are intended to increase the utility of the inputs by

FIGURE 10.2
Conceptual Diagram
of a Production System

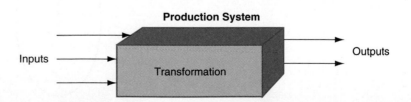

changing either the physical form of the inputs or the time or place at which the outputs are available. Operations that change the physical form of the input include factories, landscapers, restaurants, upholstery shops, ice cream shops, and laundries. Some operations provide access to special skills or improve convenience as part of their services to customers. Operations such as wholesalers, retailers, transporters, and the postal system provide materials-handling operations to change the places at which their outputs are available. Banks, public warehouses, and cold-storage plants for food or fur storage perform inventory functions to make outputs available at different times. Even though the inputs, transformations, and outputs may vary, the general characteristic of transforming inputs into more usable outputs holds true for all operations.

Manufacturing Operations   The production facilities and methods that a manufacturing company uses are sometimes referred to as its production system. A company often devises a production system to match the way it conducts its business. More specifically, this system's design is related to the stage at which the company plans to hold inventory in order to serve its customers more quickly than they could purchase all of the materials and convert them into the final product themselves. At the time a customer's order is received, the firm might hold the items to fill that order (1) as finished goods, (2) as standard modules waiting to be assembled, or (3) as basic inputs without any prior processing. The terms presented in the following paragraph characterize the degree of processing that is done after the customer's order is received.

Some companies are **make-to-stock producers** that complete products and place them in stock prior to receipt of the customer's order. The end item is shipped from finished-goods inventory after receipt of a customer order. In contrast, a **make-to-order producer** completes the end item after receipt of the customer's order. For a unique, custom-designed item, the customer will probably have to wait for the manufacturer to purchase many of the materials and perform the production work because the producer cannot anticipate what each customer might want and have the necessary raw materials and components on hand to shorten the production lead time. If it uses some components or materials frequently, however, the producer may keep some of them in stock—particularly if the lead time to purchase or produce these items is long.

The Skills Module discusses such a balancing act by a manufacturer of outdoor apparel. When a company produces standard-design, optional modules ahead of time and assembles a particular combination of these modules after the customer orders, the business is said to be an **assemble-to-order producer.**[2] An example of an assemble-to-order producer is an automobile factory that, in response to a dealer's order, provides an automatic or manual transmission, air conditioner, sound system, interior options, and specific engine options as well as a specified body style and color. The auto manufacturer would already have ordered many of the components or started them into production when the dealer placed the order. Otherwise the lead time to deliver the automobile would be much longer. With these terms in mind, we will now discuss the two major categories of production facilities and methods.

Continuous Production   A **continuous production system** arranges equipment and work stations in a sequence according to the steps to convert

SKILLS MODULE
Sport Obermeyer, Accurate Response and Product Design

INTRODUCTION

We have presented both product design and production systems as integral operations and strategy issues. Review the following situation, and then complete the skill development exercise that follows to help you develop your ability to appropriately manage product design within a production system as a component of overall strategy.

SITUATION

For more than 30 years, Sport Obermeyer's design-and-sales cycle was relatively straightforward. Production commitments for its fashion skiwear were based on firm orders, and fall delivery dates provided ample time for efficient manufacturing. The process began in March: design the product, make samples, and show the samples to retailers; in March and April, after receiving retail orders, place production orders with suppliers; in September and October, receive goods at the Denver distribution center and ship the goods immediately to retail outlets.

But the company's success and growing volume made its system obsolete by the 1980s. Unable to reserve sufficient production slots during the critical summer months, Sport Obermeyer began booking production the previous November—about a year before the goods would be sold—based on speculation about what retailers would order.

In addition, pressured by the need to reduce manufacturing costs and increase variety, the company developed a more complex supply chain. It sourced fabric and findings from three countries to be sewn in a fourth and finally delivered in the United States. This process greatly increased lead times just as earlier delivery had become paramount for dealers carrying Sport Obermeyer's new children's line; sales in the booming category were particularly strong in August, during the back-to-school season.

To deal with these problems—lengthening supply chains, limited supplier capacity, and retailers' demands for early delivery—Sport Obermeyer began a variety of quick-response initiatives to reduce lead times. The company introduced computerized systems that could process orders and compute raw-material requirements, halving the time that it had previously spent on these activities. The difficulty of reducing lead times to obtain raw materials led the company to an operational turnaround; it began to anticipate its materials requirements and preposition stocks in a warehouse in the Far East. With materials in place, Sport Obermeyer was able to begin manufacturing as soon as it received orders.

As delivery due dates approached, the company relied on air freight to expedite delivery from the Far East to Denver. By 1990, those changes had reduced delivery lead times by more than a month.

In February, Sport Obermeyer invited 25 of its largest retail customers to Aspen to preview the new fall line; persuading them to place orders earlier gave the company valuable, early insight on the likely popularity of specific styles and colors. Every year since the "Early Write" program began, its orders have accounted for about 20 percent of Sport Obermeyer's total sales.

SKILL DEVELOPMENT EXERCISE

Sport Obermeyer has successfully reduced its manufacturing and delivery lead times and solicited firm, early orders. What positive or negative effect could this strategy, especially anticipating materials needs, have on product design? If the most effective time to consider how to manufacture a product is during the design process, what role can Sport Obermeyer's product design department play to further reduce lead time?

SOURCE: Marshall L. Fisher, Janice H. Hammond, Walter R. Obermeyer, and Ananth Raman, "Making Supply Meet Demand in an Uncertain World," *Harvard Business Review*, May/June 1994, pp. 87–90.

the input raw materials into the desired component or assembly. The route of jobs are fixed, and the setup of the equipment seldom changes from one product to another. Materials flow relatively continuously during the production process. This type of production, sometimes called *repetitive manufacturing*, produces high volumes of discrete units, usually with a fixed sequence of material flow. Since the material flow path and processing steps are fixed, this type of production frequently turns out standard make-to-stock products.

Examples are production lines or assembly lines for the production of radios, televisions, refrigerators, or other products that may be produced and stocked in perhaps a few standard models. The customer selects a particular standard model. Continuous production might turn out items that are made to order or assembled to order if the volume is sufficient to justify a fixed, special-purpose production system.

Some continuous production operations produce products that blend together in bulk rather than being sold as discrete units. Some products of this type of operation include petroleum products, flour, cement, and liquid chemicals. The industries that produce these types of products are sometimes called **process industries,** particularly if some physical or chemical reaction is used. (Chemical processing can also produce batches of more specialized material; this is sometimes called *batch-process production.*)

Intermittent or Job Shop Production   An **intermittent production system** or *job shop* differs greatly from the continuous system in that it is designed to provide much more flexibility. This type of production system groups and organizes production equipment or work stations according to the functions or processes they perform. Different types of products flow in batches corresponding to individual orders. Each batch or lot might follow a different route through the functional work centers, depending on the requirements of the type of product being made. Products could be made for stock or to order, but generally this type of production is associated with make-to-order businesses.

Continuous and intermittent production systems represent opposite ends of a continuum that measures the degree of specificity of a production system (see Figure 10.3). At one end of the continuum are production facilities designed specifically to produce one particular standard item and optimized for the materials movement and production steps required to make that item. Near the other end of the continuum are job shops; they are not ideal for any single product, but are capable of producing wide varieties of items. Many production facilities embody features of both of these production approaches. They lie somewhere on the continuum between a job shop and a continuous production operation.

Lying at the flexible end of the continuum is the low-volume type of operation often referred to as a **project.** Usually, projects have relatively long durations, and the same personnel often are assigned to a project for a significant part of this time. In the manufacturing category, projects include such items as ships, bridges, buildings, and large, specialized machines.

Nonmanufacturing Operations   Nonmanufacturing operations, or service operations, do not produce tangible outputs. Like manufacturing operations,

FIGURE 10.3
Degree of Specificity
of Production Systems

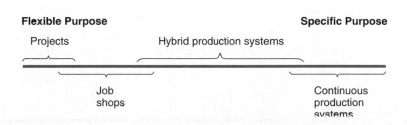

nonmanufacturing operations can be subdivided according to the degree of standardization of their outputs—that is, whether they are **standard services** or **custom services**—and/or the processes they perform. Some nonmanufacturing activities resemble projects because they involve the activities of teams of people over periods of time. A nonmanufacturing project might be a software package or a training program. Table 10.1 displays a classification system for manufacturing and nonmanufacturing operations based on the degree of standardization of their output.

TABLE 10.1

Classification of Types of Operations

Types of Operations	Manufacturing, or Goods-producing, Operations	Nonmanufacturing, or Service, Operations
Project: activity of long duration and low volume	Building a bridge, dam, or house; preparing for a banquet	Research project, development of software
Unit or batch: activity of short duration and low volume, producing custom goods or services	Job shop: making industrial hardware; printing personalized stationery; making drapes	Custom service: offering charter air or bus service; cleaning carpets; repairing autos; providing health care or counseling services; providing hair care; translating a foreign-language book for a publisher; designing costumes for a theatrical production; public warehousing; providing special-delivery mail service
Mass production: activity of short duration and high volume, producing standard goods or services	Continuous operation: making light bulbs, refrigerators, television sets, automobiles	Standard service: providing fast food, standard insurance policies, scheduled air or bus service, dry cleaning, personal checking accounts, regular mail service, distribution and wholesaling of standardized products; processing photographic film
Process industry: continuous processing of a homogeneous material	Continuous operation: processing chemicals, refining oil, milling flour, manufacturing paper	

Nonmanufacturing operations can be divided into categories according to another classification scheme that provides useful insights into the management issues they raise. Some nonmanufacturing operations deal primarily with tangible outputs, even though these operations do not manufacture the items. These types of operations, such as wholesale distributors and transportation companies, can utilize many of the same materials management principles and techniques that a manufacturing operation might use. The vital ideas of materials handling are also important in some operations that deal with tangible items.

Other nonmanufacturing operations deal in intangible products, or services, as their primary outputs. One should recognize that these service operations do not necessarily provide *only* services or *only* goods. Facilitating goods may be provided with services, and facilitating services may be provided with goods. For example, customers can obtain the same goods (although in different forms) from a grocery store or a restaurant. A grocery store seems primarily like a provider of goods. Restaurant customers primarily want services like selecting, preparing, and serving food, which is actually a tangible good. "Servicing" a car may include installation of some parts. The service is provided by someone who knows which parts to replace and how to replace them, and who spends time to perform this service.

Operations that deal primarily in services can be further divided according to the degree to which the customer participates in the process. Many services are custom services, so the customer often has some contact with the service provider. The customer does not have to be present, however, during the process for some types of services, such as having clothes laundered or watches repaired. Professor Richard Chase states that systems with more customer contact are more difficult to understand and control.[3] Table 10.2 displays a classification of nonmanufacturing operations, with some examples of each type of operation.

TABLE 10.2

Classification of Nonmanufacturing Operations

Nonmanufacturing Operations		
Providers of Tangible Products	**Providers of Services**	
Mail service	Services in which the customer is not a participant.	Services in which the customer is a participant.
Library services		
Wholesale and retail distribution	Examples:	Examples:
Examples:	Preparing tax forms	Health care
Television sets	Architectural design	Hair care
Radios	Landscaping	Travel
Watches	Cleaning clothes	Legal advice
Refrigerators	Repairing watches, automobiles, appliances, etc.	Financial advice
Air conditioners		Marriage counseling
	Rating and issuing insurance	

OPERATIONS AND STRATEGIC MANAGEMENT

Different Operations, Different Strategies

A company's overall strategy addresses many broad issues, perhaps even including plans for social responsibility, stockholder relations, and employee relations. One important aspect of the overall direction of a firm is its competitive strategy. At a very general level, one can identify some characteristics of strategies that are often associated with the types of operations functions previously introduced in this chapter. The strategy of a company with a custom product will tend to differ from that of a company with a more standardized product. Table 10.3 shows some general features of strategies for various types of operations.

Generally, companies can compete based on three primary features of their goods or services:

1. *Quality*   Do all of the characteristics of a product make it suitable and reliable for the customer's intended use?
2. *Price*   Is the cost to the customer over the life of the product affordable? Does it seem reasonable when compared to the quality of the product and other quality-to-price ratios available in the marketplace?
3. *Availability*   Can the product be obtained within a reasonable and competitive time?

To succeed in the marketplace, a product must be judged at least adequate on all three measures.

Operations: A Vital Element in Strategy

The operations function has great value as a competitive weapon in a company's strategy. Because it is the part of the firm that must produce the goods or provide the services that the consumer buys, the operations function plays an important role in implementing strategy. The operations function establishes the level of quality as a product is manufactured or as a service is provided. The operations function often encompasses the largest part of a company's human and capital assets. Thus, much of a product's cost is incurred within operations, and this cost affects the price that the firm charges and the profit margin it achieves. Finally, the ability of the operations function to perform determines to a great extent the ability of the company to have sufficient products available to meet delivery commitments.

It is clear, then, that the operations function has a critical influence on the cost, quality, and availability of the company's goods or services. In this way, operations strengths and weaknesses can have a great impact on the success of the company's overall strategy. Therefore, the capabilities of operations must be carefully considered when corporate strategy is formulated, and operations decisions must be consistent with corporate strategy so that the full potential of operations' resources can be harnessed in pursuit of the company's goals.

Strategy Decisions for Operations

Positioning Decisions   Strategy decisions at the top-management level and within the operations function affect how well the operations function contribute to the competitive effectiveness of a company. One broad strategy decision that is important in guiding and coordinating the actions of operations

TABLE 10.3			

Strategies Associated with Various Types of Operations

Type of Operation	Type of Product	Typical Process Characteristics	Typical Characteristics of Strategy
Service Project Job shop	Make to order as customer specifies	Use of broadly skilled workers and general-purpose equipment; emphasis on good initial planning of work, quality, flexibility	Selling diversity of capabilities and ability to provide features customers desire, ability to perform a quality job, ability to achieve reasonable delivery times
Continuous Process	Make for inventory a product designed to have features desired by many potential customers	Use of workers with narrower skills, specialized equipment, perhaps automation; emphasis on efficiency and cost control; good distribution system to make items readily available	Selling the desirability of features that are already designed into the product plus the desirability of the price, availability, service. Market research is important to ensure that product features are appropriate for the market.

is related to positioning. **Positioning** establishes the extent to which the production system will emphasize certain characteristics in order to achieve the greatest competitive advantage. Regardless of how desirable it may sound, no product can simultaneously be lowest in cost, highest in quality, and instantly available in abundance at numerous, convenient locations. Professor Steven Wheelwright recommends that a manufacturing company explicitly establish relative priorities for the four performance characteristics: cost efficiency, quality, dependability, and flexibility.[4] These performance characteristics can be briefly described as follows:

- *Cost efficiency*   A company that emphasizes cost efficiency will keep its capital, labor, and other operating costs low relative to those of other, similar companies.
- *Quality*   A company that emphasizes quality will consistently strive to provide a level of quality that is significantly superior to those of its competitors, even if it has to pay extra to do so. The Company Example tells how Motorola revised its operations to improve quality.

COMPANY EXAMPLE

Motorola Reverses Manufacturing Trends

Motorola tries to measure every task performed by every one of its 120,000 employees. The company calculates that this effort saved it $1.5 billion by reducing defects and simplifying processes last year.

Some of Motorola's factories have achieved such high quality that they've stopped counting defects per million units and starting working on defects per *billion*. Overall, the company's goal is to reduce its error rate tenfold every two years and to cut its cycle time tenfold every five years.

Motorola's Land Mobile Products factory in Plantation, Florida, had a long way to go back in 1990. The plant took as long as ten days to turn out a finished radio. To decide which models to make, the company's analysts churned out elaborate forecasts of consumer demand, which were rarely on target. In an effort to cut costs, Motorola began building components at a feeder plant in Malaysia, where labor costs are low, and shipping them to Plantation for final assembly.

Times have changed. Today, the plant no longer relies on forecasts or a feeder plant. Workers on Plantation's Jedi line (named after the Star Wars characters) can make a specific radio for a specific customer in just two hours. They juggle more than 500 variations.

A number of manufacturing innovations are credited for the plant's turnaround. Among them, palettes marked with binary codes now surround the U-shaped assembly line that carries the radios; the codes give instructions to the robots and the workers who monitor them. Even more important, a newly invented, computer-controlled soldering process eliminates the need for costly and time-consuming tool changes.

Motorola is now converting the two-way radio plant in Malaysia, as well as its other major operation in Ireland, into clones of Plantation's "focused flexible factory."

SOURCE: Ronald Henkoff, "Keeping Motorola on a Roll," *Fortune,* April 18, 1994, pp. 67–78.

- *Dependability* A company that stresses dependability can be relied on to have its goods available for customers or to deliver its goods or services on schedule, if at all possible.
- *Flexibility* A company that emphasizes flexibility will work to respond quickly to changes in product design, product mix, or production volume.

Positioning might be visualized as selecting a particular spot within the pyramid shown in Figure 10.4, and consistently operating within that area. The pyramid defines the relative priorities that can be assigned to each of the four performance characteristics. However, the portion of the pyramid that the company seeks to occupy is a strategic decision that must rest with the top management. If each part of a company tries to move in its own direction to respond to competitors' moves in that area, then the company's overall money, talents, and efforts will not be effectively expended. By trying to move in several directions simultaneously, such a company would fail to demonstrate a distinctive competence that would attract and retain customers, and customers could not rely on it for consistent treatment.

Although a company cannot simultaneously reach all corners of the pyramid shown in Figure 10.4, it can expand the range of the pyramid that it covers. This is quite different from bouncing inconsistently from one location to another within the pyramid. Expanding the range within the pyramid that a company consistently covers amounts to shortening one or more legs of the

FIGURE 10.4
Possible Positions of an
Operations Function

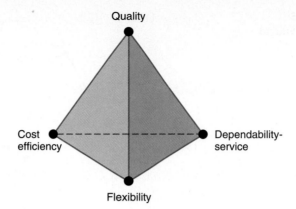

pyramid or making the pyramid smaller. A company can then cover a larger percentage of its pyramid than its competitors and leave less space for a competitor to develop a distinctive competence.

An example of shrinking the pyramid can be found in the operation of numerous Japanese companies. Through very careful and diligent efforts, these companies have controlled processes to prevent defects and have achieved superior quality. These actions have reduced the cost of screening and repairing defective work in the factory and the cost of warranty work in the field. In effect, these companies have simultaneously improved quality and cost so that they can cover a larger portion of the cost–quality leg of their pyramid. This effectively reduces the length of the cost–quality leg of the pyramid, as shown in Figure 10.5(a). Many Japanese manufacturers have also provided extensive training and cross training of their workers to develop multiskilled workers. This versatile work force, coupled with plant arrangements and equipment that can easily change over from one product to another, provides greater flexibility without a significant increase in cost. This shortens the flexibility–cost leg of the pyramid, as shown in Figure 10.5(b). Companies can employ these or other means to shrink various legs of their pyramids. Resourceful companies that succeed in shrinking their pyramids can serve their markets well, and leave their competitors few spots in which to try to establish their own distinctive competences.

Table 10.4 shows the four performance characteristics we have mentioned and some of the supporting features that are desirable in the operations function of a manufacturing company to help achieve a particular performance characteristic. Comments in the third column of the table indicate the degree to which each feature might also be appropriate to support the performance characteristic in a nonmanufacturing company.

Other Decisions   Once a company has selected its intended position and internally communicated this intention, all parts of the company can make more consistent decisions, that is, decisions that are more consistent with the company's overall decisions, and with decisions made in other parts of the company. The company will stand a better chance of achieving its strategic objectives when all of its divisions work in concert to support these objectives in all of their decisions and activities.

FIGURE 10.5
Shrinking the Pyramid

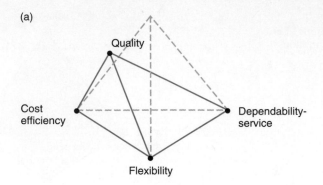

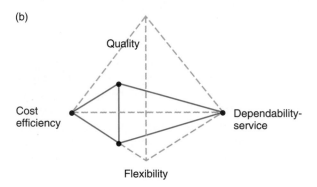

Numerous decisions within the operations function are related to the positioning decision, and to each other. Robert Hayes and Steven Wheelwright present eight major categories of strategy decisions for a manufacturing company, as shown in Table 10.5.[5] The first four categories are normally recognized as long-term decisions that are difficult to reverse and therefore more likely to be considered strategic. The last four categories appear to deal with tactical matters, that is, with more day-to-day, operating issues. It is important to recognize, however, that even these matters have long-run strategic impacts.

Product Design: An Important Strategic Factor

One of a company's basic decisions is what goods or services it will offer in the marketplace. Identifying the general type of product helps narrow the search for a niche in the market where the company might stimulate sufficient demand to achieve success. Beyond the broad question of what business it will be in, the company must address many details regarding what specific product or service it will offer and how. Decisions about the product's design specifications affect the selection of process technology (one of the decision categories in Table 10.5), which, in turn, affects the company's expenditures for equipment and facilities. Product design also affects the ease with which the product can be fabricated and assembled, so it affects operating costs. Design also affects the ease with which a product can be produced with few defects, and this influences market acceptance and the customer's perception of the company. Product design, then, has serious implications for the

TABLE 10.4

Operations Features that Support Particular Performance Characteristics

Performance Characteristic to be Emphasized	Features that Manufacturing Operations Might Provide	Applicability to Service Operations
Cost efficiency	Low overhead	Yes
	Special-purpose equipment and facilities	Yes
	High utilization of capability	Yes
	Close control of materials	Maybe
	High productivity	Yes
	Low wage rates	Yes
Quality	Skilled workers	Yes
	Adequate precision of equipment	Maybe
	Motivation for pride of workmanship	Yes
	Effective communication of standards or job requirements	Yes
Dependability	Effective scheduling system	Yes
	Low equipment failure	Yes
	Low absenteeism, low turnover, no strikes	Yes
	High inventory investment	Maybe
	Commitment of personnel to perform as required	Yes
Flexibility	Dependable, rapid suppliers	Yes
	Reserve capacity	Yes
	Multiskilled workers who can be shifted	Yes
	Effective control of work flow	Yes
	Versatile processing equipment	Yes
	Low setup time and cost	Maybe
	Integration of design and production	Maybe

TABLE 10.5

Categories of Strategy Decisions in Manufacturing Operations

1. **Capacity**—amount, timing, type
2. **Facilities**—size, location, specialization
3. **Technology**—equipment, automation, linkages
4. **Vertical integration**—direction, extent, balance
5. **Work force**—skill level, wage policies, employment security
6. **Quality**—defect prevention, monitoring, intervention
7. **Production planning materials control**—sourcing policies, centralization, decision rules
8. **Organization**—structure, control/reward systems, role of staff groups

company's long-range success, and therefore it has considerable strategic importance. The relationship between design and operating decisions differs for manufacturing and nonmanufacturing operations.

Product Design in Nonmanufacturing Operations   The product, or output, desired from the operations system of a nonmanufacturing firm will certainly affect the type of inputs it needs and the capabilities it needs to transform the inputs into the desired goods or services. The processing technology and kinds of skills that must be available in the operations function may be significantly affected, even by apparently small differences in the characteristics of the product or its delivery.[6] The decision of a food establishment to provide buffet meals rather than cafeteria-style service, for example, would reduce its need for people behind the counter to serve patrons. It would also, however, require the establishment to routinely prepare extra food, or be able to do so quickly, because management would no longer be able to control the size of each portion.

Levitz Furniture Corporation operated for years with cavernous 170,000-square-foot buildings that were combination warehouse–showrooms located near rail sidings in large cities. Customers could select furniture and haul it home. More recently, the company has added a chain of satellite stores that serve only as showrooms for warehouses located about 25 miles away. This change in merchandising strategy forced the company to keep better inventory records so the people at the showrooms would know what was available at various locations. The company also needed a more extensive fleet of vehicles and personnel to move products between locations and make deliveries to the customers.

To take another example of the operating implications that result from product design, consider a decision by the Wendy's Old-Fashioned Hamburgers chain. Wendy's had the choice of serving fresh or frozen french-fried potatoes. Serving fresh potatoes would have required each location to select, purchase, store, peel, store again, then cook and serve the potatoes. Offering preprocessed and frozen potatoes would have required each location only to store, then cook and serve the potatoes. Preprocessed potatoes also provided a more uniform product. Therefore, the chain decided to serve preprocessed, frozen french fries reducing the number of employees and the amount of space required at each location and reducing quality control and waste-disposal problems at each location.

Product Design in Manufacturing Operations   A manufacturing firm must balance the need to make its product marketable with the need to produce it economically. Product design can affect appearance, so the designer must work for an appealing look. Because some aspects of the product design may necessitate particular processes and production equipment, the best time to begin a cost-reduction program is while the product is on the drawing board. As the product is designed, managers should perform a cost–benefit evaluation, taking into account the kind and amount of materials, labor, and processing equipment that each alternative design will require. The company must also recognize that the potential consumer will also perform some sort of cost–benefit evaluation before deciding whether to purchase the product. Some processes and materials are more expensive and should be used only if the functions of the product make them necessary or the aesthetic appeal of the results justifies the expense.

Myriad alternative designs for a product are usually possible, and managers may have to choose among alternative production methods even after the product is designed. Production engineers often advise designers, helping them develop product designs that are reasonably economical to produce. A brief discussion of product design ideas will provide some appreciation of the complex nature of this topic. In selecting the raw material for a product, the designer must consider such properties as hardness, wear resistance, fatigue strength, tensile strength, weight, transparency, and ductility. Although a designer might consider the use of an inexpensive raw material, a more expensive material such as a free-machining alloy might result in a net saving when the processing costs are considered. After the material is selected, other design parameters must be evaluated. Economy can result from such ideas as:

- Using a different process to achieve a basic shape—for example; casting instead of machining.
- Requiring machined surfaces only where necessary
- Requiring close tolerances only when necessary
- Ensuring that surfaces are easily accessible to the types of processes to be used
- Considering less costly ways of joining materials, such as spot welding rather than riveting
- Requiring thinner materials or less severe bends so that light-capacity machines can be used for forming operations

As indicated earlier, the most effective time to consider how to manufacture a product is while the product is being designed. Close coordination between the design and manufacturing departments is desirable if a company wants to develop economical and effective designs. One characteristic that was found to be common during a comparison of some of America's best-managed factories was a close linkage between design and manufacturing departments, allowing them to rapidly develop easily producible designs. (Other similarities included superior ability to "build in quality, make wise choices about automation, get close to the customer, and handle their work forces."[7])

Overall, managers must keep in mind that making decisions about product design in manufacturing, as well as nonmanufacturing, situations is an extremely important aspect of strategic management. The appropriateness of such decisions a manager makes will rely heavily on his or her understanding of issues, such as how the operations function fits within an organization, how operations relates to strategic management, and how product positioning relates to product design.

SUMMARY

The operations function is performed by the people in an organization who produce the goods or services that the firm offers in the marketplace. The operations function must be compatible and consistent with other important organizational functions, such as marketing and finance, in order for any organization to succeed. Our discussion of the operations function distinguished manufacturing functions from nonmanufacturing, or service, functions. We further characterized manufacturing firms as make-to-stock, make-to-order, or assemble-to-order producers and differentiated between firms with continuous and intermittent production processes. Turning to nonmanufacturing operations, we drew a distinction between those that deal in tangible outputs that they do not manufacture and those that deal in intangible outputs, or services.

Because a firm's competitive strategy is such an important part of its overall direction, managers must understand the relationship between their operations function and their strategy. Strategy decisions determine which production characteristic(s)—cost efficiency, quality, dependability, or flexibility—the operations function will emphasize. This can also be crucial to the firm's success. Product design is a key strategy factor. It affects the selection of process technologies, the cost of equipment and facilities, the ease with which the product can be produced, the quality of the product, and hence the customer's perception of the firm.

KEY TERMS

operations function, p. 243
marketing function, p. 244
finance function, p. 244
manufacturing operations, p. 245
service operations, p. 245
make-to-stock producer, p. 247
make-to-order producer, p. 247
assemble-to-order producer, p. 247

continuous production system, p. 247
process industries, p. 249
intermittent production system, p. 249
project, p. 249
standard services, p. 250
custom services, p. 250
positioning, p. 253

CHECKLIST   Analyzing Operations in Problems and Cases

____ 1. Does the case or problem involve true production or operations issues?

____ 2. Is the operations function in the case or problem appropriately integrated with other important business functions, such as finance and marketing?

____ 3. Is the organization involved in producing goods or services? Is this fact of particular significance in the case or problem?

____ 4. If the organization is involved in manufacturing, is the production process that is used appropriate for the situation?

____ 5. If the organization is involved in a nonmanufacturing operation, is the production process that is used appropriate for the situation?

____ 6. Are the strategies employed in the case or problem consistent with the type of production function that exists?

____ 7. Is enough emphasis placed on using operations as a critical element of strategy?

____ 8. Do product positioning decisions take the operations function into account?

____ 9. Are decisions concerning such issues as capacity, facilities, technology, vertical integration, the work force, quality, production planning and materials control, and organization consistent with product positioning?

____ 10. Is product design as a strategic factor appropriately linked to operations?

Additional Readings

Belohlav, James A. "Quality, Strategy, and Competitiveness." *California Management Review,* Spring 1993, p. 55.

Garvin, David A. "Manufacturing Strategic Planning." *California Management Review,* Summer 1993, p. 85.

Harmon, Roy L., and Leroy D. Peterson. *Reinventing the Factory: Productivity Breakthroughs in Manufacturing Today.* New York: Free Press, 1989.

Hayes, Robert H., Steven C. Wheelwright, and Kim B. Clark. "The Power of Positive Manufacturing." *Across the Board,* October 1988, pp. 24–30.

Peters, Tom. "Rethinking Scale." *California Management Review,* Fall 1992, p. 7.

Schonberger, Richard J. *Japanese Manufacturing Techniques: Nine Hidden Lessons in Simplicity.* New York: Free Press, 1982.

———. *The World Class Company.* New York: Free Press, 1990.

CASE

Redner's Upends Operations

In the five years since Redner's converted from a conventional supermarket operation to a warehouse store format, sales at the Reading, Pennsylvania, company have tripled to the current level of $230 million. That's an average store-for-store increase from $100,000 to roughly $300,000 a week.

President Dick Redner has a bullish prediction that the company will be a billion-dollar operation by the end of the century and have 100 stores by 2010.

Redner's was a healthy company, its nine stores reporting industry-average sales trends and good profits. Executive interest was piqued, however, by the success of wholesalers, who sell huge volumes with hardly any advertising. One of Redner's stores was a likely prospect for a test conversion: Its 38,000-square-foot Palmyra store was the fourth operation in the small town. Even after Redner's cut its losses in half, business had not increased beyond what the previous owner had done—$90,000 to $100,000 a week. Conversion was a no-lose proposition: Operating on only a two-year lease, the chain could test the warehouse concept and, if it failed, close the store and walk away.

The transformation was completed in three days, and business immediately doubled. Despite the good customer reception, Redner's managers were troubled. "A lot of guys said, 'You know, it's not broke, so let's not fix it,' " says Dick Redner. "But as we noted the results, we just felt we couldn't be a dual operator. We were either going to stay a conventional operator or we were going all the way with the warehouse concept."

The chain converted the rest of its stores within a year, with identical results: business doubled and the sizes of the stores followed suit. As business has tripled, Redner's has built new stores, bringing its total to 15. Construction is concluding on a new 120,000-square-foot warehouse to feed the rapid growth in the company's direct-buying program, part of a drive to increase margins with the increase in volume in all departments. Other moves included eliminating sales games, gimmicks, and double coupons.

Dick Redner says the formula is simple—no deviation from the program to become a price leader in the marketplace. Everything is discounted, from produce to meat to deli products to health and beauty aids. That message is pounded home with the phrase *WAREHOUSE MARKET* printed on everything from store signs to management business cards. Redner's warehouse concept is an egoless operational philosophy that takes priority over everything, including family identity—a departure from the traditional supermarket strategy of stressing a family name and involvement.

DISCUSSION QUESTIONS

1. Which materials management principles and operations features commonly used by manufacturing operations could best be applied to Redner's service operation?

2. How much leverage has Redner's allowed itself with its low-price positioning strategy?

3. Write an operational mission statement for Redner's, focusing on how the company can best compete on quality, price, and product availability.

SOURCE: Bob Ingram, "Redner's 'Racks' Up the Volume," *Supermarket Business,* March 1994, pp. 53–56.

Notes

1. This chapter is based on Chapter 1 ("Zeroing in on Operations") and Chapter 2 ("Operations Strategy") in James B. Dilworth, *Production and Operations Management: Manufacturing and Non-manufacturing* (New York: Random House, 1986). This book is available in a 1992 version from McGraw-Hill Book Company. The authors would like to express their sincere appreciation to Professor James B. Dilworth for his important contribution to this text.

2. These terms are defined in accordance with Thomas F. Wallace, *APICS Dictionary,* 5th ed. (Falls Church, Va.: American Production and Inventory Control Society, 1984).

3. Richard B. Chase, "Where Does the Customer Fit in a Service Operation?" *Harvard Business Review,* November/December 1978, p. 138.

4. Steven C. Wheelwright, "Reflecting Corporate Strategy in Manufacturing Decisions," *Business Horizons,* February 1978, pp. 57–66.

5. Robert H. Hayes and Steven C. Wheelwright, *Restoring Our Competitive Edge* (New York: John Wiley & Sons, 1984), p. 31.

6. Dan R. E. Thomas, "Strategy Is Different in Service Businesses," *Harvard Business Review,* July/August 1980, pp. 158–165.

7. Gene Bylinsky, "America's Best-Managed Factories," *Fortune,* May 28, 1984, pp. 16–24.

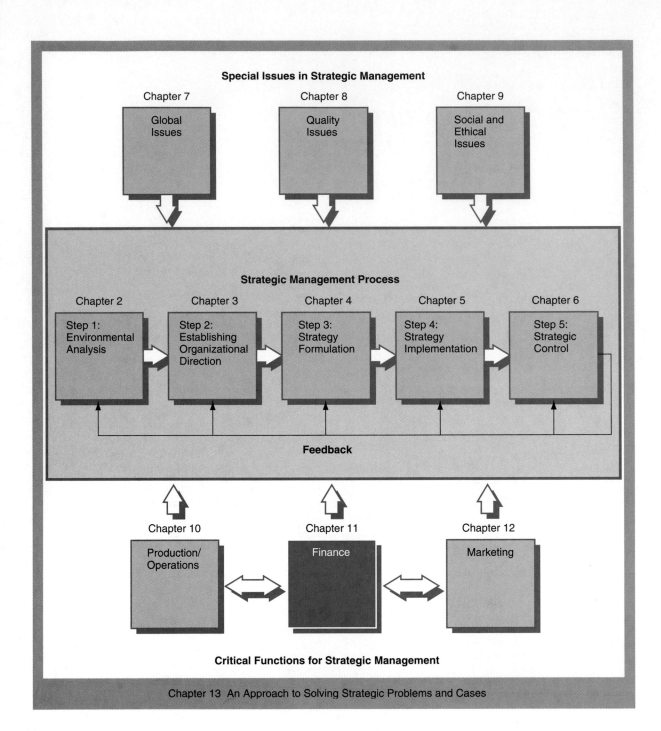

Special Issues in Strategic Management

Chapter 7

Global Issues

Chapter 8

Quality Issues

Chapter 9

Social and Ethical Issues

Strategic Management Process

Chapter 2

Step 1: Environmental Analysis

Chapter 3

Step 2: Establishing Organizational Direction

Chapter 4

Step 3: Strategy Formulation

Chapter 5

Step 4: Strategy Implementation

Chapter 6

Step 5: Strategic Control

Feedback

Chapter 10

Production/ Operations

Chapter 11

Finance

Chapter 12

Marketing

Critical Functions for Strategic Management

Chapter 13 An Approach to Solving Strategic Problems and Cases

CHAPTER 11

The Finance Function and Strategic Management

M any types of financial analyses provide useful aids for strategic decision making. In this chapter, we investigate several tools that are commonly used in analyzing strategic management problems and cases.[1] First, we discuss financial ratio analysis, which is a useful starting point for investigating the financial condition of an organization. Next, we examine break-even analysis, a simple financial tool for investigating the potential value of an investment. Finally, we describe net present value analysis, a method of examining investment alternatives.

Financial analysis is useful, most obviously, in the strategic control stage of the strategic management process, when top managers assess the bottom-line financial results of their earlier strategic decisions. However, financial tools can provide powerful help at other stages of the process. During environmental analysis, financial tools can contribute to SWOT analysis, as top managers attempt to quantify and evaluate the strengths and weaknesses of their firm in relation to those of its competitors, and to assess market opportunities and threats. At the strategy formulation stage, financial tools such as break-even and net present value analysis help managers to assess the comparative merits of different potential strategies. The Company Example illustrates the effect of financial constraints on one firm's strategic decisions.

During strategy implementation, early-stage financial analysis can often signal the need for corrective action or change. In addition, the finance function provides essential analytical tools to the other core functions—marketing and operations. In marketing, for example, financial analysis helps drive decisions about alternative distribution channels or packaging. In operations, assessments of alternative investments in plant and equipment draw upon net present value analysis and similar techniques.

These points underscore the importance of viewing an organization's operations through a cross-functional lens. In the 1990s the speed of strategic actions is critical, and a firm can enjoy great benefits if it effectively integrates its functional specialists in the strategic management process and resists outdated notions about keeping functions separated, each behind its own wall.

COMPANY EXAMPLE

Start-up Financing at Highland Energy Group

After teaming with a vendor of energy-efficient lighting to assemble a lease package for a large company, Tom Stoner says he determined that the energy savings on a five-year deal amounted to more money than the lease payments on the equipment. He decided to start a firm specializing in alternative energy. "I knew that with utilities having been a monopoly there was an opportunity to create efficiencies in this market. And where you can create efficiencies, profits can be made."

In order to sell the company to investors and customers, Stoner decided that his New England–based Highland Energy Group would not only design customized programs for conversion to energy-efficient technology but guarantee the results to large-scale energy users.

Buoyed by a friend's initial investment of more than $1 million, Stoner leveraged additional funds by structuring financing deals with architectural and engineering firms with which he worked on specific projects. A public offering put out to accumulate more capital had no takers until the company won some bids. Investors now own 70 percent of the business.

In 1992, Highland Energy sold products worth $5 million; today, it has secured utility contracts that should generate more than $20 million in revenue over the next three years. "Before, we needed capital to execute bids and set up systems, but now we need the capital to grow," says Stoner. "The dollar amount gets larger, and you always need twice as much as you think. It's like guessing the moon."

While managing growth has been a concern, the decisions to sustain that growth are the most difficult. "You could go one way and get cash-flow positive or you could get bigger, better, and more credible," he says. "Do you hire a bookkeeper at $20,000 a year or a chief financial officer at $80,000? You have to plot your commitment day in and day out, but it's like plotting a course in a vacuum."

SOURCE: Margaret Kaeter, "Buddy, Can You Spare a Million?" *Business Ethics*, May/June 1994, pp. 27–28.

FINANCIAL RATIO ANALYSIS

A useful starting point in analyzing an organization's financial condition is to perform a financial ratio analysis. A **financial ratio analysis** is based on information provided in the organization's balance sheet and income statement. These two financial statements are frequently included in strategic management cases, and performing a financial ratio analysis is a convenient way to gain insight into the condition of the firm. In this section, we first review the balance sheet and income statement and then propose a four-step process for performing a financial ratio analysis.

Table 11.1 presents the balance sheet for the MoPower Robotics Company, a manufacturer of specialized industrial robots. The **balance sheet** is a summary of the assets of an organization and the claims against its assets at a particular time. Actually, Table 11. 1 represents a **comparative balance sheet,** stating the assets and liabilities of MoPower for more than one time. Note that two types of assets are shown. **Current assets** are those that the firm expects to convert to cash within one year, whereas **fixed assets** are those that it expects to hold for a longer time. Similarly, **current liabilities** are amounts of money that it owes and expects to pay out within one year; other obligations are longer term in nature.

Table 11.2 presents MoPower's income statement. The **income statement** shows the financial results of an organization's operations during an interval

TABLE 11.1

MoPower Robotics Company Balance Sheet ($000)

ASSETS	Dec. 31, 1994	Dec. 31, 1995
Cash	$ 30	$ 25
Marketable securities	40	25
Accounts receivable	200	100
Inventories	430	700
Total current assets	$ 700	$ 850
Plant and equipment	1,000	1,500
Long-term investments	500	900
Other assets	200	250
Total assets	$2,400	$3,500

LIABILITIES AND NET WORTH		
Trade accounts payable	$ 150	$ 200
Notes payable	100	100
Accruals	25	100
Provision for federal taxes	40	50
Total current liabilities	$ 315	$ 450
Bonds	500	1,000
Debentures	85	50
Stockholders' equity	1,500	2,000
Total liabilities and stockholders' equity	$2,400	$3,500

TABLE 11.2

MoPower Robotics Company Income Statement for the Year Ending December 31, 1995 ($000)

Sales		$3,600
Cost of goods sold		2,700
Gross profit		$ 900
Less operating expenses		
Selling	$40	
General and administrative	60	100
Gross operating revenue		$ 800
Less depreciation		250
Net operating income (NOI)		$ 550
Less other expenses		50
Earnings before interest and taxes (EBIT)		$ 500
Less interest expense		200
Earnings before taxes (EBT)		$ 300
Less federal and state income taxes (40%)		120
Earnings after taxes (EAT)		$ 180

of time, usually one year. The income statement lists net sales (sales minus returns and allowances) at the top and then proceeds to subtract various amounts to determine earnings after tax (net income). The amounts subtracted from net sales on this income statement include cost of goods sold, operating expenses, depreciation, other expenses, interest, and taxes. Various organizations may have different entries and labels, but these two financial statements represent common reporting procedures.

Financial statements contain a tremendous amount of useful information for strategic managers. However, it is very difficult, based on a simple look at the statements, to determine how well the organization is doing. For example, is MoPower currently in a solid financial position, or do these financial statements suggest that the company has problems? In order to answer this question, we need a method of comparing MoPower's financial situation over time with the situations of other firms of similar size in the same industry, and with industry averages. These comparisons are the basis for financial ratio analysis.

Performing a financial ratio analysis can be divided into four steps: (1) choosing appropriate ratios, (2) calculating the ratios, (3) comparing the ratios, and (4) checking for problems and opportunities. We will discuss each of these steps in turn.

Choosing Appropriate Ratios

The many types of financial ratios include liquidity ratios, leverage ratios, activity ratios, profitability ratios, growth ratios, and valuation ratios. All have important uses in evaluating the financial well-being of an organization. Though strategic managers may use all of these types of ratios, some of them are very specialized, and applying them in a meaningful way requires an extensive financial management background.[2] However, there are several types of financial ratios that should be applied routinely in analyzing *any* strategic management case that includes financial statements. These types—the liquidity, activity, and profitability ratios—are especially useful for uncovering symptoms of problems in cases and for supporting both arguments about the major issues in the cases and proposed solutions. Each of these types includes many ratios; we will discuss only a few of the most useful ones.

Liquidity Ratios   One of the first financial considerations to consider when analyzing a strategic management case is the liquidity of the organization. *Liquidity* refers to the ability of the organization to pay its short-term obligations. If the organization cannot meet its short-term obligations, it can do little else until it corrects the problem. In other words, a firm that cannot meet its current financial obligations must resolve the problem before long-term strategic planning can be effective.

The two most commonly used ratios for investigating liquidity are the current ratio and the quick ratio (or acid test ratio). The **current ratio** is found by dividing current assets by current liabilities. It measures the overall ability of an organization to meet its current obligations. A common rule of thumb is that the current ratio should be about 2:1, although what is acceptable depends greatly on the industry and the situation.

The **quick ratio** is determined by subtracting inventory from current assets and dividing the result by current liabilities. Because inventory is the least liquid current asset, the quick ratio gives an indication of the degree to which an organization has funds readily available to meet short-term obligations. A common rule of thumb is that the quick ratio should be at least 1:1, although, again, the appropriate level depends on the industry and the situation.

Activity Ratios   Activity ratios, also called *asset management ratios,* investigate how well the organization handles its assets. For strategic management purposes, two of the most useful activity ratios measure inventory turnover and total asset utilization.

Inventory turnover is determined by dividing sales by inventories. If the firm is not turning over its inventory as rapidly as it has in the past, or as rapidly as other firms in the industry, it may have a problem. Perhaps it is tying up too much money in unproductive or obsolete inventory, or it is not marketing its products as well as it has in the past.

A second useful activity ratio is total asset utilization. **Total asset utilization** is calculated by dividing sales by total assets. It measures how productively the firm has used its assets to generate sales. If this ratio is well below the industry average, management may not be using company assets effectively.

Profitability Ratios   The profitability of an organization is an important measure of its effectiveness. Although financial analysts suggest that a firm's goal is to maximize shareholder wealth, profitability is a common yardstick for measuring success. Two key profitability ratios are profit margin on sales and return on investment (ROI). **Profit margin on sales** is calculated by dividing earnings before interest and taxes (EBIT) by sales. Serious questions about an organization should be raised if this figure is declining over time or is well below the figures for other firms in the industry.

Return on investment is calculated by dividing earnings after taxes (EAT) by total assets. This ratio is also called *return on assets,* and earnings after taxes are sometimes referred to as *profit after taxes, net profit,* or *net income.* This ratio gives an indication of how productively the organization has acquired, used, and managed assets. Return on investment is a commonly discussed measure of corporate performance.

Calculating Ratios

The next step in ratio analysis is to calculate the ratios. Below we have calculated each of the six ratios we have discussed, using data derived from the financial statements for the MoPower Robotics Company, for the year 1995.

Liquidity Ratios

$$\text{Current ratio} = \frac{\text{Current assets}}{\text{Current liabilities}} = \frac{850}{450} = 1.89$$

$$\text{Quick ratio} = \frac{\text{Current assets} - \text{Inventory}}{\text{Current liabilities}} = \frac{150}{450} = 0.33$$

Activity Ratios

$$\text{Inventory turnover} = \frac{\text{Sales}}{\text{Inventory}} = \frac{3,600}{700} = 5.14$$

$$\text{Total asset utilization} = \frac{\text{Sales}}{\text{Total assets}} = \frac{3,600}{3,500} = 1.03$$

Profitability Ratios

$$\text{Profit margin on sales} = \frac{\text{EBIT}}{\text{Sales}} = \frac{500}{3,600} = 0.14$$

$$\text{Return on investment} = \frac{\text{EAT}}{\text{Total assets}} = \frac{180}{3,500} = 0.05$$

Comparing Ratios

We cannot overemphasize the statement that no single ratio has meaning by itself. In other words, comparing ratios is critical for effective financial ratio analysis. Ratios can be compared across time for the same firm, compared with those of similar firms in the industry, or compared with industry averages. The following examples illustrate each of these different types of comparisons.

First, suppose that in 1994 MoPower had sales of $3,300,000, earnings before interest and taxes of $600,000, and earnings after taxes of $200,000. With this information, and the balance sheet information for December 31, 1994 (supplied in Table 11.1), we can compute the ratios for 1994 and then compare them with those for 1995 to investigate trends. Table 11.3 summarizes this comparison.

To compare an organization's ratios with those of similar firms in the industry or with industry averages, the analyst must look up the industry information. Sources of industry information include:[3]

1. *Annual Statement Studies.* Published by Robert Morris Associates, this work includes 16 financial ratios computed annually for over 150 lines of business. Each line of business is divided into four size categories.
2. Dun & Bradstreet provides 14 ratios calculated annually for over 100 lines of business.
3. *The Almanac of Business and Industrial Financial Ratios.* This work, published by Prentice-Hall, Inc., lists industry averages for 22 financial ratios. Approximately 170 businesses and industries are listed.
4. *The Quarterly Financial Report for Manufacturing Corporations.* This work, published jointly by the Federal Trade Commission and the Securities and Exchange Commission, contains balance-sheet and income-statement information by industry groupings and by asset-size categories.
5. Trade associations and individual companies often compute ratios for their industries and make them available to analysts.

Table 11.4 compares MoPower's 1995 ratios with those of firms of similar size in the industry and with the industry medians. (Financial sources often report the industry median rather than the mean to avoid the distorting effects of outliers, or values that lie far beyond the area where most tend to cluster.) Once the analyst has prepared comparative statements such as those shown in Table 11.3 and Table 11.4, it is time to interpret what all of the information means. This is the final step in ratio analysis.

TABLE 11.3

Comparison of Financial Ratios for MoPower Robotics Company, 1994 and 1995

	1994	1995
LIQUIDITY RATIOS		
Current ratio	2.22	1.89
Quick ratio	0.86	0.33
ACTIVITY RATIOS		
Inventory turnover	7.67	5.14
Total asset utilization	1.38	1.03
PROFITABILITY RATIOS		
Profit margin on sales	0.18	0.14
Return on investment	0.08	0.05

TABLE 11.4

Comparison of Financial Ratios for MoPower with Industry Figures

	MoPower Company	Industry Firms, Assets $1–10 Million	Industry Median
LIQUIDITY RATIOS			
Current ratio	1.88	1.80	1.80
Quick ratio	0.33	0.90	1.00
ACTIVITY RATIOS			
Inventory turnover	5.14	7.80	7.90
Total asset utilization	1.03	1.70	1.80
PROFITABILITY RATIOS			
Profit margin on sales	0.14	0.13	0.15
Return on investment	0.05	0.15	0.16

Checking for Problems and Opportunities

The comparisons between ratios shown in Tables 11.3 and 11.4 suggest that MoPower is not in a strong financial position and that its position has declined since the previous year. Although MoPower's liquidity was in good shape in 1994, its position in 1995 was not favorable. Particularly, given the quick ratio of 0.33, MoPower could be in serious trouble if its creditors were to demand quick payment. What appears to have happened is a large inventory buildup. This may mean that MoPower's products have been superseded in a market experiencing the effects of rapid technological change; they may not be selling well. Alternatively, MoPower may be building inventory for an expected increase in demand. In either case, its liquidity position needs to be improved.

The buildup in inventory is also reflected in the decrease in activity ratios. Inventory turnover and total asset utilization have slipped and are now well below industry averages. Perhaps MoPower has also accumulated some other unproductive or outdated assets that it should divest.

In terms of profitability, although profit margin on sales has decreased from 18 percent to 14 percent, it is still above the standard for firms of similar size in the industry. However, the company's return on investment is far below industry figures and has shrunk significantly. This could be a very important problem for MoPower, particularly if it is trying to attract new investors. However, much depends on other factors, such as whether MoPower is a new company that is expected to have a large increase in future earnings.

What should be clear from the foregoing analysis is that ratios offer a convenient way to investigate the financial well-being of an organization. Calculating various ratios and comparing them can alert analysts to areas that strategic managers should investigate more fully. However, financial ratios only indicate symptoms of problems; the real problems are the *reasons* for poor financial performance. To discover these underlying causes, carefully consider other information contained in a case or strategic management situation.

Finally, even when a firm's financial ratios appear to conform to industry averages, this does not mean that the firm has no financial or other strategic management problems. For example, perhaps the firm is neglecting to exploit a clear differential advantage by which it could far outstrip average industry performance. Alternatively, perhaps the firm's finances look good at the moment, but a serious competitive threat could wipe it out in the near future. In short, financial ratio analysis is a very useful tool for analyzing strategic management cases, but it cannot replace other types of analysis and careful consideration of the issues in the case.

BREAK-EVEN ANALYSIS

Break-even analysis is a simple method for investigating the potential value of a proposed investment. It is useful in the analysis of three important types of strategic management decisions:

1. In *new product decisions,* break-even analysis can help determine how much of a new product a firm must sell to achieve profitability.
2. Break-even analysis can be used as a broad framework for studying the effects of a general *expansion* in the level of a firm's operations.
3. When the firm is considering *modernization* and *automation* projects where it invests in more equipment in order to reduce variable costs, particularly the cost of labor, break-even analysis can help managers analyze the consequences of the action.[4]

The **break-even point** is the level of sales, stated in either units or dollars, at which a firm covers all costs of investing in a project. In other words, it is the level at which total sales revenue just equals the total costs necessary to achieve those sales.

In order to compute the break-even point, an analyst must obtain three values. First, the analyst needs to know the selling price per unit of the product (SP). For example, after extensive market analysis, MoPower Robotics Company plans to sell its new, multifunction industrial robot for $5,000.

Second, the analyst needs to know the level of fixed costs (FC). Fixed costs are all costs relevant to the project that do not change regardless of how many units are produced and sold. For example, whether MoPower produces and sells 1 robot or 10,000, MoPower must pay executives their salaries, purchase machinery, and construct a plant. Other fixed costs include interest payments, lease payments, and sinking fund payments. MoPower has tallied all of its fixed costs to produce the new robot and estimates the total to be $10 million.

Third, the analyst needs to know the variable costs per unit produced (VC). Variable costs, as the name implies, are those that vary directly with the number of units produced. For example, for each robot produced, MoPower must pay for electrical and mechanical components, labor to assemble the robot, and machine costs such as electricity. MoPower estimates that for each robot produced, the variable costs will be $3,000.

Armed with this information, the analyst can determine the break-even point by dividing total fixed costs by the contribution margin. The **contribution margin** is simply the difference between the selling price per unit and the variable costs per unit. Algebraically,

$$\text{Break-even point (in units)} = \frac{\text{Total fixed costs}}{\text{Contribution margin}}$$

$$= \frac{FC}{SP - VC}$$

Substituting the MoPower estimates:

$$\text{Break-even point (in units)} = \frac{10,000,000}{5,000 - 3,000}$$

$$= \frac{10,000,000}{2,000}$$

$$= 5,000 \text{ units}$$

In other words, MoPower must sell 5,000 robots in order to break even—to make its total sales equal its total costs. This is a very useful number. It informs the analyst that if sales projections at this price level are less than 5,000 units, the project may not be viable.

Alternatively, the analyst may want to know the break-even point in terms of total sales dollars rather than units. Of course, if the preceding analysis has been done, one can simply multiply the break-even point in units by the selling price: 5,000 units × $5,000 = $25 million. However, the break-even point in dollars can be computed directly with the following formula:

$$\text{Break-even point in dollars} = \frac{FC}{1 - \dfrac{VC}{SP}}$$

$$= \frac{10,000,000}{1 - \dfrac{3,000}{5,000}}$$

$$= \frac{10,000,000}{1 - 0.6}$$

$$= \$25 \text{ million}$$

Thus, MoPower must produce and sell 5,000 robots, which equals $25 million in sales, just to break even on this project. Of course, MoPower does not want to break even, but to make a profit. The logic of break-even analysis can easily be extended to include profits (P). For example, suppose that MoPower decides that a 20 percent return on fixed costs is the minimum that the project would have to generate to make it worth investing. MoPower would need 20 percent of $10 million, or $2 million in additional income to make the project worth the investment. To calculate how many units MoPower must sell to achieve this level of profits, add the profit figure to fixed costs in the foregoing formulas:

$$\text{Break-even plus profits} = \frac{FC + P}{SP - VC}$$

$$= \frac{10,000,000 + 2,000,000}{5,000 - 3,000}$$

$$= \frac{12,000,000}{2,000}$$

$$= 6,000 \text{ units}$$

In terms of the formula for sales dollars:

$$\text{Break-even plus profits} = \frac{FC + P}{1 - \dfrac{VC}{SP}}$$

$$= \frac{10,000,000 + 2,000,000}{1 - \dfrac{3,000}{5,000}}$$

$$= \frac{12,000,000}{1 - 0.6}$$

$$= \$30 \text{ million}$$

MoPower must produce and sell 6,000 robots, which equals $30 million in sales, to achieve its minimum acceptable profit level. This is a very useful figure to calculate, because it invites the analyst to consider the probability of obtaining this level of sales. For example, if the entire market were 10,000 units, is it likely that MoPower could obtain a 60 percent market share, given the competition? If so, the project would be worth investing. If not, MoPower should seek other opportunities or change its strategic plan. If the firm were to reduce the price of the robots, for example, sales increases might result in economies of scale and a profitable project.

Graphs can present a clear overall picture of break-even analysis. Figure 11.1 is a graph of our MoPower break-even example. Such a graph provides an easy-to-understand, visual representation of the various relationships among sales, fixed costs, and variable costs, and it illustrates levels of losses and profits under various conditions. The Skills Module offers you an opportunity to perform a break-even analysis.

Although break-even analysis is a useful tool, it does have limitations. For example, a whole series of break-even analyses are necessary if the analyst

FIGURE 11.1   Graphical Presentation of Break-Even Analysis

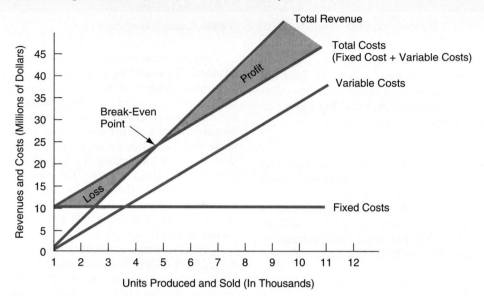

wishes to consider different price levels or different estimates of fixed or variable costs. Similarly, many costs are likely to change at different volume levels. For example, at higher volume levels, more employees may have to be hired and more machines may have to be purchased, which would change the various cost curves. Break-even analysis is useful (and in some cases, it is the only technique that can be applied), but more detailed analyses are often recommended for probing investment alternatives. One of these is net present value analysis.

NET PRESENT VALUE ANALYSIS

A detailed treatment of net present value analysis is beyond the scope of this text. Even so, we should review, in general terms, its use in strategic management analysis. **Net present value analysis** can be used to investigate the value of a proposed investment to an organization or to compare alternative investments to determine which is better from a financial point of view.

This analysis is based on the idea that money has a time value. For example, $10 today is worth more than $10 one year from today because it could be invested for the year. If the $10 were put in a money market account to earn 6 percent interest, it would be worth $10.60 a year from today. Thus, a financial analyst who is considering cash inflows and outflows that will occur in the future can use net present value analysis to discount them—that is, to reflect their value in today's dollars.

In order to calculate the net present value of an investment, the analyst needs several figures. First, the total initial cost of the investment must be determined. This includes all payments made today to begin the project. Second, the firm's cost of capital must be estimated. The cost of capital is often given in cases for which net present value analysis is appropriate. If not, one can estimate using methods suggested in financial management texts.[5] Third, the project's expected life must be determined. Fourth, the net cash flows

SKILLS MODULE
Break-Even Analysis at Sylvan Learning Systems

INTRODUCTION

We have discussed break-even analysis in some detail. Review the following situation and then complete the skill development exercise that follows to help you develop this important skill.

SITUATION

Although the partners who run Sylvan Learning Systems Inc. want to build the company into a huge enterprise, they have their work cut out for them. The Columbia, Maryland, company reported a loss of $363,833 last year on revenue of $18.1 million. Now, instead of cutting their losses, the partners are trying to avoid stagnation by branching out in a new direction.

Sylvan's main business is franchising tutoring centers where parents pay between $1,200 and $1,800 to boost their children's study skills. The company's success in that field has plateaued, however; with nearly 500 franchised units operating in the United States and Canada, there are limited desirable sites for additional franchisees.

The company is counting on two new areas to shore up its growth and improve its bottom line: computerized testing and remedial-skills contracts. The business of running remedial reading and math classes for students and employees in their schools or work sites has taken off in Baltimore. There, public school officials are using the program in eight schools under a $3.7 million program supported by federal funds targeted at disadvantaged students.

Computerized testing is the bigger growth arena. In many of its tutoring centers, Sylvan has installed electronic equipment to deliver computerized versions of standardized tests for graduate school admissions and professional licensing and certification exams. Sylvan's thrust into a new niche is having some success: its computerized tests are now mandatory for all candidates for licensing as practical nurses in the United States. The company says that it has contracts in the offing with the nonprofit Educational Testing Service to deliver computerized tests in the United States and more than 170 other countries within five years.

Sylvan recently announced that ETS had invested $1.5 million in newly issued Sylvan stock and taken options to invest another $4 million. Public investors are also high on Sylvan's strategy.

SKILL DEVELOPMENT EXERCISE

Assume that Sylvan's computerized tests have a variable cost of $15 each and that total fixed costs for its computerized testing contracts amount to $8 million. If Sylvan and its franchisees mark up the testing fee 50 percent, what is the break-even point for the test? How many computerized tests or contracts would Sylvan have to sell to make a profit of $1 million.

SOURCE: Jeffrey A. Tannenbaum, "Sylvan Learning, to Avoid Stagnation, Acts to Diversify," *The Wall Street Journal*, April 26, 1994, p. B2.

from the project must be estimated. **Net cash flows** are the net amounts (cash inflows minus cash outflows) that the firm receives from the project each year; they include earnings after taxes (net income) and depreciation.

The basic equation for calculating net present value is:

$$NPV = \frac{NCF_1}{(1 + k)^1} + \frac{NCF_2}{(1 + k)^2} + \ldots + \frac{NCF_n}{(1 + k)^n} - I$$

where

NPV	=	net present value
NCF	=	net cash flows each year of the project's life
I	=	total initial investment
k	=	cost of capital

This equation states that the net present value of an investment is equal to the net cash flows discounted at the cost of capital, minus the initial investment outlay. For example, suppose that MoPower is deciding whether to get into the market for home robots and has gathered the following financial information for the project:

Initial investment in equipment	$1,500,000
Useful life of equipment	10 years
Depreciation	10 percent per year
Salvage value	$200,000
Net income per year	$150,000
Cost of capital	10 percent

Because financial management texts include net present value tables, actually solving for the net present value is much easier than working through the formula. Table 11.5 presents the net cash flows—net income ($150,000 per year) plus depreciation ($150,000 per year) equals $300,000 and an additional $200,000 in year ten for salvage value, the appropriate discount factors for a cost of capital of 10 percent, and the present value of these cash flows. The present value of the net cash flows is $1,920,450; subtracting the initial investment of $1,500,000 results in a net present value of $420,450. The net present value is positive, so MoPower should invest in entering the home robot market.

Because the net cash flows for the first nine years are the same, it would be much easier to calculate the present value by treating these nine years as an annuity and multiplying by the total of the discount factors for nine years—that is, $300,000 × 5.7590 = $1,727,700. Adding the figure for the tenth year ($500,000 × 0.3855 = $192,750) to this amount makes it easier to obtain the present value of $1,920,450.

Net present value analysis is a useful method for examining investment alternatives. Employing it requires some background in financial management,

TABLE 11.5

Present Value Calculations for the MoPower Robotics Company

Year	Net Cash Flow	10% Discount Factor	Present Value
1	$300,000	0.9091	$ 272,730
2	300,000	0.8264	247,920
3	300,000	0.7513	225,390
4	300,000	0.6830	204,900
5	300,000	0.6209	186,270
6	300,000	0.5645	169,350
7	300,000	0.5132	153,960
8	300,000	0.4665	139,950
9	300,000	0.4241	127,230
10	500,000	0.3855	192,750
			$1,920,450

TABLE 11.6

Selected Present Value Discount Factors

Year	8%	10%	12%	14%	16%	18%
1	0.9259	0.9091	0.8929	0.8772	0.8621	0.8475
2	0.8573	0.8264	0.7972	0.7695	0.7432	0.7182
3	0.7938	0.7513	0.7118	0.6750	0.6407	0.6086
4	0.7350	0.6830	0.6355	0.5921	0.5523	0.5158
5	0.6806	0.6209	0.5674	0.5194	0.4761	0.4371
6	0.6302	0.5645	0.5066	0.4556	0.4104	0.3704
7	0.5835	0.5132	0.4523	0.3996	0.3538	0.3139
8	0.5403	0.4665	0.4039	0.3506	0.3050	0.2660
9	0.5002	0.4241	0.3606	0.3075	0.2630	0.2255
10	0.4632	0.3855	0.3220	0.2697	0.2267	0.1911

but net present value analysis should be applied to strategic management cases when the required information is available or can be estimated. Table 11.6 presents some commonly used present value discount factors; again, complete tables can be found in most financial management texts.

SUMMARY

This chapter investigated three financial tools that are useful for strategic management. We discussed ratio analysis and examined three types of financial ratios: liquidity, activity, and profitability ratios. We suggested that these types of ratios should be applied routinely to strategic management situations that include balance sheet and income statement information. We then discussed break-even analysis as a method for investigating the potential value of an investment to an organization. It enables the firm to determine at what level of sales the total revenue generated by a product just equals the costs incurred to achieve those sales. It can be extended to include desired profit levels. Finally, we presented net present value analysis as a sophisticated but useful method for analyzing investment alternatives. It enables the firm to determine the value in today's dollars of cash flows that will occur in the future.

KEY TERMS

financial ratio analysis, p. 266
balance sheet, p. 266
comparative balance sheet, p. 266
current assets, p. 266
fixed assets, p. 266
current liabilities, p. 266
income statement, p. 266
current ratio, p. 268
quick ratio, p. 268

inventory turnover, p. 269
total asset utilization, p. 269
profit margin on sales, p. 269
return on investment, p. 269
break-even analysis, p. 272
break-even point, p. 272
contribution margin, p. 273
net present value analysis, p. 275
net cash flows, p. 276

CHECKLIST

Analyzing Finances in Problems and Cases

___ 1. Does the problem or case include financial statements to provide information for ratio analysis?

___ 2. Would ratio analysis contribute to a better understanding of the firm and its problems?

___ 3. What is the financial condition of the company? That is, how does it compare with other firms in the industry in terms of such measures as liquidity, activity, and profitability ratios? What are the implications for alternatives that would solve the firm's problems?

___ 4. Does the problem or case include the information needed to perform a break-even analysis?

___ 5. Would a break-even analysis help to evaluate a proposed project for the company?

___ 6. Given a break-even point, is the firm likely to be able to sell enough units to reach that point and be profitable?

___ 7. Does the problem or case include information for a net present value analysis?

___ 8. Would a net present value analysis contribute to an analysis of the firm's investment opportunities?

___ 9. Given a positive net present value, is there any reason why the firm should not invest in the project?

___ 10. If the analyst lacks enough information to perform a break-even or net present value analysis, could such analyses be performed based on a few reasonable assumptions? For example, could one assume a cost of capital in order to perform the analysis?

Additional Readings

Brealey, Richard A., and Stewart C. Myers. *Principles of Corporate Finance,* 4th ed. New York: McGraw-Hill, 1991.

Brigham, Eugene F., and Louis C. Gapenski. *Financial Management: Theory and Practice,* 7th ed. Fort Worth, Dryden Press, 1994.

Dickerson, Bodil, B. J. Campsey, and Eugene F. Brigham. *Introduction to Financial Management,* 4th ed. Fort Worth, Dryden Press, 1995.

Rappaport, Alfred. "CFOs and Strategists: Forging a Common Framework." *Harvard Business Review,* May/June 1992, p. 84.

C A S E

Financial Analysis for Polaroid Corporation

The Polaroid Corporation designs, manufactures, and markets a variety of products primarily in instant image-recording fields. These include instant cameras and films, magnetic media, light-polarizing filters and lenses, and diversified chemical, optical, and commercial products. The principal products of the company are used in amateur and professional photography, industry, science, medicine, and education. Selected financial data for 1985 include the following (in millions):

Current assets	$1,035.7	Sales	$1,295.2
Inventory	335.0	EBIT	62.5
Total assets	1,384.7	EAT	36.9
Current liabilities	337.9		

Some of Polaroid's major products are cameras that focus and control exposure automatically. These cameras use advanced computerlike circuitry to make more than 30 complex focusing and exposure decisions within fifty-thousandths of a second. The cameras, film, accessories, and services involved are collectively called the Spectra System. This system was Polaroid's major product innovation for 1986.

DISCUSSION QUESTIONS

1. Calculate the current ratio, quick ratio, inventory turnover, total asset utilization, profit margin on sales, and return on investment for Polaroid for 1985.

2. Compare Polaroid's ratios with the following industry averages. What conclusions about Polaroid's financial condition do these comparisons suggest?

Current ratio	2.2	Total asset utilization	1.1
Quick ratio	1.0	Profit margin on sales	0.067
Inventory turnover	4.3	Return on investment	0.039

3. Suppose Polaroid were considering the development of an even more technologically advanced camera system. Say the total investment required was to be $2.5 million, and net cash flows were expected to be $750,000 for the first year, $1,500,000 for the second year, and $2,000,000 for the third year. Because the technology would be superseded after the third year, the project would end then and there would be no salvage value. If Polaroid's cost of capital were 12 percent, what would be the net present value of this investment?

SOURCE: Based on *1985 Polaroid Corporation Annual Report.*

Notes

1. This chapter is based in part on J. Paul Peter and James H. Donnelly, Jr., *Marketing Management: Knowledge and Skills,* 4th ed. (Burr Ridge, Ill.: Irwin, 1995), Section 3.

2. For cases that require detailed ratio analyses of issues such as leverage, growth, and evaluation, consult J. Fred Weston and Eugene F. Brigham, *Essentials of Managerial Finance,* 10th ed. (Fort Worth: Dryden Press, 1993), pp. 48–64.

3. This list is from James C. Van Horne, *Financial Management and Policy,* 7th ed. © 1986, pp. 767–768. Reprinted by permission of Prentice-Hall, Inc., Englewood Cliffs, New Jersey.

4. Based on Weston and Brigham, *Essentials of Managerial Finance,* p. 330.

5. Ibid., Chapter 15.

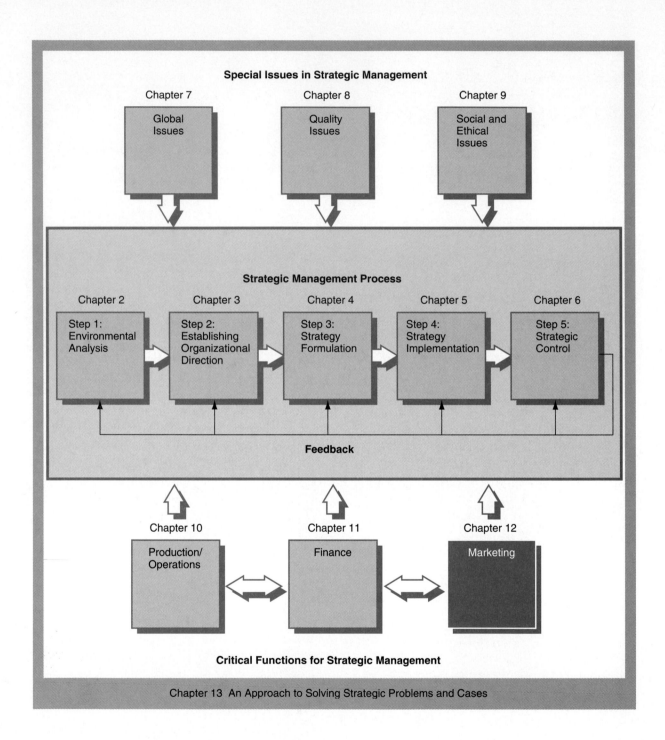

Special Issues in Strategic Management

Chapter 7

Global
Issues

Chapter 8

Quality
Issues

Chapter 9

Social and
Ethical
Issues

Strategic Management Process

Chapter 2

Step 1:
Environmental
Analysis

Chapter 3

Step 2:
Establishing
Organizational
Direction

Chapter 4

Step 3:
Strategy
Formulation

Chapter 5

Step 4:
Strategy
Implementation

Chapter 6

Step 5:
Strategic
Control

Feedback

Chapter 10

Production/
Operations

Chapter 11

Finance

Chapter 12

Marketing

Critical Functions for Strategic Management

Chapter 13 An Approach to Solving Strategic Problems and Cases

CHAPTER 12

The Marketing Function and Strategic Management

The marketing function facilitates exchanges between an organization and either industrial buyers or end users.[1] It is obviously an important function; profit-seeking organizations must develop and retain customers in order to generate sales and profits.[2] Nonprofit organizations also develop marketing strategies to attract donations of time, money, and other resources in order to maintain their operations and achieve their objectives.

Many of the strategic management issues that we have discussed in this text contribute to the creation of successful strategies for the marketing function, or marketing strategies. Environmental analysis is a critical aspect of marketing strategy development, because changes in an organization's environment can lead to both marketing opportunities and constraints on successful marketing. In particular, changes in the marketing strategies of competitors very directly affect the marketing opportunities available to an organization.

An organization's mission and objective statements provide a framework and guidance for designing marketing objectives and strategies. For example, if a firm adopts an organizational objective of increasing net profits by 15 percent per year, this goal has important implications for its efforts to develop new products and market existing products.

Finally, the development of marketing strategies involves strategic management functions such as planning, analysis, implementation, and control. Although there is no clear distinction between some aspects of strategic management and marketing strategy, marketing strategy focuses primarily on knowing, adapting to, and influencing consumers in an effort to achieve organizational objectives. Marketing strategies are usually designed to increase sales and market share in order to increase long-run profits.

In this chapter, we investigate the process of developing successful marketing strategies. We focus on those issues that are most commonly considered marketing tasks and avoid many of the more general strategic management issues discussed previously in the text. Figure 12.1 provides an overview of this process and outlines the contents of the chapter. We begin by discussing the analysis of consumer/product relationships, a critical aspect of the development of marketing strategy. Next we consider the different ways in which it is possible to segment a market, or divide it into groups of similar consumers. We then investigate the process of designing a marketing mix strategy. Finally, we examine the implementation and control of the firm's marketing strategy.

FIGURE 12.1   Strategic Marketing Process

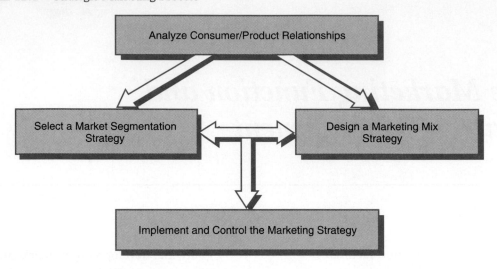

ANALYZING CONSUMER/PRODUCT RELATIONSHIPS

The first step in preparing a marketing strategy is to analyze consumer/product relationships. This analysis entails investigating why consumers buy a particular product, what the product means to them, what consequences they expect from using the product, how much they become involved in purchasing the product, and in what situations they purchase and use the product. Test marketing and primary market research may help answer these questions, and one can often gain considerable insight by investigating secondary sources of information and studying general buying habits.

In performing this analysis, it is useful first to classify products as either consumer or industrial products. **Consumer products** are those that are purchased by the final user, whereas **industrial products** are purchased to aid in the production of other products or services. Each of these types of products can be divided into the categories shown in Table 12.1. Consumer goods are commonly classified as convenience, shopping, or specialty goods on the basis of the degree of involvement consumers have with the product and how much time and effort they invest in purchasing it. Industrial goods are divided into five basic categories based on their roles in the production process. Table 12.1 also suggests some of the basic characteristics of these products and some considerations to take into account when marketing them. Simply classifying a product in this way provides some useful direction for developing marketing strategy.

Classifying products is a useful starting point in analyzing consumer/product relationships, but researching and studying the consumers of the product are critical. Consider a simple product such as toothpaste. What are some reasons why consumers buy this product? It seems clear that different consumers seek different benefits from the product. Decay prevention, fresh breath, sex appeal, whiter teeth, and plaque removal may have varying levels of importance to various consumers. Similarly, performance, economy, status, and styling vary in importance across groups of car buyers. Analysis of

TABLE 12.1

Categories of Products and Marketing Strategy Considerations

A. Consumer Products

Characteristics and Marketing Considerations	Type of Product		
	Convenience	Shopping	Specialty
CHARACTERISTICS:			
1. Time and effort devoted by consumer to shopping	Very little	Considerable	Cannot generalize; consumer may go to nearby store and buy with minimum effort or may have to go to distant store and spend much time and effort
2. Time spent planning the purchase	Very little	Considerable	Considerable
3. How soon want is satisfied after it arises	Immediately	Relatively long time	Relatively long time
4. Are price and quality compared?	No	Yes	No
5. Price	Low	High	High
6. Frequency of purchase	Usually frequent	Infrequent	Infrequent
7. Importance	Unimportant	Often very important	Cannot generalize
MARKETING CONSIDERATIONS:			
1. Length of channel	Long	Short	Short to very short
2. Importance of retailer	Any single store is relatively unimportant	Important	Very important
3. Number of outlets	As many as possible	Few	Few; often only one in a market
4. Stock turnover	High	Lower	Lower
5. Gross margin	Low	High	High
6. Responsibility for advertising	Manufacturer's	Retailer's	Joint responsibility
7. Importance of point-of-purchase display	Very important	Less important	Less important
8. Advertising used	Manufacturer's	Retailer's	Both
9. Brand or store name important	Brand name	Store name	Both
10. Importance of packaging	Very important	Less important	Less important

Continued

285

TABLE 12.1
Continued

B. Industrial Products

Characteristics and Marketing Considerations	Type of Product				
	Raw Materials	Fabricating Parts and Materials	Installations	Accessory Equipment	Operating Supplies
Example	Iron ore	Engine blocks	Blast furnaces	Storage racks	Paper clips
CHARACTERISTICS:					
1. Unit price	Very low	Low	Very high	Medium	Low
2. Length of life	Very short	Depends on final product	Very long	Long	Short
3. Quantities purchased	Large	Large	Very small	Small	Small
4. Frequency of purchase	Frequent delivery; long-term purchase contract	Infrequent purchase, but frequent delivery	Very infrequent	Medium frequency	Frequent
5. Standardization of competitive products	Very much; grading is important	Very much	Very little; custom-made	Little	Much
6. Limits on supply	Limited; supply can be increased slowly or not at all	Usually no problem	No problem	Usually no problem	Usually no problem
MARKETING CONSIDERATIONS:					
1. Nature of channel	Short; no intermediaries	Short; intermediaries only for small buyers	Short; no intermediaries	Intermediaries used	Intermediaries used
2. Negotiation period	Hard to generalize	Medium	Long	Medium	Short
3. Price competition	Important	Important	Not important	Not main factor	Important
4. Presale/postsale service	Not important	Important	Very important	Important	Very little
5. Demand stimulation	Very little	Moderate	Sales people very important	Important	Not too important
6. Brand preference	None	Generally low	High	High	Low
7. Advance buying contract	Important; long-term contracts	Important; long-term contracts	Not usually	Not usually	Not usually

SOURCE: Based on William J. Stanton, Michael J. Etzel, and Bruce J. Walker, *Fundamentals of Marketing*, 9th ed. (New York: McGraw Hill, 1991), pp. 171, 174.

SKILLS MODULE
MCI Dials Marketing Success

INTRODUCTION

Analysis of consumer/product relationships is an important starting point for developing sound marketing strategies. Review the following situation and then complete the skill development exercise to help you develop this important skill.

SITUATION

Early in 1993, MCI Communications decided to explore the untapped potential of the collect-call market. The company recognized that AT&T had all but cornered the $3-billion-a-year market by signing long-term contracts with stores, airports, and hotels with pay phones. The industry leader also benefited from its dialing formula—a simple 0 for operator and the number the caller wanted to contact.

MCI's perceptive marketing strategy to win some of the collect-call business took 11 weeks from conception to implementation. It was based on market research results that collect-calling costs were high because more than half such calls came from pay phones under long-term contracts with AT&T or other carriers. A ten-minute phone call could cost twice as much as a direct-dial call, ranging from $4.00 to $6.25, depending on where and when the call was made.

MCI research cast doubt on the assumption that the caller didn't care about the cost because the other person was paying for it. The company found that of the 300 million collect calls placed annually, 24 percent were from military personnel calling home, 33 percent were from children calling home, and 70 percent of the callers were under 30. Those findings suggested that families might encourage relatives to use a discount plan.

MCI Chairman Bert C. Roberts, Jr., approved the idea the day it was presented. The next job for MCI's marketing staff, and the most vital one, was to find an easy alternative to dialing 0 and the number. They came up with a number that is easy to recall and bypasses carriers that have contracts with pay-phone owners—1–800–COLLECT.

In addition, MCI set rates at up to 44 percent off AT&T's operator-assisted rates. Ads targeted young audiences—biplanes pulling 1–800–COLLECT banners flew over beaches and TV ads starred familiar faces from late-night television.

But the masterstroke was MCI's decision not to mention its name, so that the potential users of the service wouldn't think that only MCI subscribers could use it. The anonymity of 1–800–COLLECT bled calls from AT&T, whose research showed that half of those calling the MCI number had assumed it was run by AT&T. After the phone giant set up its own 1–800–OPERATOR number in an attempt to counter MCI's surge, it discovered that many callers needed spelling lessons; they were misdialing and punching in 1–800–OPERATER. That number was an MCI toll-free number, part of MCI's shrewd comeback in the face of AT&T's retaliatory strike. As a result, MCI handled a few hundred thousand dollars in mistaken calls. By March 1994, AT&T had started over with 1–800–CALL–ATT.

In 1993, AT&T held 75 percent of the collect-call market, MCI had 11 percent, and Sprint had 5 percent. MCI says that 18 million U.S. homes received at least one collect call through the 1–800–COLLECT program in its first year, up from 4.5 million collect calls in the prior year.

SKILL DEVELOPMENT EXERCISE

MCI was clearly successful in introducing its collect-calling campaign. 1–800–COLLECT was the result of consumer research that upended conventional wisdom about who made collect calls. Explain how you would analyze the consumer/product (or in this case, consumer/service) relationships for collect-calling services. Devise a marketing strategy for AT&T detailing where and how the company should direct its marketing efforts; include a synopsis of MCI's probable strategic response.

SOURCE: Mark Lewyn, "MCI Collects on 1-800 C-O-L-L-E-C-T," *Business Week*, June 13, 1994, p. 78.

consumer/product relationships may yield some initial idea of the appropriate market segments an organization should seek to satisfy with its products.

The Skills Module invites you to try your hand at analyzing consumer/product relationships.

SELECTING A MARKET SEGMENTATION STRATEGY

The logic of market segmentation is quite simple: it is based on the idea that a single product does not usually appeal to all consumers. Individual consumers' purchasing goals, product knowledge, involvement, and purchase behavior vary. For this reason, marketing strategists typically focus their marketing efforts on specific groups of consumers rather than on the whole population. **Market segmentation** is the process of dividing a market into groups of similar consumers and selecting the most appropriate group(s) for the organization to serve. Markets are selected on the basis of size, profit potential, and how well they can be defined and served by the organization.

Markets can be segmented on a variety of dimensions, or bases. Table 12.2 lists some of the more common dimensions for segmenting consumer and industrial markets. Often a number of these dimensions are used together to segment markets and develop profiles of the consumers in them. Typically, considerable market research is done to define particular markets very carefully. We will briefly describe four market segmentation techniques; geographic, demographic, psychographic, and benefit segmentation.

Geographic Segmentation

For many products, **geographic segmentation** offers a useful basis for initially defining markets. For example, the markets for such products as snowmobiles, ice fishing equipment, engine block heaters, and snow skiing equipment are concentrated in northern areas. Fast-food restaurants such as McDonald's and Burger King use information on population size and density to help them select restaurant locations. Because geographic data are available from public sources, collecting such information is an inexpensive way to explore market potential.

Demographic Segmentation

Demographic segmentation uses population characteristics to segment markets. Many products are designed for groups defined on the basis of sex (clothes, cosmetics), age (toys), or income (automobiles). Demographic variables are also used in conjunction with other segmentation techniques to describe particular markets more thoroughly. For example, a major market for light beer consists of men in their thirties who are eager to stay healthy and trim. In this market profile, both sex and age are demographic variables, and concerns about health and weight are psychographic variables.

Psychographic Segmentation

Psychographic segmentation, also called *lifestyle segmentation,* involves the study of consumers' activities (such as work, hobbies, and vacations), interests (such as family, job, and community), and opinions (about such things as politics, social issues, and business). Consumers are grouped together by empirical analysis of the similarity of their responses to research instruments into various lifestyle groups. A well-known psychographic segmentation system was developed at SRI International in California. This system, called VALS™ for "values and lifestyles," divided consumers in the United States into nine groups. However, while this segmentation system was commercially successful, it tended to place the majority of consumers into only one or two groups and

TABLE 12.2

Useful Segmentation Bases for Consumer and Industrial Markets

Consumer Markets	
Segmentation Base	**Base Categories**

GEOGRAPHIC SEGMENTATION

Region	Pacific, Mountain, West North Central, West South Central, East North Central, East South Central, South Atlantic, Middle Atlantic, New England
City, county, or SMSA size	Under 5,000, 5,000–19,999, 20,000–49,999, 50,000–99,999, 100,000–249,999, 250,000–499,999, 500,000–999,999, 1,000,000–3,999,999, 4,000,000 or over
Population density	Urban, suburban, rural
Climate	Warm, cold

DEMOGRAPHIC SEGMENTATION

Age	Under 6, 6–12, 13–19, 20–29, 30–39, 40–49, 50–59, 60+
Sex	Male, female
Family size	1–2, 3–4, 5+
Family life cycle	Young, single; young, married, no children; young, married, youngest child under 6; young, married, youngest child 6 or over; older, married, with children; older, married, no children under 18; older, single; other
Income	Under $5,000, $5,000–$7,999, $8,000–$9,999, $10,000– $14,999, $15,000–$24,999, $25,000–$34,999, $35,000 or over
Occupation	Professional and technical; managers, officials, and proprietors; clerical, sales; trades, supervisor, operatives; farmers; retired; students; housewives; unemployed
Education	Grade school or less, some high school, graduated high school, some college, graduated college, some graduate work, graduate degree
Religion	Catholic, Protestant, Jewish, other
Race	White, black, oriental, other
Nationality	American, British, French, German, Italian, Japanese, and so on

Continued

TABLE 12.2

Continued

Consumer Markets	
Segmentation Base	**Base Categories**

PSYCHOGRAPHIC SEGMENTATION

Social class	Lower-lower, upper-lower, lower-middle, upper-middle, lower-upper, upper-upper
Lifestyle	Traditionalist, sophisticate, swinger
Personality	Compliant, aggressive, detached

COGNITIVE AND BEHAVIORAL SEGMENTATION

Attitudes	Positive, neutral, negative
Benefits sought	Convenience, economy, prestige
Readiness stage	Unaware, aware, informed, interested, desirous . . . intention to purchase
Perceived risk	High, moderate, low
Innovativeness	Innovator, early adopter, early majority, late majority, laggard
Involvement	Low, high
Loyalty status	None, some, total
Usage rate	None, light, medium, heavy
User status	Nonuser, ex-user, potential user, current user

Industrial Markets	
Segmentation Base	**Base Categories**
Source loyalty	Purchase from one, two, three, four, or more suppliers
Size of company	Small, medium, large relative to industry
Average size of purchase	Small, medium, large
Usage rate	Light, medium, heavy
Product application	Maintenance, production, final product component, administration
Type of business	Manufacturer, wholesaler, retailer; SIC categories
Location	North, East, South, West; sales territories
Purchase status	New customer, occasional purchaser, frequent purchaser, nonpurchaser
Attribute importance	Reliability of supply, price, service, durability, convenience, reputation of supplier

SRI felt a need to update it to reflect changes in society. Thus, SRI developed a new typology called VALS 2™.[3]

VALS 2 is based on two national surveys of 2,500 consumers who responded to 43 lifestyle questions. The first survey developed the segmentation system, and the second validated it and linked it to buying and media behavior. The

FIGURE 12.2   Eight American Lifestyles in VALS 2™

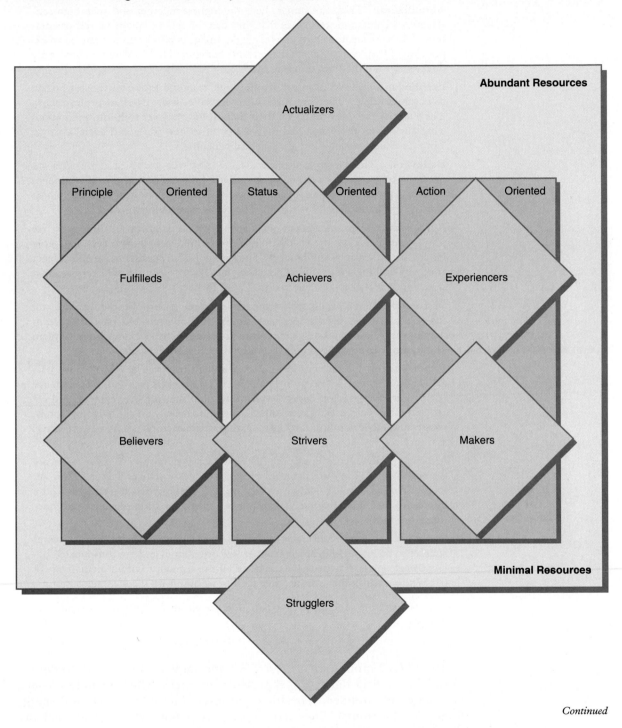

Continued

questionnaire asked consumers to agree or disagree with statements such as "My idea of fun at a national park would be to stay at an expensive lodge and dress up for dinner" and "I could stand to skin a dead animal." Consumers were then clustered into the eight groups shown and described in Figure 12.2.

FIGURE 12.2   *Continued*

Actualizers.   These consumers have the highest incomes and such high self-esteem and abundant resources that they can indulge in any or all self-orientations. They are located above the rectangle. Image is important to them as an expression of their taste, independence, and character. Their consumer choices are directed toward the finer things in life.

Fulfilleds.   These consumers are the high resource group of those who are principle-oriented. They are mature, responsible, well-educated professionals. Their leisure activities center on their homes, but they are well-informed about what goes on in the world and they are open to new ideas and social change. They have high incomes but are practical consumers.

Believers.   These consumers are the low resource group of those who are principle-oriented. They are conservative and predictable consumers who favor American products and established brands. Their lives are centered on family, church, community, and the nation. They have modest incomes.

Achievers.   These consumers are the high-resource group of those who are status-oriented. They are successful, work-oriented people who get their satisfaction from their jobs and families. They are politically conservative and respect authority and the status quo. They favor established products and services that show off their success to their peers.

Strivers.   These consumers are the low-resource group of those who are status-oriented. They have values very similar to Achievers but have fewer economic, social, and psychological resources. Style is extremely important to them as they strive to emulate people they admire and wish to be like.

Experiencers.   These consumers are the high-resource group of those who are action-oriented. They are the youngest of all the segments with a median age of 25. They have a lot of energy, which they pour into physical exercise and social activities. They are avid consumers, spending heavily on clothing, fast foods, music, and other youthful favorites—with particular emphasis on new products and services.

Makers.   These consumers are the low-resource group of those who are action-oriented. They are practical people who value self-sufficiency. They are focused on the familiar—family, work, and physical recreation—and have little interest in the broader world. As consumers, they appreciate practical and functional products.

Strugglers.   These consumers have the lowest incomes. They have too few resources to be included in any consumer self-orientation and are thus located below the rectangle. They are the oldest of all the segments with a median age of 61. Within their limited means, they tend to be brand-loyal consumers.

SOURCE: Martha Farnsworth Riche, "Psychographics for the 1990s," *American Demographics,* July 1989, pp. 24–26.

The VALS 2 groups are arranged in a rectangle measured on two dimensions. The vertical dimension represents resources, which include income, education, self-confidence, health, eagerness to buy, intelligence, and energy level. The horizontal dimension represents self-orientations and includes three different types. **Principle-oriented consumers** are guided by their views of how the world is or should be; **status-oriented consumers** are guided by the actions and opinions of others; **action-oriented consumers** are guided by a desire for social or physical activity, variety, and risk taking.

Each of the VALS 2 groups represents from 9 to 17 percent of the United States adult population. Marketers can buy VALS 2 information for a variety of products and can have it tied to a number of other consumer databases.

Benefit Segmentation

Underlying **benefit segmentation** is the concept that the benefits that people seek in consuming a given product are the real reasons for the existence of market segments. This approach attempts to measure consumer value systems and perceptions of various brands in a product class. The classic example of benefit segmentation is drawn from the toothpaste market.[4] As shown in Table 12.3, four basic segments were identified: the Sensory, Sociable, Worrier, and Independent segments.

The segments shown in Table 12.3 have important implications for many aspects of marketing strategy, including the selection of advertising copy and media, length of commercials, packaging, and new product design. For example, colorful packages might be appropriate for the Sensory segment, aqua packages (to indicate fluoride) for the Worrier group, and gleaming white packages for the Sociable segment because of their interest in white teeth. Benefit segmentation is a useful approach for investigating the meaning and value of products and brands to consumers.

Table 12.4 lists several questions that can help in analyzing consumer/product relationships and segmenting markets.

TABLE 12.3

Benefit Segmentation in the Toothpaste Market

	Sensory Segment	Sociable Segment	Worrier Segment	Independent Segment
Principal benefit sought	Flavor and product appearances	Brightness of teeth	Decay prevention	Price
Demographic strengths	Children	Teens, young people	Large families	Men
Special behavioral characteristics	Users of spearmint-flavored toothpaste	Smokers	Heavy users	Heavy users
Brands disproportionately favored	Colgate	Macleans, Ultra Brite	Crest	Cheapest brand
Lifestyle characteristics	Hedonistic	Active	Conservative	Value-oriented

SOURCE: Based on Russell I. Haley, "Benefit Segmentation: A Decision-Oriented Research Tool," *Journal of Marketing,* July 1968, pp. 30–33. From J. Paul Peter and James H. Donnelly, Jr., *Marketing Management: Knowledge and Skills,* 4th ed. (Burr Ridge, Ill.: Irwin, 1995), p. 84. Reprinted by permission.

TABLE 12.4

Some Questions to Ask When Analyzing Consumer/Product Relationships and Segmenting Markets

1. Why do consumers purchase this product?
2. What does this product mean to consumers, and how important to them is its purchase?
3. What does the product do for consumers in a functional, organizational, or social sense?
4. In what situations is the product purchased and used?
5. What are the appropriate dimensions for segmenting the market for this product?
6. Is market segmentation research necessary? If so, what are its costs and benefits?
7. Is this market segment large enough for the firm to serve profitably?
8. Can this market segment be reached efficiently, given the organization's resources?
9. Is competition too strong for the organization to attract consumers in this target market?
10. What are the implications of this analysis for marketing strategy?

DESIGNING A MARKETING MIX STRATEGY

The **marketing mix** consists of product, price, promotion, and channels of distribution (or place). These four elements are the controllable variables that organizations use to adapt to or influence market segments that they target. Organizations must develop strategies to synchronize all four of these elements so they work together to achieve the same objectives. We will discuss each of these elements in some detail, since they are the primary techniques that organizations use to obtain sales, profits, and market share.

Product Strategy

The survival of many organizations depends on developing and marketing successful new products and managing them throughout the product life cycle. In this section, we explain the process of developing and marketing new products in terms of a seven-stage **product life cycle.** This life cycle includes both stages that precede and stages that follow introduction of the product to the market. We then discuss several product characteristics that influence the success of new or existing products.

Stages in a Product's Life   The life of a successful product can be divided into seven stages, as shown in Figure 12.3. The stages from concept generation and screening to commercialization/introduction represent the process of new product development; the stages from commercialization/introduction to market decline/product deletion represent the phases of the traditional product life cycle. We will briefly describe each of these seven stages.

Concept Generation and Screening   New products start as ideas or concepts. Thus the first step in new product development involves generating concepts and screening out those that have little potential. New product concepts can come from a variety of sources, including consumers, competi-

FIGURE 12.3
Stages in a Product's
Life Cycle

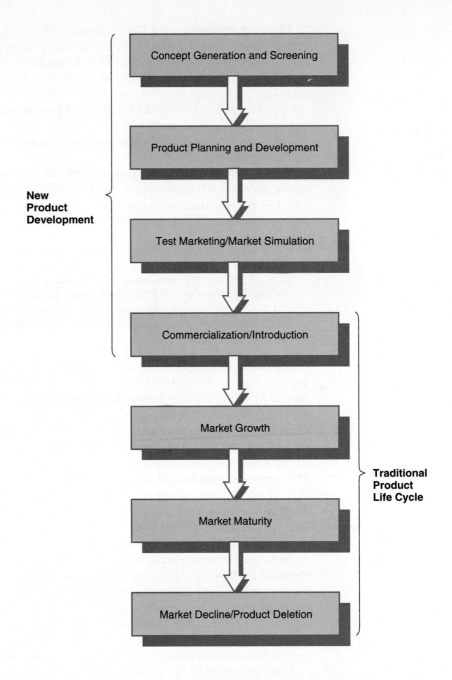

tors, salespeople, and the firm's own research and development department.
Typically, the industry a firm is in determines the types of products it seeks to
develop for consumers.

Some evidence suggests that firms are becoming more efficient at concept
generation and screening. Research on 13,000 new product introductions has
revealed that in 1968 it took an average of 58 ideas to generate one product.
In 1981, however, it took only 7 ideas to generate a product. This is partly because firms are spending more money in the earlier phases of product development, up from 10 percent to 21 percent of their total new-product dollars.[5]

Product Planning and Development   This stage involves further evaluation, planning, and development of product concepts that have passed the initial screening. These concepts are formalized into a product plan that includes cross-functional collaboration and analysis of production, marketing, financial, and competitive factors, as well as the results of prototype testing. If the product plan supports the feasibility of producing the product and results in favorable sales and profit estimates, then it is time to investigate consumer reactions to the product. This is commonly done through test marketing or market simulation.

Test Marketing/Market Simulation   In this stage, consumer reactions to the product are investigated. Traditionally, products have been test marketed in particular cities to determine their sales potential. However, as one analyst explains, there are a number of problems with test marketing:

> While a test market . . . sounds realistic, in fact almost everything can go wrong to mess up the findings. Competitors can distort the results of a test by slashing prices in the test city, promoting their brand[s] heavily, or even buying up all the items put out for the test sale, which is what happened some years ago when General Foods tried to test frozen baby food. Gerber, Libby, and Heinz bought it all. And though tests may not always be realistic, they're always expensive. They can cost up to $1.5 million.[6]

For these reasons, some firms have purchased or developed simulated market tests. Such a test is based on a small sample of the public. Members of this sample are shown ads and promotions for a variety of products, including the one being tested. The shoppers are then taken to a mock-up store or a real store where their purchases are recorded. The behavior of shoppers and their willingness to rebuy the item are then analyzed via computerized models. These models consist of sets of equations designed to simulate the market. This service ranges in cost from about $35,000 to $75,000 and can be run in eight weeks without giving competitors a look at the product. Some of these models have been credited with making very accurate predictions of product successes and failures, but their overall accuracy is sometimes disputed.

Commercialization/Introduction   If test market results and other determinations of business planning are favorable, the product is introduced to the market. This is the last stage of the new product development process and the first stage of the traditional product life cycle. The main objectives at this stage are to make consumers aware of the product and to get them to try it. Figure 12.4 shows a typical sales curve generated as a product passes through the traditional product life cycle. The tabular portion of this figure shows how several other characteristics and strategies change as the product ages.

Many estimates of the percentage of new products that fail after introduction have been offered; they range from 33 to 90 percent. However, an extensive review of this question found that about 30 to 35 percent of new consumer products fail to meet the expectations of their developers.[7]

Market Growth   In this stage, sales of the product begin to increase rapidly and the product may become profitable. The market may expand because of increased repurchases by original buyers and a large set of new buyers who have been influenced by them. As shown in Figure 12.4, a major objective at this point is to establish a strong position with distributors and users of the product.

FIGURE 12.4

Elements of Marketing Strategy in the Product Life Cycle

Stages in the Product Life Cycle

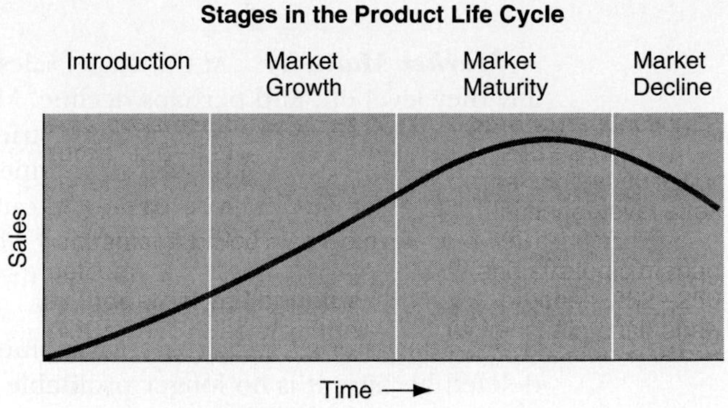

	Introduction	Market Growth	Market Maturity	Market Decline
Competition	None of importance	Some emulators	Many rivals competing for a small piece of the pie	Few in number with a rapid shakeout of weak members
Overall strategy	Market establishment; persuade early adopters to try the product	Market penetration; persuade mass market to prefer the brand	Defense of brand position; check the inroads of competition	Preparations for removal; milk the brand dry of all possible benefits
Profits	Negligible because of high production and marketing costs	Reach peak levels as a result of high prices and growing demand	Increasing competition cuts into profit margins and ultimately into total profits	Declining volume pushes costs up to levels that eliminate profits entirely
Retail prices	High, to recover some of the excessive costs of launching	High, to take advantage of heavy consumer demand	What the traffic will bear; need to avoid price wars	Low enough to permit quick liquidation of inventory
Distribution	Selective, as distribution is slowly built up	Intensive; employ small trade discounts since dealers are eager to store	Intensive; heavy trade allowances to retain shelf space	Selective; unprofitable outlets slowly phased out
Advertising strategy	Aim at the needs of early adopters	Make the mass market aware of brand benefits	Use advertising as a vehicle for differentiation among otherwise similar brands	Emphasize low price to reduce stock
Advertising emphasis	High, to generate awareness and interest among early adopters and persuade dealers to stock the brand	Moderate, to let sales rise on the sheer momentum of word-of-mouth recommendations	Moderate, since most buyers are aware of brand characteristics	Minimum expenditures required to phase out the product
Consumer sales and promotion expenditures	Heavy, to entice target groups, with samples, coupons, and other inducements, to try the brand	Moderate, to create brand preference (Advertising is best suited to do this job.)	Heavy, to encourage brand switching, hoping to convert some buyers into loyal users	Minimal, to let the brand coast by itself

SOURCE: Adapted from William Zikmund and Michael D'Amico, *Marketing*, 3d ed. (New York: John Wiley & Sons), Copyright © John Wiley & Sons, Inc. Reprinted by permission of John Wiley & Sons, Inc. and the authors.

Market Maturity   At this stage, sales begin to grow less rapidly; eventually they level off, and perhaps decline. Most of the consumers who are ever going to purchase the product have tried it and are either continuing to purchase it or have abandoned it. Competition becomes most intense at this stage and some competitors are forced out of the market or merge with other firms. As Figure 12.4 suggests, a major objective at this point is to maintain and strengthen customer loyalty to the firm's products.

Market Decline/Product Deletion   At this stage, the product has run its normal course and sales begin to decline rapidly. Eventually, the product is deleted because it is no longer profitable to maintain it. Of course, attempts can be made to revitalize the product. These attempts may include seeking new markets for the product, finding new uses for the product, or adding new features to the product. However, if opportunities to revitalize a product do exist, they should be considered long before a product is under consideration for deletion.

Reasons for Product Success   Why do some products have long, profitable lives while others are expensive failures? There is no simple answer to this question, but several factors contribute to product acceptance by consumers. Two of the most important are competitive differential advantage and product symbolism.

Competitive Differential Advantage   In marketing strategy, competitive differential advantage derives from the characteristics of a product that make it superior to competitive products. We believe that competitive differential advantage is a most important reason for product success and should be considered in any product strategy analysis.

In some situations, a competitive differential advantage can be obtained through technological developments. For example, at the product class level, RCA introduced the videodisc player that showed programs on any TV set. The disc player cost half as much as cassette machines, and the discs were cheaper than videocassettes. However, videocassettes had a competitive differential advantage over the disc player: Cassette machines could record programs and disc players could not. RCA assumed that recording ability was not an important factor to consumers—and lost more than $500 million learning otherwise.

At the brand level, however, it is often difficult to maintain a competitive differential advantage based on superior technology because competitors promptly copy new or improved technology. For example, Sony pioneered the Betamax system of videotape recorders and, in 1975, had the entire VCR market. Yet by 1982 Sony held only 14 percent of the market and was fighting for survival as competitors simply copied the technology and, having spent little on R&D, could sell at lower prices. Thus, although competitive differential advantage is a critical element of profitable marketing strategies, for such an advantage to be sustained, it often must derive from something other than technology or product modifications. One important source of sustainable competitive differential advantage is product symbolism.

Product Symbolism   Product symbolism is what the product means to consumers and what consumers experience in purchasing and using it. At the brand level, it refers to the image that a particular item evokes in the minds of consumers. Marketing researchers recognize that products have symbolic importance and that consumption of some goods may depend more on their social meaning than on their functional utility.

For many product classes, the products and brands offered are relatively homogeneous in the functions they perform for the consumer, yet these products and brands differ widely in market share. For example, it is well-known that few consumers can differentiate among the tastes of various brands of beer. Yet market shares vary dramatically, partly because of the brand images that have been created. Similarly, brands of jeans such as Levi's, Lee, and Wrangler are very similar in appearance, price, and quality. Yet it seems clear that these brand names have important meanings for consumers and symbolize different values, resulting in differences in market share. Guess? jeans obtained sales of $200 million in the first three years. A large portion of the market for these jeans consisted of teenagers who may have sought to present an identity different from that of wearers of traditional brands, such as their parents. Thus, the differential advantage of this brand of jeans may have been that Guess? products were a symbol of new generation of jeans wearers.

Product symbolism and appropriate brand images can actually be more important than technological superiority. For example, the IBM personal computer was not the fastest, most advanced PC on the market and its keyboard layout was criticized. IBM was not the first in the PC market and had little experience in marketing consumer goods. IBM dominated the PC market, however, perhaps because it had a superior company image as a computer manufacturer. IBM *meant* computers to many consumers.

Table 12.5 lists several questions that can help in analyzing product strategies. Product symbolism and brand images are often created by other elements of the marketing mix, including pricing, promotion, and channels of distribution. We will now discuss strategy in terms of each of these elements.

TABLE 12.5

Some Questions to Ask When Analyzing Product Strategies

1. What process does the organization use to develop new products?
2. How are new products evaluated?
3. What previous success has the organization had in developing new products?
4. What is the product's stage in the product life cycle?
5. What consumers make up the target market, and what are their reactions to the product?
6. What is the competitive differential advantage of this product?
7. Can this competitive differential advantage be sustained, or can it easily be copied by competitors?
8. Is product symbolism or brand image an important factor in the market, and what is the image of the organization's product among consumers?
9. What product strategies are competitors using, and how successful are they?
10. What changes in product characteristics could be made to improve the sales, profits, and market share of this product?

Pricing Strategy

Pricing strategy comes into play in three situations: (1) when an organization is introducing a new product and establishing its initial price; (2) when an organization is considering a long-term price change for an existing product; and (3) when an organization is considering a short-term price change, usually a decrease to stimulate demand. Three important influences on pricing strategy are consumer characteristics, organization characteristics, and competitive characteristics.

Consumer Characteristics   The nature of the target market and its expected reactions to a given price or price change are major considerations in pricing strategy. For some products, consumers may use price as an indicator of quality, so a low price does *not* stimulate demand. For many products, price is used to segment consumers into prestige, mass, and economy markets. Price is also used for creating product and brand images. For example, Old Milwaukee beer was promoted as tasting just as good as Budweiser at a lower price. Thus, it is positioned as a bargain for the consumer. Other products, such as Chivas Regal scotch, Cadillac automobiles, and Gucci handbags, are positioned as prestige products partly on the basis of their high prices.

Organization Characteristics   Several organization characteristics influence pricing strategies. First, the variable cost for a product usually sets the lower limit on its price. The price of a product must at least cover the variable costs of production, promotion, and distribution and should provide some profit. Second, the objectives of the organization influence pricing strategy. A common pricing objective is to achieve a target return on investment consistent with the organization's objectives. Third, the nature of the product influences pricing strategy. Distinctive products often have higher prices, for example, and perishable products must often be priced lower to promote faster sales.

Finally, the stage of the product life cycle that a product has reached may influence pricing strategy. A **skimming pricing strategy** involves setting a relatively high price early in the product life cycle and then gradually decreasing the price when competitors enter the market. Generally, skimming is used when the organization has a temporary monopoly and when demand for the product is not very sensitive to price. A **penetration pricing strategy** involves setting a relatively low price early in the product life cycle in anticipation of raising it at a later stage. Penetration is used when the firm expects competition to move in rapidly and when demand is strongly influenced by price. Penetration is also used to obtain large economies of scale and to create a large market rapidly.

Competitive Characteristics   Competitors—their number, size, cost structures, and past reactions to price changes—influence pricing strategy. An organization can price at, below, or above the competition, depending on such factors as its own cost structure, competitive differential advantage, and financial and marketing abilities.

Table 12.6 lists several questions that can help in analyzing pricing strategies.

Promotion Strategy

Designing promotion strategies involves selecting the appropriate mix of promotion tools to accomplish specific objectives. Four types of promotion tools

TABLE 12.6

Some Questions to Ask When Analyzing Pricing Strategies

1. How important is price to the target consumers of this product?
2. Do consumers of this product use price as an indicator of quality?
3. How will various prices affect the product or brand image?
4. What are the variable costs of the product, and will consumers pay a price that will cover them plus the desired level of profit?
5. What are the organization's objectives, and what price must be charged to obtain these objectives?
6. Is the product distinctive or perishable to the degree that pricing strategies are affected?
7. What is the product's life cycle stage, and what influence does this have on pricing strategy?
8. Do conditions warrant a penetration or skimming pricing strategy?
9. What are the prices of competitive products?
10. How will competition react to the initial price or to the price change contemplated?

can be used to inform, persuade, and remind consumers or industrial buyers:

1. **Advertising** is any paid form of nonpersonal presentation and promotion of ideas, goods, or services by an identified sponsor. (Examples include TV and radio commercials and magazine and newspaper ads.)
2. **Sales promotion** is a short-term incentive to encourage the purchase or sale of a product or service. (Examples include contests, games, premiums, and coupons.)
3. **Publicity** is any unpaid form of nonpersonal presentation of ideas, goods, or services. (An example is the discussion of a new product on a TV talk show.)
4. **Personal selling** is direct, face-to-face communication between sellers and potential buyers for the purpose of making an exchange.

As shown in Table 12.7, each of these promotion tools has a variety of advantages and disadvantages. No single method is always superior, and promotion mix decisions depend on several factors. For example, although sales of complex products such as insurance and computers are influenced by advertising, some personal selling is usually required to close sales.

Simpler products such as cereal and shampoo can be marketed to consumers via advertising and sales promotion, but salespeople are often required for selling the product to retailers. In general, designing promotion strategies involves three steps: determining promotion objectives, formulating the promotion plan, and developing promotion budgets.

Determining Promotion Objectives   Table 12.8 lists some general objectives of promotion. Which of these promotion objectives (or others) is appropriate depends in part on the results of the company's earlier analysis of consumer/product relationships. There are, of course, many possible relationships between consumers and products, and they lead to different promotion objectives. For example, consider the following situations:

TABLE 12.7

Advantages and Disadvantages of Major Promotion Tools

Advantages	Disadvantages
ADVERTISING	
Can reach many consumers simultaneously	May waste promotion dollars if it reaches consumers who are not potential buyers
Offers relatively low cost per exposure	Is a major target of marketing critics because of high visibility
Is excellent for creating brand images	Offers very brief exposure time for advertising message
Offers high degree of flexibility and variety of media choices; can accomplish many different types of promotion objectives	Can be quickly and easily screened out by consumers
SALES PROMOTION	
Can stimulate demand by short-term price reductions	May influence primarily brand-loyal customers to stock up at the lower price and result in few new customers
Offers a large variety of tools to choose from	May have only short-term impact
Can be effective for changing a variety of consumer behaviors	May hurt brand image and profits by overuse of price-related sales promotion tools
Can be easily tied in with other promotion tools	If effective, may be easily copied by competitors
PUBLICITY	
Can be positive and stimulate demand at no cost as "free advertising"	Content of messages cannot be completely controlled
May be perceived by consumers as more credible because it is not paid for by the seller	Not always available
May be paid more attention because messages are not quickly "screened out," as many advertisements are	Seldom a long-term promotion tool for brands, since messages are repeated only a limited number of times
	Can be negative and hurt sales as well as company, product, and brand images
PERSONAL SELLING	
Can be the most persuasive promotion tool, since salespeople can directly influence purchase behaviors	Is high in cost per contact
Allows two-way communication	Can be expensive and difficult since it involves training and motivation
Is often necessary for technically complex products	Has a poor image as a career, making recruitment difficult
Allows direct one-on-one targeting of promotional effort	Can hurt sales as well as company, product, and brand images if done poorly

TABLE 12.8

Some General Objectives of Promotion Strategies

1. Increase brand awareness
2. Increase consumer knowledge of product and brand
3. Change consumer attitudes about company
4. Change consumer attitudes about brand
5. Increase short-term sales
6. Increase long-term sales
7. Build corporate image
8. Build brand image and positioning
9. Announce a price reduction
10. Inform consumers of place of sale
11. Develop brand loyalty
12. Reassure consumers of brand quality
13. Close a sale
14. Prospect for customers
15. Obtain product trial
16. Inhibit purchase of competitive brands
17. Inform consumers of favorable credit terms
18. Increase store patronage and store loyalty
19. Reduce dissonance
20. Inform, persuade, and remind consumers

- *Situation 1: Consumers are unaware of a brand but have a need for the product.* In this situation, an appropriate promotion objective is to inform consumers of the existence of the brand and demonstrate its benefits and uses. Companies promoting new products frequently employ advertising and free samples to accomplish this objective. Promotion objectives in this situation are stated in terms of a particular percentage increase in awareness of a product.
- *Situation 2: Consumers are aware of a brand but purchase a competing brand.* In this situation, an appropriate promotion objective is to demonstrate the superiority of the firm's brand. For example, Burger King employed a series of comparative ads emphasizing the merits of flame broiling to attract McDonald's customers. Promotion objectives in this situation may be stated in terms of increases in market share or changes in consumer behavior.
- *Situation 3: Consumers are aware of a brand and purchase it, but they sometimes purchase competing brands also.* In this situation, a primary promotion objective may be to develop a higher degree of brand loyalty. For example, cereal manufacturers frequently enclose cents-off coupons in packages to encourage repeat purchases of the same brand.
- *Situation 4: Consumers are aware of a brand and purchase it consistently.* In this situation, a primary promotion objective may be to reinforce purchases via reminder advertising or phone calls. For example, automobile salespeople frequently call past customers to encourage them to rebuy the same brand. Similarly, promotion can be used to inform consumers of new uses of the product. For example, Arm & Hammer dramatically increased sales of its baking soda by demonstrating its use in freshening refrigerators and carpets.

These brief sketches of a few possible situations and appropriate promotion objectives illustrate three important points. First, objectives depend on the relationships between consumers and various products and brands. Second, promotion tools vary in their effectiveness for achieving specific objectives. Advertising is more effective for achieving awareness in a mass market, yet sales promotion and personal selling may be more effective for closing sales and developing brand loyalty. Third, promotion objectives change over time to reflect changes in consumers, competitors, and other elements of the environment. The Company Example illustrates how strategy drives the choice of promotion methods.

Formulating the Promotion Plan   At this stage, decisions are made concerning the desired structure of the promotion mix, and a promotion plan is developed. These decisions and plans are based on the objectives determined in the previous stage, which in turn depend on the analysis of consumer/product relationships.

As we have noted, the promotion mix consists of advertising, sales promotion, publicity, and personal selling. The task at this stage is to determine to what degree and in what situations each of these tools will be used. In addition, appropriate promotion messages, media choices, and schedules are formulated on the basis of the firm's promotion objectives for the product, the nature of the product, and the purchasing habits and media preferences of target consumers.

Many of these decisions depend on whether the product is new or has reached a later stage of the life cycle. If the product is new, managers must decide whether to field a sales force, what its size should be, and what territories it should cover. They must also address compensation and management issues. Similarly, for new products, they must develop appropriate brand images and appeals.

This does not mean that management of the sales force or advertising decisions can be ignored for existing products. The structure and sales organization that are already in place should be reviewed. Similarly, for an existing product, many decisions about the appropriate messages, media, and scheduling for other forms of promotion usually require careful consideration. Decision making in this situation involves investigating alternative promotion methods that could boost the efficiency of the promotion mix.

Developing Promotion Budgets   Managers establish promotion budgets by many methods. For example, some firms use the **affordable method,** which amounts to allocating to promotion as much as the firm can afford. Other firms use a **percentage of sales method,** allocating some particular percentage (such as 5 percent) of current or anticipated sales to promotion. Still others use a **competitive parity method,** setting the promotion budget to match competitors' outlays. Each of these methods has its advantages and disadvantages, but most promotion experts argue for what is called the **task method,** or *objective and task method.*

The task method takes a three-stage approach that corresponds to the three stages outlined in this section. A firm that uses the task method first determines its promotion objectives, then it formulates a promotion plan detailing the specific promotion tasks that it must perform to achieve its promotion

COMPANY EXAMPLE

Thor-Lo's Product Does the Marketing

Just as Nike and Reebok took the sneaker and re-designed it into a specialized sport shoe, Thor-Lo Inc. created sports-specific socks. Its low-key marketing—the virtues of the socks are reported mostly by word-of-mouth—helped the company earn $30 million in revenues in 1991.

Thor-Lo's foot equipment includes socks designed for 18 different sports, including tennis, aerobics, and basketball. Extra, high-density padding is placed in the areas where the foot takes the most pounding.

The socks were the brainchild of James Throneburg, the son of Thor-Lo's founders. The company, founded in 1953, was a private-label maker of socks for FootJoy, Izod, and other name-brand manufacturers. The decision in the mid-1980s to market the new, innovative socks under the company name garnered yawns from store owners. Their indifference changed when they realized how much more lucrative it was to sell a pair of Thor-Lo Padds than a competitor's socks. At about $7.50 a pair, Thor-Los are almost double the price of standard athletic socks. Using the standard markup, that placed

nearly $4 in retailers' pockets on every pair of Thor-Los they sold.

Today, most stores carry wall displays of Thor-Lo's different socks so shoppers can feel the difference between the company's high-end, padded products and their competitors.

Throneburg's innovation created an entirely new market. Sports-specific socks are now a $150-million-a-year retail business. Thor-Lo's share of that market was almost 50 percent in 1991; recognizing the success of its brand image, it discontinued all of its private-label manufacturing. During that time, the company spent just $47,000 on promotional advertising. That figure does not include Thor-Lo's one concession to modern sports marketing—hiring a celebrity spokesperson. But its use of tennis pro Martina Navratilova arose from her pursuit of the company, and she accepted far less than she could have earned from another sock endorsement.

SOURCE: Gretchen Morgenson, "The Foot's Friend," *Forbes*, April 13, 1992, pp. 60–62.

objectives. In the third step, it estimates the costs of performing all of the promotion tasks that it has selected. The sum of these costs represents the appropriate promotion budget. Of course, if the resulting figure is more than the organization can afford, or more than management is willing to invest, some reduction must be made in the planned promotion strategy.

Table 12.9 lists several questions that can help in analyzing promotion strategies.

Channel Strategy

A **channel of distribution** is the combination of institutions through which a seller markets products to industrial buyers or ultimate consumers. In **direct channels,** manufacturers sell directly to end users. In **indirect channels,** manufacturers use one or more intermediaries to sell to end users. Table 12.10 lists some of the types of marketing intermediaries that make up channels of distribution.

Manufacturers use intermediaries because intermediaries can perform marketing functions more efficiently than manufacturers or because manufacturers lack the financial resources or expertise to market directly to consumers. Table 12.11 lists the major functions performed in channels of distribution. It is important to note that, whether the manufacturer or one or more intermediaries perform these functions, all of them must usually be assumed

---

TABLE 12.9

Some Questions to Ask When Analyzing Promotion Strategies

1. What is the target market for this product, and what sources of product information do these consumers use?
2. What are the overall promotion objectives, and what are the specific objectives of each promotion tool?
3. What is the appropriate promotion mix of advertising, sales promotion, publicity, and personal selling?
4. Who is responsible for planning, organizing, implementing, and controlling the promotion strategy?
5. What should the various forms of promotion communicate about the product?
6. What are the appropriate types and combinations of personal and nonpersonal media to use? Consider salespeople, television, radio, billboards, magazines, newspapers, and direct mail.
7. How long should the firm use this promotion strategy before changing its focus or methods?
8. What is the appropriate schedule for sales calls, advertisements, sales promotions, and publicity releases?
9. How much should be spent on each of the various forms of promotion, and how much should be spent in total?
10. How will the effectiveness of promotion be measured?

---

by someone. Thus distribution requires that managers decide who will do which of these tasks.

From the consumer's viewpoint, channels provide form, time, place, and possession utility. To create **form utility** is to convert raw materials into finished goods and services that consumers seek to purchase. Creating **time utility** means making products available when consumers want to buy them. In creating **place utility,** channels make products available where consumers can purchase them. In creating **possession utility,** channels facilitate the transfer of ownership of products from manufacturers to consumers.

Given the variety of types of intermediaries, distribution functions, and types of utility provided to consumers by channels, the task of selecting and designing a channel of distribution may at first appear overwhelming. However, in many industries all competitors use essentially the same channel structure and the same types of intermediaries. In these industries, a manufacturer may *have* to use the traditional channels in order to compete in the industry. For example, nationally branded consumer food products are typically sold in a variety of grocery stores, and automobiles are typically sold through franchised dealers. These channels are likely to be highly efficient and thus appropriate for a manufacturer. In addition, no other types of intermediaries may be available to market the product. This is not to say that channel design allows no room for innovation. For example, health and beauty aids are commonly sold in a variety of retail stores. Yet Mary Kay Cosmetics sells such products door-to-door, often very profitably.

The four major concerns in designing channels of distribution are dis-

TABLE 12.10

Major Types of Marketing Intermediaries

Intermediary—independent business concern that operates as a link between producers and ultimate consumers or industrial buyers.

Merchant intermediary—intermediary who buys goods outright and takes title to them.

Agent—a business unit that negotiates purchases, sales, or both but does not take title to the goods in which it deals.

Wholesaler—merchant establishment operated by a concern that is primarily engaged in buying, taking title to, and usually storing and physically handling goods in large quantities, then reselling the goods (usually in smaller quantities) to retailers or to industrial or business users.

Retailer—merchant intermediary who is engaged primarily in selling to ultimate consumers.

Broker—intermediary that serves as a go-between for the buyer or seller; assumes no title risks, does not usually have physical custody of products, and is not looked upon as a permanent representative of either the buyer or the seller.

Sales agent—independent channel member, either an individual or a company responsible for the sale of a firm's products or services but does not take title to the goods sold.

Distributor—wholesale intermediary, especially in lines where selective or exclusive distribution is common at the wholesale level in which the manufacturer expects strong promotional support; often a synonym for *wholesaler*.

Jobber—intermediary who buys from manufacturers and sells to retailers; a wholesaler.

Facilitating agent—business firm that assists in the performance of distribution tasks other than buying, selling, and transferring title (i.e., transportation companies, warehouses, etc.).

SOURCE: Based on Peter D. Bennett (ed.), *Dictionary of Marketing Terms* (Chicago: American Marketing Association, 1988).

tribution coverage, channel control, total distribution cost, and channel flexibility.

Distribution Coverage   Because of the characteristics of the product, the environment needed to sell the product, and the needs and expectations of potential buyers, different products call for varying intensity of distribution coverage. Distribution coverage varies on a continuum from intensive through selective to exclusive distribution. **Intensive distribution** involves selling the product through as many wholesalers and retailers as possible. Intensive distribution is appropriate for most convenience goods because of their low unit value and high frequency of purchase. **Selective distribution** involves selling through a limited number of intermediaries in a particular geographic area. Appliances and home furnishings are usually distributed selectively, on the basis of the reputation and service quality of particular retailers. **Exclusive distribution** involves selling through only one intermediary in a particular territory and is commonly employed to increase the selling effort for a manufacturer's product. Automobile dealerships and beer distributors are examples of exclusive distribution arrangements.

TABLE 12.11

Marketing Functions Performed in Channels of Distribution

Buying—purchasing products from sellers for use or for resale.

Selling—promoting the sale of products to ultimate consumers or industrial buyers.

Sorting—function performed by intermediaries in order to bridge the discrepancy between the assortment of goods and services generated by the producer and the assortment demanded by the consumer. This function includes four distinct processes: sorting out, accumulating, allocating, and assorting.

Sorting out—sorting process that breaks down a heterogeneous supply into separate stocks which are relatively homogeneous.

Accumulating—sorting process that brings similar stocks from a number of sources together into a larger, homogeneous supply.

Allocating—sorting process that consists of breaking a homogeneous supply down into smaller and smaller lots.

Assorting—sorting process that consists of building an assortment of products for use in association with each other.

Concentrating—process of bringing goods from various places together in one place.

Financing—providing credit or funds to facilitate a transaction.

Storing—maintaining inventories and protecting products to provide better customer service.

Grading—classifying products into different categories on the basis of quality.

Transporting—physically moving products from where they are made to where they are purchased and used.

Risk-taking—taking on business risks involved in transporting and owning products.

Market research—collecting information concerning such things as market conditions, expected sales, consumer trends, and competitive forces.

SOURCE: Based on Peter D. Bennett (ed.), *Dictionary of Marketing Terms* (Chicago: American Marketing Association, 1988).

Channel Control   One important influence on the design of distribution channels is the amount of control an organization wants over the marketing of its products. Typically, a more direct and exclusive channel gives a manufacturer more control. Often, however, a channel is controlled by an intermediary rather than the manufacturer. For example, a large retailer such as Sears, Roebuck may control small manufacturers who produce Sears-labeled products.

Total Distribution Cost   The concept of total distribution cost suggests that channels should be designed to minimize costs, other things being equal. Thus, if a system of wholesalers and retailers can distribute a product more cheaply than marketing directly to consumers, such a system should be selected, other things equal. However, it is also important to consider the effects of a particular channel on sales, profits, the total marketing mix, and the level of consumer service that is needed to make the product successful.

Channel Flexibility   One reason why a channel strategy must be chosen so carefully is that it usually involves a long-term commitment to a particular

TABLE 12.12

Some Questions to Ask When Analyzing Channel Strategies

1. What is the target market for this product, and where do these consumers usually purchase?
2. What is the nature of the product, and what problems and opportunities does this information suggest for distribution?
3. How do competitors distribute products like this, and how successful have they been?
4. What are the total distribution costs of various channel alternatives?
5. What degree of market coverage is needed to reach the target market?
6. How competent is the organization to manage various types of channels?
7. How much control over the channel does the organization want?
8. Are appropriate intermediaries available and willing to distribute and market the product?
9. What is the relative market power of the manufacturer versus different types of intermediaries?
10. Can the manufacturer afford to perform all of the marketing functions, and can it do so efficiently?

course of action. Channels are typically not changed as frequently as other elements of the marketing mix. For example, long-term leases for retail store space and long-term agreements with wholesalers limit the flexibility of an organization. In general, more uncertainty in the environment makes channel alternatives that involve long-term commitments less favorable.

Table 12.12 lists several questions that can help in analyzing channel strategies.

IMPLEMENTING AND CONTROLLING THE MARKETING STRATEGY

Implementing a marketing strategy involves putting it into action according to a predefined schedule. Even the most carefully developed strategies often cannot be executed with perfect timing. Thus, the organization must closely monitor and coordinate implementation. In some situations, the basic strategy may need adjustments because of changes in the environment. For example, a competitor's introduction of a new product may make it desirable to speed up or delay implementation. The reaction of the market to the withdrawal of the original-formula Coke certainly required a change in planned marketing strategies for the Coca-Cola Company. In almost all situations, some fine-tuning is necessary.

Controlling the marketing strategy involves three steps. First, the results of the implemented strategy are measured. Second, the results are compared with the objectives of the strategy. Third, managers determine whether the strategy is achieving its stated objectives. If so, they must decide whether some change in strategy would improve results. If not, they must decide whether the objectives were unrealistic or the strategy is simply not effective. If the strategy is judged ineffective, a new one must be developed.

Measuring the effects of a particular strategy can involve considerable market research. For example, measuring the effects of a strategy designed to "increase awareness of the product by 25 percent" usually involves primary market research on members of the target market to estimate changes in awareness. However, marketing strategies designed to achieve other objectives, such as increases in sales, profits, or market share, can often be evaluated by examining secondary information, such as the organization's sales records.

SUMMARY

This chapter investigated the marketing function and its role in strategic management. The first step in preparing a marketing strategy is to analyze consumer/product relationships. Classifying goods as either consumer or industrial products is often helpful. Consumer products can be further divided into convenience, shopping, and specialty goods on the basis of how much trouble and expense the consumer will go to in order to purchase them. Similar classification schemes exist to help firms market industrial goods. Any research that sheds light on the reasons why consumers buy certain products can help businesses understand their target markets better.

Market segmentation is the process of dividing a market into groups of similar consumers and selecting the most appropriate group or groups to serve. For some products geographic segmentation is best. For others, the most effective segmentation is based on a demographic variable such as sex, age, or income. Segmentation based on lifestyle, or the psychographic characteristics of a market, is sometimes appropriate, as is segmentation in terms of the benefits people seek in consuming a given product.

The marketing mix consists of product, price, promotion, and channels of distribution. The product's position in the seven-stage product life cycle (from concept generation through deletion) profoundly affects the way it is marketed. Other significant factors include any competitive differential advantage that can be established either functionally or through product symbolism. Pricing strategy is influenced by consumer characteristics, organization characteristics, and competitive characteristics. Some cases call for low prices and sometimes high prices are best. The major approaches to promoting products are advertising, sales promotion, publicity, and personal selling. All suit different objectives and work best under different conditions. Choosing one or more promotion techniques is a key part of the marketing mix decision. Selecting a channel of distribution—that is, the combination of intermediaries through which the firm markets products to the consumer—is another crucial decision. Channels convert products into the forms consumers want, they make products available where and when consumers want to buy them, and they facilitate the transfer of ownership of products from manufacturers to consumers. The intermediary can sometimes be eliminated, but the functions it performs cannot.

In the course of implementing a marketing strategy, it is important to work to keep a plan on schedule and to be flexible enough to adjust it if changes in the environment make it advisable to do so. Controlling the marketing strategy involves measuring the results of the strategy, determining whether it is achieving its objectives, and then deciding what changes are needed to correct an ineffective strategy or (perhaps) to improve a successful one.

KEY TERMS

consumer product,
p. 284
industrial product,
p. 284
market segmentation,
p. 288
geographic segmenta-
tion, p. 288
demographic segmen-
tation, p. 288
psychographic seg-
mentation, p. 288
principle-oriented con-
sumer, p. 292
status-oriented con-
sumer, p. 292
action-oriented con-
sumer, p. 292
benefit segmentation,
p. 293

marketing mix, p. 294
product life cycle,
p. 294
skimming pricing strat-
egy, p. 300
penetration pricing
strategy, p. 300
advertising, p. 301
sales promotion,
p. 301
publicity, p. 301
personal selling, p. 301
affordable promotion
budgeting method,
p. 304
percentage of sales
promotion budgeting
method, p. 304
competitive parity pro-
motion budgeting

method, p. 304
task promotion bud-
geting method, p. 304
channel of distribu-
tion, p. 305.
direct channels, p. 305
indirect channels,
p. 305
form utility, p. 306
time utility, p. 306
place utility, p. 306
possession utility, p.
306
intensive distribution,
p. 307
selective distribution,
p. 307
exclusive distribution,
p. 307

CHECKLIST   Analyzing Marketing in Problems and Cases

___ 1. Does the problem or case involve relationships between an organization and consumers of the organization's product(s)?

___ 2. Why should consumers purchase the organization's product(s) rather than competitive offerings? That is, what is the organization's competitive differential advantage from the consumer's point of view?

___ 3. What are the appropriate market segments for the organization's products, and has the firm identified them?

___ 4. Are these market segments large enough to serve profitably, and can the organization serve them efficiently?

___ 5. What are the strengths and weaknesses of the organization's current marketing strategy?

___ 6. Are all elements of the marketing strategy consistent and designed to achieve the organization's objectives?

___ 7. Which elements of marketing strategy are of greatest concern in this problem or case? That is, is this a very general problem concerning the development and implementation of a marketing strategy, or is it focused on a particular type of decision?

___ 8. Does the organization have good marketing skills, and is it capable of formulating and implementing a sound marketing strategy?

___ 9. How would the marketing strategy have to change to achieve the organization's objectives?

___ 10. What is the probable long-term impact on the organization of following the current or suggested marketing strategy?

Additional Readings

Churchill, Gilbert A., Jr., and J. Paul Peter. *Marketing: Creating Value for Customers.* Burr Ridge, Ill.: Austen Press/Irwin, 1995.

Cravens, David, and Shunnon Shipp. "Market-Driven Strategies for Competitive Advantage." *Business Horizons,* January/February, 1991, pp. 54–66.

Kotler, Philip. *Marketing Management: Analysis, Planning, and Control,* 8th ed. Englewood Cliffs, N.J.: Prentice-Hall, 1994.

McCarthy, E. Jerome, and William D. Perrault. *Basic Marketing.* 11th ed. Homewood, Ill.: Irwin, 1993.

Peter, J. Paul, and James H. Donnelly, Jr. *Marketing Management: Knowledge and Skills,* 4th ed. Burr Ridge, Ill.: Irwin, 1995.

Treacy, Michael, and Fred Wiersema. "Customer Intimacy and the Other Value Disciplines." *Harvard Business Review,* January/February, 1993, p. 84.

CASE

Niche Marketing by Boston Beer

During the past decade, Jim Koch has built Boston Beer Co. into a $50 million company and the largest specialty brewer in the United States. Boston Beer has won market share by hammering away at the key weaknesses of imports—lengthy shipping times and less hearty, made-for-export formulations—while touting its own quality ingredients and brewing processes.

Indeed, Koch's beer, Samuel Adams Boston Lager, has won a number of industry awards. On four separate occasions at the Great American Beer Festival, it has been voted the Best Beer in America; it also has received six gold medals at the festival's blind tastings.

Consumer response has been strong. Sales jumped 63 percent in 1992 when the company went national and placed its beer in the bars and restaurants of 48 states.

Initially, however, Koch's marketing challenge was deceptively simple: create sales in a market that focuses as much on the image of the consumer who drinks the product or the fantasy world it creates. He had created a full-bodied beer to compete against premium imports in the high end of the beer market. Koch believed that the quality of his product would be his best sales tool.

While other microbrewers aimed their marketing at more sophisticated beer consumers, however, Koch was determined to sell directly against the imports. Koch based his marketing approach on his product, using a recipe for a pre-Prohibition beer that was heavier in taste and more full-bodied than Budweiser or Miller. His compliance with Germany's strict beer-purity laws and use of "noble" hops was aimed at attracting a select group of beer drinkers past their college days who could pay premium prices for good-tasting beer.

With only $240,000 in start-up capital, Koch hired a brewery to brew his beer; besides saving the $10 million it would cost to build a state-of-the-art brewery from scratch, this move gave Koch access to superior facilities and skills. The downside was that the beer would retail at $20 a case, roughly 15 percent more than premium imports such as Heineken. "It was a marketing nightmare," he says.

He began the slow process of convincing retailers—bars, restaurants, supermarkets, and package stores—as well as consumers to try his beer and to pay the higher price. He relied on persistent personal sales calls, occasionally visiting a potential customer 15 times before winning an agreement to carry the product. Many told him: "My customers don't drink the beer; they drink the advertising."

He responded in 1986 with a $100,000 marketing and advertising campaign that sold the beer rather than the lifestyle. No beaches, bikinis, or funny dogs were featured. Instead, print ads proclaimed that imported versions of Heineken, Beck's, and St. Pauli Girl did not pass Germany's purity standards because they contained corn starch or sugar. In addition, Koch appealed to drinker's patriotism by playing up Samuel Adams' domestic origins: "Declare your independence from foreign beer."

The brashness of the campaign garnered media attention and further established Samuel Adams' brand-name recognition. In addition, Koch redefined point-of-sale marketing. Samuel Adams table tents feature more than the Boston Beer logo. They also include the bar's name and a listing of all its beverages.

While ensuring that Boston Beer had the production capacity to supply each new market as the company expanded, Koch began hiring sales reps. In 1989, the firm had fewer than a dozen; today it has 70 across the nation— about the same as beer giant Anheuser-Busch. Highly personalized selling is still the company's hallmark; the sales force calls on 1,000 accounts a week, and each salesperson carries a supply of hops to be able to offer a sample.

DISCUSSION QUESTIONS

1. What is Boston Beer's competitive differential advantage?
2. How are environmental factors contributing to the company's success?
3. What are the marketing limits of Boston Beer's reliance on premium pricing to differentiate its product?

SOURCE: Jenny C. McCune, "Brewing Up Profits," *Management Review,* April 1994, pp. 16–20.

Notes

1. This chapter is based on J. Paul Peter and James H. Donnelley, Jr., *Marketing Management: Knowledge and Skills,* 4th ed. (Burr Ridge, Ill.: Irwin, 1995), Section 1; and J. Paul Peter and Jerry C. Olson, *Consumer Behavior and Marketing Strategy,* 3d ed. (Homewood, Ill.: Irwin, 1993), Section 5.
2. Theodore Levitt, *The Marketing Imagination* (New York: Free Press, 1983), p. 5.
3. This discussion is based on Martha Farnsworth Riche, "Psychographics for the 1990s," *American Demographics,* July 1989, pp. 24–26 ff.
4. See Russell I. Haley, "Benefit Segmentation: A Decision-Oriented Research Tool," *Journal of Marketing,* July 1968, pp. 30–35. Also see Russell I. Haley, "Benefit Segmentation—20 Years Later," *Journal of Consumer Marketing,* no. 1 (1983), pp. 5–13.
5. Jeremy Main, "Help and Hype in the New-Products Game," *Fortune,* February 7, 1983, pp. 60–64. Also see C. Merle Crawford, *New Products Management,* 4th ed. (Burr Ridge, Ill.: Irwin, 1994).
6. Ibid., p. 64.
7. See C. Merle Crawford, *New Products Management,* 4th ed. (Burr Ridge, Ill.: Richard D. Irwin, 1994).

PART V

Framework for Strategic Analysis

This part of the text explains a detailed approach to analyzing strategic management problems and cases. It is designed primarily to address analysis of comprehensive problems and cases, although the general logic of the approach can also help students to identify and analyze more specialized issues. Skilled case analysts think flexibly and adapt this approach to specific problems or cases. You will find the approach helpful when you analyze the cases in this text and when you set out to solve the actual strategic management problems you will face as a practicing manager.

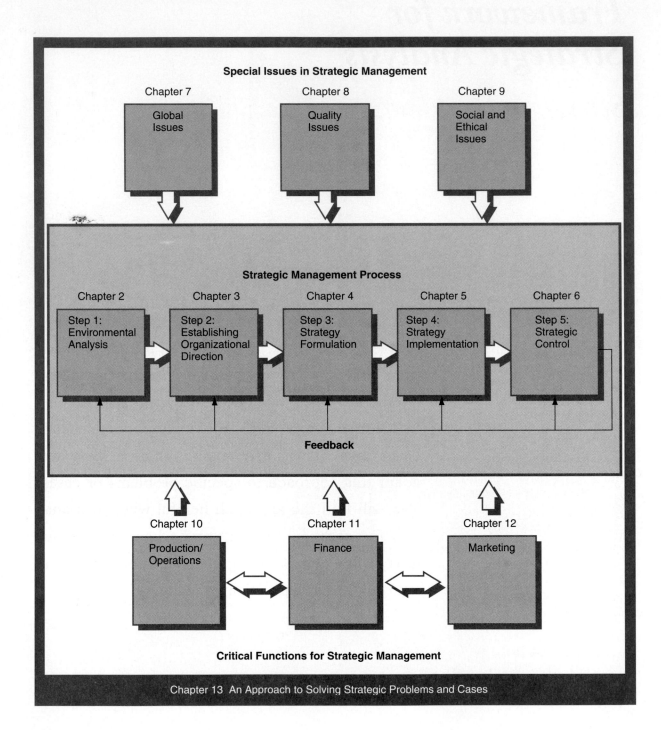

Special Issues in Strategic Management

Chapter 7

Global Issues

Chapter 8

Quality Issues

Chapter 9

Social and Ethical Issues

Strategic Management Process

Chapter 2

Step 1: Environmental Analysis

Chapter 3

Step 2: Establishing Organizational Direction

Chapter 4

Step 3: Strategy Formulation

Chapter 5

Step 4: Strategy Implementation

Chapter 6

Step 5: Strategic Control

Feedback

Chapter 10

Production/ Operations

Chapter 11

Finance

Chapter 12

Marketing

Critical Functions for Strategic Management

Chapter 13 An Approach to Solving Strategic Problems and Cases

Comprehensive Approach to Analyzing Strategic Problems and Cases

Since its development at the Harvard Business School in the 1920s, case analysis has become a major tool of management education. **Cases** are detailed descriptions or reports of strategic management problems. They are often written by trained observers who were actually involved with the organizations and problems or issues described in the cases. Cases usually include both qualitative and quantitative data that students must analyze in order to determine appropriate alternatives and solutions.

Since managers encounter many different types of strategic management problems, students encounter many different types of cases. Some cases involve large, diversified companies; others involve small, single-product companies. Some cases involve very successful companies seeking to maintain industry leadership; others focus on failing companies working to avoid bankruptcy. One case may involve a complicated mixture of strategic management problems; another may focus on a single issue.

A primary advantage of the case method is that it introduces a measure of realism into strategic management education. Rather than emphasizing concepts, the case method stresses the *application* of concepts and sound logic to real-world problems. In this way students learn to bridge the chasm between abstraction and application and to appreciate the value of both.

The purpose of this chapter is to outline a general approach to the analysis of strategic problems and cases. In addition, we suggest some common pitfalls to avoid in case analysis and some approaches to presenting cases. Remember, however, that although the approach offered here is a logical and useful way to develop sound analyses, no single approach can be applied routinely or mechanically to all cases. Cases differ widely in scope, context, and amount of information available. Analysts must always be ready to customize this approach to the particular situations they face.

For example, our approach offers a number of worksheets to assist analysts in various stages of case analysis. These worksheets are designed for broad, general cases and may have to be adapted to more specialized cases and problems. In short, there is no magic formula to guarantee an effective case analysis, and there is no substitute for logical, informed thinking on the part of the case analyst.

A major reason instructors use the case method is that analyzing cases helps students develop and improve their skills at identifying

This chapter is based on J. Paul Peter and James H. Donnelly, Jr., *A Preface to Marketing Management,* 6th ed. (Burr Ridge, Ill.: Irwin, 1994), pp. 328–342.

TABLE 13.1

A Case for Case Analysis

Cases help to bridge the gap between classroom learning and the so-called *real world* of strategic management. They provide us with an opportunity to develop, sharpen, and test our analytical skills at:

- Assessing situations
- Sorting out and organizing key information
- Asking the right questions
- Defining opportunities and problems
- Identifying and evaluating alternative courses of action
- Interpreting data
- Evaluating the results of past strategies
- Developing and defending new strategies
- Interacting with other managers
- Making decisions under conditions of uncertainty
- Critically evaluating the work of others
- Responding to criticism

SOURCE: Adapted from David W. Cravens and Charles W. Lamb, Jr., *Strategic Marketing: Cases and Applications,* 4th ed. (Burr Ridge, Ill.: Richard D. Irwin, 1993), p. 95. Reprinted by permission.

problems and creating sound solutions to them. If this process required nothing more than routinely plugging information into a formula, there would be no need for strategic managers! Managers are paid to recognize problems and to formulate and implement sound solutions to them. Having a successful career in management depends on developing these skills. Table 13.1 lists some of the skills that case analysis helps student analysts develop.

CASE ANALYSIS FRAMEWORK

The basic approach to case analysis that we propose is shown in Figure 13.1. This four-stage process suggests that analysts first clearly define the problem or issue to be resolved. Second, they should formulate reasonable alternatives that could potentially solve the problem. Third, analysts should evaluate each of the alternatives and compare them to find an effective solution. Finally, the alternative judged to be most effective and efficient should be selected and implemented to solve the problem.

When this process is carried out in a real situation, an additional step is included. Analysts would evaluate the effects of implementing the alternative to determine whether the problem had been solved. If so, they would continue to monitor the situation to ensure the sustained effectiveness of the alternative. If not, they would go back to the problem definition and begin the whole process again to continue the search for an effective solution.

This problem-solving approach to case analysis is the approach we advocate. However, for students who are not experienced in the analysis of strategic problems and cases, this basic framework may be inadequate and oversimplified because it does not explain how to approach each of these tasks.

FIGURE 13.1
Stages in Case Analysis

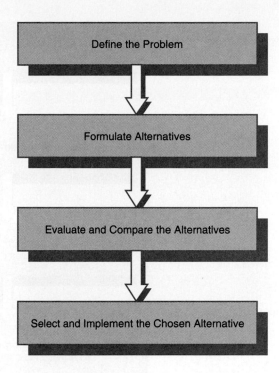

For example, consider the first stage, problem definition. What is desired here is a clear, unambiguous statement of the major problems or issues that define the case. Yet, just as in real situations that confront practicing managers, few cases offer direct statements of these pivotal problems. In fact, after initially reading a case, students often conclude that the case is no more than a description of events that present no problems or important issues for analysis. Even in cases that do include direct statements about problems or issues, the problem is almost always deeper or more complex than first meets the eye, and much more analysis must be done.

For these reasons we have developed the more detailed framework for case analysis shown in Figure 13.2. This framework is designed to help students recognize case problems and issues and sequentially devise appropriate solutions to them.

Analyze and Record the Current Situation

Whether the analysis of a strategic problem is conducted by a manager, a student, or an outside consultant, the first step is to analyze and record the current situation. This does not mean writing up a history of the organization or rewriting the case material. It involves the type of environmental analysis described in the following paragraphs.

Analyzing and recording the current situation is critical for three reasons. First, until the analyst has developed a clear understanding of the current situation, it is impossible to determine appropriate courses of action. In other words, one has no basis for deciding how to improve a situation until one knows what that situation is.

Second, the major purpose of this stage of the analysis is to investigate the current and potential problems involved in the case. By sequentially analyzing

FIGURE 13.2
Expanded Framework
for Case Analysis

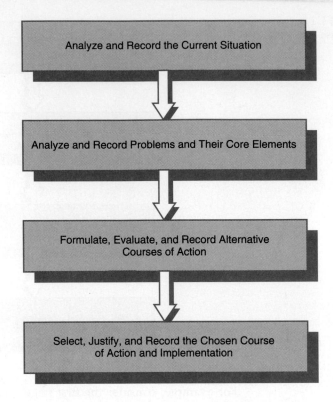

all elements of the current situation, the analyst clarifies those problems and amasses evidence that they are the central issues.

Third, this stage is useful for delineating the level of analysis for a specific case. "Level of analysis" means the overall scope of the problem. For example, some cases emphasize issues that arise at the industry level, whereas others focus on particular organizations, certain departments, individual executives, or particular strategic decisions. Clearly, determining the appropriate level of analysis is a very important aspect of case analysis.

In an effort to pinpoint case problems, it is useful to analyze sequentially each component or aspect of the general, operating, and internal environments. Table 13.2 lists these elements and the types of questions that should be asked in analyzing them.

In very few cases are all of these components or aspects crucial for the analysis. However, until each component or aspect is considered, there is no way to judge its relative importance. The analyst who considers each component and aspect in detail avoids missing critical issues. In other words, the key task at this stage of the analysis is to consider every possible environmental element in order to assess problems and opportunities in the case situation.

An analysis of any of the components or aspects of the environment may have important implications for defining case problems and for supporting appropriate solutions to the problems. Thus, keeping a detailed record of all of the relevant information uncovered in the environmental analysis is crucial. Table 13.3 presents a **worksheet** for recording this information and for further investigating its impact on the case.

TABLE 13.2

Study Areas in Environmental Analysis

GENERAL ENVIRONMENT

1. *Economic component*   What is the state of such economic variables as inflation, unemployment, and interest rates? What are the trends in these variables, and how are they relevant to the case?
2. *Social component*   What is the state of such social variables as education levels, customs, beliefs, and values? What are the trends in these variables, and how are they relevant to the case?
3. *Political component*   What is the state of such political variables as lobbying activities and government attitudes toward business? What are the trends in these variables and how are they relevant to the case?
4. *Legal component*   What is the level of such legal variables as federal, state, and local legislation? What are the trends in these variables and how are they relevant to the case?
5. *Technological component*   What is the level of technology in the industry? What technological trends are relevant to the case?
6. *Ethical component*   Does the case or problem involve ethical issues?

OPERATING ENVIRONMENT

1. *Customer component*   What are the target markets and customer profiles, and how are they relevant to the case?
2. *Competition component*   What are the major barriers to entry in this industry? What are the strengths, weaknesses, strategies, and market shares of major competitors, and how are they relevant to the case?
3. *Labor component*   What factors influence the supply of labor, and how are they relevant to the case?
4. *Supplier component*   What factors influence relationships between suppliers of resources and the firm, and how are they relevant to the case?
5. *International component*   What is the state of international factors? What international trends are relevant to the case?

INTERNAL ENVIRONMENT

1. *Organizational aspects*   What organizational or managerial issues, concepts, and analyses are relevant to the case?
2. *Marketing aspects*   What marketing issues, concepts, and analyses are relevant to the case?
3. *Financial aspects*   What financial issues, concepts, and analyses are relevant to the case?
4. *Personnel aspects*   What personnel issues, concepts, and analyses are relevant to the case?
5. *Production aspects*   What production issues, concepts, and analyses are relevant to the case?

In completing an environmental analysis, the analyst should keep six major points in mind:

1. Careful analysis is often required to separate relevant information from superfluous information. Just like the situations facing a practicing manager, cases often include information that is irrelevant to the major issues.

TABLE 13.3			

General Worksheet for Analyzing the Current Situation

Environment	Relevant Issues (Specific to Case)	Case Impact (Favorable/ Unfavorable)	Case Importance (Important/ Unimportant)
GENERAL ENVIRONMENT			
Economic component			
Social component			
Political component			
Legal component			
Technological component			
Ethical component			
OPERATING ENVIRONMENT			
Customer component			
Competition component			
Labor component			
Supplier component			
International component			
INTERNAL ENVIRONMENT			
Organizational aspects			
Marketing aspects			
Financial aspects			
Personnel aspects			

In order to get a clear understanding of the case problems, the analyst must decide what information is important and what to ignore.

2. It is important to determine the difference between symptoms of problems and current and potential problems themselves. Symptoms of problems are indicators of problems but are not problems per se. For example, a decline in sales in a particular sales territory is a symptom of a problem. The problem is the root cause of the decline in sales—perhaps the field representative stopped making sales calls on minor accounts in response to dissatisfaction with the firm's compensation plan.

3. In recording the current situation, the analyst must recognize the difference between facts and opinions. Facts are objective statements or accounts of information such as financial data reported in a balance sheet or income statement. Opinions are subjective interpretations of facts or situations. For example, when a particular executive expresses the belief that sales will increase by 20 percent next year, this is an opinion. The analyst must not place too much emphasis on unsupported opinions and must carefully consider any factors that may bias people's opinions.

4. It is often useful to collect additional information from outside the case when performing a situational analysis. Appendix 13A offers a summary of sources of secondary data from which additional information can be obtained. This information can be very useful for putting the problem in

context and for supporting an analysis. Remember, though, that the major problems are contained in the case, and the analyst should not need outside information to recognize them.

5. Regardless of how much information is contained in the case and how much additional information is collected, the analyst usually finds it impossible to characterize the current situation completely. At this point assumptions must be made. Clearly, because different analysts might make widely differing assumptions, assumptions must be stated explicitly. Doing so avoids confusion about how the analyst perceives the current situation and enables other analysts to evaluate the reasonableness and necessity of the assumptions.

6. When an analyst concludes that a certain aspect of an environmental analysis has no bearing on the case, he or she should say so explicitly. Moreover, analysts should avoid trying to force or stretch information to fit into each of the environmental components. Indeed some aspects are likely to be irrelevant to any specific case, although each must be evaluated to determine whether it is relevant.

Analyze and Record Problems and Their Core Elements

The environmental analysis just described is useful for developing a general understanding of the current situation. However, its primary purpose is to help the analyst recognize the major problems or issues. In other words, comparing the case situation with an optimal situation should highlight the inconsistencies between them. By an optimal situation, we mean a situation in which activities are performed in a manner consistent with sound managerial principles and logic.

For example, suppose analysis of a particular case revealed that although an organization had done an excellent job of setting objectives, its current strategy was not designed appropriately to accomplish these objectives. Because management principles strongly recommend that strategies flow from objectives, this inconsistency and the reasons for it should be carefully considered. The deviation in strategy is probably symptomatic of a deeper managerial problem.

Recognizing and recording problems and their core elements is crucial for a meaningful case analysis. Obviously, if the root problems are not determined and explicitly stated and understood, the remainder of the case analysis has little merit because it does not focus on the key issues.

Table 13.4 presents a worksheet to help analysts recognize and record problems. This table emphasizes the importance of providing evidence that a particular problem is a critical one. Simply stating that a particular issue is the major problem is not sufficient; analysts must also provide the reasoning by which they reached this conclusion.

Formulate, Evaluate, and Record Alternative Courses of Action

At this stage, the analyst addresses the question of what can be done to resolve the problems defined in the previous part of the analysis. Generally, several alternative courses of action that might help alleviate the problem are available. One approach to developing alternatives is to brainstorm as many as possible and then reduce the list to a workable number of the most feasible. Another

TABLE 13.4

General Worksheet for Defining Problems and Their Core Elements

MAJOR PROBLEM OR ISSUE

Description of problem or issue:

_____
_____
_____
_____

Evidence that this is a major problem or issue:

1. Facts _____
_____

2. Symptoms or other effects of the problem _____
_____

3. Opinions _____
_____

4. Assumptions _____
_____

(Repeat as necessary for cases involving several problems or issues.)

approach is to screen each alternative as it is developed, saving for further evaluation and comparison only those that meet predetermined feasibility criteria. Regardless of the method used to develop alternatives, the final list should usually include only three or four of the better solutions.

After listing a number of feasible alternatives, the analyst evaluates their strengths and weaknesses. Strengths include anything favorable about the alternative (such as increased efficiency, increased productivity, cost savings, or increased sales and profits). Weaknesses include anything unfavorable about the alternative (such as its costs in time, money, and other resources or its relative ineffectiveness at solving the problem). Table 13.5 offers a worksheet for evaluating alternative courses of action.

Sound logic and the application of managerial principles are particularly important at this stage. It is essential to avoid alternatives that might alleviate the problem but could at the same time spawn a new, more serious problem or require a greater investment of resources than solving the problem warrants. Similarly, analysts must be as objective as possible in their evaluation of alternatives. For example, it is not uncommon for analysts to ignore important weaknesses of an alternative that they favor.

Select, Justify, and Record the Chosen Course of Action and Implementation

It is now time to select the alternative that best solves the problem, while creating a minimum of new problems. This alternative is selected via careful analysis of the strengths and weaknesses of each alternative scrutinized in the previous stage. Recording the logic and reasoning that precipitated the selection of a particular alternative is very important. Regardless of what alternative is selected, the analyst must justify the choice.

TABLE 13.5

General Worksheet for Evaluating Alternative Courses of Action

ALTERNATIVE 1

Description of alternative: _____

_____

_____

Strengths of alternative: _____

_____

Weaknesses of alternative: _____

_____

Overall evaluation of alternative: _____

_____

_____

ALTERNATIVE 2

Description of alternative: _____

_____

_____

Strengths of alternative: _____

_____

Weaknesses of alternative: _____

_____

Overall evaluation of alternative: _____

_____

_____

(Repeat as necessary for each feasible alternative.)

At this stage in the analysis, an alternative has been selected, and the analyst has explained why she or he feels it is the appropriate course of action. The final phase in case analysis is to devise an action-oriented implementation plan. Analysts should describe their proposed implementation plans in as much detail as possible.

Table 13.6 offers a worksheet to use in considering implementation issues. Although cases do not always contain enough information for the analyst to answer all of these questions in detail, reasonable recommendations for implementation should be formulated. In doing so, the analyst may have to make certain assumptions about commonly used and effective methods of implementing strategic alternatives.

PITFALLS TO AVOID IN CASE ANALYSIS

Analysts commonly make a variety of errors in the process of case study. Below we discuss some of the mistakes analysts make most frequently. When evaluating your analyses or those of others, use this list as a guide to spotting potential shortcomings.

TABLE 13.6

General Worksheet for Implementing the Chosen Alternative

1. What should be done to implement the chosen alternative effectively?
Specific recommendation: _____

_____

_____

Justification: _____

_____

2. Who should be responsible for implementing the chosen alternative?
Specific recommendation: _____

_____

Justification: _____

_____

3. When and where should the chosen alternative be implemented?
Specific recommendation: _____

_____

Justification: _____

_____

4. How should the chosen alternative be evaluated for success or failure?
Specific recommendation: _____

_____

Justification: _____

_____

Inadequately Defining Problems

Analysts often recommend courses of action without adequately understanding or defining the problems that characterize the case. This sometimes occurs because analysts jump to premature conclusions upon first reading a case and then proceed to interpret everything in the case as justifying those conclusions—even factors that they should realize argue against them. Closely related is the error of analyzing symptoms without determining the root problems. A sound case analysis absolutely depends on a clear understanding of major case problems.

Searching for "The Answer"

Analysts sometimes spend a great deal of time searching through secondary sources to find out what an organization actually did in a particular case and then present this alternative as the one, right answer. However, this approach ignores the objective of undertaking a case study: to learn through exploration and discussion. There is no one official or correct answer to a case. Rather, many good analyses and solutions, as well as many poor ones, usually exist.

Assuming the Case Away

Analysts sometimes make such sweeping assumptions that the case problem is essentially assumed away. For example, suppose a case concerns a firm that has lost a major share of its market. Simply concluding that the firm will increase its market share by 10 percent per year for the next five years is an example of assuming the case away.

Not Having Enough Information

Analysts often complain that a case does not give enough information to support a good decision. However, there is good reason for not presenting all of the information in a case. In real business situations, managers and consultants seldom have all the information they would need to make an optimal decision. Reasonable assumptions and predictions have to be made, and the challenge is to arrive at intelligent solutions in spite of uncertainty and limited information.

Relying on Generalizations

Analysts sometimes discuss case problems and recommendations at such a general level that their work has little value. Case analysis calls for specific problems and recommendations, not sweeping generalizations. For example, to recommend that the structure of the firm be changed is to generalize. However, to provide a detailed plan for changing the organizational structure, to explain just what the structure should be, and to give one's reasons for this solution is to make a specific recommendation.

Postulating a Different Situation

Analysts sometimes exert considerable time and effort contending that "if the situation were different, I'd know what course of action to take" or "if the manager hadn't already fouled things up so badly, the firm wouldn't have any problems." Such reasoning ignores the fact that the events in the case have already happened and cannot be changed. Even though analysis or criticism of past events may be necessary in diagnosing problems, the situation as it exists must be addressed in the end, and decisions must be based on it.

Focusing Too Narrowly

Too often, analysts ignore the effects that a change in one area has on the rest of the situation. Although cases are sometimes labeled as concerning specific types of issues, this does not mean that other variables can be ignored. For example, changing the price of a product may well influence the appropriate methods of promotion and distribution.

Abandoning Realism

In many cases, analysts get so obsessed with solving a particular problem that their solutions become totally unrealistic. For example, designing and recommending a sound $1 million advertising program for a firm with a capital structure of $50,000 is totally unrealistic, even though, if it were possible to implement, it might solve the given problem.

Setting Up Straw Man Alternatives

Analysts sometimes offer a single viable alternative and several others that are extremely weak and untenable. The analysts then proceed with the evaluation and selection of an alternative (predictably enough) by discrediting the **straw man alternatives** and accepting the single viable solution. Such an approach to case analysis is inappropriate, because what is desired is a *set* of alternatives that it is worthwhile to evaluate. Case analysis can enhance the development of decision-making skills only when each alternative has some important strengths and analysts must make an informed choice.

Recommending Research or Consultants

Analysts sometimes offer unsatisfactory solutions to case problems by recommending either that some research be conducted to uncover problems or that a consultant be hired to do so. Although engaging in further research and hiring consultants may occasionally be useful recommendations as auxiliary steps in an analysis, it is still the analyst's job to identify the problems and decide how to solve them. When research or consultants are recommended in a case analysis, the rationale, costs, and potential benefits should be fully specified in the case report.

Rehashing Case Material

Analysts sometimes go to great lengths rewriting a history of an organization as presented in the case. This is unnecessary and wasteful: the instructor and other analysts are already familiar with this information. Similarly, student analysts sometimes copy case tables and figures and include them in written reports. This too is unnecessary. However, developing original graphs, pie charts, or other visual aids based on the case material is often a useful way to make a particular point.

Table 13.7 offers some further guidelines on approaching cases and gives an example of an effective student analysis.

Not Thinking!

By far the worst mistake analysts make is not thinking. Often analysts mistakenly assume that, having simply organized the case material in a logical format, they have done a case analysis! Similarly, although analysts usually have some general knowledge of a firm or situation, they often ignore it when working on a case. For example, suppose that a case involves a major automobile manufacturer. Although the case may say nothing about foreign imports, they may well have an important impact on the firm and should be considered. Analyzing cases requires that knowledge of management principles and sound logic from outside the case be applied.

After attempting unsuccessfully to analyze the first case or two, analysts sometimes give up and assure themselves that they cannot do case analyses. Such a conclusion is almost always unwarranted and ignores the fact that performing case analyses is a *learned* skill. To be sure, some students master case analysis much more quickly than others. Yet most students can become skillful analysts of cases and problems if they continue working hard on the cases and learning from class discussions.

COMMUNICATION OF THE CASE ANALYSIS

The final task in case analysis that we will consider here is to communicate the results of the analysis. The most comprehensive and insightful analysis has little value if it is not communicated effectively. Communication includes not only organizing the information in a logical manner but also using proper grammar and spelling. In addition, the overall appearance of a written report

TABLE 13.7

What Does Case "Analysis" Mean?

A common criticism of prepared cases goes something like this: "You repeated an awful lot of case material, but you really didn't analyze the case." At the same time, it is difficult to verbalize exactly what *analysis* means: Critics may say, "I can't explain exactly what it is, but I know it when I see it!"

It is not surprising that confusion arises, because the term *analysis* has many definitions and means different things in different contexts. In terms of case analysis, *analysis* means going beyond simply describing the case information. It includes determining the implications of the case information for developing strategy. This may involve careful mathematical analysis of sales and profit data or thoughtful interpretation of the text of the case.

One way of approaching analysis involves taking a series of three steps: synthesis, generalizations, and implications. A brief example of this process follows:

Case Material   The high growth rate of frozen pizza sales has attracted a number of large food processing firms, including Pillsbury (Totino's), Quaker Oats (Celeste), American Home Products (Chef Boy-ar-dee), Nestlé (Stouffer's), General Mills (Saluto), and H. J. Heinz (La Pizzeria). The major independents are Jeno's, Tony's, and John's. Jeno's and Totino's are the market leaders, with market shares of about 19 percent each. Celeste and Tony's have about 8 to 9 percent each, and the others have about 5 percent or less. [Excerpted from "The Pillsbury Company—Totino's Pizza," in Philip Kotler, *Principles of Marketing* (Englewood Cliffs, N.J.: Prentice-Hall, Inc., 1980), pp. 192–195.]

Synthesis   The frozen pizza market is a highly competitive and highly fragmented market.

Generalizations   In markets such as this, attempts to gain market share through lower consumer prices or heavy advertising are likely to be quickly copied by competitors and thus not be very effective.

Implications   Lowering consumer prices and spending more on advertising are likely to be poor strategies. Perhaps increasing freezer space in retail outlets could be effective; this objective might be obtained through trade discounts. Developing a superior product (such as better tasting pizza or microwave pizza) or increasing geographic coverage of the market might be better strategies for obtaining market share.

Note that none of these three steps includes any repetition of the case material. Rather, they all involve extracting the meaning of the information and, by pairing it with strategic management principles, coming up with its strategic implications.

---

and that of the presenters and visual aids in an oral report are often used by evaluators as an indication of the effort put into a project and of its overall quality.

Written Report

Good written reports usually start with outlines. We offer the framework in Table 13.8 as one useful format. This outline is fully consistent with the approach suggested in this chapter and, with a few exceptions, involves writing out in prose form the information in the various worksheets.

<table>
<tr><td colspan="2">

TABLE 13.8

</td></tr>
</table>

Outline for Written Case Reports

1. Title page	B. Description of alternative 2
2. Table of contents	a. Strengths
3. Introduction	b. Weaknesses
4. Environmental analysis	C. Description of alternative 3
A. General environment	a. Strengths
B. Operating environment	b. Weaknesses
C. Internal environment	7. Chosen alternative and implementation
D. Assumptions	A. Justification for alternative chosen
5. Problem definition	B. Implementation specifics and
A. Major problem 1 and evidence	justification
B. Major problem 2 (if applicable)	8. Summary of analysis
and evidence	9. References
C. Major problem 3 (if applicable)	10. Technical appendices
and evidence	A. Financial analyses
6. Alternative courses of action	B. Other technical information
A. Description of alternative 1	
a. Strengths	
b. Weaknesses	

Elements of a Written Report

Title Page   The title page includes the title of the case and the names of all persons who were involved in preparing the report. It is also useful to include the name and number of the course for which the case was prepared and the date the project was submitted.

Table of Contents   The table of contents lists every heading in the report and the number of the page on which that particular section begins. If a variety of exhibits are included in a case report, it may be useful to include a table of exhibits listing every exhibit and the page number on which it is located.

Introduction   The introduction of a case analysis is not a summary of the case. It is a statement of the purpose of the report and a brief description of each of its major sections.

Environmental Analysis   This section reports the results of the analysis of each environmental component. Subheadings should be used for each of the three major environments and for each relevant component or aspect listed in Table 13.3. Again, if any of the environments or categories has no relevance to a particular case, simply report that the analysis revealed nothing crucial for this particular situational element. Any assumptions made concerning the current situation should also be reported in this section.

Problem Definition   This section offers a concise statement of the major problems in the case and reviews the evidence that led to the conclusion that these are the major issues. Problems should be listed in order of their importance and should be accompanied by an account of the evidence.

Alternative Courses of Action   This section describes each of the alternatives devised for solving the major problems in the case. The strengths and weaknesses of each alternative should be clearly delineated.

Chosen Alternative and Implementation   This section reveals which alternative has been selected and explains why it is the appropriate course of action. In addition, it should include a detailed description of how the alternative will be implemented and why this method of implementation is best.

Summary of Analysis   This brief section simply restates what the report has been about. It describes what was done in preparing the report, the basic problems, and the alternative selected for solving them. It is also useful in this section to offer any additional information that supports the quality of the analysis and the value of the alternative chosen.

References   Any outside materials used in the report should be listed alphabetically in an acceptable reference style, such as that used in articles in *The Academy of Management Journal*. (Such information should also be appropriately cited in footnotes throughout the report.)

Technical Appendices   Some cases require considerable financial analysis. Typically key financial analysis is reported in the text of the report, but detailed analysis and calculations are placed here. Any other types of analysis that are too long or too detailed for the body of the report can also be placed here.

Oral Presentation

Case analyses are often presented orally in class by individuals or teams of analysts. As is true for the written report, a good outline is critical, and it is often a good idea to provide each class member with a copy of the outline and a list of any assumptions that are made. Although there is no single best way to present a case or to divide responsibility among team members, simply reading a written report is unacceptable. (It encourages boredom and interferes with all-important class discussion.) It is important to emphasize the major points of the analysis and not get bogged down in unnecessary detail. If the instructor or a class member asks for more details on a specific point, of course, the presenter must supply them.

The use of visual aids can be very helpful in presenting case analyses in class. However, simply presenting financial statements or other detailed data contained in the case is a poor use of visual media. On the other hand, taking these statements or figures and recasting them in easy-to-understand pie charts or graphs can be very effective in making specific points. Remember that any type of visual aid should be large enough so that even people sitting in the rear of the classroom can see the information clearly.

Oral presentation of case analyses is particularly helpful to students who are learning the skill of speaking to a group, a common activity in many managerial positions. In particular, the ability to handle objections and disagreements without antagonizing others is a valuable skill to develop.

SUMMARY

This chapter presented a framework for case analysis and offered some suggestions for developing and communicating high-quality case reports. Case analysis begins with analysis and recording of the current situation, including all relevant aspects of the environment, followed by analysis and recording of the problems or issues on which the case hinges. The next step is to formulate, evaluate, and record alternative courses of action in order to narrow the field to the best feasible alternatives. Then it is necessary to select one of the proposed courses of action, explain this choice, and describe how it is to be implemented.

We cautioned against several pitfalls that can plague the student (or the ill-prepared manager) engaged in case analysis, and we offered some guidelines for communicating case analyses in a written report and in an oral presentation.

Performing good case analyses takes a lot of time and effort. Analysts must be highly motivated and willing to get involved in the case and in class discussion if they expect to learn effectively and succeed in a course where cases are utilized. Analysts with only passive interest who perform "night before" analyses cheat themselves of valuable learning experiences that are critical in preparing for a successful management career.

KEY TERMS

case, p. 317   straw man alternative, p. 327
worksheet, p. 320

CHECKLIST   An Operational Approach to Case and Problem Analysis

___   1. Read the case quickly to get an overview of the situation.

___   2. Read the case again thoroughly, underlining relevant information and taking notes on potential areas of concern.

___   3. Reread and study the case until it is well-understood.

___   4. Review outside sources of information that are relevant to the case, and record important information.

___   5. Complete the General Worksheet for Analyzing the Current Situation.

___   6. Review this worksheet in search of potential problems.

___   7. List all potential problems on the General Worksheet for Defining Problems and Their Core Elements

___   8. Review this worksheet and list the major problems in order of priority.

___   9. Complete the Worksheet for Defining Problems and Their Core Elements.

___   10. Develop several feasible solutions for dealing with the major problems.

___   11. Complete the General Worksheet for Evaluating Alternative Courses of Action.

___   12. Review this worksheet and ensure that all relevant strengths and weaknesses have been considered.

___   13. Decide which alternative solves the problems most effectively.

___   14. Complete the General Worksheet for Implementing the Chosen Alternative.

___   15. Prepare a written or oral report based on the worksheets.

APPENDIX 13A   *Selected Sources of Secondary Information*

Secondary sources of data are often useful in case analysis. They provide more thorough environmental analyses and can be used to support one's recommendations and conclusions. Many of the data sources listed below can be found in business libraries. Here they are grouped under five headings: General Business and Industry Sources, Basic U.S. Statistical Sources, Financial Information Sources, Marketing Information Sources, and Indexes and Abstracts.

General Business and Industry Sources

Aerospace Facts and Figures. Aerospace Industries Association of America.

Annual Statistical Report. American Iron and Steel Institute.

Chemical Marketing Reporter. Schnell Publishing. Includes lengthy, continuing list of "Current Prices of Chemicals and Related Materials."

Computerworld. Computerworld, Inc. Last December's issue includes "Review and Forecast," an analysis of computer industry's past year and the outlook for the next year.

Construction Review. Department of Commerce. Current statistics on construction put in place, costs, and employment.

Distribution Worldwide. Chilton Co. Special annual issue, *Distribution Guide,* compiles information on transportation methods and wages.

Drugs and Cosmetic Industry. Drug Markets, Inc. Separate publication in July, *Drug and Cosmetic Catalog,* provides list of manufacturers of drugs and cosmetics and their respective products.

Electrical World. January and February issues include two-part statistical report on expenditures, construction, and other categories by region, capacity, sales, and financial statistics for the electrical industry.

Encyclopedia of Business Information Sources. Paul Wasserman et al., eds., Gale Research Company. A detailed listing of primary subjects of interest to managerial personnel, with a record of sourcebooks, periodicals, organizations, directories, handbooks, bibliographies, and other sources of information on each topic. Two vols., nearly 17,000 entries in over 1,600 subject areas.

Forest Industries. Miller Freeman Publications, Inc. The March issue includes "Forest Industries Wood-Based Panel," a review of production and sales figures for selected wood products; extra issue in May includes a statistical review of the lumber industry.

Implement and Tractor. Intertec Publishing Corporation. January issue includes equipment specifications and operating data for farm and industrial equipment. November issue includes statistics and information on the farm industry.

Industry Surveys. Standard & Poor's Corp. Continuously revised analysis of leading industries (40 industries made up of 1,300 companies). Basic analysis features company ratio comparisons and balance sheet statistics.

Adapted from J. Paul Peter and James H. Donnelly, Jr., *Marketing Management: Knowledge and Skills,* 2nd ed. (Homewood, Ill.: BPI/Irwin, 1989), pp. 907–919.

Middle Market Directory. Dun & Bradstreet. Inventories approximately 18,000 U.S. companies with indicated worth of $500,000 to $999,999, giving officers, products, standard industrial classification, approximate sales, and number of employees.

Million Dollar Directory. Dun & Bradstreet. Lists U.S. companies with an indicated worth of $1 million or more, giving officers and directors, products, standard industrial classification, sales, and number of employees.

Milutinovich, J. S. "Business Facts for Decision Makers: Where to Find Them." *Business Horizons,* March–April 1985, pp. 63–80.

Modern Brewery Age. Business Journals, Inc. February issue includes a review of sales and production figures for the brewery industry. A separate publication, *The Blue Book,* issued in May, compiles sales and consumption figures by state for the brewery industry.

National Petroleum News. McGraw-Hill, Inc. May issue includes statistics on sales and consumption of fuel oils, gasoline, and related products. Some figures are for ten years, along with ten-year projections.

Operating Results of Department and Specialty Stores. National Retail Merchants Association.

Petroleum Facts and Figures. American Petroleum Institute.

Poor's Register of Corporations, Directors, and Executives of the United States and Canada. Standard & Poor's Corp. Divided into two sections. The first gives officers, products, sales range, and number of employees for about 30,000 corporations. The second gives brief information on executives and directors.

Quick-Frozen Foods. Harcourt Brace Jovanovich Publications. October issue includes "Frozen Food Almanac," providing statistics on the frozen food industry by product.

Statistical Sources. Paul Wasserman et al., eds. Gale Research Corp., 4th ed., 1974. A subject guide to industrial, business, social, educational, and financial data, and other related topics.

Basic U.S. Statistical Sources

Business Service Checklist. Department of Commerce. Weekly guide to Department of Commerce publications, plus key business indicators.

Business Statistics. Department of Commerce. (Supplement to *Survey of Current Business.*) History of the statistical series appearing in the *Survey.* Also included are source references and useful explanatory notes.

Census of Agriculture. Department of Commerce. Data by state and county on livestock, farm characteristics, values.

Census of Manufacturers. Department of Commerce. Industry statistics, area statistics, subjects reports, locations of plants, industry descriptions arranged by Standard Industrial Classification, and a variety of ratios.

Census of Mineral Industries. Department of Commerce. Similar to *Census of Manufacturers.* Also includes capital expenditures and employment and payrolls.

Census of Retail Trade. Department of Commerce. Compiles data for states, SMSAs, counties, and cities with populations of 2,500 or more by kind of business. Data include number of establishments, sales, payroll, and personnel.

Census of Selected Services. Department of Commerce. Includes data on hotels, motels, beauty parlors, barber shops, and other retail service organizations.

Census of Transportation. Passenger Transportation Survey, Commodity Transportation Survey, Travel Inventory and Use Survey, Bus and Truck Carrier Survey.

Census Tract Reports. Department of Commerce, Bureau of Census. Detailed information on both population and housing subjects.

Census of Wholesale Trade. Department of Commerce. Similar to *Census of Retail Trade*—except information is for wholesale establishments.

County and City Data Book. Department of Commerce. Summary statistics for small geographical areas.

Current Business Reports. Department of Commerce. Reports monthly department store sales of selected items.

Economic Report of the President. Transmitted to the Congress in January (each year), together with the *Annual Report* of the Council of Economic Advisers. Statistical tables relating to income, employment, and production.

Handbook of Basic Economic Statistics. Economic Statistics Bureau of Washington, D.C. Current and historical statistics on industry, commerce, labor, and agriculture.

Statistical Abstract of the United States. Department of Commerce. Summary statistics in industrial, social, political, and economic fields in the United States. It is augmented by the *Cities Supplement, The County Data Book,* and *Historical Statistics of the United States.*

Statistics of Income: Corporation Income Tax Returns. Internal Revenue Service. Balance sheet and income statement statistics derived from corporate tax returns.

Statistics of Income: U.S. Business Tax Returns. Internal Revenue Service. Summarizes financial and economic data for proprietorships, partnerships, and small business corporations.

Survey of Current Business. Department of Commerce. Facts on industrial and business activity in the United States and statistical summary of national income and product accounts. A weekly supplement provides an up to date summary of business.

Financial Information Sources

Blue Line Investment Survey. Quarterly ratings and reports on 1,000 stocks; analysis of 60 industries and special situations analysis (monthly); supplements on new developments and editorials on conditions affecting price trends.

Commercial and Financial Chronicle. Variety of articles and news reports on business, government, and finance. Monday's issue lists new securities, dividends, and called bonds. Thursday's issue is devoted to business articles.

Dun's Review. Dun & Bradstreet. This monthly includes very useful annual financial ratios for about 125 lines of business.

Fairchild's Financial Manual of Retail Stores. Information about officers and directors, products, subsidiaries, sales, and earnings for apparel stores, mail order firms, variety chains, and supermarkets.

Federal Reserve Bulletin. Board of Governors of the Federal Reserve System. The "Financial and Business Statistics" section of each issue of this monthly bulletin is the best single source for current U.S. banking and monetary statistics.

Financial World. Articles on business activities of interest to investors, including investment opportunities and pertinent data on firms, such as earnings and dividend records.

Moody's Bank and Finance Manual; Moody's Industrial Manual; Moody's Municipal & Government Manual; Moody's Public Utility Manual; Moody's Transportation Manual; Moody's Directors Service. Brief histories of companies and their operations, subsidiaries, officers and directors, products, and balance sheet and income statements over several years.

Moody's Bond Survey. Moody's Investors Service. Weekly data on stocks and bonds, including recommendations for purchases or sale and discussions of industry trends and developments.

Moody's Handbook of Widely Held Common Stocks. Moody's Investors Service. Weekly data on stocks and bonds, including recommendations for purchases or sale and discussions of industry trends and developments.

Security Owner's Stock Guide. Standard & Poor's Corp. Standard & Poor's rating, stock price range, and other helpful information for about 4,200 common and preferred stocks.

Security Price Index. Standard & Poor's Corp. Price indexes, bond prices, sales, yields, Dow Jones averages, etc.

Standard Corporation Records. Standard & Poor's Corp. Published in looseleaf form, offers information similar to Moody's manuals. Use of this extensive service facilitates buying securities for both the individual and the institutional investor.

Marketing Information Sources

[Based in part on Gilbert A. Churchill, Jr., *Marketing Research: Methodological Foundations,* 6th ed. (Fort Worth, TX: Dryden Press, 1995), pp. 318–335.]

Advertising Age. This important advertising weekly publishes a number of annual surveys or features of special interest related to U.S. national advertising statistics.

Audits and Surveys National Total-Market Index. Contains information on various product types including total market size, brand market shares, retail inventory, distribution coverage, and out of stock.

Commercial Atlas and Marketing Guide. Skokie, Ill.: Rand-McNally & Co. Statistics on population, principal cities, business centers, trading areas, sales and manufacturing units, transportation data, and so forth.

Dun & Bradstreet Market Identifiers. Relevant marketing information on over 4.3 million establishments for constructing sales prospect files, sales territories, and sales territory potentials and isolating potential new customers with particular characteristics.

Editor and Publisher "Market Guide." Market information for 1,500 American and Canadian cities. Data include populations, households, gas meters, climates, retailing, and newspaper information.

Guide to Consumer Markets. New York: The Conference Board. This useful annual compilation of U.S. statistics on the consumer marketplace covers population, employment, income, expenditures, production, and prices.

Industrial Marketing. "Guide to Special Issues." This directory is included in each issue. Publications are listed within primary market classifications and are listed for up to three months prior to advertising closing date.

Marketing Communications (January 1968 to January 1972, formerly *Printer's Ink,* 1914–1967.) Pertinent market information on regional and local consumer markets as well as international markets to January 1972.

Marketing Information Guide. Department of Commerce. Annotations of selected current publications and reports, with basic information and statistics on marketing and distribution.

National Purchase Diary Panel (NPDP). Monthly purchase information based on the largest panel diary in the United States with detailed brand, frequency of purchase, characteristics of heavy buyers, and other market data.

Nielson Retail Index. Contains basic product turnover data, retail prices, store displays, promotional activity, and local advertising based on a national sample of supermarkets, drugstores, and mass merchandisers.

Nielson Television Index. Well-known index that provides estimates of the size and nature of the audience for individual television programs.

Population and Its Distribution: The United States Markets. J. Walter Thompson Co. New York: McGraw-Hill Book Co. A handbook of marketing facts selected from the U.S. *Census of Population* and the most recent census data on retail trade.

Sales and Marketing Management. (Formerly *Sales Management,* to October 1975.) This valuable semimonthly journal includes four useful annual statistical issues: *Survey of Buying Power* (July); *Survey of Buying Power, Part II* (October); *Survey of Industrial*

Purchasing Power (April); *Survey of Selling Costs* (January). These are excellent references for buying income, buying power index, cash income, merchandise line, manufacturing line, and retail sales.

Selling Areas Marketing Inc. Reports on warehouse withdrawals of various food products in each of 42 major markets covering 80 percent of national food sales.

Simmons Media/Marketing Service. Provides cross referencing of product usage and media exposure for magazine, television, newspaper, and radio based on a strict national probability sample.

Standard Rate and Data. Nine volumes on major media which include a variety of information in addition to prices for media in selected markets.

Starch Advertising Readership Service. Measures the reading of advertisements in magazines and newspapers and provides information on overall readership percentages, readers per dollar, and rank when grouped by product category.

Indexes and Abstracts

Accountants Digest. L. L. Briggs. A digest of articles appearing currently in accounting periodicals.

Accountants Index. American Institute of Certified Public Accountants. An index to books, pamphlets, and articles on accounting and finance.

Accounting Articles. Commerce Clearing House. Loose-leaf index to articles in accounting and business periodicals.

Advertising Age Editorial Index. Crain Communications, Inc. Index to articles in *Advertising Age.*

American Statistical Index. Congressional Information Service. A comprehensive two-part annual index to the statistical publications of the U.S. government.

Applied Science & Technology Index. H. W. Wilson Co. Reviews over 200 periodicals relevant to the applied sciences, many of which pertain to business.

Battelle Library Review. (Formerly *Battelle Technical Review* to 1962.) Battelle Memorial Institute. Annotated bibliography of books, reports, and articles on automation and automatic processes.

Bulletin of Public Affairs Information Service. Public Affairs Information Service, Inc. (Since 1915—annual index.) A selective list of the latest books, pamphlets, government publications, reports of public and private agencies, and periodicals related to economic conditions, public administration, and international relations.

Business Education Index. McGraw-Hill Book Co. (Since 1940—annual index.) Annual author and subject index of books, articles, and theses on business education.

Business Periodicals Index. H. W. Wilson Co. A subject index to the disciplines of accounting, advertising, banking, general business, insurance, labor, management, and marketing.

Catalog of United States Census Publication. Department of Commerce, Bureau of Census. Indexes all available Census Bureau data. Main divisions are agriculture, business, construction, foreign trade, government, guide to locating U.S. census information.

Computer and Information Systems. (Formerly *Information Processing Journal* to 1969.) Cambridge Communications Corporation.

Cumulative Index of NICB Publications. The National Industrial Conferences Board. Annual index of NICB books, pamphlets, and articles in the area of management of personnel.

Funk and Scott Index International. Investment Index Company. Indexes articles on foreign companies and industries from over 1,000 foreign and domestic periodicals and documents.

Guide to U.S. Government Publications. McLean, Va.: Documents Index. Annotated guide to publications of various U.S. government agencies.

International Abstracts in Operations Research. Operations Research Society of America.

International Journal of Abstracts of Statistical Methods in Industry. The Hague, Netherlands: International Statistical Institute.

Management Information Guides. Gale Research Company. Bibliographical references to information sources for various business subjects.

Management Review. American Management Association.

Monthly Catalog of U.S. Government Publications. U.S. Government Printing Office. Continuing list of federal government publications.

Monthly Checklist of State Publications. U.S. Library of Congress, Exchange and Gift Division. Record of state documents received by Library of Congress.

New York Times Index. Very detailed index of all articles in the *Times,* arranged alphabetically with many cross-references.

Psychological Abstracts. American Psychological Association.

Public Affairs Information Service. Public Affairs Information Service, Inc. A selective subject list of books, pamphlets, and government publications covering business, banking, and economics as well as subjects in the area of public affairs.

Reader's Guide to Periodical Literature. H. W. Wilson Co. Index by author and subject to selected U.S. general and nontechnical periodicals.

Sociological Abstracts. American Sociological Association.

The Wall Street Journal Index. Dow Jones & Company, Inc. An index of all articles in *The WSJ* grouped in two sections: corporate news and general news.

Index

CASE PART I

Introduction to Strategic Management

Wal-Mart, 1993

WALTER E. GREENE, *University of Texas Pan American*

THE KING IS DEAD—LONG LIVE THE KING

Can Wal-Mart continue its spectacular growth, now that its founder Sam Walton is no longer available? Can David D. Glass, President and Chief Executive Officer, with S. Robson Walton, Chairman of the Board and Donald G. Soderquist, Vice Chairman and Chief Operating Officer, maintain Wal-Mart's fabulous success?

HISTORY

No word better describes Wal-Mart than *growth*. Wal-Mart Stores, Inc., began as a small-town variety store business in 1945, when Sam Walton opened his first Ben Franklin franchises in Newport, Arkansas. Based in rural Bentonville, Arkansas, Walton, his wife Helen, and brother Bud operated the nation's most successful Ben Franklin franchises. "We were a small chain," said Walton of his sixteen-store operation. "Things were running so smoothly we even had time for our families." What more could a man want? A great deal, as it turned out.

Walton could see that the variety store was gradually dying because supermarkets and discounters were developing. Far from being secure, Walton knew that he was under siege. He decided to counterattack. He first tried to convince the top management of Ben Franklin to enter discounting. After their refusal, Walton made a quick trip around the country in search of ideas. He then began opening his own discount stores in small Arkansas towns like Bentonville and Rogers.

The company did not open its first discount department store (Wal-Mart) until November 1962. The early stores had bare tile floors and pipe racks, and Wal-Mart did not begin to revamp its image significantly until the mid-1970s. Growth in the early years was slow. However, once the company went public in 1970, sales began to increase rapidly. If one had purchased 100 shares of the stock in 1970, they would have been worth $350,000 in 1985.

Courtesy of Walter E. Green, Professor, University of Texas Pan American.

Such retailers as Target, Venture, and K-Mart provided the examples that Wal-Mart sought to emulate in its growth. The old Wal-Mart store colors, dark blue and white (too harsh), were dumped in favor of a three-tone combination of light beige, soft blue, and burnt orange. Carpeting, which had been long discarded on apparel sales floors, was put back. New racks were put into use that displayed the entire garment instead of only an edge.

Wal-Mart began to expand by taking over failing chains and "Waltonizing" them. In July 1981 Walton picked up ailing Kuhn's Big-K stores—1 warehouse and 92 locations—in effect acquiring cheap leases at a discount price. Wal-Mart assumed $19 million in debt and issued $7.5 million worth of preferred stock. Now Kuhn's has a new management team and $60 million in cash for a major facelift. Profits may pour in, as they did after Wal-Mart's only previous acquisition, the 1977 purchase of Mohr Value Stores. "We fixed them up and retrained the people, and now they're our best group," said Walton.

In 1987 Wal-Mart implemented two new concepts: Hypermarkets, 200,000-square-foot stores that sell everything including food, and Super Centers, a scaled-down supermarket. Also in 1987, Walton named David Glass as the new chief executive officer (CEO) while he remained chairman of the board.

On December 10, 1990, Wal-Mart completed the acquisition of the 14 centers of McLane Company, Inc., a national distribution system in 11 states providing over 12,500 types of grocery and non-grocery products. As of February 2, 1991, Sam's Clubs merged the 28 wholesale clubs of The Wholesale Club, Inc., of Indianapolis, Indiana, into its operations.

Wal-Mart sold its 14 Dot Discount Drug Stores in February 1990. As of the end of its 1992 fiscal year (January 31, 1993), Wal-Mart had 1,720 discount stores (including 30 supercenter stores) in 45 states and Puerto Rico, 148 Sam's Wholesale Clubs in 41 states, 3 hypermarkets, 14 McLane's distribution centers, and 13 distribution centers. (See Exhibits 1A and 1B.) In 1994, Wal-Mart plans to open approximately 150 new Wal-Mart stores and 65 Sam's Clubs. In addition, it also plans to expand or relocate approximately 100 of the older Wal-Mart stores and 25 Sam's Clubs, and to expand 40 Wal-Mart stores into combination supermarket/general merchandise Supercenters. As of January 31, 1993, Wal-Mart had approximately 434,000 full- and part-time employees, an increase of 63,000 during 1992.

CURRENT OPERATIONS

Most of the 1,880 Wal-Mart stores are located in towns of 5,000 to 25,000. There are still smaller stores for communities of 5,000 or under. The listing below shows the number of stores operated for each of the following years:

Year	Wal-Mart	Sam's Discount Hypermarkets
1974	78	
1975	104	
1976	125	
1977	153	
1978	195	
1979	229	
1980	276	
1981	330	*continued*

EXHIBIT 1A

	WAL-MART	SAM'S
ALABAMA	74	7
ARIZONA	28	
ARKANSAS	77	4
CALIFORNIA	43	3
COLORADO	32	3
CONNECTICUT	1	1
DELAWARE	2	1
FLORIDA	122	23
GEORGIA	83	9
IDAHO	5	1
ILLINOIS	97	18
INDIANA	65	12
IOWA	43	3
KANSAS	43	3
KENTUCKY	66	4
LOUISIANA	74	9
MAINE	6	2
MARYLAND	7	2
MASSACHUSETTS	2	2
MICHIGAN	22	6
MINNESOTA	27	7
MISSISSIPPI	57	3
MISSOURI	105	9
MONTANA	2	1
NEBRASKA	16	1
NEVADA	5	2
NEW HAMPSHIRE	7	2
NEW JERSEY	3	2
NEW MEXICO	19	1
NEW YORK	16	3
NORTH CAROLINA	74	8
NORTH DAKOTA	8	2
OHIO	42	16
OKLAHOMA	81	6
OREGON	12	
PENNSYLVANIA	26	5
PUERTO RICO	2	
SOUTH CAROLINA	49	5
SOUTH DAKOTA	8	1
TENNESSEE	86	7
TEXAS	229	44
UTAH	11	
VIRGINIA	37	6
WEST VIRGINIA	10	3
WISCONSIN	47	9
WYOMING	9	

table continued

Year	Wal-Mart	Sam's Discount Hypermarkets
1982	491	
1983	551	
1984	642	3
1985	745	11
1986	859	23
1987	980	49
1988	1114	84
1989	1259	105
1990	1402	123
1991	1573	148
1992	1720	208

plus 256 warehouse clubs and 64 warehouse outlets.

Growth in administrative and support functions was required to maintain sales growth through new stores and existing stores. However, a strong rein was held on operations and expense controls to permit required flexibility in

EXHIBIT 1B

TEN-YEAR FINANCIAL SUMMARY

WAL-MART STORES, INC. AND SUBSIDIARIES

(Dollar amounts in thousands except per share data.)

	1993	1992	1991	1990	1989	1988	1987	1986	1985	1984
OPERATING RESULTS										
Net sales	$55,483,771	$43,886,902	$32,601,594	$25,810,656	$20,649,001	$15,959,255	$11,909,076	$8,451,489	$6,400,861	$4,666,909
Net sales increase	26%	35%	26%	25%	29%	34%	41%	32%	37%	38%
Comparative store sales increase	11%	10%	10%	11%	12%	11%	13%	9%	15%	15%
Rentals from licensed departments and other income-net	500,793	402,521	261,814	174,644	136,867	104,783	84,623	55,127	52,167	36,031
Cost of sales	44,174,685	34,786,119	25,499,834	20,070,034	16,056,856	12,281,744	9,053,219	6,361,271	4,722,440	3,418,025
Operating, selling, and general and administrative expenses	8,320,842	6,684,304	5,152,178	4,069,695	3,267,864	2,599,367	2,007,645	1,485,210	1,181,455	892,887
Interest costs:										
Debt	142,649	113,305	42,716	20,346	36,286	25,262	10,442	1,903	5,207	4,935
Capital leases	180,049	152,558	125,920	117,725	99,395	88,995	76,367	54,640	42,506	29,946
Provision for federal and state income taxes	1,171,545	944,661	751,736	631,600	488,246	441,027	395,940	276,119	230,653	160,903
Net income	1,994,794	1,608,476	1,291,024	1,075,900	837,221	627,643	450,086	327,473	270,767	196,244
Per share of common stock*:										
Net income	.87	.70	.57	.48	.37	.28	.20	.15	.12	.09
Dividends	.11	.09	.07	.06	.04	.03	.02	.02	.01	.01
FINANCIAL POSITION										
Current assets	$10,197,590	$ 8,575,423	$ 6,414,775	$ 4,712,616	$ 3,630,987	$ 2,905,145	$ 2,353,271	$1,784,275	$1,303,254	$1,005,567
Inventories at replacement cost	9,779,981	7,856,871	6,207,852	4,750,619	3,642,696	2,854,556	2,184,847	1,528,349	1,227,264	867,155
Less LIFO reserve	511,672	472,572	399,436	322,546	291,329	202,796	153,875	140,181	123,339	121,760
Inventories at LIFO cost	9,268,309	7,384,299	5,808,416	4,428,073	3,351,367	2,651,760	2,030,972	1,388,168	1,103,925	735,395
Net property, plant, equipment and capital leases	9,792,881	6,433,801	4,712,039	3,430,059	2,661,954	2,144,852	1,676,282	1,303,450	870,309	628,151
Total assets	20,565,087	15,443,389	11,388,915	8,198,484	6,359,668	5,131,809	4,049,092	3,103,645	2,205,229	1,652,254
Current liabilities	6,754,286	5,003,775	3,990,414	2,845,315	2,065,909	1,743,763	1,340,291	992,683	688,968	502,763
Long-term debt	3,072,835	1,722,022	740,254	185,152	184,439	185,672	179,234	180,682	41,237	40,866
Long-term obligations under capital leases	1,772,152	1,555,875	1,158,621	1,087,403	1,009,046	866,972	764,128	595,205	449,886	339,930
Preferred stock with mandatory redemption provisions	—	—	—	—	—	—	—	4,902	5,874	6,411
Shareholders' equity	8,759,180	6,989,710	5,365,524	3,965,561	3,007,909	2,257,267	1,690,493	1,277,659	984,672	737,503
FINANCIAL RATIOS										
Current ratio	1.5	1.7	1.6	1.7	1.8	1.7	1.8	1.8	1.9	2.0
Inventories/working capital	2.7	2.1	2.4	2.4	2.1	2.3	2.0	1.8	1.8	1.5
Return on assets **	12.9%	14.1%	15.7%	16.9%	16.3%	15.5%	14.5%	14.8%	16.4%	16.5%
Return on shareholders' equity **	28.5%	30.0%	32.6%	35.8%	37.1%	37.1%	35.2%	33.3%	36.7%	40.2%
OTHER YEAR-END DATA										
Number of Wal-Mart Stores	1,880	1,720	1,573	1,402	1,259	1,114	980	859	745	642
Number of Sam's Clubs	256	208	148	123	105	84	49	23	11	3
Average Wal-Mart Store size	81,200	75,000	70,700	66,400	63,500	61,500	59,000	57,000	55,000	53,000
Number of Associates	434,000	371,000	328,000	271,000	223,000	183,000	141,000	104,000	81,000	62,000
Number of Shareholders	180,584	150,242	122,414	79,929	80,270	79,777	32,896	21,828	14,799	14,172

* Restated to reflect the two-for-one stock split announced January 22, 1993.
** On beginning of year balances.

reacting to sales trends. Wal-Mart's expense structure, measured as a percentage of sales, continues to be among the lowest in the industry.

Although Walton watched expenses, he does not stint on rewarding sales managers. Sales figures were available to every employee. Monthly figures for each department were ranked and made available throughout the organization. Employees who were doing better than average got rewarded with raises, bonuses, and a pat on the back. Poor performers were only rarely fired, although demotions were possible.

All employees (called "associates") had a stake in the financial performance of the company. Store managers could earn as much as $100,000 to $150,000 per year. Part-time clerks even qualified for profit sharing and stock-purchase plans. Millionaires among Wal-Mart's middle managers were not uncommon. Ideas were also solicited from all employees. Executives frequently asked employees if they had ideas for improving the organization. These ideas were noted and often put into use.

With his stock selling at 20 to 30 times earnings—an almost incredible price—Walton presided over a sizeable fortune before his death in 1992. Wal-Mart stock was 39 percent held by the Walton family. Family holdings were worth nearly $8 billion. Wal-Mart's long-term debt of $1,052,644,000 included $867 million of capital lease obligations. New stores were funded primarily through the sale of common stock and retained earnings or leaseback arrangements. Exhibits 2 through 5 cite financial data.

Walton invited over 100 analysts and institutional investors to the field-house at the University of Arkansas for the annual meeting. The mid-June occasion is a day-and-a-half session where investors meet top executives, as well as Wal-Mart district managers, buyers, and 200,000 hourly salespeople. Investors see a give-and-take meeting between buyers and district managers. Walton introduced his employees, who shouted his name and extolled him. It was an unusual sight. David Glass is continuing the rituals.

EMPLOYEE BENEFITS

Wal-Mart management had taken pride in the continued development of its people. Training was seen as critical to outstanding performance, and new programs were implemented on an ongoing basis in all areas of the company. The combination of grass-roots meetings, the open-door policy, videos, printed material, classroom and home study, year-end management meetings, and on-the-job training had enabled employees to prepare themselves for assigned advancement and added responsibilities.

Wal-Mart managers also tried to stay current with new developments and needed changes. Executives spent one week per year in hourly jobs in various stores. Walton himself once traveled at least three days per week, visiting competitors' stores and attending the opening of new stores, leading the Wal-Mart cheer, "Give me a W, give me an A . . . ."

Wal-Mart encouraged employee stock purchases; about 8 percent of Wal-Mart stock was owned by employees. Under the Stock Purchase Plan, stock may be bought by two different methods. First, an amount is deducted from each employee's check with a maximum of $62.50 per check. An additional 15 percent of the amount deducted is contributed by Wal-Mart (up to $1,800 of annual stock purchases). Second, a lump-sum purchase is allowed in April up to $1,500 with an additional 15 percent added by the company. Wal-Mart

EXHIBIT 2

CONSOLIDATED STATEMENTS OF INCOME

WAL-MART STORES, INC. AND SUBSIDIARIES

(Amounts in thousands except per share data.)

	Fiscal year ended January 31,		
	1993	1992	1991
REVENUES:			
Net sales	**$55,483,771**	$43,886,902	$32,601,594
Rentals from licensed departments	**36,035**	28,659	22,362
Other income-net	**464,758**	373,862	239,452
	55,984,564	44,289,423	32,863,408
COSTS AND EXPENSES:			
Cost of sales	**44,174,685**	34,786,119	25,499,834
Operating, selling, and general and administrative expenses	**8,320,842**	6,684,304	5,152,178
INTEREST COSTS:			
Debt	**142,649**	113,305	42,716
Capital leases	**180,049**	152,558	125,920
	52,818,225	41,736,286	30,820,648
INCOME BEFORE INCOME TAXES	**3,166,339**	2,553,137	2,042,760
PROVISION FOR FEDERAL AND STATE INCOME TAXES:			
Current	**1,136,918**	906,183	737,020
Deferred	**34,627**	38,478	14,716
	1,171,545	944,661	751,736
NET INCOME	**$ 1,994,794**	$ 1,608,476	$ 1,291,024
NET INCOME PER SHARE	**$ .87**	$ .70	$ .57

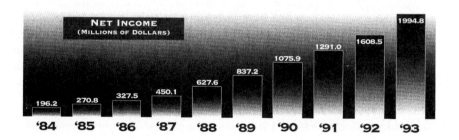

also offered an associate stock ownership plan with approximately 4,000 management associates granted stock options as of January 31, 1993.

Wal-Mart had a corporate profit-sharing plan with contributions of $98,327,000 as of January 31, 1991, $129,635,000 in 1992 and $166,035,000 in 1993. The purposes of the profit-sharing plan were to furnish an incentive for increased efficiency, to provide progressive recognition of service, and to encourage careers with the company by Wal-Mart associates. This was a trustee-administered plan, which means that the company's contributions to it are made only out of net profits of the company and are held by a trustee. The company from time to time contributes 10 percent of net profits to the trust.

Company contributions could be withdrawn only on termination. If employment with the company was terminated because of retirement, death, or permanent disability, the company contribution will be fully vested. "Fully vested" means that the entire amount is nonforfeitable. If termination of employment occurs for any other reason, the amount that is nonforfeitable depends on the number of years of service with the company. After completion

EXHIBIT 3

CONSOLIDATED BALANCE SHEETS

WAL-MART STORES, INC. AND SUBSIDIARIES

(Amounts in thousands.)

	January 31,	
	1993	1992
ASSETS		
CURRENT ASSETS:		
Cash and cash equivalents	$ 12,363	$ 30,649
Receivables	524,555	418,867
Recoverable costs from sale/leaseback	312,016	681,387
Inventories:		
At replacement cost	9,779,981	7,856,871
Less LIFO reserve	511,672	472,572
LIFO	9,268,309	7,384,299
Prepaid expenses	80,347	60,221
TOTAL CURRENT ASSETS	10,197,590	8,575,423
PROPERTY, PLANT, AND EQUIPMENT, AT COST:		
Land	1,692,510	1,077,658
Buildings and improvements	4,641,009	2,569,095
Fixtures and equipment	3,417,230	2,683,481
Transportation equipment	111,151	86,491
	9,861,900	6,416,725
Less accumulated depreciation	1,607,623	1,338,151
Net property, plant, and equipment	8,254,277	5,078,574
Property under capital leases	1,986,104	1,724,123
Less accumulated amortization	447,500	368,896
Net property under capital leases	1,538,604	1,355,227
OTHER ASSETS AND DEFERRED CHARGES	574,616	434,165
Total assets	$20,565,087	$15,443,389
LIABILITIES AND SHAREHOLDERS' EQUITY		
CURRENT LIABILITIES:		
Commercial paper	$ 1,588,825	$ 453,964
Accounts payable	3,873,331	3,453,529
Accrued liabilities	1,042,108	829,381
Accrued federal and state income taxes	190,620	226,828
Long-term debt due within one year	13,849	5,156
Obligations under capital leases due within one year	45,553	34,917
TOTAL CURRENT LIABILITIES	6,754,286	5,003,775
LONG-TERM DEBT	3,072,835	1,722,022
LONG-TERM OBLIGATIONS UNDER CAPITAL LEASES	1,772,152	1,555,875
DEFERRED INCOME TAXES	206,634	172,007
SHAREHOLDERS' EQUITY:		
Preferred stock ($.10 par value; 100,000 shares authorized, none issued)		
Common stock ($.10 par value; 5,500,000 shares authorized,		
2,299,638 and 1,149,028 issued and outstanding		
in 1993 and 1992 respectively)	229,964	114,903
Capital in excess of par value	526,647	625,669
Retained earnings	8,002,569	6,249,138
TOTAL SHAREHOLDERS' EQUITY	8,759,180	6,989,710
Total liabilities and shareholders' equity	$20,565,087	$15,443,389

of the third year of service with the company, 20 percent of each participant's account will be nonforfeitable for each subsequent year of service so that after seven years of service, a participant's account will be 100 percent vested.

Walton was admittedly old-fashioned in many respects. Since he exercised considerable control over the culture at Wal-Mart, store policies reflected many of his values. For example, store policies forbid employees from dating other employees without prior approval of the executive committee. Also, women were rare in management positions. Annual manager meetings include sessions for wives to speak out on the problems of living with a Wal-Mart manager. No women were in the ranks of Wal-Mart's top management. Walton also resisted placing women on the board of directors. Only 12 women (17 percent) had made it to the ranks of buyers. Walton was an EEOC/AA employer but had managed to get away with "apparent" discriminatory policies because most Wal-Marts were located in small rural towns in the Sun Belt states.

EXHIBIT 4

CONSOLIDATED STATEMENTS OF SHAREHOLDERS' EQUITY

WAL-MART STORES, INC. AND SUBSIDIARIES

(Amounts in thousands except per share data.)	Number of shares	Common stock	Capital in excess of par value	Retained earnings	Total
BALANCE - JANUARY 31, 1990	566,135	$ 56,614	$180,465	$3,728,482	$3,965,561
Net income				1,291,024	1,291,024
Cash dividends ($.07 per share)				(158,889)	(158,889)
Exercise of stock options	156	15	1,327		1,342
Other	(34)	(4)	(1,626)		(1,630)
Two-for-one stock split	566,257	56,625	(56,625)		
Exercise of stock options	506	51	2,427		2,478
Shares issued for McLane acquisition	10,366	1,037	273,659		274,696
Tax benefit from stock options			6,075		6,075
Purchase of stock	(1,000)	(100)	(819)	(24,907)	(25,826)
Walton Enterprises, Inc. stock exchange			14,000		14,000
Other	(104)	(10)	(3,297)		(3,307)
BALANCE - JANUARY 31, 1991	1,142,282	114,228	415,586	4,835,710	5,365,524
Net income				1,608,476	1,608,476
Cash dividends ($.09 per share)				(195,048)	(195,048)
Exercise of stock options	914	91	8,379		8,470
Shares issued for acquisition of:					
The Wholesale Club	5,190	519	161,683		162,202
Western Merchandisers	655	66	27,934		28,000
Phillips	168	17	7,983		8,000
Tax benefit from stock options			12,555		12,555
Other	(181)	(18)	(8,451)		(8,469)
BALANCE - JANUARY 31, 1992	1,149,028	114,903	625,669	6,249,138	6,989,710
Net Income				1,994,794	1,994,794
Cash dividends ($.11 per share)				(241,363)	(241,363)
Exercise of stock options	1,046	105	12,668		12,773
Two-for-one stock split	1,149,819	114,982	(114,982)		
Tax benefit from stock options			18,036		18,036
Other	(255)	(26)	(14,744)		(14,770)
BALANCE - JANUARY 31, 1993	2,299,638	$229,964	$526,647	$8,002,569	$8,759,180

MARKETING STRATEGIES

Wal-Mart had implemented many marketing strategies. It drew customers into the store via radio and television advertising, monthly circulars, and weekly newspaper ads. Television advertising was used to convey an image of everyday low prices and quality merchandise. Radio was used to a lesser degree to promote specific products that were usually in high demand. Newspaper and monthly circulars were the major contributors to the program, emphasizing deeply discounted items, and were effective at luring customers into the store.

Efforts were also made to discount corporate overhead. Visitors often mistake corporate headquarters for a warehouse owing to its limited decorating and "show." Wal-Mart executives shared hotel rooms when traveling to reduce expenses. Walton avoided spending money on consultants and marketing experts. Instead he based decisions on intuitive judgments of employees and on his assessment of the strategies of other retail chains.

Wal-Mart advertised a "Buy American" policy in an effort to keep production at home. Consequently, Wal-Mart buyers were constantly seeking vendors in grass-roots America. For example, Wal-Mart dropped Fuji for 3M film. In addition, Wal-Mart censored products that it did not like. It had banned LP's, removed magazines, and pulled albums over graphics and lyrical content as well as stopped marketing teen rock magazines.

EXHIBIT 5

CONSOLIDATED STATEMENTS OF CASH FLOWS

WAL-MART STORES, INC. AND SUBSIDIARIES

(Amounts in thousands.)	1993	1992	1991
	Fiscal year ended January 31,		
Cash flows from operating activities:			
Net income	$1,994,794	$1,608,476	$1,291,024
Adjustments to reconcile net income to			
net cash provided by operating activities:			
Depreciation and amortization	649,137	475,352	346,614
Loss (gain) from sale of assets	13,222	(8,490)	3,378
Increase in accounts receivable	(105,688)	(113,603)	(58,324)
Increase in inventories	(1,884,010)	(1,459,649)	(1,087,520)
(Increase) decrease in prepaid expenses	(20,126)	(10,686)	11,823
Increase in accounts payable	419,802	709,757	689,435
Increase in accrued liabilities	176,519	117,078	84,739
Increase in deferred income taxes	34,627	38,478	14,716
Net cash provided by operating activities	1,278,277	1,356,713	1,295,885
Cash flows from investing activities:			
Payments for property, plant, and equipment	(3,756,364)	(1,805,303)	(1,388,298)
Recoverable sale/leaseback expenditures	(25,588)	(705,697)	(235,894)
Sale/leaseback arrangements			
and other property sales	416,000	369,226	91,000
Investment in foreign ventures	(106,007)	(18,945)	–
Other investing activities	(34,365)	10,838	7,058
Net cash used in investing activities	(3,506,324)	(2,149,881)	(1,526,134)
Cash flows from financing activities:			
Increase in commercial paper	1,134,861	58,452	30,405
Proceeds from issuance of long-term debt	1,366,812	1,009,822	500,306
Exercise of stock options	16,039	12,556	4,958
Dividends paid	(241,363)	(195,048)	(158,889)
Payment of long-term debt	(7,306)	(33,292)	(109,304)
Payment of capital lease obligation	(59,282)	(41,687)	(25,177)
Other financing activities	–	–	(11,826)
Net cash provided by financing activities	2,209,761	810,803	230,473
Net increase (decrease) in cash and cash equivalents	(18,286)	17,635	224
Cash and cash equivalents at beginning of year	30,649	13,014	12,790
Cash and cash equivalents at end of year	$ 12,363	$ 30,649	$ 13,014
Supplemental disclosure of cash flow information:			
Income tax paid	$1,173,126	$ 861,853	$ 721,036
Interest paid	317,360	235,954	116,134
Capital lease obligations incurred	286,195	433,858	100,972
Liabilities assumed in acquisitions	–	176,479	513,000

GROWTH IN DISTRIBUTION CENTERS

During the 1993 fiscal year, close to 77 percent of Wal-Mart's merchandise passed through one of 22 distribution warehouses, an amount greater than K-Mart's or Sears'. These Distribution Centers are located in: three in Bentonville, Arkansas; two in Searcy, Arkansas; two in Laurens, South Carolina; and one each in Ft. Smith, Arkansas; Palestine, Texas; Cullman, Alabama; Mt. Pleasant, Iowa; Brookhaven, Mississippi; Douglas, Georgia; Plainview, Texas; New Braunfels, Texas; Loveland, Colorado; Seymour, Indiana; Poterville, California; Sutherland, Virginia; Greencastle, Indiana; Brooksville, Florida; and Grove City, Ohio. Wal-Mart has a total of 20,381,727 square feet of storage space. Sam's, unlike Wal-Mart stores, receive the majority of their merchandise via direct shipments from suppliers, rather than from the company's distribution centers.

In addition, Wal-Mart maintains warehouse space in Oklahoma, Arkansas, and Georgia that is utilized for seasonal merchandise. The McLane distribution centers primarily buy, sell, and distribute merchandise to the convenience store industry with an aggregate square footage of 4,213,430 square feet, including two distribution centers in San Bernardino, California, and Fredricksburg, Virginia, acquired in 1993 from the Southland Corporation.

Wal-Mart's distribution operations were highly automated. Terminals at each store were used to wire merchandise requests to a warehouse, which in turn either shipped immediately or placed a reorder. Wal-Mart computers were also linked directly with over 200 vendors, making deliveries even faster. "We spend a little over 2 cents for every dollar we ship out," said Walton. "For others it's around 4 cents. That's a 2 percent edge right there on gross margins." Wal-Mart had one of the world's largest private satellite communication systems to control distribution. In addition, Wal-Mart had installed point-of-sale bar-code scanning in all of its stores.

Wal-Mart owns a fleet of truck-tractors that can deliver goods to any store in 36 to 48 hours from the time the order was placed. After trucks drop off the merchandise, they frequently pick up merchandise from manufacturers on the way back to the distribution center. This back-haul rate was over 60 percent and was yet another way to cut costs.

In 1992, Wal-Mart entered into a joint venture, in which it had a 50 percent interest with CIFRA (Mexico's largest retailer). As of their annual meeting on January 31, 1993, they announced that the joint venture operated three Club Aurreras, four Bodegas discount stores, and one Aurrera combination store. This joint venture plans to add a large number of units during the coming years. Will Wal-Mart's strategy work in Mexico? At what rate and where should Wal-Mart expand in the United States? Should Wal-Mart make further acquisitions to grow even more rapidly? Should Wal-Mart expand into Canada or even Europe? What strategies would you recommend to Glass as Wal-Mart finally has become the largest retailing firm in the United States?

THE KING IS DEAD—LONG LIVE THE KING

Can Wal-Mart continue its spectacular growth, now that its founder Sam Walton is no longer available? Can David D. Glass, President and Chief Executive Officer, with S. Robson Walton, Chairman of the Board, and Donald G. Soderquist, Vice Chairman and Chief Operating Officer, maintain Wal-Mart's fabulous success?

Circle Electronics Corporation

RAYMOND M. KINNUNEN *and*
JAMES F. MOLLOY, JR., *Northeastern University*

It was July of 1991 and Jennifer Fairbanks, CEO and 20 percent stockholder in Circle Electronics Corporation, was discussing a decision she had to make. Bob Murray, the entrepreneur who had cofounded Circle with Fairbanks in 1979 and who held 80 percent of the stock, wanted out. Circle had begun as a contract manufacturer, assembling printed circuit boards, but by 1991 it had broadened operations to include procurement and some engineering design. Murray, who had a degree in aeronautical engineering, also owned Valtex, a company that designed and sold electronic valve actuators that were manufactured by Circle. Valtex was housed inside Circle's leased facilities. As Fairbanks explained the situation:

> I have an extreme loyalty and responsibility toward Bob Murray. Even though he has been a silent partner, he has contributed all the invested funds either directly or through guaranteed loans, some of which are still outstanding. Now he wants to funnel all his money and attention into Valtex, so I have to find another vehicle to fund Circle.

Fairbanks, whose college degree was in sociology, had worked her way up in management over a 7-year period from 1971 to 1978 to become a product manager for another Murray-owned company. When Murray decided to sell that company, he asked Fairbanks if she would like to help him start up a new company, Belmont Controls, whose principal product was to be an electronic

Management cooperated in the field research for this case, which was written solely for the purpose of stimulating student discussion. All events and individuals are real, but names have been disguised at the organization's request. The case has accompanying videotapes of Jennifer Fairbanks in a question-and-answer session with an Executive MBA class at Northeastern University. The tapes may be purchased from the authors at Northeastern University, College of Business, Boston, MA 02115.

actuator. Although Belmont eventually evolved into Valtex, the plans for the actuator never got off the drawing board, and Murray brought Fairbanks into Circle Electronics instead. Fairbanks commented:

> When I joined Circle in 1979, the company was doing circuit board work for a company that produced a radar detector unit. Because I knew nothing about electronic assembly, I went out and put an advertisement in the paper for electronic assemblers. Fortunately, I was able to find and hire a woman who knew everything about electronic assembly. She got me going.

At the time, people wondered why Murray had decided to back Fairbanks in this type of very competitive business. As Murray explained it:

> I like to bet on people, and I thought she was a sound bet. Basically, I was saying to her that although we were in a lousy business, because you do not have the ability to add value the way you do when you make a product and take it to the marketplace, I felt she had the capability to make things happen. I told her to pick something that she was comfortable with and I would have to accept it even though it might not be something that I was comfortable with. So when she came to me and said this is what I want to do, I went along with it. And my faith paid off.

Murray reflected further on his confidence in Fairbanks:

> She is a manager as opposed to an entrepreneur. She is in the kind of business she ought to be in for her type of skills. Management is what she is good at and that is what she is doing.

In addition to the ownership issue, Fairbanks was faced with strategic and operating decisions that needed her attention. The purchase of some new equipment would allow the company to provide another service and increase sales considerably. The purchase would require hiring and training of personnel as well as additional marketing. Upgrades in manufacturing would also be necessary. To accomplish everything would probably require external financing. The company had lost money from 1979 to 1988 but had been profitable in 1989, 1990, and 1991. (See Exhibits 1 and 2 for financial statements.)

COMPANY BACKGROUND

Circle started operations as an assembly shop. As Fairbanks explained:

> We assembled circuit boards. Customers sent us the material in a kit form and asked us to assemble it in accordance with their specifications. The only value added was labor.

Nine years later, in 1988, Circle changed its strategy and became more of a value-added manufacturer by doing procurement—purchasing parts that were needed in the manufacturing process—and some manufacturing engineering. This allowed Circle to increase efficiency and maintain high quality in manufacturing design, thus improving its profit margin. Later, Circle further sharpened its focus on procurement and manufacturing design when it began doing work for Micorp, a company that produced automobile antitheft devices. As Fairbanks put it:

> Micorp was having both quality and delivery problems with the devices, which were being manufactured overseas. Successfully redesigning Micorp's product for im-

EXHIBIT 1[1]

Balance Sheet—June 30, 1980 to June 30, 1991[2]
(Dollars in thousands)

	1991	1990	1989	1988	1987	1986	1985	1984	1983	1982	1981	1980
					Assets							
CURRENT ASSETS												
Cash	$ 36	$ 22	$ 35	$ 25	$ 9	$ 28	$ 8	$ 4	$ 9	$ 3	$ 1	$ 2
Accounts receivable	202	211	116	68	87	71	53	83	48	35	11	4
A/R affiliate	0	0	0	0	0	0	0	0	0	0	3	22
Inventories	161	138	92	57	9	10	4	10	12	6	6	4
Prepaid deposits	38	39	11	13	12	6	2	3	5	1	1	1
Total current assets	$436	$410	$253	$164	$118	$114	$ 67	$ 99	$ 74	$ 44	$ 21	$ 32
Fixed assets, net[3]	$ 16	$ 19	$ 27	$ 10	$ 8	$ 14	$ 31	$ 34	$ 25	$ 19	$ 10	$ 16
OTHER ASSETS												
Goodwill	$ 0	$ 0	$ 0	$ 11	$ 22	$ 33	$ 44	$ 55	$ 66	$ 77	$ 88	$100
Other (CVLI)[4]	54	40	34	26	18	11	1	2	1	1	1	1
Total other assets	$ 54	$ 40	$ 34	$ 37	$ 40	$ 44	$ 45	$ 57	$ 67	$ 78	$ 89	$101
Total assets	$506	$468	$314	$211	$166	$172	$144	$190	$166	$141	$119	$148
					Liabilities & Equity							
LIABILITIES												
Accounts payable	$123	$120	$ 67	$ 39	$ 37	$ 9	$ 18	$ 13	$ 9	$ 12	$ 1	$ 3
N/P trade	18	11	0	0	0	24	24	24	18	12	11	1
Accruals	79	49	53	42	26	19	13	37	21	22	9	8
Notes payable: bank	73	75	75	50	50	75	75	60	55	11	0	0
Reserves	18	6	0	0	0	0	0	0	0	0	0	0
Deposit from customer	0	56	0	0	0	0	0	0	0	0	0	0
Car and equip notes	9	0	0	0	5	10	24	22	9	13	0	0
Stockholder notes	167	234	244	485	408	321	189	137	139	151	134	128
Total liabilities	$488	$551	$440	$616	$526	$457	$342	$292	$251	$220	$154	$140
EQUITY												
Common stock	$ 20	$ 20	$ 20	$ 20	$ 20	$ 20	$ 20	$ 20	$ 20	$ 20	$ 20	$ 20
Paid-in capital	274	227	227	0	0	0	0	0	0	0	0	0
Retained earnings	(275)	(330)	(373)	(426)	(380)	(305)	(218)	(122)	(105)	(99)	(56)	(12)
Total equity	$ 19	($ 83)	($126)	($406)	($360)	($285)	($198)	($102)	($ 85)	($ 79)	($ 36)	$ 8
Total liability and equity	$506	$468	$314	$211	$166	$172	$144	$190	$166	$141	$119	$148

[1] Columns may not add due to roundoffs.

[2] Fiscal year runs from July 1 to June 30.

[3] Fixed assets, net is equal to machinery and equipment less depreciation.

[4] CVLI = Cash value of life insurance.

proved manufacturability gave Circle the opportunity to enter other arenas, and our profit position continued to improve as we moved toward total turnkey manufacturing. Our customers have shifted more and more in the direction of specialization, with the result that they now do the product engineering and design and leave the manufacturing to us.

EXHIBIT 2 [1]

Income Statement: From July 1, 1979 to June 30, 1991
(Dollars in thousands)

	1991	1990	1989	1988	1987	1986	1985	1984	1983	1982	1981	1980
Sales	$1,785	$1,618	$1,294	$918	$847	$718	$959	$887	$736	$309	$150	$101
LESS:												
Cost of goods	1,458	1,327	1,054	800	752	619	811	706	578	231	98	77
Gross profit	$ 327	$ 291	$ 239	$118	$ 95	$ 99	$148	$182	$158	$ 79	$ 52	$ 24
LESS:												
Selling expenses [2]	$ 10	$ 50	$ 6	$ 26	$ 52	$ 34	$ 27	$ 21	$ 20	$ 12	$ 4	$ 7
General and administrative	293	241	199	123	116	113	179	143	115	84	36	32
Amortization and goodwill	0	2	11	11	11	11	11	11	11	11	11	11
Management fees	0	0	0	0	0	0	0	0	0	0	37	(20)
Operating income	$ 24	($ 1)	$ 24	($ 42)	($ 85)	($ 59)	($ 69)	$ 6	$ 12	($ 29)	($ 36)	($ 6)
LESS:												
Interest expense	0	0	0	(25)	(15)	(36)	(29)	(22)	(18)	(16)	(8)	(6)
Other income and expenses	31	44	29	22	24	8	1	(1)	0	1	0	0
Net income	$ 55	$ 43	$ 53	($ 45)	($ 75)	($ 87)	($ 97)	($ 17)	($ 6)	($ 44)	($ 44)	($ 12)
Gross margin (%)	18.34	17.99	18.57	12.84	11.19	13.81	15.47	20.46	21.47	25.44	34.78	24.08

[1] Columns may not add due to roundoffs.
[2] Estimated.

INDUSTRY TRENDS

By 1988, Circle was one of approximately 200 companies nationwide offering turnkey manufacturing services (where the contractor was responsible not only for assembly but for purchasing and storing inventory to build the product), board assembly, cable and harness assembly, testing, and/or semiconductor fabrication and assembly. The combined annual sales volume of these companies was over $4 billion, and the most successful of the companies stayed competitive by making investments in new technology.

One of the most important trends in the electronic assembly industry in the late 1980s was the increasing use of *surface mount technology* (SMT), a new process that was used to expand the capability and performance of printed circuit boards (PCBs). A basic part of nearly every electronic product, PCBs provided the foundation to which a variety of electronic components were attached. With SMT, electronic components can be soldered directly onto both the front and back of the board, making it possible to attach a larger number of much smaller electronic components to each board, thereby improving performance. Before SMT, it was necessary to drill holes through the circuit boards in order to push the wire leads of electronic components through to the back of the PCB, where they were soldered.

In 1989, as Circle Electronics reported in its company business plan, 57 percent of all electronic assembly was through-hole and 43 percent was surface mount. It was projected that by 1993, these figures would be 54 percent surface mount and 46 percent through-hole. In 1991, Circle had no SMT equipment. Fairbanks said:

> You hear so many people asking for surface mount. We lost our largest customer because I cannot service their SMT needs. They said to me, "If you go surface mount now, we'll give you our business because we love dealing with you." That was enough for me to say I better start investigating SMT. Now, we have two or three other customers who are saying, "When are you going to get into surface mount technology?"

A second trend in the contract manufacturing industry was the move toward full-service providers. In 1989, 73 percent of all contract manufacturing was done on a turnkey basis. In 1991, 75 percent of Circle's business was turnkey, in which the customer provided designs and specifications and Circle delivered the finished product. Thus if customers demanded SMT technology for their product, the turnkey subcontractor had to provide it or risk losing the business. In 1991 Fairbanks was well aware of industry predictions that turnkey production would increase to 83 percent of all contract manufacturing by 1993. As she put it:

> In a nutshell, our major long-term problem is that we need to become more of a value-added manufacturer. If we remain a strictly contract manufacturer, we will become a dinosaur. We need to continue to move toward a total-service package.

A third, but more favorable, industry change was the return of some manufacturing to the United States. With SMT and anticipated future advancements in manufacturing automation, the foreign cost advantage was decreasing.

In addition, there were trends in contract manufacturing toward target market specialization. Companies could choose to focus on high-volume production, prototype and product development production only, or production focused on some specific industry, such as military/aerospace, consumer electronics, or commercial electronics. In 1991, Circle was attempting to specialize by volume, prototyping, and product development.

CUSTOMERS

Circle's five largest customers in 1991 were Micorp, Valtex, Kodak (the EPS and the ATEX divisions), Proteon, and Onset. Those customers accounted for nearly 50 percent of the almost $1.8 million in revenues that Circle generated in the fiscal year ended June 30, 1991. Circle was looking to expand its customer base. Its strategy was to develop long-term relationships with companies whose corporate philosophy included the use of outside subcontractors as an integral part of their manufacturing plan. Some of Circle's customers had been with them for a number of years and others were relatively new. (See Exhibit 3 for a customer list.)

Circle was considered a responsive subcontractor, flexible in meeting the needs of customers, which did high-quality work. It restricted customers to within a 100-mile radius of its headquarters and targeted those who could contribute at least $80,000 to its annual sales volume. The company had a comprehensive listing of sales prospects and relied heavily on frequent direct contacts with customers and potential customers. Circle was confident in projecting $2.4 million in sales for the fiscal year ending June 1992, even though the country was in a prolonged economic downturn.

EXHIBIT 3

Circle Electronics Customer List

Company	Industry	Length of the Business Relationship
Amnet	Telecommunications	4 Years
ATC Power Supply	Military power supply	< 1 Year
Atex/Kodak	Photo imaging	4 Years
Azonix	Instrumentation	3 Years
Brookstone	Mail order marketing	2 Years
Cognex	Vision machinery	3 Years
Encore Computer	Para/Process computers	5 Years
EPS/Kodak	Systems/publishing	4 Years
G.E./Ametek	Aircraft instruments	4 Years
Micorp	Auto antitheft devices	2 Years
Mod Tap	Local area networks	< 1 Year
Munin Technology	Computer controllers	< 1 Year
New Media Graphics	Systems for graphics	< 1 Year
Oak Tree	Computer peripherals	2 Years
Onset Computer	Remote data collection for marine environment	5 Years
Proteon	Local area networks	7 Years
Roll Systems	Paper feeding systems	2 Years
Valvcon	Electronic valve actuators	3 Years
Xylogics	Terminal servers and controllers	2 Years

SOURCE: Company documents.

LOCAL COMPETITION

Circle's local competition was very volatile. Three of its competitors had ceased operation in 1990 and a fourth had recently filed for bankruptcy under Chapter 11. Fairbanks identified five prominent subcontractors within the 100-mile-radius target area:

- **Phoenix Electronics,** which Fairbanks considered to be Circle's biggest competitor, had estimated annual sales of between $5 and $10 million. Phoenix was heavily automated and offered turnkey through-hole and SMT services along with cable assemblies. It was equipped with excellent testing equipment. It had a reputation as a high-quality subcontractor that offered very good prices. Phoenix was privately owned and had been founded in 1982.
- **Beacon Engineering** was expanding its facilities and had an aggressive goal of generating $10 million in 1991 sales volume from New England customers. It was also automated for through-hole work, SMT work, and in-house testing. In the past, Beacon had focused primarily on very large volume jobs and therefore did not compete directly with Circle. However, with its new and larger facility, Beacon was a threat to seek smaller jobs to fill capacity. Beacon's quality and pricing were comparable to Circle's.
- **Zenith Components** was a small firm with limited automated equipment and no testing, turnkey, or SMT capabilities. Its quality was perceived as excellent and its pricing was very low. It competed with Circle only on consignment jobs (where the customer provides all the parts), and consign-

ment work was projected to be just 25 percent of Circle's total business in the fiscal year ending June, 1991. Consignment work typically required a 2- to 3-day turnaround, whereas turnkey jobs required 6 to 8 weeks.

• **Hartwell Technology** had automated through-hole capabilities with high-quality testing equipment. It did perform turnkey work but had problems with credibility in 1991 to the extent that Circle felt that Hartwell might not survive. Fairbanks was alert to this possibility as a means of adding turnkey accounts.

• **Westford Assembly** was automated and did some turnkey work. It reportedly was for sale in 1991, but a buyer had not been found.

Despite the local competition, Fairbanks felt that Circle had a competitive edge:

> We have a good reputation. Even though Beacon is right around the corner, people still come back to us. We are not the lowest-cost producer so we are always hitting heads against everyone who is less expensive than we are. I say to my customers, "Fine, go see the competition. When they go out of business we'll be here."

In general, the market was becoming more price-sensitive in 1991 because of the poor economic climate. Some subcontractors were lowering prices to obtain work. As the economy continued to worsen, there was increasing pressure on the contract manufacturers' customers to bring all their manufacturing work in house and eliminate subcontract work entirely.

FINANCING

Turnkey subcontract manufacturing typically produced low margins. As Fairbanks explained:

> I have put together an excellent operation. But we are in a low-margin business. I sometimes feel that the greatest challenge is how to utilize what I put together in order to generate enough revenue to allow us to get into a higher-margin business.

Circle had started in 1979 with $20,000 in equity and $128,000 in stockholder debt in the form of notes. By 1991, this debt, which had been secured by Murray, was $167,300. Murray had also converted $273,900 in loans into equity. Now Murray was attempting to put his estate and financial house in order, eliminate guaranteed debt, and ensure that Fairbanks would become the majority owner in Circle.

As Fairbanks explained:

> The agreement that he and I are talking about right now is for me to gain controlling interest in the company. Bob Murray would like to be out of Circle.

One of the major concerns confronting Fairbanks was how to acquire controlling interest in Circle and, at the same time, help Murray organize his financial affairs. Because Murray had always taken care of dealings with the bank, Fairbanks had little experience in financing. She was also uncertain about how to acquire the controlling stock.

Recently, Circle had been finding it hard to raise cash to pay existing debt obligations, and Fairbanks knew that it would be very difficult for Circle to raise the cash necessary to grow and keep up with the competition. The first priority was to raise the necessary equipment funds—on the order of $250,000— for SMT equipment. Getting into SMT would mean hiring a new manager, providing training, and acquiring new inventory, and would result in incremental losses on the new business for several months. However, in Fairbanks's view, the returns would be high. She explained:

> We did an analysis and determined that in the first year, we can expect to get half a million dollars in increased sales. But, given our financing situation, who is going to lend the company any money?

> Altogether, I would need to borrow approximately $250,000. In order to get that, I would need a consistent record of profitability and some equity. In 1991 we had enough work to turn things around. That has enabled us to think about SMT in 1992.

> I've already started to talk to the bank because I want to deal with them myself.

Beyond the SMT equipment needs, Circle has some short-term financial needs. In order to meet sales objectives and to keep current facilities in working order, additions and upgrades to maufacturing and operations were necessary. Fairbanks estimated that the short-term, nonpostponable needs of the company were approximately $20,000. In the longer term, Fairbanks estimated that Circle would grow substantially, assuming the purchase of additional testing equipment and other related machines, the cost of which would be between $260,000 and $450,000. She commented:

> In fiscal 1991 we made about $54,000, which we had never done before. It looks good. Much of that profit, though, comes from the fact that we have Valtex as a captive customer.

FUTURE

Circle might move in a number of different directions in the long-range future. One option was for Circle to seek a merger with some large product organization and become the sole producer for that organization. Another option was to manufacture exclusively for Valtex. In the fiscal year ended June 1990, Valtex accounted for only 15.7 percent of Circle's sales volume, but the Valtex volume might rise dramatically. Fairbanks explained:

> Circle is coming up to a major crossroads. If Valtex really breaks out now, it could be that we'll just be absorbed by Valtex. It looks like Valtex is finally turning the corner in the marketplace. They appear to be getting an increasing number of inquiries, which are likely to be the forerunners of increased orders. They just received a large contract with Amoco for about a quarter of a million dollars, and we are now producing 800 actuators. After Amoco, it's Texaco and after Texaco it's Exxon and your name is really starting to get out there.

Circle was responsible for all the administrative and accounting work for Valtex products. In 1991, Valtex had total sales of approximately $700,000, while Circle had sales of approximately $1.8 million. The possibility that Valtex would take off was still uncertain. Fairbanks explained her dilemma:

> Circle still lacks an overall direction. There are a lot of paths we could take on the decision tree. Maybe we should be a completely separate organization from Valtex. On the other hand, Bob could say that now he needs our entire organization servicing Valtex—and forget about our other stuff. Bob deserves all the loyalty we can give him, but can we afford to wait to see how Valtex develops? My own people are

pushing hard to expand Circle's service capabilities now. We'll be a dinosaur if we can't offer full service.

Then there's me personally. I must answer the question, "Do I want to run a contract manufacturing house for the rest of my life?"

Over the next few months, Fairbanks had to make a decision on whether or not to obtain controlling ownership in Circle. Her personal financial position was not likely to support the necessary debt. Even if she *could* obtain controlling interest in Circle, Fairbanks questioned whether the long hours she might then have to devote to the company would take away too much from her family:

I get a little scared when people say to me, "You're going to have to put in a hundred hours a week with this company." I can't dedicate myself that way. I've already made that decision.

As for the potential acquisition of Murray's stock in the event of his death, the company had enough insurance on his life to pay his estate for his stock plus repay the bank loans that he had guaranteed. Without Murray's backing and with Fairbanks's limited personal assets, obtaining debt funds would be very difficult for Circle at current profit levels. Looking at 1991 profitability and beyond, however, Fairbanks was encouraged.

Wall Drug Store: Facing the 90s

PHIL FISHER, *University of Southern Indiana,*
ROBERT JOHNSON, *University of South Dakota, and*
JAMES TAYLOR, *University of South Dakota*

SIZZLING STEAK: WALL DRUG

WESTERN ART: WALL DRUG

BEAUTIFUL WESTERN ART: WALL DRUG

FREE COFFEE AND DO-NUTS FOR VIETNAM VETERANS: WALL DRUG

FREE COFFEE AND DO-NUTS FOR HONEYMOONERS: WALL DRUG

MAKE YOUR DAY: WALL DRUG

W'ALL MAKE YOU HAPPY: WALL DRUG

FREE ICE WATER: WALL DRUG

Travelers driving across the rolling prairie of western South Dakota on Interstate Highway 90 are amused, irritated and beguiled by scores of roadside signs and billboards advertising the attractions of something called Wall Drug. There are signs promising 5 cent coffee, homemade rolls, and roast beef dinners; signs intended to amuse, (HAVE YOU DUG WALL DRUG?; W-A-A-L I'LL BE DRUGGED); signs publicizing publicity, (FEATURED ON TODAY SHOW: WALL DRUG; WALL DRUG FEATURED IN PEOPLE; WALL DRUG AS TOLD BY WALL ST. JOURNAL; WALL DRUG AS TOLD BY TIME) and signs advertising Black Hills gold jewelry, cowboy boots, and camping supplies. By the time travelers reach the little (pop. 770) town of Wall, more than half of them are curious enough to exit under the friendly stare of an 80 foot, bright green, concrete brontosaurus which towers over the Wall Auto Livery, a Sinclair station. Two blocks to the left they find main street and a block long business district with a hardware store, a grocery store, a dozen gift shops, restaurants, museums, and Wall Drug, the self-proclaimed "World's Largest Drug Store."

This case was prepared by Professor Phil Fisher of the University of Southern Indiana, and Professors Emeritus Robert Johnson and James Taylor of the University of South Dakota. It was presented at the North American Case Research Meeting, 1990.

The Wall Drug Store occupies half of the east side of this block. Behind the iron hitching posts lining the curb and the pine board store front are a restaurant and twenty odd small shops selling souvenirs, western clothing, moccasins and boots, Indian pottery, western jewelry, western books, stuffed jackalopes,[1] fudge, posters, oil paintings and, of course, prescription drugs. Life-sized concrete or fiberglass old West characters lounge on benches in an enclosed mall giving tourists opportunities for photos of themselves sitting on a cowboy's lap or with an arm around a dance hall girl. Two animated, life-sized, mannequin cowboy orchestras play and sing for the crowds, and nearby a more menacing mannequin shouts out challenges to passers to try and match his quick draw in a gun fight for only fifty cents.

In back of the store is an open yard ringed with buildings featuring more animated displays, including a piano-playing gorilla, and a singing family on a Sunday drive in a restored 1908 Hupmobile. This area, termed the "back-yard," includes a six-foot stuffed rabbit, a stuffed buffalo, a stuffed bucking horse, and a large, saddled fiberglass jackalope all providing more photo opportunities for visiting tourists. An old fashioned covered well dispenses free ice water for coolers and thermos bottles from a modern faucet.

A private collection of over 300 original paintings portraying the American West is displayed on the walls of the restaurant dining rooms. Throughout the store, those walls not covered with shelves of merchandise are covered with photographs. There are old photographs of Sioux chiefs, and western characters such as Calamity Jane, General Custer, and Wild Bill Hickock. There are hundreds of photographs of less famous cowboys and homesteaders. There are photographs showing people standing in front of signs giving the mileage to Wall Drug from such places as Paris, Amsterdam, Cairo, London, New Delhi, and Tokyo. And there are pictures of the generations of the Hustead family who created, own, and manage this unique drug store which is visited each year by approximately 2 million people.

As the tourist season opened in the spring of 1990, Bill Hustead, the CEO of Wall Drug, his parents, Ted and Dorothy, his wife, Marjorie, and his sons, Rick and Ted, made last minute preparations for the flood of expected customers. At the same time they continued to consider the pros and cons of plans for the most ambitious expansion in the company's history.

WALL DRUG HISTORY

Ted Hustead graduated from the University of Nebraska with a degree in pharmacy in 1929. In December of 1931, in the depths of the depression, Ted and his wife, Dorothy, bought the drugstore in Wall, South Dakota, for $2,500. Dorothy, Ted and their four-year-old son, Bill, moved into living quarters in the back of the twenty feet of the store. Business was not good (the first month's receipts were $350) and prospects in Wall did not seem bright. Wall, South Dakota, in 1931 is described in the following selection from a book about the Wall Drug Store.

> Wall, then, a huddle of poor wooden buildings, many unpainted, housing some 300 desperate souls; a 19th century depot and wooden water tank; dirt (or mud) streets;

---

[1]Jackalopes are stuffed jackrabbits with antelope or deer antlers. Flying jackalopes have pheasant wings. These creations of taxidermy were priced from $99 to $129.

few trees; a stop on the railroad, it wasn't even on the highway. U.S. 16 and 14 went right on by, as did the tourists speeding between the Badlands and the Black Hills. There was nothing in Wall to stop for.[2]

Neither the drugstore nor the town of Wall prospered until Dorothy Hustead conceived the idea of placing a sign promising free ice water to anyone who would stop at their store. The first sign was a series of small signs along the highway that read "GET A SODA/GET A BEER/TURN NEXT CORNER/JUST AS NEAR/TO HIGHWAY 16 AND 14/FREE ICE WATER/WALL DRUG." On a blazing hot Sunday afternoon in the summer of 1936, Ted put the signs up and travelers were turning off the highway to stop at the drugstore before he got back. Located at the western edge of the Badlands National Monument, and near the major highway between the Monument and the Black Hills 50 miles further to the west, they began to draw a stream of weary, thirsty tourists into the store.

Ted began putting signs up all along the highways leading to Wall. One series read "SLOW DOWN THE OLD HACK/WALL DRUG CORNER/JUST ACROSS THE RAILROAD TRACK." The attention-catching signs were a boon to Wall Drug Store and the town of Wall prospered too. In an article in *Good Housekeeping* in 1951, the Hustead's signs were called "the most ingenious and irresistible system of signs ever devised."

Just after World War II, a friend of the Husteads, traveling across Europe for the Red Cross, got the idea of putting up Wall Drug signs overseas. The idea caught on and soon South Dakota servicemen who were familiar with the signs back home began to carry small Wall Drug signs all over the world. Many wrote the store requesting signs. For example, a sign was placed in Paris, "WALL DRUG STORE, 4278 MILES." Wall Drug signs were placed all over the world including areas near the North and South Poles, the 38th parallel in Korea and on jungle trails in Vietnam. The Husteads sent more than 200 signs to servicemen requesting them from Vietnam. These signs led to news stories and publicity which further increased the reputation of the store.

Articles about Ted Hustead and the Wall Drug Store began appearing in newspapers and magazines. In August, 1950, *Redbook Magazine* carried a story which was later condensed in *Reader's Digest*. The number of newspapers and magazines carrying feature stories or referring to Wall Drug increased over the years. As of May, 1990, Wall Drug Store files contained over 700 clippings of stories about the store. The store had also been featured on several network and cable television shows.

The store and its sales grew steadily. From 1931 to 1941, the store was in a rented building on the west side of Wall's Main Street. In 1941, the Husteads bought an old lodge hall in Wasta, S.D. (15 miles west of Wall) and moved it to a lot on the east side of the street. This building became the core around which the current store was built.

Tourist travel greatly increased after World War II, and the signs brought increasing numbers of people to the store. Bill Hustead recalls that he was embarrassed because the facilities were not large enough to service the crowds of customers. The store did not even have modern rest rooms, but sales during this period grew to $200,000 annually by 1950.

---

[2]Jennings, Dana Close; *Free Ice Water: The Story of Wall Drug;* North Plains Press; Aberdeen, South Dakota, 1969, p. 26.

In 1951, Bill Hustead, now a pharmacy graduate of South Dakota State University, joined his parents in the store. In 1953, they expanded the store into a former store room to the south. This became the Western Clothing Room. In 1954, they built an outside store on the south side of the Western Clothing Room. This resulted in a 30% increase in sales. In 1956, a self-service cafe was added on the north side of the store. The cafe expansion was built around a large cottonwood tree which remained, its trunk rising out of the center of the dining area up through the roof.

By 1958, the Wall Drug Store had two men in a truck working full time to maintain 600 signs displayed along highways throughout the Midwest. The store also gave away thousands of small signs each year to people who requested them.

In the early 1960s, Highway 16, the main east-west route across South Dakota to the Black Hills, was replaced by Interstate Highway 90. The new highway was routed near the south edge of Wall. The Husteads, who had been considering building an all new Wall Drug Store along with a gasoline service station near the old highway, did build the station, the Wall Auto Livery, at the new highway interchange.

In 1963, they added a new fireproof construction coffee shop. A new kitchen, also of fireproof construction was added to the back of the coffee shop the following year. Also in 1964 and 1965, new administrative offices and a new pharmacy were opened on a second floor over the kitchen. Another dining room and the backyard area were added in 1968. This was followed in 1971 with the Art Gallery Dining Room. By the early 70s annual sales volume had reached $1,000,000.

In 1971, the Husteads bought a theater that bordered their store on the south. The next year they demolished it and constructed a new addition, called the Wall Drug Mall. All previous expansions had been financed from profits of the business or short-term loans. Ted and Bill broke with this by borrowing $250,000 for 10 years to finance the Mall.

The Mall was designed as a miniature western town within a large enclosure. The strolling mall was designed as a street between shops fashioned like two-story frontier stores. The store fronts and interiors were made of various kinds of American wood—pine, black walnut, gumwood, cedar, hackberry, maple, and oak. The store fronts were recreated from photographs of Western towns in the 1880s. These shops stocked products which were more expensive than the souvenir merchandise of the older shops. In 1983, the mall was extended to include a half dozen more shops, a travelers' chapel modeled after one built by Trappist Monks in Dubuque, Iowa, in 1850, and a replica of the original 1931 drugstore called Hustead's Apothecary, which serves as a museum of Hustead family and Wall Drug artifacts.

The store was also expanded on the north end in 1975 and 1976 and on the south of the original Mall in 1978. Wall Drug continued to have increased sales every year until 1979. That year, a revolution in Iran started a chain of events which resulted in a doubling of the price of crude oil and temporary shortages of gasoline in the United States. This caused many service stations to experience periods of time that summer when they were out of gasoline. Travel by automobile decreased, and the Wall Drug Store was one of many businesses hit by a decrease in sales. By 1981, however, sales had recovered.

Exhibit 1 gives sales and net income after taxes for 1975 through 1989. In 1990, the store and its backyard covered 48,000 square feet and sales were $7.4 million. A map of the Wall Drug Store as it was in 1990 is shown in Exhibit 2.

EXHIBIT 1

Wall Drug Store Sales and Net Income

Year	Sales (000)	Net Income (000)
1975	2,679	118
1976	3,464	165
1977	3,777	155
1978	4,125	206
1979	3,552	33
1980	3,970	185
1981	4,821	224
1982	4,733	203
1983	4,851	257
1984	5,055	285
1985	5,273	161
1986	5,611	233
1987	6,142	249
1988	6,504	204
1989	7,419	242

SOURCE: Company Records

EXHIBIT 2

Wall Drug Store Map 1990

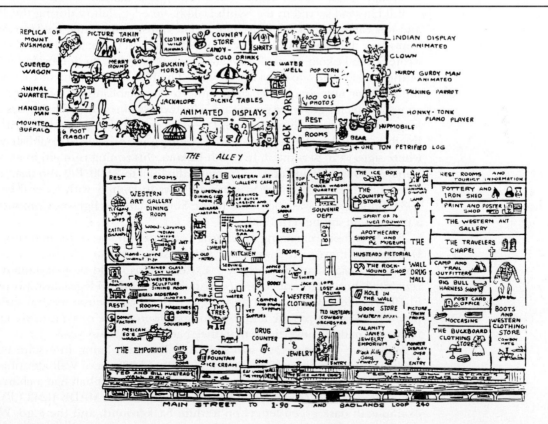

SOURCE: Company document

THE HIGHWAY BEAUTIFICATION ACT AND WALL DRUG SIGNS

In 1965, Congress passed the Highway Beautification Act, which was designed to reduce the number of roadside signs. Anticipating the removal of many Wall Drug signs, the Husteads invested in new signs that were allowed under the initial legislation. Since these signs could be no closer than 660 feet from the highway, they had to be very large and cost around $9,000 each. By the time they were installed, the laws had been amended to exclude them.

In the late 1960s, concerned about the effects of losing their roadside signs, the Husteads began advertising in unusual and unlikely places. They began taking small advertisements in the European *International Herald Tribune* and Greenwich Village's *Village Voice*. They advertised 5 cent coffee, 49 cent breakfasts and veterinary supplies. They put advertisements on double-decker buses in London, on the walls in the Paris Metro (subway), along the canals in Amsterdam and in rail stations in Kenya. These ads brought letters and telephone calls and then news articles. First, *The Village Voice* carried an article, and in 1971, the Sunday *New York Times*. Bill Hustead appeared on the network television show, "To Tell the Truth." In all, 260 articles about the store were printed in the 1970s and approximately the same number during the 1980s.

Passage of the Highway Beautification Act did not mean an end to roadside signs. Compliance with this legislation was slow in many states. Disputes over whether sign owners should be compensated for removed signs and a lack of local support for the law meant that some signs remained.

Bill Hustead served in the South Dakota state legislature during the 1960s and was Chairman of the state joint senate-house Committee on Transportation when the Highway Beautification Act was passed. He and his committee wrote South Dakota's compliance law which resulted in the removal of 22,000 of the 28,000 roadside signs in the state. The federal government then fined the state for non-compliance, objecting to the establishment of commercial zones in which signs were permitted. The owners of roadside businesses challenged this federal enforcement and were successful. The federal government finally accepted a plan which allowed county governments to establish zones where signs were permitted. In South Dakota, this zoning resulted in an additional 1,000 signs being erected bringing the total to 7,000. Bill also testified at federal and state legislative hearings on laws to comply with federal law. In 1981, Bill Hustead was appointed to the South Dakota Highway Commission, a position he still held in 1990.

By 1990, most remaining Wall Drug roadside signs were located in South Dakota, and there were fewer than 300. Existing signs were being permitted, but no new signs could be erected. Existing signs could be maintained and repainted, but could not be moved or enlarged. Federal legislation proposed in 1989 would have removed these signs without compensation, but the proposed bill was not passed; and the Husteads were more optimistic about the future of roadside advertising than they had been in many years.

Wall Drug sign coverage was still fairly intensive along Interstate 90. In 1990, a count of signs over a 250 mile stretch of I-90 east of Wall identified 86 Wall Drug signs. No two signs were alike, although about half had a characteristic design. These contained a short message, HAND MADE JEWELRY, for example, in dark green letters on a white background, and the logo, WALL DRUG, below in yellow letters on a dark green background. Other signs had a variety of colors and formats. A crew still serviced the signs twice a year, and all signs observed in 1990 were in excellent condition.

BUSINESS ENVIRONMENT

Wall is located at the northwest edge of The Badlands National Park (see Exhibit 3). The Badlands National Park is an area of 244,000 acres of barren ridges and peaks formed by centuries of erosion which exposed colorful layers of different minerals and fossil remains of prehistoric animals. Approximately one million people visit the Monument each year.

Rapid City, South Dakota, (population, 44,000) is 50 miles to the west of Wall. Rapid City is on the eastern rim of the Black Hills, a forested mountain region and one of the United States' major gold producing areas. The Black Hills is also the site of the Mount Rushmore Memorial which attracts about 2 million visitors each year. Forest Service visitation figures for the Badlands and Mount Rushmore are given in Exhibit 4.

Interstate Highway 90 is the only east-west interstate highway in South Dakota. It passes near The Badlands National Monument and through the Black Hills carrying most of the tourists who visit these areas. Exhibit 5 gives the traffic count on I-90 by month for 1988 and 1989. According to Ted Hustead, counts of traffic in the area of Wall showed that 78% of all cars which left Interstate 90 to drive a parallel road through the Badlands also entered Wall. For westbound I-90 traffic, 55% exited at Wall, and 45% of eastbound traffic turned off at the Wall exit. These counts were made during the summer months.

There were seven other gift shops in Wall, and an old west wax museum, a wild life museum, a taffy shop, and a Cactus Saloon and a Badlands Bar on

EXHIBIT 3

South Dakota: Location of Wall Drug Store

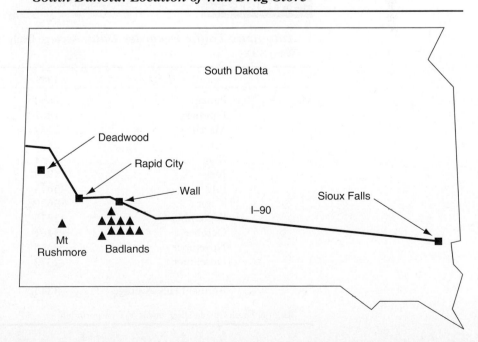

EXHIBIT 4

Annual Visitors

	Badlands National Monument	Mount Rushmore Memorial
1971	1,293,011	2,314,522
1973	1,400,000	NA
1975	1,165,161	1,994,314
1977	1,303,471	2,271,838
1979	870,000	1,642,757
1981	1,187,970	2,054,567
1983	1,038,981	1,983,710
1985	962,242	2,112,281
1987	1,186,398	1,949,902
1988	1,122,040	2,013,749
1989	1,249,956	2,075,190

SOURCE: U.S. Forest Service

Wall's Main Street. All depended primarily upon tourist business during the summer months. In the spring of 1990, the Hustead family was preparing two new gift shops for June 1 openings. These shops were across the street from the main store. They were called Dakota Mercantile and The Tumbleweed.

Voters in South Dakota approved a referendum in 1988 to permit limited betting ($5) casino gambling to be licensed in the city of Deadwood, South Dakota, (pop. 2409). Situated in the Black Hills 90 miles west of Wall and

EXHIBIT 5

Automatic Traffic Recorder Data Average Daily Traffic on I-90 near Wall, S.D.

	1988	1989
January	1674	1975
February	1867	1954
March	2184	2353
April	2567	2606
May	3361	3420
June	4919	5160
July	5615	5847
August	5629	6086
September	3875	4233
October	3401	3609
November	2675	3141
December	2372	2374
Annual Daily Average	3345	3563

SOURCE: South Dakota Department of Transportation

EXHIBIT 6

Sales Receipts (000's) Eating and Lodging Establishments

	Wall, S.D.		Deadwood, S.D.	
	Eating	Lodging	Eating	Lodging
1988				
Jan.–Feb.	$106	$ 16	$275	$172
Mar.–Apr.	118	37	285	145
May–Jun.	358	366	502	318
Jul.–Aug.	550	740	823	613
Sep.–Oct.	270	204	372	434
Nov.–Dec.	115	32	296	158
1989				
Jan.–Feb.	83	13	277	201
Mar.–Apr.	124	45	295	141
May–Jun.	385	414	538	344
Jul.–Aug.	641	911	883	724
Sep.–Oct.	328	300	434	243
Nov.–Dec.	134	54	495	265
1990				
Jan.–Feb.	103	28	715	363

SOURCE: South Dakota Department of Revenue

11 miles off Interstate Highway 90, Deadwood was founded by gold miners and is near to several still active gold mines. During the 1880s it was home to well known western characters such as Calamity Jane and Wild Bill Hickock. Hickock, in fact, was shot in the back and killed while playing poker in Deadwood. Legal gambling began again in November of 1989. While the full impact of the Deadwood gambling casinos on tourism in South Dakota could not yet be measured in early 1990, it was expected to result in an increase in traffic on Interstate 90, the most direct highway from the East. Exhibit 6 shows sales for all eating establishments and hotels and motels in Wall and Deadwood by two month periods from January 1988 through February 1990.

MANAGEMENT

Bill Hustead, 63, was the President and Chief Executive Officer of the Wall Drug Store. Bill and his wife, Marjorie owned 60 percent of the stock in the company. Marjorie was the corporation Secretary and was active in the business and in charge of merchandise buying. Ted and Dorothy Hustead owned the remaining 40 percent of the stock. Both were in their late 80s and still participated in the store management. Ted was Chairman of the Board and was involved primarily in public and employee relations. Dorothy was also an officer of the corporation and managed the store's cash receipts, accounting and banking.

Two of Bill and Marjorie's sons, Rick, 40, and Teddy, 39, were also active in store management. Rick had a Master's degree in guidance and counseling and had worked as a high school guidance counselor before joining the store in 1980. His primary responsibility was managing restaurant operations. Teddy had a degree in business and had worked for several years in the Alaskan oil fields before Rick persuaded him to join the store in 1988. He was responsible for day to day management of the shops. Both brothers participated in strategic planning and policy making for the overall business.

While neither Rick or Teddy were pharmacists, Rick's wife, Kathy, was a registered pharmacist and worked three days a week managing the store's prescription drug business. In 1990, Teddy married and his wife, Karen, was to become the newest member of the Hustead family management team. Karen was the Executive Vice President of the Badlands and Black Hills Association. This was an organization of tourism related businesses in the region. It was expected that she would start as a floating troubleshooter involved in day to day store operations to learn the business, and that she would also have a role in public and governmental relations for the store.

Bill spoke about the significant roles of his mother and wife in the success of the Wall Drug Store.

> It's known as Ted and Bill Hustead's Wall Drug, but for years Dorothy was the backbone of the store. A few years ago, Dad and I were honored at a banquet and as I sat there and listened to the speeches, a voice deep within me cried, Dorothy, Dorothy. She was the one with the idea to put up the signs. She was the one who worked behind the counter and in the restaurant.

> My wife, Marjorie, is the most valuable asset we have. After she took over the buying, we raised our net from the jewelry store by $50,000. She has a wide sphere of influence and is a stabilizing force.

If the Wall Drug Store was a family institution, it was also seen as an institution of great importance to the town of Wall and to the store's full-time employees. Bill Hustead's conversations about the Wall Drug Store frequently emphasized the importance of the business to the economy of the town of Wall, its importance as the only source of income in Wall for most of its full-time employees, and of the need to secure its continued success for the sake of the town and the store's employees. He also spoke of the business in terms of personal and family pride.

> The priest here in Wall thought I might have a calling for the priesthood, so my folks sent me to Trinity High School in Sioux City, Iowa. . . . One time I had a date with a girl who took me to her home. Some relatives, a married sister, I think, and her husband were there, and they made some slighting remarks about that "little store with all the signs." I was embarrassed. Gosh, Mom had the idea about the signs but then did Dad have to put them up all the way from Wisconsin to Montana?

> Then, when I worked in the store during the summer, I was embarrassed sometimes at some of the things customers would say about the store. Our facilities were so poor. We didn't even have indoor rest rooms.

There were two key managers who were not family members. Mike Huether worked with Rick in managing restaurant operations. The two were about the same age and had the same level of responsibility, but Bill noted that, "Mike isn't as likely to go to the mat with me." Huether was a long time employee who had worked at the Wall Drug Store since he was 18. Karen

Poppe with 16 years' experience was the personnel manager. As the store grew and the competition for seasonal employees increased, this function has become critical to the store's ability to grow or even function at the current level of operations.

The Wall Drug Store had no organization chart or written job descriptions, but all the managers belived that they had clear understandings as to their responsibilities and authority. Rick explained, "There is overlap. Ted (Teddy) and I have specific and joint responsibility. Ted's focus is more in retail. My focus is more in the restaurant. There is no organizational chart, but we spend enough time talking to each other so that our roles are defined."

Rick thought the store needed a more complete management staff but that they had made progress toward that in his ten years there. "Bill is a builder and a brilliant businessman. What I wanted to do is run the business more efficiently. It's paid off with more profits."

MANAGEMENT SUCCESSION

Asked about the difficulties of having three generations of the family active in the store management, Bill spoke of his own plans. "I went to a religious retreat earlier this month, then attended my cousin's funeral in the East and a funeral of a high school friend and I'm ten days behind in my work. Sometimes I think this darn job is killing me. I can't work ten or twelve hour days anymore."

The aspirations of his sons were a factor also. "My forty-year-old sons will have to have independence. The boys in the store (a brother and three sisters were not involved with the store) will get as much of the store as I can give them, but it's not that good a business. There's too much pressure." Asked about the fact that his father at 87 was still active in the business, he said, "I love my father. He's the best P.R. man anybody ever had."

He elaborated more on his past contributions to the business. "My plan was to work for awhile and then buy a drugstore in Jackson Hole, Wyoming, but Dad and Mom encouraged me to come here. They needed me desperately. Dad was never a floor man and they really needed someone on the floor."

Rick discussed the issue of management succession from his perspective. "We have a clear understanding with some documentation but no time table. Teddy came in with the understanding that we'd be partners. I'd like to see my Dad stay on as long as he wants. He is politically influential. He's a tremendous businessman. He's an asset to the business and to us. I hope he'll keep involved to the point he enjoys it. Control is not a major issue. If anyone is concerned about succession, it's Bill." Rick also pointed out that the family had life insurance protection to assure that the business would not be crippled by inheritance taxes should anyone in the family die.

Ted Sr. made it clear that he no longer expected to take an active role in making policy decisions. The 1989 South Dakota legislature had approved the licensing of video poker and keno machines which would accept bets up to two dollars. The Husteads had installed a few in the Western Art Gallery Dining Room where they had a liquor license and bar. Their intent was to evaluate the results and either remove them or install more depending on their profitability and their perceived contribution or detraction from the atmosphere. Asked about his attitude toward the decision to install video lottery machines, Ted said, "They don't need to ask me, and I don't want them to ask me, but if they had, I'd have said I didn't think much of them [the video lottery machines]."

Speaking of Bill's contribution to the store, Ted Sr. commented, "My son Bill is an idea man. The Mall was his. He called in an architect and gave him the plans. Bill has built the art collection. He has a great appreciation for art. I bought the first few paintings; Bill bought the rest."

STORE OPERATIONS

The Wall Drug Store had approximately 30 permanent employees. Peak summer employment would reach 225. About 100 people from the local area were employed to do seasonal work and 120 college students were recruited to complete the work force. Ninety-five percent of the local seasonal employees would be people who had worked at Wall Drug in previous years. Many were housewives and senior citizens who could begin work in May and work during September and October when the college students were not available. About forty percent of the college students each year were repeat employees from previous years, but Wall Drug had to recruit about 70 new employees each year.

Student recruiting was handled by Karen Poppe. Each year 200 colleges and universities were sent recruitment information just prior to the Christmas break. She also made recruiting trips to about six colleges and attended several "job fairs." Recruitment of seasonal employees was becoming increasingly difficult and was seen by the Wall Drug management as a potential limit to their growth.

Mrs. Poppe and the Husteads thought that Wall's remoteness was a major obstacle to recruitment of summer employees from college campuses. The nationwide increase in the tourism industry meant that there were more companies recruiting from the same source. At the job fairs, Mrs. Poppe found herself competing with such major attractions as Disney World and other theme parks, and better known vacation areas such as Yellowstone Park. This made persuading students to choose the little town of Wall on the treeless plains of South Dakota more difficult each year.

Summer employees were housed in small dormitories and houses owned by the store. The store owned a swimming pool for employees and would have social gatherings such as picnics or volleyball games. Summer employees were paid $4 an hour and worked 40 hours plus 8 hours of overtime for which they were paid time-and-a-half. They paid $25 per week for their rooms. Students who stayed through the Labor Day weekend also got a 5 percent bonus and a rent reduction of $17 per week for the entire summer.

While the gambling casinos in Deadwood, South Dakota, 90 miles to the West were expected to result in increased traffic on I-90, they also competed for seasonal employees. In 1990, unskilled casino employees in Deadwood were being paid $7 an hour.

Wall Drug had formerly hired one of every five applicants for summer jobs. By 1990, they were having difficulty filling their positions. The labor scarcity had also had an effect on their personnel policies. As Bill explained, "We would exercise discipline. We expected to send a few people home just to let everyone know that we were serious. Now we get them out here and try to make it work. If they can't make change, we try to find a place for them. And it works better. We have a better atmosphere now."

New employees were trained to be courteous and informed about the Badlands, Black Hills, and other sites of interest in the area. Karen Poppe coordinated new employee orientation, but most of the members of the Hustead family participated. Ted, Sr. studied the applications and pictures of all summer employees so that he could greet them by name when they arrived and whenever he saw them working in the store.

The Wall Drug Store and restaurant had a total area of 48,000 square feet. By comparison, the average Wal-Mart store covered a little more than 56,000 square feet. In 1989, Wall Drug merchandise sales were $5.6 million. The restaurant was a self-service restaurant with seating for 500; it had sales of $1.8 million. In 1989, the average McDonald's had $1.6 million in sales. The opening of the two new stores, Dakota Mercantile and The Tumbleweed, would add another 6,000 square feet.

Wall Drug visitors frequently asked about purchasing items by mail. For several years the store had about $50,000 in mail order sales without catalogs or order forms. In 1989, Teddy designed a simple order form with the title, "Order By Mail Year Around From WALL DRUG." It listed a few items under the categories of jewelry, western art, boots and moccasins, western wear, western books and "Etc., Etc., Etc." Items listed under this last category were jackalopes, flying jackalopes, steer skulls, rattlesnake ashtrays, horse twitches, and souvenirs galore. This one page sheet also included a map of the store but listed no prices. It was available at cash registers for customers to take with them. Mail order sales increased to over $87,000 in 1989 and sales for the first three months of 1990 were up 47 percent over 1989. Most mail order sales were for bigger ticket items such as jewelry. The store also sold over 60 jackalopes by mail in 1989.

Commenting on Teddy's success with increasing mail order sales, Rick said, "A catalog would be the next step. We talk about building a model for this business, but we need to hire the talent to run it."

The Husteads were also trying to expand their tour bus business. Bus tours were an increasingly important factor in tourism. They were especially popular with senior citizens and foreign visitors. The Husteads believed that the ability to provide fast food service from their 500 seat, self service restaurant would be a reason for bus tours to include them as a stop. They were also interested in persuading tour operators now running buses from Denver to the Black Hills to include the 100 mile round trip from Rapid City to the Badlands as part of the tour. This would also include a stop at Wall Drug. Attracting more of this business was assigned to Teddy who had increased the store's promotional efforts at bus tour operator conventions and trade shows. This had resulted in some increase in business, and about 90 buses were expected to include Wall Drug as a stop in 1990.

FINANCE

Exhibits 7 and 8 present income statements and balance sheets from 1983 through 1989. Historically, the store's growth and expansion projects had been financed through retained earnings and loans of up to ten year's duration. The long term debt of $151,000 outstanding in 1989 consisted of approximately $82,000 owed on a stock repurchase agreement and a $69,000 interest bearing note. These debts were held by Hustead family members not active in the business and were being paid in monthly installments.

EXHIBIT 7

Wall Drug Store
Income Statement (000's)

	1983	1984	1985	1986	1987	1988	1989
Net Sales	$4,851	$5,055	$5,273	$5,611	$6,142	$6,504	$7,419
Cost of Goods Sold	2,586	2,553	2,793	2,854	3,338	3,579	4,164
Gross Profit	$2,265	$2,502	$2,480	$2,757	$2,804	$2,925	$3,255
General and Administrative							
Wages and Salaries	$1,006	$1,129	$1,233	$1,274	$1,305	$1,443	$1,541
Officer's Salaries	143	154	135	151	164	155	178
Depreciation	123	136	148	149	170	168	200
Profit Sharing Contribution	100	113	119	135	126	146	157
Advertising	93	82	99	122	107	123	44
Utilities	84	111	106	124	120	129	141
Conventions and conferences	1	1	3	3	16	14	21
Other	356	424	465	501	505	534	655
Total G & A Expenses	$1,906	$2,150	$2,308	$2,459	$2,513	$2,712	$2,937
Income from Operations	$ 359	$ 352	$ 172	$ 298	$ 291	$ 213	$ 318
Dividend and Interest Income	47	57	52	68	71	69	63
Other Income and (Expenses)	16	23	8	16	6	4	7
Pre Tax Income	$ 419	$ 428	$ 230	$ 381	$ 364	$ 276	$ 374
Income Tax	162	143	69	148	115	72	132
Net Income	$ 257	$ 285	$ 161	$ 233	$ 249	$ 204	$ 242
Preferred Stock Dividend	1	1	0	2	1	1	1
Add to Retained Earnings	$ 256	$ 284	$ 161	$ 231	$ 248	$ 203	$ 241

Source: Company Records

Wall Drug had a profit sharing plan for all employees who worked more than 1000 hours during any year. At the discretion of the four senior Husteads who were the corporate officers, the plan paid up to 15% of employees' salary into a retirement trust fund managed by an independent financial institution. Profits had always been sufficient to pay the full 15 percent. The store terminated a smaller noncontributory defined benefit plan in 1988. All participating employees were fully vested in their earned benefits under the old plan.

Inventory levels are shown as of December 31. Orders for the coming season began arriving in December, but most would arrive from January through April. Peak inventory levels would reach $2.5 million. Many suppliers would post date invoices for July and August which eased the cash flow burden of financing this seasonal inventory.

The art collection was used primarily to attract customers and repeat customers. Prices for the paintings were not established. When paintings were sold the prices were negotiated. The collection was carried in the accounts as merchandise inventory and valued at cost.

A small part of the inventory consisted of gold bullion which would be sold periodically to the store's main jewelry supplier in Rapid City. This practice provided a hedge against rising gold prices. In 1990, because of the need to finance the new stores, the stocks of bullion were low.

The $300,000 reserve for self-insurance was established in 1982. The store was a self insurer for collision and comprehensive coverage of its motor vehicles, of the deductible portion of its employees' medical coverage and a

EXHIBIT 8

Wall Drug Store
Balance Sheets (000's)

Assets

				Years Ended December 31			
	1983	1984	1985	1986	1987	1988	1989
ASSETS							
Current Assets							
Cash	$ 40	$ 12	$ 18	$ 29	$ 70	$ 59	$ 267
Current Marketable Securities	205	0	0	1	1	2	0
Accounts Receivable	13	25	24	25	36	48	41
Merchandise Inventory	405	616	718	968	1,322	1,429	1,330
Prepaid Taxes and Other	33	32	114	57	68	112	52
Total Current Assets	$ 696	$ 685	$ 874	$1,080	$1,497	$1,650	$1,690
Investments and Other Assets							
Noncurrent marketable securities	402	489	600	785	739	646	487
Life Insurance and Other	7	7	7	8	14	13	79
Total Other Assets	$ 409	$ 496	$ 607	$ 793	$ 753	$ 659	$ 566
Property and Equipment							
Land	$ 174	$ 177	$ 187	$ 186	$ 171	$ 181	$ 181
Building and improvements	1,935	2,057	2,112	2,160	2,434	2,495	2,567
Equipment, furniture and fixture	1,065	1,232	1,278	1,372	1,492	1,628	1,795
Construction in Progress	0	0	0	55	0	0	148
Total Property and Equipment	$3,174	$3,466	$3,577	$3,774	$4,097	$4,304	$4,691
Less Accumulated Depreciation	1,475	1,609	1,732	1,869	2,032	2,182	2,385
Net Property and Equipment	$1,699	$1,857	$1,845	$1,905	$2,065	$2,122	$2,306
Goodwill at cost less Accumulated Amortization	16	14	12	10	9	7	5
TOTAL ASSETS	$2,820	$3,052	$3,338	$3,788	$4,324	$4,438	$4,567

continued

EXHIBIT 8

(*continued*)				Liabilities and Equity			
				Years Ended December 31			
	1983	1984	1985	1986	1987	1988	1989
LIABILITIES							
Current Liabilities							
Current maturities of long term debt	$ 40	$ 10	$ 2	$ 2	$ 2	$ 2	$ 2
Notes Payable	50	85	175	310	598	500	275
Accounts Payable	61	40	41	54	60	44	77
Taxes Payable	93	67	75	95	81	75	128
Accrued Profit Sharing Contribution	100	113	119	135	127	146	157
Accrued Pension Plan Payable	0	0	29	25	31	15	0
Accrued Payroll and Bonuses	65	50	34	48	56	56	73
Accrued Interest Payable	4	2	4	1	7	5	2
Total Current Liabilities	$ 413	$ 367	$ 479	$ 670	$ 962	$ 843	$ 714
Long Term Debt	182	173	173	172	156	154	152
Deferred Income Taxes	10	25	27	56	68	101	121
STOCKHOLDERS' EQUITY							
Preferred Stock	$ 30	$ 30	$ 30	$ 30	$ 30	$ 30	$ 30
Class A Common Stock	48	48	48	48	48	48	48
Class B Common Stock (nonvoting)	53	53	53	53	53	53	53
Capital in Excess of Par	52	52	52	52	52	52	52
Reserve for Self Insurance	300	300	300	300	300	300	300
Retained Earnings	1,732	2,004	2,176	2,407	2,654	2,857	3,097
Total Stockholders' Equity	$2,215	$2,487	$2,659	$2,890	$3,137	$3,340	$3,580
Total Liabilities and Equity	$2,820	$3,052	$3,338	$3,788	$4,322	$4,438	$4,567

SOURCE: Company Records

portion of the casualty coverage of some buildings and their contents. A portion of the store's marketable securities funded this reserve.

EXPANSION PLANS FOR THE 1990s

As he prepared for the 1990 tourist season, Bill Hustead, CEO of Wall Drug, was making plans for the store's most ambitious expansion. This expansion would include a large open mall ringed with shops to be built to the rear of the existing back yard area. Houses along the street to the rear of the store, already owned by the Husteads, would be moved or razed to make room for this expansion.

New shops with a combined floor space of nearly 15,000 square feet would include a shop selling Indian handicraft items, a poster store, a yogurt shop, a fast food hamburger shop, and a store for motorcyclists. (Sturgis, South Dakota, in the Black Hills is the site of an annual summer motorcycle rally which attracts thousands of motorcyclists from all over North America.) A major feature of the new addition would be a free gallery displaying a recently acquired collection of over 700 old photographs of cattle drives, rodeos, Indians, cowboys, and other early settlers of South Dakota and Montana. The Husteads estimated that approximately twelve to fourteen additional employees would be required to staff this expansion during the peak season.

Bill planned to build this expansion over a period of three to five years. As with previous expansions, he planned to act as his own general contractor and direct the actual construction. When the project was finished, the existing backyard would be removed. This was constructed of metal buildings and had about 3,000 square feet of floor space.

The last project being planned was to build the Wall Drug Western Art Gallery and guest house. This would be a three story mansion, a replica of an old Southern plantation house, to display the best of the Wall Drug Store's western art collection. It would also display beautiful furnishings, elegant table settings, crystal, and other accoutrements of graceful living. The Hustead art collection included 30 paintings portraying Christmas in the West. Bill planned to have a Christmas room in the mansion to display these paintings and a permanent Christmas tree with antique ornaments. The third floor was planned as a theater which would show films or videotapes about some of the artists and a film or a videotape about the Wall Drug Store. Some rooms in the mansion were to be set aside as guest quarters.

Bill planned to charge a small admission fee to the mansion. This income would be used to purchase new paintings for the art collection. Bill explained,

> There is more to business than just profit. We are aiming at sophisticated people who will get a kick out of this. Forty percent of our business is from repeat customers so we've got to keep moving in such a way as to impress people. We've got to keep forward momentum.

Bill believed that the very survival of the business and the jobs and aspirations of his full time employees depended on the Wall Drug Store's continued development.

> We are not Wal-Mart. We are in the entertainment business. We can't just sit here with what we've got and expect people to keep coming.

Bill Hustead was aware that his two sons had serious reservations about his expansion plans. Commenting on the proposed expansion, Rick said,

> Dad is more oriented to seeing the business as a real attraction—a "must stop" attraction. I'm more concerned with the nuts and bolts. I want to be profitable. I want a better handle on our inventory and labor. My concern is always that we are profitable and don't overextend or build things that won't be profitable. What he plans to do is interesting, but I have real questions about the mansion. Are we going to realize a profit? This could cost one and a half or two million dollars. Fortunately it is the farthest down the road. We should expand the food service first.

> I'm conservative. I resisted the new shops (Dakota Mercantile and The Tumbleweed) at first. The building estimates were $210,000. They cost $300,000. They are nice shops but getting personnel to run them is an issue.

The Husteads did not use a formal system of evaluating return on investment in making decisions about expansion. Rick noted, however, that these decisions were subjected to analysis. "Dad knows his expenses and his volumes. We know that we have to gross $200,000 or better in the new shops to be successful."

Bill estimated that the new stores would have a payback of approximately five years. He reported that their cost had actually been about $240,000. As to the expense of the proposed expansion plans, he said, "There is no way we are going to spend one and a half to two million dollars. The total cost of the backyard expansion and the art gallery will be between eight to nine hundred thousand and one and a half million dollars."

Teddy felt that he was somewhere in the middle on the expansion plans.

> We have got to replace the backyard and make the store more interesting, but the mansion never has made too much sense to me. I have a lot of respect for my father, but he got this idea from homes in the South. I don't know if it applies to the West. On the other hand, we are getting to have a world class collection of western art. I don't ever want to underestimate him.

Teddy also pointed out that the existing building needed extensive repairs. "The roof around the tree needs to be replaced. A few years ago the tree was trimmed back, and it died so now it has to go." Teddy estimated that these repairs would cost $200,000. He noted further that the store's administrative offices had been built in 1964 for a much smaller staff and were inadequate for current operations.

Bill commented on the objection his sons had raised to the mansion style art gallery. "People from the South settled in South Dakota and some houses of this type were built here, but it wouldn't have to a southern style mansion. It could be another type of building."

In May, the 1990 season began on a promising note. The first two weeks of sales in the Dakota Mercantile and Tumbleweed stores were very good. "It's now or never," Bill commented, reflecting on the seasonal character of their business. Sales in the main store were also running ahead of 1989's, and bus loads of travelers bound for Deadwood were stopping to eat and shop.

Cineplex Odeon Corporation

JOSEPH WOLFE, *University of Tulsa*

In mid-February 1989 Jack Valenti, head of the Motion Picture Association, reaffirmed the American film industry's basic health by citing 1988 movie theater attendance figures surpassing 1.0 billion people for the seventh year in a row. While this magnitude translated into box office revenues of over $4.4 billion, there are indications the industry is in a state of both absolute and relative decline. It is also undergoing a restructuring that is fundamentally changing the nature of competitive practices for those in the film exhibition business. In the first instance a lower proportion of America's aging population attends the movies each year partially due to the use of VCRs for film viewing, the presence of television in both its broadcast and cable versions, and to other uses of the consumer's leisure time dollars. In the second instance a great degree of owner-concentration is occurring due to separate actions by both the Hollywood producers of films and their exhibitors.

Despite the apparent decline of the motion picture theater as the major supplier of America's needs for mass entertainment, the Toronto-based firm of Cineplex Odeon has quickly become North America's second largest and most profitable theater chain through a series of shrewd and adventuresome acquisitions and the creation of a large number of upscaled, multiscreened theaters in key cities and market areas. With 482 theaters and 1,809 screens in 20 states, the Washington, DC, area, 6 Canadian provinces, and the United Kingdom, the firm posted record sales of $695.8 million and profits of $40.4 million in 1988 and is on the verge of developing and operating more than 110 screens in the United Kingdom by 1991. Central to Cineplex Odeon's success is the firm's driven and often-abrasive chairman, President and CEO, Garth Drabinsky. It is against the backdrop of the industry's fundamental changes and basic decline that Drabinsky must chart his firm's future actions to ensure its continued growth and prosperity.

Joseph Wolfe is Professor of Management at the University of Tulsa.

THE MOTION PICTURE THEATER INDUSTRY

Early Operations and Competitive Strategies

The motion picture theater industry (SIC 783) has undergone a number of radical transformations since its turn-of-the-century beginnings. The first movies were shown in cramped and hastily converted storefront locations called Nickelodeons, so-named for their five-cent admission charges. Their numbers grew rapidly because the costs of entering this industry were relatively low and a plentiful supply of films were available in both legal and illegal (pirated) versions. By 1907 it was estimated the United States had about 3,000 movie theaters concentrated in the larger cities. Rural areas were serviced by traveling film shows which made their presentations in the local town meeting halls.

The typical show lasted only 15 to 20 minutes, augmented by sing-along slides or lectures. As the film medium's novelty declined, audiences began to clamor for more lavish and ambitious productions using recognizable actors and actresses. Feature-length movies replaced one-reel short subjects and comedies in the 1910s, and the theater industry's greatest building period began. Opulent, specially built structures soon became the focal point of every major city's downtown area. Often possessing more than 5,000 seats, they came complete with a pit orchestra with vocalists and chorus, baby-sitting facilities, elevators and grand staircases to a heavenlike balcony, numerous doormen, and a watchful and attentive fleet of uniformed ushers.

By the mid-1920s over 19,000 theaters were in operation, and Hollywood's film producers began what was a continuing attempt to control the first-run exhibitors of their films via acquisitions. The battle for theaters was initially waged between Paramount and First National; but soon Loew's (MGM), Fox, and Warner Brothers joined in, with First National being the major loser. By 1935 the twin realities of the Great Depression and the advent of sound films caused the number of theaters to plummet to about 15,000. Because of the nations's bleak economic outlook many theaters had become too run-down or too costly to convert to the greater demands of sound films. Many Americans also substituted radio's free entertainment for their weekly lemminglike trek to the movies. Surviving theaters introduced the double feature to create more value for the entertainment dollar while obtaining the major source of their profits from candy, soft drink, and popcorn sales.

During World War II motion picture attendance and Hollywood's profits reached their all-time highs, with about 82 million people a week going to the nation's 20,400 theaters. This pinnacle did not last long, however, as postwar incomes were spent on new cars, television sets, and homes built in the newly emerging suburbs. Motion picture attendance began its precipitous fall in 1947, with attendance reaching its all-time low of 16 million per week in 1971. The number of theaters followed the same downward trend, although a steady increase in the number of drive-in theaters temporarily took up some of the slack.

The postwar period also saw the effects of the government's 1948 Consent Decree. By the early 1940s Hollywood's five major studios had obtained control or interests in 17% of the nation's theaters. This amounted to 70% of the important large city first-run theaters. Although certain studios were stronger in different parts of the country—Paramount dominated New England and the South, Warner Brothers the mid-Atlantic region, Loew's and RKO the New York–New Jersey area, and 20th Century-Fox the Western states—each controlled all stages of the distribution chain from its studios (manufacturing), its film exchanges (wholesaling), and its movie theaters (retailing). Under the Consent Decree the studios could either divest their studios and film exchanges or get rid of their movie theaters. Hollywood chose to sell their cinemas, thereby opting to control the supply side of the film distribution system.

In an effort to arrest the decline in attendance and to counter the relatively inexpensive and convenient medium of black and white television in the 1950s, the film studios retaliated by offering movies that dealt with subject matter considered too dangerous for home viewing, shown in formats and hues beyond television's technical capabilities. Moviegoers heard the word "virgin" uttered for the first time, women "with child" actually looked pregnant rather than merely full-skirted, and couples were shown in bed together without having to put one foot on the floor. From 1953 to 1968 about 28% of Hollywood's films were photographed and projected in a bewildering array of widescreen processes such as Cinerama, CinemaScope, RegalScope, SuperScope, Technirama, VistaVision, Panavision, Techniscope, and even three-dimensional color.

Current Competitive Conditions

As movie attendance stabilized in the mid-1980s to a little more than 20 million patrons per week, two new trends established themselves in the movie theater business: the first was the creation of multiple-screen theater sites (see Exhibit 1); the second was Hollywood's reacquisition of theaters and theater

EXHIBIT 1

Number of U.S. Movie Theaters (Selected years, 1923–1988)

Year	Theaters	Drive-ins	Total	Screens
1923	15.0	—	15.0	—
1926	19.5	—	19.5	—
1929	23.3	—	23.3	—
1935	15.3	—	15.3	—
1942	20.3	0.1	20.4	—
1946	18.7	0.3	19.0	—
1950	16.9	2.2	19.1	—
1955	14.1	4.6	18.7	—
1965	9.2	4.2	13.4	—
1974	9.6	3.5	13.2	14.4
1980	9.7	3.6	13.3	17.6
1981	11.4	3.3	14.7	18.0
1984	14.6	2.8	17.4	20.2
1985	15.1	2.8	17.9	20.7
1986	16.8	2.8	19.6	22.8
1987[1]	17.9	2.8	20.7	23.6
1988[1]	18.1	2.7	20.8	24.3

[1]Estimated.

SOURCES: Joel W. Finler, *The Hollywood Story.* New York: Crown Publishers, 1988, p. 288; "The Motion Picture Rides into Town, 1903," *The Wall Street Journal*, February 7, 1989, p. B1; *1989 U.S. Industrial Outlook.* Washington, DC: U.S. Department of Commerce/International Trade Administration, 1989, p. 57–1.

chains as part of a general consolidation within the industry. Many theater chains rediscovered the glitz and glamor of old Hollywood by rejuvenating old theaters, while existing single-screen theaters were subdivided and multiplexes were constructed from scratch in suburban malls and shopping districts. The economies of multiple-screen operations are compelling at the local level. Rather than needing a separate manager and projectionist for each theater a number of variously sized auditoriums can be combined and centrally serviced. Box office operations and concession stands can also be centrally managed and operated. The availability of a number of screens at one location also yields programming flexibility for the theater operator. A "small" film without mass appeal can often turn a profit in a room seating only 300 people, while it would be unprofitable and would be lost in a larger auditorium. Having a number of screens in operation also increases the likelihood the complex will be showing a hit film, thereby generating traffic for the other films being shown at the site. Multiple screens also allow the operator to outfit various rooms with different sound systems (the THX System by Lucasfilm versus the standard 4-track optical stereo system) and projection equipment (at least one 70mm six-track magnetic sound projector in addition to the usual 35mm projector) and thereby offer the very finest possible viewing.

The second trend toward consolidation is occurring at all levels of the film distribution chain. A number of studios recently purchased major theater chains after sensing a relaxation of the enforcement of the Consent Decree (in 1984 the Justice Department offered advance support to any studio financing a lawsuit to reenter the movie theater business) plus their promise to limit their ownership to less than 50% of any acquired chain. MCA, owner of Universal Studios, has purchased 49.7% of Cineplex Odeon; the Cannon Group purchased the Commonwealth chain; and United Artists Communications acquired the Georgia Theatre Company, the Gulf States and Litchfield chains, and, in 1988 alone, the Blair, Sameric, Commonwealth (from the Cannon Group), and Moss theater chains. Gulf & Western's Paramount Studios purchased the Mann Theaters and Festival Enterprises, while Columbia and Tri-Star (owned by Coca-Cola) bought the Loew's chain. On the retailing side Cineplex Odeon purchased the Walter Reade, Plitt, RKO, Septum, Essaness, and Sterling chains; Carmike Cinemas purchased Stewart & Everett; and AMC Entertainment purchased the Budco Theaters. Through these actions and others the top six chains now own nearly 40% of America's screens, which is a 67% increase in just three years.

Wholesaling operations were drastically reduced over the years on a scale unnoticeable to the public but very significant to those in the business. When film going was in its heyday each studio operated as many as twenty or so film exchanges in key cities across the country. Hollywood's studios have since closed many exchanges; they are now operating only five to eight branches each. Paramount recently merged its Charlotte and Jacksonville branches into its Atlanta office, while Chicago now handles the business once serviced by its Detroit, Kansas City, Des Moines, and Minneapolis branches. As observed by Michael Patrick, president of Carmike Cinemas, "As the geographical regions serviced by these offices increase, the ability of smaller exhibitors to negotiate bookings is diluted relative to the buying power of the larger circuits."[1]

---

[1] Michael W. Patrick, "Trends in Exhibition," in Wayne R. Green (ed.), *The 1987 Encyclopedia of Exhibition.* NY: National Association of Theatre Owners, 1988, p. 109.

THE INDUSTRY'S PRODUCT AND COMPETITIVE STRUCTURE

Despite the glamor associated with Hollywood, its stars, its televised Academy Award show, and such megahits as *Who Framed Roger Rabbit?*, *Rain Man*, and *Batman*, theater operators are basically in the business of running commercial enterprises dealing with a very perishable commodity. A movie is a merchandisable product made available by Hollywood and various independent producers to commercial storefront theaters at local retail locations. Given the large degree of concentration in the industry, corporate level actions entail the financing of both acquisitions and new construction, while local operations deal with the booking of films that match the moviegoing tastes of the communities being served.

To the degree a movie house merely retails someone else's product, the theater owner's success lies in the quality and not the quantity of products produced by Hollywood. Accordingly the 1987–1988 Christmas season did not produce any blockbusters, while 1987's two big hits were *Beverly Hills Cop II* and *Fatal Attraction* and 1986's hits were *Top Gun, Crocodile Dundee*, and *The Karate Kid, Part II*. Under these conditions of relatively few real money-makers the bargaining power shifts to the studios leaving the exhibitors with more screens than they can fill with high-drawing films. Although the independent producers (the "indies") such as the DeLaurentis Entertainment Group, New World, Atlantic, Concorde, and Cannon are producing proportionally more films every year and the majors are producing fewer, their product is more variable in quality and less bankable. Additionally, theaters often pay a premium for the rights to show first-run movies on an exclusive basis in a given area or film zone, such as the May 1989 release of *Indiana Jones and the Last Crusade*. This condition hurts the smaller chains especially hard, as they do not have the resources to outbid the giant circuits.

Marketing research conducted by the industry consistently found that young adults are the prime consumers of motion picture theater entertainment. This group is rather concentrated but not organized. A study by the Opinion Research Corporation in July 1986 found those under the age of 40 accounted for 86% of all admissions. Frequent moviegoers constitute only 21% of the eligible filmgoers, but they account for 83% of all admissions. A general downward attendance trend has been occurring; as shown in Exhibit 2,

---

EXHIBIT 2

Frequency of Attendance by Total Public Ages 12 and Over

Attendance	1986	1985	1984
Frequently[1]	21.0%	22.0%	23.0%
Occasionally[2]	25.0	29.0	28.0
Infrequently[3]	11.0	9.0	8.0
Never	43.0	39.0	39.0
Not reported	0.0	1.0	2.0

[1]Frequently: at least once a month.

[2]Occasionally: once in 2 to 6 months.

[3]Infrequently: less than once in 6 months.

SOURCE: *1988 International Motion Picture Almanac*. NY: Quigley Publications, 1988, p. 29A.

EXHIBIT 3

U.S. Population by Age Group for 1980 with Projections for 1990 and 2000

Age Range	Year	Number (In Millions)	Percent of Total	Percent Change
5–17	1980	47.22	20.7	—
	1990	45.14	18.1	– 4.4
	2000	49.76	18.6	10.2
18–24	1980	30.35	13.2	—
	1990	25.79	10.3	–15.0
	2000	24.60	9.2	– 4.6
25–44	1980	63.48	27.9	—
	1990	81.38	32.6	28.2
	2000	80.16	29.9	– 1.5
45–64	1980	44.49	19.5	—
	1990	46.53	18.6	4.4
	2000	60.88	22.7	31.1
65 and over	1980	25.71	11.3	—
	1990	31.70	12.8	23.3
	2000	34.92	13.0	10.2

NOTE: 1980 total: 227,705,000; 1990 total: 249,675,000; 2000 total: 267,955,000.

SOURCE: Adapted from U.S. Department of Commerce, Bureau of the Census, *Statistical Abstract of the United States, 1985.* Washington, DC: Government Printing Office, 1985, pp. 26–27.

43% of the population never attended a film in 1986. The long-term demographics also appear to be unfavorable as America's population is moving toward those age categories least likely to attend a movie. Those 40 and over make up only 14% of a typical theater's admissions, while they account for 44% of the nation's population. Those from 12–29 years of age make up 66% of admissions, while accounting for only 36% of the population.[2] See Exhibit 3.

It appears that there exist certain barriers to entry into the motion picture theater industry. Economies of scale are present, with the advantage given to operations concentrated in metropolitan areas where one omnibus newspaper advertisement covers all the chain's theaters. As shown in Exhibit 4 the largest chains in the United States lost the least during the period July 1984 to June 1985. Based on these results, scale economies appear to exist in the areas of operating costs, executive compensation, advertising, and rental expenses. Those choosing to enter the industry in recent years have done so through the use of massive conglomerate-backed capital. The possibility that an independent can open a profitable movie theater is very remote. "There's no way the small, independent operator can compete against the large screen owners these days," says John Duffy, cofounder of Cinema "N" Drafthouse International of Atlanta, Georgia.[3] As a way of carving a niche for himself, Duffy's

[2]Presented in *1988 International Motion Picture Almanac.* NY: Quigley Publications, 1988, pp. 29A–30A.
[3]Quoted in Peter Waldman, "Silver Screens Lose Some of Their Luster," *The Wall Street Journal,* February 9, 1989, p. B1.

EXHIBIT 4

Average Operating Results for Selected Motion Picture Theater Corporations by Asset Size, 7/84–6/85

Operating Results	Smaller-Sized		Middle-Sized		Larger-Sized	
Revenues	$224,171	100.0	$4,476,042	100.0	$151,545,455	100.0
Cost of operations	93,917	41.9	1,780,066	39.8	54,707,909	36.1
Operating income	130,254	58.1	2,695,976	60.2	96,837,546	63.9
Expenses:						
Compensation of officers	6,788	3.0	150,647	3.4	2,121,636	1.4
Repairs	5,497	2.5	74,134	1.7	2,438,504	1.6
Bad debts	170	.1	4,196	.1	82,661	.1
Rent	32,195	14.4	315,841	7.1	11,489,901	7.6
Taxes (excluding Federal tax)	12,904	5.8	179,881	4.0	5,689,843	3.8
Interest	8,045	3.6	117,216	2.6	8,031,909	5.3
Depreciation	8,866	4.0	269,122	6.0	8,954,959	5.9
Advertising	16,004	7.1	152,745	3.4	5,689,843	3.8
Pensions and other benefit plans	—	—	42,662	1.0	771,504	.5
Other expenses	70,971	31.7	1,682,992	37.6	55,245,207	36.5
Net profit before taxes	(31,186)	(13.9)	(293,460)	(6.6)	(3,678,421)	(2.4)
Current ratio	1.0		1.3		.7	
Quick ratio	.6		1.0		.5	
Debt ratio	140.6		52.9		74.2	
Asset turnover	3.0		1.3		1.0	

SOURCE: L. Troy, *Almanac of Business and Industrial Financial Ratios.* Englewood Cliffs, NJ: Prentice-Hall, 1988, p. 332.

chain charges $2 for an "intermediate-run" film but serves dinner and drinks during the movie, thereby garnering more than $5 in food revenue compared to a theater's average $1.25 per admission.

Despite attempts by various theater owners to make the theatergoing experience unique, customers tend to go to the most convenient theater showing the film they want to see at the time which is best for them. Accordingly a particular theater chain enjoys proprietary product differentiation to the degree that it occupies the best locations in any particular market area. Additionally, the cost of building new facilities in the most desirable areas has increased dramatically. Harold L. Vogel of Merrill Lynch, Pierce, Fenner & Smith observed the average construction cost comes to over $1.0 million per screen in areas such as New York or Los Angeles.[4]

Just as the motion picture was a substitute for vaudeville shows and minstrels at the turn of the century, radio, and now television, are the major, somewhat interchangeable substitutes for mass entertainment in America. More recently cable television, pay-per-view TV, and videocassettes have eaten into the precious leisure-time dollar. Estimates are that 49.2 million homes now subscribe to cable television, 19 million homes have pay-per-view capability, and 56 million homes have a VCR, with 20% of those homes having more than one unit. The greatest damage to theater attendance was accomplished

---

[4]Harold L. Vogel, "Theatrical Exhibition: Consolidation Continues," in Wayne R. Green (ed.), *The 1987 Encyclopedia of Exhibition.* NY: National Association of Theatre Owners, 1988, p. 62.

EXHIBIT 5

Motion Picture Exhibitors' Share of Entertainment Expenditures: Receipts as a Percent of Total for Selected Years 1929–1989

Year	Consumer Expenditures	Recreation Expenditures	Spectator Expenditures
1929	0.94	16.6	78.9
1937	1.01	20.0	82.6
1943	1.29	25.7	87.6
1951	0.64	11.3	76.3
1959	0.31	5.6	61.0
1965	0.21	3.5	51.2
1971	0.18	2.7	47.7
1977	0.56	5.8	34.8
1983	0.16	2.4	41.9
1986	0.14	1.9	37.3
1987	0.14	1.8	36.9
1988	0.13	1.8	36.5
1989[1]	0.13	1.7	36.1

[1] Estimated by the casewriter.
SOURCES: Joel W. Finler, *The Hollywood Story.* NY: Crown Publishers, 1988, p. 288; U.S. Bureau of Economic Analysis, *Survey of Current Business,* July issues; and U.S. Bureau of the Census, *Statistical Abstract of the United States: 1989* (109th ed.). Washington, DC: U.S. Government Printing Office, 1988.

by videocassettes, which deliver over 5,000 titles to viewers at a relatively low cost in the comfort of their own living rooms. Sumner Redstone, owner of the very profitable National Amusements theater chain, remarked, "Anyone who doesn't believe videocassettes are devastating competition to theaters is a fool."[5]

Although the motion picture medium has been characterized as one that provides visual mass entertainment, those going to movies must ultimately choose between alternative forms of recreation. In that regard, skiing, boating, baseball and football games, books, newspapers, and even silent contemplation, vie for the consumer's precious time. Exhibit 5 shows the movie theater industry has declined in its ability to capture both America's total recreation dollars or its thirst for passive spectator entertainment. During the period from 1984 to 1987 the greatest increases in consumer recreation expenditures were for bicycles, sports equipment, boats and pleasure aircraft, and television and radio equipment and their repair.

Different marketing strategies are being employed in an attempt to remain viable in this very competitive industry; see Exhibit 6. Some chains, such as Cinemark Theaters and Carmike Cinemas, specialize in $1 or low-price, second-run multiplex theaters in smaller towns and selected markets. In a sense they are applying Wal-Mart's original market strategy of dominating smaller, less competitive rural towns. Others, such as General Cinema, United Artists Communications, and AMC Entertainment, favor multiplex

[5] Quoted in Stratford P. Sherman, "Movie Theaters Head Back to the Future," *Fortune,* January 20, 1986, p. 91.

EXHIBIT 6

North America's Largest Theater Circuits

Circuit	Headquarters	Screens
United Artists Communications	Denver, CO	2,677
Cineplex Odeon	Toronto, CANADA	1,825
American Multi-Cinema	Kansas City, MO	1,531
General Cinema	Chestnut Hill, MA	1,359
Carmike Cinemas	Columbus, GA	742

SOURCE: 10-Ks and various stockholder's reports for 1988.

first-run theaters in major markets. Within this group AMC Entertainment has been a pioneer as a multiscreen operator. It opened its first twin theater in 1963 and its first quadplex in 1969. As of mid-1988 AMC was operating 269 complexes with 1,531 screens, with most of its expansion in the Sunbelt. General Cinema has been diversifying out of the movie theater business through its nearly 60% interest in the Neiman Marcus Group (Neiman-Marcus, Contempo Casuals, and Bergdorf Goodman) and 18.4% interest in Cadbury Schweppes. Most recently General Cinema sold off its soft drink bottling business to PepsiCo for $1.5 billion to obtain cash for investments in additional non-theater operations.

A great amount of building has occurred in the theater industry in the past few years. Since 1981 the number of screens has increased about 35% but the population proportion attending movies has actually fallen. Additionally the relatively inexpensive days of "twinning" or quadplexing existing theaters appear to be over, and the construction of totally new multiplexes is much more expensive. Exhibit 7 shows that operating profit margins peaked in 1983 at 11.7% and they have fallen dramatically since then, as the industry has taken on large amounts of debt to finance the construction of more and more screens now generating 24.6% fewer admissions per screen. Many operations are losing money although certain economies of scale exist and labor-saving devices have allowed industry employment to fall slightly while the number of screens has increased substantially. The Plitt theaters were money losers before being acquired by Cineplex Odeon, and AMC Entertainment lost $6 million

EXHIBIT 7

Per Screen Admissions, Capital Expenditures and Operating Profit Margins (Selected years, 1979–1987)

Item	1979	1981	1983	1985	1987
Tickets sold (000,000)	1,121	1,067	1,197	1,056	1,086
Average admission per screen	65,575	58,422	63,387	49,936	47,797
Capital expenditures (000,000)	$19.0	$57.4	$77.6	$164.0	$515.7
Profit margin	9.3%	9.1%	11.7%	11.6%	8.8%

SOURCE: Peter Waldman, "Silver Screens Lose Some of Their Luster," *The Wall Street Journal*, February 9, 1989, p. B1.

in 1987 and $13.8 million in 1988 on theater operations. Carmike was barely profitable in 1986, and General Cinema's earnings from its theater operations have fallen for the past three years, although the operation's assets and sales have been increasing. Generally speaking about half the nation's motion picture theaters and chains were unprofitable in the 1980s. Numerous chains have engaged in the illegal practice of "splitting," wherein theater owners in certain markets decide which one will negotiate or bid for which films offered by the various distributors available to them.

BUILDING THE CINEPLEX ODEON CORPORATION

Today's exhibition giant began in 1978 with an 18-screen complex below the parking garage of a Toronto shopping center. Garth Drabinsky, a successful entertainment lawyer and real estate investor, joined with the Canadian theater veteran Nathan Aaron (Nat) Taylor in this enterprise. After three years and dozens of new theaters, Cineplex entered the American theater market by opening a 14-screen multiplex in the very competitive and highly visible Los Angeles Beverly Center. Despite the chain's growth, however, it was only marginally profitable. When the fledgling chain went public on the Toronto Stock Exchange in 1982 it lost $12 million on sales of $14.4 million.

Cineplex nearly went bankrupt, but not through poor management by Drabinsky or Taylor. Canada's two major theater circuits, Famous Players (Paramount Studios) and the independent Odeon chain, had pressured Hollywood's major distributors into keeping their first-run films from Cineplex. But in 1983 Drabinsky, who as a lawyer had written a standard reference on Canadian motion picture law, convinced Canada's version of the U.S. Justice Department's antitrust division that Famous Players and Odeon were operating in restraint of trade. Armed with data gathered by Drabinsky, the Combines Investigative Branch forced the distributors to sign a consent decree, thus opening all films to competitive bidding. Ironically, without the protection provided by its collusive actions, the 297-screen Odeon circuit soon began to lose money, whereupon Cineplex purchased its former adversary for $22 million. The company subsequently changed its name to Cineplex Odeon.

In its development as an exhibition giant the chain always was able to attract a number of smart, deep-pocketed backers. Early investors included the since-departed Odyssey Partners, and with a 30.2% stake, Montreal-based Claridge Investments & Company, the main holding company of Montreal financier Charles Bronfman. The next major investor was the entertainment conglomerate MCA Incorporated of Universal City, California. MCA purchased 49.7% of Cineplex's stock (but is limited to a 33% voting stake because of Canadian foreign-ownership rules) in January 1986 for $106.7 million. This capital infusion gave Cineplex the funds to further pursue its aggressive expansion plans. As Drabinsky said at the time, "There's only so much you can do within the Canadian marketplace. It was only a question of when, not where, we were going to expand."[6] In short order the company became a major American exhibitor by acquiring six additional chains. See Exhibit 8. Some

[6]Quoted in David Aston, "A New Hollywood Legend Called—Garth Drabinsky?" *Business Week,* September 23, 1985, p. 61.

Garth H. Drabinsky

EXHIBIT 8

Cineplex Odeon Theater Acquisitions

Odeon
Plitt Theaters
RKO Century Warner Theaters
Walter Reade Organization
Circle Theatres
Septum
Essaness
Sterling Recreation Organization
Maybox Movie Centre Limited

rival and fearful exhibitors, because of Drabinsky's quest for growth via the acquisition route, have been tempted to call him Darth Grabinsky after the *Star Wars* protagonist.

Operating Strategy

Despite these rumblings, Cineplex Odeon reshaped the moviegoing experience for numerous North Americans. Many previous theater owners had either let their urban theaters fall into decay and disrepair or sliced larger theaters into unattractive and sterile multiplexes. Others had built new but spartan and utilitarian facilities in suburban malls and shopping centers. When building their own theaters from either the ground up or when refurbishing an acquired theater, Cineplex's strategy is to make the patron's visit to the theater a pleasurable one and thereby obtain a top-dollar return per admission.

The Olympia I & II Cinemas in New York City typify the scope of the renovations undertaken. Originally built in 1913, the theater seated 1,320 and was billed as having "the world's largest screen." In 1939 it was remodeled in an art deco style, and in 1980 it was renovated as a triplex, with a fourth screen added in 1981. As part of Cineplex's renovation the four smaller auditoriums were collapsed into two larger, 850-seat, state-of-the-art, wide-screened theaters featuring Dolby stereo sound systems and 70mm projection equipment. Its art deco design was augmented by post-modern features such as marble floors, pastel colors, and neon accents.

Whether through new construction or the renovation of acquired theaters, many Cineplex cinemas feature entry ways of terrazzo tile, marble, or glass. The newly built Cinema Egyptian in Montreal has three auditoriums and a

Cinema Egyptian, Montreal, Quebec, Canada

Cinema Egyptian,
(*continued*)

total seating capacity of 900. It is replete with mirrored ceilings and hand-painted murals rendered in the traditional Egyptian colors of Nile green, turquoise, gold, lapis, lazuli blue, and amber red. Historically accurate murals measuring 300 feet in length depict the daily life and typical activities of the ancient Egyptians.

Toronto's Canada Square office complex features a spacious, circular art deco lobby with a polished granite floor and recessed lighting highlighted by a thin band of neon encircling the high, domed ceiling. On the lobby's left side moviegoers can snack in a small cafe outfitted with marble tables, bright red chairs, and thick carpeting. In New York City the chain restored the splendor and elegance of Carnegie Hall's Recital Hall as it was originally conceived in 1891. The plaster ceilings and the original seats were completely rebuilt and refinished in the gold and red velvet colors of the great and historic Carnegie Hall.

Just to make the evening complete, and to capture the high profits realized from concession operations, patrons of a Cineplex theater can typically sip cappuccino or taste any of fourteen different blends of tea served in Rosenthal china. Those wanting heavier fare can nibble on croissant sandwiches, fudge brownies, or carrot cake, and freshly popped popcorn is always served with real butter. An unsuccessful innovation was the creation of in-theater boutiques which sold movie memorabilia. Although designed to obtain additional revenues from the moviegoer, operating costs were too high.

This glamor does not come cheaply, as the chain usually charges the highest prices in town. For those in a financial bind the American Express credit card is now honored at many of the chain's box offices. Cineplex broke New York City's $6 ticket barrier by raising its prices to $7, incurring the wrath of the then-Mayor Ed Koch, who marched on picket lines with other angry New Yorkers. Cineplex's action also caused some to suggest that the New York State Legislature pass a measure requiring all exhibitors to print admission prices in their newspaper advertisements. When justifying the increased ticket price Drabinsky said the alternative was "to continue to expose New Yorkers to filthy, rat-infested environments. We don't intend to do that."[7] Approximately $30 million was spent refurbishing Cineplex Odeon's 30 Manhattan theaters.

Another unpopular and somewhat incongruous action, given the upscale image engendered by each theater's trappings, is the running of advertisements for Club Med and the California raisins before feature films. Regardless of the anger and unpopularity created among potential patrons, Cineplex is not interested in catering to the "average" theater patron. Rather than trying to attract the mass market, the theater chain aims its massive and luxurious theaters at the aging baby-boomers, who are becoming a greater portion of America's population.

The Man Behind the Screen: Garth Drabinsky

Over the years Cineplex Odeon and Garth Drabinsky have received high marks for their creative, show business flair. As theater industry analyst Paul Kagan observed, "Garth Drabinsky is both a showman and a visionary. There were theater magnates before him, but none who radiated his charisma or generated such controversy."[8] These sentiments are reiterated by Roy L. Furman, president of Furman Selz Mager Dietz & Birney Inc., one of Drabin-

---

[7]Quoted in Richard Corliss, "Master of the Movies' Taj Mahals," *Time*, January 25, 1988, pp. 60–61.
[8]Ibid., p. 60.

sky's intermediaries in the Plitt acquisition: "Too many people see the [theater] business as just bricks and mortar. Garth has a real love for the business, a knowledge of what will work and what won't."[9] When a new Cineplex Odeon theater opens it begins with a splashy by-invitation-only party, usually with a few movie stars on hand. Besides his ability to attract smart investors, Drabinsky believes moviegoers want to be entertained by the theater's ambience as well as by the movies it shows. Accordingly about $2.8 million ($450,000 per screen) is spent when building one of the chain's larger theaters, in contrast with the usual $1.8 million for a simple, no-frills sixplex. "People don't just like coming to our theaters," says Drabinsky. "They linger afterward. They have another cup of cappuccino in the cafe or sit and read the paper. We've created a more complete experience, and it makes them return to that location."[10] This company has attempted to change the basic thinking. "We've introduced the majesty back to picture going."[11]

Drabinsky dates his fascination with the silver screen to his childhood bout with polio, which left him bedridden much of the time from the ages of 3 to 12. His illness also imbued him with a strong sense of determination; this resolution has helped to drive Cineplex Odeon forward. No one speaks for the company except Drabinsky, and he logs half a million miles a year visiting his theaters and otherwise encouraging his employees. The energetic CEO likes to drop by his theaters unannounced to talk with ushers and cashiers, and he telephones or sees 20 to 25 theater managers a week. His standards are meticulously enforced, often in a very personal and confrontational manner. He has been known to exemplify his penchant for detail by stooping in front of one of his ushers to pick up a single piece of spilled popcorn.

The combative nature that helped Drabinsky break the Famous Players and Odeon cartel in the early 1980s still resides in him. When Columbia pictures temporarily pulled its production of *The Last Emperor* out of distribution, he retaliated by canceling 140 play dates of the studio's monumental bomb, *Leonard Part 6* starring Bill Cosby. "Some people are burned by his brashness," says Al Waxman, formerly of the television series *Cagney & Lacey*. "There's no self-denial. He stands up and says, 'Here's what I'm doing.' Then he does it."[12] His longtime mentor Nat Taylor observed, "He's very forceful, and sometimes he's abrasive. I think he's so far ahead of the others that he loses patience if they can't keep up with him."[13] This nature may have long-term negative consequences for Cineplex, however, as Drabinsky recently had heated arguments with Sidney Jay Sheinberg, president of MCA Incorporated, the head of the circuit's largest shareholder group.

Other Product and Market Ventures

In addition to its motion picture theater operations, Cineplex Odeon engaged in other entertainment-related ventures such as television and film production, film distribution, and live theater. In the latter area the company

[9]Aston, op. cit., p. 62.
[10]Quoted in Alex Ben Block, "Garth Drabinsky's Pleasure Domes," *Forbes,* June 2, 1986, p. 93.
[11]Mary A. Fischer, "They're Putting Glitz Back into Movie Houses," *U.S. News & World Report,* January 25, 1988, p. 58.
[12]Block, op. cit., p. 92.
[13]Aston, op. cit., p. 63.

restored the Pantages Theatre in downtown Toronto into a legitimate theater for the housing of its $5.5 million production of Andrew Lloyd Webber's *The Phantom of the Opera.*

Cineplex also began a 414-acre motion picture entertainment and studio complex in Orlando, Florida, as a joint venture with MCA Incorporated but sold its stake to an American unit of the Rank Organization PLC for about $150 million in April 1989, after having invested some $92 million in the project. Various industry observers felt Cineplex withdrew from the potentially profitable venture to help reduce its bank debt, which had grown to $640 million.

In August 1988, the firm also created New Visions Pictures as a joint venture with a unit of Lieberman Enterprises Inc. to produce 10 films over a two-year period. Cineplex Odeon also owns Toronto International Studios, Canada's largest film center. This operation licenses its facilities to moviemakers and others for film and television production. In a related motion picture production move, Cineplex acquired The Film House Group Inc. in 1986 to process 16mm and 35mm release prints for Cineplex Odeon Films, another one of the company's divisions, and other distributors. After doubling and upgrading its capacity in 1987 it sold 49% of its interest to the Rank Organization in December 1988 for $73.5 million. Rank has a one-year option to buy the remaining portion of The Film House Group by December 1989.

The company also engaged in various motion picture distribution deals and television productions, none of which have been commercially successful. Cineplex distributed such films as Prince's *Sign o' the Times,* Paul Newman's *The Glass Menagerie, The Changeling* with George C. Scott, and *Madame Sousatzka* starring Shirley MacLaine. Its television unit contracted 41 new episodes of the revived *Alfred Hitchcock Presents* series for the 1988–89 television season. The series, however, was canceled. For future release Cineplex is financing five low-budget ($4 to $5 million each) films joint-ventured with Robert Redford's Wildwood Enterprises through Northfork Productions Inc. The five movies will be distributed through Cineplex Odeon Films.

Finances and Accounting Practices

Garth Drabinsky's financial dealings and his ability to attract capital to his firm have always been very important to its success. Serious questions have been raised, however, into the propriety of some of Cineplex's financial reporting methods. Charles Paul, a vice president of MCA Incorporated and Cineplex board member, noted that various board members are very concerned about the company's financial reporting practices and procedures. In a highly critical report distributed by Kellogg Associates, a Los Angeles accounting and consulting firm, a number of questionable practices were noted. Most frequently cited was Cineplex's treatment of the gains and losses associated with asset sales, with the overall effect creating an overstatement of operating revenues. As an example, Cineplex treated its gain of $40.4 million from the sale of The Film House Group as revenue rather than as extraordinary income. The report also criticized (1) Cineplex's $18.7 million write-off on the value of its film library, which "postponed" losses on the sale of American theaters; and (2) its inclusion of the proceeds from the sale of theaters as nonoperating income in its cash flow statement but calling it operating revenue in its profit and loss statement. In 1988 alone Cineplex reported a profit of $49.3 million from the sale of certain theater properties.

EXHIBIT 9

Cineplex Odeon's Revenue Sources 1985–1988

Revenue Source	1988	1987	1986	1985
Admissions	51.1%	62.5%	64.5%	68.0%
Concessions	16.5	18.2	20.0	20.0
Distribution and other	22.5	11.1	8.6	7.0
Property sales	9.9	8.0	6.8	5.0

SOURCE: Various 10-Ks and 1988 Annual Report.

Also of concern is the role asset sales play in the company's revenue and cash flow picture. Jeffrey Logsdon, a Crowell Weedon analyst, believes Cineplex has been selling its assets just to keep operating, citing as evidence the sale of both The Film House Group and its 50% stake in MCA's Universal Studios tour project to the Rank Organization. Exhibit 9 demonstrates how Cineplex's revenue sources have changed since 1985, with box office receipts constantly falling and property sales constantly rising. Over the period shown the sale of theater assets has increased 98% as a source of corporate revenues. Additionally, the return on those sales, based on selling price over acquisition costs, has fallen every year from a high of 139.1% in 1985 to a low of 13.3% in 1988.

There is also a question as to whether Cineplex can continue its current growth rate via acquisitions and debt financing. The cost of acquisitive growth may become more expensive, as many of the bargains have already been obtained by Cineplex or other chains. The early purchase of the Plitt Theater chain (in November 1985) cost about $125,000 per screen, although the bargain price for Plitt may have been a one-time opportunity, as it had just lost $5 million on revenues of $111 million during the nine months ending June 30, 1985. To get into the New York City RKO Century Warner Theaters chain in 1986, Cineplex had to pay $1.9 million per screen, while it paid almost $3 million a screen in 1987 for the New York City–based Walter Reade Organization. Overall, Cineplex Odeon paid about $276,000 each for the screens it acquired in 1986.

Some analysts are questioning the prices being paid for old screens as well as the wisdom of expanding operations in what many see as a declining and saturated industry. A past rule-of-thumb has been that a screen should cost 11 times its cash flow, but some experts feel a more reasonable rule should be 6 to 7 times its cash flow, given the glut of screens on the market. The changing effects of Cineplex's acquisition and debt structure since 1984 have been summarized in Exhibit 10.

Given the maturity of the North American market and Cineplex Odeon's penchant for growth, the company is currently implementing a planned expansion into Europe. Cineplex is scheduled to build 100 screens in 20 movie houses throughout the United Kingdom by 1990, with additional expansion plans in Europe and Israel for the early 1990s. Exhibit 11 lists the comparative per capita motion picture attendance rates found in various European countries. Other exhibitors are also interested in bringing multiscreen theaters to Europe. In addition to Cineplex, Warner Brothers, American Multi-Cinema, Odeon, and National Amusements have announced their intentions of opening a total of more than 450 screens in the United Kingdom.

EXHIBIT 10

Selected Summary Financial Data (in millions except when presented as percents)

	1989[1]	1988	1987	1986	1985	1984
Revenue	$710.0	$695.8	$520.2	$357.0	$124.3	$67.1
Net profit	43.0	40.4	34.6	22.5	9.1	3.5
Net profit %	6.1%	5.8%	6.6%	6.3%	7.3%	5.3%
Long-term debt	$720.0	$600.0	$464.3	$333.5	$40.7	$36.1
Interest	52.6[2]	40.2[2]	33.8	16.4	3.9	2.1
ROE %	10.2%	10.3%	11.0%	18.1%	40.7%	30.5%

[1] Estimated by Value Line.
[2] Estimated by the casewriter.
SOURCE: Value Line Report 1756 prepared December 9, 1988, and *Standard NYSE Stock Reports,* Vol. 55, No. 176, Sec. 6, September 12, 1988, p. 536F.

EXHIBIT 11

1988 Per Capita Attendance Rates

United States	4.4
Great Britain	1.4
Canada	2.8
France	1.9
West Germany	1.9
Italy	1.6

SOURCE: "Movies 'Held Firm' Last Year," *Tulsa Tribune,* February 16, 1989, p. 9C.

While few deny the attractiveness of the theaters owned and operated by Cineplex, the firm may have overextended itself both financially and operationally. Is Cineplex Odeon on the crest of a new wave of creative growth in North America and Europe, or does it stand at the edge of an abyss? Is consolidation or a thorough review of past actions in order? What moves should Garth Drabinsky and Cineplex make to continue their firm's phenomenal success story?

EXHIBIT 12

Cineplex Odeon Corporation Unaudited First Quarter Consolidated
Statement of Income (in thousands of U.S. dollars)

	1989	1988
Revenue:		
Admissions	$ 85,819	$ 80,389
Concessions	26,657	24,082
Distribution, post production and other	70,033	28,782
Sale of theatre properties	5,731	1,600
	188,240	134,853
Expenses:		
Theatre operations and other expenses	133,158	97,733
Cost of concessions	5,085	4,466
Cost of theatre properties sold	5,837	550
General and admin. expenses	8,035	6,310
Depreciation and amortization	11,207	7,923
	163,322	116,982
Income before the undernoted	24,918	17,871
Interest on long-term debt and bank indebtedness	12,257	9,138
Income before taxes	12,661	8,733
Minority interest	978	—
Income taxes	968	727
Net income	$ 10,715	$ 8,006

SOURCE: *First Quarter Report 1989*, pp. 12–13.

EXHIBIT 13

Cineplex Odeon Corporation Consolidated Statement of Income (in thousands of U.S. dollars)

	1988	1987	1986	1985
Revenue:				
Admissions	$355,645	$322,385	$230,300	$ 84,977
Concessions	114,601	101,568	71,443	24,949
Distribution, post production and other	156,372	61,216	30,846	7,825
Sale of theatre properties	69,197	34,984	24,400	6,549
	695,815	520,153	356,989	124,300
Expenses:				
Theatre operations and other expenses	464,324	371,909	258,313	89,467
Cost of concessions	21,537	18,799	13,742	5,980
Cost of theatre properties sold	61,793	21,618	11,690	2,736
General and admin. expenses	26,617	17,965	15,335	5,701
Depreciation and amortization	38,087	23,998	14,266	3,678
	612,358	454,289	313,346	107,562
Income before the undernoted	85,457	65,864	43,643	16,738
Other income	3,599	—	—	(330)
Interest on long-term debt and bank indebtedness	42,932	27,026	16,195	3,961
Income before taxes, equity earnings, pre-acquisition losses and extraordinary item	44,124	38,838	27,448	13,107
Income taxes	3,728	4,280	6,310	5,032
Income before equity earnings, pre-acquisition losses and extraordinary item	40,396	34,558	21,138	8,075
Add back: Pre-acquisition losses attributable to 50% interest Plitt not owned by the corporation	—	—	1,381	—
Equity in earnings of 50% owned companies	—	—	—	1,021
Income before extraordinary item	40,396	34,558	22,519	10,374
Extraordinary item	—	—	—	9,096
Net income	$ 40,396	$ 34,558	$ 22,519	$ 10,374

SOURCE: Company annual reports for 1987 and 1988.

EXHIBIT 14

Cineplex Odeon Corporation Unaudited First Quarter Consolidated Balance Sheet
(in thousands of U.S. dollars)

	1989	1988
ASSETS		
Current Assets:		
Accounts receivable	$ 229,961	$ 151,510
Advances to distributors and producers	18,334	26,224
Distribution costs	9,695	10,720
Inventories	7,781	7,450
Prepaid expenses and deposits	6,756	5,505
Properties held for disposition	23,833	25,557
	296,360	226,966
Property, Equipment and Leaseholds	844,107	824,836
Other Assets:		
Long-term investments and receivables	35,169	130,303
Goodwill (less amortization of $3,545; 1988—$2,758)	53,589	53,966
Deferred charges (less amortization of $8,456; 1988—$7,724)	30,222	27,100
	118,980	211,369
Total Assets	$1,259,447	$1,263,171
LIABILITIES AND SHAREHOLDERS' EQUITY		
Current Liabilities:		
Bank indebtedness	$ 37,185	$ 21,715
Accounts payable and accruals	98,876	107,532
Deferred income	38,167	21,967
Income taxes payable	3,726	5,651
Current portion of long-term debt and other obligations	12,174	10,764
	190,128	167,629
Long-Term Debt	625,640	663,844
Capitalization Lease Obligations	14,213	14,849
Deferred Income Taxes	10,920	10,436
Pension Obligations	6,847	6,326
Stockholders' Equity		
Capital stock	284,533	283,739
Translation adjustment	12,473	13,348
Retained earnings	88,571	77,856
	385,577	374,943
Total Liabilities and Shareholders' Equity	$1,259,447	$1,263,171

SOURCE: *First Quarter Report 1989,* pp. 14–15.

EXHIBIT 15

Cineplex Odeon Corporation Consolidated Balance Sheet (in thousands of U.S. dollars)

	1988	1987	1986
ASSETS			
Current Assets:			
Accounts receivable	$151,510	$42,342	$20,130
Advances to distributors and producers	26,224	10,704	4,671
Distribution costs	10,720	10,593	4,318
Inventories	7,450	8,562	6,978
Prepaid expenses and deposits	5,505	4,683	4,027
Properties held for disposition	25,557	22,704	16,620
	226,966	99,588	56,744
Property, Equipment and Leaseholds	824,836	711,523	513,411
Other Assets:			
Long-term investments and receivables	130,303	49,954	14,292
Goodwill (less amortization of $2,758; 1987—$1,878)	53,966	52,596	40,838
Deferred charges (less amortization of $7,724; 1987—$1,771)	27,100	12,015	6,591
	211,369	114,565	61,721
Total Assets	$1,263,171	$925,676	$631,876
LIABILITIES AND SHAREHOLDERS' EQUITY			
Current Liabilities:			
Bank indebtedness	$21,715	$20,672	$30
Accounts payable and accruals	107,532	74,929	$47,752
Deferred income	21,967	755	—
Income taxes payable	5,651	4,607	1,926
Current portion of long-term debt and other obligations	10,764	5,965	6,337
	167,629	106,173	55,945
Long-Term Debt	663,844	449,707	317,550
Capitalized Lease Obligations	14,849	14,565	15,928
Deferred Income Taxes	10,436	13,318	11,142
Pension Obligations	6,326	4,026	3,668
Minority Interest	25,144	—	—
Stockholders' Equity			
Capital stock	283,739	289,181	212,121
Translation adjustment	13,348	1,915	(3,591)
Retained earnings	77,856	46,791	19,113
	374,943	337,887	227,643
Total Liabilities and Shareholders' Equity	$1,263,171	$925,676	$631,876

SOURCE: Company annual reports for 1987 and 1988.

Additional References

Finler, Joel W., *The Hollywood Story*. NY: Crown Publishers, 1988.

Gertner, Richard (ed.), *1988 International Motion Picture Almanac*. NY: Quigley Publishing Co., 1988.

Green, Wayne R. (ed.), *Encyclopedia of Exhibition*. NY: National Association of Theatre Owners, 1988.

Hall, Ben M., *The Best Remaining Seats: The Story of the Golden Age of the Movie Palace*. NY: Bramhall House, 1961.

Harrigan, Kathryn Rudie, *Managing Mature Businesses*. Lexington, MA: Lexington, 1988.

Harrigan, Kathryn Rudie, "Strategies for Declining Industries," *The Journal of Business Strategy,* Vol. 1, No. 2 (Fall 1980), pp. 20–34.

Musun, Chris, *The Marketing of Motion Pictures*. Los Angeles: Chris Musun Company, 1969.

1988 International Motion Picture Almanac. NY: Quigley Publishing Co., 1988.

1989 U.S. Industrial Outlook. Washington, DC: U.S. Department of Commerce/International Trade Administration, 1989.

Tromberg, Sheldon, *Making Money, Making Movies*. NY: New Viewpoints/Vision Books, 1980.

Troy, L., *Almanac of Business and Industrial Financial Ratios*. Englewood Cliffs, NJ: Prentice-Hall, 1988.

U.S. Bureau of the Census, *Statistical Abstract of the United States: 1989* (109th ed.). Washington, DC: U.S. Government Printing Office, 1988.

U.S. Department of Commerce, Bureau of the Census, *Statistical Abstract of the United States, 1985*. Washington, DC: Government Printing Office, 1985.

Waldman, Peter, "Silver Screens Lose Some of Their Luster," *The Wall Street Journal,* February 9, 1989, p. B1.

CASE PART II

Environmental Analysis

CASE

1

Blockbuster Entertainment Corporation

JAMES A. KIDNEY, *Southern Connecticut State University*

INTRODUCTION

Seated at his desk in a rented two-story stucco executive office building in downtown Fort Lauderdale, Florida, H. Wayne Huizenga prepared to announce record revenues and net income for his chain of Blockbuster Video stores. His mid-April 1992 announcement would attribute those results to "increasing market penetration, gains in same-store revenue, and continued emphasis on cost control and increased productivity."[1] As Blockbuster Entertainment Corporation's Chairman of the Board and Chief Executive Officer, he also prepared to announce that it was now possible to pay a cash dividend to the company's 8,000 stockholders—something that had not been done before.

At the end of 1991, having achieved a 13 percent share of market, the company announced that its goal was to reach a 20 percent share of the U.S. home video market and have 3,000 Blockbuster Video stores operating in North America by 1995.[2] In some of its most mature markets, such as Atlanta, Chicago, Dallas, Detroit, and South Florida, that would mean market shares well in excess of 30 percent. Such a high share of market has been rare in specialty retailing. However, Blockbuster was the only U.S. video rental chain operating on a nationwide basis. Its next largest competitor was a regional chain, less than one tenth its size.

EXTERNAL CHALLENGES AND OPPORTUNITIES

As Huizenga optimistically pondered the company's strategic situation over the next 5 to 7 years, there were several interesting external challenges and opportunities lurking on the horizon:

- With a higher market share than all of its 300 closest competitors combined, how much further could the company's market penetration grow?

This case was prepared by Dr. James A. Kidney, Management Department, School of Business, Southern Connecticut State University, New Haven, CT 06515.

[1] Corporate news release dated April 21, 1992.

[2] The total population of video rental stores operating throughout the U.S. ranged between 25,000 and 29,000, and turnover of individual store locations was quite high during the late 1980s and early 1990s.

- Could any significant technological changes in home entertainment alter the video rental industry's attractiveness?
- What were the future implications of Philips Electronics N.V.'s recent investment in Blockbuster stock?

COMPANY HISTORY

David P. Cook, a 31 year-old Texas entrepreneur, founded the company in December 1982 as Cook Data Services, Inc., a provider of software and computer services to the oil and gas industries. Facing a sagging market for such services, Cook decided to switch over to a new, rapidly growing niche in specialty retailing—video rental stores. Cook's first store was opened during 1985, and the present corporate name was adopted one year later. From the outset, Cook recognized that an innovative superstore concept would draw many customers away from typical mom-and-pop rental stores and that well-designed computerized information systems would be advantageous for inventory planning and control as well as for customer information.

The typical mom-and-pop store had a spartan, nondescript atmosphere; short hours; a selection of fewer than 3,000 titles stressing recent hits; and empty boxes to be brought to a clerk who would have to find appropriate tapes—provided they were then in stock. Many mom-and-pops obtained significant rental revenues from X-rated videos, and that occasionally created an unwholesome image.

In comparison, Cook's idea was to have a family-oriented atmosphere with an extensive selection of children's videos, longer, more convenient hours, improved layout, quality service, faster check-in/check-out, state-of-the-art real time computer information systems, and a thoroughly trained professional staff.

ATTRACTING HUIZENGA'S ATTENTION

After only two years of operation, Blockbuster's latent potential attracted the attention of Huizenga. By that time, Cook owned 8 stores and franchised 11 more in the Dallas area. Huizenga, then 48 years old, was restless, looking for a way to come back from early retirement, after having successfully made a small fortune from several companies.

Huizenga's previous experience had been in building up businesses in a variety of dissimilar industries, such as trash bin rentals and garbage hauling, dry cleaning, lawn care, portable toilet rentals, water cooler rentals and sale of bottled water. His most notable success was Waste Management, Inc., which he had honed into the world's largest waste collection and disposal company.

There was a common denominator running throughout his past entrepreneurial ventures. Each had rendered relatively basic services, had repeat customers, required little employee training, earned a steady cash flow, and was able to expand within an industry filled with small, undercapitalized competitors. Usually, the fragmented industries he entered were ripe for consolidation, because greater firm size led to economies of scale in marketing, distribution, computerized information systems, and/or potential clout in purchasing products and services.

EXPANSION AND ACQUISITION OF STORE LOCATIONS

During 1987 Huizenga and a couple of close business associates bought out Blockbuster's founders and franchise holders for $18 million, and soon thereafter began acquiring small regional chains, such as Southern Video Partnership and Movies to Go. To help him run the new business, Huizenga hired several former upper level managers from McDonald's Corporation. His upper management group adopted the view that Blockbuster's target audience should be very similar to McDonald's broad-based restaurant clientele. Thus, Blockbuster's national expansion of its retail business was based upon McDonald's well-established growth philosophy, namely: blitz major markets, add stores quickly, use franchising to speed the process of obtaining managerial talent and operating capital, and never admit that the market is saturated.

Facing a rapid rise in VCR ownership, management tried to combine careful planning with opportunistic risk taking. An aggressive acquisition program was financed by new equity capital, in order to avoid burdensome long-term debt. Over the following four years, additional regional chains, such as Video Library Inc., Major Video Corp., Oklahoma Entertainment Inc., Vector Video Inc., Video Superstores Venture L.P., and Erol's Inc. were eagerly gobbled up.

A major international thrust was launched in early 1992, with the acquisition of Cityvision plc, the largest home video retailer in the U.K. Operating under the "Ritz" name and enjoying a 20 percent share of market, this firm had roughly 800 small stores and was considered to be an underperformer.

Around the same time, several Blockbuster Video stores were opened in Japan in a joint-venture with Fujita & Co., a retailer running over 800 McDonald's restaurants and holding a stake in Toys-'Я'-Us Japan, Ltd. Jointly they hoped to open 1,000 stores over the next ten years.

Describing the hectic, and occasionally disorganized, rush to add store locations Huizenga explained, "We felt we had to go fast because we had nothing proprietary. We had to get the locations in each area before somebody else moved in. It was a mistake, but it turned out okay. We have the locations, the people are trained, and the customers are ours. Now if somebody else comes in, they have to take it away from us."[3]

BLOCKBUSTER VIDEO'S PROFILE AS OF 1992

Blockbuster Video was a membership only club, serving more than 29 million members worldwide, who rented more than 1 million of the company's videocassettes daily. Without incurring any membership fees, patrons were provided with bar-coded membership cards which allowed for speedy computerized check-out from the issuing store. Cards were sometimes honored at other locations in the chain as well. By requiring personal photo identification and an application for membership, rather than dealing with anonymous walk-ins, the rental store was able to secure an extra measure of control over tapes which left the premises. A major credit card also had to be presented, so that the store could charge members for lost or damaged inventory.

The typical Blockbuster Video store was located in a free-standing building of approximately 6,000 square feet (560 square meters) and was open from 10:00 A.M. to midnight, seven days per week, 365 days per year. The atmosphere was bright and wholesome. Aisles were clearly marked and divided into more than 30 categories to distribute customer traffic and encourage browsing. Video boxes with tapes inside were openly displayed within easy reach. Similar categories were placed adjacent to one another, thereby increasing

[3] *The New York Times Business World Magazine,* June 9, 1991.

EXHIBIT 1

Blockbuster Entertainment Corporation Number of Blockbuster
video stores, by ownership type:

Date	Company	Franchised	Total
December 31, 1985	1	0	1
December 31, 1986	19	0	19
December 31, 1987	112	126	238
December 31, 1988	341	248	589
December 31, 1989	561	518	1,079
December 31, 1990	787	795	1,582
December 31, 1991	1,025	1,003	2,028
March 31, 1992	1,805	1,024	2,829

NOTE: The surge in company stores during the first quarter of 1992 is attributable to the Cityvision plc acquisition.
SOURCE: Blockbuster's 1991 Annual Report and 1992 press releases.

---

the potential for increase rentals. Blockbuster's superstores typically carried a
comprehensive selection of 10,000 prerecorded videocassettes, consisting of
more than 8,000 titles. The strongest months for video store rentals tended to
be December through March and June through August, with Hollywood's release schedule being a crucial variable.

Blockbuster Video stores proudly claimed to offer "More Movies Than Anyone In The World". Additionally, their relatively weak, fragmented rivals were
seldom able to match Blockbuster's advertising clout and wide array of attractions, such as: computer-driven movie selection aids; a three-evening rental policy; an attractive overnight pricing policy for new hit releases which improved
turnover and in-stock positions; a state-of-the-art management information system which tracked rentals and market trends; Microwave Popcorn and other
snack foods; promotional tie-ins with Domino's Pizza, Pepsi-Cola, Pizza Hut,
Subway, U.S. Air, and Universal Studios; drop-off boxes for fast returns; and
publicity from an annual Blockbuster Bowl football game. Nevertheless, some
competitors clearly differentiated themselves from Blockbuster by offering
lower prices, reservations, home delivery, or hard core "adult" videos.

As of March 31, 1992, there were 2,829 Blockbuster Video stores, worldwide, up from 19 just five years earlier (Exhibit 1).

LOCATIONS AND OPERATIONS

By the first quarter of 1992, 68 percent of Blockbuster's stores were located in
46 of America's 50 states, with the remaining 32 percent located in Austria,
Australia, Canada, Chile, Guam, Japan, Mexico, Puerto Rico, Spain, the United
Kingdom, and Venezuela. Nearly all of the company's retail, distribution, and
administrative facilities were rented under non-cancellable operating leases,
which in most cases contained renewal options. Blockbuster employed approximately 12,500 individuals.

There had historically tended to be a 50-50 balance between company-
owned and franchised locations. Although franchising remained beneficial
in foreign countries, where local partners made it easier to conduct business,
franchising within the U.S. became less essential once the company had an

ample cash flow and employed many competent people who could help manage ongoing growth.

The usual initial investment (i.e. franchise fee, inventory, equipment, and start-up capital) for a franchised location ranged from $700,000 to $1,000,000. Annual operating costs per location fell in the $400,000 to $500,000 range. Franchisees were provided extensive guidelines for site selection, store design and product selection, as well as customer service, and management training programs. In addition, the company furnished national and local advertising and promotional programs for the entire system. Franchisees paid royalties and other fees for those services and also routinely paid Blockbuster Entertainment for videocassette inventories, computer hardware and software.

For a typical Blockbuster Video store, cash flow payback on initial store investment occurred rapidly—generally in under three years. The average new store attained monthly revenues of $70,000 within twelve months of opening date.

Systemwide revenues, for company-owned and franchise-owned operations combined, as well as other selected financial data are shown in Exhibit 2.

EXHIBIT 2

Blockbuster Entertainment Corporation Selected annual financial data

	1991	1990	1989	1988	1987
INCOME DATA (MILLION $)					
Systemwide Revenue	1,520	1,133	663	284	98
Company Revenue	868	633	402	136	43
Operating Costs & Expenses	714	514	326	110	37
Operating Income	154	119	76	26	6
Net Income	94	69	44	17	3
Depreciation & Amortization	189	124	76	22	5
Cash Flow	283	193	120	39	8
BALANCE SHEET DATA (MILLION $)					
Total Assets	804	608	417	235	105
Cash & Cash Equivalents	48	49	40	9	7
Current Assets	163	116	93	39	27
Current Liabilities	164	110	83	49	17
Long-term Debt	134	169	118	39	22
Shareholders' Equity	483	315	208	124	59
PER SHARE DATA ($)					
Earnings Per Share	.56	.42	.28	.12	.04
Tangible Book Value	2.35	1.65	1.18	.75	.41
Stock Price—High	15.12	13.37	10.81	6.25	2.63
Stock Price—Low	7.75	6.75	4.87	1.06	.75
COMMON STOCK AND EQUIVALENTS (MILLIONS)					
Average Shares Outstanding	168	162	155	142	75

NOTES: Systemwide revenues include franchise store revenues, while company revenues do not. Operating costs and expenses include depreciation and amortization. Cash flow is net income plus depreciation and amortization. Tangible book value excludes cost of purchased businesses in excess of market value of tangible assets acquired (unamortized goodwill).

SOURCES: Blockbuster's 1991 Annual Report and Standard & Poor's Stock Report.

SOURCES OF REVENUES

During 1991, 5 percent of company revenues were derived from franchise royalties and fees, 20 percent from product sales mainly to franchisees, and 75 percent from rentals. Other than low-priced used products, outright sales of home videos were never emphasized prior to late 1991, because the largest sellers were highly competitive national discount chains like Wal-Mart and K-Mart. As a growing portion of consumer spending went towards videocassette and laser disc purchases, it became logical for video rental stores to begin taking the sell-through market more seriously.

Mr. Joseph Baczko, who headed the highly successful International Division of Toys-'Я'-Us, Inc. for eight years, was hired in 1991 as Blockbuster's new President and Chief Operating Officer. To carry out a process of "retailizing" as well as internationalizing the company, he brought several executives with significant retailing experience into the firm. Promotional and display efforts to stimulate sell-through transactions were given added emphasis under Baczko's direction. Given his background in toys, he was interested in treating child oriented movies, such as *Batman, Bambi, The Little Mermaid,* and *101 Dalmatians,* mainly as sell-through rather than rental products. Blockbuster's stores also began renting Nintendo and Sega Genesis video game products.

INDUSTRY ENVIRONMENT

Rentals and sales of home videos in the U.S. amounted to a mere $700 million in 1982. By 1991, domestic revenue for the video rental industry reached $11 billion, and Americans were spending more than twice as much to watch movies at home as they did to watch them in movie theaters. Within the marketplace for prerecorded videocassettes, movies accounted for more than 80 percent of rental revenues and at least 50 percent of dollars spent on purchases. Blockbuster Entertainment estimated that the U.S. video rental market for movies would reach $19.3 billion by the turn of the century (Exhibit 3).

In 1980, the percentage of U.S. households owning at least one television set reached 98 percent and remained at that level thereafter. By 1995, there were expected to be almost 100 million households in the U.S., and 98 percent of them were likely to own at least one color TV set. Blockbuster Entertainment expected 91 percent of those TV owning households also to own VCRs

---

EXHIBIT 3

Estimated and projected annual U.S. movie revenues, by viewing method ($ billions):

Viewing Method	1990	1995	2000
Video	10.3	15.2	19.3
Movie Theater	5.1	6.9	7.4
Pay Cable (premium channels)	5.1	6.2	7.6
Pay-per-view	.01	0.5	2.0
Total	20.6	28.8	36.3

SOURCE: Blockbuster's 1991 Annual Report.

EXHIBIT 4

Estimated and projected VCR and cable TV penetration among U.S. TV owning households (millions of TV owning households, percent with VCRs, percent with cable TV, and percent with additional pay-per-view or pay cable services, by year):

Year	No. of TV Owning Households	Percent with		
		VCR	Cable	Pay Cable
1980	76	1	20	7
1981	78	3	22	10
1982	82	6	30	16
1983	83	10	34	19
1984	84	17	39	24
1985	85	30	43	26
1986	86	42	46	27
1987	87	53	48	26
1988	89	62	49	27
1989	90	68	53	29
1990	92	72	56	29
1991	92	77	58	30
1992	93	82	61	31
1993	95	86	64	32
1994	96	89	67	34
1995	97	91	70	36

NOTE: From 1982 through 1995, it's assumed that 98 percent of all U.S. households own televisions.

SOURCES: Blockbuster's 1991 Annual Report, the Universal Almanac, and author's estimates.

(Exhibit 4), with more than 35 percent of them owning at least two machines.

VCR ownership in Europe also was growing rapidly, with household penetration rates in individual countries lagging behind the U.S. anywhere from two to five years. Total 1991 worldwide spending for home video rental and sales was $21.2 billion (Exhibit 5). Licensing, sale, and rental practices differed from one product/market to another, and in some countries most of the television viewing population remained unaware that movie videos could be rented instead of being purchased.

MOVIE PRODUCTION AND DISTRIBUTION

Approximately 390 to 450 new feature films were released annually in the U.S. Eight of the largest distributors accounted for more than 90 percent of movie theater film rentals in the U.S. and Canada. Most of them, such as Paramount, Universal, Warner, Fox, Columbia, and Disney, had been in business for more than 50 years. Leading producers and distributors of videos were usually subsidiaries of large companies which owned other leisure-time businesses. Large distributors also had prime access to international channels for distributing American made films in foreign countries. Musical, cultural, educational, exercise programs, instructional, and documentary videos tended to be handled by smaller distributors.

EXHIBIT 5

Estimated population, home video spending, VCR penetration and basic cable penetration by country, as of 1991:

Country	Population (millions)	Video Spending ($ billions)	VCRs (% of households)	Cable (% of households)
Australia	17	0.7	70	0
Canada	27	1.2	65	69
France	56	0.7	40	10
Germany	79	0.7	46	32
Italy	58	0.6	38	1
Japan	124	2.6	70	20
United Kingdom	57	1.4	70	2
United States	250	11.0	75	57
Others	4,732	2.3	n.a.	n.a.
Worldwide Total	5,400	21.2	n.a.	n.a.

NOTE: n.a. = not available

SOURCES: Blockbuster's 1991 Annual Report, *This Business of Television*, and 1992 *World Almanac*.

The time span from the point when work began on a new movie to the point when its revenue stream was largely realized often was five years or longer. Over that period, producers and distributors attempted to play out their products in a manner which gave them an optimum revenue stream.

By 1991, home video had become a major ancillary source of revenue for movie studios. For example, *Nothing But Trouble* (directed by Dan Aykroyd, 1991) grossed $8.5 million in box office receipts. The studio's share was roughly 50 percent. When released on videocassette, the same movie earned an additional $9.6 million in revenue for the studio.[4]

The sequence of each film's release depended on the nature of individual deals made by the distributor. Domestic release usually occurred somewhat ahead of international release. A typical major studio's U.S. release tended to be rolled out in the following illustrative manner:

Theatrical showings: January through April, 1992
Home video: Mid-Summer, 1992
Airline: Mid-Summer, 1992
Pay-per-view: Late-Summer or Fall, 1992
Pay cable (premium channels): Winter, 1992–93

If attractively priced, popular movies that were developed for young children were likely to achieve a sell-through market of 1.5 million or more copies. Movies that had been adult hits at the box office within the latest year were the ones most in demand for rentals, and 100,000 to 500,000 copies of them were generally sold, mostly to video rental stores. Assuming a $3 charge per rental, it normally took anywhere from 13 to 19 rentals to recover a store's initial investment in a hit movie tape.

Distributors set high initial suggested retail prices (roughly $80 to $100 on box office hits) for videotaped films they expected consumers to rent and low prices (roughly $20 to $30) for those they expected consumers to buy. Each

[4]Source: Blockbuster Entertainment 1991 Corp. Annual Report.

videocassette cost distributors about \$2 to manufacture and \$2 to market. Wholesale prices paid by Blockbuster were generally 55 to 65 percent of suggested retail prices.

WHOLESALERS

Despite the fact that movies were the mainstay of the home video business, Blockbuster Entertainment traditionally purchased its movie rental inventory from wholesalers rather than film distributors. Having achieved nationwide scope, the company could decide to bypass regional wholesalers and purchase its movies more economically directly from motion picture distributors.

TECHNOLOGICAL THREATS

During the decade from 1982 through 1991 Americans purchased 1.2 billion prerecorded and 2.2 billion blank videocassettes. They also built up a \$32 billion investment in VCR equipment. This burgeoning consumer commitment to VCR technology seemed to assure long-range demand for videocassettes. Nevertheless, the ease of duplicating and pirating videocassettes was a matter of some concern to movie producers. As laser discs began to attract a modest following, rentals and sales of video discs were being added to many video store's product offerings.

No one knew precisely when new types of home entertainment might begin to undermine home videotape viewing. Cable television was expected to become a more and more serious threat. Even though three out of five TV owning households subscribed to cable service as of 1991, only one third of those subscribers had access to movies on pay cable (e.g. HBO, Showtime, Cinemax, The Disney Channel, The Movie Channel) or pay-per-view channels.

Employing "addressable technology," pay-per-view service allowed customers to call in and have a movie, concert, or sporting event broadcast on their TV for a fee. Being transaction based, pay-per-view depended upon impulse buying. It was sold by direct mailings, advertisements, bill stuffers, and 24 hour "barker" promotional channels.

In 1992, sporting events generated almost twice as much pay-per-view business as other alternatives. As pay-per-view's market potential continued to develop, the Summer of 1992 was regarded as an important psychological turning point. Cable operators were seeking broadcasting rights for live coverage of the Olympic Games in Atlanta, Georgia, hoping that such coverage would significantly boost the number of new subscribers for pay-per-view services.

While viewers had to watch pay-per-view at a scheduled time, this service certainly provided greater convenience than having to make two round trips to a video store. The competitive threat was moderated by the fact that most new movies were released on videocassettes before they appeared on pay-per-view services or pay cable. However, that disparity could disappear rapidly, if movie distributors were enticed by cable's potential for licensing and revenue sharing arrangements.

INTERACTIVE TELEVISION

Over the long-term, advances in satellite and cable television technology and entry of regional telephone companies into the electronic home delivery arena were other potential concerns, within the U.S. market. With new developments in fiber optics and digital signal compression, expansion to 500 channels could become feasible for video delivery systems. Thus, there was a possibility that "video-on-demand" could become a reality on cable or telephone systems by the mid 1990s.

Anticipating major advances in communications, IBM and Time Warner Corp. had begun discussing ways to combine data processing and transmitting expertise with cable TV systems, TV shows, and movies. IBM believed interactive television would eventually encroach upon a wide array of existing entertainment and information product/markets, including catalog shopping, broadcast and cable advertising, home video, information services, theater, video games, electronic messaging, videoconferencing, photography, records, tapes, and CDs. Furthermore, the Federal Communications Commission (FCC) had allocated a portion of the broadcast spectrum to interactive television and intended to award licenses to investors who could serve large markets.

NERVOUS INVESTORS

Had the video rental market remained extremely fragmented, it might not have become so large and well-established. Some industry watchers predicted that Blockbuster's success in becoming a high quality specialty retail chain might impair the development of innovative competing technologies for accessing home entertainment.

Recognizing that other forms of retailing were withstanding competition from television, Baczko made the following point, "Home shopping has not taken the store away, and pay-per-view is not going to do so to video. I don't think you can ever beat a retailing environment."[5]

Nevertheless, newspaper reports of questionable depreciation accounting practices, bankruptcy filings by sizable video retailers, and media hype of future electronic home delivery systems, from time to time, stirred predictions of impending disaster for the video rental industry. Consequently, Blockbuster's common stock attracted speculators and short sellers, and the market price per share plunged every so often as frightened investors hastily bailed out to "take profits" or "stop losses." For example, the price per share reached a high of $15.125 and a low of $7.75 on the New York Stock Exchange during the first half of 1991.

STRATEGIC ALLIANCE WITH PHILIPS ELECTRONICS

During 1992, an intriguing strategic alliance began to emerge between Blockbuster Entertainment Corp. and Philips Electronics, N.V. Headquartered in the Netherlands, Philips was the world's second largest consumer electronics company after Japan's Matsushita Electric Industrial Co. Philips' decision to purchase 13 million newly issued common shares (nearly 7.2 percent of outstanding shares) suggested that the two companies might be heading toward a close working relationship.[6]

In 1991 consumer products accounted for 47 percent of Philips' $33 billion in sales revenues. The early 1990s found the U.S., Canada, Australia, the United

---

[5] *The New York Times*, February 21, 1992.
[6] These funds have been used by Blockbuster to help pay for the Cityvision plc acquisition.

EXHIBIT 6

Philips Electronics N.V. Net Sales by Product Sector and Geographical Area (millions of Guilders)

	1991	1990
PRODUCT SECTOR		
Lighting	7,351	7,026
Consumer Products	26,861	25,856
Professional Products and Systems	12,510	12,400
Components and Semiconductors	7,844	7,953
Miscellaneous	2,420	2,529
Net Sales	56,986	55,764
GEOGRAPHICAL AREA		
Netherlands	3,206	3,604
Rest of Europe	30,433	30,366
U.S.A. and Canada	12,833	11,819
Latin America	3,142	3,361
Africa	730	772
Asia	5,565	4,770
Australia and New Zealand	1,077	1,072
Net Sales	56,986	55,764

NOTE: On December 31, 1991 and 1990, respectively, one U.S. dollar equaled 1.71 and 1.69 Dutch Guilders.

SOURCE: Philips' 1991 Annual Report.

Kingdom, and Japan all experiencing economic downturns and declining consumer confidence. Stagnant demand and bloody price wars were curbing profits throughout the consumer electronics industry. Battered by stagnant demand and stiff price competition from its Japanese competitors, Philips reported a $3 billion loss in 1990. Philips' new President, Jan D. Timmer, was struggling to slash the payroll, close inefficient plants, and divest unprofitable operations. A streamlining and restructuring process initiated by Timmer, provided a $210 million profit on sales of $33 billion in 1991. Recent sales data are shown in Exhibit 6.

Some analysts, suspecting that Huizenga might be ready to move on to another new venture, speculated that Philips might be interested in acquiring a controlling interest in Blockbuster Entertainment Corp. Others expressed doubts that outright ownership and management of a captive group of rental stores would serve Philips' best interest.

Having pioneered such consumer electronics products as the videocassette recorder, audio compact disc, digital compact cassette, and high-definition television, Philips had long been a superior technological leader. Marketing agility and competitive pricing had never been Philips' strengths. Philips conceivably might be aiming for a reliable international retail base for rapid, broad distribution of future hardware and software products.

Philips owned 51 percent of Super Club Holding & Finance S.A., a poorly performing music and video retail chain. With store locations in Europe and the U.S., Super Club might benefit from a tie-in with Blockbuster. Philips also owned 80 percent of PolyGram, one of the three largest music publishing, production, marketing, and distribution companies in the world, and a major European manufacturer of compact discs. Recognizing the increasingly complementary natures of the audio and video fields, Polygram had begun producing and distributing filmed entertainment, as part of its strategy to become a multicultural, global entertainment company.

PHILIPS' MULTIMEDIA SYSTEMS

Potentially even more relevant were Philips' plans for a new Imagination Machine. Philips had developed a new Compact Disk Interactive (CD-I) entertainment system that could turn the family TV into a terminal through which one could play regular music CDs, view photo CD disks, and interact with programs rather than just watch them. Touted as the "VCR of the 21st century," Philips' Imagination Machine was one of the products that Timmer was counting on heavily to revive depressed earnings. Blending text, full-motion video, and stereo-quality sound, it called up sports statistics during live broadcasts, displayed digital snapshots, played karaoke sing-along discs, used Nintendo's new games and played movies and music videos. While CD-I had been promoted primarily to the consumer market, it was also highly suited to the educational market.

Philips utilized a special format for its CD-ROM, which was supported by several other electronics firms as well. Commodore, Apple, Toshiba, and Tandy were offering multimedia equipment with different CD formats. Sony and Panasonic (Matsushita) had not yet revealed the type of standard they might support. Having witnessed the VHS/Beta wars of the late 1970s, Philips recognized the need to insure that its CD-I standard won out over its rivals. Ultimately, the availability of appealing multimedia software would help determine which compact disc standard would dominate.

POTENTIAL NEW UNDERTAKINGS

As Blockbuster entered numerous foreign markets, its employees started to acquire increasing familiarity with markets for movies and home entertainment within many different cultures and political jurisdictions. Blockbuster's increasing knowledge of ways to formalize and expand global rental markets could help foster widespread acceptance of the rental concept for expensive multimedia CDs, such as encyclopedias, music libraries, and games. Blockbuster could thus become a leading worldwide distributor of a new generation of home entertainment products, perhaps selling and/or renting Philips' Imagination Machines and CDs.

Reacting to investor skepticism a year earlier, Huizenga had optimistically asserted, "We have the best locations in town. We've got a plain vanilla box. We can sell shoes there if we want to. Maybe we'll build a music store that's green and white. We could call it Chartbusters." [7] Such remarks indicate that someday Blockbuster Entertainment Corporation could be attracted to retailing opportunities elsewhere within the diverse, yet more and more intertwined, marketplace for home entertainment products.

[7] *The New York Times Business World Magazine,* June 9, 1991.

Chili's Restaurant

L. MIKLICHANSKY, *North Texas State University and*
B. LOGAN, *Texas Women's University*

THE STORY

It was 5:20 P.M. Norman Brinker sat in his car and put his seat belt on. "That's right, seat belts are mandatory now," he thought. He left his office building, 6820 LBJ Freeway, Dallas, still worrying about the earlier meeting.

Although Chili's had maintained its average store volumes at 1985 levels during 1986, market conditions were rather bad. With 66% of the restaurants located in the economically impacted energy-belt states, Chili's would have to concentrate its efforts on the future expansion of the company.

Traffic was heavy on LBJ Freeway. Norman turned on the radio to relax and keep his mind away from the difficult two and a half hours he had just spent with his colleagues. Bruce Springsteen was singing again, the same song, over and over. "That's enough for the day," Norman thought. "I have already heard this song three times today." He turned the radio off and decided to take advantage of the traffic jam to direct his thoughts to his business. He tried to recall the conversation he had had with his partners during the meeting.

THE COMPANY

In 1975 Larry and Jack Lavine, two brothers, opened the first Chili's restaurant on Greenville Avenue in Dallas, Texas. The Lavines were banking on a new niche in the restaurant industry between fast food and midscale restaurants. They were bent on a commitment to the quality burger. Their first restaurant offered the customer two new appealing qualities for this time period: fast, full service specializing in quality hamburgers.

Through 1982 the Lavines opened up 17 more Chili's restaurants, primarily in the Southwest. Over this period of 1975 to 1982 investors and restaurant analysts started following the growth of Chili's with interest. As of June 30, 1986, Chili's had expanded to 80 units in 12 states. (See Exhibit 1.) Chili's initial expansion strategies were that of establishing themselves in Sunbelt cities

---

This case was prepared by L. Miklichansky and B. Logan under the supervision of Professor Sexton Adams, North Texas State University, and Professor Adelaide Griffin, Texas Women's University.

EXHIBIT 1
Chili's Restaurant Units
Open as of June 30,
1986

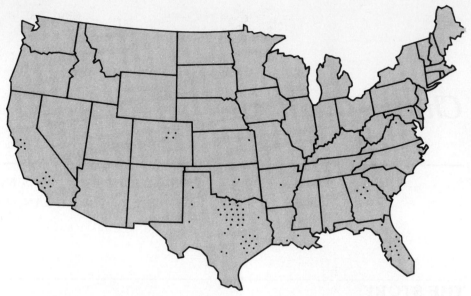

SOURCE: Chili's 1986 Annual Report.

with somewhat of a "youthful" atmosphere, for example, Dallas, Houston, Atlanta, Tampa, Orlando, Los Angeles, and San Francisco.

In 1983 Norman Brinker, a well-respected restaurant industry pioneer, paid $12 million for 35% of Chili's stock. The company up to this time was privately held by the Lavine brothers. In January 1984 Chili's had its first public stock offering on the over-the-counter exchange.

Since the initial public stock offering, the company opened more than 50 restaurants. In 1986 Chili's had 65 company-owned units, 14 joint-venture-owned units, and one franchised unit.[1] Chili's had signed two primary joint-venture agreements, one with Sunstate Restaurant Corporation in the Southeast and one with Dunkin' Ventures Corporation in the Northeast. The Sunstate agreement allowed Chili's to penetrate the Florida market. The agreement with Dunkin' was signed in October 1985. The venture would give Chili's 50% ownership in more than 50 restaurants expected to be developed in New England, eastern Canada, and upstate New York.[2,3]

In 1986 Chili's was a restaurant concept that appealed to winners. Fiscal year 1985 had been a landmark year for Chili's in terms of operating and financial results. (See Exhibit 2.) Management felt that it had been able to leverage its talents towards the expansion processes it was undergoing. Nineteen eighty-six brought menu introduction, new marketing efforts, and a 25% increase in total employment, to 4,500 employees from 3,600 employees. Chili's at this point in time was considering the following non-exclusive alternatives:

- National expansion
- Further existing market penetration
- New product introduction

[1]Donald Smith, "Romancing the Burger," *Nation's Restaurant News,* February 10, 1986, p. F9.
[2]Ibid.
[3]Don Jeffrey, "Smaller Dinner Houses Rely on Local Marketing," *Nation's Restaurant News,* March 10, 1986, p. F8.

EXHIBIT 2

Chili's Inc. Selected Financial Data *(In thousands)*

	Year Ended June 30		
	1986	1985	1984
Revenues	$106,990	$69,301	$43,157
Net income	$ 4,799	$ 4,131	$ 1,990
Weighted average shares outstanding	5,230	4,714	3,982
Working capital	$ 2,375	$ 1,453	($230)
Total assets	63,110	41,147	22,209
Long-term debt	10,739	8,483	3,528
Stockholders' equity	38,500	23,307	12,535
Number of restaurants open at year end	65	45	28

SOURCE: Chili's 1986 Annual Report.

As Chili's Chairman of the Board and Chief Executive Officer Norman Brinker said, "We have an unusually dedicated, talented group. That's the difference. A company is simply the sum total of individual efforts towards a common goal."[4]

THE ECONOMY

Industry observers saw 1986 as a year of considerable change within the restaurant industry. Oil prices had plunged, inflation was falling, and the stock market was soaring. Cheaper oil prices were hitting the Southwest harder and faster than expected. Energy companies were slashing capital spending budgets and laying off workers. Other industries both directly and indirectly related to energy were also suffering. Restaurant companies located in the economically impacted energy-belt states had reported sluggish market conditions.

Another element which presented a direct threat to the restaurant industry was the 1986 Tax Reform Act. This Act eliminated 20% of the expense-account write-off for business-related dining and also eliminated the investment tax credit. Industry analysts felt that less businessmen would eat out due to this reform. And, in the case of rapidly expanding companies, the investment tax credit meant beneficial tax savings. Chili's recognized investment tax credits of over $1.5 million in 1985 and 1986.[5]

As opposed to tightened economic conditions in the U.S. market, volatility of world politics and increased terrorism abroad persuaded many Americans to consider the advantages of traveling in the U.S. rather than in foreign countries. Industry experts considered this trend an opportunity for the U.S. hotel and restaurant businesses.

Demographers had pointed out the aging of the population. The baby boom generation had reached maturity. The tastes and values of upwardly mobile young professionals, less concerned with price than with variety and style,

[4] "The Restaurant Chain Industry," *Nation's Restaurant News,* August 11, 1986, pp. F3–F70.
[5] Chili's Annual Report, 1986.

would benefit full-service sit-down restaurants and cafeterias, industry experts believed. These restaurant categories offered a wide selection of items and an atmosphere favored by a broad section of the population. The trend was toward the "gourmet" eating experience, coupled with nutrition and weight consciousness.

Also influencing the restaurant industry was consumer retrenchment. Spending on restaurant meals was one of the first areas to be affected by changes in the financial condition of consumers. Growth in real disposable income and employment, the two key supports for restaurant sales, had moderated in 1986. When combined with relatively high debt loads and a low savings rate, the customers' propensity to eat away from home had declined.[6]

Sales of hard goods had been relatively strong in early 1986. While purchases of autos, furniture, appliances and other consumer durables obviously were substitutes for restaurant sales, they channeled an amount of buying power away from meals eaten outside the home. However, their impact on restaurant sales was expected to be short-lived since much of the strength in hard goods sales had been promotionally induced and was probably not sustainable.[7]

The differential between the cost of food prepared at home and the prices in restaurants had widened. According to *The Nation's Restaurant News,* an industry journal, the average monthly increase in 1985 in the cost of food eaten away from home was 3.9% while the average monthly increase in the cost of food eaten at home was 1.5%. In 1984 these figures were 4.2% and 3.7% respectively.[8]

The restaurant industry had become more competitive. Competition was coming from nonrestaurant food retailers as well as from other restaurants. Convenience stores, deli counters and salad bars at supermarkets, and restaurants within department stores were among the nontraditional food outlets that were capturing more of the market for food consumed outside the home by providing new alternatives for the consumer.[9]

In addition to general economic trends and consumer demand influences, direct operation factors had an impact on restaurant companies. The industry was facing rising insurance costs. Third-party liability awards and workers' compensation claims were climbing, leading to substantially higher insurance premiums. Those operators whose restaurants had a high alcohol mix had been hit especially hard. Encouraging alcoholic beverage sales was no longer commonplace in the wake of consumer awareness, such as Mothers Against Drunk Driving.[10]

According to a report by the National Restaurant Association, the nation's food-service industry will face a shortage of 1.1 million workers by 1994.[11] This industry, which employed 150,000 restaurant cashiers in 1984, will need 216,000 cashiers in 1995, a 36.7% jump. The need for cooks and chefs will ex-

[6]Don Jeffrey, p. F8.
[7]Ibid.
[8]"The Restaurant Chain Industry," pp. F3–F70.
[9]Don Jeffrey, p. F8.
[10]Ibid.
[11]"Food Service Facing Shortage of 1.1 Million Workers by 1995," *Nation's Restaurant News,* July 28, 1986, p. 61.

EXHIBIT 3

Restaurant Chain Industry Segments

Segment	Major Chains
Burger	McDonald's, Burger King
Contract	Marriott Food Service, ARA Services
Family Restaurant	Denny's, International House of Pancakes
Pizza	Pizza Hut, Domino's
Chicken	Kentucky Fried Chicken, Church's
Dinner House	Bennigan's, Red Lobster
Snack	Dairy Queen, Dunkin' Donuts
Family Steak House	Ponderosa, Western Sizzlin
Cafeteria	Luby's, Wyatt's
Fish	Long John Silver's, Captain D's

SOURCE: *Nation's Restaurant News*, August 11, 1986.

pand to 435,000 in 1995 from 331,000 in 1984, a 31.4% increase, the NRA said.

The need for bartenders will rise 29.8%, to 353,000 in 1995 from 272,000 in 1984. The industry labor shortages were exacerbated by high turnover rates in food service, according to the report, which was prepared in conjunction with the consulting firm of Arthur D. Little Inc. Food counter and fountain workers and waiter and waitress assistants all demonstrated a 43% turnover rate, followed by kitchen workers' and waiters' and waitresses' 32% rates in 1984. Even supervisors had a 24% turnover rate, the NRA said in its report. In addition, the industry was facing a labor crisis because its employment rate would swell 21.7% over the next ten years, to 8.9 million persons, while overall employment would increase only 14.9%, the NRA said. Consequently, for most operators, wage rates were being bid up and recruiting and training had intensified.

THE INDUSTRY

As of January 1986, the restaurant chain industry consisted of approximately 100,000 outlets, an increase of 9% over the previous year.[12]

The restaurant chain industry included 10 different segments (see Exhibit 3), the largest of which was the burger segment, accounting for 40% of sales dollars in the industry.[13] However, the fastest-growing segment was the pizza chains segment, registering an annual sales growth rate of 23% for 1985. Industry observers attributed this result to increased consumer demand for speed and convenience, home delivery, and variety of product. Contract feeders, snack chains and fast-food chains were all growing and reaping market share gains. Dinner houses, chicken chains, family restaurants, family steak houses and cafeterias were showing slower sales growth than the industry as a whole. (See Exhibit 4.)

[12] "The Restaurant Chain Industry," pp. F3–F70.
[13] Ibid.

EXHIBIT 4		

Burgers Do the Biggest Business . . .

Top 100 Systemwide Sale by Segment, in Billions

Burger [1]	########################\ \#################	$27.5
Contract	##############	$ 6.8
Family Restaurant	###########	$ 5.5
Pizza	##########	$ 5.4
Chicken	#########	$ 4.9
Dinner House	#######	$ 3.7
Snack	#####################	$ 9.7
Family Steak House	#####	$ 2.7
Cafeteria	###	$ 1.2
Fish	##	$ 1.1

[1] Includes roast beef.

SOURCE: *Nation's Restaurant News,* August 11, 1986.

DINNER HOUSE SEGMENT

Restaurant analysts considered Chili's within the dinner house segment, defined as the niche between the fast-food and midscale restaurants. "It is one of the most effectively positioned restaurant concepts," said Donald Smith, Professor of Hotel Restaurant and Institutional Management at Michigan State University.[14] The late 1960s saw the development of the concept, representing the birth of the American tavern. These restaurants were neighborhood eating, drinking, and meeting places, right on target for the hungry, lonely young adult audience. They emphasized casual dining atmosphere, good quality and variety accompanied by alcoholic beverages at reasonable prices.

In 1985, the top ten dinner house chains had an average of 182 units with annual sales of $2.1 million. The average guest check was $10 per person, up 0.8% from the previous years. (See Exhibit 5.)

As a result of consumer awareness programs and governmental regulations concerning alcohol sales and consumption, the new strategy in the dinner house segment was one of menu expansion to offset decreased sales of alcoholic beverages. Alcohol beverage sales in this segment ranged from 15% of total sales to 40%, but with increased awareness the norm seemed to fall off to about 20% of total sales.

HUMAN RESOURCES

Restaurant analysts saw Chili's as a very well-managed company headed by experienced and creative restaurant veterans. This dynamic outlook filtered down to the restaurant level where there was an energy and attitude present about the employees. Chili's offered a comprehensive training program and an attractive compensation and benefits package in order to develop and

[14]Donald Smith, p. F9.

... But Pizza is Growing the Fastest

Top 100 1986 Growth Rate by Segment	
#####################	13.6%
########################	15.3%
#######	5.8%
###############################	22.7%
#########	6.5%
##############	8.8%
##########	6.9%
############	8.0%
##############	9.1%
######################	14.1%

EXHIBIT 5

1985 Dinner House Segment Data

	Average Guest Check	Systemwide Sales (Millions)	Number of Units	Sales & Market Share
Red Lobster	$10.75	$ 925	400	25.09%
Bennigan's	8.40	455	223	12.34%
Chi-Chi's	7.82	435	217	11.80%
El Torito	N/A	383	196	10.39%
T.G.I. Friday's	10.00	366	123	9.93%
Steak & Ale	13.00	295	190	8.00%
Stuart Anderson's	N/A	275	120	7.46%
Ground Round	N/A	220	201	5.97%
Chili's	6.81	185	97	5.02%
Brown Derby	N/A	148	56	4.01%
		$3,687	1,823	100.00%

SOURCE: *Nation's Restaurant News*, August 11, 1986.

keep talented restaurant management. As a result, Chili's boasted a 15% management turnover rate, one of the industry's lowest.[15] In 1986 Chili's had approximately 4,500 employees, up from 3,600 in 1985.[16] Chili's organization was very structured in terms of operating autonomy. This can be seen in the Organization Chart. (See Exhibit 6.)

[15]Charles Glousky and Steven Rockwell, "Here Comes the Shakeout," *Nation's Restaurant News*, March 10, 1986, p. F37.
[16]Chili's Annual Report, 1986.

EXHIBIT 6
Chili's Organization Chart

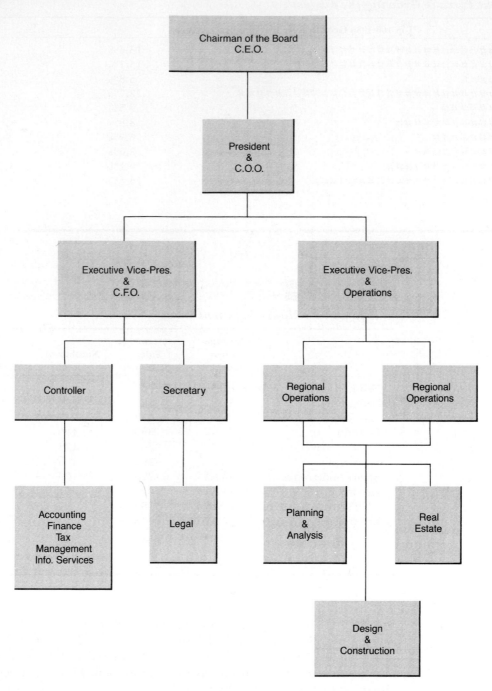

SOURCE: Company Data.

THE KEY PLAYERS

A major turning point for Chili's came in 1983 when, as previously mentioned, Norman Brinker and several other top executives were brought in to replace the Lavine brothers. The new team was known in the restaurant industry for holding aggressive marketing philosophies and growth-oriented attitudes. The key executives averaged more than 13 years of experience in the restaurant industry.

Norman Brinker, 54, joined Chili's in 1983 as Chairman of the Board and Chief Executive Officer. He had 27 years of experience in the food-service industry. In 1966, he started the Steak & Ale restaurant chain. The Bennigan's chain followed in 1976. He sold both of the chains to Pillsbury in 1976 and went to work for that company as the Chairman of Steak & Ale. He also served as Chairman and Chief Executive Officer of Burger King Corporation, a subsidiary of Pillsbury.

Ron McDougall was named President and Chief Operating Officer of Chili's in 1983, after serving as Senior Vice-President for Steak & Ale Restaurant Corporation, where he helped create the Bennigan's concept. His experience also included senior management positions with Burger King Corporation, the Pillsbury Company, Sara Lee and Procter & Gamble. Under his direction, Chili's corporate expansion strategy took on a more quantitative approach to market penetration, restaurant design/construction, site selection procedures, and advertising in the form of demographic studies, competitive studies and site selection models.

Jim Parrish, Executive Vice-President and Chief Financial Officer, joined Chili's in 1983. His prior experience included serving as Chief Financial Officer for companies in the restaurant, agricultural processing, and oil and gas industries.

Creed Ford III, who had been with Chili's since 1976, was named Director of Operations in 1978 and promoted to Executive Vice-President of Operations in 1986.

John Titus, a Real Estate and Construction Officer from Steak & Ale was elected the Vice-President of Real Estate in 1983.

Ed Palms, previously Steak & Ale Director of Design, also joined Chili's in 1983 as Vice-President of Design after serving Steak & Ale for nine years.[17]

All of the aforementioned executives were aggressive and risk taking in their management styles, restaurant analysts felt. Chili's had installed the right mixture of leadership and know-how to position themselves for the future.

CHILI'S MENU CONCEPT AND SERVICE

Chili's restaurant's distinctive building became well-established and familiar landmarks in the markets in which the company operated. Market analyses, conducted in 1984 on management's behalf, indicated that, by making some design modifications to the Chili's standardized buildings, the company could increase the appeal of the existing restaurants while significantly reducing maintenance costs. Management decided to undertake a remodeling program including the installation of effective signage, improved lighting, and

[17]Ibid.

custom-designed awnings. These changes made significant contributions to the exterior appearance and visibility of each Chili's location. Other key improvements involved a new kitchen layout to increase operational efficiency, a reconfiguration of the customer areas to raise table turnover, and a low-maintenance brick exterior.[18]

In 1986 the decor of a Chili's restaurant consisted of booth seating, tile-top tables, hanging plants, and wood and brick walls covered with interesting memorabilia. Each restaurant had a casual atmosphere and was open seven days a week, for lunch, dinner, and late-night meals. Chili's restaurants featured quick, efficient, and friendly service. Most were free-standing units of approximately 6,000 square feet with 156 to 178 dining seats.[19] Table turnover was 45 minutes.[20]

Management placed emphasis on serving customers substantial portions of high-quality food and beverages at moderate prices. Full bar service was available, with frozen margaritas offered as a specialty drink. Draft and bottled domestic and imported beers were served in frosted mugs. In 1986, Chili's introduced a premium "Top Shelf" margarita and premium wines which were available by the glass or bottle.[21] Thanks to these new drinks liquor sales had held steady at about 20% of total revenues. Although Chili's did not downplay liquor, its focus was on food and a substantial portion of alcohol sales was made to customers waiting for tables. As Ron McDougall said, "We are not a watering hole."[22]

Chili's menu was designed to be varied enough to accommodate a diverse customer group yet limited enough so that all offerings could still be "prepared from substantially fresh products each day" on the premises, said Norman Brinker.[23] Thirteen varieties of half-pound hamburgers were available with a wide range of toppings. Other selections included the ever-popular "bowl of red"; Mexican-style specialties such as nachos, soft tacos, and quesadillas; and meal-sized salads. (See Exhibit 7.)

In 1985, Chili's scored big gains with the introduction of chicken and beef fajitas, a chicken sandwich, and two new appetizers—Buffalo chicken wings and cheese fries. Seeking to broaden its market base, Chili's extended its menu early in 1986 by adding other nonburger items—the Chicken Frisco Salad, the Monterey Chicken Platter, and Country Fried Steak, and the BBQ Baby Back Ribs.

These products were targeted toward a growing consumer demand for variety, according to Chili's chairman, Norman Brinker. "Burgers are still king, but people just want more different things more often," he said.[24] Burgers, which once accounted for more than 50% of sales, according to the company, made up less than 35% by 1986.[25] Also in response to customer requests, a children's menu and desserts, which included hot fudge sundaes and a cinna-

---

[18]Chili's Annual Report, 1984.
[19]Ibid.
[20]Chili's Annual Report, 1986.
[21]Ibid.
[22]Don Jeffrey, p. F8.
[23]Charles Glousky and Steven Rockwell, p. F37.
[24]Ibid.
[25]Ibid.

EXHIBIT 7
Chili's Menu

mon apple sundae delight, were introduced.[26] New product introductions were very well received, and boosted Chili's person check average from $6.50 to $6.81.[27]

At Chili's, a new item strategy was pursued, as long as the dishes would meet the goals of high quality, simple preparation, fast service and outstanding price/value. Further, through a diversified menu, Chili's intended to maintain and enlarge its customer loyalty. Internal research had shown that more than half of the customers visited Chili's restaurants an average of three times per month.[28]

ADVERTISING CAMPAIGN

Prior to the change in management at Chili's, almost no money was spent on advertising and promotion. Success, such as it was, was due almost exclusively to word of mouth. In October 1983, Chili's engaged New York–based McCann-Erickson to handle its advertising. However, soon thereafter, in February 1984, the $1 million account was awarded to Dallas-based Levenson, Levenson, and Hill. McDougall attributed the change primarily to management's dissatisfaction with the advertising strategies taken by McCann-Erickson. Additionally, the change enabled Chili's executives to work with the top agency people as opposed to a branch office of a large agency.[29]

In mid-1984, the "No Place Else is Chili's" campaign debuted. Phase one lasted about a year and focused on both television and radio spots. March 1985 began the second phase of the campaign with two national television commercials and four new radio spots. Chili's commercials took viewers inside Chili's restaurants to eavesdrop on conversations at various tables. Scenarios

[26]Chili's Annual Report, 1986.
[27]Ibid.
[28]Ibid.
[29]D. S. Hansard, "Chili's Picks Dallas Ad Agency," *Dallas Morning News*, February 22, 1984, p. 2D.

included a couple reminiscing over old times and mutual friends, and a group of neighbors relaxing after a garage sale. According to the President of the ad agency, Bill Hill, "You can't do it by showing pretty food alone. You have to create a personality for them [the restaurants]." Levenson, Levenson, and Hill conducted market research to answer the question "What is Chili's?" The agency concluded that Chili's was an original, rather than an imitator or a fad, thus the reason for the slogan "No Place Else."[30]

In February 1986, in order to make up for its concentration in the oil-depressed Southwest, Chili's launched a two-pronged plan of new product introductions and television advertising in a stepped-up effort to stimulate sales. The advertising campaign was targeted at key oil-sensitive markets in Dallas, Houston, Austin, Denver, and Oklahoma City.[31]

FINANCE AND ADMINISTRATION

Chili's became a publicly held company on January 6, 1984. Since Chili's went public the company has posted sales gains exceeding 50% in each of the two years. Same-store sales in 1986 were relatively unchanged from 1985, although expansion of new restaurants boosted revenues. New menu items introduced in 1986 raised cost of sales by 0.4% from 27.2% in 1985. In 1984 cost of sales was 26.0%. Operating expenses, including marketing, had risen from 49.4% in 1984 to 52.5% in 1986. This cost increase was made up of first-year and start-up expenses associated with opening new restaurants and with rising insurance costs. In 1986 management believed it had positioned itself for future growth with adequate personnel and support functions in place. The growth throughout 1985 and 1986 resulted in lower general and administrative expenses as a percent of sales. The largest operating expense realized by the company in 1986 outside of salaries was rent expense, totaling $8.5 million. This, coupled with depreciation expense of $6.7 million, represented 14.2% of total sales. In 1984 the same expenses were 4.7% of sales. This 300% increase reflected 50 additional restaurant locations, a 267% increase in unit growth. Chili's profit margin in 1986 dropped to 4.5% from 6.0% in 1985. Company officials believed that they could see lower profit margins during periods of heavy growth in return for higher margins in later years.[32]

Management believed that financially Chili's was in relatively good shape in 1986. Total assets had experienced a 285% growth rate since 1984 and working capital was strong. Company officials believed that funds generated from operations, from built-to-suit agreements with landlords, and available under a revolving loan agreement and lines of credit with various Dallas banks were adequate to finance capital expenditures.[33] (See Exhibits 8 and 9.)

[30]D. S. Hansard, "Chili's Expands Ad Campaign," *Dallas Morning News,* March 15, 1985, p. 1D.
[31]David Zuckerman, "Chili's Introduces New Products, Ads," *Nation's Restaurant News,* April 28, 1986, p. 2 and p. 59.
[32]Chili's Annual Report, 1986.
[33]Ibid.

EXHIBIT 8

Chili's Inc. Consolidated Balance Sheet (In thousands)

	June 30	
	1986	1985
ASSETS		
Current assets:		
Cash & equivalent	$ 2,581	$ 308
Inventories	1,046	594
Other current assets	8,543	7,193
Total current assets	12,170	8,095
Property & equipment	54,933	34,117
Less: accumulated depreciation	(10,209)	(5,732)
Net property & equipment	44,724	28,385
Other assets	6,126	4,667
	$63,110	$41,147
LIABILITIES		
Current liabilities:		
Current portion of long-term debt	$ 362	$ 586
Accounts payable	5,842	3,558
Accrued liabilities	3,591	2,498
Total current liabilities	9,795	6,642
Long-term debt	10,739	8,483
Deferred income taxes	3,840	2,453
Deferred gain on sale & leaseback	236	262
Stockholders' equity:		
Common stock—authorized 20 million shares of $.10 par value; 5,222,818 and 4,661,038 shares issued and outstanding in 1986 and 1985, respectively	522	466
Additional paid in capital	25,847	15,509
Retained earnings	12,131	7,332
Total stockholders' equity	38,500	23,307
	$63,110	$41,147

SOURCE: Chili's 1986 Annual Report.

EXPANSION

Chili's expansion plan was twofold: first, it clustered restaurants in preexisting markets to obtain complete market penetration; and, secondly, it entered new geographic territories with one unit at a time or through joint-venture agreements with outside investors. Chili's had 20 units in Dallas/Fort Worth, 10 units in Houston, nine units in Los Angeles and four to six units each in San Francisco, Denver, Atlanta and Tampa/St. Petersburg in 1986. The biggest event in the story of Chili's expansion was an agreement signed in October 1985 with Dunkin' Ventures, operator of the world's largest donut shop chain. The 20-year agreement would allow the 50% joint venture to build and operate more

EXHIBIT 9

Chili's Inc. Consolidated Statement of Income (*In thousands, except per share data*)

	Year Ended June 30		
	1986	**1985**	**1984**
REVENUES			
	$106,990	$69,301	$43,157
COSTS & EXPENSES			
Costs of Sales	29,504	$18,882	$11,200
Operating expenses	56,165	34,891	21,320
General & administrative	7,483	5,887	4,880
Depreciation & amortization	6,730	3,378	2,040
Interest	470	301	774
	100,352	62,339	40,214
Income before taxes	6,638	5,962	2,943
Income taxes	1,839	1,831	953
Net income	$ 4,799	$ 4,131	$ 1,990
Net income per share	$ 0.92	$ 0.88	$ 0.50
Weighted average shares outstanding	5,230	4,714	3,982

SOURCE: Chili's 1986 Annual Report.

than 50 Chili's in New England and Canada. Norman Brinker said that Chili's management was impressed with Dunkin's food service operations and expansion plans. The first unit should open in the Boston area in fiscal 1987.[34,35]

In 1986 Chili's also had joint-venture agreements with Chesapeake Seafood Co. in the Washington, D.C. area and with Tampa-based Sunstate Restaurant Corporation. Chesapeake operated nine units and Sunstate operated 10 units in 1986. The strategy behind the joint-venture agreements allowed Chili's to approach unfamiliar territories with limited financial risk.

At the start of fiscal 1986 Chili's plan was to grow to 80 restaurants by June 30, 1986. This goal was accomplished through a systematic, disciplined approach to expansion. (See Exhibits 10 and 11.) Chili's Vice Presidents of Design and Construction and Real Estate employed sophisticated site models in the selection of Chili's restaurant locations. In addition, rigorous financial analyses and experienced managerial instincts were used.

FUTURE DIRECTIONS

The future of the restaurant industry was not very glamorous by the fall of 1986. According to *Standard & Poor,* profits of restaurants and lodging compa-

---

[34]Ibid.
[35]J. Fine, "Chili's Franchise Agreement Fits In with Its Long-Range Expansion Plan," *Dallas Business Courier,* October 14, 1985, p. 3.

EXHIBIT 10
Chili's Inc. Sales
Growth

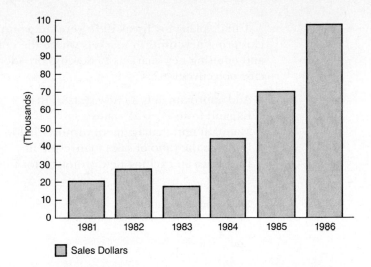

SOURCE: Chili's 1986 Annual Report.

EXHIBIT 11
Chili's Inc. Unit
Growth

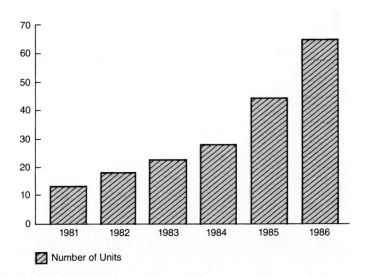

SOURCE: Chili's 1986 Annual Report.

nies had dropped 22% during 1986, third quarter, in comparison with 1985, same period. This result was mainly due to increase competition among restaurant chains and to an increase in the popularity of cheaper ready-made packaged foods that people could eat at home.[36] Some chains had been forced to close units; others had reckoned on introduction of new menu items; and others were seeking geographical expansion.

[36]Laurie Baum, "Profits Look Muscular—But Not for Long," *Business Week,* November 17, 1986, p. 175.

Chili's plans for fiscal 1987 were the continuation of national expansion, clustering new units in markets where the company already had restaurants, and entering new markets to develop broader national exposure. Chili's specific objectives were:[37]

- Add approximately 35 new restaurants
- Expand from 12 to 22 states
- Maintain unit management turnover below 17%
- Improve the ratio of sales to investment
- Introduce an exciting new prototype for future Chili's restaurants.

[37]Chili's Annual Report, 1986.

Food Lion Comes to Tulsa . . . "Hello, I'm Diane Sawyer"

JOSEPH WOLFE, *University of Tulsa*

On Thursday evening November 5, 1992 Diane Sawyer of the ABC network's top-rated investigative program *PrimeTime Live* leveled her hazel-eyed gaze into the television cameras and announced

> Tonight we have a story about what the consumer sees in the supermarket and what goes on behind the scenes . . . a *PrimeTime* investigation.
>
> Food Lion is the fastest growing grocery chain in the nation, a remarkable success story in an industry where profit margins tend to be perilously low. But six months ago we started talking to current and former employees. Seventy agreed to go on the record. People from different states, who didn't know each other, yet [all] told us similar stories about sanitation and food handling in some departments in their stores.
>
> Before we begin, a word about the Food Lion employees that were filmed with hidden cameras. They're hard working people who care about their jobs. But what this report will show is the kind of thing that *can* happen when the pressure for profit is great and you break the rules.

With that introduction to the segments shown that evening and the following week, Food Lion was thrown into a maelstrom of negative publicity and harsh market reactions. The next day its two stocks respectively plummeted 10.8% and 13.8% as the NASDAQ's most active over-the-counter issues. Overnight the company's parent corporation's stock fell 6.2% in very heavy trading in the Brussels stock exchange as many questioned the basis for the company's amazing success in the highly competitive and low growth supermarket grocery industry. By early March, 1993 Standard & Poor placed up to $500.0 million of Food Lion's credit for review and later that month Moody's Investors Service lowered the chain's senior long-term debt rating. In taking this action

---

Joseph Wolfe is Professor of Management at the University of Tulsa.

This case does not exemplify either correct or incorrect managerial decisions or actions taken but is instead intended to facilitate a discussion and analysis of the issues involved.

Moody Vice President Pam Stubing cited the investigation's negative publicity, the company's falling sales and growth rates, and the fact that the swift recovery Moody's felt would occur after the expose ". . . isn't happening and further pressures on earnings could occur."

Moreover, the televised expose could not have come at a worse time for the company's struggling Southwestern expansion. After opening 42 stores in the Dallas/Fort Worth area to disappointing sales in 1991, its entry into the Tulsa, Oklahoma market with seven new stores would be accomplished the following week and the chain would be facing strong local and national competition in that city. Company officials in both Tulsa and its Salisbury, North Carolina headquarters tried to minimize the television program's long-term consequences but they admitted short-term problems were causing concern. The company continued to press its earlier September, 1992 lawsuit against Capital Cities/ABC Inc. over the methods used in preparing its investigation and in April, 1993 the suit was amended to a civil racketeering (RICO) action for damages amounting to at least $30.0 million.

Over the entire period, however, numerous forces from both within Food Lion itself and the grocery industry had begun to exert themselves. The chain's same-store sales had been falling at an increasing rate over the past number of years and it had made a number of low growth, "defensive expansions" to ward off new competition in its home territories. Although Food Lion felt it was both targeted and blameless regarding the food handling and employment practices detailed in the expose, various industry observers believed the report merely highlighted the harsh realities of doing business in the supermarket industry and the exploitative practices the company had employed in its quest for growth at all costs.

FOOD LION, INC.

Today's food giant was started by Ralph Ketner, Brown Ketner, and Wilson Smith in 1957 as a one-store independent called Food Town (SIC 5411). All former Winn-Dixie employees, they struggled for the next ten years attempting to find a place for their company in its home state of North Carolina. A number of stores were opened and closed as the small 16-unit chain strived for survival. It was only after Ralph Ketner began a policy of everyday low prices that the chain began to experience stability and sales growth. Food Town went public in 1970 and four years later the Belgium grocery combine of Etablissements Delhaize Freres et Cie (Delhaize Le Lion) purchased a controlling stock interest in the company and currently occupies half of its Board seats. Upon the entry of Delhaize Le Lion rapid expansion ensued. The chain changed its name to Food Lion when it expanded into a territory in 1983 already having a number of stores called Food Town.

Delhaize Le Lion Group   Delhaize Le Lion is Belgium's second largest retailing conglomerate. It is also that country's most internationally oriented company with over 60.0% of its sales coming from outside the country—principally the United States. The company adopted its overseas diversification strategy mainly due to Belgium's 1975 "loi de cadenas" or padlock law. This legislation attempted to protect the country's small, independent retailers by controlling the expansions of its larger retail chains.

Before a group of entrepreneurs in June, 1981 Delhaize Le Lion's Guy Beckers spoke of his company's thinking at the time of the law's passage. Because it was a Belgium-based supermarket chain the company concluded

the number of domestic supermarkets could not increase indefinitely and that the rate of increase of the turnover of existing supermarkets would diminish some time or another. First, we took it for granted that manufacturing was not our job. We looked at the situation in a number of European countries. Everywhere the same constraints were evident—control by the State, pressure from the trade unions, and not many potential openings as far as sales points were concerned. This made us look toward the United States. We were looking for a region with a growing population and an expanding economy. We chose the Sun Belt, which fulfilled these requirements: (1) lower energy consumption—with air-conditioning there is no problem about heat affecting the quality of work; (2) unemployment—the South is better situated from this point of view than other regions of the United States; (3) the population—the South is the best region for lower wage scales; (4) increase of population—the South comes at the top of the list; (5) the South is at the top of the list for capital investments for equipment and next to the top for nonresidential investments.

Within Belgium, Delhaize Le Lion operates over 100 of its own supermarkets and has 144 franchisees and affiliates which include 64 AD Delhaize supermarkets, 41 neighborhood Delhaize food stores, a number of traditional stores with whom it has long-term supply agreements, the Dial chain of 51 discount stores, and a chain of over 60 DI drug stores. Exhibit 1 summarizes the holdings and operations of this conglomerate in both Western Europe and the United States.

Operational control of Food Lion rests within an American group headed by Tom E. Smith, the company's current CEO. His first affiliation with Food Lion came from working in the company's first store as a bagboy in 1958 when he was 17. After graduating from Catawba College in 1964 with an A.B. in Business Administration he worked for Del Monte Foods for six years and subsequently became Food Lion's only buyer. It was at this time Smith developed the company's strategy of mass buying at discount prices and simplifying store operations by stocking fewer brands and sizes than the chain's competitors. He became the company's Vice-President for Distribution in 1974 and its Executive Vice-President in 1977. Smith, at the age of 39, became Food Lion's President in 1981 and its CEO in 1986. In 1992 his company-related compensation amounted to the dividends on his 1,534,089 shares of Food Lion stock as well as his base salary of $628,788 (a 20.0% raise from the previous year) plus a $272,955 performance bonus voted him by the board of directors in December 1991 upon the accomplishment of that year's record earnings. In late December, 1991 the company's Class A and B stocks were trading for $25.125 each.

Food Lion Operating Characteristics   Food Lion has operated as a regional chain primarily in the Southeastern section of the United States although it is now spreading North into Pennsylvania and Southwest into Louisiana, Texas, and Oklahoma. In making its original expansions its average store had approximated 25,515 square feet with a typical trading area of fewer than 7,000 people. The simplicity and standardization of store operations has been a key factor in the company's success. Stores usually do not carry nonfood

EXHIBIT 1

Delhaize Le Lion Business Activities and Holdings

Belgium retail and wholesale operations:

- 106 Delhaize Le Lion company-owned supermarkets
- 64 AD Delhaize franchised supermarkets
- 41 Delhaize neighborhood food stores
- 39 independent stores supplied through food distribution arrangements
- 51 Dial discount food stores
- 62 DI drug stores
- 4 warehouses operated by Delhaize Le Lion Coordination Center SA

Full or partial operating control through ownership interests:

DELIMMO—A real estate company providing long-term leases to 14 of its supermarkets in Belgium. Owned by Delhaize Le Lion SA through a 99.9% stock interest.

DELNED—A holding corporation 100.0% owned by Delimmo. Through Delned (BV Delhaize The Lion Nederland) Delimmo has a 50.0% interest in Shipp's Corner Shopping Center, Virginia Beach, Virginia and the Debarry Center, Jacksonville, Florida.

WAMBACQ & PEETERS—A transportation company delivering goods from Delhaize Le Lion's Belgium distribution centers; Controlled by Delhaize through a 55.0% stock ownership.

PINGO DOCE—A 31-store supermarket chain operating in the Portuguese cities of Lisbon and Porto of which Delimmo has a 38.8% stock interest.

ARTIP SA—An airline ticket reseller 33.14% owned by Delhaize Le Lion.

DEFICOM SA—An affiliate of the Defi holding company in the telecommunications industry of which Delhaize Le Lion has a 10.0% ownership interest.

FOOD LION INC. USA—Controlled by Delhaize Le Lion's 50.3% ownership of Food Lion's Class A non-voting shares and a 44.2% ownership of its Class B voting shares either directly or indirectly through its wholly-owned American subsidiary Delhaize The Lion America Inc. USA.

DELHAIZE THE LION AMERICA—A wholly-owned company of Delhaize Le Lion SA (Detla).

SUPER DISCOUNT MARKETS INC.—A seven-superstore food chain operating in Atlanta, Georgia under the name Cub Foods of which Delhaize The Lion America Inc. USA has 60.0% ownership.

SOURCE: Summarized from "Retailer Profile No. 1: Delhaize Le Lion," *Marketing in Europe*. Brussels: Economist Intelligence Unit, July, 1990, pp. 95–99.

EXHIBIT 2

Stores in Operation

Characteristic	Year				
	1992	1991	1990	1989	1988
Number of stores	1,012	881	778	663	567
Total square footage (000)	26,428	22,480	19,424	16,326	13,695
Scanning stores	1,012	801	508	315	130

SOURCE: *1991–1992 Annual Reports,* pp. 4–5 and Press Release, February 11, 1993, p. 3.

items and they shelve approximately 16,000 stock keeping units (SKUs). Food Lion's stores have averaged 25,000 square feet of selling space or roughly 20.0%–35.0% less than its competitors such as Winn-Dixie or Kroger. Because of their size and simplicity the stores are also cheaper to build—about $650,000 each versus $1.5 million for the average supermarket. Exhibit 2 presents the number of stores operated by Food Lion both today and in the recent past.

Until lately Food Lion had been able to lease its stores after having them built by local construction companies but in 1991 the company began owning its new stores. Tom Smith attributed the shift in its construction/ownership policy to "a credit crunch that has made it difficult, if not impossible, for developers to build Food Lion stores and lease them to us as they have done in the past." Accordingly the chain used its own funds to build its Dallas/Fort Worth, Texas stores and has indicated it will continue to use debt to finance future store growth. In 1992 approximately $200.0 million was spent on building and owning new stores as well as for the refurbishment of some of its older units.

Many other methods are employed to bring about efficient operations. When building its distribution centers it looks for railroad access and gets about 25.0% of its goods by rail, more than for most firms. In 1991 it opened three new combined 700,000 square foot dry/refrigerated facilities, and through an additional expansion in 1992, its total amount of distribution center space amounted to 8.7 million square feet found in the following centers:

Salisbury, North Carolina
Dunn, North Carolina
Prince George County, Virginia
Elloree, South Carolina
Green Cove Springs, Florida
Plant City, Florida
Greencastle, Pennsylvania
Roanoke, Texas
Clinton, Tennessee

Food Lion also carefully nurtures its reputation for being a low cost, efficient operation that translates its low operating costs into savings for its customers. Company lore states the firm's name was changed from Food Town to Food Lion because only two letters had to be changed on its store signs. All advertisements are prepared in-house thereby keeping marketing costs to .5 percent of sales rather than the industry's average of 1.1 per cent. Tom Smith himself appears in about one-half of the company's advertisements extolling

"At Food Lion, when we save, you save" thereby drawing customers with everyday low prices rather than costly weekly price-special advertisements. As one competitor acknowledges, "They do a good job of promoting their everyday low-price image. They promise to deliver one thing—price—and they do, on groceries and frozens." He also added, however, "Their feature prices on produce are not that dramatic."

Other methods and procedures contribute further to lower store level operating costs. When resetting or remodeling older stores Food Lion places an adhesive covering over its old shelves thus saving up to $10,000 a store. This method has also sped up new store opening schedules from three to two weeks thereby saving an additional $4,000 per opening. By 1992 Food Lion had converted all its stores to front-end scanning operations. In addition to using its scanners in the normal fashion, store visits by brokers and direct sales representatives are recorded on the store's computer thereby insuring each one is visited every four weeks as requested. To minimize "shrinkage" or theft the company is currently testing an electronic article surveillance (EAS) system in 25 of its stores. Food Lion's Director of Loss Prevention, Clayton Edwards, says "We tagged health and beauty aids, cigarettes, meat, and, where applicable, wine." In an earlier test in six stores it was found that "After six months, our gross profits were up nearly 10.0%. The biggest change was in the attitude of store management. With EAS, they feel as if they finally have a way of fighting theft." Edwards also observes that customers seem to like the system. "It makes for a safer shopping environment. We found that once word gets out—and it gets out very quickly—that a particular store is using EAS, the 'bad apples' or undesirable tend to go elsewhere. I think that supermarkets willing to invest in electronic tagging systems will definitely have a competitive advantage in years to come."

At the headquarters level all buying is centralized and all stores are run in the same fashion throughout the chain thereby resulting in the operation of a tightly disciplined, consistent, centralized operation. Centralized buying has resulted in both lower procurement costs and food prices for the chain. As one of its vendors has said Food Lion has ". . . the best buyers in the business. They will buy a year's worth of product if they can cut a deal and hold the price. Individual buyers have the authority to buy millions of dollars worth of a product with no second opinions needed. There is no buying committee. It's awesome." All stores are relatively small, layouts are almost identical, and store and district managers are told exactly what to do. As one competitor observes, Food Lion's "store managers have a checklist of what they should do, and they had better follow it. There's only one way to do things. Managers may have some leeway in supporting local charities, but that's about it. You can go into a Food Lion store in Florida and find the same end displays and planograms as in a store in North Carolina." Through both its low overhead costs, which ultimately must be supported at the store level, and efficient store operations a typical Food Lion unit can make a profit on weekly volumes as low as $100,000.

To insure conformity within its system Food Lion offers one of the industry's most liberal employee benefits package. Its stock purchase plan is open to all full-time employees over 18 and all part-timers who have been employed for at least one year. Other benefits include a profit-sharing plan, vision care, and a comprehensive medical and dental plan. While many laud the company's progressive benefits some believe its overall management system encourages loyalty but that it also discourages initiative. It has been reported that many managers have quit the company after a few years "because they felt the company was cold and impersonal, and they had no real feeling of security there." Others have claimed Food Lion saves money by causing workers to be dismissed before they are fully vested in the company's profit-sharing plan or, as in the case of Rickey Bryant who has filed a civil action suit against Food Lion with the help of the United Food and Commercial Workers Union (UFCW), that the company does not provide dismissed workers with an extension of their health insurance coverage as required by federal law.

Expansion Activities and Plans   Over the past five years Food Lion has added over 100 stores per year to its chain. The method employed in entering new markets can be illustrated in its experience in Jacksonville, Florida. In August, 1987 Smith blanketed the market with ads warning shoppers "Food Lion is coming to town, and prices will be going down." After operating there for one year Food Lion's five Jacksonville stores had 2.4% of the market and by 1991 the company had added 32 more stores and had obtained a 14.0% share. The chain's entry into the market, however, did not go unchallenged. Months before Food Lion entered the market Winn-Dixie had lowered its prices 5.0% across the board and by the time Food Lion had opened its stores the entire market's prices were down almost 15.0%. Although Food Lion obtained market share Winn-Dixie still led with 36.0% and after Food Lion completed its Jacksonville expansion Winn-Dixie's market share fell an additional 8.3%.

Given Winn-Dixie's experience with Food Lion others have begun to learn how to withstand the company's entry into their markets. When Food Lion came to the already crowded Dallas/Fort Worth area in December, 1990 many competitors had already reacted to earlier news announcements of the company's expansion plans. Some local grocers pursued the areas where they felt Food Lion was vulnerable. Because Food Lion does not emphasize service many went to 24-hour operations, promoted home delivery, and added such services as FAX machines, Western Union money transfers, and money orders. Some emphasized the selection and variety of food offered especially perishables and deli/bakery sections where Food Lion was felt to be at a competitive disadvantage. Most, however, engaged in price competition in one form or another. This was done through tactics of everyday low prices, advertising hot specials in weekly shopping guides, running one-cent sales, or offering triple coupons. For all market participants advertising and promotional costs were increased. Endcap displays, banners, and flags compared the store's own prices to Food Lion's, others advertised they would meet Food Lion's prices on comparable items, and many, such as Tom Thumb Food Stores and Kroger, ran advertisements twice a week rather than weekly. Kroger additionally guaranteed the lowest milk prices in town or triple the difference in cash.

Although customers may temporarily enjoy food prices other harmful and longer-term aspects of Food Lion's market entry strategies have been noted. The Organization for Economic Cooperation and Development (OECD) has received formal complaints since 1985 against Delhaize/Food Lion as fair marketing practices have not been employed and these practices have threatened the host country's standard of living. The OECD asked its Trade Union Advisory Committee to investigate and its summary findings were:

> Food Lion routinely opens a store in a town and launches a competitive war based on lower prices in order to take the market away from the already established

supermarkets. The already established grocers are forced into closure or to lower their prices, which they can only do by lowering wages and benefits they pay in line with the level set by Food Lion.

After one year in the Dallas/Fort Worth market, and its attendant price war, Food Lion had garnered a 4.0% market share which was less than half of its ultimate 10.0% objective. Although Food Lion's management expressed initial pleasure with its results others feel the company's success has been mixed. As observed by Cleve Park, a local Russell-Moss real estate broker, "In 75.0% of their stores they are extremely pleased, but in 25.0% they are extremely unhappy. They are in some terrible locations." It has also been noted that many of the company's successes have come in rural markets or less affluent communities with less sophisticated shoppers and weaker competition. To some extent this has been acknowledged by Vince Watkins, Food Lion's operations vice president. Referring to the chain's relatively weak results in Texas, "The competition out there was much better organized in preparing for our entry than perhaps they had been in other areas." Additionally, because of his chain's obsession with standardization its stores failed to recognize local food preferences and stocked popular Eastern brands unknown to those in the Southwest. After much delay Food Lion subsequently added to its Dallas/Fort Worth stores regional favorites such as ranch beans, various peppers, corn husks, plantain, and a select grade of beef popular with Texans.

Despite these results Food Lion has designated its "primary expansion areas" for the 1990s as being Kansas, Louisiana, Oklahoma, Missouri, Arkansas, Mississippi, and Alabama. The general mobilizing cry of "2,000 by 2,000" can be heard throughout the chain. Exhibit 3 presents economic and population growth data for the company's current and projected operating states, Exhibit 4 profiles the national competition Food Lion currently and potentially faces when it moves into its projected new markets, and Exhibit 5 presents the operating results of those competitors.

To maintain its expansion program Food Lion needs a constant pool of new employees. The company's goal has been to have 80.0% of new store management coming from existing operations but it is actually getting only about 50.0% at this time. For 1993 Food Lion plans on opening about 110 new stores primarily in Virginia, Maryland, West Virginia, and Texas. The estimated capital expenditures for those stores can be found in Exhibit 6.

Company Corporate Responsibility and Community Relations Efforts   Given the chain's destabilizing effects on local markets it has been no stranger to controversy. Food Lion, however, is proud of its recognition as a good corporate citizen. In 1986 the company received the Martin Luther King Award for its humanitarian efforts. One of its actions which led to the award was the donation of its trucks to aid Southeastern farmers during their 1985 drought. With these trucks farmers were able to transport hay from Indiana to save their cattle. The company has also been praised for providing equal opportunity employment and for establishing express lanes for handicapped customers.

When dealing with controversy the company has traditionally met the criticism head on. During one attack by Winn-Dixie in the Jacksonville, Florida market Food Lion produced a television advertisement featuring Tom Smith

EXHIBIT 3

Population Statistics for Present and Projected Store Operations

Operations	1990 Per/Capita Income	1991 Population (1,000)	1991 Population Rank	1980–1990 Percent Growth	2000 Projected Population*
CURRENT STATES:					
Delaware	$20,039	680	46	12.1	802
Florida	18,586	13,277	4	32.7	16,315
Georgia	16,944	6,623	11	18.6	8,005
Kentucky	14,929	3,713	24	0.7	3,689
Maryland	21,864	4,860	19	13.4	5,608
North Carolina	16,203	6,737	10	12.7	7,717
Pennsylvania	18,672	11,961	5	0.1	12,069
South Carolina	15,099	3,560	25	11.7	3,962
Tennessee	15,978	4,953	18	6.2	5,424
Texas	16,769	17,349	3	19.4	17,828
Virginia	19,746	6,286	12	15.7	7,275
West Virginia	13,747	1,801	34	−8.0	1,651
PROJECTED STATES:					
Alabama	$14,826	4,089	22	3.8	4,358
Arkansas	14,218	2,372	33	2.8	2,509
Kansas	17,986	2,495	32	4.8	2,534
Louisiana	14,391	4,252	21	0.3	4,141
Mississippi	12,735	2,592	31	2.1	2,772
Missouri	17,497	5,158	15	4.1	5,473
Oklahoma	15,444	3,175	28	4.0	2,924

*Series A migration assumptions employed.

SOURCES: *Statistical Abstract of the United States 1992.* Washington, DC: U.S. Department of Commerce, Economics and Statistics Administration, Bureau of the Census, 1992, pp. 22–23; *Current Population Reports: Population Estimates and Projections. Series P-25.* Washington, DC: U.S. Department of Commerce, Social and Economic Statistics Administration, Bureau of the Census, 1989, p. 13; *Information Please Almanac 1992.* NY: Dan Golenpaul Associates, 1993, p. 52.

EXHIBIT 4

Selected Actual and Potential Food Lion Competitors

ALBERTSON'S INC.—Operates over 650 grocery stores in 19 Western and Southern states. Store formats include about 250 combination food/drugstores employing approximately 58,000 square feet of selling space per store, 250 superstores of about 42,000 square feet each, 118 27,000 square ft. conventional supermarkets, and 32 warehouse stores. The company operates 9 full-line distribution centers which handle about 65.0% of the merchandise carried in its stores. In May, 1992 Albertson's acquired 74 Jewel Osco stores. Future sales growth is expected to come from store space expansions planned at about 10.0% a year and population increases found in its Florida and West Coast markets. The company competes through a strong private brand program, everyday low pricing, and superior service. Albertson's is 40.0% unionized.

BRUNO'S INC.—This Southern chain has more than 250 supermarkets operating in Alabama, Florida, Georgia, Mississippi, and Tennessee under the names Food World, Consumer Warehouse, Bruno's, Food

(continued)

EXHIBIT 4

Continued

Max, and Piggly Wiggly. Its stores average about 35,000 square feet each. In 1992 same-store sales fell 1.0% and it has been buffeted by high store opening costs and increased advertising expenditures caused by increased competition in some of its hotly-contested markets. Bruno's plans to open 33 new units in 1993 and will be installing in-store computers to reduce inventory shrinkage and increase labor productivity.

DELCHAMPS, INC.—Is affiliated with the Topco cooperative grocery purchasing organization. The chain operates 115 supermarkets along the Gulf Coasts of Alabama, Florida, Louisiana, and Mississippi as well as 10 liquor stores in Florida. All stores are leased under long-term agreements and measure about 35,345 square feet each. Sales fell in 1992 due to food price deflation and competitive pressures. Delchamps responded to heavy local competition by doubling the value of coupons up to 60 cents and by making cash donations to schools equalling 1.0% of the cash receipts collected by the schools. The chain has begun to reduce its selling costs by cutting its nighttime store hours and obtaining greater labor productivity.

GIANT FOOD—This is a highly integrated chain of 154 supermarkets concentrated in Washington, DC and Baltimore and their adjoining areas in Virginia and Maryland. It has its own warehouses and distribution network and a construction and maintenance company. Giant Food also produces its own privately-labelled ice cream, baked goods, dairy products, soft drinks, and ice cubes. Same-store sales, which have averaged about $22.7 million per store, fell in 1992 but the chain's high degree of vertical integration adds about 1.0% to its overall margins.

THE KROGER, CO.—America's largest grocery chain with major market shares in the Midwest, South, and West. Kroger operates about 1,265 stores of which 657 are combination food and drug units and 520 are superstores. The chain also operates over 940 convenience stores. Kroger acquired the Mini-Mart Convenience store chain in 1987 and sold its free-standing drug stores in the same year. In October, 1988 it accomplished a major restructuring. To foil a takeover bid at that time Kroger declared a special dividend which left the company with much debt. Much of its current cashflow is now being used to retire that debt. Kroger processes food at 37 plants and offers over 4,000 privately labelled goods. The company is heavily unionized and has faced stiff competition in Houston, Cincinnati, Dayton, and Tennessee.

WEIS MARKETS—Has most of its 127 food outlets in Southern Pennsylvania but also a few units in Maryland, Virginia, West Virginia, and New York. Other food retailers, including a number of low-price warehouse club chains, have moved into Weis' markets forcing it to cut prices. Same-store sales and operating margins have fallen annually for the past few years. Weis owns about 55.0% of its sites, is debt free, and sells nationally branded merchandise plus 1,800 items under its trademarks Big Top, Carnival, and Weis Quality. The company also operates five Amity House Ice Cream Shoppes and the Weis Food Service institutional supply company.

WINN-DIXIE STORES—This company is America's fifth largest grocery chain and the largest one in the Sunbelt. It operates about 1,200 31,400 square foot supermarkets under the names Winn-Dixie and Marketplace. The chain is nonunionized and has its own distribution centers, processing and manufacturing plants, and a fleet of trucks. In 1990 Winn-Dixie began emphasizing everyday low prices in addition to its usual high service orientation.

in his office assuring consumers that "Winn-Dixie would have you believe that Food Lion's low prices are going to crumble and blow away. Let me assure you that as long as you keep shopping at Food Lion, our lower prices are to stay right where they belong—in Jacksonville." In 1984 Smith reacted quickly when a number of rumors in eastern Tennessee linked the Food

EXHIBIT 5

1992 National and Regional Chain Comparisons

	Albertson's	Bruno's	Delchamps	Giant Food	Kroger	Weis Markets	Winn-Dixie
Sales	10,095.0	2,618.2	949.8	3,550.0	22,085.0	1,320.0	10,074.0
Gross Margin	26.0%	22.2%	26.5%	31.5%	22.5%	27.7%	22.8%
Net Profit Margin	2.67%	2.34%	.60%	1.85%	.37%	5.90%	2.09%
Inventory Turnover	13.0	11.2	10.0	16.0	15.0	14.5	10.9
Long-Term Debt	575.0	172.2	42.2	255.0	4,250.0	0.0	90.3
Net Worth	1,340.0	422.4	112.8	650.0	−2,749.0	692.0	952.2

NOTE: All data in millions of dollars except for margin percentages and inventory turns per year.
SOURCES: *Value Line* Company Surveys, November 20, 1992, pp. 1498, 1501, 1503–1505, 1508, 1515–1516.

Lion logotype to Satanic worship. Grand Ole Opry star Minnie Pearl was hired by the company to appear in local advertisements until the stories disappeared.

Recent Operating Results   Food Lion has stated its general plans are still in effect and that Tom Smith plans on doubling revenues by 1997. The CEO's near-term sales and profit projections have recently been less optimistic. As shown in Exhibits 7 and 8 the chain's long-term and near-term same-store sales have been falling and the American economy is not very robust despite the Clinton administration's early efforts at stimulating economic growth. The chain's new real estate development strategy was a major factor in raising its long-term debt from 27.0% of capital to 35.0% last year. This debt load should increase as Food Lion owned as many as 90 of the new stores built in 1992. Smith intends, however, to start selling and leasing back the new stores in 1994 when he hopes the real estate market will have rebounded. Exhibits 9–10 present the company's balance sheets and income statements for 1989–1992 while Exhibit 11 presents comparative quarterly sales and profit results for periods concurrent with the PrimeTime Live expose.

EXHIBIT 6

1993 Estimated New Store Expenditures

Capital Item	Expenditure (000,000)
Construction	$ 60.0
Store Equipment	85.0
Land Costs and Distribution Center Expansion	10.0
Total	$155.0

EXHIBIT 7

Same-Store Sales Volume Changes

Year	Growth
1989	8.6%
1990	4.5
1991	2.7
1992	−0.4

EXHIBIT 8

Monthly 1992–1993 Same-Store Sales

Period	Decrease
November, 1992	9.5%
December, 1992	6.2
January, 1993	7.6
February, 1993	5.4
March, 1993	5.7

SOURCE: *Food Lion, Inc. 1992 Annual Report.* p. 15.

THE GROCERY INDUSTRY

The grocery or supermarket industry has always been hotly contested. The more recent trends of greater degrees of participant concentration, the overlapping of market and trading areas caused by suburban scrawl, the quest for sustained profits, falling real income for many American families, and the effects of the two-career household on at-home food preparation have caused this industry to be even more competitive and challenging. Although Americans consume more than 750 million meals a day Exhibit 12 shows that the grocery store has been an ever-declining provisioner of the nation's food. In order to cater to changing tastes and shopping patterns the industry's chains have responded by extending operating hours, increasing their assortments of prepared and ready-to-eat foods, and offering convenience services which help to build customer traffic while simultaneously providing greater markups than can be obtained from food retailing alone. Exhibit 13 displays the sales and food mix obtained by the nation's largest chains in 1991 while Exhibit 14 shows the great variety of services offered by those responding to *Progressive Grocer*'s 1992 industry survey.

Because of the shrinking sales base caused by out-of-home eating and dining, America's declining population growth, and increasing inter-chain competition which has driven down prices and profit margins, most grocery chains are also attempting to reduce both store operating expenses and chain-wide corporate expenses. Capital outlays have been made on in-store computer systems so that about 85.0% of all stores possess scanning systems. These systems track inventory levels, check-out customers more quickly, and efficiently

EXHIBIT 9

Food Lion Balance Sheets (000,000)

	Fiscal Year Ending Nearest Saturday to December 31			
	1992	1991	1990	1989
ASSETS				
Current Assets:				
Cash and Cash Equivalents	$ 105.1	$ 4.3	$ 10.4	$ 15.7
Receivables	96.0	97.1	77.0	72.9
Income Tax Receivable	2.2	0.0	0.0	0.0
Inventories	896.4	844.5	673.6	577.9
Prepaid Expenses	15.5	36.5	6.7	4.7
Total Current Assets	1,115.2	982.5	767.7	671.2
Property at Cost less Depreciation and Amortization	1,373.6	1,036.8	791.8	610.5
Total Assets	2,488.8	2,032.1	1,559.5	1,281.7
LIABILITIES AND SHAREHOLDERS' EQUITY				
Current Liabilities:				
Notes Payable	459.6	122.5	127.5	131.7
Accounts Payable, Trade	324.1	343.2	290.1	237.0
Accrued Expenses	196.8	184.0	148.9	104.3
Long-Term Debt—Current	.6	1.1	3.4	12.8
Capital Lease Obligations—Current	5.1	4.1	3.1	3.2
Income Taxes Payable	0.0	22.0	29.8	21.8
Total Current Liabilities	986.3	676.8	602.8	510.8
Long-Term Debt	248.1	247.2	97.9	99.9
Capital Lease Obligations	245.7	195.2	153.8	95.0
Deferred Charges/Income	51.4	67.4	36.3	37.4
Deferred Compensation	1.7	1.7	0.0	0.0
Total Liabilities	1,533.1	1,188.2	890.9	743.2
Shareholders' Equity:				
Common Stock Net Common	241.9	161.2	161.1	161.0
Capital Surplus	.2	2.0	1.2	.7
Retained Earnings	713.6	667.9	506.3	376.7
Total Shareholders' Equity	955.7	826.6	668.6	538.5
Total Liabilities and Shareholders' Equity	$2,488.8	$2,019.3	$1,559.5	$1,281.7
Dividends Paid	$ 53.8	$ 48.0	$ 43.0	$ 32.5

SOURCES: Company 10-K Report, February 11, 1993 press release, Shareholder's Reports for 1991–1992.

schedule employees based on sales volumes and store traffic patterns. Also at the store level a greater amount of staffing is done via part-time labor. This labor is cheaper, more flexible, and not prone to unionization efforts.

At the area or district level many chains have begun to concentrate their stores within selected greater-metropolitan areas to secure advertising economies of scale and to minimize and consolidate shipping distances from centrally-located

EXHIBIT 10

Food Lion Statements of Income (000,000)

| | Fiscal Year Ending Nearest Saturday to December 31 | | | |
	1992	1991	1990	1989
Net Sales	$7,196.0	$6,438.5	$5,584.4	$4,717.1
Cost of Goods Sold	5,760.0	5,103.0	4,447.2	3,772.5
Gross Profit	1,436.4	1,335.5	1,137.2	944.6
Selling and Administrative Expenses	975.1	855.8	738.7	619.9
Interest Expense	49.1	34.4	32.6	29.2
Depreciation and Amortization	121.6	104.6	81.4	65.0
Income Before Taxes	290.6	340.7	294.5	230.5
Provision for Income Taxes	112.6	135.5	111.9	90.7
Net Income	$ 178.0	$ 205.2	$ 172.6	$ 139.8

SOURCE: Company 10-K Report and February 11, 1993 press release.

food distribution centers. At the corporate level buying operations are often centralized to obtain dedicated, advanced buying volume discounts. Corporate-level real estate departments have often been successful in renegotiating store site leases, covenants, and/or payment terms and schedules. Exhibit 15 presents typical operating characteristics for the industry's stores. Over the past few years productivity levels per employee and square foot of selling space have been increasing slowly despite longer store operating hours, greater inventory levels, and larger store sizes.

In the face of the lingering 1991–1992 recession and falling real incomes America's grocery chains have had to deal with the fact that shoppers have been trading down for the past few years. Through this process customers have been avoiding discretionary or impulse purchases as well as substituting lower-priced, often generic or unbranded, items for more expensive ones which carry more profit. Warehouse clubs offer lower prices for those who can buy in large quantities and they have increased their market shares in many

EXHIBIT 11

Near-Term Sales and Income Results (000,000)

Quarter	Sales	Net Income
4/1991	$2,300.0	$60.8
4/1992	2,020.0	27.3
1/1992	$1,600.0	$49.6
1/1993	1,660.0	21.9

SOURCES: "Food Lion's Payout Is Delayed Following Fallout of News Story," *The Wall Street Journal* (February 3, 1993), p. B2 and "Firm Posts 56% Decrease In 1st-Quarter Earnings," *The Wall Street Journal* (April 8, 1993), p. C6.

EXHIBIT 12
U.S. Food Expenditures

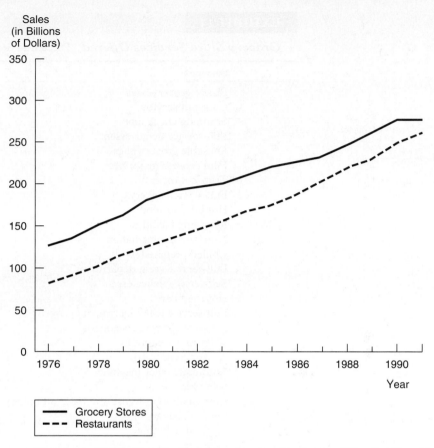

SOURCE: From graphed data in Eben Shapiro, "A Page from Fast-Food's Menu," *New York Times* (October 14, 1991), p. D1.

metropolitan areas. Club members typically pay an annual fee to shop for goods priced about 25.0% lower than in most supermarkets. Both the warehouse's operator and its patrons purchase products in bulk sizes providing both with many cost advantages and savings. Items are stocked on pallets and placed on industrial-type shelves by forklift trucks rather than being stocked

EXHIBIT 13

1991 Food Chain Sales Proportions by Merchandise Type

Grocery	49.0%
Meat	15.0
Dairy	8.0
General merchandise/Health & beauty aids	7.0
Produce	7.0
Frozen food	6.0
Service delicatessen	3.0
In-store bakery	2.0
Other	3.0

SOURCE: "How Supermarkets Are Measuring Up," *Progressive Grocer 59th Annual Report,* April, 1992, p. 37.

EXHIBIT 14

Grocery Store Services Offered (Percent of Stores Surveyed)

Service	Percent
*Plastic grocery bags	90.0%
*Carryout service	82.0
*Scanning checkouts	77.0
*Full-service delicatessen	76.0
Reusable grocery bags	69.0
Film processing service	62.0
*Trim-cut meat	60.0
*Full-service bakery	56.0
*Hot takeout food	55.0
Recycling facilities	51.0
Nutritional information	48.0
Chilled prepared foods	47.0
Full-service meat department	45.0
*Self-service delicatessen	42.0
Hot food bars	37.0
Full-service fish department	36.0
Separate cheese department	34.0
Videocassette rentals	33.0
Accept credit cards	28.0
*Automatic teller machines	25.0
Salad bar	24.0
*Combination in-house and bake-off bakery	24.0
Bake-off bakery only	22.0
Coupon scanning	20.0
Catering	20.0
Sit-down eating	18.0
FAX ordering	18.0
Pharmacy	16.0
Accept debit cards	12.0
Frequent shopper programs	12.0
Scratch/mix bakery	10.0
Fruit/juice bar	8.0
Ethnic prepared foods	8.0

*Services offered by Tulsa Food Lion stores.

SOURCE: "How Supermarkets Are Measuring Up," *Progressive Grocer 59th Annual Report*, April, 1992, p. 36.

individually by hand. Many buying clubs also inventory general merchandise items. This results in more sales per customer thus spreading operating expenses over a larger revenue base. Warehouse club sales amounted to $34.0 billion in 1992. In 1983 there were 15 warehouse club stores in operation in the United States and their number had grown to 577 by 1992. At this time Sam's Wholesale Clubs, Price Company, and Costco Wholesale are the largest chains of this type in the United States.

A number of tactics to either combat or join this trend have been engaged in by supermarketers. Some now stock bulk-sized, "big box" items and others have increased their service levels to include home or office delivery, FAXed

EXHIBIT 15

1991 Grocery Chain Operating Results and Characteristics

Sales Volume

Weekly Sales per Checkout	$26,375
Weekly Sales per Employee	$ 3,768
Sales per Employee Hour	$ 94.42
Weekly Sales per Square Foot	$ 8.65
Average Transaction Size	$ 17.71
Annual Inventory Turns	13.9

Front-End Measures

Percent of Scanning Stores	85.0%
Number of Weekly Transactions	13,082
Number of Checkouts	8.8

Physical Measures

Average Sq. Ft. Selling Area	26,656
Average Total Area Sq. Ft.	34,012
Items Stocked	20,372
Store Inventory value (000)	$ 702.0

Store Hours

Average Hours Open per Week	127
Percent Open 24 Hours All Week	31.0%

SOURCE: "How Supermarkets Are Measuring Up," *Progressive Grocer 59th Annual Report*, April, 1992, p. 37.

orders, and food clubs. A relatively few have opened their own warehouse-type markets. As difficult as supermarket competition has been in the past it is believed it will become even more competitive in the future. The new competition will be waged less and less against small, under-capitalized independents but more often by big, well-capitalized chains as they intrude on each other's market areas. And despite the relatively low profits obtained by the nation's major chains shown in Exhibit 16 new cash infusions or totally new entrants

EXHIBIT 16

Grocery Store Industry Financial Results

	1988	1989	1990	1991	1992	1993
Revenues	$97,401.0	$107,325.0	$113,019.0	$115,940.0	$120,400.0	$130,800.0
Cost of Goods Sold	73,148.2	80,279.1	84,199.2	86,259.4	89,336.8	96,792.0
Operating Profit	24,252.8	27,045.9	28,819.8	29,680.6	31,063.2	34,008.0
Overhead Expense	22,517.6	25,164.5	26,261.0	26,998.1	27,996.5	30,222.9
Pretax Income	1,735.3	1,881.4	2,558.9	2,682.6	3,066.7	3,785.1
Income Taxes	682.0	777.0	1,041.5	1,081.1	1,226.7	1,495.1
Net Profit	$ 1,053.3	$ 1,104.4	$ 1,517.4	$ 1,601.5	$ 1,840.0	$ 2,290.0

SOURCE: Philip S. Mulqueen, "Grocery Store Industry," *Value Line*, November 20, 1992, p. 1497. Includes the operating results only of those companies studied by *Value Line*.

are appearing. Wal-Mart, a super retailer in the general merchandise field, has recently entered the supermarket industry and companies from the United Kingdom, Germany, and Belgium have acquired controlling interests in various American food chains.

ABC *PRIMETIME LIVE*'S EXPOSE

The food handling and sanitation practices at Food Lion were first brought to *PrimeTime Live*'s attention by the Government Accountability Project, a group which provides support to company whistle-blowers. Subsequently ABC producer Lynn Neufer Litt began to gather materials for the expose by talking to 70 current and past Food Lion employees who had worked at 200 different company stores. To obtain independent confirmation of the various employee claims several investigators, one of whom was Lynn Neufer Litt, applied for jobs in over 20 different Food Lion stores. Two were hired and worked in three stores in two meat departments and a deli. Via both Neufer Litt's hidden-camera footage, and employee interviews conducted by Diane Sawyer, viewers were provided a behind-the-scenes look at Food Lion's food-handling methods, deceptive labelling practices, pressures to protect profit margins, and unsanitary short-cuts employees pursued to survive under the company's time management system.

Food Freshness, and Food-Handling Practices   With profit margins very slim due to price competition supermarkets must squeeze profits from every dollar spent. Given its merchandise costs are about 79.0% of its total expenses any savings found in this area are of major importance. Accordingly upper management went to great lengths to demonstrate frugality and the conservation of profit margins. Area managers and even vice presidents would get into trash barrels and dumpsters to retrieve discarded food stating "You're throwing away profits." Bryan Rogers, an ex-produce manager told Diane Sawyer, "I've seen them *in* the dumpster, not just leaning over into it, climb *in* it, I mean be up in it" to get merchandise and have it recycled. "Just take a head of cauliflower, for instance, I mean to where it's just got tiny little black spots all over the top of it, and they'd bring it back in and want you to take a, like a Brillo pad type of thing, and scrub it to get the little black stuff off and stick it in a tray and reduce it and try to get something for it."

As stated by a meat manager. "We try to sell everything we can to keep from throwing anything away" while another worker, shown trimming off discolored portions of out-dated pork announced, "OK, these are conversions; they look just as good as fresh." Jean Bull, a meat wrapper who had worked in twelve different Food Lion stores over a thirteen year period said,

> I have seen my supervisor take chicken back out of the bone can, make us wash it, and put it back out, and it was rotten. It's just unreal what they'll do to save a dime. They take *that* pork that's already starting to get a slime to it, it gets what they call a halo to it, a kind of a green tinge to it, and they take and put that into a grinder with sausage mixture, and they put it back out for anywhere from 7–10 days as fresh, home-made sausage. And it's *rotten*.

Another tale of trimming away spoilage and of the pressures placed on employees to perform was told by Larry Worley, an ex-market manager. "We'd have this pack of cheese, sliced American cheese, and rats would get up on top of that and just eat, eat like the whole corner off of it. You'd have to trim it up and put it back out. You *had* to because if we didn't make our gross profit we were out the door."

Other methods were presented on how Food Lion extended the shelf-life of out-dated products through re-packaging or reformulation. Whole ham that is two weeks past the meat packer's "sell-by" date is sliced up, placed in new number ten trays and put on sale as fresh meat while another worker is observed unwrapping old ground beef and mixing it with fresh ground beef to be sold as new. Bleach was used in a creative fashion. Bonnie Simpson, a five year Food Lion veteran meat wrapper, said they first soaked out-dated ham in Clorox to remove its foul odor and then cut it into small squares and sold it as cubed pork. Fish received a different treatment:

> Fish has a three day shelf life. OK? After three days you're supposed to reduce it and sell it or throw it away. But we didn't do that. We soaked the fish in baking soda and then we'd squirt lemon juice on it. Then put it back in the case and sell them for three more days on it. The fish would be *so* rotten it would crumble in your hand.

The most elaborate method for dealing with out-dated product was found in one manager's handling of "Country Pride" chicken parts. In an on-camera segment he was shown working with some cellophane-wrapped packages while saying, "Open them up and put a soaking pad, a couple of them in the tray. This way we can put three days' date on them." He then proceeded to spread barbecue sauce on the chicken parts and sent them to the gourmet section for sale at full price.

Despite these practices Diane Sawyer noted that no cases of food poisoning have been connected to Food Lion or any other grocery chain in North Carolina where these practices were observed. And Johanna Reese, of the state's Division of Environmental Health, said Food Lion has an "average to above-average record" regarding health inspections.

Time Management and Unsanitary Work Practices   In addition to squeezing as much profit as possible from the merchandise it procures for re-sale Food Lion has attempted to be as labor-efficient as possible. To accomplish these efficiencies a time management system called "Effective Scheduling" was developed by a consulting firm. Under this system all work has been timed and standards established dictating the work's pace. For example a meat cutter must cut one box of meat every 32 minutes and a meat wrapper has one hour to unload and stock 50 boxes of product. Based on these standards each store receives from headquarters a schedule mandating the work each department should accomplish in 40 hours. Through this system Tom Smith believes "We don't work our employees hard. We work them smart."

Unfortunately many employees have found it impossible to complete the work in the allotted time and have resorted to forgoing work breaks and working illegally "off-the-clock." For three workers interviewed by Diane Sawyer on camera their weekly unpaid work amounted to 10–25 hours each and the work-pace was grueling. Mark Riggs, who had been a manager of two Food Lion stores, felt pressured by higher management to get performance from his employees and he knew he was asking too much from them. "I felt guilty, incredible guilt for the things I made people do. It was the biggest reason for me leaving [Food Lion]. I couldn't look at myself in the mirror at the end of the day. You had to push people, push people."

Employees also took many short-cuts to save time and these short-cuts led to unsanitary workplace conditions. In one meat department the ground beef grinder was not cleaned either that evening or morning and the department's bandsaw blades and wheels were not disassembled each evening to eliminate spending time reassembling them in the morning. In these instances meat residues rotted overnight and were later deposited on newly-ground meat the next day. One deli clerk, casting a baleful eye around her work station's area, commented after the hidden camera showed dirty trays and baking tins and a meat cutter "ice skating" on a grease-covered floor:

> Well, the floor and the meat slicer . . . God, comin' into a place and the gunk on the slicer is thick. The floor's got all kinds of crap all over it. I don't think it's real appealing for a deli.

Another expose segment pointed out shipping problems associated with Food Lion's vaunted advance purchasing system. Although centralized advance purchases and volume buying resulted in lower initial product costs shipping delays or problems getting merchandise from distribution centers in a timely manner caused many meat products to arrive in stores near their "sell-by" dates. In one on-camera sequence the following dialogue transpired:

Meat manager: You *know* that the lamb that you cut on Monday is not gonna run, is not gonna go through Wednesday. Because the damn stuff is old when it comes in.

PrimeTime: What do you mean it's old when it comes in?

Meat manager: It's ———— lamb. I been on their ass for three years to get some decent lamb, if they want to sell lamb.

Food Lion Responds   Prior to its broadcast *PrimeTime Live* had provided Food Lion with a report on its investigation and had invited a company spokesperson to be an interview subject. Rather than appearing under *PrimeTime*'s conditions Food Lion immediately began running television advertisements. Tom Smith was shown strolling through a Food Lion store where he mentioned the company's "A" sanitation rating and the chain's pride in its cleanliness standards. On the morning of the telecast employees in Salisbury held a rally where pro-company petitions and letters were prepared and these expressions of opinion were subsequently sent to congressional members and Capital Cities/ABC Inc. And in the Tulsa market a story was published the same morning anticipating the program's effect on its new stores. Vince Watkins was quoted, "It is our understanding that this program will make some very serious and potentially devastating allegations about our company. These allegations will make excellent television but they will not be the truth."

The next day Food Lion distributed a media "Fact Sheet" outlining its position regarding food handling and employee scheduling practices. The company began visiting each store shown in the segment and to interview the employees involved. The announcement promised to quickly accomplish the following:

1. Establish more stringent periodic testing of employees to ensure complete and clear understanding of all of Food Lion's policies and procedures.
2. Increase internal and external audits and internal inspections by management to ensure that these policies and procedures are rigorously implemented.

3. Continue to ensure that if there is ever any problem in any of our stores, anywhere, at any time, we fix it.

Other operating procedures were changed immediately. The company's previous meat-handling policy had been to open the packages on their "sell-by" date to check for freshness. Any spoiled meat was to be discarded while still-fresh meat would be repackaged and sold at a discount. Now "so as not to create any further suspicions" about repackaging, Michael Mozingo said price reductions would be taken while the meat remained in the case at which time it could be sold for only one day longer.

Although the chain expressed a belief the furor would quickly subside such was not the case. Mike Mozingo admitted, "Our stock is down, but we expected that to happen and we expect it to go back up to its previous level. The reason Food Lion has been so successful is because our customers are happy with the job we're doing." In an effort to stem the company's sliding stock value Tom Smith made a 50-minute conference call to stock analysts charging most of the program's sources lacked credibility and were union sympathizers. He also made a television commercial where he said, in part, "You've heard some shocking stories about Food Lion. We do have sound policies and procedures. However, occasionally a problem can exist." And within the chain itself another public relations strategy was tried. 60,000 video tapes of Food Lion's responses to the broadcast were sent to employees and they were urged to show them to their family, friends, and local groups. Vincent Watkins also suggested that along with the tapes ". . . they might want to have a party with their friends and serve them food from Food Lion's delis."

During the ensuing weeks Food Lion launched a counter-offensive in both the press and via television against what it considered was unfair, careless, and dishonest reporting. As expressed by Vince Watkins, "When unwarranted attacks are made on a company, you don't say, 'We'll take our hit and move on.' You come back with the truth." Food Lion questioned whether the out-of-date meat loaf was actually nine days old as it would have become visibly black to the television cameras after only four days. Various products were displayed in one televised sequence, such as Colombo yogurt and Healthy Choice Lunch meats, which were never carried by Food Lion. Also Beef America products were shown but it was Montford Beef that was shipped 6–7 weeks old in vacuum sealed packages. The time period on those products was well within the allotted 12–14 week freshness period. And in the very damaging barbecue sauce segment the chicken products changed from scene to scene.

Additionally, the union's integrity, as well as the motivations of three of the program's interviewees, were questioned. Sixty-five of the seventy people interviewed by *PrimeTime Live* were supplied by the UFCW and six of the seven people identified in the story were involved in UFCW-initiated lawsuits against Food Lion. Joe Sultan, the former perishables manager, was reprimanded for poor conditions in his department and has been fired for requiring off-the-clock work from his people. Bryan Rogers, while denigrating the company's produce in the telecast, had shopped at a Food Lion the night of the *Prime-Time* program. Jean Bull, who talked about selling slime-covered pork, shops with her family at Food Lion each week. She has been reprimanded for passing bad checks and has a lawsuit against Food Lion.

Numerous legal actions were also begun by Food Lion. The company filed its first suit in connection with the program by charging the network with fraud as ABC's producers lied to Food Lion to get jobs at its stores. Through this lawsuit Food Lion gained access to the program's unedited footage as well as the right to question Lynn Neufer Litt, the segment's producer. As observed by Mike Mozingo, "Some of the things we are finding out from our depositions make it plain to us they engaged in extensive illegal acts and violated state and federal laws in doing so." Accordingly the chain's original suit was amended in April, 1993 with allegations that the network violated federal racketeering laws in conducting its expose. Food Lion now includes in its suit accusations of racketeering, trespassing, illicit eavesdropping, and wire fraud. It was now also allowed to collect triple damages. ABC's response to this emendation noted that "Food Lion does not challenge the truth of the ABC report. It challenges only the undercover methods used by ABC. We believe Food Lion's charges of racketeering are outrageous. We believe this is a legally baseless complaint."

In another lawsuit filed February 12, 1993 against the UFCW, Food Lion alleges the union has waged a smear campaign in an attempt to have it unionized. In seeking actual and punitive damages Food Lion has charged the union with the (1) "abuse of process," (2) use of "economic guerrilla tactics" to tarnish its image, and (3) filing of frivolous lawsuits to obtain proprietary information about company operations and finances.

In the face of all these legal actions some, such as John Small of Fort Worth's Strategic Retail Consulting firm, have questioned the wisdom of Food Lion's public relations strategy. "From a public relations standpoint, they were their own worst enemy. I would have advised a massive *mea culpa* as opposed to the defensive posture that they're taking." Food Lion, however, believes it is pursuing the right strategy and takes comfort in General Motors' vindication after it had been severely damaged in an NBC *Dateline* expose of safety hazards associated with its pickup trucks. Referring to GM's defense, and to television sensationalism in general, Vince Watkins said the debacle only "illustrates that TV tabloid-type programs will go to extraordinary lengths to concoct or stage events."

Although Food Lion has often employed court actions to remedy challenges to its survival, numerous court actions have in turn been begun against it. The company began meeting with the U.S. Labor Department in January, 1993 to head off federal charges of child-labor and overtime violations. These charges resulted from a 183-person class action suit filed on September 11, 1991 with the help of the UFCW. The suit seeks $388.0 million in back pay and damages although none in the action are members of the UFCW. Francis D. Carpenter, who claims to have regularly worked 60- and 70-hour weeks during his seven years at Food Lion's Southern Pine, NC grocery store, said, "It got to the point where I just couldn't take it anymore. My supervisor would always say, 'Do what you have to do to get the job done, but don't let me catch you working off the clock.' I took that to mean 'Work off the clock, but don't get caught.'" In its suit the union concluded employees often worked up to 13 hours a week in such a fashion. Food Lion has already lost one decision of this nature where a North Carolina U.S. District Court Judge ordered Food Lion to pay two former employees a total of $53,000 in overtime wages and damages.

Food Lion is also being investigated by the Labor Department for about 1,400 alleged violations of child-labor laws including 1,200 involving teenagers working with or near potentially dangerous equipment. If the chain is ultimately charged all violations it would be the largest case of its kind involving a single employer. Whereas Food Lion Vice President Vince Watkins did not know the investigation's details he understood that about 90.0% were related to teenagers putting cardboard boxes into package balers that were turned off. He noted the ban on teenagers doing that type of work had gone into effect less than a year ago and the grocery industry as a whole is fighting the ban's breadth. Food Lion's company policy states teenagers must sign statements acknowledging the ban. They must also wear a blue dot on their name tags so they will not be asked to perform forbidden work. Watkins said, "I don't think anybody violated it intentionally and I don't think anyone in management asked them to do it."

FOOD LION'S TULSA OPERATIONS

Over a short period Food Lion opened its seven stores in the Tulsa metropolitan area as shown in Exhibit 17. These stores were built in the city's fastest-growing localities and each faced different combinations of competitors within

EXHIBIT 17
Tulsa Metropolitan
Area

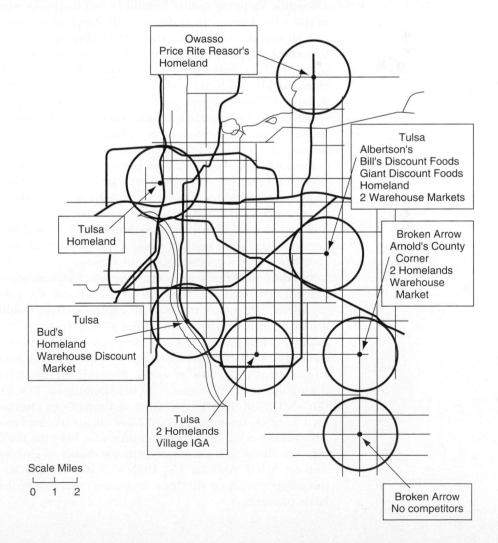

Owasso
Price Rite Reasor's
Homeland

Tulsa
Albertson's
Bill's Discount Foods
Giant Discount Foods
Homeland
2 Warehouse Markets

Tulsa
Homeland

Broken Arrow
Arnold's County
Corner
2 Homelands
Warehouse
Market

Tulsa
Bud's
Homeland
Warehouse Discount
Market

Tulsa
2 Homelands
Village IGA

Scale Miles
0   1   2

Broken Arrow
No competitors

EXHIBIT 18

Food Lion's Supermarket Competition

Company	Stores
Albertson's	4
Bud's Food Stores	4
Consumer's IGA	2
Homeland	25
Payless Food Store	2
Price Mart	3
Price Rite Reasor's Reasor's Foods	2
Super H Discount Foods	5
Warehouse Market	12

a two-mile shopping radius. Exhibit 18 lists the major supermarkets operating in the Tulsa market. In addition to the large number of Warehouse Markets and Homelands blanketing the area, additional competition comes from at least three warehouse clubs and 135 convenience stores.

Food Lion's stores were open from 7:00 am to 11:00 pm and they were clean, well-lit, easily accessed, and utilitarian in their appearance. They were 28,000 to 32,000 square foot stores and cost $1.0–$2.0 million each to construct depending primarily on the real estate values associated with each unit. All were similarly configured as in Exhibit 19 with the only difference being the use of 13 aisles in their smaller Broken Arrow and Owasso stores. The company employed its usual low price strategy which was announced through comparative advertising of the type in Exhibit 20. Well in advance of Food Lion's store openings, however, its competitors had begun cutting prices and featuring cent-off end displays and shelf-specials. Other competitors renewed double redemptions on coupons, a practice that had been previously discontinued in the Tulsa market, while some guaranteed they would match Food Lion's prices on a product-by-product basis.

In addition to the actions taken by other supermarkets Food Lion was also immediately challenged by the UFCW's Local 76. John Stone, the local's president, felt the *PrimeTime Live* expose's effect would be short-lived and would be effective for about three weeks. To keep its message before the public Stone's union mailed "informational literature" to households in each store's ZIP-code area and passed out leaflets at each store's parking lot entrance for a number of weeks. Postcard literature mailed to households during the week of December 3, 1992 headlined "FOOD LION IS FOREIGN OWNED!" and that "Every Dollar in Profit Goes Overseas to Belgium!" The card went on by stating, "Food Lion cheats its employees to gain an illegal advantage over American businessmen who obey the law!" and ended with the message, "Don't let a foreign company dump its garbage on American consumers! SHOP AMERICAN! DON'T SHOP AT FOOD LION!" The leaflet campaign continued the "Buy American" theme and the company's abusive labor practices.

EXHIBIT 19
Typical Tulsa Food Lion Store Layout

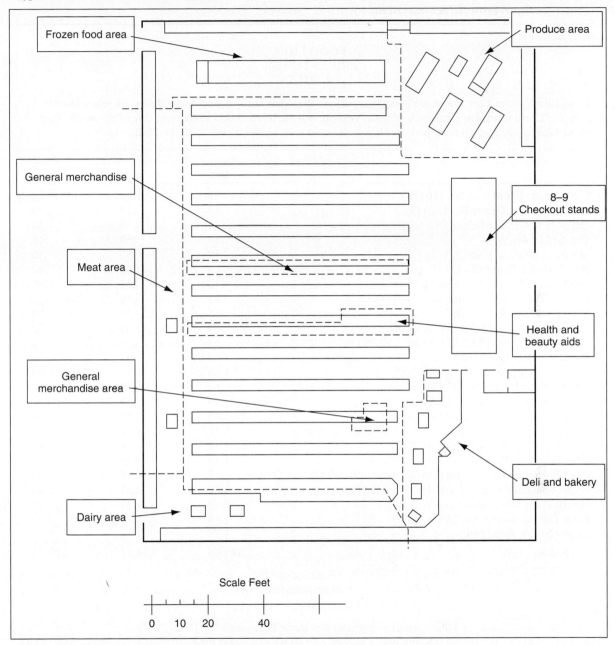

NOTE: All other areas are dedicated to Groceries.

WHAT NOW?

In addressing his company's shareholders Tom Smith acknowledged that problems have arisen over its Southwestern market expansion, of which Tulsa only serves as an example.

EXHIBIT 20

Price Comparison Advertisement

Comparison reveals

FOOD LION
PRICES LOWER
IN TULSA

Food Lion's Extra Low Prices are lower everyday on the items families buy most. Below are just a few examples. These represent thousands of items you can buy for less at Food Lion every day of the week. Visit Food Lion today and discover how much you can save each week on your total food bill.

	Price Mart	Homeland	Food Lion
Libby's Lite Sliced Peaches (16 Oz.)	.89	1.19	.79
Del Monte Cut Green Beans (8 Oz.)	.43	.53	.34
Del Monte Creamed Corn (8.75 Oz.)	.43	.53	.34
Veg All (16 Oz.)	.59	.59	.48
Del Monte Green Peas (8.5 Oz.)	.43	.53	.30
Bush's Baked Beans (16 Oz.)	.69	.69	.50
Van Camp's Beanee Weenees (7.75 Oz.)	.74	.85	.55
Hunt's Whole Peeled Tomatoes (14.5 Oz.)	.73	.79	.48
Mahatma Yello Rice (5 Oz.)	.41	.39	.33
Campbell's Vegetable Soup (10.5 Oz.)	.64	.65	.55
Campbell's Cream of Chicken Soup (10.75 Oz.)	.69	.75	.64
Spam Deviled Spread (3 Oz.)	.59	.65	.56
Underwood's Deviled Ham (4.5 Oz.)	1.29	1.39	1.09
Libby's Vienna Sausages (5 Oz.)	.63	.75	.43
Bush's Hot Chili Beans (16 Oz.)	.49	.55	.38
Franco American Spaghetti (14.75 Oz.)	.65	.69	.50
Franco American Spaghetti O's W/Meatballs (14.75 Oz.)	1.13	1.16	.89
Chef Boyardee Beef-O-Getti (15 Oz.)	1.13	1.16	.89
Chef Boyardee Beef Ravioli (15 Oz.)	1.13	1.16	.79
Chef Boyardee Micro. Spaghetti W/Meatballs (7.5 Oz.)	.99	1.09	.79
Prego Spaghetti Sauce W/Mushrooms (30 Oz.)	1.89	2.27	1.69
Old El Paso Taco Dinner (12/9.75 Oz.)	2.39	2.59	1.99
Kraft Deluxe Macaroni (14 Oz.)	1.69	1.77	1.39
Crisco Shortening (16 Oz.)	1.28	1.39	1.23
TOTALS	$21.95	$24.11	$17.92

America's
Fastest Growing
Supermarket Chain

This price comparison was made December 17, 1992.
Some prices may have changed since that time.

Operating results in this market have been less than originally expected and are significantly below the average for the Company's stores in other markets. We will closely monitor and evaluate performance in this market in light of the Company's performance objectives and will continue to do all things reasonably necessary to increase performance. However, at the present time, the Company does not plan any significant additional growth in the Southwest and is studying alternative strategies for this market.

Asked what Smith's remarks meant, Vince Watkins scoffed at any idea of selling its Southwestern stores along with their 1.1 million square-foot Roanoke, Texas distribution center. "We intend to battle hard for market share out there."

Meanwhile the company disclosed in late-April, 1993 the filing of three shareholder suits against it. One suit alleges Food Lion's top executives conspired to inflate the market price of the company's securities. The second lawsuit maintains executives made misstatements or omissions in its company reports dating back to September, 1991, and the third claims the company's 1992 proxy statement was false and misleading when it failed to disclose the improper food handling procedures documented by *PrimeTime Live*.

APPENDIX A   *How To Handle The Media*

Progressive Grocer has provided a number of general guidelines on how a food chain should handle inquiries from the media. Those guidelines and their rationales are as follows:

1. Be prompt
    If you cannot give an immediate and informed answer to the media do not attempt to stall by replying "No comment" which raises a red flag to most reporters. State you will have to look into the matter and that you will get back as soon as possible with a complete and conversant response.
    Have someone return all media calls as soon as possible. Do not assume by not responding the problem will go away as with or without your company's response the media will run the story regardless.
2. Be informative
    Do not consider the media a collective enemy but instead consider the situation one in which you have an opportunity to explain your side of the story or event.
    Be sure the media understands the conditions under which your industry operates as well as the various pressures to which your firm must respond.
3. Be prepared
    Have a formal program which details how the media will be handled by all store personnel regardless of their position. This formal program is administered best through a public affairs or communications department with individuals assigned to specific media liaison duties.
    Be sure your employees know what they can and cannot say to the media.
4. Don't lie
    Try to determine why the media is interested in your company. The question may be about food retailing in general and your company may have just been a convenient source of information, or it may be about your particular firm and therefore a company-specific response is required.
    If the query is about something negative try to present a positive action that has already commenced, if such is the case, or state that corrective action will be taken if further investigation indicates that such action is required.
    Never lie to reporters as they invariably have more information about the particular issue than you do at the time of the query.

Summarized from Steve Weinstein, "How to Handle the Media," *Progressive Grocer* (September 1991), pp. 90–93.

CASE 4

L.A. Gear, Inc.

A. J. ALMANEY, S. GREEN, S. SLOTKIN, *and* **H. SPEER,** *DePaul University*

OVERVIEW

In February 1989, Robert Y. Greenberg stood on the floor of the New York Stock Exchange and watched as the letters "LA" flashed across the ticker tape for the very first time after L.A. Gear was listed on the Big Board. "It was my proudest moment. It was my dream," Greenberg said. "You see, I always wanted to be the president of a company on the New York Stock Exchange,"[1] he added.

For over 14 years, L.A. Gear promoted the Southern-California lifestyle with attractively styled shoes designed primarily for women. Later, however, the company altered its focus to include products that appealed to the men's performance athletic market. The company continued to produce fashion shoes for women, but its core business became the performance athletic market where sales were not as dependent on swings in consumer tastes. The company achieved its position as the number three brand maker of footwear products when it surpassed Converse, Inc. in 1989. Greenberg set his sights at the number one position in the industry by challenging Nike and Reebok.

However, L.A. Gear began to experience financial difficulties in 1991. Its market share dropped from a high of 12% in 1990, to 8% in 1991, and to 5% in 1992. And its net sales declined from $820 million in 1990, to $619 million in 1991, and to $430 million in 1992. The company incurred losses of $45 million in 1991 and $72 million in 1992. As a result, L.A. Gear was unable to obtain credit from its lenders. To enhance its credit rating, L.A. Gear managed to lure a new investor, Trefoil Capital Investors L.P. who, in September 1991, paid $100 million for a 34% stake in the company.

Since the Trefoil deal, L.A. Gear's internal operations underwent major restructuring. As part of the restructuring, the Trefoil team replaced L.A. Gear's

Presented and accepted by the refereed Midwest Society for Case Research. All rights reserved to the authors and the MSCR. Copyright © 1993 by A. J. Almaney (312) 362–6785.

This case was prepared by A. J. Almaney, S. Green, S. Slotkin, and H. Speer of DePaul University and is intended to be used as a basis for class discussion rather than to illustrate either effective or ineffective handling of the situation.

A. J. Almaney is Professor of Management at DePaul University.

top management—including the company's founder, Robert Y. Greenberg. Stanley P. Gold, managing director of Trefoil Capital Investors L.P., and Mark R. Goldston, former Reebok executive, took over. Gold succeeded Greenberg as the company's new chairman and chief executive officer, and Goldston was appointed president and chief operating officer.

Gold and Goldston developed a survival strategy to nurse the ailing L.A. Gear back to health. At the core of the turnaround strategy was a new advertising campaign built around the theme, "Get in Gear." In an effort to create a clear identity for L.A. Gear, Goldston reorganized product lines into three groups: athletic, lifestyle, and children. The new management also launched a restructuring program aimed at paring the company's costs.

In their letter to the shareholders, Gold and Goldston stated, "We believe that the accomplishments of the past year have laid the groundwork upon which we can build to achieve our ultimate objective—to make L.A. Gear a leader in the footwear industry and one of the most admired companies in America." But, will they be able to accomplish their objective in this highly competitive industry?

HISTORY

Robert Y. Greenberg, L.A. Gear's founder, had a knack for selling. First, it was wigs. Later it was roller skates and jeans for the trendy residents of Venice Beach, California. Then it was sneakers. As one analyst described him, "Greenberg is the quintessential salesman."[2]

Greenberg's story is a 1980s financial fairy tale with a 1990s climax: A street-smart shoemaker who always feared being poor would create a pair of sneakers that brought him fortune. As a kid working in the Brooklyn's family produce business and reading his father's copies of *Forbes* magazine, Greenberg set his sights on starting his own company. He took his first step toward that goal by enrolling in a beauty school. After graduation, he opened a chain of hair salons in Brooklyn in the mid 1960s. Later, he started a wig-importing business. As that venture petered out, Greenberg spotted another trend—fashion jeans—and began importing them from South Korea. By 1979, the jeans business had started to fade, and Greenberg decided to pack up for Southern California.

His next inspiration came soon after his arrival in Los Angeles, as he waited three hours at Venice Beach to rent roller skates for his wife and kids. "I figured the guy must be taking in $4,000 to $5,000 a day," he said. So, Greenberg walked out of that skate shop and immediately plunked $40,000 into his own, which soon expanded to nine locations. Not only did he sell skates through the stores, but he established a skate-manufacturing business. The market for skates quickly soured, though. As a result, Greenberg opened a clothing store on Melrose Avenue which he named L.A. Gear. By 1985, the L.A. Gear store was losing money.

Greenberg started looking for the next trend to ride. Having watched Reebok storm the market a year earlier with its fashionable aerobics shoes, Greenberg went chasing after Reebok with his own candy-colored sneakers, all aimed at a market he knew: trend-conscious teenage girls. In what proved to be a brilliant marketing strategy, he opted to sell his shoes not just to sporting-goods stores but to big department stores like Nordstrom, May Co, and Bullock's. L.A. Gear's big break came the following year, 1987, when Reebok underestimated the demand for its wildly popular black-and-white athletic shoes. Greenberg stepped in to meet the demand by marketing "The Workout," a simple canvas shoe that became the flagship of the company.

During Greenberg's Venice Beach tenure, he had become friends with Sandy Saemann, who was making skating-safety equipment while Greenberg was hawking skates. After Saemann launched his own advertising agency, Greenberg brought him into the company to help craft L.A. Gear's frothy image of sun and sex.

The Greenberg-Saemann combination worked. L.A. Gear soon became a highly profitable operation. Sales mushroomed from $200,000 per month at the beginning of 1985 to 1.8 million per month by mid-year. As the company grew to an operation of 51 employees, it needed outside funds for more development and opted for an initial public offering which was completed on July 1, 1986.

The company used the $16.5 million in proceeds from the offering to fund its growing working capital requirements and to fund a hefty advertising and promotion budget. The initial single style of footwear developed into 150 styles, and L.A. Gear's preeminence in the youth market expanded to include footwear for customers of all ages. In 1986, L.A. Gear launched lines for men, children, and infants and expanded its women's line to include athletic shoes for basketball, aerobics, and crosstrainers.

In 1989, sales rocketed to $617 million from $71 million in 1987, and the company surpassed Converse Inc. to become the nation's third-largest seller of athletic shoes. In 1989, L.A. Gear's stock switched from trading in the over-the-counter market to the Big Board. L.A. Gear's stock price in 1988 was $10.94 with $224 million in sales. By early December 1989, L.A. Gear's stock had climbed more than 178%, more than any Big Board stock.[3] The *Wall Street Journal, Business Week,* and *Fortune Magazine* named L.A. Gear the best performing stock on the New York Stock Exchange in 1989. Greenberg boasted that he would push L.A. Gear past Reebok and Nike by 1991. Mark R. Goldston, L.A. Gear's current president, described the company's early success as a phenomenon achieved by innovative styling and a unique ability to have their ear to the market and respond quickly.

In 1990, however, the company's stock price started to decline, and investors became concerned that L.A. Gear was losing its appeal to fashion-conscious young women. Some analysts marked the beginning of L.A. Gear's troubles with the failure of its Michael Jackson shoes.[4] In 1989, Sandy Saemann, executive vice president, signed a $20 million contract with Michael Jackson for endorsement of a line of black, silver-buckled shoes. But the shoes proved to be a failure. Other signs of trouble included reports of stock selling by insiders as well as the Justice Department's investigation of alleged underpayment of custom duties.[5]

In April 1991, L.A. Gear posted a fiscal first-quarter loss of $12.5 million. Sales fell 8.8% to $171 million from $187 million. L.A. Gear posted a tangible net worth of $193 million as of February 28, 1991.[6]

In May 1991, L.A. Gear agreed to sell a 30% stake to Roy E. Disney's Trefoil Capital Investors L.P. for $100 million. Under the agreement, Trefoil would also receive three seats on L.A. Gear's board of directors and the opportunity to have first option to buy shares of Greenberg's 3.5 million in common shares should Greenberg decide to sell. L.A. Gear also agreed to hire Disney's Shamrock Capital Advisors Inc. as consultants for three years, paying fees of $500,000 the first year, $600,000 the second year, and $700,000 the third year.

Shortly after the Trefoil agreement was initiated, Sandy Saemann—a flamboyant, gold–chain decked executive vice president—resigned. Saemann was the architect of L.A. Gear's sexy marketing campaign which often featured scantily clad models. He was also credited with gathering celebrity endorsers for L.A. Gear. Saemann agreed to provide consulting services to L.A. Gear for 2.5 years. Analysts said Saemann resigned because his flamboyant personality conflicted with the Trefoil team.[7] Kevin Ventrudo, 32, senior vice president of administration and a board member, also resigned. Mark R. Goldston succeeded Robert Greenberg as president. Greenberg remained chairman and chief executive.

On January 27, 1992, Robert Greenberg, L.A. Gear's founder, was eased out as chairman and chief executive and a director, along with Gil N. Schwartzberg, vice chairman. Stanley P. Gold, 50, managing director of Trefoil was appointed as the new chairman and chief executive officer of L.A. Gear.

BOARD OF DIRECTORS

As shown in Exhibit 1, the board of directors was composed of 11 members. Three of them were insiders, while the others were outsiders. One of the outside directors was a woman, Ann E. Meyers, who worked as a sports commentator. The chairman of the board was Stanley P. Gold who also served as the chief executive officer (CEO) of the firm. The board carried out its duties through the Executive and Nominating Committees. The Executive Committee consisted of Stanley Gold, R. Rudolph Reinfrank, and Mark Goldston. Reinfrank served as chairman of the Executive Committee. The Nominating Committee consisted of Stephen A. Koffler, Robert G. Moskowitz and Mark Goldston. Koffler served as the chairman of the Nominating Committee.

TOP MANAGEMENT

L.A. Gear's top management underwent major changes since the consummation of Trefoil's $100 million investment in the company. Below is a profile of each of the key executives.

Stanley P. Gold: Stanley Gold, 50 years old, succeeded Greenberg as chairman and chief executive officer of L.A. Gear, Inc. Formerly, he was president and chief executive officer of Shamrock Holdings, Inc., a Burbank, California-based company wholly owned by the Roy Disney Family. Gold was considered to be a turnaround expert. He proved himself by helping revive Walt Disney Co., oil driller Enterra, and soybean processor Central Soyal. Prior to assuming his positions at Shamrock, Gold was a managing partner of Gange, Tyre, Ramer & Brown, Inc., a prominent Los Angeles law firm he joined in 1968. For a number of years, he specialized in corporate acquisitions, sales, and financing. Earlier in his legal career, he served as a trial lawyer in major corporate and civil litigation.[8]

A native of Los Angeles, California, Gold first studied at the University of California at Berkeley and subsequently graduated from the University of California at Los Angeles with an A.B. degree in political science. After receiving

EXHIBIT 1

L.A. Gear's Board of Directors

Stanley P. Gold
Chairman of the Board and Chief Executive Officer
L.A. Gear, Inc.
President and Managing Director
Trefoil Investors, Inc. and Shamrock Capital
  Advisors, Inc.

Mark R. Goldston
President and Chief Operating Officer
L.A. Gear, Inc.

Richard W. Schubert
General Counsel and Secretary
L.A. Gear, Inc.

Alan E. Dashling
Chairman of the Board and Chief Executive Officer
Sterling West Bancorp.

Willie D. Davis
President and Chief Executive Officer
All-Pro Broadcasting

Stephen A. Koffler
Executive Vice President and Director of
  Investment Banking
Sutro & Co., Inc.

Ann E. Meyers
Sports Commentator
KMPC Radio, Prime Ticket, ESPN,
  Sportschannel, and ABC

Clifford A. Miller
Chairman
The Clifford Group, Inc.

Robert G. Moskowitz
Managing Director
Trefoil Investors, Inc. and Shamrock Capital
  Advisors, Inc.

R. Rudolph Reinfrank
Executive Vice President
Shamrock Holdings, Inc.

Vappalak A. Ravindran
Chief Executive Officer
Paracor Company
President
Elders Finance, Inc.

SOURCE: L.A. Gear, *1992 Annual Report*, p. 29.

his J.D. degree from the University of Southern California Law School in 1967, he did postgraduate work at Cambridge University in England.[9] Gold's professional and civic affiliations included the American Bar Association and the Copyright Society. He served as a guest lecturer at the Wharton School at the University of Pennsylvania. He was Chairman of the Board of Governors of Hebrew Union College, a Trustee of the Center Theater Group in Los Angeles, The George C. Marshall Foundation, and a member of the USC Law Center Board of Councilors.

Mark R. Goldston: Mark Goldston, 38 years old, succeeded Robert Y. Greenberg, the company's founder, as president and chief operating officer. Greenberg was also eased out as chairman, chief executive, and a director at a board meeting in an apparent effort by the company's largest investor, Trefoil Capital Investors L.P., to bury the "old" L.A. Gear.[10] Despite Greenberg's assertions that "the company is left in great hands," the ouster capped a four-month battle between the laid-back Greenberg and the buttoned-down Trefoil team for the soul of L.A. Gear.[11]

Goldston was a principal of Odyssey partners, a leverage buyout and investment firm. At Odyssey, Goldston was part of an internal operating unit that supervised the management of certain portfolio companies. His responsibilities included the development, execution, and management of operating plans and the evaluation of strategic alternatives for those portfolio companies. Prior to joining Odyssey, Goldston was senior and chief marketing officer of Reebok International, Ltd. where he spearheaded the marketing effort for "The Pump," a $500 million line of athletic footwear products. As one of the inventors of the Reebok "Visible Energy Return System Technology," Goldston was on the U.S. patent for that technology. Additionally, Goldston was involved in the development of the Hexalite and Energaire product lines for Reebok. Prior to joining Reebok, Goldston was president of Faberge USA, Inc., a cosmetics and personal care products company. During his tenure there, the company's U.S. sales increased about 50%.

Goldston was on the J.L. Kellogg Graduate School of Management Dean's Advisory Board at Northwestern University. In addition, he sat on the board of directors of Revel/Monogram, Inc., ABCO Markets, and Collection Clothing Corp. Goldston's book, entitled *The Turnaround Prescription*, detailing a step-by-step blueprint for effecting a corporate marketing turnaround was published in 1992.[12]

In his new position as president and chief operating officer, Goldston brought in fresh talent by hiring former Reebok employees—Gordie Nye, Robert Apatoff and Christopher Walsh. Gordie Nye, Vice President of Marketing Athletic Footwear, joined the company in December 1991. Previously, he was at Reebok where he was Senior Director of Fitness Marketing, with responsibility for marketing men's and women's fitness products.

Christopher Walsh: Christopher Walsh was 43 years old. He joined L.A. Gear as senior vice president of operations in December 1991. Previously, he was vice president of production at Reebok for three years, where he was in charge of worldwide supply sources. Prior to joining Reebok, he spent two years at Toddler University, a children's shoe manufacturer as vice president of operations. Prior to that, he worked as a senior consultant for Kurt Satmon Associates for two years, focusing on strategic planning. Earlier in his career, he worked at Nike for ten years in production and sourcing.[13]

William L. Benford: William L. Benford, 50 years old, was appointed chief financial officer in September 1991.[14] Prior to that, he was senior vice president and chief financial officer of Central Soya company. Before that he was vice president and treasurer of Dekalb, Inc. He was also affiliated with Shamrock Holdings, Inc., an investment company for the Roy E. Disney Family. Shamrock Holdings, Inc. bought Central Soya company in 1985, turned it around, and sold the company two years later at a profit of about $125 million.

MISSION

L.A. Gear defined its mission as follows:

The Company's principal business activity involves the design, development, and marketing of a broad range of quality athletic and casual/lifestyle footwear. Since its inception, the Company has expanded its product line from its original concentration on fashionable women's footwear to diversified collections of footwear for men, women, and children. The Company is organized into two primary marketing divisions: Athletic (including men's and women's basketball, fitness, walking, tennis, and aerobics) and Lifestyle (casual footwear styles intended for non-athletic use). All of the Company's footwear products are manufactured to its specifications by independent producers located primarily in South Korea, Indonesia, Taiwan and the People's Republic of China.[15]

OBJECTIVES AND STRATEGIES

L.A. Gear's short-term objective was to streamline its operations over the next two years. In the long-term, the company would attempt to achieve the following objectives:

- To provide a broad range of quality athletic and casual/lifestyle footwear, primarily in the "mid" price range (i.e., $30 to $65 retail).
- To improve relations with, and increase shelf space at, full-margin retailers.
- To improve production and quality control practices.
- To increase international sales and profitability.

In attaining these objectives, L.A. Gear adopted a retrenchment/turnaround strategy that involved a comprehensive restructuring of its operations. Thus, in 1992 the company's staff was reduced by 613 employees, or about 45%. In addition, the company reduced its occupancy of about 200,000 square feet of leased office space in five buildings to about 116,000 square feet in two buildings. Further, the general and administrative expenses were reduced in 1992 by $42.7 million, or 21.2%, to $158.7 million from $201.4 million in 1991. The company also discontinued its apparel marketing and design operations which had a pre-tax operating loss of $14.2 million in 1991.

The company's restructuring was augmented with a product development strategy. The product strategy involved developing a broad range of innovative new products for the athletic, lifestyle, and children's line. Grouping products into three well identified divisions was well received by analysts of the footwear industry. Bob McAllister, West Coast market editor for *Footwear News,* said, "In the past, there was no rhyme or reason to L.A. Gear's different styles. Now, the company has introduced new lines that are cleanly divided into athletic, lifestyles and kids."[16]

The company also sought to differentiate its products from its competitors. Goldston was confident that L.A. Gear would increase its market share by using materials in a unique way to carve a specific niche for its products. According to Goldston, "L.A. Gear is committed to designing shoes that do not resemble its competition."[17] While pursuing retrenchment and product development strategies, L.A. Gear launched a marketing campaign that focused on projecting a consistent brand image across varying retail price points and distribution channels.

PRODUCTION

L.A. Gear's footwear was manufactured to its specifications by independent producers located primarily in The People's Republic of China, Indonesia, South Korea, and Taiwan. In 1992, manufacturers in these countries supplied 34%, 32%, 30%, and 4% of total pairs of footwear purchased by the company respectively.

The footwear products imported into the U.S. by the company were subject to customs duties, ranging from 6% to 48% of production costs. Duty rates depended on the construction of the shoe and whether the principal component was leather or some other material.

The use of foreign manufacturing facilities subjected the company to the customary risks of doing business abroad, including fluctuations in the value of currencies, export duties, import controls, trade barriers, restrictions on the transfer of funds, work stoppage, and political instability. Thus far, these factors, however, did not seem to have had an adverse impact on the company's operations.

PRODUCTS

L.A. Gear's product lines were organized into three marketing categories: Athletic, Lifestyle, and Children's. Athletic footwear included fitness, walking, tennis, cross-training, and basketball shoes, as well as the recently introduced Light Gear CrossRunner and Dance Training shoes. These products were marketed under two brand names: L.A. Gear, with suggested domestic retail prices under $70; and L.A. Tech, the newly released, which were a higher priced premium brand.

The Lifestyle lines included men's and women's casual footwear styles that included the Street Hiker, Vintage Series, and Fashion Athletic and Casual Collections. The Children's footwear incorporated features from the Athletic and Lifestyle lines plus products specifically developed for children. L.A. Lights, lighted shoes for children introduced in June 1992, became one of the largest selling children's shoes in the company's history. The age of the company's target market for the adult products was 14 to 35 years, and for children 5 to 13.[18] Some of L.A. Gear's products and the technologies incorporated in the Athletic, Lifestyle, and Children's lines are described in Exhibit 2.

PRODUCT QUALITY

In 1990, L.A. Gear committed a grave marketing blunder in the process of launching its new line of basketball shoes. In a scramble to launch the new shoes, the company outfitted the Marquette University team with handmade pairs, since molds were not completed yet for the large sizes the team members required. As TV cameras zeroed in on one player, the bottom of his sneaker peeled away from the top. This and other cases of poor quality served to seriously tarnish the company's brand image. In an effort to improve quality, L.A. Gear reduced the number of foreign manufacturers from 44 in 1991 to 29 in 1992, retaining only those known for their quality products. The company also engaged a "sourcing" agent with the responsibility of inspecting finished goods prior to shipment by the manufacturer, supervising production management, and facilitating the shipment of goods.

ADVERTISING

Sandy Saemann, Greenberg's second in command, was the architect of L.A. Gear's early advertising campaign. His success in signing such celebrities as Paula Abdul and Kareem Abdul–Jabbar was responsible for the phenomenal increase in the company's sales between 1985 and 1990. Saemann fit the image of the laid-back California executive perfectly—right down to the silver necklace. And his flamboyant vision proved perfect for peddling flashy sneakers.

EXHIBIT 2

L.A. Gear's Products and Their Technologies

Athletic	Description
Catapult	A midsole system consisting of a carbon graphite spring to provide cushioning and shock absorption
Encapsole Air	A cushioning system which uses air chambers built into the outsole to provide shock absorption
Light Gear	Shoes incorporating battery–powered lights in the outsole that flash upon impact

Lifestyle	Description
Street Hiker	A light-weight casual hiking shoe
Vintage Series	Footwear based on classic athletic styles

Children's	Description
L.A. Gear (Galactica for boys; L.A. Twilight for girls; Nightcrawlers for infants)	Shoes incorporating motion activated battery–powered lights in the outsole that flash with movement
Regulator	Shoes with an adjustable fit and support system using an air inflation device to cushion the foot over the midfoot area
Bendables	Flexible shoes for infants
Clear Gear	Shoes with a clear outsole in flexible plastic with an assortment of designs printed on the midsole

SOURCE: L.A. Gear, *1992 10-K Form,* p. 4.

Saemann represented L.A. Gear's brash, entrepreneurial roots by producing virtually all of the company's ads and commercials himself without the help of Madison Avenue. However, L.A. Gear's tumble began, ironically, with its biggest advertising deal ever. In 1989, Saemann was able to sign megastar Michael Jackson in what was described as the largest endorsement contract ever: $20 million. L.A. Gear had hoped to time the release of a new line of shoes to an upcoming Michael Jackson greatest-hits album, but the album never materialized. Teenagers everywhere thumbed their noses at the black, buckle–laden shoes. The company was eventually forced to discontinue the entire line, taking a loss of several million dollars.

Since the failure of the Michael Jackson advertising campaign, L.A. Gear stopped contracting for the endorsement of its products by entertainment celebrities. Instead, the company chose to contract endorsements with athletic stars such as Karl "The Mailman" Malone of the Utah Jazz, Hakeem Olajuwon of the Houston Rockets, and Joe Montana of the San Francisco Forty-Niners. A new slogan, "Get in Gear," was used in the campaign.

Under the new management, L.A. Gear changed the focus of many of its advertising campaigns from promoting a fashionable shoe to promoting a performance shoe. Performance was emphasized with the advertisement tag line for the Catapult performance shoe, "It's not just a shoe, it's a machine."[19] L.A. Gear's most successful commercial was the use of the tag line "Anything else is just hot air" to promote the Catapult shoe, with its hightech, carbon-fiber soles. The ad was an indirect attack at Nike who made the Air Jordan shoes, endorsed by Chicago Bulls' star Michael Jordan. NBC refused to run the television ads, and the ensuing exposure received by coverage of NBC's refusal was worth millions to L.A. Gear.[20] In promoting the $110 Catapult shoe, the new management decided to drop the L.A. Gear logo, believing that the L.A. Gear name was a liability in performance shoes.

The new management team subdivided the marketing of the company's products on the basis of price. Shoes costing less than $70 per pair retained the L.A. Gear name and logo, and shoes priced over $70 per pair carried the L.A. Tech name. L.A. Gear's management believed that the L.A. Tech name would help establish the line as a high technology and performance product. The lowest-cost L.A. Gear shoe retailed for approximately $30 per pair, whereas the top of the line L.A. Tech shoe, the Catapult, topped out at about $150 per pair.[21] L.A. Gear's budget amounted to between 10% to 15% of total sales.

RESEARCH AND DEVELOPMENT

In designing its products, L.A. Gear conducted comprehensive market research, using a variety of conventional research techniques. Primarily, the company depended on focus groups, product testing, and interviews with consumers and retailers. These methods allowed the company to accurately gauge the image and reputation of L.A. Gear's products and to incorporate changes demanded by the public.

SALES

The phenomenal rise in L.A. Gear's sales between 1985 and 1990 was due to Greenberg's ability to create a clear-cut image for the company with brightly colored shoes and sexy ads aimed at teenage girls. The company's spectacular success led Greenberg to set a higher objective for the company, $1 billion in sales. To achieve this objective, Greenberg tried to challenge Nike and Reebok directly by adding a line of men's performance shoes. The move was too much, too fast. Venturing into the men's performance shoes blurred L.A. Gear's image. According to one analyst, "When L.A. Gear moved into the performance side, it lost its way." Greenberg, however, was unwilling to lay the company's problems on the men's shoes. Instead, he maintained that "in any battle you're gonna get a little bruised or battered. And we're playing with a couple of billion-dollar companies that don't need us around."

The rapid growth also placed an enormous strain on the company. Employees had to push hard to attain the new growth objective. As a result, the company's internal controls got out of hand. A shareholders' class action lawsuit called those controls "chaotic and virtually nonexistent."

As a result of the relentless push for fast growth, product-quality problems, and the attendant bad publicity, L.A. Gear saw its share of the overall athletic shoe market drop from a high of 12% in 1990 to 5% in 1992. The company net sales, as shown in Exhibit 3, declined from $820 in 1990 to $619 in 1991 and to $430 in 1992. The 1992 sales figure represented a 31% decline from 1991. The company incurred losses of $72 million in 1992 and $45 million in 1991. Net international sales, which accounted for about 28% of the company's total net sales, decreased by 6.7% from 1991.

According to management, the overall decline in net sales for 1992 was principally due to a drop in the number of pairs sold worldwide resulting from

EXHIBIT 3

Net Sales (dollars in thousands)

	1992		1991		1990	
	$	%	$	%	$	%
Domestic Footwear						
Women's	112,990	26	178,481	29	285,709	35
Men's	104,593	24	176,238	28	196,969	24
Children's	90,997	21	134,485	22	174,486	21
Other	2,688	1	2,517	—	4,217	1
Total Domestic Net Sales	311,268	72	491,721	79	661,381	81
International Footwear	118,926	28	127,454	21	158,220	19
Total Net Sales	430,194	100	619,175	100	819,601	100

SOURCE: L.A. Gear, *1992 10-K Form*, p. 5.

decreased customer demand, and, to a lesser extent, to an average decrease of $1.52 in the selling price per pair. The decline was also due to the continuing effects of the recession and price reductions by the company's principal competitors, which resulted in increased competition at lower prices.

Another factor that contributed to the drop in the 1992 sales volume was delivery delays. As part of its restructuring program in 1992, the company changed the manufacturers from which it purchased products. These changes contributed to the company's difficulties in meeting its delivery deadlines on orders for its back-to school season.

INTERNATIONAL STRATEGY

In recent years, sales of athletic and casual/lifestyle footwear in many international markets grew at a faster rate than in the United States. However, L.A. Gear's own sales in the international market declined from $158 million in 1990, to $127 million in 1991, and to $119 million in 1992.

In an effort to stem this decline in sales, L.A. Gear decided to increase its investment in the international market through joint ventures, acquisitions of distributors, and the creation of wholly-owned foreign subsidiaries. By selling its products directly abroad (as opposed to the company's historical reliance on independent distributors in those markets), the company sought to increase sales by adopting more competitive marketing and distribution programs. In March 1992, the company established its first foreign subsidiary to conduct direct sales of its products in France.

L.A. Gear also began to focus on Asia for its potential as a retail sales market. "We see Asia as a huge market. You have basically got two billion pairs of feet out here," said Goldston. Consequently, the company began investigating promotional alliances and equity partnerships with Asian companies.

DISTRIBUTION

L.A. Gear distributed its products out of a one million square foot warehouse/distribution center in Ontario, California. The company's products were sold in the U.S. to about 4,000 distributors that included department, sporting goods, athletic footwear and shoe stores, and wholesale distributors.

In recent years, L.A. Gear relied on extensive distribution through whole-sale distributors who sold into deep-discount outlets. This policy tarnished the company's image and, as a result, several key retail accounts ceased or reduced their business with the company in 1991. To improve relations with full-margin retailers, the company began to distribute its products through specific channels, using what it called the "Gear Strategy Classification System." In line with this system, distribution channels were grouped in terms of "Image," "Mainstream," "Volume," and "Value." The Image channels were used to market the most technologically advanced and expensive high-performance products such as the L.A. Tech. The Mainstream and Volume channels were used to market "2nd Gear" and "1st Gear" products which incorporated fewer technological and aesthetic features. The Value channels were intended only for the distribution of inventory that could not be sold through the other channels. As part of the Value channels, the company planned to open a limited number of outlet stores.

Under Greenberg, the company maintained a next-day (at once) open stock system, where retailers could order products and have them shipped within 24 hours. This system forced inventory expenses to skyrocket. To mitigate this problem, the company also adopted a "futures" ordering system which provided discounts to retailers who ordered products four to six months in advance of shipment. It was hoped that the new program would enable the company to improve inventory management.

Internationally, L.A. Gear distributed its product in about 60 countries, primarily through agreements with independent distributors. The distribution agreements were intended to maintain a consistent product offering and brand image throughout the world. However, this arrangement afforded the company little or no control over the ultimate retail price of its footwear. It also restricted both profit and growth potential.

RESEARCH AND DEVELOPMENT

L.A. Gear maintained close ties with firms that conducted basic materials research. For example, L.A. Gear had an alliance with U.T.I. Chemicals Corporation of California. U.T.I. developed a new outsole material known as Z-thane which was a patented plastic compound that outlasted similar materials already in the marketplace.[22] L.A. Gear also applied older materials to their shoe lines, such as the innovative use of carbon fiber heel protectors in its performance shoes. With the Catapult, L.A. Gear hoped to challenge the high performance image of Nike and Reebok by luring the performance oriented buyer away from these market leaders.

L.A. Gear, however, lagged behind its competitors in product innovation. For example, the company introduced a "pump" style shoe almost two years after Nike and Reebok introduced their versions of this technology. Ironically, former CEO Robert Greenberg once boasted that the company spent a fraction of what its competition spent on research and development.[23] The company's "catch-up" R&D practices damaged its relations with retailers. For example, one shoe buyer to a large department-store chain said: "We saw Nike and Reebok 1993 spring lines in May or June of 1992 and started committing for product in July. We didn't see L.A. Gear's product until mid-August."[24]

HUMAN RESOURCES

L.A. Gear employs 753 full-time employees. In 1991, the company embarked on a restructuring program to reduce its workforce. By 1992, 613 employees ceased employment with the company, 152 of whom were associated with the company's discontinued apparel design and marketing operations. This represented a 45% reduction in staff and reduced the company's monthly payroll expense from $4.8 million in 1991 to $3.4 million in 1992. The company's employees were not covered by any collective bargaining agreement, but management considered the company's relations with its employees to be satisfactory. The company offered its employees 401(k) retirement savings programs and had an employee stock option plan (ESOP) in place. The ESOP program was instituted as an incentive program for employees and management.

COMMUNICATION AND CORPORATE CULTURE

As L.A. Gear grew bigger, it had to hire more employees to handle the new functions. In 1985, 50 people turned out the product; by 1992, that figure swelled to 1,200. As a result, the company which was characterized by an informal communication system and corporate culture, splintered into departmental fiefdoms scattered in several buildings. The new structure eroded the informal relationships that existed among L.A. Gear's management and employees. In the early days, for instance, Greenberg and Saemann worked just across the hall from each other, and their basic form of communication was to yell back and forth. Greenberg, who had a passion for tropical fish and kept a large tank in his office, would often march across the hall to see Saemann with a dripping net in one hand and a new sneaker design in the other.

The new management brought with it buttoned-down seriousness. Coats and ties were now a regular sight at L.A. Gear. Gone were the days when Greenberg would slip each of his employees $100 bills in pink envelopes whenever the company turned a profit. Now, employees carried around black coffee mugs that read ATTACK BUSINESS COSTS.

LEGAL ISSUES

In 1990 and 1991, three class action lawsuits were brought against L.A. Gear by shareholders. The shareholders claimed that the company violated the U.S. securities laws by inflating sales by tens of millions of dollars in 1990 when it counted as revenues merchandise that was being stored in L.A. Gear's warehouses and docks. In settling these lawsuits, the company recorded a $23 million pre-tax charge against its 1992 earnings.

In October 1992, L.A. Gear reached an agreement with the U.S. Attorney for the District of Massachusetts regarding the resolution of all customs claims arising from the importation of footwear from Taiwan in 1986 and 1987. Accordingly, L.A. Gear entered a guilty plea with respect to two counts charging underpayment of duties on such shipments. A sentencing hearing was scheduled in 1993. In addition, the company paid $1.3 million in settlement of all potential civil claims arising from underpayment of duties on the 1986 and 1987 shipments from Taiwan.

In November 1992, L.A. Gear settled a patent infringement lawsuit brought against it by Reebok International Ltd, alleging that certain footwear products marketed by the company infringed on a patent issued to Reebok covering "inflatable bladder" shoe technology. L.A. Gear paid Reebok $1 million to settle the lawsuit. As part of the settlement, L.A. Gear entered into a license agreement under which Reebok granted the company a four-year non-exclusive worldwide license to manufacture, use, and sell footwear utilizing the "inflatable bladder." The license agreement, however, did not grant L.A. Gear access to Reebok's technology.

Another legal issue involved L.A. Gear's relationship with entertainer Michael Jackson. In September 1992, the company filed a complaint against Jackson alleging, among other things, fraud, breach of contract, and breach of good faith. The company's claims arose from contracts between the company and the defendant which granted the company the exclusive right to use Jackson's name and likeness in advertising and promoting the company's shoes and apparel as well as the right to develop and market a Michael Jackson athletic shoe line. Michael Jackson countered with a lawsuit, alleging fraud and breach of good faith on the part of the company. No settlement of this dispute has been reached yet.

FINANCE AND ACCOUNTING

L.A. Gear's gross profit declined from $286 million in 1990, to $170 million in 1991, and to $109 million in 1992. While the company earned a net income of $31 million in 1990, it lost $66 million and $72 million in 1991 and 1992 respectively.

Because of an imbalance between inventory purchases and sales, L.A. Gear accumulated inventory greater than that necessary for its business. The introduction of the company's new product lines also resulted in a greater number of styles being discontinued than would otherwise have been the case. As a result, as part of an inventory reduction program, the company sold inventory at significant discounts resulting in lower margins. As was the custom in the footwear industry, substantial changes to the current product lines were made at least twice a year (i.e., for the spring and back-to-school seasons). As a result, a certain number of styles were usually discontinued.

In September 1991, Trefoil Capital Investors, L.P. invested $100 million in L.A. Gear in the form of a new issue of Series A Cumulative Convertible Preferred Stock, the net proceeds of which were used to repay indebtedness. In November 1992, the company had cash and cash equivalent balances of $84 million. In addition, the company expected to receive income tax refunds in 1993 of about $25 million.

INDUSTRY

The U.S. general footwear market was valued at about $12 billion. The athletic shoe market comprised about $6 billion. According to *Footwear News*, the domestic retail shoe market was expected to continue to grow at a rate of 5.5% at least until the year 2000.[25]

A 1987 Census of Manufactures conducted by the U.S. Bureau of the Census revealed that over 100 companies participated in the men's and women's footwear industries.[26] During 1992 there were two dozen companies competing in the U.S. branded footwear market.[27] Domestically, the two largest athletic shoe makers were Nike and Reebok with a combined share of the market totaling 50%.[28] Although Nike and Reebok, as well as L.A. Gear, were head-quartered in the U.S., the majority of their products was manufactured in Asian, European, and South American countries. A shoe that retailed for $100 cost the company between $20 and $25 if manufactured in foreign countries. Markups to the retailer and consumer were nearly 100%.

The footwear industry was not cyclical but did show some seasonality with back-to-school sales in August and September. Although profitability and sales for footwear companies fluctuated, these fluctuations were attributable not to economic cycles but to changes in advertising expenditures, price, product quality, and overall market trends such as consumer preferences for fashion versus performance shoes.

Entry into the footwear industry was rather difficult. This was due to the fact that success in this industry depended to a great extent on heavy advertising, brand awareness, and intensive research and development. In the high-performance athletic shoe market, advertising was critical to footwear producers as a means of promoting new styles and creating brand awareness. Footwear companies spent vast sums to get popular athletes to endorse certain shoes. Nike and Reebok, for example, spent $200 million on advertising and promotion in 1992. This medium was cost prohibitive to smaller firms whose revenues were often too small to mount effective marketing campaigns. Another barrier to entry was brand awareness. Consumers purchased shoes based on either how well they perceived a brand to perform or on its fashion characteristics. On the average, when selecting a shoe, men tended to look at sole cushioning and how well an inner structure supported the foot—not fashion or style. Women's purchases, however, were determined more by the design or style of the shoe.[29]

An even greater entry barrier in the footwear industry was the excessive capital required for research and development. Nike, Reebok, and L.A. Gear allocated large budgets toward R&D. Each of the top three competitors had a highly advanced technology. Nike had its Air Jordan; Reebok had the Pump and Insta Pump; and L.A. Gear had its Catapult and Regulator shoes that incorporated high-tech carbon fiber soles.

In the highly competitive discount-athletic footwear market, barriers to entry were less formidable. Volume companies (mass producers) tended to carve out a niche through brands they licensed or created on their own. According to Footwear News, "the mass market usually followed where the better-grade merchandise had already beaten a path. Volume sources capitalized on the consumer appetite for branded-athletic footwear generated by the sophisticated marketing of companies such as Nike, Reebok, and L.A. Gear." According to the Sporting Goods Manufacturers Association, discount stores commanded $3.4 billion of the athletic shoe market.[30]

The U.S. footwear industry was maturing and analysts expected that consumers would purchase more non-athletic footwear than athletic footwear. With the domestic market maturing, many footwear companies began expanding overseas where the market was expected to grow at a rate of 23% a year in the next decade.[31]

The appeal of overseas markets to U.S. footwear companies stemmed not only from their sheer size but also from the cheap advertising common in such markets. Furthermore, a growing number of consumers overseas were becoming increasingly interested in U.S. sports generally and in basketball in particular. Actually, U.S. basketball was now a close second to soccer in worldwide popularity.[32] As a result, footwear companies discovered that their big endorsers, like Michael Jordan for Nike, translated well across borders.

COMPETITORS

The athletic and athletic-style footwear industry was highly competitive in the U.S. and on a worldwide basis. L.A. Gear's competitors included both specialized athletic shoe companies and companies with diversified footwear product lines. The company's primary competitors in the domestic athletic and athletic-style markets were Nike and Reebok. These companies were more established than L.A. Gear and had greater financial, distribution, and marketing resources, as well as greater brand awareness, than the company. Internationally, L.A. Gear's major competitor was Adidas. Below is a brief profile of each of L.A. Gear's major competitors.

Nike: Nike was a publicly held sports and fitness company with a 26% share of the domestic market. Nike was the first company in the sports and fitness industry to exceed $2 billion in U.S. revenues and $3 billion worldwide. The company accomplished this in 1991. The diversity of Nike's product lines was far reaching. The company designed and marketed athletic footwear, apparel, and related items for competitive and recreational uses. To promote this breadth of product line, Nike was successful with advertisements that used high-profile athletes. Nike had an impressive stable of endorsers with Michael Jordan, Bo Jackson, David Robinson, and Andre Agassi. The success of these advertising campaigns enabled Nike to command a higher price for its shoes than its competitors.

To add to their image as one of the premier athletic footwear companies, Nike began to open a series of high-tech futuristic looking, company-owned outlets around the world called Nike Town. This outlet was a tribute to Nike's innovative flair and marketing genius.[33] The design concept incorporated sports, fitness, entertainment, history, and product innovation.

Nike spent more than its competitors on research and development. Nike learned the hard way to push its technology. In 1987, Nike was surpassed by rival Reebok as the number one domestic footwear company. At this time, Nike was concentrating on marketing its apparel and fashion shoes instead of promoting its air cushioning system. Within eighteen months of being surpassed by Reebok, Nike regained the number one spot by marketing its Nike Air Jordan shoes. Now, Nike's engineers began to call the shots—not its fashion designers.

Reebok: Reebok International Ltd. was a designer and marketer of active lifestyle and performance products, including footwear and apparel. Reebok held 24% of the domestic footwear market. According to industry sources, Reebok was the company best positioned to take advantage of the developing worldwide sneaker market.[34] Reebok announced in early 1992 that it had established a new worldwide sports marketing unit and that it would spend 25% more on advertising. Additionally, international sales soared 75% to $832.6 million from $475.2 in 1990. The sports marketing unit worked in conjunction with the fitness and casual units to deliver the best products and programs to consumers and retailers worldwide.

In 1988, Reebok acquired Avia and Rockport—two fast-growing companies. Paul Fireman, chairman and chief executive officer, believed that Avia and Rockport exemplified a "sense of aliveness" which was a characteristic of Reebok.[35] In 1991, Avia's sales rose 4.3% to $161 million, and Rockport's sales grew 8.5% to $251.3 million. Rockport produced products primarily for the walking shoe market while Avia competed directly with the Reebok brand for the athletic footwear market.

Reebok replaced its ineffective advertising with a cause-related campaign aimed at supporting philanthropic organizations while promoting its own products. In 1990, industry sources noted that Reebok was lacking a winning advertising campaign. In that year, two consecutive advertising campaigns flopped. In 1991 and 1992, Reebok reversed this trend with its cause-related advertising. Practitioners maintained that cause-related advertising could be risky, but when handled carefully, could supply the best of all promotional worlds: higher visibility, a unique image niche resulting from association with worthy projects, and stronger ties to the community.[36] As part of its cause-related marketing, Reebok gave financial support to Amnesty International's Human Rights Now tour. Angel Martinez, Vice President of business development at Reebok's Los Angeles office, said that, "the tour was an extension of our value system as a company. We believe in freedom of expression and wanted to do something of importance, beyond selling sneakers."[37] Reebok's President, Joseph LaBonte, added: "We both believe very strongly in the freedom to do what you want."

To remain competitive with Nike, Reebok also planned to contract endorsements with high-profile athletes. Even though the Insta-Pump would not be available to consumers until January 1993, Reebok hoped to get a lot of promotional mileage by putting the shoes on several Olympic track-and-field stars at the 1992 summer games in Barcelona, Spain.

Adidas and Puma: A decade ago, most athletic shoes sold in Europe were made by Adidas or its smaller rival, Puma. For years, the two German companies controlled about 75% of Europe's athletic shoe and apparel market, and they were also strong in the U.S. Things changed, however. Now, Nike and Reebok, and to a lesser degree L.A. Gear, made spectacular inroads in Europe. Although Adidas continued to be No. 1 with $1.6 billion in revenues, Nike ranked second with $500 million and Reebok ranked third with $380 million. L.A. Gear's sales were less than $119 million.

Both Nike and Reebok profited from long-term problems at Adidas and Puma. In the past five years, both German companies reported steady streams of losses because of unfocused marketing, high costs, and a glut of products. At Adidas, the confusion was acute: In footwear alone, it had 1,200 different variations and styles. "We had everything," said Michel Perrauding, Adidas' manager for logistics, "even shoes for left-handed bowlers."

Adidas' poorly coordinated marketing in Europe angered many distributors who started to desert to Nike and Reebok. And in the U.S. where Adidas was once No. 1 in athletic shoes, chronic delivery problems and a failure to spot the trend to more comfortable shoes led to huge losses and a dramatic drop in market share.

Nike and Reebok, however, might have to confront the possibility that Adidas and Puma might fight back. A Swedish company took full control of

Puma and planned to pump cash into it. At Adidas, a new French owner slashed its product range in shoes and apparel to several hundred from several thousand, retired hundreds of employees, and started a network of more efficient purchasing and production facilities in Asia. Adidas launched a new line, Equipment, featuring no-frills shoes for such sports as soccer, tennis, and track. There was also a new Adidas series of hiking and outdoors shoes. Nevertheless, Adidas and Puma lacked the deep pockets of Nike and Reebok to enable them to spend as much on advertising as the two U.S. companies.

CUSTOMERS

L.A. Gear sold to retail stores, specialty shoe stores, and sporting goods stores but their ultimate customer was the individual retail consumer. L.A. Gear's customers historically were young fashion minded girls. Under Greenberg, the company promoted the young Southern-California lifestyle. Its advertisements were of young blondes on the beach in stylish L.A. Gear shoes. Under the new management, the company repositioned itself. Former CEO Robert Greenberg said that they knew that in order to grow they would eventually have to enter the men's market and that meant more technically-oriented footwear.[38] Fashion athletics was now only a part of L.A. Gear.

GOVERNMENT REGULATIONS

In 1990, the U.S. Congress passed the Textile, Apparel, and Footwear Trade Act (the "Textile Act") which would have set highly restrictive global quotas on imported textile, apparel, and footwear products. This legislation was vetoed by President Bush, and the veto was sustained by the House of Representatives.

There was a possibility that a similar legislation would be proposed in the future. If such a legislation was enacted into law, L.A. Gear could face restrictions on its ability to import into the U.S. its footwear products manufactured abroad.

In 1992, the U.S. placed L.A. Gear's suppliers in Taiwan, China, Indonesia, and South Korea on a "priority watch list" for engaging in unfair trade practices. If such countries were proved to be engaged in unfair trade practices, the U.S. might retaliate against them, which could result in increases in the cost, or reductions in the supply, of footwear generally and L.A. Gear's footwear in particular.

DEMOGRAPHICS

The U.S. population, which totaled 250 million in 1990, was expected to reach 283 million by the year 2010. That was an increase of about 13%. Perhaps more significant to the footwear industry was the rise in the size of baby boom generation, born between 1946 and 1964. A prime target of footwear companies, this segment, which comprised 18% of the population in 1990, was expected to grow by about 9% by the year 2010.

CULTURE

Lifestyle changes in the U.S., as well as in many other countries, were propitious for footwear producers. An increasing segment of the population was becoming more health conscious, engaging in athletic activities such as jogging and walking. Because of the increasing popularity of walking, the walking-shoes market was expected to be the largest growth segment of the footwear industry. According to industry sources, 75% of the walking-shoes market consisted of women in their mid-30s and up.[39]

ECONOMY

In 1991 and 1992, the Federal Reserve Board laid the groundwork for an economic recovery by keeping prime interest rates low and gradually expanding the money supply. The Fed was able, at the same time, to keep inflation at less than 4%. Depressed consumer confidence in economic recovery, however, continued to be a major obstacle to increased consumer and business spending. The slow start of President Clinton's economic program served only to slow a long-awaited growth in the nation's economy.

TECHNOLOGY

Counterfeiting is the perennial enemy of brand-name producers in Asia. Recognizing the danger to his company's technology, Goldston, L.A. Gear's president said, "The major focus of our agreements with new manufacturers is on integrity. Our technology innovation will be protected."[40] However, an L.A. Gear executive said the means available to foreign shoe manufacturers for protecting patents were limited. As a result, athletic-shoe makers could find their most nagging competitors were not each other but the companies who filled their orders. Such companies as L.A. Gear "tend to stumble when faced with competition, and this time it will come from say, . . . a factory in Indonesia that has acquired the technology to make a good jogging shoe."[41]

POLITICS

With political changes occurring in Eastern Europe and the Soviet Union, markets that were previously closed to Western companies were now fairly wide open.

The enactment of NAFTA (North American Free Trade Agreement) among the U.S., Canada, and Mexico, was likely to strengthen U.S. exports. According to estimates made by the U.S. Trade Representative, the tariff reductions alone, if undertaken by all countries, could raise U.S. real GNP by 3% by the year 2000.[42]

CONCLUSION

As they implement their turnaround strategy, Gold and Goldston have their work cut out for them. What should they do next? And will their strategic moves be sufficient to restore L.A. Gear to its heyday or will they cause the company to disappear?

APPENDIX A   *Consolidated Balance Sheet, as of November 30 (in thousands)*

	1992	1991
ASSETS		
Current assets:		
Cash and cash equivalents	$ 55,027	$ 1,422
Collateralized cash	28,955	—
Accounts receivable, net	56,369	111,470
Inventories	61,923	141,115
Prepaid expenses and other current assets	2,557	8,506
Refundable income taxes	25,269	22,795
Deferred income taxes	—	11,763
Total current assets	230,100	297,071
Property and equipment, net	17,667	26,869
Other assets	1,735	1,631
Total assets	$249,502	$325,571
LIABILITIES, MANDATORILY REDEEMABLE PREFERRED STOCK AND SHAREHOLDERS' EQUITY		
Current liabilities:		
Borrowing under line of credit	$ —	$ 20,000
Accounts payable and accrued liabilities	49,753	55,856
Dividends payable on mandatorily redeemable preferred stock	7,746	—
Costs related to discontinued operations	4,552	18,000
Total current liabilities	62,051	93,856
Mandatorily redeemable preferred stock:		
7.5% Series A Cumulative Convertible Preferred Stock, $100 stated value; 1,000,000 shares authorized, issued and outstanding; redemption value of $100 per share	100,000	100,000
Shareholders' equity:		
Common stock, no par value; 80,000,000 shares authorized; 22,898,182 shares issued and outstanding at November 30, 1992 (19,542,513 shares issued and outstanding at November 30, 1991)	127,714	92,331
Preferred stock, no stated value; 9,000,000 shares authorized; no shares issued	—	—
Retained earnings (accumulated deficit)	(40,263)	39,384
Total shareholders' equity	87,451	131,715
Commitments and contingencies	—	—
	$249,502	$325,571

SOURCE: L.A. Gear, *1992 Annual Report*, p. 17.

APPENDIX B   *Consolidated Statements of Cash Flows, as of November 30 (in thousands)*

	1992	1991	1990
Operating activities:			
Net income (loss)	($71,901)	$(66,200)	$31,338
Adjustment to reconcile net income (loss) to net cash			
provided by (used in) operating activities:	17,075	—	—
Shareholders' litigation settlements			
Depreciation and amortization	7,107	7,182	3,394
Provision for loss on discontinued operations	—	18,000	—
Loss on sale or abandonment of property and equipment	1,871	4,146	—
Issuance of shares to employee stock savings plan	233	382	—
(Increase) decrease in: Accounts receivable, net	55,101	44,431	(52,969)
Inventories	79,192	19,553	(21,152)
Prepaids and other assets	6,343	1,565	(998)
Refundable and deferred income taxes	8,791	(26,174)	(3,795)
Increase (decrease) in:			
Accounts payable and accrued liabilities	(6,103)	(8,222)	3,143
Costs related to discontinued operations	(8,343)	—	—
Net cash provided by (used in) operating activities	89,366	(5,337)	(41,039)
Investing activities-capital expenditures	(4,881)	(14,188)	(18,939)
Financing activities:	—	92,511	—
Net proceeds from issuance of mandatorily redeemable preferred stock			
Payment of dividends on mandatorily redeemable preferred stock	—	(1,265)	—
Exercise of stock options and warrants	1,986	414	908
Tax benefits arising from the disposition/exercise of incentive stock options	2,089	356	5,408
Proceeds from issuance of common stock	14,000	—	—
Net borrowing (repayment) under line of credit agreement	(20,000)	(74,000)	56,600
Net cash provided by (used in) financing activities	(1,925)	17,656	62,916
Net increase (decrease) in cash and and cash equivalents	82,560	(1,869)	2,938
Cash at beginning of year	1,422	3,291	353
Cash and cash equivalents at end of year, including collateralized cash	$83,982	$ 1,422	$ 3,291

SOURCE: L.A. Gear, *1992 Annual Report*, p. 20.

Endnotes

1. "L.A. Gear," *Los Angeles Magazine,* December 1991, p. 116.
2. "L.A. Gear Calls in a Cobbler," *Business Week,* September 16, 1991, p. 78.
3. "L.A. Gear +184.6%," *Institutional Investor,* March 1990, pp. 52, 53.
4. "L.A. Gear Co-Founder Saemann Quits in Wake of Firms Deal with Trefoil," *The Wall Street Journal,* June 13, 1991, p. B1.
5. "The Best and Worst Stocks of 1989," *Fortune,* January 29, 1990, p. 114.
6. "L.A. Gear Inc.," *The Wall Street Journal,* April 4, 1991, p. B1.
7. "L.A. Gear Co-Founder Saemann Quits in Wake of Firms Deal with Trefoil," *The Wall Street Journal,* June 13, 1991, p. B1.
8. "Stanley P. Gold L.A. Gear Chairman & Chief Executive Officer," L.A. Gear Press Release, January 24, 1992.
9. *Ibid.*
10. "L.A. Gear Inc. Investor Steps in With New Team," *The Wall Street Journal,* January 27, 1992, pp. B1, B5.
11. *Ibid.*
12. "L.A. Gear Inc. Investor Steps in With New Team," *The Wall Street Journal,* January 27, 1992, pp. B1, B5.
13. *Ibid.*
14. "L.A. Gear, Several Changes at Senior Level," *The Wall Street Journal,* September 17, 1991, p. A22.
15. L.A. Gear, *Form 10-K,* 1991, p. 2.
16. *Ibid.*
17. *Ibid.*
18. L.A. Gear Inc., *1990 Annual Report* (Los Angeles, CA: L.A. Gear Inc.), p. 7.
19. B. Horivitz, "Some Companies Find They Get More," *Los Angeles Times,* February 5, 1991, p. D6.
20. "L.A. Gear Says High Inventories May Affect 1992 Earnings," *Bloomberg News,* March 3, 1992.
21. *Ibid.,* p. B5.
22. L.A. Gear Inc., 1990 Annual Report (Los Angeles, CA: L.A. Gear Inc.), p. 8.
23. "The Goldston Prescription," *Footwear News,* January 27, 1992, pp. 11–12.
24. "L.A. Gear Still Looks Like an Also-Ran," *Business Week,* December 21, 1992, p. 37.
25. "Footwear (Men's, Women's, Boys' and Girls')," *Fairchild Fact File,* 1990, pp. 5–9.
26. *Ibid.,* pp. 5–9.
27. F. Meeds, "The Sneaker Game," *Forbes,* October 22, 1990, p. 114.
28. J. Schlax, "The Shoe as Hero," *Forbes,* August 20, 1990, p. 77.
29. K. Kerwin, "L.A. Gear is Going where the Boys Are," *Business Week,* June 19, 1989, p. 54.
30. *Ibid.,* p. 52.
31. M. Grimm, "To Munich and Back With Nike and L.A. Gear," *Adweek's Marketing Week,* February 18, 1991, p. 21.
32. *Ibid.,* p. 22.
33. M. Wilson, "Nike Town Goes Back to the Future," *Chain Store Age Executive,* February, 1991, pp. 82–83.
34. M. Tedeschi, "Reebok Splits U.S. Int'l Setups," *Footwear News,* November 26, 1990, p. 12.
35. S. Gannes, "America's Fastest-Growing Companies," *Fortune,* May 23, 1988, p. 37.
36. A. Shell, "Cause-Related Marketing: Big Risks, Big Potential," *Public Relations Journal,* July, 1989, pp. 8, 13.
37. *Ibid.,* p. 8.
38. M. Rottman, "L.A. Gear Catapults Into Technology," *Footwear News,* February 18, 1991, pp. 12, 14.
39. D. McKay, "Walk This Way," *Footwear News,* September 9, 1991, pp. 14–15.
40. "L.A. Gear President Says Shoe Maker Will Recover and Will Focus on Asia," *The Wall Street Journal,* October 16, 1992, p. B7.
41. *Ibid.*
42. *OECD Economic Survey,* United States, 1990/1991, pp. 60–65.

CASE PART III

Establishing Organizational Direction: Vision, Mission, Objectives

Liz Claiborne, 1993: Troubled Times for the Woman's Retail Giant

SHARON UNGAR LANE, PATRICIA BILAFER, MARY FANDEL,
BARBARA GOTTFRIED, *and* ALAN N. HOFFMAN, *Bentley College*

In 1986, Liz Claiborne, Inc. became the first company started by a woman to make the Fortune 500. Described by Working Woman magazine as "the wizard of the working woman's wardrobe,"[1] Liz Claiborne, Inc. provides quality career and casual clothing, accessories, and fragrances at prices working women can afford. In fact, the company's philosophy, to produce "simple, straightforward fashion designed for women who have more important things to think about than what to wear,"[2] has made it the largest women's apparel manufacturer in the world. In 1993, Liz Claiborne sold 65 million garments, and more than 20 million accessories.

THE EARLY YEARS

The daughter of a banker at Morgan Guaranty Trust Company, Liz Claiborne spent her early childhood in Brussels before moving with her family to New Orleans in 1934. She never finished high school, but after the War, her father sent her to Europe to study at the Art School in Brussels, and then to the Academie in Nice, France to study fine arts. She returned to the United States only to discover that her family opposed her desire to work in the fashion industry. Nevertheless, Liz entered a sketch of a woman's high-collared coat in a design contest sponsored by Harper's Bazaar, and won. At twenty-one, she began her career as a sketcher, model, and later, designer on "Fashion Avenue," the insiders' name for New York's Seventh Avenue garment district, where much of America's ready-to-wear is designed, and was, at one time, produced. Soon afterward, while working at Rhea Manufacturing Company in Milwaukee, she met Arthur Ortenberg, a design executive, whom she married in 1957.

The authors would like to thank Jane Moreno, Jeffrey Shuman, and Sally Strawn for their valuable contributions to this case. Photographic contribution by Scott Lane.

Please address all correspondence to Dr. Alan N. Hoffman, Department of Management, AGC320, Bentley College, 175 Forest Street, Waltham, MA 02154–4705.

In 1960, Liz Claiborne embarked on a fifteen-year career as the chief designer for Youth Guild, the junior dress division of Jonathan Logan. It was during these years that the seeds of Liz Claiborne, Inc. were sown: more and more women were entering the work force, and Liz perceived that there was an opening in the market for tasteful, moderately priced career clothes. She could not sell Youth Guild on her vision of a mix-and-match sportswear line to fill that gap, so she decided to set up her own company.

Liz Claiborne, Inc. was launched on January 19, 1976. Financed by $50,000 in personal savings and $200,000 from family, friends, and business associates, the company began small, with Liz Claiborne as President and head designer, and her husband, Arthur Ortenberg, an expert in textiles and business administration, as Secretary and Treasurer of the corporation, and later, Chairman. A third partner, Leonard Boxer, contributed production expertise, and in 1977, Jerome Chazen, a personal friend, was named Vice President of Marketing. Within its first year, the company was operating in the black, with sales of over $2 million. In 1985, sales reached the half billion dollar mark; the next year, retail sales surpassed $1.2 billion, and Liz Claiborne, Inc. made it into the Fortune 500.

In February 1989, Liz Claiborne and Arthur Ortenberg announced their retirement from active management of the company to pursue environmental, social, and other interests. Jerome Chazen, one of the company's original partners was named CEO, and Jay Margolis was hired as Vice Chair and President of Women's Sportswear, Liz Claiborne, Inc.'s core division. Committed to taking Liz Claiborne into the 1990's debt-free, they and a team of designers have expanded product lines, adding accessories and fragrances to meet customer demand. They also purchased Russ Togs company to sustain company growth. Today Liz Claiborne can claim a full 2% of the women's apparel market—more than any other publicly held company.

THE FASHION INDUSTRY

The fashion industry is highly competitive. The maturing market for women's clothing is dominated by Liz Claiborne and its major competitors: Jones New York, Chaus, Evan Picone, JH Collectibles, and VF Corporation. Retailers, the interface between the fashion industry and the consumer, have suffered in recent years from the recession and volatile consumer tastes, necessitating major restructuring which has had a significant impact on the fashion industry. Mergers, acquisitions, and bankruptcies of major retailers have created powerful retail rivals with the financial resources to create large economies of scale and withstand new entrants, strict governmental regulation, and technological advances. For instance, when Macy's, which had accounted for a significant percentage of Liz Claiborne sales, went bankrupt in 1992, Liz Claiborne's sales figures suffered in the ensuing bankruptcy settlement.

The retail clothing industry is also highly vulnerable to shifting tastes. Predicting fashion is risky and expensive because what is considered stylish today may be out tomorrow. Yet significant lead time is required to bring new styles to market. A company may invest a year or more in the design and production stages of a new design concept only to have the line fail upon introduction. In fact, clothing lines are usually either complete successes or fail altogether, yet at the same time, inventory levels for successful lines must be adequate to meet consumer demand, which doesn't leave much margin for error. Establishing name recognition is a priority for designers. Consumers consistently shop their favorite designers, and remain loyal to those whose clothes fit best. Indeed, strong designer loyalty dominates the retail industry. Thus fashion industry marketing strategies must take many contingencies into account at all times, while remaining flexible enough to respond to continually shifting consumer tastes.

PRODUCT LINES

Liz Claiborne's principal lines are designed to meet the work and leisure clothing needs of working women. Today 57.7% of all women in the United States work outside the home; and women with children under the age of six are the fastest growing segment of the workforce. The dual income family has become the norm, and stay-at-home moms the exception rather than the rule. Consequently many women no longer have the kind of leisure time they once had to shop; rather they prefer to maximize any shopping outing. Liz Claiborne, Inc. has carved out a niche for itself by targeting these women as its primary constituency, designing mix-and-match coordinating outfits, rather than separates, that can be variously combined to suit individual needs and tastes, simplifying both shopping and dressing for the busy lifestyles of working women. To market this concept, Liz Claiborne was one of the first companies to merchandise their clothing lines as outfits rather than single items, arranging them on the display floor to demonstrate that they can dress the customer from head to toe, rather than displaying single garments by classification. Furthermore, the clothes are modern classic rather than trendy, designed with practicality, style and fashion longevity in mind. Liz Claiborne's goal is to offer clothing and accessories that are not only aesthetically and technically well designed, but which make the customer feel confident, addressing all the needs of her busy life.

As of 1993, Liz Claiborne, Inc. had 18 divisions (Exhibit 1) offering various products aimed at specific target markets and covering a wide gamut of career, active wear and accessories for women, as well as for men. Liz Claiborne is continually adding new products to their apparel line, such as the women's suits introduced in 1991, not simply to increase sales, but to garner more department store space. Their perfume, "Liz Claiborne," has been particularly successful. The versatile scent was conceived to be worn around the clock, at work or out on the town, and based on Liz Claiborne's instinctive preferences rather than on market research, as was the triangle-shaped logo and the red, yellow and blue color scheme for the packaging. The company also carved out a niche for itself marketing to the "forgotten" woman. Over 30% of adult women are overweight. Liz Claiborne, Inc. entered the large-sized women's clothing market with its "Elisabeth" line, which successfully serves a long-neglected group of consumers by offering large-sized sportswear that provides the excellent fit, fashion and quality of its regular sportswear lines. The gambit has paid off, and Liz Claiborne, Inc. has plans to continue extending the "Elisabeth" line. In yet another ploy to extend its markets and increase its sales, Liz Claiborne Inc. has ignored the industry standard of four seasons and has opted for six seasonal lines to offer women clothes they can wear right away and to allow for a constant flow of new merchandise to generate consumer interest. The net result of the company's versatility and market savvy: Liz Claiborne outfits more women than any other designer.

To stay on top of the huge volume of its business, Liz Claiborne uses both direct customer feedback and a unique computerized system, SURF (System Updated Retail Feedback), which provides weekly sales trends reports on what

EXHIBIT 1
Liz Claiborne, Inc.'s
Product Line Overview

SPORTSWEAR:

Includes Collection, Lizsport, Lizwear and Petite Sportswear.
Liz Claiborne Inc. launched into the fashion industry with its sportswear line in 1976. Designed to be modern classic rather than trendy so as to ensure fashion longevity, the sportswear division divided into three distinct lines. The first, COLLECTION, is primarily a career-oriented, tailored, and professional line. LIZSPORT provides sportswear for leisure time as well as for more casual work environments, while LIZWEAR is a highly denim-driven sportswear division. Our PETITE sportswear was developed in 1982 to fulfill an unmet need in the market for the 5'4"and under customer. Petite sizes are offered in all three sportswear lifestyles.

DRESSES:

Misses and Petite.
Misses' dresses were launched in 1982, followed by Petite in 1985. Our dresses include a wide range of fabrications and styles, from career to knit to social occasion dresses. Furthermore, the dress division offers a large selection of dresses that can be worn from day-to-dinner, encompassing the ease and professionalism necessary for a work environment with the style and fun for an evening on the town.

SUITS:

In 1991 Liz Claiborne Inc. ventured into the Suits market. The division differentiates itself by offering a wide variety of skirt and jacket lengths, seasonless fabrics, pant suits, and day-to-dinner designs.

LIZ & CO.:

Liz & Co., launched in 1989, consists primarily of comfortable and coordinated knitwear separates with a relaxed fit and a youthful attitude.

DANA BUCHMAN:

Sportswear, Petite Sportswear, and Dresses.
Founded in 1987, Dana Buchman is our bridge sportswear division with prices that range from better sportswear to designer merchandise. It offers sophisticated styles of the highest quality fabrics with an exceptional attention to detail. Dana Buchman's distribution is selective.

ELISABETH:

Sportswear, Petite Sportswear, and Dresses.
In response to a previously neglected market, Liz Claiborne Inc. developed its large size division called Elisabeth in 1989. The line includes a wide range of products from activewear to career clothing to evening dressing in sizes 14–24 and 14P–22P. Through Elisabeth's high attention to design, quality, and fit, it has become a market leader.

CLAIBORNE:

Men's Sportswear and Men's Furnishings.
Liz Claiborne Inc. launched into the men's market in 1985 with our Claiborne sportswear division and in 1987 with men's furnishings. Furnishings include men's dress shirts and ties, while our men's sportswear incorporates

the same high level of fashion and quality as offered in our women's sportswear areas.

CRAZY HORSE:

Acquired in 1992, Crazy Horse is a casual line with a young and modern attitude that is merchandised in department and specialty stores. Its fashion-forward appearance appeals to a younger customer.

RUSS:

Also acquired in 1992, Russ offers career as well as casual dressing and is displayed in the moderate areas of department stores.

THE VILLAGER:

The Villager, acquired in 1992 along with Crazy Horse and Russ, focuses on career clothing but offers some casual wear as well. It will be distributed to national and regional chain department stores. Thus, with these three new labels, Liz Claiborne Inc. has expanded both its product offerings and its distribution to include moderate career and casual dressing.

ACCESSORIES:

Includes Handbags/Small Leather Goods and Fashion Accessories.
Our fashion accessories, organized in 1980, include scarves, belts, hats, tights, socks, and hair accessories. Also introduced in 1980 were Liz Claiborne handbags and small leather goods. Many of the Liz Claiborne accessories are designed and developed to coordinate with our sportswear and can be used for anything from work to play. Recently, the Accessories division launched our bodywear, offering the same fit, fashion, and quality of all Liz Claiborne products.

SHOES:

Shoes and Sportshoes.
Also designed to coordinate and complement our sportswear, Liz Claiborne Inc. moved into the shoe market in 1981. This division includes casual shoes, dress shoes, and as of 1991, fashionable and athletic sportshoes. Of course, like all our apparel divisions, all styles are comfortable and of the highest fashion sense.

JEWELRY:

Liz Claiborne Inc. also offers a wide range of fashion jewelry designed for both casual and go-to-work. Many of the designs coordinate with the seasonal apparel trends and color ways. Introduced in 1990, this division offers a full range of jewelry including earrings, necklaces, bracelets, and pins.

COSMETICS:

Our Cosmetics division was launched in 1987 and consists of a collection of fragrances that captures and completes the whole Liz Claiborne attitude. The first, our signature fragrance, is entitled LIZ CLAIBORNE and is bottled in Liz Claiborne's trademark triangle. CLAIBORNE for men was developed in 1989, followed by REALITIES in 1990. In the Fall of 1993, Liz Claiborne Inc. will be launching its new fragrance, VIVID. Various complementary fragrance items are also carried in the lines, including shampoo, conditioners, and body lotion to name a few.

is and isn't selling nationwide. At the end of each week, data on sales, styles, sizes, and colors are reviewed by division heads to determine both short and long term planning needs. Most importantly, SURF allows the company to respond quickly to mistakes. For example, for the spring, 1988 season, Liz Claiborne had decided to fall in line with current trends—and market miniskirts. When it became obvious through SURF that the company's regular customers had no intention of baring their thighs, Liz Claiborne was able to adjust their fall 1988 designs quickly and order longer skirts for the fall fashion season to avoid losing loyal customers.

Nevertheless, Liz Claiborne, Inc. has had a few disappointments, such as its girls' line for 5–12 year olds begun in 1984, but phased out in 1987. Also, 1992 sales of the men's sportswear and furnishings lines were a big disappointment, falling 24.6%; as a result, the "Claiborne" collection of men's sportswear, originally styled for young customers, has shifted to a more upscale, conservative look.

While saturation is always a possibility, especially as the core sportswear line matures, Liz Claiborne works hard to stay one step ahead of the game. Recently the company saw in the moderate market, which targets working women with more sophisticated, yet reasonably priced clothes than those at the GAP or Limited stores, the potential for new business and a broadened customer base. In 1992 Liz Claiborne entered the moderate women's sportswear market by acquiring Russ Togs (Russ, Crazy Horse and The Villager labels), which broadened their distribution by expanding Liz Claiborne's position in both national and regional chain department stores, in addition to the moderate areas of traditional department stores.

LIZ CLAIBORNE: 1993

Liz Claiborne Inc. markets its various lines primarily through 3,500 leading department stores such as Bloomingdale's, Filenes, Lord & Taylor, Macy's, and Jordan Marsh, delivering a consistent product at a fair price. The company usually sets up "Liz Claiborne boutiques" within these stores which carry the full line of Liz merchandise to allow for one-stop shopping for women who don't have time to shop (the store within a store concept pioneered by Ralph Lauren).

However, because many of its best retailers were in financial trouble, Liz Claiborne made an ambitious move into retailing. By 1993, the company had opened 16 Liz Claiborne company-owned retail stores, 39 First Issue stores, and 55 outlet stores nationwide. The 16 company-owned retail stores help give "Liz Claiborne" fashions a unique identity, and play an important role in testing new products and new merchandising ideas, functioning as "laboratories" to observe consumer taste and measure reactions to such elements as fit, selling, size, group, and fabric. The company also owns three Elisabeth retail stores.

The 39 First Issue stores, opened in 1993, are designed to compete with retailers like The Limited and The Gap. The stores exclusively market First Issue merchandise, related separates and basics similar to Liz Claiborne sportswear but less career oriented, designed by a separate team and priced approximately 15% lower than the Liz Claiborne label lines.

Liz Claiborne also has 55 outlet stores where they sell unsold merchandise from previous seasons, providing the company with control over the disposition of unsold inventories. The outlets are deliberately located at some distance from the department and specialty stores where Liz products are regularly sold in order to preserve brand image.

Since many segments of the U.S. fashion industry are maturing, overseas markets represent new and substantial sources of growth for U.S. designers. An internationally recognized brand name and worldwide advertising campaign are critical to competing successfully in European and Asian markets. To effectively market its products outside the U.S., Liz Claiborne, Inc. is tailoring its sales strategies specifically for each country. To date, Liz Claiborne has met with some success in Canada and England, where women tend to shop and dress like Americans, but less success in other parts of the world. One problem lies in the fact that Liz Claiborne is essentially a department store line in the United States, while in Europe most business is done in small boutiques. In some British stores, Liz Claiborne is leasing space and selling their goods themselves. In Japan the company is selling through a mail order catalog in addition to the two Liz Claiborne stores that were opened in Tokyo during fall, 1993. International expansion has, however, suffered the adverse impact of recessions in both Europe and Japan.

INTERNATIONAL MANUFACTURING

Currently, 100% of Liz Claiborne's product lines are manufactured overseas. Global outsourcing is widespread in the textile industry to capitalize on lower labor and production costs at overseas manufacturing sites. Outsourcing creates the flexibility to shift production to various sites depending on wage differentials. Yet many of these sites are high risk due to the political and economic instability of developing and Third World countries. Nevertheless, very few firms have manufacturing facilities in the U.S., so they vary their sources by using a combination of domestic, Caribbean and foreign sources to insure minimal instability. However, scattered production sites can jeopardize quality control. In addition, reliance on foreign suppliers is not without its disadvantages, since those suppliers are not always consistent, and cannot be easily relied upon to operate on the tight schedules necessitated by the time pressures of an industry that turns around four to six seasonal lines a year.

U.S. import regulations are currently favorable for retailers, which further contributes to the marketing of goods made overseas; however, these conditions are subject to change. As imports rise, quota restrictions are more strictly enforced; and recently, the government has shifted to a more protectionist policy. The garment industry has been criticized both for exporting U.S. manufacturing jobs and for exploiting foreign labor. Indeed, the shift of clothing production to overseas sites has been economically significant for the U.S. because "apparel production alone employs more people than the entire printing and publishing field and more than the automobile manufacturing industry."[8]

WOMEN'S WORK

Liz Claiborne, Inc. has a long-standing commitment to the welfare of others, especially women. In the past, the Liz Claiborne Foundation, funded by company profits, actively assisted organizations involved in social welfare programs, e.g., helping the homeless, serving people with AIDS and their families, and enhancing opportunities for underprivileged children. The company also strongly encourages its employees to volunteer and support local non-profit organizations.

Over the years Liz Claiborne has learned a great deal about the lives of the women who buy their products—about their careers, their dreams, and their struggles outside of work. The company wanted both to give something back to the millions of women who had contributed to the company's success, and to contribute to social change by making a difference in people's lives. To do so, Liz Claiborne Inc. recently developed "Women's Work." "Women's Work" develops and funds multiyear, nationwide programs designed to heighten awareness of social problems and encourage positive social change with regard to issues of particular concern to women and their families, such as domestic violence and work-family conflicts.

The specific "Women's Work" project supported in each target community is based on issues of particular concern to that community: domestic violence in San Francisco, Boston, and Miami; the needs and concerns of working mothers in Chicago. In each city, Liz Claiborne builds innovative, collaborative partnerships with organizations active in confronting domestic violence. In Chicago, a local artist and children from a local elementary school published a book that addresses the impact of working mothers on their families, especially their children. All proceeds resulting from the sale of the book are donated to literacy programs nationwide.

In 1993, to coincide with National Domestic Violence Awareness Month, Liz Claiborne launched domestic violence awareness programs in Boston and Miami, and formed a partnership with the Jane Doe Safety Fund sponsored by the Massachusetts Coalition of Battered Women. To raise money for the fund, Claiborne solicited the help of Barbara Kruger, a contemporary artist whose work advocates social change. The Fund's public awareness campaign on domestic violence includes billboards, city bus signs, transit stop posters, and educational brochures (Exhibits 2a and 2b), as well as broadcast and print public service announcements. Additionally, Liz Claiborne launched a collection of special commemorative products (Exhibit 3), which can be purchased at local Liz Claiborne stores, participating department stores, or through a special toll-free number, whose proceeds will be donated to domestic violence programs such as the Jane Doe Safety Fund in Boston. Liz Claiborne has also donated money to establish the first centralized 24-hour domestic violence hot line, which the company hopes will become permanent with the support of local foundations and organizations.

"Women's Work" is a way for Liz Claiborne Inc. to give something back to communities and the American women who have contributed to Liz Claiborne's success by funding programs for the future welfare of women. In addition, Liz Claiborne Inc. is exploring the possibility of sponsoring educational programs about the detection and treatment of breast cancer, and already offers free mammograms to all its women employees. While the company acknowledges that they do not expect sales to increase as a result of the Liz Claiborne Foundation or "Women's Work," they hope that by responding to concerns important to women and their families, "Women's Work" will reinforce Liz Claiborne, Inc.'s reputation as a company that cares.

1993: THE WRONG PRODUCT—AND TOO MUCH OF IT

By the late 1980s, Liz Claiborne had branched beyond clothes for working women into petites, large sizes, accessories, fragrances, men's clothing, and

EXHIBIT 2A

PHOTO BY SCOTT LANE

EXHIBIT 2B

other lines. With so much to watch over, managers began to lose their focus on the core merchandise. Customers yawned at many outfits, which too often repeated past styles. Retailers, who had allowed Liz Claiborne's presence in their stores to reach King Kong-like proportions, say top managers were slow to admit the problem. According to a former senior Claiborne executive: "If the product didn't sell, it was always someone else's fault. The buyers didn't show it right, or it wasn't delivered in the right way. They didn't allow themselves to think that maybe they just weren't listening to the customer."[7]

1993 was a difficult year for Liz Claiborne. A weak retail environment, conservative buying by customers, the start-up costs associated with the Russ Division, and the surprise resignation of Jay Margolis in July 1993 led industry

EXHIBIT 3

WOMEN'S WORK
Liz claiborne, inc.

Contact: Maria Kalligeros/Lisa Schmidt
Patrice Tanaka & Company, Inc.
(212) 505-9332

<u>LIZ CLAIBORNE, INC. TO LAUNCH COMMEMORATIVE COLLECTION;
PROCEEDS WILL BENEFIT DOMESTIC VIOLENCE ORGANIZATIONS</u>

Items Feature Special Images by Artist Barbara Kruger

COMMEMORATIVE COLLECTION	To increase awareness of domestic violence, Liz Claiborne, Inc. will be launching a special collection of products, proceeds from which will raise funds for domestic violence organizations. Each piece in the collection features contemporary artist **Barbara Kruger**'s striking red, black and white images and the message, "DON'T DIE FOR LOVE – STOP DOMESTIC VIOLENCE," specially commissioned by Liz Claiborne, Inc. for this program. Startling statistics, running across the top and bottom of the image, read – "Every 12 seconds a woman is beaten in the U.S." and "52% of female murder victims are killed by their partners."
ITEMS AVAILABLE VIA PHONE ORDER	<u>T-Shirt</u> ($12) in white 100% cotton. Available in X-large with the image silk screened on the front.
	<u>Tote Bag</u> ($20) in natural color canvas (15" x 13" x 5") silk screened with the image on the front. Natural color twill straps, a zippered center section and two zippered interior compartments.

Over...

THE WOMEN'S WORK PROGRAM IS SUPPORTED AND FUNDED BY LIZ CLAIBORNE, INC.

WOMEN'S WORK. c/o PT&Co..141 Fifth Avenue, New York, NY 10010 212-505-9332 Fax 212-505-9928

(continued)

analysts to question the strength of Liz Claiborne, Inc. Sales were flat for the first nine months of 1993 and earnings dropped by 40% in the third quarter after double digit declines in the first and second quarters. The consensus opinion on the problem: the wrong product and too much of it.

The following excerpt appeared in the January, 1994 edition of Smart-Money Magazine:

In late 1992, Louis Lowenstein, a Claiborne director, bragged that the apparel maker's balance sheet was so solid it would bring tears to [his] mother's eyes. Save the hanky. Investors watched Liz's earnings slide all year. The company overestimated shoppers' appetites after a strong 1992 Christmas season and made too many clothes. Then its uninspired 1993 fashion collections failed to entice thrift shoppers. The inventory overload prevented Liz from being able to react quickly to the slow retail environment, causing profits to slide an estimated 40% for the year. Liz Claiborne's stock traded at $42.38 on January 7, 1993 and was $18.13 on October 21,1993.

Clearly, 1993 was a disappointing year for Liz Claiborne, Inc.

EXHIBIT 3
Continued

LIZ CLAIBORNE, INC. COMMEMORATIVE COLLECTION/FACT SHEET   page 2

	Baseball Cap ($10) in black twill with the Kruger message silk screened in red and white above the brim. Available in adjustable one-size-fits-all.
PHONE ORDERING INFORMATION	The collection can be ordered by calling 1-800-449-STOP (1-800-449-7867). American Express, VISA, Mastercard, checks or money orders will be accepted; New York/New Jersey residents must add sales tax. Shipping is not included. Consumers should allow four to six weeks for delivery.
ITEMS AVAILABLE AT RETAIL	The T-shirt, tote bag, baseball cap and:
	Mug ($6) in white featuring the Kruger image in red and black.
	Sunglasses ($15) are a classic black frame with the Kruger message displayed on the outside of each lens. View is unobstructed for the wearer.

RETAIL LOCATIONS

- several Boston-area Filene's
- Burdines stores in Miami's Dade and Broward Counties
- Museum shops nationwide
- Liz Claiborne Stores:
    -Copley Place, Boston, MA
    -Town Center, Boca Raton, FL
- Selected campus stores

WHO DO PROCEEDS BENEFIT?

- Through 800 #: The Family Violence Prevention Fund, a national, non-profit organization devoted to public policy, education and advocacy.
- In Miami: The Women's Fund of Dade County which will administer grants to local domestic violence programs.
- In Boston: The Jane Doe Safety Fund, a statewide fundraising and public education campaign of the Massachusetts Coalition of Battered Women Service Groups.

# # #

THE OUTLOOK FOR THE FUTURE

Consumers today are demanding more and are adamant about paying less. A global economy has given them a "sultan's power to command exactly what they want, the way they want it, when they want it, and at a price that will make [companies] weep."[9] Companies will have to either meet these expectations or be forced out of business by those competitors that do.

The prolonged recession, low consumer confidence, a four year national decline in per capita clothing spending and numerous bankruptcies among several of the nation's largest department stores have wreaked havoc in the apparel industry. Many companies are cutting costs through sophisticated inventory control systems and computer aided design and manufacturing, as well as enhanced fabric production systems. But the industry must also comply with federal legislation which regulates competition and requires product labeling with content and care instructions designed to protect consumers, both of which contribute to higher costs.

At the same time, Americans are changing the way they shop. Many designers, including Liz Claiborne, rely on large department stores located in shopping malls for a large percentage of their sales. However, the appeal of shopping malls is diminishing and the trend is toward specialty stores. Consumers, especially women, have less time to shop, so convenience is becoming even more important than it already was.

Consolidated Balance Sheets Liz Claiborne, Inc. and Subsidiaries
(All amounts in thousands except share data)

	December 25, 1993	December 26, 1992
ASSETS		
Current Assets:		
Cash and cash equivalents	$ 104,720	$ 130,721
Marketable securities	204,571	294,892
Accounts receivable—trade	174,435	200,183
Inventories	436,593	385,879
Deferred income tax benefits	15,065	13,907
Other current assets	69,055	55,384
Total current assets	1,004,439	1,080,966
Property and Equipment—net	202,068	145,695
Other Assets	29,831	29,647
	$1,236,338	$1,256,308
LIABILITIES AND STOCKHOLDERS' EQUITY		
Current Liabilities:		
Accounts payable	$ 141,126	$ 138,738
Accrued expenses	97,765	87,330
Income taxes payable	15,547	22,109
Total current liabilities	254,438	248,177
Long-Term Debt	1,334	1,434
Deferred Income Taxes	2,275	8,922
Commitments and Contingencies		
Stockholder's Equity:		
Preferred stock, $.01 par value, authorized shares—50,000,000, issued shares—none	—	—
Common stock, $1 par value, authorized shares—250,000,000, issued shares—88,218,617	88,219	88,219
Capital in excess of par value	56,699	55,528
Retained earnings	1,123,413	1,034,280
Cumulative translation adjustment	(1,279)	(1,410)
	1,267,052	1,176,617
Common stock in treasury, at cost—9,371,217 shares in 1993 and 5,436,864 shares in 1992	(288,761)	(178,842)
Total stockholders' equity	978,291	997,775
	$1,236,338	$1,256,308

The accompanying notes to consolidated financial statements are an integral part of these statements.

Clearly, for 1994, questions abound. Liz Claiborne, Inc. must re-think both its product lines and its entire marketing strategy, considering whether it has grown too fast, spread itself too thin, and/or set itself up to compete with itself by branching out into retailing lines under other labels which are too similar to its own name-brand lines. And the company must consider how best to fill the void left by the departure of Liz Claiborne herself, clearly a visionary who carved out a fashion empire which may now be on the brink of decline.

Consolidated Statements of Income Liz Claiborne, Inc. and Subsidiaries *(All dollar amounts in thousands except per common share data)*

	Fiscal Years Ended		
	December 25, 1993	December 26, 1992	December 28, 1991
Net Sales	$2,204,297	$2,194,330	$2,007,177
Cost of goods sold	1,453,381	1,364,214	1,207,502
Gross Profit	750,916	830,116	799,675
Selling, general and administrative expenses	568,286	507,541	471,060
Operating Income	182,630	322,575	328,615
Investment and other income—net	16,151	19,349	22,133
Income Before Provision for Income Taxes and Cumulative Effect of a Change in Accounting Principle	198,781	341,924	350,748
Provision for Income Taxes	73.500	123,100	128,000
Income Before Cumulative Effect of a Change in Accounting Principle	125,281	218,824	222,748
Cumulative effect of a change in the method of accounting for income taxes	1,643	—	—
Net Income	$ 126,924	$ 218,824	$ 222,748
Earnings per Common Share:			
Income Before Cumulative Effect of a Change in Accounting Principle	$1.54	$2.61	$2.61
Cumulative effect of a change in the method of accounting for income taxes	.02	—	—
Net Income per Common Share	$1.56	$2.61	$2.61
Dividends Paid per Common Share	$ .44	$ .39	$ .33

The accompanying notes to consolidated financial statements are an integral part of these statements.

Liz Claiborne Five Year Sales, Net Income, & EPS Summary (000)

Year	Sales	Net Income	EPS
1993	$2,204,297	$126,924	$1.56
1992	$2,194,330	$218,824	$2.61
1991	$2,007,177	$222,748	$2.61
1990	$1,728,868	$205,800	$2.37
1989	$1,410,677	$164,591	$1.87
5-year Growth Rate	11.8	−6.2	−4.4

Endnotes

1. Morris, Michele, "The Wizard of Working Women's Wardrobe," *Working Women*, June 1988, p. 74
2. Better, Nancy Marx, "The Secret of Liz Claiborne's Success," *Working Women*, April 1992, p. 68
3. Liz Claiborne Inc., *Current Biography*, June 1989, p. 8
4. Jacob, Rahul, "Beyond Quality and Value," *Fortune*, Autumn/Winter 1993, p. 8
5. Gillam, M., First Call Industry Report, June 16, 1993
6. Smith, Adam, "How Liz Claiborne Designed an Empire," *Esquire*, January 1986, p. 78–89
7. Caminiti, Susan, "Liz Claiborne: How to Get Focused Again," *Fortune*, January 24, 1994, p. 85
8. Guenciro, Miriam and Jeannette Jarnow, *Inside the Fashion Industry*, Macmillan Publishing Company, New York, 5th Edition, 1991, p. 5
9. Jacob, p. 8
10. Anonymous, "Underachiever's Club Disappointments of 1993: These Wall Street Favorites Burned Investors Bad," *Smart Money*, January 1994, p. 29

Ryka, Inc.: The Athletic Shoe with a "Soul"

VALERIE J. PORCIELLO, ALAN N. HOFFMAN, *and* **BARBARA GOTTFRIED,** *Bentley College*

THE ULTIMATE LIGHTWEIGHT SHOE FOR THE ACTIVE WOMAN

Rykä shoes are made for top performance. You'll find that Rykä shoes will help you look good and feel great, no matter how demanding your fitness program.

Rykä shoes are designed, engineered, and manufactured by women for women. Because a woman's needs in a comfortable, attractive, high performance athletic shoe are different from a man's.

As you lace up for your first workout in your new Rykä shoes, you'll feel the difference. With every pair of Rykä shoes goes the positive energy of women who believe in other women.

Step forward with confidence, and be your best.

Sheri Poe

Sheri Poe
Founder and President

RYKÄ®

Specially designed for stepping, the RYKA STEP shoe has special flex channels placed in the forefoot providing the flexibility necessary for stepping while still maintaining excellent forefoot cushioning for aerobics.

Whether it's high impact, low impact or step aerobics, RYKA's STEP shoes are superior in cushioning, shock absorption, stability and performance.

RYKA's STEP shoes are made with the highest performance midsole and outsole materials available— Nitrogen Ultra-Lite.

161

"Ryka has a great story to tell. We are the only athletic footwear company that is exclusively for women, by women, and now supporting women."—SHERI POE

It was the day after Christmas, 1990, and Sheri Poe, president and chief executive officer of Ryka, Inc., knew she was on the verge of the marketing break she'd been waiting for. During the past year, Poe had sent several free pairs of Ryka athletic shoes to Oprah Winfrey. Now Poe was going to be featured as a successful female entrepreneur on Winfrey's popular talk-show, with a television viewing audience numbering in the tens of millions—almost entirely women. Ryka's new line of Ultra-Lite aerobic shoes had just begun to penetrate the retail market. Poe could not have planned for a better advertising spot than Winfrey tossing pairs of Ryka shoes into the studio audience exclaiming, "Can you believe how light these are?"

After the "Oprah" broadcast, the Ultra-Lite line became an overnight success. Lady Footlocker immediately put the Ultra-Lite shoe line in 200 stores, up from the 50 that had been carrying Ryka's regular line of athletic shoes. Retailers were swamped by consumer requests for Ryka products, and the sharp upturn in consumer demand quickly exhausted their inventories. It took Poe over three months to catch up with the orders. Many industry analysts believe that the shot in the arm provided by the Ultra-Lite sales literally saved the company.

Ryka, Inc. designs, develops and markets athletic footwear for women, including aerobic, aerobic/step, cross-training, walk-run, and walking shoes. The company's products are sold all over the world in sporting goods, athletic footwear specialty, and department stores.

As a new entrant in the highly competitive athletic footwear industry, an industry with very deep pockets, the fledgling Ryka Corporation had no choice but to rely on low-budget, "guerrilla marketing" tactics such as the "Oprah" show appearance. Since that time, however, Ryka has turned to more traditional marketing techniques such as radio and glossy magazine advertising. Ryka print ads appear regularly in *City Sports, Shape, American Fitness, Elle,* and *Idea Today,* magazines that particularly target women aged 21–25, who care not just about how they look, but are serious about physical fitness.

COMPANY BACKGROUND

Ryka was first organized in 1986 as ABE Corporation, but changed its name to Ryka in February, 1987 when it commenced operations. The company was co-founded by Martin P. Birrittella and his wife, Sheri Poe. Prior to founding Ryka, Birrittella had worked at Matrix International Industries as a vice president of sales and marketing from 1980 to 1986. At Matrix, he was responsible for developing and marketing footwear and health and fitness products, and has two patents pending for shoe designs that have been assigned to Matrix. From 1982 to 1985, Sheri Poe was national sales manager for Matrix. She then moved to TMC Group, a $15 million giftware maker based in New Hampshire, where she was national accounts manager from May 1986 to June 1987.

The authors would like to thank Jeffrey Shuman, Holly Fowler, Maura Riley, Liliana Prado, Christine Forkus, and Mary Fandel for their valuable contributions to this case.
Please send all correspondence to: Dr. Alan N. Hoffman, Adamian Graduate Center 320, Bentley College, 175 Forest Street, Waltham, MA 02154.

Sheri Poe, Ryka's current president and chief executive officer, is one of only two women CEOs in the state of Massachusetts. Poe admits being an exercise fanatic who really knew nothing about making athletic shoes when she co-founded Ryka. In 1986 Poe had injured her back in an aerobics class and was convinced that the injury had been caused by her shoes, which had never fit properly. After an exhaustive search for footwear that would not stress her body, Poe realized that many other women were probably having the same trouble as she was finding a shoe that really fit, and decided to start her own women's athletic footwear company. As she conceived it, what would make Ryka distinctive was that rather than adapting men's athletic shoes for women, Ryka would design athletic shoes especially suited for women's feet and bodies. Despite heavy odds, Poe was able to realize her goal: Ryka introduced its first two styles of athletic shoes in September, 1987, and began shipping the shoes in March, 1988.

In 1987, Poe had considerable difficulty obtaining venture capital to start a women's athletic shoe company. Potential investors questioned her ability to compete with industry leaders such as Nike and Reebok, given that she had no money and no retail experience—then turned down her requests for loans. Ironically, some of those same venture capitalists now call Poe to ask how they can get in on her $8 million business.

Since she couldn't get anything out of the venture capitalists, Poe leveraged her own house, then turned to family and friends to help finance the company. She also continued to search for more open-minded commercial investors and eventually discovered a Denver investment banker who was willing to do an initial public offering. Poe got a $250,000 bridge loan before the initial public offering—which happened to be about the time the stock market crashed in October, 1987. Nevertheless, Ryka went public on April 15, 1988, and despite the unstable market, 4 million shares in the company were sold at one dollar each in less than a week. The Denver firm completed a second offering before failing. Poe then turned to Paulson Capital Corporation in Oregon for a third offering in mid-1990.

SHERI POE

Sheri Poe believes that the fact that Ryka's president is a woman inspires other women to buy the company's products. As she points out, "we're the only company that can tell women that the person running the company is a woman who works out every day." Even Nike doesn't have a woman making all its product decisions.

In fact, Poe's image and profile are the most critical components in Ryka's marketing strategy. Rather than using professional models, Ryka's print advertisements feature Poe working out; and in the company's recent venture into television advertising spots, Poe is the company spokesperson. The caption on a 1992 ad for Ryka's 900-series aerobic shoes reads, "Our president knows that if you huff and puff, jump up and down, and throw your weight around you eventually get what you want," cleverly referring to Poe's own determination to succeed, and including her audience as co-conspirators who know how hard it is for a woman to make it in the business world because they have "been there" themselves.

As part of Ryka's unique marketing strategy, Poe appears on regional television and radio shows throughout the country, and has been interviewed by numerous magazines and newspapers. Feature articles on Poe and Ryka have appeared in *Entrepreneurial Woman, Executive Female,* and *Working Woman.* Poe has successfully worked the woman angle: she particularly appeals to today's working women because although she has become something of a celebrity, she considers herself a down-to-earth woman who also happens to be a successful executive, and a [divorced, and now remarried] mother. A *Boston Business Journal* article describes her as a CEO whose title "does not cramp [her] style . . . she eschews power suits for miniskirts and jeans, drives herself to work, and lets calls from her kids interrupt her meetings."

THE ATHLETIC FOOTWEAR INDUSTRY

The $11 billion athletic footwear industry is highly competitive. Three major firms control the market: Nike, Reebok, and L.A. Gear. Second string competitors include Adidas, Avia, Asics, and Converse. All of these companies have greater financial strength and more resources than Ryka. While Ryka's sales were $12.1 million in 1992, Nike's were $3.4 billion, Reebok's $3.0 billion, and L.A. Gear's $430 million.

In 1987, the industry as a whole grew at a rate of 20%; but by 1991, its annual growth rate had shrunk to approximately 4%. The athletic footwear market is now considered a mature market. Despite the subdued growth characteristics of the overall industry, however, a number of its sub-markets are expanding via high specialization, technological innovation, and image and fashion appeal.

Product Specialization

The athletic footwear industry is divided into various sub-markets by specialization. Product use categories include: basketball, tennis, running, aerobic, cross-training, and walking, etc. Ryka competes only in the latter three markets: aerobic, cross training, and walking shoes.

Aerobic Segment   The aerobic segment of the athletic shoe industry accounts for approximately $500 million in annual sales. Reebok pioneered the segment and continues to be the industry leader. The market is primarily made up of women and has grown rapidly in recent years. Ryka's number one market is aerobics; in 1991, 80% of Ryka's sales resulted from the Ultra-Lite and step aerobic lines.

Walking Segment   The second major market Ryka competes in is the walking segment. This high growth market is now the fourth largest product category in the athletic shoe industry. In 1991, 70 million people walked for exercise and sales reached $1.7 billion. Reebok leads this market and is concentrating its marketing efforts on young women. Nevertheless, while the male and younger female walking markets have experienced some growth, the walking segment is primarily focused on women 45–55 years old. Ten percent of Ryka's sales are derived from its Series 500 walking shoe, and the company expects the walking shoe segment to be its greatest growth category.

Cross-Training Segment   Ryka also competes in the cross-training segment of the athletic shoe market. Cross-training shoes are popular because they can be used for a variety of activities. Nike created this segment, and maintains the lead in market share. Overall sales for the segment are currently at $1.2 billion, and growth is strong. Ryka earns 10% of its revenues from its cross-training shoes.

Technological Innovation

Reebok and Nike are fast moving toward the goal of identifying themselves as the most technologically advanced producers of performance shoes. Ryka understands that it must keep up with research and development to survive. In October 1988, Ryka introduced its nitrogen footwear system, "Nitrogen/ES"—the "ES" stands for Energy Spheres. The system was developed over a two-year period by a design team with over 35 patents in shoe design and state-of-the-art composite plastics. The idea is that the ES ambient air compression spheres contain nitrogen microballoons that provide significantly more energy return than the systems of any of Ryka's major competitors. Consumer response to the Nitrogen/ES shoe was overwhelming, and in 1989 Ryka discontinued sales of a number of models that did not include this special feature.

Two patents were filed for the Nitrogen/ES System. One has been granted; the other is pending. Although patents are intended to provide legal protection, the cost of defending patents can be quite high. With the vast resources available to Ryka's competition, it would be easy for Reebok or Nike to adopt Ryka's technology at little or no risk of an infringement suit. Ryka's limited financial resources would disable them from enforcing its rights in an infringement action.

Fashion

Ryka has focused on performance rather than fashion because Poe believes that fashion-athletic footwear is susceptible to trends and the economy, but performance shoes will not be affected because women always need to protect their bodies. Nevertheless, a large segment of athletic footwear consumers purchase products based on looks rather than function. In fact, the fashion market is a mainstay of Ryka's major competitors, especially Reebok, the originators of the fashion aerobic shoe market; 80 to 90% of fashion aerobic shoe buyers do not participate in the sport.

Although Ryka shoes are as technologically advanced as Reebok, Nike or L.A. Gear's, they are often overlooked by fashion-conscious consumers unfamiliar with the Ryka name. Despite the fact that Ryka's sales have grown even during these recessionary times, retailers haven't always carried Ryka shoes because they prefer to stock only those brands which are easily recognizable. The lack of a nationally recognized name is a serious concern for any company; thus for Ryka, as for its competitors, expensive, leading edge advertising campaigns have played an essential part in its marketing initiatives.

A ROCKY START

Given the saturation of the athletic footwear market, athletic shoe companies need more than a good product to stay alive; they need powerful marketing and advertising. Ryka concentrates much of its energies on marketing. As a new manufacturer in an already crowded industry, Poe understands the possibility of being marketed right out of business by big competitors with deep pockets like Nike and Reebok. Ryka's approach is to offer similar products, but focus on the most cost-effective ways to reach a target market, thus carving out a niche that the industry giants have overlooked.

To protect a niche, it is critical to stay one step ahead of the competition. Unfortunately for Ryka, Poe had to learn this lesson the hard way. When the company was first founded, it tried unsuccessfully to challenge the brand name manufacturers in all product categories, including running, tennis, aerobics, walking, and cross-training shoes. However, given its limited capital and the huge advertising budgets of Reebok, Nike, and L.A. Gear, Ryka could not compete in all of these different markets at once. Instead, Ryka cut back and chose to focus on aerobic shoes, and secondarily on their walking shoe line. Thus, in addition to limiting product line breadth, Ryka has designed its marketing approach to attract a specific set of customers rather than a broad audience. Poe does not believe that Ryka has to be a giant to succeed. Rather, she contends that Ryka needs to maximize its ability to perform in a particular niche within a large industry.

A NEW DIRECTION

In the already-crowded athletic footwear industry, the various competitors are continually jockeying for a better market position, and competitive edge. Currently, women are, and will probably continue to be, the fastest growing segment of the athletic footwear market. Women's athletic footwear accounts for 55% of Reebok's sales, 60% of Avia's, 45% of L.A. Gear's, and 17% of Nike's $2.2 billion in domestic sales. In recent years, Reebok and Nike have fought for the number one spot in the women's market, and Reebok initially prevailed; but in each of the past two years, Nike has posted a 30% growth in the market. This unparalleled growth in the women's athletic footwear market is the most important trend in the sporting goods industry today, and it is on this niche that Ryka is staking its future.

An important part of the Ryka mission stems from the fact that their shoes are specifically made for women. While the big name shoe companies were merely making smaller sizes of men's shoes made on men's lasts, Ryka developed a fitness shoe built specifically for women with a patented design for better shock absorption and durability. Ryka had a first mover advantage in this segment and has a sustained competitive advantage in that none of the other companies in the athletic shoe industry can boast having a business strategy focused on women. All other contenders have other lines or are concentrated in other niches. Ultimately, however, it is the Ultra-Lite mid-sole, Ryka's most significant and successful product advancement, that keeps Ryka up with its competition in its market. The Ryka Ultra-Lite aerobics shoe weighs 7.7 ounces, or roughly 30% of the weight of a regular aerobic shoe. Within two months of its introduction in December 1990, the company had sold all of its Ultra-Lites at a unit price of $70 a pair (retail). It took three months before additional shoe orders could be filled. Some investment firms were concerned that Ryka might not be able to capitalize on the success of its new line given its difficulty keeping retailers supplied with sufficient quantities. Eventually, Ryka did lose some ground to Nike and Reebok—both of which quickly jumped into the lightweight aerobic shoe market. Despite the competition, however, Ryka's Ultra-Lite lines are a success, accounting for close to 90% of its total sales for 1991.

After establishing a solid foundation in the aerobics category, Ryka again turned its attention to product differentiation. Its current product line includes the Series 900 Aerobic/Step shoes, the Series 700 Aerobic shoes, the Series 800/Cross Training shoes, and the Series 500 Walking shoes. To make sure its shoes were not perceived as "too specialized," Ryka designed the Aerobic Step 50/50 and a lightweight version of it, the Step-Lite 50/50, each of which can be worn for both high-impact and step aerobics. Ryka also designed a dual purpose WALK/RUN shoe, the 570, for women who complement their walking routine with running, but don't want to own shoes for every activity. Ryka is now considering entering the medical footwear market because an increasing number of podiatrists and chiropractors are recommending Ryka walking shoes to their patients.

THE RYKA ROSE FOUNDATION

The Ryka ROSE (Regaining One's Self Esteem) Foundation is a not-for-profit organization created by Sheri Poe to help women who have been the victims of violent crimes. The foundation was launched in September, 1992, and Poe herself personally pledged $250,000. Poe founded the ROSE Foundation because she was raped at age 19. The trauma resulting from the rape led to further suffering from bulimia. She sees herself as a survivor who needed to do something to help fellow victims: "For me, having a company that just made a product was not enough. I wanted to do something more."

Ryka has made a commitment to donate 7% of its pre-tax profits to the foundation and sponsor special fundraising events to help strengthen community prevention and treatment programs for women who are the victims of violent crimes. Ryka includes information on the foundation in brochures that are packaged with each box of shoes in the hope that its social conscience may favorably influence some consumers. But for Poe, it is more than a marketing ploy. She considers Ryka's financial commitment to the ROSE Foundation a natural extension of the company's commitment to women.

The foundation has created alliances with health clubs, non-profit organizations, and corporations in an effort to reach women directly with educational materials and programs. In addition, the ROSE Foundation funds a $25,000 grants program to encourage organizations to develop creative solutions to the widespread problem of violence against women. One of the foundation's beneficiaries, the National Victim Center, received an award of $10,000 to set up a toll-free (800) telephone number for victims and their families through which they can obtain immediate information, referrals, and other types of assistance.

Poe hopes that the foundation will act as a catalyst for coalition-building to help stop violence against women. But she also envisions the foundation as a means of involving retailers in marketing socially-responsible programs directly to women. Lady Foot Locker has taken advantage of this opportunity and became the first retailer to join forces with the ROSE Foundation. In October, Lady Foot Locker conducted a two-week promotional campaign in their 550 United States stores in conjunction with the ROSE Foundation. The retailer distributed free education brochures and held a special sweepstakes contest to raise awareness about the issue of violence against women. Customer response was overwhelmingly positive, and Lady Foot Locker is considering a future partnership with the ROSE Foundation. Foot Locker, Champs and Athletic X-press have also expressed interest in the foundation.

MVP Sports, a New England retailer, has also participated in Ryka's activities to help stop violence against women. The company, which operates eight stores in the New England area, sponsored a two-week information-based campaign featuring Sheri Poe that included radio, TV and newspaper advertisements. In addition, Doug Barron, president of MVP Sports, was so impressed with the concept and progressive thinking of the Ryka ROSE Foundation that he decided his company would donate $2 to the foundation for each pair of Ryka athletic shoes sold during the 1992 holiday season. Poe sees MVP Sports' support as an important first step toward actively involving retailers in Ryka's efforts to help prevent violence against women, and is reaching out to other retailers who she hopes will follow suit.

Poe considers Ryka and its foundation unique. As she sees it, the company has a great story to tell. It is the only athletic footwear company that is exclusively for women, by women, and now supporting women, "the first athletic shoe with a 'soul.'" And Poe is banking on her hunch that the foundation will appeal to Ryka customers who appreciate the idea that their buying power is helping women less fortunate than they are.

Nevertheless, Poe's choice to make Ryka a socially responsible company right from the beginning, rather than waiting until the company is fully established, has had consequences for its financial status. Some industry analysts have suggested that Ryka would be better off funneling any extra cash back into the company until it is completely solvent, and its product lines and name recognition automatic. But others argue that the reputation Ryka has garnered as an ethical company, as concerned about social issues as about the "bottom line," effectively appeals to kind hearted women consumers. For them, the ROSE Foundation is worth in "good press" whatever it has cost the company in terms of actual investment dollars, because the company has effectively carved out a niche that speaks on many different levels to women's ethical and consumer concerns.

MARKETING

Ryka's promotional strategy is aimed at creating both brand awareness and sales at the retail level. By garnering the support of professional sports organizations early on, Ryka acquired instant name recognition in a variety of key audiences. In 1988, Ryka entered into a six-figure, eight-year licensing agreement with the U.S. Ski Team which permitted Ryka to market its products as the official training shoes of the Team. Also in 1988, the American Aerobics Association International boosted Ryka's brand name recognition when it replaced Avia with Ryka as the association's preferred aerobics shoes. The next year, *Shape* magazine labeled Ryka number one in its aerobic shoe category.

Ryka has also begun sponsoring both aerobics teams and aerobics competitions. In July, 1992, twenty-five countries competed in the World Aerobic championships in Las Vegas, Nevada. The Canadian Team was sponsored by Ryka Athletic Footwear. In September, 1992, Ryka was the premier sponsor and the official shoe of the Canadian National Aerobic championship held in Vancouver, BC. To ensure the success of the event and build awareness for the sport of competitive aerobics, Ryka successfully promoted the nationals through retailers, athletic clubs, and individuals. Given that virtually every previous aerobics competition world-wide had been sponsored by Reebok, Canada's selection of Ryka as their official sponsor marked a significant milestone for Ryka, as well as marking Ryka's international recognition as a core brand in the women's athletic market.

The Ryka Training Body

Early on, Sheri Roe determined that the most effective way to reach Ryka's female aerobics niche would be through marketing to aerobics instructors, and targeted Ryka's advertising accordingly. In fact, Ryka spends almost as much as industry leaders on print advertisements in aerobics instructors' magazines, and very little on print advertising elsewhere. On the other hand, unlike its big competitors, Ryka does not use celebrity endorsements to sell its products, because the company markets on the theory that women will care more about what feels good on their feet than about what any particular celebrity has to say.

Beyond advertising in aerobics magazines, Ryka has successfully used direct mail marketing techniques to target aerobics instructors The Ryka Training Body is comprised of more than 40,000 women employed as fitness instructors and personal trainers throughout the country. They receive product information four to six times per year, as well as discounts on shoes. Ryka also has a group of its instructors tied to specific local retailers The instructors direct their students to those retailers, who then offer discounts to the students. Finally, Ryka-affiliated instructors offer demonstrations to educate consumers about what to look for in an aerobics shoe.

In addition to increasing sales, the relationship between Ryka and the aerobics profession has led to significant product design innovations. Aerobics instructors' suggestions, based on their own experience, as well as on feedback from students in their classes, has led to improvements such as more effective cushioning and better arch support in the shoes. Poe considers these teachers as the link to Ryka's customers. In fact, as a direct result of instructor feedback, Ryka was the first manufacturer to respond to the new step aerobics trend by developing and marketing lightweight shoes specifically designed to support up and down step motions.

Salespeople

Ryka's marketing efforts are also aimed at the people who sell Ryka products. In Ryka's early days, Poe and her advertising manager, Laurie Ruddy, personally visited retail stores to meet salespeople and "sell" them on Ryka products. Now, the Vice President of Sales and Marketing maintains contact with retailers using incentive programs, give-aways, and small monetary bonuses to keep salespeople excited. The company also provides premiums, such as fanny packs or water bottles for customers.

Advertising Budget

Given the highly competitive nature of the athletic footwear industry, effective advertising is crucial in distinguishing among brands and creating brand preference. As a two-year old company in 1989, Ryka was particularly capital-intensive, given that it was trying to penetrate the athletic shoe market. Its $3.5 million loss that year is largely attributable to advertising spending of approximately $2.5 million, but that amount was nothing compared to Nike, Reebok, and L.A. Gear who, combined, spent more than $100 million on advertising during the same period.

At that time, Ryka advertised only in trade publications; therefore recognition among consumers was lagging. Since then, Ryka ads have appeared in *Shape, City Sports, American Fitness, Elle,* and *Idea Today* magazines. By 1992 Poe could claim that Ryka's brand recognition had grown dramatically, even though Ryka's advertising and marketing budget was only about 9% of sales. Poe attributes Ryka's marketing success to its direct marketing techniques, especially its targeting of certified aerobic instructors to wear Ryka shoes.

In October, 1992, after three successive quarters of record sales and little profitability, Poe announced that Ryka was going to expand its direct marketing to consumers, even if it required increased spending to penetrate the marketplace beyond aerobics instructors. But Ryka is still in another league compared to industry giants when it comes to budgets. Ryka's total advertising budget is estimated at approximately $1.5 million, while Nike could afford to spend $20 million on a 1991 pan-European campaign to launch a single product; and Reebok is currently spending $28 million on its "I Believe . . ." ad campaign which specifically targets women.

OPERATIONS

As is common in the athletic-footwear industry, Ryka shoes are made by independent manufacturers in Europe and the Far East, including South Korea and Taiwan, according to Ryka product specifications. Ryka's first three years were rough, in large part because of the poor quality of the products provided by its manufacturer in Taiwan. Now, however, the shoes are made in Korea with strict quality-controls measures in effect. The company relies on a Far Eastern buying agent, under Ryka's direction, for the selection of suppliers, inspection of goods prior to shipment, and shipment of finished goods.

Ryka's management believes that this sourcing of footwear products minimizes company investment in fixed assets as well as reducing cost and risk. Given the extent of the underutilized factory manufacturing capacity in countries outside of South Korea and Taiwan, Ryka's management believes that alternative sources of product manufacturing are readily available, should the company have need of them. Because of the volatility of international and economic relations in today's global marketplace, and in order to protect itself from complete dependence on one supplier, Ryka has resolved to keep itself free of any long-term contract with manufacturers beyond the terms of purchase orders issued. Orders are placed on a volume basis through its agent and Ryka receives finished products within 120 days of an order. If necessary, Ryka may pay a premium to reduce the time required to deliver finished goods from the factory to meet customer demand.

The principal raw materials in Ryka shoes are leather, rubber, ethylvinyl acetate, polyurethane, cambrelle, and pigskin, all of which are readily available both in the United States and abroad. Nevertheless, even though Ryka could locate new sources of raw materials within a relatively short period of time if it needed to for its overseas manufacturers, its business could be dev-astated by any interruption in operations, whereas Reebok and Nike have large stockpiles of inventory and would be less affected by any difficulties with suppliers.

Distribution

Ryka products are sold in sporting-goods stores, athletic-footwear stores, se-lected high-end department stores, and sport-specialty retailers including Foot Locker, Lady Foot Locker, Athlete's Foot Store, Foot Action, US Athlet-ics, Oshman's and Nordstroms.

Ryka's major distribution relationship is with the 476 Lady Foot Locker stores in the United States and 250 Lady Foot Locker stores in Canada. In No-vember, 1992, Ryka announced that in early 1993, 400 Lady Foot Locker stores would display permanent Ryka signage, identifying Ryka as a brand es-pecially promoted by Foot Locker. Both Sheri Poe and Amy Schecter, Vice President of Retail Marketing for Lady Foot Locker, agree that Ryka shoes have seen solid sales in Lady Foot Locker stores, and the Lady Foot Locker's display of permanent Ryka signage expresses the confidence Lady Foot Locker has in Ryka's future success.

During the spring of 1992, FOOTACTION USA, a division of the Melville Corporation, and the second largest specialty footwear retailer in the country, began selling Ryka athletic shoes on a trial basis in 40 stores. The trial was so successful, FOOTACTION agreed to purchase five styles of Ryka shoes for its stores, and in September, 1992, Ryka announced that 150 FOOTACTION stores would begin to carry its products nationally.

On November 3, 1992, Ryka announced that it had received orders from three large retail sporting goods chains, adding well over 200 store outlets to its distribution network. The twelfth largest sporting goods retailer in the country, MC Sporting Goods, based in Grand Rapids, Michigan, now carries five styles of Ryka athletic shoes in each of its 73 stores. In addition, Ryka has received orders from the Tampa, Florida-based Sports and Recreation, which will sell four styles of Ryka athletic shoes in all of its 23 sporting goods stores. Charlie Burks, head footwear buyer for Sports and Recreation, based his deci-sion to stock Ryka shoes on his sense that the chain's customers are looking for new, exciting styles of athletic shoes at affordable prices, and that Ryka de-livers on performance, fashion and value. Ryka shoes are also carried in more than 135 Athletic Express stores.

In the competitive athletic footwear industry, distributors and retailers have considerable clout. In 1989, Lady Foot Locker and Foot Locker retailers accounted for 13 percent of Ryka's net sales. But the company realized it needed a broader pool of retailers. More recently, Ryka has managed to con-trol its customer base such that no single customer or group under common control accounts for more than 10% of its total revenue.

Human Resources

When Ryka was in its early stages, Poe set out to gain credibility through human resources. The company offered industry-standard salaries, stock op-tions, and the opportunity for significant input into the day-to-day operations of the company. In addition, Poe attracted four top executives from Reebok for positions in sales, advertising, and public relations. This high-powered team performed so effectively that sales doubled between Ryka's first and second years. But, total executive compensation was too much for the young company. Poe realized that a change in strategy was necessary, and three of the four Reebok veterans have since left.

Early on, in 1988, Ryka had only four employees. Ryka now employs 22 people at its Norwood headquarters, as well as 35 sales representatives across the country. Ryka's small size gives it a certain flexibility, enabling the company to concentrate on continual streamlining and improvement, so that new ideas and adjustments can be implemented and in the stores within 120 days.

In November, 1992, Ryka appointed Roy S. Kelvin as Vice President and Chief Financial Officer to reinforce its commitment to the financial community. Poe sees Kelvin, a former New York investment banker, as instrumental to helping the company grow, but there is also a sense in which Poe's appointment of Kelvin is her acknowledgment of the fact that she's competing for funds in an "old-boy's" network, so it is extremely valuable to have an "old-boy" to help build up her list of contacts. Kelvin's main priorities are helping to secure domestic financing, reduce operating expenses, and improve profit margins.

FINANCIALS

Ryka originally financed its operations principally through public stock offerings, warrant exercises, and other private sales of its common stock, netting an aggregate of approximately $7.2 million. In July, 1990, Ryka completed its public stock offering, which raised net proceeds of $3.5 million, allowing the company to market its products aggressively during the fall of 1990 and beyond. So far, Ryka has sold shares to private investors who control 65% of the shares.

In September, 1992, Ryka extended the date for redemption of its outstanding common stock purchase warrant issues in the company's 1990 public offering another two weeks in response to requests made from warrant holders. Poe was very pleased with the response to the warrant solicitation and agreed to the extension to allow the maximum number of holders to exercise their warrants. If all public and underwriter warrants are exercised, the company will receive approximately $6.3 million in gross proceeds.

In 1991, Ryka signed an agreement with its Korean trading company to increase its line of credit from $2.5 million to $3.5 million. In addition, working capital resources come from a letter of credit financing agreement, coupled with an accounts receivable line to credit.

Ryka's product costs are higher than those of the industry leaders for several reasons. First of all, because Ryka is significantly smaller than the industry leaders, it cannot take advantage of volume production discounts. Secondly, the company has opted to pay somewhat higher prices for its products than would be charged by alternate suppliers in order to achieve and maintain higher quality. Finally, higher production costs have resulted from Ryka's inventory financing arrangement with its Korean trading company, which includes financing costs, commissions, and fees as part of cost of sales.

Ryka has taken on some formidable competition in the form of Nike and Reebok. For Ryka to prosper, Sheri Poe must successfully carve out a niche in the women's athletic shoe market before they run out of money. Time is becoming increasingly scarce.

EXHIBIT 1

Ryka, Inc. Summary of 1992 Results

| | Year Ended December 31 | | Percent Change |
	1992	1991[1]	
Gross sales	$13,329,777	$8,838,911	50.8%
Discounts, returns and allowances	1,136,134	860,986	32.0%
Net sales	12,193,643	7,977,925	52.8%
Cost of goods sold	8,867,375	5,231,346	69.5%
Gross profit	3,326,268	2,746,579	21.1%
OPERATING EXPENSES			
General and administrative	1,239,245[2]	1,287,925	−3.8%
Marketing	1,722,618	1,396,769	23.3%
Research and development	148,958	155,576	−4.3%
Total operating expenses	3,110,821	2,840,270	9.5%
Operating income (loss)	215,447	(93,691.00)	
OTHER (INCOME) EXPENSE:			
Interest expense	516,455	418,469	23.4%
Interest income	(4,196)	(12,648)	−66.8%
Total other (income) expense	512,259	405,821	26.2%
Net loss	(296,812)	(499,512)	−40.6%
Net loss per share	($0.01)	($0.03)	
Weighted average shares outstanding	19,847,283	18,110,923	
Cash and cash equivalents	$1,029,161	$ 166,030	519.9%
Current assets	$8,199,411	$4,367,255	87.7%
Total assets	$8,306,262	$4,498,021	84.7%
Current liabilities	$4,134,974	$3,623,668	14.1%
Stockholder's equity	$4,153,410	$ 834,902	397.5%

1. To provide comparability with the current year presentation, $410,000 of 1991 product financing expenses have been reclassified from Cost of goods sold to Interest expense.
2. General & administrative expense includes a charge of $138,000 to reserve a receivable relating to the liquidation of the Company's licensed distributor in the U.K.

EXHIBIT 2

Ryka, Inc. Financial Data 1988–1992

	Year Ended December 31				
	1992	**1991**	**1990**	**1989**	**1988**
STATEMENT OF OPERATIONS DATA:					
Net sales	$12,193,643	$7,977,925	$4,701,538	$4,916,542	$991,684
Gross profit before inventory write-down	3,326,268	2,746,579	1,013,445	1,364,340	308,901
Inventory write-down to lower of cost or market			906,657		
Gross profit	3,326,268	2,746,579	106,888	1,364,340	308,901
Costs and expenses	3,110,821	2,840,270	3,598,728	4,368,774	1,687,806
Operating income (loss)	215,447	(93,691)	(3,491,840)	(3,004,434)	(1,378,905)
Interest expense, net	512,260	405,821	218,817	548,149	148,485
Expenses incurred in connection with termination of merger agreement			377,855		
Net loss	$(296,813)	$(499,512)	$(4,088,512)	$(3,552,583)	$(1,527,390)
Net loss per share	$(0.01)	$(0.03)	$(0.27)	$(0.31)	$(0.16)
Weighted average shares outstanding	19,847,283	18,110,923	15,336,074	11,616,088	9,397,360
Number of common shares outstanding	23,101,948	18,136,142	18,005,142	13,242,500	10,252,500
BALANCE SHEET DATA:					
Total assets	$8,319,229	$4,498,021	$2,711,713	$3,553,000	$2,073,058
Total debt	410,673	68,256	86,149	974,521	247,340
Net working capital	4,077,404	743,587	1,097,827	1,643,352	1,140,173
Stockholders' equity	4,166,377	834,902	1,299,264	1,848,059	1,341,858

EXHIBIT 3

Ryka's Stock Price 1992/1991

	1992		1991	
Calendar Period	**High**	**Low**	**High**	**Low**
First Quarter	$2.31	$0.53	$1.06	$0.22
Second Quarter	$2.44	$1.19	$0.87	$0.50
Third Quarter	$1.69	$1.19	$0.90	$0.56
Fourth Quarter	$1.89	$0.97	$0.78	$0.56

Ryka's Common Stock is Traded on NASDAQ.

The company does not pay dividends to its stockholders and does not plan to pay dividends in the foreseeable future.

Works Consulted

Colter, Gene, "On target: athletic shoes just for women; Women's awareness of athletic shoes; Special super show athletics issue," *Footwear News*, February 18, 1991.

Dutter, Greg, "Making strides," *Sporting Goods Business*, March 1992, v25, n3, p34(1).

Fucini, Suzy, "A women's game: Women have become the hottest focus of today's marketing," *Sporting Goods Dealer*, August 1992, p 34(3).

Goodman, Doug, "Reebok chief looks beyond Nike," *Advertising Age*, January 29, 1990, v61, n5, p57(1).

Grimm, Matthew, "Nike targets women with print campaign," *Adweek's Marketing Week*, December 10, 1990, v33, nl2, p12(1).

Hower, Wendy, "Gender gap: The executive suite is still wilderness for women," *Boston Business Journal*, July 27, 1992, v12, n23, sec2, p5(2).

Kelly, Craig T., "Fashion sells aerobics shoes," January 1990, v23, n1, p39(1).

Lee, Sharon; McAllister, Robert; Rooney, Ellen; Tedeschi, Mark, "Community ties nourish growth of aerobic sales; Aerobic programs boost sales of aerobic shoes," *Footwear News*, October 7, 1991, v31, n33, p17(1).

Magiera, Marcy, "Nike again registers no.1 performance," *Advertising Age*, May 7, 1990, v61, n19, p4(1).

Magiera, Marcy, "Nike again registers no.1 performance," *Advertising Age*, January 29, 1990, v61, n5, p16(1).

"New England retailer joins Ryka in fight against domestic violence," *Business Wire*, November 13, 1991.

"Nike takes Reebok's edge: advertising expenditures of top sports shoes manufactures," LEXIS "mrktng," April 16, 1992, p10(1).

Poe, Sheri, "To compete with giants, choose your niche," *Nation's Business*, July 1992, v80, n7, p6(1).

Powell, Robert J., "Ryka is off and running," *Boston Business Journal*, February 29, 1988, v8, n1, p3.

"Ryka adds 100 stores to distribution network," *Business Wire*, November 3, 1992.

"Ryka announces extension for warrant redemption," *Business Wire*, September 11, 1992.

"Ryka announces record first quarter 1991 results," *Business Wire*, April 24, 1991.

"Ryka completes $ 4.7 million offering," *Business Wire*, July 24, 1990.

"Ryka introduces new nitrogen system," *Business Wire*, October 20, 1988.

"Ryka launches ROSE Foundation to help stop violence against women," Ryka Inc., News Release, September, 28, 1992.

Ryka 1991 in Review, Annual Report, Ryka Inc.

"A Ryka rose: Sheri Poe on career, family and purpose," *Sporting Goods Dealer*, September 1992.

"Ryka to expand its presence in Footlocker Stores," *Business Wire*, June 4, 1992.

"Ryka vaults to $8M in its lightweight sneaks," *Boston Business Journal*, March 30, 1992, v12, n6, p9.

Simon, Ruth, "The no-P/E stocks," *Forbes*, October 2, 1989, p40.

Touby, Laurel Allison, "Creativity vs. cash" *Working Woman*, November 1991, v16, n11, p73(4).

Witt, Louise, "Ryka turns to aerobics for toehold in market," *Boston Business Journal*, April 1, 1991, v11, n6, p6.

Wolfensberger, Beth, "Shoe markers have itch to enter niche markets," *Boston Business Journal*, March 19, 1990, v10, n4, p7.

Nike, Inc.

RANDALL K. WHITE, *Auburn University—Montgomery*

INTRODUCTION

In his letter to shareholders in the 1991 annual report, Philip H. Knight, Chairman and CEO, projected his outlook for the company:

> Around the world, people of all cultures are increasing their participation in fitness activities. All are motivated by the common desire for athletic and personal excellence.

> Nike—a simple sneaker company to many newspaper readers—is transforming into an international consumer products company. Companies attacking international markets generally will take one of two approaches: (1) lay a solid infrastructure and build off of it forever, or (2) cream it without regard to the long term. Obviously, we have chosen the first approach.

> Specifically, over the past decade, we have built an international management team of more than 1500 people. In Western Europe, we own the distribution rights over 90% of our sales. Nike has hired more than 1000 people in the last 12 months, mostly dictated by our desire to service and support our international growth.

> Shortly after the middle of the decade, Nike will be a bigger company outside the United States than inside. Given the speed and power of global communications, there will no longer be a different brand leading the market in each hemisphere. There will be one world leader in sports and fitness. You can easily guess which brand gets my vote.

> The payoff from overcoming all these challenges can be seen in our 1991 international growth of 80% to $862 million in revenues. We are at last, after many sometimes comical fits and starts, after 10 years of hard work, a serious threat not only in Europe, but in Asia as well.

Reflecting Knight's comments, Nike experienced continued growth in net income, from $167 million in 1989 to $243 million in 1990 to over $287 million in 1991, an increase of over 71% since 1989. This impressive growth was in sharp contrast to the reported income of $36 million in 1987. The company

---

Courtesy of Randall K. White, Auburn University—Montgomery.

reported that the decline in 1987 was due to three factors: the "decrease in volume of Air Jordan basketball products, the elimination in 1987 revenues from the company's unprofitable Japanese subsidiary which was sold, and increased competition. . ." [1]. However, profits rebounded to over $101 million in 1988.

> . . . partly because of a swing in buyer's tastes. After years of preferring stylish Reeboks, the trendsetters are now clamoring for "performance" shoes such as Nike's. [4]

Sales followed a relatively similar pattern. From 1989 to 1990, revenues climbed from over $1.7 billion to about $2.2 billion, a 29% increase. The following year, 1991, revenues exceeded $3 billion, a 34% increase.

The company's inventory position increased from $309 million in 1990 to about $586 million in 1991, a $277 million increase. Approximately $157 million of this increase was in domestic footwear, while international inventories increased $102 million to handle the increased demand.

Nevertheless, as it faced stiff challenges in its various market segments, the question remained whether Nike could respond fast enough to remain a top athletic shoe manufacturer. Other strategic questions were facing the company. (a) Nike was a low-cost producer with overseas manufacturing facilities in Asia—notably South Korea, Thailand, and Taiwan where 51%, 15%, and 13%, respectively, of shoes were produced. About 43% of the company's apparel production was also located in Asia and in South America. Could the potential political risks, increasing costs, and a declining U.S. dollar compel the company to retrench and make other sourcing arrangements? (b) Did it have the financial muscle and customer franchise to counter such strong competitors as Reebok, L.A. Gear, and others? (c) Would the intense competition in the industry compel the company to sell its high-quality athletic footwear as private-branded products for major retailing chains? Or, should it position itself as the premier athletic shoe company?

BRIEF HISTORY

Incorporated in 1968 in Oregon, Nike began years earlier "when Knight, a former college miler, sold running shoes from the back of his station wagon at track meets" [2]. A native of Oregon and born in 1938, Knight graduated from the University of Oregon in 1959 with a BBA and later received his MBA from Stanford in 1962. His interests in running shoes remained strong during this period after visiting Japan, which he felt would become a major player in the athletic shoe market. Knight joined Coopers & Lybrand as an accountant from 1963 to 1964 and then moved to Price Waterhouse from 1964 to 1967. He later became an assistant professor in business administration at Portland State University from 1967 to 1969. Both *Fortune* and *Business Week* magazines provided interesting personal glimpses of Knight:

> He is no match for Bo Jackson, the pro football and baseball player who displays a stunning athletic versatility in the ubiquitous TV ads for Nike shoes. But for a middle-aged CEO who gently complains about "old bones," Phil Knight, 51, does all right. He runs 18 to 30 miles a week, lifts weights, plays tennis. [4]

> Philip H. Knight, shy? In private, yes. A foot twitches nervously while the blond, bearded chief executive officer of Nike Inc. talks about himself. But watch the former college runner in competition, and "shy" is not a word anyone would dare

hang on Phil Knight. He is emotional about Nike, even prone to watery eyes during his employee pep talks. And when a guy like that gets beat, he usually gets even. [4]

Knight and his track coach, William Bowerman of the University of Oregon, formed Blue Ribbon Sports on an initial investment of $500 each and began importing Tiger brand shoes from Japan. The venture enjoyed considerable success as sales surged from its modest beginning of $3 million in 1972 to fiscal year-end 1988, when sales exceeded $1 billion. However, disputes with the company's large supplier led the company to design and market its own shoes, which the founders named Nike, after the Greek goddess of victory.

Highly regarded within the company as the driving entrepreneurial force that ultimately transformed Nike into a world-class athletic footwear manufacturer, Knight visualized the company focusing on three core areas: shoes, related clothing, and accessories. At the same time, he viewed timely acquisitions as a way to strengthen the company's position in the highly competitive athletic footwear market. Moreover, Knight envisioned the company primarily as a producer of performance-oriented shoes, not a fashion shoe company.

ORGANIZATION

Nike's organizational structure is shown in Exhibit 1. Although generally regarded as a company with a deliberately lean structure intended to foster autonomy and an entrepreneurial climate, Nike has a formalized management structure that defines accountability and responsibility. This presumably freed Knight to deal with long-term strategic issues.

EXHIBIT 1

Nike Management Organization Chart

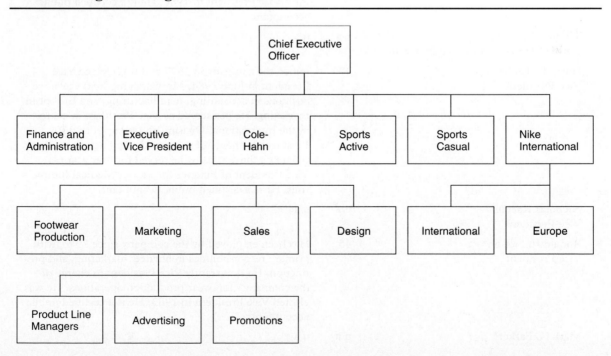

The company's experienced executive officers and the board of directors are listed in Exhibit 2. Outsiders accounted for one-half of the board membership; in addition, six of its officers, including Knight, are CPAs.

Nike's basic mission is the design, development, and worldwide merchandising of high-quality footwear and apparel products for a wide range of sport, athletic, and leisure activities. Nike does not see itself as a manufacturer but

EXHIBIT 2

Nike, Inc. Officers and Directors

Name	Age	Position with Nike, Principal Occupation, and Business Experience
Philip H. Knight*,**(1) Chairman and CEO	50	Co-founder of the company and has served as its Chairman of the Boardand, except for the period June 1983 through September 1984, as its President since its organization in 1968.
Richard K. Donahue*,**(1) President and Chief Operating Officer	n/a	Partner, Donahue & Donahue, Attorneys, Lowell, Massachusetts.
William J. Bowerman*,**(2) Deputy Chairman of the Board of Directors and Senior Vice President	77	Co-founder of the company, has served as Sr. Vice President and a Director since 1968 and was elected Senior Vice President and Deputy Chairman of the Board in 1980.
Delbert J. Hayes*,**(4) Executive Vice President	53	Joined the company as Treasurer and Executive and became a Director in 1975. He thereafter served as Treasurer and in a number of executive positions, primarily in manufacturing, until his election as Executive Vice President in 1980. He is a certified public accountant.
Thomas E. Clarke* General Manager and Vice President	n/a	n/a
Harry C. Carsh* Vice President	49	Joined the company in 1977 and was elected Vice President in June 1984. Mr. Carsh has held executive positions in accounting, manufacturing, and European marketing. He has served as Vice President in charge of the International Division and is currently Vice President in charge of merchandising operations. Prior to joining the company, he served for four years as Vice President of Finance for Laneet Medical Industries. He is a certified public accountant.
Nicholas Kartalis* Vice President	n/a	n/a
Ronald E. Nelson* Vice President	45	Has been employed by the company since 1976, with primary responsibilities in finance, marketing, and production. He is currently Vice President in charge of the company's footwear production operations. He was elected Vice President in 1983. He is a certified public accountant.
Mark G. Parker*	n/a	n/a

more a market-driven company. Consequently, it does a number of things very well—for example, maintaining and nurturing the ability to pinpoint future trends in the industry, continuing to strengthen its R&D capability for new and technologically superior athletic footwear, and cultivating its existing and potential relationships with its various domestic and international contract manufacturers in order to ensure product quality.

EXHIBIT 2

Nike, Inc. Officers and Directors

Name	Age	Position with Nike, Principal Occupation, and Business Experience
George E. Porter* Vice President—Finance	57	Joined the company as Vice President in 1982 and has held executive positions in administration, research and development, and footwear. He became Vice President—Finance in February 1985. Prior to joining the company, he was employed for nine years by Evans Products Company, Portland, Oregon, as Vice President and Controller. He is a certified public accountant.
David B. Taylor* Vice President	n/a	n/a
John E. Jaqua*,**(3)(5) Secretary	67	Has been Secretary and a Director of the company since 1968. He has been a principal in the law firm of Jaqua, Wheatley, Gallagher and Holland, P.C., Eugene, Oregon since 1962.
Lindsay D. Stewart* Vice President & Corporate Counsel	n/a	n/a
Thomas Niebergall* Assistant Secretary	n/a	n/a
Jill K. Conway**(2)	n/a	Visiting Scholar, Massachusetts Institute of Technology, Boston, Massachusetts.
Robert T. Davis**(2)	n/a	Professor of Marketing, Stanford University, Palo Alto, California.
Robert D. DeNuncio** (3)(4)(5)	n/a	n/a
Douglas G. Houser**(2)	n/a	Assistant Secretary, Nike, Inc.; Partner—Bullivant, Houser, Bailey, Pendergrass & Hoffman, Attorneys, Portland, Oregon.
Thomas O. Paine**(3)(5)	n/a	Chairman, Thomas Paine Associates, Los Angeles, California.
Charles W. Robinson**(4)	n/a	Chairman, Energy Transition Corporation, Santa Fe, New Mexico.
John R. Thompson, Jr.**(3)	n/a	Head Basketball Coach, Georgetown University.

  * Officers, annual report.
 ** Directors
(1) Member—Executive Committee
(2) Member—Audit Committee
(3) Member—Personnel Committee
(4) Member—Finance Committee
(5) Member—Stock Option Committee

In effect, Nike, as well as many other U.S. companies, has essentially become a marketer for foreign producers; that is, a company such as Nike, which designs, develops, and markets products worldwide, does not manufacture anything! In contrast to traditional manufacturers, these firms are labeled "hollow corporations" [14, p. 57]. As many U.S. firms move to low-cost overseas producers (e.g., Taiwan, South Korea, and others), this continued outsourcing could bring about a decline in U.S. manufacturing capability. Some see these "hollow corporations" as "network companies"—that is, companies that depend on other firms for manufacturing and other functional support.

MARKETING

Product

Although the company's footwear products are targeted for athletic use, many buyers tend to wear them also for casual and leisure purposes. To complement its footwear merchandise and round out its athletic image, Nike produces a variety of accessory and apparel items such as athletic bags, hats, socks, jackets, warm-up suits, shorts, T-shirts, and tank tops. The company also introduced the Nike Monitor, an electronic monitoring training aid.

Jones [2] reported that Nike may need to diversify to stay ahead in the highly competitive and mature running shoe market, and perhaps, "to change its image from a running shoe company to a total-fitness-oriented operation." However, it was unlikely it would abandon the running shoe market—a unique Nike strength.

To protect its market share from fast-growing fashion-oriented competitors such as Reebok and L.A. Gear, Nike introduced, in late 1988, a new line called Side One,

> . . . a nontechnical shoe for teenager girls who buy athletic, or athletic-looking shoes, to make a fashion statement. Those customers are the core of Keds' and L.A. Gear's business. [7]

The company missed the shift in consumer preferences toward fashion and sport-styled shoes, and consumer desire to stay fit through a variety of such activities as running, weightlifting, aerobics, tennis, and other sports activities [3]. To meet this need, Nike developed the cross-training shoe, which was a natural product evolution for the company, whose prime attention was directed toward specialized products. The company pinpointed the product's marketing message toward the shoe's economy and the convenience of buying, wearing, and carrying only one pair of shoes for diverse fitness activities. The shoe was a result of the company's commitment to thorough research of the foot's biomechanical movements. To convey the cross-trainer's technical qualities, Nike contracted with 100 of the top U.S. fitness instructors and provided them with samples of the product to influence their students as well as to take part in trade shows and other sales activities [15].

To further expand its product lines, Nike acquired, in May 1988, Cole-Hahn Holdings, Inc., "a leading designer and marketer of high quality casual and dress shoes." Nike paid for the acquisition with $89.2 million in cash and the issuance of 243,713 shares of Nike stock, which had a market value of $5.8 million, for the remainder [1]. Knight estimated the company's efforts to broaden its lines would increase sales by $150 million and would position Nike with the "most prestigious brands at both ends of the footwear spectrum" [8]. Knight added that about "69% of the company's shoe sales come from models costing between $44 and $73 a pair" [8].

Promotion

Advertising and promotion expenditures steadily increased, from $135 million in 1989 to $190 million in 1990 (a 40% increase), then doubled from 1989 to 1991, to $286 million. Promotional activities include brochures, print and TV advertising, as well as point-of-purchase displays. Posters are used to depict new footwear models promoted by the company.

Other promotional efforts have included publication of the book *Walk On,* which was co-authored by the former sports research laboratory director and a senior editor of *American Health Magazine.* Containing extensive information on walking—a potentially large growth area for the company—the book provided relevant consumer and product information. Back-to-school campaigns broadened the children's line of such new products as the Air Jordan, Air Max, and the Air Trainer; these were competitively promoted in the "fifty-dollar" range. Other new children's shoes were designed exclusively for children's activities such as skateboarding and biking. In addition, a licensing arrangement with Major League Baseball allowed the company to market specially designed baseball apparel; this unique opportunity would enable Nike to transfer its favorable sports image to both on and off the field.

Nike has also developed a co-op advertising program whereby a retailer can accumulate a 1% to 3% credit allowance based on its total footwear purchases. For example, assuming a 1% allowance on $100,000 of footwear purchases, the retailer could build up $1,000 of credit with Nike whereby it could use this "credit" to buy certain promotional items such as watches, sunglasses, and ankle weights. The applicable percentage for the retailer is based on population and buying power data.

To a large extent, Nike relies heavily on endorsements by prominent athletes from a variety of sports such as running, walking, track, tennis, basketball, football, baseball, and racquetball, and from such general fitness activities as aerobics. Hence, the high performance of Nike is consistently advertised by these top athletes. The company's Air Ace tennis shoe achieved a milestone when it received the first endorsement of a U.S.-based shoe manufacturer by a Soviet sports federation; this allowed the company to introduce its products into the Soviet Union. The company has also promoted the higher-priced cross-training shoe, the Air Trainer, as one shoe for all purposes! To further develop this concept, the company signed Bo Jackson, the versatile NFL (Los Angeles Raiders) and Major League Baseball (Chicago White Sox) superstar to endorse the cross-training line [6].

The company achieved a milestone in 1985, when it signed Chicago Bulls basketball star Michael Jordan to a contract. Jordan, who had just completed an outstanding rookie year in the National Basketball Association, was hired to introduce the new Air Jordan leather basketball shoe [9]. This shoe, which had a special gas pocket in its sole, provided extra spring and better protection from serious injuries usually encountered by the professional basketball athlete to the foot, leg, and back. The Air Jordan was cited as one of several "new products" for the year by *Fortune* magazine [10]. Nike also signed Charles Barkley of the Phoenix Suns [9].

Distribution

Domestic   The company's approximately 17,000 retail accounts racked up over $2 billion in sales in 1991, about 71% of total revenues. Retailers included department, footwear, and sporting goods stores as well as tennis and golf shops and other specialty retailers. The three largest retail customers accounted for about 30% of domestic sales; military sales were handled in-house.

Independent regional sales representatives are assigned several associate representatives and specific accounts within their jurisdictions. These associate representatives, who work solely on commission, are especially careful to ensure that retailer orders are handled promptly and within monthly deadlines. To establish and maintain a solid loyal dealer network as well as control the demands placed on the company's transportation and delivery system, Nike set up its innovative Futures ordering program whereby retailers could place their orders five to six months in advance and Nike would guarantee that 90% of their orders would be delivered on a set date at a fixed price. The Futures program has had some success in controlling inventory; for example, 81% of domestic footwear shipments in 1991 (excluding Cole-Hahn) were made under this program compared to 82% and 79% in 1990 and 1989, respectively [1]. As ocean and air carriers are used to transport products produced overseas into the United States, Nike exerts much effort to work closely with U.S. Customs Service to avoid the inspections and seizures other importers face. This working relationship also helps the company to detect counterfeiters of athletic footwear, apparel, and sports bags [16]. Additionally, imported products are subject to duties collected by the Customs Service.

Another innovation is Nike's next-day guarantee shipment for certain "team accounts" such as colleges and universities. According to one source, if the university faces an emergency when a few athletes require a certain size or type of shoe, the institution can contact Nike's Promotional Division for a special shipment of this equipment. The shoes are shipped via Federal Express. The program is reported to be very successful because of the high degree of loyalty these accounts provide Nike. Team accounts also have access to Nike's Futures program; for example, orders placed in December will be delivered by June or July of the following year. Regional distribution centers for footwear are located in Wilsonville and Beaverton, Oregon; Memphis, Tennessee; Greenland, New Hampshire; and Yarmouth, Maine. Apparel goods are shipped exclusively from Memphis.

The company also has 40 wholly owned retail outlets. *Chain Store Age Executives,* a trade publication, described one of Nike's innovative retail outlets. It cited the store's attractive display of styles and colors for footwear and clothing, which are geared toward a variety of sports. Knowledgeable sales personnel staff the store; they know the product, can explain it, and use it themselves. Shoes are turned upside down to show their soles, thus differentiating the various types of athletic footwear. Apparently, Nike capitalized on the simple idea that customers prefer to buy from salespeople who really know what they sell [17].

Twenty-two outlets sell primarily "B grade" and closeout merchandise. "B grade" merchandise has "cosmetic" defects such as discoloration, poor stitching, and so on and is therefore not first quality. As this merchandise is not first line, these products are sold in plain white boxes marked "blemished."

Foreign   Nike markets its products through independent distributors, licensees, subsidiaries, and branch offices located in about 66 countries outside the United States. Foreign sales accounted for 29% of revenues in 1991, compared to 21% and 20% for 1990 and 1989, respectively. Branch offices are located in Canada, Brazil, Belgium, Denmark, France, Great Britain, Hong Kong, Italy, Norway, South Korea, Spain, Sweden, Taiwan, West Germany, the Netherlands, Indonesia, Malaysia, Singapore, and Thailand. Since 1972, the Japanese trading company Nissho Iwai American Corporation (NIAC) has provided Nike with substantial financing and export-import services, enabling Nike to buy through NIAC almost all of its athletic footwear and apparel for U.S. and European sales. Nike also bought goods for other foreign sales through NIAC. In 1991, the largest single foreign supplier outside the United States accounted for about 7% of total production.

RESEARCH AND DEVELOPMENT

The company takes an aggressive stance in designing and marketing innovative footwear products based on such customer benefits as performance, reliability, quality, and reduction or prevention of injury—factors that appeal to both the professional and nonprofessional athlete. In-house specialists come from a variety of such backgrounds as "biomechanics, exercise physiology, engineering, industrial design and related fields" [1, p. 2]. The company set up advisory boards and research committees to review designs, materials, and product concepts; these groups included a broad range of experts such as athletes, coaches, trainers, equipment managers, orthopedists, podiatrists, and other professionals. R&D expenditures averaged over $8.4 million from 1989 to 1991.

Its Sports Research Lab, reputedly one of the most sophisticated among shoe manufacturers, is equipped to do biomechanical and anatomical checks on footwear "using the latest traction-testing devices and high-speed video cameras." Through careful testing procedures, Nike evaluates shoes in diverse locations under varying climatic conditions. Over a 90-day period, testers log reports of "total miles and terrain traversed, reporting every 2 weeks on cushioning, flexibility, perception of weight, and durability" [18]. The company's advanced product engineers, regarded as the cornerstone of their R&D efforts, "devised the multisport cross-trainer shoe and conceived what became the aqua sock," now used widely by swimmers. Compounds and molds for footwear are also tested in a rubber laboratory; the molds for soles are constructed in a model shop, after which samples are manufactured by a small-scale shoe factory. A physical testing lab also evaluates shoe tension and adhesion.

Nike has an exclusive worldwide license to manufacture and sell footwear using its technology to deliver the ultimate cushioning agent: compressed air. According to *Science Digest,* Nike Air shoes feature

> gas-filled mattresses encapsulated in polyurethane. The walls of the mattress's inflated plastic tubes are supposed to be virtually leak-proof. The gas never breaks down, and it returns to the foot much of the energy of additional impact, acting somewhat like a trampoline. [19, p.80]

Additional stability for the shoe is provided by using denser polyurethane, which collars the heel, plus a wider sole "along the inside of the foot near the arch." This feature helps to prevent the "foot's natural tendency to roll inward after landing," a tendency called pronation. E. C. Frederick, Nike's former director of the Sports Research Lab, called pronation the "'herpes' of the running crowd" [20]. This Air Revolution, as Nike called it, helped to introduce twelve new Nike-Air models. The research lab also pioneered other new materials such as durathane, a synthetic, and washable leather.

To protect itself from patent infringement, the company registered its Nike trademark and the well-known "Swoosh" design in over 70 countries. The company felt that these distinctive marks were important in marketing its products as well as distinguishing them from competitors' goods.

MANUFACTURING

In fiscal 1991, about 47% of Nike's apparel production was manufactured in the United States, by independent contract manufacturers located primarily in the southern states. The balance was manufactured by independent contractors in Asia and in South America, mainly in Hong Kong, Malaysia, Singapore, Taiwan, Thailand, Chile, and Peru. Almost all of its footwear is produced by Asian contractors in Taiwan, Indonesia, South Korea, and Thailand. Management contracts also exist with independent factories in Brazil, Hungary, Italy, Mexico, and the United States. Nike also has a management contract with the People's Republic of China (PRC) and has experienced no stoppages at these plants. The Chinese produce about 11% of its shoes [8, 1].

As mentioned earlier, South Korean, Thai, and Taiwanese contractors account for 51%, 15%, and 13%, respectively, of the company's total footwear production. Considering the magnitude of the company's dependence on Korean manufacturers, Nike's financial condition could be seriously affected by any disruptions in delivery of their products. However, the company has indicated that it has the ability to develop over a period of time alternative sources of supply for its products. Moreover, Nike claims that at the present time, it is not materially affected by this risk. Still another risk Nike faces with certain Asian manufacturers is increasing labor costs.

Management contracts are a critical part of Nike's overall strategy to provide its 17,000 retail accounts with a reliable delivery system. Moreover, these contracts allow the company to solidify its Futures program and enable Nike to guarantee retailers' orders by a set date and a fixed price. Additionally, the company is better able to refine its sales forecasts and, equally important, control inventory build-up and the subsequent costs. These independent domestic and foreign contractors provide Nike with two advantages: greater flexibility to take advantage of low-cost foreign labor and less capital requirements. Yet, foreign sourcing could cause the company a number of problems such as political instability, currency fluctuations, and the inability to repatriate profits.

Because of the volume of overseas production, Nike maintains a keen interest regarding any legislation passed by Congress that would impose quotas on certain countries that have been cited as having unfair trading practices. For example, Japan has been cited as having restrictive trade barriers that deny U.S. firms access to the Japanese market. Hence, the U.S. could assess an increase in duty rates on certain Japanese products imported into the United States. In addition, legislation has been introduced that could revoke the "most favored nation" status of the PRC and, consequently, result in a significant increase in tariffs on goods imported from China.

Raw materials such as canvas, rubber, nylon, and leather used in Nike's footwear products are purchased in bulk and are generally available in the countries where these products are manufactured. The company also acquired Tetra Plastics, Inc., in 1991, its only supplier for the air-sole cushioning components used in footwear. Hence, Nike encounters little difficulty in meeting its raw materials requirements. Moreover, to assure uniform product quality, Nike provides its contractors with exacting product guidelines, which, according to one source, are closely monitored through on-site expatriate quality control personnel. It should be noted that there is an industry trend to move from relatively high labor cost countries such as Taiwan and South Korea to other low-cost Asian countries.

THE COMPETITION

Several firms can be identified as competitors in the U.S. athletic shoe market (see Exhibits 3 and 4). This $5.8 billion wholesale market in 1991 was characterized as one with a shoe for any occasion. According to *Marketing and Media Decisions,* about 80% of the athletic shoes purchased are not used for the activity they are designed for; hence, the shoes' look counts. Moreover, basketball shoes are the largest segment, with a 28% share of the market, claimed the Sporting Goods Manufacturers Association [21]. Exhibits 5 through 9 show the financial picture for Nike, followed by Exhibits 10 through 13, which detail the financial picture for its competitors.

Reebok International, Ltd.

A closely held firm (about 60%) and a major competitor of Nike, Reebok was founded in 1979 when it acquired exclusive use of the name in North America—it brought the original English Reebok firm later, in mid-1985. The company was incorporated in Massachusetts to design, develop, and market athletic shoes and related accessories. It was initially a successful marketer of women's fashion aerobic shoes; however, in order to grow, the company needed to expand into men's performance athletic footwear such as basketball and tennis shoes. Exhibits 10 and 11 provide financial and operating data.

According to Steve Race, its general manager of athletic footwear, a shoe

---

EXHIBIT 3

Athletic Footwear World Market Share, 1991

Nike*	20.72%
Reebok*	16.18
Adidas	9.89
L.A. Gear*	5.23
ASICS (Tiger)	4.95
Aritmos (includes Etonic, Puma)	3.51
Keds*	3.14
Converse*	3.09
Others (includes licenses)	33.29

*U.S.-based company.

SOURCE: *Sporting Goods Intelligence,* as cited in *The Wall Street Journal,* July 11, 1992, p. 417.

EXHIBIT 4

Financial Data, 1989–1991 (in millions)

	1989	1990	1991
Net Sales			
Nike	$1710.8	$2235.2	$3003.6
Reebok	1822.1	2159.2	2734.5
L.A. Gear	617.1	902.2	618.1
Net Income			
Nike	167.1	243.0	287.1
Reebok	175.0	176.6	234.7
L.A. Gear	55.1	31.3	d45.0
Net Profit Margin			
Nike	9.8%	10.9%	9.6%
Reebok	9.6%	8.2%	8.6%
L.A. Gear	8.9%	3.5%	NMF
% Earned Net Worth			
Nike	29.7%	31.0%	27.8%
Reebok	20.7%	17.7%	28.5%
L.A. Gear	32.7%	15.2%	NMF

SOURCE: Value Line.

EXHIBIT 5

Nike Revenues by Product Categories for the Fiscal Years Ended May 31, 1991, 1990, 1989

	1991	Percent Change	1990 (in thousands)	Percent Change	1989	Percent Change
Domestic footwear	$1,676,400	22	$1,368,900	29	$1,058,400	40
Domestic apparel	325,700	22	266,100	28	208,200	46
Other brands	139,400	16	120,500	26	95,500	—
Total United States	2,141,500	22	1,755,500	29	1,362,100	51
International						
Europe	664,700	99	334,300	38	241,400	3
Canada	98,100	7	92,100	76	52,200	66
Other	99,300	86	53,300	(3)	55,100	45
Total International	862,100	80	479,700	38	348,700	15
Total Nike	$3,003,600	34	$2,235,200	31	$1,710,800	42

SOURCE: 1991 Annual Report.

could have fashion and performance; moreover, fashion is "a very important function of our performance shoes. And in fashion shoes, performance in terms of comfort is a very important element" [21]. To stress performance, the company contracted with such professional athletes as Dominique Wilkins of the NBA's Atlanta Hawks and PGA professional Greg Norman. The company also added children's shoes to its product lines.

EXHIBIT 6

Nike, Inc. Consolidated Balance Sheet As of Fiscal Years
May 31, 1991, 1990 (in thousands)

	1991	1990
Assets		
Current Assets		
Cash and equivalents	$ 119,804	$ 90,449
Accounts receivable, less allowance for doubtful accounts of $14,288 and $10,624	521,588	400,877
Inventories	586,594	309,476
Deferred income taxes	25,536	17,029
Prepaid expenses	26,738	19,851
Total current assets	1,280,260	837,682
Property, plant and equipment	397,601	238,461
Less accumulated depreciation	105,138	78,797
	292,463	159,664
Goodwill	114,710	81,021
Other assets	20,997	16,185
	$1,708,430	$1,094,552
Liabilities and Shareholders' Equity		
Current Liabilities		
Current portion of long-term debt	$ 580	$ 8,792
Notes payable	300,364	31,102
Accounts payable	165,912	107,423
Accrued liabilities	115,824	94,939
Income taxes payable	45,792	30,905
Total current liabilities	628,472	273,161
Long-term debt	29,992	25,941
Non-current deferred income taxes and purchased tax benefits	16,877	10,931
Commitments and contingencies	—	—
Redeemable preferred stock	300	300
Shareholders' equity		
Common Stock at stated value:		
Class A convertible—27,438 and 28,102 shares outstanding	164	168
Class B—47,858 and 46,870 shares outstanding	2,712	2,706
Capital in excess of stated value	84,681	78,582
Foreign currency translation adjustment	(4,428)	1,035
Retailed earnings	949,660	701,728
	1,032,789	784,219
	$1,708,430	$1,094,552

SOURCE: 1991 Annual Report.

EXHIBIT 7

Nike, Inc. Consolidated Statement of Income Fiscal Years Ended May 31, 1989, 1990, and 1991 (in thousands, except per share data)

	1991	1990	1989
Revenues	$3,003,610	$2,235,244	$1,710,803
Costs and expenses:			
Cost of sales	1,850,530	1,384,172	1,074,831
Selling and administrative	664,061	454,521	354,825
Interest	12,316	10,457	13,949
Other (income) expense	(43)	(7,264)	(3,449)
	2,541,864	1,841,886	1,440,156
Income before income taxes	461,746	393,358	270,647
Income taxes	174,700	150,400	103,600
Net income	$ 287,046	$ 242,958	$ 167,047
Net income per common share	$ 3.77	$ 3.21	$ 2.22
Average number of common and common equivalent shares	76,067	75,668	75,144

SOURCE: 1991 Annual Report.

EXHIBIT 8

Nike, Inc. Selected Financial Data Year Ended May 31, 1987 through 1991 (in thousands, except per share data)

	1991	1990	1989	1988	1987
Revenues	$3,003,610	$2,235,244	$1,710,803	$1,203,440	$877,357
Net income	287,046	242,958	167,047	101,695	35,879
Net income per common share	3.77	3.21	2.22	1.35	.46
Cash dividends declared per common share	.52	.38	.27	.20	.20
Working capital	$ 651,788	$ 564,521	$ 422,478	$ 298,816	$325,200
Total assets	1,708,430	1,094,552	825,410	709,095	511,843
Long-term debt	29,992	25,941	34,051	30,306	35,202
Redeemable preferred stock	300	300	300	300	300
Common shareholders' equity	1,032,789	784,219	561,804	411,774	338,017

SOURCE: 1991 Annual Report.

NOTE: All per common share amounts have been adjusted to reflect the 2-for-1 stock split paid October 5, 1990. The company's class B common stock is listed on the New York and the Pacific Stock Exchanges and trades under the symbol NKE. At May 31, 1991, there were approximately 4,500 shareholders of record.

EXHIBIT 9

Nike, Inc. Operations by Geographic Areas Fiscal Years Ended May 31, 1991, 1990, and 1989 (in thousands)

	1991	1990	1989
Revenues from unrelated entities			
United States	$2,141,461	$1,755,496	$1,362,148
Europe	664,747	334,275	241,380
Other international	197,402	145,473	107,275
	$3,003,610	$2,235,244	$1,710,803
Intergeographic revenues			
United States	$ 9,111	$ 4,765	$ 1,757
Europe	—	—	—
Other international	11,892	5,628	4,323
	$ 21,003	$ 10,393	$ 6,080
Total revenues			
United States	$2,150,572	$1,760,261	$1,363,905
Europe	664,747	334,275	241,380
Other international	209,294	151,101	111,598
Less intergeographic revenues	(21,003)	(10,393)	(6,080)
	$3,003,610	$2,235,244	$1,710,803
Operating income			
United States	$ 325,257	$ 315,246	$ 230,156
Europe	134,069	55,098	35,376
Other international	51,745	42,880	30,173
Less corporate, interest, and other income (expense) and eliminations	(49,325)	(19,866)	(25,058)
	$ 461,746	$ 393,358	$ 270,647
Assets			
United States	$1,156,091	$ 786,775	$ 600,629
Europe	370,104	162,383	102,744
Other international	94,212	74,329	50,756
Total identifiable assets	1,620,407	1,023,487	754,129
Corporate cash and eliminations	88,023	71,065	71,281
	$1,708,430	$1,094,552	$ 825,410

SOURCE: 1991 Annual Report.

Reebok acquired the Rockport Company, a major walking and leisure shoe manufacturer, for about $119 million cash in late 1986 and followed with another major acquisition, for about $180 million in early 1987, of Avia Group International, a premium priced athletic footwear and hiking shoes producer. Other acquisitions included the North American operations of the Italian Ellesses International for about $60 million; Ellesses manufactures premium-

EXHIBIT 10

Reebok International, Ltd. Consolidated Balance Sheet As of December 31, 1990 ($000)

	1990	1989
Assets		
Cash & cash equivalents	227,140	171,424
Accounts receivable, net	391,288[a]	289,363[a]
Inventory	367,233	276,911
Deferred income taxes	31,673	34,845
Prepaid expenses	12,328	11,735
Total current assets	1,029,662	784,278
Gross property & equipment	160,132	136,776
Less: Accumulated depreciation & amortization	49,017	30,542
Property & equipment, net	111,115	106,234
Intangibles, net of amortization	255,051	261,398
Other noncurrent assets	7,397	14,457
Total noncurrent assets	373,563	382,089
Total assets	1,403,225	1,166,367
Liabilities		
Notes payable to banks	8,855	1,651
Commercial paper	59,805	—
Current maturity of long-term debt	1,411	598
Accounts payable & accrued expenses	166,061	148,360
Income taxes payable	49,071	43,834
Dividends payable	8,576	8,538
Total current liabilities	293,779	202,981
Long-term debt, net current maturity	105,752	110,302
Deferred income taxes	6,975	7,788
Common stock	1,144[b]	1,139[b]
Additional paid-in capital	281,478	275,336
Retained earnings	707,336	564,987
Unearned compensation	dr 191	dr 524
Foreign currency translation adjusted	cr 6,962	cr 3,358
Stockholders' equity	996,729	844,296
Total liability and stockholders' equity	1,403,225	1,166,367
Net current assets	735,883	581,297
Book value	$6.48	$5.12

[a]Allowance for doubtful accounts: 1990, $33,730,000; 1989, $28,704,000.
[b]Par value $.01; Auth sns: 1990, 250,000,000; 1989, 250,000,000.
SOURCE: Reebok Annual Reports.

EXHIBIT 11

Reebok International, Ltd. Consolidated Income Account Years Ended December 31, 1990, 1989, 1988 ($000)

	1990	1989	1988[a]
Net sales	2,159,243	1,822,092	1,785,935
Other income (exp)	dr 893	11,377	dr 1,351
Gross operating revenues	2,158,350	1,833,469	1,784,584
Cost of sales	1,288,314	1,071,751	1,122,226
Selling expenses	353,983	278,939	260,891
General & administrative expenses	202,352	174,972	149,195
Amortization of intangibles	15,646	14,427	14,216
Interest expense	18,857	15,554	14,129
Interest income	15,637	12,953	6,633
Total costs & expenses	1,863,515	1,542,690	1,554,024
Income before income taxes	294,835	290,779	230,560
Income taxes	118,229	115,781	93,558
Net income	176,606	174,998	137,002
Previous retained earnings	564,987	424,002	320,886
Dividends declared	34,257	34,013	33,886
Retained earnings	707,336	564,987	424,002
Earnings per common share	$1.54	$1.53	$1.20
Common shares (000):			
Year end	114,428	113,856	112,951
Average	114,654	114,176	113,757
Depreciation & amortization	20,156	13,512	8,850

[a]Reclassified to conform to current presentation.
SOURCE: Reebok Annual Reports.

priced tennis shoes and ski fashions. Other acquisitions were the John A. Frye Company, a boot and loafer manufacturer, and Boston Whaler, a power boat firm[11, 12].

Six plants are located in Massachusetts and one in Oregon, the home state of Nike. The company sources over 70% of its footwear with contract manufacturers in South Korea, in addition to other plants located in Taiwan and the Philippines.

Sales grew steadily, from over $1.7 billion in 1988 to about $1.8 billion in 1989, then exceeded to $2.1 billion in 1990. Net income increased from $137 million in 1988 to over $174 million in 1989, a 20% increase; this was followed by another increase of over 18% from 1989 to 1990.

L.A. Gear, Inc. [13]

Robert Y. Greenberg, CEO and owner of 25% of the company's stock, founded L.A. Gear in 1985. L.A. Gear carved its niche as a developer, designer, and marketer of stylish, high-quality, and youthful shoes for aerobics, athletics, and leisure. The line was later expanded to include a variety of other footwear, such as walking, tennis, and overall fitness shoes, for children and men. Sales surged from over $223 million in 1988 to $902 million in 1990, a threefold increase. Although net income rose 15%, from $22 million in 1988 to over $55 million in 1989, it then declined 43% from 1989 to 1990. Exhibits 12 and 13 provide financial and operating data.

EXHIBIT 12

L.A. Gear, Inc. Consolidated Balance Sheet As of November 30, 1990, 1989 (in thousands of dollars)

	1990	1989
Assets		
Cash	$ 3,291	$ 353
Accounts receivable, net	156,391	100,290
Inventory	160,668	139,516
Prepaid expenses & other current assets	16,912	12,466
Deferred tax charges	1,097	4,589
Total current assets	338,359	257,214
Gross property & equipment	28,599	9,888
Accumulated depreciation	4,975	1,809
Property & equipment, net	23,624	8,079
Other assets	1,972	1,265
Total assets	363,955	266,558
Liabilities		
Line of credit	94,000	37,400
Accounts payable	22,056	25,619
Accrued expenses & other current liability	39,672	17,627
Accrued compensation	2,350	16,906
Income taxes payable	—	783
Total current liabilities	158,078	98,335
Common stock	91,179[a]	84,363[a]
Retained earnings	114,698	83,360
Total shareholders' equity	205,877	168,223
Total liabilities & stock equity	363,955	266,558
Net current assets	180,281	158,879
Book value	$10.61	$8.80

[a]No par value: Auth shs: 1990, 80,000,000; 1989, 80,000,000.
SOURCE: L.A. Gear Annual Reports.

The company moved into the highly competitive "60% chunk of the $4.2 billion U.S. athletic-shoe market" in basketball and running, a market dominated by Nike and Reebok. Skeptics were doubtful about the success of L.A. Gear's shoes for the male-dominated basketball segment, as males typically paid less attention to style and leaned more toward the inner structure of the shoe supporting the feet. Commented a competitor, technology was the fashion. However, to promote its acceptance in this market, the company signed 42-year-old Kareem Abdul-Jabbar, the retired superstar of the Los Angeles Lakers. As one analyst remarked, this was a move to the "geriatric crowd." Later, other notable basketball athletes were signed to contracts—Akeem Alajuwan of the Houston Rockets and Karl Malone of the Utah Jazz. Michael Jackson was also contracted to design shoes and apparel [21].

The company's footwear is sold principally in department, shoe, sporting goods, and athletic footwear stores, while its apparel is distributed through de-

EXHIBIT 13

L.A. Gear Inc. Consolidated Income Statement Years Ended November 30, 1990, 1989, 1988 (in thousands of dollars)

	1990	1989	1988
Net sales	902,225	617,080	223,713
Cost of sales	591,740	358,482	129,103
Gross profit	310,485	258,598	94,610
Sell, general & administrative expenses	240,596	154,449	53,168
Interest expense, net	18,515	12,304	4,102
Earned income before taxes	51,374	91,845	37,340
Income tax expense	20,036	36,786	15,310
Net earnings	31,338	55,059	22,030
Previous retained earnings	83,360	28,301	6,271
Retained earnings	114,698	83,360	28,301
Earnings per common share	$1.56	$3.01 [a]	$1.29 [b]
Common shares (000):			
Year-end	19,395	19,109 [a]	16,374 [b]
Average	20,041	18,308 [a]	17,110 [b]

[a] 2-for-1 stock split, 9/25/89.
[b] Reclassified to conform to 1989 presentation.
SOURCE: L.A. Gear Annual Reports.

partment, specialty, and sporting goods stores. Products are also distributed through independent distributors in 20 countries, primarily in Japan, Canada, and West Germany. Manufacturing is done by 13 suppliers in South Korea and 2 in Taiwan; both countries also manufacture Nike footwear. The company maintains offices in both countries.

To further expand its product offerings, L.A. Gear has ventured into the jeans and watch markets where, presumably, its brand name and distribution network will enhance its market position.

THE INDUSTRY

Exhibit 14 depicts a growing sales trend for the shoe industry from 1989 to 1992. Other data in the exhibit show varying performances for this same period.

Generally regarding athletic footwear as discretionary items, consumers would be likely to limit their spending for these products during an economic

EXHIBIT 14

Selected Industry Composite Indicators, 1989–1992

	1989	1990	1991 [a]	1992 [a]
Sales ($ Mil)	7762.8	8905.2	10365.0	11250.0
Operating margin (%)	12.7	12.1	10.5	11.0
Net profit margin (%)	6.7	6.2	5.9	6.5
Return on net worth (%)	20.9	19.1	20.5	21.0

[a] Estimated.

downturn. Moreover, with rising consumer debt and decreasing personal savings, buyers' confidence could be seriously affected. At the same time, buyers would prefer footwear that is not only durable but also suitable for a variety of activities.

The long-term prospects for the industry appear promising. The trend toward physical fitness should accelerate as it becomes a pastime for increasing numbers of buyers. Also, certain demographic changes favor continued industry growth; for example, Census Bureau projections for adults in the 25–44 age segment—major buyers for sporting and athletic equipment—are estimated to approximate 82 million people by 1992, about one-third of the total population. Moreover, this age group is forecasted to grow at twice the rate for the total population. Another important buyer segment is the 45–54 age group, projected to increase annually by 3.6% between 1987 and 1992 in contrast to a 1% growth for the total population.

Other key growth indicators include the increasing participation of women in sports, not only to improve their physical fitness, but also for recreation and competition. According to a National Sporting Goods Association study, women were the major participants in 10 of 45 activities it surveyed; these activities include aerobic exercise, gymnastics, and exercise walking. Additionally, the increasing presence of women in the work force and decisions to delay childbearing and have fewer children, should bring about higher household incomes, thus allowing for more discretionary spending and more leisure time available for recreation. In essence, greater emphasis may be directed toward fitness-related products.

As mentioned earlier in the case, there is a continuing movement by U.S. manufacturers to produce overseas through manufacturing contracts. However, as these newly industrialized countries become more developed—which exerts upward pressure on production costs—manufacturers will be compelled to seek other low-cost producer countries.

THE FUTURE

Nike management faces a number of challenges for the future. Can Nike move fast enough in a rapidly changing market with strong competitors such as Reebok, L.A. Gear, and others to remain the premier athletic shoe manufacturer? Given Nike's low-cost production in Taiwan, South Korea, and the People's Republic of China, will recent political demonstrations in the latter two countries compel Nike to seek other low-cost Asian producers or increase its U.S. domestic manufacturing? Should Nike consider manufacturing private-branded products for major retailing chains?

References

1. Annual Reports, various years, and Forms 10–K.
2. Lynn Strong in Dodds, "Heading Back on the Fast Track," *Financial World*, August 21–September 3, 1985, p. 90. See also *Who's Who in Finance & Industry*, 1983–84, p. 431.
3. Sheryl Franklin, "The Other Side," *Bank Marketing*, August 1987, p. 62.
4. Barbara Buell, "Nike Catches Up with the Trendy Frontrunner," *Business Week*, October 24, 1988, p. 88. See also "Walking on Air at Nike," *Fortune*, January 1, 1990, p. 72.
5. See reference 11.
6. Marcy Magiera, and Pat Sloan, "Sneaker Attack," *Advertising Age*, June 20, 1988, p. 3.

7. Marcy Magiera, ". . . As Nike Flexes Its Fashion Sense," *Advertising Age,* January 30, 1989, p. 76.

8. James P. Miller, "Nike Chairman Concurs with Estimates of Net Rise for Year of as Much as 65%," *The Wall Street Journal,* July 7, 1989, p. A5A. See also "Increase in Sales Expected by Nike," *New York Times,* February 11, 1989, p. 37; Dori Jones Yang, "Setting Up Shop in China: Three Paths to Success," *Business Week,* October 19, 1987, p. 74.

9. "Nike Pairs Michael Jordan with a Down-to-Earth Guy," *New York Times,* February 14, 1989, p. D7.

10. Carri Gottlieb, "Products of the Year," *Fortune,* December 9, 1985, p. 112. See also Jon Wiener, "Exploitation and the Revolution," *Advertising Age,* June 29, 1987, p. 18.

11. Douglas C. McGill, "Reebok's New Models, Fully Loaded," *New York Times,* February 14, 1989, pp. D1–D2.

12. Christopher Chipello, "Reebok to Buy CML Unit for $42 Million, Signalling Expansion of Product Line," *The Wall Street Journal,* August 8, 1989, p. A4.

13. Kathleen Kerwin, "L.A. Gear Is Going Where the Boys Are," *Business Week,* June 19, 1989, p. 54. See also "The Best of 1989 so Far," *Business Week,* June 26, 1989, p. 112.

14. "The Hollow Corporation," *Business Week,* March 3, 1986, pp. 57–85.

15. Sheryl Franklin, "'Word of Foot' Helps Nike Stay One Step Ahead," *Bank Marketing,* August 1987, p. 62.

16. "Nike Outdoes Competition in Delivery to Customers," *Global Trade,* March 1988, p. 8. See also *U.S. Industrial Outlook,* 1988, pp. 49–9.

17. "The Nike Store Breaks New Ground," *Chain Store Age Executive,* July 1990, pp. 90–91.

18. Dori Jones Yang, "Step by Step with Nike," *Business Week,* August 13, 1990, pp. 116–117. See also "When Your Feet Are Spending the Day Underwater," *Business Week,* February 27, 1989, p. 136.

19. Tom Yulsman, "Anatomy of the High-Tech Running Shoe," *Science Digest,* April 1985, pp. 46, 80, 83. See also Jean Sherman, "No Pain, No Gain," *Working Woman,* May 1987, p. 82.

20. *Ibid.*

21. Brian Bagot, "Shoeboom!" *Marketing and Medium Decisions,* June 1990, pp. 61–65.

The Walt Disney Company

NEIL H. SNYDER, *University of Virginia*

HISTORY OF THE COMPANY

Walt Elias Disney, the creative genius and founder of what is today an international entertainment conglomerate, was born in 1901 into a struggling midwestern farm family. Fueled by clever concepts and an innovative spark, young Walt worked as a cartoonist for a Kansas City newspaper and created animated shorts for local movie theaters.[1] However, when his early business ventures failed, the twenty-one year old dreamer left for Hollywood.[2]

Once in Los Angeles, Walt went into business with his older brother Roy, who was recovering from a bout with tuberculosis. Although Roy's only exposure to business had entailed a short stint as a bank teller, he had a better grasp of numbers than Walt.[3] Together they formed the "Disney Brothers" and immediately began work on their first series of shorts. From the beginning, it was Walt who handled the production of cartoons while Roy was relegated to the secondary, but necessary, role of arranging the financing for Disney Brothers animation.[4] Inspired by the moderate success of their first series, entitled "Alice in Cartoonland," the brothers next created "Oswald the Rabbit."[5] However, disaster struck when a New York distributor stole the series along with all of its animators.[6]

Disappointed but not defeated, the Disneys renewed their search for concepts and animators. It was Walt who developed the idea for Disney's earliest character, Mickey Mouse.[7] Ironically, New York distributors were uninterested in "Plane Crazy," the first silent short to spotlight the mouse that would become one of Disney's most endearing and timeless characters.[8] Nonetheless, the brothers persevered and featured Mickey in a new film the following year. In the enormously successful "Steamboat Willie," the Disney Brothers were the first production company to employ sound in an animated short.[9] Walt alone had provided the inspiration for the studio's first major hit, and it came as no surprise when he renamed the company "Walt Disney Productions."[10]

This case was prepared by Joanna Blattberg under the direction of Neil H. Snyder, Ralph A. Beeton Professor of Free Enterprise at the University of Virginia's McIntire School of Commerce. Ms. Blattberg is a student at the University of Virginia School of Law. The case is designed to be used as a basis for discussion rather than to illustrate effective or ineffective handling of an administrative situation.

The Studio of Walt Disney Productions

Under Walt's control, the new studio was characterized by attention to detail and constant striving for improvement and innovation, even during times of financial difficulty. Studio animators were trained at an elaborate art school and thereafter encouraged to experiment with lavish cartoons and new techniques at any expense.[11]

Disney quickly became the leading studio in innovative animation. For example, the studio pioneered the use of full color and synchronized sound in cartoons.[12] In 1937 Disney produced "Snow White," the first full-length animated film ever released.[13] The movie also featured the use of a revolutionary multi-plane camera which produced the illusion of depth in the figures on screen.[14] The studio had a similar commitment to innovation in its true life adventure movies. In preparation for the films, Walt required naturalist cameramen and artists to study the anatomy and locomotion of animals in their natural habitat.[15]

The single-minded pursuit of quality and innovation in the studio meant, however, that during the early years Disney operated on borrowed money. On the brink of bankruptcy, the company's leaders responded to crisis with flexibility. In order to alleviate the burden of bank loans, Disney went public in 1940. It was during these early financial difficulties that Disney first implemented its cross-promotional efforts by licensing Mickey Mouse and other cartoon characters.[16] Creative business planning coupled with quality products pulled Disney out of debt. The studio was in full swing by 1964 when it grossed over $45 million after the release of its first animated and live action musical, "Mary Poppins."[17]

Disneyland

Shortly after the formation of the family business, Walt had begun to develop his dream of building an amusement park for the enjoyment of honest American families. For over twenty years he worked on the concept as a hobby until he had produced a sketch for the theme park in 1952. Roy, however, would invest only $10,000 of Disney Studio money in the risky project.[18] Determined to realize his vision, Walt came up with the rest of the capital he needed by borrowing on his life insurance policy.[19]

The goal at Disneyland was to ensure that guests enjoyed an educational and friendly escape. To that end, the attention to detail and quality was as apparent at the theme park as it was in the studio. Walt spared no expense in demanding that the rides be authentic and the audio-animatronic figures as life-like as possible.[20] Disney characters at the park were required to undergo days of training and indoctrination before appearing in public to entertain guests.[21] Characters such as Mickey Mouse, Pluto and Donald Duck were also featured in a successful weekly television show, "Disneyland," that promoted the theme park as well as Disney-licensed consumer products.[22] Within one year of its opening, the gross annual revenues from Disneyland totalled $10 million and accounted for roughly one-third of overall sales at Disney.[23]

DISNEY UNDER NEW MANAGEMENT: THE TROIKA

Over the years the division of labor between the creative "Walt men" and the financial "Roy men" intensified and often resulted in severe disagreements, generally over whether to invest company money in risky new ventures.[24] Fortunately, the brothers had reconciled after a decade of feuding when Walt died of lung cancer in 1966. Although Walt had neglected to lay out a succession plan, seventy-three year old Roy was the obvious successor.[25]

The management team which emerged promptly replaced the autocratic style of Walt's leadership with a committee-rule approach.[26] Roy, previously president of Disney, became the chairman of a new "Troika." The former executive vice-president of administration, Don Tatum, moved into the position of president. Tatum, a quiet and intelligent Oxford-educated man, had risen under the direction of Roy through the ranks of Disney's financial side.[27] On the other hand, Card Walker, who left his position as head of marketing to become executive vice-president in charge of operations, was clearly an impulsive and outgoing "Walt man." Walker had first worked at Disney as a mail-room messenger in 1938, then with Walt as a cameraman on "Fantasia."[28] Later, as he rose through the marketing division, Walker had become one of Walt's closest confidantes.[29]

Walt Disney World

Under the reign of Roy, Tatum and Walker, gross revenues at Walt Disney Productions grew dramatically, more than doubling over six years. The completion of Walt Disney World, a dream on which Walt had begun to focus a few years before his death, accounted for one source of the revenues. The complex, which included rides, themed attractions, restaurants, and shops, was built in 1971 on 29,000 acres of land just outside of Orlando, Florida.[30] The futuristic park, featuring not employees and customers but rather "castmembers" and "guests" was an immediate success.[31]

To accommodate guests of the park, Disney later developed eight resort hotels, a complex of houses and villas, and a camping and recreational facility.[32] The company went on to build the Disney Village Marketplace, which serviced guests at the resort with a blend of shopping, dining, clubhouse, conference center, and entertainment facilities.[33]

Roy died within a year of the opening of Walt Disney World. Until that point, either Walt or Roy had overseen every aspect of the operation of the family business.[34] It was unclear whether the company could produce leaders capable of leading Disney into the 1970s with the innovation and imagination that had characterized Disney from the start.

DISNEY PRODUCTIONS IN TRANSITION

In the aftermath of Roy's death, Walker moved into the position of president. Four years later he made it clear that he was in control at Disney when he added to his title of president that of chief executive officer.[35] Walker viewed himself as a corporate heir entrusted with the founder's legacy and, accordingly, insisted on a rather rigid adherence to traditional Disney formulas.[36] According to top executives at Disney, the company's mission was to nurture the imaginations of children around the world as well as to celebrate American values. Under Walker's direction, the studio delivered predictable and wholesome entertainment which generated increasing revenues for several years.[37]

However, by 1979 the studio's market share had fallen to a mere 4%.[38] One explanation was that while American moviegoers had changed, particularly in their taste for more violent films, Disney insisted on adherence to old formulas.[39] Without the leadership of Walt, company executives resisted engaging in uncertain and imaginative ventures. Moreover, Disney routinely lost top projects because of an unwillingness to pay the huge salaries that had become customary in the movie industry.[40]

These changes in the film division troubled Roy E. Disney, who was Roy Disney's son, a principal shareholder, and a member of the executive committee. Roy was disturbed by the deferential philosophy that had come to prevail in the film division, as well as by the back seat that the studio had been taking with respect to the company's other projects.[41] He believed that instead of producing silly comedies and sequels, the studio should concentrate on producing updated versions of the inventive, high-quality films that had been central to its successes of the past.[42] However, the widespread belief at the studio was that Roy was "the idiot nephew."[43] Frustrated by the lack of response to his suggestions, Roy resigned in 1977.

Internal discord at the company continued into 1980 when Walker, without the consent of the board, selected Ron Miller for the position of president and chief operating officer.[44] Several years after his marriage to Walt's daughter, Diane, Miller had been invited by his father-in-law to join the company's studio operations. Miller immediately abandoned his position as tight end for the Los Angeles Rams and began his career as a second assistant director.[45] Though unassertive and inexperienced, Miller received special attention and training from Walt as he moved up the ranks of Disney's production division.[46] When Miller became head of production in 1976, critics attributed his success to his close ties with Walt, who had no sons of his own.

Though Miller may indeed have lacked the experience necessary to direct corporate strategy, by the 1970s he had nonetheless realized that Disney's approach to film-making was outdated.[47] Finally out from under his father-in-law's shadow, Miller attempted to implement changes at the company. He directed Thomas Wilhite, Disney's publicity director, to take control of creative development in the studio.[48] Wilhite's first priority would be to broaden the appeal of the Disney brand of family entertainment. However, Wilhite's tenure as head of the new film operations was unfruitful, and foreseeably so; although he had been exposed to the film industry through Disney's marketing department, he had never before produced films.[49] His contemporary movies, marketed towards a more mature audience, were opposed by Walker and poorly received by moviegoers.

To make matters worse, the company had taken on a huge amount of debt to finance construction work at the Environmental Prototype Community of Tomorrow. EPCOT would be divided into two themed areas.[50] Pavilions in "Future World" would dramatize significant historical trends and explore resulting energy, health, communication and cultural issues.[51] World Showcase exhibits, on the other hand, would feature exhibits that surveyed cultural traditions and accomplishments of foreign nations.[52]

Disney was determined to open EPCOT by 1982, but costs had risen unexpectedly because of design difficulties and labor shortages.[53] Moreover, the sharp rise in gas prices in the 1970s and the downturn in the economy in the early 1980s led to falling attendance at Disneyland and Walt Disney World.[54]

Faced with mounting problems, Disney's leaders failed to implement the flexible business plans that had characterized the company's recovery from hard financial times under Walt's guidance. In order to preserve Disney's friendly reputation, Walker refused to increase ticket prices for admission to theme parks and rejected proposals that advertising be permitted.[55] At the same time, Disney management scaled back on necessary upkeep at the aging theme parks.[56]

Disney Under Miller and Watson

Before retiring, Walker, whose confidence in Miller had dwindled, appointed Ray Watson as vice-chairman. Watson was an architect with extensive experience in real estate development resulting from years of converting farmland into planned communities. Watson's background in real estate, coupled with his creative training as an architect, made him especially valuable to Walt.[57] He had worked as a consultant to Disney on real estate development issues for several decades and clearly understood the Disney culture.[58]

As newly appointed vice-chairman, Watson inherited a company plagued by falling stock. Though rich with Florida real estate, massive theme park complexes and a treasury of cartoons and classic films, Disney had failed to exploit its assets. Dwindling confidence among the investment community in the Disney management team pushed the company into crisis by 1984.[59]

The possibility of a hostile takeover was too great to ignore when the board noted unusually heavy trading of Disney stock in March.[60] By the end of that month, Watson learned that Saul Steinberg, one of America's most aggressive corporate raiders, had been acquiring Disney stock for several weeks.[61] Not surprisingly, many Americans viewed the threat of a takeover as unpatriotic. One journalist in Hollywood wrote that

> while Steinberg and his ilk are making millions by threatening to tear down what took years to build, Disney and other creative institutions still are developing ideas, tangible products—and jobs. Steinberg apparently thought nothing of dissolving an American original, a monument to ingenuity and quality.[62]

In order to prevent a Steinberg takeover, the company began to strengthen its position through mergers and acquisitions. Disney first bought Arvida, a solid real estate and development company specializing in resorts and apartment buildings in Florida.[63] Disney next acquired Gibson, a greeting card company.[64] Watson believed that the acquisitions made solid business sense not only because they reduced Steinberg's stake in Disney from 12.1% to 11.1%, but also because ownership of Arvida would facilitate aggressive development of the Disney's Orlando property.[65]

Of course, the acquisitions diluted Roy Disney's holdings in the company as well. In response, Roy and a group of his business allies known as the "brain trust" hired Drexel Burnham Lambert junk bond guru Michael Milken to structure the financing for a takeover battle. However, the brain trust backed down when they realized that the risky venture, if successful, would result in the dismemberment of the company.[66] Milken then took the same package to Steinberg, who eagerly accepted and publicly announced his tender offer on June 8.[67] Instead of a self-tender, proxy fight, or direct appeal to shareholders, Disney's managers responded with a strategy which would most effectively keep the company intact; they paid "greenmail" and bought back Steinberg's stock at a premium.[68]

Although Disney had survived the attempts by corporate raiders, its management team was in desperate need of revitalization as its stock continued to fall steadily. In the aftermath of the takeover attempt, stockholders, members of both factions of the Disney family and potential investors showed little confidence in Disney's management. The company had preserved its independence, but many in the investment community questioned the propriety of the greenmail payment since Disney had not offered to buy the shares of other stockholders at the same premium that Steinberg had received.[69]

The Gibson deal was another source of criticism, particularly from Roy Disney and his lawyer and financial advisor, Stan Gold. When the board refused to respond to pressure to bail out on the deal, Roy and Gold approached the company with a request to be incorporated into the management team. After the managers rejected the proposal, Roy initiated a lawsuit against the board on the grounds that Disney's acquisition of Gibson had not been in the best interests of its shareholders. In addition, Gold threatened to bring the Gibson issue before the shareholders for a vote.[70]

Disney found itself once again in a vulnerable position. Disney's management team was widely perceived to be weak, ineffectual and divided. A shareholder vote against Gibson would exacerbate heightening skepticism about management's ability to perform. Despite the release of "Splash," the studio's most successful film ever, and the improved earnings that resulted from the hit movie, the financial industry remained unenthusiastic about Disney's ability to bounce back in the wake of the takeover attempts.[71]

In order to ward off the pending law suit, stabilize the company and harmonize the two factions of the Disney family, Watson agreed to appease Roy.[72] First, Watson gave him three board seats, which went to Roy Disney, Gold, and advertising executive Peter Dailey, Roy's brother-in-law.[73] Before dropping the suit Roy demanded that Walker and Tatum be forced off the executive committee; Roy apparently wanted revenge for the decades he had spent with the company in vain.[74]

Once back on the board of directors, Roy focused on the rejuvenation of the film division, which he saw as the company's most important asset.[75] This would mean an increase in production and a search for a new creative leader.[76] Gold agreed that the studio should be restored to primacy under a creative, high-powered management team.[77]

The search for new leadership coincided with widespread critique of Miller's leadership. Financial analysts blamed the decline of the film division, the greenmail maneuver and the Gibson deal on weak leadership by Miller, who was becoming increasingly dispensable. In a memorandum dated July 28, Watson wrote that "Disney's primary support historically comes from the Disney family and the institutional investors. Today that support is at best precarious."[78] Watson went on to write that institutional investors viewed Disney as "a rudderless boat caught in a violent storm" and concluded that the company needed "to resolve the [Ron Miller] issue as soon as possible. Perceived lack of leadership hurts all alternatives."[79] The board soon agreed that a decisive change in management was needed to send a clear message to Wall Street that the company was ready to begin rebuilding; Ron Miller was an easy scapegoat for the problems that had been plaguing the company during his tenure.[80] On September 7, the board unanimously voted to ask for Miller's resignation.[81]

REVIVAL UNDER TEAM DISNEY

Eisner and Wells Join Disney

In the wake of Miller's resentful resignation, Watson faced the ominous task of configuring a new executive management team that would appease the board, both branches of the Disney family, and the shareholders.[82] Gold argued the most suitable leaders for a creative institution like Disney were "creative crazies."[83] Watson was inclined to agree, at least to the extent that Disney's chief executive ought to be a "Walt man."[84] In the meantime, Michael Eisner, president of Paramount Pictures Corporation, and Peter Wells, a consultant to Warner Brothers, had decided to campaign for the Disney job as a team: Eisner as chairman and chief executive and Wells as president and chief operating officer.[85]

Eisner was born into an established New York family and was raised amid the affluence of Park Avenue. His father, a Harvard-trained attorney who had served as an executive housing official under Eisenhower, believed not only in the value of the dollar, but also of discipline, culture and formality. Eisner's exposure to the world of arts and entertainment was cultivated as his family attended the theater to celebrate every special occasion.

Like Walt, Eisner was a man driven by ideas. After several futile attempts to act while a student at Dennison University, in 1963 Eisner got his first show business job with NBC. At the network, he worked as an usher, clerk, and traffic reporter for the radio station. Eisner's big break came when he was hired by Barry Diller at ABC, then in third place among the three major networks. Eisner took charge of Saturday morning programming and captured the top position within three years. He then was given responsibility for the prime time schedule at ABC, and again under his guidance ABC became the top ranked network.

In 1976, Eisner left ABC to begin work at Paramount Pictures, where he again joined forces with Barry Diller. The two creative executives spent eight years at Paramount, during which time the studio produced a remarkable string of box office hits. Eisner, it turned out, had the common touch: a natural aptitude for pop programming through simple storytelling techniques.[86] Like Walt, he had a creative flair as well as the ability to recognize mass appeal. In fact, Eisner was widely perceived as one of the most creative executives in Hollywood.

On the other hand, Wells, who was detail oriented and pragmatic, had the business sense to translate Eisner's concepts into profitable realities. Wells was bred in a blue-collar family, and from an early age he learned the importance of hard work and commitment from his father, a Navy Commander.[87] Wells was a dedicated student who graduated Phi Beta Kappa from Pomona College, studied as a Rhodes Scholar at Oxford and edited the law review at Stanford Law School.[88] Upon graduation from Stanford, he went to work for the entertainment law firm, Gang, Tyre & Brown, where he was eventually made a partner.[89]

Wells left the legal profession to take over Warner Brothers' west coast business operations in 1969. Within 8 years he became co-chief executive and president of Warner Brothers. After running the business side of the company for five years, Wells unexpectedly left his job to pursue a lifelong dream of climbing the tallest mountain on each of the seven continents. Unfortunately, just before reaching the top of the seventh mountain, Mount Everest, he was forced to turn back because of a severe storm.[90] When he returned he was given a position as consultant to Warner Brothers, where he remained until 1984.[91]

Eisner and Wells were an attractive and suitable combination for the task of resurrecting Disney, particularly because of their resemblance to the founding brothers. When campaigning for the position, Eisner reasoned with one of

Disney's largest shareholders: "It's going to take a creative person to run this company. . . . Look at the history of America's companies. They have always gotten into trouble when the creative people are replaced by the managers."[92] Wells was the perfect counterpart to Eisner. He once said to Ray Watson: "I love the business of business."[93]

The Disney Board had finally found a high-powered team of executives to update the business while maintaining its traditional commitment to quality and innovation. Perhaps to underscore such high expectations, the two executives were offered uncharacteristically attractive compensation packages. In addition to signing and performance bonuses, options and portfolios, Eisner and Wells would receive $750,000 and $400,000 a year, respectively.[94] The signing of the contracts marked the company's newfound willingness to pay for talent as well as the beginning of an impressive comeback.

Studio Leadership

Eisner and Wells began by assembling a group of talented executives from the entertainment and financial industries. In order to lure the best, they secured a promise from the Board to approve higher salaries and bonuses than ever before.[95] That commitment proved worthwhile when, only a week after Eisner had taken over, Disney signed Paramount executive Jeffrey Katzenberg as president of the Studio.

Like Eisner, Katzenberg grew up on Park Avenue. The son of a stockbroker, he developed an interest in politics at an early age and dropped out of New York University after two years to become a full time member of Mayor John Lindsay's staff. Through his political connections, Katzenberg eventually met Barry Diller who hired him as an assistant at Paramount in 1975.[96]

In Hollywood, Katzenberg was known as the "golden retriever" because of his uncanny aptitude for sniffing out directors and agents with hot scripts. Renowned for his tough negotiating and relentless work ethic, Katzenberg routinely arrived at work before 7 A.M., even on holidays and weekends.[97] He advanced quickly through Paramount's marketing division, television network and eventually productions, where he became Eisner's closest confidante.[98] It therefore came as no surprise when Katzenberg joined Disney only a week after Eisner.

Finance Department

The 1984 fiasco had revealed weaknesses not only in the studio, but in the company's finance department as well. Eisner was well aware that a public company in the 1980s by necessity operated in a more threatening investment environment.[99] It would no longer be enough for Disney's leaders to simply provide wholesome family entertainment.[100] To remain competitive Disney's leaders needed to confidently promote the company image to investors.[101] In a maneuver symbolic of Disney's new approach to the investment community, at the 1986 annual meeting the name "Walt Disney Productions" was dropped in favor of "The Walt Disney Company."[102]

Unlike Ron Miller, Eisner and Wells had the wherewithal to cultivate Wall Street, and they sought a new chief financial officer who could structure the necessary creative financial deals.[103] Gary Wilson, CFO at Marriott for twelve years, was the strongest candidate for the position. Under Wilson's leadership,

Marriott had grown dramatically, its revenues increasing over five times in just a decade. To inspire that growth, Wilson had pioneered the pattern of raising funds through limited partnerships, then selling off the hotels to investors while retaining the revenue-generating contracts for Marriott.[104] To lure Wilson, Disney offered the Marriott executive an immense compensation package complete with stock options. Wilson accepted and became the highest paid CFO in the industry.[105]

Emphasis on Group Creativity

In addition to bringing in top flight executives from the entertainment and financial industries, Eisner began to change the management style at Disney. He placed a greater emphasis on group encounter meetings in order to more efficiently generate ideas for movie scripts and creative business strategies. Typically, a group of the company's most creative talents would meet on Sunday mornings to brainstorm.[106] During the meetings, which came to be known as "gong shows," a head executive would require each attendant to offer a new idea. Those which fell below group standards would be rejected with a gong.[107]

By infusing the company with new executives, a fresh approach to the investment community, and a highly creative format for generating new ideas, Disney's leaders had positioned the company to expand its studio, theme park complexes, and consumer product divisions into the 1990s.

THE WALT DISNEY STUDIOS

Katzenberg, who had epitomized the work ethic at Paramount, revamped the management culture at Disney and infused the leadership team with dozens of Paramount executives. Among the new Team Disney members were Helene Hahn, who took over the legal affairs department for the film division, Bill Mechanic, previously in charge of Paramount's pay television, and Ricardo Mestres, one of Katzenberg's most impressive production assistants.[108] Katzenberg's relentless work ethic became the model for these and other studio executives who were expected to arrive early, stay late, and work weekends.[109]

Furthermore, innovative financing was essential to the studio's turnaround. In producing its films Disney not only showed restraint and efficiency but also proved that its retreat from creative corporate structures had merely been temporary. Significantly, the studio began to rely heavily on investors to fund its film projects. The company was thereby able to increase output while relinquishing neither control nor high returns.[110]

Updated Film Division

During Ron Miller's tenure, Disney had created a second label, Touchstone Pictures, under which Disney could produce racier movies that were preferred by American audiences. Katzenberg began his reign at the studio by exploiting the new label; he signed a deal for Disney's first R-rated film, "Down and Out in Beverly Hills," which was released in December 1985.[111] The film quickly replaced "Splash" as Disney's most successful movie and marked the beginning of the studio's ascent to the top of the industry.[112]

Critics of Disney's more daring approach to film-making charged that the movies, though highly successful, were losing the unique Disney flavor and had come to resemble the ordinary films routinely turned out by the other major studios.[113] Supporters, on the other hand, argued that Disney's new direction was in fact more consistent with the company's fundamental commitment to creativity and innovation.[114] Under any account, the film division had become a profitable and resourceful division of the company.

However, Eisner was not satisfied. In a drive to create new assets, he encouraged the film division to begin work on new Disney characters. Before long, animators had come up with an idea that developed into the central character of Disney's next live action animated film. Innovative and fast-paced, "Who Framed Roger Rabbit" was an immense success for the studio. Similarly, Disney's next character, featured in "The Little Mermaid," was reminiscent of the Disney classics and was heavily promoted in the consumer product as well as the theme park industry. Under the leadership of Eisner and Katzenberg, Disney was once turning out fresh and marketable assets.

The studio's insistence on long hours, good scripts and fresh ideas paid off. By late 1988, Disney was making and marketing traditional family-oriented films as well as 12 films per year under the Touchstone label. Eisner and Katzenberg wanted to increase the number of movies it was producing, but they knew that studios which grew too large inevitably sacrificed quality.[115] As a result, they launched Hollywood Pictures, a third Disney film unit that, like Touchstone, would produce light adult entertainment with simple story lines and tight budgets.[116]

Disney's overall film division has produced a steady stream of successful films featuring top talent, strong writing and original formats. Moreover, Touchstone Pictures has also done well at the international box office; in particular, Disney made millions with its successful 1991 international release of "Pretty Woman," which was even more popular with foreign than American moviegoers.[117]

That year, Walt Disney Pictures produced another major success, "Beauty and the Beast." Eisner compared the immensely successful "Beauty and the Beast" with "Snow White" in that each classic was a wellspring for consumer products, videos, and theme park rides.[118] Katzenberg called the musical, whose star is uncharacteristically sophisticated and spunky, the Disney animation team's "greatest artistic achievement."[119] "Beauty and the Beast" had the most successful opening weekend for an animated film of all time, grossing $9.6 million.[120]

Film Slump and the Studio's Response

Notwithstanding the success of "Beauty and the Beast," Disney had its first noticeable film slump in 1991. Eisner justified the studio's problems by reference to the downturn in America's economy and to industry-wide falling box office revenues. It seems that Disney, third in total box office in 1991, was not immune to the trend towards skyrocketing production costs and resulting decreases in overall profitability.[121]

Katzenberg responded to the slump by cutting back on costs involved in making and marketing Disney films. In a 1991 memorandum to his staff, Katzenberg wrote: "We have slowly drifted away from our original vision of how to run a movie business."[122] He went on to articulate the studio's revised mission: to return to "the kind of modest, story-driven movies we tended to make in our salad days."[123]

The studio began to implement the policy of producing films with tight budgets and correspondingly reasonable returns rather than hit-or-miss blockbusters, like "Dick Tracy," that cost $100 million to make and market.[124] At Hollywood Pictures, the average film budget was cut from $20 million to $15 million.[125] The overall strategy is to avoid making expensive flops by sticking to budgets that fall below Disney's average budget in previous years as well as below the industry averages.[126]

Diversification Strategy: Home Videos

Under Katzenberg, the studio has pursued a strategy of diversification, with a steady expansion into home video, network, cable and syndicated television, and radio. Disney distributes home video versions of its studio releases into domestic and foreign markets. Since 1988, Disney Video has captured and maintained the largest market share in the domestic home video industry.[127] In addition to releasing mainstream feature films on video, the company has been squeezing value out of its previously underexploited library of animated classics. 500,000 copies of the videocassette "Pinocchio" were sold within one year of its release, making it one of the industry's most successful videos.[128] Classic Disney animated films subsequently released and skillfully marketed on home video have included "101 Dalmatians," "The Jungle Book," and "Fantasia."[129]

Disney's video division has benefitted from a revival of wholesome family entertainment. The cartoon videocassettes are especially popular with the post-war generation that grew up with Disney and is now having children of its own.[130] Much of Disney Video's success over the last several years can also be credited to "sell-through titles" which are sold at low prices to encourage purchase rather than rental by consumers.[131]

Network Television and KCAL-TV

Not surprisingly in view of Eisner's background in television programming, Disney has been remarkably successful in the network TV industry.[132] Under the labels Touchstone Television and Walt Disney Television, Disney produces TV programs which it distributes to the major networks and other broadcasters.[133] The TV division has made an aggressive drive to distribute half-hour situation comedies for prime-time broadcast and its Saturday morning animated cartoon series.[134] In 1991, Disney placed a total of twelve programs, more than any other Hollywood studio, on the major networks. Among its successes are "Golden Girls," "Empty Nest," "Home Improvement," and "Blossom."[135]

Disney has also been successful in the international syndicated television market. A series of programs, known as Disney Clubs, airs segments before 50 million viewers. The programs, produced in Italy, Venezuela and Australia, serve generally to promote the Disney spirit, and specifically to advertise Euro Disneyland.[136] In addition, 135 million viewers from Poland, Czechoslovakia, Hungary and what was once the Soviet Union watch top ranked "Walt Disney Presents," the only American show that appears in all four Eastern European markets.[137]

Disney also earns revenues from advertising sales tied to its independent radio station.[138] KCAL, which broadcasts in Southern California, offers news, entertainment and sports.[139]

Disney Cable Channel

The company's pay television programming service has 6 million subscribers nationwide.[140] While other cable channels are struggling to maintain their market share, since 1984 Disney has seen a 300% increase in the number of subscribers to its pay-cable services.[141] Disney attributes the success of its cable division to its varied programming, a blend which offers educational, dramatic, comedy, adventure and documentary programs for children, teenagers and adults.[142]

Emphasis on Expansion

Disney is eager to accelerate its distribution of television shows and movies. Manic deal-making is expected to continue, but Katzenberg has made it clear that efficiency and restraint will continue to be important values at the studio. Furthermore, studio management has suggested that an evolving hands-off policy will lead to more autonomy for Disney executives and a more dynamic creative process.

Although it has been rumored that Eisner is considering the addition of a second cable channel,[143] he has said that an expensive acquisition is not Disney's mission:

> It's not to be the biggest, to have the most toys, to own things writers think are important and sexy like networks, cable companies, satellites and countries. Our mission is to grow our own. We can have a nice respectable 20% without having to impress anybody.[144]

Nonetheless, there has also been some speculation that, given the expected reform of federal antitrust regulations, Disney will seriously consider a merger with a major television network which would provide Disney with a powerful distribution network for its already strong programming.[145]

WALT DISNEY ATTRACTIONS: THEME PARK AND RESORT COMPLEXES

Tokyo Disneyland

Expansion of theme parks and resorts under Team Disney has emphasized the increasing importance and attractiveness of foreign markets. The company capitalized on the prospects for growth abroad by opening its first international theme park, Tokyo Disneyland. Disney and Oriental Land, a Japanese corporation, came together in 1979 to establish the theme park in Tokyo.[146] Under the terms of their agreement, Oriental Land would pay for construction and provide the land, while Disney would receive royalties on the revenues generated: 10% of ticket sales, 5% of concession sales, and 10% of corporate sponsorship agreements.[147]

Tokyo Disneyland, located on a 600-acre landfill in Tokyo Bay, opened in April, 1983. The park, which features traditional Disney rides, restaurants, shops and entertainment, also showcases Japanese cultural traditions.[148] More than 10 million people visited the park during its first year in operation. From the start, attendance at Tokyo Disneyland threatened to surpass that at Disneyland, and it has continued to climb, setting records along the way.[149] The park had its most successful year in 1991 with a record 16 million guests.[150] Indeed, the success of Tokyo Disneyland has proven that Disney's brand of family entertainment is marketable worldwide.[151]

Euro Disneyland

Eight years before Eisner joined Disney, the theme park division had begun to study the population and demographic projections of Europe following Card Walker's suggestion that the company look into building a resort complex on the Continent.[152] Although Ray Watson supported the idea, the project was put on the back burner while the company was defending itself against corporate raiders.[153]

By 1984, there was an inviting European market for Disney theme parks and products. An estimated 2 million Europeans visited American theme parks annually.[154] Furthermore, roughly 25% of Disney trinkets, magazines and t-shirts were sold in Europe.[155] In September Eisner and Wells enthusiastically endorsed a search for a European theme park site. Disney officials selected Marne-la-Valle, France, mainly because of its demographic advantages.[156] The theme park would be located 20 miles east of Paris, which has a population of 10 million people.[157] Paris, in turn, is well-located in relation to major European population centers; 68 million people are within four hours by car, and 300 million within two hours by plane.[158]

Eisner and Wells believed that Disney had sacrificed too many profits in negotiating the Tokyo deal and were determined to retain control as well as a healthy share of the profits generated by the new European park.[159] But they also wanted to minimize its risk by sharing costs with a maximum number of participants. To do so the company would have to rely on a new corporate structure.[160] In yet another innovative financing maneuver directed by Gary Wilson, Disney set up a French version of a limited partnership to be managed by Euro Disneyland, a publicly held French company in which Disney now owns a 49% equity interest.[161]

The complex is expected to generate substantial licensing royalties and management fees for Disney.[162] As with the Tokyo project, Disney is entitled to 10% of ticket sales and 5% of merchandise and food sales.[163] Furthermore, just as in Wilson's Marriott schemes, Disney will manage the complex.[164] Under a 30-year agreement, in exchange for running the park Disney will receive 3% of the profits for five years and 6% during each subsequent year.[165]

From a tax standpoint, the deal that was ultimately negotiated with the French government is extremely favorable to Disney. Disney will have to pay only 7% tax on the cost of goods sold rather than the 18.6% that other French companies pay.[166] Also, the buildings will be depreciated over 10 instead of the usual 20 years.[167] Moreover, the host country committed to a major expansion of its roads as well as its commuter rail line.[168] Finally, the French government agreed to lend the project 40% of the cost of the project, roughly $770 million.[169]

Construction of Euro Disneyland began in 1988, and the $3.6 billion theme park is scheduled to open on April 12, 1992. Euro Disneyland is an ultra-modern version of Disney's Magic Kingdom with a European flair. In the 1991 Annual Report, Eisner calls Euro Disneyland "the most wonderful project we have ever done, . . . [a] theme park jewel, a creative extension of Walt's first park utilizing new technology. . . ."[170] The rides were built by Walt Disney

Imagineering, a group of design specialists, writers, artists, and engineers that design Disney attractions worldwide.[171] To ensure smooth operation, the Imagineers have built indoor arcades to connect the 29 attractions.[172]

Disney applied its Orlando strategy to Euro Disney by providing lodging for guests of all income levels. The park is surrounded by six hotels with distinctly American themes and a campground with 414 cabins. For further entertainment, the park contains Festival Disney, a complex of shops, restaurants, discotheques and a 27-hole golf course.[173] Finally, Wells has referred to Euro Disneyland as the linchpin for Disney's other divisions.[174] Long-term plans for Euro Disney include building 15 additional hotels with 13,000 additional rooms.[175]

Other Development Projects

In addition to building theme parks and resorts abroad, Disney has improved its existing complexes and embarked on new projects. First, however, Disney streamlined its operations by selling Arvida, the real estate development company it had purchased during the 1984 crisis. By 1986, Disney's real estate division had begun to reassess its acquisition of Arvida. Eisner in particular thought that Disney should develop only its own hotels.[176] He also worried that Arvida's Florida land was a liability considering the volatile and increasingly soft real estate market.[177] In 1987, Disney sold Arvida to JMB Realty Corporation in a move that reflected the company's financial flexibility and willingness to shed assets that no longer suited its long-term plans.[178]

In 1989 Disney added to the Walt Disney World Complex the Disney-MGM Studios Theme Park and an accompanying production facility.[179] The park contains themed attractions, backstage tours, restaurants and shops based on Hollywood's golden age of the 1930's and 1940's.[180] Next, the company built three new resort hotels with 2,222 rooms and 51,000 square feet of conference space to its already existing accommodations.[181] Disney has also begun to develop more moderately priced accommodations, including one 2,048 room resort, at Walt Disney World.[182]

Finally, in 1991 the Disney Development Company, which plans new projects related to properties in California, Florida and Europe, introduced the Disney Vacation Club. Under the unique plan, members pay a fee, purchase a real estate interest in Walt Disney World vacation accommodations and thereby acquire the right to stay at vacation resorts around the world.[183]

Disney's Response to Falling Attendance

While 1991 was a good year for Disney's moderately priced hotels, with a 94% room occupancy rate, Disney's theme park and resort division showed decreases in overall revenues and profits. Wells and Eisner attributed the 1991 fall in profits to the recession, lower levels of domestic and international travel resulting from the Persian Gulf War, and the cost of additional Walt Disney World hotels and attractions.[184] Even though 1991 operating profits fell 23% from 1990, Eisner explained, Disney's operations are healthy in comparison to an overall decline in performance by other hotel operators in the travel and leisure industry.[185]

Team Disney management addressed the problem of falling attendance at its theme parks in a cautious but effective and often resourceful manner. First, the company departed from former policy and raised ticket prices. The cost was raised in small increments in order to avoid negative publicity. As a result, instead of tarnishing Disney's friendly image and thus exacerbating the decline in attendance, the strategy led to soaring revenues. However, critics contend that ticket prices cannot be acceptably increased beyond the $33 that it now costs for a one-day adult ticket to Walt Disney World.[186]

Furthermore, management called for the creation of new theme park attractions which would appeal to teenagers. The new attractions designed by the Imagineering team include "Captain Eo," a 3-D short produced by George Lucas, directed by Francis Ford Coppola and starring Michael Jackson. The successful twelve minute film became a permanent addition to Disneyland and Epcot.[187]

Management also sought to augment attendance by aggressively investing in advertising campaigns. Eisner, wearing Mickey Mouse ears, has appeared in advertisements to encourage the use of Walt Disney World for business conventions.[188] In another break with tradition, Disney began discounting. Guests at the Disney-MGM Studios in Orlando receive free videos of Fantasia, while visitors holding $25 receipts from Vons Grocery Store in Southern California gain free admission to Disneyland.[189]

Future Expansion of Theme Parks Complexes

The theme park division will remain the central focus at Disney. At a 1990 press conference, Eisner announced Team Disney's intent to "do nothing less than reinvent the Disney theme park experience."[190] Imagineers continue to work on revolutionary, high-tech rides. To ensure continued creativity, Eisner has also encouraged Team Disney executives to develop the "Disney Institute," a think tank in Orlando, and "The Workplace," an entertainment and educational facility focusing on manufacturing plants.[191]

Disney anticipates the construction of several new theme parks including one each in Southern California, Florida, and Japan. Disney Imagineers have drawn up plans for an Anaheim theme park which, like Epcot Center, will feature exhibits from around the world and corporate-sponsored pavilions.[192] The new theme park, expected to be six times as large as Disneyland, will be Disney's first project of this scale to be built in an existing urban area.[193] With the expectation of building time-share resort villas near its California amusement parks, the company has been lobbying to amend a California law that regulates such resorts.

Likewise, in 1990 Disney announced plans to build "Dream City," a 5,200 acres just southwest of Walt Disney World.[194] The high-tech city, which is expected to cost more than $2.5 billion and take 25 years to complete, will consist of 15,000 apartments, 6,300 mid-priced homes, an upscale shopping mall, museums and commercial high-rise office buildings.[195]

In October 1990, Eisner and Wells also made a proposal to Oriental Land to build a new theme park similar to MGM Studios next to Tokyo Disneyland.[196] Analysts have predicted that Disney might seek an equity position in the new park rather than simply an entitlement to royalties.[197]

HOLLYWOOD RECORDS

With the formation of Hollywood Records in 1991, Disney entered the mainstream music business, a $25-billion-a-year industry characterized by low overhead and comparatively high rewards.[198] Disney's participation in the popular music business is guided by a pursuit of both fresh talent as well as more established and expensive groups like "Queen."[199]

In furtherance of its goal to become a major competitor in the worldwide pop music business, Hollywood Records opened an office in Great Britain.[200] Disney executives anticipate a dramatic expansion of the international music industry, and as a result Hollywood Records entered licensing agreements in Germany, Italy, Spain, Scandinavia, Japan, Australia and New Zealand.

WALT DISNEY CONSUMER PRODUCTS

The sale of consumer products in both domestic and foreign markets not only generates significant revenues for the company, but also promotes Disney resorts, theme parks, and characters. In addition, Disney receives major media exposure for its ventures through tie-ins with companies like Mattel and Nestlè.[201]

Disney Stores

Disney has 123 stores including four successful international divisions. The stores, most of which can be found in shopping malls and retail complexes, promote Disney's other businesses and carry Disney-related merchandise. Specialty retail products include Disney Babies infant products, Baby Mickey & Co. infant apparel, merchandise drawn from animated characters, and Mattel toys. In spite of increasing competition from other entertainment giants like Time Warner Inc. and a depressed retail environment, same-store sales show a steady increase.[202]

Disney intends to set up and operate 100 stores in Japan, the first of which is expected to open in May 1992.[203] The chain will sell toys, games and clothing, and possibly food inspired by Disney characters.[204] Based on soaring profits at Tokyo Disneyland, executives in the Consumer Products division estimate 50 billion yen per year in sales.[205]

Licensing

The company licenses the name "Walt Disney" as well as its characters, literary and visual properties, and music to consumer manufacturers, publishers and retailers around the world.[206] In particular, Disney-licensed products enjoy great popularity in Japan, the world's second largest toy market.[207]

Royalties are generally based on a fixed percentage of the retail or wholesale selling price of the product bearing a Disney trademark.[208] Disney oversees the development, approval and generations of licensed products featuring classic and newly created characters. Licensed merchandise includes toys, apparel, watches and housewares.[209] Books, magazines and comic strips are examples of licensed publications.[210] The company also licenses software products for video machines and educational products such as teaching aids.[211]

Publications and Discover Magazine

Disney built on its extensive experience in licensing by starting a new publishing venture, Hyperion Press, which offers trade books for adults.[212] Under Walt Disney Publications, the company publishes books, comics and magazines for children in the United States and Italy.[213]

In addition, in September, 1991, Disney bought the rights from Family Media to "Discover," a wholesome science news monthly magazine.[214] The acquisition broadened Disney's focus on science and marked the company's entry into the general-interest magazine business.[215] Disney plans to redesign and update the packaging of the science magazine and may go on to publish a children's version.[216] According to Eisner, Disney may buy more magazines, but only those with a family-oriented image.[217] Executives in the publishing unit anticipate building a profitable, vertically integrated publishing company.[218]

Music and Audio

Disney has long been a participant in the children's music business. In fact, Walt Disney Records is the largest children's label in the world.[219] The bulk of revenues in the music and audio division is from the domestic retail sales of audio cassettes and records.[220]

Mattel Alliance

Disney has recently announced plans to enter a long-term agreement with Mattel Inc. under which the latter will sponsor attractions and develop toys to be sold in special retail stores at Disney parks.[221] The companies also expect to concentrate on foreign markets and to expand their toy-licensing pact, sales from which topped $200 million in 1991.[222] Wells pointed to the enormous potential for growth in Europe to explain a heightening interest in the international market:

> More of Mattel's growth, like our own, will be coming from the international market rather than the more mature domestic market. . . . If you look at projections, the enormity of growth in Europe exceeds that of any other geographic section in the World.[223]

Thus, the Mattel alliance underscores Disney's commitment to its merchandising operations in international markets.

Despite a recession in the domestic retail market, Disney's Consumer Products division showed an increase in overall profits in 1991. Retail sales, consistently strong in the European market, reached $2 billion in 1991.[224] The success is in large part due to increasingly popular Disney Stores and outstanding merchandise and publishing sales in Asia and Europe.[225]

Eisner, referring to the 1990s as the "Disney Decade," has said that only "a lack of continued creativity and nerve can impede us as we move into the 90s."[226] Indeed, management has pledged to continue a strategy of diversification, expansion of foreign projects, commitment to excellence and innovation, and concentration on theme parks as a wellspring for Disney's other services and products in an increasingly globalized economy.

Exhibit 1 is a financial review of the Walt Disney Company that was obtained from the company's 1991 Annual Report.

Endnotes

1. Ron Grover, *The Disney Touch: How a Daring Management Team Revived an Entertainment Empire* (Homewood, IL: Richard D. Irwin, Inc., 1991) p. 5.
2. William E. Fulmer and Robert M. Fulmer, "Walt Disney Productions" (Charlottesville, VA: Darden Graduate School Foundation, 1986) p. 2.

3. The Disney Touch, p. 6.

4. John Taylor, *Storming the Magic Kingdom* (New York: Alfred A. Knopf, 1987) p. 7.

5. Storming the Magic Kingdom, p. 7.

6. Darden case, p. 2.

7. Storming the Magic Kingdom, p. 7.

8. Darden case, p. 2.

9. Storming the Magic Kingdom, p.7.

10. Storming the Magic Kingdom, p. 8.

11. Darden case, p. 5.

12. The Disney Touch, p. 7.

13. The Disney Touch, p. 7.

14. Darden case, p. 5.

15. Darden case, p. 7.

16. The Disney touch, p. 7.

17. Storming the Magic Kingdom, p. 13.

18. Storming the Magic Kingdom, p. 9.

19. Storming the Magic Kingdom, p. 9.

20. Darden case, p. 10.

21. Darden case, p. 11.

22. The Disney Touch, p. 8.

23. The Disney Touch, p. 8.

24. The Disney Touch, p. 10.

25. The Disney Touch, p. 10.

26. Storming the Magic Kingdom, p. 12.

27. Storming the Magic Kingdom, p. 12.

28. The Disney Touch, p. 11.

29. The Disney Touch, p. 11.

30. 1991 Walt Disney Company Form 10-K, p. 1.

31. 1991 10-K, p. 1.

32. 1991 10-K, p. 2.

33. 1991 10-K, p. 2.

34. The Disney Touch, p. 11.

35. Storming the Magic Kingdom, p. 12.

36. Storming the Magic Kingdom, p. 14.

37. The Disney Touch, p. 11.

38. The Disney Touch, p. 12.

39. The Disney Touch, p. 11.

40. The Disney Touch, p. 12.

41. Storming the Magic Kingdom, p. 13.

42. Storming the Magic Kingdom, p. 14.

43. Storming the Magic Kingdom, p. 14.

44. Storming the Magic Kingdom, p. 23.

45. Storming the Magic Kingdom, p. 19.

46. Storming the Magic Kingdom, pp. 19–20.

47. Storming the Magic Kingdom, p. 23.

48. Storming the Magic Kingdom, p. 23.

49. The Disney Touch, p. 16.

50. 1991 10-K, p. 1.

51. 1991 10-K, p. 1.

52. 1991 10-K, p. 1.

53. The Disney Touch, p. 13.

54. The Disney Touch, p. 13.
55. The Disney Touch, p. 14.
56. The Disney Touch, p. 13.
57. The Disney Touch, p. 15.
58. The Disney Touch, p. 15.
59. The Disney Touch, p. 15.
60. Storming the Magic Kingdom, p. 54.
61. Storming the Magic Kingdom, p. 58.
62. Darden case, p. 26.
63. Storming the Magic Kingdom, p. 81.
64. Storming the Magic Kingdom, p. 111.
65. The Disney Touch, p. 18.
66. Storming the Magic Kingdom, p. 119.
67. Storming the Magic Kingdom, p. 119.
68. Storming the Magic Kingdom, p. 132.
69. Storming the Magic Kingdom, p. 137.
70. Storming the Magic Kingdom, p. 145.
71. Storming the Magic Kingdom, p. 142.
72. Storming the Magic Kingdom, pp. 149, 164.
73. The Disney Touch, p. 19.
74. Storming the Magic Kingdom, p. 149.
75. Storming the Magic Kingdom, p. 184.
76. Storming the Magic Kingdom, p. 188.
77. Storming the Magic Kingdom, p. 185.
78. Storming the Magic Kingdom, pp. 178–9.
79. Storming the Magic Kingdom, pp. 178–9.
80. The Disney Touch, p. 19–20.
81. Storming the Magic Kingdom, p. 211.
82. Storming the Magic Kingdom, p. 220.
83. Storming the Magic Kingdom, pp. 220–221.
84. Storming the Magic Kingdom, p. 225.
85. The Disney Touch, pp. 22–23.
86. The Disney Touch, p. 30.
87. The Disney Touch, p. 32.
88. The Disney Touch, p. 33.
89. The Disney Touch, p. 33.
90. The Disney Touch, p. 34.
91. The Disney Touch, p. 17.
92. The Disney Touch, p. 23.
93. The Disney Touch, pp. 22–23.
94. Storming the Magic Kingdom, p. 233.
95. The Disney Touch, p. 50.
96. The Disney Touch, p. 54.
97. The Disney Touch, p. 53.
98. The Disney Touch, p. 54.
99. Storming the Magic Kingdom, p. 243.
100. Storming the Magic Kingdom, p. 247.
101. Storming the Magic Kingdom, p. 247.
102. Storming the Magic Kingdom, pp. 242–243.
103. The Disney Touch, pp. 59–61.
104. The Disney Touch, pp. 59–61.

105. The Disney Touch, pp. 59–61.

106. The Disney Touch, p. 61.

107. The Disney Touch, p. 62.

108. The Disney Touch, p. 57.

109. The Disney Touch, p. 62.

110. The Wall Street Journal, November 12, 1991, pp. A-1, A-10.

111. Storming the Magic Kingdom, p. 240.

112. Storming the Magic Kingdom, p. 240.

113. Storming the Magic Kingdom, p. 241.

114. Storming the Magic Kingdom, p. 241.

115. The Disney Touch, p. 220.

116. The Disney Touch, p. 222.

117. 1991 Walt Disney Company Annual Report, pp. 21–22.

118. 1991 Annual Report, p. 1.

119. Newsweek, November 18, 1991, pp. 56–57.

120. 1991 Annual Report, p. 21.

121. 1991 Annual Report, Eisner's letter, p. 1.

122. The Disney Touch, p. 281 (from Jeffrey Katzenberg memo to staff, "The World is Changing: Some Thoughts on Our Business," January 11, 1991).

123. The Disney Touch, p. 281 (from Jeffrey Katzenberg memo to staff, "The World is Changing: Some Thoughts on Our Business," January 11, 1991).

124. WSJ, November 12, 1991, pp. A-1, A-10.

125. WSJ, November 11, 1991, pp. A-1, A-10.

126. 1991 Annual Report, p. 21.

127. 1991 Annual Report, p. 27.

128. Storming the Magic Kingdom, p. 248.

129. 1991 Annual Report, p. 2.

130. Storming the Magic Kingdom, p. 248.

131. 1991 Annual Report, p. 27.

132. 1991 Annual Report, p. 3.

133. 1991 10-K, p. 4.

134. 1991 10-K, p. 4.

135. 1991 Annual Report, p. 3.

136. 1991 Annual Report, p. 27.

137. 1991 Annual Report, p. 27.

138. 1991 10-K, p. 4.

139. 1991 Annual Report, p. 28.

140. 1991 10-K, p. 5.

141. 1991 Annual Report, p. 27.

142. 1991 Annual Report, p. 27.

143. The Disney Touch, p. 281.

144. WSJ, November 12, 1991, pp. A-1, p. A-10.

145. The Disney Touch, p. 281.

146. Nikkei Weekly, August 17, 1991, pp. 1, 8.

147. Nikkei Weekly, August 17, 1991, pp. 1, 8.

148. 1984 Annual Report, p. 9.

149. 1984 Annual Report, p. 9.

150. 1991 Annual Report, p. 19.

151. 1984 Annual Report, p. 9.

152. 1991 Annual Report, p. 3.

153. The Disney Touch, p. 186.

154. The Disney Touch, p. 186.

155. The Disney Touch, p. 187.

156. The Disney Touch, p. 188.

157. The Disney Touch, p. 188.

158. The Disney Touch, p. 188.

159. The Disney Touch, p. 190.

160. The Disney Touch, p. 190.

161. 1991 10-K, pp. 2–3.

162. 1991 10-K, p. 3.

163. The Disney Touch, p. 191.

164. The Disney Touch, p. 191.

165. The Disney Touch, p. 191.

166. The Disney Touch, p. 192.

167. The Disney Touch, p. 192.

168. The Disney Touch, p. 192.

169. The Disney Touch, p. 192.

170. 1991 Annual Report, p. 4.

171. 1991 Annual Report, p. 36.

172. The Disney Touch, p. 197.

173. 1991 Annual Report, p. 6.

174. WSJ, November 12, 1991, pp. B-1, B-6.

175. The Disney Touch, p. 198.

176. The Disney Touch, p. 211.

177. The Disney Touch, pp. 211–212.

178. The Disney Touch, p. 212.

179. 1991 10-K, p. 1.

180. 1991 10-K, p. 1.

181. 1991 Annual Report, p. 3.

182. 1991 Annual Report, p. 3.

183. 1991 Annual Report, p. 38.

184. Orlando Sentinel (FL), July 26, 1991, pp. C-1, C-6.

185. 1991 Annual Report, p. 5.

186. WSJ, November 12, 1991, pp. A-1, A-10.

187. Storming the Magic Kingdom, p. 242.

188. Storming the Magic Kingdom, p. 242.

189. WSJ, November 12, 1991, pp. A-1, A-10.

190. The Disney Touch, p. 270 (from Michael Eisner, press conference, Swan Hotel, Orlando, Florida, January 14, 1990).

191. The Disney Touch, p. 276 (from Robin Benedick, Disney Serious about Making Osceola Dream City a Reality," Orlando Sentinel, July 25, 1990, p. 1).

192. The Disney Touch, p. 275.

193. The Daily Progress (Charlottesville, VA), December 14, 1991, p. B-6.

194. The Disney Touch, p. 276.

195. The Disney Touch, p. 276.

196. Nikkei Weekly, August 17, 1991, pp. 1, 8.

197. Nikkei Weekly, August 17, 1991, pp. 1, 8.

198. 1991 Annual Report, p. 3.

199. 1991 Annual Report, p. 40.

200. 1991 Annual Report, p. 40.

201. 1991 Annual Report, p. 35.

202. The Wall Street Journal, November 11, 1991, pp. A-1, A-10; 1991 Annual Report, p. 3.

203. Nikkei Weekly, August 17, 1991, p. 8.
204. Nikkei Weekly, August 17, 1991, p. 8.
205. Nikkei Weekly, August 17, 1991, p. 8.
206. 1991 10-K, p. 5.
207. WSJ, November 12, 1991, pp. B-1, B-6.
208. 1991 10-K, p. 5.
209. 1991 10-K, p. 5.
210. 1991 10-K, p. 5.
211. 1991 10-K, p. 6.
212. 1991 Annual Report, p. 3.
213. 1991 10-K, p. 5.
214. 1991 Annual Report, p. 4.
215. Los Angeles Times (CA) September 6, 1991, p. D-3.
216. 1991 Annual Report, p. 4.
217. WSJ, September 6, 1991, p. B-1.
218. WSJ, September 6, 1991, p. B-1.
219. 1991 Annual Report, p. 3.
220. 1991 10-K, p. 6.
221. WSJ, November 12, 1991, pp. B-1, B-6.
222. WSJ, November 12, 1991, pp. B-1, B-6.
223. WSJ, November 12, 1991, pp. B-1, B-6.
224. 1991 Annual Report, p. 32.
225. 1991 Annual Report, p. 31.
226. The Disney Touch, p. 270 (from Michael Eisner, press conference, Swan Hotel, Orlando, Florida, January 14, 1990), 274.

EXHIBIT 1   Walt Disney Company 1991 Annual Report

FINANCIAL REVIEW

Richard D. Nanula
Senior Vice President and
Chief Financial Officer

TABLE OF CONTENTS

OBJECTIVES

The Walt Disney Company has several strategic and financial objectives that guide management decision-making in creating value for its shareholders. The overriding objective is to sustain Disney as the world's premier entertainment company from a creative, strategic and financial standpoint.

The Company's financial objectives are to achieve 20% earnings growth over any five-year period and, through profitable reinvestment of cash flow, 20% annual return on stockholders' equity. The Company met its earnings objective for the five-year period ending with 1991, achieving a 25% compound annual EPS growth from continuing operations. The Company fell short, however, of its ROE objective in 1991, with lower earnings resulting in a return on equity of 17% for the year. The decline in earnings experienced in 1991, if coupled with a continued weak economy in 1992, would make it difficult for the Company to achieve its EPS objective in the short term. However, on a going-forward basis from 1991, the Company continues to view 20% earnings growth over future five-year periods and 20% annual return on equity as realistic financial objectives.

EARNINGS PER SHARE

RETURN ON EQUITY

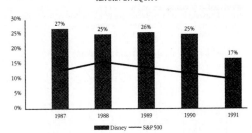

Another objective is to maintain and build upon the integrity of the Disney name and franchise. The Disney "brand" is an asset of considerable value which the Company continues to enhance and protect.

And finally, it is the Company's goal to accomplish all of the above while preserving the basic Disney values—quality, imagination, guest service—which have enabled The Walt Disney Company to entertain billions of people around the world for decades.

STOCK PRICE PERFORMANCE

On September 30, 1991, the Company's stock closed at $114 on the New York Stock Exchange. As shown on the following chart, long-term investors in Disney stock have experienced returns superior to those generated by the market. Over the last five years, the annualized return on Disney stock was a full eight percentage points higher than the S&P 500. A hypothetical investment of $1000 in Disney stock in fiscal year 1987, including dividends paid, would have been worth $2,669 as of September 30, 1991.

65

FINANCIAL REVIEW

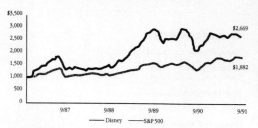

RETURN ON DISNEY COMMON STOCK VERSUS S&P 500

STOCK REPURCHASES

It has been The Walt Disney Company's practice to increase shareholder value by repurchasing Disney stock at attractive levels when the Company's excess cash or debt capacity enables it to do so efficiently. Since the adoption of a program to repurchase shares was approved by the Board of Directors early in fiscal year 1985, Disney has repurchased 13 million shares at an aggregate cost of $780 million, an average price of $60 per share. If valued on September 30, 1991, at the NYSE closing price, these shares would have a market valuation of approximately $1.5 billion.

DEBT RATING

Currently, Disney's long-term Moody's/Standard & Poor's senior unsecured debt ratings are Aa3/A+. Over the long term, Disney's objective is to maintain an A or better credit rating. With this in mind, the Company will strive to maintain conservative levels of leverage in relation to its ability to service its debt.

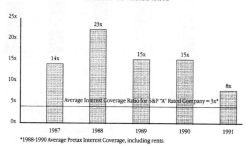

INTEREST COVERAGE RATIO

*1988-1990 Average Pretax Interest Coverage, including rents.

CASH FLOW AND CAPITAL SPENDING

As shown by the chart below, Disney continues to have strong cash generating capabilities. Even in difficult economic times, it was able to generate a record $1.5 billion in cash flow from operations in 1991, achieving a five-year annualized growth rate of 18%.

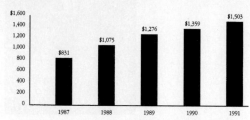

CASH FLOW FROM OPERATIONS
(in Millions)

Disney puts its capital to work both in existing businesses and new projects, thereby creating long-term value and contributing to future growth. Approximately $70 million of total 1991 capital spending was incurred to ensure that theme park and other assets remain well maintained, fresh and state-of-the-art. The rest of the spending was investment in existing businesses and new projects.

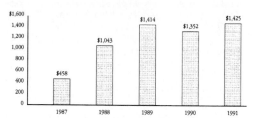

CAPITAL SPENDING
(in Millions)

As the bulk of this spending is discretionary, The Walt Disney Company has generated substantial free cash flow in each of the last five years.

FINANCIAL REVIEW

NEW PROJECTS

All Disney projects are carefully analyzed and are expected to make a positive contribution on a net present value basis against a risk-adjusted discount rate. New projects developed since 1987, such as the hotel build-out at Walt Disney World Resorts, the self-distribution of home video product and The Disney Stores, contributed over $1.7 billion (or over 28%) of fiscal 1991 revenues, having grown from virtually zero five years ago.

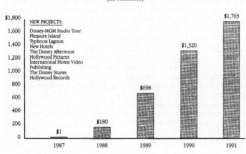

ANNUAL REVENUES GENERATED BY NEW PROJECTS
(In Millions)

NEW PROJECTS:
Disney-MGM Studio Tour
Pleasure Island
Typhoon Lagoon
New Hotels
The Disney Afternoon
Hollywood Pictures
International Home Video
Publishing
The Disney Stores
Hollywood Records

RECENT FINANCINGS

Innovative financings create value for the Company by reducing the potential volatility of its earnings. Consistent with the philosophy of allowing partners to share in the upside from film successes, while helping to limit the downside, Disney closed Touchwood Pacific Partners I, L.P., in fiscal year 1991. Touchwood raised $600 million for Walt Disney, Touchstone and Hollywood Pictures film production, with $420 million in non-recourse debt financing provided by a consortium of banks and $180 million in limited partnership units raised largely from Japanese institutions. Since 1985, the Company has raised over $1.5 billion in funds for film financing.

INTERNATIONAL

Over the last several years, The Walt Disney Company's business has become increasingly global, with approximately 22% of fiscal year 1991 revenues coming from foreign sources.

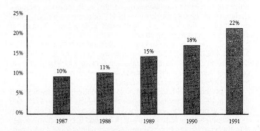

TOTAL REVENUE CONTRIBUTION BY
INTERNATIONAL OPERATIONS

While Disney products are well-recognized and sought after worldwide, the Company believes it has substantial room for increased penetration in international markets. Therefore, future overseas business represents a key growth opportunity. The demand for Disney products is expected to be especially strong in Europe over the next several years, fueled by the opening of Euro Disney in April, 1992, and expanded film and television activity.

International expansion has made foreign exchange management increasingly important to the Company. Disney monitors and manages its economic exposure to foreign currency fluctuations within a five-year planning horizon, and seeks to minimize the impact of changes in exchange rates on the Company's financial performance.

MANAGEMENT'S DISCUSSION AND ANALYSIS

OPERATIONS

1991 vs. 1990

Worldwide revenues increased in 1991 by 6% to $6.2 billion from 1990 levels. The increase resulted primarily from greater activity in the home video and television businesses and expansion of The Disney Stores together with the start-up of several new initiatives within the Consumer Products segment. The increase in revenues was partially offset by the impact of decreased park attendance. Additionally, theatrical revenues declined from 1990 levels. Revenues of $1.3 billion from foreign operations in all business segments represented 22% of total revenues, an increase of 4 percentage points over 1990.

Consolidated operating income for 1991 fell by 18% to $1.2 billion from $1.4 billion in 1990. The decrease was caused by several factors discussed in the individual business segments below. The decline in operating income generally reflected lower levels of domestic travel and tourism caused by the economic recession.

Net income for 1991 decreased by 23% to $636.6 million from $824.0 million in 1990 and earnings per share fell 20% from $6.00 to $4.78. The decrease in net income was impacted by lower net interest and investment income and the start-up costs of Hollywood Records. Earnings per share benefited from a lower number of shares outstanding due to share repurchases made under the Company's repurchase program. (See Note 9 to Consolidated Financial Statements.)

1990 vs. 1989

In 1990, the Company generated revenues of $5.8 billion, an increase of 27% over 1989. The increase was attributable to record attendance at the theme parks, higher resort occupancy, the success of certain theatrical and home video releases and increased merchandise licensing. Foreign revenues of $1.0 billion constituted 18% of total revenues compared with 14% or $665 million in 1989 as the Company expanded its international businesses.

Operating income increased 16% to $1.4 billion from $1.2 billion in 1989. Each of the operating business segments contributed to the record performance in 1990. Theme Parks and Resorts results reflected higher per capita guest spending at the parks and resorts, expanded resort operations and the benefit of our 49% investment in Euro Disney S.C.A. Filmed Entertainment benefited from the growth in home video, syndication and pay television. Continuing demand for Disney licensed products in international and domestic markets and the expansion of the Company's publishing business in Europe all contributed to the growth in Consumer Products operating income as compared to 1989.

Net income for 1990 increased to $824.0 million or 17% over 1989. Earnings per share of $6.00 which increased 18% over 1989, benefited from the Company's share repurchases. (See Note 9 to Consolidated Financial Statements.)

Theme Parks and Resorts

1991 vs. 1990

Revenues for 1991 of $2.9 billion were 5% lower than 1990. This decrease was primarily attributable to lower theme park attendance caused by the economic recession and resulting weakness in domestic travel and tourism. The decline in attendance was more severe at Walt Disney World than at Disneyland Park due in part to the greater reliance on tourism versus local resident attendance. Decreased attendance revenues were partially offset by higher per capita spending, primarily due to price increases.

Operating income of $617.0 million in 1991 was 31% lower than the prior year. The total number of occupied rooms at the resorts in 1991 was slightly higher compared to 1990, but the increased capacity resulting from the openings of the Yacht and Beach Club resort hotels and the Port Orleans hotel caused overall occupancy rates to fall. Revenues generated by the increase in the total number of occupied rooms were insufficient to cover all incremental costs from additional room capacity.

Attendance at Tokyo Disneyland reached record levels in 1991 for the seventh consecutive year, and the Company's 49% investment in Euro Disney S.C.A. generated a benefit in 1991. (See Note 4 to Consolidated Financial Statements.)

Increased design and development costs incurred to support future expansion of the theme parks and resorts contributed to lower operating income in this segment.

1990 vs. 1989

Record revenues of $3.0 billion were achieved in fiscal 1990, representing an increase of 16% over fiscal 1989. Operating income was $889.3 million or 13% higher than the prior year. Results benefited from higher per capita guest spending primarily due to price increases, increased resort occupancy and increased theme park attendance. Combined 1990 attendance at the Disney theme parks was the highest in the Company's history. The results benefited from the first full year of operations of the Disney-MGM Studios Theme Park which opened in May 1989. Attendance in 1990 at Disneyland Park decreased slightly from the prior year due to weakening West Coast tourism in the latter part of the year. In fiscal 1990, occupancy rates and occupied rooms at the resorts increased over the prior year.

Attendance at Tokyo Disneyland reached a record high in 1990 for the sixth consecutive year. Contributing to results in 1990 was the benefit from the Company's 49% investment in Euro Disney S.C.A. Also included in results for 1990 were higher design and development costs incurred to support future expansion.

Filmed Entertainment

1991 vs. 1990

Revenues of $2.6 billion in 1991 were 15% higher than the $2.3 billion generated in 1990 and reflected growth in both the international and domestic home video markets. Domestic theatrical revenues declined in 1991 reflecting the weak performance of several of the Company's live-action films.

Domestic home video releases included *Jungle Book*, *Robin Hood*, *Pretty Woman*, *Rescuers Down Under* and *Dick Tracy*. Domestic television revenues reflected the continued growth of The Disney Channel along with increased activity in network television, pay television and syndication.

Films making a significant contribution to domestic theatrical revenues included *What About Bob?*, *Three Men and a Little Lady*, and the re-release of *101 Dalmatians*. International theatrical releases included *Pretty Woman*, *The Little Mermaid* and *Three Men and a Little Lady*.

As a result of the Company's expanded international business, foreign revenues increased from 29% in 1990 to 36% of total Filmed Entertainment segment revenues in 1991. The increase was largely a result of higher sales of home video releases internationally, together with increased activity in the foreign theatrical and international television syndication markets.

Operating income was $318.1 million, or 2% higher than the $313.0 million reported in 1990. Results benefited primarily from the growth in home video and television distribution. The highly successful domestic home video releases of the library titles *Jungle Book* and *Robin Hood* together with the theatrical re-release of *101 Dalmatians* had a favorable impact on operating income. Library titles generate higher operating margins because most production and distribution costs have already been amortized. Partially offsetting these results were the weak domestic theatrical performances of *True Identity*, *V.I. Warshawski*, *The Marrying Man*, *Run*, *Scenes From a Mall* and *One Good Cop*.

1990 vs. 1989

Revenues of $2.3 billion increased 42% from $1.6 billion in 1989 and reflected significant growth in worldwide home video sales. Home video releases in 1990 included *Peter Pan*, *The Little Mermaid*, *Honey, I Shrunk the Kids* and *Who Framed Roger Rabbit*.

MANAGEMENT'S DISCUSSION AND ANALYSIS

Theatrical results in 1990 reflected the strength of *Pretty Woman*, *Dick Tracy* and *The Little Mermaid* domestically, and *Dead Poets Society* and *Pretty Woman* internationally.

Television results in 1990 and 1989 benefited from higher pay and syndication television sales and continuing subscriber growth at The Disney Channel.

Operating income rose to $313.0 million, or 22%, over the $256.5 million generated in the prior year. Operating margins in 1989 were favorably impacted by the higher concentration of library versus new product released, while 1990 operating results reflected the weak performance in the domestic theatrical market of *Blaze*, *Firebirds*, *An Innocent Man* and *Taking Care of Business*.

Consumer Products

1991 vs. 1990

Revenues in 1991 were $724.0 million or 26% higher than the $573.8 million generated in 1990. The expansion of The Disney Stores from 69 to 113 in 1991, combined with increased revenues in Asia/Pacific and Europe and new publishing initiatives contributed to the growth in revenue. Results in Europe and Asia/Pacific also benefited from favorable foreign exchange rates.

Operating income of $229.8 million was 3% greater than the $223.2 million generated in the prior year. As expected, operating margins declined reflecting further expansion into lower margin businesses of direct publishing, retail and catalog merchandising and The Disney Stores. Start-up costs associated with new initiatives in publishing, computer software and audio entertainment negatively impacted results, together with the weak performance of the catalog business. Strong sales of *The Little Mermaid* merchandise contributed to the growth in operating income in 1991.

Evident in the Company's results was the increasing contribution made by our overseas businesses. In 1991, 73% of operating income came from outside the United States compared to 62% in 1990.

1990 vs. 1989

Revenues of $573.8 million were up 40% from the $411.3 million generated in 1989. At September 30, 1990, there were 69 Disney Stores open, compared to 34 one year earlier. The expansion of The Disney Stores, together with the strength of licensed product sales in apparel, toys and publications and European direct publishing, all contributed significantly to the increase in worldwide revenues. Sales of *The Little Mermaid* soundtrack and *Dick Tracy* merchandise contributed to growth in revenues.

Operating income of $223.2 million in 1990 was 19% higher than in 1989. Both years benefited from the increasing value of major foreign currencies in relation to the U.S. dollar. Operating margins in 1990 were lower than in 1989 due to the shifting of business mix into lower margin businesses such as direct publishing, retail and catalog merchandising.

Corporate Activities
General and Administrative Expenses

1991 vs. 1990

General and administrative expenses of $160.8 million increased 16% over the prior year, and reflected the start-up costs and operating losses generated by Hollywood Records.

1990 vs. 1989

General and administrative expenses for 1990 were $138.5 million, representing a 16% increase over the 1989 total of $119.6 million. The increase resulted primarily from the additional costs incurred to support the growth in the Company's operations and performance-related incentive programs.

Investment and Interest Income and Interest Expense

1991 vs. 1990

Investment and interest income for 1991 was $119.4 million, which was 48% higher than 1990. The increase was primarily attributable to the gain on sales of certain marketable securities. An increase in the average balances of interest-bearing investments, together with an increase in the average interest rate also contributed to the higher income in 1991.

Total interest expense for 1991 was $105.0 million, which was 144% higher than 1990. This resulted from higher average borrowing balances in 1991 compared to 1990. The average borrowing rate decreased from 6.9% in 1990 to 6.5% in 1991, partially mitigating the effects of the higher borrowing balances. Capitalized interest, which reduces interest expense, was lower in 1991 than in 1990 due to the lower average balances in projects in progress.

1990 vs. 1989

Total investment and interest income for 1990 was $80.8 million, which was 20% higher than 1989, resulting from higher average balances of interest-bearing investments.

Interest expense increased from $23.9 million in 1989 to $43.1 million in 1990, primarily due to increased average borrowings. The decline in the average borrowing rate during 1990 partially offset higher borrowing balances. The decrease in the average rate reflected the issuance of subordinated debt which has an effective interest rate of 6.2%. Capitalized interest decreased in 1990 due to lower average balances on projects in progress, contributing to the higher levels of interest expense.

LIQUIDITY AND CAPITAL RESOURCES

The Company generates significant liquidity from operations. Cash flow from operating activities amounted to $1.5 billion in 1991. The Company raised an additional $500 million in proceeds from the issuance of medium term notes during 1991. The Company also entered into an agreement with Touchwood Pacific Partners I, L.P. which provides for up to $600 million to finance a portion of the production of a minimum of 20 feature-length theatrical films over the next two years.

In 1991, the Company used $924.6 million of funds to further develop the theme parks and new resort properties, primarily the Dixie Landings Hotel, the Yacht and Beach Club resort hotels and to refurbish the Disneyland Hotel. In addition, the Company used $486.8 million of funds in development and production of film and television properties.

During 1991, the Company repurchased 1,973,000 shares at a cost of $181.1 million as part of the previously authorized stock repurchase program.

The Company's financial condition remains strong and the Company has the resources necessary to meet future anticipated funding requirements. In addition to cash flow from operations, the Company has sufficient unused debt capacity, including a $375 million unused line of credit, to finance its ongoing capital investment programs and to take advantage of internal and external development and acquisition opportunities. The Company continues to explore potential sources of additional funding, both domestically and internationally, as opportunities arise.

In order to reduce the Company's exposure to risks arising from foreign currency fluctuations and its variable interest rate debt, management has adopted an extensive hedging program and it continually monitors the status of its hedging activities. As a result of these programs, the Company actively manages its currency and interest rate risk. (See Notes 1, 2 and 5 to Consolidated Financial Statements.)

CONSOLIDATED STATEMENT OF INCOME

(In millions, except per share data)

Year ended September 30	1991	1990	1989
Revenues			
Theme parks and resorts	**$2,864.7**	$3,019.6	$2,595.4
Filmed entertainment	**2,593.7**	2,250.3	1,587.6
Consumer products	**724.0**	573.8	411.3
	6,182.4	5,843.7	4,594.3
Costs and Expenses			
Theme parks and resorts	**2,247.7**	2,130.3	1,810.0
Filmed entertainment	**2,275.6**	1,937.3	1,331.1
Consumer products	**494.2**	350.6	224.2
	5,017.5	4,418.2	3,365.3
Operating Income			
Theme parks and resorts	**617.0**	889.3	785.4
Filmed entertainment	**318.1**	313.0	256.5
Consumer products	**229.8**	223.2	187.1
	1,164.9	1,425.5	1,229.0
Corporate Activities			
General and administrative expenses	**160.8**	138.5	119.6
Interest expense	**105.0**	43.1	23.9
Investment and interest income	**(119.4)**	(80.8)	(67.4)
	146.4	100.8	76.1
Income Before Income Taxes	**1,018.5**	1,324.7	1,152.9
Income taxes	**381.9**	500.7	449.6
Net Income	**$ 636.6**	$ 824.0	$ 703.3
Earnings Per Share	**$ 4.78**	$ 6.00	$ 5.10
Average Number of Common and Common Equivalent Shares Outstanding	**133.2**	137.2	138.0

See Notes to Consolidated Financial Statements

50

CONSOLIDATED BALANCE SHEET

(In millions)

September 30	1991	1990
Assets		
Cash and cash equivalents	$ 886.1	$ 819.8
Marketable securities	782.4	588.1
Receivables	1,128.2	851.5
Merchandise inventories	311.6	269.2
Film and television costs	596.9	641.1
Theme parks, resorts and other property, at cost		
Attractions, buildings and equipment	5,628.1	4,654.6
Accumulated depreciation	(1,667.8)	(1,405.1)
	3,960.3	3,249.5
Projects in progress	540.9	594.0
Land	70.4	67.0
	4,571.6	3,910.5
Other assets	1,151.7	942.1
	$9,428.5	$8,022.3
Liabilities and Stockholders' Equity		
Accounts payable and other accrued liabilities	$1,433.8	$1,158.1
Income taxes payable	296.2	200.3
Borrowings	2,213.8	1,584.6
Unearned royalty and other advances	859.5	841.9
Deferred income taxes	753.9	748.8
Stockholders' equity		
Preferred stock, $.10 par value		
Authorized — 5.0 million shares		
Issued — none		
Common stock, $.10 par value		
Authorized-300.0 million shares		
Issued — 137.2 million shares and 136.8 million shares	549.7	502.8
Retained earnings	3,950.5	3,401.1
Cumulative translation adjustments	35.2	67.7
	4,535.4	3,971.6
Less treasury stock, at cost — 7.0 million shares and 5.0 million shares	664.1	483.0
	3,871.3	3,488.6
	$9,428.5	$8,022.3

See Notes to Consolidated Financial Statements

51

CONSOLIDATED STATEMENT OF CASH FLOWS

Year ended September 30	1991	1990	1989
Cash Provided by Operations Before Income Taxes	$1,764.5	$1,780.3	$1,688.8
Income taxes paid	(261.2)	(421.4)	(413.2)
	1,503.3	1,358.9	1,275.6
Investing Activities			
Theme parks, resorts and other property, net	924.6	716.3	749.6
Film and television costs	486.8	533.0	426.7
Acquisitions	13.8	103.1	237.3
Marketable securities, net	194.3	(74.2)	(6.3)
Euro Disney and other	113.4	(96.3)	321.9
	1,732.9	1,181.9	1,729.2
Financing Activities			
Borrowings	641.9	965.0	452.3
Reduction of borrowings	(124.6)	(255.9)	(27.2)
Repurchases of common stock	(181.1)	(427.5)	(14.4)
Cash dividends	(87.2)	(74.1)	(61.8)
Other	46.9	54.5	57.5
	295.9	262.0	406.4
Increase (Decrease) in Cash and Cash Equivalents	66.3	439.0	(47.2)
Cash and Cash Equivalents, Beginning of Year	819.8	380.8	428.0
Cash and Cash Equivalents, End of Year	$ 886.1	$ 819.8	$ 380.8

The difference between Income Before Income Taxes as shown on the Consolidated Statement of Income and Cash Provided By Operations Before Income Taxes is explained as follows.

Income Before Income Taxes	$1,018.5	$1,324.7	$1,152.9
Charges to Income Not Requiring Cash Outlays:			
Depreciation	263.5	203.1	191.5
Amortization of film and television costs	531.0	335.2	272.1
Other	29.7	(36.7)	24.1
Changes in:			
Receivables	(266.8)	(166.2)	(131.4)
Merchandise inventories	(42.4)	(44.9)	(64.4)
Prepaid expenses	(46.9)	(64.1)	(15.0)
Accounts payable and other accrued liabilities	280.1	300.0	169.6
Unearned royalty and other advances	(2.2)	(70.8)	89.4
	746.0	455.6	535.9
Cash Provided by Operations Before Income Taxes	$1,764.5	$1,780.3	$1,688.8
Supplemental Cash Flow Information:			
Interest paid	$ 69.8	$ 67.3	$ 66.9

See Notes to Consolidated Financial Statements

MANAGEMENT'S RESPONSIBILITY FOR FINANCIAL STATEMENTS

Management is responsible for the preparation of the Company's consolidated financial statements and related information appearing in this annual report. Management believes that the consolidated financial statements fairly reflect the form and substance of transactions and that the financial statements reasonably present the Company's financial position and results of operations in conformity with generally accepted accounting principles. Management also has included in the Company's financial statements amounts that are based on estimates and judgments which it believes are reasonable under the circumstances.

The independent accountants audit the Company's consolidated financial statements in accordance with generally accepted auditing standards and provide an objective, independent review of the fairness of reported operating results and financial position.

The Board of Directors of the Company has an Audit Review Committee composed of five non-management Directors. The Committee meets periodically with financial management, the internal auditors and the independent accountants to review accounting, control, auditing and financial reporting matters.

REPORT OF INDEPENDENT ACCOUNTANTS

To the Board of Directors and Stockholders of
The Walt Disney Company

In our opinion, the consolidated balance sheet (page 51) and the related consolidated statements of income (page 50) and of cash flows (page 52) present fairly, in all material respects, the financial position of The Walt Disney Company and its subsidiaries at September 30, 1991 and 1990, and the results of their operations and their cash flows for each of the three years in the period ended September 30, 1991, in conformity with generally accepted accounting principles. These financial statements are the responsibility of the Company's management; our responsibility is to express an opinion on these financial statements based on our audits. We conducted our audits of these statements in accordance with generally accepted auditing standards which require that we plan and perform the audits to obtain reasonable assurance about whether the financial statements are free of material misstatement. An audit includes examining, on a test basis, evidence supporting the amounts and disclosures in the financial statements, assessing the accounting principles used and significant estimates made by management, and evaluating the overall financial statement presentation. We believe that our audits provide a reasonable basis for the opinion expressed above.

Price Waterhouse

Los Angeles, California
November 25, 1991

NOTES TO CONSOLIDATED FINANCIAL STATEMENTS

(Tabular dollars in millions, except per share amounts)

DESCRIPTION OF THE BUSINESS AND SUMMARY OF SIGNIFICANT ACCOUNTING POLICIES

THE WALT DISNEY COMPANY and its subsidiaries (the Company) is a diversified international entertainment company with operations in the following business segments.

THEME PARKS AND RESORTS

The Company owns and operates the Disneyland theme park, Disneyland Hotel and other attractions in California and the Walt Disney World destination resort in Florida. Walt Disney World includes the Magic Kingdom, Epcot Center, the Disney-MGM Studios Theme Park, nine hotels and villas, a nighttime entertainment complex, shopping villages, conference centers, campgrounds, golf courses and other recreational facilities. The Company earns royalties on revenues generated by the Tokyo Disneyland theme park near Tokyo, Japan, which is owned and operated by an unrelated Japanese corporation. The Company is an equity investor in Euro Disney which is currently under construction near Paris, France. The Company owns and operates Walt Disney Imagineering and Disney Development Company, which design and develop new theme park attractions and resort properties.

FILMED ENTERTAINMENT

The Company produces and acquires live action and animated motion pictures for distribution to the theatrical, television and home video markets. Original television product is also produced for network and first run syndication markets. The Company distributes its filmed product through its own distribution and marketing companies in the United States and through both its own subsidiaries and foreign distribution companies throughout the rest of the world. The Company invests in programming for and operates The Disney Channel, a pay television programming service and a Los Angeles television station.

CONSUMER PRODUCTS

The Company licenses the name Walt Disney, its characters, literary properties, songs and music to various manufacturers, retailers, printers and publishers. Audio products are produced primarily for the children's market, while film, audio and computer software products are produced for the educational market. The Company also operates several catalog businesses primarily for the children's market. These products are licensed and distributed throughout the world.

The Company also has direct publishing operations in the United States in both the children's and adult markets, and in Europe primarily in the children's market. In addition, the Company owns and operates The Disney Stores, which are retail outlets for the Company's merchandise, in selected markets throughout the United States and Great Britain.

NOTES TO CONSOLIDATED FINANCIAL STATEMENTS

The following is a summary of the Company's significant accounting policies.

Principles of Consolidation

The consolidated financial statements of the Company include the accounts of The Walt Disney Company and its subsidiaries after elimination of intercompany accounts and transactions. Investments in affiliated companies are accounted for using the equity method.

Revenue Recognition

Revenues from the theatrical distribution of motion pictures are recognized in domestic markets when motion pictures are exhibited and in foreign markets when revenues are reported by distributors. Television licensing revenues are recorded when the program material is available for telecasting by the licensee and when certain other conditions are met.

Revenues from participants/sponsors at the theme parks are recorded over the period of the applicable agreements commencing with the opening of the attraction.

Cash, Cash Equivalents and Marketable Securities

Cash and cash equivalents consist of cash on hand and marketable securities with original maturities of three months or less.

Debt securities are carried at cost, adjusted for unamortized premium or discount, which approximates market. Marketable equity securities are carried at the lower of aggregate cost or market. Realized gains and losses are determined on an average cost basis.

Merchandise Inventories

Cost of merchandise, materials and supplies inventories are generally determined on a moving average cost basis and are stated at the lower of cost or market.

Film and Television Costs

Film production and participation costs for each production are expensed based on the ratio of the current period's gross revenues to estimated total gross revenues from all sources on an individual production basis. Estimates of total gross revenues are reviewed periodically and amortization is adjusted accordingly.

Television broadcast rights are amortized principally on an accelerated basis over the estimated useful lives of the programs.

Theme Parks, Resorts and Other Property

Depreciation is computed on the straight-line method based upon estimated useful lives ranging from three to fifty years.

Other Assets

Rights to the name, likeness and portrait of Walt Disney, goodwill and other intangible assets are being amortized over periods ranging from five to forty years.

Hedging Contracts

In the normal course of business, the Company employs a variety of off-balance-sheet financial instruments to reduce its exposure to fluctuations in interest and foreign currency exchange rates, including interest rate swap agreements and foreign currency forward exchange contracts and options. The Company designates interest rate swaps as hedges of investments and debt, and accrues the differential to be paid or received under the agreements as interest rates change over the life of the contracts. Gains and losses arising from foreign currency forward exchange contracts and options offset gains and losses resulting from the underlying hedged transactions.

The Company continually monitors its positions with, and the credit quality of, the major international financial institutions which are counterparties to its off-balance-sheet financial instruments, and does not anticipate nonperformance by the counterparties.

At September 30, 1991, the Company had approximately $1.9 billion (notional amount) of foreign currency hedge contracts outstanding, consisting principally of option strategies providing for the sale of foreign currencies. The contracts reflect the selective hedging of French franc, German mark, Japanese yen and other foreign currency exposures over a multi-year horizon, extending up to six years.

Reclassifications

Certain reclassifications have been made in the 1990 and 1989 financial statements to conform to the 1991 presentation.

2 CASH, CASH EQUIVALENTS AND MARKETABLE SECURITIES

At September 30, 1991, the cost and market value of marketable equity securities were $103.6 million and $107.7 million, respectively. At September 30, 1990, the cost and market value of marketable equity securities were $168.2 million and $177.5 million, respectively. For both 1991 and 1990, cost approximates market value for marketable securities other than marketable equity securities.

Interest rate swap agreements related to certain foreign currency denominated investments converted $120 million of fixed rate securities to variable rate investments. At September 30, 1991, the Company received interest at the three-month LIBOR rate and paid interest at a weighted average fixed rate of 11.87%. The agreements expire in approximately seven years.

The Company entered into interest rate swap agreements expiring in three to five years, which effectively converted $600 million of variable rate investment securities to fixed rate instruments. Under these swap agreements, the Company received interest on the $600 million notional amount at a weighted average fixed rate of 8.3% and paid interest at the one-month commercial paper rate at September 30, 1991.

54

NOTES TO CONSOLIDATED FINANCIAL STATEMENTS

3 FILM AND TELEVISION COSTS

	1991	1990
Theatrical Film Costs		
Released, less amortization	**$111.7**	$ 90.6
In process	**85.4**	167.6
	197.1	258.2
Television Costs		
Released, less amortization	**131.3**	138.9
Completed but not released	**—**	3.2
In process	**112.0**	77.3
	243.3	219.4
Television Broadcast Rights	**156.5**	163.5
	$596.9	$641.1

Based on management's total gross revenue estimates as of September 30, 1991, approximately 84% of unamortized film production costs applicable to released theatrical and television productions are expected to be amortized during the next three years.

4 INVESTMENT IN EURO DISNEY

Euro Disney is a theme park and resort complex being developed on a 4,800-acre site near Paris, France. Euro Disney S.C.A., a publicly traded French company, owns and will operate the complex which is scheduled to open in April 1992.

The Company has a 49% ownership interest in Euro Disney S.C.A. and is using the equity method of accounting for its investment. At September 30, 1991 and 1990, the investment in and advances to Euro Disney S.C.A. were $581 million and $464 million, respectively.

In October 1989, Euro Disney S.C.A. completed a public equity offering of approximately $1 billion. As a result of the offering, the Company's share of the net assets of Euro Disney S.C.A. exceeded its investment by approximately $375 million. The Company is recognizing this difference ratably over an eight-year period, which represents the Company's contractual obligation to manage the development and operation of the complex and maintain an ownership interest of at least 17%.

In June 1991, Euro Disney S.C.A. completed a public offering of convertible bonds of approximately $670 million. The bonds are convertible into common stock of Euro Disney S.C.A. at any time before they become due in 2001. If all of the holders of the bonds exercised this conversion option, the Company's ownership interest in Euro Disney S.C.A. would decrease to 42%.

At September 30, 1991, Euro Disney S.C.A. had investment and project assets of $4.0 billion financed by equity capital of $1.3 billion and borrowings of $2.7 billion and generated $64 million in earnings for the fiscal year ended September 30, 1991. The market value of the Company's investment in Euro Disney S.C.A. exceeded its accreted carrying value at September 30, 1991 by approximately $1.6 billion.

The Company has agreed, under certain circumstances, to provide or obtain additional financing of up to $160 million and provide indemnification of up to $95 million in connection with the development of Euro Disney. The Company does not expect to incur any obligation with respect to these agreements.

5 BORROWINGS

	Effective Interest Rate	Fiscal Year Maturity	1991	1990
Subordinated notes(a)	6.2%	2005	**$1,091.9**	$ 980.0
Medium term notes(b)	5.4	1992-1995	**500.0**	—
Commercial paper(c)	5.7	1992	**128.9**	230.0
Securities sold under agreements to repurchase(d)	11.2	1992	**127.3**	—
Unsecured loans(e)	13.0	1998-1999	**101.8**	104.5
Swiss franc bonds(f)	6.1	1997	**64.7**	64.7
ECU notes(f,g)	6.5	1995	**49.9**	62.4
Euroyen notes	6.6	1996	**49.5**	49.5
ECU notes(f,h)	7.1	1994	**43.2**	48.6
Other	9.8		**56.6**	44.9
	6.7%		**$2,213.8**	$1,584.6

(a) During 1990, the Company issued $2.3 billion zero coupon subordinated notes which resulted in gross proceeds of $965 million. Holders may redeem the notes at their option for the issuance price plus accrued interest at the end of five and ten years, and upon a change in control of the Company, as defined, or at any time exchange the notes for the U.S. dollar equivalent of 19.651 shares of Euro Disney S.C.A. which is listed on the Paris Bourse. The Company has the right to call the notes at their issuance price plus accrued interest after two years. The Company has designated a portion of its Euro Disney S.C.A. shares as a hedge offsetting the contingent liability that may arise due to the exchangeability of the notes.

(b) The Company has executed interest rate swap agreements to convert all medium term notes to commercial paper-based floating rate instruments. The effect of these swaps has been reflected in the effective interest rate.

(c) The Company has available through 1992 an unsecured revolving line of bank credit of up to $375 million for general corporate purposes, including the support of commercial paper borrowings. The Company has the option to borrow at various interest rates not to exceed LIBOR plus 1/4%.

(d) Securities sold under agreements to repurchase are collateralized by certain marketable securities.

(e) Principal is due in varying annual installments.

(f) Foreign currency swaps effectively converted $158 million of foreign debt issuances to Japanese yen or dollar obligations. The effect of these swaps has been reflected in the effective interest rate. The Company hedges the obligations converted to yen borrowings with a portion of its yen royalty receipts.

(g) Principal is payable in annual installments of $12.5 million.

(h) Principal is payable in annual installments of $5.4 million with the balance due at maturity.

Borrowings, excluding commercial paper and securities sold under agreements to repurchase, have the following scheduled maturities.

1992	$ 139.5
1993	202.5
1994	164.1
1995	132.1
1996	60.1

The Company capitalizes interest on assets constructed for its theme parks, resorts and other developments, and on theatrical and television productions in process. In 1991, 1990 and 1989, respectively, total interest costs incurred were $142.4, $90.7 and $76.0 million, of which $37.4, $47.6 and $52.1 million were capitalized.

NOTES TO CONSOLIDATED FINANCIAL STATEMENTS

6 UNEARNED ROYALTY AND OTHER ADVANCES

	1991	1990
Tokyo Disneyland royalty advances	$545.8	$559.4
Other	313.7	282.5
	$859.5	$841.9

In 1988, the Company monetized a substantial portion of its royalties through 2008 from certain Tokyo Disneyland operations. The Company has certain ongoing obligations under its contract with the owner and operator of Tokyo Disneyland and, accordingly royalty advances are being amortized through 2008. Included in royalty advances is $145 million which is the maximum amount the Company may be required to fund under certain circumstances under the monetization agreement. The Company does not anticipate funding any significant amount under this agreement.

7 INCOME TAXES

	1991	1990	1989
Income Before Income Taxes			
Domestic (including U.S. exports)	$ 952.4	$1,270.2	$1,102.5
Foreign subsidiaries	66.1	54.5	50.4
	$1,018.5	$1,324.7	$1,152.9
Income Tax Provision (Benefit)			
Current			
Federal	$ 248.3	$ 260.4	$ 356.6
State	34.0	50.2	55.8
Foreign subsidiaries	30.5	25.0	21.4
Other foreign	44.5	34.9	26.0
	357.3	370.5	459.8
Deferred			
Federal	10.5	110.4	(23.4)
State	14.1	19.8	13.2
	24.6	130.2	(10.2)
	$ 381.9	$ 500.7	$ 449.6
Components of Provision for Deferred Income Taxes			
Depreciation and amortization	$ 56.6	$ 49.9	$ 42.3
Licensing revenues	11.3	29.5	(23.5)
Capitalized interest and property taxes	8.9	13.1	(1.6)
Royalty expenses	(51.8)	(2.2)	(15.8)
Other	(0.4)	39.9	(11.6)
	$ 24.6	$ 130.2	$ (10.2)

Reconciliation of Effective Income Tax Rate

Federal income tax rate	34.0%	34.0%	34.0%
State income taxes, net of Federal income tax benefit	3.3	3.6	4.0
Other	0.2	0.2	1.0
	37.5%	37.8%	39.0%

Due to the Financial Accounting Standards Board's ongoing deliberations with respect to the requirements and effective date of Statement of Financial Accounting Standards No. 96, Accounting for Income Taxes, the Company is unable to reasonably estimate the effects of adopting the Standard at its ultimate effective date.

8 PENSION AND OTHER BENEFIT PROGRAMS

The Company contributes to various pension plans under union and industry-wide agreements. Contributions are based upon the hours worked or gross wages paid to covered employees. In 1991, 1990 and 1989, the cost recognized under these plans was $12.9, $6.1 and $5.5 million, respectively. The Company's share of the unfunded liability, if any, related to these multi-employer plans is not material.

The Company also maintains pension plans covering most of its domestic salaried and hourly employees not covered by union or industry-wide pension plans and a non-qualified, unfunded retirement plan for key employees.

With respect to the defined benefit pension plans, the Company's policy is to fund, at a minimum, the amount necessary on an actuarial basis to provide for benefits in accordance with the requirements of ERISA. Benefits are generally based on years of service and/or compensation.

Pension cost is summarized as follows.

	1991	1990	1989
Service cost of current period	$37.1	$25.4	$21.1
Interest cost on projected benefit obligations	21.5	17.9	16.5
Gain on plan assets	(18.2)	(30.8)	(14.5)
Net amortization and deferral	(1.4)	16.2	.7
Net pension cost	$39.0	$28.7	$23.8

For 1991, 1990 and 1989 the weighted average discount rate was 9.5% and the expected long-term rate of return on plan assets was 9.5%. The rate of increase in compensation level was 6.6% for 1991 and 6.5% for 1990 and 1989.

NOTES TO CONSOLIDATED FINANCIAL STATEMENTS

The funded status of the plans and the amounts included in the Company's consolidated balance sheet were as follows.

	1991	1990
Plan assets at fair value, primarily publicly traded stocks and bonds	**$270.9**	$235.6
Actuarial present value of projected benefit obligations		
Accumulated benefit obligations		
Vested	**(228.5)**	(195.4)
Non-vested	**(10.4)**	(8.6)
Provision for future salary increases	**(37.7)**	(26.0)
Plan assets greater (less) than projected benefit obligations	**(5.7)**	5.6
Unrecognized net loss	**27.9**	10.3
Unrecognized prior service cost	**3.8**	3.6
Unrecognized net obligation	**4.4**	4.6
Prepaid pension cost	**$ 30.4**	$ 24.1

The Company sponsors a plan to provide postretirement medical benefits to most of its domestic salaried and hourly employees, and contributes to multi-employer welfare plans to provide similar benefits to certain employees under collective bargaining agreements.

In December 1990, the Financial Accounting Standards Board issued Statement of Financial Accounting Standards No. 106, Employer's Accounting for Postretirement Benefits Other Than Pensions (SFAS 106), which will require accruals of postretirement benefit costs to actuarially allocate such costs to the years during which employees render qualifying service. SFAS 106 also requires recognition no later than the fiscal year ending September 30, 1994 of the unfunded and previously unrecognized accumulated postretirement benefit obligation for all participants in the Company-sponsored plan as of the plan's implementation date. This "transition obligation" may be charged immediately to operations or amortized over the longer of the average remaining service period of active plan participants, or twenty years. Although an adoption date and method have not been determined, the Company does not anticipate that its transition obligation or ongoing expense pursuant to SFAS 106 will be material to its financial condition.

9 STOCKHOLDERS' EQUITY

(Shares in millions)	Shares	Common Stock	Paid-in Capital	Retained Earnings
Balance at September 30, 1988	134.1	$13.3	$377.4	$2,009.7
Exercise of stock options, net	2.2	.2	57.4	
Dividends ($.46 per share)				(61.8)
Net income				703.3
Balance at September 30, 1989	136.3	13.5	434.8	2,651.2
Exercise of stock options, net	.5	.1	54.4	
Dividends ($.555 per share)				(74.1)
Net income				824.0
Balance at September 30, 1990	136.8	13.6	489.2	3,401.1
Exercise of stock options, net	.4	.1	46.8	
Dividends ($.67 per share)				(87.2)
Net income				636.6
Balance at September 30, 1991	137.2	$13.7	$536.0	$3,950.5

In June 1989, the Company adopted a stockholders' rights plan. The plan becomes operative in certain events involving the acquisition of 25% or more of the Company's common stock by any person or group in a transaction not approved by the Company's Board of Directors. Upon the occurrence of such an event, each right, unless redeemed by the Board, entitles its holder to purchase for $350 an amount of common stock of the Company, or in certain circumstances the acquiror, having a market value of twice the purchase price.

In connection with the rights plan, 1.8 million shares of preferred stock were reserved.

In 1991 and 1990, the Company recorded cumulative foreign currency translation adjustments of $35.2 million and $67.7 million, net of deferred taxes of $19.5 million and $41.3 million, respectively.

Treasury stock activity for the three years ended September 30, 1991 was as follows.

(Shares in millions)	Shares	Treasury Stock
Balance at September 30, 1988	.9	$ 41.1
Common stock repurchases	.1	14.4
Balance at September 30, 1989	1.0	55.5
Common stock repurchases	4.0	427.5
Balance at September 30, 1990	5.0	483.0
Common stock repurchases	2.0	181.1
Balance at September 30, 1991	7.0	$664.1

In November 1984, the Company adopted a program to repurchase up to 14 million shares. In December 1990, the Company increased the authorized share repurchase amount to 22.5 million shares. Under this program, the Company repurchased 2.0 million shares during the year ended September 30, 1991. Since adoption of the program, a total of 13.0 million shares have been repurchased at prevailing market prices.

NOTES TO CONSOLIDATED FINANCIAL STATEMENTS

10 STOCK INCENTIVE PLANS

Under various plans, the Company may grant stock option and other awards to key executive, management and creative personnel. Transactions under the various stock option and incentive plans during 1991 were as follows.

(Shares in millions)	1991	1990	1989
Outstanding at beginning of year	10.8	9.7	7.5
Awards cancelled	(0.2)	(0.1)	(0.1)
Awards granted	1.0	1.7	4.5
Awards exercised	(0.4)	(0.5)	(2.2)
Outstanding at September 30	11.2	10.8	9.7
Exercisable at September 30	4.4	3.5	2.2

Stock option awards are granted at prices equal to at least market price on the date of grant. Options outstanding at September 30, 1991 and 1990, respectively, ranged in price from $12.93 to $130.62 and $12.57 to $130.62 per share. Options exercised during the period ranged in price from $12.57 to $123.00 per share in 1991, from $12.93 to $92.75 per share in 1990, and from $9.42 to $64.19 per share in 1989. Shares available for future option grants at September 30, 1991 were 7.9 million.

11 DETAIL OF CERTAIN BALANCE SHEET ACCOUNTS

	1991	1990
Receivables		
Trade, net of allowances	$ 969.7	$ 719.8
Euro Disney advances and other	158.5	131.7
	$1,128.2	$ 851.5
Other Assets		
Intangibles	$ 332.0	$ 345.2
Euro Disney and other	819.7	596.9
	$1,151.7	$ 942.1
Accounts Payable and Other Accrued Liabilities		
Accounts payable	$1,111.5	$ 861.0
Payroll and employee benefits	303.4	261.1
Other	18.9	36.0
	$1,433.8	$1,158.1

12 BUSINESS SEGMENTS

	1991	1990	1989
Capital Expenditures			
Theme parks and resorts	$ 790.1	$ 519.8	$ 665.4
Filmed entertainment	50.1	39.5	27.2
Consumer products	35.5	34.3	21.6
Corporate	48.9	122.7	35.4
	$ 924.6	$ 716.3	$ 749.6
Depreciation Expense			
Theme parks and resorts	$ 213.2	$ 177.4	$ 172.4
Filmed entertainment	23.9	12.9	12.2
Consumer products	12.4	5.8	3.1
Corporate	14.0	7.0	3.8
	$ 263.5	$ 203.1	$ 191.5
Identifiable Assets			
Theme parks and resorts	$5,165.7	$4,420.3	$4,066.9
Filmed entertainment	1,878.2	1,672.8	1,252.1
Consumer products	351.4	236.4	193.1
Corporate	2,033.2	1,692.8	1,145.1
	$9,428.5	$8,022.3	$6,657.2
Supplemental Revenue Data			
Theme Parks and Resorts			
Admissions	$1,093.0	$1,179.9	$1,021.7
Merchandise, food and beverage	1,048.0	1,113.5	1,019.5
Filmed Entertainment			
Theatrical product	1,776.9	1,545.7	1,090.1
Export revenues	1,267.1	938.8	653.3

13 COMMITMENTS AND CONTINGENCIES

The Company, together with, in some instances, certain of its directors and officers, is a defendant or co-defendant in various legal actions involving antitrust, copyright, breach of contract and various other claims incident to the conduct of its businesses. Management does not expect the Company to suffer any material liability by reason of such actions.

In December 1990, the Company entered into a joint venture with Touchwood Pacific Partners I, L.P. (Touchwood) whereby Touchwood will provide financing totalling approximately $600 million to fund at least a portion of the production of a minimum of 20 theatrical feature films. Under certain circumstances, the Company may be liable to reimburse Touchwood for a portion of its production costs related to these films. No liability existed as of September 30, 1991.

QUARTERLY FINANCIAL SUMMARY

(In millions, except per share data)
(Unaudited)

	December 31	March 31	June 30	September 30
1991				
Revenues	$1,492.4	$1,439.0	$1,511.6	$1,739.4
Operating income	307.7	231.9	302.0	323.3
Net income	170.4	126.6	165.5	174.1
Earnings per share	1.28	.95	1.24	1.31
Dividends per share	.145	.175	.175	.175
Market price per share				
High	108¾	129¾	123¾	127⅞
Low	86	93⅝	110⅛	110¼
1990				
Revenues	$1,288.2	$1,303.7	$1,539.5	$1,712.3
Operating income	309.2	311.5	407.8	397.0
Net income	174.4	178.5	238.4	232.7
Earnings per share	1.26	1.29	1.75	1.72
Dividends per share	.12	.145	.145	.145
Market price per share				
High	136¼	117¾	132¾	136½
Low	105¾	101½	109¼	86⅞

SELECTED FINANCIAL DATA

(In millions, except per share and other data)

	1991	1990	1989	1988	1987
Statement of Income					
Revenues	**$6,182.4**	$5,843.7	$4,594.3	$3,438.2	$2,876.8
Operating income	**1,164.9**	1,425.5	1,229.0	884.8	776.8
Interest expense	**105.0**	43.1	23.9	5.8	29.1
Income from continuing operations	**636.6**	824.0	703.3	522.0	392.3
Net income	**636.6**	824.0	703.3	522.0	444.7
Per Share					
Net income					
Continuing operations	**$4.78**	$6.00	$5.10	$3.80	$2.85
Total	**4.78**	6.00	5.10	3.80	3.23
Cash dividends	**.67**	.555	.46	.38	.32
Balance Sheet					
Total assets	**$9,428.5**	$8,022.3	$6,657.2	$5,108.9	$3,806.3
Borrowings	**2,213.8**	1,584.6	860.6	435.5	584.5
Stockholders' equity	**3,871.3**	3,488.6	3,044.0	2,359.3	1,845.4
Statement of Cash Flows					
Cash flow from operations	**$1,503.3**	$1,358.9	$1,275.6	$1,075.4*	$830.6
Investing activities	**(1,732.9)**	(1,181.9)	(1,729.2)	(1,909.5)	(506.8)
Financing activities	**295.9**	262.0	406.4	(245.8)	44.7
Other Data					
Stockholders at year-end	**189,000**	175,000	143,000	124,000	101,000
Employees at year-end	**58,000**	52,000	47,000	39,000	31,000

* Excludes $722.6 million unearned royalty advances.

CASE PART IV

Strategy Formulation

Kentucky Fried Chicken and the Global Fast-Food Industry

JEFFREY A. KRUG, *The College of William & Mary*
and **W. HARVEY HEGARTY,** *Indiana University*

During the 1960s and 1970s, Kentucky Fried Chicken Corporation (KFC) pursued an aggressive strategy of restaurant expansion, quickly establishing itself as one of the first fast-food restaurant chains in the U.S. (see Exhibit 1). KFC was also one of the first U.S. fast-food restaurant chains to expand overseas. By 1990, restaurants located outside of the U.S. were generating over 50 percent of KFC's total profits. By the end of 1993, KFC was operating in over 63 foreign countries and was one of the three largest fast-food restaurant chains operating outside of the United States.

Japan, Australia, and the United Kingdom accounted for the greatest share of KFC's international expansion during the 1970s and 1980s. However, as KFC entered the 1990s, a number of other international markets offered significant opportunities for growth. China, with a population of over one billion, and Europe, with a population roughly equal to the U.S., offered such opportunities. Latin America also offered a unique opportunity because of the size of its markets, its common language and culture, and its geographical proximity to the United States.

By 1994, KFC was operating successful subsidiaries in Mexico and Puerto Rico. A third subsidiary was established in Venezuela in 1993. The majority of KFC's restaurants in Mexico and Puerto Rico were company-owned. However, KFC had established 21 new franchises in Mexico by the end of 1993, following enactment of Mexico's new franchise law in 1990. KFC anticipated that much of its future growth in Mexico would be through franchises rather than company-owned restaurants. KFC was only one of many U.S. fast-food, retail, and hotel chains to begin franchising in Mexico following the new franchise law. In addition to Mexico, KFC was operating franchises in 42 other countries throughout the Caribbean, and Central and South America by mid-1994.

Courtesy of Jeffrey A. Krug, The College of William & Mary and W. Harvey Hegarty, Indiana University.

EXHIBIT 1

Leading U.S. Fast-Food Chains

Chain	Parent	U.S. Sales ($M) 1993(e)	1992	1992 % CHG	Units
McDonald's	McDonald's Corporation	13,992	13,243	5.7%	8,959
Burger King	Grand Metropolitan PLC	6,500	6,400	1.6%	5,705
Pizza Hut	PepsiCo, Inc.	4,781	4,265	12.1%	7,608
Hardee's	Imasco Ltd.	4,149	3,898	6.4%	3,313
Taco Bell	PepsiCo, Inc.	3,643	3,139	16.1%	4,078
Wendy's	Wendy's International Inc.	3,608	3,289	9.7%	3,607
KFC	PepsiCo, Inc.	3,600	3,400	5.9%	5,089
Little Caesars	Little Caesar Enterprises	2,311	2,160	7.0%	4,575
Domino's Pizza	Domino's Pizza Inc.	2,201	2,358	−6.7%	5,301
Subway	Doctor's Associates Inc.	2,200	1,800	22.2%	7,000
Dairy Queen	International Dairy Queen	2,114	2,091	1.1%	4,780
Denny's	Flagstar Cos. Inc.	1,730	1,600	8.1%	1,391
Red Lobster	General Mills Inc.	1,688	1,610	4.9%	581
Arby's	DWG Corp.	1,536	1,452	5.8%	2,382
Shoney's	Shoney's Inc.	1,345	1,218	10.4%	855
Dunkin' Donuts	Allied-Lyons PLC	1,228	1,076	14.1%	2,342
Olive Garden	General Mills Inc.	1,091	928	17.5%	379
Big Boy	Elias Bros. Restaurants	1,064	1,118	−4.8%	934
Jack in the Box	Foodmaker Inc.	1,008	1,049	−3.9%	1,155
Long John Silver's	Long John Silver's Rest.	946	889	6.4%	1,437
Chili's	Brinker International	786	684	14.9%	314
Sizzler	Sizzler International Inc.	775	764	1.5%	597
Ponderosa	Metromedia Steakhouses	762	756	0.8%	792
Roy Rogers	Imasco Ltd.	751	702	7.0%	650
Sonic Drive-In	Sonic Corp.	690	600	15.0%	1,191
T.G.I. Friday's	Carlson Cos.	676	577	17.1%	195
Carl's Jr.	Carl Karcher Enterprises	625	599	4.4%	623
Cracker Barrel	Cracker Barrel	575	515	11.7%	152
Applebee's	Applebee's Int'l Inc.	575	404	42.3%	250
Perkins	Tennessee Rest. Cos.	572	543	5.3%	413
Total		67,521	63,125	7.0%	76,648

SOURCE: Nation's Restaurant News. (e) 1993 sales estimated.

COMPANY HISTORY

Fast-food franchising was still in its infancy in 1954 when Harland Sanders began his travels across the United States to speak with prospective franchisees about his "Colonel Sanders Recipe Kentucky Fried Chicken." By 1960, "Colonel" Sanders had granted KFC franchises to over 200 take-home retail outlets and restaurants across the United States. He had also succeeded in establishing a number of franchises in Canada. By 1963, the number of KFC franchises had risen to over 300 and revenues had reached $500,000.

By 1964, at the age of 74, the Colonel had tired of running the day-to-day operations of his business and was eager to concentrate on public relations issues. Therefore, he sought out potential buyers, eventually deciding to sell the business to two Louisville businessmen—Jack Massey and John Young Brown Jr.—for $2 million. Massey was named chairman of the board and Brown, who would later become Governor of Kentucky, was named president. The Colonel stayed on as a public relations man and goodwill ambassador for the company.

During the next five years, Massey and Brown concentrated on growing KFC's franchise system across the United States. In 1966, they took KFC public and the company was listed on the New York Stock Exchange. By the late 1960s, a strong foothold had been established in the United States, and Massey and Brown turned their attention to international markets. In 1969, a joint venture was signed with Mitsuoishi Shoji Kaisha, Ltd. in Japan, and the rights to operate 14 existing KFC franchises in England were acquired. Subsidiaries were also established in Hong Kong, South Africa, Australia, New Zealand, and Mexico. By 1971, KFC had 2,450 franchises and 600 company-owned restaurants worldwide, and was operating in 48 countries.

Heublein, Inc.

In 1971, KFC entered negotiations with Heublein, Inc. to discuss a possible merger. The decision to seek a merger candidate was partially driven by Brown's desire to pursue other interests, including a political career (Brown was elected Governor of Kentucky in 1977). On April 10, Heublein announced that an agreement had been reached. Shareholders approved the merger on May 27, and KFC was merged into a subsidiary of Heublein.

Heublein was in the business of producing vodka, mixed cocktails, dry gin, cordials, beer, and other alcoholic beverages. It was also the exclusive distributor of a variety of imported alcoholic beverages. Heublein had little experience in the restaurant business. Conflicts quickly erupted between Colonel Sanders, who continued to act in a public relations capacity, and Heublein management. In particular, Colonel Sanders became increasingly distraught over quality control issues and restaurant cleanliness, By 1977, new restaurant openings had slowed to about twenty per year (in 1993, KFC opened a new restaurant on average every two days). Restaurants were not being remodeled and service quality was declining.

In 1977, Heublein sent in a new management team to redirect KFC's strategy. Richard P. Mayer, who later became chairman and chief executive officer, was part of this team (Mayer remained with KFC until 1989, when he left to become president of General Foods USA). A "back-to-the-basics" strategy was immediately implemented. New unit construction was discontinued until existing restaurants could be upgraded and operating problems eliminated. Restaurants were refurbished, an emphasis was placed on cleanliness and service, marginal products were eliminated, and product consistency was reestablished. By 1982, KFC had succeeded in establishing a successful strategic focus and was again aggressively building new units.

R.J. Reynolds Industries, Inc.

On October 12, 1982, R.J. Reynolds Industries, Inc. (RJR) announced that it would merge Heublein into a wholly-owned subsidiary. The merger with Heublein represented part of RJR's overall corporate strategy of diversifying into unrelated businesses. RJR's objective was to reduce its dependence on the tobacco industry, which had driven RJR sales since its founding in North

Carolina in 1875. Sales of cigarettes and tobacco products, while profitable, were declining because of reduced consumption in the U.S., due mainly to the increased awareness among Americans regarding the negative health consequences of smoking.

RJR's diversification strategy included the acquisition of a variety of companies in the energy, transportation, and food and restaurant industries. RJR had no more experience in the restaurant business than did Heublein when Heublein purchased KFC in 1971. However, RJR decided to take a hands-off approach to managing KFC. Whereas Heublein had installed its own top management at KFC headquarters, RJR left KFC management largely intact, believing that existing KFC managers were better qualified to operate KFC's businesses than were its own managers. By doing so, RJR avoided many of the operating problems that Heublein had experienced during its management of KFC. This strategy paid off for RJR, as KFC continued to expand aggressively and profitably under RJR's ownership.

In 1985, RJR acquired Nabisco Corporation for $4.9 billion. Nabisco sold a variety of well-known cookies, crackers, cereals, confectioneries, snacks and other grocery products. In October 1986, Kentucky Fried Chicken was sold to PepsiCo, Inc.

PEPSICO, INC.

Corporate Strategy

PepsiCo, Inc. (PepsiCo) was first incorporated in Delaware in 1919 as Loft, Inc. In 1938, Loft acquired the Pepsi-Cola Co., a manufacturer of soft drinks and soft drink concentrates. Pepsi-Cola's traditional business has been the sale of its soft drink concentrates to licensed independent and company-owned bottlers, which manufacture, sell, and distribute Pepsi-Cola soft drinks. Today, Pepsi-Cola's best known trademarks are Pepsi-Cola, Diet Pepsi, Mountain Dew, and Slice. Shortly after its acquisition of Pepsi-Cola, Loft changed its name to Pepsi-Cola Co. On June 30, 1965, Pepsi-Cola Co. acquired Frito-Lay Inc. for three million shares, thereby creating one of the largest consumer companies in the United States. At that time, the present name of PepsiCo, Inc. was adopted. Frito-Lay manufactures and sells a variety of snack foods. Its best known trademarks are Fritos brand Corn Chips, Lay's and Ruffles brand Potato Chips, Doritos and Tostitos Chips, and Chee-tos brand Cheese Flavored Snacks. In 1992, 63 percent of PepsiCo's net sales were generated by its soft drink and snack food businesses (see Exhibit 2).

EXHIBIT 2

PepsiCo, Inc.—1992 Operating Results ($ millions)

	Beverages	Snack Foods	Restaurants	Total
Net Sales	$7,605.6	$6,132.1	$8,232.2	$21,970.0
Operating Profit	798.6	984.7	718.5	2,501.8
% Net Sales	10.5%	16.1%	8.7%	11.4%
Assets	$7,857.5	$4,628.0	$5,097.1	$17,582.6
Capital Spending	343.7	446.2	757.2	1,565.1*

*Includes corporate spending of $18.0 million.

Beginning in the late 1960s, PepsiCo began an aggressive acquisition program. Initially, PepsiCo pursued an acquisition strategy similar to that pursued by RJR during the 1980s, buying a number of companies in areas unrelated to its major businesses. For example, North American Van Lines was acquired in June 1968. Wilson Sporting Goods was merged into the company in 1972 and Lee Way Motor Freight was acquired in 1976. However, success in operating these businesses failed to live up to expectations, mainly because the management skills required to operate these businesses lay outside of PepsiCo's area of expertise.

In 1984, then-chairman and chief executive officer Don Kendall decided to restructure PepsiCo's operations. Most importantly, PepsiCo would divest those businesses which did not support PepsiCo's consumer product orientation. PepsiCo sold Lee Way Motor Freight in 1984. In 1985, Wilson Sporting Goods and North American Van Lines were sold. Additionally, PepsiCo's foreign bottling operations were sold to local businesspeople who better understood the cultural and business conditions operating in their respective countries. Lastly, Kendall reorganized PepsiCo along three lines: soft drinks, snack foods, and restaurants (see Exhibit 3). All future investment would be directed at strengthening PepsiCo's performance in these three related areas.

Restaurant Business and Acquisition of Kentucky Fried Chicken

PepsiCo first entered the restaurant business in 1977 when it acquired Pizza Hut's 3,200 unit restaurant system. Taco Bell was merged into a division of PepsiCo in 1978. The restaurant business complemented PepsiCo's consumer product orientation. The marketing of fast-food followed much of the same patterns as the marketing of soft drinks and snack foods. Therefore, PepsiCo's management skills could easily be transferred among its three business segments. This was compatible with PepsiCo's practice of frequently moving managers among its business units as a way of developing future top executives. PepsiCo's restaurant chains also provided an additional outlet for the sale of Pepsi soft drink products. In addition, Pepsi soft drinks and fast-food

---

EXHIBIT 3

PepsiCo, Inc.—Principal Divisions

Executive Offices: Purchase, New York

Beverage Segment	Snack Food Segment	Restaurants
Pepsi-Cola North America Somers, New York	PepsiCo Worldwide Foods Plano, Texas	Kentucky Fried Chicken Louisville, Kentucky
Pepsi-Cola International Somers, New York	Frito-Lay, Inc. Plano, Texas	Pizza Hut Worldwide Wichita, Kansas
	PepsiCo Foods International Plano, Texas	Taco Bell Worldwide Irvine, California
		PepsiCo Food Systems Dallas, Texas

products could be marketed together in the same television and radio segments, thereby providing higher returns for each advertising dollar.

To complete its diversification into the restaurant segment, PepsiCo acquired Kentucky Fried Chicken Corporation from RJR-Nabisco in 1986 for $841 million. The acquisition of KFC gave PepsiCo the leading market share in three of the four largest and fastest-growing segments within the U.S. quick-service industry. At the end of 1992, Pizza Hut held a 25 percent share of the $16 billion U.S. pizza segment, Taco Bell held 70 percent of the $4.6 billion Mexican food segment, and KFC held 49 percent of the $7.0 billion U.S. chicken segment. In an analysis of PepsiCo's restaurant business in 1989, Shearson Lehman Hutton analyst Caroline Levy commented that "on balance, PepsiCo's restaurants are clearly outperforming the industry and most of the major chains." (See Exhibits 2 and 4 for business segment financial data and restaurant count.)

PepsiCo's success during the late 1980s and early 1990s can be seen by its upward trend in *Fortune* magazine's annual survey of "America's Most Admired Corporations." By 1991, PepsiCo was labeled the 5th most admired corporation overall (of 306 corporations included in the survey), rising from a 6th place finish in 1990. In particular, PepsiCo was ranked high in value as a long-term investment, innovativeness, wise use of corporate assets, quality of management, and quality of products/services offered.

PepsiCo
Ranking

1994—26
1993—14
1992— 9
1991— 5
1990— 6
1989— 7
1988—14
1987—24
1986—25

However, PepsiCo's ranking fell to 9th place in 1992, 14th place in 1993, and 26th place in 1994. PepsiCo's fall in the 1994 rankings appears on the surface to be significant. However, PepsiCo's fall in the rankings is partially the

EXHIBIT 4

PepsiCo, Inc.—Number of Units Worldwide

Year	KFC	Pizza Hut	Taco Bell*	Total
1987	7,522	6,210	2,738	16,470
1988	7,761	6,662	2,930	17,353
1989	7,948	7,502	3,125	18,575
1990	8,187	8,220	3,349	19,756
1991	8,480	8,837	3,670	20,987
1992	8,729	9,454	4,153	22,336
Five-Year Compounded Annual Growth Rate				
	3.0%	8.8%	8.7%	6.3%

*Taco Bell units include Hot 'n Now chain acquired in 1990.

result of changes made in the way *Fortune* conducted its 1994 survey. In particular, it increased the number of companies surveyed from 311 to 404, increased the number of industry groups from 32 to 42 (e.g., by adding computer services and entertainment), and divided some industry groups up into their components (e.g., by dividing the transportation group into airlines, trucking, and railroads). Home Depot, Microsoft, and Walt Disney, which were added to the survey in 1994, were all ranked in the top ten most admired corporations in America.

FAST-FOOD INDUSTRY

U.S. Quick-Service Market

According to the National Restaurant Association (NRA), 1994 food-service sales will top $275 billion for the approximately 500,000 restaurants and other food outlets making up the U.S. restaurant industry. The NRA estimates that sales in the fast-food segment of the food industry will grow 6.3 percent to approximately $86 billion in the United States in 1994, up from $81 million in 1993. This would mark the first time that fast-food sales exceeded sales in the full-service segment, which is expected to grow to $85.5 billion in 1994. The growth in fast-food sales reflects the long, gradual change in the restaurant industry from an industry once dominated by independently-operated sit-down restaurants to an industry fast becoming dominated by fast-food restaurant chains. The U.S. restaurant industry as a whole is projected to grow by 3.9 percent.

Sales data for the top 30 fast-food restaurant chains are shown in Exhibit 1. Most striking is the dominance of McDonald's. Sales for 1993 are estimated at $14.0 billion, which would represent 17.3 percent of industry sales, or 20.7 percent of sales of the top 30 fast-food chains. McDonald's strong per restaurant sales are more striking given that McDonald's accounts for under 12 percent of the industry's total outlets. U.S. sales for the PepsiCo system, which includes KFC, Pizza Hut and Taco Bell, are estimated to reach $12.0 billion in 1993, which would represent 14.9 percent of the fast-food industry and 17.8 percent of the top 30 fast-food chains. The PepsiCo system grew to 16,775 restaurants by the end of 1992. McDonald's holds the number one spot in the hamburger segment, while PepsiCo holds the leading market share in the chicken (KFC), Mexican (Taco Bell), and pizza (Pizza Hut) segments.

Major Business Segments

Six major business segments make up the fast-food market within the food service industry. Exhibit 5 shows sales for the top 64 fast-food chains in the six major segments for the years 1991 through 1993, as compiled by *Nation's Restaurant News*. Sandwich chains make up the largest segment, reaching estimated sales in 1993 of $42.4 billion. Of the 17 restaurant chains making up the sandwich segment, McDonald's holds a 33 percent market share. Sandwich chains, faced by slowed sales growth, have turned to new menu offerings, emphasized customer service, and established non-traditional units in unconventional locations to beef up sales. Hardee's and McDonald's have successfully introduced fried chicken, which will challenge KFC, the chicken chain market share leader. Burger King has introduced fried clams and shrimp to its dinner menu in some locations and Jack-in-the-Box has introduced chicken

EXHIBIT 5

U.S. Sales of the Top Fast-Food Chains by Business Segment ($ billions)

Business Segment	#Chains	1991	1992	1993(e)
Sandwich Chains (McDonald's, Burger King, Hardee's, Taco Bell, Wendy's, Subway, Dairy Queen, Arby's, Jack-in-the-Box, Roy Rogers, Sonic Drive-In, Carl's Jr., Rally's, Whataburger, White Castle, Krystal, Del Taco)	17	$36.7	$39.7	$42.4
Pizza Chains (Pizza Hut, Little Caesars, Domino's, Chuck E. Cheese's, Sberro The Italian Eatery, Round Table Pizza, Godfather's Pizza, Pizza Inn)	8	9.6	10.4	10.8
Family Restaurants (Denny's, Shoney's, Big Boy, Cracker Barrel, Perkins, Friendly's, Int'l House of Pancakes, Bob Evan's, Bakers Square, Waffle House, Village Inn, Marie Callender's, Country Kitchen)	13	7.0	7.7	8.2
Dinner Houses (Red Lobster, Olive Garden, Chili's, T.G.I. Friday's, Applebee's, Bennigan's, Chi-Chi's, Outback Steakhouse, Ruby Tuesday, Ground Round, El Torito, Stuart Anderson's Black Angus, Steak and Ale, Tony Roma's, Red Robin)	15	6.3	6.9	7.8
Chicken Chains (KFC, Popeyes, Church's, Chick-fil-A)	4	4.5	4.7	5.0
Steak Restaurants (Sizzler, Ponderosa, Golden Corral, Ryan's, Western Sizzlin', Quincy's, Bonanza)	7	3.5	3.3	3.4
Top Fast-Food Chains	64	$67.6	$72.7	$77.6

SOURCE: Nation's Restaurant News. (e) 1993 sales figures estimated.

and teriyaki with rice in its Sacramento, California units, in order to appeal to its Asian-American audience. Other issues of growing importance for the sandwich chains are franchise relations, increasingly tough government regulations (e.g., secondhand smoke), and food safety and handling.

The second largest fast-food segment is pizza, long dominated by Pizza Hut. Pizza Hut expects sales to top $4.8 billion in 1993, which would represent a 44 percent market share among the eight competitors making up the pizza segment. Little Caesars has now overtaken Domino's as the second largest pizza chain, despite the fact that Domino's operates more outlets. Little Caesars is the only pizza chain to remain exclusively a take-out chain. Increased competition within the pizza segment and pressures to appeal to a wider customer base have led pizza chains to diversify into non-pizza menu items, to develop non-traditional units (e.g., airport kiosks), and to offer special promotions. Among the many new product offerings, Domino's has introduced submarine sandwiches, Little Caesars is offering spaghetti and bread sticks, and Pizza Hut has rolled out deep-dish pizza. Many of the pizza chains have also begun intensive advertising for giant-sized pizzas. Godfather's was the first pizza chain to introduce a giant pizza—its 18-inch Jumbo Combo. The top three pizza chains quickly followed suit. Pizza Hut has introduced its 24-slice Big Foot (one foot by two feet), Little Caesars offers its Big, Big deal 24-slice pizza made of two pies, and Domino's has introduced The Dominator, a 30-slice pizza.

The highest growth business segment in 1992 was the dinner house segment, for which 1992 sales exceeded 1991 sales by 10.4 percent. The dinner house segment is again expected to lead all food segments in 1993, growing by an estimated 12.5 percent, about twice as fast as the next fastest-growing segment. Red Lobster remains the largest dinner house and is expected to surpass $1.7 billion in sales for its fiscal year ending May 1994. The would make Red Lobster the 15th largest chain among the top 100. Olive Garden is expected to hit the $1 billion sales mark when its fiscal year ends May 1994. Olive Garden is currently running a strong second place within the dinner house segment behind Red Lobster. Olive Garden's sales in 1993/1994 are expected to grow by 12.5 percent over the previous year, compared to a growth rate of 4.9 percent for the segment leader.

The dinner house segment should continue to outpace the other five fast-food segments for a variety of reasons. Major chains still have low penetration in this segment, though General Mills (Red Lobster and Olive Garden) and PepsiCo, Inc. (Fresh-Mex) are poised to dominate a large portion of this segment. A maturing population is already increasing demand for full-service, sit-down restaurants. Seven of the fifteen dinner houses in this segment posted growth rates in sales of over 14 percent in 1992. Outback Steakhouse, Applebee's Neighborhood Grill & Bar, Red Robin Burger & Spirits Emporium, and Chili's Grill & Bar grew at rates of 114, 40, 19, and 19 percent in 1992, respectively.

KFC continues to dominate the chicken segment, with projected 1993 sales of $3.6 billion. Its nearest competitor, Popeyes, is a distant second with projected sales of $568.8 million. Church's and Chick-fil-A follow with projected sales of $428.1 and $375.0 million, respectively. KFC continues to hold a market share of over 72 percent in the chicken segment and accounts for about one-half of all sales by chicken franchises. Other competitors within the chicken market are Bojangle's, El Pollo Loco, Grandy's, Pudgie's, and Boston Chicken.

Industry Consolidation

Although the restaurant industry has outpaced the overall economy in recent years, there are indications that the U.S. market is slowly becoming saturated. According to the U.S. Bureau of Labor, sales of U.S. eating and drinking establishments increased by 2.7 percent in 1992. Following a period of rapid expansion and intense restaurant building in the U.S. during the 1970s and 1980s, the fast-food industry has apparently begun to consolidate. In January 1990, Grand Metropolitan, a British company, purchased Pillsbury Co. for $5.7 billion. Included in the purchase was Pillsbury's Burger King chain. Grand Met has already begun to strengthen the franchise by upgrading existing restaurants and has eliminated several levels of management in order to cut costs. This should give Burger King a long-needed boost in improving its position against McDonald's, its largest competitor in the U.S. market. In 1988, Grand Met purchased Wienerwald, a West German chicken chain, and the Spaghetti Factory, a Swiss chain.

Within the chicken segment, a number of acquisitions have intensified competition behind KFC. In particular, the second largest chicken segment restaurant chain, Church's, was acquired by Al Copeland Enterprises in 1989 for $392 million. Copeland also owns Popeyes Famous Fried Chicken, which has since replaced Church's as the second largest restaurant in the chicken segment. In 1992, Popeye's had worldwide sales of $580 million, compared to KFC's worldwide sales of $6.7 billion and Church's worldwide sales of $510 million. Following the Church's acquisition, Copeland converted 303 of Church's 1,368 restaurants into Popeyes franchises, bringing the Popeyes restaurant system to a total of 1,030. This made Popeyes the second largest chicken chain in the U.S. Several hundred Church's units were scheduled to be sold to raise cash to pay for the Church's acquisition. Although the Church's acquisition enlarged the competitive base controlled by Copeland, the Copeland restaurant system is still dwarfed by KFC, which ended 1992 with 8,729 restaurants worldwide.

Perhaps more important to KFC was Hardee's acquisition of 600 Roy Rogers restaurants from Marriott Corporation in early 1990. Hardee's immediately began to convert these restaurants to Hardee's units and quickly introduced "Roy Rogers" fried chicken to its menu. By the end of 1993, Hardee's had introduced fried chicken into most of its 3,313 domestic restaurants. While Hardee's is unlikely to destroy the customer loyalty that KFC has long enjoyed, it has already cut into KFC's sales as its widened menu selection appeals to a variety of family eating preferences.

The effect of these and other recent mergers and acquisitions on the industry has been powerful. The top ten restaurant chains now control over 50 percent of all fast-food sales in the U.S. The consolidation of a number of these firms within larger, financially more powerful firms should give these restaurant chains the financial and managerial resources they need to outgrow their small competitors.

Demographic Trends

Intense marketing by the leading fast-food chains will likely continue to stimulate demand for fast-food in the U.S. during the 1990s. However, a number of demographic and societal changes are likely to affect the future demand for fast-food in different directions. One such change is the rise in single-person households, which has steadily increased from 17 percent of all U.S. households in 1970 to approximately 25 percent today. In addition, disposable household income should continue to increase, mainly because more women are working than ever before. According to Standard & Poor's *Industry Surveys,* Americans spent 52 percent of their food dollars at restaurants in 1992, up from 34 percent in 1970. Most of this increase came from increased consumption, while the balance came mainly from higher prices.

In addition to these demographic trends, a number of societal changes may also affect future demand for fast-food. For example, microwaves have now been introduced into approximately 70 percent of all U.S. homes. This has already resulted in a significant shift in the types of products sold in supermarkets and convenience restaurants, which have introduced a variety of products that can be quickly and easily prepared in microwaves. In addition, the aging of America's Baby Boomers may change the frequency with which people patronize more upscale restaurants. Lastly, birth rates are projected to rise in the 1990s. This is likely to affect whether families eat out or stay home. Therefore, these various demographic and societal trends are likely to affect the future demand for fast-food in different ways.

International Quick-Service Market

Because of the aggressive pace of new restaurant construction in the U.S. during the 1970s and 1980s, future growth resulting from new restaurant construction in the U.S. may be limited. In any case, the cost of finding prime locations is rising, increasing the pressure on restaurant chains to increase per restaurant sales in order to cover higher initial investment costs. One alternative to continued investment in the U.S. market is expansion into international markets, which offers large customer bases and comparatively little competition. However, few U.S. restaurant chains have yet defined aggressive strategies for penetrating international markets.

Three restaurant chains which have established aggressive international strategies are McDonald's, Pizza Hut, and Kentucky Fried Chicken. McDonald's currently operates the most units within the U.S. market. McDonald's also operates the largest number of fast-food chains outside of the United States (4,041), recently overtaking KFC, which long dominated the fast-food industry outside of the U.S. KFC ended 1992 with 3,640 restaurants outside of the U.S., 401 restaurants fewer than McDonald's. However, KFC remains the most internationalized of all fast-food chains, operating almost 42 percent of its total units outside of the U.S. In comparison, McDonald's operates slightly more than 31 percent of its units outside of the U.S. Pizza Hut presently operates in the most countries (73). However, over 83 percent of its units are still located in the U.S.

Exhibit 6 shows *Hotels'* 1993 list of the world's twenty largest fast-food restaurant chains. Several important observations may be made from these data. First, eighteen of the twenty largest restaurant chains are headquartered in the U.S. Only one non-U.S. company appears in the largest eighteen restaurant chains. This may be partially explained by the fact that U.S. firms account for over 25 percent of the world's foreign direct investment. As a result, U.S. firms have historically been more likely to invest assets abroad. However, while both Kentucky Fried Chicken and McDonald's operate over 3,600 units abroad, no other restaurant chain, U.S. or foreign, has more than 1,500 units outside of the U.S. In fact, most chains have fewer than 500 foreign units and operate in less than twenty countries.

There are a number of possible explanations for the relative scarcity of fast-food restaurant chains outside of the U.S. First, the U.S. represents the largest consumer market in the world, accounting for almost one-fourth of the world's GNP. Therefore, the U.S. has traditionally been the strategic focus of the largest restaurant chains. In addition, Americans have been more quick to accept the fast-food concept. Many other cultures have strong culinary traditions which have not been easy to break down. The Europeans, for example, have long histories of frequenting more mid-scale restaurants, where they may

EXHIBIT 6

The World's 20 Largest Fast-Food Chains (year-end 1992)

Franchise	Location	Units	Countries
1 McDonald's	Oakbrook, IL	13,000	65
2 Pizza Hut	Wichita, KS	9,078	73
3 Kentucky Fried Chicken	Louisville, KY	8,729	63
4 Subway Sandwiches	Milford, CT	7,327	15
5 Burger King	Miami, FL	6,648	47
6 Domino's Pizza	Ann Arbor, MI	5,300	31
7 Dairy Queen	Minneapolis, MN	5,293	20
8 Whitbread	Luton, U.K.	4,943	7
9 Little Caesars Pizza	Detroit, MI	4,500	3
10 Hardee's	Rocky Mount, NC	4,015	11
11 Wendy's International	Dublin, OH	4,000	29
12 Taco Bell	Irvine, CA	4,000	15
13 Baskin-Robbins	Glendale, CA	3,484	45
14 Dunkin' Donuts	Randolph, MA	3,000	24
15 Arby's Roast Beef	Miami Beach, FL	2,606	12
16 Long John Silvers	Lexington, KY	1,461	4
17 Denny's	Spartansburg, SC	1,460	9
18 Jack-in-the-Box	San Diego, CA	1,155	3
19 Kyotaru Co	Tokyo, Japan	1,144	3
20 Church's Fried Chicken	Atlanta, GA	1,072	4

SOURCE: *Hotels,* May 1993.

spend several hours in a formal setting enjoying native dishes and beverages. While KFC is again building restaurants in Germany, it previously failed to penetrate the German market because Germans were not accustomed to take-out food or to ordering food over the counter. McDonald's has had greater success penetrating the German market because it has made a number of changes in its menu and operating procedures in order to better appeal to German culture. For example, German beer is served in all of McDonald's German restaurants. KFC has had more success in Asia, where chicken is a traditional dish.

Aside from cultural factors, international business carries risks not present in the U.S. market. Long distances between headquarters and foreign franchises often make it difficult to control the quality of individual franchises. Large distances can also cause servicing and support problems. Transportation and other resource costs may also be higher than in the domestic market. In addition, time, cultural, and language differences can increase communication and operational problems. Therefore, it is reasonable to expect U.S. restaurant chains to expand domestically as long as they can achieve corporate profit and growth objectives. However, as the U.S. market becomes more saturated, and companies gain additional expertise in international business, we should expect more companies to turn to profitable international markets as a means of expanding restaurant bases and increasing sales, profits, and market share.

KENTUCKY FRIED CHICKEN CORPORATION

Management

One of PepsiCo's greatest challenges when it acquired Kentucky Fried Chicken in 1986 was how to mold two distinct corporate cultures. When R.J. Reynolds acquired KFC in 1982, it realized that it knew very little about the fast-food business. Therefore, it relied on existing KFC management to manage the company. As a result, there was little need for mixing the cultures of the two companies. However, one of PepsiCo's major concerns when considering the purchase of KFC was whether it had the management skills required to successfully operate KFC using PepsiCo's managers. PepsiCo had already acquired considerable experience managing fast-food businesses through its Pizza Hut and Taco Bell operations. Therefore, it was anxious to pursue strategic changes within KFC which would improve performance. However, replacing KFC with PepsiCo managers could easily cause conflicts between managers in both companies, who were accustomed to different operating procedures and working conditions.

PepsiCo's corporate culture has long been based heavily on a "fast-track" New York approach to management. It hires the country's top business and engineering graduates and promotes them based on performance. As a result, top performers expect to move up through the ranks quickly and to be paid well for their efforts. However, this competitive environment often results in intense rivalries among young managers. If one fails to perform, there is always another top performer waiting in the wings. As a result, employee loyalty is sometimes lost and turnover tends to be higher than in other companies.

The corporate culture at Kentucky Fried Chicken in 1986 contrasted sharply with that at PepsiCo. KFC's culture was built largely on Colonel Sander's laid-back approach to management. As well, employees enjoyed relatively good employment stability and security. Over the years, a strong loyalty had been created among KFC employees and franchisees, mainly because of the efforts of Colonel Sanders to provide for his employees' benefits, pension, and other non-income needs. In addition, the Southern environment of Louisville resulted in a friendly, relaxed atmosphere at KFC's corporate offices. This corporate culture was left essentially unchanged during the Heublein and RJR years.

When PepsiCo acquired KFC, it began to restructure the KFC organization, replacing most of KFC's top managers with its own. By the summer of 1990, all of KFC's top positions were occupied by PepsiCo executives. In July 1989, KFC's president and chief executive officer, Richard P. Mayer, left KFC to become president of General Foods USA. Mayer had been at KFC since 1977, when KFC was still owned by Heublein. PepsiCo replaced Mayer with John Cranor III, the former president of Pepsi-Cola East, a Pepsi-Cola unit. In November 1989, Martin Redgrave moved from PepsiCo to become KFC's new chief financial officer. In the summer of 1990, Bill McDonald, a Pizza Hut and Frito Lay marketing executive, was named senior vice president of marketing. Two months before, PepsiCo had named Kyle Craig, a former Pillsbury executive, as president of KFC's USA operations.

Most of PepsiCo's initial management changes in 1987 focused on KFC's corporate offices and USA operations. In 1988, attention was turned to KFC's international division. During 1988, PepsiCo replaced KFC International's top managers with its own. First, it lured Don Pierce away from Burger King and

EXHIBIT 7

KFC Organizational Chart

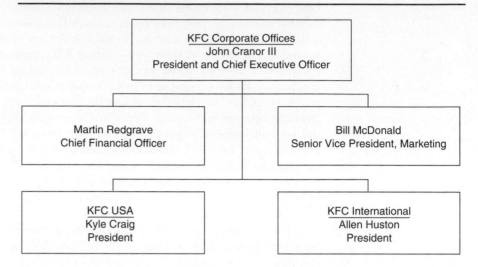

made Pierce president of KFC International. However, Pierce left KFC in early 1990 to become president of Pentagram Corporation, a restaurant operation in Hawaii. Pierce commented that he wished to change jobs partly to decrease the amount of time he spent traveling. PepsiCo replaced Pierce with Allan Huston, who was formerly senior vice president of operations at Pizza Hut. In late 1988, PepsiCo also brought in Robert Briggs, former director of finance at Pepsi-Cola International, as vice president of international finance. Briggs left KFC for a position at Arby's in 1993. (see Exhibit 7 for current organization chart.)

An example of the type of conflict faced by PepsiCo in attempting to implement changes within KFC occurred in August 1989. A month after becoming president and chief executive officer, Cranor addressed KFC's franchisees in Louisville, in order to explain the details of a new franchise contract. This was the first contract change in thirteen years. The new contract gave PepsiCo management greater power to take over weak franchises, to relocate restaurants, and to make changes in existing restaurants. In addition, existing restaurants would no longer be protected from competition from new KFC restaurants. The contract also gave management the right to raise royalty fees on existing restaurants as contracts came up for renewal. After Cranor finished his address, there was an uproar among the attending franchisees, who jumped to their feet to protest the changes. The franchisees had long been accustomed to relatively little interference from management in their day-to-day operations. This type of interference, of course, was a strong part of PepsiCo's philosophy of demanding change.

Operating Results

KFC's recent operating results are shown in Exhibit 8. In 1992, worldwide sales, which represent sales of both company-owned and franchised restaurants, reached $6.7 billion. Since 1987, worldwide sales have grown at a compounded annual growth rate of 10.3 percent. KFC's market share remained at

EXHIBIT 8

KFC Operating Results

	Worldwide Sales ($B)	KFC Corp.* Sales ($B)	KFC Corp.* Profit ($M)	Percent of Sales
1987	$4.1	$1.1	$ 90.0	8.3%
1988	5.0	1.2	116.5	9.6
1989	5.4	1.3	100.0	7.5
1990	5.8	1.5	126.9	8.3
1991	6.2	1.8	80.5	4.4
1992	6.7	2.2	168.8	7.8
CAGR %	10.3%			

SOURCE: PepsiCo annual reports for 1988, 1989, 1990, 1991, and 1992.
*KFC corporate figures include company restaurants and franchise royalties and fees.

about one-half of the $7.0 billion U.S. market in 1992. KFC corporate sales, which include company-owned restaurants and royalties from franchised units, reached $2.2 billion, up 18 percent from 1991 sales of $1.8 billion. New restaurants contributed $345 million to sales, while the translation effects of a weaker dollar lowered reported sales by $22 million.

KFC's worldwide profits increased by 110 percent to $169 million in 1992. KFC's operating profits were split equally between its domestic and international operations. Domestically, KFC's profits rose as a result of additional units, lower headquarters administrative expenses from a restructuring program implemented in early 1992, a sales mix change to higher margin products such as Popcorn Chicken, and higher volumes. Domestic profits were lowered slightly as a result of a higher level of sales promotions. Internationally, profits benefitted from higher franchise royalty revenues and growth in Canada and Mexico. Profits were partially offset by lower profits in Australia, mainly the result of lower volumes and a negative currency translation effect.

BUSINESS LEVEL STRATEGIES

Marketing

As KFC entered 1994, it grappled with a number of important issues. During the 1980s, consumers began to demand healthier foods and KFC was faced with a limited menu consisting mainly of fried foods. In order to reduce KFC's image as a fried chicken chain, it changed its logo from Kentucky Fried Chicken to KFC in 1991. In addition, it responded to consumer demands for greater variety by introducing a variety of new products. Consumers have also become more mobile, demanding fast-food in a variety of non-traditional locations such as grocery stores, restaurants, airports, and outdoor events. This has forced fast-food restaurant chains in general to investigate non-traditional distribution channels and restaurant designs. In addition, families continue to seek greater value in the food they buy, further increasing the pressure on fast-food chains to reduce operating costs and prices.

Many of KFC's problems during the late 1980s surrounded its limited menu and its inability to quickly bring new products to market. The popularity of its Original Recipe fried chicken allowed KFC to expand through the

1980s without significant competition from other chicken competitors. As a result, new product introductions were never an important part of KFC strategy. However, the introduction of chicken sandwiches and fried chicken by hamburger chains has changed the make-up of KFC's competitors. Most importantly, McDonald's introduced its McChicken sandwich in the U.S. market in 1989 while KFC was still testing its new sandwich. By beating KFC to the market, McDonald's was able to develop a strong consumer awareness for its sandwich. This significantly increased KFC's cost of developing consumer awareness for its chicken sandwich, which was introduced several months later.

The increased popularity of healthier foods and consumers' increasing demand for better variety has led to a number of changes in KFC's menu offerings. In 1992, KFC introduced Oriental Wings, Popcorn Chicken, and Honey BBQ Chicken as alternatives to its Original Recipe fried chicken. It also introduced a dessert menu, which included a variety of pies and cookies. In 1993, KFC rolled out its Rotisserie Chicken and began to promote its lunch and dinner buffet. The buffet, which includes 30 items, had been introduced into almost 1,600 KFC restaurants in 27 states by the end of 1993.

One of KFC's most aggressive strategies was the introduction of its "Neighborhood Program." By mid-1993, almost 500 company-owned restaurants in New York, Chicago, Philadelphia, Washington D.C., St. Louis, Los Angeles, Houston and Dallas had been outfitted with special menu offerings to appeal exclusively to the Black community. Menus were beefed up with side dishes such as greens, macaroni and cheese, peach cobbler, sweet-potato pie, and red beans and rice. In addition, restaurant employees have been outfitted with African-inspired uniforms. The introduction of the Neighborhood Program has increased sales by 5 to 30 percent in restaurants appealing directly to the Black community. KFC is currently testing thirteen Hispanic-oriented restaurants in the Miami area, which offer such side dishes as fried plantains, flan and tres leches.

As the growth in sales of traditional, free-standing fast-food restaurants has slowed during the last decade, consumers have demanded fast-food in a greater variety of non-traditional locations. As a result, distribution has taken on increasing importance for fast-food chains. KFC is relying on non-traditional units to spur much of its future growth. Distribution channels which offer significant opportunities are shopping malls and other high-traffic areas which have not traditionally been exploited by fast-food chains. Increasingly, shopping malls are developing food areas where several fast-food restaurant chains compete against each other. Universities and hospitals also offer opportunities for KFC and other chains to improve distribution. KFC is currently testing a variety of non-traditional outlets, including drive-thru & carry-out units; snack shops in cafeterias; kiosks in airports, stadiums, amusement parks, and office buildings; mobile units that can be transported to outdoor concerts and fairs; and scaled-down outlets for supermarkets. In order to help its KFC, Taco Bell, and Pizza Hut units more quickly expand into these non-traditional distribution channels, PepsiCo acquired a partial share of Carts of Colorado, Inc., a manufacturer of mobil merchandising carts, in 1992.

Operating Efficiencies

While marketing strategies traditionally improve a firm's profit picture indirectly through increased sales, improved operating efficiencies can directly affect operating profit. As pressure continues to build on fast-food chains to limit price increases in the U.S. market, restaurant chains continue to search for ways of reducing overhead and other operating costs in order to improve profit margins. In 1989, KFC reorganized its U.S. operations in order to eliminate overhead costs and to increase efficiency. Included in this reorganization was a revision of KFC's crew training programs and operating standards. A renewed emphasis has been placed on improving customer service, cleaner restaurants, faster and friendlier service, and continued high-quality products. In 1992, KFC reorganized its middle management ranks, eliminating 250 of the 1,500 management positions at KFC's corporate headquarters. More responsibility was assigned to restaurant franchisees and marketing managers and pay was more closely aligned with customer service and restaurant performance.

Restaurant Expansion and International Operations

While marketing and operating strategies can improve sales and profitability in existing outlets, an important part of success in the quick-service industry is investment growth. Much of the success of the top ten competitors within the industry during the late 1980s and early 1990s can be found in aggressive building strategies. In particular, a restaurant chain is often able to discourage competition by being the first to build in a low population area which can only support a single fast-food chain. Additionally, it is equally important to beat a competitor into more largely-populated areas, where location is of prime importance.

Internationally, KFC was operating 3,640 restaurants outside of the U.S. at the end of 1992. In 1993, KFC expanded into two new countries—France and Brazil—bringing the total number of countries in which KFC has a presence to 63. KFC is now the third largest quick-service, and largest chicken, restaurant system in the world. In 1992, KFC's international operations contributed 50 percent to KFC's overall operating profit. In the future, KFC's international operations will be called on to provide an increasing percentage of KFC's overall sales and profit growth as the U.S. market continues to saturate.

MEXICO AND LATIN AMERICA

KFC was one of the first restaurant chains to recognize the importance of international markets. In Latin America, KFC was operating 187 company-owned restaurants in Mexico, Puerto Rico, the Virgin Islands, and Trinidad as of April 1994. In addition, KFC had 108 franchisees in 42 countries throughout Latin America, bringing the total number of KFC restaurants in operation in Latin America to 295 (see Exhibit 9).

Through 1990, KFC concentrated its company operations in Mexico and Puerto Rico and focused its franchised operations in the Caribbean and Central America. However, by 1994, KFC had altered its Latin American strategy in a number of ways. First, it began franchising in Mexico, mainly as a result of Mexico's new franchise law, which was enacted in 1990. Second, it expanded its company-owned restaurants into the Virgin Islands and Trinidad. Third, it reestablished a subsidiary in Venezuela in 1993. KFC had closed its Venezuelan operations in 1989 because of the high fixed costs associated with running the small subsidiary. Last, it decided to expand its franchise operations beyond Central America. In 1990, a franchise was opened in Chile and in 1993, a new franchise was opened in Brazil.

EXHIBIT 9

KFC (Latin America) Restaurant Count of January 31, 1994

	Company Restaurants	Franchise Restaurants	Total Restaurants
Mexico	108	21	129
Puerto Rico	55	0	55
Virgin Islands	7	0	7
Trinidad	17	0	17
Franchises	-	87	87
Total	187	108	295

Franchising

Through 1989, KFC relied exclusively on the operation of company-owned restaurants in Mexico. While franchising was popular in the United States, it was virtually unknown in Mexico until 1990, mainly because of the absence of a law protecting patents, information, and technology transferred to the Mexican franchise. In addition, royalties were limited. As a result, most fast-food chains opted to invest in Mexico using company-owned restaurants rather than through franchising.

In January 1990, Mexico enacted a new law which provided for the protection of technology transferred into Mexico. Under the new legislation, the franchisor and franchisee are free to set their own terms. Royalties are also allowed under the new law. Royalties are currently taxed at a 15 percent rate on technology assistance and know-how and 35 percent for other royalty categories. The advent of the new franchise law has resulted in an explosion of franchises in fast-food, services, hotels, and retail outlets. In 1992, franchises had an estimated $750 million in sales in over 1,200 outlets throughout Mexico.

At the end of 1989, KFC was operating company-owned restaurants in three regions: Mexico City, Guadalajara, and Monterrey. By limiting operations to company-owned restaurants in these three regions, KFC was better able to coordinate operations and minimize costs of distribution to individual restaurants. However, the new franchise legislation gave KFC and other fast-food chains the opportunity to more easily expand their restaurant bases to other regions of Mexico, where responsibility for management could be handled by individual franchisees.

Economic and Political Environment

Many factors make Mexico a potentially profitable location for U.S. direct investment and trade. Mexico's population of 89.5 million people is approximately one-third as large as the U.S. This represents a large market for U.S. goods. Because of its geographical proximity to the U.S., transportation costs from the United States are minimal. This increases the competitiveness of U.S. goods in comparison with European and Asian goods, which must be transported at substantial cost across the Atlantic or Pacific Ocean. The pas-

EXHIBIT 10

Mexico's Major Trading Partners (% Total Exports and Imports)

	1988		1990		1992	
	% Total Exports	% Total Imports	% Total Exports	% Total Imports	% Total Exports	% Total Imports
USA	72.9%	74.9%	69.3%	68.0%	68.7%	65.2%
Japan	4.9	6.4	5.8	4.5	3.2	6.3
West Germany	1.3	3.5	1.4 (1)	4.2 (1)	N/A	5.1
France	1.8	2.0	3.5	2.3	2.0	2.7
Other	19.1	13.2	20.0	21.0	26.1	20.7
% Total	100.0%	100.0%	100.0%	100.0%	100.0%	100.0%
Value ($M)	20,658	18,903	26,773	29,799	46,196	62,129

SOURCE: Business International, 1994. (1) Data include East Germany.

sage of the North American Free Trade Agreement (NAFTA) will result in further opportunities as tariffs and non-tariff barriers are eliminated and restrictions on foreign investment are eased. The United States is, in fact, Mexico's largest trading partner. Over 65 percent of Mexico's imports come from the U.S., while 69 percent of Mexico's exports are to the U.S. market (see Exhibit 10). In addition, low wage rates make Mexico an attractive location for production. By producing in Mexico, U.S. firms may reduce labor costs and increase the cost competitiveness of their goods in world markets.

Despite the importance of the U.S. market to Mexico, Mexico still represents a small percentage of overall U.S. trade and investment. Since the early 1900s, the portion of U.S. exports to Latin America has declined. Instead, U.S. exports to Canada and Asia, where economic growth has outpaced growth in Mexico, have increased more quickly. Canada is the largest importer of U.S. goods. Japan is the largest exporter of goods to the U.S., with Canada close behind. While the value of Mexico's exports to the U.S. has increased during the last two decades, mainly because of the rise in the price of oil, Mexico still represents a small percentage of overall U.S. trade. U.S. investment in Mexico has also been small, mainly because of government restrictions on foreign investment. Instead, most U.S. foreign investment has been in Europe, Canada, and Asia.

The lack of U.S. investment in and trade with Mexico during this century is mainly the result of Mexico's long history of restricting trade and foreign direct investment in Mexico. In particular, the Institutional Revolutionary Party (PRI), which came to power in Mexico during the 1930s, has traditionally pursued protectionist economic policies in order to shield its people and economy from foreign firms and goods. Industries have been predominately government-owned or controlled and production has been pursued for the domestic market only. High tariffs and other trade barriers have restricted imports into Mexico and foreign ownership of assets in Mexico has been largely prohibited or heavily restricted.

In addition, a dictatorial and entrenched government bureaucracy, corrupt labor unions, and a long tradition of anti-Americanism among many government officials and intellectuals has reduced the motivation of U.S. firms

EXHIBIT 11

Economic Data for Mexico

	1989	1990	1991	1992
Population (Millions)	84.5	86.2	87.8	89.5
GDP (Billions of New Pesos)	507.5	686.4	865.2	1,033.2
Real GDP Growth Rate (%)	3.3	4.4	3.6	2.7
Exchange Rate (New Pesos/$)	2.641	2.945	3.071	3.115
Inflation (%)	20.0	26.7	22.7	15.5
Current Account ($ Billions)	(4.0)	(7.1)	(13.8)	(22.8)
Reserves (Excl Gold $ Bil)	6.3	9.9	17.7	18.9

SOURCE: *International Financial Statistics,* International Monetary Fund.

for investing in Mexico. As well, the 1982 nationalization of Mexico's banks led to higher real interest rates and lower investor confidence. Since then, the Mexican government has battled high inflation, high interest rates, labor unrest, and lost consumer purchasing power (see Exhibit 11). Total foreign debt, which stood at $125.9 billion at the end of 1993, remains a problem.

Investor confidence in Mexico has, however, improved since December 1988, when Carlos Salinas de Gortari was elected President of Mexico. Following his election, Salinas embarked on an ambitious restructuring of the Mexican economy. In particular, Salinas initiated policies to strengthen the free market components of the economy. Top marginal tax rates were lowered to 36 percent in 1990, down from 60 percent in 1986, and new legislation has eliminated many restrictions on foreign investment. Foreign firms are now allowed to buy up to 100 percent of the equity in many Mexico firms. Previously, foreign ownership of Mexican firms was limited to 49 percent. Many government-owned companies have been sold to private investors in order to eliminate government bureaucracy and improve efficiency. In addition, the elimination of trade barriers and interest surrounding NAFTA has resulted in increased trade with the U.S. during the past five years. U.S. exports to Mexico reached $40 billion in 1992, while imports from Mexico exceeded $42 billion.

Import Controls

Prior to 1989, Mexico levied high tariffs on most imported goods. In addition, many other goods were subjected to quotas, licensing requirements, and other non-tariff trade barriers. In 1986, Mexico joined the General Agreement on Tariffs and Trade (GATT), a world trade organization designed to eliminate barriers to trade among member nations. As a member of GATT, Mexico is obligated to apply its system of tariffs to all member nations equally. As a result of its membership in GATT, Mexico has since dropped tariff rates on a variety of imported goods. In addition, import license requirements have been dropped for all but 300 imported items. Since President Salinas took office in 1988, tariffs have fallen from 100 percent on some items to an average of 11 percent.

Privatization

The privatization of government-owned companies has come to symbolize the restructuring of Mexico's economy. On May 14, 1990, legislation was passed to privatize all government-run banks. By the end of 1992, over 800 of some 1,200 government-owned companies had been sold, including Mexicana and AeroMexico, the two largest airline companies in Mexico. At least 40 more companies were scheduled to be privatized in 1993. However, more than 350 companies remain under government ownership. These represent a significant portion of the assets owned by the state at the start of 1988. Therefore, the sale of government-owned companies, in terms of asset value, has been moderate. A large percentage of the remaining government-owned assets are controlled by government-run companies in certain strategic industries such as steel, electricity, and petroleum. These industries have long been protected by government ownership. As a result, additional privatization of government-owned enterprises until 1993 was limited. However, in 1993, President Salinas opened up the electricity sector to independent power producers and Petroleos Mexicanos (Pemex), the state-run petrochemical monopoly, initiated a program to sell off may of its non-strategic assets to private and foreign buyers. This was motivated mainly by a desire by Pemex to concentrate on its basic petrochemical businesses.

Prices, Wages, and Foreign Exchange

Between December 20, 1982 and November 11, 1991, a two-tiered exchange rate system was in force in Mexico. The system consisted of a controlled rate and a free market rate. A controlled rate was used for imports, foreign debt payments, and conversion of export proceeds. An estimated 70 percent of all foreign transactions were covered by the controlled rate. A free market rate was used for other transactions. On January 1, 1989, President Salinas instituted a policy of allowing the peso to depreciate against the dollar by one peso per day. The result was a grossly overvalued peso. This lowered the price of imports and led to an increase in imports of over 23 percent in 1989. At the same time, Mexican exports became less competitive on world markets.

Effective November 11, 1991, the controlled rate was abolished and replaced with an official free rate. In order to limit the range of fluctuations in the value of the peso, the government fixed the rate at which it would buy or sell pesos. A floor (the maximum price at which pesos may be purchased) was initially established at Ps 3056.20 and remains fixed. A ceiling (the maximum price at which the peso may be sold) was initially established at Ps 3,056.40 and and allowed to move upward by Ps 0.20 per day. This was later revised to Ps 0.40 per day. On January 1, 1993, a new currency was issued—called the new peso—with three fewer zeros. The new currency was designed to simplify transactions and to reduce the cost of printing currency.

Labor Problems

One of KFC's primary concerns is the stability of Mexico's labor markets. Labor is relatively plentiful and cheap in Mexico, though much of the work force is still relatively unskilled. While KFC benefits from lower labor costs, labor unrest, low job retention, absenteeism, and punctuality continue to be significant problems. A good part of the problem with absenteeism and punctuality is cultural. However, problems with worker retention and labor unrest are mainly the result of workers' frustration over the loss of their purchasing power due to inflation and past government controls on wage increases. *Business Latin America* estimated that purchasing power fell by 35 percent in Mexico between January 1988 and June 1990. Though absenteeism is on the decline due to job security fears, it is still high at approximately 8 to 14 percent of the labor force. Turnover also continues to be a problem. Turnover of production line personnel is currently running at 5 to 12 percent per month. Therefore, employee screening and internal training continue to be important issues for foreign firms investing in Mexico.

RISK AND OPPORTUNITIES

Managers in KFC Mexico were hopeful that the government's new economic policies would continue to keep inflation under control and promote growth in Mexico's economy. They also hoped that greater economic stability would help eliminate much of the labor unrest that has plagued Mexico during the last several years. Of greatest concern was KFC's market share in Mexico, which stood at around 10 percent in 1990. McDonald's and Arby's both signed franchise agreements in early 1990. While neither company had a significant market share in Mexico at that time, KFC feared that its market share gains could easily be lost if it were to slow its building program in Mexico. KFC planned to counter McDonald's and other competitors by expanding its franchise base in Mexico and relying less heavily on company-owned restaurants as it had in the past. By 1994, KFC had built 21 franchises in Mexico.

KFC also worried that the gains by President Salinas during the last five years, namely in stabilizing the Mexican economy, reducing restrictions on foreign investment in Mexico, and privatizing government assets, might be lost. On January 1, 1994, the day the North American Free Trade Agreement (NAFTA) went into effect, rebels (descendants of the Mayans) rebelled in the southern Mexican province of Chiapas on the Guatemalan border. After four days of fighting, Mexican troops had driven the rebels out of several towns earlier seized by the rebels. Around 150—mostly rebels—were killed. The uprising symbolized many of the fears of the poor in Mexico. While Salinas' economic programs have increased economic growth and wealth in Mexico, many of Mexico's poorest feel left out. For Mexico's farmers, lower tariffs on imported agricultural goods from the United States could drive many farmers out of business. Therefore, social unrest from Mexico's Indians, farmers, and the poor could unravel much of the success that Salinas has had economically, by creating a politically and socially unstable environment in Mexico.

Further, Salinas' hand-picked successor for president, Louis Donaldo Colosio, was assassinated on March 23, 1994 while campaigning in Tijuana. Of greatest concern to Salinas and his Institutional Revolutionary Party is the possibility that the assassin—Mario Aburto Martinez, a 23-year old mechanic and migrant worker—was affiliated with a dissident group upset with the PRI's economic reforms and the fact that the PRI has not lost a presidential election in seven decades. The possible existence of a dissident group has raised fears of further political violence in the future. The PRI quickly named Ernesto Zedillo, a 42 year old economist with little political experience or name recognition, as their new presidential candidate. Presidential elections are scheduled for August 1994. Further political violence by dissident groups, discontentment among the poor, fear among Mexico's farmers that NAFTA will destroy their businesses, and the lack of name recognition of the PRI's new presidential candidate mean that a PRI victory in the August elections is no longer a certainty. A victory by the Party of the Democratic Revolution (PRD), the main opposition party of the left, could result in the reversal of many of the free market reforms pursed by President Salinas since 1988.

KFC's alternative was to approach investment in Mexico more conservatively, until greater economic and political stability could be achieved. Instead, resources could be directed at other investment areas with less risk, such as Japan, Australia, China, and Europe. At the same time, significant opportunities existed for KFC to expand its franchise base throughout the Caribbean and South America. However, PepsiCo's commitments to these other markets were unlikely to be affected by its investment decisions in Mexico, as PepsiCo's large internal cash flows could satisfy the investment needs of KFC's other international subsidiaries, regardless of its investments in Mexico. The danger in taking a conservative approach in Mexico was the potential loss of market share in a large market where KFC enjoys enormous popularity.

PepsiCo and the Fast-Food Industry

JOSEPH WOLFE, *University of Tulsa*

As the PepsiCo Corporation entered the early 1990s Wayne Calloway, the company's Board Chairman and Chief Executive Officer, had every right to be optimistic. From 1991 to 1992 sales had increased 14.0%, earnings were up 21.0%, and per share dividends increased 20.0%. Moreover the firm's major industry segments of soft drinks, snack foods, and restaurants had obtained respective 10.0%, 17.0%, and 16.0% sales hikes. Taking a five year perspective since 1987 PepsiCo's compounded annual sales had increased 16.8% and its income from continuing operations had grown at an 18.4% rate. With these results Calloway now set a new goal for the corporation's 338,000 employees by asking the question "How does a $20.0 billion company add another $20.0 billion in just five years?"

Based on his review of the situation the CEO identified two major growth opportunities. PepsiCo's $20.0 billion growth was to come from (1) global expansion, and (2) a redefinition of the company's basic businesses. As Calloway stated,

> Not too long ago we would have described ourselves as a company in the business of soft drinks, snack chips and quick service restaurants. Today, we're in the business of beverages, snack foods and quick service food distribution. A soft drink company sells only carbonated colas and the like; a beverage company might sell things like water and tea or fruit based drinks. Also, a restaurant company is constricted to certain physical locations. A food distribution company can take its products wherever there's a customer, without necessarily making an investment in a large restaurant. We also reconsidered our geographic limitations. Up until a few years ago, we were basically a strong U.S. company with a solid but limited international presence. Not so today. In 1991, nearly one out of every four sales dollars came from our international operations. When you consider that 95.0% of the world's population is outside the U.S., you can see what that means in terms of opportunity. And this is doubly true for our kinds of products, which are in great demand everywhere on earth, with almost no economic or cultural barriers.

Although numerous opportunities appear to exist for PepsiCo many industry observers have noted overall domestic soft drink industry sales increases

Joseph Wolfe is Professor of Management at the University of Tulsa.

have been marginal and the cola segment has just about been played out. Even though the cola market amounted to $34.0 billion in 1992 its growth was only 1.5%, far lower than the 5.0% to 7.0% annual growth rates experienced in the 1980s despite changes in packaging, logotypes and advertising campaigns by both Coke and Pepsi. The market share for diet soft drinks, for years a growth segment, showed their first annual drop from 29.8% in 1991 to 29.4% in 1992, and overall consumption rose only marginally from 47.8 gallons to 48.0 gallons per capita. In the United States Coca-Cola maintained its 40.7% share of the soft-drink market while PepsiCo slipped from 31.5% to 31.3% in 1992. Additionally, the first mover advantages claimed by Pepsi in the former Warsaw-Pact nations quickly evaporated after Coca-Cola began its 18-month, $400.0 million assault in Central Europe's post-Socialist countries in "Operation Jumpstart." Health concerns have generally affected the sales of both snack foods and fast-food dining and have strong implications for PepsiCo's other two divisions. Although new product formulations have been introduced by snack chip and cracker manufacturers, and new, leaner burgers and menu assortments have been launched by all America's national chains, these innovations have met with mixed success.

In charting his company's future Wayne Calloway knows he must interpret the source of PepsiCo's growth prospects while carefully balancing the resource needs of the various divisions, businesses, and products at his disposal. Known worldwide for its soft drinks, in reality more sales, or about 36.0% of its revenues, are obtained from its restaurant operations. Although these operations increased their sales the division's costs and profit performances have been spotty. What can be done to correct this situation? Again Calloway is optimistic for at least his company's Pizza Hut and Taco Bell systems.

> A steadily growing interest in eating away from home and the continued gravitation to convenience foods are creating an atmosphere of excitement for our restaurants. Our strategy is to take advantage of these trends by accelerating our growth in existing markets and introducing our products to new markets. At Pizza Hut, we'll continue to expand delivery aggressively. We're testing alternatives to our traditional dine-in concept and we're adding innovative distribution channels. Taco Bell is also continuing its break with tradition. Alternative distribution points and the increasing use of technology to drive costs down make Taco Bell the market innovator. The situation at KFC in the U.S. is challenging. We're in the process of restructuring our business to greatly improve productivity and customer service. We're reorganizing our kitchens, upgrading our units and adding nontraditional distribution points.

PEPSICO INC.

PepsiCo is an international company currently operating in three industries—soft drinks, snack foods, and restaurants. As shown in Exhibit 1, it has followed an evolutionary path to its current status as an annual $20.0 billion revenue giant. Begun in 1893 as a soda fountain drink known in New Bern, North Carolina as "Brad's drink," the trademark Pepsi-Cola was created in 1902 when the Pepsi-Cola Company became a North Carolina corporation. Profitable operations ensued until heavy losses on sugar inventories caused its bankruptcy in 1922. A new "Pepsi-Cola Corporation" was formed the following year and all operations were moved to Richmond, Virginia. The new Virginia corporation lost money for the next five years and then was only marginally profitable until it too went bankrupt in June, 1931.

Using the assets and borrowing power of the New York-based Loft, Inc. candy company, Charles Guth subsequently purchased Pepsi-Cola's proprietary rights for $10,500. The drink was reformulated to Guth's tastes, Pepsi's syrup was sold mainly to Loft's own candy stores, but the operation continued to lose money. Mired in the depths of the Great Depression the company began to bottle its soft drink in used 12 oz. beer bottles and promoted the slogan "Two large glasses in each bottle." Through this move Pepsi offered almost twice as much for the same 5¢ price charged by Coca-Cola in its 6½ oz. container. Sales and profits rose dramatically. With this revival in profits court battles were soon waged against the firm on two fronts. The Loft Company's management, with the help of its major stockholder Phoenix Securities, sued Guth for the company's control while Coca-Cola simultaneously filed a trademark infringement suit over Pepsi's use of the word "Cola." After four years of court-appointed management Charles Guth lost all his claims. In the intervening period Coca-Cola also lost its lawsuit against Pepsi after successfully suing many other soft drink manufacturers for the same violation and having seen more than 1,100 other cola manufacturers go out of business.

For the next 20 years the company operated as a soft drink firm battling against the firmly entrenched Coca-Cola company. Another bankruptcy was narrowly averted in 1950 and various conglomerate diversifications were attempted or consummated from the late 1950s to the mid-1960s. Upon its merger with Frito-Lay in 1965 the company became PepsiCo, Incorporated and obtained its subsequent growth through concentric acquisitions, new product introductions, and product line extensions.

Today in 1993 PepsiCo's soft drink division markets Pepsi-Cola, Mountain Dew, and Slice in regular and diet versions in both the American and international market, and 7UP in non-American markets. In this division the company also operates various soft drink joint bottling and distribution ventures such as those with Ocean Spray and Lipton Tea in the United States, Canada's Avalon spring water in United States' Eastern seaboard, A&W's root beer, cream soda, Squirt and Vernors brands in Asia, and Kas brands with Knorr Elorza SA in Spain. Crystal Pepsi and Diet Crystal Pepsi, the firm's clear, uncolored "New Age" soft drink, was introduced during Super Bowl XXVII with 90 seconds of advertising at $28,000 a second and it slowly rolled out All Sport as it tried to crack America's $800.0 million-a-year sports-drink category.

The company's snack foods division makes and distributes its products throughout the world. Its major offerings are Lay's Potato Chips, Cheetos, Doritos, Crunch Tators, Tostitos, Ruffles, Rold Gold Pretzels, Fritos, and Santitas Tortilla Chips. New snack and chip products include Sunchips multigrain snacks, Suprimos wheat-based snack chips, McCracken's cracker crisps, and the Sonric sweet snack in Mexico. In a related move Frito-Lay has introduced a line of salsa and picante sauces which garnered an 11.0% share of 1992's $496.8 million market. In Spring, 1993 the division rolled out a premium brand of salsa and picante named after its popular Tostitos restaurant-style chips. Major manufacturing and processing operations can be found in the United Kingdom, Spain, Mexico, Portugal, and Brazil. Joint ventures are underway in various countries such as in Mexico with the Gamesa Company in the cookie business, with Poland's Wedel in the sweet snack segment, and the

EXHIBIT 1

Significant Company Events

1893   "Brad's Drink" concocted in Caleb B. Bradham's pharmacy in New Bern, North Carolina.

1902   Pepsi-Cola Company Incorporated in North Carolina.

1908   First bottling franchise created.

1920   Sugar prices rise dramatically from $5\frac{1}{2}$¢ to $26\frac{1}{2}$ per pound. Bradham invests heavily in sugar inventories. Prices drop to $3\frac{1}{2}$ per pound in December and the company reports a $150,000 loss on operations.

1922   Company files for bankruptcy. Bradham forced to resign and R.C. Megargel & Company forms "The Pepsi-Cola Company" as a wholly-owned Delaware Corporation. This company lapses on March 18, 1925 for nonpayment of taxes.

1923   Craven Holding Corporation of North Carolina purchases all of Pepsi-Cola's assets and trademark. Roy C. Megargel forms the "Pepsi-Cola Corporation" in Richmond, VA after purchasing Pepsi's trademark, business, and goodwill from the Craven Holding Corporation for $35,000. Operations in New Bern closed and moved to Richmond.

1928   Company is merged with the "National Pepsi-Cola Corporation" which was 90.0% owned by Megargel.

1931   Company goes bankrupt. Charles Guth uses $10,500 from the Loft, Inc. candy and candy store company to buy Pepsi's proprietary rights. A new Pepsi-Cola Company is founded in Long Island City and loses money for the next three years.

1933   Company begins to bottle its soft drinks in used 12 oz. beer bottles. Within five months over 1,000 cases a day are being sold.

1935   Loft, with support from Phoenix Securities Corporation, sues Guth for control of Pepsi-Cola. Guth loses the suit but appeals the decision. Company is managed by a court-appointed team during the appeal process.

1938   Coca-Cola files a trademark violation suit against Pepsi over its use of the word Cola. Coke loses the lawsuit.

1939   Charles Guth loses his appeal. All legal and financial control of the company reverts to Phoenix Securities which has a dominant stock interest in Loft. "Pepsi-Cola hits the spot" jingle created.

1941   Pepsi jingle played on over 469 radio stations and voted America's best-known tune in 1942.

1946   Sales level off at about $45.0 million for the next few years and earnings drop 70.0%.

1950   Pepsi nears bankruptcy. Alfred N. Steele leaves Coca-Cola to become Pepsi's President and vows to "Beat Coke." Pepsi's Cuban sugar plantation sold for $6.0 million. Over the next five years $38.0 million is invested in new plants and equipment.

1955   Steele marries film star Joan Crawford. Pepsi's advertising budget is $14.0 million or 18.0% of the industry's total. Advertising theme is "Be Sociable with Light Refreshment." Sales have risen 112.0% since 1950. Company owns 120 plants in over 50 countries.

1958   Steele attempts to merge company with Pabst Brewing Company.

1959   Steele dies of a heart attack after completing "Adorama," a $200,000 national sales promotion tour. Donald Kendall, head of Pepsi's overseas operations, photographs Nikita Khrushchev drinking six cupfuls of Pepsi at a Moscow trade fair. Drink becomes an instant hit with the Russians and the East European world.

1962   Advertising theme is "Now, it's Pepsi, for those who think young."

1963   Coke introduces diet Tab and Pepsi-Cola introduces Patio Diet Cola and later Diet Pepsi to fill low calorie segment pioneered by Royal Crown's Diet Rite Cola.

Significant Company Events (continued)

1964   Advertising theme is "Come Alive, You're in the Pepsi Generation." Company establishes the Pepsi-Cola Equipment Corp. to lease trucks and equipment to bottlers. Company later acquires and adds to this unit Lease Plan International, a trucking concern, National Trailer Convoy, North American Van Lines, Lee Way Motor Freight, and Chandler Leasing. Pepsi-Cola United Bottlers buys Rheingold Breweries for $26.0 million; PepsiCo later acquires a 51.0% interest in the United Bottlers operation. Company acquires Tip Corp., the Virginia manufacturer of Mountain Dew.

1965   Develops Devil Shake to compete with the Yoo-Hoo chocolate drink. Company attempts to buy controlling interest in Miller Brewing Co. Company purchases Wilson Sporting Goods from LTV. Pepsi-Cola Company merges with Frito-Lay of Dallas to become PepsiCo, Inc. Herman W. Lay becomes PepsiCo's largest stockholder and Chairman of its Board.

1966   Advertising theme is "Taste That Beats the Others Cold . . . Pepsi Pours It On." Company closes its up-state New York sugar refinery after losing $12.0 million on operations.

1969   Pepsi's late-year advertising theme becomes "You've Got a Lot to Live, and Pepsi's Got a Lot to Give." Soft drink sales are $940.0 million compared to Coke's $1.3 billion.

1970   Corporation moves from its Manhattan Headquarters to the suburb of Purchase, New York.

1974   Company fined $50,000 for conspiring to fix sugar cane prices in 1972 and 1973.

1977   Company acquires Pizza Hut for about $300.0 million. Coca-Cola outbids PepsiCo for Taylor Wines of New York for $96.0 million. Pepsi's management admits that its overseas executives have made $1.7 million in questionable payments to local officials; Coke's questionable payments had been $1.3 million.

1978   Company acquires Taco Bell, Inc., the nation's largest Mexican fast food chain, for $148.0 million in stock.

1982   Lee Way Motor Freight loses $12.8 million.

1984   Taco Bell unit experiments with La Petite Boulangerie, a franchised chain of bakeries. Introduces Slice to compete in the "natural fruit" drink segment. Sells Lee Way Motor Freight for a $15.0 million after tax loss.

1985   Sells North American Van Lines for an after tax gain of $139.0 million. Sells Wilson Sporting Goods for an $18.0 million after tax loss.

1986   Acquires Kentucky Fried Chicken, the world's largest chicken chain. Acquired Mug Root Beer, and 7UP for distribution in all non-U.S. markets.

1989   Acquires the United Kingdom's Smiths Crisps Limited and Walkers Crisps Holdings Limited for $1.34 billion. Acquires General Cinema's domestic bottling operations for $1.77 billion.

1991   Taco Bell acquires Hot 'n Now hamburger franchiser.

1992   Acquires Evercrisp Snack Productos de Chile SA and Mexico's Kas SA and Knorr Elorza SA. Buys out joint venture partners Hostess Frito-Lay in Canada and Gamesa Cookies in Mexico. Acquired a 50.0% interest in California Pizza Kitchen Inc. and an equity position in Carts of Colorado, Inc.

1993   Pepsi-Cola International begins to distribute Cadbury Schweppes products in Central Europe through a franchise partnership. Increased distribution of H2Oh! sparkling water and Avalon still water in the United States. PepsiCo creates a $600.0 million European snack food joint venture with General Mills after failing in its bid to purchase the company's European operations. PepsiCo's snack companies in Spain, Portugal and Greece are joined with General Mills' French, Belgium, and Dutch operations into Snack Ventures Europe.

EXHIBIT 2

PepsiCo Corporation Income Statements (000,000)

	Years Ending			
	12/26/92	12/28/91	12/29/90	12/31/89
Net Sales	$21,970.9	$19,607.9	$17,802.7	$15,242.4
Cost of Goods Sold	10,492.6	9,395.5	8,549.4	7,421.7
Gross Profit	11,477.4	10,212.4	9,253.3	7,820.7
Selling and General Administration	8,840.3	7,880.8	7,008.6	5,887.4
Pretax Operating Income	2,637.1	2,331.6	2,244.7	1,933.3
Non-Operating Income	113.7	(45.4)	111.2	26.8
Interest Expense	586.1	615.9	688.5	609.6
Pretax Income	2,164.7	1,670.3	1,667.4	1,350.5
Provision for Taxes	597.1	590.1	576.8	449.1
Less Exceptional Item and Discontinued Operations*	1,193.3	-0-	13.7	-0-
Net Income	$ 374.3	$ 1,080.2	$ 1,076.9	$ 901.4

*1990 net charges for discontinued operations; 1992 net charges for required accounting changes for retiree health benefits and income taxes.

SOURCE: Adapted from company 10-K report and *News from PepsiCo Inc.*, February 2, 1993, p. 2.

---

complete ownership of the Arnotts snacks and cracker company in Australia after initially operating as a joint venture.

PepsiCo also operates the world's largest system of restaurants through its Pizza Hut, Taco Bell, and KFC chains. Included in this division are the sales of PepsiCo Food Systems Worldwide (PFS) which supplies all company-owned and franchised units with everything from food, paper goods, equipment, and promotional materials. The division's revenues come from company-owned store sales, initial franchising fees, royalty and rental payments from franchisees, and net wholesale sales to franchisees by PFS. Although already a worldwide presence new markets for Pizza Hut have been opened in Aruba, Cyprus, and Gibraltar, for KFC in France and Chile, and Taco Bell in Aruba, Korea, and Saudi Arabia. In total Pizza Hut and KFC each operate in over 60 countries and Taco Bell is in eleven countries with 20 more countries being investigated. Within the United States Taco Bell is experimenting in Charleston, South Carolina and Fresno, California with its Hot 'n Now acquisition, an express drive through burger concept, as well as additions to the fare served in its three major restaurant systems. Exhibits 2–3 present the corporation's Income Statements and Balance Sheets for the fiscal years 1988–1992, Exhibit 4 indicates PepsiCo's degree of international sales involvement, and Exhibits 5–6 present each segment's overall performance and their assigned assets and geographic areas of concentration. Exhibit 7 indicates recent one-time and unusual expenditures associated with PepsiCo's industry segments.

EXHIBIT 3

PepsiCo Corporation Balance Sheets (000,000)

	Years Ending			
	12/26/92	12/28/91	12/29/90	12/31/89
ASSETS:				
Cash	$ 169.6	$ 186.7	$ 170.8	$ 76.2
Marketable Securities	1,888.5	1,849.3	1,644.9	1,457.7
Receivables	1,588.5	1,481.7	1,414.7	1,239.7
Inventories	768.8	661.5	585.8	546.1
Other Current Assets	426.6	386.9	265.2	231.1
Total Current Assets	4,842.3	4,566.1	4,081.4	3,550.8
Property, Plant and Equipment	7,442.0	6,594.7	5,710.9	5,130.2
Advances to Subsidiaries	1,707.0	1,681.9	1,505.9	970.8
Intangibles	6,959.0	5,932.4	5,845.2	5,474.9
Total Assets	$20,951.2	$18,775.1	$17,143.4	$15,126.7
LIABILITIES:				
Notes Payable	$ 706.8	$ 228.2	$ 1,626.5	$ 866.3
Accounts Payable	1,164.8	1,196.6	1,116.3	1,054.5
Income Taxes	387.9	492.4	443.7	313.7
Other Current Liabilities	2,064.9	1,804.9	1,584.0	1,457.3
Total Current Liabilities	4,324.4	3,722.1	4,770.5	3,691.8
Deferred Charges	1,682.3	1,070.1	942.8	856.9
Long Term Debt	7,964.8	7,806.2	5,600.1	5,777.1
Other Long Term Liabilities	1,624.0	631.3	925.8	909.8
Total Liabilities	15,595.5	13,229.7	12,239.2	11,235.6
Common Stock	14.4	14.4	14.4	14.4
Capital Surplus	667.6	476.6	365.0	323.9
Retained Earnings	5,439.7	5,470.0	4,753.0	3,978.4
Less Treasury Stock	667.0	745.9	611.4	491.8
Currency Adjustment	(99.0)	330.3	383.2	66.2
Shareholder Equity	5,355.7	5,545.4	4,904.2	3,891.1
Total Liabilities and Net Worth	$20,951.2	$18,775.1	$17,143.4	$15,126.7
Dividends Paid	$ 395.5	$ 343.2	$ 293.9	$ 241.9

SOURCE: Adapted from company 10-K report and *1992 Stockholder's Report*, pp. 32 and 46.

THE FAST-FOOD INDUSTRY

Americans eat about 750 million meals a day but over the years the proportion of food consumed in the home has declined. In the battle for "stomach share" Exhibit 8 shows by 1991 almost as much, or about $262.0 billion, was spent on restaurant fare as was spent for prepared and non-prepared grocery store food. Considering prepared food, which is a growth industry because of the two-person working family and the provision of an escape from cooking chores, Exhibit 9 demonstrates fast-food restaurants have increased their mar-

EXHIBIT 4

PepsiCo Sales and Profits by Geographic Area (000,000)

	Net Sales				Operating Profit			
Area	1992	1991	1990	1989	1992	1991	1990	1989
United States	$16,551.0	$15,167.8	$14,046.9	$12,519.4	$2,059.6	$1,842.2	$1,853.3	$1,601.9
Europe	1,349.0	1,486.0	1,057.5	771.7	52.6	61.8	108.5	53.8
Canada and Mexico	2,214.2	1,434.7	1,089.2	899.0	251.0	198.7	164.2	117.1
Other	1,855.8	1,519.4	1,321.9	1,052.3	138.6	123.8	98.4	122.9
Total	$21,970.0	$19,607.9	$17,515.5	$15,242.4	$2,501.8	$2,226.5	$2,224.4	$1,895.7

SOURCE: *1990 and 1991 Stockholder's Reports*, p. 35 and *1992 Stockholder's Report*, p. 29.

EXHIBIT 5

Domestic and International Segment Sales and Profits (000,000)

	Net Sales				Operating Profit			
Segment	1992	1991	1990	1989	1992	1991	1990	1989
Beverages								
Domestic	$ 5,485.3	$ 5,171.5	$ 5,034.5	$ 4,623.3	$ 686.3	$ 746.2	$ 673.8	$ 577.6
International	2,120.4	1,743.7	1,488.5	1,153.4	112.3	117.1	93.8	98.6
Total	7,605.6	6,915.2	6,523.0	5,776.7	798.6	863.3	767.6	676.2
Snack Foods								
Domestic	3,950.4	3,737.9	3,471.5	3,211.3	775.5	616.6	732.3	667.8
International	2,181.7	1,827.9	1,295.3	1,003.7	209.2	271.0	202.1	137.4
Total	6,132.7	5,565.8	4,766.8	4,215.0	984.7	787.6	934.4	805.2
Restaurants								
Domestic	7,115.4	6,258.4	5,504.0	4,684.8	597.8	479.4	447.2	356.5
International	1,116.9	868.5	684.8	565.9	120.7	96.2	75.2	57.8
Total	8,232.3	7,126.9	6,225.7	5,250.7	718.5	575.6	522.4	414.3
Total								
Domestic	16,551.0	15,167.8	14,046.9	12,519.4	2,059.6	1,842.2	1,853.3	1,601.9
International	5,419.0	4,440.1	3,468.6	2,723.0	442.2	384.3	371.1	293.8
Grand Total	$21,970.0	$19,607.9	$17,515.5	$15,242.4	$2,501.8	$2,226.5	$2,224.4	$1,895.7

SOURCE: *1990 and 1991 Stockholder's Reports,* p. 35 and *News from PepsiCo, Inc.,* February 2, 1993, p. 5.

ket share while the table-service or "white linen" restaurant share has declined. In 1993 restaurant spending will amount to more than $268.0 billion and meals will be served both on and off the restaurant's premises as displayed in Exhibit 10.

The 1980s was a decade of high industry growth with average sales increases amounting to 8.7% a year. Lately, however, real growth and the industry's returns on net worth have declined. See Exhibit 11 for the combined actual and estimated operating profits for a number of restaurant chains. After

EXHIBIT 6

Identifiable Assets by Division and Geographic Area (000,000)

Division and Area	1992	1991	1990	1989
Soft Drinks	$ 7,857.5	$ 6,832.6	$ 6,465.2	$ 6,198.1
Snack Foods	4,628.0	4,114.3	3,892.4	3,310.0
Restaurants	5,097.1	4,254.2	3,448.9	3,070.6
Total	$17,582.6	$15,201.1	$13,806.5	$12,578.7
United States	$11,957.0	$10,777.8	$ 9,980.7	$ 9,593.4
Europe	1,948.4	2,367.3	2,255.2	1,767.2
Canada and Mexico	2,395.2	917.3	689.5	409.5
Other	1,282.0	1,138.7	881.1	808.6
Total	$17,582.6	$15,201.1	$13,806.5	$12,578.7

SOURCE: *1990 and 1991 Stockholder's Reports*, p. 35 and *1992 Stockholder's Report*, p. 29.

EXHIBIT 7

Assorted Restaurant Division Charges (000,000)

Pizza Hut	1990—$9.0 for closing underperforming domestic units; $8.0 to consolidate domestic field operations; $2.4 to relocate headquarters
Taco Bell	1989—$5.5 to consolidate domestic field operations 1990—$4.0 for closing underperforming domestic units
KFC	1989—$8.0 reorganization 1990—$4.0 for closing underperforming domestic units $0.6 for closing underperforming international units 1991—$32.8 to restructure domestic operations $1.2 to restructure international operations $9.0 for delay of Skinfree Crispy introduction

SOURCE: *1990 and 1991 Stockholder's Reports*, p. 35.

adjusting for inflation total 1991 to 1992 industry sales increased only 1.8% and price wars have periodically broken out in response to outlet proliferation and the lingering 1991 recession. Discounting has been employed extensively to generate traffic but the major chains are now redefining the nature of a "bargain." This new definition regards "value" through the use of combination meals which guide the customer to higher markup food items while simultaneously emphasizing the food's quality and the restaurant's service and atmosphere.

While overall growth has declined various growth segments and food delivery concepts exist. From 1985 to 1990 the fast-food industry's sandwich segment rose from 4.9% of total sales to 5.7% of sales while hamburger chain sales fell from 53.4% to 50.5% of all sales. Sandwich segment sales amounted to about $5.3 billion in 1992 or .8% more than in 1991. In 1991 America's 100 largest restaurant chains added only 413 hamburger outlets but pizza makers opened 1,095 additional restaurants. By the beginning of 1992 the nation had

EXHIBIT 8

U.S. Consumer Food Expenditures

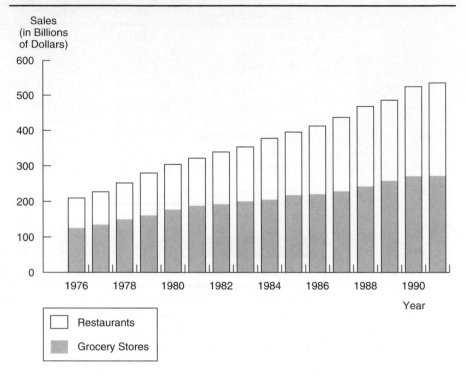

SOURCE: Derived from graph data presented in Eben Shapiro, "A Page From Fast-Food's Menu," *New York Times* (October 14, 1991), p. D1.

EXHIBIT 9

America's Sources of Prepared Food

Year	Fast-Food Restaurants	Table-Service Restaurants	Supermarkets	Other
1991	51.0%	23.0%	14.0%	12.0%
1990	46.0	27.0	14.0	13.0
1989	41.0	33.0	12.0	14.0

SOURCE: Adapted from Charles S. Clark, "Fast-Food Shake-Up," *CQ Researcher*, Vol. 1, No. 25 (November 8, 1991), p. 837.

about 18,600 pizza and 26,600 burger restaurants. Ice cream and yogurt outlets were ranked third in number but this food segment had a net loss of 142 outlets in 1991. Contributing to the pizza category's growth are a number of factors. Technomic President Ronald Paul says "Pizza's a very friendly product." He observes crusts can vary in thickness and can be crunchy or chewy, the pizza's cheese base is rich in protein, and a great variety of toppings can

EXHIBIT 10

Where America Ate Its Restaurant Food In 1991

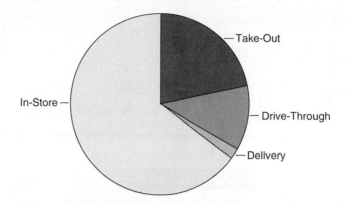

SOURCE: From data and graphs in "Forget Candlelight, Flowers—and Tips: More Restaurants Tout Takeout Service," *The Wall Street Journal*, (June 18, 1992), p. B1.

EXHIBIT 11

Restaurant Industry Income and Expenses (000,000)

	1989	1990	1991	1992*	1993*	1995–1997*
Sales	$12,048.0	$12,943.0	$13,330.0	$14,085.0	$15,315.0	$21,275.0
Cost of Sales	9,445.6	10,017.9	10,277.4	10,845.5	11,716.0	16,062.6
Gross Profit	2,602.4	2,925.1	3,052.6	3,239.6	3,599.0	5,212.4
Adm. Overhead	426.0	459.1	473.0	325.8	401.0	640.7
Depreciation	604.9	758.9	800.8	845.0	895.0	1,155.0
Pretax Profit	1,571.5	1,707.1	1,778.1	2,068.7	2,303.0	3,416.7
Less Taxes	573.6	602.6	601.2	713.7	783.0	1.161.7
Net Profit	$ 997.9	$ 1,104.5	$ 1,177.5	$ 1,355.0	$ 1,520.0	$ 2,255.0
Net Worth	$ 4,937.7	$ 5,762.3	$ 6,624.8	$ 7,640.0	$ 8,860.0	$13,075.0

*Estimated.

NOTE: Summary results for Bob Evans Farms, Carl Karcher Enterprises, Frisch's Restaurants, International Dairy Queen, JB's Restaurant, Luby's Cafeterias, McDonald's, Morrison Restaurant, National Pizza, Perkins Family Restaurant, Piccadilly Cafeterias, Ryan's Family Steak Houses, Shoney's, Sizzler International, TCBY Enterprises, Vicorp Restaurants, and Wendy's International.
SOURCE: William G. Barr, "Restaurant Industry," *Value Line* (September 25, 1992), p. 295.

be applied. Moreover, given the trend to more takeout and home delivery, pizza holds up better over further distances than either burgers or fries. Exhibit 12 displays the current high growth food segments while Exhibit 13 lists America's fastest growing fast-food chains.

Although the upscale, casual dining segment has lost market share in recent years each unit generates relatively high profits. Rather than relying on the fast-food restaurant's "table turn" for profits, white linen restaurants obtain profits by serving more highly marked up meals, generating bar and table

EXHIBIT 12

Growth Food Segments in 1991

Segment	Growth
Pizza	5.4%
Chicken	6.8
Fish	11.6
Mexican	12.6
Oriental	28.4

SOURCE: Adapted from *1991 PepsiCo, Inc. Stockholder's Report*, p. 31.

EXHIBIT 13

Fastest Growing Fast-Food Chains

Chain	Menu/Theme	1990 Sales ($000,000)
Taco Bell	Inexpensive Mexican food	2,600.0
Subway	Deli-style submarine sandwiches	1,400.0
Sonic	1950s-style drive-ins	515.0
Sbarro	Fast Italian food	277.0
Rally's	Double drive-through burgers	216.0

SOURCE: Lois Therrien, "The Upstart's Teaching McDonald's a Thing or Two," *Business Week* (October 21, 1991), p. 122.

liquor sales, and the serving of multi-course meals rather than finger food and limited combos. General Mills, Inc. has been especially successful in the casual dining, ethnic food restaurant segment. To supplement its aging Red Lobster seafood restaurant chain in 1982 General Mills simultaneously created the Olive Garden based on an Italian theme, purchased Darryl's, a North Carolina fern-bar restaurant chain, a California health-food restaurant called The Good Earth, and Casa Gallardo, a Mexican-food chain. Of the four concepts the Olive Garden appeared to have the greatest potential as market research found that Italian cuisine was America's most identifiable ethnic food. In 1985 seven more restaurants were opened and by 1992 the chain had grown to 320 stores with sales of $808.0 million. Success did not come easily, however, as management spent five years and about $28.0 million before settling on the chain's optimal recipes, flavorings, and decor. Although uniformity and consistency are the hallmarks of fast-food operations, the Olive Garden found it had to recognize regional taste differences if it was to cater to the white-collar, evening dinner crowd. It discovered through taste tests and trial menus that chunky tomato sauce did not do very well in St. Louis but patrons in California loved it and customers in Rhode Island uniquely favored veal saltimbocca.

Based on General Mills' success with its Olive Garden it is now in its third year of testing Chinese cuisine at its China Coast restaurant in Orlando, Florida. The company first tried oriental cuisine with its Minneapolis-based Leeann Chin buffet and takeout chain seven years ago after extensive testing. When this failed the company hired Terry Cheng, a Chinese-American chef and food biologist, to produce a more satisfying menu for American tastes. The result has been the creation of six main dishes revolving around moo goo gai pan, fried rice, egg rolls, and sweet-and-sour chicken but definitely not authentic Chinese dishes such as chicken feet, jellyfish, and bird's nest soup. Exhibit 14 presents an array of national chains employing various ethnic segments and upscaled dining accommodations along with their ratings from a 1992 *Consumer Reports* reader survey.

In addition to price wars and niche hunting as strategies for dealing with the fast-food industry's declining growth other methods are being tried to continue the industry's development. These strategies entail the creation of more convenient outlets, alternative food delivery methods, greater attempts to capture the after-six eating crowd, and an increasing reliance on foreign or internationally-derived sales.

Because so many people need and want to avoid spending time preparing meals in their own kitchens more meals are purchased in restaurants, more people are buying prepared and semiprepared foods in grocery stores, and more are using restaurant takeout, drive-through, and delivery service. This latter service group is called off-premises dining which grew 5.9% in 1991 while the fast-food restaurant industry's on-premises sales were flat. Prepared foods represented a $63.5 billion business in 1989 and the market research firm Find/SVP projects this market will increase to $88.7 billion by 1994 with the supermarkets' share increasing to 16.5% at the expense of fast-food restaurant sales.

Over the years certain chains have been more successful than others in obtaining off-premises sales. These sales accounted for 65.0% of Wendy's volume in 1992, a 30.0% increase since 1988, and they accounted for 70.0% of Burger King's sales. Despite the growth of this food delivery method certain dangers are involved. As George Rice, chairman of GDR Enterprises says "Off-premises sales are a great opportunity, but they can also screw up your business." He recommends owners should view it as a separate business and ask such questions as "Who's going to take orders? How's the kitchen going to integrate takeout with on-premises orders? Where are takeout customers going to stand while they wait? Will they make the restaurant look crowded?" Other sit-down restauranteurs resist doing takeouts as they have been using their ambiance as a competitive weapon against the plastic-boothed and spartan-appearing fast-food chains. Ann Durning of the Olive Garden chain observes "We make takeout available, but our feeling is that there's more to a full service restaurant than food. There is also good service, Italian music and fresh flowers on the table."

An innovation which eliminates the problems of offering both on and off-premises dining from the same location is the creation of restaurants that prepare meals exclusively for off-premises consumption. Pizza Hut has opened Fastino's, a chain that sells pasta and pizza on a takeout and drive-through basis only. Pizza Hut's Vice President of Development Pat Williamson predicts Fastino's will eventually become as big as its 8,000 unit Pizza Hut chain. A variant of this concept is the use of double drive-throughs. McDonald's is experimenting with this concept in Raleigh, NC which uses tandem drive-through windows on the side of a small food preparation and cashiering building. The store has no counter or seating, is one-third the size of a typical McDonald's 4,500 square foot outlet, and the number of employees per unit falls from 60 to about 35. To accelerate food preparation and simplify order-taking a limited

EXHIBIT 14

Selected National Restaurant Chains by Type

Family Restaurants

Big Boy	963 units. Originally known for its hamburgers but now offers a variety of meals and a soup, salad, and fruit bar. Worst rated restaurant in this category. Value and prices were average.
Denny's	1,391 units. 24-hour service, well-known for breakfast menu and grilled sandwiches. Menus for senior citizens and children. Alcohol served at many locations. Food taste and selection rated less than average for average-priced fare.
Int. House of Pancakes	500 units. Traditional breakfast stop with a wide variety of all day meals of average value and price. Menus for seniors and children. Most patrons were seated immediately.
Po Folks	137 units. Large portions of "home style cookin'." Special menus for seniors and children. Has a takeout service and catering facilities. Considered a good value with lower than average prices. Received the highest overall rating in this category of restaurants.
Village Inn	229 units. Focuses mainly on breakfast with a limited selection of lunch and dinner meals. Senior citizen discount and low fat/calorie breakfasts. Most diners were seated immediately.

Steak/Buffet Restaurants

Golden Corral	458 units. Mostly steak but limited grilled chicken and seafood. Food, salad, and dessert bar with over 100 items. Menus for seniors and children. Bar. Prices and food value judged better than average.
Mr. Steak	60 units. Steak, chicken, and seafood. Takeout service and a children's menu. Received the highest rating for this type of restaurant.
Sizzler	634 units. Features chicken, steak, and seafood with a large salad, soup, taco, and pasta bar. Senior citizen and children's menus. Entertainment lounge and wine. Takeout service. Taste, food selection, price and value rated average.

Casual Dinner Houses

Bennigan's	223 units. Menu varies throughout the U.S. but emphasizes Southwestern dishes and finger foods. Children's menu. Takeout. Bar. Received the lowest ratings for this type of

menu is used that excludes salads and breakfast entrees such as pancakes. Other companies experimenting with this concept are Taco Bell and Arby's which respectively bought the Hot 'n Now and Daddy-O's Express Drive-Thru chains in 1991.

Other trends attempting to capitalize on the desire for off-premises dining, as well as compensating for the scarcity of prime sites for full-scale restaurants in various markets, are the creation of smaller outlets and greater access to fast-food from alternative locations. One smaller outlet form is the use of kiosks and portable food carts. Basically a one-person operation Taco Bell has operated kiosks in supermarkets in Phoenix, and Taco Bell's first Mexico City outlet was a two-person food cart started in June, 1992 with two more locations planned for Mexico City and one in Tijuana. Pizza Hut, which already has 500 carts in operation, has plans to set up more than 10,000 carts in the United States and more than 100,000 in overseas locations. KFC has opened a cart-unit in a General Motors plant in January, 1992 with plans for carts in train stations, office buildings, sports stadiums, and amusement parks. Pep-

EXHIBIT 14

Selected National Restaurant Chains by Type (continued)

	restaurant. Value and prices were much worse than average although the atmosphere was rated much better than average.
Chili's	267 units. Southwest grill, Tex-Mex, burgers, and salads. Seniors and children's menus. Bar. Fare was rated above average in tastiness. Rated about average for this group.
El Torito	169 units. Clearly Mexican featuring fajitas, quesadillas, and chimichangas and daily specials. Sunday brunch. Bar. Dinner portions were considered larger than average.
Houlihan's	54 units. Steaks, burgers, and fajitas. Kids' menu. Bar and lounge. Value and prices were rated much worse than average for this group.
Olive Garden	Homemade pasta, regional Italian meat and seafood specialties. Large Italian wine list. Children's menu, takeout service and catering. The highest rated restaurant in this category with much better than average taste and better than average menu selection. Dinner portions were larger than average and the food's quality was more consistent. At least 25.0% of the raters had to wait more than 10 minutes to be seated for dinner.
Red Lobster	550 units. Seafood, chicken, and steak with catch-of-the-day specials. Children's menu, takeout service, and bar. Prices rated much higher than average although its fare was rated above average in taste and selection. 25.0% of the raters had to wait more than 10 minutes to be seated.
Ruby Tuesday	151 units. Menu varies throughout the U.S. with international appetizers and main courses. Salad bar and weekend brunch. Senior citizen discounts and children's menus. Bar. Rated below average for price and value.
Steak and Ale	158 units. Well appointed atmosphere featuring steak, seafood, pasta, and chicken. Salad bar. Bar. Food rated much tastier than average and above average in selection. Prices were much higher than average. Rated the second highest restaurant in this group.
T.G.I. Friday's	202 units. Very eclectic menu. Also has "lite" and children's menus. Takeout service and bar. Prices were much higher than average although tastiness and selection were better than average.
Tony Roma's	122 units. Barbecued ribs and chicken entrées. Takeout, bar, and children's menu. Food rated higher than average in tastiness although rated below average in value and cost.

SOURCE: Adapted from "Best Meals Best Deals," *Consumer Reports,* Vol. 57, No. 6 (June, 1992), pp. 361–362.

siCo is also negotiating with Wal-Mart to put its units in the mass merchandiser's chain throughout the United States. As an indication of the company's commitment to this concept PepsiCo purchased a strong minority interest in Carts of Colorado Inc. in February, 1992.

Others are also looking for additional stores. McDonald's is attempting to develop "niche" outlets in such places as airports and hospitals, as well as in small, rural towns by opening smaller-sized units called Golden Arch Cafes. These cafes are about half the size of a standard McDonald's, seat about 50 people, and offer counter service. Other examples of the "niche" location is the presence of Wendy's in the downtown Atlanta Day's Inn lobby and Marriott Hotels' provision of Pizza Hut room service from its own kitchens despite the fact that most of its hotels have restaurants and it once owned the Gino's and Roy Rogers restaurant chains. Hotels and motels find they can charge more for the franchised products they offer than their own because of their instant brand name recognition. As of early 1992 Pizza Hut's offerings were available in about 40 Marriott Hotels with 25 more scheduled for July, 1992.

Economy hotels, which usually do not have dining facilities or are losing money on them, are now the fast-food industry's target. Economy or budget hotels account for about 38.0% of the nation's 44,500 hotels and motels and are the lodging industry's fastest growing segment.

Another attempt to increase sales in the fast-food industry has come with its revival of its attack on attracting the dinner crowd and to profit from the rise of the "casual dining out experience." Many customers want to relax and spend more time over dinner than they do at breakfast or lunch. Norman K. Stevens, former marketing chief for Hardee's explains "People's expectations at dinner are totally different than at lunch" and that dinner is more of a leisurely event, a destination, and not something to be gotten over with as quickly as possible. As an example of this trend 1991 sales at sit-down ethnic restaurants totaled $8.0 billion, a 10.0% increase over l990's sales. It is difficult, however, to change a nation's fast-food eating habits or to change a chain's food delivery system or concept. McDonald's attempted to expand upon its successful lunch trade by offering its Egg McMuffin in 1975 to the breakfast segment. It was unsuccessful with the category until 11 years later when it introduced a variety of breakfast sandwiches. Upon the establishment of its breakfast menu the chain created a "Mac Tonight" promotion featuring a piano-playing Moonman character in 1987 to induce customers to have an evening meal at a McDonald's. The campaign was not very successful as only about 20.0% of McDonald's sales come after 4:00 pm today.

Burger King has initiated a dinner menu and table service to revive its stagnant sales and attract a different dinner customer. Although it serves about 2.0 million Whoppers a day it realized its customers were switching to other menu items late in the day. Burger King's Cory Zywotow also found their customers said "They'd like to relax and spend more time" over dinner. In certain outlets tablecloths and napkin rings are provided to heighten the ambiance. Starting at 4:00 pm each Burger King offers four main courses priced between $3.00 to $5.00—a hamburger, steak sandwich, fried shrimp, or fried chicken filet in a dinner basket with either a baked potato or french fries, and a salad or cole slaw. Customers are given a tray, beverage cups and a numbered plastic marker along with free popcorn. When their order is ready it is brought to them at their table. Management believes its sit-down dinner service was a major factor in increasing the company's operating profit over 9.0% from 1991 to 1992. While table service is an innovation for a fast-food restaurant the role of a different evening menu should not be over-estimated as about 65.0% and 73.0% of KFC's and Pizza Hut's respective sales are at the dinner hour despite the lack of both table service and special dinner items.

Because of the decline in industry sales growth and saturation in various food segments and geographic markets many chains have turned to overseas operations. Looking at the franchising field in general a survey of 366 franchisers conducted by Arthur Andersen & Co. in 1992 found that only about one-third of them have foreign outlets but nearly half of those without foreign operations intend to grow internationally in the next five years. Gary L. Copp, President of Spee-Dee Oil Change Systems, Inc. speaks for many when he reasons, "Why take on Chicago when I can go to Brazil and find a virgin market?"

In the fast-food industry international sales have become very important and very profitable. McDonald's first-quarter 1992 international sales rose 14.0% to $1.9 billion or 39.0% of its total revenue and 42.0% of its total operating profits. Steven A. Rockwell of Alex. Brown & Sons estimates the company's overseas profits will surpass domestic profits by 1995 due to both the number of units operated and the high unit volumes they produce. In early 1992 McDonald's added 50 restaurants to its system of which most were in foreign countries and as many as 450 new overseas units were planned for the year. By April, 1992 McDonald's had 8,772 American and 3,696 foreign restaurants. In that month it also opened its biggest store—700 seat facility in Beijing.

Other chains have also profited from foreign operations. KFC posted a 26.0% third-quarter world-wide profit increase while its same-store U.S. sales declined 1.0%. Its first East European store was opened in Budapest, Hungary, in partnership with the Hungarian franchisee Hemingway Holding AG, in October, 1992 after working nearly two years to develop local suppliers. Pizza Hut opened two restaurants in Moscow in September 1990 with one selling pizzas for hard currency and the other selling them for rubles. About 20,000 customers are served a week, about the amount sold by 10 American-based Pizza Huts.

As profitable as foreign operations are for the fast-food franchisers, numerous problems accompany the application of their global strategies and standardized operating systems in foreign cultures. McDonald's American success has come from its routinized manufacturing and operating skills. Its operations manual is 600 pages long and the company demands mass production techniques and absolute uniformity. A crew person must get a manager's approval before replacing a malted drink order or a spilled soft drink. Dressing a hamburger is always done in the same order—mustard first, then ketchup, then onions, and then two pickles. The result is a Big Mac that looks and tastes the same in Tokyo as in Tacoma. In coming to Hungary, however, McDonald's found the country's native potatoes were dark and did not fry "golden brown" and the requisite iceberg lettuce was not home-grown. To replicate the chain's eye appeal and taste standard entire B-747 airplane loads of potatoes and shredded lettuce were initially flown to Budapest when it opened its first restaurant on the corners of V. Aranykéz and Régiposta streets.

While the fast-food industry's participants have employed numerous strategies to accommodate its lower growth, two long-term concerns have continued to haunt the industry. One concern deals fast-food's nutritional value and this concern has accelerated with America's greater awareness of the health and diet issues associated with its aging population. The other concern deals with franchisee/franchisor relations. Although these relations have often been contentious, many franchisees have been hit hard by franchiser actions taken to maintain sales growth at the unit level. Accordingly, in the early 1990s they have developed a new militancy which often frustrates the designs of the national chains.

To many consumers fast-food has always meant "bad food." PepsiCo has attempted to avoid this stereotype of fast not being good by calling their chains "quick service" restaurants. Others, such as McDonald's, emphasize the enjoyment of eating fast, tasty meals with friends, family, and co-workers. America's health concerns are real, however, and the national chains have begun to introduce low-fat and low-calories items to their standard fare as well as emphasizing the nutritional value of fast-food dining. In early 1990 McDonald's introduced its McLean Deluxe, a 91.0% fat-free hamburger containing carrageenan, a seaweed-based additive, to wide acclaim. Unfortunately its sales were not sizzling. Two years later, as part of a nutritional, public information effort, the company aired a dozen animated 55-second televised spot announcements called "What's on Your Plate." These announcements attempted to explain the basics of well-balanced eating and how it could be accomplished. In each restaurant McDonald's posts nutritional information on all its fare and leaflets about its food are available for the asking. Burger King displays posters with the calorie, fat, cholesterol, and sodium content of all its food. The company is also test marketing, in 350 of its stores, menus exclusively based on Weight Watchers foods as well as experimenting with foods under 300 calories including chicken on angel-hair pasta and chocolate mocha pie. About 60.0% of Taco Bell's company-owned outlets offer complete nutritional product information while Wendy's has taken the position of matching its competition regarding the amount of information it supplies.

Many critics, however, are dissatisfied with the industry's efforts at providing a healthy diet. Michael Jacobson, Executive Director of the Center for Science in the Public Interest, feels the fast-food industry could do more. "The charts and posters don't convey much to the average person. The information is presented as a matrix with 10 or 15 numbers for every food. Most people aren't going to lose their places in line to read about nutritional values."

Both nutritionists and industry participants emphasize the role of self-choice in making food purchases mixed with a bit of cynicism regarding America's eating intentions versus its actions. Sandwich shops have capitalized on the desire for greater nutrition. Many customers believe deli meats sandwiched between two slices of fresh bread is healthier than a quarter-pound burger on a bun. Subway's "fattiest" sandwich is a six-inch meatball sub. "[I]t's not particularly healthy," observes Bonnie Liebman, Director of Nutrition at the Center for Science in the Public Interest, "but it has only half as much fat as a McDonald's Big Mac." As another example of the role of self-choice, Michael Evans of Burger King notes that by eating a Whopper without mayonnaise the customer saves 140 calories. With mayonnaise, which is the way most people have it served, it has 619 calories. Accordingly many chain operators are frustrated regarding the health issue. Maurice Bridges, Hardee's Director of Public Affairs says, "After spending millions on research, we found, just by listening to the consumer, that people are talking nutrition, but they buy on taste." And industry observer Rajan Chaudhry of *Restaurants and Institutions* magazine believes, "People talk healthy but what they're really looking for is something to let them off the hook and let them believe they're eating healthier than they were otherwise."

Exhibit 15 displays the results of eating typical fast-food restaurant fare for an entire day. The average adult needs between 1,200 and 3,000 daily calories for weight maintenance. Approximately 50.0%–60.0% of those calories should come from carbohydrates, 15.0%–20.0% from protein, and 25.0%–30.0% should come from fat. It is also recommended that healthy adults limit their sodium intake to 3,000 milligrams per day and cholesterol to 300 daily milligrams.

Since the early 1960s McDonald's has exemplified the virtues of franchising as a form for rapid business development. Frandata Corp. of Washington, DC, estimates there are more than 3,000 franchisers in the United States operating about 540,000 franchised outlets. And according to the International Franchise Association a new outlet of some type opens about every 16 minutes. Accordingly franchised business sales have risen dramatically and rose 6.1% in 1991 to $757.8 billion or more than 35.0% of all retail sales. Although some franchisees experience long hours, hard work, and often little profits, franchising makes business sense in many cases. In four of five industries sur-

EXHIBIT 15

A Day of Fast-Food Dining

Meal	Nutrition				
	Carbo-hydrates	Protein	Fat	Choles-terol	Cal-ories
Breakfast at McDonald's					
Orange Juice	19	1	0	0	80
McMuffin Sausage/Egg	28	23	27	263	440
Hashbrown Potatoes	15	1	7	9	130
Total	62	25	34	272	650
Lunch at Pizza Hut					
3 Slices Medium size					
Pepperoni Pizza	75	42	36	75	750
1 Regular Pepsi	40	0	0	0	159
Total	115	42	36	75	909
Supper at KFC					
3 Drumsticks	12	39	27	201	438
Cole Slaw	13	2	7	5	119
2 Buttermilk Biscuits	56	10	24	2	470
1 Regular Pepsi	40	0	0	0	159
Total	121	51	58	208	1,186
Grand Total	298	118	128	555	2,745

NOTE: Carbohydrates, Protein, Fat, and Cholesterol listed in grams.

SOURCE: *Eating Out Made Simple*. Tulsa, OK: St. Francis Hospital, 1991, pp. 16–17, 22, 25–26.

veyed by Francorp, an Olympia Fields, Illinois consulting firm, a franchisee's 1991 per store sales grew faster or declined less than their industry's national average. Restaurants, which constitute the franchising industry's largest single group, found their 1991 per-store sales increased 6.2% versus an overall restaurant industry growth rate of 3.0%.

Despite these generally favorable results many restaurant franchisees have become increasingly dissatisfied with their franchisers. When Britain's Grand Metropolitan PLC purchased Burger King from the Pillsbury Co. in 1989 it ordered changes in floor tile designs, background music, and cutbacks in field management help. It also created an advertising campaign that many franchisees felt was unsuccessful. Burger King's management group now faces a very disgruntled, 1,300 National Franchisee Association Inc., which it met in 1991 for the first time in seven years. The association's grievances were so great it even explored buying Burger King from Grand Met.

Other militant franchisee associations have entered the fray. Almost all of Taco Bell's franchisees joined an independent group in January, 1992 to oppose PepsiCo's aggressive price-cutting strategy and to challenge a contract clause which allows PepsiCo to open company-owned stores within a franchisee's market. In protest against the advertised prices PepsiCo sets for their company-owned stores about 30.0% of the franchised units priced their products higher than the nationally promoted prices in September 1992. Taco Bell officials said in March 1992, however, it would maintain the .59 cent, low-price strategy that many believed started the industry's price war in late-1988. Although the chain rang up 50.0% sales increases to $2.4 billion in two years, its profit growth dropped rapidly. Earnings increases of 108.0% and 19.0% for 1991's first two quarters sank to 2.0% and 5.0% in the following two quarters. As a result of Taco Bell's discounting, McDonald's engaged in retaliatory price-cutting in 1991 and in Joseph S. Capser's experience, a Tampa, Florida licensee with 29 McDonald's restaurants, price-cutting increased his customer count 15.0% but overall sales increased only 4.0% to 5.0% and profits fell 10.0% to 15.0%.

Accordingly, many franchisees feel they are bearing the brunt of the price wars being conducted at their chain's headquarters level. The Taco Bell franchisees want higher priced items featured in its advertisements but Tim Ryan, the system's Senior Vice President of Marketing, says "Our customers' focus on price is unchanged. Value continues to be the primary driver." Accordingly he is testing a Value Menu that is priced 10 cents lower. Actions by Taco Bell's Hot 'n Now management group have engendered a similar response by some of its franchisees. All Hot 'n Now units have been encouraged to feature 39¢ prices for hamburgers, french fries and soft drinks that have upset many of the chain's independent franchisees. Because they say they cannot make a profit with these prices and the company's advertisements are confusing, 15 franchisees formed an independent association to stand up to PepsiCo in October, 1992.

PEPSICO'S QUICK SERVICE RESTAURANT DIVISION

Under Wayne Calloway's leadership PepsiCo's success has been attributed to "Love change. Learn to dance. And leave J. Edgar Hoover behind." By this he means change is inevitable so it is better to initiate change rather than reacting to a situation. "The worst rule of management is 'If it ain't broke, don't fix it.' In today's economy, if it ain't broke, you might as well break it yourself, because it soon will be." By "learning to dance" the CEO wants PepsiCo to deal with customers in new ways and "leaving J. Edgar Hoover behind" means practicing a "hands off" management style the former FBI chief would have detested. This loose style has allowed each chain a wide degree of latitude although Calloway is not against moving people around when necessary and setting high financial goals for each operation. He brought John Cranor over from Frito-Lay in 1991 to fix the Kentucky Fried Chicken operation and sent Pepsi's Worldwide Beverages chief Roger Enrico to head the snack division after he suffered a mild heart attack in Turkey. To accomplish this latter move he created a new unit for Michael Jordan after Enrico replaced him and within the past eight years three senior soft drink sales and marketing vice presidents have left the company after falling off their career ladders.

Although much of the public's attention has been focussed on the cola wars, Calloway has set his mind on a different priority which is to double his company's quick service business within the decade. "For us the restaurant business is the most compelling action around. We're not going to prosper if we just wait for busy people to come to our restaurants. We want to move toward the day when pizzas, chicken, and tacos are as convenient and readily available as a bag of Doritos is now." To help accomplish his goals the following top executives have been assembled and they are dealing with the operating results found in Exhibits 16–19:

EXHIBIT 16

Same-Store Sales Growth by Chain

Chain	1992	1991	1990	1989
Pizza Hut	0.0%	0.5%	5.5%	9.2%
Taco Bell	6.0	4.1	11.5	15.3
KFC	0.0	0.0	7.0	2.0

SOURCE: Derived from E. S. Ely, "Some High Hurdles Loom for Pepsico's Fast-Food Hotshots," *New York Times* (February 16, 1992), Section 3, p. 5 and *News from PepsiCo, Inc.*, February 2, 1993, pp. 7–9.

EXIIIBIT 17

Restaurant Division's 1992 U.S. Market Shares by Food Category

PepsiCo Chain	Food Category	Market Share	Total Market (In billions)
KFC	Chicken	48.6%	$ 7.4
Pizza Hut	Italian	26.2%	$16.4
Taco Bell	Mexican	69.6%	$ 4.6

SOURCE: Based on data presented in *1992 Stockholder's Report*, p. 23.

EXHIBIT 18

1992 Unit Ownership by Area and Chain

Area	Pizza Hut	Taco Bell	KFC
United States:			
Company-owned	4,301	2,498	1,994
Licensed	402	134	21
Franchised	2,905	1,446	3,074
Total	7,264	3,616	5,056
Overseas:			
Company-owned	539	51	726
Joint Venture	370	- 0 -	474
Franchised	937	24	2,440
Total	1,846	75	3,640
Grand Total	9,454	4,153	8,729

NOTE: Unit totals include 477 primarily Pizza Hut kiosks and 293 other special concept units. Taco Bell U.S. unit count includes 99 company-owned and 38 franchised Hot 'n Now restaurants. U.S. count does not include 29 California Pizza Kitchen, Inc. units.
SOURCE: Abstracted from *1992 Stockholder's Report*, p. 24.

EXHIBIT 19

Results by Restaurant Chain (000,000)

Chain	Net Sales				Operating Profit			
	1992	1991	1990	1989	1992	1991	1990	1989
Pizza Hut	$3,603.5	$3,258.3	$2,949.9	$2,453.5	$335.4	$314.5	$245.9	$205.5
Taco Bell	2,460.0	2,038.1	1,745.5	1,465.9	214.3	180.6	149.6	109.4
KFC	2,168.8	1.830.5	1.530.3	1,331.3	168.8	80.5	126.9	99.4
Total	$8,232.3	$7,126.9	$6,225.7	$5,250.7	$718.5	$575.6	$522.4	$414.3

SOURCE: Data found in *1990 and 1991 Stockholder's Reports*, p. 35 and *News from PepsiCo, Inc.*, February 2, 1993, p. 6.

Kentucky Fried Chicken Corporation
Louisville, Kentucky
John M. Cranor III, President and Chief Executive Officer, 46,
15 years PepsiCo service

Taco Bell Worldwide
Irvine, California
John E. Martin, President and Chief Executive Officer, 47,
9 years PepsiCo service

Pizza Hut Worldwide
Wichita, Kansas
Steven S. Reinemund, President and Chief Executive Officer, 44,
8 years PepsiCo service

Kentucky Fried Chicken Corporation   As shown in Exhibit 16 this chain's same-store sales have not risen for the past two years and it has met with a number of failures as it has attempted to diversify its offerings away from fried chicken-on-the-bone. A number of factors, however, should help John Cranor in his attempts to turn this operation around. Michael Mueller, restaurant analyst with Montgomery Securities observes, "Regular hamburger customers, for health and variety, are switching to chicken." Within the restaurant industry itself chicken entree and sandwich sales climbed to 12.4% of all transactions in 1990 from 10.9% in 1987 while hamburgers fell from 19.0% to 17.0% during the same period. Moreover the chain's nearest rivals, Church's and Popeye's, recently merged and were ultimately forced into bankruptcy.

KFC dominates America's chicken segment with at least a 50.0% market share, as shown in Exhibit 17, but many fast-food chains have entered the marketplace with their own chicken-based meals. Wendy's has introduced a grilled chicken sandwich and Burger King has come out with its BK Broiler. McDonald's began offering chicken fajitas in mid-year 1991 and it has been testing both grilled sandwiches and oven-baked chicken-on-the-bone. Closer to home additional competition is coming from within the PepsiCo family itself. Taco Bell introduced four chicken products in April, 1991 and Pizza Hut began testing marinated, rotisserie-cooked chicken in mid 1992. Two of Taco Bell's items were 79¢ chicken tacos and 99¢ chicken-and-cheese filled tortillas called MexiMelts. Elliot Bloom of Taco Bell insisted his chicken products would not steal business from KFC. "You're talking about apples and oranges. What we're offering fills a void, a different niche."

Many see KFC's reliance on fried chicken products as its main menu problem. Although chicken itself is lean and potentially healthy, the batters and frying processes employed usually offset those advantages. The chain has renamed itself KFC to eliminate the "fried" from its logotype and a new skinless, but still fried, product called Lite 'N Crispy was introduced in Spring, 1991. It suffered a number of embarrassing marketplace setbacks as it was too expensive, tasteless, and the division's franchisees protested its low margins. Initially announced as a phased national introduction it had to be renamed Skinfree Crispy and withdrawn until 1992 due to its production and taste problems. The delay ultimately resulted in charges of $9.0 million against domestic operations in 1991. For some industry observers Lite 'N Crispy's flop is indicative of the entire KFC operation. "There doesn't seem to be a strategic direction. There is a disjointedness, and the skin-free chicken is a microcosm of that" states Emanuel Goldman of Paine Webber Inc. Moreover Lite 'N Crispy's failure is particularly significant as John Cranor intended it to be the bridge from flavored chicken, such as lemon, barbecue, and teriyaki, to other non-fried fare.

This experience has also caused the division to back off from other new product introductions although it introduced Popcorn Chicken in July, 1992. Popcorn Chicken consists of small pieces of marinated, breaded and fried chicken. The Center for Science in the Public Interest, however, in its *Nutrition Action Healthletter* described it as "nuggets of grease-drenched breading that are oozing with fat and salt." A standard 5.3 ounce serving contains 45 grams of fat, almost twice as much as in two Big Macs, and 1,775 mg of sodium. Other new products have been stalled in KFC's test kitchens and a line of eight new sandwiches failed while in test market. The sandwiches, including barbecue, spicy, and chicken salad designed for the lunch trade, increased sales only when heavily promoted. Moreover, they cannibalized KFC's higher-margin chicken-on-the-bone sales.

William McDonald, KFC's senior marketing vice president, says reformulating the chicken is not easy. "It's not a no-brainer. We've learned a product has got to be unbelievably indulgent, special and unique and not eminently substitutable at home." The chain has been trying hard to come up with a non-fried chicken—first trying to bake it, then trying open-hearth grilling. When those two methods were unsatisfactory KFC tried char-grilling and then broiling the product. It has recently scrapped Monterey Broil, its most recent effort, and is starting over again to make it stand out from home-prepared chicken by spicing up its flavor. Doctoring this product's recipe could take another one and a half years to complete.

The chain has also been working on its image in addition to making menu changes. By early 1992 85.0% of its U.S. stores had invested an average of $7,500 for new landscaping, new atriums, a coat of fresh red roof paint, and brighter wallpaper. John McDonald says, "KFC has a '60s image and it's the '90s. We've got to turbo-charge." Beginning in Spring, 1992, KFC's advertising became focused on the make-believe town of Lake Edna and its single KFC restaurant. The campaign's purpose was to capture the positive, feel-good aspects associated with good food and the traditional values and security found in small towns. Colin Moore, KFC's senior marketing vice president said in defense of the campaign's strategy, "Clearly we were looking for a 'campaign-able' idea. And we think we've found it. Lake Edna is obviously a fictitious place that is simultaneously nowhere and everywhere. This notion of a small town is as much a state of mind as a physical location." KFC spent almost $120.0 million on advertising in 1991. In that same year McDonald's spent $387.3 million, $118.4 and $92.7 million was respectively paid by Pizza Hut and Taco Bell.

Various economy and efficiency actions have also been undertaken and John Cranor has recruited a number of Pizza Hut executives to teach him the fast-food business. As a first step KFC has begun to use more frozen products in its cooking to reduce in-house chicken preparation labor costs. At the chain's administrative level $43.0 million was spent in 1991 on a restructuring which could save the division up to $25.0 million a year. The move eliminated about 750 or one-half the company's managers and support staff at both the 800-employee Louisville, Kentucky headquarters and its 700-employee field management offices. After the restructuring the remaining middle managers supervised more stores, and headquarters became more involved in field operations. Although KFC admitted the restructuring was necessary and the division had become bloated, Ron Paul, president of Technomic Inc. observes "All this does is improve their margins in the short run. It does not fundamentally change the menu and the way consumers view the store."

In attempting to turn the KFC operation around John Cranor has been faced by another source of problems. Its franchisees, who own about two-thirds of KFC's American outlets, are an independent minded group with many of their outlets in middle- or low-income neighborhoods where customers are less concerned about nutrition and are partial to fried food. Besides many are loyal to Col. Sanders' original Kentucky Fried Chicken concept, which is why they initially purchased their franchises and are antagonistic towards some of the new products headquarters has created for them. Their antagonism has been expressed many ways and they have had PepsiCo in court for three years over various contract disputes. PepsiCo has begun to buy out some of its franchisees as at least a partial method for dealing with these frustrations.

When asked how KFC's turnaround has progressed under his leadership Cranor responded, "I didn't expect turning KFC around was going to be an easy proposition. We're all impatient with everything. We need direction, we need a unified focus. We just want to make sure we don't screw up a $6.0 billion business while we decide how to get from there to $10.0 billion." Gary Stibel, of the New England Consulting Group, agrees the division's president has the right idea. For KFC "the marketing challenge is a matter of attracting new users without losing their current loyal following."

Pizza Hut Worldwide   Steven S. Reinemund, division president and former Marriott Corporation executive, believes he heads a pizza distribution company. Accordingly Pizza Hut has been very creative in finding alternative methods for obtaining off- and on-premises pizza sales. It began delivering pizza in 1987 and has built the most units dedicated to delivery and carryout. Says George Rice, chairman of a food-service consulting firm, "Since 1984 the entire growth in restaurant sales has been in takeout, delivery, and other consumption outside the stores. That makes Pizza Hut one of the industry's best-positioned companies." Although Pizza Hut has captured about 25.0% of the pizza delivery market it is well behind Domino's and just even with Little Caesars in the number of stores devoted to takeout and delivery service. Moreover, Little Caesars is adding domestic units of this type to its chain at a faster rate than is Pizza Hut.

In 1992 a strategic shift was implemented by Steven Reinemund in reaction to a long-term trend in operating results. By the third quarter of 1991 Pizza Hut's delivery sale increases were not compensating for the declining sit-down sales it was experiencing. Therefore it began to refocus on its in-store business. Part of this effort has been the installation of all-you-can-eat buffets.

The buffets were tested for four months at Pizza Huts in Dallas, Indianapolis, Savannah, and Tulsa, and were later installed in 2,000 restaurants in 1992 at a cost of tens of millions of dollars. "We're into it hot and heavy" said Reinemund. "It is phase one of our effort to revitalize our dine-in business." For $3.99, patrons can load their plates at a 14-foot table spread with pastas, salads, and pizza. Although its buffets were initially open only for lunch it is possible that dinner buffets will be added. Certain risks, however, are involved with buffet service. As observed by Michael Mueller, a restaurant analyst with Montgomery Securities, "It's not an easy business to operate well. The risk is the quality of the food you offer." To maintain product quality Pizza Hut designed a screen that sits inside a pan and allows air to circulate around the pizza. By this method pizzas can stay hot and fresh at the buffet table for as long as 20 minutes.

Steven Reinemund is also exploring the upscale pizza market with a concept called Pizza Hut Cafes. The chain believes a market exists for this concept although the field is already crowded with others offering pastas, desserts, and gourmet pizzas in casual dining atmospheres. Its cafe, which has been tested in Wichita, Kansas, featured table cloths, desserts, sauteed chicken, and a wider variety of pizzas than found in regular Pizza Huts.

Taco Bell Worldwide   Under John Martin's leadership Taco Bell has become the fast-food industry's value leader. In late-1988 the chain introduced its 59¢ Value Menu. Sales rose 50.0% in two years to $2.4 billion causing McDonald's and Burger King to retaliate in late-1990 but to their disadvantage as their operations are not as efficient as Taco Bell's. Continuing the trend of offering everyday bargains, in Fall, 1990 Martin reorganized most of his menu into three price tiers—59¢, 79¢ and 99¢. Although he ultimately had to back off the rigid enforcement of these tiers due to franchisee pressures for margins, he believes offering value menus is his chain's key to success and he feels Taco Bell alone can be as big as the entire PepsiCo corporation is today. In responding to questions about his low price strategy Martin responds, "Radical thought, huh? Low prices are what got our business started. The other guy has gotten away from it."

To be a low-cost producer Taco Bell began to shift as much food preparation to outside suppliers as possible and to rationalize its production methods in the mid-1980s. Its ground beef is pre-cooked outside the store and then reheated, its tortillas are already fried, pre-cooked dishes are placed in boil bags, and all its onions are pre-diced in a factory. The result of these actions has been the slicing of 15 daily man-hours from every outlet and the reduction of kitchen space from 70% to 30% of a typical building. "Our entire Taco Bell restaurant can fit into a McDonald's kitchen," says Elliot Bloom.

Other operating efficiencies have come from greater automation and simplified food production. This has enabled Taco Bell to permanently slash prices on its 69¢ 29-item core menu. Martin has refigured the menu to emphasize plain tacos and burritos which take only eight seconds to make versus the 20 seconds needed to make a Mexican pizza or a taco salad. Through various efficiencies a new Taco Bell restaurant can handle twice the volume of five years ago with half the labor and it is currently testing taco-making robots in its quest for lower operating costs.

While being the industry's low-price leader various industry analysts question Taco Bell's strategy. They point out that low pricing hurts profit margins, cannibalizes the sales of full meals, can leave customers unfilled, and creates an image of low quality. Hugh Zurkuhlen of Weiss, Peck & Greer says the chain is ". . . a potential victim of their own success" and would have a difficult time abandoning that image when facing the ultimate pressures of rising ingredient and labor costs.

1993 AND BEYOND

As 1993 begins Wayne Calloway's overall goal for PepsiCo ". . . is simply to be the best consumer products company in the world." He went on to explain, "In 1992 we took dramatic steps to keep us on a strong growth path. Our domestic beverage division is being completely restructured to serve our customers better. And our aggressive acquisition activity, over 50 in all, is doing a lot to expand and strengthen our core businesses. We're entering 1993 with solid momentum and well positioned to address changing consumer needs. Low cost Mexican food is still a novelty to most Americans, there are more ways to sell pizza, and new products and value combinations at KFC will bring customers back more often." Jay Nelson, an analyst with Brown Brothers Harriman, observes that "PepsiCo doesn't participate in rapid-growth industries with favorable demographic trends. But managers there think it's their destiny to win." The question is what must PepsiCo do to continue its phenomenal growth in sales and profits? What contributions can PepsiCo's restaurant operations make as the corporation attempts to double its sales in the next five years?

APPENDIX A   Annual Per Capita Consumption of Various Consumer Goods and Wealth for Selected Countries

Country	Soft Drinks[a]	Income[b]	TVs[c]	Newspapers[d]	Literacy[e]
United States	770	$19,678	769	255	99.0%
Mexico	512	2,222	123	142	88.0
Australia	403	14,994	500	308	99.0
Germany[f]	255	19,637	385	417	99.0
Japan	75	21,845	244	569	99.0
CIS	46	3,606	313	345	99.0
India	3	339	16	16	36.0

[a] 1991 Per capita 8 oz. servings per year

[b] 1988 GDP per capita in U.S. dollars

[c] Television sets per 1,000

[d] Newspaper circulation per 1,000

[e] Percent literacy rate

[f] Former Federal Republic of Germany

SOURCES: Adapted from data in *1992 PepsiCo Stockholder's Report*, pp. 9, 15; *The World Almanac and Book of Facts, 1991*, NY: Pharos Books, pp. 687, 712, 718, 723, 733, 760, 765; "Indicators of Market Size for 117 Countries," *Business International* (July 30, 1990), pp. 248, 250.

APPENDIX B   Current and Estimated PepsiCo Sales and Operating Results From Continuing Operations

	1988	1989	1990	1991	1992*	1993*	1995–1997*
Sales	$13,007.0	$15,242.0	$17,803.0	$19,608.0	$22,200.0	$24,500.0	$32,500.0
Cost of Sales	11,016.9	12,681.3	14,847.7	16,274.6	18,426.0	20,212.5	26,650.0
Operating Profit	1,990.1	2,560.7	2,955.3	3,333.4	3,774.0	4,287.5	5,850.0
General Overhead	598.6	902.3	1,021.3	1,098.7	1,234.0	1,357.5	1,775.0
Depreciation	629.3	772.0	884.0	1,034.5	1,100.0	1,250.0	1,600.0
Pretax Profit	762.2	886.4	1,050.0	1,200.2	1,440.0	1,680.0	2,475.0
Income Taxes	251.5	295.2	346.5	417.7	504.0	588.0	866.3
Posttax Profit	$ 510.7	$ 591.2	$ 703.5	$ 782.5	$ 936.0	$ 1,092.0	$ 1,608.8

*Estimate

SOURCE: Stephen Sanborn, "PepsiCo, Inc.," *Value Line*, November 20, 1992, p. 1539.

Post Machinery Company, Inc.

MICHAEL J. MERENDA *and* WILLIAM NAUMES, *University of New Hampshire,*
with the assistance of PETER GOWELL

As the snow lashed against his office window, Bob Hopkins, President and owner of Post Machinery was beside himself. He had just been given the latest financials from Marcel Binette, Post's controller. Bob did not like what he saw.

> "I am in the middle of some really exciting things here at Post. Paxall wants to re-negotiate its note; the new computerized, folder-gluer is almost ready for introduction; and I have an opportunity to enter into an exclusive marketing arrangement with a full-line Italian manufacturer of converting equipment. How can I do any of these things with stagnant sales and inflated inventory!"

Bob noted his concerns with sales:

> "It is February and with five months to go we are already significantly behind our 1986 sales goal of $11,000,000. Now Marcel wants to revise the goal to $10.5 million. I will never reach $20 million by 1989! Furthermore, the auditors and Marcel are now telling me we could incur an unfavorable manufacturing adjustment of $400,000 to cost of goods sold for last fiscal year. I know we had to go outside for inventory when the machinists went on strike, but look at the financials. Inventory levels are out of sight!"

Post was founded in Beverly, Massachusetts in 1921 as a specialty tools manufacturer. In the late 1940s, after near bankruptcy, Post began manufacturing folding and gluing machinery for the box making industry. The company's machines (known as folder-gluers) were designed to convert paperboard into corrugated and folding carton boxes. Box companies were Post's major customers and were known in the industry as converters because they converted paperboard into boxes used in shipping or retail packaging.

In 1975 Post moved from Beverly, MA to Portsmouth, NH. In 1979, Post introduced a line of specialty folder-gluer machinery for the corrugated box business. Specialty referred to the type and range of boxes that could be folded and glued on a converting machine. The vast majority of the box companies

By Michael J. Merenda and William Naumes of the University of New Hampshire, with the assistance of Peter Gowell.

An earlier version of the case was presented at the North American Case Research Association Annual Conference and was the recipient of the Curtis E. Tate, Jr. Award. The case is based on actual events and individuals and is meant to stimulate discussion and critical thinking pertaining to the study of business. The case is not intended to demonstrate either effective or ineffective handling of management practices or issues.

produced "RSCs"—regular slotted cartons—which were nothing more than an ordinary brown shipping or packing box. Corrugated boxes were usually made on machines designed to produce standard boxes with long production runs. A specialty machine could be changed over to make several different "custom" boxes. Because the corrugated box manufacturer could respond to custom orders with shorter production runs with a specialty machine, higher prices could be charged. A custom box could have designed into it one or more unique features either in its graphics, shape, or function. With Post's specialty machines, the corrugated box companies had an opportunity to compete with the higher value, higher margin boxes of the folding carton companies.

Post was acquired in the early seventies by the Paxall Group, Inc., a publicly held Chicago based holding company. Paxall viewed the Post acquisition as a means to expand and diversify their competitive position in the packaging industry. When Paxall encountered severe cash flow problems in the early eighties, their creditors forced them to restructure their balance sheet. In 1983, Paxall earnings per share was a negative $4.12. While Post was unprofitable at the time, it had strong, positive net worth, and the management group believed that without Paxall's overhead and control, Post could become profitable. Paxall's cash starved management decided to sell Post to a management and investment group, led by Hopkins. Hopkins received his MBA from the University of Chicago. After working several years with an industrial valve company, followed by working as an acquisition manager for a major oil company, he joined Paxall Group as its treasurer in 1982.

POST: AN OVERVIEW

Management

Post Machinery Company had just over 100 people employed in Portsmouth. The company's top management included the president, manufacturing manager, engineering manager, marketing manager, controller, and more recently the manager of material control and purchasing. Each top manager received a base salary and participated in a newly created bonus program. The bonus was based on the achievement of the manager's agreed upon objectives and a share of company profits. An equal share of ten percent of all profits over $100,000 was placed in a bonus pool and distributed among the top six managers. Hopkins stated, "I know I'm taking quite a risk by establishing the incentive program, but I believe we're all in this together. The incentive program will help us motivate performance and it will keep us on the right track."

Post manufacturing, marketing, administrative and support operations (e.g., engineering, customer service) were housed in a 42,500 square foot building. The building was constructed in 1975 and was financed by industrial revenue bonds. Post research and development activities, along with the assembly operations and administrative support for carpet systems, were housed in a leased building at the same location.

Post had sold over 1,000 machines since the late 1940s. Along with machine sales, Post conducted a significant parts, accessories, and field service business. In addition to box equipment, Post sold carpet handling machinery under its carpet system product line. In 1985 Carpet Systems represented less than 3% of total sales and was not profitable. (See latest financials, Exhibits One and Two.) Post's organization chart is contained in Exhibit Three.

EXHIBIT 1

Post Machinery Company, Inc. Balance Sheet (in thousands of dollars)

	Jan. 31, 1986	June 30, 1985
Assets		
Cash	4,001	3,383
Accounts Receivable	805,430	1,580,059
Notes Receivable	16,856	32,356
Other Receivables	102,958	34,795
Inventory	4,375,250	2,710,278
Prepaid Assets	193,310	34,359
Other Current Assets	—	35,828
Total Current Assets	5,497,805	4,431,058
Long-Term		
Notes Receivable L.T.	304,434	297,144
Fixed Assets—Net	1,482.764	1,598,502
Organizational Costs	231,220	268,845
Total Other Assets	2,018,418	2,164,491
Total Assets	7,516,223	6,595,549
Liabilities		
Accounts Payable	1,072,920	306,743
Current Portion L.T.D.	77,936	77,936
Customer Deposits	403,252	188,685
Accrued Expenses	292,163	551,135
Current Portion of Capital Lease Obligation	—	29,172
Total Current Liabilities	1,846,271	1,153,671
Capital Leases	100,094	86,430
Industrial Revenue Bonds	1,063,193	2,714,532
Bank Revolver[1]	2,836,473	1,176,695
Total Senior Long Term Debt	3,999,760	3,977,657
Paxall Sec'd Subord. Note	1,250,000	1,250,000
PMCI Unsec'd Subord. Debenture	65,769	—
Promissory Note—Fergnani	9,566	—
Total Subordinated Debt	1,325,335	1,250,000
Deferred Taxes	1,350	1,350
Stockholder's Equity		
Capital Stock	2,500	2,500
Current Year's Income	130,637	210,371
Retained Earnings	210,370	—
Total Stockholder's Equity	343,507	212,871
Total Liabilities/Stockholders Equity	7,516,223	6,595,549

[1]The company has a $3,000,000 line of credit through a bank at 1 3/4%–2 1/2% above the prime rate with interest payable monthly, secured by inventories and receivables. As of June 30, 1985, $2,714,532 had been borrowed against this line of credit.

EXHIBIT 2

Post Machinery Company*** Income Statements(in thousands of dollars)

	30 Jun-85 Actual*	1985/86 Budgeted	31 Jan-86 7 Month
Net Sales	9,396	11,000	5,217
Cost Goods Sold	6,433	6,850	3,315
G.M. Standard	2,963	4,150	1,902
Warranty Manuf. Variance			
S.G.& A. Expenses			
Administrative		1,198	739
Selling & Commis.		1,720	727
Research & Development	★★	★★	★★
Totals S.G.& A. Exp.	2,137	2,918	1,466
Operating Income	826	1,232	436
Other Exp. (-Inc.)	–76	40	–18
Incentive Compens.	—	—	—
Interest Expense	500	540	323
Total Other Exp.	424	580	305
Inc. Before Taxes	402	652	131
Income Tax	192		
Net Income	210		

Notes

  *Includes two months as a division of Paxall—July 1, 1984 to June 30, 1985.

  **Amount included in administrative expense.

  ***Post was purchased by Robert Hopkins and investment group on September 6, 1984.

Company Goals

Hopkins stated in early 1986 his goals for the company: "The short-term goals are profitability and cash flow at levels adequate to service debt, and to maintain a strong position in the specialty corrugated machinery market. The longer term goals are to strengthen its position in the industry by offering a full product line of converting equipment, and to find a counter cyclical product."

Hopkins' concern for profitability was evident: "Right now the water's deep," the economy is strong and capital equipment expenditures are at an all time high, but can we survive when the water is shallow? The river bed can be awfully rocky."

Sales

Dick MacLeod, Post's Marketing Manager, estimated that the company held over 60% market share of the specialty corrugated folder-gluer machine market. MacLeod estimated that Post sold 97 of the 161 specialty corrugated folder gluers operating in box companies. MacLeod expected that as Post's

EXHIBIT 3 Organization Chart of Post Machinery Company

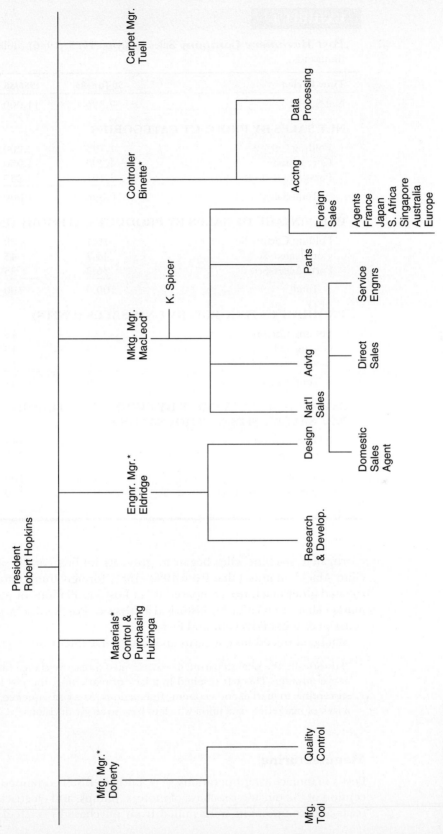

*Participates in Bonus Plan

EXHIBIT 4

Post Machinery Company Sales Analysis (1985–1986) (dollars in thousands).

Time Period	30 Jun-85	1985/86	31 Jan-86
Net Sales	9,396	11,000	5,217
NET SALES BY PRODUCT CATEGORIES			
Folding Carton	1,795	2,200	783
Corrugated	4,200	4,950	2,504
Parts/Accessories	3,401	3,850	1,930
Total Sales	9,396	11,000	5,217
PERCENTAGE OF SALES BY PRODUCT CATEGORY (IN %)			
Folding Carton %	19.1	20	15
Corrugated %	44.7	45	48
Parts/Accessories	36.2	35	37
Total	100.0	100	100
PRODUCT CATEGORIES BY UNIT SALES (UNITS)			
Folding Carton	14	15	5
Corrugated	14	15	7
Accessories	10	11	6
Total Units	38	41	18
AVERAGE SELLING PRICE BY PRODUCT CATEGORY NET SALES/UNITS (IN THOUSANDS $)			
Folding Carton	128	147	157
Corrugated	300	330	358
Total Employees	98	100	102
Sales per Employee (in thousands $)	96	110	51

corrugated machine sales began to grow, its folding carton sales would decline. MacLeod noted that from 1982–1985, foreign competitors sold 27 corrugated gluer machines compared to 47 Post installations or a slip from 85% market share to 63.5%. An historical analysis of Post's sales by product line is contained in Exhibits Four and Five.

MacLeod voiced his concerns about his department:

"Historically, the sales department has assumed a reactive stance rather than a proactive position. This has resulted in a lack of marketing, thereby leaving us more susceptible to market and economy fluctuations. As a consequence, there has been a lack of marketing data upon which to base strategic decisions."

Manufacturing

Post's manufacturing operations were fairly well self-contained. With the exception of the outside purchase of motors, pumps, and electrical products, all parts and components were milled from purchased raw steel. A significant

EXHIBIT 5

Post Machinery Company Division of the Paxall Group, Inc.
Sales Analysis (1980–1984) (dollars in thousands)

	31 Oct-80	31 Oct-81	31 Oct-82	31 Oct-83	31 Oct-84
Net Sales	8,515	8,775	7,773	7,725	9,228
NET SALES BY PRODUCT CATEGORIES					
Folding Carton	2,359	2,483	2,379	2,194	2,233
Corrugated	4,019	3,563	2,930	2,619	3,710
Parts/Accessories	2,137	2,729	2,464	2,912	3,285
Total Sales	8,515	8,775	7,773	7,725	9,228
PERCENTAGE OF SALES BY PRODUCT CATEGORY (IN PERCENTAGE)					
Folding Carton	27.7	28.3	30.6	28.4	24.2
Corrugated	47.2	40.6	37.7	33.9	40.2
Parts/Accessories	25.1	31.1	31.7	37.7	35.6
Total %	100.0	100.0	100.0	100.0	100.0
PRODUCT CATEGORIES BY UNIT SALES (UNITS)					
Folding Carton	18	23	21	15	16
Corrugated	24	14	11	11	12
Accessories	3	3	4	10	10
Total Units	45	40	36	36	38
AVERAGE SELLING PRICE BY PRODUCT CATEGORY (IN THOUSANDS)					
Folding Carton	131	108	113	146	140
Corrugated	167	254	266	238	309
Employees	108	106	105	97	101
Sales per Employee (in thousands)	79	83	74	80	91

portion of machine parts and inventory were processed on several numerically controlled machines. All support and assembly were handled in-house by 59 production (direct labor) employees, all represented by the International Association of Machinists (IAM). The current contract had recently been negotiated after a strike with the IAM and was not due to expire until June, 1988. Management did not anticipate further labor problems despite the recent strike.

Post's manufacturing capacity was determined by the "mix" of machines being produced. In 1980, Post produced 45 units (Exhibit Five). According to J. Huizinga, material control and purchasing manager, those 45 units strained plant capacity— "some of the machines were being shipped 80% complete."

Post's in-house manufacturing capacity had expanded since 1983 through increased use of vendors. According to Huizinga, "manufacturing is extremely flexible in that many of the parts and components now milled in-house could be purchased from local vendors if justified economically and approved by the union." Obtaining union approval was one of the main factors behind the recent strike and still was a cause of concern for the union, according to Huizinga.

THE CONVERTING INDUSTRY[1]

The box industry involved the fabrication and manufacture of boxes (cartons) and other containers from paperboard. Paperboard, the basic raw material of the boxboard container industry, was a fibrous material made from pulp. Pulp was produced from the cellulose fibers in wood, rags or other vegetable materials— such as straw. These materials were broken down into pulp by mechanical or chemical means.[2] The conversion of paperboard into containers required several steps, including but not limited to: (1) paperboard preparation, (2) die cutting, (3) printing or laminating, (4) folding, and (5) gluing (see Appendix A). Generally, converters or box makers could be classified by: type of containers (shipping or retailing containers); material (folding carton or corrugated); and size (large vertically integrated to small privately held companies).

Corrugated Containers[3]

Corrugated paperboard, or containerboard, was one of the most versatile and inexpensive packaging materials. Consisting of a fluted sheet glued to one or more liners, corrugated board could be made into exceptionally strong and rigid constructions for use as relatively lightweight heavy-duty shipping containers.

Most corrugated board today was used for shipping containers, which were often designed to convert to point-of-purchase displays at retail outlets. Recent advances in folder-gluer equipment technology, such as the introduction of Post's specialty corrugated folder-gluer in 1979, had accelerated the trend toward a single corrugated box used in shipping and retail packaging. This trend had positioned the corrugated box as a direct threat to the folding carton box, the mainstay of retail packaging.

The low cost, lightness and durability of corrugated containers made them ideally suited for use in nationwide and worldwide distribution systems. Corrugated shipping containers could withstand the rigors of freight, express and parcel post shipment better than other paperboard containers and protect products ranging from delicate glassware to heavy machinery. Corrugated paperboard also was the most compatible packaging material available for the newly introduced automated equipment. Corrugated boxes could be rigid (set-up box) or collapsed (flat) for shipment to their users.

There were two types of corrugated container manufacturing facilities. A corrugator plant operated one or more corrugated combining machines to produce containerboard sheets. The sheets were then cut, scored, creased, folded, glued and/or stitched to form various types of containers.

A sheet plant produced corrugated containers from the containerboard sheet it purchased from the corrugator plant. The sheet plant did not operate a corrugating machine. Owners of sheet plants bought sheets from several corrugating plants, allowing them to run orders that required different containerboard weights as well as fast customer service. Sheet plants were potentially large customers of specialty converting equipment. Most of the larger boxmakers owned paperboard mills that supplied at least half the needs of their own box plants. See Exhibit Six (A) for a listing of the ten largest corrugated producers by type of plants.

Folding Cartons[4]

Folding cartons were paper boxes made of paperboard that were precisely printed, cut, creased and glued. Folding cartons were shipped flat or were

EXHIBIT 6 (A)

Top 10 Corrugated Producers by Number of Plants in the United States—1983

Total Plants	Corrugated Plants	Sheet Plants
Champion International	25	1843
Stone Container Corporation	28	432
Weyerhaeuser Company	31	031
Container Corporation of America	28	028
International Paper Company	28	533
Packaging Corporation of America	21	324
Inland Container Corporation	26	228
Union Camp Corporation	23	225
Owens-Illinois Forest Products Div.	21	223
Georgia-Pacific Corporation	28	331

SOURCE: Fibre Box Association. Contained in "Market Profile: 1984–1985," *Container Magazine*, December 1984.

collapsed for shipment to their users. The user set up, filled and sealed the cartons.

Folding cartons have had strong competition from such materials as corrugated containerboard, flexible wraps and plastic containers in recent years. Still, folding cartons had several distinct advantages. They could be manufactured and filled at high speeds; save transportation and storage costs because they remain flat until used; be beautifully printed to create attractive displays and quick brand identification. Brand identification was particularly important in supermarket merchandising where more than three-fourths of all folding cartons and their contents were sold to the consumer. The largest folding carton producers by number of plants are listed in Exhibit Six (B).

EXHIBIT 6 (B)

Largest Folding Carton Producers According to Number of Plants—1983

Company	No. of plants
Rock-Tenn Co.	16
Container Corporation of America	14
James River Corporation	9
Federal Paper Board Company	9
Simkins Industries, Inc.	8
Champion Packaging	7
Jefferson Smurfit	7
Packaging Corporation of America	6
International Paper Company	6

SOURCE: Fibre Box Association. Contained in "Market Profile: 1984–1985," *Container Magazine*, December 1984.

DEMAND FOR CONTAINERBOARD

Approximately 6% of the value of all manufactured goods went toward packaging. Of the total packaging cost, 20% went to the shipping containers (usually corrugated cartons) and 80% to the retail containers (usually folding carton boxes). For example, $.01 and $.05 of a product valued at $1.00 was spent on shipping and retail containers, respectively. The *U.S. Census of Manufacturers* identified five standard industrial classifications (SICs) for paperboard containers: corrugated and fibre boxes (SIC 2653), folding cartons (SIC 2651), sanitary food containers (SIC 2654), fibre cans, tubes, drums (SIC 2655), and setup boxes (SIC 2652). In 1985, total value of shipments for corrugated and solid fiber containers (SIC 2653) was $14.7 billion.[5] The 1985 value of shipments for folding cartons (SIC 2651) was $4.5 billion.[6] Corrugated and folding cartons represented approximately 75% of the total dollar value of shipments for all containerboard in 1985.[7] The historical value of shipments for corrugated and folding cartons is found in Exhibit Seven.[8]

Demand for Corrugated Containers

The demand for corrugated and folding carton containers was based on the overall strength of the economy, especially the economic health of several basic industries, such as: textile, automobile parts, housing materials, food and electronics. Analysts were predicting that the 1986 economic climate should be relatively strong compared to the flat growth in 1985 and the long-term industry prospects for corrugated containers appeared reasonably bright:

> The corrugating industry's 1986–1990 outlook is for a 2.5% compounded annual rate of growth. Industry progress will be marked by continuing development of multi-ply box technology, increased use of flexography in color printing, further improvements in graphic design, greater use of pre-printed linerboard in box construction, further computerization and automation of plant operations.[9]

While the box converting equipment industry was characterized as a mature, cyclical industry, with long equipment life (some converting equipment had been in operation for over 35 years) it was expected that expenditures for converting equipment should grow because of recent trends in the containerboard industry:

> The present course in the industry is in the direction of increasing automation and computerization, higher-speed machinery, improved marketing techniques, reducing energy costs, better product quality, and effective competition versus _ other packaging mediums, especially plastics.[10]

EXHIBIT 7

Historical Performance Sales Value of Boxboard Containers (in billions of dollars)

	1982	1983	1984	1985
Corrugated and Fiber Boxes	10.5	11.4	13.0	14.7
Folding Paperboard Boxes	3.9	3.9	4.4	4.5

SOURCE: 1986 *U.S. Industrial Outlook*, U.S. Department of Commerce, January 1986.

Demand for Folding Carton Containers

Contrary to the *U.S. Industrial Outlook* modest 1985 increase, *Boxboard Container* reported the dollar value of shipments of folding cartons declined by about 1% in 1985. The decline was attributed to a drop in sales of packaged nondurables, the major end-use market for folding cartons:

> . . . major end users of folding cartons such as beverages, dry foods, textiles, sporting goods and toys, hardware, candy, and cosmetics showed significant year-to-year declines in real growth, while the market for paper goods either grew slightly or remained fairly level. . . . Industry growth has also been retarded by slow growth in the packaged food and beverage sector.[11]

The long-term outlook for folding carton shipments was a modest 1.2% compound annual rate of real growth for 1986–1990:

> This outlook is based on continuing, albeit slow, growth in the consumer nondurables sector, a gradual rise in consumer disposable income and spending, continued moderation in the inflation rate, and constraints on the rising costs of energy, raw materials and labor.

> The trend toward greater consumption of single-portion meals is expected to continue, as an outgrowth of changing demographic patterns in which single-person home occupancy has been on the rise. As a result, the industry will direct more of its efforts toward the packaging market for fast food and convenience-type foods.[12]

Folder Gluer Equipment Estimates

The demand for converting equipment was based on the demand for corrugated and folding carton containers. The folder-gluer equipment industry was divided into manufacturers of folding carton and corrugated machinery. Obtaining sales estimates for folder-gluer machinery was complicated by the fact that there were no converting equipment industry trade associations or publications reporting the number of machines installed or sold annually. Exhibit Eight lists total U.S. sheet, corrugator and folding carton plants in operation from 1980 through 1985. In 1985 there were 1,434 corrugator and sheet plants and 446 folding carton plants. The number of corrugator and sheet plants had slightly increased over the last three years while the number of folding carton plants had slightly decreased. Post's marketing people estimated that there was

---

EXHIBIT 8

Post Machinery Company U.S. Paperboard Plants 1981–1985

	1981	1982	1983	1984	1985
Sheet Plants	748	764	756	814	818
Corrugator Plants	631	623	614	615	616
Sub Total	1,379	1,387	1,370	1,429	1,434
Folding Carton Plants	479	485	459	450	446
Total Plants	1,858	1,872	1,829	1,879	1,880

SOURCE: "Forecast '86," *Boxboard Container Magazine*, December 1985. "Market Profile: 1984–1985," *Boxboard Container Magazine*, December 1983.

at least one folder-gluer in each corrugator and sheet plant and four folder-gluers in each folding carton plant. If correct, then there would be 3,236 folder-gluers in operation in 1985. Post's management estimated that approximately 5% of folder-gluers in corrugator and sheet plants were specialty machines

COMPETITION

Competitors were basically the same in both the corrugated and folding carton specialty machine market. Major competitors were Bobst, Jagenberg, Gandossi and Fossati and Vega (four European firms) and Tanabi from Japan. The only domestic manufacturer, in addition to Post, was International Paper Box Machine Company. IPBM competed exclusively in the folding carton folder-gluer machine market. The following is a brief overview of Post's major competitors according to Post's Marketing Manager, Dick MacLeod.

Bobst

Bobst was headquartered in Switzerland and had a worldwide reputation for outstanding quality and after-sales service. It was a full line converting equipment manufacturer, offering a whole range of machines, including: cutting and creasing presses, printing equipment, diecutters, and folder-gluers. Bobst's high quality was reflected in the high price of its machines. Its folder-gluers were the most complex and were the highest priced machines in the market. Its full line of products allowed them to quote prices on complete converting systems consisting of several machines. Bobst offered its customers large discounts for multi-machine purchases. By 1985, Bobst had yet to make a significant impact in the U.S. specialty folder-gluer market though it dominated the U.S. market in large, printing machinery. Bobst utilized an extensive advertising campaign aimed at promoting the Bobst brand name rather than concentrating on any one of its extensive array of products. The company had secured a high level of brand recognition in the United States.

Jagenberg

A German based subsidiary of Rhine-Metal, Jagenberg was now undertaking a strong marketing effort to break into the U.S., after considerable worldwide success. Jagenberg's major advantages were its technical expertise, financial resources, and ability to offer a full line of converting equipment, similar to Bobst. Post's marketing people believed Jagenberg's lack of a U.S. machine base and its customers' perception that their machines were complicated to operate and expensive were considerable disadvantages to them. Jagenberg's medium visibility advertising campaign aimed at promotion of its full line of "Diana," specialty folder-gluers, was expected to change with a major advertising campaign being planned. Jagenberg maintains an assembly and warehouse facility in Connecticut.

Gandossi & Fossati

Prior to filing for bankruptcy in the summer of 1985, this Italian firm had given Post its strongest competition in the U.S. specialty folder-gluer market. Aided by a strong U.S. dollar, G&F had been able to successfully penetrate the U.S. market and was beginning to establish a strong installed machine base. With the help of an aggressive sales agent located on the East Coast, G&F was rapidly becoming a formidable competitor in the specialty corrugated machine market. Internally, Post had questioned G&F's ability to remain price competitive in the United States, considering the import tax and shipping costs from Italy. However, in the past three years Post had lost several machine sales to Gandossi & Fossati. G&F's advertising campaign focused on promoting its CS 1800 model specialty folder-gluers, diecutters and flexo folder-gluers.

Vega

To date this Italian company was the least significant competitor in the U.S. corrugated folder-gluer market. Vega competed strictly on price as their equipment lacked the technical sophistication to be competitive, and as such, their U.S. success had been negligible. Lacking technical expertise, Vega's attempt to copy existing technology had not been successful. Unlike its competitors, Vega had not utilized any media advertising campaigns in the United States.

Tanabi

A Japanese firm, Tanabi had made considerable progress in the corrugated folder-gluer market. Recently, the company had completed the development of a computerized, folder-gluer capable of handling a wide range of corrugated cartons. Through reverse engineering, Tanabi had taken many of the technical innovations introduced by Post and incorporated them into their machines. Tanabi's new computerized folder-gluer had been successfully marketed on the West Coast, and also successfully competed with Post machines in Southeast Asia and Australia. Tanabi's equipment contained all the capabilities offered in Post's corrugated machinery, but was considered far more sophisticated because of its extensive use of computerization. Its folder-gluers were considered to be the most technologically advanced machines in the market and competitively priced. Tanabi had its first U.S. installations on the West Coast in early 1985. It had recently begun an extensive West Coast advertising campaign, concentrating on its computerized folder-gluer.

International Paper Box Machine Company

A U.S. firm located in Nashua, N.H., International competed solely in the specialty folding carton equipment market. It was the oldest company in the folder-gluer machine business. IPBM had recently begun to lose market share through increased competition, and a lack of product upgrades, and a management in transition. IPBM though still enjoyed a significant parts and service business. IPBM employed a highly visible and recognizable advertising campaign featuring a bright yellow advertisement promoting its wide range of specialty folding carton folder-gluers. IPBM was a family controlled company. There had been recent rumors that IPBM might be up for sale.

POST'S STRATEGIC POSITIONING

Post's Acquisition by Hopkins

Paxall, after experiencing severe cash flow problems, assigned Hopkins the task of selling Post. Hopkins was promised the General Manager's position of Paxall, Ltd., a foreign division headquartered in London, after he handled

EXHIBIT 9

Post Machinery Company Division of the Paxall Group, Inc.
Income Statements (in thousands of dollars)

	31 Oct-80	31 Oct-81	31 Oct-82	31 Oct-83	31 Oct-84 ***
Net Sales	8,515	8,775	7,773	7,725	9,228
Cost Goods Sold	6,127	6,158	5,466	5,430	6,054
G.M. Standard	2,388	2,617	2,307	2,295	3,174
Warranty	124	89	116	173	142
Manuf. Variance	101	341	752	436	326
G.M. Actual	2,163	2,187	1,439	1,686	2,706
S.G & A. EXPENSES					
Administrative	1,104	715	729	653	655
Selling & Commis.	*	497	557	648	908
Amortiz/Intangibles				35	32
Research & Development	*	40	57	84	99
Total S.G.& A. Exp.	1,104	1,252	1,343	1,420	1,704
Operating Income	1,059	935	96	266	1,002
Other Exp. (-Inc.)	−57	−75	−5	133	
Incentive Compens.	79	20	18		
Paxall Ser. Chg. **		176	155	154	184
Interest Expense					93
Total Other Exp.	22	121	168	287	277
Inc. Before Taxes	1,037	814	−72	−21	725
Income Tax	316	66			250
Net Income	721	748	−72	−21	475

NOTES

*Amount included in administrative expense.

**Paxall service charge calculated at 2% of sales.

***Post was purchased by Robert Hopkins and investment group on September 6, 1984.

Post's divestiture. It quickly became quite evident to him that the Post assignment was going to take more time than originally planned. In his first months in Portsmouth, Hopkins fired Post's General Manager, familiarized himself with the overall operations, and began to find buyers for the company. At the same time, the economy improved, and Post's sales began to pick up. The more Bob became involved, the more he liked what he saw (see Exhibit Nine). He became convinced that beyond some rather easily identifiable problems, there existed a great deal of opportunity at Post.

By December 1983, Bob began to entertain the idea that he might personally be able to arrange a leveraged buyout of Post. In February, 1984, Bob hired a consultant to prepare a business plan to be distributed to potential investors who might be interested in acquiring Post. This plan would also provide him some objectivity in his beliefs about Post's future prospects. While the plan identified several critical issues facing the company it also revealed that:

... Post was able to operate at near breakeven (relative to bottom line) in 1982 and 1983, even with the following adverse circumstances: (1) abnormally high manufacturer's variance of $752,000 and $436,000 (in 1982 and 1983) respectively,* (2) depressed demand for capital goods, (3) poor in-house production scheduling, planning and control, and (4) losses of $150,000 attributed to carpet systems, a product line assigned to Post by Paxall.

Furthermore, the consultant concluded:

... as management improves production efficiencies, Post should be able to sustain profitability even during depressed economic times.

Through the Spring of 1984, negotiations with various bankers and investment brokers gave Bob a package he thought worthy of consideration by Paxall top management. On September 4, 1984, after lengthy delays in negotiations, Post was acquired by Robert Hopkins. The buyout was highly leveraged with all but $100,000 of the final $4,700,000 selling price being financed through debt. Bob invested $50,000 and retained 80% of the common shares of the new company. The remaining shares were held by the investment banking firm (see Exhibit Ten).

Reflecting on his feelings about acquiring Post, Bob noted that:

I realize there is a difficult transition to make in shifting from a treasury function to general manager function, but by stressing open communication channels with employees, I can make the transition. When I came to Post the left hand didn't know what the right hand was doing. I consider myself an opportunist. I've had opportunities before and passed them up for whatever reason and have regretted it. I didn't want to let this one get away.

SALES AND MARKETING

Post's worldwide sales organization was composed of a marketing manager, three direct salesmen, field service, a parts and accessories salesman, in-house customer service, and several manufacturer's sales agents.

Post's marketing stressed product durability and productivity. The specialty corrugated folder-gluer was targeted to value added box making companies. Value added was based on custom orders of boxes that could be produced at high speed with improved customer service. It was not uncommon for specialty, corrugated boxes to be folded and glued at rates exceeding 20,000 per hour. Post's machines were designed to allow fast set-up times to meet customer orders quickly. All boxes were collapsed or flat when they came off Post machines.

In the folding carton box market the majority of Post's recent sales had been for replacement of older less productive equipment. Commenting on Post's marketing efforts, Norman Beaulieu, recently retired Post salesman, stated:

Post is manufacturing a folding carton gluer that in terms of appearance is the same piece of equipment that has been marketed over the last thirty years. Our ability to survive as a manufacturer of folding carton equipment has come as a result of a good reputation, durable produce and very competent sales force.

---

*The company defined manufacturer's variance as a charge to Cost of Goods Sold resulting from the auditor's valuation of inventory versus the company's periodic valuation of inventory. An unfavorable manufacturer's variance means that Cost of Goods Sold Expense account is understated by the amount of the manufacturer's variance and the Asset Inventory account is overstated by a like amount. A variance can occur from inadequate or poor inventory and financial controls.

EXHIBIT 10

Post Leveraged Buyout Financing

Post Asking Price from Paxall:	$4,700,000
Total Financing Needed:	$4,700,000

NOTES

(1) Notes payable to Paxall	$1,250,000
(2) Industrial Revenue Bonds	1,183,745
(3) Note payable—private party	57,399
(4) Line of credit—IHB	2,158,856
Robert Hopkins—Equity Contribution	50,000
Total Debt and Equity	$4,700,000

(1) Prime + 2% note payable to Paxall in quarterly installment, principal payable annually in installments of $208,333 commencing on February 29, 1988, secured by all assets of the company.   **$1,250,000**

(2) 8% bond payable to a bank in quarterly installments of $19,281, including principal and interest, through January, 1993, secured by real estate.   **$583,944**

   6.175% bond payable to a bank in quarterly installments of $19,951, including principal and interest, through September, 1995, secured by real estate.   **$ 599,801**

(3) 25% note payable to an investment banker, payable in single installment on September 3, 1994, with interest compounded annually from September 4, 1984 (date of note origination), unsecured. The investment bank provided this note at time of closing when Hopkins was unable to meet his original $100,000 equity contribution. The investment banking firm also received a position on Post's Board of Directors, as a condition of the note.   **$57,399**

(4) The company has a $3,000,000 line of credit through a bank at 1 3/4%–2 1/2% above the prime rate with interest payable monthly, beginning December 31, 1984, secured by inventories and receivables.[a]

[a]Prime rate: September 1984 was 12 percent.

The ability (of Post's salesmen) to make a good machine presentation that reflects well on the company exists at Post, where it does not exist at IPBMC. The foreign competitors in the folding carton industry are also not represented well by their sales staffs and agents in the U.S. Finally, the high productivity and fast set-up times are also considered key reasons why converters (box companies) buy Post machinery.

Beaulieu felt that in the corrugated industry, Post was able to corner the lion's share of the market for the specialty folder-gluer because they were the first company to introduce the machine. Beaulieu noted, "Our pricing structure was based on the higher margins our machines offered the specialty converters" (a Post 90 or 115 machine sells for well over $300,000).* Dick MacLeod noted: "The value added business has proven very lucrative for those in it and as a result other

*The 90″ and 115″ defines the width of the machine and the size of a box that can be folded and glued. The larger the machine the greater range of boxes it can handle, from very small to large.

converters want to capture a piece of that market. Post was, and still is, in a position to exploit their corrugated line of folder-gluers." MacLeod continued:

> The corrugated machines, much like the folding carton equipment, are extremely durable and were designed with the operator in mind. The specialty box market is characterized by very short runs of cartons. The average lot size ranges between 5,000 cartons and 10,000 cartons. As a result, machine set-up becomes a critical issue. Post was able to take advantage of their technical knowledge gained in the folding carton equipment industry and design it into the corrugated line. The set-up time on Post corrugated equipment is quite low when compared to the competition. In addition to the durability and productivity strengths, the corrugated equipment also thrives as a result of Post's overall reputation in the industry. Our ability to be innovative and offer a strong service capability is recognized within the industry.

Foreign Sales Representatives and Exports: Post used two sales agents (one based in Australia and one based in England) to cover worldwide markets. Export sales to date had been disappointing, occurring in a very sporadic and often haphazard manner.

The agents, in responding to a Post survey asking them their reasons why they were unable to secure greater international sales for Post, responded:

  i. the strength of the U.S. dollar over the last two years.
 ii. Post's noncompetitive price abroad when freight, tariffs and agents' commissions are taken into consideration. (Tariff for European market was 4.4%)
iii. the lack of sufficient sales aids supplied by Post: for example, foreign language brochures, machine videos and visits by Post sales personnel.

MacLeod felt that a full examination of Post's overseas sales needed to be undertaken. He noted that "WIFAC, Post's European agent, is tied to a three-year revolving sales agreement and they have failed to secure an order for more than a year."

Marketing Reorganization

Marketing, Bob Hopkins felt, had been one of his biggest disappointments. The group simply had not reached its full potential. The sales personnel had continued to experience an inability to meet company sales goals. Bob realized that total industry sales had been lower than estimated, and felt the competitive environment was shifting—and not for the better. The name of the game to survive in the market of the future was going to be hustle, something he thought was lacking in the present sales force. Bob felt a relaxed attitude toward sales existed and this could have a damaging effect on new machines sales, product development, parts sales, and customer service. If the salesman waited for the customer to call him, he was not motivated to find new ways to better serve the customer, either by improving the machinery or service.

To overhaul the sales department and inject some aggressiveness, Bob brought to Portsmouth, Ken Spicer, Post's Australian sales agent. Bob did not consult with any of his key managers in hiring Ken. Ken's charge was to improve sales. One possible way to do this, according to Spicer, was to make the sales territory the sales agent covered smaller. "If a salesman has a smaller market he's going to have to hustle more," Spicer observed, "unless he wants his revenue from commissions to drop." Therefore, Spicer continued, "this method of creating smaller sales territories will improve the level and type of feedback the marketing department receives from the field."

Hopkins was also keen on developing one of Dick MacLeod's ideas. Dick felt there was potential in selling Post's specialty folder-gluers as part of a complete system or package. A folder-gluer would be sold along with a rotary diecutter, flexo folder-gluer, improved service contracts, and packaging consulting. Dick estimated this approach would increase sales to $20–$25 million in three years. Post's strongest competitors in the specialty folder-gluer market (Bobst, Jagenberg, and Tanabi) all had the capability to offer complete systems or package deals, and this bothered him. Dick commented:

> "If competitors began to heavily promote this sales strategy, customers would start to forsake Post's specialty folder-gluers in order to gain the economies of having a complete equipment package offered by one company, as well as to cash in on the discounts that no doubt would be offered. As one industry analyst had noted, brand loyalty in the converting industry lasts as long as the next machine sale."

New Products

As MacLeod had pointed out repeatedly, the competition in Post's traditionally dominant market (corrugated specialty machinery) had intensified rapidly. Bobst and Jagenberg had strengthened their efforts in this area, and Tanabi had recently thrown its hat into the ring. Thus, Dick and Bob felt it would be extremely difficult to draw a significantly greater level of sales just from specialty corrugated folder-gluers. As a result, Dick, at the urging of Bob, had been investigating two potential areas for growth: the rotary diecutter equipment market and the flexo folder-gluer equipment market.

Diecutting Equipment Market.   A study Hopkins had requested from his marketing staff showed the diecutting equipment market to be strong, with estimated 1985 industry sales of $114 million on 190 total units. A diecutter was a machine that prepared a corrugated sheet for folding and gluing by cutting or stamping out sections of the sheet enabling it to be folded. There were two types of diecutters—rotary and flatbed. A rotary diecutter used knives that spin or rotate as the sheet passes under them. A rotary diecutter could be built into a folder-gluer machine thus integrating the operation into a system. A flatbed diecutter stamped out the desired pattern similar to a cookie cutter. The flatbed diecutter equipment market was dominated by Bobst. The rotary diecutter market was dominated by two manufacturers—Ward and Staley with 70% worldwide market share. The remainder of the rotary diecutter market was divided among eighteen other firms. The future of the market looked bright according to the study, as continued product development had positioned the "rotary" diecutter close to (in regards to quality) "flatbed" diecutters, the current standard for the industry. A scan of recent trade journals by MacLeod revealed that in the next five years there was a potential for 422 new units or $253,200,000 in additional "rotary" diecutter equipment sales.

Flexo Folder-Gluer Equipment Market.   According to the market study, the flexo folder-gluer market consisted of seven manufacturers (Action, Bobst, Langston, S. A. Matin, SIS, Staley and Ward) all battling for position in a surprisingly strong market. A flexo folder-gluer was a folder gluer that had the capacity to diecut and print directly on the paperboard as sheets were passed through the folder-gluer machine. The printing was usually in one or two colors and was used to mark or label the container as it was fed through the folder-gluer. In fact, demand was such that Bobst was reported as having difficulty filling orders. *Boxboard* pegged the market's annual sales of flexo folder-gluers for 1985 at close to $149 million. The forecast for growth over the next five years was equally impressive, with an estimated potential of over 600 new units or $360 million in additional sales. Acquisition of both a diecutting line and a flexo folder-gluer line would move Post closer to being a full line equipment manufacturer. (Appendix A diagrams the basic operation involved in both flexo folder-gluer and rotary die cutter equipment.)

ENGINEERING

Post engineering staff consisted of four design engineers, five field service engineers and a Vice President of engineering. The engineering staff was responsible for product field support and handled all design and development of new products, the maintenance of all bills of materials, and problem solving and trouble shooting in the plant and field.

Charlie Eldridge, V.P. of Engineering, stated: "Currently we are in the developmental stages of a major redesign of the existing folding carton and corrugated product lines." Eldridge noted that according to marketing, "We've got to have a new image. We're marketing a machine, which to the average box maker "looks" not much different from a thirty-five year old model. We've got to upgrade the product lines." He went on:

> We will incorporate many things we have learned over the years into this new design. Post introduced a large corrugated machine (90″ and 115″) in 1979 which was a "new look" when compared to conventional Post folder-gluers, and we will use some of the general design parameters we used on the 90″ and 115″ corrugated machines. We will eliminate major differences between folding carton and corrugated machinery. The thickness of the paper line determines the type of material you're able to run. By being able to change the thickness of the paper line, you will be able to run folding carton and corrugated material on the same piece of equipment. This is certainly a unique and innovative concept. Although cost reduction is always an objective, it is not the major priority. The major emphasis will be placed on ease of operation, through easier (operator) accessibility, further reduction of set-up times and durability.

FINANCE AND ACCOUNTING

Commenting on the current financial situation, Marcel Binette, Post's controller, reported:

> Under the present ownership arrangement Post does not have the luxury of a parent organization to lean on if business falls off. Cash management has to become a major priority. The debt to equity ratio will resemble more that of a bank than a capital goods manufacturer, and we all know who has the safer assets. With the cyclical nature of our business, steps must be taken to insure adequate cash flow during down years. Bob has a strong financial background as the treasurer for two very large firms. My background has dealt primarily with asset management. I feel I can exploit some of my talents and put this company back on solid financial ground.

Continuing, Marcel stated:

> The most critical issue we are faced with presently is inventory build-up. The effects of the strike in the 3rd quarter requiring us to purchase from outside suppliers also had a major impact on inventory levels over the last year. We will not be able to survive for long with inventory turns of less than two. The average inventory turns for most manufacturers in the capital goods industry is about 3.8. If we are able to manage the inventory more effectively we will be able to reduce our level of debt with the bank thus putting less pressure on everyone.

Regarding Post's line of credit with its bank, Marcel stated:

> We have what we feel is an adequate line of credit to get the company through some of the slower periods when cash flow is down. Our relationship with our bank is very good and I'm sure if they see we are working hard to resolve some of our internal problems and we hit a period where even the best managed capital goods manufacturer would have a hard time, the bank would stand behind us. They are well aware of the fact that we are worth more to them as a going concern than at liquidation value.

Binette noted:

> In addition to dealing with the inventory build-up and decline in machine orders my major concerns are finding the money to buy back the Paxall note and overseeing any financing associated with the G&F proposal. Tom, Paxall's Vice President of Finance, called me just yesterday. Paxall is still short of cash and wants to sell us the note at a considerable discount. Paxall is willing to take a 40% discount on the note; that's a savings of $500,000. Our revolving line of credit is at $2.8 million and while they'll probably work with us, I doubt that the bank will increase our line of credit much above the $3,000,000 limit.

Marcel was also involved with negotiating a new G&F proposal. If the deal went through, he would have to finance up to $750,000 in equipment plus $150,000 in upgrades and marketing expenses in 1986.

NEW GANDOSSI AND FOSSATI

Gandossi and Fossati (G&F) the Italian converting equipment manufacturer filed for bankruptcy in the summer of 1985. Reports from Europe indicated that while G&F converting machinery business was profitable, the company's machine tool business had significant financial problems. G&F had offered a full-line of folder-gluers, flexo folder-gluers, and rotary diecutters. While Bob felt entry into flexo folder-gluer and rotary diecutter market was desirable, he realized Post did not have the time or engineering staff to develop its own machines. Entry into this market would most likely come through an acquisition, joint venture, or other arrangements.

G&F's only direct competitive threat to Post was its corrugated CS 1800 folder-gluer which competed directly with Post's top seller—its Model 74. After building a strong reputation in Europe, G&F entered the U.S. market in 1980 capitalizing on a strong dollar and aggressive marketing techniques to quickly capture sales. Some of Post's salesmen felt G&F "underpriced" their machines in order to capture a foothold in the U.S. marketplace. By the time it had pulled out in 1985, G&F had annual sales in the U.S. of approximately $11.4 million (estimated to be 15 machines), parts (estimated to be 20% of sales), and service (10% sales).

In the fall, 1985, Bob was approached by Mario Rossati, a major vendor and creditor to G&F. Upon G&F's bankruptcy, Rossati entered into an agreement with the Italian Bankruptcy court. This agreement gave him the rights to 40%

of the G&F assets, primarily those assets related to G&F's converting machinery business. Rossati figured he could resurrect G&F and was looking for a partner in the States. Rossati wanted Bob to enter into an exclusive marketing arrangement with NG&F (New Gandossi and Fossati) where Post would undertake the marketing and distribution of G&F equipment in the states. As part of the agreement, Bob would buy from NG&F a minimum of $750,000 in equipment in 1986. This minimum would be raised per year depending on an agreed annual sales forecast. If Post failed to meet the minimum sales level in any one year, NG&F could revoke the exclusive marketing arrangement.

Rossati estimated that he could deliver a flexo folder-gluer in the United States for approximately $400,000. The going market price for this type of flexo folder-gluer in the U.S. was about $650,000 per unit. Terms of the purchase and sales agreement for each flexo gluer sold to Post from NG&F would be 20% at time of order, 40% FOB Portsmouth, net (40%) ninety days from date of receipt by Post. Rossati would share equally in any engineering costs to "Americanize" the machine (estimated to be approximately $100,000 the first year). Bob would bear all sales and marketing expenses in the United States.

MacLeod, after talking to some existing Post customers relative to the merits of acquiring the rights to sell NG&F equipment reported:

> The customers' comments on G&F machines were generally positive. G&F were considered to offer high value for the customer's investment dollar. The rotary diecutter, in particular, was considered to be technically superior to the most costly market leaders. However, this is not to say the equipment was without problems. Customers had repeatedly experienced trouble with the electronic components. Many felt the root of this particular problem was that G&F engineered the equipment for European standards and not American. This, in turn, was believed to be the result of a bigger problem, G&F's inability to understand the problems faced by the typical American converter. Yet, despite the glitch, customers did not become discouraged. In fact, many expressed a willingness to pay more for an improved G&F machine.

Hopkins, in conjunction with MacLeod, figured the initial cost to market and sell two machines would be approximately $100,000 the first year. This figure included the cost of an additional salesman. Rossati informed Hopkins that G&F's rotary diecutters would not be available for sale in the states until late 1986 at the earliest. Rossati wanted to move quickly; he expected an answer from Hopkins by the end of March.

Final Thoughts

Commenting on the direction he wanted to take the company Bob responded:

> This company's strengths are in the folder-gluer industry. We need to capitalize on this strength. We have to remain visible in the industry as a technological leader. I feel this is imperative and we are right now trying to shore up our engineering staff to give us even greater technical ability. I expect to run this company in a professional manner. If there is something I'm not happy with it will be addressed immediately.

Concerning his thoughts about G&F, Bob stated:

> With effective asset management, this company will be able to withstand virtually any downturn in the capital goods market. I feel we need to look for a countercyclical business over the long run, but presently we need to get our act together in our primary line of business, namely folder-gluers. I have been completely absorbed by the recent G&F proposal and have not been able to spend the time I would like to around here in operations. When I bought Post I knew nothing about the industry

or the company. My decision to buy was based purely on the numbers. Now I must decide what to do with the company and G&F.

Bob, leaning back in his chair, as the snow came down heavier outside, thought out loud: "What direction should I take this company?" He recalled a quote from one of his professors at Chicago: "Any road will get you there if you don't know where you're going. What road should I travel?"

Notes

1. Background information on the converting industry was excerpted from: "Market Profile: 1984–1985," *Boxboard Container Magazine*, December 1984, pp. 4–17.
2. *Ibid.* p. 5.
3. *Ibid.* p. 6.
4. *Ibid.* pp. 4–6; 16–20.
5. *Ibid.* p. 4.
6. "Forecast '86," *Boxboard Container Magazine*, December 1985, pp. 19–23.
7. *1986 U.S. Industrial Outlook*, U.S. Department of Commerce, January 1986, p. 6.
8. *Ibid.* p. 9.
9. "Forecast '86," *Boxboard Container Magazine*, December 1985, p. 21.
10. *Ibid.* p. 21.
11. *Ibid.* p. 22.
12. *Ibid.* p. 23.

APPENDIX A   *Typical Converting Equipment Configurations*

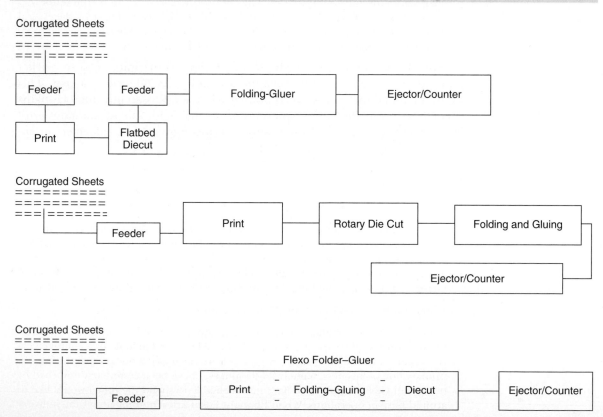

United States Gypsum Corporation

A.J. ALMANEY, *DePaul University*

INTRODUCTION

United States Gypsum Corporation is a Fortune 200 company that manufactures building materials and other products for use in the repair and construction industries in the United States and Canada. The corporation is composed of six units: United States Gypsum Company, USG Interiors Company, L&W Supply Company, DAP Inc., Canadian Gypsum Co., Inc. (CGC), and USG International Ltd.

Producing gypsum and gypsum related products is the major function of the United States Gypsum, L&W, and CGC subsidiaries. In this arena, the major competitors in North America are National Gypsum Company, Domtar, Inc., Georgia Pacific Corporation and the Celotex Corporation. In 1989, United States Gypsum Company had a U.S. market share of 34%, and was labeled the leading gypsum producer in the world, supported by L&W Supply and Canada-based CGC.[1] Gypsum accounted for 57% of USG's 1989 sales and 75% of its profits.[2]

USG Corporation's subsidiary, USG Interiors, and a portion of CGC, Inc. are responsible for producing building interiors. CGC is the leading gypsum board producer in Eastern Canada. In 1989, USG Interiors was cited for the success of its ceiling tile sales to Europe, a market which is expected to grow 20% over the next few years. DAP's primary responsibility is the manufacture of materials for remodelling and repair purposes. DAP boasts several leading competitive brands. For the interiors market, the major competitors are Celotex Corporation, National Rolling Mills, Armstrong World Industries, and the Chicago Metallic Corporation. These non-gypsum producing entities are responsible for approximately 40% of USG's total sales and are expected to grow by approximately 10% in 1990, due to USG's presence in Europe and the Far East.[3] USG International, Ltd., is responsible for the corporation's global operations.

This case was prepared by A. J. Almaney, Professor of Management at DePaul University, Chicago and the following graduate students: J. Jenkins, K. Landauer, R. Pekosh, and D. Schacht and is intended to be used as a basis for class discussion rather than to illustrate either effective or ineffective handling of the situation.

The primary products generated by the gypsum producing unit, the company's core business, include: wallboard, sheathing, baseboard, mobile home board, lay-in panels, soffit board, lawn and garden gypsum, agricultural gypsum, plaster, industrial gypsum cements and fillers, spray textured finish, textured panels, cement board and joint compound.[4]

The past few years have been relatively unkind for USG Corporation. It has faced numerous lawsuits for asbestos-related illnesses, price-fixing, and violation of employees' rights. In the mid 1980s, USG's stock price began to fall and one of USG's stockholders, Desert Partners Ltd., threatened to take over the company. USG's board of directors and management opposed the hostile bid and decided to fight back through recapitalization.

In the third and fourth quarters of 1990, USG experienced an $11 million loss. This resulted from the slump in new home and building construction which has been going on for the past four years[5] and which is expected to continue for the next decade, particularly in large cities.[6] In the meantime, USG's inventories are accumulating, forcing its plants to operate only six days a week rather than the usual seven. What can USG do in response? Can USG resolve its dilemma by divesting some of the company's assets? Or is filing for bankruptcy the only possible alternative?

HISTORY OF GYPSUM

To place USG's current problem in a meaningful perspective, it is necessary to provide a brief history of the company, beginning with the history of its core product, namely, gypsum.

Gypsum is a mineral that is found in mines and quarries around the world. Known as the "mineral with memory," gypsum can be melted down and processed into any form. Legend has it that a Chinese shepherd built his campfire on white rock (which was gypsum). The fire removed the water from the gypsum (gypsum is 28% water by weight) and left a white powder. The next morning the shepherd dumped water on the embers of the campfire. The water mixed with the white powder into a fluid that later hardened into rock (gypsum). At the time, the shepherd thought that he witnessed a miracle; however, it is essentially the process used today to change gypsum into plaster. Historical evidence indicates that gypsum was used 5,000 years ago in pyramids in Egypt. Artists such as Leonardo da Vinci created works on gypsum plaster in palaces. In the late 1700s Lavoisier, a French chemist, worked with gypsum (also referred to as plaster of paris) to determine its secrets.[7]

In the U.S., the first very large scale use of gypsum in buildings was in the 1893 World's Columbian Exposition in Chicago where several model buildings were completely structured with gypsum. In the early 1900s, gypsum board was used for partitions in New York City's buildings.[8] Gypsum's near fireproof quality made it a prime candidate for building construction.

HISTORY OF UNITED STATES GYPSUM CORPORATION

United States Gypsum Company was founded in 1902, and was comprised of a group of small gypsum suppliers. It was incorporated in Illinois in 1920, and reincorporated in Delaware in 1966 and again in 1985. USG's original mission at the time of its founding in 1902 was to "develop and produce gypsum products of such consistent quality and performance that they would become the industry standard of excellence".[9]

In 1906, USG's president, Sewell Avery, was largely responsible for recruiting a competent staff and implementing modern manufacturing and marketing policies needed to develop USG. USG hired geologists to search for gypsum deposits, skilled engineers to mine the mineral, and researchers to experiment to find its best uses. In the early years, USG prided itself on its efficient production processes and a concern for employee safety that was uncommon in the early 1900s.[10]

The year 1915 marked the beginning of USG's product line expansion. It began producing lime and sheetrock gypsum wallboard. Sheetrock paved the way for development of gypsum sheathing, drywall, and panels. Two of gypsum's biggest assets are its ease and speed in construction and near fireproof quality. These features led the U.S. government to contract with USG during both world wars. In World War II, USG supplied over one billion square feet of wallboard for military facilities.[11]

Through the years, USG continued to expand product lines through innovation and diversification. The company began producing acoustical wood fiber, metal insulation, roofing and water resistant gypsum core. Today, gypsum wallboard has replaced plaster in almost all new office buildings and homes.[12] In its diversification efforts, USG has acquired a myriad of companies and resold several of them, including: BPB Industries, Ltd., London, England; United Cement Company of Alabama; Warren Paint and Color Company in Nashville; Kinkead Aluminum Industries; Float-Away Door Company; Chicago Mastic Company; and Hollytex Carpet Mills of California.[13]

THE BOARD OF DIRECTORS

The board of directors is composed of five USG officers and nine outside directors. The board also has a representative from BPB Industries, a London-based construction company. Board functions are performed by six committees: executive, compensation, audit, public affairs, finance, and director nomination. The board meets on a regular basis to review company operations and counsel the chief executive officer concerning the corporation's future direction.

MANAGEMENT

Eugene B. Connolly, the Chief Executive Officer of USG, was born in 1932 in New York. He received a bachelor's degree in management in 1954 and an M.B.A. degree in marketing in 1964, both from Hofstra University. From 1955 to 1958, Connolly served as an officer in the U.S. Navy.

Connolly joined United States Gypsum Company in May 1958. He has served in a variety of management positions, including President and Chief Executive Officer of USG Corporation, Executive Vice President of USG Corporation, President and Chief Executive Officer of USG Interiors, Inc., President and Chief Executive Officer of DAP Inc., President and Chief Operating Officer of U.S. Gypsum Company.[14]

Connolly follows a participative decision-making style. He often meets with various managers and seeks the advice of members of the board before making a decision.

USG's executive officers are all between the ages of 45 and 65; some have both a legal and a business background. All have held senior positions in various areas of the corporation for five or more years. Some also serve on boards of other corporations.

CORPORATE CULTURE

USG's corporate culture is built around the notion of providing customers high-quality products and consistent, reliable service. The essence of the culture is captured in what the company executives refer to as "The USG Franchise."

Four ingredients make up "The USG Franchise." First is safety which has been firmly ingrained in every employee. Considered the most important part of every manufacturing job, safety extends from the plant to the construction site. Second is USG's customer service orientation. Customers are treated in a way that guarantees repeat business and encourages loyalty to USG products. Third, USG emphasizes high ethical standards. These standards apply to every aspect of the Corporation's business. The fourth ingredient of the corporate culture is USG's commitment to technological innovation. Being on the forefront of technology has enabled USG to increase productivity, lower operating costs, reduce lead time, and increase market share.

Supporting "The USG Franchise" is a philosophy that permeates the organization, namely, the Corporation is committed to maintaining and expanding its leadership position in its core businesses. This goal is accomplished by using expertise in product and process development, a comprehensive sales and distribution network, low-cost manufacturing facilities, and the ability to deliver consistently high-quality building products at low prices.

USG UNITS

United States Gypsum Company.   United States Gypsum Company is the largest manufacturer of gypsum in North America. The company holds a 34% market share of total gypsum board sales in the United States. This makes the company a leading player in the industry followed by National Gypsum with 25%, Georgia Pacific with 12%, Domtar with 11%, and Celotex with 7%. The remaining 11% is shared by several smaller companies.

In 1990, net sales and profits of USG declined. The primary reason for the decline was an 8% lower selling price for gypsum wallboard which management attributed to growing industry overcapacity. During 1990, about 14% or 3.5 billion square feet of gypsum wallboard manufacturing capacity in the industry remained unused, compared to about 2% during the peak year of 1986.[15]

USG Interiors, Inc.   USG Interiors, Inc. manufactures and markets a diverse product line of ceiling, wall and floor systems. Specifically, it produces ceiling tile and suspension systems for commercial and residential applications, access floors, and relocatable wall systems. Since 1987, USG Interiors' operating profit has risen 28% but profits from nonresidential business have declined by over 7%.

During 1990, USG Interiors implemented an operational improvement effort, known as The Quality Way, among its hourly and salaried employees. Quality Improvement Teams (QITs) were established at every USG Interiors office and plant location. Under the direction of its QIT, each location controls its own training, problem solving, and employee participation. According to management, the program resulted in noticeable improvement in product quality.[16]

L&W Supply Corporation. L&W Supply Corporation is the nation's largest distributor of gypsum board and other building materials. It operates 128 distribution centers in 33 states and supplies about 9% of all gypsum board sold in the United States. In 1990, both net sales and operating profit of L&W were lower than those of 1989.

In 1991, L&W will continue to be adversely affected by declining housing starts, lower gypsum board prices, and overcapacity in distribution.

Canadian Gypsum Co., Inc. CGC Inc. is 76% owned by USG Corporation and is the leading gypsum board producer in eastern Canada. CGC had 1990 total sales of $173 million in U.S. dollars, which compared with $208 million for 1989. Operating profit in 1990 totaled $27 million in U.S. dollars, compared with $49 million in 1989. The decline in operating profit was due primarily to sharply lower volume and selling prices for wallboard. An extended commercial construction trade strike in Ontario also contributed to the earnings decline.

CGC and two of its competitors began a cooperative program in 1990 to accept scrap wallboard from new construction for recycling. With landfills rapidly reaching capacity levels, the city of Toronto has banned the dumping of wallboard scrap in landfills. Under the new program, CGC's Hagersville, Ontario, plant is expected to receive between 20,000 and 30,000 tons of wallboard scrap per year for recycling.

USG expects the current Canadian economic recession to continue throughout 1991. High interest rates, a new value-added tax and a depressed economy have contributed to extremely soft housing and nonresidential construction activity.

DAP Inc. DAP Inc. is the nation's leading manufacturer of caulks and sealants and holds strong market positions in a variety of products for the new remodel segments of the construction industry. DAP products also include adhesives, wood preservatives, paints and coatings, grouts and mortars, glazing and spackling compounds, and other specialty products. In 1990, poor economic conditions and a slowdown in growth of personal disposable income led to a drop in the company's sales and operating profits.

In May 1991, USG put DAP Inc. on the market to raise funds necessary to cover interest charges.

USG International, Ltd. In 1990, USG Corporation formed a separate operating unit called USG International, Ltd. to manage the Corporation's international business. The new unit was charged with the responsibility of formulating and implementing the Corporation's strategy of becoming a global leader in the development, manufacturing, and marketing of building systems.

USG International combines the previous international marketing and manufacturing operations of USG Interiors, the export functions of United States Gypsum Company and its investment in Thai Gypsum into one operation.

The global market is viewed by USG as offering a substantial opportunity. To capitalize on this market, the Corporation established an acoustical ceiling

TABLE 1

Sales and Profits of USG Units (in millions)

	Sales		Profits	
	1990	1989	1990	1989
USG	$ 928	$1,032	$ 115	$ 173
USG Interiors	564	549	NA	NA
L&W	478	485	4	7
CGC	173	208	27	49
DAP	181	186	10	12
USG International	184	NA	NA	NA

tile plant in Aubang, Belgium, in addition to its facilities in Australia, Mexico, New Zealand and Malaysia.[17]

As a result, sales outside of the United States and Canada grew to $184 million or 10% of total sales in 1990. Including Canada, total international sales in 1990 accounted for 18.6% of total net sales. The Corporation's long-term goal is not only to sell products in the international market but also to market its business expertise and technology. For data on sales and profits of USG units, see Table 1.

HOSTILE TAKEOVER BID

In October, 1987 one of USG's common shareholders, Desert Partners, Ltd., indicated that it had purchased 9.8% of USG common shares and proposed a leveraged buy-out which USG rejected. In February 1988, Desert Partners offered to purchase 21.5 million shares of common stock at $42 per share. The tender offer was later amended to increase the amount of common stock subject to purchase to 39 million shares. The USG board refused the offer and searched for ways to make the hostile buy-out difficult to carry out. Toward that end, USG developed a recapitalization plan in May of 1988 which offered each shareholder $37.00 per share in cash, $5.00 pay-in-kind securities and one new share of common stock in the new company for each old share. Although the deal was valued at $49.00 per share compared to $42.00 per share from Desert Partners, this promise to shareholders caused USG to take on $2.6 billion in debt.[18]

USG sought to finance this debt by acquiring $1.6 billion from foreign and domestic banks, by divesting some divisions, and by strictly managing cash flow. In 1988, the company sold its Masonite division for $400 million, the Kinkead division for $58 million, and the Marlite division for $18 million. The company also sold its corporate headquarters to Manufacturers Life Insurance Co. of Toronto for $60 million and received $6.4 million for sale of its corporate jet.[19] Cash proceeds from these divestitures and sales were used to repay its loan debt.

Further cutbacks included:

• DAP's closure of two plants in California and Georgia
• L&W Supply's closure or consolidation of 18 distribution centers and a new policy of leasing rather than buying cars and trucks for transport
• CGC's consolidation of ceiling and acoustical tile into one division called CGC Interiors.[20]

In addition, more than 550 salaried positions were eliminated during 1990, bringing the total number of employee reductions since mid-1987 to nearly 1,600 (excluding eliminations resulting from asset sales). These reductions eliminated one in four salaried positions resulting in an annual overhead reduction of about $65 million. Despite these efforts, USG was still left with a total debt of $2.4 billion.

Some financial analysts questioned USG's recapitalization decision. First, the company based its decision on expectations of steady housing starts, growth from remodeling and increased nonresidential construction. USG's ten year forecast failed to include a contingency plan which addressed the possibility of a recession. Second, the company expected to receive more money from the sale of its three businesses than it actually did. Analysts believe that one positive aspect of the recapitalization is that employees now own a much larger share of the company which may protect USG from another hostile takeover threat.[21]

As of October 30, 1990, USG's common stock was selling for less than $2.00 per share, which is largely due to the company's current financial condition. USG's bond prices have also dropped as a result of National Gypsum's and Celotex's recent filings for Chapter 11. Additionally, USG is paying high interest expense for the loans used to recapitalize the company. Recent articles report that USG suffered an $11 million net loss during the current quarter and will be forced to further restructure its organization and implement even tighter cash flow solutions.[22]

MARKETING

USG maintains a long-standing policy of producing high quality products along with a total commitment to excellence in providing consistently reliable customer service before and after the sale. USG's products, however, are seasonal. Sales are generally greater from the middle of spring through the middle of autumn than during the remaining part of the year. The business is also affected by the cyclical behavior of the new residential and nonresidential construction markets.

The company's gypsum board product is distributed by L&W Supply Corporation, a USG subsidiary, which operates 128 distributorships strategically located throughout the U.S. The specific distribution channels which L&W relies upon include mass merchandising, building material dealers, contractors, and industrial and agricultural users. A computer-generated distribution program introduced at U.S. Gypsum enabled the company to refine product distribution. This program resulted in lower distribution costs without affecting customer service and delivery schedules. During the first year of full operation, the program increased wallboard profitability by more than $10 million.

As was noted earlier, gypsum product prices have declined steadily since 1987. This price decline has been due in part to both greater industry-wide production and recent depressed construction activity levels.

PRODUCTION

Gypsum is the corporation's major raw material and is obtained from the Corporation's mines and quarries throughout North America. USG's mines and quarries provide the essential raw material for manufacturing gypsum wallboard.

EXHIBIT 1

Locations of USG's Production Facilities

United States

Baltimore, Maryland	Gypsum, Ohio	Shoals, Indiana
Boston (Charlestown), Massachusetts	Jacksonville, Florida	Sigurd, Utah
Detroit (River Rouge), Michigan	New Orleans, Louisiana	Southard, Oklahoma
East Chicago, Indiana	Norfolk, Virginia	Sperry, Iowa
Empire (Gerlach), Nevada	Oakfield, N.Y.	Stony Point, N.Y.
Fort Dodge, Iowa	Plaster City, California	Sweetwater, Texas
Fremont, California	Plasterco (Saltville), Virginia	
Galena Park, Texas	Santa Fe Springs, California	

Canada   **Mexico**

Hagersville, Ontario	Puebla, Puebla
Montreal, Quebe	(two locations)
St. Jerome, Quebec	

Proven reserves contain about 249 million tons of which about 69% are located in the United States and 31% in Canada. The Corporation's total average annual production of crude gypsum in the United States and Canada between 1985 and 1990 was 9.4 million tons. For the locations of USG's production facilities, see Exhibit 1.[23]

The Corporation maintains an active program of finding and developing new reserves, with corporate geologists estimating that recoverable reserves of gypsum are sufficient for more than 30 years of operation based on recent average annual production.

The other major component of drywall is paper for outer coating and this is produced from waste paper which is in abundant supply. The waste paper and other raw materials used in this industry are purchased from numerous local and national firms.

USG's gypsum and other plants are substantial users of thermal energy. The company uses primarily six major fuel types in the following order: natural gas 74%, electricity 10%, coal 6%, oil 5%, coke (coal by-product) 4%, and steam 1%. These fuels come from various suppliers and USG feels that there will be sufficient supplies for the foreseeable future.[24] No shortages of raw materials used by the Corporation are expected for the foreseeable future.

The company's North Kansas City, Mo., paper plant was recognized for initiating and promoting sound waste management practices and awarded the Missouri Waste Control Coalition's Outstanding Achievement Award in the recycling and resource recovery category. The Shoals, Ind., mine received the mining industry's top safety award in the underground nonmetal category for the sixth time. Two other U.S. gypsum mines, in Oakfield, N.Y., and Sperry, Iowa, placed second and third, respectively.

Expenditures for plant modernization increased to $46 million for 1989 even though total corporate capital spending was down by 7% from $84 million in 1988 to $78 in 1989. The emphasis on plant modernization was prompted by the company's desire to enhance quality control and to maintain its reputation of providing high quality products. The plants, however, remained underutilized due to weak demand. As a result, production has been reduced to six days per week.

The company is now studying the possibility of using computer models of the gypsum wallboard manufacturing process. The purpose of such models is to assist in pinpointing trouble spots and fine-tuning the manufacturing process.

RESEARCH & DEVELOPMENT

USG owns three research facilities: one in Libertyville, Illinois, which focuses on product development, one in Avon, Ohio, which focuses on interior products, and one in Dayton, Ohio, which concentrates on sealant products. Due to USG's recapitalization and the recent weakened gypsum market, research expenditures were reduced from $24 million in 1987 to $19 million in 1989.

Despite the cut in R&D budget, USG introduced in 1990 DUROCK underlayment, a water-resistant tile substrate created especially for floors and counter tops. The new product is 2/10 inch thinner than standard DUROCK interior panels and is designed to compete with traditional lightweight, wood-based underlayments.[25]

The company also introduced SHEETROCK lightweight setting-type joint compounds, a line of chemically setting powder compounds for drywall interiors and exteriors. Unlike conventional setting-type compounds, this product sands easily and allows for same-day joint finishing with next-day decoration, thereby speeding job completion, saving time and money. Also introduced were TUF-TEX wall and ceiling spray texture and tinted PLUS 3 joint compound.

HUMAN RESOURCES

USG employed 12,700 people in 1990, down from 13,400 in 1989. The decline resulted from the company's efforts to streamline operations and pay off debt. Employee layoffs eliminated one in four salaried positions, resulting in an annual overhead reduction of about $65 million. One positive aspect of the hostile takeover bid was the company's effort to provide financial incentives to employees to purchase the company's outstanding common stock. As a result, employees became the company's largest group of shareholders—26%.

Employee ownership, in turn, resulted in improved corporate communication. Said Eugene B. Connolly, the company CEO, "We had to expand communications with our employees to directly share the good and the disappointing news, the challenges, strategies, and goals we need to attain."[26] The company developed five ways to keep employees informed, including: *USG Bulletin,* a daily publication of urgent messages; *Looking Ahead,* a bi-monthly publication that deals with company's debt; *USG Today,* a 1–800 telephone number for updated information on USG; *USG Employee Communications Guide,* a tool which USG officers and managers use to make presentations to employees; and *Video News,* a financial reference for USG.

Prior to these efforts, the company's communication program left much to be desired. During the restructuring phase, for example, USG came under severe criticism from employees for not keeping them abreast of what was going on. Employees were forced to find out through rumors and the press where cuts were being made, and whose jobs were affected.[27]

The new, improved communication, however, proved inadequate in mollifying employees' ire over a company policy ordering the employees of USG's

Acoustical Products unit to stop smoking on the job and at home, or they would lose their jobs. This policy was inspired by the fact that USG was named in numerous asbestos-related lawsuits. The company chose this route as one of the measures to protect itself against future lawsuits from workers who might develop lung cancer. The policy was based on information obtained from the World Health Organization which indicated that smokers who worked in an asbestos-laden environment were more likely than non-smokers to get lung cancer. Because the affected workers did not have a union, they could be forced to accept the policy at work, which was stated to them formally, in writing and in person. However, many employees and activist groups felt that trying to enforce non-smoking at home would not only be impossible, but would infringe on people's rights so USG backed down on the policy.[28]

LEGAL PROBLEMS

In 1975, USG together with National Gypsum and Georgia Pacific were accused by the U.S. Justice Department of price-fixing. The charges were dropped in 1980 in exchange for a $2.9 million tax settlement that USG paid to the Internal Revenue Service.[29]

One of the Corporation's subsidiaries, United States Gypsum, is among numerous defendants in lawsuits that seek to recover compensatory and in many cases punitive damages for costs associated with maintenance or removal and replacement of products containing asbestos that were installed in buildings more than a decade ago when U.S. Gypsum ceased manufacturing such products.

The lawsuits have been brought by a variety of plaintiffs, including school districts, state and local governments, colleges and universities, hospitals, and private property owners. Two of these cases have been certified as class actions and others request such certification. U.S. Gypsum has settled property damage claims of about 140 plaintiffs, including three cases involving 83 school district plaintiffs. Nineteen cases have been tried in the courts, 12 were won by U.S. Gypsum and seven lost. In the cases lost, compensatory damage awards totalled $3.5 million. Punitive damages totaling $1.5 million were entered against U.S. Gypsum in three trials which US Gypsum has appealed. As of December 31, 1990, 124 damage cases were pending against U.S. Gypsum.

FINANCE

As of December 31, 1990, total current liabilities exceeded total current assets by $2.2 billion and the ratio of current assets to current liabilities was 0.24 to 1, compared to 1.09 to 1 as of December 31, 1989 when current assets exceeded current liabilities by $51 million. Current liabilities in 1990 increased significantly due to the reclassification of the outstanding balance of the term loan, as well as most other long-term debt issues, to current liabilities.

In February 1991, USG defaulted on about $40 million in interest payments. Skipping a payment could, in theory, have prompted lenders to force USG into involuntary bankruptcy, or it could have triggered a Chapter 11 bankruptcy filing by the company if it wanted to seek protection from creditors. USG, however, expected creditors to provide it with a grace period and did not plan on filing for bankruptcy . In the meantime, and according to Sheryl Van Winkle, a Merrill Lynch analyst, the company continues to be, "in a very, very horrible position."[30] For financial data, see Appendixes A, B, C, and D.

INDUSTRY

The gypsum industry is dependent on new residential and nonresidential markets as well as the repair and remodel market. These markets are tied to the economy, interest rates, inflation, and availability of credit. Thus, the building materials industry is cyclical. It slacks off when the economy is poor and picks up when the economy improves. Also, "sales of gypsum products are seasonal to the extent that sales are generally greater from middle of spring through the middle of autumn than during the remaining part of the year."[31]

The outlook for the building materials industry for 1991 looks bleak. *Value Line Investment Survey* states:

> Improvements in the building materials industry doesn't look to be at hand. Weak demand in the new housing market, coupled with economic weakness in many parts of the country and stricter lending standards, is likely to prevent any gains in the residential and commercial construction sectors of the economy.[32]

Value Line goes on to state that even though unemployment "has been fairly stable and at a relatively low level for some time now, we sense a certain uneasiness among potential home buyers about the course of the economy. This skittishness will likely keep the new residential construction market in a slump into 1991."[33]

Iraq's invasion of Kuwait in August, 1990 exacerbated the situation. The invasion caused the price of crude oil to more than double in just two and a half months. The invasion created more uneasiness among potential home buyers about the future of the economy. In fact, new home construction "slumped for an eighth straight month in September" creating "the longest slide since statistics were first kept in 1959, and activity slowed nationally to a recession-era pace."[34]

Another event that hurt the building material industry has been the Savings and Loan crisis. "The home building industry, which drives the building materials segment, relies on massive amounts of credit to buy land and purchase materials for building houses. The S&L crisis, however, has spawned new regulations that prevent S&L's from lending large amounts to any one creditor in the real estate industry."[35]

Overall, the industry in which USG competes is headed for hard times in the future. The Iraqi invasion, the S&L crisis, legal problems, and predictions of an economic recession may all combine to reduce the size of the market in which USG operates.

COMPETITORS

National Gypsum.   National Gypsum is an integrated, diversified manufacturer and supplier of products and services for the building, construction and shelter markets.[36] The company has three business segments. The first is the Gold Bond Building Products Division which produces gypsum wallboard and related products. Second, the Austin Company provides design, engineering and construction services. The third segment encompasses specialty items including a limestone quarry and plant, two vinyl manufacturing plants, and a metal products plant. The company is estimated to have 25% of the U.S. gypsum products market.[37]

The company has gypsum manufacturing plants in Arizona, California, Georgia, Illinois, Indiana, Iowa, Louisiana, Maryland, Michigan, New Hampshire,

> ### TABLE 2
>
> *Sales and Net Income of National Gypsum*
>
> | | 1991 ($000) | 1990 ($000) | 1989 ($000) |
> |---|---|---|---|
> | Sales | 1,136 | 1,332 | 1,364 |
> | Net Income | −95 | −529 | −58 |
>
> SOURCE: National Gypsum Co., *10-K Form, 1991.*

New Jersey, New York, North Carolina, Ohio and Texas. National Gypsum owns several mines in the U.S., one in Mexico and one in Nova Scotia. It has enough estimated recoverable gypsum to last approximately 67 years based on 1988 production. It also owns three mills that manufacture paper used in the production of wallboard. The company estimates that it operates at a 96% annual utilization of its optimum production capacity.[38]

Table 2 presents data on the sales and net income of National Gypsum Co.

Georgia-Pacific.   Georgia-Pacific is an integrated manufacturer and distributor of a wide range of building products and pulp and paper products. It sells these products through 144 distribution centers located in the U.S. Gypsum products are sold by the corporation's distribution centers to building supply retailers ranging form traditional lumber yards to consumer-oriented home centers. These distribution centers enable Georgia-Pacific's manufacturing plants to operate at efficient rates of output by providing outlets for the plant's full production.[39]

Georgia-Pacific ranks third in the manufacture of gypsum products in the U.S., accounting for approximately 12% of the total domestic production. The company owns gypsum mines, quarries and deposits in Iowa, Kansas, Michigan, Nevada, Texas, Utah, Wyoming and Nova Scotia. It owns ten gypsum board plants located adjacent to these deposits or on ports served from the Nova Scotia quarry ocean vessels. The gypsum plants are running at approximately 78% of capacity. The company estimates that its current reserves are sufficient for a 45 year supply. Gypsum research is based in Decatur, Georgia. Laboratories at universities and other institutions are also utilized in the development of new products.[40]

The company employs approximately 44,000 people. The majority of the hourly workers are members of unions. The company considers its relationship with employees to be good.[41]

Georgia-Pacific has had a long-standing concern for environmental quality. The company's operations are subject to extensive regulation by federal, state and local agencies for environmental compliance. In the past, Georgia-Pacific has made significant capital expenditures to comply with such regulations and expects to make significant expenditures in the future to maintain compliance. Capital expenditures for pollution control facilities were approximately $39 million in 1989 (.4% of 1% of net sales) and budgeted for $66 million in 1990.[42]

Table 3 provides data on the sales and net income of Georgia-Pacific Corp.

Domtar.   Domtar Inc. is a Canadian based company that manufactures and markets a wide range of products through four operating groups: Pulp &

TABLE 3

Sales and Net Income of Georgia-Pacific Corp.

	1991 ($000)	1990 ($000)	1989 ($000)
Sales	11,524	12,665	10,171
Net Income	142	365	661

SOURCE: Georgia-Pacific Corp., *10-K Form, 1991.*

Paper Products, Packaging, Chemicals and Construction Materials. It has 16,000 employees and operates 61 facilities in Canada and 14 in the U.S. Operations are supported by a network of warehouses and sales offices across Canada and in certain areas of the U.S. as well as representatives abroad. Twenty-nine percent of consolidated sales comes from the Construction Materials Group, with gypsum products as the largest component.[43]

The company holds approximately 11% of the U.S. gypsum market and 35% of the Canadian market. It produces gypsum board at five plants in Canada and eight plants in the US. Eight of the plants are integrated with their own rock supply. Domtar estimates that its current reserves of gypsum are ample for 25 years at current and anticipated production levels.[44] Domtar's sales and net income are presented in Table 4.

Celotex.   The Celotex Corporation is a subsidiary of Jim Walter Corporation which in turn is owned by Hillsborough Holdings Corporation. Jim Walter Corporation is a diversified company that started in the business of selling, constructing, and financing shell-type and partially-finished homes. It has expanded into the manufacturing and distributing of a wide range of building materials for residential, commercial and renovation/remodeling uses, products for industrial uses, products for water and waste transmission and the development of natural resources including coal, marble, granite, limestone, oil, gas and gypsum. The company's other businesses include production of industrial chemicals, distribution of a full line of fine printing papers, retail and wholesale credit jewelry operations, and insurance services.[45]

The Celotex Building Products Division manufactures foam insulation, gypsum board, mineral ceiling tiles, lay-in panels and fiberboard sheathing. It markets its products primarily to building materials dealers and wholesalers, distributors and specialized applicators. The company employs 16,750 people.

TABLE 4

Sales and Net Income of Domtar, Inc.

	1991 ($000)	1990 ($000)	1989 ($000)
Sales	1,804	2,314	2,515
Net Income	−148	−294	33

SOURCE: Domtar, Inc. *Ontario Securities Commission Filings,* December 31, 1991.

Celotex's policy is to own its plants and facilities and mineral deposits. Its gypsum reserves are located at three gypsum plants estimated to be sufficient for more than 50 years at present and projected annual rates of consumption.[46] Data of sales and income for Celotex are not available.

CUSTOMERS

USG's customers vary from large to small. Products are distributed through different channels to mass merchandisers, building material dealers, contractors, distributors and industrial and agricultural users. USG's export sales to foreign unaffiliated customers represented less than 10% of consolidated net sales. Also, no single customer accounted for more than 4% of consolidated net sales.[47]

GOVERNMENT REGULATORS

As a generator of hazardous substances, the industry in which USG operates is highly regulated. Owners of sites containing hazardous waste are subject to claims brought by state and federal regulatory agencies pursuant to statutory authority. Since 1981, the EPA has sought compensation and remedial action from waste generators, site owners and operators, and others under the Comprehensive Environmental Response, Compensation, and Liability Act of 1980 ("CERCLA" or "Superfund") which authorizes such action by the EPA regardless of fault or the legality of the original disposal.[48]

DEMOGRAPHICS

Based on U.S. Census Bureau statistics, housing starts are expected to decline in the 1990s. The housing industry contributed nearly $220 billion to the Gross National Product (GNP) of the U.S. in 1988. However, a decrease of 100,000 housing starts will result in a drop of $12.5 billion in the GNP. The number of new housing units started dropped from 1.8 million in 1986 to 1.4 million in 1989. This drop reflects about a $50 billion drop in the GNP in the last four years. Economists expect that trend to continue with an estimated 1.2 million housing starts in 1990 and 1.0 million in 1991.[49] The dramatic decline in housing starts is attributed to the fact that fewer young people will be demanding homes. Americans from 25 to 34 years old make up the age group most likely to be first-time home buyers. In the U.S. this age group is expected to decline from 43.3 million in 1987 to 36.2 million in the year 2000.[50]

Other factors that decrease the demand for housing include: Americans are marrying at a later age, divorcing less frequently, and staying in their parents' homes longer. Also, the Bureau of Labor Statistics calculates that inflation-adjusted investment in residential construction will increase just 0.4% annually during the 1990s compared to 3.9% in the 1970s and 1.2% in the 1980s.[51] Canadian sales volumes of gypsum board products have been hurt by a drop in housing starts more severe than in the U.S.[52]

ECONOMY

The gypsum industry is cyclical as well as seasonal. Recently, demand for gypsum products has declined due to the lackluster new residential construction market. The reduced demand, in turn, led to a reduction in price. One manufacturer, for example, lowered its price from $89.93 per thousand square feet in 1988 to $87.36 in 1989. The price peaked at $127.50 per thousand square feet in the fourth quarter of 1985 and hit the previous cyclical bottom of $74.73 in 1982. The 1989 prices were below the 1982 price level when adjusted for inflation.[53]

Another contributing factor to the soft demand for gypsum is the weak office building market, evidenced by a 17% vacancy rate nationwide. Cities such as Chicago, Cleveland, Washington, D.C., and New York are particularly over-built. The demand for gypsum products in the repair and remodeling market, which tends not to be cyclical, has been strong, but not strong enough to make up for the weakness in the residential and non-residential/commercial markets. The repair and remodeling market continues to grow and command a larger share of the total demand annually.[54]

Economic forecasts that the economy is likely to slide into a severe recession does not bode well for USG or the industry.

TECHNOLOGY

New sources of gypsum have been found as a result of companies' efforts to control acid rain which came to be viewed as a serious environmental threat in the U.S. as well as in Canada. Efforts to reduce the amount of sulphur emissions from coal burning power stations have resulted in a new supply of gypsum. One desirable by-product from the process of scrubbing sulphur that is sent up the power station chimneys is gypsum. The desulphurization process removes at least 90% of the sulphur dioxide while it produces gypsum that is 95% pure which makes it suitable for commerical use.[55]

Northern Indiana Public Service Company (NIPSCO), prompted by impending federal acid-rain legislation and U.S. Energy Department monetary contributions, is installing what could become the prototype scrubber for other urban-area electric generators in the 1990s. The NIPSCO scrubber is scheduled to open in mid-1992 and will produce 150,000 tons of gypsum annually—enough gypsum for 150 million square feet of wallboard which is enough for 18,750 single family homes. USG is negotiating to purchase NIPSCO's gypsum, a move that could save USG the 900 mile rail transportation costs from their nearest gypsum mine, in addition to mining costs.[56]

The scrubber, however, may have a limited application. First, gypsum is abundant in most parts of the U.S. which is reflected in the dirt-cheap price of $2.00 a ton. Second, gypsum is a heavy mineral and transportation is the most expensive component of the cost in the gypsum wallboard industry. Thus, potential power plants that could economically use scrubbers need to be near large metropolitan areas that use large quantities of wallboard. Currently, only three of five electric generators that produce gypsum can sell their output. The other two either produce inferior quality gypsum or cannot find buyers. The U.S. Environmental Protection Agency has identified 115 power plants that will fail to comply with recent federal acid rain legislation. Some utilities will likely switch to low-sulphur coal and others will shut down. Experts predict that an average of ten new scrubbers a year will open either on existing plants or will be incorporated into new plants in the 1990s.[57]

European efforts to curtail acid rain are ahead of the U.S. The Central Electricity Generating Board (CEGB) in Britain has one desulphurization plant that produces 1.1 million tons of gypsum annually. BPB Industries controls 96% of the British gypsum market and mines 3 million tons of gypsum a year. If the CEGB includes similar plants at other power stations, it will have the capacity to produce as much gypsum as BPB mines annually. In West Germany, the power stations produce so much gypsum that they pay plaster board manufacturers to take the gypsum off their hands.[58]

USG has recently developed a new wallboard product called fiber gypsum board. Fiber gypsum board does not need the two sheets of paper liner used on typical gypsum board which represent about 30% of the cost of making wallboard. Instead it uses wood fiber within the board which should give the board greater strength, better soundproofing, and enhanced fire-retardant properties than typical wallboard. Also, the new technology reduces evergy costs per unit of production.[59] The new technology should give USG a significant cost advantage over its next largest competitor, National Gypsum.

SUMMARY

Up until 1987, USG was one of the most profitable and respected corporations in the U.S. In that year, however, the company's "good times" came to an end when one of its shareholders, Desert Partners, Ltd., purchased 9.8% of its common stock and made an offer to acquire the company through a leveraged buy-out.

USG's top management and the board of directors rejected the offer and began exploring ways to thwart the hostile buy-out. As a result, the company developed a recapitalization plan in 1988 which offered each shareholder $49 per share compared to $42 per share from Desert Partners. This strategy caused USG to take on $2.6 billion in debt.

USG sought to finance the debt by divesting some of its divisions, selling assets, and laying off salaried employees. The company also based its recapitalization plan on a continued growth in the economy and a steady increase in residential and non-residential construction. USG's forecast of the future did not pan out, however. Instead of the hoped-for growth, the economy began to sink into a severe recession, causing its common stock to fall to less than $2 per share. The company is now hemorrhaging red ink and unless something is done to assuage the creditors USG could very well file for bankruptcy.

APPENDIX A	*USG Corporation's Consolidated Balance Sheet, as of December 31*

(All dollar amounts in millions)

	1990
ASSETS	
Current Assets:	
Cash and cash equivalents (primarily time deposits)	$ 175
Receivables (net of reserves, 1990—$8; 1989—$11)	282
Inventories	103
Net assets of discontinued operations	137
Total current assets	697
Property, Plant and Equipment, Net	825
Purchased Goodwill, Net	75
Other Assets	78
Total assets	1,675
LIABILITIES AND STOCKHOLDERS' EQUITY	
Current Liabilities:	
Accounts payable	104
Commercial paper and notes payable	—
Accrued expenses	
Interest	60
Payrolls	12
Taxes other than taxes on income	12
Recapitalization and restructuring	18
Reserve for DAP Inc. planned divestiture	43
Other	113
Notes payable	156
Long-term debt maturing within one year	268
Long-term debt and debentures classified as current	2,104
Taxes on income	5
Dividends payable	—
Total current liabilities	2,895
Long-Term Debt	72
Deferred Income Taxes	213
Minority Interest in subsidiaries	13
Stockholders' Equity/(Deficit):	
Preferred Stock—$1 par value; authorized 36,000,000-shares	
$1.80 Convertible Preferred Stock (initial series)—outstanding at December 31, 1990	
Common Stock—$0.10 par value: authorized 300,000,000-shares; outstanding at December 31, 1990—55,097,676-shares	5
Capital received in excess of par value	23
Deferred currency translation	(3)
Reinvested earnings/(deficit)	(1,546)
Total stockholders' equity/(deficit)	(1,518)
Total liabilities and stockholders' equity	1,675

Source: United States Gypsum Corporation, *1990 Annual Report,* p. 18.

APPENDIX B	*USG Corporation's Consolidated Balance Sheet, as of December 31* (All dollar amounts in millions)

	1989
ASSETS	
Current Assets:	
Cash and cash equivalents (primarily time deposits)	$ 67
Receivables (net of reserves, 1990—$8; 1989—$11)	275
Inventories	109
Net assets of discontinued operations	139
Total current assets	590
Property, Plant and Equipment, Net	837
Purchased Goodwill, Net	75
Other Assets	81
Total assets	1,585
LIABILITIES AND STOCKHOLDERS' EQUITY	
Current Liabilities:	
Accounts payable	123
Commercial paper and notes payable	—
Accrued expenses	
Interest	70
Payrolls	21
Taxes other than taxes on income	14
Recapitalization and restructuring	12
Reserve for DAP Inc. planned divestiture	—
Other	121
Notes payable	1
Long-term debt maturing within one year	168
Long-term debt and debentures classified as current	—
Taxes on income	9
Total current liabilities	539
Long-Term Debt	2,259
Deferred Income Taxes	211
Minority Interest in subsidiaries	14
Stockholders' Equity/(Deficit):	
Preferred Stock—$1 par value; authorized 36,000,000-shares $1.80 Convertible Preferred Stock (initial series)—outstanding at December 31, 1989—none	—
Common Stock—$0.10 par value: authorized 300,000,000-shares; outstanding at December 31, 1989—54,155,686-shares (after deducting 422,043 and 102,467 shares respectively, held in treasury)	5
Capital received in excess of par value	15
Deferred currency translation	(3)
Reinvested earnings/(deficit)	(1,455)
Total stockholders' equity/(deficit)	(1,438)
Total liabilities and stockholders' equity	1,585

SOURCE: United States Gypsum Corporation, *1990 Annual Report*, p. 18.

APPENDIX C	**USG Corporation's Consolidated Balance Sheet, as of December 31**

(All dollar amounts in thousands except per-share figures)

	1988

ASSETS

Current Assets:

Cash and cash equivalents (primarily time deposits)	$ 250,045
Receivables (net of reserves, 1990—$8; 1989—$11)	278,288
Inventories	124,608
Net assets of discontinued operations	20,412
Total current assets	673,353
Property, Plant and Equipment, Net	906,382
Purchased Goodwill, Net	146,469
Other Assets	94,974
Total assets	1,821,178

LIABILITIES AND STOCKHOLDERS' EQUITY

Current Liabilities:

Accounts payables	125,411
Commercial paper and notes payable	1,308
Accrued expenses	
Interest	72,672
Payrolls	25,879
Taxes other than taxes on income	16,140
Recapitalization and restructuring	30,112
Other	112,089
Long-term debt maturing within one year	259,314
Taxes on income	23,027
Dividends payable	15,657
Total current liabilities	681,609
Long-Term Debt	2,384,326
Deferred Income Taxes	206,200
Minority Interest in subsidiaries	19,988

Stockholders' Equity/(Deficit):

Preferred Stock—$1 par value; authorized 36,000,000-shares $1.80 Convertible Preferred Stock (initial series) outstanding at December 31, 1988	—
Common Stock—$0.10 par value: authorized 300,000,000-shares; outstanding at December 31, 1988 (after deducting 11,810 shares held in treasury)	5,397
Capital received in excess of par value	12,183
Deferred currency translation	(5,830)
Reinvested earnings/(deficit)	(1,482,695)
Total stockholders' equity/(deficit)	(1,470,945)
Total liabilities and stockholders' equity	1,821,178

SOURCE: United States Gypsum Corporation, *1988 Annual Report,* p. 20.

APPENDIX D   *USG Corporation's Consolidated Balance Sheet, as of December 31*

(All dollar amounts in thousands except per-share figures)

	1987
ASSETS	
Current Assets:	
Cash and cash equivalents (primarily time deposits)	$ 31,309
Receivables (net of reserves, 1990—$8; 1989—$11)	274,051
Inventories	144,107
Net assets of discontinued operations	415,100
Total current assets	864,567
Property, Plant and Equipment, Net	909,078
Purchased Goodwill, Net	148,896
Other Assets	34,980
Total Assets	1,957,521
LIABILITIES AND STOCKHOLDERS' EQUITY	
Current Liabilities:	
Accounts payables	141,553
Commercial paper and notes payable	38,830
Accrued expenses	
Interest	12,550
Payrolls	25,509
Taxes other than taxes on income	18,429
Recapitalization and restructuring	47,681
Reserve for DAP Inc. and planned divestiture	—
Other	84,008
Long-term debt maturing within one year	32,043
Taxes on income	14,761
Dividends payable	—
Total current liabilities	416,604
Long-Term Debt	724,938
Deferred Income Taxes	193,600
Minority Interest in subsidiaries	12,786
Stockholders' Equity/(Deficit):	
Preferred Stock—$1 par value; authorized 36,000,000-shares $1.80 Convertible Preferred Stock (initial-series) outstanding at December 31, 1987	68
Common Stock—$0.10 par value; authorized 300,000,000-shares; outstanding at December 31, 1987—51,632,623 shares (after deducting 15,993,754 shares held in treasury)	206,530
Capital received in excess of par value	5,410
Deferred currency translation	(9,077)
Reinvested earnings/(deficit)	406,908
Total stockholders' equity/(deficit)	609,833
Total liabilities and stockholders' equity	1,957,521

SOURCE: United States Gypsum Corporation, *1988 Annual Report,* p. 20.

Endnotes

1. United States Gypsum Corporation, *1989 Annual Report,* p. 10.

2. Stuart J. Benway, "Building Materials, " *Value Line Survey,* (New York, N.Y., 1990), Vol. 45, Part 3, p. 877.

3. *Ibid.*

4. United States Gypsum Corporation, *1989 10-K Report,* p. 5.

5. "11 Million Net Loss Prompts USG Layoffs," *Chicago Tribune,* October 24, 1990, Section 3, p. 1.

6. "Chicago's Office Glut Could Outlast Decade," *Crain's Chicago Business,* October 26, 1990, p. 56.

7. "Products and Processes," *USG Corporation Training Manual,* (Chicago, IL.: USG Corporation, 1990), pp. 5–9.

8. *Ibid.,* p. 8.

9. *Ibid,* p. 5.

10. *Ibid.*

11. *Ibid.,* p. 7.

12. "Wall to Wall," *Forbes,* July 2, 1984, p. 45.

13. *Moody's Industrial Manual, 1990,* pp. 6400–6401.

14. *Standard and Poor's Register of Corporate Directors* (New York: Standard and Poors, 1990), p. 286, and USG Corporation, *Biography of Eugene B. Connolly,* June 1991.

15. United States Gypsum Corporation, *1990 Annual Report,* p. 7.

16. *Ibid.,* p. 9.

17. *1990 USG Annual Report, op. cit.,* p. 5.

18. *Chicago Tribune, op. cit.*

19. *1989 USG Annual Report,, op. cit.,* p. 4.

20. *Ibid.*

21. "A Vote for Readers," *Financial World,* December 27, 1988, pp. 10–11.

22. "National Gypsum and Parent Seek Chapter 11 Status," *The Wall Street Journal,* October 30, 1990, p. B8.

23. *1990 USG Annual Report, op. cit.,* p. 7.

24. *1989 USG 10-K Report, op. cit.,* pp. 5 and 8.

25. *Ibid.,* p. 8.

26. *1989 USG Annual Report, op. cit.,* p. 2.

27. "Lending an Ear to Employee Relations," *Chicago Tribune,* June 29, 1989, Section 3, p. 4.

28. "Hup 2–3–4! No Smoking," *Industry Week,* February 9, 1987, pp. 24–25.

29. *Moody's Industrial Manual, op. cit.,* p. 5.

30. David Greising, "USG's Remodeling May Mean Gutting the House," *Business Week,* January 21, 1991, pp. 54–55.

31. *1989 USG 10-K Report, op. cit.,* p. 5.

32. Stuart J. Benway, *op. cit.*

33. *Ibid.*

34. *1989 USG 10-K Report, op. cit.,* p. 5.

35. "Midwest Bucks Housing Slide," *Chicago Tribune,* October 18, 1990, Section 3, pp. 1 and 5.

36. Stuart J. Benway, *op. cit.,* p. 851

37. *Moody's Industrial Manual, 1990,* p. 314.

38. *1988 USG 10-K Report,* pp. 2–5.

39. *Ibid.*

40. *Moody's Industrial Manual, 1990, op. cit.,* p. 314.

41. National Gypsum Co., *1988 10-K Report,* p. 4.

42. *Ibid.*

43. *Ibid.*

44. Domtar, *1989 10-K Report,* p. 4.

45. *Ibid.,* p. 16.

46. Jim Walter Corporation, *1987 10-K Report*, p. 2.

47. *Ibid.*, p. 7.

48. *1989 USG Annual Report, op. cit.*, p. 30.

49. *1988 USG 10-K Report, op. cit.*, p. 30.

50. *Construction Review,* July/August 1990, p. 9.

51. "What's Pulling the Rug Out from Under Housing," *Business Week,* January 23, 1989, p. 104–105.

52. *Ibid.*

53. Stuart J. Benway, *op. cit.*, p. 877.

54. "Gypsum also in the Doldrums," *Industry Surveys-Building and Forest Products,* December 14, 1989, p. B87.

55. *Ibid.*

56. "Utility to Generate Walls as Well as Watts," *Chicago Tribune,* April 22, 1990, Section 7, pp. 1–2.

57. *Ibid.*

58. *Ibid.*

59. "Gypsum: Acid Cloud, Silver Lining," *Economist,* October 15, 1988, pp. 73–74.

CASE PART V

Strategy Formulation in Service Organizations

CASE

1

Mesa Airlines, Inc.

ROY A. COOK *and* JEREMY J. COLEMAN, *Fort Lewis College*

INTRODUCTION

Mesa Airlines is a regional carrier, headquartered in Farmington, N.M., providing local passenger service to the Rocky Mountain, Southwest, and Midwest regions of the U.S. Regularly scheduled flights feed passengers into the company's primary hubs of Denver, Albuquerque, Phoenix, and Milwaukee. Exhibit 1 shows the system route maps of the cities and towns served by Mesa Airlines and its subsidiaries from their respective hub cities. The company's routes to and from these hubs are served on scheduled flights under three separate names: Mesa Airlines, United Express, and Skyway Airlines.

Founder, President, and CEO Larry L. Risley has shepherded Mesa's meteoric growth from one aircraft serving two cities to a fleet of 42 aircraft serving 61 cities in the ten years between 1980 and 1990. In fact, during the past five years, Mesa's revenues have grown at an average annual rate of over 46%, with growth in net earnings equaling or exceeding these increases. Mesa's growth has been fueled by a dual strategy consisting of internal expansions and acquisitions. "Mesa operates as a low cost, low fare, high frequency carrier offering one-class seating, advanced ticketing, and courtesy baggage handling, with emphasis on customer service."[1] These growth figures are especially impressive when compared to those of both major and many regional carriers who have at best experienced only single digit growth percentages.[2,3]

BACKGROUND

According to Larry L. Risley, President and Chief Executive Officer, "Mesa Airlines is absolutely a product of a deregulated environment."[4] Although the concept for regional airlines such as Mesa was originated in 1967 with inaugural short-haul flights and smaller craft by US Air, it was not until the Airline

This case was prepared by Professors Roy A. Cook and Jeremy J. Coleman of Fort Lewis College, and is intended to be used as a basis for class discussion rather than to illustrate either effective or ineffective handling of the situation.

This case was presented at the 1991 Midwest Society for Case Research Workshop and appears in *Annual Advances in Business Cases, 1991,* edited by Robert E. Meadows.

EXHIBIT 1   Mesa Airlines, Inc., Route Systems

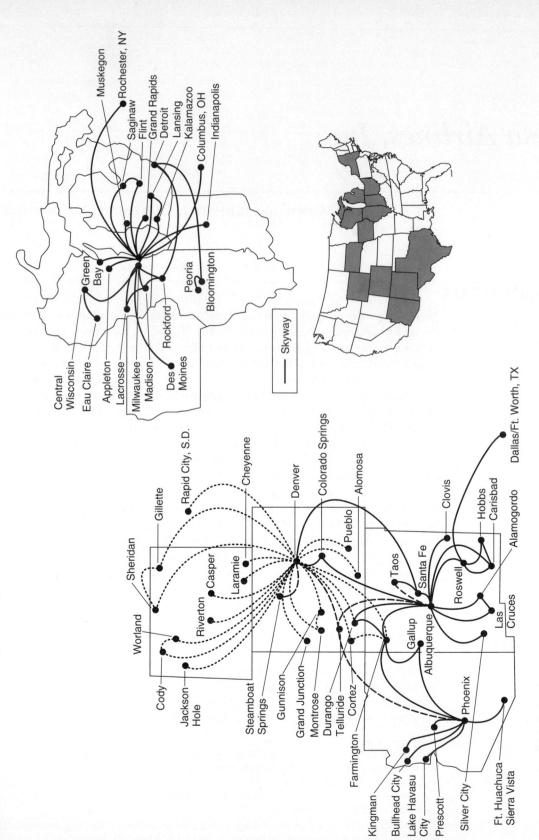

Deregulation Act of 1978 that the commuter airline industry began to flourish. "Regional carriers' revenue passenger miles grew to 7.61 billion in 1990 from 2.09 billion in 1981. But even so, the entire regional industry represents just 2% of the total 457.9 billion scheduled passenger miles flown by U.S. airlines in 1990."[5]

The Airline Deregulation Act of 1978 was designed to create a competitive environment where market forces could freely operate to provide an efficient and effective air transportation system. Through this Act, air routes were openly available to all providers and new carriers were encouraged to provide a variety of low-priced services and schedules. "Deregulation was supposed to open the door to new airlines. But faced with huge fixed costs and cyclical demands, most startups were overwhelmed by the established carriers."[6] The Act specifically resulted in the following changes:

1. Prior to 1978, air carriers had little, if any, pricing freedom. The simple fare structure was based on a three-tier pricing structure: economy, coach, and first class. Since deregulation, the fare structure has become incredibly complex with literally thousands of published fares.
2. Prior to 1978, airlines planning to begin services to one or more new cities had to apply to the Civil Aeronautics Board (CAB) for approval. In the current environment, there is little to prevent a carrier from entering a new market other than the capacity of the airport in that market to handle safely the increased traffic.
3. Prior to deregulation, airlines wishing to discontinue service to a city had to apply for and obtain formal approval from the CAB, ninety days in advance. The CAB, in turn, could require the airline to continue service until an alternate carrier was found for that city.
4. As part of the deregulation of the airline industry, the Essential Air Service Program designed to provide guaranteed levels of service to specified cities was placed under the administration of the U.S. Department of Transportation (DOT). Under this program, the DOT may authorize subsidies to compensate designated carriers for providing service to unprofitable markets.

Competition has intensified and resulted in industry consolidation as operators have adjusted to the realities of a deregulated environment. In fact, the number of regional carriers has decreased from a record 246 in 1981 to only 150 by the end of 1990.[7]

In the wake of deregulation, the air transportation system in the United States has been developed around the hub and spoke concept with major carriers dominating key hub cities and the regional airlines feeding into these hubs. The hub and spoke system allows passengers to fly with the same airline from point of origin to destination. As the hub system has evolved, the major carriers have structured their scheduling so that regional airlines can feed passengers into hub cities under a code-sharing system. Code-sharing agreements with dominant carriers in key hub cities are so important that "the success or failure of any regional carrier . . . is tied to the performance of the major carrier to which it is aligned."[8]

Most carriers have established affiliations with regional airlines to provide air service between the major carriers' hubs and medium-sized and smaller communities. These affiliations benefit both the major carriers by enabling them to market air service from their hubs to medium-sized and smaller cities, some of which cannot support large jet air service, and the regional airlines by enabling them to publish their flights under the major carriers' two-letter designator codes in computer reservations systems. These arrangements provide the airline with a competitive advantage in booking passengers who make connections at hub airports served by the affiliated major carrier.[9]

Code-sharing allows a passenger to purchase through one airline a single ticket for all segments of one's flight. The regional airlines not only share common reservation systems but also company logos and other identifying service marks of their code-sharing major airline partners such as US Air, United, Continental, TWA, and American. Although Mesa Airlines has encountered some marketing turbulence in this deregulated environment, it has been able to overcome these rough spots by capitalizing on new opportunities.

HISTORY

In 1979, when Larry and Janie Risley moved to Farmington, New Mexico, to begin running a fixed base operation (FBO), starting scheduled airline service was not a part of their long-range plans. Fixed base operators serve such needs of private aircraft owners and renters as refueling, tiedown and hanger services. In addition, they also provide flight instruction and charter services. Due to the early lack of success in this business, the Risleys began to search for additional ways to generate revenues and utilize their aircraft.

Based on suggestions from friends, in October 1980 Risley began his "scheduled operation" using a single-engine Piper Saratoga. This was a four-times-a-day, fair-weather shuttle between Farmington, a city of 25,000 in northwestern New Mexico, and Albuquerque, 200 miles to the southeast. According to Risley, "In those early days, if the weather got bad, I didn't fly and I don't know what the passengers did because I didn't ask them."[10] Thus, as a part of a fixed base operation, the Mesa Air Shuttle was born. Although Risley served as president of the company, he had no ownership position at this time. He was merely operating the company for his brother-in-law, whose primary interests were in the oil and gas business.[11]

August of 1982 marked a milestone in the history of the present company. At that time, fixed base operations were eliminated and the primary business of Mesa became passenger service. In addition, the original partners who had financed the fixed base operations decided that the financial returns for the passenger service business were too marginal for the risk involved. Faced with a loss of his financial backing, Risley was forced to search for sufficient capital to continue operations. He found it by mortgaging the Risley home and car. This mortgage provided enough capital to purchase the aircraft and the right to use the name Mesa Air Shuttle.[12]

During the first year of operation under Risley's control, Mesa Air Shuttle carried 10,000 passengers between Farmington and Albuquerque. In comparison, just nine years later, Mesa was serving 61 cities and was carrying approximately 650,000 passengers per year. Operations expanded rapidly due to the origination in April 1989 of the Milwaukee, Wisconsin-based Skyway operations and the code-sharing agreement reached with United Airlines in April 1990 to operate United Express into Denver. These two additions to Mesa's operating system doubled the number of passengers carried. As a consequence of its success, Mesa Airlines has quadrupled in size over the past five years and it had successfully driven its largest competitor, Air Midwest, out of the New Mexico market.[13,14]

Mesa's growth has not been without mistakes. One of the more turbulent periods in its growth occurred in 1987. During 1987, Mesa purchased the routes of Centennial Airline, a regional carrier serving Riverton, WY. This was the first time Mesa had operated in a competitive environment containing code-sharing carriers. Mesa, operating as an independent carrier, found itself to be non-competitive with its code-sharing rival, Continental Express. Mesa was unable to generate sufficient volume to achieve profitability on the newly acquired Centennial routes. Since 85% of all reservations are made on the first screen of computerized reservations systems, and as an independent, its flights were listed on the third screen of the system, Mesa found itself at a competitive disadvantage. Even though Mesa offered better fares and connections than its on-line rival, the traveling public was unaware of these services due to the peculiarities of airline reservation systems. "That's where we learned not to compete with a code-sharing carrier unless you have the same power to deal with him."[15]

In all, 1987 proved to be an eventful year for Mesa Airlines. In addition to the ill-fated acquisition of the Centennial Airline routes, Mesa also went public and changed its name from Mesa Air Shuttle to Mesa Airlines, Inc. The year 1989 proved to be another action packed period with Mesa fighting off a takeover attempt by States West Airlines and launching an initial attempt to acquire Wichita, Kansas-based Air Midwest.[16] The attempted acquisition of Air Midwest was aborted when an amicable solution to the details of the takeover agreement could not be reached. This is in keeping with Risley's stated policy of avoiding engaging in hostile takeovers.

MARKETING

When Mesa Air Shuttle began serving the Farmington and Albuquerque markets, it was in direct competition with four other commuter airlines serving the market with a total of twenty-three flights a day. The initially intense competition among these carriers resulted in fares dropping to as low as $25 one-way. In the face of this competition, the fare on Mesa flights was lowered to $24. By comparison, a comparable fare today is quoted at $69.00 one-way. According to Risley, "That's where I found I had a competitive edge over the competition and that I had a business that just happened to be an airline."[17]

By focusing on a strategy of developing a low-cost business rather than an airline which is typically a high-cost operation, Mesa was able to offer these $24 fares on a profitable basis. Mesa's low-cost strategy consisting of low fares/high volume, cross-utilization of employees, high frequency of service, and sizing aircraft to the market allowed it to survive in a very competitive market place serving many small, widely dispersed cities. Shortly after these fare wars began, competitors began to raise their prices, while Mesa retained its lower prices, thus allowing it to increase its market share and eventually drive all of its competitors out of the Farmington-Albuquerque market.[18] Mesa's low-cost strategy has allowed it to attain the lowest cost structure of any publicly-held commuter airlines in the U.S.

These early battles for survival and market share have helped shape Mesa's competitive posture. "Where Mesa faces competition, it will compete aggressively by lowering fares, increasing frequency, and scheduling competitive aircraft for flights that occur at the same time as those of the competitors."[19]

Although Mesa has proven its ability to compete successfully in crowded markets, it also has a stated strategy "to provide service between medium-sized and small cities that do not have other scheduled airline service or where the Company believes other service [is] insufficient."[20]

The operating strategy used by Mesa as it enters new markets is to first test these markets by inaugurating scheduled service with smaller aircraft. Then, based on the level of demand, larger aircraft and/or more frequent service may be added on these new routes. At the same time, if demand decreases or does not materialize, a similar reverse strategy is utilized, thus conserving resources.

Although Mesa's preference is to operate as an independent carrier under its YV (Yankee Victor) code in the computer reservation system, it realizes the importance to a regional carrier of name recognition in primary hub cities afforded by code-share arrangements. Through code-share agreements, regional carriers are listed in the computer reservation systems under the primary carrier's code. Mesa was initially precluded from entering code-share agreements with any of the major carriers in its geographic service areas because these major carriers already had existing contracts with feeder airline partners.

In 1989, an opportunity presented itself to purchase the routes of Aspen Airways, a United Express code-share carrier in the Denver market. Mesa entered into the purchase agreement for Aspen's routes realizing that UA was not obligated to extend the use of its computer reservation code to Mesa. To convince UA to code-share, Mesa first had to demonstrate how it could improve UA's Denver market share. Mesa was able to accomplish this task by providing a consistent and dependable level of service and by acquiring four 30-passenger Brasilia aircraft from Air Midwest to serve this market. Based on its demonstrated levels of performance, Mesa was able to eventually enter into a 5-year code-share agreement with UA to serve as a feeder into its Denver hub.[21]

Mesa, like most other scheduled airlines, depends heavily on an effective hub and spoke system, reservations generated through travel agencies, and the steady repeat patronage of business travelers. Much of Mesa's marketing success can be attributed to focusing on these three key areas. Management has estimated that approximately 60% of its passengers make interline connections in Albuquerque, Denver, or Phoenix, 55% of its business is generated through travel agencies, and 80% of its passengers are business travelers.[22,23]

OPERATIONS

According to Risley, "Mesa Airlines only hires people; [it] doesn't hire pilots, ticket agents, [or] presidents. While [an employee's] primary job might be to fly an airplane or work on an airplane, they are there to perform whatever service is needed to accommodate the passenger."[24] Based on this concept, Mesa has been able to gain a competitive advantage because its employees can be cross-utilized in all operational positions. "Cross-utilization of employees, a tradition dating back to the days when Larry and Janie did everything, helps keep costs down."[25]

Management of Mesa Airlines can be typified as being hands-on. In fact, Risley himself is a qualified mechanic and still serves as maintenance director. The hierarchial management layers between the president/CEO and operating ground crews are limited. Decision-making is centralized at the top level of the company with very limited latitude in decision-making at the lower levels of the organization.

Even in the face of its rapid expansion, Mesa has retained a very lean management staff which is beginning to show the strains of its explosive growth. According to Risley, "We don't have the depth of experience we need. We doubled our fleet and our pilots and maintenance staff, but the management and administrative staff increased by only 13%."[26] Jonathan Ornstein, Mesa's Vice President, Planning and Scheduling, echoes this sentiment by noting that "[w]e're all entrepreneurial and everyone in management hates to give up any responsibilities."[27]

Mesa Airlines prides itself on its relationships with aircraft manufacturers and its ability to perform its own maintenance work. During 1989, the level of training of its mechanics was enhanced and additional equipment expenditures were made so that maintenance service on its fleet could be retained in-house. In-house maintenance combined with a limited variety of aircraft in its fleet has also contributed to the company's ability to achieve its low cost strategy. The configuration of Mesa's current fleet which is the most modern in the industry can be seen in Table 1.

The driving force behind Mesa's spectacular growth is 46-year old President, Chief Executive Officer, and Chairman of the Board of Directors Larry L. Risley. Prior to the incorporation of the company in 1983, Risley served as President of Mesa Aviation Services Incorporated, the predecessor fixed base operator of the present company. Risley and his wife Janie, who serves as Executive Vice President and also sits on the Board of Directors, together control over 27% of Mesa's outstanding common stock.

FINANCE

The need for additional capital to fuel its rapid growth caused Mesa to enter the public financial markets in 1987. Prior to this time, growth had been fueled through internally generated and privately borrowed funds. The strong demand for initial public offerings during 1987 prompted Mesa to tap this funding source. According to Risley, going public encompassed the good, the bad, and the ugly. "The good side is [that we] got a lot of money. The bad side is [that you] hang all your laundry out for everybody to look at and the competition knows exactly the condition of the airline. The ugly [is that you] have

TABLE 1

Mesa Airlines, Inc. Flight Equipment* (As of August 1990)

Type of Aircraft	Passenger Capacity	Number in Fleet
Beechcraft 1900	19	19#
Beechcraft 1300	13	10
Cessna Caravan	9	2
Embraer Brasilia	30	2

*Approximate average age of fleet less than two years
#Represents oldest aircraft in fleet, ranging from 1 to 5 years

---

EXHIBIT 2

Mesa Airlines, Inc. Consolidated Balance Sheets (000 omitted)

Fiscal Year Ending	9/30/90	9/30/89	9/30/88
ASSETS			
Current Assets:			
Cash & Mkt. Sec.	$ 4,143	$ 4,606	$ 2,361
Receivables	5,487	2,186	1,556
Inventories	1,123	923	573
Other Current Assets	398	253	156
Total Current Assets	$11,151	$ 7,967	$ 4,646
Fixed Assets:			
Property, Plant & Equipment	16,433	15,686	17,982
Other Assets	5,502	1,467	1,673
Total Assets	$33,086	$25,120	$24,301
LIABILITIES AND STOCKHOLDERS' EQUITY			
Accounts Payable	$ 1,789	$ 1,100	$ 784
Current Long-Term Debt	921	1,043	1,175
Accrued Expenses	1,333	362	326
Income Taxes	511	43	—
Other Current Liab	1,358	575	381
Total Current Liabilities	$ 5,912	$ 3,123	$ 2,666
Long-Term Debt	9,608	11,921	13,875
Deferred Charges	5,377	1,560	335
Total Liabilities	$20,897	$16,604	$16,876
Stockholders' Equity	12,189	8,516	7,425
Total Liabilities & Stockholders' Equity	$33,086	$25,120	$24,301

stockholders. [We now] have basically 400 owners of Mesa Airlines. About 396 of those are great people. The other four are a pain in the ass."[28]

Mesa once again tapped the financial markets in December 1990 completing a secondary public offering consisting of 862,500 shares of new common stock which sold at $7.25 per share, yielding $5,400,000. Consolidated Balance Sheets and Statements of Income for Mesa Airlines, Inc. are presented in Exhibits 2 and 3.

GROWTH THROUGH ACQUISITIONS

The Airline Deregulation Act has resulted in a free entry market and, according to Risley, "We're here to provide a level of service to those communities that can't justify [the type of] service that they feel they need. Mesa Airlines built its business on sizing aircraft to market. We're dedicated to providing

EXHIBIT 3

Mesa Airlines, Inc. Consolidated Statements of Income (000 omitted)

Fiscal Year Ending	9/30/90	9/30/89	9/30/88
Net Sales	$45,954	$22,508	$17,509
Cost of Goods	22,740	9,583	6,749
Gross Profit	$23,214	$12,924	$10,760
Sell Gen. & Adm. Exp.	15,435	7,887	6,366
Income from Operations	$ 7,779	$ 5,038	$ 4,394
Depr. & Amort.	1,854	3,138	2,421
Nonoperating Income	385	1,467	232
Interest Expense	1,119	1,690	1,564
Income before Taxes	$ 5,191	$ 1,677	$ 641
Income Taxes	2,018	636	238
Net Inc. before Extraordinary Items	$3,173	$1,041	$403
Extraordinary Items	455	-0-	-0-
Net Income	$3,628	$1,041	$403
Outstanding Shares	1,675,065	1,669,140	1,654,765

whatever service a community can prove it can support."[29] Regional air carriers have continued to grow at a faster pace than the major airlines by focusing on routes that average less than 200 miles in length; regionals posted a 12.4% increase in revenue passenger miles compared to a 5.7% increase in revenue passenger miles for the entire airline industry during 1990.[30] Mesa Airlines has been able to grow and prosper in an environment that has proven to be hostile to many startup airlines such as People Express, Air Florida, World Airways, Metro Airlines, and Midway Airlines.

As Larry Risley charts the future for Mesa Airlines, he seeks growth through acquisitions. In a renewed bid to execute this strategy, on January 24, 1991, Mesa once again attempted to expand its service areas by launching a friendly offer for Wichita, Kansas-based Air Midwest. The offer includes a package of cash and stock valued at approximately $27 million. This is the equivalent of $8 per share for all of Air Midwest's outstanding common stock.[31] At the time of the offer, the 52-week trading range for Air Midwest stock ranged from a low of $3 3/8 to a high of $6 1/4. On the date of the offer, Air Midwest stock closed at $6 per share.

The offering price of $8 a share for all outstanding Air Midwest common stock is structured to yield $1 per share in cash and between .63 and .82 shares of newly issued Mesa common stock. The exact distribution of common stock is to be based on the average closing bid/ask price of Air Midwest stock on the five trading days prior to the close of the transaction. If Air Midwest is trading at below $8 1/2, then .82 shares will be issued. On the other hand, if Air Midwest is trading at or above $11 1/8, then .63 shares will be issued. If the closing price falls between these two quotes, then the number of shares issued will be factored based on the actual closing price. The proposed Air Midwest acquisition provides Mesa with many opportunities and threats in an expanded market area.

BACKGROUND INFORMATION ON AIR MIDWEST

In May of 1990, Air Midwest celebrated its twenty-fifth anniversary of operations. As can be seen from the Consolidated Balance Sheets and Statements of Income presented in Exhibits 4 and 5, 1989 was a year of extreme turmoil resulting from the $1,200,000 loss in passenger revenue due to the bankruptcy of its code-share partner in the Kansas City market, Braniff Inc. In addition, "the company faced operating seven 30-passenger aircraft and thirteen 17-passenger aircraft in the Kansas City-based market where connecting traffic had disappeared."[32] Subsequently the company was able to downsize its fleet to the current configuration shown in Table 2. Regularly scheduled flights for Air Midwest feed passengers into its primary hubs of Kansas City and St. Louis, MO. Exhibit 6 shows the system route maps of the cities and towns served from these two hub cities.

EXHIBIT 4

Air Midwest, Inc. Consolidated Balance Sheets (000 omitted)

Fiscal Year Ending	12/31/89	12/31/88	12/31/87
ASSETS			
Current Assets:			
Cash & Mkt. Sec.	$ 2,101	$ 2,096	$ 2,642
Receivables	4,533	2,166	2,959
Inventories	7,194	8,228	6,698
Other Current Assets	478	684	515
Total Current Assets	$14,307	$13,174	$12,814
Net Property, Plant & Equipment	38,882	49,782	58,120
Other Assets	5,472	4,340	4,128
Total Assets	$58,661	$67,296	$75,062
LIABILITIES AND STOCKHOLDERS' EQUITY			
Current Liabilities:			
Payables	$9,912	$10,370	$10,783
LTD (Current)	1,021	2,184	2,453
Leases (Current)	2,557	3,228	2,841
Accrued Expenses	1,857	1,502	1,695
Income Taxes	-0-	-0-	-0-
Other Current Liab.	2,205	1,066	1,272
Total Current Liabilities	$17,552	$18,350	$19,046
Debt:			
LTD	5,814	10,368	12,552
Deferrals	1,502	506	210
Capital Leases & Other Liab.	18,646	20,614	24,434
Total Liab.	$43,514	$49,838	$56,242
Stockholders' Eq.	15,147	17,458	18,820
Total Liab. & Stockholders' Eq.	$58,661	$67,296	$75,062

EXHIBIT 5

Air Midwest, Inc. Consolidated Statements of Income (000 omitted)

Fiscal Year Ending	12/31/89	12/31/88	12/31/87
Net Sales	$81,100	$74,099	$83,314
Cost of Goods	51,031	62,997	69,225
Gross Profit	$30,069	$11,102	$14,089
Sell Gen. & Adm. Exp.	24,644	2,740	3,968
Income from Operations	$5,426	$8,362	$10,121
Depr. & Amort.	4,227	5,016	6,139
Non-operating Income	420	552	531
Interest Expense	4,012	5,281	5,731
Income before Taxes	$(2,393)	$(1,383)	$(1,218)
Income Taxes	-0-	-0-	-0-
Net Inc. before Extraordinary Items	$(2,393)	$(1,383)	$(1,218)
Extraordinary Items	-0-	-0-	-0-
Net Income	$(2,393)	$(1,383)	$(1,218)
Outstanding Shares	3,913,509	3,891,541	3,837,298

LOOKING INTO THE FUTURE

As Mesa enters 1991, many questions about its future growth and success remain to be answered. Can the rapid growth rate in sales and markets served be maintained? Will the acquisition strategy continue to be effective? What role will changes in aircraft technology play in the future of the company? How far should Mesa Airlines expand its operations outside of its current market areas? Can the company continue to maintain its low cost strategy in light of its anticipated growth? What changes, if any, will need to be made in the company's management structure and administrative policies and procedures? These and many more questions face management as decisions are made to prepare Mesa Airlines to face the turbulent 21st century.

TABLE 2

Air Midwest, Inc. Flight Equipment* (As of December 1989)

Type of Aircraft	Passenger Capacity	Number in Fleet
Fairchild Metro II	17	19#
Fairchild Metro II–A	17–19	2#
Jetstream Super 31	19	5
Saab-Fairchild 340	30	5
Embraer Brasilia	30	8

*Approximate average age of fleet greater than six years
#Represents oldest aircraft in fleet, averaging 10 or more years

EXHIBIT 6 Air Midwest, System Route Map, Effective February 1, 1990

air midwest

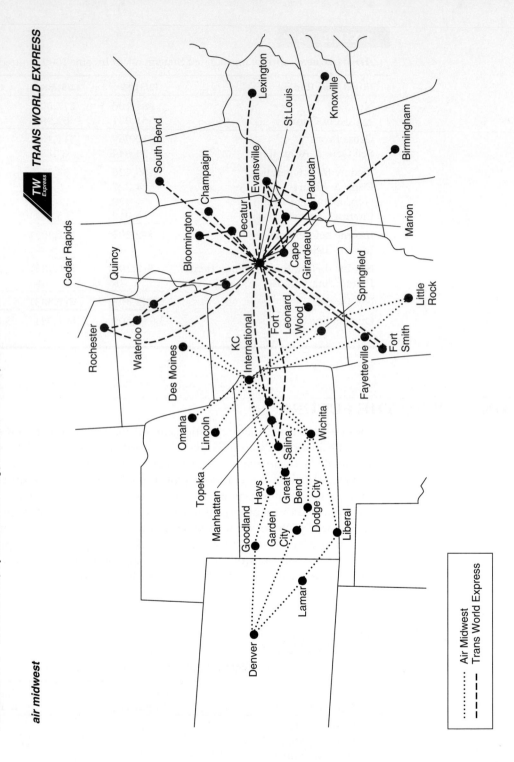

End Notes

1. Mesa Airlines, Inc. Form 10-K. 1989, p.2.

2. "Flying Fortresses." *The Economist,* 314, March 10, 1990, pp. 72–74.

3. Conlin, Joseph. "Puddle Jumpers." *Successful Meetings,* December 1990, pp. 89–95.

4. Presentation by Larry L. Risley, CEO, Mesa Airlines. (1990). Executive Speaker Series: Fort Lewis College, Durango, CO.

5. Kramer, Farrell. "Small Airlines Hit Turbulence But Stay Aloft." *Investor's Daily,* April 5, 1991, p. 34.

6. Schain, Eric; Maremont, Mark; and Ellis, James E. "Can These Startup Airlines Handle the Heavy Weather?" *Business Week,* October 1, 1990, pp. 122–123.

7. Kramer, 1991.

8. Kramer, 1991.

9. Air Midwest, Inc., Form 10-K, 1989, p.6.

10. Presentation by Larry L. Risley, CEO, Mesa Airlines, 1990.

11. Presentation by Larry L. Risley, CEO, Mesa Airlines, 1990.

12. Presentation by Larry L. Risley, CEO, Mesa Airlines, 1990.

13. Mesa Airline, Inc. 1990 Annual Report, p.5.

14. Henderson, Danna K. "Mesa Airlines Embraces Code Sharing." *Air Transport World,* 27, September 1990, pp. 178–185.

15. Presentation by Larry L. Risley, CEO, Mesa Airlines, 1990.

16. Henderson, 1990.

17. Presentation by Larry L. Risley, CEO, Mesa Airlines, 1990.

18. Presentation by Larry L. Risley, CEO, Mesa Airlines, 1990.

19. Mesa Airlines Inc., Form 10-K, 1989, p. 7.

20. Mesa Airlines Inc., Form 10-K, 1989, p. 7.

21. Presentation by Larry L. Risley, CEO, Mesa Airlines, 1990.

22. Presentation by Larry L. Risley, CEO, Mesa Airlines, 1990.

23. Mesa Airlines Inc., Form 10-K, 1989, p. 2.

24. Presentation by Larry L. Risley, CEO, Mesa Airlines, 1990.

25. Henderson, 1990, p. 180.

26. Henderson, 1990, p. 180.

27. Henderson, 1990, p. 180.

28. Presentation by Larry L. Risley, CEO, Mesa Airlines, 1990.

29. Presentation by Larry L. Risley, CEO, Mesa Airlines, 1990.

30. Kramer, 1991.

31. "Mesa Airlines Launches Offer for Air Midwest." *Denver Post,* January 25, 1991, p. C1.

32. *Annual Report,* Air Midwest, 1989, p. 1.

Circus Circus Enterprises, Inc. 1994

JOHN K. ROSS III, MIKE KEEFFE, and BILL MIDDLEBROOK,

Southwest Texas State University

The sun bears down as you travel across the desert searching for your destination. The heat causes the air to rise in waves towards the sky as you carefully examine the horizon for the first glimpse of the "PYRAMID." At last, above the sand dunes shimmering in the heat, you see the top of the fabled pyramid. Even at this distance you can tell it's bigger than anything you imagined. The closer you get to the desert oasis where the pyramid is located, the bigger it seems in this land of dreams. Finally you stand at the base of the pyramid, at the foot of the great sphinx, anxious to explore the huge complex before you. Then the sphinx flashes its eyes at you—and you enter. Flashes its eyes? Yes, for this is Las Vegas—and you have entered the land of Circus Circus Enterprises, Inc.

Although Circus Circus Enterprises, Inc. (hereafter Circus) describes itself as a merchant and compares its stores to supermarkets and shopping malls, its products are hardly those one finds on the typical store shelves. The merchandise of Circus is "entertainment" and the stores are huge pink and white striped concrete circus tents, a 600-foot-long riverboat replica, a giant castle and the latest addition—a great pyramid. Their areas of operation are the glitzy vacation and convention meccas of Las Vegas, Reno and Laughlin, Nevada, as well as other locations in the U.S. and abroad. Circus' marketing of its products has been called "right out of the bargain basement," and has catered to "low rollers," although Circus now aims more at the middle income gambler and family-oriented vacationers wanting more than a conventional gambling-oriented vacation.

Circus was purchased in 1974 for $50,000 as a small and unprofitable casino operation by partners William G. Bennett, an aggressive cost-cutter who ran furniture stores before entering the gaming industry in 1965, and William N. Pennington (see Figure 1 for Board of Directors and top managers). The partners were able to rejuvenate Circus back to profitability, went public with a stock offering in October 1983, and since that time have achieved an average growth rate in earnings per share of more than 21 percent per year. Today, Circus is the largest casino-hotel operator in both the

---

Dr. John K. Ross III, Dr. Mike Keeffe, and Dr. Bill Middlebrook are all of the Department of Management and Marketing at Southwest Texas State University.

FIGURE 1
Circus Circus Enter-
prises, Inc.—Directors

Name	Age	Title
William G. Bennett	69	Chairman of the Board and CEO Circus Circus Enterprises
William P. Pennington	71	Co-founder, Circus Circus Enterprises
Clyde T. Turner	56	Chief Executive Officer and President, Circus Circus Enterprises
Fred W. Smith	60	President and CEO, Donrey Media Group
James Cashman III	45	President, Cashman Equipment and VP, Cashman Cadillac, Inc.
Tony Coelho	51	Managing Director, Wertheim Schroder & Co., Inc.
Carl F. Dodge	78	Former Chairman, Nevada Gaming Commission, Retired
Arthur M. Smith, Jr.	72	Chairman of the Board, Retired, First Interstate Bank of Nevada
Kurt D. Sullivan	42	Executive Vice President and COO

Circus Circus Enterprises, Inc.—Top Management

William G. Bennett	Chairman of the Board
Clyde T. Turner	Chief Executive Officer and President
Kurt D. Sullivan	Executive Vice President and Chief Operating Officer
Daniel N. Copp	Chief Financial Officer and Executive Vice President
Terry L. Caudill	VP, Chief Accounting Officer & Treasurer
Mike Sloan VP	General Counsel & Secretary

SOURCE: Notice of Annual Meeting of Stockholders, May 2, 1994.

Las Vegas and Laughlin markets in terms of square footage of casino space and number of hotel rooms, despite the incredible growth in both markets. For instance, Laughlin has experienced over 100 percent growth in total hotel rooms, yet Circus continues to operate nearly 30 percent of that total. Casino gaming operations provide over one-half of total revenues for Circus (see Figure 2) and in 1994 they reported a net income of more than $130 million and employed more than 18,000 people.

CIRCUS CIRCUS OPERATIONS

Circus defines entertainment as pure play and fun, and it goes out of the way to see that customers have plenty of opportunity for both. Each of Circus' "stores" has a distinctive personality. Circus Circus–Las Vegas is the world of the Big Top, where live circus acts perform free every thirty minutes. Kids may cluster around video games while the adults migrate to nickel slot machines and dollar game tables. The latest addition to the original casino is the $90 million "Grand Slam Canyon Adventuredome," a five-acre glass enclosed theme park

FIGURE 2
Circus Circus
Enterprises, Inc.
—Sources of Revenue

Casinos	56.4%
Food & Beverage	16.0%
Hotel	18.4%
Other	12.3%

SOURCE: Circus Circus Annual Report, 1994.

including a four-loop roller coaster. Recent soft results at the Las Vegas property have induced management to include more rides, with the first phase completed by the summer of 1994 at a cost of approximately $10 million.

Luxor—the newest Circus property—opened on October 15, 1993, when 10,000 people entered to play the 2,517 slot and video poker games and 82 table games in the 100,000-square-foot casino in the hotel atrium (reported to be the world's largest). By the end of the opening weekend 40,000 people per day were visiting the 36 story bronze pyramid that encases the hotel and entertainment facilities.

Circus management is gambling that over 11 million visitors will tour the Luxor in the first year. In the Luxor you step back to the days of the pharaohs with a cruise on one of eleven barges down an 18,000 foot River Nile amid the obelisk and sphinx, see a show in the 1,100 seat dinner theater, dine in one of the seven restaurants, exercise in the state-of-the-art health spa, or play the slots. During the first three and one-half months of operations, the Luxor contributed $89.3 million to the company's revenues and $27.6 million to operating cash flow.

Circus operates nine properties in all (see Figure 3). At one end of the Vegas strip is Circus Circus–Las Vegas, a circus big-top which covers 795 hotel rooms, shopping areas, two restaurants, a buffet with seating for 1,100, fast-food specialty shops, cocktail lounges, video arcades, 110,000 square feet of casino, live circus acts and the Grand Slam Canyon. Guests who stay in the facility's other 1,998 rooms travel by elevated monorail from the adjacent Circus Skyrise and Circus Manor, or from the nearby Circusland RV Park.

Located next to the Luxor, Excalibur is one of the first sights travelers see as they exit interstate highway fifteen. (Management was confident that the sight of a giant, colorful medieval castle would make a lasting impression on mainstream tourists and vacationing families arriving in Las Vegas.) Guests cross a drawbridge, with moat, onto a cobblestone walkway where multicolored spires, turrets and battlements loom above. The castle walls are four 28-story hotel towers containing a total of 4,032 rooms. Inside is a medieval world complete with a Fantasy Faire inhabited by strolling jugglers, fire eaters and acrobats, as well as a Royal Village complete with peasants, serfs, and ladies-in-waiting around medieval theme shops. The 100,000-square-foot casino encompasses 2,600 slot machines, more than 100 game tables, a sports book, and a poker and keno area. There are twelve restaurants, capable of feeding more than 20,000 people daily, and a 900-seat amphitheater. Excalibur, which opened in June 1990, was built for $294 million, primarily financed with internally generated funds and contributed 30 percent of the organization's revenues in the year ending January 31, 1994, down from 33 percent in 1993.

FIGURE 3
Circus Circus
Enterprises, Inc.

Properties	Percent Revenues		
	1994	93	92
Circus Circus–Las Vegas	36%	39%	40%
Circus Circus–Reno			
Excalibur	30%	33%	33%
Luxor	9%	na	na
The Colorado Belle	21%	23%	23%
The Edgewater			

Situated between the two anchors on the Las Vegas strip are two smaller casinos which are also operated by Circus. The Silver City Casino and Slots-A-Fun primarily depend on the foot traffic along the strip for their gambling patrons.

All of Circus' operations do well in the city of Las Vegas. However, Circus' 1993 and 1994 operational earnings have remained relatively flat, reflecting the general economic turndown. Circus' hotel room occupancy rates in Las Vegas are typically 98 to 100 percent, due, in part, to low room rates ($30 to $50 at Circus Circus–Las Vegas) and popular buffets. Seating over 3,000, the restaurants at Excalibur alone are able to offer the most meals per day of any single site commercial establishment in the world. Although Circus loses fifty cents on each meal it serves, the popular buffets generate enough cash flow each year to cover debt obligations nearly six times.

The company's other big top facility is Circus Circus–Reno. With the addition of Skyway Tower in 1985, this big top now offers a total of 1,625 hotel rooms, 60,600-square-feet of casino, a buffet which can seat 700 people, shops, video arcades, cocktail lounges, midway games and circus acts. As a project, Circus Circus–Reno had several marginal years, but has become one of the leaders in that market.

The Colorado Belle and The Edgewater Hotel are located in Laughlin, Nevada, a city 90 miles south of Las Vegas on the banks of the Colorado River. The Colorado Belle, opened in 1987, features a huge paddle wheel river boat replica, buffet, cocktail lounges and shops. The Edgewater, acquired in 1983, has a southwestern motif, a 57,000-square-foot casino, a bowling center, buffet and cocktail lounges. Combined, these two properties contain 2,700 rooms and over 120,000-square-feet of casino. Together these two operations contributed 21 percent of the company's revenues in the year ended January 31, 1994.

Circus has achieved success through an aggressive growth strategy and a corporate structure designed to enhance that growth (see Figure 4). Since 1984, Circus has increased its available hotel rooms from approximately 2,500 to more than 13,000. Casino space has increased from 165,000 square feet to more than 536,000 square feet during the same period. A strong cash position, innovative ideas, and attention to cost control has allowed Circus to satisfy the bottom line during a period when competitors were typically taking on large debt obligations to finance new projects (see Tables 1, 2, 3, and 4). Yet the market is changing.

New Ventures

Gambling, of all kinds, has spread across the country; no longer does the average individual need to go to Las Vegas or New Jersey. Instead, gambling can be found as close as the local quick market (lottery), bingo hall, many Indian reservations, the Mississippi river and others. In order to maintain a competitive edge, Circus has recently announced several projects that will take it beyond the bounds of Nevada.

Circus has decided to join the Mississippi gambling development by creating a riverboat casino site less than 20 miles from Memphis. Circus will own and operate one of three dockside casinos at the site and should open in late summer 1994 at an estimated cost of $80 million. In May 1994, Circus was granted a license to operate a riverboat casino in Chalmette, Louisiana, just fifteen minutes from downtown New Orleans. This is a 50 percent partnership with American Entertainment Corporation to build a 30,000-square-foot riverboat to be

FIGURE 4   Circus Circus Enterprises—Management Structure

18 October, 1993

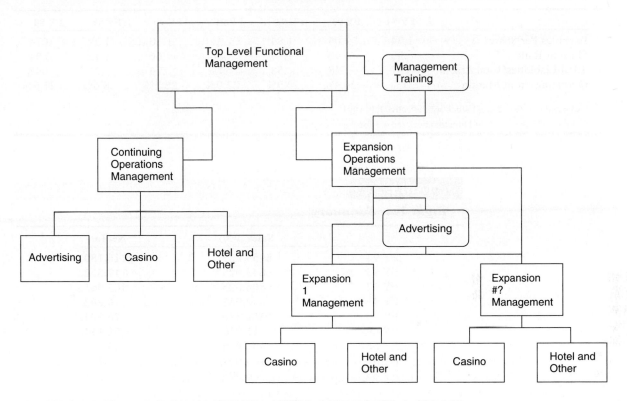

opened in December 1994. As an additional river operation, Circus is attempting to secure a riverboat license from the Indiana Gaming Commission for the town of Michigan City. Gambling is, of course, not limited to the U.S. and Circus is attempting to expand internationally by joining with Press Holdings Limited and Nine Network Australia to bid on a proposed casino license in Sydney, Australia. Circus recently announced they were unsuccessful in this bid.

Closer to home, Circus was successful in a bid to build a casino project in Windsor, Canada. This will be a joint arrangement with Caesar's World, Inc. and Hilton Hotels to build a 75,000-square-foot casino, a 1,000 seat showroom, three dining areas and a 300 room hotel. Expected to open in 1996, this project will cost an estimated $250–$275 million. Each partner will provide approximately $60–$90 million, with the balance financed.

Even closer to home, in May, 1993, Circus formed a joint partnership with Eldorado Hotel/Casino to develop and operate "Project C" in downtown Reno. This will be a theme project depicting an elaborate silver mining theme complete with an automated 120-foot mining rig covered by a 180-foot dome. The facility will include 1,700 hotel rooms and 76,000-square-feet of casino space with numerous restaurants, bars and entertainment areas at an estimated cost of $310 million.

Circus' projects are being tailored to attract mainstream tourists and family vacationers. Prices and credit limits are low, while the diversity of potential entertainment activities is substantial.

TABLE 1

Selected Financial Information

	FY 94	FY 93	FY 92	FY 91	FY 90	FY 89	FY 88
Earnings Per Share*	1.34	2.05	1.84	1.39	1.30	1.29	074
Current Ratio	.95	.90	1.14	.88	.66	1.12	2.34
Total Liabilities/Total Assets	.57	.48	.58	.77	.76	.72	047
Operating Profit Margin	21%	24.4%	24.9%	22.9%	28.7%	28.6%	27.6%

*Adjusted to reflect 2-for-1 stock split effective July 1991.
In June 1993 the Board of Directors declared a 3-for-2 stock split.

TABLE 2

Eight Year Summary

	Sales (000)	Net Inc
FY 94	$954,923.	$116,189.
FY 93	843,025.	117,322.
FY 92	806,023.	103,348.
FY 91	692,052.	76,292.
FY 90	522,376.	76,604.
FY 89	511,960.	81,714.
FY 88	458,856.	55,900.
FY 87	373,967.	28,198.
FY 86	306,993.	37,375.

TABLE 3

Circus Circus Enterprises, Inc.—Annual Income (000)

Fiscal Year Ending	1/31/94	1/31/93	1/31/92	1/31/91	1/31/90	1/31/89	1/31/88
Net Sales	954,923	843,025	806,023	692,052	522,376	511,960	458,856
Cost of Goods	437,601	386,971	346,663	313,269	227,942	217,891	200,005
Gross Profit	517,322	456,054	441,360	378,783	294,434	294,069	258,851
Sell. Gen. & Adm. Exp.	258,156	204,022	193,584	179,309	124,228	125,380	113,361
Inc. Bef. Dep. & Amort.	259,166	252,032	247,776	199,474	170,206	168,689	145,490
Depreciation & Amort.	58,105	46,550	47,385	40,998	31,216	31,800	29,134
Non-operating Inc.	(683)	820	245	(570)	1,030	1,493	4,113
Interest Expense	17,770	22,989	43,632	42,048	26,818	28,425	19,733
Income Before Tax	182,608	183,313	157,004	115,858	113,202	109,957	100,736
Prov. for Inc. Taxes	66,419	62,330	53,656	39,566	38,138	37,478	38,809
Net Inc. Bef. Ex. Items	116,189	120,983	103,348	76,292	75,064	72,479	61,927
Ex. Items & Disc. Ops.	0	(3,661)	0	0	0	9,235	(6,027)
Net Income	116,189	117,322	103,348	76,292	75,064	81,714	55,900
Outstanding Shares	85,686	58,167	56,600	54,977	62,572	57,814	75,814

TABLE 4

Circus Circus Enterprises, Inc.—Balance Sheet

ANNUAL ASSETS (000)

Fiscal Year Ending	1/31/94	1/31/93	1/31/92	1/31/91	1/31/90	1/31/89	1/31/88
Cash	39,110	43,415	34,158	18,134	19,411	20,667	14,212
Marketable Securities	0	0	0	0	0	0	60,097
Receivables	8,673	3,977	4,171	5,977	2,156	3,197	3,319
Inventories	20,057	16,565	15,894	16,573	9,337	15,714	10,861
Other Current Assets	20,062	14,478	13,687	13,601	10,323	8,212	8,734
Total Current Assets	87,902	78,435	695,154	717,466	41,227	47,790	97,223
Prop. Plant & Equip.	1,183,164	851,463	695,154	717,466	612,905	455,074	413,745
Deferred Charges	16,658	9,997	9,080	9,438	9,252	0	0
Intangibles	10,200	10,563	10,927	11,290	11,654	12,328	11,198
Deposits & Other Assets	0	0	0	0	0	8,920	6,891
Total Assets	1,297,924	950,458	783,071	792,479	675,038	524,112	529,057

ANNUAL LIABILITIES (000)

Fiscal Year Ending	1/31/94	1/31/93	1/31/92	1/31/91	1/31/90	1/31/89	1/31/88
Accounts Payable	14,804	11,473	11,814	16,048	23,690	9,578	7,177
Cur. Long Term Debt	169	154	941	938	935	1,485	2,053
Accrued Expenses	59,438	47,397	45,558	43,652	35,104	29,326	30,822
Income Taxes	3,806	708	1,185	818	2,345	2,168	1,420
Total Current Liabilities	92,061	87,494	59,498	48,750	62,074	42,557	41,472
Deferred Charges/Inc.	78,568	64,123	58,830	48,209	42,586	38,933	39,529
Long Term Debt	567,345	308,092	337,680	496,750	408,314	296,316	168,339
Non-Cur. Cap. Leases	0	0	0	0	0	0	485
Other Long Term Liability	1,415	740	867	1,221	1,340	1,394	1,174
Total Liabilities	737,974	460,449	326,196	184,843	514,314	379,200	250,999
Common Stock Net	1,603	1,599	1,590	1,571	1,912	1,907	1,903
Capital Surplus	120,135	111,516	84,026	52,302	47,376	42,273	42,035
Retained Earnings	618,446	502,257	384,935	281,587	205,295	130,370	237,290
Treasury Stock	(180,234)	(125,353)	(144,355)	(150,617)	93,859	30,638	3,170
Shareholder Equity	559,950	490,009	326,196	184,843	160,724	144,912	278,058
Total Liab. & Net Worth	1,297,924	950,458	783,071	792,479	675,038	524,112	529,057

MARKETPLACES

Laughlin: Laughlin represents a market quite distinct from that of Las Vegas and Reno. It is a city with a population of 4,791, compared with 741,459 in Las Vegas and 139,900 in Reno. Laughlin caters to the day travelers from nearby Arizona and Southern California population centers and attracted more than four million visitors in 1992. Ten casinos opened in Laughlin during the period between 1986 and 1993 with some expansion to the current 9,000 hotel rooms underway. Such construction activities have been, at times, a disruptive factor to the tourism business due to the strain placed on the city's housing, schools and water supplies. Laughlin has been described as the industry's fastest growing market with gaming revenues of about $507 million in 1993 compared to $40 million in 1985. Its future, however, depends on the extent to which it becomes a destination resort, as contrasted to a day trip resort.

Although Circus' facilities must compete with eight major casinos, they are able to maintain a 95 percent occupancy rate.

Las Vegas: Las Vegas is a more established gambling market, although growth has recently been quite explosive. Over 70 casinos operate in the Las Vegas area and in 1993 collected close to $3.6 billion. On the "Strip," well-known casinos such as Caesar's World, Harrah's and The Golden Nugget brought in about 80 percent of the strip's winnings and more than one-third of the state-wide totals. Many cater to the upscale gambler, offering big name entertainment, free drinks for gamblers, easy credit and glamorous surroundings. Las Vegas draws clientele largely from Southern California and the rest of the Southwestern United States. It ranks as one of the most popular convention locations in the nation and is becoming more popular for tours from Asia and Europe.

Several new casino-hotels have opened in Las Vegas during 1989–1993 such as the Mirage, Excalibur, and O'Sheas. Openings in the last three months of 1993 included not only the Luxor, but the Mirage Resorts' Treasure Island as well as the MGM Grand Hotel and Theme Park. The MGM operation is the most ambitious of the three projects costing over $1 billion and adding 5,000 hotel rooms. This rapid growth in Las Vegas has some observers worried; however, most expect it to be readily absorbed by the current market and increased tourism. The expected increase in family vacationers may end up exerting pressures on the more traditional 'gambling only' casino operations forcing them to compete with the theme resorts. All the new properties seem to be doing very well and the older, upper-tier properties have not lost any significant revenue.

Reno: In Reno, recent growth has been much more modest with total gambling revenues about $678 million, up 4.8 percent over last year. Like Las Vegas, Reno is a relatively established gaming market with twelve major casinos catering to the upscale gambler. It draws clientele largely from Northern California and the rest of the Northwestern United States.

THE GAMING INDUSTRY

By 1994 the gaming industry had captured a large amount of the vacation/leisure time dollars spent in the U.S. Gamblers lost over $29.9 billion in 1992 on legal wagering, including wagers at racetracks, bingo parlors, lotteries and casinos. This figure does not include dollars spent on lodging, food, transportation and other related expenditures associated with visits to gaming facilities. Casino gambling accounts for 76 percent of all legal gambling expenditures, far surpassing second place lotteries at 7.4 percent. The popularity of casino gambling may be credited to more frequent and somewhat higher payout as compared to lotteries and racetracks; however, as winnings are recycled, the multiplier effect restores a high return to casino operators.

Riverboat and limited casino initiatives have continued to make headway in a number of states throughout 1994. Where states have allowed casino operations to commence, casino developers and operators have been very quick to take advantage. New casino building is at a particularly frantic pace in selected areas along the Mississippi river and the Gulf coast. In states without casino gambling, industry supported groups lobby heavily for legalization. For example in Florida, five different pro-casino groups, such as the Proposition for Limited Casinos Inc. and Safe Bet For Florida Committee, are battling anti-casino groups for this potentially lucrative state. Gaming industry watchers believe that the number of different pro-casino groups and propositions may be counter productive with many groups looking out for their own interest.

Two geographical areas, the state of Nevada and Atlantic City, New Jersey, currently dominate the gaming industry, being the only established areas allowing full-fledged casino gambling. Nevada accounted for $6.02 billion in casino revenues in 1993 as compared to Atlantic City's $3.3 billion. It is believed that Nevada generates more revenue and higher profitability due to two factors: lower interest expense because of old debt, and lower regulatory and labor costs. Limited gaming activity (such as floating casinos, bingo, poker parlors, video gambling, lotteries and parimutuel betting) is allowed in other states but significant expansion beyond these two areas is expected to be slow due to legal constraints in these jurisdictions.

Besides geographical separation, the primary differences in the two markets reflect the different types of consumers frequenting these markets. While Las Vegas attracts overnight resort-seeking vacationers, Atlantic City's clientele are predominantly day-trippers traveling by automobile or bus. According to the Las Vegas convention and Visitor Authority, Las Vegas is a destination market with most visitors planning their trip more than a week in advance (81 percent), arriving by car (47 percent) or airplane (42 percent), and staying in a hotel (72 percent). Gamblers are typically return visitors (77 percent), averaging 2.2 trips per year and like playing the slots (65 percent).

Development of new and existing markets will determine the industry's future. New theme resorts are being introduced to differentiate the market and are expected to capture most of the increase in gaming revenues. Atlantic City is expanding transportation and lodging accommodations to better enable it to attract resort and convention-related business, but it will be some time, if ever, before it can compare with Nevada.

The gaming industry is led by ten companies which account for more than 60 percent of total gaming revenues. According to Standard & Poors Industry Surveys, the Trump Organization, Caesar's World and Promus were the leaders in gaming revenues in calendar year 1992 (see Figure 5). Other revenue leaders

FIGURE 5
Major U.S. Casino Operators

Company	Fiscal 1993
Caesar's World	772
Promus Companies	712
Mirage	534
Bally Manufacturing	478
Trump Organization	959
Aztar	432
Circus Circus	495
Hilton Hotels	439
Showboat	313
Resorts International	246
Boyd Group	308
Clairidge	155
Hollywood Casino	247
Sahara Gaming	151
TOTALS	6,241

(SOURCE: Standard & Poor's Industry Surveys, March 17, 1994.)

are Bally Manufacturing, Mirage, Circus Circus, Hilton Hotels, and Aztar. All of the top eight companies have casino operations in Nevada except Trump.

MAJOR INDUSTRY PLAYERS

Bally Manufacturing Corporation: Bally Manufacturing Corporation is a diversified organization that operates casinos and fitness centers and produces and distributes gaming products. Bally is currently enjoying a recovery in its casino operations in both Atlantic City and Nevada. Through the first half of 1993 both the Park Place and Bally Grand saw increased revenue through winnings with the Park Place reestablishing its position in the upper tier of Atlantic casinos. Bally Manufacturing has acquired 40 percent of the stock of Bally's Grand in Nevada through bankruptcy proceedings.

In addition to casinos, Bally's Scientific Games manufactures gaming equipment and services. They produce German wall machines and coin-operated gaming equipment and recently were the first to sell slot machines to the Soviet Union. Producing and selling paper ticket lottery games is another of Bally's gaming segments with customers in the U.S. as well as Costa Rica, Guatemala and Venezuela. Finally, Bally operates 315 fitness centers and manufactures exercise bicycles among other items for the health care market.

Caesar's World Inc.:   In 1992 Caesar's World was listed as the top gaming revenue-producing-casino operator (in absolute dollars) in the U.S. Caesar's owns and operates three casino-hotels: Caesar's Palace in Las Vegas, Caesar's Taho and Caesar's Atlantic City. Altogether these properties offer 223,000-square-feet of casino space and 2,600 rooms with an average 84 percent occupancy (86 percent in Las Vegas). Caesar's probably will be adversely impacted by the opening of the new theme park/casinos/hotels in Las Vegas and Trump's Taj Mahal in Atlantic City. Caesar's reacted to competitive pressures by renovating and adding on to its properties in all three locations. In addition, it began operation of its first cruise/casino called "Caesar's Palace at Sea," aboard a Japanese-owned luxury cruise liner. Another cruise/casino is already under construction and should be operating in the near future.

Capitalizing on the Caesar's name are two other subsidiaries, Caesar's World Resorts and Caesar's World Merchandising. Caesar's World Resorts owns and operates four non-gaming resorts in the Pocono Mountains, Pennsylvania. In addition, Caesar's has an agreement with a Japanese firm to manage a new non-casino resort to open in 1992 in Henderson, Nevada. Caesar's World Merchandising, Inc. markets private-label apparel, accessories, gifts and fragrances.

Mirage Resorts (formally Golden Nugget Inc.):   All of Mirage's gaming operations are located in Nevada. It owns and operates the Golden Nugget–Downtown, Las Vegas (which may be spun off), the Mirage on the strip in Las Vegas, and the Golden Nugget–Laughlin. The Mirage, an extremely ambitious resort venture with 3,056 hotel rooms and 95,000-square-feet of casino space became Vegas' top attraction when it opened in 1989. Constructed around a tropical theme, it offers a 20,000 gallon aquarium, a 54-foot-high volcano that erupts with pina colada scented fumes every fifteen minutes, rare white tigers in a jungle scene, tropical gardens, a multitude of restaurants, bars and shops, and an adjacent 16,000-seat outdoor sports arena. The Mirage was the first of the tourist-family-oriented theme resorts in Las Vegas. The project cost more than $615 million and was largely financed with borrowed money.

Mirage's latest venture is "Treasure Island," a pirate-theme casino-resort which opened in October, 1993. Adding 3,000 rooms to the Las Vegas market the project cost an estimated $430 million. Visitors will have the opportunity to watch a ship sunk during a pirate battle in front of the resort and are expected to add significantly to Mirage's profitability during 1994.

Hilton Hotels Corporation: The Hilton family name is well known around the world for fine hotels. Hilton owns five casino-hotels: the Las Vegas Hilton and Flamingo Hiltons in Las Vegas, two in Reno and one in Laughlin, Nevada. These casino-hotels have 12,557 guest rooms with an 85 percent average occupancy rate. Casinos brought in revenues of $438 million in 1992 with 57 percent of those revenues derived from gaming.

Producing slightly less revenues are the 243 other hotels and inns owned, managed or franchised by Hilton. While experiencing a slight improvement in occupancy rate in 1993, almost all of the earnings growth occurred in the gaming operations. Hilton is moving rapidly into the riverboat gaming venue with boats operating out of New Orleans and Kansas City.

Promus Companies Inc.:   A relatively new company, Promus is a spin-off of Holiday Corporation (the transaction occurred in February 1990). Promus has both casino-hotel and hotel only operations. Promus operates Harrah's casino-hotels in Reno, Lake Taho, and Laughlin, Nevada, Harrah's in Atlantic City, Holiday Casino and Holiday Inn Hotel in Las Vegas, and Bill's Lake Taho, Nevada. Promus has also ventured into the riverboat gambling market with one boat operating out of Joliet, Illinois and has won the rights to co-operate the only land based casino complex in New Orleans, Louisiana. Plans call for a 120,000-square-foot casino to be completed by the end of 1994. Gaming operations contributed 80 percent to revenues and 81 percent to operating income in 1992.

Promus' hotel segment develops real estate for the purpose of selling it while retaining franchise and management contracts. It operates 454 hotels under the names of Embassy Suites, Hampton Inn and Homewood Suites. Only 104 are owned/managed through a management contract and the remaining 350 are licensed to franchise owners and other investors.

MGM Grand Inc.:   MGM Grand Inc. has undergone numerous changes in recent months to prepare for the opening of its largest and potentially most profitable gamble. Although the MGM Grand Air Inc. subsidiary has been a drain on the corporation, MGM Grand has been able to sell off its MGM Sands and Desert Inn holdings, purchase and close the Marina Hotel and Casino and the Tropicana Country Club in Las Vegas and finance the construction of the MGM Grand Hotel and Theme Park. Situated on 115 acres directly across from the Excalibur, the MGM Grand Hotel and Theme Park has been erected at an estimated cost of over $1 billion. This complex will be the world's largest hotel with 5,011 rooms, a 170,000-square-foot casino and will feature a 35-acre theme park. Built around the Wizard of Oz theme, visitors walk under a 109-foot-tall gold lion and up the yellow brick road into Emerald City, an entertainment area. Staged performances on three levels will entertain visitors riding the 50-passenger elevator.

THE LEGAL ENVIRONMENT

Within the gaming industry all current operators must consider compliance with extensive gaming regulations as a primary concern. Gambling operations are subject to regulatory control by the Nevada State Gaming Control Board, the Clark County Nevada Gaming and Liquor Licensing Board, and by city governments. Gaming companies must submit detailed operating and financial reports to authorities. Nearly all financial transactions, including loans, leases and the sale of securities must be reported. Some financial activities are subject to approval by regulatory agencies. As Circus moves into other locations outside of Nevada, they will need to adhere to local regulations.

Although Circus can expect to exert only limited influence on regulatory matters, it took a step in 1989 to strengthen its ability to deal with regulatory concerns by electing Carl F. Dodge to its Board of Directors. Mr. Dodge is a former chairman of the Nevada Gaming Commission.

THE FUTURE FOR CIRCUS CIRCUS

Circus intends to continue its growth in the Nevada markets by further innovation in theme-oriented entertainment, but is also expanding to other gambling locations.

Circus has done well by introducing theme-oriented entertainment "megastores," and can be expected to innovate more on that concept. Likewise, its focus on serving middle income tourists by delivering family entertainment at relatively low prices (room prices range up from $39) has been effective in capturing market share. Excalibur and Luxor represent a move upscale in the target market, and it is not yet clear whether future projects will cater to the lower or upper-middle class tourists. Circus believes that customer loyalty in the gaming industry is closely tied to the merchant's ingenuity and management believes that the philosophy which brought them this far can be expected to carry them into the future. Circus is considering ventures outside Las Vegas and Nevada as they arise and has set aggressive performance targets for itself, including exceeding 20 percent in both the average annual growth rate in earnings per share, and in return on equity, as well as sustaining its industry-leading profit margin and return on invested capital.

Bibliography

"Casinos Move into New Areas," *Standard and Poors Industry Surveys*, March 11, 1993, pp. L35–L41.

Circus Circus Enterprises, Inc., *Annual Report to Shareholders*, January 31, 1989, January 31, 1990, and January 31, 1993.

"Circus Circus Rakes in the Bread," *Business Week*, February 27, 1990.

"Circus Circus Enterprises, Inc.," *The Wall Street Journal*, August 31, 1990.

Corning, Blair, "Luxor: Egypt Opens in Vegas," *San Antonio Express News*, October 24, 1993.

Kennedy, John, "Support for Casinos Falters in New Survey," *The Orlando Sentinel*, May 26, 1994.

Koselka, Rita, "The Last Pharaoh," *Forbes*, April 11, 1994, pp. 118–119.

Lalli, Sergio, "Excalibur Awaiteth," *Hotel and Motel Management*, June 11, 1990.

"When You're Hot, You're Hot," *Time*, July 2, 1990.

Yoshihashi, Pauline, "Circus Circus Stock Falls on Forecast of Profit; Other Casino Shares Tumble," *The Wall Street Journal*, October 21, 1992.

CASE

3

Orthopedic Services, Inc.

ROBERT J. PAVAN, *Rutgers University*

On Thursday, March 19, 1992, Jeffrey S. Levitt, President of Orthopedic Services, Inc. (OSI) was in his office at 7:30 a.m. as usual. The morning newspaper, open to the NASDAQ National Market Quotations, showed OSI had closed the day before at 32⅞, selling at 73 times earnings. It was the last listing of OSI, for on the nineteenth of March the shareholders of NovaCare, Inc., listed on the New York Stock Exchange, had approved a merger with OSI and OSI had become a subsidiary of NovaCare at the close of business. NovaCare was a leading national provider of contract rehabilitation services to health care institutions, offering speech-language pathology, occupational therapy, and physical therapy, as well as operating seven comprehensive medical rehabilitation hospitals, one hospital-based rehabilitation unit, and six community-based transitional care programs.

OSI, in less than 5 years, had gone from a concept to become the nation's largest provider of orthotic and prosthetic patient care services. Its 104 branches in 20 states from the East to the West coasts generated $55 million in sales. The next 5 years had promised to be different for OSI and for Jeff. As President, he had seen that he would have to manage what he called a "jump shift" in emphasis from the acquisition psychology that had excited and motivated OSI's managers to an internal growth psychology if they were to achieve the objective of 60 percent revenue growth in 1992. The jump shift was needed, he felt, because industry growth was projected at 6 to 7 percent and after OSI's forty-one acquisitions the remaining acquirable practices were few and small in size. Also, with an almost 200 percent increase in net income planned, productivity would have to improve. And, of course, OSI would have to continue seeking to influence as favorably as possible future changes in health care reimbursement. Now all would have to be done in the context of NovaCare as a parent.

THE O & P INDUSTRY

The orthotics and prosthetics (O & P) industry was part of the $19 billion medical rehabilitation market. Orthotics involves the design, fitting, and fabrication of custom-made braces and support devices for the treatment of musculoskeletal conditions resulting from illness, injury, or congenital anomalies. Prosthetics involves the design, fitting, and fabrication of custom-made artificial limbs typically required by people who have suffered the loss of a limb from vascular disease, diabetes, cancer, or traumatic injuries. In 1992, the market for O & P patient care was estimated at $750 million with 6 to 7 percent annual growth.

Traditionally, O & P practices had been small, highly profitable, family-run businesses which capitalized on strong demand for their expertise and the limited supply of qualified professionals. The American Orthotic and Prosthetic Association (AOPA) estimated there were about 1500 local practices averaging less than $500,000 per year in revenue, five regional firms, and two multiregional firms. OSI and AOPA estimated O & P market shares as follows: 76 percent for independents, 5 percent for the five regionals, 3 percent for Hanger Orthopedic Group, 9 percent for OSI, and 7 percent for other providers (drugstores, etc.).

The supply of certified O & P practitioners at the end of 1990 was 2780, with expansion at 3 to 4 percent per year. Certification in both orthotics and prosthetics could take up to 7 years, including a 4-year baccalaureate degree. Fewer than ten schools offered certification programs, and two of the largest (New York University and the University of California—Los Angeles) had closed their O & P programs recently because of a lack of federal funding.

The O & P industry generated high gross margins (see Exhibit 1) and was more profitable than most other health care businesses. This was seen as a result of the custom nature of the devices; the technical expertise of the practitioner; the three-stage service, which consisted of fitting, fabrication, and delivery; the limited supply of certified practitioners; and the more favorable payer mix. Nearly all O & P services were billed to third-party payers—payers other than the patients.

EXHIBIT 1
Typical Gross Margins of Five of the Most Profitable Health Care Businesses

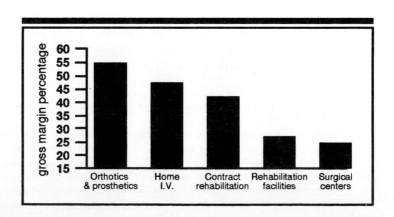

For 1990, the O & P payer mix was 71 percent from private and third-party insurance companies; 19 percent from Medicare, 10 percent from Medicaid, and 4 percent from the Veterans Administration. With the increase in the elderly portion of the patient population, the proportion of industry revenue coming from Medicare would increase from its current level of 19 percent. Until 1990, O & P services had been subject to Medicare reimbursement amounts defined by the rules for durable medical equipment (DME). DME rules, however, failed to recognize either the custom nature of the devices or the care component of O & P. In 1990, Medicare reimbursement for O & P was removed from the DME schedule, and the Health Care Financing Administration (HCFA) worked with the industry to devise a new reimbursement plan. The new plan developed maximum allowable charges for each of 10 geographic regions (instead of limits set by each state), but in no case would the amount be less than 85 percent or more than 195 percent of the national average charge. The plan would be phased in starting January 1, 1992, using weighted averages of local and regional fees to determine the total allowable charge, and be fully in place for 1994. Barring any legislative action, the O & P industry knew what to expect in regard to Medicare reimbursement levels for the next few years.

Normal industry sales growth was estimated at 6 to 7 percent a year, with 2 percent from yearly price increases and 4 to 5 percent from normal volume expansion. The following factors were identified by OSI as driving the unit growth rate in the future:

Societal demand.   Many handicapped individuals aggressively seek to regain independence through rehabilitation programs. Studies by major insurance carriers and the federal government have demonstrated that investment in rehabilitation dramatically reduces ongoing health care expenses.

Aging population.   The 65 and over age group is expected to increase from approximately 32 million in 1990 to approximately 34 million in 1995. Vascular disorders and musculoskeletal conditions in this age group often result in the need for an orthotic or prosthetic device.

High value-added.   Patients generally value O & P products and services highly because (1) most are custom devices, (2) individualized services and technical expertise are important components of the price for products and services, and (3) ongoing patient care involving adjustments, refittings, and replacements is provided.

Technology and materials.   Significant advances in both have resulted in lighter, more sophisticated, and more comfortable devices, which, while frequently more expensive, are applicable to a wider range of patients.

Underserved market.   OSI's analysis of the businesses it has acquired shows that the O & P businesses have not actively marketed their services in various health settings, such as nursing homes, the home health care system, and rural environments, but have instead relied on relationships with hospital-based referral sources and with physicians. The unsophisticated sales and marketing programs and dearth of adequate consumer and referral source education, along with a shortage of O & P practitioners, suggested an unmet need of $250 million a year.

COMPANY HISTORY

The concept for OSI originated in 1986, when John H. Foster, of Foster Management Company, a venture capital firm he founded in 1972, followed the suggestion of an investor to "look into the O & P industry." Foster hired a consultant to research the industry economics, identify the leaders, and determine if there was an opportunity for consolidation. The report showed that the O & P industry had a high gross margin and was highly fragmented, with no one attempting consolidation. With a list of the ten largest companies in hand, the acquisition quest began.

Early Acquisitions

OSI had begun operations on August 1, 1987, upon completing the acquisition of Missouri Valley Orthotics and Prosthetic Center, Inc., the fourth largest regional company. Located in Omaha, Nebraska, Missouri Valley had three offices each in Nebraska and Kansas, plus two in South Dakota. On December 4, 1987, Foster acquired Orthopedic Service Center, Inc., adding its Kansas office. The third acquisition, on May 31, 1988, was Orthomedics, Inc. Orthomedics, based in Brea, California, was the second largest regional company, with nineteen offices in California and two in Washington. The initial goal of acquiring "platform companies" had been achieved.

As President Jeffrey S. Levitt explained:

> What John did then, basically, was draw a 500-mile radius around the Midwest and West platforms. With input from the former owners, John then identified which firms to acquire in order to "densify." It was very important to start with industry leaders. To acquire two of the largest, OSI paid up. There was a larger component of cash used to acquire these businesses than in later deals.

Exhibit 2 summarizes the acquisitions completed from 1987 through 1991.

Later Acquisitions

Jeff described the desirable acquisition candidate as: (1) a private practice with a reputation for quality care; (2) at least $1 million in revenue with the potential for quickly achieving a minimum 20 percent operating margin; (3) key practitioners who were willing to help sustain the practice and preserve referral sources and work with OSI to implement its systems and vision; and (4) respected practitioners who would serve as magnets to attract other motivated sellers who like themselves sought an opportunity to expand their practices as part of OSI. He said, "Our experience is that these sellers typically fall into three broad categories: (1) professionals in business many years who are seeking an exit strategy without retiring; (2) those lacking management or capital resources to expand but who have the drive and talent to do so; and, (3) owners frustrated with the increasing administrative burden placed on them by third party payers."

By mid-March of 1992, OSI had closed 41 deals, after looking at 275 potential acquisitions. "We have been able to close most of the deals we wanted," claimed Levitt. "Many of the practices are too small, and some are dying businesses. There are also the family businesses that don't want to sell because 'Grandpa started this business and we can't let him down.' The second, fourth and fifth largest private practices are examples. There have only been three or four sellers who sold to someone else who was willing to pay more."

EXHIBIT 2

OSI Acquisitions 1987–1991

	1987	1988	1989	1990	1991	Total
West						
Arizona				2	3	5
California		21		6	14	41
Oregon					6	6
Washington		2			1	3
	0	23	0	8	24	55
Midwest						
Colorado				2	3	5
Iowa		2			1	3
Kansas	4			1		5
Missouri			4	2		6
Nebraska	3					3
Oklahoma						2
South Dakota	2					2
Texas					6	6
	9	2	5	6	10	32
East						
Connecticut					2	2
Georgia					1	1
Kentucky				1	2	3
Massachusetts				1	1	2
Maine					1	1
New Hampshire					5	5
Tennessee				4	2	6
	0	0	0	6	14	20
No. of locations	9	25	5	20	48	107
No. of companies	2	3	3	13	18	39

SOURCE: OSI, excludes start-ups and branch consolidations.

Typically, OSI paid a price about equal to "trailing annual sales," defined as sales for the 12 months prior to the acquisition agreement. For a business with the potential for quickly achieving a 20 percent pretax margin, that was five times potential pretax earnings. As Jeff noted, "Many family-owned firms report lower pretax margins because of higher owner salaries, related benefits, and discretionary expenses which often run through the business."

Usually, the price paid exceeded the value of the assets acquired. Payment was a combination of cash, 5-year notes, and OSI stock. The agreements included 3- to 5-year employment contracts for the principals with financial incentives if the acquired practices met or exceeded performance targets.

For all of its eighteen acquisitions in 1991, OSI paid 87 percent of trailing revenues, according to Jeff. "As to payment, OSI would prefer to pay 100 percent in stock, while the seller would like all in cash, so we negotiate."

The average 1991 deal provided 30 percent in cash at closing, 10 percent in OSI 5-year 7 percent notes, and 60 percent earnout over 5 years, paid in a combination of cash and stock. (Earnout is that portion of the purchase price paid during the 5 years after acquisition, and is dependent upon the acquired business achieving an agreed-upon sales threshold.)

Integration of the Acquisitions

OSI had developed a systematic approach to the integration of its acquisitions. Integration began before the transaction closed, with the regional president explaining employee responsibilities, benefits, and opportunities to the owners and key employees. Following the closing, OSI typically maintained a regional management presence on site for 30 to 90 days to enhance integration.

"We have found," said Jeff, "that having someone immediately available to answer questions before they become problems is critical. There are many issues which seem small to an outsider that can affect employee attitudes if left unanswered, such as 'Mr. Jones always gave us our birthdays off with pay; will OSI?'"

Most acquired practices carried roughly 52 percent gross margins as compared to OSI's existing locations which typically ran 57 percent. To improve the gross margin, OSI worked on reducing expenses, improving efficiency, and expanding revenues. All superfluous functions and expenses were eliminated. OSI's proprietary management information system, TOPS (Total Orthotic and Prosthetic System), was installed to connect the local offices with the regional headquarters for the management of cash, receivables, and other administrative tasks required of small businesses. Regional purchasing of components and supplies was installed where economies of scale were possible. A materials management system was introduced to reduce inventory and improve inventory turnover. Where feasible, fabrication of O & P devices was regionally centralized.

On the revenue side, billing procedures were reviewed and revised when necessary to ensure that all services rendered were properly classified. Professional marketing programs were instituted. In order to retain the goodwill of acquired businesses, OSI's policy was to initially operate sites under their existing names and to slowly shift name recognition to that of OSI. The ability of practitioners to provide services and generate revenues was enhanced not only by reducing the time formerly devoted to administrative tasks, but also by OSI instituting education and training programs for O & P assistants and technicians who could attend to more routine professional services for the practitioner.

OSI's experience was that within a few months after acquisition, they were able to add 2 to 3 percentage points to a typical branch's gross margin. In the subsequent 6 to 12 months, further margin improvement was derived from changes in practitioner productivity and billing efficiency. Simultaneously, OSI's marketing initiatives and recruiting efforts helped the branches pursue revenue growth more aggressively than previously possible.

A strategic plan for each acquired business was worked out by OSI with the former owners. The plan accommodated the particular nature of the specific practice, while adhering to OSI's overall corporate strategy of enhancing both patient care and productivity. It was Jeff's belief that "issues involving the consistent delivery of high-quality care and physician and patient satisfaction are given as much attention as those relating to financial and operational procedures."

COMPANY OPERATIONS

Management Personnel

OSI had sought to create a strong, seasoned management team (see Exhibit 3). Founder John Foster had been involved in the rehabilitation services industry for a decade. Jeffrey Levitt and Alan Vinick had extensive experience in identifying and integrating acquisitions in the health care delivery field. Barry Roth was experienced in monitoring the reimbursement environment. As a certified orthotist, Thomas Bart provided sensitivity at the top levels of management to practitioner needs.

The three regional presidents, Brian Murphy, Bill Pastor, and Rick Taylor, all had considerable experience with national health care companies and had

EXHIBIT 3
Orthopedic Services,
Inc., Management
Team (March 1992)

John H. Foster, B.A., M.B.A. (49): Founder, Chairman, CEO (1987-present)
Williams College and Amos Tuck School of Business Administration; Morgan Guarantee Trust (1967–72), venture capital, left as Assistant Vice President; Founder, Chairman, CEO (1972–present), Foster Management Co., venture capital; Founder, Chairman (1979–83) The Aviation Group, Inc., all cargo carrier, Director (1979–86) until sold; Founder, Chairman, CEO (1980–84) Foster Medical Corp. until sold to Avon Products, Inc.

Jeffrey S. Levitt, B.S., J.D., C.P.A. (43): President, COO (1989–present)
University of Pennsylvania and Villanova University; Arthur Anderson & Co. (1974–77), Senior Tax Accountant; V.P. (1977–82) Johnson Rents, Inc., medical equipment; President (1982–84) Home Health Care Division, Foster Medical Corp; President (1984–86) Home Health Care Division, Avon Products, Inc.; President, COO (1986–89) Heritage Health Systems, Inc., owner and manager of health maintenance organizations.

Thomas R. Bart, Certified Orthotist (46): V.P. Development (1989–present)
Chairman, President (1978–87), Missouri Valley Orthotic & Prosthetic Center, Inc.; President, OSI Midwest Region (1987–89); former President, American Orthotics and Prosthetics Association.

Barry M. Roth, B.S., L.L.B. (48): V.P. Regulatory Affairs, General Counsel, Secretary (1990–present)
V.P., General Counsel (1984–87) Foster Medical Corp.; V.P. Government Affairs (1987–88), V.P. General Counsel (1988–90) Heritage Health Systems, Inc.

Alan N. Vinick, B.S., M.B.A. (48): V.P., CFO, Treasurer (1990–present)
V.P., CFO, Heritage Health Systems, Inc. (1988–90); V.P., CFO, John Hancock Health Plans (1984–88).

Marilyn J. Twombley, B.S., M.S., R.N. (45): Director—Marketing (1987–present)
Director—Marketing (1982–87), Foster Medical Corp.; prior position, Director, Stein Medical, home health care equipment and respiratory business.

Scott Kessler, B.S. in Business Administration (34): Director—Reimbursement (1991–present)
American Express, Director of Reimbursement Services (1986–91); Foster Medical Corp., Director of Claims Administration (1980–85); Accountant/Controller (1975–80).

John Gardner, B.S. in Business Administration (35): Director—Human Resources (1991–present)
Manager—Human Resources (1983–91), Decision Data, Inc.; Manager—Human Resources (1978–83), United Engineers & Contractors, Inc.

Jeffrey Allgood, B.S. in Industrial Engineering, M.B.A. in Marketing (40): Director—Logistics (1991–present)
Manager-Purchasing, Managing Buyer, Customer Service and Distribution (1979–91), Johnson and Johnson.

William Torzolini, B.S. in Business Administration, C.P.A. (31): Director—Finance (1990–present)
Peat, Marwick, Main & Co. (1981–84); Senior Auditor (1984–87), Alco Standard Corp., Director—Finance (1987–90) Chilton Co./Capital Cities ABC.

William McGinnis, B.S. in Business Administration, C.P.A. (32): Controller (1990–present)
Senior Manager (1984–90), Pannell Kerr Forster CPAs; Senior Auditor (1982–84), Peat, Marwick, Main & Co.

Brian G. Murphy, B.S. in Health Education (31): President, Midwest Region (1989–present)
Prior positions: President, AmeriPlan Health Services; President—Heritage Health Plans; Director—Development, Partners National Health Plans.

Floyd W. Pastor, B.S. (51): President, East Region (1991–present)
Group Vice President (1985–89) Foster Medical Corp.; District Manager (1965–85) United Parcel Service.

Richmond L. Taylor, B.S. in International Affairs (43): President, West Region (1989–present)
V.P. (1984–88), Home Health Care Division, Avon Products, Inc.; V.P. Sales (1988–89) Integrated Medical Systems, Inc., developer of medical information systems; currently Director, California Orthotics and Prosthetics Association.

William M. Clover, Jr., B.A., M.A. (46): President, Products Division (1990–present)
Director, Engineering (1984–88), V.P. Operations (1988–89), Products Division, Orthomedics, Inc.

worked with Foster and Levitt in other businesses. Bill Clover, president of the Products Division, combined engineering and administrative experience. The additions, within the past year, of directors for marketing, reimbursement, human resources, and logistics were intended to provide greater depth to OSI's corporate management.

The headquarters executives, despite their professional experience, perhaps because of their relative youth (most were in their forties) and OSI's rapid growth, appeared to interact in an informal manner. A visitor on a Saturday morning found standard office decor, office doors open, and people popping in and out of each other's office. Half the offices were in use, with their occupants casually dressed, including Jeff Levitt in his warmup suit. A shared story was that at OSI, there were three types of people: certified orthotists, certified prosthetists, and overhead—with Jeff Levitt as certified overhead! If you were overhead, the question was, "What have you done to help an orthotist or prosthetist today?"

MANAGEMENT STYLE AND SYSTEMS

"This is a people business, so the focus is on people in how we manage," Jeff stated. "I see my job as creating an atmosphere of winning. I keep a checklist of the top 50 people at OSI with the aim of spending, at a minimum, one to two quality hours per quarter talking to each one in person. I actually keep track of who I have talked to. The idea is to have a 'quality time' chat, not a broad discussion of 'how is your job going?' We focus on 'where are you today in your career plan?' and 'how can I help you succeed?' Each regional president is encouraged to do the same with a checklist of the top 30 people in their region. This is really important considering how fast we are moving. Our voice mail also helps. We have 95 people on that system. It has eliminated interoffice memos for communications."

Jeff genuinely enjoyed talking to people at all levels in the organization. "I think I'm good at listening and people like to talk to me. I'll hear of a problem from an employee and ask, 'What should we do about it?' Often the initial look is, 'Do you really want to know?' but after reassuring them that I do, they respond. I listen and then get the views of others on the suggestion. This probably comes from when I was a kid working at all the low-level jobs in the meat packing plan my father managed. At home I would hear the management responses to union demands, and then at work, hear the worker reactions. Workers were not dumb. They knew what would and would not work, and whether management was sincere or not." OSI had a formal review and bonus system with quarterly reviews by the president. A quarterly bonus was determined for the regional presidents and corporate officers with financial goals and MBO goals (the agreed-upon set of "to dos") weighted equally, while for regional officers and corporate staff financial goals carried a 30 percent weight and MBO goals 70 percent. The bonus for branch managers was a function of specific branch key success variables including sales growth, cash collection, material cost percentage, and turnover rate. OSI believed that a quarterly bonus evened out performance and made sure that the business and strategic plans were used.

The overall business plan set up what Jeff called quarterly "to dos." Managers submitted their own list of "to dos," and an agreed-upon set of goals was negotiated. Each week Jeff received a status report on the "to dos." Jeff, in turn, reported weekly to John Foster. An end-of-the-quarter review was conducted with written comments. John Foster, at year end, received written reviews of Jeff from the regional presidents and corporate vice presidents.

As Jeff said:

> We all get our report cards. The system provides discipline and detail. Tons of feedback, but on what is important, not just a "data dump." Each person gets a one-page form telling: here is where I am; here is where I am off; here is what I have to do. I have never had a person who was unclear on where they stood. The system is self-policing. Nonperformers replace themselves.

Organization

"Corporate executives have to learn not to run local health care businesses from their centralized corporate offices. Our decentralized philosophy enables management to be more responsive in providing prompt follow-up and decision making so that local practitioners can provide high-quality patient care services in their local branches. This approach also allows for the efficient and rapid integration of acquired businesses," explained Jeff Levitt.

OSI had no formal organization chart. It preferred to emphasize its "conceptual" organization chart (see Exhibit 4), which reflected the philosophy that it was the practitioner at the branch level who made money for OSI while every-

EXHIBIT 4
OSI Conceptual
Organizational Chart

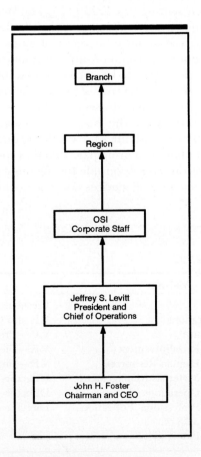

SOURCE: Orthopedic Services, Inc.

TABLE 1

Branch Management

Region	Managers Not Principal	Managers Principal	Assistant Managers Not Principal	Without Manager	Total Branches
East	14	6	0	1	21
Midwest	23	13	0	1	37
West	31	11	2	2	46
	68	30	2	4	104

one else was overhead. The purpose of all overhead was to assist the branch-level practitioners in providing patient care most efficiently while maintaining quality. The knowledge and resources available at what are traditionally viewed as "higher" organization levels were of value only to the extent that they supported the task of the practitioner.

When fully developed, the Eastern, Midwestern, and Western operating regions were intended to be stand-alone businesses with a complete staff providing all support functions, including accounting, information systems, professional services, operations, central fabrication, and sales. In early 1992, the regions varied in their staffing (see Exhibit 5). The Western region had a full-scale fabrication center to serve all branches, while the Midwest region fabrication center only served about 60 percent of its patient care centers. The Eastern region had not yet focused on the development of its fabrication capability, as it was the last region to be started by OSI in January, 1990.

The regions also varied in their use of principals from acquired companies to head up patient care centers, as seen in Table 1. Among the principals shown in the table were two in the West who managed two branches, while both the East and Midwest had one who was doing double duty. The Midwest also had one branch where two principals served as co-managers.

The Products Division was responsible for the design and manufacture of a line of noncustomized O & P devices for sale to OSI branches, non-OSI

EXHIBIT 5

OSI Regional Staffing—As of March, 1992

East	Midwest	West
President	President	President
V.P.—Professional Development	V.P.—Operations	V.P. and General Manager
V.P.—Operations	V.P.—Finance	V.P.—Professional Development
V.P.—Finance	Director—Reimbursement	V.P.—Field Operations
Director—Materials Management	Director—Human Resources	V.P.—Finance and Administration
Director—MIS	Director—Materials Management	Director—Customer Fabrication
Director—Human Resources	Director—Operations (3)	Director—Sales/Operations (2)
Director—Operations (2)	Director—Professional Education	Director—MIS
Director—Reimbursement	Director—MIS	
	Director—Fabrication	

branches, orthopedic surgeons, and international markets. The Products Division manufactured both customized and noncustomized O & P devices, but its principal product line was a family of standard low-end orthotic braces. Current division sales were approximately $3.5 million and were 90 percent to external customers. The gross margin ran 70 percent.

A critical success factor in the O & P industry, OSI had concluded, was branch location and not the number of facilities. This impacted on decisions concerning acquisitions and branch operations. Take, for example, a situation in which an acquiree had two branches, one of which duplicated an OSI branch. Since the earnout contract with an acquiree set a minimum sales threshold, OSI, when it changed the acquiree's business, adjusted the threshold. If it ended up closing the second branch, it reduced the threshold; if the decision was to close an existing OSI branch, OSI increased the threshold.

The TOPS system generated for each branch a monthly operating statistics report for the past 12 months (see Exhibit 6). The report helped identify areas of needed corrective action(s). If, from the TOPS systems, a branch showed declining revenues for 5 to 6 months, closing the branch was considered.

Sales and Marketing

To increase its referral base, OSI had introduced sales and marketing, a largely unheard of activity in the O & P industry. The typical small practice depended upon walk-in trade. OSI employed a variety of mailed promotions directed at principal referral sources—physicians, hospitals, and managed care organizations. It also used a professionally trained sales force to actively call on the same referral sources. The marketing efforts aimed to project a reputation for quality, increase a referral source's comfort with Orthopedic Services, and lure referrals away from competing practitioners.

The company also conducted a patient-focused marketing program, including patient feedback and follow-up systems. The objectives were to retain patients and to inform them about applicable technological developments.

Orthotics services accounted for roughly half of OSI revenues. Of this, 50 percent was for injury victims and represented nonrecurring business; the balance was for congenital defects and age-related disorders, which tended to generate long-term patients. Prosthetic services provided 42 percent of OSI sales. The patient base was relatively small, but revenue contribution was disproportionately large. O & P products and their services represented the balance of the company's revenue.

Finance

On July 17, 1990, Lehman Brothers and Paribas Corporation successfully co-managed OSI's initial public offering (IPO). Originally scheduled to sell 3,000,000 shares at $19.00 per share, the underwriters sold 3,450,000 shares. The net proceeds of $49,311,000 were used by OSI to repay about $5 million in bank debt, and to redeem Foster Management's more than $18 million in notes with accrued interest and almost $4 million in cumulative preferred stock and unpaid dividends.

At the time of the IPO, the company had issued 3,610,804 common shares for approximately $450,000 to the Foster Management partnerships, plus another 60,000 common shares for $7200 to these investors for their guarantee

EXHIBIT 6

TOPS Monthly Operating Statistics Report

ORTHOPEDIC SERVICES, INC.
BRANCH OPERATIONAL STATISTICS
REGION:
BRANCH:

	1991 MAR	APR	MAY	JUN	JUL	AUG	SEP	OCT	NOV	DEC	1992 JAN	FEB	1992 YTD	1991 FULL YEAR	FEB 1992 ACTUAL	FEB 1992 BUDGET	VARIANCE +/(−)
ADJUSTED NET REVENUES:																	
ORTHOTICS	$49,806	$57,174	$58,966	$40,752	$47,909	$50,347	$32,922	$34,066	$47,322	$35,244	$26,427	$27,781	$54,208	$532,481	$27,781	$21,446	$6,335
PROSTHETICS	3,532	4,854	23,849	6,777	25,373	8,651	15,473	28,140	13,407	15,221	4,102	18,942	23,044	174,726	18,942	5,130	13,812
OTHER	1,544	3,495	1,923	1,560	1,699	1,567	1,271	631	1,833	1,092	483	593	1,076	20,238	593	1,966	(1,373)
TOTAL NET REVENUES	$54,882	$65,523	$84,738	$49,089	$74,981	$60,565	$49,666	$62,837	$62,562	$51,557	$31,012	$47,316	$78,328	$727,445	$47,316	$28,542	$18,774
# OF BILLED PATIENTS:																	
ORTHOTICS	70	88	68	70	80	68	60	53	61	67	51	52	103	832	52	33	19
PROSTHETICS	4	9	14	5	5	6	10	10	6	9	11	12	23	92	12	3	9
OTHER	12	22	18	10	12	14	12	6	10	9	5	7	12	165	7	16	(9)
TOTAL BILLED PATIENTS	86	119	100	85	97	88	82	69	77	85	67	71	138	1,089	71	52	19
TOTAL PATIENT VISITS	141	190	178	187	254	207	206	198	195	NA	213	205	418	NA	205	92	113
# OF WORK DAYS	21	22	22	20	22	22	20	23	19	21	22	20	42	254	20	20	0
FTE'S:																	
# OF PRACTITIONERS	2.0	3.0	3.0	2.0	3.0	3.0	3.0	1.0	1.0	1.0	2.0	2.0	2.0	2.2	2.0	3.0	(1.0)
# OF BOARD ELIGIBLES	0.0	0.0	0.0	0.0	0.0	0.0	0.0	1.0	2.0	2.0	1.0	1.0	1.0	0.4	1.0	0.0	1.0
# OF PRACT. ASSTS.	0.0	0.0	0.0	0.0	0.0	0.0	0.0	0.0	0.0	0.0	0.0	0.0	0.0	0.0	0.0	0.0	0.0
TOTAL PRACTITIONERS	2.0	3.0	3.0	2.0	3.0	3.0	3.0	2.0	3.0	3.0	3.0	3.0	3.0	2.6	3.0	3.0	0.0
# OF TECHNICIANS	0.0	0.0	0.0	0.0	0.0	0.0	0.0	0.0	0.0	0.0	0.0	0.0	0.0	0.0	0.0	0.0	0.0
# OF ADMINISTRATIVE	1.0	1.0	1.0	1.0	1.0	1.0	1.0	1.0	1.0	1.0	1.0	1.0	1.0	1.0	1.0	1.5	(0.5)
TOTAL FTE'S	3.0	4.0	4.0	3.0	4.0	4.0	4.0	3.0	4.0	4.0	4.0	4.0	4.0	3.6	4.0	4.5	(0.5)
REVENUE PER BILLED PATIENT:																	
ORTHOTICS	$712	$650	$867	$582	$599	$740	$549	$643	$776	$526	$518	$534	$526	$640	$534	$646	($112)
PROSTHETICS	$883	$539	$1,704	$1,355	$5,075	$1,442	$1,547	$2,814	$2,235	$1,691	$373	$1,579	$1,002	$1,699	$1,579	$1,918	($340)
OTHER	$129	$159	$107	$158	$142	$112	$106	$105	$183	$121	$97	$85	$90	$123	$85	$124	($39)
TOTAL	$638	$551	$847	$578	$773	$688	$606	$911	$812	$607	$463	$666	$568	$668	$666	$552	$115
REVENUE PER PRACTITIONER	$27,441	$21,841	$28,246	$24,545	$24,994	$20,188	$16,555	$31,419	$20,854	$17,186	$10,337	$15,772	$156,656	$281,592	$15,772	$9,514	$6,258
REVENUE PER FTE	$18,294	$16,381	$21,185	$16,363	$18,745	$15,141	$12,417	$20,946	$15,641	$12,889	$7,753	$11,829	$117,492	$203,008	$11,829	$6,343	$5,486
PATIENTS SEEN PER PRAC	71	63	59	94	85	69	69	99	65	0	71	68	139	0	68	31	38
PATIENTS SEEN PER PRAC/PER DAY	3.4	2.9	2.7	4.7	3.8	3.1	3.4	4.3	3.4	0.0	3.2	3.4	3.3	0.0	3.4	1.5	1.9
PATIENTS BILLED PER PRAC	43	40	33	43	32	29	27	35	26	28	22	24	46	422	24	17	6
PATIENTS BILLED PER PRAC/PER DAY	2.0	1.8	1.5	2.1	1.5	1.3	1.4	1.5	1.4	1.3	1.0	1.2	1.1	1.7	1.2	−0.9	0.3
PATIENT CONVERSION RATIO	1.6	1.6	1.8	2.2	2.6	2.4	2.5	2.9	2.5	0.0	3.2	2.9	3.0	0.0	2.9	1.8	1.1

to repay a $20 million bank line of credit extended to OSI. In addition, 217,111 common shares were issued for $25,000 in connection with the first seven acquisitions. The Foster Management partnerships also paid $3.6 million for 36,000 shares of 10 percent cumulation preferred stock.

Following the IPO, management believed it was amply funded to pursue its acquisition plans. Projections indicated that cash flow would just about cover operational needs and notes due in 1991 and 1992 of $1.9 million and $2.7 million, respectively. Consolidated statements of operations and balance sheets are shown in Exhibits 7 and 8.

OSI and NovaCare, Inc., jointly announced on November 19, 1991, an agreement to merge, with OSI to become a wholly owned subsidiary. Each outstanding share of OSI common was to be converted into 1.3 shares of NovaCare common stock which was listed on the New York Stock Exchange. The exchange was to be treated as a pooling of interests and a tax-free reorganization subject to the approvals of each company's board of directors and of two-thirds of NovaCare common stockholders and a majority of OSI common stockholders. Shares beneficially owned by John Foster in each company were excluded from voting. The merger was completed on March 19, 1992.

John Foster, Chairman and CEO of both NovaCare and OSI, stated, "Driven by a desire to improve patient care, enhance financial performance, and

EXHIBIT 7

OSI Consolidated Statement of Operations—Year Ended December 31[1]
(Dollars in thousands)

	1987[2]	1988	1989	1990	1991[3]	1992E
Net sales	3,134	16,158	22,754	35,049	55,002	87,969
Direct cost: products and services sold	1,475	7,086	9,778	15,860	25,003	38,737
Gross profit	1,659	9,072	12,976	19,189	29,999	49,232
Selling and indirect	310	2,067	2,930	4,285	7,223	10,867
General and administrative	965	4,386	7,212	10,803	15,812	24,188
Operations income	384	2,619	2,834	4,101	6,964	14,177
Interest expense	291	1,843	2,692	2,025	895	1,025
Interest income	(19)	(41)	(40)	(713)	(866)	(236)
Amortization: excess cost over net assets acquired[4]	69	356	514	723	1,050	1,604
Other expense (income)	0	(1)	130	14		
Income (loss) before minority interest and income taxes	43	462	(462)	2,052	5,885	11,784
Minority interest in income	0	221	237	299	143	164
Income (loss) before income taxes	43	241	(699)	1,753	5,742	11,620
Income tax (benefit)	7	193	(85)	648	1,797	3,835
Net income (loss)	36	48	(614)	1,105	3,945	7,785
Shares outstanding at year end (in thousands)	3,866	3,979	4,037	7,654	7,654	N.A.

[1]Includes results of businesses acquired from effective date of each acquisition.
[2]Includes results of Missouri Valley from August 1, 1987.
[3]1991 pro forma excludes merger related expenses with NovaCare.
[4]Excess of cost over the fair value of net assets acquired is amortized on a straight-line basis over 40-year period.
SOURCE: July 10, 1990, prospectus and 1990 Annual Report prepared by Price Waterhouse, and OSI 1991 pro forma and 1992 estimate.

EXHIBIT 8

OSI Consolidated Balance Sheet—Year Ended December 31
(Dollars in thousands)

	1987	1988	1989	1990	1991[1]
Assets					
Cash	495	216	1,821	21,830	9,363
Accounts receivable	810	3,110	3,325	7,020	12,406
Doubtful accounts receivable	(142)	(229)	(317)	(886)	(1,198)
Income tax recoverable	89	312	96	107	104
Inventories	501	1,570	1,803	3,423	5,752
Other	143	156	251	404	763
Total current assets	1,896	5,135	6,979	31,898	27,190
Net property, plant, and equipment	586	4,272	4,263	4,724	5,569
Excess cost over net assets acquired	7,403	19,659	20,061	30,600	53,250
Other assets	173	250	325	438	448
Total Assets	10,058	29,316	31,628	67,660	86,457
Liabilities and Stockholders' Equity					
Notes payable—bank	2,931	65	0	0	0
Accounts payable	220	445	679	1,223	2,443
Accrued expenses and liabilities[2]	598	1,134	2,324	3,576	5,972
Long-term debt (current)	328	512	1,385	1,727	1,903
Income tax payable	27	0	0	363	1,814
Total current liabilities	4,104	2,156	4,388	6,889	12,132
Long-term debt	5,381	25,624	22,290	8,812	10,356
Deferred income tax	0	547	217	0	0
Other liabilities	0	64	806	1,625	4,812
Total Liabilities	9,485	28,391	27,701	17,326	27,300
Minority interest	0	290	299	351	146
Stockholders' equity	573	635	3,628	49,983	59,011
Total liabilities and equity	10,058	29,316	31,628	67,660	86,457

[1]1991 pro forma excludes merger-related expenses with NovaCare.

[2]Lease expense for office space and vehicles and equipment charged to operations was $727,000, $1,085,000, and $1,571,000 in 1988, 1989, and 1990.

SOURCE: July 10, 1990, prospectus and 1990 *Annual Report* prepared by Price Waterhouse, and OSI 1991 pro forma.

reduce reimbursement risk, the rehabilitation industry will continue to undergo dramatic consolidation. NovaCare will lead the industry in that consolidation. The merger with OSI is another important step in that process."

NOVACARE, INC.

Founded in 1985 as InSpeech, Inc., by John H. Foster, NovaCare's initial strategic plan was to consolidate the high-margin, highly fragmented market for the provision of speech-language pathology (SP) services to nursing homes on a contract basis. Nursing homes were a receptive market: SP was the least cost-effective therapy for a nursing home's own staff to provide, since the average 190-bed nursing home generated relatively low demand.

Having gained entry into nursing homes, Foster added physical and, later, occupational therapy to further serve his nursing home clients. Expansion into these therapy services was by acquisition (19 in 19 months). By including these diverse services in one company and by introducing professional management techniques, economies of scale were sought and new treatment programs were developed.

In recognition of these changes, the company name was changed to NovaCare in 1988. The financial management organization was strengthened to further improve economies of scale, cash management, and the timeliness and accuracy of financial reporting. In the following fiscal year a president and chief operating officer was appointed. In 1991, the top management positions were chairman and CEO; president and chief operating officer; senior vice president—finance and administration and chief financial officer; vice president—MIS and customer accounting; vice president and controller; vice president—regulatory affairs; vice president—professional services; vice president—human resources; and vice president—operations.

As NovaCare grew, it learned that therapists are not motivated by money alone. They need to work for an organization that first and foremost is concerned with the quality of care delivered. In 1988–89, the company implemented many programs to improve hiring and retention of therapists. By fall of 1989 the company had decentralized into four geographic operating division, empowering regional and district supervisors (most of whom were therapists) to solve problems and create programs to enhance productivity of the therapists and the well-being of their patients. It also had integrated physical, speech, and occupational therapists into multidisciplinary teams to provide a level of cooperative, comprehensive care, previously available only in acute care and rehabilitation hospitals.

In fiscal 1989 NovaCare revenues were $70 million; in fiscal 1990 revenue had grown to $102 million, with net income as a percent of sales increasing from 7.3 percent to 19.1 percent. (See Exhibits 9 and 10 for financial statements.) The annual average number of full-time equivalent therapists (FTEs) for fiscal 1990 had increased to almost two thousand (1975), but the average annual therapist turnover rate was at 32 percent. NovaCare had discovered an industry truth: nursing homes are very difficult places for which to recruit talented professionals such as therapists because geriatric patients rarely experience full recovery.

NovaCare was well on its way to dominating the contract rehabilitation market. Fiscal 1991 closed with over 1900 rehabilitation contracts in 34 states; $191 million in revenue; return on sales 19.4 percent; and average FTE therapists at 1,929 with turnover rate down to 27 percent. Diversification of its patient base and reduction of dependence on Medicare appeared desirable. On August 9, 1991, NovaCare acquired Rehab Systems Company (RSC), which operated seven rehabilitation hospitals, an inpatient rehab unit in an acute care hospital, and six transitional living centers. In all, RSC had 463 licensed beds. Its revenue for the 12 months ended July 30, 1991, was $65 million. Its payer base included more private-pay patients and fewer Medicare-dependent patients than NovaCare's. RSC's patient base was younger and more acutely ill than

EXHIBIT 9

NovaCare, Inc., Consolidated Operations—Year Ended June 30[1]
(Dollars in thousands)

	1987	1988	1989	1990	1991
Net revenues	$26,869	$56,612	$69,975	$102,110	$151,532
Cost of services	15,364	35,941	44,389	62,632	95,129
Gross profit	11,505	20,671	25,586	39,478	56,403
Selling, general, and administrative expenses	6,645	17,509	16,587	19,944	25,935
Merger expenses	. . .	. . .	. . .	. . .	593
Income from operations	4,860	3,162	8,999	19,534	29,875
Interest expense	(696)	(1,516)	(1,636)	(1,383)	(552)
Interest and dividend income	1,357	1,416	1,358	1,750	2,293
Amortization of excess cost of net assets acquired	(341)	(887)	(886)	(905)	(960)
Loss on marketable securities	(710)	(2,468)			
Income (loss) before income taxes and extraordinary item	4,470	(293)	7,835	18,996	30,656
Income taxes	2,157	752	2,728	6,614	10,341
Income (loss) before extraordinary item	2,313	(1,045)	5,107	12,382	20,315
Extraordinary item: tax benefit from utilization of net operating loss carryforward	566				
Net income (loss)	$ 2,879	$(1,045)	$ 5,107	$ 12,382	$ 20,315
Shares outstanding[2] (at year end, in thousands)	13,215	13,376	26,764	26,945	32,060

[1]Includes results of acquisitions from effective date of acquisition.
[2]Stock splits of 2 for 1 in June 1987 and July 1991.
SOURCE: Annual reports; prepared by Price Waterhouse.

the nursing home patient base and thus more challenging and satisfying to therapists. "Additionally," as John Foster noted, "NovaCare generates cash and has virtually no debt, while RSC requires a capital to continue its expansion."

NovaCare saw itself as a national provider of comprehensive medical rehabilitation services. The rehabilitative therapy industry in the United States was estimated in 1989 to exceed $3.7 billion in annual revenues. With an aging population and advancing medical technology, experts projected annual growth exceeding 10 percent, with 1993 revenue of about $5.5 billion. It viewed the rehabilitation industry as consisting of seven primary settings on a spectrum from greater to lesser intensity of care:

• Acute care hospital
• Dedicated in-patient rehabilitation hospital
• Long-term hospitals
• Transitional care units
• Nursing homes
• Out-patient clinics
• Home care

EXHIBIT 10

NovaCare, Inc., Consolidated Balance Sheet—Year Ended June 30 (Dollars in thousands)

	1987	1988	1989	1990	1991
Assets					
Cash and cash equivalents	$ 1,053	$ 2,760	$19,668	$22,713	$ 25,799
Marketable securities	0	20,486	1,953	5,067	7,311
Accounts receivable, net	8,445	15,303	18,460	25,899	43,394
Income taxes receivable	. . .	. . .	. . .	. . .	1,793
Other current assets	1,416	1,011	951	975	1,245
Deferred income taxes	0	1,019	338	811	378
Total current assets	10,914	40,597	41,370	55,465	79,920
Marketable securities	25,197	. . .	. . .	. . .	14,205
Property and equipment, net	1,291	1,907	1,753	2,219	2,584
Excess cost of net assets acquired, net of accumulated amortization	20,451	29,900	30,152	29,295	28,291
Other assets	252	. . .	. . .	933	2,389
Total assets	$58,105	$72,386	$73,275	$87,912	$127,489
Liabilities and Stockholders' Equity					
Current portion long-term debt and credit agreement	$ 1,179	$ 1,456	$ 1,385	$ 3,159	$ 634
Accounts payable and accrued expenses	3,733	6,462	6,293	8,552	12,565
Income taxes payable	612	1,146	478	1,667	. . .
Deferred income taxes	1,110	0	0	407	. . .
Total current liabilities	6,634	9,064	8,156	13,785	13,199
Long-term debt and credit agreement, net of current portion	8,337	17,459	14,523	10,916	403
Deferred income tax	121	1,158	818	406	373
Total liabilities	15,092	27,781	23,497	25,107	13,975
Commitments and contingencies					
Stockholders' equity					
Common stock, $0.01 per value;[1]	132	134	134	269	321
Additional paid in capital	41,317	43,914	43,955	44,605	74,947
Retained earnings	1,638	593	5,700	18,082	38,397
	43,087	44,641	49,789	62,956	113,665
Less: common stock in treasury (at cost)[2]	(74)	(36)	(11)	(151)	(151)
Total stockholders' equity	43,013	44,605	49,778	62,805	113,514
Total liabilities and stockholders' equity	$58,105	$72,386	$73,275	$87,912	$127,489

[1]Authorized 50,000,000 shares; issued 32,060,440 shares in 1991 and 26,945,402 shares in 1990.

[2]204,372 shares in 1991 and 1990.

SOURCE: Annual reports; prepared by Price Waterhouse.

Patients moved through the system according to their specific needs and progress.

Each of these primary settings was served by ancillary service segments, such as orthotics and prosthetics, clinical supplies, and psychological, social, and audiological services. Many of these segments were seen as economically attractive. Insurance sources varied from segment to segment, and most were characterized by a shortage of qualified clinical professionals.

NovaCare's strategy was to integrate the most profitable and logical rehabilitation segments which leverage local management and corporate infrastructure, thus providing broadened patient care, diversified revenue sources, and attractive, long-term career opportunities for care givers. The goal was for 1993 revenue of $275 million and a 5 percent market share. John Foster firmly believed:

> There is going to emerge over the next five or ten years a company which is the leader in rehabilitation, and that company will provide a full range of services. That is where I'm going. That is my vision. We're all betting that we will be part of the team that will be the Johnson & Johnson of rehabilitation services.

OSI: THE NEXT FIVE YEARS

In less than 5 years, OSI had established itself as the largest provider of orthotic and prosthetic patient care services in the United States, an attractive niche within the dynamic medical rehabilitation industry. Basic to its growth was a very aggressive and, management believed, well thought out acquisition program. It saw its management structure, operations systems, and policies as the most sophisticated in the industry. With OSI's reputation for quality care, size, access to capital, and management systems, the base was in place to achieve $190 million in sales in 1994. The next 5 years would be interesting and challenging.

OSI and the "Jump Shift"

"Our acquisition plans for 1992 through 1994 are to acquire some fifteen companies a year," explained Jeff Levitt. He went on to add, "Although we can enunciate an acquisition strategy, are there enough companies out there willing to be acquired at an economical price? Only six did more than $5 million a year and three of them joined OSI. The others are family-owned and somewhat resistant to selling. Periodically, we talk to them to remind them, in a friendly way, of our interest."

Beyond the largest firms were the 1300 practices which shared 76 percent of O & P revenues, with an average annual revenue of less than $500,000.

The second 5 years also raised the question of what to do with the former owners of previously acquired companies who were coming to the end of their 5-year employment contracts. OSI faced this issue for the first time in 1992, with thirteen cases. Did OSI want them to stay? Did they want to stay? Some had indicated yes, if they could get a premium to "re-up." This seemed more likely to be the case with minority owners who had spent the money they received when their business was first acquired. Jeff's initial reaction was, "They want us to buy them a second time, now that they see what we have accomplished!"

Employment agreements contained a covenant not to compete in the area for 2 years after leaving OSI. If anyone tried to ignore this constraint, OSI's legal counsel and the lawyer side of Jeff felt the company should legally enforce the covenant. The business manager side of Jeff wondered about the risk of adverse local publicity.

> I can see the possibility of local news stories that focus on the small local guy vs. the distant big guy. Remember, competition among providers for referrals occurs at the local level . . .

> Of course a person could move and open a small shop in a new market. If they do that, we think they will find they have lost touch with the management side of the practice, which was the weakness for many of them in the first place. Also, they now have the use of the TOPS computer system which is proprietary, and support of all of the professional programs we developed. Don't forget—they must also replicate a central fabrication capability as well. It's not an easy decision if OSI has done its job right.

Though acquisitions were fundamental to OSI's strategy in the first 5 years. OSI had from the beginning sought internal growth through the integration of its acquisitions. It saw integration as differentiating OSI from its only competition in consolidating the O & P industry nationally. The competition's strategy appeared to be to "only build a confederation." For OSI to achieve its growth goal, internal growth would have to play an increasingly greater role. The company's record on revenue gains by businesses acquired at least one year earlier is given in Table 2.

Managing what Jeff called the "jump shift" from acquisitions psychology to internal growth psychology would be critical. As he reviewed the accomplishments of OSI, Jeff was pleased but concerned: "I think we are a great group of business builders. We have shown that we can acquire businesses successfully, but we need to marry that ability with the ability to operate a multisite franchise-like business." He had been looking for a vice president—operations and found, "When I interview applicants from companies like Sears or Pizza Hut and describe our regional and branch operations they seem very comfortable with our needs. Do we have the ability to be business operators as well as business builders? Will our people find it is as exciting and fun to operate as it is to build a business?" As John Foster had observed, "The idea is to benefit from economies of scale. It sounds easy. Well, we can all cook a hamburger, but there's only one McDonald's."

TABLE 2

Internal Growth

Region	1989	1990	1991
Midwest	+8%	+11%	+10%
West	—	+13%	+13%
East	—	—	+19%
	+8%	+12%	+12%

OSI and the Industry Dynamics

A new dimension of OSI's marketing was its commitment to become a major sponsor of two national disabled ski events hosted by National Handicapped Sports (NHS), the "Ski Spectacular" and the U.S. Disabled Ski Championships. NHS was the nation's largest sports and recreation program for the disabled. Its 66 community-based chapters served annually an estimated 55,000 people of all ages. The NHS press release hailed its partnership with Orthopedic Services, Inc., because ". . . they share our philosophy of excellence in service to disabled people. The quality of a prosthesis can mean the difference for a disabled person between a full and active life or one that is doomed to reclusiveness and inactivity." When "Good Morning America" on January 6, 1992, covered the U.S. Disabled Ski Championship, the OSI logo was prominently displayed. A segment of the program showing a high-tech leg prosthesis was conducted in front of an Orthopedic Services, Inc., banner.

The "Good Morning America" segment showed that computers could analyze how an amputee would walk if the person had real legs and then design "artificial legs that will work almost as well." The computer created a custom-designed tight-fitting plastic socket and a carbon-fiber knee mechanism that eliminated knee buckling when the user walked. The "foot," with its linked carbon-fiber components, simulated the movement of foot bones. The leg and foot were very lightweight, and the foot mechanism and materials were designed to store energy (in contrast to old-style solid models, which lost energy), allowing the amputee to push off.

OSI believed that developing a reputation for introducing and using leading-edge O & P devices would enhance its competitive position. In fact, because of OSI's marketing efforts, it had received calls from manufacturers and universities about possibly working together in this area. However, when it pushed for commitment, OSI found that the other parties were not ready to move.

Research and development on new O & P products was fragmented. Companies such as DuPont did research on materials which were or might be used in prosthesis, and colleges did some research on components. Most development was done by small practitioners who created what they thought was needed, without any systematic way to determine the market's needs. OSI, with 66,000 orthotic and 19,000 prosthetic patients (annualized fourth-quarter 1991 rate), felt it was in a position to better identify market needs. OSI knew that it was capable of partnering in new product development, testing a device on a sample of patients, and publishing a joint paper, but OSI wanted to be in on the initial product specifications as well.

In the past few years as OSI had grown, it had met with its twenty-five largest vendors, seeking distributor status, with mixed results. It seemed to Jeff that manufacturers, distributors, and practitioners were all making money with the status quo and saw no reason to change. In addition to the strategic advantage of leadership in new product development, Jeff saw potential operational advantages: "It would be great if we could go from inventorying 8000 different items to 1000 items."

Promoting OSI nationally also intensified the "brand name" question. Regional policies in identifying branches varied. In the West, branches carried the Orthomedics name together with either a geographic location or the name of another acquired company—e.g. Orthomedics—San Diego and Orthomedics—Barnhart; Midwestern branches mostly carried the OSI name;

TABLE 3				

Regional Branch Name Policy (March 2, 1992)

Region	OSI	Various Acquiree	Orthomedics- Geographic	Orthomedics- Acquiree
East	0	21	0	0
Midwest	31	6	0	0
West	0	0	17	29
	31	27	17	29

and in the East all carried the name of the acquired company. Regional practices are shown in Table 3.

With the shortage of O & P practitioners, firms expected that practitioner compensation would increase faster than inflation. Successful recruiting and retention of practitioners would be essential for competitors to remain viable and grow. Historically, the industrywide retention rate was high; i.e., once certified, few persons left the profession. OSI's turnover figures showed steady improvement, from 19.5 percent in 1989, to 7.5 percent in 1990, and 6.5 percent in 1991. The 1992 operating goal was 5.0 percent.

To improve its retention rate (and aid in recruiting), OSI had adopted a number of policies and practices. A clear career path had been established with defined levels of technician and assistant responsibilities, coupled with promotions from within and transfer of individuals to accommodate personal circumstances. OSI provided on-the-job training for practitioners who had yet to obtain certification and might then offer sponsorship to accredited schools. It ran mock testing clinics to better prepare individuals for their exams. To date, all who had participated in these clinics had passed their exams. The adoption in 1991 of the *OSI Vision* (see Exhibit 11) after 15 months of companywide discussions was thought to contribute greatly to improving retention. The *Vision* was promoted throughout OSI, using video tape, literature, and group meetings.

Recruiting was increasingly treated as a "professionalized" activity. The company offered a formal residency program and actively recruited recent graduates from accredited schools to complete their residency requirements at OSI. It supported its practitioners in meeting their continuing education requirements by reimbursing them for attendance at national and regional industry and supplier-sponsored training programs and by offering company-sponsored education programs.

An issue increasingly discussed by OSI management was whether OSI should become even more directly involved in the education business, to expand the number of practitioners that would be needed as demand grew, particularly as the "unmet need" was tapped. Should OSI set up a school? A joint venture with a school? Was it in OSI's interest to increase the total supply of practitioners? Perhaps OSI might gain a competitive advantage from a practitioner shortage by advancing its recruiting and retention capabilities relative to the competition. As the well-staffed competitor, OSI would be best positioned to provide high-quality services, continuity of care, and increased access, which might prove particularly attractive to contracting managed care organi-

EXHIBIT 11

Vision

Patients are our most important priority.

  We treat them professionally with compassion, respect, and dignity in a
  manner that makes a positive difference in their lives. To this end, we provide
  the highest levels of quality care that meet the patients' needs.

Employees are OSI's most valuable resource.

  In our pursuit of excellence, we create a challenging and rewarding
  atmosphere that encourages personal and professional growth. By providing
  an environment of mutual respect and teamwork, we attract the best people
  in the industry.

Referral sources are the lifeblood of our company.

  Mutual concern for our patients' well-being fosters a partnership
  between us. We enhance the value of that partnership by contributing our
  unique professional expertise.

We commit to providing the highest quality, most cost-effective services.

**We distinguish ourselves through our leadership in the profession
and the industry.**

  OSI is a community of people living this VISION.

Orthopedic Services, Inc.

© copyright 1991

---

zations. OSI had over 200 exclusive provider agreements, including the Oregon Health Sciences University Hospital in Portland, Oregon, a premier teaching institution.

OSI had also pursued increased revenues by opening nineteen new branches. Start-up branches were in response to excess demand at an existing center or to an invitation from a referral source. Before opening a new branch, regional headquarters had to answer the "buy or build" question. The market had to clearly show sufficient demand from a strong referral base and availability of qualified personnel. Start-ups were viewed as a high return-on-investment activity.

A typical start-up required leased space and computer hardware, office furniture, and tools. With OSI's regional fabrication and warehousing, the space and tools needed were less than for an independent practice. A recent start-up had required an initial investment of $43,000. Working capital needs would be primarily for personnel, 55 days of accounts receivable, and leasing costs. The rent for the 1500-square-foot branch was $10 per square foot annually. Salaries were $50,000 for a practitioner, $25,000 for a practitioner assistant, and $20,000 for an office administrator (plus 20 percent for benefits and taxes). Staffing needs based on past experience were related as shown in Table 4.

Revenue expectations were an annual rate of $200,000 by the end of 19 months; $400,000 by 24 months; and $600,000 by 36 to 48 months, which was average for a mature branch.

TABLE 4			

Typical Branch Start-up Staffing Needs

Revenue ($000)	Practitioner	Practitioner Assistant	Office Administrator
0–100	1	0	1
100–300	1	0.5	1
300–500	1	1	1
500–700	1	2	2
700–900	2	3	2

OSI and Productivity

Besides working to expand the demand for its products and services, gain a larger share of the market, and increase the number of practitioners, management believed it also needed to improve productivity. Materials were slightly less than 50 percent of the cost of sales; practitioner compensation was the balance.

OSI was unique in its focus on materials management. The two principal areas of focus were: (1) the development of efficient central fabrication (i.e., production and/or assembly) capability within each region, and (2) better material purchasing from third-party manufacturers and distributors.

The Western region operated the most comprehensive fabrication center, acquired as part of the 1988 Orthomedics acquisition, which in part accounted for its above-average profit margin. The Midwest region fabrication center served only some of the branches in its area.

Patients were treated in a multistep process involving consultation between the O & P practitioner, the physician, and the patient to assess the individual's needs and rehabilitative goals. The practitioner then made a cast of the patient's affected area, took measurements, and/or made drawings to assure an intimate fit of the device. A custom device was designed and fabricated by trained technicians using an increasing array of materials and technologies. Next, the patient was carefully fitted and trained in the use and care of the device by the practitioner. For prosthetic patients, the practitioner might use gait analysis, which involved videotaping the patient walking. Patient follow-up with the practitioner included adjustments, refittings, or replacement as needed, along with follow-up reporting to the physician and assistance with insurance paperwork and billing.

The initial increase in practitioner productivity was achieved by freeing practitioners from certain nonclinical tasks by transferring those tasks to the regional or corporate headquarters, thereby maximizing the time available for branch practitioners to provide patient care. Further increase in productivity could be obtained through greater use of supervised practitioner assistants for less complex care. OSI continued to study other staffing models for health care provision, e.g., group practitioner dentistry. A current OSI model of staffing to improve productivity at the branch level is shown in Table 5.

Practitioner productivity at OSI, measured as revenue per practitioner, had increased yearly: $195,000 in 1988; $225,000 in 1989; $285,000 in 1990; and $305,000 in 1991. "We have learned that beyond the structural changes to

	TABLE 5	

Branch Staffing for $1 Million in Revenue

	OSI Model	Industry Model
Certified practitioners	2	3–4
Practitioner assistants	3–4	0
Technicians	0	3–4
Office administration	2–3	3–4
	7–9	9–12
Central fabrication	Yes	No

improve practitioner productivity, you can't say 'work harder' or set sales and/or output quotas. Practitioners are professionals who care about their patients," Jeff noted. "What you can say is 'Are there any other patients who could have benefited from our services today and need it?' The impact of the *OSI Vision* has been remarkable." Continuing education programs in the design and use of increasingly sophisticated O & P technology also contributed.

OSI and the Reimbursement Environment

Productivity gains were sought in part to offset future expected pressure from payers, in all health care fields, to reduce payments. With perhaps some exaggeration, John Foster commented, "Health care is a strange business. It's the only business where you provide the service first, then see how much you can get paid for it later."

OSI, a major proponent of regional pricing for Medicare patients, with experienced reimbursement professionals, expected to implement the new HCFA rules in a timely fashion. TOPS would allow OSI to update reimbursement data at both branch and state levels as each phase occurred, while less proficient providers might face delays in reimbursement while the new system was digested, adversely affecting cash flow.

In addition, OSI would continue its effort to improve reimbursement levels on a state-by-state basis by challenging the data upon which state reimbursement limits were set. In a few states, OSI had achieved a 20 percent increase in allowable charges. The company's activity in the reimbursement area promised to be vigorous.

OSI AND NOVACARE

Both OSI and NovaCare expected to benefit from the merger. OSI's expectations were access to management systems and expertise; capital availability; new market opportunities; and better administrative cost leverage. For its part, NovaCare looked forward to seeing corporate selling, general, and administrative (SG&A) expenses spread over a larger sales base; Medicare dependence reduced and mitigated; expanded market opportunities; increased local scale/leverage economies; and diversification of customer base.

To reach OSI's goals of $150 million in 1994 revenue and 15 percent of an expanded market, Jeff Levitt believed he would have to go back to the public market for funds. NovaCare had committed to supplying capital. There were also opportunities for savings, e.g., the approximately $500,000 a year it cost OSI to satisfy the reporting requirements of a listing on the NASDAQ Market.

OSI and NovaCare operations overlapped in more than forty geographic markets, but until now OSI had only begun to serve the needs of NovaCare's in-patient clients, in only one of those markets. Nor had OSI yet tapped NovaCare's nursing home clients in those markets. Overlap selling was expected to increase. OSI also expected to establish branches that would be advantageously positioned to obtain referrals from NovaCare's 1991 acquisition of Rehab Systems Company (RSC). The expectation was that branches adjacent to RSC facilities should be able to obtain referrals more economically than the strategy of capturing market share through acquisitions.

Access by OSI to NovaCare's management system and expertise was highly valued by Jeff: "NovaCare has highly skilled senior staff in place, which we can benefit from as we manage the jump shift from an acquisition emphasis to an integration emphasis. We would like advice from their consultants, much as we would like our regions to provide consulting help and services to our branches. An OSI branch manager is free to use the services of the regional staff or go outside." Exhibit 12 shows the services offered by one of OSI's regional service centers to its branches.

In contrast, spreading corporate SG&A over a larger sales base was seen by NovaCare as a means of achieving integrated operating control. As Jeff stated: "They have a well-run machine. They have a disciplined model set up of how to operate, and their staff feels we should adopt their systems. We agree that there should be technical integration of NovaCare and OSI systems, but as to content, OSI, for example, needs its own inventory and cost accounting systems. Tell us what the end game is—what output information does NovaCare need from the systems we use?"

Also to be decided was whether OSI would develop its own systems or NovaCare would do it. If NovaCare did it, would OSI run into conflict with other NovaCare subsidiaries for its highly valuable systems development resources?

Differences had arisen in regard to the legal function. Barry Roth, OSI's general counsel, had developed a relationship of trust, credibility, and responsiveness with the regional and branch managers, and they felt comfortable calling upon him. OSI had recently hired a staff attorney to assist Barry. NovaCare thought their corporate general counsel staff should be expanded to handle all legal matters of the subsidiaries. OSI's general counsel was proud of his accomplishments in serving growing OSI branches, handling acquisitions, and successfully dealing with the Securities and Exchange Commission for the initial public offering of OSI shares. The relationship with the NovaCare general counsel office remained to be determined.

NovaCare and OSI were also different in regard to human resource management and compensation. NovaCare used a consulting firm which specialized in job evaluation and prepared for each position a salary schedule with steps. The management at NovaCare, using their Performance Planning and Review System (PPR), met with a subordinate at the beginning of the year to review his or her job description and reach agreement on expected achievement that year. John Foster saw PPR as the company's way of making good on its commitment to the employee. He thought OSI should use PPR.

OSI did not have well-delineated or communicated job descriptions. Throughout the company, it was felt that before OSI could integrate into a

EXHIBIT 12

Service Listing: OSI Regional Center

OSI East Region Services

We serve the needs of our people who serve the needs of our patients.

Dear Partner:

The OSI Regional Service Center has developed this service menu to show you the wide range of resources which we make available to you. We hope it will be helpful to you in becoming familiar with the services the Regional Center has to offer in furthering our continued success in the O & P profession!

ORTHOPEDIC SERVICES, INC.

BUSINESS MANAGEMENT AND REPORTING

Financial Reporting and Analysis
At the OSI Regional Service Center, we prepare monthly, quarterly and annual reports on your operations and provide business analysis of various plans and programs which drive your business.

Business Planning
We will support you in preparing your annual business plan, including goals, objectives, and financial statements. We also prepare special proforma analysis including sales growth trends, "what if?" analysis, fabrication cost, alternative staffing levels, and other factors you may specify.

Accounts Payable Processing
The Regional Service Center handles all payments to your vendors, and responds to communications between vendors and your branch.

Daily Cash Management
• We will manage your daily bank deposits and pool your excess cash balances for investment.
• We will fund weekly payrolls, vendor payments, and petty cash needs through the Service Center.
• For newly acquired businesses and start ups, we advance funds to meet working capital needs.

Business Loans
The Regional Service Center provides funds needed for building improvements, equipment and other asset additions.

Accounts Receivable Management and Training
We provide hands-on training in these areas:
• Working effectively with patients
• Accelerating collections
• Establishing goals and communicating results
We also establish and maintain national contracts with "pre-collect" and "collection" services.

Reimbursement Management
We provide training and guidance in insurance carrier relations. And, we monitor changes in government programs and communicate that information to you.

Physical Inventories and Pricing
We monitor and analyze the movement of your inventory, and we help you to establish the inventory levels best suited for your branch. We also will assist with organizing and taking periodic physical inventories and compiling these results.

ORTHOPEDIC SERVICES, INC.

EXHIBIT 12 (CONT.)

MANAGEMENT INFORMATION SYSTEMS

TOPS System Conversion
We offer initial training and assistance in converting existing billing systems to the OSI TOPS system for maximum efficiency.

User Training
Training programs are established for all system users. The Regional Center provides system overviews to branch managers, and, for each individual, sets up needed training programs.

TOPS System Upgrades and Modifications
• We coordinate system enhancement requests from user committees.
• We provide demonstrations and training in periodic new system release information.

24 Hour Telephone Support
We provide 24 hour system support to all users and resolve all errors in a timely manner. And, we acknowledge the receipt of an error within one hour of the time that it comes to our attention.

PROFESSIONAL DEVELOPMENT

Practitioner Education Programs
We provide inservices, educational materials and other continued education opportunities such as professional seminars and workshops.

Representation at Professional Societies
The Regional Service Center is actively involved with ABC, AOPA and AAOP on a national, regional, and local level.

Nationwide Professional Recruitment
Recruitment is provided on a nationwide basis in order to hire needed practitioners and technicians.

Practitioner Certification
We assist in certification preparation up to, and including a mock examination.

Quality Assurance Program Development and Implementation
The Regional Service Center assists with the implementation of local and national quality assurance initiatives.

OPERATIONS

Patient Programs
We implement programs for our branches in which patients are routinely asked to rate the services we provide them. This is done through questionnaires sent to each patient and ranking results. This program helps to measure our patients' preceptions of our services and will help to resolve potential problems early on.

Sales and Marketing Program Development
The Regional Center can assist in implementing a patient recall program, patient follow-up program, and physician follow-up program. These are all done as part of our automated revenue system. And, patient service representatives may be hired to help further develop the market.

Legal Assistance
We provide access to corporate legal counsel both inside and outside. We also make arrangements for local counsel to represent the company in any legal actions or legal matters.

HUMAN RESOURCES

Benefits Administration
The Regional Service Center monitors and processes all employee enrollments and disenrollments for health, life, disability and 401K programs. We work with employees on resolving any outstanding employee insurance and workers' compensation claims. We handle all COBRA conversions.

Payroll Processing
We process bi-weekly payroll checks and update any employee changes such as their address, W-4 rate, etc. We also offer employees the choice of direct deposit.

Employee Recordkeeping
The Regional Service Center maintains and updates employee personnel files, employment applications, performance review information, and personnel action reports. We also track employee vacations and sick time.

Training and Employee Development
Through human resource programs, we offer employee training and development programs.

OPERATIONS

Material Management System Development and Implementation
We assist in developing policies and procedures for purchasing, shipping and receiving to ensure patients receive the highest level of service available.

National and Regional Materials Discount Negotiation
Assistance is provided in negotiating discounts with vendors. We offer OSI's national purchasing power and our discount arrangements to each branch that becomes part of the OSI system.

Facilities Management Assistance
The Regional Service Center can help with the review of facility layouts, appearance as it relates to our patients, equipment capabilities and lease renewals.

BUSINESS GROWTH

Acquisition Candidate Analysis
The Regional Service Center provides both financial and operational evaluations of potential acquisition candidates.

Acquisition Negotiations and Deal Closings
We facilitate all contract negotiations and closings of a potential acquisition.

Business Integration
The Center provides a detailed integration plan for each acquired company, which includes a business plan. We convert many of the financial functions to the Regional Service Center and enhance our branches' ability to service their patients and generate revenues.

PPR process, it would have to roll out standardized job descriptions and gain widespread acceptance and understanding of these job descriptions deeply within the company. Yet there were many other tasks with higher priority. When John Gardner, OSI's director of human resources, tried to discuss job descriptions with regional and branch managers, he found they wanted to talk about more immediate needs.

At NovaCare a human resources information system was in operation. OSI did not have such a system. John Gardner had agreed with the NovaCare staff on such a project, but then found no one was available from NovaCare to work with him. OSI wanted help in the form of actual staff assistance, but felt what it was getting was an attitude of "we know best" which showed disrespect for the OSI staff.

The NovaCare staff also believed its compensation plan should be used in OSI for senior managers. It saw OSI's regional presidents as comparable to NovaCare's regional vice presidents since they, in broad terms, managed similar amounts of sales revenue. OSI's view was that its regional presidents were general managers with control over their own profit-and-loss statements and capital budgets—with, in effect, accountability for their own decentralized business—whereas NovaCare's regional vice presidents did not have those financial responsibilities.

"NovaCare looks at OSI as an $85 million company in 1992, whereas I see OSI as forty to fifty small companies. There is a great difference of cultures. For the most part, NovaCare has evolved to be run by professional managers and operators, while we are still in the entrepreneurial phase. We don't want to lose our locker-room spirit too quickly," Jeff stated. OSI's corporate group felt it must be a buffer and translator between those regional companies and NovaCare. Moreover, it felt its decentralization model was necessary to further build OSI. With a smile, Jeff noted, "We, for the first time, are feeling what probably every other company we acquired has felt."

Jeff believed that John Foster shared his view. He had worked with John before, and was pleased that John had named him a senior vice president of NovaCare and had included him in his Office of the Chairman to help facilitate fitting OSI into NovaCare. Of course, the issues might be complicated by NovaCare's relationships with companies acquired in its other health care businesses. Frederick C. Powell, President and CEO of RSC, for example, would undoubtedly be watching to see if the NovaCare compensation system was applied only to RSC.

Carnival Corporation:1994

MICHAEL J. KEEFFE, JOHN K. ROSS III, *and* BILL J. MIDDLEBROOK,
Southwest Texas State University

Carnival Corporation, although only twenty-two years young, is considered the leader and innovator in the cruise travel industry. From inauspicious beginnings, Carnival grew from two converted ocean liners to an organization with two cruise divisions (and a joint venture to operate a third cruise line), a chain of Alaskan resorts and hotels with corporate revenues of $1.577 billion and income from operations of $318 million. Carnival became the first cruise line to carry five million passengers when Mrs. Missy Rechel passed through embarkation at the Port of Miami, and the first cruise company to carry over one million passengers in a single year.

The company is prepared to maintain their reputation as the leader and innovator in the industry. Carnival's new President, Mr. Bob Dickinson, states:

> " . . . A new chapter in the Carnival Cruise Lines story has just begun. For the first time in the company's history the names of two ships will no longer appear in our fleet roster. The Marti Gras, the original "Fun Ship" is on her way to a new life cruising the Eastern Mediterranean as the Olympic of Epirotiki Lines. Her long time fleet-mate, the Carnivale, is also beginning a new life as the Fiestamarina—the first ship of what we plan will be a great line of ships serving an international Spanish-speaking clientele under the banner of a new member of the Carnival family of companies, FiestaMarina Cruises. Carnival will now have the newest fleet of any major cruise line. With four new ships scheduled to be delivered in the next four years, Carnival will continue to offer consumers a variety of exciting new cruise vacations."

Strategically and tactically, Carnival seems to have made all the right moves at all the right times, sometimes in direct opposition to trends identified by industry observers and market analysts. When passenger growth in the industry slowed to 3.8% in 1989, Carnival increased their already aggressive advertising and promotional campaign to attract new passengers. All ships averaged near 100% occupancy for their sailing dates. When other cruise lines started a mini "discounting war" in 1989 and 1990 (fare cuts of up to 60% off published fares), Carnival refused to jeopardize their operations and discounted only

Dr. Michael J. Keeffe, Dr. John K. Ross III, and Dr. Bill J. Middlebrook are all of the Department of Management and Marketing, Southwest Texas State University. This case was prepared for classroom purposes only, and was not designed to show effective or ineffective handling of administrative situations.

during the off-season or for ships with less than popular itineraries, and instituted "supersaver" fares for passengers who booked their cruise more than six months in advance. While industry analysts are emphasizing the dangers of industry overcapacity due to the explosive shipbuilding of recent years, Carnival proceeded with one of the most ambitious building and renovation campaigns to keep the title of having the largest and newest fleet of any major cruise operator in the world.

THE EVOLUTION OF CRUISING

With the replacement of ocean liners by aircraft in the 1960s as the primary means of transoceanic travel, the opportunity for developing the modern cruise industry was created. Ships which were no longer required to ferry passengers from destination to destination became available to investors with visions of a new vacation alternative to complement the increasing affluence of Americans. Cruising, once the purview of the rich and leisure class, was targeted to the middle class, with service and amenities similar to the grand days of first-class ocean travel.

According to Robert Meyers, Editor and Publisher of *Cruise Travel* magazine, the increasing popularity of taking a cruise as a vacation can be traced to two events that were serendipitiously timed. First, television's "Love Boat" series dispelled many myths associated with cruising and depicted people of all ages and backgrounds enjoying the cruise experience. This show was among the top ten shows on television for many years according to Nielsen ratings, and provided extensive publicity for cruise operators. Second, the increasing affluence of Americans and the increased participation of women in the work force gave couples and families more disposable income for discretionary purposes, especially vacations. As the myths were dispelled and disposable income grew, younger couples and families "turned on" to the benefits of cruising as a vacation alternative, creating a large new target market for the cruise product which accelerated the growth in the number of Americans taking cruises as a vacation. In 1989 the Boston Consulting Group estimated the potential of the cruise market to exceed $50 billion.

CARNIVAL HISTORY

In 1972 Ted Arison, backed by American Travel Services, Inc. (AITS), purchased an aging ocean liner from Canadian Pacific Empress Lines for $6.5 million. The new AITS subsidiary, Carnival Cruise Line, refurbished the vessel from bow to stern and renamed it the Marti Gras to capture the party spirit. (Also included in the deal was another ship later renamed the Carnivale.) The company start was not promising, however, as on the first voyage the Marti Gras, with over 300 invited travel agents aboard, ran aground in Miami Harbor. The ship was slow and guzzled expensive fuel, limiting the number of ports of call and lengthening the minimum stay of passengers on the ship to break-even. Arison then bought another old ocean vessel from Union Castle Lines to complement the Marti Gras and the Carnivale and named it the Festivale. To attract customers, Arison began adding diversions on-board such as planned activities, a casino, nightclubs, discos, and other forms of entertainment designed to enhance the shipboard experience.

Carnival lost money for the next three years and in late 1974 Ted Arison bought out the Carnival Cruise subsidiary of AITS, Inc. for $1 cash and the assumption of $5 million in debt. One month later, the Marti Gras began showing a profit and through the remainder of 1975 operated at more than 100% capacity. (Normal ship capacity is determined by the number of fixed berths available. Ships, like hotels, can operate beyond this fixed capacity by using rollaway beds, pullmans, and upper bunks.) Carnival Cruise Lines, with Ted Arison at the helm, was about to become one of the great corporate success stories as one of the pioneers of the modern cruise vacation alternative.

Ted Arison (Chairman), along with Bob Dickinson (who was then Vice President of Sales and Marketing) and his son Micky Arison (President of Carnival), began to alter the current approach to cruise vacations. Carnival went after first-time and younger cruisers with a moderately priced vacation package that included air fare to the port of embarkation and home after the cruise. Per diem rates were very competitive with other vacation packages and Carnival offered passage to multiple exotic Caribbean ports, several meals served daily with premier restaurant service, and all forms of entertainment and activities included in the base fare. The only things not included in the fare were items of a personal nature, liquor purchases, gambling, and tips for the cabin steward, table waiter, and busboy. Carnival continued to add to the shipboard experience with a greater variety of activities, nightclubs, and other forms of entertainment and varied ports of call to increase its attractiveness to potential customers. They were the first modern cruise operator to use multimedia advertising promotions and established the theme of "Fun Ship" cruises, primarily promoting the ship as the destination and ports of call as secondary. Carnival told the public that it was throwing a shipboard party and everyone was invited. Today, the "Fun Ship" theme still permeates all Carnival Cruise ships.

Throughout the 1980s, Carnival was able to maintain a growth rate of approximately 30%, about three times that of the industry as a whole, and between 1982 and 1988 its ships sailed with an average of 104% capacity (currently they operate at 96 to 100% capacity). Targeting younger, first time passengers by promoting the ship as a destination proved to be extremely successful. Carnivals' 1987 customer profile showed that 80% of the passengers were first-time cruisers, 20% experienced cruisers with 9% Carnival repeaters. In 1994 that profile has changed to 58% first-timers, 42% experienced cruisers with 20% Carnival repeaters.

In 1987, Ted Arison sold 20% of his shares in Carnival Cruise Lines and immediately generated over $400 million for further expansion. In 1988, Carnival acquired the Holland America Line which had four cruise ships with 4,500 berths. Holland America was positioned to the higher-income travelers with cruise prices averaging 25–35% more than similar Carnival cruises. The deal also included two Holland America subsidiaries, Windstar Sail Cruises and Holland America Westours. This success, and the foresight of management, allowed Carnival to begin an aggressive "superliner" building campaign for their core subsidiary.

In the late 1980s, Carnival decided to further diversify its holdings and built the Crystal Palace Resort and Casino, a $250 million resort situated on 250 acres in the Bahamas. The project was completed in 1989. Also in 1989 the cruise segments carried over 750,000 passengers in one year, a "first" in the cruise industry.

EXHIBIT 1

Board Members and Corporate Officers of Carnival Cruise Lines, Inc.

BOARD OF DIRECTORS:

Micky Arison
Chairman of the Board/CEO
Carnival Cruise Lines, Inc.

Uzi Zucher
Managing Director
Bear Stearns & Co., Inc.

Maks Birnbach
Chairman of the Board
Fullcut Manufacturers

Robert H. Dickinson
President
Carnival Cruise Lines, Inc.

Howard S. Frank
Senior V.P. Finance/CFO
Carnival Cruise Lines, Inc.

A. Kirk Lanterman
President/CEO
Holland America–Westours

Harvey Levinson
Chair of the Investment Committee
U.S. Security Insurance Co., Inc.

William S. Ruben
President
William Ruben, Inc.

Stuart Subotnick
General Partner & Exec. V.P.
Metromedia Company

Sherwood M. Weiser
Chairman of the Board/CEO
The Continental Companies/TCC

Meshulam Zonis
Senior V.P. Operations
Carnival Cruise Lines, Inc.

CORPORATE OFFICERS:

Micky Arison
Chairman of the Board/CEO

Robert H. Dickinson
President/COO—CCL. Inc.

A. Kirk Lanterman
President/CEO—HAL

Howard S. Frank
Vice Chairman of the Board

Robert B. Sturges
Vice President–Resorts/Gaming

Lowell Zemnick
Vice President & Treasurer

Meshulam Zonis
Senior V.P.–Operations

SOURCE: Carnival Annual Report—1993.

The company's product positioning stems from its belief that the cruise market is actually comprised of three primary segments with different passenger demographics, passenger characteristics, and growth requirements. The three segments are the contemporary, premium, and luxury segments. The contemporary segment is served by Carnival ships for cruises that are seven days or shorter in length and feature a casual ambience. The premium segment, served by Holland America, serves the seven day and longer market and appeals to more affluent consumers. The luxury segment, while considerably smaller than the other segments, caters to experienced cruisers for seven day and longer sailings.

Corporate structure is built around the "profit center" concept and is updated periodically when new acquisitions are brought under the corporate umbrella. The cruise subsidiaries of Carnival Corporation gives the corporation a presence in most of the major cruise segments and provides for world-wide operations.

Carnival has always placed a high priority on marketing in an attempt to promote cruises as an alternative to land-based vacations. It wants customers to know that the ship in itself is the destination and the ports of call are important, but secondary, to the cruise experience. Education and the creation of awareness are critical to corporate marketing efforts; John Godsman of Cruise Lines International Association (an industry association promoting cruises as a vacation) estimates that only 5–10% of the potential market has been tapped. To reach new customers, Carnival was the first cruise line to successfully break away from traditional print media and use television to reach a broader market. Even though other lines have followed Carnival's lead in selecting promotional media, the organization still leads all cruise competitors in advertising expenditures.

Carnival wants to remain the leader and innovator in the cruise industry and intends to do this with sophisticated promotional efforts and by gaining loyalty from former cruisers by refurbishing ships, building new ships, varying activities and ports of call, and being innovative in all aspects of ship operations. Management intends to build on the theme of the ship as a destination given their historical success with this promotional effort.

FINANCIAL PERFORMANCE

Carnival Corporation retains Price Waterhouse as independent accountants, the First Union National Bank of North Carolina as the registrar and stock transfer agent, and their Class A Common stock trades on the New York Stock Exchange under the symbol CCL. The company has also issued 4 1/2% Convertible Subordinated notes (due January 1, 1997) which also trade on the New York Stock Exchange. Carnival maintains a five-year, $500 million revolving line of credit for short-term working capital purposes. As of fiscal 1993, the company has $248 million outstanding under this line.

The consolidated financial statements for Carnival Corporation are shown in Exhibits 2 & 3 and selected financial data are presented in Exhibit 4.

Property and equipment on the financial statements are stated at cost. Depreciation and amortization is calculated using the straight line method over the following estimated useful lives: vessels 15–25 years, buildings 10–35 years, equipment 2–20 years and leasehold improvements at the shorter of the "term of lease" or "related asset life". Goodwill of $274 million resulting from the acquisition of HAL Antillen, N.V. (Holland America Lines) is being amortized using the straight line method over 40 years.

On June 29, 1990, Carnival issued $602 million (aggregate principal amount at maturity) of zero coupon convertible subordinated notes due 2005, and received $195 million, net of underwriting costs and expenses. The $1000 denomination notes, which accrue interest at 7.5% per annum, were convertible into 12.174 shares of Class A Common stock per note. On June 19, 1992, Carnival redeemed its outstanding notes at an aggregate redemption price of approximately $207.7 million. Roughly $13 million of the notes were converted into shares of Class A Common stock prior to the redemption date. The company then issued Convertible Subordinated Notes (4 1/2%) due in 1997 and raised $113 million to repay various bank loans.

EXHIBIT 2

Income Statement—Carnival Corporation, for Years 1990–1993 (in thousands)

	1993	1992	1991	1990
Revenues	$1,556,919	$1,473,614	$1,404,704	$1,253,756
COSTS & EXPENSES				
Operating Expenses	907,925	865,587	810,317	708,308
Selling & Admin	207,995	194,298	193,316	181,731
Deprec & Amortiz	93,333	88,833	85,166	72,404
Operating Income	347,666	324,896	315,905	291,313
OTHER INCOME (EXPENSE)				
Interest Income	11,527	16,946	10,596	10,044
Int Expense	(34,325)	(53,792)	(65,428)	(61,848)
Other Income (Exp)	(1,201)	2,731	1,746	(532)
Income Tax Expense	(5,497)	(9,008)	(8,995)	(4,546)
Total Income	318,170	281,773	253,824	234,431
DISCONTINUED OPERATIONS				
Hotel Casino Operating Loss			(33,373)	(28,229)
Est Loss on Disposal			(135,463)	
Extraordinary Item**		(5,189)		
Net Income	$ 318,170	$ 276,584	$ 84,998	$ 206,202

**Loss on the early extinguishment of debt.

SOURCE: Form 100–Securities & Exchange Commission & Carnival Annual Report—1993.

During 1991, Carnival decided to dispose of the Crystal Palace Resort & Casino. A provision for the loss on disposal of Crystal Palace of approximately $135 million was recorded in 1991. The loss represents a write-down of $95 million to record the property at its net realizable value and a provision of $40 million for the possible funding for Crystal Palace which might be required prior to disposal. During fiscal 1992, the company incurred approximately $3.2 million of cash losses at the properties. Carnival is near agreement with a European investment group for the sale of 81% of the remaining properties.

Also in July 1991, Carnival issued 5,588,750 shares of Class A Common stock and received proceeds of approximately $115 million, net of underwriting costs and expenses. The proceeds were used to increase working capital and fund the continued expansion of the cruise business.

According to the Internal Revenue Code of 1986, Carnival is considered a "controlled foreign corporation (CFC)" since 50% of its stock is held by individuals who are residents of foreign countries and its countries of incorporation exempt shipping operations of U.S. persons from income tax. Because of the CFC status, Carnival expects that all of its income (with the exception of U.S. source income from the transportation, hotel and tour businesses of Holland America) to be exempt from U.S. Federal income taxes at the corporate level.

One financial consideration of importance to Carnival management is the control of costs, both fixed and variable, for the maintenance of a healthy

EXHIBIT 3

Consolidated Balance Sheet—Carnival Corporation, 1991–1993
(in thousands)

	Aug 31, 1993	Nov 30, 1992	Nov 30, 1991
ASSETS			
Current Assets			
Cash & Equivalents	$ 60,243	$ 115,014	$ 221,708
Short-Term Investments	88,677	111,048	56,428
Accounts Receivable	19,310	21,624	12,508
Consumable Inventory	37,245	31,618	34,136
Prepaid Expenses & Other	48,323	32,120	39,008
Total Current	253,798	311,424	363,788
Property and Equipment—			
at cost, less accum			
depreciation/amort	2,588,009	1,961,402	1,920,009
Other Assets—Goodwill, less			
accumulated amortization	237,327	244,789	254,110
Net Assets (Discontinued Ops)	89,553	89,553	89,553
Other	50,233	38,439	22,702
Total Assets	$3,218,920	2,645,607	2,650,252
LIABILITIES & SHAREHOLDERS EQUITY			
Current Liabilities			
Current Portion of LT Debt	$ 91,621	$ 97,931	$ 178,137
Accounts Payable	81,374	71,473	76,890
Accrued Liabilities	94,830	69,919	70,260
Customer Deposits	228,153	178,945	167,723
Dividends Payable	19,763	19,750	18,277
Reserve for Discontinued Ops	34,253	36,763	40,000
Total Current	549,994	474,781	551,287
Long Term Debt	1,031,221	776,600	921,689
Other Long Term Liabilities	10,499	9,381	6,147
Shareholders Equity			
Class A Common (1 vote/share)	1,137	1,136	1,131
Class B Common (5 vote/share)	275	275	275
Paid-in Capital	542,606	539,622	525,492
Retained Earnings	1,089,323	850,193	652,482
Less—Stock shares to be vested	(6,135)	(6,381)	(8,251)
Total Shareholders Equity	1,627,206	1,384,845	1,171,129
Total Liabilities & Equity	$3,218,920	2,645,607	2,650,252

SOURCE: Carnival Corporation Annual Report—1993.

EXHIBIT 4

Selected Financial Data by Segment—Carnival Corporation,
1990–1993 (in thousands)

Years Ended November 30,	1993	1992	1991
REVENUES			
Cruise	$1,381,473	$1,292,587	$1,224,700
Tour	214,382	215,194	212,753
Intersegment Revenues	(38,936)	(34,167)	(32,569)
Totals	1,556,919	1,473,614	1,404,704
GROSS OPERATING PROFIT			
Cruise	598,642	552,669	539,313
Tour	50,352	55,358	55,074
Totals	648,994	608,027	594,387
DEPRECIATION & AMORTIZATION			
Cruise	84,228	79,743	76,468
Tour	9,105	9,090	8,698
Totals	93,333	88,833	85,166
OPERATING INCOME			
Cruise	333,392	301,845	292,149
Tour	14,274	23,051	23,756
Totals	347,666	324,896	315,905
IDENTIFIABLE ASSETS			
Cruise	2,995,221	2,415,547	2,415,829
Tour	134,146	140,507	144,870
Discount Resort & Casino	89,553	89,553	89,553
Totals	3,218,920	2,645,607	2,650,252
CAPITAL EXPENDITURES			
Cruise	705,196	111,766	108,425
Tour	10,281	11,400	11,324
Totals	715,477	123,166	119,749

SOURCE: Carnival Corporation Annual Report—1993.

profit margin. Carnival has the lowest break-even point of any organization in the cruise industry (ships break-even at approximately 60% capacity) due to operational experience and economies of scale. Unfortunately, fixed costs, including depreciation, fuel, insurance, port charges, and crew costs, which represent more than 25% of the company's operating expenses, cannot be significantly reduced in relation to decreases in passenger loads and aggregate passenger ticket revenue. (Major expense items are air fare (25–30%), travel agent fees (10–15%), and labor (13–15%).) Increases in these costs could negatively affect the profitability of the organization.

PRINCIPLE SUBSIDIARIES

Carnival Cruise Line

At the end of fiscal 1993, Carnival operated eight ships with a total berth capacity of 12,716. Carnival operates principally in the Caribbean and has an assortment of ships and ports of call serving the 3–, 4–, and 7–day cruise markets. (See Exhibit 5.)

EXHIBIT 5

Ships of the Carnival Fleet

CARNIVAL CRUISE SHIPS

Ship Name	GRT	Days	Area	Home Port
Fantasy	70,367	3–4	Bahamas	Canaveral
Ecstacy	70,367	3–4	Bahamas	Miami
Fascination	70,367	7	S. Caribbean	San Juan
Sensation	70,000	7	E/W Caribbean	Miami
Celebration	47,262	7	E. Caribbean	Miami
Holiday	46,052	7	W. Caribbean	Miami
Jubilee	47,262	7	Mex Riviera	Los Angeles
Tropicale	36,674	7	W. Caribbean	Tampa/N.O.

HOLLAND AMERICA SHIPS*

Ship Name	GRT	Passengers
Maasdam	55,000	1,266
Nieuw Amsterdam	33,930	1,214
Noordam	33,930	1,214
Rotterdam	38,000	1,070
Statendam	50,000	1,266
Westerdam	53,872	1,494

FIESTAMARINA SHIP

Ship Name	GRT	Passengers
Fiestamarina	27,250	950

WINDSTAR SAIL SHIPS**

Ship Name	Length	Passengers
Wind Song	440′	148
Wind Spirit	440′	148
Wind Star	440′	148

SEABORNE CRUISE LINES

Ship Name	GRT	Passengers
Seaborne Pride	10,000	204
Seaborne Spirit	10,000	204

*Holland America Ships cruise Alaska during the summer months and the Caribbean during the winter. Other destinations include Europe, Panama Canal cruises, South Pacific, and Worldwide.

**Windstar sails the Caribbean, Europe, the South Pacific, and Southeast Asia.

SOURCE: Cruise Line Directory, *Cruise Travel*, Feb. 1994.

Each ship is a floating resort including a full maritime staff, shopkeepers and casino operators, entertainers, and complete hotel staff. At various ports-of-call, passengers can also take advantage of tours, shore excursions, and duty-free shopping at their own expense.

Shipboard operations are designed to provide maximum entertainment, activities, and service while pursuing a low-cost producer strategy. Size has allowed Carnival to achieve various economies of scale, and management is very cost-conscious. Estimates are that the company begins to break-even at 60% of berth capacity and approximately 14% of corporate revenue is generated from shipboard activity such as casino operations, liquor sales, and gift shop items.

Although Carnival is increasing their presence in the shorter cruise markets, their general marketing strategy is to use 3-, 4-, or 7-day moderately price cruises to fit the time and budget constraints of the middle class. Shorter cruises can cost less than $500 per person (depending on accommodations) up to roughly $3000 per person in a luxury suite on a seven day cruise, including port charges. (Per diem rates for shorter cruises are slightly higher, on average, than per diem rates for seven-day cruises.) Average rates per day are approximately $180, excluding gambling, liquor and soft drinks, and items of a personal nature. Guests are expected to tip their cabin steward and waiter at a suggested rate of $3 per person/per day, and the bus boy at $1.50 per person/per day.

Some 99% of all Carnival cruises are sold through travel agents who receive between 10% and 15% commission. Carnival works extensively with travel agents to help promote cruises as an alternative to a Disney or European vacation. In addition to training travel agents from nonaffiliated travel/vacation firms to sell cruises, a special group of 90 employees regularly visits travel agents posing as prospective clients. If the agent recommends a cruise before another vacation option, he or she receives $10. If the travel agent specifies a Carnival cruise before other options, they receive $1000 on the spot. As of 1989, Carnival had awarded over $500,000 on this promotion which helps develop travel agent loyalty. During fiscal 1992, Carnival took reservations from about 28,500 of the approximately 39,000 travel agencies in the U.S. and no one travel agency accounted for more than one-half of one percent of Carnival revenues. (Agents receive more commissions from selling cruises than from selling airline tickets and hotel rooms.)

On-board service is labor intensive, employing help from some 51 nations—mostly Third World countries—with reasonable returns to employees. For example, waiters on the Jubilee can earn approximately $18,000 to $27,000 per year (base salary and tips), significantly greater than could be earned in their home country for similar employment. Waiters typically work 10–12 hours per day with approximately one day off per week for up to ten straight months. Carnival records show that employees remain with the company for approximately eight years and that applicants exceed demand for all cruise positions. Nonetheless, the American Maritime union has cited Carnival (and other cruise operators) several times for exploitation of its crew.

Holland America Lines

On January 17, 1989, Carnival acquired all the outstanding stock of HAL Antillen N.V. from Holland America Lines N.V. for $625 million in cash. Carnival financed the purchase through $250 million in retained earnings (cash account) and borrowed the other $375 million from banks at .25% over the prime rate. Carnival received the assets and operations of the Holland America Lines, Westours, Westmark Hotels, and Windstar Sail Cruises. Holland America currently has six cruise ships with a capacity of 7,529 berths with new ships to be delivered in the future.

Founded in 1873, Holland America Lines is an upscale (it charges an average of 27% more than similar Carnival cruises) line with principal destinations in Alaska during the fall and winter months and the Caribbean during the summer. Holland America targets an older, more sophisticated cruiser with fewer youth-oriented activities and an emphasis on the beauty of the Alaskan wilderness. On Holland America ships, passengers can dance to the sounds of the Big Band era and avoid the discos of Carnival ships. Passengers on Holland America ships enjoy more service (a higher staff-to-passenger ratio than Carnival) and have more cabin and public space per person, and a "no tipping" shipboard policy. Holland America has not enjoyed the spectacular growth of Carnival cruise ships, but has sustained constant growth over the decade of the 1980s and early 1990s with high occupancy. The operation of these ships and the structure of the crew is similar to the Carnival cruise ship model, and the acquisition of the line gave the corporation a presence in the Alaskan market where it had none before.

Holland America Westours is the largest tour operator in Alaska and the Canadian Rockies and provides vacation synergy with Holland America cruises. The transportation division of Westours includes over 280 motorcoaches comprised of the Gray Line of Alaska, the Gray Line of Seattle, Westours motorcoaches, the McKinley Explorer railroad coaches, and four dayboats for tours to glaciers and other points of interest. Carnival management believes that Alaskan cruises and tours should increase in the future due to a number of factors. These include the aging population wanting relaxing vacations with scenic beauty coupled with the fact that Alaska is a U.S. destination.

Westmark Hotels consists of 16 hotels in Alaska and the Yukon territories, and also provides synergy with cruise operations and Westours. Westmark is the largest group of hotels in the region providing moderately priced rooms for the vacationer.

Windstar Sail Cruises was acquired by Holland America Lines in 1988 and consists of three computer controlled sailing vessels with a berth capacity of 444. Windstar is very upscale and offers an alternative to traditional cruise liners with a more intimate, activity-oriented cruise. The ships operate primarily in the Mediterranean and the South Pacific. Although catering to a small segment of the cruise vacation industry, Windstar helps with Carnival's commitment to participate in all segments of the cruise industry.

Seaborne Cruise Lines

Seaborne targets the luxury market with two vessels providing 200 passengers per ship with all-suite accommodations. Seaborne is considered the "Rolls Royce" of the cruise industry and in 1992 was named the "World's Best Cruise Line" by the prestigious Cond'e Naste Traveler's Fifth Annual Readers Choice poll. Seaborne cruises the Americas, Europe, Scandinavia, the Mediterranean and the Far East.

INDUSTRY CONSIDERATIONS

The cruise industry is a maturing industry with several strong competitors. (See Exhibit 6 for a description of major competitors.) Industry consolidation has been the norm for the last 12 years in order to gain economies of scale and to gain entry into the various sub-segments of the cruise market. Not only are cruise operators continuing to contract for the building of new ships, but buyouts, mergers and acquisitions have changed the nature of competitive forces in the industry. Kloster Cruise Ltd., parent of Norwegian Cruise Lines, bought Royal Viking Lines to enter the upscale market. Carnival bought Holland America which previously bought Windstar Sail Cruises. Eastern, Western and Sundance Lines consolidated and formed Admiral Cruises, which later merged with Royal Caribbean Cruise Lines under the parent company of Royal Admiral Cruises. (Royal Admiral Ltd. is run as a 50/50 venture by Oslo-based Anders Wilhelmsen & Co. and a group headed by the Pritzker family of Chicago, which owns Hyatt Hotels.) Wilhelmsen formally owned 20% of Admiral Cruises and paid $500 million for the 50/50 split. Princess Cruises (subsidiary of P&O Lines) bought Sitmar Cruise Lines. Rederi Effjohn AB, a Finnish company that owns Scandinavian-based cruise ferries (Silja Lines) and Miami-based Commodore Cruise Lines, bought Bermuda Star Lines. Although further mergers, acquisitions and other strategic alliances are anticipated, the larger competitors are growing primarily through new shipbuilding strategies. (See Exhibit 7 for ships under construction.)

The amount of shipbuilding, the expected emergence of new competitors (the Japanese already build cruise ships for existing operators and are studying the feasibility of entering the North American and Southern Pacific markets), and the slowing of the rate of industry growth provide some interesting scenarios for cruise operators. During the late 1980s, several industry analysts predicted the growth in industry capacity would cause a supply/demand imbalance. Instead, supply seemed to create its own demand. The new wave of shipbuilding scheduled for the 1990s has rejuvenated this argument. Between 1990 and 1993 industry capacity grew at over 20% and there is a 14% increase anticipated for the remainder of the decade. Many industry observers expect passenger growth to be less than growth in industry capacity, straining the profitability of cruise competitors. Even with a $50 billion market potential identified by a Boston Consulting Group study in the 1980s, management must pay careful attention to the growth in industry capacity, demand patterns, and cruise ship occupancy levels.

With the number of repeat passengers (loyalty is approximately 40% for various firms and loyalty to cruising is estimated to be 60–70%), cruise lines are rotating ships and ports of call to provide fresh destinations. In the Caribbean market, growth and rotations are straining the infrastructure of many nations, and the League of Women Voters in St. Thomas has been campaigning to limit the number of cruise ships docking at Charlotte Amalie in St. Thomas, U.S. Virgin Islands.

There are currently two bills under consideration by the United States Congress which could affect cruise operators if enacted into law. The first, H.R. 1517 (also known as the Clay Bill) would extend certain U.S. labor laws, including the right to organize and minimum wage provisions, to foreign-registered vessels which call on U.S. ports. This bill would substantially increase operating costs of cruise lines.

EXHIBIT 6

Major Industry Competitors

CHANDRIS FANTASY CRUISES, 4470 Biscayne Blvd., Miami, FL 33137

Chandris offers five- and seven-day Eastern and Western Caribbean, Mexico, South America, Panama, and Nassau cruises on reconditioned trans-Atlantic ships and new cruise vessels as well as one- and two-night weekend cruises to Bermuda. Chandris's niche has always been value for the money—offering a little more for the dollar than other competitors.

COSTA CRUISE LINES, P.O. Box 019614, Miami, FL 33101

Costa promotes itself as the Italian Cruise Line offering a strictly Italian experience. The decor, amenities, food, and activities are designed to enhance the ethnic flavor of its ships. Costa has six refurbished ships that offer Caribbean and Mediterranean cruises for seven days or longer. Costa's mix of ships and destinations appeal to a wide spectrum of people: first-time cruisers, young adults, and seasoned cruise passengers.

NORWEGIAN CRUISE LINES, 2 Alhambra Pl., Coral Gables, FL 33134

Norwegian Cruise Lines (NCL), formally Norwegian Caribbean Lines, was the first to base a modern fleet of cruise ships in the Port of Miami. It operates seven ships on three-, four-, and seven-day Eastern and Western Caribbean cruises and cruises to Bermuda. A wide variety of activities and entertainment attracts a diverse array of customers. The Norway and the Seaward offer Broadway shows at sea and there is an active schedule of theme cruises on every ship. NCL offers many sports and leisure activities both onboard and ashore, such as the Dive-In snorkeling program, and owns a private Bahamian Out Island where passengers are treated to a private beach party.

PREMIER CRUISE LINES, P.O. Box 573, Cape Canaveral, FL 32930

A former subsidiary of the Greyhound Corporation, Premier became a major player in the industry when it was named the official cruise line of Walt Disney World. Premier and Walt Disney offer joint Disney-cruise vacations for seven or more days to include a Hertz rental car, a Walt Disney World Passport, admission to the Kennedy Space Center, and a three- or four-day Caribbean cruise. Premier attracts families with children as well as traditional cruise passengers.

PRINCESS CRUISES, 2029 Century Pk. East, Los Angeles, CA 90067

Princess Cruises, with its fleet of eight "Love Boats", offers seven-day and extended cruises to the Caribbean, Alaska, and Europe. Princess' primary market is the upscale 50-plus experienced traveler, according to Mike Hannan, Senior Vice President for Marketing Services. Princess ships have an ambiance best described as casual elegance and are famous for their Italian-style dining rooms and onboard entertainment.

ROYAL CARIBBEAN CRUISE LINES, 9303 S. Am Way, Miami, FL 33132

RCCL's nine ships have consistently been given high marks by passengers and travel agents over the past twenty-one years. In fact, repeat passengers comprise approximately 30% of passengers. RCCL's ships are built for the contemporary market, are large and modern, and offer three-, four-, and seven-day as well as extended cruises and also has a private island for beach parties. RCCL prides itself on service and exceptional cuisine.

Other Industry Competitors (Partial List)

American Family Cruises	(2 Ships—Alaska, Caribbean)
American Hawaii Cruises	(2 Ships—Hawaiian Islands)
Celebrity Cruises	(3 Ships—Caribbean, Bermuda)
Club Med	(2 Ships—Europe, Caribbean)
Commodore Cruise Line	(1 Ship —Caribbean)
Cunard Line	(9 Ships—Caribbean, Worldwide)
Dolphin Cruise Line	(3 Ships—Caribbean, Bermuda)
Epirotiki Cruises	(9 Ships—Caribbean, Worldwide)
Fantasy Cruises	(2 Ships—Caribbean, Bahamas)
Regency Cruises	(5 Ships—Caribbean, Alaska, WW)
Royal Cruise Lines	(4 Ships—Caribbean, Alaska, WW)

SOURCE: Cruise Line International Association.

EXHIBIT 7

Cruise Ships under Construction

1994

Cruise Line	Ship Name	GRT	Capacity	Cost
Silversea	Silver Cloud	15,000	310	$125M
Carnival	Fascination	70,400	2,600	$315M
Holland America	Ryndam	55,000	1,266	$250M

1995

Delta Queen Steam	America Queen	3,500	420	$60M
Silversea	Silverwind	15,000	310	$125M
P&O (Princess)	Oriana	67,000	1,975	$350M
Carnival	Imagination	70,400	2,600	$330M
Swedish American	Radisson K	15,000	232	$150M
Crystal	Symphony	48,000	960	$200M
P&O (Princess)	Sun Princess	77,000	1,950	$300M
Royal Caribbean	Project Vision	65,000	1,800	$325M
Celebrity	Not Named	70,000	1,750	$225M

1996

Carnival	Not Named	95,000	3,300	$400M
Royal Caribbean	Project Vision	65,000	1,800	$325M
Celebrity	Not Named	70,000	1,740	$225M

SOURCE: Cruise Line International Association.

The second bill, known as the Trade Reform Act of 1993 (the Gibbons Bill), provides for the listing by the Secretary of Commerce of countries which provide subsidies for the construction of vessels ("Subsidizing Countries"). Under this Bill, sanctions are to be applied to vessels which are flagged or owned by citizens of a Subsidizing Country. The nature and form of the sanctions have not been specified and if enacted, the bill would affect the cost of current operations and affect construction costs of new ships.

Carnival, and all other cruise operators that sail to Alaska, have been informed of an investigation by federal authorities with respect to the operations of casinos on cruise ships in Alaskan waters. Carnival does not believe their Holland America ships are in contravention of the law and feel that cessation of casino activities would have a material impact on Alaskan cruise operations.

CASE PART VI

Strategy Implementation and Control

Dell Computer Corporation

BILL J. MIDDLEBROOK, MICHAEL J. KEEFFE, *and* JOHN K. ROSS III,

Southwest Texas State University

Customer satisfaction and customer service are two of the most repeated catch phrases in major corporations, especially from the producer rather than the consumer side of the equation. Michael Dell does not want service and satisfaction to simply be repeated by his corporate employees and support staffs; he requires them to practice what he preaches. In fact the corporate culture—as clearly stated by Michael Dell (Personal Selling Power, March, 1993)— "... is very simple. Responsive, customer focus, high intensity level."

Dell's commitment to this concept of customer satisfaction and service—known at Dell as Direct Relationship Marketing—can be shown through the policies of the corporation. First, there is an unconditional, thirty-day money-back guarantee for all of Dell's computer systems and a "no questions asked" return policy.

Second, Dell's toll-free technical support organization is available from 7:00 a.m. to 7:00 p.m., coast to coast (including Mexico). These technicians solve 95 percent of customer problems in less than six minutes. Additionally, a TechFax system is available twenty-four hours a day, seven days a week. Customers can request technical information through a fax catalogue, and problem-solving instructions are returned by fax. A third-party network of on-site service representatives can be dispatched when problems are not solved over the phone. If necessary, unresolved problems are expedited to the design engineers to ensure complete customer satisfaction. Dell users can also access an on-line technical support group via CompuServe. Finally, Michael Dell openly invites customers to write or call him with comments about the quality of Dell's products and the level of support received from service and support personnel.

This emphasis on quality and service has won accolades from customers and industry analysts. Dell has consistently been recognized as the best in customer support and satisfaction, ahead of all other computer manufacturers.

Dr. Bill J. Middlebrook, Dr. Michael J. Keeffe, and Dr. John K. Ross III are all of the Department of Management and Marketing, Southwest Texas State University.

J. D. Power and Associates, known for their automobile rankings, again this year rated Dell number one in customer satisfaction in its third annual end-user survey for the computer industry.

The most publicized story of a company start-up in the computer industry is that of Steven Jobs and Stephen Wozniak designing and marketing Apple computers. These young entrepreneurs took a concept from a garage manufacturing arena and evolved Apple into a multimillion-dollar organization. The story of Michael Dell and the development of the Dell Computer Corporation rivals that of Jobs and Wozniak.

In 1983 Dell, then a freshman pre-med student at the University of Texas, decided to earn additional money by selling disk-drive kits and random access memory (RAM) chips at computer user meetings in Austin, Texas. Within a few months he had sufficient funds to acquire excess personal computers (PCs) at reasonable prices from IBM dealers having difficulties meeting their sales quotas. He modified these machines and began selling them through contacts in the local area and was reported to be grossing approximately $80,000 per month by April 1984. In May 1984 Dell formed the Dell Computer Corporation to sell PC's Limited brand computers and conducted operations out of his dormitory room. After dropping out of school (against his parents' wishes) he began attending computer trade fairs where he sold these IBM PC-compatible computers, one of the first custom "clones" on the market.

The results of Dell's endeavors were immediate. During the first year of business, sales were approximately $6 million and grew to $257 million within the next four years. In 1988 the brand name was changed to Dell and sales continued to grow such that by 1990 the organization had sold $546 million in PC compatible and peripheral equipment and $2.1 billion in fiscal 1993 (Dell's fiscal year ends February).

In 1987 Dell established its first international subsidiary in the United Kingdom to enter the growing European computer market. European countries had a lower PC saturation rate than the United States, and there were no large PC manufacturers in Europe. From 1988 to 1991 the organization developed wholly owned subsidiaries in Canada, France, Italy, Sweden, Germany, Finland, and the Netherlands and is in the process of launching other subsidiaries in Europe. An Irish manufacturing facility opened in 1991 to provide systems for the European market. In addition, a support center located in Amsterdam provides technical support throughout Europe. Dell reported that fourth-quarter 1991 international sales were up 109 percent over the same quarter in 1990. By February of 1993 European sales totaled $240 million and constituted 30 percent of total sales. Currently, 40 percent of sales are derived from international subsidiaries after only five years of operations.

In January, 1993, Dell made a bold move by entering the Japanese Market. Dell Computer of Japan employs a staff of forty workers to provide a full range of sales, service and technical assistance. Telephone sales are supplemented with an outside sales force and through two major retailers in Tokyo. As the first to attempt telemarketing in Japan, Dell was met with skepticism by some industry observers. Initial reports indicate that the Japanese are very enthusiastic about the marketing approach and are responding in greater numbers than originally forecasted. In fact, the forty (40) people in the Tokyo office are being tested in their ability to handle requests. Although successful, Dell is expected to have less than 1 percent of the Japanese market in 1993.

FIGURE 1
Dell Computer
Corporation

OFFICERS

Name	Age	Position
Dell, Michael S.	28	Chairman of the Board, CEO
Kocher, Joel J.	36	President, Worldwide Mkt., Sal & Ser
Henry, G. Glenn	50	Senior Vice-President
Flaig, L. Scott	48	Senior Vice-President
Meredith, Thomas J.	42	Chief Financial Officer, Treasurer
Thomas, Thomas L.	43	Chief Information Officer
Ferrales, Savino R.	42	Vice-President
Salwen, Richard E.	47	Vice-President, Legal Counsel
Medica, John	34	Vice-President, Portable Products Gp.

DIRECTORS

Name	Age	Position
Dell, Michael S.	28	Chairman of the Board, CEO
Hirschbiel, Paul Jr.	40	
Luce, Thomas W. III	52	
Inman, Bobby R.	62	Nominee
Kozmetsky, George	75	Nominee
Jordan, Michael H.	56	Nominee
Malone, Claudine B.	57	

Dell Computer Corporation is headquartered in Austin, Texas, with approximately 4200 employees worldwide. Dell had the foresight to surround himself with people having expertise in computer engineering and marketing, and he serves as both chief executive officer (CEO) and chairman of the board of directors (see Figure 1 for corporate officers and members of the board of directors). The company still operates on the principles espoused by Dell during its inception: customer service and a personal relationship with Dell system users.

PERSONAL COMPUTER INDUSTRY OVERVIEW

The short history of the PC industry is one of booms and slumps. The stellar performance of the industry during the early to mid-1980s was followed by a consolidation of existing companies and a slowdown in sales during the 1986–1987 period. Industry sales increased through 1990, and projections show that corporate capital-equipment spending should grow at a 7 to 8 percent annual rate into the early 1990s. Some analysts contend that the growth rate of the PC industry is uncertain as the growth rate of the economy slows. For example, Volpe & Covington, a San Francisco-based PC investment consulting firm, believes that a 15 percent long-term growth in revenues for high-end PCs and a 12 percent compound growth rate for the industry is a reasonable assumption. Other analysts contended that PC sales would grow at only 5 to 7 percent in the 1990s, less than half as fast as sales grew in the late 1980s. In 1992 computer and peripheral sales totaled over $142 billion. This amount grew to $155 billion in 1993 and is projected to exceed $167 billion in 1994.

PC Industry Strategies

Two macroindustry strategies for competing in the PC industry can be combined with two macrosegments of the PC market to assess competitors and competitive approaches. First, PC manufacturers can approach the market as either innovators or imitators. IBM is the accepted innovation leader as both computer manufacturers and customers watch IBM's product development and base production and purchase decisions on current IBM products. Other computer manufacturers approach the market as innovators by developing hardware and software to satisfy specific market segments.

Most firms approach the market building clone PCs. These firms (sometimes called value-added remarketers) use the base MS-DOS technology of innovators and attempt to improve on the system configuration and/or differentiate their product on some basis such as marketing channel used, service and support, product reliability, and/or price. Essentially, value-added remarketers buy components and software from various vendors to configure systems sold under their own brand labels. The success of the imitative approaches is evidenced by the performance of companies such as Compaq, Prime Computer, Inc., CompuAdd, and Dell. Many clone firms believe that to be successful in the PC industry they must be concerned with market pressures to reduce price, and thus they constantly monitor costs and search for ways to reduce those costs.

PC Markets

Macrosegments in the PC industry are usually defined as business, home, government, or education users. Business users want high performance, reliability, and value in a system for their computing needs. State-of-the-art technology, the ability to network and communicate with other systems, customer service and support, and cost are primary purchase determinants for the business user. One of the fastest-growing segments in the business market is the portables market, which is expected to grow at an annualized rate of 20 percent for the next few years.

Home market demand was initially created by innovators, early adopters, and the early majority groups of the adoption or diffusion of innovation cycle. Most home users are price conscious, planning to spend less than $1,200 for a system, and they value ease of operation and service as well as support from the manufacturer. This market should not be as lucrative as it was in the early to mid-1980s, but replacement sales (sales to previous PC owners) and sales to those still intending to buy a home PC should make this market moderately attractive.

Government and education users comprise the remaining macrosegments of the PC market. Both of these segments represent large, important segments yet typically yield lower margins than either the business or home markets. Typical purchase decisions are based on a bidding system, with the contract going to the lowest qualified bidder. The education market was considered important for its proposed ability to generate long-term brand loyalty among early users (students). Apple was one of the earliest entrants into this market. It is questionable, however, if the long-term benefits of brand loyalty by early users is actually realized.

This segment, like the business segment, is interested in integrated systems designed to perform to buyers' specific needs. Increased competition for this market has led to increased downward pressures on prices.

Competitors

Major competitors of Dell include most traditional PC manufacturers such as IBM, Compaq, Zenith, and Tandy. These firms rely on selling through a professional sales force or through retail outlets. Competitors of Dell using a direct marketing and/or retailing approach (primarily value-added remarketers) include CompuAdd, which offers a full line of machines; Northgate, which offers machines similar to Dell at savings of up to $2,000 over Dell equipment; and Everex, which offers machines similar to Dell but claims that they are faster than Dell PCs. CompuAdd is located in Austin, Texas; Northgate in Plymouth, Minnesota; and Everex in Freemont, California. None of these firms have the service and satisfaction reputation of Dell.

Changes in the industry will be driven by several factors as the market matures. First, the Gartner Group, a market research firm, estimates that the number of customers replacing their outdated systems is expected to outnumber first-time purchasers by 1995.

Second, an investment report on the PC distribution industry shows that PC saturation rates are relatively low. Only about 33 percent of white-collar workers use PCs on the job, and only 17 percent of all domestic households have a PC. This becomes more important when one considers that the largest growth opportunities are in small to medium-sized accounts (businesses with fewer than 500 employees) that employ more than 70 percent of white-collar workers.

Third, the ratio of price to performance for equivalent functions continues to improve approximately 20 to 25 percent per year, which makes the purchase of state-of-the-art machines more attractive to many segments. And fourth, competition should intensify. Value-added remarketers more than doubled during the 1988–1989 period, with the number of firms increasing from 350 to more than 1,000. Coupled with increased demand by business users, improved software and networking capabilities, and increased competition through differentiation and focus-oriented marketing strategies, industry analysts forecast additional changes in both market approaches used by major competitors and further segmentation of the market. The 1990s should be a period change for the industry, rivaling changes that occurred during the 1980s.

DELL COMPUTER OPERATIONS

Dell's success can be attributed to its commitment to customer service and satisfaction and the marketing of state-of-the-art systems to business users through direct marketing strategies.

Product Line

Dell offers an extensive and competitive product line ranging from inexpensive "first time user" computers to those with the latest technological developments. This strategy has resulted in a continuing evaluation and modification of Dell's product line with new products constantly being offered and other products being discontinued. Currently Dell is working with Microsoft to deliver factory installed Windows NT in high end workstations and networks as the software becomes available. Dell also plans to sell IBM's competing OS/2 operating system preinstalled. The ever changing demands of computer technology and the market have made product forecasting and planning difficult and risky. For example, during the last quarter of fiscal 1989, Dell overestimated demand and had considerable surplus inventories of finished goods. It attacked this problem and reduced inventories by $36 million in fiscal 1990. Inventory levels for the third and fourth quarters of 1991, respectively, were between 8.6 and 10.3 weeks of sales, below industry averages. In 1993, Dell reported a loss of $75.7 on sales of $700.6 million. This was after taking $71 million in unusual charges relating to the restructure of European operations. Also included in this loss was the value of inventories and the costs related to notebook computer projects. Michael Dell is predicting a revenue growth of about 70 percent in FY 1994, according to the March 10, 1993 *Wall Street Journal*.

Manufacturing

Dell's computers for the domestic market are manufactured in facilities in Austin, Texas. The purchase of a 126,000 square-foot manufacturing facility in 1989 doubled Dell's manufacturing capability. The 135,000-square-foot facility in Limerick, Ireland, is expected to satisfy the growing international demand for Dell Systems.

The manufacturing strategy utilized at Dell is one of building each computer system to the buyer's specifications. Buyers can add options to customize their system for their own needs. The order is then assembled and shipped with peripherals and upgrades requested by the customer. Manufacturing at Dell actually consists of the assembly and testing of vendor-procured parts, assemblies, and subassemblies. The assembly line is not automated at present, and Dell has not indicated plans to automate. In addition, Dell utilizes a total quality approach where enthusiastic workers compete in product-quality competitions for bonuses and recognition.

Marketing

One factor leading to Dell's success is the organization's marketing style. Dell approaches the market from a service and customer satisfaction standpoint combined with lower prices than comparable brands. Sales leads are generated through several sources, the primary source being advertising in PC and business publications. An outside sales force located in major markets addresses the needs of large corporate customers.

Dell's sales force is channelized according to the market it serves: small/medium business and home users, corporate buyers, and government/education/medical. Each of these sales channels is supported by its own marketing, customer service, and technical support organization. This organizational structure ensures high accountability for the satisfaction of each customer, as well as feedback from daily direct contact with the customer. PC makers dealing through the retail channel do not have this advantage and are not able to respond as quickly to market and service demands as the direct channel. Additional face-to-face exposure occurs at industry shows.

Dell's entire product line is sold by telephone sales representatives who answer more than 8,000 incoming calls on a busy day. In addition to answering customer-initiated calls, the Austin-based sales force responds to sales leads and supports the efforts of its team members in the field.

Sales orders are downloaded to the manufacturing facility several times each day, and all systems are custom-configured according to the customer's

FIGURE 2
Percentage of
Consolidated Sales—
Year Ended

	Jan 30 1994	Jan 31 1993	Feb 2 1992
NET SALES:			
North America (U.S. & Can.)	68.1%	68.9%	69.6%
Europe	27.2	27.5	27.2
Other international	4.7	3.6	3.2
Consolidated net sales	100.0	100.0	100.0
Cost of sales	84.9	77.7	68.3
Gross profit	15.1	22.3	31.7
OPERATING EXPENSES			
Selling, general & admin.	14.7	13.3	20.5
Research, dev. & engr.	1.7	2.1	3.7
Total operating expenses	16.4	15.4	24.2
Operating income (loss)	(1.3)	6.9	7.5
Net financing & other income (expense)	—	0.2	0.7
Income (loss) before income taxes	(1.3)	7.1	8.2
Provision for taxes (benefit)	(0.1)	2.1	2.5
Net income (loss)	(1.2)	5.0	5.7
Preferred stock dividends	(0.1)	—	—
Net income (loss) app to com stockholdrs	(1.3%)	5.0%	5.7%

SOURCE: Dell form 10-K fiscal year ended January 30, 1994.

specifications. Trucks load at Dell's manufacturing facility throughout the day, and overnight services are utilized for expedited orders. Lead times on systems vary from three to seven days.

Internationally, Dell is similar in marketing approach and culture to its domestic operation. Dell's wholly owned subsidiaries give it access to over 70 percent of the available worldwide market for PCs (see Figures 2 and 3).

Dell sells to major buyers through a small (twenty-five-person) sales force located in major metropolitan areas throughout the United States and services those accounts with management teams consisting of sales, customer service, and technical support representatives. Dell believes that the small to medium-sized business represents the greatest growth potential for PC-based systems.

Dell has also arranged to sell its systems through integrators like Electronic Data Systems (EDS) and Anderson Consulting, which will increase its sales potential. This move from traditional channels was prompted by the fact that

FIGURE 3
Five Year Summary

Date	Sales (000)	Net Income	EPS
1993	2,873,165	(39,576)	(1.06)
1992	2,013,924	101,642	2.59
1991	889,939	50,911	1.40
1990	546,235	27,232	0.91
1989	388,558	5,114	0.18

the mail-order market is only 16 percent of a $35 to $40 billion market, less than one-fifth the size of sales of computer stores. Dell currently has 25 percent of the mail-order market.

RETAIL

In 1990 Dell contracted with CompUSA, Inc., a Dallas-based chain of twenty superstores, to sell Dell products through 1993. CompUSA is a computer version of Toys-R-Us, with approximately 21,000 square feet of retail space per store, a service center with a fast service pickup for corporate clients, and over 5,000 items at discount prices. CEO Nathan Morton, a former senior executive with Home Depot and Target Stores, expected sales to top $1 billion in 1991 after only two years of operations. CompUSA is adding new stores in major metropolitan areas and sells Dell systems for the same prices as Dell's direct sales.

Dell added Staples Office Supply Superstores to its mass merchandising channel in mid-1991 as well. Staples markets to a less sophisticated computer user than does CompUSA. Although Dell systems are sold through this superstore channel, Dell maintains its same level of customer support to these buyers. Users who purchase Dell systems through CompUSA and Staples are entered into Dell's customer data base as if they had ordered directly through Dell.

Dell's mass merchandising move may provide a serendipitous opportunity for the company even though computer retailing is seen by some industry analysts as posed for a shakeout. Dataquest, Inc., believes that traditional retailers will see their share of PC sales shrink through 1994. Analysts state that marketers will have to move toward the ends of the retail spectrum by either concentrating on high-volume, low-price selling or specializing in market niches or other customized services that mass marketers neglect in order to be successful. Smaller operations that emphasize service along with price are already showing the greatest gains. Superstores may be one retail format that not only survives the shakeout but prospers. In 1993 Dell began selling its Precision Line of Computers through Sam's Clubs, a division of Wal-Mart Stores Incorporated. This move is in addition to the agreement with Price Club, another mass merchandising chain.

Research and Development

During the last few years, Dell's revenue growth has allowed the organization to devote considerable resources to building a first-class technological capability. Research and development spending in fiscal 1989 increased 29 percent over the previous year, doubled in fiscal 1990, and was estimated to be more than $18 million in 1991. Dell's efforts are enhanced since Intel added Dell to its preferred purchaser list in 1989.

During fiscal 1990, the first products to utilize the Dell proprietary integrated circuit chip were shipped to customers. Dell is no longer restricted to standard vendor technologies when customizing its machines for specific usages. In 1990 Dell filed forty-five patent applications to protect Dell-developed technologies and designs.

Finance

Financial summaries of Dell are presented in Figure 4. The organization does not pay dividends to investors, instead relying on appreciation of stock price.

FIGURE 4 Dell Computer Corporation— Condensed Consolidated Balance Sheet (in thousands)	Jan 30 1994	Jan 31 1993	Feb 2 1992
ASSETS			
Current Assets:			
Cash & cash equivalents	$3,355	$14,948	$55,460
Accounts receivable, net	$410,774	$374,013	$164,960
Inventories	$220,265	$303,220	$126,554
Other current assets	$80,323	$80,239	$65,814
Total current assets	$1,048,384	$852,787	$512,180
Property and equipment, net	$86,892	$70,464	$44,661
Other assets	$5,204	$3,756	$2,722
Total assets	$1,140,480	$927,005	$559,563
LIABILITIES AND STOCKHOLDER'S EQUITY			
Current Liabilities:			
Notes payable			
Accounts payable	$282,708	$295,133	$97,389
Other current liabilities	$255,279	$198,706	$132,145
Total current liabilities	$537,987	$493,839	$229,534
Long-term debt	$100,000	$48,373	$41,450
Other liabilities	$31,385	$15,593	$14,399
Common stock	$379	$369	$358
Additional paid in capital	$320,041	$177,978	$165,745
Retained earnings	$170,790	$208,544	$106,902
Obligations under capital leases			
Deferred income taxes			
Redeemable convertible preferred stock			
Stockholders' equity	$471,108	$369,200	$274,180
Cumulative translation adjustment	($23,345)	($17,691)	$1,175
Total liabilities & net worth	$1,140,480	$927,005	$559,563

It has experienced good sales and profit growth, especially after instituting tighter inventory controls following the overstock of 1989. The 1989 inventory problem caused the stock price to drop 42 percent, from a high of $12 to $7 per share. Dell is currently searching for ways to reduce costs without sacrificing customer service and technological performance of its systems.

ISSUES AND CONCERNS

The most pressing concern of investors regarding Dell operations is Michael Dell. Dell has been very successful in building his organization with an entrepreneurial style of management. On a scale of one to ten, Dell rates himself ten as a competitor, innovator, goal setter, entrepreneur and exporter. He rates himself lowest in the areas of production and finance. Although Dell was cited as Entrepreneur of the Year by *Inc.* magazine, his critics wonder if he is capable of making the transition of moving the corporation from a Stage 1 entrepreneurial mode to a Stage 2 professional management company.

Another concern is Dell's current move to include retail sales in addition to its traditional strength of telemarketing. This move is designed to broaden

Dell's appeal to small businesses and the home PC user, but retailers historically have not shown loyalty to any particular brand of machine and may stock several different brands in their stores. Additionally, Dell's emphasis on telemarketing is a double-edged sword. Telemarketing does reduce the need for a field sales force and eliminates channel markups, but Dell is considered by some to be little more than a dim, dusty warehouse that sells cheap, undistinguished PCs.

Lastly, the question also arises whether Dell can continue to grow as quickly as it would like and still have the same emphasis on service, performance, and satisfaction. There is also the situation of more intense competition as the industry matures and growth slows. Dell is still one of the infants in an industry populated by giants, and it must be wary of these financial and technological colossuses potentially entering its market niche.

C A S E

2

Ben & Jerry's Homemade Ice Cream, Inc.

NEIL H. SNYDER, *University of Virginia*

One evening in early 1990, company founders Ben Cohen and Jerry Greenfield sat at a local pub trading stories of the early years at Ben & Jerry's Homemade Ice Cream, Inc. In regretful voices they questioned the virtually overnight success of their company and the changes that had come about in their once "weird, free-spirited" adventure. Middle management alienation, more structured outside managers and lack of corporate direction threatened Ben & Jerry's original mission, and they wondered if they really could be a big business with a "weird and fun" mentality. Inwardly, both Ben and Jerry questioned their changing role within the company, their ability to provide a corporate vision, and ultimately, whether they should sell out and pursue less structured ventures.

HISTORY

Ben & Jerry's Homemade Ice Cream, Inc. makes Ben & Jerry's super premium ice cream, ice cream novelties, and Ben & Jerry's Light super premium ice milk. The first "scoop shop" opened on May 5, 1978 in a renovated gas station in Burlington, Vermont. Two lifelong best friends Ben Cohen and Jerry Greenfield, invested $12,000 of their own capital and borrowed an additional $4,000 to launch their entrepreneurial venture. Initially, the only equipment used amounted to an old-fashioned rock salt ice-cream maker, and the owners' ice cream expertise consisted of a $5 correspondence course in ice-cream making from Penn State.

Despite these meager beginnings, the company quickly developed a reputation for making chunky, delicious, unusual flavors made solely from Vermont milk and cream. Local popularity gave way to larger markets, and by 1980, they were delivering Ben & Jerry's ice cream to grocery stores and restaurants.

This case was prepared by Angela Clontz, Billy Deakyne, Johnna Duncan, and Michael Chung under the direction of Neil H. Snyder, Ralph A. Beeton Professor of Free Enterprise at the University of Virginia's McIntire School of Commerce. This case was designed for use in classroom discussion and is not intended to demonstrate either effective or ineffective handling of administrative situations.

Time magazine discovered th e company in 1981 and hailed it the "best ice cream in the world," helping the company's further expansion.

In 1985, Ben & Jerry's moved its corporate headquarters and ice cream factory from Burlington to Waterbury, Vermont. This new 43,000 square foot facility possessed production capacity of 400,000 gallons of ice cream per month. A similar facility came on line in 1988 in Springfield, Vermont, to expand product lines into ice cream novelties and Peace Pops.

BEN & JERRY'S UNIQUE BUSINESS PHILOSOPHY

Cohen and Greenfield, both products of the 1960s and 1970s, approached business from a unique perspective. They transformed their personal free-spirited lifestyles into a business adventure. Ben & Jerry's is dedicated to the creation and demonstration of this new corporate concept of linked prosperity. The corporate mission consists of three interrelated parts:

- *Product Mission*—To make, distribute, and sell the finest quality, all-natural ice cream and related products in a wide variety of innovative flavors made from Vermont dairy products.
- *Social Mission*—To operate the company in a way that actively recognizes the central role that business plays in the solitude of society by initiating innovative ways to improve the quality of life of a broad community—local, national, and international.
- *Economic Mission*—To operate the company on a sound financial basis of profitable growth, increasing value for our shareholders, and creating career opportunities and financial rewards for our employees.

Ben Cohen comments on the Ben & Jerry's approach to corporate operations.

It is our objective to run Ben & Jerry's for long term financial and social gain. We continue to refuse to run our business to make the short term quarterly numbers look good. We are becoming more comfortable and adept at functioning with a two-part bottom line, where our company's success is measured by both our financial and our social performance.

This dedication to dual success measures goes beyond lip service. The company's annual report consists of both a financial audit as well as a social audit. By interrelating financial and social performance, the company believes it further improves its financial performance—and it has. Ben & Jerry's has saved millions of dollars in public relations and marketing expenses by providing the media with publicity generating, noteworthy "stunts." Furthermore, Cohen and Greenfield share deep and sincere respect for all individuals and the community. Through Ben & Jerry's, they exercise their belief that business and government have a dual responsibility to devote resources to solve the problems of our society, especially concerning the environment, children, the family, the handicapped and peace issues.

THE BEN & JERRY'S FOUNDATION, INC.

To aid in carrying out this corporate mission, the company established The Ben & Jerry's Foundation, Inc. in September 1985 with Jerry as chairman. Jerry believes the charity foundation seeks to "empower people to take action and to feel effective in their communities and in their lives." The foundation receives 7.5% of Ben & Jerry's pre-tax earnings, which in 1989 amounted to $288,971 appropriated among 78 groups.

1% for Peace

Through the foundation, Ben & Jerry's is heavily involved in "1% for Peace" which seeks to redirect 1% of the U. S. Defense Budget toward building understanding between the nations of the world. In 1989, the company contributed $35,433 to the peace movement through earnings from its new "Peace Pop" product.

SOCIAL CONCERNS

International Expansion

In line with the company's and the Foundation's goals, Ben & Jerry's plans to open a "scoop shop" in the Soviet Union. The goals of this project are to (1) demonstrate a model of small scale private enterprise in the Soviet Union and (2) to use business resources to further peace through understanding between the Soviet Union and the United States. All profits from the venture will fund citizen exchange programs between the two countries.

Bovine Growth Hormone

A current concern is the use of Bovine Growth Hormone (BGH) which is a controversial new bio-engineered hormone designed to increase milk production in dairy cattle. The company voiced its opposition to the drug on 6 million of its ice cream cartons, emphasizing the threat the drug poses for small, family-owned dairy farmers.

People Encouraging People

Ben & Jerry's dedicated a store franchise worth $21,000 to People Encouraging People. This non-profit program offers community support to mentally ill people and other emotionally handicapped individuals.

Social Mission through Suppliers

Ben & Jerry's also seeks suppliers who share enlightened views on the role of business in the community of the world. With over 300 regular suppliers, the company seeks to spread its social mission. For example, Greystone Bakery, which supplies the brownies for the Chocolate Fudge Brownie flavor ice cream, employs homeless and economically at-risk people. In addition, St. Albans Cooperative Creamery is the company's sole supplier of milk and cream, receiving 23% of Ben & Jerry's annual payments to vendors. This farmer-owned Vermont cooperative is a successful model of dairy farmers sharing in the profits derived through joint marketing and illustrates Ben & Jerry's commitment to Vermont's farmers.

ENVIRONMENTAL CONCERNS

Ben & Jerry's takes several steps to be environmentally aware and safe. In 1989, the company created the position of Manager of Environmental Development to analyze the corporate environmental practices and develop alternatives and solutions to current practices.

Recycling efforts remain a major thrust of waste concerns for Ben & Jerry's. Approximately 60% of office paper is recycled and all packaging materials are recyclable. In addition, the company works in combination with Vermont Republic Industries, which employs physically and emotionally handicapped people to recycle plastic ice cream pails.

Other environmental steps include Ben & Jerry's construction of a water treatment plant in 1989 and energy conservation within the manufacturing process.

Most notably, Ben & Jerry's developed a special product, Rain Forest Crunch, to call attention to the destruction of South America's rain forests and to work for their preservation. The product contains Brazil and cashew nuts purchased from Cultural Survival, a human rights organization, which is using the profits to set up cooperative Brazil nut processing plants owned and operated by indigenous forest peoples. Introduced in 1989, 40% of Rain Forest Crunch's profits are donated to such preservation groups.

KEY MANAGEMENT

Ben Cohen, Chairman of the Board at 40, is far from the typical business executive. He dropped out of Colgate College and entered Skidmore where he studied pottery and jewelry. Feeling too restrained he entered Skidmore's "University Without Walls" program, an unstructured college degree program, but again quit school never to return. Ben is a self-professed "hippie" whose free spirit led him through various activities before co-founding Ben & Jerry's.

Jerry Greenfield, 38 and head of Ben & Jerry's Foundation, is another free spirit. He studied pre-medicine at Oberlin College but was unable to gain acceptance to medical school. He drifted about for several years before teaming with Ben on their venture.

Fred Lager, fondly called "Chico," was hired in 1982 as the Chief Executive Officer. A University of Southern California MBA, he is described as the company's fiscal soul, the balance to Ben Cohen. Under his direction the company has slashed costs, boosted production and drastically improved earnings to its current level of $2.05 million.

Both Ben and Jerry now spend most of their time travelling and doing marketing promotions for the company, leaving Fred to handle operations.

EMPLOYEES AND WORK ENVIRONMENT

Ben & Jerry's views its 250 employees as valuable resources. The company supports its people and the community by hiring the handicapped and providing free therapy sessions—including anonymous drug and alcohol counseling—to any employee who needs it. Employees are actively involved in developing, integrating and carrying out the company's goals. The company holds monthly staff meetings where all employees—owners, managers and line workers—congregate over refreshments to discuss projects, performance, changes and overall "fun" in the work place.

Ben & Jerry's is the antithesis of the typical corporate culture. "Fun" and a laid back atmosphere are valued at Ben & Jerry's where the young, dedicated employees dress casually, know each other, and promote "weird" behavior.

Furthermore, the company uses a 5 to 1 salary ratio, which limits the top salary to five times that of the lowest-paid employee. Top salary in 1988 amounted to approximately $89,000.

BEN & JERRY'S MARKETING

Ben & Jerry's marketing strategy focuses on innovative, nontraditional methods of promotion and totals to 5% of annual sales. By emphasizing its all-natural, high quality ingredients and "down home Vermont" image on all packaging, sales material and promotional campaigns, Ben & Jerry's differentiates itself from competitors. Ben Cohen and Jerry Greenfield are also very prominent in defining the products' image. These two "real people" appear on all packaging and make personal appearances to further the company's social mission.

Ben & Jerry's has avoided traditional mass media and opted for less costly and more creative means of obtaining publicity. Innovative techniques provide unpaid newspaper, magazine, radio and television news coverage. For example, Ben & Jerry's sponsors many community events, the Newport Folk Festival in Newport, Rhode Island, the new Museum of American Folk Art in New York City, and various charity concerts. Preparations for a Ben & Jerry's "scoop shop" in the Soviet Union have also provided free publicity while furthering the corporate mission.

In addition, Ben & Jerry's conducts guided tours of its ice cream production facility in Waterbury, Vermont. In 1989, approximately 167,000 people visited the plant, making it one of Vermont's prime tourist attractions.

Franchise Program

In addition to sales through grocery stores and restaurants, Ben & Jerry's has expanded its store ownership beyond its original "scoop shops" beginnings. Additional stores have been added in Golchester, Williston, Montpelier and Waterbury, Vermont to enhance both sales, community presence and name recognition. Ben & Jerry's also has over 80 licensed franchises ("scoop shops") in California, Connecticut, the District of Columbia, Florida, Georgia, Illinois, Indiana, Maine, Maryland, Massachusetts, New Hampshire, New Jersey, New York, North Carolina, Ohio, Pennsylvania, Rhode Island, Vermont, Virginia, Canada and Israel. Franchises cost $25,000 initially with a yearly advertising fee of 4% of sales.

Distribution

Distribution is critical to the ice cream industry and especially to a small business like Ben & Jerry's which is entering new and geographically diverse markets. The company primarily uses independent regional ice cream distributors in New England and Florida, and Dreyer's Grand Ice Cream, Inc. handles markets outside these areas. In addition, Ben & Jerry's owns six trucks which distribute products in the Vermont and upstate New York region.

THE ICE CREAM INDUSTRY AND COMPETITION

The ice cream industry ranges from super premium to black label ice cream products and has wholesale factory shipments of approximately $500 million per year. Ben & Jerry's competes in the highly competitive super premium ice cream and frozen dessert market. From 1982 to 1985 this segment grew 25% to 30% annually, yet growth has since slowed to approximately 15%.

The principal players are The Haagen-Dazs Company, Inc., Frusen Gladje, Steve's Homemade Ice Cream, Dreyer's Grand Ice Cream, Inc. and Ben & Jerry's. Haagen-Dazs, the super premium industry leader, is owned by the Pillsbury Company, which is now a subsidiary of Grand Metropolitan PLC, a British food and liquor conglomerate. Haagen-Dazs has also developed its own line of "chunky" flavors in response to market demand.

Frusen Gladje is owned by Kraft, Inc., a subsidiary of Philip Morris Companies, a tobacco and food conglomerate. Both Grand Metropolitan and Philip Morris are huge, diversified corporations with resources far beyond those of Ben & Jerry's.

Steve's, run by aggressive, streetwise marketer Richard Smith, is the most similar to Ben & Jerry's in its product offerings. Steve's has also recently acquired a majority interest in American Glace, a manufacturer of fat and cholesterol-free frozen desserts.

Dreyer's, with over 1,000 people, manufactures and distributes a line of premium quality ice cream and sherbet products sold to supermarkets, convenience stores, restaurants and ice cream parlors.

Ben & Jerry's has also recently marketed its Ben & Jerry's Light which is all-natural with 1/3 less fat and less cholesterol than normal ice cream. Significant promotion and sales dollars have been invested since its 1989 introduction to gain market share from competition such as Steve's Ice Milk and frozen yogurt. In addition, Monsanto, another highly diversified corporation, plans to market its own light, frozen dessert, Simple Pleasures, using its Simplesse fat substitute.

Further competition comes from the ice cream novelty segment which includes Dove Bars, Snickers Ice Cream Bars and other frozen desserts.

Given this wide product offering, shelf space remains limited, and expanding franchises in malls and cities leads to more intensified competition. Ben & Jerry's continued sales growth is attributed to geographic market expansion combined with market penetration in the New England segment. Currently, Ben & Jerry's is the best selling super premium ice cream in New England, but this market remains highly competitive as well.

Exhibit 1 shows the major players in the ice cream industry along with their total assets, sales and return on sales.

FINANCIAL PERFORMANCE

Industry Position

In the food processing industry Ben & Jerry's ranks 11th in Earnings Per Share growth at 25.4%. Its sales growth of 56.1% over the last four years places the company 9th in the industry, while Return on Equity of 15.3% ranks 38th.

Capital Structure

Ben & Jerry's is a publicly traded company with 8,887 shareholders and 2,614,000 shares outstanding. During the early years, much of the company's growth was financed through debt. Ben & Jerry's has been working to decrease its long term debt and now has a debt to equity ratio of 72% and a long

---

EXHIBIT 1

Market Players

	Total Assets (000)	Sales (000)	ROS
Ben and Jerry's Homemade Inc.	$ 28,139	$ 58,463	3.5
Dreyer's Grand Ice Cream Inc.	$139,408	$227,286	4.6
Steve's Homemade Ice Cream Inc.	$ 21,304	$ 33,429	4.3
International Yogurt Company	$ 3,464	$ 4,864	−18.7
Tofruzen Inc.	$ 2,001	$ 1,165	−81.5
Larry's Ice Cream Inc.	$ 1,986	$ 2,176	−35.3

Ben and Jerry's Ownership Distribution

Type of Investor	#	Percentage
Institutions	17	11.63%
5% owners	2	30.81%
Insiders	4	21.52%

---

term debt to capitalization of 33%. As of December 1989, the stock sold for $15.00 with a Price to Earnings ratio of 17.63 with no dividends paid due to a bank loan covenant. Ownership proportions are given in Exhibit 1.

Liquidity

Despite its substantial debt, Ben & Jerry's covers its financing costs with a Quick Ratio of 1.27 and a Current Ratio of 2.24. Recent cash expenditures have been primarily financed through cash flows generated from operations.

Sales

Sales growth doubled each year from 1980 to 1986 and grew an average of 50% per year from 1986 to 1988, reaching nearly $20 million. From 1988 to 1989 sales increased 23% to nearly $58.5 million. Several factors contributed to this improvement. Unit sales volume rose 18%, price per unit rose 7%, and better franchise management improved profitability. Sales remain decidedly seasonal, peaking in the summer and bottoming out in the winter. Exhibit 2 shows Ben & Jerry's increases in earnings and sales for 1986 to 1989.

EXHIBIT 2

Percentage Increase in Earnings and Sales—1986–1989

	1986	1987	1988	1989
Sales	102%	59%	49%	22%
Earnings	84%	42%	11%	26%

Cost of Goods Sold

Higher dairy ingredients costs and increased manufacturing costs contributed to a 23% increase in costs from 1988 to 1989. The ingredient costs are forecasted to subside and are heavily controlled by supply and demand conditions. The manufacturing expenses, however, will remain and adversely impact the operating margin into the future.

Earnings

Ben & Jerry's earnings growth remains impressive, totalling $551,000 in 1985 and then growing 84% to just over $1 million in 1986. Since then, net income has grown an average of 28% per year to over $2 million in 1989. In addition, Earnings Per Share has grown to $.78 per share as shares outstanding has remained relatively constant since 1986.

Exhibit 3 shows Ben & Jerry's financial highlights for 1985 to 1989. Exhibit 4 shows the firm's distribution percentages for 1989. Exhibit 5 presents Ben & Jerry's financial ratios. Exhibit 6 shows Ben & Jerry's income statements for 1988–89 and pro forma statements for 1990–95. The firm's balance sheet for 1989 is presented in Exhibit 7.

EXHIBIT 3

Ben and Jerry's Five Year Financial Highlights from 1985 to 1989 (in thousands except per share data)

| | Year Ended | | | | |
	1989	1988	1987	1986	1985
Net Sales	$58,464	$47,561	$31,838	$19,954	$9,858
Cost of Sales	$41,660	$33,935	$22,673	$14,144	$7,321
Gross profit	$16,804	$13,627	$9,185	$5,810	$2,537
S&A expenses	$13,009	$10,655	$6,774	$4,101	$1,812
Operating income	$3,795	$2,972	$2,391	$1,709	$725
Other income	($362)	($274)	$ 305	$ 208	($31)
Income before income taxes	$3,433	$2,698	$2,696	$1,917	$694
Income taxes	$1,380	$1,079	$1,251	$901	$143
Net income	$2,053	$1,628	$1,445	$1,016	$551
Net income per common share	0.79	0.63	0.56	0.40	0.28
Avg common shares outstanding	2599	2579	2572	2565	1991
BALANCE SHEET DATA	**1989**	**1988**	**1987**	**1986**	**1985**
Working capital	$5,829	$5,614	$3,902	$3,678	$4,955
Total assets	$28,139	$26,307	$20,160	$12,805	$11,076
Long-term debt	$9,328	$9,670	$8,330	$2,442	$2,582

EXHIBIT 4

Ben and Jerry's Distribution % of Net Sales for the Fiscal Year Ended December 1989

Wholesale sales to distributors	90.3%
Wholesale sales to franchisees	3.8%
Retail sales at company-owned parlors	5.9%
	100%

EXHIBIT 5

Ben and Jerry's Financial Ratios

	1987	1988	1989
Quick ratio	1.98	1.43	1.27
Current ratio	2.78	2.19	2.24
LT debt to equity	0.92	0.89	0.72
Interest coverage	22.24	4.48	5.33
Inventory turnover	19.91	15.42	14.63
ROE	15.6	14.4	15.3
ROA	7.2	6.2	7.3

MID-GROWTH CONCERNS

In late 1982, bewildered by the company's success and impending structure, Jerry left the company. He felt unable and unwilling to be a "businessman," but did return in 1985 to head the Foundation.

By this time, Fed Lager's leadership had transformed Ben & Jerry's from a small operation to a multi-million dollar enterprise which had doubled in size each year through 1986. Ben Cohen, too, felt uneasy about this rapid growth and pursued options to sell the company. Ben disliked the negative aspects of a large bureaucracy and felt that he could no longer exercise hands-on management. The growth of Ben & Jerry's, however, enhanced his and the company's ability to follow its social mission to benefit the community. For this reason he decided against selling the company, took it public (initially only offering shares to Vermonters) and pursued growth in hopes of redistributing the wealth throughout the community.

Ben and Fred realized that by growing they would confront further competition so they aggressively moved into eight new markets, including Atlanta and Los Angeles, in only nine months. This move pushed sales up 40% and sent the company scurrying to hire more people and find new facilities to meet demand.

EXHIBIT 6

Ben and Jerry's Pro Forma Income Statement Income Statement 1987–1989

Growth rate	49% 1988	22% 1989	20% 1990	20% 1991	15% 1992	15% 1993	15% 1994	15% 1995
Net sales	$47,561,416	$58,463,864	$70,156,637	$84,187,964	$96,816,159	$111,338,583	$128,039,370	$147,245,275
Cost of sales	$33,934,736	$41,659,596	$49,991,515	$59,989,818	$68,988,291	$79,536,535	$91,667,015	$105,617,067
Gross profit	$13,626,680	$16,804,268	$20,165,122	$24,198,146	$27,827,868	$32,002,048	$36,802,355	$42,322,708
Administrative exp	$10,654,747	$13,008,951	$15,610,741	$18,732,889	$21,542,823	$24,774,246	$28,490,383	$32,763,941
Operating income	$2,971,933	$3,795,317	$4,554,380	$5,465,256	$6,285,045	$7,227,802	$8,311,972	$9,558,768
OTHER INCOME								
Interest income	$355,352	$227,331	$272,797	$327,357	$376,460	$432,929	$497,869	$572,549
Interest expense	($775,533)	($792,566)	($951,079)	($1,141,295)	($1,312,489)	($1,509,363)	($1,735,767)	($1,996,132)
Other	$145,839	$203,643	$244,372	$293,246	$337,233	$387,818	$445,990	$512,889
	($274,342)	($361,592)	($433,910)	($520,692)	($598,796)	($688,616)	($791,908)	($910,694)
Income bef taxes	$2,697,591	$3,433,725	$4,120,470	$4,944,564	$5,686,249	$6,539,186	$7,520,064	$8,648,073
Income taxes	$1,079,187	$1,380,412	$1,656,494	$1,987,793	$2,285,962	$2,628,857	$3,023,185	$3,476,663
Net income	$1,618,404	$2,053,313	$2,463,976	$2,836,771	$3,280,286	$3,790,329	$4,376,879	$5,051,410
Avg common shares	2578701	2599194	2599194	2600000	2600112	2601126	2601126	2601126
EPS	0.63	0.79	0.95	1.09	1.26	1.46	1.68	1.94
Market share	9.51%	11.69%	14.03%	16.84%	19.36%	22.27%	25.61%	29.45%
	Actual		Pro Forma					

EXHIBIT 7	

Ben and Jerry's Homemade, Inc.—Balance Sheet

	1989
Current Assets	
Cash	$2,393,313
Accounts receivable	$3,669,878
Income taxes refundable	$58,119
Inventories	$3,996,550
Prepaid expenses	$190,289
Deferred income taxes	$204,000
Total Current Assets	$10,512,149
Property plant and equipment	$21,704,132
Less accumulated depreciation	$4,666,904
Other assets	$589,641
	$28,139,018
Current Liabilities	
Current capital leases	$329,393
Accounts payable	$2,777,655
Accrued payroll	$454,201
Accrued expenses	$745,510
Franchise deposits	$376,000
Total Current Liabilities	$4,682,759
Long term debt	$9,327,867
Deferred income taxes	$723,000
Stockholder's equity	$900
Class A common stock	$67,261
Class B common stock	$19,209
Additional paid-in capital	$6,386,671
Retained earnings	$6,960,493
Class A treasury stock	($29,142)
Total Stockholder's Equity	$13,405,392
	$28,139,01

GROWTH REPERCUSSIONS

Ben & Jerry's rapid growth brought many, often unwanted changes to the old corporate culture. The weird, family atmosphere fell prey to controls, departments and memos. Flexibility declined as more and more approvals stalled product introductions. No longer did the employees all know each other, celebrate employee birthdays and feel connected. One five year employee and shift supervisor explained, "It's hard to feel you're a part of a big family if you don't know the brothers and sisters."

The forces that had sent Ben & Jerry's into the spotlight as a lean and nimble enterprise had fallen out of balance. Ben described how once small tasks had become unmanageable for the understaffed company.

> We didn't have good systems or standard operating systems. So every time we had to do something that was pretty much a repetitive process, it would get started from the beginning— instead of just pulling out the procedure and following it. Eventually we'd get the job done, but it took a whole lot more energy.

Flexibility limitations in the areas of distribution and ingredients due to Ben & Jerry's social selectivity also placed pressure on the company's ability to meet demand. Facilities produced at nearly full capacity, without plans for added plants in the near future. Employees found themselves spending time putting out small fires in various areas as growth placed stress on all of the company's internal operations.

MIDDLE MANAGEMENT DISCONTENT

By 1986, management and line workers alike complained of confusion over corporate objectives. Ben and Jerry called for heightened social contributions, yet remained uneasy about further growth. Growth continued, almost magically, leaving the management team fragmented as to the true direction of the company. No longer were the employees 100% behind the company's social mission or content with such a "weird and free spirited" approach to business. Furthermore, managers' discontent with the 5 to 1 salary limitation became more vocal as responsibility widened with sales growth. The internal organization needed restructuring and more support services to satisfy the added products and markets.

The growing competition and the slowed growth in the super premium market heightened the need for a cohesive, lean and efficient Ben & Jerry's organization. Ben and Jerry fretted over the erosion of their corporate culture and wondered if they could somehow reinstall their values despite the explosive growth. Many at the company, however, questioned whether Ben and Jerry could provide the corporate vision and leadership necessary for prosperity through the 1990s.

Sun Microsystems: A High Growth, Loosely Organized Giant in a Constrained, Technology Intensive Environment

WALTER E. GREENE, *University of Texas Pan American*
and WILLIAM C. HOUSE, *University of Arkansas—Fayetteville*

INTRODUCTION

In 1982, four individuals, who were twenty-seven years old, combined forces to found Sun Microsystems, with the objective of producing and marketing computer workstations to scientists and engineers. Two of the four were Stanford MBA graduates—Michigan born Scott McNealy, and Vinod Khosla, a native of India. They were joined by Andreas Bechtolsheim, a Stanford engineering graduate who had constructed a computer workstation with spare parts in order to perform numerical analysis, and Unix software expert, William Joy from the Berkeley campus. Sun's founders believed there was demand for a desktop computer workstation costing between $10,000 and $20,000 in a market niche ignored by minicomputer makers IBM, Data General, DEC, and Hewlett-Packard.

Sun Microsystems is the market leader in the fast growing workstation industry, expecting sales revenue growth of 30% annually during the next five years compared to 5 to 10% for the personal computer industry. Workstations can be used in stand-alone fashion or as part of networked configurations. The product lines produced range from low priced diskless units to higher powered graphics oriented stations at the top of the line.

In contrast to personal computers, workstations are characterized by 32 bit instead of 16 bit microprocessors, a strong tendency to use the UNIX operating system instead of MS/DOS, more sophisticated software and graphics capabilities, larger storage capacities, faster processing speeds and the ability to function effectively in a networking environment. The principal users of workstations have been engineers and scientists. However, price reductions and

The research and written case information was prepared by Wm. C. House of the University of Arkansas—Fayetteville, and Walter E. Greene, Professor, University of Texas Pan American for presentation at the North American Case Research Association Symposium (Atlanta, 1991).

technological improvements have broadened the appeal of workstations so that they are finding use in financial trading, desktop publishing, animation, mapping, and medical imaging applications.

Sun, the fastest growing company in the computer hardware industry, has revenues that are increasing at a five year compounded rate of 85% and income increasing at a 67% rate from 1985 to 1990 (Markoff, 1991). For fiscal year 1991, Sun's revenues were 3.2 billion dollars and net income was 190 million (Zachary, 1991). The company's rapid growth rate has severely drained its cash resources.

CHAIRMAN AND CEO OF SUN MICROSYSTEMS

Scott McNealy, the current chairman of Sun, is a native of Detroit and grew up on the fringes of the U.S. automobile industry. Originally rejected by both Harvard and Stanford Business Schools, he graduated from Harvard with a major in economics. In 1981, at the age of 26, McNealy became manufacturing director at Onyx systems, a small minicomputer maker. The company was faced with serious quality problems. In two months, the operation showed drastic improvement as McNealy probed work rules and production bottlenecks, encouraging workers to identify problems and overcome obstacles on the way toward improving workplace efficiency.

In 1982, former Stanford classmates Andy Bechtolsheim and Vinod Khosla asked him to join them as Director of Operations in a new company to be called Sun Microsystems. Two years later, McNealy was chosen by the Board of Directors to be CEO over Paul Ely, now Executive Vice-President of Unisys. During the first month after he became CEO, one of the three cofounders resigned, the company lost $500,000 on 2 million in sales, and two-thirds of its computers didn't work.

He is a workaholic, working from daylight to dark, seven days a week, rarely finding time for recreation activities. The frantic pace at Sun engendered by McNealy is sometimes referred to as Sunburn. There is a tendency for Sun executives to take on too many projects at once, thereby creating tremendous internal pressure and organizational chaos.

McNealy's philosophy can be capsuled in these company sayings (9):

1. On Decision-making—Consensus if possible, but participation for sure.
2. On Management Cooperation—Agree and commit, disagree and commit, or just get the hell out of the way.
3. On Market Response—The right answer is the best answer. The wrong answer is second best. No answer is the worst.
4. On Individual Initiative—To ask permission is to seek denial.

He has stated that company is trying to achieve four goals— significant increases in revenue and book value, improved product acceptance, and higher profit margins.

CHIEF COMPUTER DESIGNER

Andreas Bechtolsheim, chief computer designer, was one of Sun's cofounders. At age 35 he has the title of Vice President of technology. A native of West Germany, Bechtolsheim designed his first computer in 1980 while still a graduate student at Stanford University. It was a workstation designed for scientists and engineers. However, he was unable to sell the idea to any computer company then in existence. Shortly thereafter, he joined Joy, Khosla, and McNealy in founding Sun Microsystems and the company's first product was based on his machine.

Initially, Bechtolsheim persuaded Sun to use off-the-shelf products to develop its workstations instead of following the usual industry practice of utilizing proprietary components. This meant that company products would be easy for competitors to copy, but it also allowed quick entry into the market place. As nonproprietary open systems came to be more widely accepted, competitors such as Apollo, DEC, and IBM encountered problems in keeping pace with product lines that lacked the flexibility and performance of Sun's products. When Steve Jobs formed Next, Inc. and announced the development of a desktop workstation, Bechtolsheim urged Sun officials to build a truly desktop computer. There was considerable resistance to the project, and he almost left the company at that point. Because the company has had a culture based on building bigger boxes, the new sparcstation was widely criticized within the company as being too small. However, Bechtolsheim stubbornly refused to change the specifications and eventually prevailed.

FIELD OPERATIONS DIRECTOR

Carol Bartz, National Sales Director and the number two executive at Sun Microsystems, has about half of the company's 12,000 employees reporting to her. Bartz attended the University of Wisconsin, receiving a Bachelor of Computer Science degree in 1971. After that, she spent seven years with Digital Equipment Corporation. Since joining Sun in 1983, she has become intimately involved in supervising field support activities and a subdivision that sells to federal governmental agencies. According to Bob Herwick, an investment analyst, Bartz is a very effective problem solver, turning around a sluggish service organization and ensuring that the company fully exploited the market potential in the government market (5).

TEAM AND CONSENSUS MANAGEMENT AT SUN

McNealy, current Sun chairman, attended Cranbrook, a North Detroit prep school. While there, he excelled in a variety of activities including music, tennis, golf, and ice hockey. According to Alan De Clerk, a high school classmate, McNealy developed a strong self-image and competitive spirit as a result of participating in sports activities and competing with two brothers and a sister. Through the years he has approached all activities as if they were team sports.

McNealy's efforts to build consensus among executives before a decision is made have become famous throughout the company. As he has stated, "Give me a draw and I'll make the decision but I won't issue an edict if a large majority is in favor of an alternative proposal" (9). A frequently quoted example occurred in 1988 when he stubbornly resisted changing prices at a time when rapidly increasing memory costs were reducing profit margins. With a consensus arrayed against him, he finally agreed to some product price increases which were enacted without reducing sales. In fact, he has a hard time saying no to any project pushed by one or more company groups. He demands complete loyalty within his concept of teamwork and becomes very angry if he believes that individuals or teams have let him down (9).

PRODUCT LINE FOCUS

The Sparcstation I was introduced in April 1989 at a stripped down price of $9,000. A lower priced version was introduced in May of 1990, costing $5,000. The machine processes data at 12 mips and runs about twice as fast as personal computers. Sun expected the lower price to facilitate sales to large companies who base computer purchases on quantity discounts. However, the low end sparc station does not have disk drives, color monitors, or add in slots. Therefore, it must be networked and cannot be used as a stand alone unit.

An improved version of Sparc I was introduced in the summer of 1990 with an improved graphical interface, a color monitor, and sales price of $10,000. Sun has asserted that a personal computer with the same characteristics as the IPC would cost $15,000 to $20,000 and would have only about one third the processing power of this workstation model. The Sparcstation is now Sun's top seller among all its product lines and Sparcstation products produce 80 to 90% of total company revenues.

Table One shows prices, specmarks (a measure of processing power and speed) for two Sun models as well as for the latest Hewlett Packard and IBM workstation models. From this table, the relative performance of the Sun computers in terms of computing power per dollar can be compared with its major competitors.

COMPANY STRATEGY

Early on, Sun executives believed that they only had a short time to focus on growing demand for computer workstations from scientists and engineers before large companies such as IBM, DEC, and Hewlett Packard would aggressively move into that market niche. Therefore, company strategy was designed to emphasize gaining market share, concentrating on all out sales growth, no matter what the cost. At one point, the organization was adding more than 300 employees and a new sales office each month. Company engineers developed a steady stream of innovative but sometimes impractical prototypes.

TABLE 1

A Comparison of Performance Measures for Major Workstation Makers

	Price	Specmarks	Price Per Specmark
Hewlett Packard 9000	11,990	55.5	216.00
Sun Sparcstation ELC	4,995	20.1	248.50
IBM RS/6000	13,992	32.8	426.50
Sun Sparcstation IPX	13,495	24.2	557.60

SOURCE: J. A. Savage, "Price Takes Backseat with Users," *Computerworld*, September 2, 1991, p. 4.

Products were sold largely by word of mouth with virtually no formal sales promotion programs.

As part of the market share focus, in the mid-80s the company began creating autonomous divisions to develop and market its products. This policy allowed rapid movement into such market areas as sales to government agencies, universities, and financial institutions. The autonomous groups did create unnecessary duplication and contributed to development costs that were almost twice the industry average. When attempts were made to consolidate functions, fierce turf battles resulted and top executives were forced to step in and referee the conflicts.

The market share/sales growth emphasis created many unexpected problems. Needed investments in customer service and data processing activities had to be postponed. The existence of independent, autonomous divisions caused numerous difficulties for both sales and manufacturing activities. At one point, the company had more than 10,000 computer and option combinations to keep track of. Three different product lines based on three different microprocessors—Sparc, Motorola 68000, and Intel 386 required excessive investment and extensive coordination to ensure that they all worked on the same network. Overlaps and duplications in marketing and finance made forecasting all but impossible. At its current size the company can no longer scramble madly to meet shipping deadlines at the last minute.

By the summer of 1989, the company was experiencing production bottlenecks as discounted sales of older products mushroomed. Demand for newer products also increased faster than expected. Large backlogs of sales orders were not being entered in the inventory control system, preventing the company from knowing how many or what kinds of products it needed to produce.

In the last quarter of 1989, Sun experienced a 20 million dollar loss due to misjudging consumer demand for its new Sparcstation and incurring parts shortages. A new management information system produced inaccurate parts forecasts which contributed to order snafus and lower earnings. However, it posted a 5 million dollar profit in the first quarter of 1990. Sun produced revenues of 2.5 billion in fiscal 1990 and expected to achieve revenues of 3.3 billion in 1991 (8). Sun is now changing its approach to place more emphasis on profitability and less on growth, on expanding customer service and hiring fewer employees. Sun President McNealy has recently tied executive pay to before tax return on investment. In the 1989 annual report he stated that he desired performance to be judged on the basis of significant increases in revenues, acceptance of new products, improvements in profit margins, and increases in book value.

McNealy was one of the early pioneers pushing open systems which would allow computers of many different manufacturers to be linked together in networks. In fact, Sun has actually encouraged competition with itself through its focus on open systems development and invited the industry to build Sparc based clones in order to expand the position of the workstation industry. As the percentage of total Sparc based computers sold by Sun has begun to decline, Sun appears to be changing its position on clones. Recently, it told its own dealers they would incur Sun's displeasure if they sold Sun clones along with Sun workstations. Many of these dealers are angry at what they perceive to be Sun's arrogance.

Sun has consistently maintained a narrow product line focus. It has gradually phased all out microprocessors except Sparc and has concentrated on low end workstations with the greatest market share growth possibilities. It has avoided entering markets for higher priced lines and the personal computer segment with emphasis on low price and compactness. However, recently Sun announced plans to move into high end workstation markets where processing speed and power requirements necessitate linking a series of microprocessors and using sophisticated software. Sun may encounter problems in this market similar to those it experienced in product upgrades of its lower level models, since it does not have a good record in managing product introductions.

As workstations become more powerful and less expensive, workstation manufacturers face a serious challenge in maintaining profit margins. Current models now combine high functionality with high volume, in contrast to an earlier focus on producing highly functional units in small quantities. Extensive use of application specific integrated circuits with fewer components reduces system size, increases reliability, and lowers product costs. Sun and other companies increasingly follow the practice of involving manufacturing representatives in the design process as early as possible in order to minimize manufacturing problems. Increased attention is also being paid to maintaining product quality and improving product testing before systems are shipped.

In past years, Sun's strategies have included focusing on lower prices, well developed marketing programs and third party software development. From 1,500 to 2,000 applications are available for the Sun Sparcstation compared to approximately 1,000 for Hewlett Packard and DEC. The company is licensing its Sparc chip to third party clone companies with the desire of expanding the installed RISC computer base. The overall company goal is to deliver a complete processing solution, including graphics, input/output, software, and networking.

DISTRIBUTION CHANNELS AND CUSTOMER SERVICE

Workstation makers have traditionally sold their units using manufacturers sales forces and specialized hardware resellers, who repackage specialized software with other companies' workstations. Sun has about 300 VARS (i.e. value added resellers) compared to more than 500 for Hewlett Packard with Digital and IBM falling somewhere in between. Some authorities think the majority of VARs are not capable of selling workstations (11). Sun is now considering the possibility of selling some of its models through retailers such as Microage in manner similar to personal computer sales now made by IBM, COMPAQ, and Apple. Such a move would reduce selling and inventory costs but is meeting initial resistance from dealers unaccustomed to handling complex workstation models.

Sun still sells a large number of workstations through its 1,000 person salesforce. In July 1990, Sun selected 200 dealers from three retail chains and gave them training in selling workstations. The company expects to sell 30 million dollars of workstations through retail dealers in Fiscal 1990, but a full fledged dealer network may require several years to develop. Because of the higher average selling prices and of greater product differentiation and uniqueness of workstations compared to personal computers, many PC vendors are expressing interest in handling workstations in spite of the small volumes generated.

One area of concern has been Sun's field service organization which has not been very effective in supporting customer software. Bartz has stated that the company wants to improve on customer service without making large monetary expenditures or building a dinosaur service group (2). In line with this, Sun has announced plans to start using company trained, third party service personnel who can be dispatched to customer locations on demand.

CUSTOMER CATEGORIES

The workstation market for engineers and scientists is rapidly becoming saturated. About one-third of Sun's customers now come from the commercial side, up from only 10% several years ago. The company is now concentrating more of its efforts on airlines, banks, insurance and finance companies, trying to persuade users to utilize Sun workstations to solve new problems. Sun Vice-President Eric Schmidt says that Sun tends to get early adopters of new technology (7). Often, by starting with a pilot program that proves successful, workstations can be expanded to other areas in a customer's operations. Eastman Kodak began using Sun workstations in engineering design and soon expanded their use of marketing databases and mailroom operations.

Sun machines are being used by Wall Street firms Merrill Lynch, Shearson/Lehman/Hutton and Bear/Sterns on the trading floor. Northwest Airlines uses 500 workstations an Minneapolis to monitor ticket usage, checking the correctness of air fare charges and the impact of flight delays or cancellations on revenues and profits. To increase customer satisfaction, Sun has had to change product designs, to make its machines easier to install, and to improve understandability of product manuals. As Sun has discovered, commercial customers need more help than engineers.

Dataquest says that by 1994, 29.1% of workstation sales will be made to commercial users as opposed to Scientific/Engineering users in a market expected to reach 22 billion dollars (16). Workstation makers are moving into the personal computer area by offering Unix versions that will run on both workstations and on personal computers. Workstations provide much greater computing power at a lower cost than would be required to enhance a personal computer so that it possessed the equivalent capability of a typical workstation. Workstations seem to be making their biggest inroads into CPU intensive applications formerly done on mainframes (e.g., stock transactions, airline reservations).

Sun's first major TV advertising effort occurred in April 1991 and took the form of a 30 second commercial seen on CNN, ESPN, and the three major TV networks. The commercial was not directed specifically at a consumer audience, but instead was an attempt to get broad exposure for a new message beamed at the business market. Sun expected the advertisement to reach 59% of U.S. households and 42% of the target market of senior level corporate and computer executives. The campaign also included an eight page insert in *The Wall Street Journal.*

Sun's advertising budget of approximately 4.6 million in 1990 was spent on computer and general interest business publications. Sun's advertising budget is only about 0.25% of sales revenues compared to 1.0 to 1.5% spent by its major competitors. Some observers have questioned the cost-effectiveness of a high priced TV advertisement by a company which sells high priced computers to a limited group of customers.

SOFTWARE DEVELOPMENTS

Availability of software still remains a major problem in expanding sales of workstations. Only about 5% to 10% of UNIX based software is designed for business and commercial applications. Sun is trying to sign up software developers to produce UNIX based versions of many common personal computer products. It now has UNIX based versions of popular PC software, including Lotus 1–2–3 and DBASE IV. It hopes the increased availability of software plus the narrowing cost gap between low end workstations and high end personal computers will help it penetrate the personal computer market. However, it must sell users on the benefit/cost performance of workstations compared to personal computers and also needs to expand its existing base of software developers.

The type of software to be run is often the determining factor in deciding between a personal computer or workstation. For productivity and business applications, PCs can be more cost efficient. For technical and graphics applications, workstations are more appropriate. Differences in costs are no longer a differentiating factor.

An entrenched personal computer MS/DOS operating system base and lack of commercial workstation software have hampered a switch from high end personal computers to workstations. MS/DOS based computers appear adequate for a majority of user needs, especially with the advent of the WINDOWS operating environment. PC users are more likely to change if complex applications such as multimedia, integrated data base, or windowing become desirable rather than on the basis of price alone. Workstations may become less attractive if 80846 based personal computers with considerably more computing power than today's systems become more widely available.

Product/price performance is no longer as important a differentiating factor as it used to be. Software availability and usability are increasing in importance. In recognition of this, Sun has formed two software subsidiaries—one for application software and one to concentrate on improvements in the Unix operating system. The Open Look Graphical Interface has been added to make Sun products more user friendly. The key to maintaining market position seems to be improving systems software and selling software developers and users on the benefits of workstations over other hardware options.

Sun has announced that it will release a new version of its operating system designed to run on Intel based personal computers. Some analysts say that Sun will face a stiff test in competing with Microsoft's DOS/Windows combination and that it is a defensive move, made in realization that Sun no longer can generate enough revenue from its own machines to meet its growth goals. McNealy denies that the Sun announcement is defensive, saying that high powered PC owners will move to Sun's operating systems to take advantage of advanced capabilities (e.g., running multiple programs simultaneously) which is something that has been vaguely promised by Microsoft's Windows new NT versions (13). McNealy has sharply criticized Windows NT version, referring to it as illusionary or not there.

Sun's Solaris operating system will not be available until mid-1991, and will work on both Intel's X86 series and Sun's Sparc processors. The new operating system will make it easier for Sun's customers to link Sun workstations with other computers in a network and increase the number of Sun users. Sun hopes that this will encourage independent software houses to write new programs for Sun OS. So far, approximately 3,500 application programs are available for Sun OS compared with more than 20,000 for IBM-compatible personal computers (12).

COMPETITION IN THE MARKETPLACE

Although still the market leader, Sun is facing increasing competition from much larger computer companies. Sun shipped 146,000 workstations in 1990 (39% of the market) out of a total of 376,000 and is expected to ship 200,000 in 1991 (4). Having fully absorbed Apollo into its organization, Hewlett Packard is selling about two-thirds as many workstations as Sun, with about 20% of the market and DEC, which has completely reworked its product lines, has about 17% of the workstation market. Hewlett Packard has also introduced a new work station model comparable in price to the sparcstation which runs about twice as fast as Sun's current model. Exhibit One in Appendix A shows the 1989 and 1990 market shares for the major firms in the workstation market.

IBM has made a significant comeback in the workstation market with the RS/6000, after its first workstation model proved to be a slow seller. In 1990, IBM shifted more than 25,000 workstations, producing revenue of 1 billion dollars and attaining a market share of 6.6%, or more than double its 1989 market share (4). In 1991, some analysts estimate IBM will sell between 2 and 3 billion dollars of workstations. IBM has a stated goal of overtaking Sun by 1993, achieving a 30% market share, although some experts predict it is more likely to achieve a 15% market share by that date (14).

With the workstation market expected to exceed 20 billion dollars by the mid-1990s, competition is expected to be fierce. IBM's late entry, entrenched positions of competitors in the market, lack of a low-priced entry level model, and the use of nonstandard operating and graphics environments are likely to hamper its efforts to achieve a market share much above 15% (6). IBM's service and sales reputation, its large reseller base, and strong position in commercial markets should give the company leverage to enter the fast growing markets for network servers and small or branch office multiuser systems. However, if IBM focuses its efforts on penetrating these markets with its RS/6000, it runs a serious risk of undercutting sales of the AS/400.

Cost no longer seems to be the primary factor in decisions to acquire workstations. Workers must become more accustomed to graphic as opposed to character based systems before adoption by current PC becomes more widespread. Some companies feel that workstations have yet to demonstrate significant productivity advantages over personal computers. The biggest shortcomings of workstations are lack of application software and integration difficulties.

FINANCIAL ANALYSIS

Exhibit Two in Appendix A shows revenues, expenses, and income for the five year period 1986 to 1990. Revenues have increased at a more rapid rate than net income during the period being considered. Return on sales has declined significantly to 4.5% from the peak of almost 7% in 1987 with revenue per shipment also declining in 1990 compared to 1989 and 1988. Book value per share and unit shipments have increased significantly during the five years.

Table One (Appendix A) indicates that Sun's sales, income and asset growth are higher than the industry average in 1990 and 1989 with market value/equity also above the industry average. However, net income/sales was below the industry average in 1989 and slightly above the industry average in 1990. As Table Two indicates, Sun appears to be very close to the industry average in terms of two common productivity measures, sales/assets and sales/employee. In reviewing the common leverage measures, Sun is well above the industry average for R&D expenses/revenues and R&D expenses/employee.

End Notes

1. Susan E. Fisher, "Vendors Court Reseller Partners As Workstations Go Mainstream," PC WEEK, July 30, 1990.
2. Jonathan B. Levine, "High Noon for Sun," BUSINESS WEEK, July 24, 1989, pp. 71, 74.
3. John Markoff, "The Smart Alecs at Sun Are Regrouping," NEW YORK TIMES, April 28, 1991.
4. Andrew Ould, "IBM Challenges Sun in Workstation Market," PC WEEK, February 28, 1991.
5. Andrew Ould, "Carol Bartz: Star Is Still Rising for Hard Driving Executive," PC WEEK, September 3, 1990.
6. Andrew Ould, "What's Behind Lower Workstation Prices," UNIX WORLD, July 1990.
7. Julie Pitta, "The Trojan Horse Approach," FORBES, April 15, 1991.
8. Kathy Rebello, "Sun Microsystems on the Rise Again," USA TODAY, April 20, 1990.
9. "Sun Microsystems Turn on the Afterburners," BUSINESS WEEK, July 18, 1988.
10. G. Paschal Zachary, "Sparc-station's Success Is Doubly Street for Sun Microsystem's Bechtolsheim," THE WALL STREET JOURNAL, May 29, 1990.
11. Susan E. Fisher, "Vendors Court Resellers as Workstations Go Mainstream," PC WEEK, July 30, 1990.
12. Robert D. Hof, "Why Sun Can't Afford to Shine Alone," BUSINESS WEEK, September 9, 1991.
13. G. Paschal Zachary, "Sun Challenges Microsoft's Hold Over Software," THE WALL STREET JOURNAL, September 4, 1991.
14. Bob Francis, "Big Blue's Red Hot Workstation," DATAMATION, October 15, 1990.
15. Lawrence Curran, "HP Speeds Up Workstation Race," ELECTRONICS, April 1991.
16. "Getting Down to Business," INFORMATION WEEK, January 14, 1991.

APPENDIX A   *Exhibit One—Computer Workstation Market Shares*

Company	1989	1990
Sun Microsystems	30.4%	38.8%
Hewlett Packard	26.1%	20.1%
Digital Equipment	26.6%	17.0%
Intergraph	7.0%	3.8%
IBM	1.2%	4.5%
Silicon Graphics	5.1%	2.6%
Sony	—	3.3%
Next	—	2.6%
Other	3.6%	7.0%
Total	100.0	100.0

Exhibit Two—Revenues, Expenses, and Income for Five Years

(Billions of $)	1990	1989	1988	1987	1986
Net Revenues	2,466	1,765	1,052	538	210
Cost of Sales	1,399	1,010	550	273	102
Gross Profit	1,067	755	502	265	108
R&D Outlays	302	234	140	70	31
Selling, Adm. & General Expenses	588	433	250	127	57
Total	890	667	390	197	88
Operating Income	177	88	111	68	20
Interest Income	(23)	(10)	(302)	834	369
Income Taxes	43	17	44	33	9
Net Income	111	61	66	36	11
Net Income/Sales	4.5%	3.4%	6.3%	6.8%	5.3%
Net Income/Share	1.21	0.76	0.89	0.55	0.21
Book Value/Share	9.82	7.77	4.75	3.57	2.04
Unit Shipment (000'S)	118.3	80.7	48.4	24.6	9.9
Revenue/Unit Shipped (000'S)	20.8	21.9	21.7	21.8	21.2

SOURCE: Adapted from 1990 Annual Report.

Table One—Computer Industry Data for Years 1989 and 1990

Company	Sales Growth 1990	1989	Income Growth 1990	1989	Asset Growth 1990	1989	Net Inc/ Sales 1990	1989	Mkt Value/ Equity 1990	1989
Apple	1.07	1.21	1.14	1.05	1.12	1.24	8.7	8.2	4.81	3.21
Compaq	1.25	1.39	1.36	1.31	1.30	1.31	12.6	11.6	3.26	3.31
Dec	1.01	1.05	0.00	0.72	1.03	1.10	−.72	6.8	1.21	1.13
Hew Pck	1.10	1.20	0.95	0.97	1.09	1.31	5.7	6.6	1.83	1.98
Intrgrph	1.21	1.07	0.79	0.80	1.06	0.97	6.0	9.2	1.79	1.73
IBM	1.10	1.05	1.60	0.68	1.30	1.06	8.7	6.0	1.75	1.62
NCR	1.06	0.99	0.90	0.94	1.01	0.95	5.9	6.9	3.54	3.40
Silgrphs	1.41	1.73	1.97	1.94	1.37	0.94	8.3	5.9	3.57	4.30
Sun Mcrs	1.34	1.41	318.	0.40	1.49	1.50	5.5	1.8	2.72	1.41
Wang	0.87	0.90	0.00	0.00	0.72	0.87	−6.7	−13.9	1.27	0.87
Avg	1.14	1.20	32.7	0.88	1.15	1.12	5.4	4.9	2.58	2.37

SOURCE: Business Week 1000 Companies, 1991, 1990.

Table Two—Computer Industry Data for Years 1989 and 1988

Company	Sales/ Assets 1990	1989	Sales/ Employee 1989	1988	Adv Exps/ Sales 1989	1988	R&D Exps/ Sales 1989	1988	R&D Exps/ Employee 1989	1988
Apple	1.82	1.91	364	377	7.34	8.30	8.0	6.7	28937	25233
Compaq	1.32	1.38	303	289	1.75	2.87	4.6	3.6	13945	10849
Dec	1.13	1.15	101	94	1.38	1.01	12.0	11.4	12123	10753
Hew Pck	1.22	1.21	125	113	2.69	2.35	10.7	10.4	13358	11713
Intrgrph	1.20	1.07	105	110	1.00	1.00	10.6	11.1	11157	12216
IBM	0.79	0.81	164	154	1.17	0.44	8.3	7.4	13572	11415
NCR	1.38	1.32	106	100	1.06	0.53	7.5	7.0	7964	6940
Silgrphs	1.22	1.19	180	105	1.00	1.00	11.9	15.8	21150	21908
Sun Mcrs	1.27	1.41	172	148	1.00	0.74	13.3	13.3	22934	19733
Wang	1.35	1.12	109	97	1.00	1.02	9.8	8.7	10543	8510
AVG	1.27	1.26	173	159	2.64	1.93	9.7	9.5	15568	14027

Source: Business Week 1000, 1991, 1991; Innovation in America, Special Business Week Issues, 1990, 1988.

Bermo, Inc.

MELVIN J. STANFORD, *Mankato State University, Minnesota*
and **SHAILENDRA JHA,** *Wilfrid Laurier University, Ontario, Canada*

In early October, 1990, Dan Berdass, President of Bermo, Inc., was reviewing the operations of the company and thinking about Bermo's strategy and goals. Business had been good, and it seemed to Dan that everyone in the company was working harder. Dan himself was feeling some fatigue. He was concerned that many orders were being shipped later than scheduled, and some important customers were becoming unhappy with delivery dates. He believed that the Bermo plant was running at near-capacity despite the recent purchase of three new metal stamping presses, and he was concerned about the backlog of work in the plant. Dan looked at the computer screen on his desk and saw unshipped orders totaling $9.6 million. He estimated that Bermo's current shipment rate was running about $2 million a month. Dan thought that three months' backlog was about industry average. In December 1989, the backlog at Bermo had been $4.5 million, with shipments running about $1.5 million per month. Also in December 1989 Bermo had about 160 employees, and that number had risen to around 200 by October 1990.

Bermo was a job shop, doing both low and high volume production orders. Dan Berdass estimated that about 10% of the work, and 10% of the backlog, was low volume, and about 90% was high volume. Customers wanted to cut costs for high volume work, which was more competitive to obtain than smaller-lot custom work. Mr. Berdass believed that Bermo's recognized expertise in design and tool work, along with its modern equipment in Computer-aided design (CAD) and Computer-aided manufacturing (CAM) and robotics, were advantages for the company in both small lot-custom work and higher volume production runs.

Dan wondered, How could Bermo get more production to utilize and cover the cost of its large investment in modern machinery and technology? How could the company lower costs? Give faster delivery? Should Bermo add capacity? If so, how much, and where? How could both short-run, low-volume and long-run, high-volume work best be done in the plant? How much of both kinds of business could the plant do? To what extent did these two kinds of work complement or conflict with each other in the plant? How much of each kind of work should Bermo continue to seek?

THE PRECISION METAL FORMING INDUSTRY

Precision metal forming included the operations of stamping-cutting-bending (with heavy duty precision presses and tool and die facilities), machining, welding, brazing, plating, heat treating, painting and assembling. The Standard Industrial Code (SIC) for precision metal forming was 3469. This industry was made up of establishments primarily engaged in manufacturing metal stampings and spun products, including porcelain enameled products. There were in 1987 a total of 2,815 establishments in S.I.C. 3469, according to the 1987 Census of Manufactures. Total industry value of shipments (sales) for 1987 was reported as $8.33 billion (see Exhibit 1).

"Key Business Ratios," published by Dun's Analytical Services, showed the following solvency ratios for 1373 establishments in S.I.C. 3469 for the year 1989:

	Upper Quartile	Median	Lower Quartile
Quick Ratio (times)	2.7	1.3	0.8
Current Ratio (times)	4.3	2.2	1.4
Current Liab. to Net Worth (%)	19.1	47.6	106.3
Current Liab. to Inventory (%)	76.2	136.8	237.9
Total Liab. to Net Worth (%)	27.2	73.2	164.9
Fixed Assets to Net Worth (%)	22.8	48.3	100.8

EXHIBIT 1

Bermo, Inc. Metal Stampings Industry Data (S.I.C. 3469)

	1972	1977	1982	1987
All establishments (number)	2,356	2,663	2,843	2,815
Total employees (thousands)	92.0	103.2	100.4	95.5
Payroll ($ millions)	781.0	1,225.4	1,782.7	2,131.9
Production workers (thousands)	74.2	82.0	75.6	73.2
Production hours (millions)	146.5	161.2	146.3	146.2
Wages ($ millions)	554.8	842.5	1,154.0	1,402.0
Value of shipments ($ millions)	2,688.8	4,735.7	6,437.7	8,331.1
New capital expenditures ($ millions)	76.7	154.7	200.1	268.9
Establishments with an average of				
1 to 4 employees			639	633
5 to 9 employees			465	459
10 to 19 employees			582	561
20 to 49 employees			664	658
50 to 99 employees			296	296
100 to 249 employees			150	163
250 to 499 employees			38	35
500 to 999 employees			5	9
1,000 to 2,499 employees			3	1
2,500 or more employees			1	—

SOURCE: *Census of Manufactures, 1982 and 1987*, U.S. Department of Commerce.

The Precision Metalforming Association (PMA) directory for 1989 listed 950 members. Many industry participants were specialized and did only selected operations, such as machining or work involving tools, dies and presses. An industry outlook for the 1990s was expressed in an editorial of the December 1989 issue of the PMA publication METALFORMING:

> We're entering an era of truly global economic competition—and global opportunities—where struggles for markets will replace wars for territory. EC '92 has been on our minds, but suddenly the concept of a single market stretching from the Atlantic to Vladivostok becomes a possibility. In metalforming, the trends of the 1980s are clear. Competition is intensifying. Technology and training are key. There will be winners and losers.

> Above all, in this age of high technology and instantaneous information, ideas take hold and events move much faster than ever before. Market opportunities also change more rapidly, requiring that we act—and react—faster.

> If the 1980s have taught us anything, it is that speed in adapting to change will become an increasingly important weapon.

Larger firms in the PM industry were generally more profitable, according to a survey conducted by the PMA in 1989 (see Exhibit 2). Costs of sales appeared to be the main differentiation between the companies that reported to its banker and to PMA but otherwise kept its income statements confidential for competitive reasons. PMA provided comparative cost information for its members on a periodic basis (see Exhibit 3). Robert Mycka, Bermo Vice President for Finance and Administration, and his staff monitored the PMA reports and periodically discussed them with Dan Berdass, along with cost information from the plant.

COMPETITION

Rivalry among "stampers" (precision metal manufacturers) was seen by Bermo executives as becoming increasingly worldwide, with a lot of offshore competition for U. S. firms. Dan Berdass identified in the PMA directory, which showed the services performed by each member firm, some competitors in the U. S. who often bid against Bermo (see Exhibit 4). All of these competitors did stamping as well as the other operations listed for each of them, but none of them except Bermo, so far as Dan was aware, did plastic injection molding.

There were other competitors who were not PMA members. Dan knew of one stamper in the St. Paul area who sometimes underbid Bermo. This firm had old equipment but had total assets of more than $9 million. Dan said: "His costs are lower than ours, and he spends only $50,000 a year on new capital investment, but he isn't keeping up with technology. Bermo has spent more than $1.5 million this year in new technology" (such as CAD/CAM, robots, and new machine tools).

"Stamping" is cutting and forming metal parts with dies in a heavy duty press (one of Bermo's presses had a force of 400 tons). Dies (tooling) were made of hardened metal and could be used to stamp out large numbers of parts. Substitutes for metal stamping included metal die casting, plastic extrusion, and structural foam. Stamping was generally less expensive than these substitutes, which were not considered by Dan to be much of a threat to Bermo's market. Bermo did some plastic injection molding for customers who wanted it as component parts of their products that contained metal stamp-

EXHIBIT 2

Bermo, Inc. Precision Metalforming Association 1989 Operational Cost Survey—Association Wide 1988 Costs and Profits as % of Sales

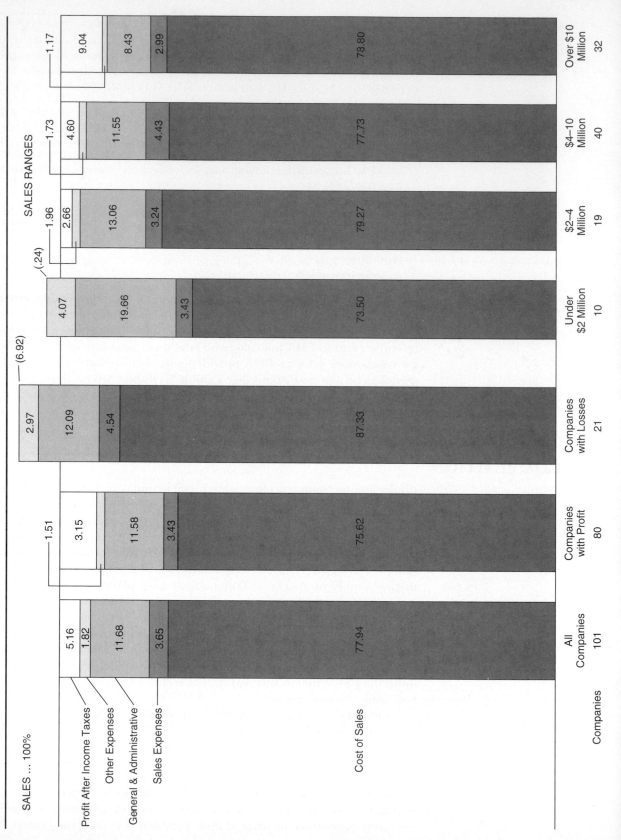

EXHIBIT 3

[omitted]

EXHIBIT 4

Bermo, Inc. Some U.S. Competitors and Their Services

| | Services* (In addition to stamping, done by all firms) | | | | | | | |
Firm & Location	1	2	3	4	5	6	7	8
Bermo, Inc., MN	X	X	X	X	op	op	X	X
Schulze Mfg., CA	X	-	X	X	-	-	X	X
Krasberg Corp., IL	X	X	X	X	-	X	X	X
O.D.M. Tool & Mfg., IL	X	-	-	X	-	-	X	X
R. Olson Mfg., IL	X	X	-	X	X	X	X	X
Parkview Metal, IL	X	-	-	-	X	-	X	X
P.K. Tool & Mfg., IL	X	-	-	X	-	-	X	X
Service Stampiongs, IL	X	-	X	X	X	X	X	X
Triton Industries, IL	X	X	-	X	X	X	X	X
Wisconsin Tool & Stamping, IL	X	-	X	-	X	X	X	X
Arvin Industries, IN	X	-	X	-	X	X	X	X
Larson Tool, MA	X	X	-	-	X	-	X	X
Mercury Metal Products, MA	X	-	-	-	-	-	X	X
McAlpin Industries, NY	X	X	-	X	X	X	X	X
Ervite, PA	X	-	-	-	X	X	-	X

★

1. Assembling
2. Brazing
3. Heat treating
4. Machining
5. Painting (op = outside purchase)
6. Plating
7. Tool and Die Facilities
8. Welding

SOURCE: *Sources 1989*, Precision Metalforming Association.

ings. Bermo assembled stamped metal parts, sometimes including plastic components, for some of its customers. Plastic work was relatively less important than metal and was done as an accommodation for customers, who were "always a competitive threat . . . they muscle Bermo constantly," said Dan. Many of Bermo's customers could do "in house" (that is, in the customer's own facilities) at least some of the work they ordered from Bermo.

Suppliers were rarely seen as a competitive threat. "We muscle them!" said Dan, referring to price or delivery concessions obtained through negotiation. The materials and supplies purchased by Bermo were readily available from a large number of suppliers. Bermo bought from three suppliers of steel: Keeler Steel and Juster Steel were local, and Triumph Steel was in Chicago. All three supplied steel of standard specifications. Bermo had only one subcontractor (Fotomark) for painting and one (Superior Plating) for metal plating. There were about 20 other minor suppliers. Dan considered all of Bermo's suppliers to be satisfactory as to quality, delivery, and price.

Potential new entrants to the precision metalforming industry were not considered by Bermo executives to be much of a threat to existing firms. Barriers to entry were described as quite high, with about $8 million needed for equipment, plus CAD/CAM ability, training, software and expertise in toolmaking. Small market niches for specialized parts could be entered by a new competitor who didn't have a full line of equipment, but broader competition for major customers was seen as requiring substantial equipment and capability that was expensive to acquire and maintain.

BERMO BACKGROUND AND ORGANIZATION

Bermo, Inc. was started in 1947 by Fred Berdass and Joe Moses (the brother of Fred's wife, Margo). The business "had its ups and downs," as Dan expressed it, but made progress. In 1963, Fred bought out Joe's interest, and that put a burden of debt on the company for several years. The payout to Joe Moses was completed in 1988. By the 1980s, the company was operating above $10 million annual sales and was profitable.

Fred Berdass had come to the United States from Germany in 1941. He learned the machine tool trade in the U.S. As Bermo grew, Fred's sons, Dan and Jeff, began to work in the business with him. Dan Berdass studied at Mankato State University, where he received a baccalaureate degree in 1969. Progressing through a variety of responsible positions, Dan became President of Bermo in 1987 and managed the operations of the business. He enjoyed the work and kept involved in it to a point of spending 12 to 14 hours a day at the plant, six and sometimes seven days a week.

Fred Berdass continued to serve as Chairman of the board of Directors. He often came in to his office at the plant and was involved in technical matters and capital equipment decisions. Other members of the board of Directors reflected the family ownership and control of Bermo: Fred's wife, Margo Berdass, Dan Berdass and his wife Nancy, and Dan's brother, Jeff Berdass.

Bermo was organized around manufacturing. Sales and engineering functions were the responsibility of one vice president, Jerome Atherton, who reported directly to Dan Berdass (see organization chart, Exhibit 5). This combination of responsibilities was intended to provide good coordination of service to Bermo's customers. There was a strong organizational relationship between sales and engineering, manufacturing, and quality control. Mr. Atherton had previously served as plant manager, and in quality control. The plant manager who succeeded him, Keith Monson, had previously been responsible for quality control. Dan Berdass did not agree with the idea of quality control being independent but rather saw it as a part of production. He said, "Quality Control really reports to the Plant Manager, but customers want to see it on the chart as responsible to the President."

As Bermo grew in size from year to year, manufacturing operations needed more space. The original plant in Bloomington, Minnesota, was not big enough, so in 1987 a second location was purchased in the vicinity. Three years previous to that expansion, a plastic molding operation was started in order to give more complete service to Bermo's metal products customers. The three locations in the Bloomington area served Bermo's needs but also became crowded as business grew. Eventually there was not enough room for inventory within the plant buildings, so a number of semi trailers were rented, parked outside the main plant and used to store inventory.

Bermo Inc., Organization Chart

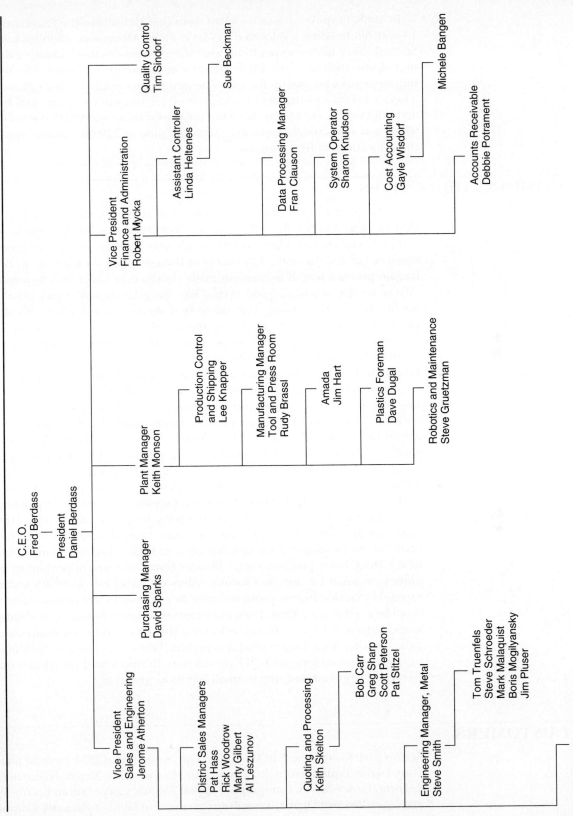

C.E.O.
Fred Berdass

President
Daniel Berdass

Vice President Sales and Engineering
Jerome Atherton

District Sales Managers
Pat Hass
Rick Woodrow
Marty Gilbert
Al Leszunov

Quoting and Processing
Keith Skelton

Bob Carr
Greg Sharp
Scott Peterson
Pat Stitzel

Engineering Manager, Metal
Steve Smith

Tom Truenfels
Steve Schroeder
Mark Malaquist
Boris Mogilyansky
Jim Pluser

Engineering Manager, Plastic
Jeff Berdass

Purchasing Manager
David Sparks

Plant Manager
Keith Monson

Production Control and Shipping
Lee Knapper

Manufacturing Manager
Tool and Press Room
Rudy Brassl

Amada
Jim Hart

Plastics Foreman
Dave Dugal

Robotics and Maintenance
Steve Gruetzman

Vice President Finance and Administration
Robert Mycka

Quality Control
Tim Sindorf

Assistant Controller
Linda Heltenes

Sue Beckman

Data Processing Manager
Fran Clauson

System Operator
Sharon Knudson

Cost Accounting
Gayle Wisdorf

Michele Bangen

Accounts Receivable
Debbie Potrament

In 1988, Bermo purchased a plant from Ball Manufacturing Company. The 13-year old building was located in Circle Pines, Minnesota, 15 miles north of St. Paul. All of Bermo's operations were moved from the three plants in Bloomington into the one Circle Pines building in the summer of 1988. The Bloomington plants were put up for sale. The new facility in Circle Pines allowed for a better manufacturing layout, adequate office and storage space, and had 55 acres of land for expansion. Total building floor space was 186,000 square feet, which was substantially more than the aggregate of 110,000 square feet in all three locations in Bloomington.

COMPANY OBJECTIVES

After the operations in the new location had stabilized somewhat, Fred and Dan Berdass and Jerome Atherton and Robert Mycka, worked out a set of company objectives (see Exhibit 6), which were then known to those four executives but not distributed to others in the company. As a job shop, Bermo had no product line of its own but made products to order for its customers. "We're service oriented," said Fred. "We compete on lead time, price, and quality. Bermo does more than make to customer specification. We design products and design some of the tooling to meet the customer's needs."

Bermo had a strong involvement in automation, which included the use of robots. "Automation in the industry has a lead time of 18 to 36 months," said Fred Berdass. "We have a lead time of 13 months. We want our robots to interface with other machine tools, and early in the 80s we built a unit to facilitate that interface. Once we put it to work, we paid for that first robot in 3 months." Bermo had 17 robots operating in the plant in 1990. They were used in production and in materials handling. "We learned how to use robots for small production quantities. The top of our horizon is a million pieces," Fred observed. Dan estimated the average size of a Bermo production run at about 5,000 pieces. Some of Bermo's customers were ordering on a just-in-time (JIT) inventory basis. Dan said, "They want smaller batches to keep inventory down. That involves more setup cost per part. Some customers want 500 not 5,000 but they don't want to pay for the setup. Our job is to figure out how to do it. We are looking at a way of reducing a six-hour setup to 15 minutes. It's a neat system, but it may not work!" Shorter setup time was important to make money on small lot service. Custom orders for small lots were attractive because they carried higher profit margins. Bermo usually got custom orders for small lots, without bidding, from customers who knew Bermo's capability. An attractiveness of larger volume orders was the greatly reduced setup cost per part resulting from longer production runs. When capacity was tight and setups were too costly to justify JIT production, Bermo would sometimes manufacture in large lots and ship in small lots from inventory.

CUSTOMERS

Bermo had 40 customers in late 1990. The list included IBM (several plants), Toro, Digital Equipment, John Deere, Sun Microsystems, Xerox, National Cash Register, Pitney-Bowes, Intergraph, Nippon Electric Corporation, Epson, Westinghouse, Western Digital, Texas Instruments, and Hewlett-Packard. Computer

EXHIBIT 6

4501 BALL ROAD NORTHEAST
CIRCLE PINES, MINNESOTA 55014
TELEPHONE: (612) 786-7676
FAX: (612) 785-2159

May 11, 1989

COMPANY OBJECTIVES

Become the world wide leading fabricator of pressed metal stampings, assemblies
and molded plastics. Improve market share for stability, growth and profitability.
To serve our clients by delivering highest quality at lowest cost in timely
fashion.

SPECIFIC OBJECTIVES

ENGINEERING

To expand our training of shop employees. To employ their manufacturing
skills to design, estimating and processing. To continue updating and improving our CAD/CAM facilities to compress the design to build time and obtain
error free design. To train sales engineers with experience to assist in
early vendor design programs. To be able to offer suggestions to improve
manufacturability, quality, and reduce cost.

TOOLING

Adopt tooling construction strategies to serve effective on all levels of
production. From proto to high volume. Under current consideration are
laser driven technologies. Employ the best machine tools available and to
search for better methods of tool fabrication.

MANUFACTURING & QUALITY CONTROL

To heighten awareness of process and quality. To expand training and company
culture for participative climate and communication. For quality of less
500/million reject and production standards that are accepted and met. To
bring the competive market in to our work place so that we are able to measure
our performance. Install our computer schedule to improve our delivery to
better than 95%. Expand our quick change set up by 60%. Tie manufacturing
to our computer system to eliminate paper flow, and time collection. Expand
our technology in robotics for greater reliability and ease of toil. Expand
SPC to bring responsibility to the operator for documented buy off and
accountability.

ADMINISTRATION/SALES

Simplify work flow processing, streamline computer generated reports, enabling
management to respond with maximum flexibility. Purchasing, install vendor
SPC and write program to monitor performance. & goals to be established after
we obtain baseline. Develop vendors who will deliver J.I.T To maintain
inventory levels to acceptable levels. Implement programs for customary
entry orders and change orders by E.D.I., as well as invoicing and other
communication. Finally develop programs and processes that compress response
time relating to costing and pricing.

HIGH **IQ** PARTS / METAL STAMPINGS, WELDMENTS, INJECTION MOLDED PLASTICS
MECHANICAL AND ELECTRO-MECHANICAL ASSEMBLIES.

cabinets were one of the products most often made for these customers. Some
sales effort was being concentrated on Japanese manufacturers, such as NEC,
who were assembling electronic components in the U. S.

The Berdasses also wanted to focus on electronics (including such products as cabinets for electronic equipment), not just computers. Bermo also
had some component part business in lawn and garden equipment (from
Toro and Deere). Earlier in the spring of 1990, Jerome Atherton, VP for Engineering and Sales, remarked, "We never turn down a job if we can bid on it."
He had estimated then that 90% or more of Bermo's jobs were delivered on
time and that about 30% of new orders were "rush," with a trend toward more.
He thought that about half of the rush work was price-sensitive. "A couple of
key factors allow us to not have to be a low-cost producer now," said Mr. Atherton. "First, we're real good with CAD" (computer-aided design). "Second,
quick turnaround—we're a fourth the time of many competitors. And if we
can't get the large runs, we'll cut costs on the shorter ones. We're after the
'ones,' the prototypes. We'll get the volume later."

FINANCING

Bermo had financed its growth and machinery for its automated capability primarily out of earnings, with some bank borrowing as needed. Total assets of the Company as of September 30, 1989, were nearly $8.5 million (see Balance Sheets, Exhibit 7). The Circle Pines plant had cost $1.8 million, including the land. Payments on the plant financing were $13,000 per month at 6.5% interest. The building was energy efficient: lights and machinery heated the plant without using the heating system. In the summer, however, air conditioning was run during hot weather.

TOOLMAKING

Bermo did two major types of work: toolmaking and production of parts. When a customer wished to design and prototype a new part, it invited bids from Bermo and other suppliers that had the needed expertise and reputation. Price and delivery time were major considerations in competing for an order. There wasn't any profit in the tooling, because Bermo followed the industry practice of bidding tooling at breakeven cost so as to be more competitive for the production order. When Bermo won a contract, its designers would work with the customer to design the tools (dies and punches, usually) needed to produce the part. However, a few Bermo contracts did not require toolmaking, because the tooling was supplied by the customer; such contracts usually did involve parts that a customer already manufactured in-house but did not have enough capacity to produce all it needed.

Traditional toolmaking in the industry typically would be done by an intuitive genius toolmaker who would eyeball a customer's prints and specifications and then machine the dies to produce the parts. When the toolmaker is ready, the tools are set up in a stamping press (on the production floor if a heavy press were required) and a prototype piece is produced and measured. If it's not quite right (which can happen for a lot of reasons), the tools are pulled, and the toolmaker rebuilds or modifies them until he's ready to try again and the right press is available again. This kind of procedure was followed by many firms, small shops or those who could not afford the large investment in modern design technology.

Dan Berdass considered Bermo to be on the leading edge of technology in tool design, production, and parts manufacturing: "One of the most advanced in the country," as he described it. Bermo used Computer Aided Design (CAD) software to design the tooling. The CAD software ran on powerful microcomputers called workstations, located between the business offices and the toolroom on the south side of the plant (see Exhibit 8). The CAD software allowed the designers to view prospective designs in two and three dimensions without having to build a physical prototype. Design errors and production difficulties could thus be corrected relatively quickly and inexpensively, compared to trial and error using manual drafting and physical models.

Once Bermo and the customer agreed upon a design, Bermo input the design specifications into Computer Aided Manufacturing (CAM) software. This software generated code to guide the Computer Numerical Control (CNC) machine, located in the adjacent toolroom with a controlled (temperature, humidity, and dust-free) environment, which would cut the tool or die from a block of high grade steel. This expensive CNC machine utilized "traveling-

EXHIBIT 7

Bermo, Inc. Balance Sheets, 1984–1989

($000)	1984	1985	1986	1987	1988	1989
ASSETS						
Cash	197	194	279	131	475	(189)
Accounts receivable (net)	1,634	1,266	1,066	1,772	1,616	1,998
Inventories	1,289	779	814	1,463	1,684	1,928
Other	298	815	178	141	289	22
Total Current Assets	3,418	3,054	2,336	3,058	4,064	3,760
Property and Equipment	5,231	6,511	6,866	8,083	8,791	9,569
Less accumulated depreciation	(2,244)	(2,999)	(3,704)	(4,515)	(4,659)	(5,319)
Other Assets	14	22	444	540	31	294
TOTAL ASSETS	6,418	6,588	5,905	7,616	8,227	8,303
LIABILITIES						
Current Liabilities	2,909	2,633	1,724	2,135	2,658	2,623
Long-term debt (less current due)	63	398	353	1,008	922	884
Deferred Income Tax Credits	132	242	300	557	637	–
TOTAL LIABILITIES	3,104	3,273	2,377	3,700	4,217	3,507
STOCKHOLDERS' EQUITY						
Common Stock	20	20	20	20	20	20
Additional paid-in capital	6	6	6	6	6	6
Retained Earnings	3,288	3,288	3,502	3,891	3,984	4,770
TOTAL STOCKHOLDERS' EQUITY	3,314	3,315	3,528	3,916	4,009	4,796
	6,418	6,588	5,905	7,616	8,227	8,303

SOURCE: Company records.

wire electrical discharge machining" which was able to hold very tight toler-ances while cutting difficult shapes (as tools often had) from hard-to-work metals. After being cut on the machine, the tooling was inspected to make sure that it met specified tolerances. The machining technology was so accu-rate that rework and scrap were negligible.

Customers left the tooling for a part with Bermo for the duration of a con-tract. Usually, Bermo would make the part over the life of the contract, which ranged from a few weeks to several years. For new parts, initial production quan-tities were usually low but could grow rapidly if the part achieved commercial success for quantity use. However, as orders for a part grew bigger, customers typically demanded price concessions, and some vertically integrated customers with their own machine shops could even take their business in-house to save money. Customers owned the tools and could take them whenever they wanted to. Although rare, such loss of business was more likely during recessions when these customers tried to avoid layoffs by reducing their reliance on subcontrac-tors such as Bermo, who would assess a cancellation charge to a customer if Bermo had incurred costs on an order which was not completed.

EXHIBIT 8

Bermo, Inc. Circle Pines Plant

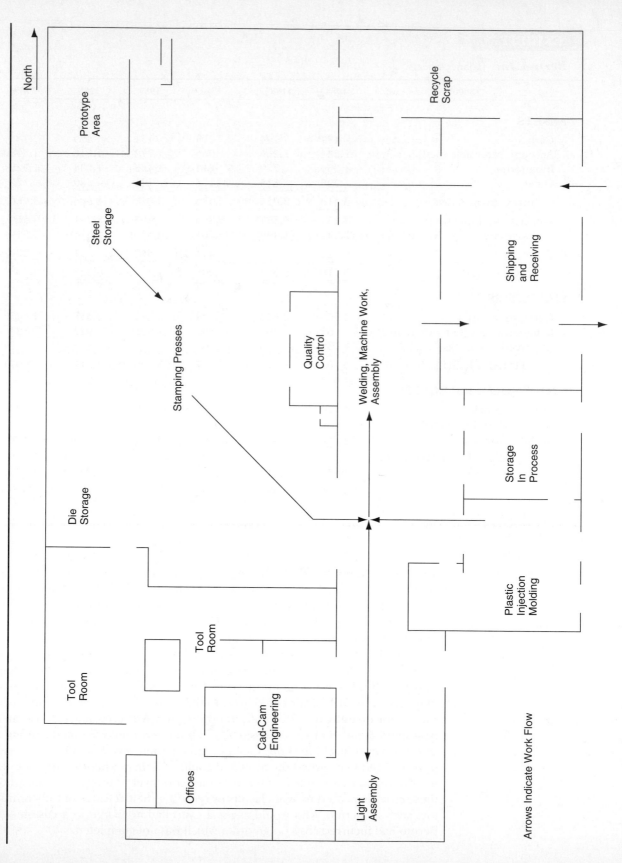

North

Prototype Area

Recycle Scrap

Steel Storage

Stamping Presses

Quality Control

Welding, Machine Work, Assembly

Shipping and Receiving

Die Storage

Storage In Process

Tool Room

Tool Room

Cad-Cam Engineering

Plastic Injection Molding

Offices

Light Assembly

Arrows Indicate Work Flow

PARTS PRODUCTION

Once the necessary tooling was ready, parts production could begin. Most low to medium volume orders were machined in the Welding, Machine work, Assembly area in the east center of the plant. Large orders were stamped by the stamping presses on the west side of the plant. Stocks of various grades and thicknesses of sheet steel used in stamping were kept in the steel storage area adjacent to the stamping presses (see Exhibit 8).

There was considerable variety in the routing of orders which required different sets of operations from one another. Therefore, jobs followed a variety of paths among the work centers in the plant. As a result, bottlenecks shifted almost daily as the mix on the shop floor changed, with little predictability. Dan Bergass noted that almost all jobs in the plant required tooling and stamping, with other operations estimated as follows:

Operation	Percentage of jobs requiring the operation	
Stamping	90%	
Assembling	30%	
Brazing	1%	
Heat treating	1%	
Machining	10%	
Painting	50%	(outside purchase)
Plating	50%	(outside purchase)
Tool and Die making	100%	
Welding	40%	
Plastic Injection molding	10%	

Although everything else was done in its own plant, Bermo sent painting and plating to outside subcontractors, because good quality, delivery, and prices were available on these procedures. To do them satisfactorily in-house would involve an estimated investment of over $1.5 million.

QUALITY CONTROL

Each order specified the "tolerance limits" for the part, i.e., the range of values within which certain part dimensions had to be. These limits were agreed upon by Bermo when it entered into a contract with a customer. Some customers even involved Bermo in setting the tolerances so as to avoid unnecessarily hard-to-make part designs. Parts with dimensions outside tolerance limits, or with faulty welds, assembly, or surface finish, were classified as defective. Increasingly, Bermo's customers required that all pieces shipped to them be nondefective. While this was especially true for customers in the computer and electronics industries, the allowable percent defective was also low and shrinking for Bermo's customers in the garden equipment industries.

For operations on larger jobs, Bermo used statistical process control, carried out at each work station. For very small jobs, "first piece, last piece" inspection was used, in which the operator determined that the first piece was good quality and then ran the job and inspected the last piece. If the last piece was also good, there was no need to inspect the rest, because the chance was negligible that the manufacturing process would have made any defective pieces between the first and last pieces. If the last piece was defective, then the job was 100% inspected and rectified.

Bermo had developed proprietary technology to automate inspections requiring very high precision or a large number of measurements. This was done to eliminate inspection errors caused by human variability and fatigue. Bermo's innovation coupled a microcomputer with a camera "eye," such that the camera lens would capture the image of the object to be inspected. The dimensions of the object would be calculated by Bermo's proprietary software and compared with its ideal dimensions and tolerance limits as stored in the computer's memory. "Off-spec" pieces would be detected and their defects identified.

Such process innovation was rare in job shops like Bermo, and it had become a sales advantage when prospective quality-oriented, blue-ribbon customers such as Hewlett-Packard toured Bermo's plant before deciding which supplier should get their business. Fred Berdass attributed the innovative spirit of Bermo (as evident in CAD/CAM, robotics, and automation of quality control) to the company's practice, over the past several years, of hiring engineering students from the University of Minnesota for summer and co-op jobs, rather than relying solely on technicians. Some of these students later chose after graduation to work at Bermo (instead of joining larger corporations), attracted by Bermo's lack of bureaucracy and the freedom to try new things. Fred believed that Bermo employed more engineers per dollar of sales than any of its competitors and that this gave Bermo a competitive edge.

MANUFACTURING LAYOUT AND SCHEDULING

On a typical day Bermo received between five and ten new orders from both existing and first-time customers. It was Bermo's policy not to accept customer lead times longer than 90 days. That was an industry-wide "rule of thumb," according to Dan, which was intended to cut work in process. Orders with requested lead times of less than 3–4 weeks were considered rush orders, and Bermo charged a premium price for such jobs so as to cover the higher cost they generated, e.g., interrupted machine set-ups on other jobs, overtime, and so on.

Bermo had the following major types of machinery and operators in its plant:

Operation	Number of Machines	Number of Qualified Operators
Stamping	25	40
Assembling	25	40
Brazing	3	1
Machining	6	4
Tool and Die	20	30
Welding	8	10
Plastic injection molding	12	15

Bermo had chosen to have most of its machines mobile rather than fixed in place, resulting in a very flexible plant layout. This flexibility enabled Bermo to frequently construct temporary manufacturing cells for high volume orders. Such a cell would consist of the necessary machines needed to run a particular order, and would be dedicated to that order. Advantages of this arrangement included reduced handling cost for work in progress and more streamlined material flow. It enabled an operator to set up the next machine for a job while the job was running, so that the job could flow with minimal stoppages from machine to machine. Once the order was finished, the cell would be dismantled and the machines freed up for other uses. Equipment that was fixed in place included the heavier stamping presses, which were all in one line on the west side of the plant (see Exhibit 8).

Changes to the production schedule at Bermo were the rule rather than the exception. Scheduling was made difficult by highly unpredictable demand and complex production conditions. On the demand side, it was very difficult to forecast the number and arrival times of rush jobs. Regular or non-rush jobs were easier to forecast, as these frequently were repeat orders from existing customers. In fact, many regular orders were high volume orders to be delivered in installments, with a specified weekly delivery time and quantity. Unfortunately, the benefit of this greater predictability for planning and scheduling was reduced by two factors: order rescheduling and engineering changes. Customers requested, and were allowed to make, drastic changes in both order size and delivery dates. Nearly every order Bermo processed was rescheduled at least once by the customer, and between five and ten rescheduling requests were accommodated daily. In addition, customers made engineering changes affecting their orders. Such changes altered the nature and sequence of processing operations required for the order. One such engineering change, on the average, was made each day to some order on Bermo's schedule.

The disruption caused to Bermo's schedule by rescheduling and engineering changes was further aggravated by the processing of rush orders, which were allowed to interrupt regular orders that were running on machines needed by the rush orders. Such schedule disruptions delayed the job that was interrupted as well as all jobs following it on the machine in question and also necessitated a costly extra setup for the interrupted job. The loss in production capacity due to these extra setups was often considerable, as some setups could take as much as ten hours to complete. In order to reduce costly setups on some high volume orders for customers who requested delivery in small lots, some such orders were manufactured in larger lots than they were shipped, with the effect of increasing finished goods inventories and the variety of job sizes on the factory floor.

The complexity of the manufacturing environment also made scheduling difficult. Most production workers tended several machines simultaneously, by setting up one machine while another machine was running a job. This was possible because nearly all the manufacturing equipment was either semi-automated or fully automated. However, it also meant that the scheduler had to decide several times each day which machine a worker should operate next and which job should be run on that machine. Given the enormous number of possible answers to these two scheduling questions, it was not possible for the scheduler to evaluate all feasible schedules and choose the "best" one according to some criterion (e.g., on-time delivery). In fact, at Bermo the scheduler made these two choices without consistently using any decision rule (an example of a decision rule: assign a worker to the machine that has the most jobs waiting).

Scheduling at Bermo was, therefore, done informally. Orders were released to the shop floor as soon as they were accepted by Bermo, and each operation on an order was started as soon as possible. Generally, jobs were processed on a first-come, first-served basis on each machine. With five to ten new jobs arriving every day, and frequently inaccurate estimates of job processing times, it seemed to be a futile exercise to develop a detailed schedule specifying who would run what job, when, and on which machine. Such a detailed schedule would have been made obsolete several times each day by rush orders, order rescheduling, and engineering changes.

FUTURE STRATEGIES

Dan Berdass was satisfied with continuing toward the objectives that Bermo had adopted. He wondered how big and how fast Bermo should try to grow. He felt that it would be hard to bring a big-company culture into a small company. Dan and the Berdass family wanted to maintain and enhance Bermo's reputation for leadership in automated manufacturing. Although volume work was attractive, the custom production of smaller lots was something which Bermo did well and which was quite profitable. In recent months, Fred Berdass had been talking with Dan about raising prices and turning away some orders. Dan was concerned about losing customers, but Fred thought that Bermo could be more selective in the orders it accepted, maintain sales volume with fewer customers, and improve its delivery time. Fred observed that company supervisors had been stretched by the expansion. He believed that an important strategy issue for Bermo was the question, "Whom to sell to?" Fred was interested in selling more to Japanese customers in the U.S., which was attractive because of the dollar-yen exchange rate (i.e, the high yen made Bermo's prices lower than those of the traditional Japanese suppliers of these U.S.-based Japanese customers). He reasoned that if Bermo cut back on orders they could replace customers, if necessary, later on. "If you have a good facility and do good work," he said, "there will be enough business. The U.S. stamping market is about 8 billion dollars. If half of that is automotive, and if a billion of the other half is accessible to Bermo, then 30 million is a small market segment."

Later in the morning of October 8, Dan Berdass held a meeting in his office about an order being negotiated with a customer. Present at the meeting were Jerome Atherton, Pat Haas—a District Sales Manager, Mel Houle—Manager of Plastics, and Jeff Berdass—Engineering Manager for Plastics. The order involved $150,000 worth of tooling to be made at customer expense and used by Bermo to manufacture products for the customer. It was estimated that potential sales to that customer (following completion of the tooling) could be about $450,000 worth of product per year. After some discussion, it was decided by Dan that the customer should pay Bermo "what we've got in it" (i.e. Bermo's direct cost of making the tools) by the time the tooling is completed and the balance of the $150,000 in six equal monthly payments after that.

Following the meeting, Dan and Jerry had lunch with a visitor and reflected on the strategy of Bermo. Several factors were thought to be important in being able to maintain a competitive advantage. They were interested in emphasizing low cost production of high-quality custom products, with a focus on the market segments Bermo was serving. Technological leadership was seen as the key to cost reduction, quality, and timely delivery. Another factor was labor costs. Bermo's average hourly labor charge to a job was about $28, which included machine costs. Labor and benefits alone were around $20 per hour, Dan estimated.

With labor costs in mind, Dan had visited Tijuana, Mexico, several times in recent months and had talked with the Tijuana Chamber of Commerce about the possibility of establishing a plant there. Labor costs in Tijuana were about $1 per hour, including benefits. However, productivity of Mexican labor was generally considered to be lower than that of American labor. Dan was aware that extensive training and supervision would be necessary for Mexican workers in order for them to work with highly technical processes such as Bermo utilized. Government regulation of business in Mexico was seen as minimal as compared to the United States. The fact that Bermo had no customers in Mexico led Jerry Atherton to feel disinclined to operate there.

Several of Bermo's major customers had indicated their dissatisfaction with schedule delays, and Dan realized that corrective action was required to prevent things from getting worse. If prolonged schedule delays became chronic, then customers might begin to counter with actions that could create further problems for Bermo. They could demand rush order deliveries earlier than needed (to allow for expected schedule delays), thereby exacerbating Bermo's schedule disruptions. They could release routine orders to Bermo earlier (to allow for longer lead times), thereby increasing Bermo's work load in the short run and causing even longer lead times, resulting in even earlier order release by some customers, and so on. Customers also could take their business elsewhere.

While the backlog problem had to be dealt with promptly, Dan recognized that its successful solution could depend on decisions about other strategic matters. How much should Bermo expand capacity, and where? Why was the backlog of orders increasing at the plant, and could manufacturing and scheduling be improved enough to make a difference? What would happen if Bermo raised prices and declined some orders? What kind of orders? And how did all these choices fit with Bermo's overall objectives? These questions were on Dan's mind as he and Jerry returned to the plant for a busy afternoon of work that could last into the evening.

Harley-Davidson, Inc.—
Motorcycle Division[1]

J. PAUL PETER, *University of Wisconsin—Madison*

Harley-Davidson, Inc. is a diversified company with corporate headquarters at 3700 Juneau Avenue, Milwaukee, Wisconsin. Its three major business segments include (1) motorcycles and related products, (2) transportation vehicles including both recreational and commercial vehicles, and (3) defense and other businesses. In 1990, the company experienced another record year of growth. In the *Business Week 1000* ranking of the top U.S. companies, Harley-Davidson, Inc., with a market value of $515 million, moved from the 973d to the 865th largest U.S. company. Richard F. Teerlink, President and Chief Executive Officer of the company, offered the following introduction to the company's 1990 annual report:

> Fellow Shareholder: I am again pleased to announce a record year at Harley-Davidson, Inc. in terms of revenues, profits and earnings. I'm especially proud this year because we were able to deliver very impressive results despite the fact that 1990—the third and fourth quarters, especially—was tough on most American manufacturers.
>
> Revenues for 1990 totaled $864.6 million, an increase of 9.3 percent over 1989. Net income was $37.8 million, a 14.8 percent increase and net earnings per share increased 11.0 percent to $2.12. Since 1987, revenues, net income and net earnings per share have increased 33.8, 78.3 and 29.3 percent, respectively. Considering where we were as recently as five years ago, these are tremendous results.

Indeed, these were tremendous results given that the company is the only US motorcycle manufacturer still in business, although there were once more than 140 competitors. In addition, the company had tremendous difficulties surviving the 1970s and early 80s and few analysts thought it would survive. In fact, the company would have gone bankrupt in 1985 had it not gotten refinancing with only days to spare.

---

[1]Copyright © 1991 by J. Paul Peter.

J. Paul Peter is the James R. McManus-Bascom Professor in Marketing at the University of Wisconsin—Madison. All factual information in the case is taken from public sources.

COMPANY BACKGROUND AND OPERATIONS

Harley-Davidson was established in 1903 and had a virtual monopoly on the heavyweight motorcycle market by the 1960s.[2] In the early 60s Japanese manufacturers entered the marketplace with lightweight motorcycles that did not directly compete with Harley-Davidson. The influx of the Japanese products backed by huge marketing programs caused the demand for motorcycles to expand rapidly.

Recognizing the potential for profitability in the motorcycle market, American Machine and Foundry (AMF, Inc.) purchased Harley-Davidson in 1969. AMF almost tripled production to 75,000 units annually over a four year period to meet the increases in demand. Unfortunately, product quality deteriorated significantly as over half the cycles came off the assembly line missing parts and dealers had to fix them up in order to make sales. Little money was invested in improving design or engineering. The motorcycles leaked oil, vibrated, and could not match the excellent performance of the Japanese products. While hard-core motorcycle enthusiasts were willing to fix up their Harleys and modify them for better performance, new motorcycle buyers had neither the devotion nor skill to do so. If Harley-Davidson was to remain in business, it desperately needed to improve quality and update its engine designs. Japanese manufacturers also moved into the heavyweight motorcycle market and began selling Harley look-alike motorcycles. Yamaha was the first company to do so and was soon followed by the three other major Japanese manufacturers, Honda, Suzuki, and Kawasaki. Their products looked so similar to Harley's that it was difficult to tell the difference without reading the name on the gas tank. The Japanese companies also copied the style of the Harley advertisements. As one Harley executive put it, "We weren't flattered."

In late 1975 AMF appointed Vaughn Beals in charge of Harley-Davidson. He set up a quality control and inspection program that began to eliminate the worst of the production problems. However, the cost of the program was high. For example, the company had to spend about $1,000 extra per bike to get the first hundred into shape for dealers to sell at around $4,000. Beals along with other senior managers began to develop a long-range product strategy—the first time the company had looked ten years ahead. They recognized the need to upgrade the quality and performance of their products to compete with the faster, high-performance Japanese bikes. However, they also recognized that such changes would require years to accomplish and a huge capital investment.

In order to stay in business while the necessary changes in design and production were being accomplished, the executives turned to William G. Davidson, Harley's styling vice-president. Known as "Willie G." and a grandson of one of the company founders, he frequently mingled with bikers and with his beard, black leather and jeans was well-accepted by them. Willie G. understood Harley customers and stated:

> They really know what they want on their bikes: the kind of instrumentation, the style of bars, the cosmetics of the engine, the look of the exhaust pipes and so on. Every little piece on a Harley is exposed, and it has to look just right. A tube curve

---

[2]This section is based on "How Harley Beat Back the Japanese," *Fortune*, September 25, 1989, pp. 155–164.

or the shape of a timing case can generate enthusiasm or be a total turnoff. It's almost like being in the fashion business.[3]

Willie G. designed a number of new models by combining components from existing models. These included the Super Glide, the Electra Glide, the Wide Glide and the Low Rider. Each model was successful and other Harley executives credit Davidson's skill with saving the company. One senior executive said of Willie G., "The guy is an artistic genius. In the five years before we could bring new engines on-stream, he performed miracles with decals and paint. A line here and a line there and we'd have a new model. It's what enabled us to survive."

Still Harley-Davidson was losing market share to its Japanese competitors who continued to pour new bikes into the heavyweight market. By 1980, AMF was losing interest in investing in the recreational market and decided to focus its efforts on its industrial product lines. Since AMF could not find a buyer for Harley-Davidson, it sold the company to 13 senior Harley executives in an $81.5 million leveraged buyout financed by Citicorp on June 16, 1981.

In 1982 things turned worse than ever for Harley-Davidson. Overall demand for motorcycles dropped dramatically and Harley's market share of this smaller market also continued to drop. The company had a large inventory of unsold products and could not continue in business with its level of production and expenses. Production was cut drastically and more than 1,800 of the 4,000 employees were let go.

The Japanese manufacturers continued producing and exporting to the United States at rates well above what the market could endure. Harley-Davidson was able to prove to the International Trade Commission (ITC) that there was an eighteen-month finished-goods inventory of Japanese motorcycles that fell well below fair market value and asked for protection. The ITC can offer protection to a U.S. industry being threatened by a foreign competitor. In 1983, President Reagan increased the tariffs on large Japanese motorcycles from 4.4 percent to 49.4 percent, but these would decline each year and be effective for only five years. While this did decrease the imports somewhat and gave Harley some protection, Japanese manufacturers found ways to evade most of the tariffs, for example, by assembling more of their heavyweight bikes in their U.S. plants. Harley-Davidson's market share in the 1983 heavyweight motorcycle market slipped to 23 percent, the lowest ever, although it did earn a slight profit. By 1984, it had sales of $294 million and earned $2.9 million; it has continued to increase sales and profits through the early 1990s.

Manufacturing Changes

From the late 1970s Harley-Davidson executives recognized that the only way to achieve the quality of Japanese motorcycles was to adopt many of the manufacturing techniques used by them. The manufacturing systems changes that were instituted included a just-in-time manufacturing program and a statistical operator control system.[4]

---

[3]Ibid., p. 156.

[4]This section is based on Thomas Gelb, "Overhauling Corporate Engine Drives Winning Strategy," *Journal of Business Strategy,* November/December 1989, pp. 8–12.

The just-in-time manufacturing program was renamed MAN which stood for Materials As Needed. When the program was discussed with managers and employees at the York, Pennsylvania manufacturing facility, many of them reacted in disbelief. The York plant already had a modern computer-based control system with overhead conveyors and high-rise parts store and the new system would replace all of this with push carts! However, the MAN system eliminates the mountains of costly parts inventory and handling systems, speeds up set-up time, and can solve other manufacturing problems. For example, parts at the York facility were made in large batches for long production runs. They were stored until needed and then loaded on a 3.5 mile conveyor that rattled endlessly around the plant. In some cases, parts couldn't be found, or when they were, they were rusted or damaged. In other cases, there had been engineering changes since the parts were made and they simply no longer fit. The MAN system consists of containers that travel between the place where the parts are made and where they are to be used. The containers serve as a signal at each end to either "feed me" or "empty me." This system is credited with reducing work-in-process inventory by $22 million.

The statistical operator control (SOC) system allows continuous process improvements to reduce costs. The system involves teaching machine operators to use simple statistics to analyze measurements taken from parts to determine dimensional accuracy and quality. The system helps identify problems that occur during production early enough that they can be corrected before many parts are produced.

Human Resource Changes

In designing the new manufacturing processes, Harley executives recognized the importance of employee involvement.[5] In 1978 the company was among the first in the U.S. to institute a company-wide employee involvement program. Harley-Davidson was the second U.S. company to begin a quality circles program which permits employees to contribute their ideas, solve problems, and improve the efficiency and quality of their work. Prior to these changes, engineers would figure out how to improve the manufacturing process and then tell operating employees what changes they needed to make. Naturally, the engineering plans were not flawless but the operating employees would not lift a finger to help solve the problems and would simply blame the engineers for screwing up again.

The changes in manufacturing and human resource strategy were credited with a 36 percent reduction in warranty cost; a 46 percent increase in defect-free vehicles received by dealers since 1982; inventory turnover up 500 percent; and productivity per employee up 50 percent.

Marketing Changes

By 1983 Harley executives recognized that they had become too internally-oriented and needed to pay greater attention to customers.[6] They recognized that they would not be able to compete effectively with the Japanese manufac-

---

[5]Same as footnotes 2 and 3.

[6]Same as footnotes 2 and 3.

turers by offering a complete product line of motorcycles but rather would have to find a niche and defend it successfully. They decided to focus all of their efforts on the superheavyweight motorcycle market (850cc or greater) and adopted a "close-to-the-customer" philosophy. This involved several unique marketing strategies. First, Harley executives actively sought out and discussed motorcycle improvement issues with customers. Second, it started the Harley Owner Group (HOG) to bring together Harley riders and company management in informal settings to expand the social atmosphere of motorcycling. The club is factory-sponsored and is open to all Harley owners. It sponsors national rallies and local events and gives customers a reason to ride a Harley and involves them in a social group whose main activities revolve around the product.

Third, it began a Demo Ride program in which fleets of new Harleys were taken to motorcycle events and rallies and licensed motorcyclists were encouraged to ride them. This program was felt to be critical for convincing potential new customers that Harley-Davidson motorcycles were of excellent quality and not the rattling, leaking bikes of the 1970s. The program was renamed Super-Ride and $3 million was committed to it. A series of TV commercials was purchased to invite bikers to come to any of Harley's over 600 dealers for a ride on a new Harley. Over three weekends, 90,000 rides were given to 40,000 people, half of whom owned other brands. While sales from the program did not immediately cover costs, many of the riders came back a year or two later and purchased a Harley.

Fourth, the company invited several manufacturing publications to visit the plant and publish articles on quality improvement programs. These articles reached the manufacturing trade audience and the national media as well. Finally, recognizing that many dealers viewed their business as a hobby and did not know how to sell, the company increased its sales force by 50 percent to give sales representatives more time to train dealers in how to sell Harleys.

Financial Changes

Although Harley-Davidson was improving its quality, reducing its breakeven point, catching up with competitors in the superheavyweight market and marketing more aggressively, Citicorp was concerned about the economy and what would happen to Harley-Davidson when the tariffs on Japanese bikes were lifted in 1988.[7] The bank decided it wanted to recover its loans and quit being a source of funds for the company. After a number of negotiations, Citicorp took a $10 million write-off which might have facilitated Harley obtaining new financing. However, other bankers felt that the company must have been in really bad shape if Citicorp took a write-off and refused financial assistance. While lawyers were drawing up a bankruptcy plan, Harley executives continued to seek refinancing. Finally, several banks did agree to pay off Citicorp and refinance the company with $49.5 million.

Harley-Davidson went public with a stock sale on the American Stock Exchange in 1986. The company hoped to raise an additional $65 million and obtained over $90 million with the sale of common stock and high yielding bonds. It then was in an excellent cash position and purchased Holiday Rambler Corporation, at that time the largest privately held recreational vehicle

[7]Same as footnotes 2 and 3.

EXHIBIT 1

Harley-Davidson, Inc. Selected Financial Data

(In thousands, except share and per share amounts)	1990	1989	1988	1987	1986
INCOME STATEMENT DATA:					
Net sales	$864,600	$790,967	$709,360	$645,966	$295,322
Cost of goods sold	635,551	596,940	533,448	487,205	219,167
Gross profit	229,049	194,027	175,912	158,761	76,155
Selling, administrative, and engineering	145,674	127,606	111,582	104,672	60,059
Income from operations	83,375	66,421	64,330	54,089	16,096
Other income (expense):					
Interest expense, net	(9,701)	(14,322)	(18,463)	(21,092)	(8,373)
Lawsuit judgement	(7,200)	—	—	—	—
Other	(3,857)	910	165	(2,143)	(388)
	(20,758)	(13,412)	(18,298)	(23,235)	(8,761)
Income from continuing operations before income taxes and extraordinary items	62,617	53,009	46,032	30,854	7,335
Provision for income taxes	24,309	20,399	18,863	13,181	3,028
Income from continuing operations before extraordinary items	38,308	32,610	27,169	17,673	4,307
Discontinued operation, net of tax	—	3,590	(13)	—	—
Income before extraordinary items	38,308	36,200	27,156	17,673	4,307
Extraordinary items	(478)	(3,258)	(3,244)	3,542	564
Net income	$ 37,830	$ 32,942	$ 23,912	$ 21,215	$ 4,871
Weighted average common shares outstanding	17,787,788	17,274,120	15,912,624	12,990,466	10,470,460
PER COMMON SHARE:					
Income from continuing operations	$2.15	$1.89	$1.70	$1.36	$0.41
Discontinued operation	—	0.21	—	—	—
Extraordinary items	(.03)	(.19)	(.20)	0.28	0.05
Net income	$2.12	$1.91	$1.50	$1.64	$0.46
BALANCE SHEET DATA:					
Working capital	$ 50,152	$ 51,313	$ 74,904	$ 64,222	$ 38,552
Total assets	407,467	378,929	401,114	380,872	328,499
Short-term debt, including current maturities of long-term debt	23,859	26,932	33,229	28,335	18,090
Long-term debt, less current maturities	48,339	74,795	135,176	178,762	191,594
Total debt	72,198	101,727	168,405	207,097	209,684
Stockholders' equity	198,775	156,247	121,648	62,913	26,159

In December 1986, the Company acquired Holiday Rambler Corporation. Holiday Rambler Corporation's results of operations are not included in the income statement data for 1986.

SOURCE: *Harley-Davidson, Inc. Annual Report 1990*, p. 29.

company in the United States. Holiday Rambler is similar to Harley-Davidson in that it is a niche marketer that produces premium-priced products for customers whose lives revolve around their recreational activities. In 1987 the company moved to the New York Stock Exchange and made two additional stock market offerings. Selected financial data for Harley-Davidson is contained in Exhibits 1 through 4.

EXHIBIT 2

Harley-Davidson, Inc. Consolidated Statement of Income

(In thousands, except per share amounts)

Years ended December 31	1990	1989	1988
Net sales	$864,600	$790,967	$709,360
OPERATING COSTS AND EXPENSES:			
Cost of goods sold	635,551	596,940	533,448
Selling, administrative, and engineering	145,674	127,606	111,582
	781,225	724,546	645,030
Income from operations	83,3753	66,421	64,330
Interest income	1,736	3,634	4,149
Interest expense	(11,437)	(17,956)	(22,612)
Lawsuit judgement	(7,200)	—	—
Other—net	(3,857)	910	165
Income from continuing operations before provision for income taxes and extraordinary items	62,617	53,009	46,032
Provisions for income taxes	24,309	20,399	18,863
Income from continuing operations before extraordinary items	38,308	32,610	27,169
DISCONTINUED OPERATION, NET OF TAX:			
Income (loss) from discontinued operation	—	154	(13)
Gain on disposal of discontinued operation	—	3,436	—
Income before extraordinary items	38,308	36,200	27,156
EXTRAORDINARY ITEMS:			
Loss on debt repurchases, net of taxes	(478)	(1,434)	(1,468)
Additional cost of 1983 AMF settlement, net of taxes	—	(1,824)	(1,776)
Net income	$37,830	$32,942	$23,912
EARNINGS PER COMMON SHARE:			
Income from continuing operations	$2.15	$1.89	$1.70
Discontinued operation	—	.21	—
Extraordinary items	(.03)	(.19)	(.20)
Net income	$2.12	$1.91	$1.50

The accompanying notes are an integral part of the consolidated financial statements.
SOURCE: *Harley-Davidson, Inc. Annual Report 1990*, p. 34.

EXHIBIT 3

Harley-Davidson, Inc. Consolidated Balance Sheet

(In thousands, except share amounts)

December 31	1990	1989
ASSETS		
Current assets:		
Cash and cash equivalents	$ 14,001	$ 39,076
Accounts receivable, net of allowance for		
doubtful accounts	51,897	45,565
Inventories	109,878	87,540
Deferred income taxes	14,447	9,682
Prepaid expenses	6,460	5,811
Total current assets	196,683	187,674
Property, plant and equipment, net	136,052	115,700
Goodwill	63,082	66,190
Other assets	11,650	9,365
	$407,467	$378,929
LIABILITIES AND STOCKHOLDERS' EQUITY		
Current liabilities:		
Notes payable	$ 22,351	$ 22,789
Current maturities of long-term debt	1,508	4,143
Accounts payable	50,412	40,095
Accrued expenses and other liabilities	72,260	69,334
Total current liabilities	146,531	136,361
Long-term debt	48,339	74,795
Other long-term liabilities	9,194	5,273
Deferred income taxes	4,628	6,253
Commitments and contingencies (Note 6)		
Stockholders' equity:		
Series A Junior Participating preferred stock, 1,000,000 shares authorized, none issued	—	—
Common stock, 18,310,000 and 9,155,000 shares issued in 1990 and 1989, respectively	183	92
Additional paid-in capital	87,115	79,681
Retained earnings	115,093	77,352
Cumulative foreign currency translation adjustment	995	508
	203,386	157,633
Less:		
Treasury stock (539,694 and 447,091 shares in 1990 and 1989, respectively), at cost	(771)	(112)
Unearned compensation	(3,840)	(1,274)
Total stockholders' equity	198,775	156,247
	$407,467	$378,929

SOURCE: *Harley-Davidson, Inc. Annual Report 1990*, p. 33.

EXHIBIT 4

Harley-Davidson, Inc. Business Segments and Foreign Operations

A. Business Segments	1990	1989	1988
NET SALES:			
Motorcycles and Related Products	$595,319	$495,961	$397,774
Transportation Vehicles	240,573	273,961	303,969
Defense and Other Businesses	28,708	21,045	7,617
	$864,600	$790,967	$709,360
INCOME FROM OPERATIONS:			
Motorcycles and Related Products	$ 87,844	$ 60,917	$ 49,688
Transportation Vehicles	825	12,791	20,495
Defense and Other Businesses	2,375	2,236	755
General corporate expenses	(7,669)	(9,523)	(6,608)
	83,375	66,421	64,330
Interest expense, net	(9,701)	(14,322)	(18,463)
Other	(11,057)	910	165
Income from continuing operations before provision for income taxes and extraordinary items	$62,617	$53,009	$46,032

	Motorcycles and Related Products	Trans-portation Vehicles	Defense and Other Businesses	Corporate	Consolidated
1988					
Identifiable assets	$180,727	$215,592	$2,863	$1,932	$401,114
Depreciation and amortization	10,601	6,958	3	396	17,958
Net capital expenditures	14,121	6,693	66	29	20,909
1989					
Identifiable assets	192,087	176,813	7,018	3,011	378,929
Depreciation and amortization	9,786	7,282	1,125	1,814	20,007
Net capital expenditures	18,705	3,524	1,190	200	23,619
1990					
Identifiable assets	220,656	177,498	7,163	2,150	407,467
Depreciation and amortization	13,722	6,925	1,166	618	22,431
Net capital expenditure	34,099	2,547	1,257	490	38,393

There were no sales between business segments for the years ended December 31, 1990, 1989 and 1988.

B. Foreign Operations (In thousands)	1990	1989	1988
Assets	$25,853	$18,065	$ 6,557
Liabilities	17,717	15,814	3,761
Net sales	82,811	39,653	22,061
Net income	5,555	2,281	1,941

Export sales of domestic subsidiaries to nonaffiliated customers were $93.0 million, $75.4 million and $56.8 million in 1990, 1989 and 1988, respectively.

SOURCE: *Harley-Davidson, Inc. Annual Report 1990*, p. 43.

By 1987, Harley-Davidson was doing so well that it asked to have the tariffs on Japanese bikes removed a year ahead of schedule. On its 85th birthday in 1988, the company held a huge motorcycle rally involving over 40,000 motorcyclists from as far away as San Francisco and Orlando, Florida. All attendees were asked to donate $10 to the Muscular Dystrophy Association and Harley memorabilia was auctioned off. The event raised over $500,000 for charity. The final ceremonies included over 24,000 bikers whose demonstration of product loyalty is unrivaled for any other product in the world.

MOTORCYCLE DIVISION—EARLY 1990s

Exhibit 5 shows the motorcycle division's growth in unit sales. In 1990, Harley-Davidson dominated the superheavyweight motorcycle market with a 62.3 percent share while Honda had 16.2 percent, Yamaha had 7.2 percent, Kawasaki had 6.7 percent, Suzuki had 5.1 percent and BMW had 2.5 percent. Net sales for the division were $595.3 million with parts and accessories accounting for $110 million of this figure. Production could not keep up with demand for Harley-Davidson motorcycles although a $23 million paint center at the York, Pennsylvania plant was nearing completion and would increase production to 300 bikes per day.[8]

Approximately 31 percent of Harley-Davidson's 1990 motorcycle sales were overseas. The company worked hard at developing a number of international markets. For example, anticipating the consolidation of Western European economies in 1992, a European Parts and Accessories warehouse was established in Frankfurt, Germany in 1990. After entering a joint venture in 1989 with a Japanese distributor, the company bought out all rights for distribution in Japan in 1990. Revenue from international operations grew from $40.9 million in 1986 to $175.8 million in 1990.

EXHIBIT 5

Harley-Davidson Motorcycle Unit Sales 1983–1990

Year	Total Units	Domestic Units	Export Units	Export Percentages
1990	62,458	43,138	19,320	30.9
1989	58,925	43,637	15,288	25.9
1988	50,517	38,941	11,576	22.9
1987	43,315	34,729	8,586	19.8
1986	36,735	29,910	6,825	18.6
1985	34,815	29,196	5,619	16.1
1984	39,224	33,141	6,083	15.5
1983	35,885	31,140	4,745	13.2

SOURCE: Adapted from *Harley-Davidson, Inc. Annual Report 1990*, p. 20.

[8]*Harley-Davidson, Inc. Annual Report 1990*, p. 12

Product Line

For 1991, Harley-Davidson offered a line of 20 motorcycles shown in Exhibit 6. Other than the XLH Sportster 883 and XLH Sportster 883 Hugger which had chain drives, all models were belt driven; all models had a five speed transmission. Three of the Sportster models had an 883cc engine and one had a 1200cc engine; all of the remaining models had a 1340cc engine. The first five models listed in Exhibit 6 were touring models while the remaining bikes were standard and cruising types. All of the models exhibited impressive painting and classic styling attributes visually reminiscent of Harley-Davidson motorcycles from the 50s and 60s.

Motorcycle magazine articles commonly were favorable toward Harley-Davidson products but pointed out weaknesses in various models. For example, a review of the XLH Sportster 1200 in the December 1990 edition of *Cycle* reported:

> But Harley undeniably has its corporate finger on the pulse of Sportster owners, and knows what they want. All of the complaints—poor suspension, high-effort brakes, awkward riding position, short fuel range, engine vibration, and poor seat—have echoed through the halls of 3700 Juneau Ave. for more than a decade, yet have had seemingly little effect on XL sales. H-D sold 24,000 Sportsters over the past two years, and these complaints have been common knowledge to anyone who's cared enough to listen.[9]

EXHIBIT 6

Harley-Davidson, Inc. 1991 Product Line and Suggested Retail Prices

Model	Suggested Retail Price
FLTC Tour Glide Ultra Classic	$13,895
FLHTC Electra Glide Ultra Classic	$13,895
FLTC Tour Glide Classic	$11,745
FLHTC Electra Glide Classic	$11,745
FLHS Electra Glide Sport	$10,200
FXDB Sturgis	$11,520
FLSTC Heritage Softail Classic	$11,495
FLSTF Fat Boy	$11,245
FXSTS Springer Softail	$11,335
FXSTC Softail Custom	$10,895
FXLR Low Rider Custom	$10,295
FXRT Sport Glide	$10,595
FXRS Low Rider Convertible	$10,445
FXRS SP Low Rider Sport Edition	$10,295
FXRS Low Rider	$10,195
FXR Super Glide	$ 8,995
XLH Sportster 1200	$ 6,095
XLH Sportster 883 Deluxe	$ 5,395
XLH Sportster 883 Hugger	$ 4,800
XLH Sportster 883	$ 4,395

SOURCE: Adapted from *Cycle World 1991 Motorcycle Buyer's Guide*, pp. 76–82.

[9]"Harley-Davidson 1200 Sportster," *Cycle*, December 1990, p. 90.

The article, however, was very complimentary of the newly designed engine and new five speed transmission and concluded that "This is the best Sportster ever to roll down an assembly line."

A review of the same model in *Cycle World 1991 Motorcycle Buyer's Guide* pointed out a number of the same problems but concluded:

> Yet the bike's appeal is undeniable. A stab at the starter button rumbles it into instant life, and as the engine settles into its characteristically syncopated idle, the bike is transformed into one of the best platforms anywhere from which to Just Cruise. And that means anything from cruising your immediate neighborhood to cruising (with appropriate gas and rest stops) into the next state.
>
> This the bike is more than willing to do, with its premium tires and seemingly bulletproof reliability. The important thing is to not ask the Sportster 1200 to be something it isn't. What it is is a Sportster, much as Sportsters always have been.
>
> This is merely the best one yet.[10]

Pricing

The suggested retail prices for 1991 Harley-Davidson motorcycles are also shown in Exhibit 6. These products were premium-priced although the low-end XLH Sportster 883 and XLH Sportster 883 Hugger were less so in order that new motorcyclists could buy them and then trade-up at a later time to larger, more expensive models. In fact, in 1987 and 1988, the company offered to take any Sportster sold in trade on a bigger Harley-Davidson at a later time.

The prices for Harleys can be compared with competitive products.[11] For example, the three 1991 Honda Gold Wing touring models with larger 1520cc engines had suggested retail prices of $8998, $11,998 and $13,998. A Harley look-alike, the Kawasaki Vulcan 88, had a 1470cc engine and a suggested retail selling price of $6599; a Kawasaki Voyager XII with a 1196cc engine had a suggested retail selling price of $9099. Another Harley look-alike, the Suzuki Intruder 1400, had a 1360cc engine and a suggested retail selling price of $6599. The Yamaha Virago 1100, another Harley look-alike, had a 1063cc engine and also had a suggested retail selling price of $6599.

Promotional Activities

Kathleen Demitros, Vice-President—Marketing for the Motorcycle Division, discussed a problem in designing advertising for Harley-Davidson motorcycles:

> One of the problems was that we had such a hard-core image out there that it was turning off a lot of people, even though people basically approved of Harley-Davidson. We had to find a way to balance our image more, without turning it into 'white bread' and making it bland. Our goal was to get as close to our Harley riders as possible and communicate with them very personally.[12]

In addition to print advertising in general magazines, and Harley's own quarterly magazine, called *Enthusiast,* Harley has its own catalogs with full

---

[10]Harley-Davidson Sportster 1200—Improving on Tradition," *Cycle World 1991 Motorcycle Buyer's Guide,* April–May 1991, p. 27.

[11]All prices are taken from the same reference as footnote 9.

[12]Kate Fitzgerald, "Kathleen Demitros Helps Spark Comeback at Harley-Davidson," *Advertising Age,* January 8, 1990, p. 3.

color pictures and descriptions of each model and discussions of Harley-Davidson products. For example, below is an excerpt from the 1991 Harley-Davidson catalog:

> To the average citizen, it's a motorcycle. To the average motorcyclist, it's a Harley. To the Harley owner, it's something else entirely, something special. Once you've got your Harley, it's much more than a piece of machinery or a way to get around. In a sense, it actually owns you. It occupies you even when you're not riding it. It's part of your life. And while you might not ever be able to explain it to anyone who doesn't know, you know; the trip certainly doesn't end after the road does. Different? Most wouldn't have it any other way.

In 1990 the Harley Owner Group had 650 chapters and 134,000 members with expected growth in 1991 of 15 percent and an additional 55 chapters.[13] In addition to national, regional and state rallies and other events, meetings between HOG members and Harley management continued to provide suggestions for product improvements. HOG groups have "adopted" various scenic highways and have taken responsibility for their upkeep. In the ten years Harley-Davidson and its owner groups have been involved, they have raised over $8.6 million for the Muscular Dystrophy Association.

Dealer Improvements

Several years earlier Harley-Davidson instituted a Designer Store program to improve the appearance, image, and merchandising of its products at the retail level. By the end of 1990, more than 310 of the company's 851 domestic and international motorcycle dealerships had completed major store renovation projects or had agreed to do them in 1991. Some dealers reported receiving full return on the renovation investment within 12 to 18 months due to increased sales brought about by a more inviting shopping environment.

Market Information

The traditional U.S. motorcyclist is an 18 to 24 year old male.[14] Since 1980, the number of men in this age group has declined from 42.4 million to 35.3 million. By 2000 the number is expected to be only slightly higher, at 36.1 million. Women are buying motorcycles in increasing numbers and sales to them have doubled. However, they still account for only 6 percent of the total motorcycles purchased. Motorcycle manufacturers have responded to this market, however, by designing bikes that are lower slung and easier for women to ride. The Harley-Davidson XLH Sportster 883 Hugger was designed in part for this market.

The sale of motorcycles, including three and four wheel off-road vehicles, peaked in 1984 at 1,310,240 units. Five years later sales had dropped to 483,005 units. Sales dropped in all categories, although dirt bikes had the largest sales losses. Sales of larger motorcycles, which tend to be purchased by older buyers for use on highways, represented 12.2 percent of sales in 1984 but increased to 21.3 percent of sales five years later.

[13]This discussion is based on *Harley-Davidson, Inc. Annual Report 1990*, pp. 15–26.

[14]This discussion is based on Doron P. Levin, "Motorcycle Makers Shift Tactics," *The New York Times*, September 16, 1989.

As less affluent young men have drifted away from motorcycling, the sport has been taken up by professionals and businesspeople in their 40s and 50s. Likely, the late Malcolm S. Forbes, motorcycle enthusiast and wealthy magazine publisher, influenced this market, which is older and more conservative, to often ride long distances with their spouses on luxury vehicles.

There is some evidence that many motorcycle owners do not use their bikes very often, some only for a ride or two in the summer. Although the number of fatal accidents involving motorcycles declined 9 percent in a recent year, this decrease was likely because of decreased usage. The Insurance Institute for Highway Safety reported that in a crash, a person was 17 times more likely to die on a motorcycle than in a car.

Competition

Exhibit 7 shows changes in overall market share percentages for the five major competitors in the U.S. motorcycle market.[15] Honda clearly lost the greatest share and its sales decreased from $1.1 billion in fiscal 1985 to $230 million in fiscal 1990. However, motorcycle sales represent less than 1 percent of Honda's worldwide revenues.

Honda's plan to battle its sagging sales involved the introduction of more expensive, technologically-advanced bikes. However, with an increase in the value of the yen from 250 to the dollar in 1987 to 120 by 1988, all Japanese competitors had to raise prices. Honda had to raise their prices even more to cover their new expensive models and became less price competitive. In fact, nearly 600 Honda motorcycle dealers went out of business since 1985, leaving the company with 1,200 dealers in North America. Honda's Maryville, Ohio plant had so much excess capacity that executives considered transforming much of it to production of auto-parts.

Honda's 1990 strategy included cutting back prices and a $75 million advertising campaign to reintroduce the "wholesome" angle of cycling to reach new market segments. Promotional emphasis was also given to encouraging Americans to use motorcycles for commuting as an alternative to cars as is done in Europe and the Far East. High levels of air pollution, increased traffic, and rising fuel costs supported Honda's strategy. The advertising campaign

EXHIBIT 7

U.S. Motorcycle Market Shares for Major Manufacturers

Company	1985	1987	1989
Honda	58.5	50.8	28.9
Yamaha	15.5	19.8	27.7
Kawasaki	10.2	10.2	15.6
Suzuki	9.9	11.6	14.2
Harley-Davidson	4.0	6.3	13.9

SOURCE: R.L. Polk & Co., as reported in "That 'Vroom!' You Hear Is Honda Motorcycles," *Business Week*, September 3, 1990, p. 74.

[15]This discussion is based on "7That 'Vroom!' You Hear Is Honda Motorcycles," *Business Week*, September 3, 1990, pp. 74, 76.

was oriented less to selling individual products than to selling the idea that motorcycling is fun. Honda also offered free rides in shopping malls, sponsors races, and paid for Honda buyers to be trained at Motorcycle Safety Centers throughout the country.

In 1991, Honda's motorcycle product line included 25 models with displacements from 49 to 1520cc's including sportbikes, touring, cruisers, standards and dual purpose types. It also included four models of 4-wheel all terrain vehicles (ATV's). Kawasaki's line included 23 motorcycle models in a variety of types and four 4-wheel models. Suzuki offered 24 models of motorcycles and eight 4-wheel models. Yamaha offered 25 motorcycle models and seven 4-wheel models. Other smaller competitors in the U.S. market included ATK, BMW, Ducati, Husqvarna, KTM and Moto Guzzi.

The Future

Rich Teerlink and the other Harley executives have much to be proud of in bringing back the company to a profitable position. However, they must also plan for the future, a future that is uncertain and fraught with problems. For example, the company faces much larger, well-financed competitors in the industry. The company faces increasing legislation on motorcycle helmet use and noise abatement laws that could decrease industry sales.

The company clearly recognizes the fact that the motorcycle industry has contracted greatly since the mid 1980s. It faces the problem of judging how much to increase supply of Harley-Davidson motorcycles given that it is a mature product whose future is uncertain. It faces decisions concerning how much should be invested in such an uncertain market and what marketing approaches are the most appropriate given this situation.

CASE

6

Cincinnati Milacron

JOSEPH WOLFE, *University of Tulsa*

The decade of the 1980s was supposed to have been one of high earnings recovery and the realization of new growth and market plans for Cincinnati Milacron (CM). Industry analysts and "the Mill's" top management team believed it had all the requisites for success. It was the largest machine tool company in the United States and it could afford to develop and market the new manufacturing technologies needed for the factories of the future. CM had a diversified customer base and was not dependent on the capital investment swings and fortunes of just one industry. It also had a strong reputation in plastics molding equipment and plastics were rapidly replacing metals in many applications. Most importantly the company had especially bright prospects for its newly developed, "cutting edge" line of robots and computer-controlled manufacturing systems.

The period's realities were much more harsh. Instead of obtaining high earnings Cincinnati Milacron operated in the red over the years of 1981–1991 and lost as much as $80.0 million in 1987. After starting the decade as America's largest machine tool company it ended it as merely "one of America's largest" after turning its top managers over in 1988 and eliminating the jobs of almost half of its employees. Moreover, Milacron found itself outclassed and outmaneuvered in its high-tech diversifications into robots, lasers, and semiconductor wafers which were supposed to protect it from the fearsome competitive strength of Japan's machine tool companies. The robotics industry, which was expected to amount to $4.0 billion in American sales by 1990 never took off and the company's profits and market responsiveness were hampered by production inefficiencies, rigid assembly techniques, and a slow, cumbersome management system. After suffering high losses on the robotics line it was sold in April 1990 to the Swedish-Swiss manufacturer Asea Brown Boveri after failing to find a manufacturing partner for its excellently designed equipment.

As 1992 begins Cincinnati Milacron's new strategy is to return to its core business of standard machine tools. While this strategy pits the firm squarely against the mainly Japanese competition they attempted to avoid in the first place, Daniel J. Meyer, the company's chief executive officer, says it is the correct path to follow because "we had more confidence in machine tools." More importantly for the company's long-term fortunes "we have a 107-year reputation in

Joseph Wolfe is Professor of Management at the University of Tulsa.

EXHIBIT 1

Major Categories and Manufacturers of Metal-working Machinery and Tools

---

Machine Tools

As a general class machine tools are power-driven metal-working devices that shape or form metal by using cutting, sawing, pressing, pounding, or electrical discharges.

Within this general class there are two types of machine tools classified by their operating method—metal-cutting and metal-forming machines. Metal-cutting machines shape metal by cutting away the material not wanted in the final product. This carving can be accomplished by any of the following methods alone or in combination:

1. Turnings—These machines turn or spin the object being shaped against a cutting edge. Examples of these types of machines are lathes, automatic bar machines, and screw machines.

2. Boring—Machines that cut circles or cylindrical shapes into metal from either a horizontal or vertical plane.

3. Planing and shaping—Machines that shear metal in continuous strokes.

4. Drilling—Smaller-diameter holes that are pierced through the metal by a continuous rotating action.

5. Grinding and honing—Shaping the metal through the use of abrasives.

Metal-forming machines operate through the actions of forging, shearing, hammering, extruding (stretching), bending, die casting, or pressing. The automobile industry is the largest market for these types of machines. As plastics, ceramics and exotic materials have begun to be used more frequently in cars and other products, these tools have been modified or applied to those applications. America's largest manufacturers of machine tools are Cross & Trecker, Cincinnati Milacron, Giddings & Lewis, Industrial Automation Systems (Litton Industries), and Ingersoll Milling Machine.

Automatic, Numerically Controlled Machine Tools

Numerically controlled (NC) machine tools use some type of medium to control the tool being used. This degree of automation eliminates human mistakes, lowers labor costs, and allows the machine to easily switch jobs. Three kinds of NC tools are currently available:

1. Conventional NC systems—Also known as hard-wired NC tools, the functions of these machines are pre-coded into a fixed and unalterable routine or activity sequence.

2. Computerized Numerical Control (CNC) systems—Also known as soft-wired NCs, a small computer is used to control the machine tool's functions. A set of programs controlling those functions are stored in the computer's memory and these programs can be called upon by the machine's operator when desired. While conventional NC systems are still the major sellers in this market, CNCs have been rapidly increasing their market shares through the availability of low-cost, free-standing minicomputers in the late 1960s.

---

manufacturing, and the opportunity for success is still there, based on the history we have. We're not going to lose."

MACHINE TOOLS AND THE MACHINE TOOL INDUSTRY

The machine tool industry (SIC 3541) consists of metal cutting and metal forming power machinery. It is the business which makes the machines that make the machines of industry as almost all manufacturing processes require these tools. A nation's manufacturing capabilities are highly dependent on the quantity and quality of its machine tools. Accordingly this industry is of strate-

EXHIBIT 1

Continued

3. Direct Numerical Control (DNC)—In this system a main computer simultaneously controls the actions and functions of a number of machine tools. Rather than using punched cards, paper or magnetic tape to control the machine's actions, jobs and routines are called and corrected through the use of a display screen.

The principal manufacturers of these types of machines are General Electric, Allen-Bradley (Rockwell International), and Fanuc of Japan. Cincinnati Milacron, Cross & Trecker, Monarch Machine Tool, Giddings & Lewis, and Ex-Cell-O Corporation (Textron, Inc.) are also major players in this industry's segment.

Expendables and Accessories

These are products or supplies employed during the metal-working process. These are taps, dies, twist drills, chucks, gauges, reamers, and jigs. Because these products wear out in proportion to their use the demand for these products is closely tied to industry's level of activity. National Twist Drill, Acme-Cleveland, and Vermont American are the largest manufacturers of twist drills while the major manufacturers of taps, dies, and gauges are United-Greenfield, TRW Geometric Tools (TRW, Inc.), and Ex-Cell-O Corporation.

Hand Tools and Mechanics' Precision Tools

Hand tools can employ either human or electrical/mechanical energy to accomplish their task. Hand tools are pliers, hammers, screw drivers, tool boxes, and interchangeable socket wrenches. These are primarily manufactured by Snap-On Tools, Stanley Works, McDonough Co., and Triangle Corporation. Power-driven hand tools are of two power types—portable pneumatic tools and portable electric tools. The pneumatic, air-driven tools, which include drills, screw drivers, nut setters, ratchet wrenches, hoists, grinders, sanders, polishers, and shipping and riveting hammers, are usually made to customer specifications and are sold to mass production assemblers. America's largest manufacturer of these types of tools is Chicago Pneumatic Tools followed by Ingersoll-Rand and Thor Power Tool (Stewart-Warner).

Portable electric tools are used for both metal and woodworking and for home maintenance purposes. Professional electric tools include electric drills, saws, sanders, polishers, hammers, lawn and garden tools, and chain saws. Black & Decker is the largest producer of these types of tools. Other manufacturers are Rockwell International, McGraw-Edison (Cooper Industries), and Ingersoll-Rand.

When accomplishing their tasks mechanics employ various measuring devices. These hand-operated devices include micrometers, steel rules, steel combination squares, calipers, verniers, and protractors. Among many manufacturers in the United States the largest are Brown & Sharpe, L.S. Starrett, and the Triangle Corporation.

SOURCES: "Machinery Outlook," *Standard & Poor's Industry Surveys: Steel and Heavy Machinery,* Vol. 158, No. 30, Sect. 1 (August 9, 1990), p. 28 and various Value Line Machine Tool Industry overviews, 1980 to 1991.

gic importance to a country's ability to compete internationally. The major users of machine tools are the auto industry (roughly 20.0% to 40.0% of annual sales orders), the oil and gas industry, and the makers of farm and industrial machinery, appliances, aircraft, and electronic equipment. Exhibit 1 describes the various machine tools manufactured by this industry as well as citing America's major machine tool suppliers. Exhibit 2 displays the value of domestic and foreign machine tool shipments by major category.

While firms using metals and plastics as part of their manufacturing processes are the consumers of machine tools, the basic demand for them is derived from a number of production-related factors. Machine tools can alter

EXHIBIT 2

Shipments of Complete Machine Tools ($000,000)

Tool Type	1979	1980	1981	1982	1983	1984	1985	1986	1987	1988	1989
Metal-Cutting											
Domestic	2,606	3,206	3,550	2,599	1,200	1,484	1,538	1,685	1,499	1,400	2,059
Foreign	324	475	551	296	172	123	194	206	178	174	299
Total	2,930	3,681	4,101	2,985	1,372	1,607	1,732	1,891	1,677	1,574	2,358
Metal-Forming											
Domestic	860	878	824	600	430	608	744	621	538	702	704
Foreign	87	133	167	110	43	71	60	67	109	122	133
Total	947	1011	991	710	473	679	804	688	647	824	837

SOURCE: *The Economic Handbook of the Machine Tool Industry.* National Machine Tool Builder's Association (The Association for Manufacturing Technology), various years.

and number of machinists needed to operate them. Therefore the demand for machine tools is dependent on the (1) sales expectations for the products the tools support, and (2) supply and cost of skilled labor. The role of sales expectations and projected factory utilization rates can be seen in Exhibit 3. When capacity utilization rates begin to rise above the 85.0% mark the demand for machine tools tends to rise. This relationship is somewhat delayed, however, depending on the complexity of the machinery being produced and labor/capital substitution considerations. The historical lag between orders and shipments graphed in Exhibit 4 shows it ranges from five to six business quarters. When Detroit's car manufacturers planned for the production of their redesigned transmissions and engines for the 1991 and 1992 model years the machine tools for them were ordered in late-1987 and nearly all of 1988. The lag, however, between orders and shipments is much shorter for standard, commodity-like machine tools. These are sold "off-the-shelf" from inventories with no customizing and little manufacturer's service or support.

EXHIBIT 3

Machine Tool Shipments and Net Orders

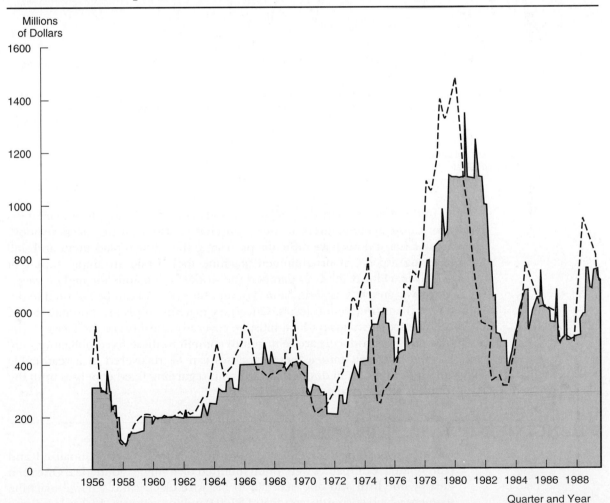

EXHIBIT 4

Machine Tool Orders vs. Factory Operating Rates

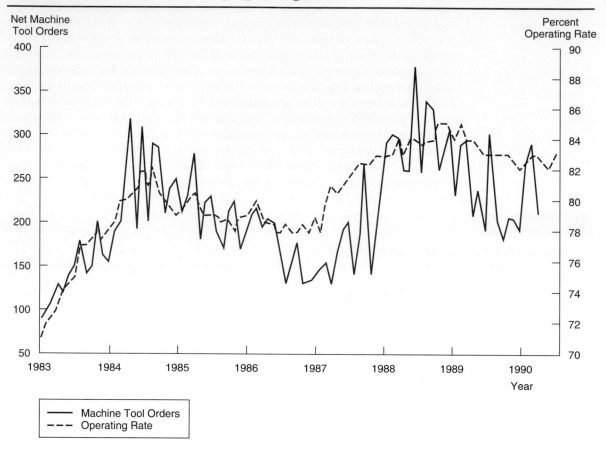

In the short term weakened labor unions or an ample supply of machinists may cause manufacturers to delay purchasing labor-saving machine tools. Weak labor unions have difficulty protesting the labor replacement and skill lowering aspects of programmed machine tools while an ample supply of skilled machinists tends to dampen the worker's demands for higher wages. Moreover, in the long term, labor is a variable cost and can be adjusted to different plant production levels. Once new machine tools are purchased they become fixed expenses which must be covered regardless of the factory's utilization rate. Producers are reluctant to commit to these fixed obligations unless there is a guarantee these expenses can be recovered in a reasonable amount of time. If in doubt many will wait regarding fixed expenses until the future is more certain.

CHANGING INDUSTRY STRUCTURE

America's machine tool industry has traditionally been fractionalized and craft-related. Companies were often founded on a single, good idea. One such idea by one firm and one man led to the wire electrical discharge machine segment which currently has sales of $700.0 million per year. Victor Harding's job during World War II was to remove broken bits of metal left in the grooves of newly-threaded pieces. By rigging a spark-producing copper electrode to his machine he found the sparks eroded the metal, thereby loosening waste material. Because his employer was not interested in his innovation Harding started his own company and by the mid-1960s his Elox Corporation was selling an entire line of "electron drills."

Product and entrepreneurial patterns such as this resulted in an industry comprised of a large number of small firms producing a few, particular machine tools. It was a highly segmented industry and its manufacturers had limited economies of scale. Despite this fractionalized nature, America's producers were the world's leaders as they possessed the most advanced technology and almost one-third of the world's sales.

In the late 1970s, however, the introduction of NC and CNC machine tools began to change the industry's economics. The new technologies of electronics and computers were added to the machine tool manufacturer's production matrix. Higher capital investments, new skills, and plant retooling expenses had to be financed and those operating on a small scale were unable to do so. Also coming into play were learning curve effects associated with high technology electronics. Being basically small, single-line producers, many firms could not upgrade or acquire these skills or capture these learning curve effects. To stay in business many gravitated toward the market's lower and technologically simpler end comprising standard machine tool products.

For many American companies this was a disastrous strategy. Japan's machine tool firms had just come on the domestic scene and they were pursuing the same market niche. Many U.S. firms were quickly overwhelmed by that country's superior, lower-priced products. By the mid-1980s Japan had captured 80.0% of new sales in the American NC lathe and machining center market after only having entered it in 1976. The fate of Victor Harding's Elox Corporation is an example in miniature. It is now a small-time player in the segment it created as over 80.0% of America's market in wire electrical discharge machines has been captured by the Japanese firms of Mitsubishi, Fujitsu Fanuc, Sodick, and Hitachi.

On the international scene America's machine tool firms experienced similar problems during this period. Japan's share of world exports of machine tools grew from 3.5% in 1970 to 15.0% in 1983 while America's share fell from 11.7% to 4.8%.

JAPAN'S MACHINE TOOL INDUSTRY POLICY

How did this sweep of the American machine tool industry come about? What did the Japanese do to overwhelm an industry which had the United States as its leading participant?

As part of its economic revival in the 1950s the Japanese government's policies have been guided by "developmental capitalism." Under this system the state works hand-in-hand with private enterprise to further the nation's economic development. Through its Ministry of International Trade and Industry (MITI) various "vision" statements are intermittently authored. These statements generally specify the strategies and the industries to be targeted for special emphasis. As early as 1956 MITI recognized the strategic value of the machine tool industry by passing the Extraordinary Measures Law for the Promotion of Specified Machinery Industries.

Teeth were soon put into MITI's vision for Japan's machine tool industry. To obtain rationalization and economic efficiency within the domestic industry itself it recommended the following:

1. Japanese domestic firms would stop manufacturing any product line whose Japanese market share was less than 5.0%; or
2. Firms would stop manufacturing any product line that was less then 20.0% of the firm's total production. Once rationalization was achieved within the industry, then
3. All machine tool firms would concentrate on NC tools. This machine tool type should account for over 50.0% of the industry's total output by 1980.

After having accomplished rationalization within its own industry by the early 1970s, new policies were adopted to promote overseas sales with the United States being a prime target. Exhibit 5 summarizes these policies and actions while Exhibit 6 summarizes the competitive strategies employed by Japan's machine tool companies.

As the Japanese have succeeded in the United States via the relatively safe strategy of exporting their machines into the country they are now establishing deeper roots and greater equity commitments on American soil. These roots and commitments have taken the following form:

• Joint Ventures—Fujitsu Fanuc Ltd.-General Motors; Okuma Machinery Works Ltd.-DeVlieg; Toyoda-Bendix; Toshiba-Cross & Trecker; Yokogawa Electric Manufacturing-Gould; Dijet Industrial-Kennametal

EXHIBIT 5

MITI's Policies and Maneuvers for the Machine Tool Industry

Policy	Maneuvers
Industry Structure	Rationalization of the machine tool industry through forced or encouraged mergers, the divestment of extraneous or non-strategic product lines, and the achievement of economies of scale.
Product Line	Concentration on NC machine tools. This type to be at least 50.0% of all output by 1980. Certain companies would specialize in particular products. Export cartels created to facilitate joint export activities. Government research funds and tax credits provided for joint research in earmarked technologies. All activities coordinated by a machine tool industry association.
Customer Financing	Small businesses receive loans and special depreciation allowances made to firms purchasing machine tools. Leasing of Japanese-made robots subsidized by Japan Robot Leasing Authority.
Exports	Export cartel set floor prices on NC lathes and machining centers exported to U.S., Canada and the EEC. Expenses shared regarding exporting, market research and international marketing information.

SOURCE: Adapted from Ravi Sarathy, "The Interplay of Industrial Policy and International Strategy: Japan's Machine Tool Industry," *California Management Review* (Spring, 1989), pp. 138–141.

EXHIBIT 6

Japanese Machine Tool Competitive Strategy

Strategy	Implementation
Company Cost Structure	Lower the company's manufacturing cost through high volume production of standardized products in capital-intensive factories. From 1975–1986 Japan's major machine tool manufacturers reduced their labor expenses from 25.0% to 12.2% and general overhead from 16.2% to 14.2% of sales. This was accomplished by heavy capital investment per employee. Capital stock increased from ¥2.15 million in 1975 to ¥6.19 million by 1986 resulting in greater productivity. Sales per employee were ¥9.83 million in 1975 and they increased to ¥34.76 million by 1986.
Product/Market Niches	Sell standardized, off-the-shelf machine tools to small and medium-sized firms. Designed small, cheaper, and lower performance CNC lathes for Japan's own medium and smaller-sized firms. These standard products were subsequently widely distributed in the U.S. through independent dealers rather than through company-controlled sales engineers who were only needed for custom-fitted machine tool applications.
R&D	Efforts aimed at simplifying the product and making it easier to manufacture and be produced in large volumes via assembly-line techniques.
Pricing	Sell the product for less. By 1982 Japan's prices were lower by 19.0% on 25 hp horizontal spindles, 39.0% for 50 hp horizontal spindles, 32.0% for vertical spindle lathes, and 44.0% for horizontal spindles with a y-axis of over 40.0 inches. Machining centers were 30.0% to 41.0% lower in price.
Delivery and Distribution	Standardized, off-the-shelf products easier to warehouse and deliver during boom times. Import penetration tends to increase when domestic order backlogs exceed 9.5 months. Japan's products were immediately available from stockpiled warehouses and they made large inroads. Heavy use of distributors rather than direct customer sales.
Foreign Direct Investment	Obtain an American manufacturing presence through either transplants, acquisitions, or joint ventures. The American firm LeBlond was acquired by Makino allowing it to manufacture machining centers in the U.S. with Japanese parts. Mori Seiki, OSG Manufacturing, Sonoike Manufacturing, and Hitachi have created American subsidiaries. Joint ventures have been established between General Motors and Fanuc, Okuma with DeVlieg, Toyoda and Bendix, Toshiba and Cross & Trecker, Gould and Yokogawa Electric Manufacturing, and Dijet Industrial with Kennametal.

SOURCE: Adapted from Ravi Sarathy, "The Interplay of Industrial Policy and International Strategy: Japan's Machine Tool Industry," *California Management Review* (Spring, 1989), pp. 149–153

- United States subsidiary operations—U.S. Mazak, a subsidiary of Yamazaki; Mori Seiki, OSG Manufacturing, Sonoike Manufacturing, Hitachi
- Acquisition—Makino acquired LeBlond

These strategies and commitments have been so effective that about 30.0% of America's machine tool capacity is now provided by the Japanese firms of Mazak Corp., LeBlond Makino Machine Tool Co., and Okuma Machinery Works, Ltd. This presence will be even greater in the early 1990s. In July 1990 Mitsubishi Heavy Industries America Inc. opened a plant in Hopkinsville, Kentucky to make horizontal and vertical machining centers and NC lathes. Mazak completed a $55.0 million expansion of its Florence, Kentucky plant in March 1990 and this raises its monthly capacity from 80–85 units to 100–120 units.

CURRENT INDUSTRY CONDITIONS

The composite results for a number of benchmark American machine tool companies indicates the difficulties they experienced in the 1980s. Exhibit 7 shows combined losses in 1987–88 and 1990 for Acme-Cleveland, Brown & Sharpe, Cincinnati Milacron, Cross & Trecker, Gleason Works, and the Monarch Machine Tool Company. Future profits are expected to be relatively low. The health of today's firms appears to be partially related to their past strategies. As described in Exhibit 8 some companies attempted to diversify away from the extremely competitive machine tool industry while others tried to apply their core strengths to exotic applications. During the past decade about half of America's machine tool companies went out of business and a large number of consolidations occurred. Despite the resulting greater industry concentration the average U.S. tool firm has less than $3.0 million in annual sales and fewer than 25 employees. It can be expected that more casualties will be experienced in the 1990s.

Industry observers have cited two sets of factors which could improve the industry's prospects. The first set of factors are historical and demographic in nature. A historically weakening dollar has made American goods more price competitive with foreign goods. This could generally give American manufacturers an incentive to increase their capacity and for the machine tool manufacturers themselves it means American-built machine tools will continue to be price competitive with those built overseas. Regarding demographics America's aging population and declining birth rate translates into a shortage of industrial skilled labor. This shortage of skilled labor can be compensated for by "smarter" machine tools which also have the advantage of being depreciated.

The second set of factors are competitive in nature. American firms are under continuing pressure to lower costs and raise the quality. Efficient and accurate machine tools are at least a partial solution. Much of America's manufacturing equipment is more than twenty years old and it needs replacement. Due to inefficiencies in the face of foreign competition these factories must retool to survive. Improvements in computer and manufacturing technology are also occurring more rapidly and these could force an industry's remaining

EXHIBIT 7

Composite Machine Tool Industry Results ($000,000)

	1987	1988	1989	1990	1991	1992	1994–96*
Sales	1882.8	1944.2	1945.5	1933.4	1945.0	2038.0	2645.0
OperatingProfit	90.4	108.9	118.7	97.7	97.3	132.3	277.7
Depreciation	80.5	71.9	58.7	59.1	60.0	65.0	90.0
Net Profit	−111.2	−26.2	−6.3	−34.5	11.0	44.0	115.0

*Estimated by Value Line

NOTE: Composite companies are Acme-Cleveland, Brown & Sharpe, Cincinnati Milacron, Cross & Trecker, Gleason Works, and Monarch Machine Tool Company.

SOURCE: Theresa Brophy, "Machine Tool Industry," *Value Line Industrial Survey* (May 17, 1991), p. 1336.

EXHIBIT 8

Company Profiles

Cross & Trecker—In the 1980s Cross & Trecker emphasized the machine tool market's more specialized end. This did not work out well. Companies pursuing this strategy take all the risks of designing customized tools but this does not guarantee their ultimate sale. This strategy has the attendant problems of estimating expenses and therefore many contracts are underpriced and unprofitable. Cross & Trecker had to suspend its first dividend in 1986 and in 1987 took a large charge against earnings to consolidate operations and write down old equipment and inventories. Dislocations caused by its corporate restructuring hampered sales in 1989 and it has been struggling for a number of years. Giddings & Lewis will finalize its acquisition of this company in Fall, 1991.

Giddings & Lewis—The AMCA International Corporation acquired this company in 1982. After losing $6.1 and $138.1 millions in 1986 and 1987 it was sold off in July, 1989. Giddings & Lewis quickly earned a profit of $17.1 million in 1989 after increasing its revenues 38.0% in one year. By August, 1990 the company had no long term debt and it generated cash in excess of capital spending and normal needs. Giddings has been very successful with large, yet flexible integrated manufacturing systems selling for up to $30.0 million each. Chairman William J. Fife, Jr. vows, "We're not going into competition with the Japanese. [They] move low-end machine tools by the truckload. We're going to stay away from truckload sales." As one of America's most profitable machine tool companies it will be the industry's largest firm after it completes its acquisition of Cross & Trecker.

Gleason Works—In the mid-1980s Gleason attempted to capitalize on its dominance of the bevel gear grinding industry. It soon lost money marketing a complex differential for sports cars. It has subsequently retrenched to its gear-making specialty. As of May, 1991 its new line of simplified computer controlled gear production machinery is generating relatively healthy company earnings. Gleason has also begun to reduce design and manufacturing costs by using standardized parts. The company is basically a niche manufacturer as it dominates the worldwide market for bevel gear making machinery. Its sales are concentrated on the automobile industry.

Monarch Machine Tool—This venerable company was established in Sidney, Ohio in 1909. It produces highly computerized yet standardized lathes and machining centers in antiquated plants in Sidney and Cortland, New York. Monarch was very profitable in the early 1980s when it earned as much as $19.0 million on sales of $139.0 million in 1981. Losses occurred shortly thereafter. To save money management stopped all "unnecessary" spending including dividends, research and development, and new shop floor machinery. Only old, used equipment was purchased which pushed further back Monarch's already outdated manufacturing operations. The company has relatively little exposure to the auto industry and CEO Robert Siewert says they will focus on customer service. "We haven't done business that way in the past. It was forced upon us by the Japanese. It was our way of staying in business."

Newell Company and Stanley Works—Along with Vermont American these companies cater to the relatively healthy do-it-yourself and equipment maintenance markets. In late 1991 the Newell Company announced its intentions of buying up to 15% of Stanley Works' common stock with later aim of making a complete acquisition.

Norton—This company is a high-tech materials and grinding wheel manufacturer. It began to benefit from a cost reduction program it launched in 1986. In the late 1980s Norton restructured itself and it has been carried by profits from its non-machine tool operations.

firms to use these technologies as competitive weapons. Computer prices have fallen drastically thus lowering the costs of various CNC and DNC units. This means factories can adopt "cutting edge" technology at a lower cost.

Many U.S. companies are finally realizing they must modernize if they are to succeed. Caterpillar Inc. will have spent about $3–4 billion from 1986 to 1992 to build its new automated "Plant With A Future." When completed it will produce more heavy duty equipment than ever but with 3.0 million square feet less manufacturing space. Pressures for modernization should also increase when Europe completes its unification plans in 1992 and Japan completes its current capital improvement program. Additional markets will be opening with the emergence of Eastern and Central Europe as invigorated customers. In June 1990 the Coordinating Committee on Multilateral Export Controls, of which the United States is a major partner, agreed to ease its 41-year old embargo on the sale of machine tools to the Eastern bloc countries.

Because America's automobile manufacturers are the machine tool industry's single largest customer, trends and expectations in that industry are extremely important. Japan's superiority in engine design and transmissions may force Detroit to re-tool their plants even though the motor city's sales prospects and capacity utilization rates for the mid-1990s are not that bright. Japan has taken the lead in producing multi-valve engines and electronically-controlled transmissions. The engines boost performance without increasing pollution or diminishing fuel economy and electronically controlled five-speed automatic transmissions provide better fuel economy and smoother gearshifts. Regardless of what the Japanese do the U.S. government is redefining its automobile emission standards and Detroit will probably want to invest in new drive train programs for their 1993 and 1994 models.

Detroit's automobile manufacturers currently have excess capacity so they will probably not build new plants but will instead attempt to make given capacity more efficient. Ford has indicated it has about 20.0% more capacity than it needs. Instead it will spend about $600.0 million to re-tool and "prep" its Van Dyke plant in Sterling Heights, Michigan to produce four- and five-speed automatic front-wheel-drive transmissions for cars and light trucks.

While many are hoping for a rosy future for the machine tool industry a number of unsettling factors remain. The dollar must remain weak if mere price competitiveness is to be employed by the American machine tool manufacturers. Moreover, neither the weak dollar nor the trade restrictions the American government has placed on foreign machine tool manufacturers have kept the Japanese manufacturers from making serious inroads into the U.S. machine tool market. Regarding the capital/labor substitution effects associated with the installation of labor saving machine tools, there are other less expensive and more flexible ways to increase a factory's efficiency. Quality circles and just-in-time methods can increase efficiency and these methods can be quickly turned on or off depending upon the company's needs for efficiency.

Closer to home within the American automobile industry itself, the Japanese have begun to produce and assemble their cars in transplants. When this is done the tendency has been to employ their own country's machine tool equipment in their factories rather than purchasing American machine tools. The Japanese nameplates of Honda, Toyota, Nissan, Mazda, Mitsubishi and others garnered a 31.0% share of America's 1991 automobile sales and this was an 11.0% increase over their 1990 share. To circumvent the import restrictions that have been placed on them more and more of these cars are being manufactured in the United States. While an opportunity exists for American machine tool to be used in Japan's transplant, sales to them have been difficult. Most Japanese manufacturers are part owners of the machine tool companies they use. They find it financially and culturally beneficial to continue these relationships regardless of the comparative quality or cost of the tools themselves.

Strategies for handling the foreign competition, especially the Japanese with the most efficient manufacturing facilities in the world, are varied. Some companies emphasize the "Made in America" label while others emphasize service which may be a disguised method of taking advantage of foreign producer's unfamiliarity with American customs, values and decision making methods. The standardized products segment, where service is not of great importance, has all but been surrendered to the Japanese. American companies have tended to concentrate on the highly sophisticated, CNC machines priced from $300,000 to $2.0 million. As noted by Henry Mamlok, President of Jacobson Tool & Manufacturing Corp., "The Japanese are awfully hard to beat in the commodity end of the business. We focus on customized tools made to fill a special need with prices up to $500,000 or so."

Some companies have emphasized a niching strategy. Harvey Rohmiller of the Lodge & Shipley Division of Manuflex Corporation says

> To be successful, American companies—even the small ones—have to get better at defining their markets more narrowly and deciding what products will fit that market. Twenty years ago, a company like ours was manufacturing driven. We'd produce a new tool with the confidence it would soon have wide appeal. With so much more engineering and technology in the industry today, the stakes are higher and we've all had to become market-driven.

Then there is the last group of companies. They feel their fortunes are tied to the degree they can capitalize on whatever eventualities occur with their product's major users. Accordingly they are attempting to hold on and keep their options open.

CINCINNATI MILACRON

Within the machine tool industry Cincinnati Milacron currently manufactures and sells industrial process equipment and systems. These products are gathered into three groups with independent profit accountability:

- Machine Tool Group—Machine tools, composites processing equipment, advanced manufacturing systems and electronic controls. The machine tool product lines include vertical and horizontal machining centers, turning centers, aerospace profilers and routers, bridge and portal mills, die and mold making machines, horizontal boring machines, grinding machines and special machines.
- Plastics Machinery Group—Reaction injection molding machines, systems for extrusion, blow molding and blown film, auxiliary equipment, and contract services.
- Industrial Products Group—*Cimcool* metalworking fluids, precision grinding wheels, and LK measurement and inspection systems.

This product array is far different, however, from the one pursued just ten years before and came about after much soul searching and upheaval. In late February, 1991 Milacron's management explained the rationale for their newest strategy.

> For several decades in the post-World War II era, Milacron's strategy was diversification and we brought to market new manufacturing technologies in many fields: electronics, plastics, robotics, laser and flexible manufacturing systems, to name only a few. Certain new product lines, such as plastics machinery, were highly successful. However, the widely predicted large markets for other technologies never

evolved. So, for the 1990s, we have honed a new strategy. We are channeling and focusing all Milacron's creativity, innovation and entrepreneurial spirit directly into our core businesses, which are products and services for the metalworking and the plastics processing industries.

Today, global markets for machine tools and plastics machinery are large and growing steadily. Annual worldwide sales of machine tools have doubled since the mid-1980s and now exceed $40.0 billion. The world market for plastics processing machinery, although smaller, is growing even faster. It is currently approaching $8.0 billion, with a real growth rate higher than the GNP. These are the primary markets Milacron is targeting in the 1990s.

In the late 1970s and early 1980s, facing record-high demand for capital equipment, fierce foreign competition and the over-valued dollar, Milacron and other U.S. machine tool builders moved away from producing *standard* machine tool products, i.e., basic machining centers and turning centers. Instead, we concentrated on highly engineered and custom-designed machines and systems for automotive, aerospace and other important industries. The standard machine business, however, offers excellent economies of scale in manufacturing and the benefits of a broad marketing network. So now Milacron is going back after the standard machine tool market, not only in the U.S. but throughout the world. And we're doing it by building cost-competitive all-metric machines with world-class quality and features.

In pursuing its original diversification strategy the company jettisoned its original stodgy name of the Cincinnati Milling Machine Company and became the space-age sounding company called Cincinnati Milacron. Donald Shively, who would later be passed over for the company's top spot because he was too much a machine tool man, recalled, "The board decided we were beating a dead horse with machine tools, so the decision was made to more or less abdicate the standard line." Exhibit 9 lists the various diversifications and acquisitions the company made as it implemented this strategy. The exhibit also lists the ultimate deposition of many of those activities.

As the 1980s proceeded management took solace that it often did not perform as badly as other firms in the machine tool industry. In 1981 Milacron's orders did not fall as much as the industry's because of its strong position in the less cyclical special machine tool market rather than in commodity-type tools. Additionally the company was able to offer attractive credit terms to its customers through its financial subsidiary and it also benefitted from close ties to its customers through its direct marketing channels. A year later management stated "Although our operating results were down for the year, it should be kept in mind that Milacron performed better than many capital goods companies, and while the size of our markets declined, we gained share in our major product lines." In 1990 the company observed that orders for the American machine tool industry had declined 27.0% while its own orders declined only 14.0%. Exhibit 10 plots Cincinnati Milacron's net profits versus those obtained by its major competitors for the years 1981 to 1992. Exhibit 11 reports the company's overall profits and expenses for the same period.

To provide better guidance top management enunciated various goals and predictions for the firm during the mid-1980s. In 1985 James A.D. Geier, then-Chairman and CEO, forecast Milacron's sales would surpass $1.0 billion before 1990 and that plastics machinery revenues would be more than $300.0 million by that year. To provide a level of financial comfort management's goal for 1989 was to produce a debt to total capital ratio in the low- to mid-30s. In December, 1986 this ratio was 43.0% and it was deemed inappropriate.

EXHIBIT 9

Diversifications, Acquisitions, and Divestitures

Diversifications	Acquisitions	Divestitures, Plant Closings and Liquidations
Pre-1976—Small business systems. 1976—Computer controlled industrial robots. 1978—Silicon wafers and circuit board composite material. 1986—Plastic packaging film. 1987—Expert Systems software and PC-based shop floor management software.	1983—Purchased a line of injection molding machines from Emhart Corporation's Farrel Rochester Division. 1984—Purchased LK Tool Company, Ltd. of England, a manufacturer of coordinate measuring machines. 1986—Purchased Laser Machines Corporation of Indianapolis, Indiana. 1986—Purchased Sano Design and Machine Co., Inc., a manufacturer of plastic packaging films. 1988—Purchased Chesapeake Laser Systems, Inc. as a complement to the LK Tool Company. 1989—Acquired a line of plastics extrusion blow molding machines from the Bemis Company's Hayssen Manufacturing Co. 1990—Bought SL Abrasives, Inc., a grinding wheel manufacturer. 1990—Acquired from Pratt & Whitney its die and mold product line.	1978—Liquidated its German machine tool manufacturing subsidiary at a loss of $3.6 million. 1982—$10.0 million write-down on the closing of a British machine tool plant. 1988—Sold metals fabrication division to Cast-Fab Technologies, Inc. 1989—Semiconductor materials business sold to a subsidiary of Japan's Osaka Titanium Co., Ltd. 1990—Sold all laser operations to The 600 Group, PLC for a $4.5 million loss. 1990—Sold entire robot line to Asea Brown Boveri for a $1.7 million loss. 1990—Closed Vlaardingen, Holland machine tool plant.

More importantly, asset usage was to be realigned according to the schedule shown in Exhibit 12. Between 1980 and 1985 the company closed five plants and reduced its machine tool workforce by 46.0%. In 1981 65.7% of its assets were dedicated to machine tools and this had been cut back 21.0% by 1985. Still there was too much capacity in this money-losing line. In 1986 operations were discontinued in one of its Cincinnati plants, in the robot plant in Greenville, South Carolina, and at its turning center in Wilmington, Ohio. Overall over 200 pieces of equipment were taken out of production that year. Exhibits 13 and 14 respectively show Milacron's capital expenses and asset maneuvers from 1985 to 1991 and the recent operating results of its two latest divestitures.

In carrying out its reallocations Cincinnati Milacron established the following new investment or new product criteria in 1985:

1. The investment or product had to provide now, or provide by 1990, at least $100.0 million in revenues and good profits.
2. They exist in a product area where Milacron already has a leadership position.
3. They be sold on the basis of technology and service rather than on price alone.

EXHIBIT 10

Net Profits for Cincinnati Milacron vs. Benchmark Machine Tool Companies

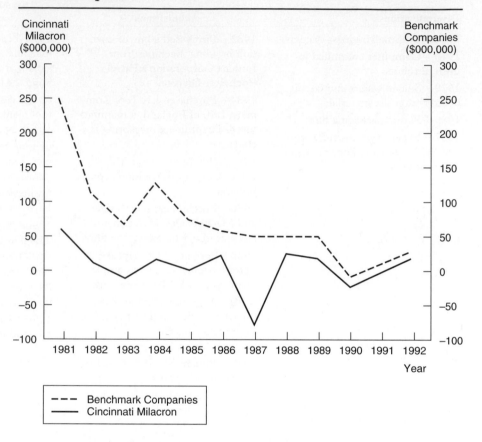

Cincinnati
Milacron
($000,000)

Benchmark
Companies
($000,000)

Year

- - - Benchmark Companies
——— Cincinnati Milacron

Accordingly the product areas to be emphasized would be process plastics, flexible manufacturing cells and systems, special machinery for advanced applications, automation for advanced composites, metrology and inspection systems, and silicon epitaxial wafers.

With a firmer grasp on the products to be pursued the company turned next to rationalizing its production facilities. This was spelled out in its most ambitious and comprehensive reorganization plan approved by the Board February 16, 1988. A number of "focus factories" were created. These factories were to operate as independent business units with full profit and loss responsibility. Each was dedicated to manufacturing and marketing similar or complementary product lines. This reorganization's goal was a reduction of the company's burdensome and over-centralized bureaucracy and faster responses to the market place. The following "focus factories" were created at this time and they were to be fully operational by mid-1989:

1. Robots—Factory in Greenwood, South Carolina with support functions being moved from Cincinnati to Greenwood. Liaison with the American automobile industry would be continued through its technical center in Detroit.

EXHIBIT 11

Cincinnati Milacron Sales, Expenses and Earnings ($000,000)

	1981	1982	1983	1984	1985	1986	1987	1988	1989	1990	1991*	1992*
Sales	934.4	759.7	559.0	660.5	732.2	850.0	828.0	857.8	850.6	837.7	850.0	985.0
Cost of Goods Sold	691.5	569.8	458.4	535.0	549.2	595.0	612.7	637.3	625.3	647.5	646.0	712.3
Gross Profit	242.9	189.9	100.6	125.5	183.0	255.0	215.3	220.5	225.9	190.2	204.0	272.7
General Administration	142.4	121.6	57.6	48.4	115.3	163.5	229.7	135.3	152.5	156.4	154.5	158.2
R&D	22.4	35.7	30.2	36.3	36.6	40.0	35.6	35.2	31.5	34.3	31.5	32.7
Depreciation	17.3	20.4	23.1	26.0	29.6	28.3	30.0	25.0	22.9	23.7	23.0	24.0
Profit before Taxes	60.8	12.2	-10.3	14.8	1.5	23.3	-80.0	25.0	18.5	-24.3	-5.0	57.8
Taxes	25.4	6.5	0.0	4.1	0.0	6.9	0.0	10.7	8.8	-11.6	0.0	36.8
Profit after Taxes	35.4	5.7	-10.3	10.7	1.5	16.4	-80.0	14.3	9.7	-12.7	-5.0	21.0

*Estimated from Value Line data.

SOURCE: Reconstructed from annual August Value Line reports.

EXHIBIT 12

Actual and Target Percent of Assets Employed by Product Division

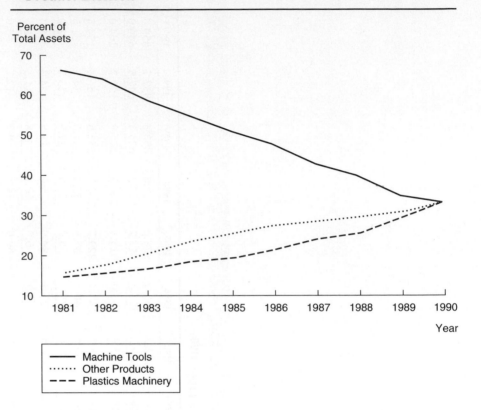

Percent of Total Assets

Legend:
— Machine Tools
······ Other Products
--- Plastics Machinery

2. Aerospace and special-purpose machines—Cincinnati, Ohio.
3. Turning centers—Wilmington, Ohio.
4. Machining centers—Fountain Inn, South Carolina and Birmingham, England.
5. Grinding machines—Worchester, Massachusetts.
6. Service parts—Cincinnati, Ohio.
7. Plastics machinery—Most products produced in Afton, Ohio with the systems for extrusion, reheat blow molding and thermoforming moved to a plant in Cincinnati, Ohio.

In early 1990 Milacron had created a specific process for developing new products. Initially called "team engineering" but now termed Wolfpack Projects, the idea is to create world-class products designed simultaneously for marketability and "manufacturability." The anticipated outcomes from creating new product development teams were a shortened product development cycle, lower product manufacturing costs, an improved machine tool performance and quality, and increased market share. Top management also spelled out the process for creating a Wolfpack Project.

1. Create a team of personnel relevant to the production, sale, and service of a product. The team members would typically come from the departments

---

EXHIBIT 13

Asset Changes and R&D Activities ($000,000)

	1991*	1990	1989	1988	1987	1986	1985
Capital Expenditures:							
Machine Tools	15.0	16.1	17.0	9.9	8.0	11.8	9.2
Plastics Machinery	12.0	14.0	14.0	4.7	3.4	10.6	11.6
Industrial Products	3.0	4.0	2.6	6.9	4.3	6.9	23.6
Total	30.0	34.1	33.6	21.5	15.7	29.3	44.4
Write-Downs, Reorganization, Charges, and Liquidation Losses:							
Machine Tools	90.0	34.0			54.0		46.3
Plastics Machinery							
Industrial Products			4.5		24.0		
Headquarters					5.0		27.2
Total	90.0	34.0	4.5		83.0		74.4
Research and Development	37.0	34.4	31.4	35.3	35.6	39.6	36.8

*Projected by management.

EXHIBIT 14

Operating Performance of Industrial Robots and Laser Machines ($000)

	1990	1989	1988
Sales			
Industrial Robots	$31,182	$30,527	$38,697
Laser Machines	—	3,180	7,036
	31,182	33,707	45,733
Net Loss from Operations			
Industrial Robots	−441	−588	−911
Laser Machines	—	−2,313	−1,459
	441	−2,901	−2,370
Net Loss on Sale of Assets	−1,700	−4,474	—

SOURCE: 1990 Company 10-K.

---

of design engineering, production, marketing, purchasing, cost analysis, manufacturing engineering, assembly, and inventory control.

2. Analyze and conduct market research on all competitive products. The features, design, materials, electronics, and performance of all products are studied as well as citing the reasons why the competitive products are succeeding or failing.

3. Apply the principles of "simultaneous" or "concurrent" engineering to work with potential customers and suppliers. To be approved for commecializa-

tion a Wolfpack Project's product must demonstrate that it can (a) capture significant new market share in existing or new markets, and (b) provide at least a 30.0% manufacturing cost savings over the product it would replace in the line. Through concurrent engineering the company will create products that fill a place in the market and are easier and less costly to manufacture.

As of February, 1991 the Wolfpack program had slashed Milacron's manufacturing costs on standard machine tools by as much as 40.0%. About 20.0% of its standard tools can match the foreign competition's prices and quality. Overall manufacturing costs have been reduced about 30.0% by using fewer and standard, off-the-shelf parts in the product's assembly. The typical, newly-designed tool has about two-thirds of its parts outsourced where before it was less than half. The results are also lower warranty and installation costs.

Management has already introduced a new line of simplified plastics injection-molding machines and is the country's lowest-cost producer of these tools. The *Vista* line has been very successful and additional products have made it the broadest line available from an American manufacturer. In 1988 the plastics operation was increased by 100,000 square feet with a capital infusion of $4.7 million; in 1989 an additional $14.5 million was budgeted with about 70.0% of that amount going into a 78,000 square foot expansion of its Mt. Orab, Ohio plastics parts plant. While management is pleased with the results it has obtained through Wolfpack programs, it does not believe their outcomes will be fully realized until the mid-1990s. On this basis top management is optimistic about the company's future.

Management also believes problems caused by its past reorganization efforts and production "bugs" are over. In 1985 sales of $17.8 million were lost on machine tools alone. The tools scheduled for shipment used new designs, innovative software, and higher precision and performance standards resulting in longer than anticipated production times. Sales for that year had to be delayed until early 1986. The company also experienced serious bottlenecks in making grinding machine shipments in November, 1989. These bottlenecks caused lost sales through cancellations. It also did not allow the company to obtain part of the $45.0 million per year savings it had projected from its most recent reorganization effort. Additional bottlenecks occurred in February, 1990 as production and equipment were shifted between plants to create its numerous "focus factories."

1992 AND BEYOND

As part of its new strategy to make competitively priced $100,000 standard machine tools, Cincinnati Milacron points with pride to its Cincinnati-based "incubator" demonstration plant. The factory makes the company's *Talon* computer-controlled turning centers and uses the most efficient production and management techniques available. It employs just-in-time parts deliveries, the *Talons* use only 16 outside vendors, and they need 60.0% fewer parts. More importantly, they can be made for 40.0% less. C. William Murray, Milacron's Division Manager for standard machine tools says, however, that it might take five years for the techniques used in this 19-person plant to spread to the company's other plants and employees. Others are more pessimistic about this and other company actions.

Manufacturers in the Cincinnati area have noticed that Milacron is losing key people and that morale has sagged badly in recent months. Based on the number of resumes and job inquiries many of the "Mill's" middle managers fear they may lose their jobs in another reorganization move or that they may be pushed onto the shop floor. Cincinnati Milacron's recently retired Chief Technical Officer, Richard C. Messinger, says, "They've got the basic technology and capability, but they have had a problem in that it's very difficult to change the culture and direction of that kind of organization."

It has also been noted that of its 27 current Wolfpack projects several are actually imported products and many of its "American-made" tools use almost 50.0% foreign parts. To Jack Addy, an independent Detroit machine tool distributor, this makes Milacron's "Made in the U.S.A." label a fraud. He says the company is "importing just like the Japanese, and what they're importing are not good machines."

The quality of the company's new products may also suffer in the long term. To save money Milacron has not increased its engineering staff, which would be needed to implement future plant efficiencies like those found in the "incubator" plant, and it is spending only 4.1% of sales on research and development. Leading firms such as Giddings & Lewis spend about 10.0% on similar efforts. As an additional money-saving move the company has retreated from its promise to its distributors to spend $250.0 million on machine tools over the next five years.

Given plastics machinery has been a highlight of the company's operations it takes pride in noting that it has helped lower Japan's market share in plastics machinery. That country's sales have fallen 20.0% since 1987 to about 50.0% of the American market. By cutting prices on the *Vista* line Milacron was able to win back the business of General Motors and the Toyota Motor Corporation of America. Financial analysts, however, are pessimistic about Cincinnati Milacron's near-term and long-term prospects. Both Moody's Investors Service and Standard & Poor's downgraded Milacron's debt in early October, 1991. In making its judgment on the firm's financial security Standard & Poor's particularly noted the company's debt level of 55.0% to 60.0% of total capital and they questioned the wisdom of the new strategy being pursued by the company. As observed by David Sutliff, an S.G. Warburg & Company analyst, "I give them credit for giving it the old college try, but I don't think it's too smart. They're going into the most competitive sector again, where the Japanese sell tools like cookies."

Additional Readings

Murphy, H. Lee, "Machine Tool Marketers Emerge from 'Drought,' " *Business Marketing,* November, 1988, pp. 36–38.

Sarathy, Ravi, "The Interplay of Industrial Policy and International Strategy: Japan's Machine Tool Industry," *California Management Review,* Spring, 1989, pp. 132–160.

Sciberras, E., and J. Payne, *Machine Tool Industry: Technical Change and International Competitiveness.* Essex: Longman, 1985.

Slutsker, Gary (Ed.), "Struggling Against the Tide," *Forbes,* November 12, 1990, pp. 312–320.

Yoffie, David B., "Protecting World Markets," in Tom McCraw (Ed.), *America Versus Japan: A Comparative Study in Business Government Relations.* Boston: Harvard Business School Press, 1986.

Yoffie, David B., and Helen V. Milner, "An Alternative to Free Trade or Protectionism: Why Corporations Seek Strategic Trade Policy," *California Management Review,* Summer, 1989, pp. 111–131.

APPENDIX   *Operating Margins by Product Group*

Product Group	1981	1982	1983	1984	1985	1986	1987	1988	1989	1990	1991
Machine Tools	83.1	42.8	−14.5	−8.1	−30.0	11.0	−47.9	20.2	−7.6	4.3	−2.2
Plastic Machines	11.5	−8.6	0.0	20.8	17.7	26.3	25.5	30.9	35.0	18.0	8.3
Industrial Products	9.5	−5.1	−7.4	4.0	5.0	26.3	−12.0	19.1	18.7	16.7	13.0
Total	104.1	26.1	−21.9	16.7	−7.3	63.6	−54.4	70.2	46.1	39.0	19.1

Cincinnati Milacron Quarterly Income Statements ($000)

	6/15/91	3/23/91	10/6/90	6/16/90
Net Sales	173,069	181,054	233,959	204,804
Cost of Goods	136,571	143,840	177,702	159,233
Gross Profit	36,498	37,214	56,257	45,571
R&D Expenditures	n.a.	n.a.	n.a.	n.a.
Selling, General and Administration	36,946	37,465	48,430	36,643
Income before Depreciation and Amortization	−448	−251	7,827	8,928
Depreciation and Amortization	n.a.	n.a.	n.a.	n.a.
Non-Operating Income	853	−131	1,217	810
Interest Expense	4,389	4,452	5,830	4,916
Income before Taxes	−3,984	−4,834	3,214	4,822
Provision for Income Taxes	541	1,078	1,155	1,708
Net Income before Extra Items	−4,525	−5,912	2,059	3,114
Extra Items and Discontinued Operations	n.a.	n.a.	−515	n.a.
Net Income	−4,525	−5,912	1,544	3,114

SOURCE: Company 10-K.

Cincinnati Milacron Balance Sheets—Fiscal Years Ending in December ($000)

	1990	1989	1988
ASSETS			
Cash	45,188	32,894	17,868
Receivables	196,953	198,512	235,823
Inventories	233,396	249,642	254,070
Other Current Assets	14,139	18,160	20,155
Total Current Assets	489,676	499,208	527,916
Net Property & Equipment	159,234	146,478	152,683
Deposits and Other Assets	44,072	40,484	40,881
Total Assets	692,982	686,170	721,480

Cincinnati Milacron Balance Sheets—Fiscal Years Ending in December ($000) (continued)

	1990	1989	1988
LIABILITIES			
Notes Payable	10,753	13,604	15,902
Accounts Payable	72,764	65,385	80,723
Current Long Term Debt Due	1,408	16,080	4,386
Accrued Expenses	99,168	93,546	106,459
Income Taxes	9,741	13,580	15,837
Other Current Liabilities	42,317	37,956	35,224
Total Current Liabilities	236,151	240,151	258,531
Deferred Charges	8,799	11,461	11,365
Long Term Debt	157,273	165,831	42,171
Other Long Term Liabilities	43,089	42,148	182,122
Total Liabilities	445,312	459,591	494,189
Preferred Stock	6,000	6,000	6,000
Common Stock Net	27,303	24,327	24,202
Capital Surplus	139,430	90,360	88,968
Retained Earnings	68,842	111,992	112,376
Other Liabilities	6,095	−6,099	−4,254
Shareholder Equity	247,670	226,579	227,291
Total Liabilities and Net Worth	692,982	686,170	721,480

SOURCE: Company 10-K.

Cincinnati Milacron Quarterly Balance Sheets ($000)

	6/15/91	3/23/91	10/6/90	6/16/90
ASSETS				
Cash	15,031	15,780	22,607	16,810
Receivables	171,124	181,347	185,377	191,752
Inventories	229,074	231,282	292,501	269,458
Raw Materials	9,394	9,401	8,737	8,750
Work in Progress	173,406	169,708	229,594	215,516
Finished Goods	46,274	52,173	54,170	45,192
Other Current Assets	11,638	14,183	16,028	12,918
Total Current Assets	426,867	442,592	516,513	490,938
Property, Plant & Equipment	428,397	440,688	435,087	422,567
Accumulated Depreciation	282,010	283,069	283,041	273,047
Net Property & Equipment	146,387	157,619	152,046	149,520
Deposits and Other Assets	43,758	44,285	44,494	43,486
Total Assets	617,012	644,496	713,053	683,944

Cincinnati Milacron Quarterly Balance Sheets ($000)

(continued)

	6/15/91	3/23/91	10/6/90	6/16/90
LIABILITIES				
Notes Payable	8,255	9,452	12,972	36,446
Accounts Payable	42,139	54,479	57,987	55,126
Accrued Expenses	95,644	90,778	85,013	101,796
Income Taxes	7,177	10,713	8,826	n.a.
Other Current Liabilities	45,496	41,607	48,083	46,996
Total Current Liabilities	198,711	207,029	212,881	240,364
Deferred Charges	7,852	8,408	13,214	13,329
Long Term Debt	156,960	157,148	162,297	162,169
Other Long Term Liabilities	38,901	40,887	41,116	41,969
Total Liabilities	402,424	413,472	429,508	457,558
Preferred Stock	n.a.	n.a.	n.a.	n.a.
Common Stock Net	173,654	173,642	n.a.	n.a.
Capital Surplus	n.a.	n.a.	173,174	121,892
Retained Earnings	48,436	57,945	105,271	108,717
Other Liabilities	−7,502	−563	5,100	−4,223
Shareholder Equity	214,588	231,024	283,545	226,386
Total Liabilities and Net Worth	617,012	644,496	713,053	683,944

SOURCE: Company 10-K.

Cincinnati Milacron Income Statements—Fiscal Years Ending in December ($000)

	1990	1989	1988
Net Sales	837,689	820,087	850,794
Cost of Goods	647,759	625,403	637,324
Gross Profit	189,930	194,684	213,324
R&D Expenditures	n.a.	n.a.	n.a.
Selling, General and Administration	157,185	143,426	149,396
Income before Depreciation and Amortization	32,745	51,258	64,074
Depreciation and Amortization	n.a.	n.a.	n.a.
Non-Operating Income	−30,807	7,372	4,003
Interest Expense	19,734	22,460	22,048
Income before Taxes	−17,796	36,170	46,029
Provision for Income Taxes	4,351	17,139	19,595
Net Income before Extra Items	−22,147	19,031	26,434
Extra Items and Discontinued Operations	−2,141	−1,663	10,655
Net Income	−24,288	17,368	37,089

SOURCE: Company 10-K.

CASE PART VII

Strategic Management and International Operations

Cadbury Schweppes

FRANZ T. LOHRKE, JAMES G. COMBS, and GARY J. CASTROGIOVANNI,
Louisiana State University

"All large (food) companies have broken out of their product boundaries. They are no longer the bread, beer, meat, milk or confectionery companies they were a relatively short time ago—they are food and drink companies."—SIR ADRIAN CADBURY, CHAIRMAN, (RETIRED) CADBURY SCHWEPPES, PLC. (SMITH, CHILD, & ROWLINSON, 1990:9)

In the early l990s, Cadbury Schweppes, PLC embodied the archetypical modern food conglomerate. With extensive international operations in confectionery products and soft drinks, the company maintained a diversified global presence. Although Cadbury had enjoyed a relatively stable competitive environment through much of the company's history, contemporary developments in the international arena presented Cadbury management with many different and critical challenges.

THE HISTORY OF CADBURY

The company began in 1831 when John Cadbury began processing cocoa and chocolate in the United Kingdom (UK) to be used in beverages. In 1847, the company became Cadbury Brothers, and in 1866, it enjoyed its first major achievement when the second generation of Cadburys found a better way to process cocoa. By using an imported cocoa press to remove unpalatable cocoa butter from the company's hot cocoa drink mix instead of adding large quantities of sweeteners, Cadbury capitalized on a growing public concern for adulterated food.

The company further prospered when it later found that cocoa butter could be used in recipes for edible chocolates. In 1905, Cadbury introduced Cadbury Dairy Milk (CDM) as a challenge to Swiss firms' virtual monopoly in British milk chocolate sales. A year later, the firm scored another success with

---

FIGURE 1

Cadbury's Foreign Direct Investment

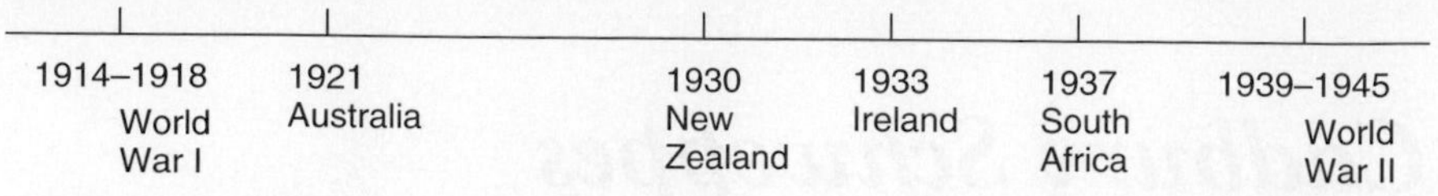

1914–1918	1921		1930	1933	1937	1939–1945
World War I	Australia		New Zealand	Ireland	South Africa	World War II

(SOURCE: Jones, 1986).

---

the introduction of a new hot chocolate drink mix, Bournville Cocoa. These two brands provided much of the impetus for Cadbury's early prosperity (Jones, 1986).

Cadbury faced rather benign competition throughout many of the firm's early years. In fact, at one point, Cadbury provided inputs for the UK operations of the American firm, Mars, Inc. (Smith, Child, and Rowlinson, 1990). Cadbury also formed trade associations with its UK counterparts, J. S. Fry and Rowntree & Co., for the purpose of, among other things, reducing uncertainty in cocoa prices. The company later merged financial interests with J. S. Fry, but spurned offers to consolidate with Rowntree in 1921 and 1930 (Jones, 1986).

Facing growing protectionist threats in overseas markets following World War I, Cadbury began manufacturing outside the UK, primarily in Commonwealth countries (see Figure 1). This international growth was also prompted by increasing competition. For example, by 1932 Cadbury management considered the Swiss company, Nestlē, as their primary competitor in the international arena (Jones, 1986).

In 1969, Cadbury merged with Schweppes, the worldwide maker of soft drinks and mixers. The merger offered both companies an array of advantages, both defensive and offensive. First of all, both companies faced potential takeover threats from larger firms, so the merger placed the new company in a better defensive posture to ward off unwanted suitors. On the offensive side, the marriage allowed the new company to compete better on a worldwide scale. Cadbury had invested primarily in Commonwealth countries, and Schweppes had branched out into Europe and North America, so the new company enjoyed greater geographic dispersion. The increased international presence also allowed the company to defray product development costs over a wider geographic base. Furthermore, the new company enjoyed greater bargaining power from suppliers. For example, following the merger, Cadbury Schweppes became the largest UK purchaser of sugar (Smith, Child, & Rowlinson, 1990).

The British confectionery companies historically pursued a different strategy than their American counterparts. While U.S. companies, such as Mars, Inc., manufactured narrow product lines and employed centralized production, Cadbury maintained 237 confectionery products until World War II forced the company to scale back to 29. While faced with a lack of intense competition, Cadbury's brand proliferation strategy could be undertaken. As rivalry heated up in the mid-1970s, though, Cadbury's share of the UK chocolate market fell from 31.1 percent to 26.2 between 1975 and 1977. Management then began to realize that the lower cost, American-style strategy of rationalized product lines and centralized production provided the only viable means to compete (Child & Smith, 1987).

TABLE 1

Assorted Major Brand Names of Cadbury Schweppes and Its Confectionery Competition

CADBURY SCHWEPPES

Cadbury Dairy Milk (CDM)	Whole Nut
Milk Tray	Roses
Crunchie	Fruit and Nut
Whispa	Trebor

NESTLĒ

Nestlē Crunch bar	Polo
Kit Kat	Quality Street
Smarties	Yorkie
After Eight	Aero
Rolo	Black Magic
Dairy Box	Fruit Pastilles
Butterfinger	Baby Ruth

M&M/MARS, INC.

Mars Bar	Galaxy
Twix	Maltesers
Bounty	Milky Way
M&Ms	Snickers

HERSHEYS

Hershey bars	Reece's Peanut Butter Cup
Hershey Kisses	Reece's Pieces
Mounds	Almond Joy

PHILIP MORRIS

Milka
Toberlone
E. J. Brachs candy

Cadbury had long been famous for its unique management style. "Cadburyism" drew influence from the founders' Quaker heritage, providing for worker welfare and harmonious community relations. Following Cadbury's reorientation toward core products and rationalized production, though, the company's old management style underwent a transformation. Confectionery manufacturing personnel were reduced from 8565 to 4508 between 1978 and 1985 (Child & Smith, 1987). In the process, management's traditional close relationship with workers, which had been built through years of maintaining employment stability, began to erode as worker reduction became a professed goal of Cadbury executives.

THE ENVIRONMENT

As is the case with several products in the food industry, many of Cadbury's product lines enjoyed very long product life cycles. (See Table 1 for assorted confectionery products of Cadbury and its rivals.) Food and beverage companies derived substantial benefit from their long-established products, such as Cadbury's CDM bar, and the occasional new product introductions required little in the way of technological investment. The food companies, therefore, competed primarily by seeking cost reduction through process improvements such as automation, by finding alternative inputs to replace expensive cocoa, and by introducing creative packaging and marketing (Child & Smith, 1987).

Successful new product introductions remained sporadic, and many of the most successful confectionery products, such as Mars Bar and Rowntree's Kit Kat, had been around since the 1930s (Tisdall, 1982). Some unsatisfied demands seemed to persist, however, as was evidenced by Rowntree's successful 1976 launch of its Yorkie bar, Mars' profitable introduction of Twix a few years later, Cadbury's notable 1984 launch in the UK of its Whispa bar, and Hershey's 1988 introduction of Bar None (Weber, 1989).

Nevertheless, new brand introductions required immense investments in development and marketing costs with only limited possibilities for success. For instance, various research suggests that approximately 60 percent of new food product introductions have been withdrawn inside of five years, and this figure may be an underestimate (Smith, Child, & Rowlinson, 1990). Consequently, established brands with customer loyalty represented crucial assets for food and beverage companies.

MODERN CADBURY SCHWEPPES

Expansion was key to Cadbury's plans to improve its international position. Chief Executive Officer Dominic Cadbury commented, "If you're not operating in terms of world market share, you're unlikely to have the investment needed to support your brands" (Borrus, Sassen, & Harris, 1986: 132). In 1986, Cadbury shared third place in the world with Rowntree and Hershey, each having approximately 5 percent of the market. Nestlé held second place with about 7.5 percent, while Mars dominated internationally with approximately 13 percent (van de Vliet, 1986: 44–45).

To generate its necessary worldwide expansion, Cadbury had two primary markets in which to gain positions. Enjoying a dominant position in its home market, the company realized that the United States and the remaining countries of the European Economic Community (those besides the UK) provided critical markets for a worldwide standing. According to Terry Organ, director of international confectionery, "Rightly or wrongly . . . we decided to tackle the U.S. first" (van de Vliet, 1986: 45). Earlier, Cadbury had taken steps toward competing more vigorously in the U.S. by acquiring Peter Paul in 1978. By 1980, however, the company still controlled only about 3.5 percent of the U.S. confectionery market, far eclipsed by its bigger rivals, Hershey and Mars.

Cadbury did not have sufficient size to employ the sales force of its competitors. The company, therefore, had to rely on food brokers to push products to wholesalers, which left the firm far removed from the consumer. Further, the company could be easily outspent in advertising by its two larger rivals (Borrus, et. al., 1986).

To compound problems, the company also committed two marketing blunders in the U.S. market. When Cadbury introduced Whispa, the company's marketing success of the decade in the UK, management did not realize that distribution channels in the U.S. were longer than in the UK. Consequently,

TABLE 2

Top Five Soft Drink Companies in U.S. (percent of total market)

	1986	1987	1988	1989	1990
COCA-COLA, CO.	**39.8**	**39.9**	**39.8**	**40.0**	**40.4**
Classic	19.1	19.8	19.9	19.5	19.4
Diet Coke	7.2	7.7	8.1	8.8	9.1
Sprite	3.6	3.6	3.6	3.6	3.6
PEPSICO	**30.6**	**30.8**	**31.3**	**31.7**	**31.8**
Pepsi-Cola	18.6	18.6	18.4	17.8	17.3
Diet Pepsi	4.4	4.8	5.2	5.7	6.2
Mountain Dew	3.0	3.3	3.4	3.6	3.8
DR PEPPER	**4.8**	**5.0**	**5.3**	**5.6**	**5.8**
Dr Pepper	3.9	4.0	4.3	4.6	4.8
Diet Dr Pepper	.4	.4	.4	.4	.4
SEVEN-UP	**5.0**	**5.1**	**4.7**	**4.3**	**4.0**
7-Up	3.5	3.4	3.1	3.0	2.9
Diet 7-Up	1.4	1.0	1.0	.9	.9
CADBURY SCHWEPPES	**4.2**	**3.7**	**3.5**	**3.1**	**3.2**
Canada Dry	1.4	1.4	1.4	1.3	1.2
Sunkist	.9	.7	.7	.7	.7
Schweppes prod.	.5	.5	.5	.6	.6
Crush	1.4	1.0	.8	.6	.6
Total Market Share of Top Five	84.5	84.5	84.5	84.6	85.2

(SOURCE: *Standard and Poor's Industry Surveys,* 1991)

the candy bars aged seven to nine months by the time they reached test markets in New England, and consumers reacted accordingly.

The company's second mistake occurred following an effort to standardize its candy bar size across countries. When Cadbury first introduced its CDM bar in the U.S., the bar commanded a higher price than its U.S. rivals. Since CDM was also larger than U.S. competitors' regular bars, consumers were willing to pay a little extra. When Cadbury reduced the size, management discovered that given the choice between CDM and American confectionery products of equal size and price, U.S. consumers usually chose the more familiar American products (van de Vliet, 1986). According to one former Cadbury executive, "What happened in the U.S. was a gigantic, gargantuan cock-up, and the fact that London (Cadbury headquarters) did not know what was happening is a sheer disgrace" (Gofton, 1986: 20).

Not all the news from the other side of the Atlantic was bad for the UK company, however. Although Peter Paul Cadbury only commanded a small slice of the market, some products such as Coconut Mounds and York Peppermint Patties dominated their segments. Cadbury's Creme Eggs also enjoyed seasonal success. Moreover, the company's acquisition of Canada Dry from R.J. Reynolds provided Cadbury Schweppes with a strong position in the carbonated mixers market in the U.S. and many other countries (see Table 2

| TABLE 3 | | | |

Top Five Companies in the $8 Billion U.S. Confectionery Market
(percent of total market)

1980		1988	
Company	**Market Share**	**Company**	**Market Share**
Mars	17.0	Hershey	20.5
Hershey	15.3	Mars	18.5
Nabisco	7.1	Jacobs Suchard	6.7
E.J. Brachs	6.4	Nestlē	6.7
Peter/Paul Cadbury	3.5	Leaf	5.6

(SOURCE: Weber, 1989)

for U.S. market shares). For example, although Cadbury Schweppes only commanded about a 3 percent market share in the $43 billion U.S. soft drink industry, the company sold Canada Dry, the number one ginger ale and club soda in the U.S., and Schweppes, the leading tonic water in the American market (Winters, 1990). Additionally, the cola giants, Coca-Cola and PepsiCo, did not (as yet) vigorously market products in segments dominated by Cadbury Schweppes. Overall, though, the company faced an uphill struggle in many segments of the U.S. market.

In an effort to remedy some of the company's problems in the U.S. confectionery market, Cadbury decided to sell its manufacturing assets to Hershey in 1988, catapulting the Pennsylvania company to the dominant position in the U.S. market (see Table 3). Cadbury also granted Hershey licenses to manufacture and sell its Peter Paul products including Mounds, Almond Joy, and York Peppermint Patties. Under this arrangement, Cadbury gained the benefit of Hershey's marketing muscle behind the Peter Paul products (Swarns & Toran, 1988).

Cadbury faced additional challenges to building market share in the European Economic Community (EEC). Schweppes' beverages enjoyed success on the Continent (Borrus, et. al., 1986), but Europe's confectionery industry proved difficult to break into since the market remained dominated by family-owned firms and suffered from overcapacity (van de Vliet, 1986). Successful expansion in the EEC, however, was crucial to Cadbury's remaining a dominant player in the worldwide food and beverage industries.

CONTEMPORARY CHALLENGES

The 1990s brought about radical shifts in the industries in which Cadbury Schweppes competed. First, corporate leaders (and stock markets) discovered that food and beverage enterprises with established brand names were not mundane investments offering only lackluster financial returns. Purchasing popular brands or taking over companies that had portfolios full of well known products often provided a safer and more economical avenue for growth than attempting to develop entirely new products. In 1985, for instance, Philip Morris acquired General Foods for $5.75 billion, approximately three times book value, while R. J. Reynolds laid out $4.9 billion for Nabisco Brands (van de Vliet, 1986).

TABLE 4

The United States (U.S.) and the European Economic Community (EEC)

	U.S.	EEC
Population	243.8 million	323.6 million
Gross National Product (GNP) (in 1987 $U.S.)	4.436 trillion	3.782 trillion
Per capita GNP	$18,200	$11,690
Inflation	3.7%	3.1%
Unemployment	6.1%	11.0%

(SOURCE: House, 1989)

NOTE: EEC members include the UK (England, Scotland, Wales, Northern Ireland), Ireland, Denmark, Germany, France, Belgium, the Netherlands, Luxembourg, Portugal, Spain, Italy, and Greece.

These attempts to acquire popular brands were also dictated by dramatic industry-wide changes which altered the nature of competition faced by the international food and beverage enterprises. First, the push by the 12 countries of the European Economic Community (EEC) to remove trade barriers among the member nations by 1992 sparked a buying frenzy of European food companies with established brand names (see Table 4 for a comparison of the North American and EEC market). Many non-European companies feared that the EEC would eventually increase tariff barriers for products from outside the Community, which could have effectively closed foreign companies out of the market. This anticipation of "Fortress Europe" sent companies without EEC operations scurrying to acquire European enterprises.

Second, the common perception that only the largest companies in most industries would survive in Europe as well as internationally contributed to the takeover hysteria. To become big quickly, companies began aggressively acquiring rival food companies. For example, Nestlé scored a major victory in July 1988 when it outbid its Swiss counterpart, Jacobs Suchard, to acquire Cadbury's long time UK competitor, Rowntree. In the process, Nestlé moved from a minor status in the EEC confectionery market into a first place duel with Mars. In the UK market, Nestlé's acquisition positioned the company in a second place battle with Mars and within striking distance of first place Cadbury (*Mergers and Acquisitions,* 1989). In January 1992, Nestlé also attempted to continue its acquisition binge by launching a hostile takeover bid for the French mineral water company, Source Perrier.

Other major food conglomerates, such as Philip Morris (U.S.) and Unilever Group (UK/Netherlands) were also rumored to be on the prowl for acquisitions in Europe (Browning & Studer, 1992). These heavyweights not only presented medium-sized food and beverage companies like Cadbury with increased competition in the marketplace, they also represented potential bidders in any acquisitions attempted by Cadbury. This increased competition threatened to drive up acquisition prices through cutthroat bidding for popular brand names. In fact, as the takeover battles became more heated, stock market analysts speculated that Cadbury and other medium-sized companies could find themselves targets of acquisition attempts (Browning & Studer, 1992).

TABLE 5

Food Sales—Europe (Including the UK)

Nestlē	$15.1 billion
Unilever	12.2
Phillip Morris*	8.0
BSN	7.8
Mars	4.1
Cadbury Schweppes	3.1.

*Includes Jacobs Suchard
(SOURCE: Templeman & Melcher, 1990)

The European food and beverage industries were undergoing other changes along with the acquisition binges. At the end of the food and beverage distribution pipeline, for example, many European supermarkets were also consolidating. In April 1990, eight EEC grocery chains formed an alliance to combine buying power and promote house brands. As these supermarket companies combined forces, they greatly enhanced their bargaining power against the food and beverage companies. This increased power threatened future profits of food and beverage companies since the grocery chains' ability to demand price concessions from the companies was enhanced by the stores' consolidation. Furthermore, since supermarkets only wanted to carry the top two or three brands for each product type, food and beverage companies faced the option of acquiring popular brands or risking lost shelf space in stores (Templeman & Melcher, 1990).

In response to these massive changes in the industry, Cadbury also began acquiring name brand products and searching for strategic alliances. In 1986, for example, the company decided to end its bottling agreement with Pepsi to form a joint venture with Coke in the UK (Gofton, 1986). In 1990, Cadbury purchased the European soft drink operations of Source Perrier (Templeman & Melcher, 1990), and in 1991, the company formed a joint venture with Appolinarus Brunnen AG, a German bottler of sparkling water.

TABLE 6

Cadbury Schweppes' 1990 Worldwide Sales (In £ million*)

Region	Total Sales	Confectionery	Beverages
United Kingdom	1,476.0	715.4	760.6
Continental Europe	638.0	195.6	442.4
Americas	403.7	18.3	373.5
Pacific Rim	495.5†	N/A	N/A
Africa and other	132.9	91.2	38.8

*1 £ = $1.93
†Sales primarily in Australia/New Zealand
N/A: not available
NOTE: Total Sales will not always equal Confectionery plus Beverages. In the U.S. (Americas region), for example, Cadbury Schweppes also generated sales from its Mott's subsidiary.
(SOURCE: Compact Disclosure; *The Wall Street Journal.*)

TABLE 7

Financials (In £000)

BALANCE SHEET

Fiscal Year Ending	12/29/90	12/30/89	12/31/88
ASSETS			
Cash	62,600	57,400	41,300
Marketable Securities	118,000	33,300	200,700
Receivables	554,100	548,200	434,500
Inventories	328,200	334,800	253,400
TOTAL CURRENT ASSETS	1,062,900	973,700	929,900
Net Prop, Plant, Equip	978,800	822,500	602,200
Other Long term assets	320,700	332,600	20,700
TOTAL ASSETS	2,362,400	2,128,800	1,552,800
LIABILITIES			
Notes Payable	60,100	57,400	92,200
Accounts Payable	272,100	263,900	409,500
Current Capital Leases	76,200	76,300	21,900
Accrued Expenses	320,900	305,900	52,100
Income Taxes	78,200	95,800	81,800
Other Current Liab	154,700	143,600	118,800
TOTAL CURRENT LIAB	962,200	942,900	776,300
Long term debt	407,900	381,400	124,700
Other Long term Liab	108,401	124,000	74,600
TOTAL LIABILITIES	1,478,500	1,448,300	975,600
Preferred Stock	300	N/A	3,300
Net Common Stock	174,400	173,600	150,400
Capital Surplus	95,800	36,700	33,000
Retained Earnings	115,800	167,600	88,800
Miscellaneous	381,600	217,400	210,500
TOTAL SHAREHOLDERS EQ	767,900	595,300	486,000
Minority Interest	116,000	85,200	91,200
TOT LIAB & NET WORTH	2,362,400	2,128,800	1,552,800
1 £ =	$1.93	$1.61	$1.81

INCOME STATEMENT (In £ 000)

Fiscal Year Ending	12/29/90	12/30/89	12/31/88
Net Sales	3,146,100	2,766,700	2,381,600
Cost of Goods Sold	1,738,400	1,596,900	1,365,000
Gross Profit	1,407,700	1,179,800	1,016,600
Sell Gen & Admin Exp	1,074,700	907,500	787,800
Income Before Int & Tax	333,000	272,300	228,800
Non-Operating Inc	3,800	3,100	4,400
Interest Expense	57,200	31,100	17,500
Income Before Taxes	279,600	244,300	215,700
Taxes & Misc Expenses	100,200	85,500	75,200
Income Before Ex Items	179,400	157,800	140,500
Extraordinary Items	N/A	15,200	28,400
NET INCOME	179,400	173,000	168,900
1 £ =	$1.93	$1.61	$1.81

(SOURCE: Compact Disclosure; *The Wall Street Journal*)

N/A: not applicable

With the competitive environment heating up, Cadbury management faced a number of crucial questions. Could the company continue to compete independently against the food and beverage mega-corporations that were forming or should Cadbury merge with another company before being faced with a hostile takeover attempt? Did Cadbury have the resources to acquire more brand names or should management continue to investigate the joint venture route? Should the company reduce emphasis on Europe and instead attempt to exploit new opportunities in the underdeveloped Asian market? Whatever Cadbury Schweppes management decided to do, they had to move quickly. The choices of popular name brand food and beverage products on the table were being cleared away fast.

References

Borrus, A., Sassen, J., & Harris, M. A. 1986. Why Cadbury Schweppes looks sweet to the raiders. *Business Week,* January 13: 132–133.

Browning, E. S., & Studer, M. 1992. Nestlé and Indosuez launch hostile bid for Perrier in contest with Agnellis. *The Wall Street Journal,* January 21: A3.

Child, J., & Smith, C. 1987. The context and process of organizational transformation—Cadbury Limited in its sector. *Journal of Management Studies,* 24: 565–593.

Gofton, K. 1986. Has Cadbury got his finger on the button? *Marketing,* July 31: 20–25.

House, K. E. 1989. The 90s & beyond: The U.S. stands to retain its global leadership. *The Wall Street Journal,* January 23: A8.

Jones, G. 1986. The chocolate multinationals: Cadbury, Fry and Rowntree 1918–1939. In G. Jones (Ed.), *British Multinationals: Origins, Management and Performance:* 96–118. Brookfield, VT: Gower Publishing Co.

Mergers and Acquisitions. 1989. The Nestlé-Rowntree deal: Bitter battle, sweet result. September/October: 66–67.

Smith, C., Child, J., & Rowlinson, M. 1990. *Reshaping work: the Cadbury experience.* Cambridge: Cambridge University Press.

Standard and Poor's Industry Surveys. 1991. Food, beverages, and tobacco. June 27: F23–F27.

Swarns, R. L., & Toran, B. 1988. Hershey to buy U.S. business from Cadbury. *The Wall Street Journal,* July 25: 30.

Templeman, J., & Melcher, R. A. 1990. Supermarket Darwinism: The survival of the fattest. *Business Week,* July 9: 42.

Tisdall, P. 1982. Chocolate soldiers clash. *Marketing,* July 29: 30–34.

van de Vliet, A. 1986. Bittersweet at Cadbury. *Management Today,* March: 42–49.

The Wall Street Journal. Various issues.

Weber, J. 1989. Why Hershey is smacking its lips. *Business Week,* October 30: 140.

Winters, P. 1990. Cadbury Schweppes' plan: Skirt cola giants. *Advertising Age,* August 13: 22–23.

Teléfonos de Mexico:
The Privatization Decision (A)

RAVI RAMAMURTI, *Northeastern University*

"Privatization will be the means for realizing the commitment to modernize Teléfonos de Mexico . . . "
—PRESIDENT CARLOS SALINAS DE GORTARI, SEPTEMBER 1989

On September 18, 1989, nine months after assuming office as president of Mexico, 40-year old Carlos Salinas de Gortari announced at the annual meeting of the telephone workers union (STRM) that the state-owned telephone company, Teléfonos de Mexico (Telmex), would be privatized. The announcement came as a surprise to many Mexicans, since Telmex was one of the largest state enterprises and there had been no talk of privatizing it earlier. However, the leader of the STRM, Francisco Hernández Juárez, knew the announcement was forthcoming and had already agreed to support it. Indeed, in April 1989, his union had made several concessions while renegotiating its labor agreement with Telmex, paving the way for privatization. At the September meeting, the workers voted unanimously to support the government's decision.

Jacques Rogozinski (Ph.D. Economics, University of Colorado), Director of the Office for Privatization of State-Owned Enterprises in the Ministry of Finance, had primary responsibility for organizing the Telmex privatization. For more than 6 months prior to Salinas's announcement, he and a select group of colleagues from the Ministry of Communications, the Ministry of Transportation, the Ministry of Commerce and Industry, and Telmex had been studying the matter. Yet, three months after the president's announcement,

Copyright Ravi Ramamurti and the *Case Research Journal* (a publication of the North American Case Research Association). This case was written with the cooperation of management, based on published information and field research in Mexico, solely for the purpose of stimulating student discussion. Partially supported by the Harvard Institute for International Development. Produced originally for use at the 1992 Harvard University Public Enterprise Workshop. All events and individuals are real. Reproduced with permission.

in December 1989, they remained divided on many issues. There were different points of view on whether Telmex should be divided before privatization, whether it should be permitted to diversify, how much equity ought to be given to workers, what role foreign capital ought to play in Telmex, how buyers might be found, and whether its monopoly rights ought to be preserved after privatization, and, if so, for how long.

Rogozinski was scheduled to discuss these and other issues the following Monday with his boss, Finance Minister Pedro Aspe Armella (Ph.D. Economics, MIT), who expected the Telmex privatization to be concluded within a year of the president's announcement, that is, by September 1990.

THE TELECOMMUNICATIONS INDUSTRY

Technology

A telecommunications system consists of three parts: customer-premise equipment, such as telephones and private branch exchanges (PBXs); transmission equipment, such as the cables connecting individual phones to the local exchange or lines connecting exchanges to one another; and the exchanges themselves, where telephone calls are completed by linking one telephone to another.

Over the years, technological change had affected all three parts. Exchanges that relied on human operators to complete phone calls were replaced first by electromechanical switches, then by electronic exchanges in which computers managed the network, and, most recently, by digital exchanges. With each successive technology, the telephone system's quality, reliability, versatility, and cost-effectiveness improved.

Initially, all transmission—local and long distance—was via copper wires or cables that physically tied the system together. In more recent years, fiberoptic technology had permitted far greater amounts of information to be transmitted in a single cable and with far greater reliability than ever before. In addition, alternative methods of transmission, such as microwave and satellite systems, had become available. Like mobile (cellular) telephones, satellite and microwave systems did away with cables and wires and were therefore more economical; they found extensive use in long-distance transmission. Yet even in the 1990s, in most countries the local network—which connected phones to the nearest exchange—relied almost entirely on wires and cables. Industry experts believed that the day was not far away when wires and cables could be done away with altogether, and everyone could own a portable phone.

Finally, the choice of customer-premise equipment had broadened from the "plain old rotary telephone" to products such as push-button telephones, fax machines, answering machines, and networked computers.

Another trend affecting the telephone industry was the growing interdependence between the technologies for communication and computing. Business users, such as banks, retail outlets, and multinational companies, demanded an integrated solution for their computing and communication needs so that they could freely input, transmit, and process messages of all kinds—voice, text, data, and images—within a dispersed but interconnected computer system. (The term "telecommunications" referred to a system that could handle the full range of messages mentioned rather than just voice messages.) Telephone companies around the world were straining—and, in some cases, failing—to satisfy these emerging needs.

Industrialized countries undertook massive investments to convert to digital systems increasingly linked by fiber-optic cables. Developing countries, on the other hand, were torn between extending basic service to a wider segment of the population and offering modern systems for business users. One common solution was to create a digital system on top of the traditional network to serve business customers. Another was to permit large users to bypass the existing network through satellite-based communications.

Deregulation and Privatization

In the early 1980s, the telephone system was state-owned in most rich and poor countries. Even among the exceptions to this rule, such as the United States, Barbados, the Dominican Republic, Hong Kong, and Puerto Rico, governments tightly regulated the private phone companies. However in the 1980s, several countries began to deregulate and/or privatize the telecommunications industry.

The deregulation trend had been led by the United States, where privately owned AT&T (known more commonly as the Bell system) had monopolized the sector for decades. In 1968, the Federal Communications Commission (FCC) allowed customers to connect non-Bell phones to the system for the first time. A year later, the FCC allowed alternative long-distance microwave carriers to interconnect with AT&T's network, though only for private use. In the late 1970s, a company called MCI fought and obtained the right to convert its private-line, microwave network into a public service that would compete with AT&T in the long-distance business. Finally, in 1984, AT&T and U.S. regulators reached an agreement to break up the Bell system into eight parts. Seven of these, the so-called Baby Bells, would offer local service in the assigned regions but would be barred from long-distance service (outside their territories), equipment manufacture, and enhanced information services, such as voice mail or electronic yellow pages. The regional companies would be regulated by state-level agencies on matters such as pricing, quality of service, etc. The eighth company, to be called AT&T, would offer domestic and international long-distance service, manufacture equipment, and retain control over the world-famous Bell Labs. In addition, the new AT&T would be permitted to diversify into other businesses, including computers, from which it had been barred in 1956.[1]

By 1990, these measures had resulted in a sharp fall in long-distance rates in the United States, a rise in the rates for local service (which had previously been cross-subsidized by long-distance charges—paid mostly by businesses), a wider choice of telephone equipment for the regional Bells as well as for telephone users (cordless telephones, fax machines, etc.), and access to new voice and data services for business customers. The two biggest rivals of AT&T in the domestic long-distance business, MCI and Sprint, had garnered small but significant shares of that market by 1990.

The most celebrated case of privatization probably occurred in the United Kingdom in 1984, when Prime Minister Margaret Thatcher sold 51 percent of British Telecom (BT) for 3.9 billion British pounds through a global stock offering, the largest of its kind until then. The government appointed a new chairman and president for the company—both from the private sector—before privatization. No single investor, British or foreign, was permitted to own more than 15 percent of the voting stock, while the government retained a "golden share" (worth only 1 British pound) that gave it the right to appoint some directors and approve changes to the company's charter. Simultaneously, the government permitted another long-distance company to compete with BT but barred additional competitors for the next 7 years. Under the license granted to BT, the company was permitted to continue offering both local and long-distance service, to manufacture equipment, and to offer enhanced information services. BT was also permitted to raise its prices periodically for a basket of services by the rate of inflation (as measured by the retail price index) less 3 percent. A new, independent agency, Oftel, was created to regulate the telecom industry.

In 1985, Japan sold a minority share in its state-owned company, NTT, but barred foreigners from participating in the sale. The government's share was supposed to fall eventually to 33 percent. The new law ended NTT's legal monopoly over telephone service, but no serious competitor had emerged by 1989. Elsewhere in the industrialized world, the New Zealand government was expected to sell 49.9 percent of its telephone company to two Baby Bells, Bell Atlantic and Ameritech, for over US$2.0 billion, and planned to divest the rest of its shares through an international stock offering in 1991.

Toward the end of the 1980s, the idea of privatizing telecommunications firms had gathered steam in the developing world. Several countries were turning their telephone departments into joint stock companies. Others, like Malaysia and Fiji, were planning public stock offerings. Several small countries had sold big blocks of shares to foreign telecommunications firms: France Cable et Radio, a subsidiary of state-owned France Telecom, owned between 25 and 48 percent of the shares of telecommunications firms in many francophone nations in Africa, while Cable and Wireless of the U.K. held similar positions in former British colonies. In Latin America, Chile privatized its telephone company in 1988, while Argentina, Mexico, and Venezuela were in the process of doing the same. Chile had two state enterprises in the telephone sector, one devoted to local service (CTC) and the other to long distance service (ENTEL). Fifty-two percent of CTC was sold to an Australian group with no experience in the telephone business, while 30 percent of ENTEL was sold to a consortium consisting of the Spanish state-owned telephone company, Teléfonica, together with Chase Manhattan Bank. Argentina, on the other hand, was reportedly planning to divide the telephone company along geographical lines (north and south), with a third company for long-distance service that would be jointly owned by the two regional companies. The capital city of Buenos Aires, in which almost two-thirds of the telephone lines were installed, was to be divided equally between the regional companies.

In most developing countries, the state-owned telephone company or agency was unable to keep up with demand: waiting times of 2 to 10 years for new connections were not unusual. Rumor had it that it cost US$2000 to US$3000 under the table for a connection in downtown Bangkok, while in Indonesia retiring telephone employees reportedly received not golden watches but a telephone line! While industrialized countries had 40 to 50 telephone lines per 100 persons, developing countries seldom had more than 5 to 10 per 100 persons. In China, the ratio was 1:100, in India 1:160 (with only 1:3500

EXHIBIT 1

Telephone System Performance, Comparative Data on Selected Measures

Country	Lines per 100 Population	Workers per 1000 Lines	Waiting Time for Lines, Years	Lines with Failures, %
Mexico	5.2	10	2–3	10
Argentina	9.6	14	22	45
Brazil	5.5	11	na	5
Chile	4.6	8	na	7
Venezuela	7.5	11	8	na
Tanzania	0.2	69	11	na
India	0.5	96	na	13
Indonesia	0.4	50	8	17
United States	51	6.6	few days	less than 1
Japan	40	6.6	few days	less than 1

SOURCE: Various publications.

in rural areas), and in Tanzania 1:500. Further, service tended to be very poor when judged by measures such as the call completion rate or the percentage of lines that were down at any time. At the same time, the telephone companies tended to be overstaffed by developed country standards—in some cases by a factor of 500. (Exhibit 1 contains comparative data on these measures for a few countries, including Mexico.)

State-owned telephone organizations in developing countries tended to be profitable, despite low rates for local service and a considerable amount of underbilling and corruption on the part of employees. Indeed, in many cases surpluses generated by the telephone companies were diverted by governments to other sectors. Some policymakers viewed telephone service as a luxury in the context of poor countries, hence meriting lower priority than sectors such as health, housing, and education. Telephone service was also a capital-intensive proposition, requiring on average US$1000 to US$1500 per new line, with much of that consisting of imported equipment. However, others argued that a good telephone system was essential for promoting domestic commerce, exports, and international competitiveness. They pointed to the example of countries like Barbados and Jamaica that had benefitted from modern telecommunications systems: Barbados had set up an international teleport facility, while Jamaica had set up an office park with an international teleport that provided high-speed, high quality voice and data links with the United States.

A World Bank report had this to say on telecommunications privatization in developing countries:

The arguments in favor of some private participation in telecommunications are compelling. Additional financial, technical, and managerial resources—desperately needed in most developing countries—can be provided by private telecom firms. Under increased competitive pressure, private operators of telecom networks can be expected to lower costs by restructuring the work force, introducing new technologies, and procuring components in greater volumes, thus reducing the unit cost of inputs. Commercially minded firms would also increase their responsiveness toward customers and work toward expanding coverage of telecommunications services.[2]

Opponents of privatization argued that telephone companies ought to be government-owned because they were natural monopolies. Technology may have made it possible to create competition in long-distance service, but local service was without doubt still a natural monopoly. Private telephone companies could be counted on to exploit their customers and deny service in remote areas. "Just because governments are financially broke," said one policymaker, "it doesn't mean they should sell their crown jewels at throwaway prices to the highest bidder, including foreigners. How can privatization be a good idea for poor countries when so many rich countries, including France, Germany, Italy, and Spain, have not yet privatized their phone companies?"

THE MEXICAN ECONOMY IN 1989

As president of Mexico, Salinas presided over one of the largest economies in the developing world (population 85 million; GNP US$160 billion). It was also one of the richer developing countries, with per capita income of US$1900. Since the adoption of a new constitution in 1917, Salinas's party, the PRI, had dominated Mexican politics. The PRI encompassed almost all segments of Mexican society, including teachers, workers, labor unions under the Confederation of Mexican Workers (CTM), and business interests. Until the 1988 elections, PRI had not lost the presidency nor any of the thirty-one state governorships or sixty-four seats. Elections for president, accompanied by smooth transitions of power, had occurred every 6 years. Presidents were limited to one term, but enjoyed broad powers, including primacy over the legislature and the judiciary.[3]

Like many other developing countries, Mexico pursued a policy of import-substituting industrialization after World War II. In the 1950s and 1960s, GNP and per capita income grew at impressive levels. In the 1970s, Mexico profited from the oil boom, and the new riches led to ambitious public programs under presidents Luis Echeverria (1970–76) and José López Portillo (1976–82). Public spending outpaced the increase in government revenues, leading to fiscal deficits and foreign borrowing. Between 1979 and 1989, Mexico's foreign debt grew from US$40 billion to more than US$100 billion. As oil prices began to fall and interest rates on foreign loans rose, Mexico defaulted on its external debt in August 1982, triggering the global debt crisis. Rich Mexicans, losing confidence in the economy, began to take money out of the country. López Portillo responded by nationalizing the country's large, private banks and instituting exchange controls. Private businessmen, including, of course, the former owners of the big banks, were irate.

Portillo's successor, Miguel de la Madrid Hurtado, a graduate of the Kennedy School of Government at Harvard University, had to administer "hard medicine" to get the Mexican economy back on its feet. He also began Mexico's shift from an inward-looking economy to one that would be more outward-looking. To get the budget deficit under control, he cut subsidies, raised taxes, and reduced public investment in real terms. To open up the economy, he allowed the peso to depreciate, lowered import barriers, relaxed some of the rules governing foreign investment and made Mexico a signatory of the GATT. He also launched a program of "disincorporating" state enterprises, a term that implied not merely privatization but also the liquidation of enterprises or their transfer from the federal government to state or local governments. Between 1982 and 1988, nearly 600 small state enterprises, accounting for about 10 percent of the state enterprise sector's budget, were disincorporated. These measures began to improve Mexico's balance of payments, but at a high social cost. Real per capita income fell by 40 percent and unemployment hit 20 percent. Inflation remained high (150 percent in 1987) and took its toll on the poor, whose number was believed to have swelled. Meanwhile, the richest 5 percent of the population earned 25 percent of the national income. To contain inflation, De la Madrid convinced workers and private businesses to sign an Economic Solidarity Pact in December 1987, which provided for restrictive fiscal and monetary policies and the reduction of trade barriers. After substantial increases in public-sector prices and utility rates, price controls were also introduced.

In 1987, Carlos Salinas de Gortari, Secretary of Programming and Budgeting, was named the PRI's candidate for the 1988 election. Salinas had never before held elected office. Barely 40 years old, he had a master's degree and a doctorate in political economy from the Kennedy School of Government. Salinas promised to continue the reforms started by De la Madrid.

By the time of the July 1988 election, Mexico's economy was looking far better than at any time in the recent past. Real gross domestic product (GDP) registered its second straight year of growth, inflation was expected to fall to the 50 percent range, the government deficit was less than 10 percent of GDP (compared with a peak of 17 percent in 1982), and both exports and foreign direct investment were on the upswing. On all these measures, 1989 and 1990 were expected to be even better. Nevertheless, Salinas barely won the presidency with 51 percent of the vote in an election marred by charges of fraud. In previous elections, the PRI's candidate had garnered at least 75 percent of the vote.

Within days of assuming office in December 1988, Salinas surprised everyone by arresting the powerful, entrenched leader of the oil workers union (known popularly as "La Quina") and having him replaced with a more acceptable person. Soon thereafter he arrested a notorious drug trafficker and several private businessmen for securities fraud. This earned him the reputation of a tough and determined leader. He also renewed the pact signed earlier between the government, unions, and business groups—this time under the name Pact for Stability and Economic Growth.

Besides continuing many of De la Madrid's economic policies, Salinas pushed harder on trade reform, deregulation of the economy, and privatization. In May 1989, Salinas liberalized the rules governing foreign direct investment, allowing 100 percent foreign ownership under specified conditions, and eliminating government approval for foreign investments under US$100 million. In July, he negotiated a major agreement with international creditors that was expected to reduce Mexico's outflows on foreign debt servicing by US$3 to US$4 billion a year for the next few years. A few months later, he visited the United States to "cement his honeymoon with President Bush," who was reportedly "pleased with [Mexico's] dismantling of protectionist barriers, privatization, and revision of rules for foreign investment.[4] At about this time, the government also announced its desire to enter into a free trade agreement with the United States along the lines of the U.S.–Canada Free-Trade Agreement. Such an agreement would be a major triumph for the Salinas administration and, in the view of some, make his economic reforms irreversible.

THE TELMEX ANNOUNCEMENT

It was in this context that Salinas announced before the telephone workers in September of 1989 that Telmex was to be privatized. Salinas laid out six premises under which the privatization would be carried out:

1. The government would continue to maintain oversight of telecommunications in the country.
2. Telmex would radically improve telephone service for Mexican citizens.
3. The rights of workers would be ensured.
4. The telephone system would be expanded.
5. Telmex would participate in scientific and technical research to strengthen the sovereignty of the country.
6. Majority control of Telmex would remain in Mexican hands.

The president further said that the privatized company would invest US$10 billion between 1989 and 1994 to improve and expand the system.

Two days later, the Secretariat of Communications and Transport (SCT), which supervised Telmex, announced that after privatization the telephone network would be expanded at the rate of 12 percent per year, compared to 6 percent in the recent past. As a result, the current density of 5 lines per 100 people would double to 10 lines by 1994 and quadruple to 20 lines by the year 2000. Specific targets were also announced for the replacement of obsolete exchanges with digital ones, and for the development of new microwave, optical fiber, and satellite systems. The Secretariat of Communications and Transport also announced that workers would participate in the capital of the company, but did not indicate how much. Foreign investors would be allowed to hold up to 49 percent of the privatized company, although no single foreigner, firm or individual, could own more than 10 percent of the total stock. At the time of the announcement, 25 percent of Telmex stock was already in foreign hands and traded in the United States in the over-the-counter market.[5] (Telmex was the only Mexican stock traded in the United States at the time.)

One newspaper noted: "Salinas de Gortari was careful not to provoke a confrontation with the workers this time, in contrast with some previous privatizations. It was significant, indeed, that he chose to make his announcement at a union meeting, where he offered workers a share of the company, and clearly after an agreement had been reached with the usually combative leader of the STRM."[6]

However, the country's political left protested loudly. One influential Congressman complained that problems such as low efficiency and underinvestment by state enterprises were "aggravated by the policy of privatization, which prefers to consent to vices and to delay solutions in the public sector, and then uses the consequent loss of prestige to justify privatizing."

The country's business groups cheered the government's decision. On the day following Salinas's announcement, Telmex accounted for fully forty percent of the shares traded on the Mexican stock exchange. Between the first and last quarters of 1989, Telmex stock had risen from US$0.34 per share to US$0.91 per share.

THE GOVERNMENT'S ROLE IN THE MEXICAN TELEPHONE INDUSTRY

The government first became involved with the telephone sector when it granted concessions to two foreign-owned companies in the late nineteenth century. One firm was started by American investors, the other by the Swedish firm, L.M. Ericsson. Both foreign owners, in fact, were primarily manufacturers of telephone equipment but entered the telephone service business in many foreign markets to promote sales of their equipment. By the early 1900s, each had created a telephone equipment manufacturing subsidiary in Mexico. By 1958, the two telephone service companies had merged under the name Teléfonos de Mexico, and control had moved into the hands of a group of Mexican investors, who owned 73 percent of the stock. Among other things, the government set telephone rates to yield a 12 percent return on equity.

In the mid-1950s, Telmex sought the government's help in raising additional funds for growth and expansion. Unwilling to raise prices, the government agreed that Telmex could give preference in the allocation of new lines to subscribers who bought a stipulated number of shares and bonds issued by the company. (Many new subscribers preferred to sell the Telmex shares and bonds they had been forced to buy, thus spawning the Mexican stock market.)

In addition, the government agreed to impose a telephone tax on users that would be reinvested fully and automatically in Telmex in exchange for bonds yielding a low 6 percent return. Two consequences followed: First, the Mexican controlling group's equity in the company got diluted as subscribers acquired new shares, and, second, Telmex's balance sheet became debt-heavy, as the government continued to accumulate bonds in exchange for reinvesting the telephone tax. To solve the latter problem, in the mid-1960s the government converted its bonds into non voting preferred stock carrying a tax-deductible 6 percent dividend.

By 1972 the government's preferred stock represented 48 percent of Telmex's total equity. President Echeverria's government decided that it was time to stop pretending that Telmex was a private company. He decided that the government should convert its preferred shares into voting shares, acquire additional shares in the market, and assume majority control of Telmex. Under the veiled threat that Telmex's license would not be renewed when it expired in 1976, the government got the private shareholders to amend the company's by-laws to create a special class of AA voting shares that could only be owned by the government and which had to represent at least 51 percent of the total equity at all times. The other type, A shares, could be owned by anyone, including foreigners. In August 1972, the government's shares were converted to AA shares and Telmex became a state-controlled, mixed enterprise. In 1976, the Secretariat of Communications and Transportation issued Telmex a new 30-year license.

Although after 1972 the majority of the board's thirteen directors, including the president, were appointed by the government, and the chairman was the minister of communications, Telmex reportedly ran like a private company, at least for the first few years. Many of the government directors were secretaries or senior officials from various ministries; Salinas himself had served as a director of Telmex from 1981 to 1986. For 13 years (from 1974 to 1987), the same individual, Emilio Carillo Gamboa, the son of a highly respected former minister, served as Telmex's president. By the standards of the public sector, Telmex was regarded as a well-run organization, and many of its senior managers were highly qualified.

The practice of coercing new subscribers to buy Telmex shares and bonds continued. In 1988, for instance, a new residential subscriber paid US$475 in installation charges and had to buy over US$500 worth of Telmex stock to get a connection; commercial customers had to pay even more. Over the years, the telephone tax also went up; it was doubled in 1974, but only 50 percent of the new tax was earmarked by the government for reinvestment in Telmex. As the government became increasingly strapped for funds in the 1980s, the telephone tax crept upward and the portion earmarked for Telmex crept downward, reaching 40 percent in 1981 and even less thereafter. In addition, in 1989, customers paid the standard 15 percent value-added tax on their phone bills—which already included the telephone tax. In all, of every 100 pesos that went to Telmex, 60 pesos went to the government in telephone and value-added taxes.

Between 1976 and 1989, Telmex's sales grew in real terms at about 6 percent and the company was consistently profitable. In 1989, the company had sales of US$2 billion and net income after taxes of US$450 million. (See Exhibit 2 for financial data on Telmex.) Although the government was reluctant to raise the price of local service, which affected the average citizen most, it did raise prices for long-distance service, especially international, which mostly affected businesses. (Residential customers accounted for more than 50 percent of local call-minutes billed but only 20 percent of domestic and international long-distance call-minutes billed.) International calling was priced in U.S. dollars rather than pesos, so that Telmex's international rates went up automatically as the peso depreciated. By 1988, international calls accounted for only 5 percent of all calls but more than 50 percent of Telmex's revenues. That same year, the monthly rent for a residential telephone was about US$2.40 and local calls beyond the first 150 calls per month were charged less than 1 American cent each. Some local exchanges were not equipped to measure the number of calls made.

High international rates also turned Telmex into a major foreign exchange earner for the country. Since a United States–Mexico call originating in Mexico cost more than twice as much as the same call originating in the United States, the vast majority of United States–Mexico calls originated in the United States, making Mexico a net exporter of telephone service to the United States. In 1989, Telmex received about US$500 million from AT&T at settlement time for this reason. However, Mexico was under pressure from the United States to lower Mexican rates for calls to the United States.

Although Telmex remained profitable and the government helped to finance its growth by reinvesting a portion of the telephone tax, the company could not keep pace with the demand for modernization and expansion. In real terms, Telmex's investment was steady through the late 1970s and 1980s; indeed, it had risen significantly from 1987 to 1989. But the waiting list for telephone connections still had 1.5 million names in 1988, which at past rates

EXHIBIT 2

Telmex Financial Data, 1985–1989 Actuals and Projections for 1990–92 (All Figures in Millions of U.S. Dollars) [1]

	Actuals					Projections [2]		
	1985	1986	1987	1988	1989	1990	1991	1992
Income Statement Data								
Long Distance								
International	478	515	564	710	907	861	992	1116
National	303	237	309	449	709	1322	1599	1934
Local service	182	116	153	315	442	1131	1331	1566
Other services	31	22	18	25	57	173	241	324
Total revenues	994	890	1045	1499	2115	3488	4164	4940
Net income after taxes	119	113	206	628	450	1068	1431	1773
Balance Sheet Data								
Total assets	3040	3102	3730	5825	6999	7874	9626	11560
Debt and other liabilities	1586	1658	2156	2612	2892	3757	4199	7230
Equity	1454	1445	1573	3211	4107	4117	5427	4330
Sources and Uses of Funds								
Sources								
Cash flow from operations	404	308	385	449	833	1520	1907	2383
Outside financing	452	504	1064	699	638	575	524	256
Total sources	856	812	1449	1148	1471	2095	2431	2639
Uses								
Investment in plant and equipment	576	499	531	746	955	1741	1917	2130
Debt amortization	29	45	73	148	129	92	112	117
Others	251	268	845	254	387	262	402	392
Per Share Data								
Shares outstanding (millions)	4257	4257	4257	4257	4257	4257	4257	4257
Earnings per share (US$/share)	0.06	0.04	0.06	0.16	0.11	0.25	0.34	0.42

[1]Totals may not add exactly due to rounding off.

[2]Projections for 1990, 1991, and 1992 are based on a stock analyst's report and assume that revenue per line will increase from US$450 in less 1989 to US$661 in 1990 and US$700 in 1991. The number of lines in service is projected to grow at 10.4 percent in 1990 and 12.1 percent in 1991.

of expansion would take 3 to 4 years to satisfy even if no new names were added to the list.

Telmex had also invested funds to modernize the system. By 1981, 99 percent of the exchanges were automatic. Since 1982, only digital exchanges had been added to the system, thereby raising the percentage of digital lines from almost zero in that year to 22.0 percent in 1989. Practically all of the exchange equipment was supplied on a turnkey basis by the Mexican affiliates of two companies, Ericsson (Sweden) and Alcatel (France). Telmex first introduced fiber-optic transmission in 1981, but optical fiber accounted for less than

1 percent of the transmission capacity in 1990. In 1988, Telmex introduced an 800 service for the first time, and the following year extended the 800 service to calls to and from the United States. In 1989, the company initiated the first phase of a digital overlay network that would encompass the eight largest cities within 2 years and another seventeen cities thereafter. Several large customers, including banks, export-oriented firms, and tourism organizations connected into this network through dedicated private circuits. A research and development center, which employed 160 technicians and held 40 patents, designed improvements to the Telmex network. In 1989, the company also opened the Center for Advanced Telecommunications to work exclusively on digital communications.

Telmex provided domestic long-distance transmission via cable, microwave links, and through geostationary satellites. Part of the microwave network belonged to the Ministry of Communications and Transport and was leased to Telmex. Mexico was linked to North America by microwave and to other countries through international satellites.

Union management relations were reasonably good, although workers had gone on strike at times. Telmex's work force grew at the rate of 8 percent per annum from 1984 to 1988, while the number of lines added grew at 5 to 6 percent per annum in the same period. In 1989, however, the work force contracted by about 1 percent due to "retirements, voluntary resignations of employees, and by the termination of contracts of temporary employees that did not justify renewals".[7] By 1989, Telmex employed 49,000 persons, of whom 41,000 were unionized. Telmex workers were considered well paid and enjoyed good benefits. The union was believed to have gained influence over the years and, by 1989, had eroded management's authority in several operational areas, such as job rotation and hiring. For instance, in the case of recruitment, management had to choose from within a slate of three candidates proposed by the union.

READYING TELMEX FOR PRIVATIZATION

Most enterprises privatized by the Office of Privatization had been sold "as is," because that was faster and the government preferred that the new owners decide how to restructure the firms. However, in the case of large companies such as Aeromexico, Mexicana Airlines, and Telmex, the government preferred to restructure before privatization.

Aeromexico, for instance, had been sold in November 1988 after a bitter struggle with the unions. The airline was considered overstaffed, and the government had chosen to close down the company and start a new one that rehired only a third of the original workers. The government cleaned up the company's balance sheet and then sold it to a group of Mexican investors.

In the case of Telmex, the Office of Privatization created committees with representatives from the Ministry of Communications, the Ministry of Commerce and Industry, the Ministry of Finance, and Telmex itself. In addition, the investment banking division of a local bank (Banco Internacional) and an American investment banking firm (Goldman Sachs) were hired to advise on financial issues. Jacques Rogozinski was associated with all the committees. Preparatory work fell into three areas: reorganization of Telmex; legal reforms, including changes to the Telmex license and telecommunications regulations; and financial planning to ensure the sale would be a success.

CORPORATE REORGANIZATION

Within a month of Salinas's announcement, the Ministry of Finance took over control of Telmex from the Secretariat of Communications and Transportation. This had become standard practice by 1989: firms to be disincorporated were first moved to the Ministry of Finance. Finance minister Pedro Aspe became Telmex's chairman, and Alfredo Baranda García, a former ambassador to Spain, was appointed president with the charge of readying the company for privatization.

The new labor contract signed with the STRM in April 1989 prepared the way for "cleaning up" the company's labor relations. In that agreement, the STRM agreed to sign a single contract for all unionized employees rather than 57 separate agreements as in the past. The union also agreed to reduce the number of job classifications from 500 to only 41 and provided management with the flexibility to introduce new technology. Some observers suggested that Telmex was overstaffed by about 30 percent, but Baranda did not plan to lay off any workers.

Another of Baranda's responsibilities was to move ahead with Telmex's plans for modernization and expansion pending privatization. The company estimated that the expansion goals announced by the government would require investment of US$11 billion between 1989 and 1994—two to three times the past rates of investment.

Finally, Baranda worked to make Telmex's balance sheet more attractive to private investors by borrowing U.S. dollars (against the settlement charges owed by AT&T for international calls) to buy back some of the company's foreign debt, which was selling in secondary markets at a deep discount.

LEGAL AND INSTITUTIONAL ISSUES

On the legal front, there were at least two challenges. One was to finalize a revised license agreement for Telmex. The second challenge was to revamp the government's archaic telecommunications regulations to clarify the rules that would govern entry, operations, and competition in the telecommunications sector in the future. Fortunately, the constitution itself would not have to be amended, since it permitted private provision of telephone service, unlike telegraph service and satellite communication, which were reserved for the state. However, Mexico's foreign investment rules limited foreign ownership of telephone service companies to 49 percent.

The task of redrafting Telmex's license opened up a messy set of interconnected issues. Pricing was particularly thorny. Everyone agreed that the heavy cross-subsidization of local service by long-distance service had to end—as it had in the United States. If competition were to be permitted in long-distance, Telmex would be forced to lower those rates, but could the company afford to do that without raising local rates? At any rate, American officials were already forcing down Telmex's prices for calls to the United States, which accounted for more than 80 percent of Mexico's international calling. Then there was the question of how quickly the cross-subsidization should be ended. If Mexican rates were raised to match those in the United States in one swift adjustment, the monthly rent for residential users might have to be increased from US$2.40 to US$15 or US$20, and the charge per local call raised from 1 cent to 8 or 10 cents. How would the public react to such a sharp increase? And might that derail the government's plan to extend the Pact for Stability and Economic Growth with unions and business groups for another stint when it expired in March 1990? A sharp increase in telephone rates could single-handedly add 1 to 2 percentage points to the consumer price index.

On the other hand, the ambitious targets announced by the Secretariat of Communications and Transport for Telmex in September 1989 might not be achievable without higher prices. Financial advisers to the government noted repeatedly that higher prices for telephone service would mean that the government would be able to sell Telmex for a higher price, a point that was not lost on officials from the Ministry of Finance. Indeed, there was under consideration a proposal to revise Telmex's rates as follows starting January 1, 1990:

• Raise the monthly rent for residential users to US$3.60
• Raise the charge per local call drastically, from 1 cent to 10 cents
• Raise rates for an average domestic long-distance call by 55 percent (in real terms)
• Lower international rates by 34 percent (in real terms)

To reduce the impact on consumers, however, it was proposed that the telephone tax—one of the highest in the world—be abolished. The combined effect of these changes would be to increase Telmex's annual revenue per line by 47 percent, from US$450 to US$660. The proposal was met with great skepticism by some officials, who feared that it would provide too much of a windfall income for the future owners who might not put it to good use. Another said, "I thought the whole point of privatization was to attract private investment into the telephone sector. If prices can be raised this much, why privatize at all?"

Representatives of the Ministry of Commerce and Industry, on the other hand, were more concerned with the question of deregulation. They proposed, for instance, that the new telecommunications regulations should simplify and liberalize the rules governing the connection of products such as fax or answering machines to the Telmex network. Their most controversial proposal, however, was that Telmex ought to be divided into at least two parts (north and south) before privatization. Even though the two parts would not compete directly, in many ways they might compete indirectly, as in Argentina. Opponents of the idea argued that it might take two or more years to divide Telmex into regional parts. Besides, who would get Mexico City, which had one-third of all the lines in the country? If Mexico City also had to be divided up, might that further worsen service in the capital? Moreover, would anybody want to buy the system in the south, where economic growth and income levels were much lower than in the booming north? Experts brought in by Telmex from the United States argued against breaking up the company, as did the investment bankers, who feared a divided company might not be nearly as attractive to private investors. Officials from the Ministry of Commerce argued that if a geographical break-up was too difficult, a solution might be to divide the firm into a local service company and a long-distance service company, as in Chile.

In the same realm was the question of whether or not to grant Telmex exclusivity in long-distance service for some length of time. Local service had always been open to new entrants, but, as one observer put it, "you would have to be a fool to get into that lousy segment." Domestic and international long-distance service, on the other hand, could actually attract new entrants if opened up. Rumor had it that AT&T and MCI were already exploring opportunities in Mexico. The Ministry of Commerce was impressed by the gains from competition in the long-distance business in the United States and favored the same in Mexico. However, Telmex officials, supported by the financial advisers, argued that the company needed some time—say, 8 to 10 years—to prepare for competition. Britain had restricted competition in long-distance for 7 years, and so had Argentina. Pressing the opposite side, one official remarked: "If Telmex actually invests US$10 billion to modernize and expand the system over the next 5 years, no one will be able to challenge them in long-distance. Telmex will get even more entrenched."

The government's financial advisers introduced an additional issue along the way. Based on discussions with prospective investors in Mexico and abroad, they had discovered a strong sentiment that the microwave system owned by the Ministry of Communications should be sold to Telmex. Investors seemed uncomfortable with the idea that the ministry, which was responsible for regulating Telmex, would in a sense also be a competitor to Telmex if it continued to own part of the national microwave network. The idea was quite fiercely opposed by the Ministry of Communications and by officials from the Ministry of Commerce, who were keen to cut Telmex down to size before privatization rather than strengthen it further.

Another issue dogging the policymakers was whether or not Telmex should be permitted to diversify into areas such as cellular telephone service, value-added service, telephone equipment manufacture, customer premise equipment, computers, and so on, all of which had high growth potential. In 1989, Telmex's nineteen subsidiaries had total revenues of US$56 million and produced telephone directories, yellow pages, and public pay phones, and installed cables and telephone equipment in customer premises. British telecommunications had been permitted to diversify in this manner so long as these activities were carried out by independent subsidiaries without cross-subsidization by the telephone service business. In the United States, the Baby Bells were permitted to offer cellular telephone service but were barred from diversifying into other areas.

Officials from the Secretariat of Communications and Transport were concerned about public service goals that might get ignored by the future management. In particular, they wanted Telmex to quadruple the density of public telephones—from 1 per 10,000 persons to 4 per 10,000 in 1995—and to ensure that all 10,000 towns in Mexico with 500 or more persons had telephone service by the year 2000. They felt that the revised license ought to stipulate specific targets in these areas as well as measurable targets for quality of service (call completion rates, repair time, percentage of lines down, etc.). And if the targets were missed, the company ought to pay a financial penalty.

FINANCIAL ISSUES

On the financial side, there were at least three sets of issues. First, since the president's guidelines as well as prevailing foreign investment regulations forbade foreign control of Telmex, the company would somehow have to be made affordable to Mexicans. The government was strongly inclined to turn control of the firm over to an identifiable Mexican business group rather than sell shares to dispersed investors. The question then arose, How many business groups could raise the funds necessary to buy Telmex?

The answer would depend in part on the price Telmex fetched. Based on the price of Telmex shares in December 1989, the government's 2.3 billion AA shares (representing 55 percent of the capital), were worth about US$2 billion. On the other hand, in December 1989, the book value of Telmex's assets was US$7 billion. These sums seemed beyond the reach of even the six or seven largest business groups in Mexico. Several experts seemed to feel that no group would be willing or able to assemble more than a billion dollars to buy Telmex. One way around this might be to permit Mexican groups to team up with foreign investors to form a trust in which Mexicans had at least 51 percent ownership. The Mexican-controlled trust might be permitted to buy the government's controlling interest—and this could be taken to mean that Telmex was still under Mexican control. But if the price of Telmex stock doubled in 1990 as it had in 1989, even this approach might not work. It was important for the government to receive multiple bids, so that it could not be accused of giving away the company to the only bidder, yet it was likely that some of the large groups would wait to buy one of the other firms scheduled to be privatized, not Telmex. (See Exhibit 2 for Telmex's projected results for 1990, 1991, and 1992.)

That led to the second set of issues. Would foreign investors want to invest in Telmex? In particular, would foreign telephone companies, which had the technical expertise to improve Telmex, be interested, even though none of them could own more than a 10 percent stake in Telmex? Would they care to be junior partners in a consortium led by Mexican entrepreneurs with whom they had never before done business? To be sure, Mexico had recently done away with the income tax on dividends and capital gains earned by foreign investors, and freed up the repatriation of profits and capital, but could these incentives make up for the restrictions on foreign control that still applied to telephone service? In any case, would U.S. regulators permit the Baby Bells to invest in Mexico? And was it acceptable, from Mexico's standpoint, if telephone companies from France, Spain, or Italy—all of which were government-owned—bid for Telmex? Should the government consider allowing debt-for-equity swaps as a way of enticing foreign investors, especially multinational banks that were holding Mexican debt? And what if some consortiums wanted to buy less than the government's entire 55 percent? Could the government's remaining shares be unloaded on the Mexican stock exchange? Or might they be marketable in foreign stock markets, even though no Mexican company had ever floated shares abroad until then?

Finally, some shares had to be set aside for Telmex workers. How much ought that to be? Should they be sold to the workers or given away? Should the shares be voting or nonvoting? And should workers be given a seat on the board?

OTHER ISSUES

A more fundamental question was how to regulate telephone prices after privatization. What rules ought to govern pricing? In the past, the Secretariat of Communications and Transport had approved prices for each service on a regular basis after examining Telmex's costs and assets to yield a "fair rate of return," similar to the method widely used in the United States. Others argued for more decentralized pricing, such as the system used in Britain when British telecommunications had been privatized.

A related but more general issue was whether the Secretariat of Communications and Transport would be able to regulate Telmex effectively after privatization. Did it have the kind of people it needed? Did it have the funding and autonomy to hire good people and to keep them? Or would it be no match for the expertise and resources controlled by Telmex? Indeed, executives within Telmex had helped a great deal in the analysis and planning for privatization; could the government count on similar cooperation from the firm when other policy issues affecting the telecommunications sector arose down the road? In this context, was it desirable for the government to have one or more seats on the board after privatization? Or should the government retain a "golden share," as the British and Malaysian governments had done?

Sitting in his office in the grand Palacio Nacional in downtown Mexico City, Rogozinski reflected on the status of the Telmex privatization. Over the next 9 months, several policy tangles would have to be sorted out, tough political questions tackled, and a buyer found. There was a lot riding on the Telmex privatization. A successful sale would give the country and Salinas's program a new credibility. That could solidify the mood of optimism building in Mexico, attract additional foreign capital, and lure back the billions of dollars held abroad by rich Mexicans. It might even increase the chances of signing a free-trade agreement with the United States and Canada. Rogozinski took a clean sheet of paper and began making notes for his forthcoming meeting with finance minister Aspe.

References

1. U.S. experience based on Richard H.K. Vietor, "Government Regulation of Business," *Harvard Business School Division of Research Working Paper No. 92027,* pp. 45–47.
2. Ambrose et al., 1990, p. 9.
3. See Helen Shapiro, "Mexico: Escaping from the Debt Crisis," Harvard Business School case 390–174.
4. *Latin American Weekly Report,* 10/26/89, p. 7.
5. *Latin American Weekly Report,* 10/5/89, p. 8.
6. *Latin American Weekly Report,* 10/5/89, p. 8.
7. Telmex, *Annual Report 1989,* p. 27.

Csepel Machine Tool Company

JOSEPH WOLFE, *University of Tulsa and* JOZSEF POOR,
formerly of the International Management Center, Budapest, Hungary

From many appearances, 1989 seemed to have been a good year for the Csepel Machine Tool Company. More importantly it had been part of a tumultuous, yet basically successful decade. Since 1985 sales had increased an average of 7.5 percent a year and the company had successfully weathered the financial crisis which had hindered its managerial freedom in the early 1980s. More recently management had been able to lessen the firm's dependency on domestic sales, doubly important because of Hungary's stagnant economy, and it had increased its vital hard currency sales 23 percent in just one year. Moreover, it appeared the firm's strategy of customizing its products as much as possible to suit the unique needs of various customer groups, especially those in the People's Republic of China, was a viable way to operate in an industry which had been only marginally profitable in other advanced industrial countries.

Something, however, was seriously wrong as numerous fears and misgivings were held in various quarters within Csepel. Profits were falling and the company's sales had been erratic for the past four years. Yet, after allowing for Hungary's double-digit inflation, many felt sales revenues were actually falling. Accordingly, top management was forecasting that 1990 revenues would range from 2.05 billion to 2.19 billion forints and profits would run between −55.6 million and 66.6 million forints for the three alternative pro forma income statements developed by top management in Exhibit 1. Various managers questioned whether Csepel should continue pursuing its customizing strategy, with its attendant high manufacturing costs and operations within a market easily accessed by superior Japanese machine tool technology, without instituting strict cost controls and modernizing the company's aging product line. As the decade of the 1990s began, Csepel's top management faced a number of thorny issues and problems and a clear course of action did not seem to be in existence.

This case, written by Joseph Wolfe, Professor of Management at the University of Tulsa, does not describe either correct or incorrect managerial actions or decisions but instead is intended to facilitate an understanding of the organizational and strategic management issues involved. The authors gratefully acknowledge the use of materials and consulting reports created by Maria Raboczki Bordané, Éva Tihanyi, Andras Farkas, and Anna Jakab Baané.

EXHIBIT 1

Csepel Machine Tool Company 1990 Pro Forma Income Statements under Three Scenarios (in millions of forints)

	A	B	C
REVENUES			
Domestic	407.0	430.0	450.0
Exports			
CMEA ruble market	648.0	231.4	130.0
Hard currency	993.2	1,428.0	1,610.0
Total	2,048.2	2,089.4	2,190.0
MANUFACTURING COST			
Direct	1,124.1	1,145.2	1,182.6
Overhead	900.0	900.0	900.0
Total	2,024.1	2,045.2	2,082.6
OTHER INCOME			
U.S.-dollar support	0.0	0.0	32.2
Ruble export	−86.3	−30.0	−13.0
Profit before taxes	−55.6	34.2	66.6
Less taxes	0.0	17.1	33.3
Profit after taxes	−55.6	17.1	33.3

SOURCE: Company internal forecast.

MACHINE TOOLS AND THE MACHINE TOOL INDUSTRY

The basic principle of using rotary motion to smooth, sharpen, or otherwise machine surfaces has been linked to the bow and arrow. The bow lathe and its near relative, the pole lathe, did not produce a steady, continuous motion, but the basic principle of rotary cutting to smooth, bore, or drill hard materials had been discovered. Progress in the technology's development was relatively slow as the wheel-driven lathe, which provided continuous rotation by either hand or foot, was not invented until the 14th century. Although the French were cutting screw-threads by the late 1500s, the lathe's efficiency and accuracy were not increased until Henry Maudslay invented the slide rest in 1794. Due to England's Industrial Revolution, machine tools of ever-increasing accuracy were soon required. Maudslay's screw-cutting lathe of 1800 and Eli Whitney's development of the capstan lathe did much to improve the speed and accuracy of this popular device.

While the lathe is still today's most widely used machine tool, other tools mill, drill, bore, plane, cut, and shape steel and castings into their final form. The demand for these tools is highly dependent on the amount of metal working activity conducted in both heavy and light industry. Perhaps the machine tool industry's largest customers are the automobile manufacturers and their parts and subassembly suppliers, followed by the aircraft industry and all others who finish, grind, or stamp metal. Accordingly the demand for machine tools (lagged by sometimes over a year for the manufacture of today's more-sophisticated machinery) is quite high in Western Europe and Japan and among Japanese automobile manufacturers regardless of the location of

EXHIBIT 2

EXHIBIT 2

American Machine Tool Industry Performance

Measure	1985	1986	1987	1988	1989	1990	1993
Sales ($billions)	$ 3.2	$ 3.3	$ 3.4	$ 3.7	$ 4.0	$ 4.3	$ 5.6
Operating margin	8.5%	9.3%	9.2%	9.6%	9.5%	9.0%	12.0%
Net profits ($ millions)	$28.8	$80.9	−$31.3	$76.4	$105.0	$185.0	$300.0
Net profit margin	0.9%	2.5%	−0.9%	2.1%	2.6%	4.3%	5.4%

NOTES: Results for 1989 and 1990 are estimates; performance figures for 1993 are mean estimates of the years 1992 to 1994.
SOURCE: T. Brophy, "Machine Tool Industry," *Value Line Investment Survey,* November 17, 1989, p. 1,336.

their plants. Alternatively the demand for these tools in Detroit and the Big Three's plants scattered throughout the United States, Canada, and Mexico has been relatively low during the past decade. In the near term, industry experts believe the American automobile industry will defer its purchases of the larger, more sophisticated flexible manufacturing systems due to the losses incurred by both Ford and General Motors in 1989 and the plant closings transpiring at Chrysler Motors as it tries to reverse its sagging fortunes.

Composite statistics for the American machine tool industry for the past seven years are presented in Exhibit 2. Sales growth has been less than GNP growth in the United States and net profit margins have only been 2.03 percent of sales during that period. A number of firms have restructured themselves such as Cross & Trecker, Acme-Cleveland, and Cincinnati Milacron, while others have attempted diversifications out of the industry. Certain Japanese machine tool manufacturers, such as Yamazaki Mazak Corporation, Okuma Machinery Inc., and Toyoda Machinery USA are very bullish about the industry's prospects. Yamazaki Mazak plans to enter a variety of world markets with innovative, cost-cutting machine tool stations which enhance end-user value by justifying their purchase as an investment in efficiency and higher end-product quality. Okuma, Toyoda, and other Japanese manufacturers are broadening the product lines being exported to the United States to include grinders and screw machines, which are machine tool categories not included in the industry's 1986 voluntary restraint agreements. Exhibit 3 outlines the nature of the machine tool industry's technology and the degree its technology has been diffused in most technologically advanced nations. Exhibit 4 presents data on the dollar value of worldwide production of machine tools by selected capitalist and socialist countries.

THE CSEPEL MACHINE TOOL COMPANY

Today's Csepel Machine Tool Company is an outgrowth of what was once the Manfred Weiss manufacturing complex. Although it began operations in 1882 as a can manufacturer, the firm began manufacturing military ordnance in 1889 and shortly thereafter an iron and steel plant was built. The Manfred Weiss Company began bicycle and automobile production in 1925 and airplane engine production was added to its industrial empire in 1927. Its machine tool business began in 1929 as an in-house supplier of its own needs, but one year later the firm began to sell its tools to outside firms in both Hungary

EXHIBIT 3
Two Decades of
Technological Progress
in the Machine
Tool/Production
Engineering Industry

By the early 1980s extensive software had been developed which fully automated and optimized all steps in the manufacture of a component. These programs select the machining sequence, selection of machine tools, clamping, selection of the operations sequence, tool selection, choose the optimum cutting conditions, and numerically control the entire machining operation. Programs and machines of this type were in wide use in many industries.

By the mid-1980s fully self-optimizing adaptive control of machine tools had been developed, and on-line process identification and on-line optimization were in general use in manufacturing plants. Work preparation in the form of machine loading and scheduling is being accomplished by computers in over 75.0 percent of all American factories.

In the 1990s standardized computer software systems will be commercially available. About 70.0 percent of industry will be using group technology in its manufacturing processes. The machine industry's traditional lathes, boring mills, and broaching machines are being rapidly replaced by plastic machinery, flexible manufacturing machinery, and advanced composite machinery to reflect the new materials which are being introduced as replacements for iron and steel.

SOURCE: Adapted from M.E. Merchant, "Delphi-Type Forecast of the Future of Production Engineering," *CIRP Annals* 20, no. 3 (1971), p. 213; and *U. S. Manufacturing Competitiveness—Profiles in Competitive Success* (Chicago: A.T. Kearney, 1989), p.10.

EXHIBIT 4

World Production of Machine Tools (selected years in $millions)

Country	1975	1980	1984	1985
United States	$ 2,451.7	$ 4,812.3	$ 2,423.2	$ 2,575.0
West Germany	2,403.6	4,707.6	2,803.7	3,123.1
Japan	1,060.6	3,826.1	4,473.3	5,269.7
Italy	873.1	1,728.1	996.0	1,056.4
Great Britain	728.3	1,395.8	674.9	722.9
Switzerland	535.9	994.1	759.2	956.7
France	678.6	957.9	465.5	468.5
Total	$ 8,731.8	$18,421.9	$12,595.8	$14,172.3
Soviet Union	$ 1,984.4	$ 3,065.0	$ 2,776.4	$ 3,015.0
East Germany	585.2	891.5	789.1	789.3
Rumania	106.0	590.0	353.0	324.1
Czechoslovakia	305.4	331.5	325.2	334.4
Poland	422.8	605.0	120.7	97.3
Yugoslavia	65.0	231.8	225.9	238.6
Hungary	50.0	421.3	198.1	160.0
Bulgaria	25.5	43.0	192.5	192.5
Total	$ 3,544.3	$ 6,179.1	$ 4,980.9	$ 5,151.2
World total	$12,276.1	$24,601.0	$17,576.7	$19,323.5

SOURCE: Cited by Istvan Nemeth, "Machine Tools Export for the Hard Currency Market," unpublished dissertation, University of Economics, Budapest, 1987.

and abroad. Over the years it developed a solid reputation by offering a series of innovative, high-precision products.

After supplying the Axis war effort in the 1940s, temporarily as in the guise of the Hermann Goring Werke after the forced withdrawal of the Jewish-born Weiss family, the firm was nationalized in 1946. Upon becoming state-owned the company became known as the Csepel Iron and Metalworking Trust, so named for its location on Csepel island in the Danube River south of Budapest. Various Soviet industrial organization concepts were quickly introduced over the years. Rather than continuing the Taylorism which had been used by Manfred Weiss since its introduction in the 1930s by consultants from the German Method Time Measurement Association (RETA), a planning orientation comprised of a series of three- and five-year national plans was strictly applied. Workers were encouraged to over-fill the individual plans which were created for them, shops were given greater autonomy through the addition of staff support, and a new management level was added to monitor the company's conformity to the centralized plan.

The state government assumed control of the company's import/export effort through its Ministry of Commerce and its research and development function was removed to be housed within the Institution for Mechanical Industry Research in Budapest. From its nationalization in 1946 until 1968 the company quadrupled its number of shops while adding 112,800 square feet of factory space and a new office building to its manufacturing complex. Since that period Exhibit 5 demonstrates that the company's general product mix has become more diversified after a heavy period of concentration in drilling and milling machines in the 1960s.

In late 1983 the company reorganized itself into an independent, state-owned company called the Machine Tools Factory of the Csepel Works. Its debut was inauspicious as the new entity was burdened by nearly 700 million forints worth of debt and delinquent accounts receivables of 500 million. The company's resulting low working capital forced it to abandon its ambitious modernization program and to find new sources of cash in an effort to stabilize operations. A manufacturing building was sold in 1986 and, more importantly, the company obtained equity financing by transforming itself into a publicly held shareholders' corporation. In this regard, Csepel became a pioneer within the Hungarian economy and this action became a model for others to emulate. The company split itself into two stock corporations in October 1988; the larger of the two was capitalized at 860 million forints and

EXHIBIT 5

Production by General Machine Tool Groups

Product	1946	1960	1970	1980	1989
Drilling machines	110	500	700	500	172
Milling machines (including NC and CNC)	100	660	295	100	67
Lathe machines (including NC and CNC)	n.a.[a]	n.a.	40	240	93
Grinding and other high-precision machines	n.a.	1	29	160	36

[a]Product was not manufactured at this time.
SOURCE: *90 Years of the Csepel Iron and Metal Company* (Budapest: Csepel Iron and Metal Company, 1982).

EXHIBIT 6

Major Hungarian Machine Tool Manufacturers in 1987

Company	Employees	Revenue (million forints)	Fixed Assets (million forints)
Csepel Machine Tool Company	2,500	2,500.0	1,800.0
SZIM Machine Tool Company	15,000	10,000.0	2,590.0
DIGEP Mechanical Factory	3,000	300.0	910.0

SOURCE: Istvan Nemeth, "Machine Tools Export for the Hard Currency Market," unpublished dissertation, University of Economics, Budapest, 1987, p 27.

became known as the Csepel Machine Tool Company, while the smaller one, called the Csepel Fixture and Tool Corporation, was capitalized at 160 million forints. In making this division, the Csepel Machine Tool Company retained its original interests in manufacturing and providing parts for its lathes, machining centers, and drilling and milling machines, while the Csepel Fixture and Tool Corporation currently manufactures small fixtures, tools, and parts. Within the Hungarian economy itself, Csepel is only one of three manufacturers available. As shown in Exhibit 6, the company is much smaller than the SZIM Machine Tools Company while DIGEP (Deutsche Industrieanlagen GmbH) has a minor claim to the market.

Although the Csepel Machine Tool Corporation has been able to retrench and stabilize its operations, Exhibit 7 shows the firm's profits peaked in 1987 while sales have continued their upward climb to about 2.6 billion forints in 1989. Over the next three to four years Csepel expects to boost its sales to over 3.5 billion while simultaneously changing its sales composition to that displayed in Exhibit 8. The 700 million new forint sales in parts contracts are planned as joint ventures with western companies. This has been planned as a revival of the once-flourishing business the firm had with the West in the 1970s. A large slump in demand in the early 1980s had caused this market to diminish significantly. Exhibit 9 displays the source of Csepel's sales by general market areas for 1985 through 1989.

Products and New Product Development

The Csepel Machine Tool Corporation produces the finished products listed in Exhibit 10. Its current product line consists of five basic types of equipment—radial drilling machines, computer numerically controlled (CNC) machining centers, CNC lathes, precision equipment, and special-purpose machinery. The radial drilling machines come in three different sizes with a moveable column and varying operating lever lengths. Ten years ago these units had annual sales of about 1,000 per year. Csepel's CNC machining centers consist of four different models. The first is the Yasda model which comes in three different sizes whose design was purchased in 1979 from the Yasda Company. The next model, the MK-500, was created by Csepel itself and is a small machining center. The third set of models is the "M" family, consisting of the model numbers MVI-6-11 and MVI-10-11. These models come in both horizontal and vertical versions.

Csepel makes four different kinds of lathes. The first is a tailor-made shaft and pulley lathe made under a licensing agreement with Heid. The next was

EXHIBIT 7
Csepel Machine Tool
Company Sales and
Profits, 1985–1989

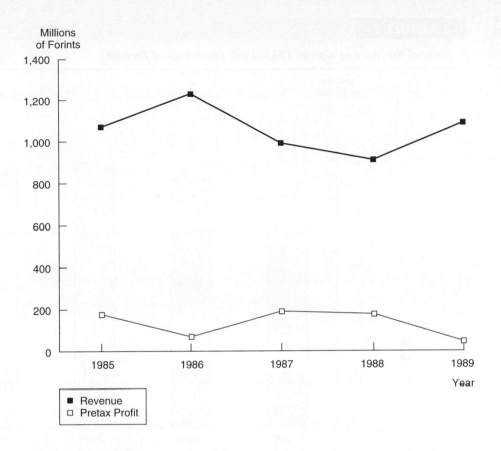

Millions
of Forints

Revenue
Pretax Profit

EXHIBIT 8

Planned Sales Compositions, 1988 versus 1993 (billions of forints)

Product or Service	1988	1993
Finished products	2.38	2.63
Services	0.08	0.00
Tools	0.05	0.00
Parts production	0.00	0.70
Other	0.00	0.18
Total	2.50	3.50

SOURCE: Consultant's report and company interviews.

designed by Csepel and meets the needs of the precision instrument industry. The third model in this group is the TCFM-100, which is used for training purposes as well as being able to produce both revolution solids and box-shaped parts.

The company's next set of products is a high-precision gear-cutting system which comes with a twist-drill attachment and programmable logic control, and the UP-1, which is a small precision lathe. The last two products, the PTC-71-180 and SMC-71-180, are special-purpose systems currently being exported solely to the Soviet Union.

EXHIBIT 9

Csepel Sources of Sales, 1985–1989 (millions of forints)

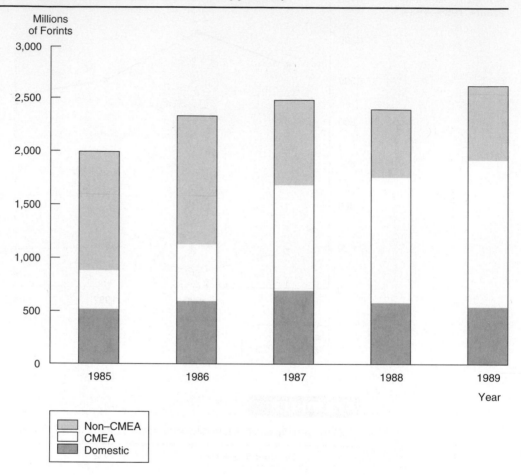

In commenting on the number of Csepel products in the late stages of their life cycles as well as the general lack of new products coming on-stream, Levente Godri, the Central Plant's Chief Designer, explained,

> We don't have enough engineers in the first place and those we do have get too involved in daily operations—so much so they don't have any time to do new product development. We could hire some good people from the Technical University in Budapest and they could staff a new R&D department but I don't know if that would really solve our problem.
>
> I see two ways to get more new products for us. We could use a project manager approach. We could pick out two to three projects to be pursued for the next year and we'd select project leaders who could hire personnel from those that are available within the company. These leaders would stay in charge of the project as long as they stayed within the budget. Another way would be to set up an independent engineering bureau to operate on its own or jointly with another firm.
>
> Whatever we're doing we have to do a better job than we're doing now. Unfortunately our bonus system is based on the on-time delivery of machines so our R&D people spend time in the shop helping to get orders delivered instead of spending time developing new products.

Csepel 1989 Product Mix and Product Prices by Geographic Market

Machine Type	Model Number	Product Price (thousands of forints)			Annual Production	Life Cycle Position	Competitive Strength
		Hungarian	U.S. Dollar	CMEA Countries			
Radial drilling machines	RF-50	747.7	577.5	577.9	200 for entire group	All very late	All are weak
	RFh-75	1,449.4	1,116.4	909.6			
	RFh-100	2,015.7	2,056.1	1,558.2			
CNC machining centers	Yasda	n.a.[a]	23,951.4	n.a.	30 to 40	Early	Average
	MK-500	11,683.4	9,460.0	12,072.9	35 to 55	Early	Average
	MVI6	10,903.6	n.a.	n.a.	10 to 15	Relatively late	Weak
	MVI10	11,989.6	13,294.9	n.a.	6 to 8	Relatively early	Average
CNC lathes	SDNC610 1000	8,951.5	10,581.9	6,566.2	35 to 50	Relatively early	Strong
	SDNC610 1500	n.a.	4,742.4	8,464.1	35 to 50	Relatively early	Strong
	RS-100	5,516.3	9,258.8	n.a.	15 to 25	Very early	Average
	TCFM-100	1,616.2	n.a.	2,047.2	25 to 30	Very early	Strong
High-precision systems	FKP-326-10	7,315.5	10,851.5	7,259.4	35 to 40	Mature	Weak
	UP-1	15,726.0	n.a.	n.a.	5 to 10	Very early	Strong
Special-purpose systems	PTC-71-180	n.a.	n.a.	4,431.7	10 to 15	Mature	Weak
	SMC-71-180	n.a.	n.a.	5,539.8	10 to 15	Mature	Weak

[a]Product not available in this market.

SOURCE: Company internal records and consultant's estimates.

EXHIBIT 11

Csepel R&D Expenditures (millions of forints)

1985	1986	1987	1988	1989	1990[a]
37.4	27.1	81.2	55.7	18.7	15.0

[a]Planned.
SOURCE: Company records.

The company's Research and Development expenditures for the past five years in addition to its planned budget for 1990 are presented in Exhibit 11.

As if to underscore Godri's observations about being saddled with plant production problems, the leader of the NC Assembly and Machining Shop interrupted the conversation by telephone demanding that an engineer be sent immediately to the production unit to make a substitute part in the Maintenance Department to replace a part which had not been delivered by a supplier. This call was made even though each shop has an on-duty technical assistant to handle these minor crises. Levente later explained these problems could be completely avoided if substitute parts could be identified and used, but Csepel's part numbering system does not disclose or cross-reference part substitutions.

In addition to producing machines for its finished goods inventory, Csepel willingly works to special customer specifications. As shown in Exhibit 12, the proportion of these special orders varies by product type. Overall, the firm has little trouble obtaining equipment orders as it attempts to satisfy each customer's unique requirements. It has also obtained a reputation for quality products and low prices.

Factories and Manufacturing Operations

The company manufactures its machine tools and parts in two factories. The Central Plant, which also houses its executive offices, is in Budapest, while its second plant is in Nyirbator, a countryside city of about 30,000 inhabitants in the northeastern section of Hungary's Great Plain. Because of the high degree of specialization existing within the company, neither plant can make an

EXHIBIT 12

Proportions of Special Order Work by Product Line

Product Line	Proportion
Radial drilling machines	2 to 3%
CNC machining centers	30 to 50
CNC lathes	20 to 40
High-precision systems	
FKP-326-10	5 to 10
UP-1	100
Special-purpose systems	100

SOURCE: Consultant's report.

EXHIBIT 13

Production Equipment State of Repair

Repair State	Proportion of Equipment
Good	46.3%
Average	48.0
Poor	5.7

SOURCE: Consulting report.

entire machine tool. While the Nyirbator facility features a better plant layout because it is relatively new, outside experts generally agree Csepel's factories leave much to be desired. About 15 percent of its production equipment is zero to 10 years old, another 37 percent is 11 to 20 years old, and almost half is over 20 years of age. Overall the firm has only 24 numerically controlled machines of its own and about 59 percent of its equipment has been depreciated to scrap value. It is believed that an investment of $4.7 to $6.0 million would be needed to modernize Csepel's production equipment while an additional $12.0 million would be needed to introduce extensions to its current product lines and to acquire and introduce advanced production control and information systems. Exhibit 13 displays a repair status summary of the company's equipment.

Despite using technology which is frequently 20 to 25 years old, the technological gap has often been bridged by engineering know-how and exceptionally skilled and dedicated workers. In recent years, however, the Central Plant has begun to lose both its highly qualified and cross-trained senior factory technicians, as well as its younger trainees to local private-sector machine shops and small factories. This is due to their superior working conditions and freedom from forced overtime work near the end of the business year. Ironically they often work with old equipment sold to the private-sector machine shop by Csepel itself. Because of the lack of alternative employment opportunities in the Nyirbator area, a similar loss of blue-collar workers has not occurred at that facility.

Central Plant Operations

Due to the nature of the products being manufactured and the availability of various types of equipment, the manufacturing process in the Central Plant, as shown in Exhibit 14, is more complex than that found at Nyirbator. The Central Plant's formal organization, which also includes the firm's headquarters personnel, is also more elaborate. See Exhibit 15 for Csepel's Budapest Central Plant organization chart.

A conversation with Arpad Koknya, Deputy General Director in charge of the Central Plant's manufacturing operations, revealed both the complexity of the production control process and certain problems that have not been resolved.

> Every quarter for each month and each shop my department produces a production plan. We also do this for Nyirbator. On the basis of this plan our department assembles a portfolio of shop cards, raw materials requisitions, and time and labor charges by order number. If everything is all right the portfolio goes to the Production

EXHIBIT 14
Central Plant
Manufacturing
Sequence

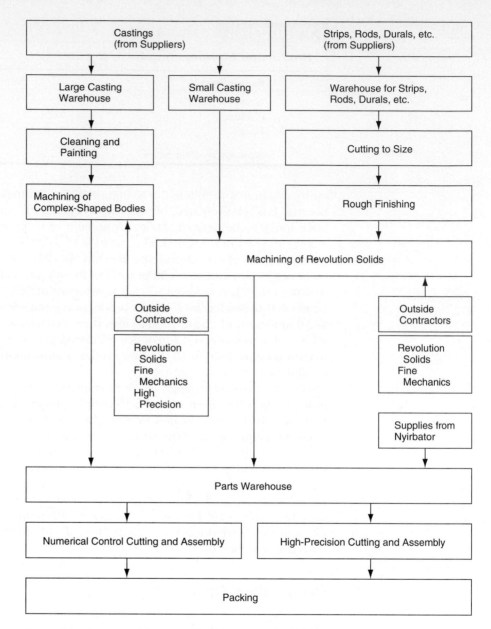

NOTE: About 5 percent of the company's 24,000 parts and subassemblies are manufactured in the Central Plant. The plant handles parts requiring extreme accuracy and/or state-of-the-art technologies. Its layout is not very rational, although efforts are being made to create a more orderly plant configuration.

Department. That department then launches a new shop order. When the shop manager gets the portfolios he assigns them to various foremen who have the workers get the tools and raw materials bill. That's the normal process.

When his assignment is completed each worker signs off on the bill. But we have a stupid quality control system that works well for simple, small things, but for complicated subassemblies like ours it doesn't work so well. It can really cause big problems if the assembly is produced in a number of steps.

Our quality control system is a mixture of worker self-inspection and staff department quality control inspection. Under worker self-inspection the worker himself

EXHIBIT 15

Organization Chart for Csepel Machine Tool Company

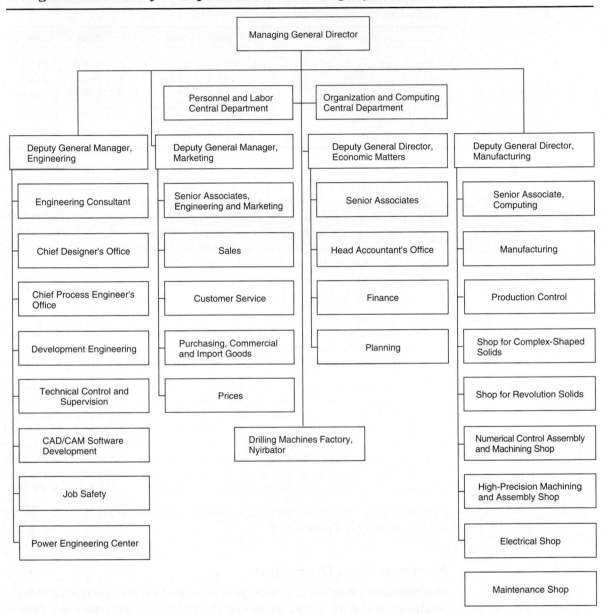

says whether the work is good or not while the quality control department looks at the entire subassembly when it's been completed. Many of our workers sign off that their work is up to standard, but it isn't—and we don't find out about it until it shows up in the final subassembly. Or what's worse, after it's been delivered and we have to field service it ourselves. We should really punish these guys, but the present employment situation doesn't allow us to do this. We also have a quantitative bonus system in the production of parts and this also adds to our problems.

Another part of our production problem also has something to do with parts. Each month our department sets up a so-called parts shortage list (PSL). The PSL has a

EXHIBIT 16

*Csepel Machine Tool Company Inventory Levels
(thousands of forints)*

Inventory Type	1985	1986	1987	1988	1989
Purchased stocks and raw materials	450.6	678.6	610.9	551.8	777.5
Goods in process	185.5	139.8	171.6	192.3	216.5
Finished goods	15.5	17.4	31.8	36.3	10.0
Total	651.7	635.2	814.3	780.4	1,017.4

SOURCE: Internal company records.

list of final products on the left side and on the right side the number of missing parts for that product with the part's identification number. This list is a key input into the parts manufacturing operation. They have a production schedule which deals with making parts for the PSL and parts for things currently being assembled. Those items on the PSL get a higher priority. Unfortunately because of a bad, six-plus one-digit code system, which looks like this,

our computer system can't handle it so a lot of parts searches kick out out-of-stock messages even though they're really in stock. Too often we're making parts we don't need and their higher priority slows up our regular production runs.

The creation of our production plan for assembly operations isn't so complicated but it's coordinating the production that's difficult. Because of how our sales orders come in we only have to deliver about 20 units per month in the first part of the year but about 60 to 100 units a month in the last part. Because we have a limited number of assembly workers they get very overworked by the end of the year—sometimes our best workers get sick from stress. But life isn't so easy for management either. These swings in production cause headaches for everybody. If the sales department could just forecast sales better we'd have fewer problems down the line.

Exhibit 16 presents data on the various inventory levels carried by Csepel within the various stages of production.

Nyirbator Plant Operations

The Nyirbator plant was originally created to manufacture parts for all Csepel products, as well as serving as part of the Hungarian government's plan to bring industrial economic development to the country's rural areas. Accordingly the original labor supply was drawn from unskilled agricultural workers who had to be intensively trained in company-run technical training programs. Over the years Csepel has been a strong supporter of the city's technical school, which has now become the firm's major source of skilled labor. In 1989 the plant employed about 740 people and it generated sales of 649.1 million forints.

Currently the plant has moved from producing only parts to that of a manufacturer of both parts and the company's basic drilling machines. See Exhibits 17 and 18 for presentations of Nyirbator's production system and organiza-

EXHIBIT 17
Nyirbator Manu-
facturing Sequence

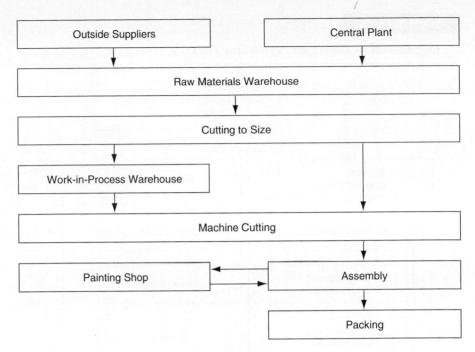

NOTES: Almost 90 percent of Csepel's parts and subassemblies are manufactured in this factory. The process technology is simpler compared to that used in the Central Plant. Nyirbator's products are easier to assemble than those produced in the Central Plant, but their unit value is significantly lower. Except for high-precision parts, the plant is self-sufficient.

tion chart. Although the plant is more modern in its layout, various Nyirbator managers feel that constraints placed on them by headquarters rob them of their chances to be more profitable. The drilling machine plant's director of economic matters, Janos Fazekas, expressed it in the following manner.

> First of all our plant has to manufacture Csepel's low-profit items. As bad as that is many times we get urgent orders by fax from the Central Plant which forces us to shut down our machines to supply them. We argue about these things all the time.
>
> We want to be more independent and to have more power in these discussions with Production Control and Planning. These departments consider us to be their slaves and don't consider our specific bottleneck problems and they continue to bother us with their special orders which overuse our special machines.
>
> Also headquarters' sales operations are very slow in processing domestic orders. We could do a faster job on these sales if we could set up our own sales department.

Nyirbator's engineering director, Istvan Szatmari, also thinks the plant should have more freedom, if only to develop a line of more profitable products for the facility.

> In recent years we've brought in new engineers for new product development, but all their time is spent in operations. They want to design new tools but can't. We're also in conflict with the Central Plant's R&D operations because they won't give us the freedom to operate on our own.

As much as Nyirbator's management feels shackled, they have occasionally taken advantage of the poor telephone communications between their two cities and the lack of tight internal auditing controls existing at headquarters.

EXHIBIT 18

Organization Chart for Nyirbator Factory

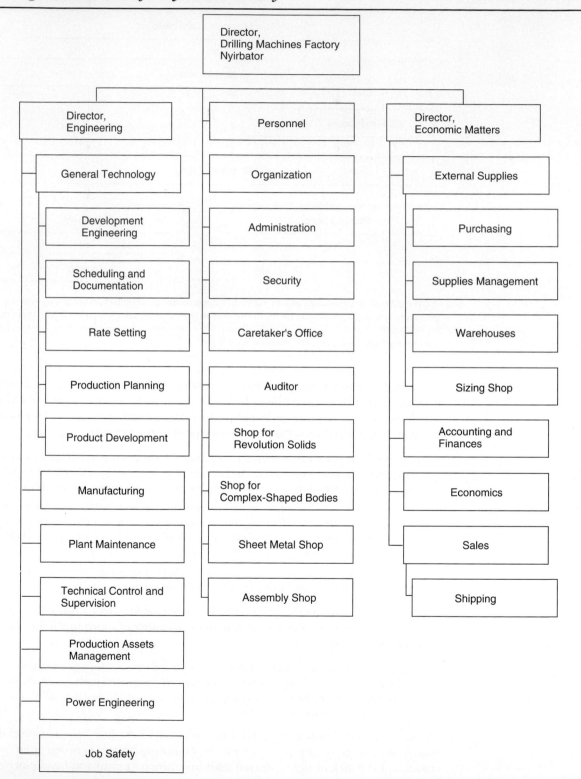

By falsely listing desired equipment as production parts, they have been able to purchase non-authorized office equipment at times. In one instance it was a prized Xerox machine.

Headquarters Operations

Csepel's headquarters is staffed predominantly by people who have been promoted from within and they all have graduated from production operations after many years of service. The one exception is Istvan Rakoczy, the head of the company's computer services. Top management's pace and style appear to be dictated by that practiced by Gabor Hajnoczy, Csepel's managing general director. Two or three mornings a week beginning just after the shift opens, he tours the Central Plant's shops with Arpad Koknya. These rounds, which are conducted both here and occasionally at Nyirbator, can last up to three hours and can occur more often, should problems be plaguing a particular production run. Hajnoczy is very familiar with plant operations and its workers, and he knows many employees on a personal and first-name basis. Should he see something that appears to be wrong he will immediately order a change in either the production method or the order's schedule.

Later in the day, while holding a two-hour discussion in Gabor Hajnoczy's office, he was interrupted many times by short telephone calls from plant personnel and brief conferences with his secretary. He also had to sign a number of technical orders as well as a request for computer supplies. Several very lengthy telephone calls dealt with decisions about where pieces of shop equipment should be placed for a shop-floor layout change that was underway.

Although some appreciate top management's intimate working knowledge of plant operations and its accessibility, others see it as "always having someone breathing down our necks" or showing too much concern for production and the bonuses attached to on-time production deliveries. The head of the Central Plant's sales department, Gabor Nagy, commented that

> Top management's manufacturing bias is the company's major problem—it keeps us from being flexible. This company doesn't have its own selling rights because it must trade through Technoimpex. This was all right at one time because Technoimpex had traditionally been machine-tools oriented. Now Technoimpex wants to buy and sell a whole range of products so it doesn't represent us as well as it once did—their representatives can't emphasize us like they did before because they have so many other companies to represent and they really don't want to emphasize our machine tools any longer. To cover ourselves on this we now have service representatives, who can also help us with our sales, in such places as Rumania, West Germany, and the United States. Where we don't have our own people we use Austria's Intertrade which specializes in steel and machine tools.

The general manager's plant tours not only disturb many production workers, they also appear to interfere with the operations of other company functions. As an example, Nagy observed that,

> Sometimes our General Manager gets orders on his own when he's out in the field . . . and when he comes back he simply gives these orders directly to the production department. This is bad for us in Sales because we can't tell how effective we've been. We don't know if we got the order because of him or because we had been developing the same customer over the past few months. By doing things this way we can't tell why the sale was ever made.

LOOKING TO THE FUTURE

For the head of the organization and computing department, 1990 and beyond were going to be exciting years. Istvan was proud to say,

> I've recently convinced top management they should buy the MAS-MCS (Management Accounting System-Management Control System) integrated software package from the British software firm Hoykens. It's being introduced at the Hungarian firms VIDETON, BHG, and SZIM and it's a system that can manage the MIS problems for a company our size—production planning, all the paperwork controls, operations scheduling, and operations finance.

> We bought a used IBM 4361 from a German firm late last year and 70 workstations, as well as some in Nyirbator, are being installed right now. It's the first time we've tried to implement a real integrated management system. It'll cost the company nearly 100 million forints but it should be completed in 1991. If this implementation is successful I'd like to make the department into a separate money-making operation. This would allow us to serve Csepel, keep our own people busy, and help them earn more money.

For Peter Toth, general manager of economic matters, the future was a bit more cloudy. As for Csepel's current situation, he noted the order book was very low in general and even more so for domestic clients. Overall prices were rising, the government was cutting its support for CMEA exports, and optimal production lot sizes have not been established. His suggestions for improving 1990 company performance entailed the following:

- Dismiss 15 percent of all personnel or about 200 employees
- Raise the salaries of all remaining personnel by 20 percent
- Reduce costs in general, including the stock level of various finished goods
- Investigate opportunities for new ruble exports
- Maintain the company's traditionally good relations with its creditors
- Accelerate the rate at which products are delivered to customers
- Find a joint venture partner

APPENDIX A   Csepel Machine Tool Company Balance Sheets (unaudited; millions of forints)

	1988	1989
ASSETS		
Current assets		
Cash	1,139	3,230
Bank account	32,646	16,276
Additional accounts	13,896	–32,949
Bonds	0	0
Domestic buyer	203,731	192,807
Foreign buyer	666,332	978,162
Total current assets	917,744	1,157,526
Employee fund	657	0
State budget fund	0	2,882
Total	870,720	1,173,851

APPENDIX A

	1988	1989
ASSETS (continued)		
Inventories		
Goods in process	192,216	216,533
Finished goods	36,315	23,362
Total	229,687	239,895
Raw material	428,644	678,293
Purchased stocks	123,201	99,229
Total inventories	551,845	777,522
Total	781,532	1,017,417
Contingency fund	0	0
Other active accounts	257,231	45,158
Temporary account	0	0
Total	257,231	45,158
Shares held	6,000	228,000
Assets held	0	0
Foreign investments	6,000	228,000
Fixed plant and equipment	928,097	1,091,681
Less depreciation	735,634	786,716
Plant additions	22,559	82,249
Net book value	215,022	387,214
Total assets	2,177,030	2,838,030
LIABILITIES		
Accounts payable	0	840,399
Domestic deliverer	812,413	188,014
Foreign deliverer	89,070	221,510
Investment deliverer	24,962	12,935
Factoring	30,000	113,810
Creditors	308	36,144
Salaries payable	10,511	17,933
Social security payable	21,747	34,077
Prepaid taxes	−125,762	−33,389
Other accounts	200,270	262,972
Total	1,063,519	1,694,405
Paid-in capital	835,000	835,000
Retained earnings	−99	323,344
Total	834,901	1,158,344
Income tax liability	−35,910	−53,613
Profit account	−3,716	−22,428
Profit	318,236	61,489
Total liabilities	2,177,030	2,838,197

APPENDIX B   *Hungarian Economic Deflators by Activity Segment*

Market	1985	1986	1987	1988	1989[a]
Domestic[b]	100.0	104.4	112.1	111.2	117.4
CMEA[c]	100.0	107.2	110.1	110.1	110.0
Non-CMEA[d]	100.0	116.5	137.3	157.5	177.0

[a]Preliminary estimate by the Central Statistical Office.
[b]Domestic Sales Price Indices—Machine Tool and Machine Equipment Industry, *1988 Statistical Yearbook for Industry* (Budapest: Central Statistical Office, 1988), p.134
[c]Sales in CMEA Relations—Machine Tool and Machine Equipment Industry, *1988 Statistical Yearbook for Industry* (Budapest: Central Statistical Office, 1988), p. 130.
[d]Non-CMEA Foreign Trade Sales Price Indices—Machine Tool and Machine Equipment Industry, *1988 Statistical Yearbook for Industry* (Budapest: Central Statistical Office, 1988) p. 132.

APPENDIX C   *Csepel Machine Tool Company Income Statements (unaudited; thousands of forints)*

	1985	1986	1987	1988	1989
Revenues					
Domestic	484.7	605.8	814.2	567.0	542.5
Exports					
CMEA ruble market	352.8	466.4	694.7	981.4	1,058.9
Hard currency	1,151.0	1,263.6	982.2	898.1	1,016.9
Total	1,988.6	2,335.8	2,491.1	2,446.5	2,618.3
Direct manufacturing cost	1,044.4	1,173.7	1,277.8	1,294.7	1,385.8
Operating profit	944.2	1,162.2	1,213.3	1,151.8	1,232.5
Overhead cost					
Factory overhead	351.2	478.0	478.4	282.0	352.6
Administrative overhead	325.5	293.8	299.2	505.8	689.8
R&D expense	37.3	27.1	81.2	55.7	18.7
Customer service	11.3	16.2	12.5	22.1	17.0
Land rent	4.0	3.7	0.0	0.0	0.0
Miscellaneous	53.4	64.9	70.4	97.1	8.1
Total	782.7	883.7	941.7	962.7	1,086.2
Additional expenses	156.3	129.8	107.4	62.9	137.2
Other income					
Export support	123.0	16.0	60.7	0.0	0.0
Ministry support	2.1	35.7	79.1	129.2	35.1
R&D subsidy	5.0	0.0	51.2	35.7	5.9
Vendor penalties	6.1	2.4	2.4	0.0	3.4
Other	2.5	5.7	3.0	0.0	8.3
Total	138.7	59.8	196.4	164.9	52.7
Profit before taxes	143.9	208.4	360.6	291.1	61.8
Taxes	109.6	133.1	151.4	49.3	.3
Profit after taxes	34.1	75.3	209.2	241.8	61.5

Caterpillar Responds to the Komatsu Challenge in Latin America

ROBERT P. VICHAS, *Texas A&M University*
and **TOMASZ MROCZKOWSKI,** *American University*

Although Caterpillar's presence in Latin America dated to 1914, when the U.S.-based multinational corporation opened its first dealership in Panama, manufacturing in Latin America did not commence until 1960, when the company initiated assembly operations in Brazil, its fourth national market.

A giant in the global construction equipment industry, Caterpillar was challenged in the early 1980s by Komatsu Ltd, a Japanese multinational corporation. Having grown from a weak rival one-tenth the size of Caterpillar in 1961 to the world's second largest supplier of construction equipment, Komatsu confronted Caterpillar on the latter's home turf in the U.S. as Caterpillar had done 20 years earlier in Japan.

In 1988 Komatsu renewed its assault by forming a strategic alliance with Dresser Industries of Dallas, Texas. The Komatsu-Dresser joint venture presented the latest threat to Caterpillar's Latin American markets. Although Caterpillar, with a strategy of competitive renewal and its "plant with a future," had successfully defended itself from Komatsu's strategic thrusts in the 1980s, the U.S. MNC would face a new set of challenges in the 1990s.

CATERPILLAR, INC.

A U.S. multinational corporation headquartered in Peoria, Illinois, Caterpillar could trace its origins to two inventors who, in the late 1800s, independently had developed leading-edge technology of that era. Their inventions led to automation of agricultural production in the state of California. Subsequently the two formed the Caterpillar Tractor Co.

Robert P. Vichas is Professor of International Business, Graduate School of International Trade & Business Administration, Texas A&M International University, and Visiting Scholar and Fulbright Professor, Kaunas Technological University, Panevezys, Lithuania.

This case is not intended to represent either good or bad management practices or decisions of any firm mentioned; it has been designed and organized to facilitate discussion of strategic management principles and illustrate challenges of international business.

Although for years the company had exported its products from the United States, globalization began in 1950 when the firm announced formation of its first foreign subsidiary in the United Kingdom. By the end of the 1950s, it had established manufacturing subsidiaries in the United Kingdom, Australia, and Brazil. Before the end of the 1960s, the MNC had expanded operations into France, Belgium, South Africa, and Mexico, with sales subsidiaries in Europe and the Far East to service those dealerships.

Historically, Caterpillar had led the global construction equipment industry with a strategy of broad and deep market penetration within two main categories of heavy equipment: (a) earthmoving, construction, and materials handling machinery; and (b) engines. Several subsidiaries serviced the Latin American markets.

Caterpillar Americas Co.

To support its 34 dealers who sold Caterpillar machines, engines, lift trucks, paving products, parts, and repair service in Latin America and the Caribbean, Caterpillar Americas Co. (also headquartered in Peoria, Illinois) controlled four district offices.

Two of these district offices were located in Plantation, Florida. The Northern District Office supported dealers in Colombia (1985), Ecuador (1925), French Guiana (1973), Guyana (1975), Netherland Antilles (1987), Suriname (1941), and Venezuela (1927). (Numbers in parentheses represent year dealership was established.) The Caribbean/Central America District Office serviced sixteen dealers, the first of whom was appointed in Panama (1914), the most recent in Jamaica (1987).

In Santiago, Chile, a third district office served dealers in Argentina (1971), Bolivia (1969), Chile (1940), Paraguay (1951), Peru (1942), and Uruguay (1927). Located in Houston, Texas, the fourth district office assisted customers and dealers in Mexico.

Caterpillar Americas Exporting Company (CAMEC)

Yet another subsidiary, CAMEC, called Florida home. The Miami Lakes operation exported Caterpillar parts on behalf of its Latin American and Caribbean dealers. These replacement parts and components might have been manufactured in Latin America, shipped to the United States, and then reexported to still another Latin American country.

Caterpillar World Trading Corporation

Another subsidiary, Caterpillar World Trading Corporation, arranged for the acquisition of Caterpillar products through countertrade or barter for a variety of products. This type of trade permitted Caterpillar to penetrate markets where inconvertibility of foreign currency remained a problem.

Of its fifteen manufacturing plants outside of the United States, both Brazilian and Mexican subsidiaries were wholly owned. The only other Latin American manufacturing plant, an independent manufacturer in Argentina, produced under a licensing agreement with Caterpillar. Altogether, the MNC marketed over 100 models of earthmoving, construction, materials-handling machines, 40 paving/compaction products, 80 lift truck models, and 25 basic engine models.

Brazil

Caterpillar Brazil S.A. (CBSA) opened a parts distribution center in 1954 Santo Amaro. To support Brazilian exports, it initiated assembly operations in 1960. Inaugurated in 1976 in Piracicaba, a second plant manufactured track-type tractors, motor graders, wheel loaders, and scrapers. Brazil represented the MNC's fourth largest national market.[1]

To maintain market dominance, Caterpillar Brazil strengthened its manufacturing presence during the latter 1970s in response to competitive challenges of Komatsu, Dresser Industries, Case, Fiatallis, VME, and TEREX. Caterpillar expanded both manufacturing capacity and product lines. In 1973, it had purchased nearly 1,000 acres of land, about one-half of the new industrial park, Unidade Industrial Unileste, north of Piracicaba, which was the largest land acquisition Caterpillar had ever made outside of the United States.[2]

By 1989, the firm had enlarged the Piracicaba operation to almost 1 million square feet with ambitions nearly to double the physical size again by 1992, at which time it planned to close the Santo Amaro plant. Altogether the two facilities in Brazil employed about 5,000 persons.

CBSA management had to cope not only with the competitive thrusts of Komatsu and Dresser but also with various constraints imposed by Brazilian government policies and regulations, such as local content laws. In order to obtain more duty- and tax-free import privileges, which benefits its competitors were already receiving, CBSA signed an accord with the government in 1980. CBSA agreed to export $2 billion worth of equipment between 1980 and 1990. (Note: All monetary values are stated in U.S. dollars.) The commitment was predicated on projections that domestic and export demand for the 1980s would at least equal or better the 1970s.

However, demand declined. CBSA Project Manager Bill Cook said that the world market for construction equipment collapsed after Caterpillar had entered into the agreement. "Both the export market and the domestic market declined. So we couldn't export what we said we would, nor did we need to import what we thought."

Of the 1980 export pact, CBSA Vice President Don Coonan said, "There was a very real threat there. We had a contractual agreement that we weren't meeting. In fact, it looked like we would only get about 40 percent of that amount. We agreed we ought to have a strategy for CBSA."

Facing a potential penalty of $335 million for not meeting the export target, management had to reevaluate its goals and strategy. Of its several short- and long-term goals, the following ranked highest:

1. Become more cost-effective.
2. Increase management effectiveness.
3. Emphasize quality in the production processes.
4. Develop a more export-driven organization.
5. Comply with local content laws.
6. Meet aggressive market challenges of Komatsu and Dresser.

Several task forces were created. Coonan headed an export task force. Its objective was to increase exports from Brazil. Another group focused on a new strategy for CBSA. They found that CBSA had noncurrent products,

---

[1] "A Letter for Caterpillar Management," (April 1989), p. 4. (Internal document.)

[2] "Cat Unit Merges Brazilian Facilities," *Journal Star* (Peoria, Illinois) (December 10, 1988), p. C9.

volatile demand, complex operations, deteriorating manufacturing facilities, and excess costs.

During the mid-1980s, corporate headquarters had compiled an in-depth study and evaluation of Komatsu. Management reevaluated its Latin American presence. Caterpillar had realized a 16 percent gain for all of Latin America during 1986; much of that headway was attributable to the Brazilian operations. In 1987, corporate headquarters opted to strengthen its commitment in Brazil and support changes required by CBSA.

The new strategy embraced several significant elements. First, the new strategy called for renegotiation of the contract with the Brazilian government. CBSA management succeeded in renegotiating export requirements from $2 billion down to $816 million.

Second, to meet the goal of making CBSA a more export-driven organization, Brazil would become the new world source for scraper bowls (except elevating scrapers). A new motor grader series, as well as the D4H along with a newer model of the track-type tractor, would be dual-sourced with Brazil designated as one of two manufacturing sites. Also, CBSA would manufacture the 3116 engine and countershaft transmission for use in Brazilian-built machines. Over the long term CBSA wanted its exports to account for 35 percent of total sales.

Third, modernization to achieve better cost and quality control became part of the manufacturing plan. Consolidation included expansion of the Piracicaba plant to accommodate increased production. Chuck Gladson, technical director, said, "We upgraded and simplified our processes through use of technology and layout." Factories were reorganized to improve materials handling. Cook said, "We positioned ourselves with new manufacturing philosophies."

Fourth, because cost effectiveness was essential to remain competitive, CBSA planned to reduce the number of different models it built. At that time CBSA built two distinct versions of each model: one for the domestic market that complied with local content requirements, another version for export.

Fifth, in order to increase the allowable volume of products for domestic sale, CBSA intended to improve supplier capabilities in Brazil. Cook said, "We explained to our suppliers that we're looking at things from a world class perspective—that means higher volumes, lower costs and high expectations for quality and reliability from them." Reaching its local content goal would permit CBSA to expand Brazilian sales. Without greater domestic sales, CBSA's earning power would be considerably restricted.

Sixth, to meet efficiency goals, CBSA management reorganized its reporting structure in 1988 to implement consolidation of the two-plant operations. The departments of manufacturing, industrial relations, quality control, and materials at each plant were merged under one department head, who held simultaneous responsibility for the departments in both plants. Management created the new organizational structure in Exhibit 1 to improve accountability and efficiency.

Implementation of the new strategy, consolidation, modernization, and new-product programs was scheduled over a five-year period. However, CBSA faced a number of environmental challenges.

1. A volatile Brazilian market.
2. Inflation of 1,000 percent a year.

EXHIBIT 1

Partial Organization Chart of CBSA, 1988

Technical Director Chuck Gladson	Administrative Director Luiz Palotino	Logistics Director Jose Ribiero Cunha Netto	Finance Director Carlos Alberto Serafini	Commercial Director Tony Walker
—Manufacturing —Planning —Plant Engineering & Tooling —Quality	—Employee Relations —Human Resources —Communications —Tax & Legal —AQI	—Purchasing —Production & Scheduling Control —Data Processing	—Accounting —Auditing —Business Economics —Treasury	—Business Units —Sales & Dealer Administration —Export & Finance —Market Support —Parts Distribution

SOURCE: "A Letter for Caterpillar Management," (April 1989), p. 3.

---

3. Price controls that limited prices of final outputs but not necessarily the cost of raw material inputs and labor.
4. Government-owned and -protected industries.
5. Brazilian debt crisis that restricted availability of foreign exchange for imports and profit repatriation.
6. Local content regulations.
7. A massive governmental bureaucracy.
8. Political uncertainty and capital flight.
9. An aggressive foreign competitor, Komatsu.

On the positive side, Brazil, the world's seventh largest economy with abundant natural resources, offered potential opportunities in mining, agricultural and construction markets, as well as growing infrastructure needs. Brazil had the highest developed industrial structure in South America; many MNCs considered it a potentially attractive investment; and should Brazil resolve its political and fiscal problems, established companies would have first crack at newly emerging opportunities. However, even from a perspective of late 1988, realization of market projections were subject to considerable variance. Since uncertainties continued into 1989 for Brazil, Mexico seemed to offer greater promise.

Mexico

During the early part of the decade of the 1980s, the U.S. MNC suffered a precipitous decline in Mexican sales due in part to lower oil prices. (Mexico was a net exporter of petroleum, an important generator of foreign exchange.) Caterpillar blamed a challenging economic environment, high foreign debt, and high interest rates in the U.S. for its problems in Latin America.

Despite operating losses, Caterpillar preserved a strong relationship with its Mexican dealers in Chihuahua (1945), Monterrey (1981), Ciudad Obregon (1929), Mexico City (1926), and Guadalajara (1974). This established dealership network was costly to sustain. Caterpillar typically turned around requests for parts within 48 hours—an important consideration in the purchase of heavy equipment—and offered service that competitors could not always match. In addition to its dealerships, the firm maintained manufacturing facilities in Monterrey.

Of Caterpillar's seven wholly owned foreign subsidiaries, two were located in Latin America: one in Brazil, the other, Conek SA de CV, in Mexico. For the first time in company history Caterpillar had accepted a minority interest of 49 percent in a joint venture formed in 1981 with the Mexican chemical producer, CYDSA, which owned the other 51 percent of Conek. The name, Conek, derived from two words: construction plus equipment. Caterpillar believed that a partnership with CYDSA was a good match; CYDSA had operations throughout Mexico; and Mexican law required a local partner.

Caterpillar had decided to locate the plant in Monterrey, Nuevo Leon, for several reasons.

1. CYDSA recommended the location.
2. Monterrey was the second largest industrial city in Mexico.
3. It was near raw material sources: natural gas, steel, and trained labor and technical people educated at Monterrey Institute of Technology.
4. There was stability of state and local governments.
5. Fewer labor problems arose here than in some border areas where organized labor had disrupted work.
6. The work ethic and business philosophy seemed more akin to the U.S.

With the crash of the Mexican economy in 1982, CYDSA found itself under financial constraints due to its U.S. dollar-denominated debts and wanted to divest its interest in Conek. Caterpillar searched for a new Mexican partner. Partners which Caterpillar preferred had insufficient capital; those who came forward with sufficient capital Caterpillar did not want. Consequently, in December 1983, Caterpillar requested exemption from Mexican law and permission from the government for 100 percent ownership of the subsidiary. (Note: Current Mexican law allows 100 percent foreign ownership; however, for foreign investments exceeding $100 million, the foreign investor must have a Mexican partner.)

In August 1984 the government gave its permission for the company to assume 100 percent ownership of its Mexican subsidiary. In November 1984 Caterpillar completed the transaction and acquired CYDSA's interest in Conek; in that month Conek became a wholly owned subsidiary of Caterpillar, Inc. in Peoria, Illinois. Until that point in time, Conek's operations had been essentially an assembly plant. Beginning in early 1985, the subsidiary began full-scale manufacturing to produce components and parts primarily for sale to the United States.

Conek chiefly shipped its output to corporate headquarters in Illinois or to other Caterpillar sales companies in the United States for reexport. By mid-1989, export production at Conek was about 40 percent finished products and 40 percent components and replacement parts; the remaining 20 percent of manufacture was destined for production of lift trucks and parts for the Mexican market. Local content varied according to the product; heavy manufactures requiring substantial steel usage might have 99 percent local content.

Products were transported by truck to Texas. Ing. Adan J. Pena Guerrero, treasury manager at Conek, said that by clearing customs in Monterrey prior to shipment, the paperwork required about 24 hours versus three days at the Texas border. He also said that with anticipated construction of the Colombia

Bridge between Nuevo Leon and Texas, built exclusively for the expedient movement of exports and imports, the new 10-mile bridge near Laredo would save the firm considerable time and money. Currently, strong labor unions required expensive and time-consuming off-loading and reloading to cross the border. Additionally, the Mexican government sought private investors to construct a 15-mile toll highway direct to the bridge to bypass Nuevo Laredo.

Caterpillar maintained three industrial locations near Monterrey. Nearly 3.3 million square feet, the main manufacturing plant sat on 272 acres of industrial land. A second location, used for parts warehousing and some electronics manufacture, comprised almost 100 acres; a third site at Santa Catarina was about half that size.

With a 1989 total of 1700 office and plant workers (whose average age was 23) on a three-shift schedule, Conek operated at full capacity. Ing. Pena Guerrero proudly pointed out that office workers followed the American system of 8:00 to 5:00 with a 30-minute lunch break in the plant cafeteria. He said, "Most office employees usually arrive 15 or 20 minutes before 8 and do not leave until 10 or 15 minutes after 5." This contrasted sharply with Mexico City where the workday traditionally might begin at 9:00, with a two-hour mid-afternoon lunch, and end at 7:00 P.M.

Although Ing. Pena Guerrero was born in Monterrey, he preferred the efficiency of a U.S.-styled system. He had earned his M.S. degree in engineering at the Monterrey Institute of Technology (ITSEM), a private university, and an M.B.A. from the University of Wisconsin at Milwaukee. At age 31, he managed five supervisors and a total of 42 employees over whom he kept a watchful eye. He reported directly to another Mexican, Juan Gamez, finance manager, who, in turn, reported to the general manager, Jim Palmer.

Conek paid plant workers slightly above market rates and generated employee loyalty and cooperation by:

1. Using a complaint and suggestion box, to which management usually reacted within one week.
2. Publishing a monthly employee newsletter, titled, "Conexion."
3. Holding periodic one-hour plant-wide meetings to inform employees of news, progress, and events.
4. Maintaining close supervision over all employees.
5. Creating an intense training program to improve quality and productivity.
6. Offering free bus service to employees from the city to the plant.

Because the manufacturing facility was some distance from urban Monterrey, a daily bus picked up employees at designated points and times. Several advantages derived from this program:

1. Employee costs for transportation were reduced.
2. People arrived at work on time.
3. Riders could either rest or develop friendships during the ride.
4. Employees were less likely to talk casually with unionized workers from other plants.

The training program helped achieve goals of greater productivity (lower costs of production) and higher quality. For example, welders must be adept at using a technique not employed in typical manufacturing. Conek required an intense six-week training course. Pena said that Conek had sent some employees to Texas for special welding training. After two weeks the welding school had sent them back to Mexico, because Conek had already trained them better for specific tasks than the school could. Pena added, "Conek also pays employees for college courses and for M.B.A. degrees."

Conek used Just-in-Time (JIT) inventory control and Duran Quality Control techniques. To resolve minor problems at the shop level, small quality control (QC) circles were activated. For larger problems Conek employed an annual quality improvement program (QIP), which, according to Pena, excelled over QC. Functioning like a task force, QIP focused on specific problems and on how to save money. All this effort had paid off for the manufacturer. Pena said, "Conek has had no delivery or quality problems [since 1986]."

In Mexico, Caterpillar's chief competitor, Komatsu, was number two in the construction equipment market. Clark Equipment ranked as an unimportant third-place competitor, and all remaining competitors together represented only a minor threat to Caterpillar.

Conek and its parent had many strengths: It was well established in the market. It maintained a costly dealership network. It had built an international reputation. Its trademark, CAT, and the distinct yellow color of its equipment were instantly recognizable. Conek, as one of several sourcing points for components in a worldwide network, was assured of continued demand for its manufactures. Additionally, in its manufacture of finished products and components, Conek:

1. Used a high grade heavy steel, from a Mexican source, not readily available everywhere.
2. Maintained very good relations with its local steel supplier and had experienced no sourcing problems.
3. Manufactured high-quality products which required less refabrication, and, therefore, lowered overall costs.
4. Tested all equipment thoroughly at the plant site and before shipment.
5. Maintained careful quality control in its highly integrated operations.
6. Insisted upon quality workmanship (e.g., welding) not necessarily found in all competing products.
7. Achieved good cost control and continued to strive for higher productivity to maintain price competitiveness.

Financially, the operation had not achieved payback of investment, due to large start-up costs. A typical payback period in this industry would be on the order of 10 to 15 years. CYDSA, Conek's former partner, used payback projections of 18 years. By taking advantage of its experience curve, training employees for quality and productivity, and achieving a careful mix of exports and imports, Caterpillar expected to shorten the payback period of its Mexican subsidiary.

To test possibilities of diversification, Conek modestly invested in a small plant to assemble tractor electronics. The project had not been financially successful, due, in part, to sourcing problems for electronic chips. Its foreign source provided chips only twice yearly, which generated an inventory problem between overinvesting in inventory or a stock-out which would shut down the production line. The chip manufacturer needed longer production runs to bring down its costs. Since Conek was not a major purchaser, it has little influence on the supplier.

In early 1989 Peter Donis, president of Caterpillar, had said that profitability was constrained by higher material costs, higher start-up costs incurred by the factory modernization program, and higher-than-expected short-term interest rates to finance working capital needs.

Nevertheless, with a turnaround in the Mexican economy expected by 1990, Caterpillar anticipated an increase in sales of construction machinery. The new president of Mexico seemed to have considerable popular support for his economic development strategy, which was to: (a) open the economy to foreign competition; (b) privatize most public enterprises; (c) move toward creating a market economy; and (d) encourage foreign direct investment. Despite Caterpillar's aggressive stance, Komatsu's yellow (in imitation of CAT products) bulldozers could be seen excavating sites for construction of new commercial buildings in the heart of Monterrey, not many miles from Caterpillar's production facilities.

KOMATSU, LTD.

Caterpillar's chief competitor was the Japanese multinational corporation, Komatsu Ltd. Within most Latin American markets, Caterpillar and Komatsu's other competitors were frequently a distant number three or four in a particular country, often market spoilers; but altogether they did account for a respectable volume of business. Komatsu had to concern itself not only with Caterpillar but also with those competitors whose presence in individual markets was most threatening to the Japanese firm.

Originating as the Takeuchi Mining Factory in 1894, Komatsu Ltd. manufactured and marketed a full line of construction equipment, industrial presses, and machinery such as robots and laser machines to customers in over 150 countries. The parent organization of the Komatsu Group, comprised of 60 affiliated companies, Komatsu Ltd., maintained world headquarters in Tokyo, Japan.

Komatsu had faced a major crisis in 1961 when Caterpillar announced a joint venture in Japan with Mitsubishi Heavy Industries Ltd. With one-tenth the sales of Caterpillar, Komatsu recognized that survival was problematic unless the prices and quality of its products were competitive. Komatsu signed a license agreement with Cummins Engine Inc. (U.S.) to manufacture and sell diesel engines, and subsequently entered into several other joint venture agreements with U.S. firms (which were later terminated).

Nevertheless, Komatsu did not establish its first foreign subsidiary until 1967: N.V. Komatsu Europe S.A. in Belgium. Global expansion began in earnest with the creation of Komatsu America Corp. and the establishment of Brazilian and German subsidiaries. Bulldozer production commenced at Komatsu do Brasil in 1975, at Dina Komatsu Nacional S.A. in Mexico in 1976, and at P.T. Komatsu Indonesia in 1983.

Brazil

Formed in 1970 in Sao Paulo, Komatsu do Brasil initiated the first overseas bulldozer production in 1975. In those early years the Brazilian operation did not figure prominently in Komatsu's corporate global plans, and it had not been successful financially. Because corporate net income in 1983 had declined about 20 percent from 1982, management blamed the Brazilian subsidiary for a significant share of those corporate losses and attributed them to unfavorable economic conditions in Brazil.

Of Third World countries, Shoji Nogawa (president of Komatsu) wrote: "Developing Countries, also important markets for the industry, generally experienced economic difficulties, with their burdens of extensive debt further aggravated by the high level of U.S. interest rates."[3] (The Middle East had been Komatsu's most important foreign market.)

Corporate management said, in 1985, "Internationalization for Komatsu means not only establishing more efficient corporate management in overseas marketplaces but, more importantly, pursuing more effective customer-focused operations as the Company continues to expand its worldwide customer portfolio."[4] Despite management's stated commitment to globalization, the firm continued to manufacture principally in Japan for export to its foreign markets. Even as late as 1986, foreign manufacturing represented only 5 percent of company total, while 95 percent of manufacturing was still done in Japan.

Then, in 1987, under leadership of Komatsu's new corporate president, Masao Tanaka, the company sped up globalization of its operations. Setting a new target, management wanted foreign manufacturing to account for 35 percent of total production and pushed to integrate its manufacturing bases in Brazil, Mexico, and Indonesia into a framework of strategically defined roles.

Mexico

Komatsu's Mexican subsidiary, Dina Komatsu Nacional, SA de CV, also experienced a change during 1987 when the Japanese MNC's share in this joint venture rose from 40 to 68 percent ownership.[5] Dina Komatsu Nacional, a joint venture with Nacional Financiera, the government-owned Mexican development bank, began to manufacture bulldozers in 1976; but it produced no profit in its nearly 13-year history. The Mexican government, under President Salinas de Gotari, had been trying to privatize much of the public sector and divest itself of unprofitable joint ventures. Although the government's investment in Komatsu had been on the sale block since early 1988, potential private investors showed little interest in the offer.

Primarily, Komatsu's global strategy had been one of export development. The Mexican venture figured in a defensive move to counter Caterpillar in Mexico. Perceiving the Mexican market as a subunit of the larger North and South American market, Komatsu chose to do battle on U.S. soil and in 1988 sought to strengthen its presence in the Americas' markets with a joint venture (JV).

The United States

Management of the world's second largest integrated maker of construction machinery stated that competitive strength "lies in its versatile technological base and its tradition of quality first." Entry into the U.S. construction equipment market was a cornerstone in Komatsu's global market penetration strategy.[6]

---

[3]Komatsu *Annual Report 1983*, p. 3.

[4]Komatsu *Annual Report 1984*, p. 10.

[5]"Komatsu Raises Stake in Mexico Venture," *Japanese Economic Journal*, v. 25 (August 29, 1987), p. 6.

[6]"Komatsu Digs Deeper into the U.S.," *Business Week* (September 22, 1985).

When Komatsu opened its manufacturing facility in Chattanooga, Tennessee, in 1985, it had an 8 percent share of the U.S. market, which it had hoped to double. Nobuo Murai, president of Komatsu America Corp., said, "Our goal is a market share of 15 percent in the near term and 20-to-25 percent in the long term."[7] Komatsu faced increasing obstacles in its exports to the United States due to the depreciated value of the dollar coupled with trade conflict issues between the U.S. and Japan.

In 1988 Masao Tanaka (corporate president) wrote: "Strategically, we are committed to establish a competitive operational system on a global scale, by setting up a worldwide manufacturing/sales network capable of flexibly and effectively responding to changes in the economic climate.[8]

To strengthen its competitive position in both North and South America, Komatsu and Texas-based Dresser Industries, Inc. announced in February 1988 the formation of a strategic alliance in which the two companies would combine their construction equipment manufacturing and engineering facilities in the U.S., Canada, and Latin America. Operationalized September 1, 1988, the 50–50 JV, Komatsu Dresser Company, constituted an initial capitalization of $200 million for machinery and automation plus $50 million to refurbish manufacturing plants. Sales for 1989 were projected at $1.5 billion. The strategic alliance also called for the creation of Komatsu Dresser Finance Division to finance sales to both wholesale and retail customers.[9]

Essential elements of the agreement were: Komatsu and Dresser would share equally in the management of Komatsu Dresser, which had exclusive manufacturing and marketing rights for North, Central, and South America. The JV also would distribute replacement parts, engage in engineering, and establish training and test centers as well as sales and administrative offices.[10]

The new alliance also required consolidation of three foreign subsidiaries—Komatsu America Corp., Komatsu America Manufacturing Corp., and Komatsu do Brasil—together with Dresser's Construction Equipment and Haulpak Divisions and Dresser's manufacturing subsidiary in Brazil. Of this 1988 joint venture, Komatsu management wrote:

> The venture clearly symbolizes one successful outcome of Komatsu's internationalization strategy to establish the three-core comprehensive operations in Japan, the U.S. and Europe. It also advances Komatsu's commitment to further promote international cooperation with other firms for mutual business expansion as an equal partner.[11] [p. 8]

Based in Libertyville, Illinois, a Chicago suburb, Komatsu Dresser Company began operations in late 1988 with 5,000 workers employed at eight plants in the United States, Canada, and Brazil. It had more than 3.5 million square feet of factory space. One of these plants, the Haulpak Division (which produced mining trucks), was only 22 blocks down Adams Street from Caterpillar's Peoria, Illinois, corporate headquarters.

The new strategic alliance allowed Komatsu to shift much final assembly from Japan to the Americas and fight the battle for Brazil and the rest of Latin

[7]Clyde Farnsworth, "Chattanooga Reviving Itself with Foreign Capital," *Chattanooga Times* (October 18, 1985).

[8]Komatsu [Quarterly] *Financial Report* (March 31, 1988), p. 2.

[9]*The Wall Street Journal* (August 18, 1988).

[10]"Dresser, Komatsu Form Joint Venture," *Pit & Quarry* (March 1988), p. 121.

[11]Komatsu *Annual Report 1987*.

America right in Illinois. The new company would become number two in the Americas in the construction equipment industry.

FIGHTING FOR MARKET DOMINANCE

When battle lines between the two firms were drawn in 1961, Komatsu developed Total Quality Control (TQC) to become competitive in price and quality, broadened its product offerings to match Caterpillar's, reduced manufacturing costs, increased exports, and, by 1980, became recognized as the world's second largest manufacturer of construction machinery. It dominated the Japanese market with a 60 percent share.

Generally, in every country-market the Japanese had entered in recent decades, they applied a market-share pricing strategy, which meant using a low entry price to build market share and, in the long run, dominate the targeted market. However, shifts in exchange rates and the debt-laden economies of Brazil and Mexico dampened that success pattern for Komatsu.

Komatsu's exports to the U.S. had doubled in 1983. Its world market share rose to around 20 percent; and its U.S. market share had been expanded to 8 percent by the mid-1980s. The Japanese firm had managed to boost volume by 40 percent with very little escalation in employment by the heavy application of robotics. Management was spending $80 million a year alone on automation while continuing to diversify products in order to become a major producer of automated production systems and robots. By 1985, the firm had erected three large R & D laboratories, established five foreign production facilities—including a plant in the United States and in the United Kingdom—and added plastics, electronics, robots, metal presses, and other products to its line.

Prior to 1985 a high dollar exchange rate and price-cutting strategy gave Komatsu a 40 percent price advantage over Caterpillar. Its export ratio was 64 percent. But environmental factors swung against Komatsu. The dollar-yen relationship turned in favor of the dollar. Due to the strong yen, export-oriented Komatsu had to raise prices by 18 percent in 1986, while Caterpillar raised their prices an average 3 percent, the first increase since 1984; Komatsu lost 2 percent market share to Caterpillar. Komatsu's 1986 profits plummeted by 33 percent, exports fell nearly 5 percent, and in 1987 its president, Shoji Nogawa, resigned in the midst of unfavorable rumors. Komatsu's battle cry had been MARU 'C' (or encircle CAT) to put Caterpillar in a defensive position. However, Caterpillar maintained a solid financial position, held significant leadership in many areas of construction equipment technology, and by its size and global network was well positioned to take an offensive, rather than a defensive, position. Management initiated a strategic analysis.

Asked to assess strengths and weaknesses of Caterpillar and Komatsu, middle managers from various functional activities developed a comparative competitive analysis between Japan and the U.S. By rating the two firms on a seven-point scale, they developed comparative analysis on 17 factors. Professors Tomasz Mroczkowski and Marek Wermus tabulated the summary of responses appearing in Exhibit 2. On the seven-point scale, a rating of one was most favorable to Komatsu; a rating of seven, most favorable to Caterpillar. The arithmetic mean represented the management group's averages. Additional statistics are included in the table.

Caterpillar's managers perceived Komatsu as operating in a lower labor cost environment and enjoying access to lower cost capital, a cooperative in-

EXHIBIT 2

Komatsu vs. Caterpillar: Competitive Advantages as Perceived by U.S. Executives

(Summary of Responses)

Area	Advantage/Sample Mean (KOMATSU 1-3 / CATERPILLAR 4-7)	$S_{\bar{x}}$	Mc	M
1. Cooperative labor-management relations	1.52	.16	1.25	1.00 (18)
2. Cooperative business government relations	1.59	.15	1.34	1.00 (16)
3. Labor costs	1.82	.26	1.34	1.00 (16)
4. Workforce trained in stat & quality control	2.07	.17	2.05	2.00 (10)
5. Strong organizational culture	2.22	.25	1.02	1.00 (11)
6. Pressure of management for short-term profit	2.64	.26	2.43	2.00 (7)
7. Better trained blue-collar	2.92	.32	3.69	4.00 (8)
8. Capital charges	3.32	.27	3.68	4.00 (11)
9. Responses to international markets	3.65	.29	3.79	4.00 (7)
10. Better trained white-collar	3.67	.32	3.60	4.00 (8)
11. Overall management	4.04	.25	4.06	4.00 (8)
12. Superior marketing intelligence	4.52	.36	4.63	4.00 (6)
13. Modern equipment & machinery	4.78	.21	4.71	4.00 (17)
14. Advanced manufacturing technology	5.15	.28	5.64	6.00 (17)
15. Product research & development	5.78	.19	5.94	6.00 (17)
16. Technologically more advanced products	5.96	.16	6.03	6.00 (16)
17. Superior design & product development capabilities	6.00	.21	6.13	6.00 (12)

SOURCE: Tomasz Mroczkowski and Marek Wermus, "Improving Competitiveness Survey."

dustry-government relationship, a cooperative labor force that had extensive skills in statistical process control, and that Komatsu's managers were not under pressures to produce short-term profits.

Caterpillar's managers saw their own superiority in design and product development, R & D, technological level of products, and a worldwide reputation for quality products supported by a dealer network.

To counteract Komatsu's drive, Caterpillar reduced production capacity 25 percent, cut inventories 37 percent, slimmed down its labor force, and closed plants. With plant closures Caterpillar was no longer a vertically integrated company. It defended market share with deep price discounts, and offered smaller machines to smaller-sized contractors. The heart of the turnaround decision was to (a) cut operating costs by 22 percent; (b) give more price authority to local managers; and (c) diversify into other product areas.

PLANT WITH A FUTURE

In October 1986, Caterpillar President Peter Donis said:

> Although we've reduced costs by more than 20 percent, we're not stopping there. We've returned to profitability, but we expect cost and price pressures to continue. Our costs are still 15-to-10 percent higher than our foreign competitor's, and in spite of the dollar weakening, transaction prices for our products are about the same now that they were in 1981. So, Caterpillar's long-term profitability will not be secure until we do, in fact, become the industry's low cost producer. We've developed a strategy for achieving the additional cost reduction. We call it our Plant with a Future.[12]

For Caterpillar, the Plant with a Future (PWAF) concept portrayed in Exhibit 3 embraced all elements of manufacturing as well as product design, supplier relationships, and logistics. Although this new manufacturing strategy went beyond simple cost cutting, its implementation and integration of facilities would continue for the rest of this century. At the heart of PWAF was automation, new factory layouts, and continuous work flow. Caterpillar Executive Vice President, Pierre Gueridon, said, "We believe computer-integrated manufacturing is our supreme weapon for cost reduction. It's the area where we have the largest long term advantage over the Japanese."

Based on a cell manufacturing concept, plants and equipment were arranged to process families of components from start to finish. For example, machining, welding, heat treating, and painting might all be functions within a single cell. Work flow was continuous. Since all cells fed the assembly line just in time, it required JIT delivery to the cells. Immediate objectives were to simplify and integrate.

Computer integrated manufacturing (CIM) linked self-contained manufacturing cells (i.e., independent islands of automation) to a material, tooling, and information network to allow for electronic communication between engineering, logistics, and the factory floor. By the next decade, interplant communication would be routine through a corporate information center coupled with global marketing and financial data bases. With complete implementation of the strategy and integration of operations, all systems, from the plant's host computer to personal computers on the shop floor, could com-

---

[12]Speech by Peter Donis at the General Electric/Northwestern University Executive Dialog Series on October 14, 1986.

EXHIBIT 3

PWAF and Its Three Basic Components

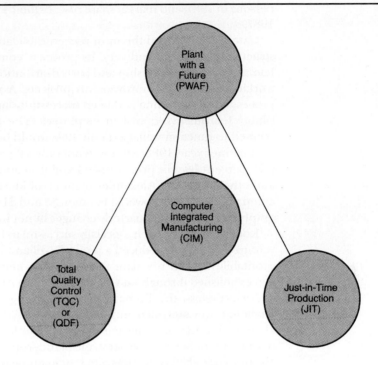

municate to result in unprecedented coordination and optimization of all manufacturing functions: supplier delivery, scheduling of equipment, tooling, quality control, maintenance, and troubleshooting.

Gueridon said, "At our Gosselies [Belgium] plant, for example, we expect PWAF changes to result in a 22 percent reduction in material costs and a 31 percent reduction in labor costs by 1990."

Conek, the Mexican subsidiary, exemplified successful execution of this new strategy. Management implemented JIT and Duran quality control techniques, small QC circles at the shop level, and an annual QIP to resolve bigger challenges. Critical to success at Monterrey were cost and quality control.

On the other hand, CBSA, the Brazilian subsidiary, best reflected "gradualism": Caterpillar's chief approach to automation and implementation of the PWAF. PWAF automation was conceived as a self-financing program with highest priorities for capital investments. Funds generated from reduced inventories and improvement in efficiencies would finance these investments. Caterpillar management expected its manufacturing plants to migrate from present systems, to a hybrid system, and to end up with PWAF, a purely customer-driven manufacturing philosophy.

RETURN TO PROFITABILITY AND A NEW CHALLENGE

The Japanese invader was not invincible. Komatsu's exports decreased because most were dollar-dominated; and the dollar was overpriced in terms of yen. Its profits fell by a third in 1986.

On the other hand, Caterpillar's competitive position sharply improved. Profits in 1986 were $76 million ($0.77 per share), and, in 1987, $350 million ($3.51 per share). Sales were up; employment at Caterpillar increased by 732 persons in 1987; and market share rose. Exhibit 4 depicts global market shares in 1987.

Caterpillar still had the most recognizable and respected name in the construction equipment industry. Its products commanded a price premium. It had a worldwide dealership and parts distribution network. Project teams were working on quality improvements projects. A massive program of statistical process control training had been successfully launched to transfer the responsibility for quality control to employees. The PWAF strategy, now in place, seemed to function well. Certainly 1988 would be a good and trouble-free year.

A banner year, 1988, witnessed not only a 25 percent rise in revenue but also a 76 percent leap in profits. (See Exhibits 5 and 6 for summary financial data and other statistics.) Alexander Blanton, of Merrill Lynch, said, "I estimate the company's earnings power at between $8 and $10 per share by 1990." Exhibit 7 graphically illustrates quarterly changes in net income during the decade.

Komatsu had not been especially successful in Latin America. Its Mexican joint venture had never produced a profit. Brazilian losses severely affected corporate profitability. It did not have the dealership network that Caterpillar had long ago established throughout Central and South America as well as the Caribbean.

Nevertheless, the Komatsu Dresser strategic alliance presented a serious challenge to Caterpillar in Latin America. With both Komatsu and Dresser, along with Caterpillar, having a strong manufacturing presence in Brazil, this market might become the strategic battleground for Latin America. Although all companies had older, less efficient manufacturing facilities, Caterpillar had already initiated its program of modernization to cut costs, improve quality, and consolidate product line—the PWAF strategy.

In its 1988 JV agreement, Komatsu would give up to $300 million to Dresser to upgrade factories, which prior to the agreement had been running at 50

EXHIBIT 4

Estimated Shares of World Construction Machinery Sales, 1987

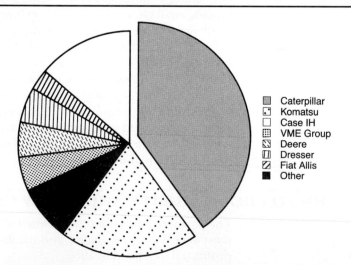

- Caterpillar
- Komatsu
- Case IH
- VME Group
- Deere
- Dresser
- Fiat Allis
- Other

EXHIBIT 5

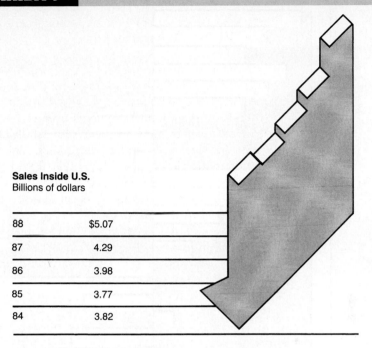

Sales Inside U.S.
Billions of dollars

88	$5.07
87	4.29
86	3.98
85	3.77
84	3.82

EXHIBIT 6

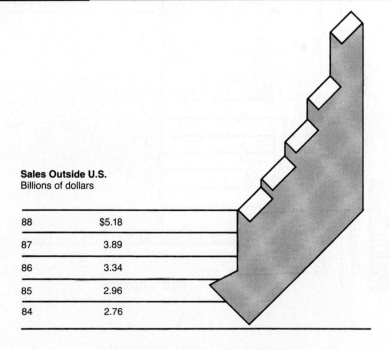

Sales Outside U.S.
Billions of dollars

88	$5.18
87	3.89
86	3.34
85	2.96
84	2.76

EXHIBIT 7

Caterpillar Quarterly Net Income

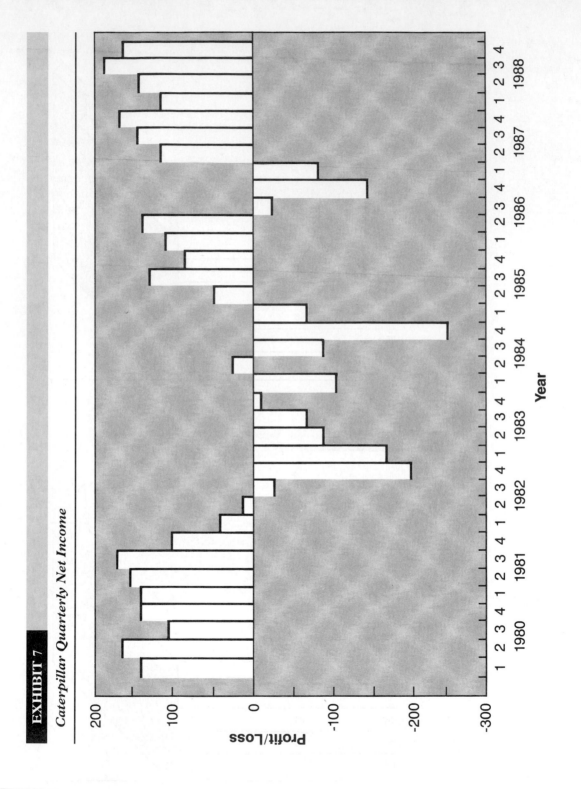

percent capacity. Although both Komatsu and Dresser continued to introduce new products, they maintained separate, yet competing, dealerships.

By July 1989, Caterpillar had registered strong gains in sales outside of the U.S.; approximately 52 percent of business now derived from foreign sources. (See data in Exhibits 5 and 6 for foreign versus domestic sales, 1984–1988.) Global revenues of $5.7 billion marked a 15 percent increase over the comparable six-month period in 1988. Net income for the first half of 1989 of $282 million resulted in $2.78 profit per share of common stock compared to $2.60 per share the first six months of 1988. Employment rose to 60,881.[13]

Early 1989 recorded no further major changes in the Latin American environments for either MNC. Considerable uncertainty reined in most key Latin American markets. Argentina experienced yet another economic crisis as a new president was about to assume office. Peru's hyperinflation and communist terrorism produced a chaotic situation as the country entered a campaign year for the presidency. Brazil's economic condition continued to deteriorate; national elections were scheduled for late 1989. The most stable economies appeared to be Chile, which had successfully implemented a program partially consistent with free market philosophy, and Mexico, which was trying to move toward a market economy. Chile would elect a new president by year's end; and Mexico's president was still in the first half of his term.

Caterpillar had parried Komatsu's strategic thrust but not without difficulties. For instance, for the three-year 1986–1988 period, decreases in production costs fell short of the targeted 5 percent annual rate of reduction. Part of the problem could be attributed to translation losses due to unfavorable swings in foreign exchange rates. During 1989 the PWAF program experienced cost overruns exceeding $300 million. Uncertainty still characterized Latin American markets. A new competitor, Komatsu Dresser Company, was in training for yet another round. In early 1989, the Strategic Planning Committee, comprised of senior managers from various functional areas, was charged with the task of evaluating strategic options for the 1990s. The challenge to Caterpillar continued.

APPENDIX   *Summary Financial Data and Other Statistics for Caterpillar*

EXHIBIT 8

Caterpillar Consolidated Financial Position at December 31, 19— (in millions of U.S. dollars)

ITEM	1980	1981	1982	1983	1984	1985	1986	1987	1988
Current assets	2933	3544	3433	3383	2915	2982	3363	4006	5317
Intangible assets	—	147	117	99	96	77	60	47	71
Other fixed assets	3165	3594	3651	3486	3212	2957	2865	3578	4198
TOTAL ASSETS	6098	7285	7201	6968	6223	6016	6288	7631	9686
Current liabilities	1711	2369	1197	1576	1939	1742	2180	2758	3435
Long-term debt	955	1059	2508	2055	1432	1206	959	1308	2138
Equity	3432	3657	3496	3337	2852	3068	3149	3565	4113
TOTAL DEBT/EQUITY	6098	7285	7201	6968	6223	6016	6288	7631	9686

[13]Caterpillar 1989 Quarterly Financial Reports.

EXHIBIT 9

Consolidated Income Statement at December 31, 19—(in millions of dollars)

ITEM	1980	1981	1982	1983	1984	1985	1986	1987	1988
Revenue	8598	9154	6469	5424	6576	6725	7321	8180	10,255
Operating profit	831	903	(253)	(310)	(339)	233	137	498	924
Net profit (loss)	565	579	(180)	(345)	(428)	198	76	350	616
Dividends per share of common stock ($)	2.325	2.40	2.40	1.50	1.25	0.50	0.50	0.50	0.75
Average number of employees	86,350	83,455	73,249	58,402	61,624	53,616	53,731	54,463	60,558

SOURCE: Figures derived from annual reports.

CASE PART VIII

Strategic Management—
Social and Ethical
Dimensions

The Boston YWCA: 1991

DONNA M. GALLO, *University of Massachusetts—Amherst,*
BARBARA GOTTFRIED, *Bentley College,*
and **ALAN N. HOFFMAN,** *Bentley College*

In the summer of 1991 Mary Kinsell, controller and chief financial officer for the Boston YWCA, briefed her successor, Carolyn Rosen, and Marti Wilson-Taylor, the YWCA's new Executive Director. Deeply aware of the organization's financial crisis, Kinsell noted that the past 20 years had created many difficulties for the once predominant Boston YWCA. Especially pressing was the need to seek out new sources of funding because of significant cuts in federal funding to non-profits, increased demand and competition in the fitness and day-care industries, and increased real estate costs. In addition, the YWCA faced questions about how to deal with several aging YWCA buildings, located in prime neighborhoods of Boston but unmodernized and slowly deteriorating. Ms. Kinsell warned, "The Boston YWCA is like a dowager from an old Boston family that has seen better days: it is 'building rich' and 'cash poor.' Leveraging equity from its buildings is difficult and making operations generate enough cash flow to maintain the buildings seems almost impossible." The YWCA must now meet these challenges or it will be forced to cut back its activities, and may even face bankruptcy.

THE FIRST 100 YEARS

The Young Women's Christian Association (YWCA) is a non-profit organization whose original mission was "To provide for the physical, moral, and spiritual welfare of young women in Boston." For more than 12 decades it has done just that: meeting the changing needs of women in the community by providing services, opportunities, and support in an environment of shared sisterhood.

In 1866, a group of affluent women formed the Boston Young Women's Christian Association to rent rooms to women and children whom the Indus-

---

*The authors would like to thank Mary Kinsell, Carolyn Rosen, Juanita Wade and Gail Healy for their valuable contributions to this project.

trial Revolution had forced to leave their failing farms for work in city factories. Not only were their working conditions deplorable, but their living conditions consisted almost entirely of unsafe slums and unsanitary tenements. The Boston YWCA offered a clean, safe alternative to these living conditions, as well as recreation, companionship, and an employment referral network for women. The success of the facility led to the opening of the Berkeley Residence (40 Berkeley Street, Boston) in 1884, with accommodations for 200 residents and an employment and training bureau. It also housed the first YWCA gymnasium in America, a crucial part of its mission to "empower women through fitness, health care, and independent employment opportunities." At this early date in the YWCA's history, most of the funding for the YWCA's facilities and services was raised by wealthy women patrons both through their family connections and from among their friends and acquaintances. From its inception, the YWCA, unlike the larger, more well-known, and more aggressive YMCA, which easily garnered bank loans and donations, had to struggle to fund its projects.

In the ensuing decades, the Boston YWCA opened The School of Domestic Science to train women as institutional housekeepers and managers, and started a secretarial training program, and other training and educational programs for women. In 1911, the Boston YWCA became affiliated with the other YWCA's in the United States. By this time, the YWCA was no longer merely a philanthropic association run by upper class women for women of a lower class, but an association of working women meeting the needs of other working women in the home and in the marketplace. Nevertheless, the continued support of wealthy patrons was crucial to the YWCA's viability as a community resource.

In the early 1920s, the "Y" initiated a capital campaign under the slogan, "Every Girl Needs the YWCA," to raise funds for another building. Over $1 million in contributions was received by subscription from among donors of both the middle and upper classes, and in 1927 ground was broken at the corner of Clarendon and Stuart Streets for the Boston YWCA's new headquarters. The new building, including recreational facilities, a swimming pool, classrooms, meeting rooms, and offices for the staff, was dedicated in 1929 and has served as headquarters for the association ever since.

During World War II, the YWCA contributed to the war effort by sponsoring educational lectures and forums such as "Fix-It-Yourself" for the wives of servicemen, offering housing to women doing war work, and providing recreation and entertainment to men and women in the armed services. During this time the YWCA continued to be managed and funded primarily by women, for women.

After the war, YWCA administrators made a concerted effort to reach out to immigrant women. An interracial charter was adopted at the national convention which called for the integration and participation of minority groups in every aspect of the association, the community, and the nation. In addition, rapid post-war population growth in the suburbs west of Boston led to the opening in 1964 of the West Suburban Branch of the "Y" in Natick, Massachusetts, 20 miles west of Boston. The Natick "Y" focussed its energies on the needs and wants of suburban women and their children. Additionally, advocates formed a lobbying group, the YWCA Public Affairs Committee, to focus on the areas of housing and family planning, and to call attention to the needs of those women, especially mothers, that were not being met by traditional social service organizations.

Throughout its first 100 years, the Boston YWCA, staffed and funded almost entirely by women, worked to empower women by helping them take charge of their lives, plan for their futures, and become economically independent and self-supporting.

RECENT HISTORY

"In 1886, the Boston YWCA became the first YWCA in the nation. Today we are part of the oldest and largest women's organization in the world, serving all people regardless of sex, race, religion or income. Our One Imperative is the elimination of racism."— Mary L. Reed, Former Executive Director, 1986

The 1960s were a time of social and cultural upheaval, especially with regard to civil rights, the movement whose goal was equality for all races. In support of the civil rights movement, the YWCA made a commitment to fight racism and integrate its programs and services at every level, initiating a special two-year action plan in 1963. The operating budget for the plan provided for two staff members and support services to become more involved and with other community groups working in the areas of fair housing, voter registration, and literacy programs. In 1967, the YWCA's first black president, Mrs. Robert W. Clayton, was elected at the National Convention. In 1968 the Boston YWCA opened Aswalos house in Dorchester, Massachusetts, especially to meet the needs of women in the inner city. As a fitting ending to the 1960s the *One Imperative,* "To eliminate racism wherever it exists and by any means necessary" was adopted and added to the statement of purpose as the philosophical basis for the YWCA in coming years.

Although fighting racism remained important, in the 1970s the YWCA shifted its attention to issues raised by the changing roles of women in American society. The 1960s and 1970s were decades of the revival and growth of the feminist movement in the United States and throughout the world. The social and political arena in which the Boston and other YWCAs were operating was changing rapidly. More and more women were working outside the home while raising children. The number of women living at or near the poverty level was on the rise. Classes and programs at the YWCA had to be redesigned to meet changing demands. For instance, the "Y" offered instruction in survival skills for urban living; but more radically, because non-traditional jobs for women were on the rise, in 1977 the "Y" launched its first non-traditional training program, funded by the federal government, to train women to work in the construction industry. Thus, in the 1970s, federal, state and local governments became increasingly involved in social welfare, whereas in the past these needs had been met by private charitable and voluntary organizations. At the same time that the YWCA began to rely more on government funding and less on private donations, the YWCA's Board of Directors in the 1960s and 1970s changed to reflect the racial and class diversity of the women in the communities the YWCA served. While the new Board members helped the YWCA respond effectively to the immediate needs of the inner city community, they lost touch with the monied constituency which had formerly been the YWCA's base of support, and that monied constituency in turn shifted its attention and support to other causes.

THE CHANGING ENVIRONMENT

The late 1970s saw a dramatic rise in the number of unwed mothers, teen pregnancy, and teen parenting. At the same time, more and more state and federal funds became available for social programs, and many non-profits directed their energies to establishing themselves as vendors or service providers to win government contracts. The Boston YWCA became a major vendor in the areas of child care, employment training, teen services, and domestic abuse programming. As a result of the YWCA's strong advocacy efforts, major federal and state contracts were awarded to the YWCA for further study of issues related to teen pregnancy. However, the YWCA's redirecting of its efforts toward securing government funding significantly eroded its base of private support, especially among those upper crust women who had, for generations, been the primary source of funds for the YWCA in Boston, and the YWCA which had for a long time been one of a few non-profits, became one of many contending for the same funds.

As the decade came to a close, the outlook for the Boston YWCA began to shift. Given the community's growing need for services and their own aging facilities, the management team of the Boston YWCA realized they would have to make some tough decisions about allocating funds that were beginning to get more scarce. If they were to decide that a major outlay of cash or large loans for facilities were necessary, they would have to pull funds from the programs and services the association provided to the community at a time when the need for community services was greater than ever and funds for these services were scarcer than they had been for some time. However, if the YWCA's management team continued to allocate funds for services and programs while making only minimal allocations for facility maintenance, they risked incurring the cost either of major repairs further down the line, or the serious deterioration of their major assets. Though the management team did not want to lose sight of the YWCA's commitment to the women and children in the community, the "Y's" financial crisis would require foresight, careful planning, and some hard choices.

THE ECONOMIC CRUNCH

In the early 1980s the need for social services grew, increasing the number of non-profit organizations competing for the same funds. At the same time the Reagan Administration cut back federal funding, and non-profits were forced to go back to raising funds through private donations, grants, bequests, and the United Way. The mid-1980s, however, were prosperous years, especially in the Boston area. Individuals and companies gave more generously than in past years to non-profits, and in response to the limited availability of federal funds for social services during the Reagan era, non-profits increasingly directed their resources to funding everything from homeless shelters and food pantries to drug and alcohol rehabilitation centers.

However, the economic downturn in late 1987 immediately cut into the funding flow for non-profits. Corporations and the general public became more discerning about where they directed their charitable contributions. Many people lost their jobs; a high debt lifestyle caught up with others: in short, people's disposable income dropped off. It became increasingly difficult to raise the funds necessary to keep up the facilities and to provide the services the community continued to demand. As the economy worsened, the need for services increased proportionately and at a more rapid rate than the Boston YWCA had ever witnessed. At the same time, the YWCA had to contend both with its old "mainstream" image in the face of the proliferation of more "chic" non-profits such as homeless shelters, battered women's shelters or "safe houses," etc. and with the growing misperception of the YWCA as an organization run primarily by women of color for women of color.

The climate for the banking industry in Boston during the late 1980s also altered dramatically. Many banks were in financial trouble and those that had lent freely in the mid-1980s now scrutinized every loan request and rejected a large majority of those they received. Funds for capital improvements and construction were not looked upon favorably by most Boston area banks; and money to fund new projects and large renovations became nearly impossible to obtain. These negative trends have only worsened so far in the 1990s, as the YWCA faces the absolute necessity of making some hard decisions regarding the allocation of its shrinking resources.

SOURCES OF FUNDING

Revenue for the Boston YWCA comes from three sources:

1. *Support Funds*—funds from the United Way of Massachusetts Bay, contributions, grants, legacies, and bequests.
2. *Operating Revenue*—money from program fees, government sponsored programs, membership dues, housing and food services.
3. *Non-Operating Revenue*—income from leasing of office space to outside concerns, investment income, and net realized gain on investments.

Table 1 shows the percentage each has contributed to the total revenue for the past five years.

From 1985 to 1989 the United Way accounted for 70–80 percent of the support funds revenue. But like all non-profit organizations in the late 1980s, the United Way was under fire for its operational procedures and found itself in a fiercely competitive fundraising environment. The United Way anticipated a 30 percent drop in fundraising for 1991, which would affect all the agencies it funded, including the Boston YWCA. At the same time, operating revenues for the YWCA dropped off in 1990 as well, so that more, rather than less support funding was needed to operate. Since support funding is expected to continue to decrease in the next three to five years, the Boston YWCA must discover new sources of funding to maintain its services and meet its operational expenses.

TABLE 1

Percentage Breakdown—Sources of Funding

	1985	1986	1987	1988	1989	1990
Support Funds	22%	22%	23%	21%	24%	33%
Operating Revenue	67%	66%	65%	67%	63%	54%
Non-Operating Revenue	11%	12%	12%	12%	13%	13%

FACILITIES

In 1987, the Boston YWCA was operating from four facilities in neighborhoods of Boston and one in a western suburb of the city. During 1987, the Boston Redevelopment Authority, a commission which oversees all real estate development in the city, awarded a parcel of land to the YWCA for $1.00 on which to build a new facility as part of the city's redevelopment plan. The new facility would replace the old Dorchester YWCA, Aswalos House, which a grant would then convert to transitional housing for unwed mothers and their children. Since the YWCA now had a new parcel of land, and other existing facilities in need of maintenance and repair, the management team embarked on a three-year study to analyze its programs and services, and its properties. Most importantly, they decided to implement an aggressive renovation schedule designed to modernize all facilities, to protect the value of the YWCA's major assets, its buildings.

As part of this renovation, repair, and maintenance program, the association's management team had to perform a thorough review of its programs and services. The programs most beneficial to the agency in terms of revenue and those the community had the greatest need for had to be assessed for future expectations of growth and space requirements. New programs would have to be accommodated and those programs that were no longer financially feasible or in demand would have to be eliminated. The management team planned to complete their research and decision-making prior to implementing any expansion or renovation of the buildings.

I. West Suburban Program Center

When the YWCA expanded, and opened a branch in Natick, Massachusetts, a suburb located 20 miles west of Boston in 1964, it bought a building which quickly became inadequate to the YWCA's needs, and in 1981 the center moved to a new facility. The resources for women at this branch were designed to serve its suburban constituency, and included programs for women reentering the job market after years of parenting, training programs for displaced workers, spousal and family abuse programs, divorce support groups, and counseling for women suffering from breast cancer. However, in 1988, after much research and years of restructuring the services offered at the West Suburban Program Center, its inability to support itself financially through its operations led to a decision to close down the facility.

II. Aswalos House

Aswalos House, located in Dorchester, Massachusetts, an urban center within the jurisdiction of the City of Boston, was originally opened in 1968. Until 1989, it housed an After School Enrichment Program and a Teen Development Program which offered training for word processing and clerical work, and GED preparation courses. Later, Aswalos House added a program for teen mothers.

In 1989, the receipt of a $100,000 HUD grant transformed Aswalos House into transitional housing for teenage mothers and their children, and existing programs were transferred to other facilities. Originally the programs were to be transferred to the new Dorchester Branch planned for the parcel acquired from the City of Boston. However, that parcel was never developed because development costs were estimated at \$1.5–\$2 million, but the YWCA was only able to raise \$300,000. Consequently, the parcel of land was returned to the City of Boston.

The new Aswalos House for teen mothers opened in October, 1990, and provided transitional housing for 10 mothers and their children. Prospective occupants have to be between 16 and 20 and demonstrate severe financial need. Counseling services are provided, and a staff case worker arranges for schooling and job training for the teenagers. In addition, a staff housing advocate coordinates permanent housing for the mothers and their children.

Half the expense of running the facility is covered by a federal grant to the Boston YWCA. The remaining half is made up by fees paid by the teen mothers from their welfare income, and by contributions from the United Way and private donations.

III. YWCA Child Care Center

The YWCA Child Care Center is rather inconveniently located in downtown Boston on the fringe of the commercial district, and is rented rather than owned by the YWCA. To be licensed as a day care center in the Commonwealth of Massachusetts, it had to undergo extensive renovations. The owner of the property contributed a substantial portion of the cost of the renovation work, and the balance of the expense was covered by a private grant so that no loans were necessary to complete the project.

The center, a licensed pre-school, provides day-care for 50 children at fees of \$110 a week per toddler and \$150 a week per child for children under three. Some scholarships are available for families who are unable to pay. When the center first opened, many of its clients were on state funded day care vouchers. Participation has now dropped considerably, however, because a significant percentage of state-funded day care vouchers were cut form the state budget. To compensate for the loss of clients, the center went into the infant care business, caring for children from six months to two years, but it continues to run at less than capacity.

IV. The Berkeley Residence

The Berkeley Residence was opened in 1884 in downtown Boston to serve as housing for women of all ages. Originally there was housing for 100 residents, an employment and training bureau, and a gymnasium, the first in the country for women. In 1907, 35 rooms and a meeting hall were added to the facility.

In 1985 the Berkeley Residence was cited by Boston's Building Code Department because it did not meet current safety and fire codes of the city or the Commonwealth. Major repairs and renovations estimated at \$1 million were necessary to bring the building up to healthy, safe, and legal standards. In 1986 a construction loan for the full amount was secured at 10 percent interest amortized over 25 years. Once the project was completed, payments would come to approximately \$100,000 annually. Work began in 1988. Repairs were needed to the infrastructure of the building, and included a conversion from oil heat to gas, a sprinkler system and smoke detector system wired throughout the building, new elevators, as well as many other repairs and maintenance work of a less costly nature. Tenants were not displaced during construction, a major concern at the beginning of the project's planning stage.

After completion of the renovation work in the spring of 1991, the facility now rents 215 rooms which provide long-term and short-term housing for women of all ages. The Berkeley Residence offers inexpensive rent and meals, an answering service, and maid service. Other services located at the facility include a referral network for jobs and services, social services, tourist information, and emergency services. The building is open and staffed 24 hours a day, seven days a week, providing safe, secure housing at reasonable rates for single women in the city.

V. Boston YWCA Headquarters at 140 Clarendon Street

Constructed between 1927 and 1929, the headquarters for the Boston YWCA is advantageously located at the corners of Clarendon and Stuart Streets on the edge of one of the city's most prestigious retail districts, Newbury and Boylston Streets and Copley Place in the heart of Boston's Back Bay business district. The area offers the finest in upscale retail stores and desirable office space, including the John Hancock Building and the Prudential Center. The Clarendon Headquarters, a 13-story brick and steel building, sits on approximately 13,860 square feet of land and includes approximately 167,400 square feet of space. It currently houses the YWCA administration offices, the Parlin House Apartments, the Melnea Cass Branch of the YWCA, and several commercial tenants. The Melnea Cass Branch operates health and fitness facilities which include a swimming pool, and employment training programs. The Parlin Apartments occupy floors 9–13 and are comprised of studio, one- and two-bedroom apartments rented at market rates.

The building has not been significantly renovated since its completion in 1929, and no longer complies with city and state building codes. In 1987, the building elevators desperately needed repairs at an estimated cost of $270,000. The building also needs a new sprinkler system to insure the safety of its residents and tenants and to bring the building up to code. The Parlin Apartments also require major renovations to achieve an acceptable standard of safety, appearance, and comfort. The Apartments currently use common electric meters, and need to be rewired so tenants can control the electricity to their individual units, and pay accordingly. The YWCA's administrative offices also require improvements and repairs.

The health and fitness facilities also require significant repairs, updating, and renovation. Old, dreary locker rooms are unattractive to current and potential members, and a larger men's locker room is needed to accommodate male members. In addition, to keep up with new trends in the fitness industry, the YWCA needs to refurbish its space for aerobics classes and purchase new weight training equipment. During this time, the YWCA has also been forced to close the pool for repairs, and the pool building itself needs significant exterior work. Cost estimates for the work on the pool and pool building are in excess of $200,000. At the same time, a decrease in demand for health and fitness clubs and an increase in competition in both the daycare and health and fitness industries has had a negative impact on revenues for this facility.

Because the YWCA's Clarendon headquarters is in such a state of disrepair, it has become very costly to maintain and operate the building. In years past, the Board of Directors has chosen to funnel their scarce available resources into their programs rather than into general repairs and maintenance of the facilities, with the result that the building at 140 Clarendon Street is currently running at a net loss in excess of $200,000 a year.

In 1988 a certified appraiser valued the Clarendon property at $16 million. (However, the real estate market in the Boston area has since declined significantly.) The Boston YWCA's Board of Directors then sought a $7 million loan for the proposed renovations from several major Boston area banking and financial institutions, but most of these institutions did not respond favorably to the loan request. While there were a number of valid reasons for the banks' refusing to loan the YWCA the funds necessary for the renovations, including the YWCA's own uncertainty about how the changes would impact revenues, the fact that the YWCA is a women's organization without connections in the "old-boy" network of the banking establishment contributed to the YWCA's lack of financial credibility. Finally, although the Clarendon building's excess value would cover the loan to value ratio, the banks raised serious questions about whether the YWCA's existing and potential cash flow could meet the debt service obligation.

The executive committee of the Boston YWCA is now faced with a serious dilemma. It must decide what to do with a deteriorating facility that not only serves as its headquarters, but also as a flagship of services offered by all the area YWCAs. After several years of study, review, and debate they are considering the following options for the Clarendon headquarters:

1. Sell the building with a guaranteed lease back for its facilities and offices.
2. Sell the building to an interested local insurance company and rent space for the administrative offices in a nearby office building.
3. Bring in an equity partner to fund the renovations for a percentage of ownership in the facility.
4. Continue with minimal renovations and operate as they have in the past.

INCREASING COMPETITION IN FITNESS SERVICES

In 1989, the management team of the Boston YWCA hired a consulting firm to review their Health Promotion Services division, housed at 140 Clarendon Street, one of the YWCA's primary sources of both operating revenue and expense, and to assist them in finding ways to enhance this branch of their services. The consultants surveyed current, former, and potential members about the strengths and weaknesses of the YWCA's Health Promotion Services including appearance, cleanliness, scheduling, products (ie., equipment, classes, swimming pool, etc.), and overall management of the facility. This study also noted that there is considerable competition from the following vendors in the area of health and fitness:

1. Bally's Holiday Fitness Centers
2. Healthworks
3. Fitcorp
4. BostonSports
5. SkyClub
6. The Mount Auburn Club
7. Nautilus Plus

8. Fitness International
9. Fitness First
10. The Club at Charles River Park
11. Mike's Gym
12. Fitness Unlimited
13. Gold's Gym

The health club marketplace is, for the most part, a standardized industry in terms of the products and services offered at the various facilities. Most clubs offer free weights, weight equipment, exercise and aerobics classes, locker rooms, and showers with towels available. During the 1980s many new health clubs opened and the health club market became increasingly competitive. These clubs went to great expense to promote elaborate grand openings and fund extensive advertising campaigns to attract new members. The consultants' study found that 15 other health and fitness facilities within the city are in direct competition with the YWCA. However, among the competition, the YWCA does fill a unique niche because it is affordable, strongly emphasizes fitness in a non-competitive and non-commercial environment, appeals to a diverse cross-section of people, and is conveniently located. Other clubs are perceived as more commercial and competitive than the YWCA, with a greater emphasis on social interaction and frills such as saunas, racquetball and squash courts, eating facilities, etc. A comparison of the YWCA's Health Promotion Services to other health clubs in the city shows the YWCA to be in a price range somewhere between the commercial clubs and the no-frills gymnasiums. The commercial clubs range from $800–$1,200 a year, plus a one-time initiation fee of from $100–$1,200; the no-frills gymnasiums range from $300–$400 per year; and the YWCA costs between $420 and $600 a year, plus an annual membership fee of $35.

The YWCA is comparable in size to the competition, but its space is not as well laid out as at other clubs. Most of the other clubs are air-conditioned but the YWCA isn't and its membership drops significantly during the summer months, while for other clubs summer is the peak season. The YWCA also ranked behind the top four clubs in cleanliness, and members noted that its dreary atmosphere contributed to their sense of its uncleanliness. The YWCA's weight lifting equipment and weight machines are not quite up to the standards of the competition and the YWCA lacks the staffing and supervision other clubs provide. On the other hand, the YWCA can boast a swimming pool, an indoor track, and day care. Only one other club has a pool that comes close in size to the YWCA's, and only two other clubs offer indoor tracks or day care.

According to the consultants' study, current users of the YWCA's Health Promotion Services joined because the YWCA is convenient, provides a caring environment that promotes interaction, and is relatively inexpensive. A current user profile revealed that members are generally seeking a health and fitness experience for themselves as individuals rather than a social atmosphere and that what mattered to them additionally was sensible class schedules, adequate staffing, communication with the members, timely information, affordable pricing, an atmosphere without pressure, and an open, caring, and diverse environment. The complaint most often cited among current users was the lack of communication with members with regard to scheduling changes for classes, changes in the hours of operation, class cancellations, pool closings, and changes in procedures and policies of the club. Other factors that concerned current members were: lack of cleanliness, dreary appearance, small men's locker room, poor management of the staff, poor management of class capacity, inadequate maintenance of equipment, poor scheduling, poor layout of the facility, and the lack of public relations and advertising to attract new members.

Former members were also surveyed to determine why they did not renew. Their reasons mirrored the complaints of current members:

- Poor communications with members
- Equipment breakdowns
- Untimely equipment repairs
- Poor upkeep/cleanliness
- Poor ventilation
- Dreary appearance
- Dissatisfaction with staff (no personal attention)
- Rigid schedules
- Lack of air conditioning
- Overall deterioration of the facility

The study also concluded that marketing and promotion of the Health Promotion Services is minimal, with little effort put into attracting new members, making it nearly invisible in the community.

Marti Wilson-Taylor, the new executive director and Carolyn Rosen, the new chief financial officer, quickly realized as they took control of the Boston YWCA in 1991 that several major decisions concerning the YWCA's physical facilities and programs and services had to be made. However, first and foremost, it was necessary for them to determine the strategic direction of the YWCA for the remainder of the decade. In an environment of increasing competition and shrinking resources the challenge facing them is great.

FIGURE 1
Detailed Analysis of
YWCA Revenues 1991

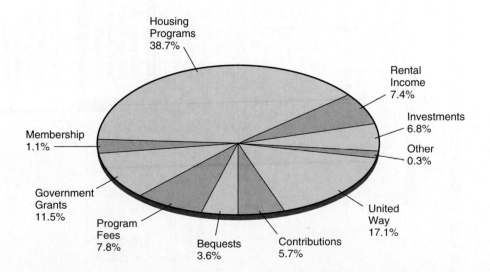

Housing Programs 38.7%

Rental Income 7.4%

Investments 6.8%

Other 0.3%

Membership 1.1%

Government Grants 11.5%

Program Fees 7.8%

Bequests 3.6%

Contributions 5.7%

United Way 17.1%

FIGURE 2 Boston YWCA—1991 Table of Organization

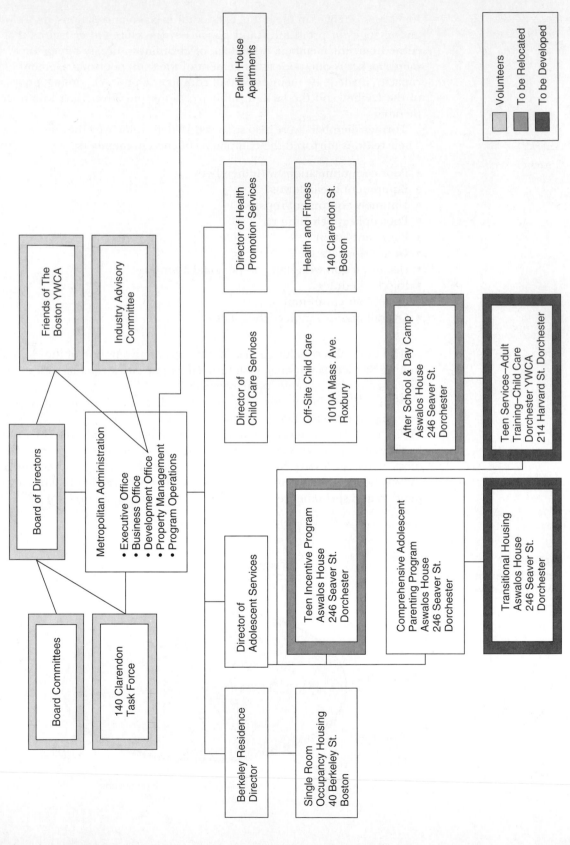

TABLE 1

Boston Young Women's Christian Association Balance Sheet June 30, 1991 (With comparative totals as of June 30, 1990)

	Current Fund	Plant Fund	Endowment Fund	June 30, 1991 Totals	June 30, 1990 Totals
ASSETS					
Current assets:					
Cash	$ 137,469	66,292	—	203,761	110,684
Cash in escrow and security deposits	40,642	—	—	40,642	37,932
Accounts receivable, (less allowance for doubtful accounts of $3,500 in 1991 and $2,687 in 1990)	102,334	—	—	102,334	166,245
Supplies and prepaid expenses	54,452	—	—	54,452	73,613
Total current assets	334,897	66,292	—	401,189	388,474
Pooled investments	1,793,198	—	3,180,303	4,973,501	4,775,252
Land, buildings and equipment, net	—	2,147,155	—	2,147,155	1,869,963
Deferred charges	—	349,638	—	349,638	349,638
	1,793,198	2,496,793	3,180,303	7,470,294	6,994,853
	$2,128,095	2,563,085	3,180,303	7,871,483	7,383,327
LIABILITIES AND FUND BALANCES (DEFICIT)					
Current liabilities:					
Current maturities of long-term notes payable	—	18,979	—	18,979	17,524
Accounts payable and accrued expenses	254,757	—	—	254,757	201,581
Deferred revenue	182,073	—	—	182,073	202,717
Total current liabilities	436,830	18,979	—	455,809	421,822
Long-term notes payable, less current maturities	—	1,196,746	—	1,196,746	910,443
Loan payable to endowment fund	—	—	—	—	143,841
Total liabilities	436,830	1,215,725	—	1,652,555	1,476,106
Fund balances (deficit):					
Unrestricted:					
Designated by governing board to function as endowment	1,507,135	—	—	1,507,135	1,453,867
Undesignated	(101,933)	—	—	(101,933)	(354,084)
	1,405,202	—	—	1,405,202	1,099,783
Restricted—nonexpendable	286,063	223,798	3,180,303	3,690,164	3,545,183
Net investment in plant	—	1,123,562	—	1,123,562	1,262,255
Total fund balances	1,691,265	1,347,360	3,180,303	6,218,928	5,907,221
	$2,128,095	2,563,085	3,180,303	7,871,483	7,383,327

TABLE 3

Boston YWCA Statement of Support and Revenue, Expenses, Capital Additions and Changes in Fund Balances Year Ended June 30, 1991 (With comparative totals for the year ended June 30, 1990)

	Current Fund	Plant Fund	Endowment Fund	June 30, 1991 Totals	June 30, 1990 Totals
SUPPORT AND REVENUE					
Support:					
United Way	$ 703,643	—	—	$ 703,643	$ 713,500
Contributions and grants	233,264	—	—	233,264	197,700
Legacies and bequests	150,386	—	—	150,386	537,540
	1,087,293	—	—	1,087,293	1,448,740
Operating revenue:					
Program fees	320,611	—	—	320,611	355,170
Government-sponsored programs	471,615	—	—	471,615	411,050
Membership	45,674	—	—	45,674	71,579
Housing and food service	1,589,587	—	—	1,589,587	1,586,553
	2,427,487	—	—	2,427,487	2,424,352
Non-operating revenue:					
Rental income	302,641	—	—	302,641	298,036
Investment income	278,982	—	—	278,982	244,224
Net realized gain on investments	41,392	—	—	41,392	2,308
Other revenue	7,967	—	—	7,967	43,790
	630,982	—	—	630,982	588,358
Total support and revenue	$4,145,762	—	—	$4,145,762	$4,461,450
EXPENSES					
Program services:					
Aswalos House	$ 250,621	$ 14,782	—	$ 265,403	$ 384,776
Berkeley Residence	1,053,131	86,465	—	1,139,596	1,054,106
Cass Branch	1,216,544	128,673	—	1,345,217	1,394,075
Childcare	422,411	2,030	—	424,441	344,011
Harvard	6,132	—	—	6,132	—
	2,948,839	231,950	—	3,180,789	3,176,968
Supporting services:					
General and administration	632,657	15,364	—	648,021	793,861
Fundraising	287,448	6,981	—	294,429	135,978
	920,105	22,345	—	942,450	929,839
Total expenses	$3,868,944	$ 254,295	—	$4,123,239	$4,106,807
Excess (deficiency) of support and revenue over expenses before capital additions	$ 276,818	$ (254,295)	—	$ 22,523	$ 354,643

continued

TABLE 3

Continued

	Current Fund	Plant Fund	Endowment Fund	June 30, 1991 Totals	June 30, 1990 Totals
CAPITAL ADDITIONS					
Grants and gifts	106,495	38,985	—	145,480	314,798
Investment income	—	5,529	65,598	71,127	68,018
Net realized gain on investment transactions	—	—	72,577	72,577	63,874
Write-off of deferred charges	—	—	—	—	(305,312)
Loss on sale of asset	—	—	—	—	(11,856)
Total capital additions	106,495	44,514	138,175	289,184	129,522
Excess (deficiency) of support and revenue over expenses after capital additions	383,313	(209,781)	138,175	311,707	484,165
Fund balances, beginning of year	1,379,040	1,486,053	3,042,128	5,907,221	5,423,056
Transfers between funds:					
Plant acquisition	(274,155)	274,155	—	—	—
Principal repayment on loan payable to endowment fund	(143,841)	143,841	—	—	—
Permanent fund transfer	346,908	(346,908)	—	—	—
	(71,088)	71,088	—	—	—
Fund balances, end of year	$1,691,265	$1,347,360	$3,180,303	$6,218,928	$5,907,221

BASF's Proposed Paint Plant:
A Community's Reaction

MAX E. DOUGLAS, *Indiana State University*

INTRODUCTION

In early 1988, BASF Corporation, a member of the international German-based BASF Group, released plans for a five-year $2 billion capital expansion program. BASF Corporation is one of the largest chemical companies in North America. In 1988, net sales equalled $5 billion while net income amounted to $149 million. Nearly 22,000 people are employed by the four divisions of BASF Corporation. Its diversified product mix includes the following: basic, intermediate and specialty chemicals, colorants, dispersions, fiber raw materials, fibers, automotive coatings, printing inks, urethane specialties and chemicals, plastics, advanced composite materials, antifreeze, crop protection products, pharmaceuticals, vitamins, fragrances, and audio, video, and computer recording media.

On March 10, 1988, BASF officials announced that the company intended to build a manufacturing facility somewhere in the American Midwest. Three cities were selected as finalists: Terre Haute, Indiana (located in Vigo County), Evansville, Indiana and Portsmouth, Ohio. Terre Haute's drawing card was an undeveloped county industrial park comprised of 1,476 acres of land. Terre Haute has a population of roughly 57,483 and is located in the west central part of Indiana. As a community, Terre Haute was in dire need of expanded employment opportunities since several major companies had exited the area over the past decade. Statistics published by the local Chamber of Commerce showed that between 1979–1987, the community suffered a net loss of 6,062 jobs. However, data published by the local Democratic Party reported that 6,102 jobs had been created in the community between 1986–1991. (See Exhibit 1.)

Presented and accepted by the refereed Midwest Society for Case Research. All rights reserved to the author and the MSCR.

Copyright © 1991 by Max E. Douglas.

Max E. Douglas is Professor of Management at Indiana State University. This case is intended to be used as a basis for class discussion rather than to illustrate either effective or ineffective handling of the situation.

On March 28, 1988, the Vigo County Commissioners signed a licensing agreement with BASF allowing the company to inspect and conduct soil tests at the county industrial park located south of Terre Haute. Approximately a month later, BASF released more precise information regarding the nature of the plant facility. Tentative plans called for a $150 million automotive paint plant that would employ approximately 500 local people. This economic data encouraged city and county government officials to court BASF Corporation. In mid-June an entourage of local government officials and business leaders visited a BASF plant in Gainsville, Ohio. On July 6, 1988, BASF announced that the soil tests at the industrial park were affirmative and that the company was initiating procedures to "option" land at the Vigo County industrial park. Further discussion between company and county government officials revealed that a small 30 acre parcel of land within the industrial park was still owned by the federal government. BASF stressed that the company would need this 30 acres to develop its plant operations. The Vigo County Commissioners eventually purchased this acreage from the General Services Administration in order to accommodate BASF.

CONTROVERSY DEVELOPS

On August 10, 1988, Jack Wehman, Midwest Venture Director for BASF, announced that the company planned to build a hazardous waste incinerator and establish a landfill in addition to building its paint manufacturing plant. The proposed incinerator and landfill would handle on-site wastes and imported wastes trucked to the site from other BASF plants. following this news release, Evansville Mayor, Frank McDonald, indicated that his city would no longer pursue the BASF plant. Terre Haute Mayor, Pete Chalos, and Portsmouth, Ohio Mayor, Roger Bussey, indicated that their communities were still positive about the BASF plant regardless of the implications of the incinerator and landfill.

In contrast to the favorable reception of the August 10th BASF announcement by Terre Haute's mayor and other BASF supporters, a local community action group, Citizens for a Clean County (CCC), organized to begin an anti-BASF campaign. The initial purpose of the CCC was to stop BASF from building the waste treatment facility on the site and from importing waste to the incinerator/landfill. The CCC eventually became the primary opponent to BASF although other BASF adversaries expressed their opposition regarding the importation of toxic wastes. For example, one local entrepreneur, Jim Shanks, mailed out 8,000 letters and petitions to Vigo County residents living in the southern and eastern parts of the county enlisting their opposition to BASF. His letter, shown in Exhibit 2, demonstrated his concern for the environmental impact of BASF's incinerator/landfill proposal, especially the windfall pattern of emissions. In reaction to the growing anti-BASF sentiment, BASF Corporation hired Fleishman Hilliard, a St. Louis opinion research firm, to conduct community focus groups to solicit views regarding the proposed automotive paint plant, hazardous waste incinerator and landfill. In addition, BASF launched a letter writing campaign to reach local citizens. These letters attempted to provide facts to help diffuse controversy over the proposed paint plant and waste management facility. (See Exhibits 3, 4, & 5.) As can be seen from the content of these letters, BASF officials stressed the economic benefits their plant would bring to the community although one letter does address BASF's concern for the environmental impact of their proposed facility.

ECONOMIC DEVELOPMENT PLAN STIRS PUBLIC DEBATE

While this controversy was dominating the community news, the local governmental officials continued to pursue a plan for the economic development of the industrial park. The Vigo County Council created the Vigo County Redevelopment Commission to oversee the development of the 1,505 acre industrial park. The County Redevelopment Commission hired the Terre Haute Department of Redevelopment to draw up a detailed Economic Development Plan for the industrial park. The existence of an Economic Development Plan for the park was a prerequisite for qualifying for federal funds to underwrite the development of infrastructure such as sewer and water lines. The final Economic Development Plan proposal called for $6 million in improvements to the property in order to make it suitable for industrial development. On November 28, 1988, the Vigo County Redevelopment Commission declared that the industrial park was an economic development and tax allocation area despite opposition from area residents. Following this official declaration, the Redevelopment Commission submitted the proposed Economic Development Plan to the Vigo County Area Planning Commission. The Area Planning Commission was charged with determining whether the proposed Economic Development Plan conformed with the comprehensive land usage plan for the entire county. On December 7, 1988, a public meeting at a local high school was conducted by the Area Planning Commission. Despite much opposition from the audience, the Economic Development Plan was approved by *this* commission 11–3.

Following this vote of approval by the Area Planning Commission, the Redevelopment Commission scheduled public hearings regarding the industrial park economic development plan. Some thirty hours of testimony were heard over three days. Spearheading the anti-BASF forces was the Citizens for a Clean Community. Members of the CCC hired outside consultants to speak at the hearings.

One spokesperson, Hugh Kaufman, an employee of the Environmental Protection Agency, expressed concerns about the BASF incineration/hazardous waste landfill proposal. According to Kaufman, hazardous waste facilities inhibit industrial and economic growth rather than promote it. Costs and burdens fall on local governments, which may have additional liabilities if waste from incinerators enters public water and sewage systems. Kaufman further stressed that increased industrial traffic and repairs, chemical spills, and the expanded need for continual training of emergency response teams add additional concerns and costs for taxpayers.

Another environmentalist, John Blair, gave testimony during the marathon hearings. Blair was being paid $125 per diem by the Oil, Chemical, and Atomic Workers local in Geismar, Louisiana to help promote opposition to the BASF plant. OCAW had been engaged in a bitter four-year lockout with BASF at the Geismar plant. Blair said evidence suggests that BASF often acts in an immoral fashion. He claimed that BASF's real intentions were to locate a hazardous treatment plant using the paint plant as a carrot. Blair further charged that the economic development plan under consideration had no enforcement provisions. Blair claimed that Terre Haute would become a "national sacrifice zone" if it begins accepting hazardous waste from other areas.

In addition to the above "expert" testimony, several citizens presented personal position statements. One opponent, Eva Kor, a survivor of Nazi Germany's World War II Auschwitz concentration camp, claimed that BASF was one of three companies formed out of the ashes of the German company I. G. Farben. Kor claimed that Farben used slave labor from the Auschwitz camp until "they were used up." She opposed BASF locating in Terre Haute and suggested a referendum be held to resolve the issue. Harold Cox, CCC member, reported that more than one half of the polled respondents in a local survey opposed a hazardous waste facility. Although in the minority, BASF supporters cited the tremendous economic boost that the company would provide for the community. In addition, BASF advocates labeled the CCC as a biased group more interested in protecting their property values than in stopping the importation of toxic waste. Nevertheless, the majority of statements presented during the thirty hours of public hearings conducted by the Vigo County Redevelopment Commission demonstrated opposition to the establishment of an incinerator and landfill adjacent to the automotive paint plant as well as the importation of hazardous wastes from other BASF plants for disposal in Terre Haute.

Subsequent to the public hearings, the Redevelopment Commission reviewed all written testimony regarding the Economic Development Plan. On January 19, 1989, the Redevelopment Commission conducted its final session to determine the fate of the proposed plan for the industrial park. One of the commissioners, Linda Burger, expressed concern that this plan would allow the importation of several truckloads of hazardous wastes into the community. Ms. Burger indicated further concern about the high cancer rates that already existed in Vigo County. Burger proposed an amendment to the economic development plan that would ban importation of toxic wastes into Vigo County. The amendment was rejected 3–2. The Economic Development Plan was finally approved 4–1.

LEGAL ACTION TAKEN

Shortly following the approval of the Economic Development Plan by the Redevelopment Commission, the CCC and 16 other people living near the industrial park filed a legal petition for judicial review against the Redevelopment Commission, the Vigo County Commissioners and Vigo County. The petition made the following charges:

1. The Economic Development Plan was adopted by using impermissible procedures alleged to be a) inadequate notice of when the Redevelopment Commission would meet; b) holding meetings in rooms too small to accommodate interested parties; c) curtailment of public comment.
2. The Redevelopment Commission was wrong to meet during regular business hours because that precluded some people from attending.
3. Four out of five Commission members had conflicts of interest.
4. The Economic Development Plan jeopardized the public health, safety, and welfare of the community.

Coinciding with the filing of the legal petition by the CCC et al. was the public introduction of a BASF visitation team. The team consisted of employees from various areas of the company such as human resources, operations, and plant safety. BASF provided biographical sketches of each member and indicated they were sent to discuss the quality of work life at BASF and to share their experience with the environmental safety of BASF at other plant locations. Jack Wehman, Midwest Venture Director for BASF, indicated that the presence of this team did not mean BASF had decided on Terre Haute. That decision, according to Wehman, depended on the outcome of the litigation over the industrial park. Wehman stressed that the visitation team's purpose was to gather and disseminate information pertaining to the proposed paint plant.

Shortly following the above two events (CCC's legal petition and the arrival of BASF's visitation team) the Mayor of Terre Haute, Pete Chalos, expressed displeasure that a legal petition had been filed to disaffirm the Economic Development Plan for the county industrial park. Mayor Chalos stated:

> I think that there are some people on the loose here that want to take us back 20 years and put Terre Haute in the position of being called an injunction city. I certainly hope cooler heads and wiser people take a leading role in making sure BASF comes here.

During March, 1989, the litigation and personal charges filed to disaffirm the approved Economic Development Plan intensified. On March 1, the coalition of the CCC and local property owners filed an amended court petition claiming that the adoption of the Economic Development Plan by the Redevelopment Commission on January 19, 1989, should be canceled because county commissioners failed to adopt an ordinance establishing the Redevelopment Commission. Hugh Kaufman, an EPA employee, charged that the purchase of the 30 acre tract of land for the Vigo County Industrial Park from the GSA was fraudulent. Kaufman contended that the GSA should have determined the environmental impact of potential development before selling federal land. He further implied that a new impact study should have been conducted rather than relying on the original assessment covering the 1476 acres sold to Vigo County in 1986. County government officials responded that they had followed appropriate legal advice in purchasing the additional 30 acres for $50,000 at a public auction held on August 19, 1988.

ECONOMIC DEVELOPMENT PLAN DECLARED NULL AND VOID

By mid-March, 1989, Judge Frank Nardi conducted a pre-trial conference in an attempt to resolve questions and issues raised by the plaintiffs. Judge Nardi indicated he would review all inclusive evidence about the way the Vigo County Redevelopment Commission was formed and the procedures used to reach its decision. Following Federal court hearings, Judge Nardi gave the CCC and Vigo County adequate time to file written briefs. The core of the plaintiffs' position was as follows: the Economic Development Plan was written especially for BASF, was adopted in violation of certain aspects of state law and was approved by government officials without giving proper consideration to all factors, including environmental impact issues. The defendants (county officials) testified that plaintiffs were given full rein during public hearings and that the plan was a reasonable one, designed with BASF in mind, seeking economic development by attracting not only BASF but other industry as well to the industrial park. Defendants also contended that monitoring the environment was a state and federal responsibility and that the incineration of waste from other BASF plants was permissible as part of the industrial park. On July 1, 1989 Judge Nardi ruled that the Economic Development Plan approved by the Redevelopment Commission was null and void. Nardi cited the following reasons:

1. questions of propriety regarding payments and alliances that suggested possible conflicts of interest among the commissioners
2. prejudgment of the decision before the Vigo County Redevelopment Commission was formed

As a result of these findings, the Economic Development Plan was remanded to the Vigo County Commissioners for further action.

MEANWHILE BACK AT THE RANCH

While Judge Nardi was analyzing the data contesting the approval of the Economic Development Plan (approximately April 1–July 1, 1989) another controversy was brewing. BASF opponents expressed concern that the company had not produced a complete list of chemicals that would be imported, burned and/or buried at its selected Midwest facility. Company officials indicated that the amount of waste handled, if Vigo County is selected, would be strictly limited by the redevelopment plan. BASF stressed that it would act responsibly and show concern for the short-run and long-run impact on the environment. BASF officials reassured the community that no third party wastes would be imported. It was also pointed out that BASF was following common corporate practice in that partial lists were seldom released. According to BASF management, most large companies do not release lists of chemicals until they apply for a state permit for incineration operations.

Unfortunately for BASF officials, their responses were jaded by an analysis of data conducted by a local Indiana State University chemistry professor, Dr. John Corrigan. A reporter of the Sullivan Daily Times (a local community newspaper 30 miles south of Terre Haute) asked Professor Corrigan to analyze some unpublished BASF documents. Data revealed that BASF intended to incinerate up to 152 chemicals—waste residues from 33 plants in 14 states in 1991–92. Corrigan reported that metals for incineration included cadmium, chromium, lead, and barium, among others; these chemicals cannot be destroyed or rendered harmless by incineration. BASF officials responded that the data were not current and were subject to revision. Jack Wehman, Midwest Venture Director for BASF, responded to the community concern by saying that following Judge Nardi's decision, BASF would begin the permitting process and make a full disclosure of chemicals to be disposed of at the Vigo County facility. The controversy over the chemical list at this point remained unresolved. A major factor contributing to the impasse was the ruling by U.S. District Court Judge Nardi declaring the Economic Development Plan null and void.

POST ECONOMIC DEVELOPMENT PLAN

Subsequent to Judge Nardi's ruling declaring the Economic Development Plan for the industrial park null and void, controversy continued regarding the possible sale of industrial park land to BASF. A joint meeting of the Vigo County Commissioners, seven County Councilmen, and the five members of the Redevelopment Commission, resulted in a consensus not to appeal Judge Nardi's ruling on the plight of the Economic Development Plan. County Commissioners expressed concern that deed restrictions might have to accompany the sale of industrial park acreage in order to protect the environment. Special concern about importation of hazardous waste was expressed. John Scott, president of the Commission, indicated that he was worried that BASF had not yet published a list of what wastes would be imported. On July 15, 1989, anti-BASF groups met with County Commissioners to share their views about the future of the industrial park. Harold Cox, representative of the CCC, said that a new Economic Development Plan would be written to attract a wider spectrum of potential buyers. It was stressed that Vigo County needs to market to industries that do not present environmental health risks. The commissioners responded that they welcomed ideas for marketing land but emphasized that the industrial park was still for sale but no specific time frame had been established to offer the property for public bid. About a month after this meeting, the Vigo County Commissioners sought legal advice regarding the disposal of the industrial park. The commissioners also stated that public hearings would be conducted. BASF opponents hoped that the new hearings would result in a plan that would restrict activities that are ecologically unsound while promoting safe economic development on the industrial park.

BASF MODIFIES PLANS

On August 31, 1989, BASF Midwest Venture Director, Jack Wehman, announced that his corporation would be scaling down its plans for an industrial plant in Vigo County. He stated:

> Our new plan calls for the construction of a stand-alone automotive plant with the necessary waste-management facilities for only the paint plant. This means that the waste-management facility will handle only the waste from the site's paint plant. These are on-site generated wastes.

Wehman further explained that the waste-management operations would include a wastewater treatment facility, an incinerator system, and a landfill for the incinerated ash, all of which would dispose of on-site wastes. These revisions would require only 200–300 acres of land and about 300 local employees at a cost of roughly $100 million. Wehman further projected that these 300 local employees would complement 100 "imported" workers each earning about $10.15 per hour or about $8.4 million in annual income. In addition, Wehman estimated that the 2000 construction workers employed for the two-year project would generate about $40 million per year in payroll. Wehman concluded by stressing the need to negotiate sale of needed land in the park within the next six weeks so that the plant could be operational by the end of 1992.

The Vigo County Commissioners reacted favorably to BASF's revised plan and indicated that selling appropriate acreage with a clear title within six weeks seemed feasible. At this point, the Commissioners stated that public hearings regarding the sale of the land seemed unnecessary especially since wastes would not be imported into the community.

On the flip side, however, many community members still questioned the integrity of BASF's proposed revision. A member of one anti-BASF coalition, Mothers Against Toxic Chemical Hazards, indicated that opposition to BASF continues because the revision still proposes a toxic waste incinerator and landfill for the site. Harold Cox, president of the CCC, stated that the proposed landfill was not allowed according to Vigo County's comprehensive land use plan. Other opponents voiced concern that the industrial park had not been appropriately marketed. BASF adversaries stressed the previous "bait and switch" tactics in which the company initially announced plans for a paint plant and later added the hazardous waste facilities to its agenda. A staunch critic of BASF opponents was Terre Haute City Mayor, Pete Chalos. Mr. Chalos criticized environmental groups who had previously said they would accept BASF if toxic waste was not imported. Mayor Chalos indicated he had studied BASF's new proposal and was optimistic that the County Commissioners would accommodate BASF.

Two days after announcing their revised plan for the paint plant operations, BASF released two bound volumes of printed material explaining in detail the list of chemicals that could be treated and disposed of at its Midwestern paint plant. BASF officials assured the community that all of the tested materials would be handled using procedures that protect the safety, health and environmental welfare of the citizens.

BASF'S BID FOR INDUSTRIAL PARK LAND APPROVED BY COUNTY

On October 27, 1989, approximately six weeks following its announced plant revision, BASF submitted a bid of $500,000 for 296.7 acres of industrial park land. Jack Wehman expressed hope for a successful culmination of the sale and stated that his company would begin a skills inventory of the local workforce. The skills inventory was quite successful as 1836 people completed surveys. BASF officials emphasized that the survey wasn't a job application; it was a tool to give BASF an idea of what skills local people have and what training would be needed.

At first it appeared that BASF was on the road to Terre Haute. But on November 2, 1989, four local anti-BASF groups united to form the Terre Haute Environmental Rights Coalition (TERC). TERC's attorney, Mike Kendall, wrote a letter to county attorney, Robert Wright, advising him that the terms of the BASF bid for the 296 acres of industrial park were extremely biased in favor of the company. Kendall said the county should reject the conditions of the BASF offer; Kendall reinforced TERC's opposition by stating that they would take whatever legal steps are necessary to prevent the sale.

Controversy heightened because BASF filed an amendment to its original bid that had substantial changes regarding its property rights at the industrial park if the sale was consummated. TERC's legal counsel indicated that BASF's amended bid may have violated the pubic bid law and expressed concern that the substantive changes made by the amendment may be a *de facto* new bid. Kendall also pointed out that the original bid was the only one available to the public from October 30–November 14.

On November 20, 1989, a public hearing on the BASF bid proposal sparked heated debate. Several BASF officials made presentations of the company plans and fielded questions from the public and county officials. TERC's attorney, Mike Kendall, stated the following summary position:

> We are not against having a facility such as the one described per se, but BASF's revised bid is not enough. We question the legality of negotiating a revised bid and the granting of easements which the BASF facility would require. County Commissioners do not have authority to accept an amended bid except one that raises the price and then only after certain other notice provisions have been complied with.

Other BASF adversaries continued to remind county officials that the industrial park had never been properly marketed and that no such plan existed. Advocates of BASF stressed that the Vigo County area was in desperate need of jobs.

Despite the threats of TERC and other sundry opponents, on November 22, 1989, the Vigo County Commissioners and Vigo County Council voted unanimously to accept BASF's bid for 296.7 acres of land in the industrial park. Selected parts of the sale order were as follows:

1. The Board of Commissioners finds that the county has no other need for the real estate; Vigo County has severe economic stagnation; the use of real estate for industrial development would help alleviate problems of unemployment and economic stagnation; the soil conditions of the real estate are appropriate for the manufacturing facility, incinerator and landfill.
2. The Commissioners are satisfied that the proposed facility will not threaten the health of local residents as long as the incinerator and landfill are operated in accordance with federal, state, and local laws, ordinances, regulations, and rulings.

A few days after Vigo County approved the sale of land to BASF, the company announced a formation of a Community Awareness Panel to provide information to the Vigo County region about BASF's plans and actions. Jack Wehman reported that the panel would meet monthly to discuss topics such as plant facilities, environmental standards, safety and emergency procedures, employment training and social commitments. Wehman stressed that the agenda was open and that panel members were their own people—not expected to be ambassadors for BASF. Although Wehman claimed that the Awareness Panel was a balanced representation of the community, he pointed out that anti-BASF people declined to serve. Two prominent leaders of the CCC, Harold Cox and John Strecker, rebutted Wehman's comments stating that they had not been asked to serve. Cox pointed out that the makeup of the Awareness Panel was skewed in favor of BASF.

TERC FILES LAWSUIT

On April 10, 1990, the Terre Haute Environmental Rights Coalition filed a lawsuit in U.S. District Court charging the following:

1. The Government Services Administration violated the National Environmental Policy Act by selling land to Vigo County without requiring an environmental impact study before each of two land sales to the county. TERC requested that the sales be declared null and void and that the title to the industrial park land revert back to the U.S. government. The suit also requested that the GSA be required to conduct an environmental impact study in light of the intended use of the land—e.g., a hazardous waste landfill and incinerator.
2. TERC also filed a motion for an injunction stopping the county from selling the 296 acres to BASF until the lawsuit is resolved.

TERC legal counsel, Mike Kendall, also stated that the lawsuits would be filed against county officials for failing to disclose the true use of the property to the GSA—a violation of the Racketeer and Corrupt Organizations Act. In response to the charge that GSA was negligent in failing to conduct an environmental impact study, Assistant U.S. Attorney Sue Bailey filed a motion to dismiss the TERC lawsuit based on the position that the action taken by the federal government was several years old and the property no longer belonged to the federal government. Jack Wehman, Midwest Venture Director for BASF issued a position statement:

> The frivolous filing of two federal lawsuits against the county and federal government by the Environmental Rights Coalition brings into question whether this group is concerned about the health and economic welfare of the citizens of Vigo County. BASF is not a defendant in either of the two lawsuits but, as a partner in the economic development of the community, we are disappointed in these self-serving delaying tactics. BASF is steadfast in its interest to invest more than $100 million in an automotive plant facility which will bring new jobs to Vigo County. BASF remains confident that the county and federal attorneys will resolve this matter to the satisfaction of the great majority of Vigo County residents.

Continued debate followed TERC's legal action. A countersuit was eventually filed by Vigo County Commissioners charging that TERC's complaint was "frivolous, unreasonable, and groundless." The countersuit further claimed that members of TERC were negligently and maliciously interfering with a contractual relationship simply to fulfill a goal of stopping the sale of land to BASF.

TERC responded with the following position statement:

> Some local government officials put all the public's marbles in one basket with BASF for less than 300 jobs. Instead of going after BASF, the commissioners should have spent the last two years enticing good corporate citizens with sound environmental records that would have provided hundreds of additional jobs. Having evaded the requirement for an environmental impact study and faced with a fickle BASF, the Vigo County Commissioners are in danger of being left with an empty plot of land, legal fees, and no jobs for our people.

In response to this legal impasse, Jack Wehman stated in mid-June, 1990, that if the federal lawsuit wasn't settled by September 1, 1990, BASF may decide to locate elsewhere. Wehman stressed that BASF must get its plant on line by the end of 1992.

BASF BREAKS OFF COURTSHIP

On September 4, 1990, Jack Wehman announced that BASF corporate officials in Germany had decided that the corporation would no longer consider land at the Vigo County industrial park as an option for its automotive plant. A big stumbling block to the marriage of BASF and Vigo County was the unresolved litigation filed by TERC claiming that the original sale of federal land by the GSA to Vigo County failed to comply with environmental regulations. Mixed emotions were recorded in the community ranging from bitter disappointment to jubilation. City and county officials faced the dilemma of developing a new marketing plan for the industrial park in order to attract new companies and create jobs. BASF executives wondered what they could have done to avoid the confrontation and how their location strategy should be changed in the future. TERC's legal counsel, Michael Kendall, stressed that BASF's decision is not an issue about a group of people who allegedly kept a company out of Vigo County. It is about a victory for environmental integrity.

Bibliography and References

"A Company At Work," *BASF Corporation,* January 1, 1989, 35 pages.

"An Economic Development Plan for the Vigo County Industrial Park," *Vigo County Redevelopment Commission,* November, 1988, 21 pages.

Annual Report, BASF Corporation, 1988, 28 pages.

———, "BASF Pulls Out of Wabash Valley," *Terre Haute Tribune Star,* September 10, 1990, p. A 1.

"BASF Corporation: Proposed Midwest Facility for Terre Haute," *BASF Corporation,* 1988, 9 pages.

"BASF Corporation: Proposed Midwest Facility for Terre Haute," *BASF Corporation,* January 1989, 10 pages.

Cox, Harold and Duffy, Pat, "Court Rules Against Plan," *CCC Newsletter,* Vol. 1, #3, Fall, 1989, p.1.

"GSA Disputes Kaufman's Claim," *Terre Haute Tribune Star,* March 14, 1989, p. A 3.

Halladay, John, "BASF Lawsuit Gaining Weight," *Terre Haute Tribune Star,* March 15, 1989, p. A 4.

———, "BASF's Efforts to Avoid Court Stopped by Judge," *Terre Haute Tribune Star,* March 16, 1989, p. A 1.

———, "Testimony Ends in BASF Lawsuit," *Terre Haute Tribune Star,* March 24,1989, p. A 1.

———, "BASF Hearings Sham, Foes Charge in Post-Trial Brief," *Terre Haute Tribune Star,* May 24, 1989, p. A 3.

———, "BASF Battle Heats Up Again," *Terre Haute Tribune Star,* July 6, 1989, p. A 1.

———, "Development-Environmental Tie Possible," *Terre Haute Tribune Star,* July 13, 1989, p. A 1.

———, "Officials Schedule New Hearings on Industrial Park," *Terre Haute Tribune Star,* August 26, 1989, p. A.1.

"Hazard Waste Incinerators," *Greenpeace,* 1987, 4 pages.

"Hazardous Waste Incineration: Questions and Answers, *U.S. Environmental Protection Agency,* April 5, 1988, 53 pages.

Heldman, Deborah D., "BASF Breaks Off Courtship With Vigo," *Terre Haute Tribune Star,* September 5, 1990, p. A 1.

Igo, Becky, "Chalos Says BASF Loss Could Hurt," *Terre Haute Tribune Star,* June 20, 1990, p. A 3.

———, "Counterclaim Filed On BASF Land Sale," *Terre Haute Tribune Star,* June 23, 1990, p. A 1.

———, "BASF Foes Call County's Legal Retaliation Intimidation," *Terre Haute Tribune Star,* June 26, 1990, p. A 3.

———, "TERC Files Opposition To Dismissal Request," *Terre Haute Tribune Star,* July 24, 1990, p. A 4.

LeBar, Gregg, "Chemical Industry: Regulatory Crunch Coming," *Occupational Hazards,* November, 1988, pp. 36–39.

Loughlin, Sue, "BASF Foes Ask Delay In Sale," *Terre Haute Tribune Star,* July 16, 1989, p. A 1.

———, "Several Foes Remain Opposed To BASF's Plans," *Terre Haute Tribune Star,* August 31, 1989, p. A 1.

———, "Community Leaders Beaming: Mayor Critical of Environmental Groups," *Terre Haute Tribune Star,* August 31, 1989, p. A 3.

———, "Federal Judge Thinking Over TERC Request," *Terre Haute Tribune Star,* April 13, 1990, p. A 1.

Petiprin, Amy, "More Than 1800 Fill Out Survey: BASF Completes First Step In Hiring Process," *Terre Haute Tribune Star,* November 5, 1989, p. A 1.

Porter, Kelley, "Too Secret or Just Not Ready?" *Terre Haute Tribune Star,* June 25, 1989, p. A 1.

———, "BASF's Chemicals List Still Not Complete," *Terre Haute Tribune Star,* April 7, 1989, p. A 1.

———, "Prof More Worried Now After Studying Incineration Data," *Terre Haute Tribune Star,* June 26, 1989, p. A 3.

———, "Judge Voids Economic Plan; Cites Conflicts," *Terre Haute Tribune Star,* July 1, 1989, p. A 1.

———, "Wright's Statements Labeled Speculative," *Terre Haute Tribune Star,* July 12, 1989, p. A 1.

———, "BASF Scales Back Its Plant Plans," *Terre Haute Tribune Star,* August 31, 1989, p. A 1.

———, "BASF Releases Chemical List in Continued Spirit of Sharing Facts," *Terre Haute Tribune Star,* September 2, 1989, p. A 1.

Robinson, Dick, "Commissioners Confident They Can Meet Land Deadline," *Terre Haute Tribune Star,* August 31, 1989, p. A 1.

Walters, Gordon, "BASF Submits $500,000 Bid For Industrial Land," *Terre Haute Tribune Star,* October 28, 1989, p. A 1.

———, "Environmentalists Form Anti-BASF Coalition," *Terre Haute Tribune Star,* November 3, 1989, p. A 1.

———, "BASF Bid Meeting Postponed," *Terre Haute Tribune Star,* November 15, 1989, p. A 1.

———, "Coalition Promises To Sue Commissioners," *Terre Haute Tribune Star,* November 21, 1989, p. A 1.

———, "County Approves Offer To Sell Land To BASF," *Terre Haute Tribune Star,* November 23, 1989, p. A 1.

———, "BASF Fulfills Panel Promises," *Terre Haute Tribune Star,* November 29, 1989, p. A 1.

Wardell, George, "Loss of Jobs Hurts Local Businesses," *Terre Haute Tribune Star,* February 26, 1989, p. J 4.

APPENDIX

EXHIBIT 1

Major Industrial Development Activity—Terre Haute, Indiana 1986–1991

Company	New Investment ($ In Millions)	New Jobs
★ Accurate Glass	+$ 4.0	+ 20
★ Alcan	+$95.0	−0−
★ Ampacet	+$25.5	+130
★ Avganics	+$ 3.0	+ 20
★ Bemis	+$71.0	+300
★ BF Goodrich	+$19.0	+ 50
★ CBS	+$24.9	+150
Coca-Cola	+$ 2.0	−0−

EXHIBIT 1

Continued

Company	New Investment ($ In Millions)	New Jobs
★ Dadc	+$30.0	+125
★ Distr. Term. Corp.	+$ .4	+ 2
★ Donnelley	+$ 2.0	+ 65
General Housewares	+$ .4	+ 20
Green Leaf	+$ 1.3	+ 35
★ Hercules	+$30.0	+ 90
★ Ivy Hill	+$ 5.0	+125
★ Jadcore	+$ 7.0	+ 75
★ Kyoto Foods	+$ 4.0	+100
★ Numerical Concepts	+$ 1.7	+ 45
Pfizer	+$55.0	–0–
★ Pillsbury	+$ 4.0	–0–
★ Pitman-Moore, Inc.	+$60.0	–0–
★ Shenango	+$ 4.0	+125
★ Snacktime	+$ 6.0	+170
★ Specialty Blanks	+$ 2.5	+ 34
Standard Register	+$ 3.0	+ 9
★ Tredegar	+$14.4	+ 60
★ Tri Industries	+$ 4.5	+205
★ Wabash Fiber Box	+$ 3.0	–0–
★ Western Tar	+$ .5	+ 5
★ Weston Paper	+$30.0	+ 5
★ Winslow Scale	$ .4	12
Totals	$511 Million	(+)1977

Major Commercial Development Activity—Terre Haute, Indiana 1986–1991

Company	New Investment ($ In Millions)	New Jobs
★ Boston Connection	+$ 2.0	+144
★ Conway Trucking	+$ 2.5	+ 22
★ Farmer's Market (s)	+$ .8	+ 48
Honey Creek Square	+$ 2.5	–0–
★ IBM	+$ 2.0	–0–
Indiana-AM. Water Co.	+$ .8	–0–
Merchants National Bank	+$ 3.0	+ 18
★ Miller Business Forms	+$ .4	+ 9
★ MRI	+$ 2.8	+ 5
OSCO (Ft. Harrison)	+$ 1.3	+ 22
Pharmor	+$ .9	+ 71
★ Plaza No. Shopping Ctr.	+$ 1.6	+125
Sam's Wholesale	+$ 2.2	+120
★ T.H. First National Bank	+$10.0	+ 65
T.H. Savings Bank	+$ .9	+ 6
Toys "R" Us	+$ 2.0	+ 75
★ Tribune Star	+$ 1.0	+ 10
★ Wabash Commission	+$ .5	–0–
Wal-Mart	$ 1.6	+175
Totals	$38 Million	(+)915

EXHIBIT 1

continued

Company	New Investment ($ In Millions)	New Jobs
* A.P.& S. Clinic	+$ 5.5	+20
Charter Hospital	+$ 4.6	+120
* Hamilton Center	+$ 2.7	–0–
* Regional Hospital	+$21.2	+244
* Union Hospital	+$20.1	+400
* ISU	+$51.4	–0–
IVY Tech	+$ 5.0	+56
Rose Hulman Inst.	+$14.0	+122
St. Mary's/Woods	+$ 2.0	–0–
* Vigo Co. School Corp.	+$30.0	–0–
* Airport Auth.	+$13.5	–0–
Federal Penitentiary	+$ 1.4	+41
Army Reserve	+$ 3.0	–0–
Natl. Guard-Air	+$ 4.0	+230
VFW Post 972	$ .6	–0–
Totals	$179 Million	(+)1233
Total New Investment	$729.5 Million	
Total New Jobs		4,125

(*) Denotes Companies Assisted by the City of Terre Haute

EXHIBIT 2

November 8, 1988

Dear Neighbor:

I am opposed to the BASF toxic waste incinerator and dump in Vigo County for reasons which I invite you to review, briefly summarized in this letter.

I have lived most of my life here, having owned and operated an automobile agency for thirty-six years. The economic and environmental health of this community is of crucial importance to me and to members of my family.

Recently, Vigo County officials wisely purchased a 1,500-acre tract close to Fowler Park to be used as a large, set-aside site for industrial development. This property is an absolute county jewel and we can be proud that our local representatives had the wisdom and foresight to acquire it. This site was reviewed by Toyota as the possible location for a large manufacturing complex which would have employed over 3,500 people. Although Toyota chose to locate in Kentucky, we surely now have, or will have, other good prospects for this land.

Currently the German-owned BASF Chemical conglomerate, the direct corporate offspring of I G Farben, has expressed interest in the site. Originally, they indicated their intention to build a paint and industrial coatings factory which would employ 400 local people. Months later, almost as an afterthought, BASF told us that they also planned to use the property as a collection area for hazardous wastes to be shipped to Vigo County from many other out-of-state BASF, factory locations. They have proposed that these wastes are to be incinerated here and buried on the 1,500-acre site.

If our goal in acquiring this prime industrial property is to maximize our opportunity for large-scale employment growth, I believe the sale of this tract to BASF, with the promise of only 400 jobs, represents an inefficient use of this important county asset. *We can and should do much better.* We must not now lose our nerve and become anxious to sell to the first possible buyer without seriously evaluating the long-term economic and environmental impact of such a sale.

My second objection to the BASF proposal concerns what I believe to be the negative tax effect which the incineration and dump operations would have on county taxes. Because BASF would be exempt from local property taxes on their waste disposal operations, it would mean that Vigo County taxpayers would, in effect, be subsidizing the BASF toxic waste operation. We would be receiving, processing, and storing toxic wastes here from other BASF plants whose host communities are permitted to enjoy the fruits of BASF payroll *and* property taxes. These communities would suffer none of the liabilities and dangers associated with BASF effluents. It's a terrific deal for BASF—with local tax exemptions we would actually help finance their disposal of wastes from other locations. At the same time, we in Vigo County would lose the potential for large-scale employment and property tax development and forever lose control of our 1,500-acre industrial development area.

My most serious concern is environmental. Indications are that BASF will be processing approximately 36 million pounds of hazardous waste annually— *and that may be only the beginning.* I believe that large-scale processing of toxic waste materials here represents a risk to our entire community which we must not take. These toxic wastes will have to be carried to our community by trucks or railroad cars with the attendant deadly danger of accidental spills; moreover, independent environmental experts appear to agree that toxic waste incineration can be dangerous to health. This would be particularly true here since our

EXHIBIT 2

Continued

---

prevailing wind direction would carry smokestack emissions over large and un-predictable parts of Vigo County. *Schools, parks, and homes are not exempt from the poisons carried by wind from incinerator smokestacks.*

It would also seem logical to assume that clay and plastic barriers used in the dump areas will eventually leak, permitting a gradual infusion of toxic sub-stances into our vital underground water supplies. One needs also to consider the effect on the dump of even a mild earthquake.

The immediate and potential environmental dangers of a BASF toxic waste facility in Vigo County would also adversely influence our ability to at-tract additional industry. It seems only reasonable to assume that industry deci-sion-makers would not knowingly move into an environmentally crippled com-munity. Environmental disasters associated with toxic waste disposal such as those at Hooker Chemical's Love Canal, and Velsicol Chemical's Marshall, Illi-nois plant should signal caution to us in Vigo County. Neither should we forget the suffering and death caused by Union Carbide's Bhopal, India factory and by Dow Chemical's Agent Orange.

We need to act immediately before decisions and commitments are irrevo-cable. If you agree with me that as a community we deserve better than to be-come a hazardous waste disposal center, I urge you to do three things:

1. Sign a petition opposing the BASF toxic waste operation. The attached paper is such a petition. Please sign it, indicating your address, and ask your friends and neighbors to join you. Return it, please, to me at the address shown below. We need to let our political officials know where we stand!

2. Write or call the following government officials—your representatives—and voice your objection to the BASF toxic waste operation:

County Councilmen

Councilman John Walsh 1711 So. Brown Ave., Terre Haute, IN 47803 Ph. 238–9440 (At Large)

Councilman Clyde Kersey R.R. 51, Box 508, Terre Haute, IN 47805 Ph. 877–2211 (1st District)

Councilman Robert Lawson P.O. Box 516, Terre Haute, IN 47808 Ph. 232–8686 (3rd District)

Councilman Charles Fouty 98 Antelope Drive, Terre Haute, IN 47802 Ph. 299–1227 (4th District)

Councilman Thomas Fitzpatrick R.R. 11, Box 606, West Terre Haute, IN 47885 Ph. 533–2273 (At Large)

Councilman Frank Kaperak R.R. 32, Box 14, Terre Haute, IN 47803 Ph. 877–9538 (At Large)

County Commissioners

Commissioner John Scott 529 Paris Avenue, West Terre Haute, IN 47885 Ph. 533–2278 (2nd District)

Commissioner James Diehl 6412 North 32nd Street, Terre Haute IN 47805 Ph. 466–2942 (3rd District)

Commissioner James Adams R.R. 52, Box 455, Terre Haute, IN 47805 Ph. 877–1638 (1st District)

EXHIBIT 2

Continued

> Mayor P. Pete Chalos
> City Hall, 17 Harding Avenue, Terre Haute, IN 47807 Ph. 232–9467
>
> 3. Attend an informational meeting Saturday, November 12, at Woodrow
> Wilson Jr. High School featuring an outstanding expert in the field of envi-
> ronmental hazard, Mr. Hugh Kaufman, Environmental Protection Special-
> ist Hazardous Site Control Division, Environmental Protection Agency. So-
> cial hour starts at 7:30 p.m. Meeting starts at 8:00 p.m.

Thank you for your time.

Sincerely,

Jim Shanks
R.R. 22, Box 550
Terre Haute, IN 47802
299–4474

WINDFALL?

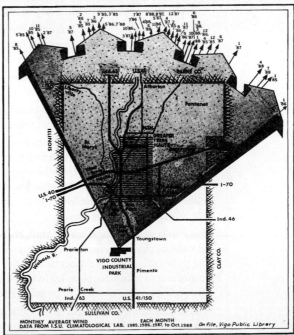

THE FALLOUT ZONE

Most of the toxic gases or particles that escape
the proposed BASF hazardous waste incinerator
will blow this way.

SOURCE: Personal letter and map received by the case author, November 10, 1988.

EXHIBIT 3

BASF Corporation   **BASF**
PO Box 234, Terre Haute, Indiana 47808
November 18, 1988
Dear Friend:

As you know, BASF, an American corporation, is seeking a site in the Midwest for a major new manufacturing facility. Vigo County is one of the locations under consideration.

The initial manufacturing plant will be an automotive paint plant although it is anticipated that many other manufacturing plants will follow in years to come.

During this year, we have spoken to dozens of community organizations and met hundreds of Vigo County residents to share our plans for development in the Midwest. Since I cannot reach everyone personally, I am writing to you with information about our project.

In future mailings we will address all aspects of the paint plant, the materials we intend to use at the site, the recycling of by-products, the waste materials, the processes of waste management, safety and health, and what future expansions can be expected. You deserve to know the *FACTS* in light of misinformation and distortions currently being distributed in your community.

If Vigo County becomes the prime site for our Midwest facility, the county and residents will gain the benefits including:

- $150 million of immediate capital investment. As future plants are constructed this figure will multiply many times.

- 500 skilled jobs, with at least 400 hired locally. These will be quality jobs with competitive wages, ones you can take pride in to support your family. The work force will grow with each new plant constructed.

- 3,500 new on-site/off-site construction jobs will be created during the erection of the facility.

- 1,000 new jobs available in the community to service the on-going operation of the initial paint plant and operations.

The positive statistics are numbers to consider in the economic development of your city and county. Keep in mind tens of millions of dollars in salaries will spill over into all sectors of this economy. More homes will be built, more cars sold and maintained, more clothes purchased. Service station owners, grocers, religious institutions—nearly everyone will receive some benefit from our positive impact on the economy.

You can certainly count on a significantly expanded tax-base that will benefit all public-supported institutions such as schools, libraries, hospitals and clinics, police and fire departments, and the like. There will be benefits for your community's infrastructure, including more money for road systems, utilities, airport expansion and future building projects.

These economic advantages are for the long term. BASF is not a company that makes business decisions or takes commitments lightly. Once a site is chosen, that community will share in the growth and lasting commitment of its new corporate citizen—BASF.

Jack M. Wehman
Venture Director
BASF Corporation

SOURCE: Personal letter received by the case author, November 21, 1988.

EXHIBIT 4

BASF Corporation   **BASF**
PO Box 234, Terre Haute, Indiana 47808

December 5, 1988

Dear Friend:

In my last letter, I highlighted the significant economic benefits that can be expected if BASF locates its new major manufacturing facility in Vigo County.

Today I want to focus on the important issues of long-term site development and environmental management. In spite of what others have alleged about BASF, I know that you are interested in the truth. Here are the *FACTS:*

- BASF desires to purchase 1,000 acres for immediate and *future* development. Most of the area will be utilized by manufacturing facilities, with the initial paint plant occupying more than 100 acres.

- Future installations considered for the site include an ink plant, an engineering plastics plant to service the auto industry, a facility to manufacture value-added or specialty chemical type products, a distribution and packaging center as well as a blending facility for agricultural products.

- About 200 acres in the southwest corner of the site will be maintained as a wildlife preserve in concert with our positive attitude toward environmental quality. BASF will also provide a 300–500 foot setback from the perimeter property line as a green buffer zone between us and our neighbors.

- It is expected that less than 25 acres will be required for the permanent storage of BASF wastes over the next 25 years. As new techniques are developed and implemented, it is forecast that less than 50 acres will be required for this over the next 100 years.

- Even after programs of waste minimization and recycling of materials, some wastes will inevitably be produced. BASF accepts its responsibility for quality waste management.

- BASF will treat and dispose *ONLY* BASF wastes. We are *NOT* a commercial waste treatment company, nor will we become one.

- We plan to build a high-tech incinerator system to treat certain waste materials. These will be burned at temperatures in excess of 2,000 degrees Fahrenheit under conditions that destroy even steel drums.

- Gases from the incineration system are cleaned in five unique purification steps (rapid cooling, liquid quench, electrostatic precipitation, filtration, two stage scrubbing) before discharge. The incineration system produces *NO* odors and poses *NO* health hazards.

- The incineration system has *NO* liquid discharges, only cleaned gases (such as carbon dioxide) and disposable ash. Incineration ensures the toxic nature of waste is destroyed, and it reduces the volume of waste by 90 percent.

- BASF will *NOT* burn or dispose of PCBs or radioactive wastes. No dioxin will be handled.

- BASF plans to construct and permanently monitor an *above-ground* hazardous waste landfill for disposal of certain solid materials, including ash. The ash will be combined with a cement-like substance resulting in solid rock-like material.

- No liquids will be placed in the landfill. In fact, the active use area will be covered by a moveable roof preventing rain and snow from entering the storage cells.

EXHIBIT 4

Continued

- Multiple barriers, both natural and synthetic, will isolate the above-ground storage cells from the ground water, preventing environmental contamination now and in the future.

- The incineration/landfill systems represent the latest state-of-the-art technology. They not only meet the letter of the environmental regulations, but the spirit as well.

- BASF will handle *ONLY* BASF wastes. Primary input of wastes to the incinerator will come from the site operation, but until the site is totally developed with other manufacturing plants, BASF plans to transport certain materials from other BASF locations for incineration and landfilling. As more plants come on line, the outside BASF wastes will diminish.

- The initial logistic operations at the Midwest site, including all raw materials, finished products and waste materials, will require only 20 truck movements per day. This is very minor in comparison to the 40,000 vehicles that daily use Indiana Route 41. Proper training and modern equipment will ensure safe transportation.

The promise we make, and accept accountability for, is to develop a major manufacturing campus that any community would be proud to have. That means a facility that provides good jobs, a growing opportunity and a bright future. And it means a facility that minimizes/recycles its waste and treats/disposes of it in a responsible, safe manner short-term and long-term.

BASF will build a facility that environmentalists as well as the chemical industry will see as a quality model for future country-wide implementation and development.

I am certain that the citizens of Vigo County will listen to the facts, recognize the truth and support BASF. In future letters, I will highlight other facts about our project.

In the meantime, I invite you to obtain a copy of a publication entitled, *Hazardous Waste Incineration: Questions and Answers,* published by the U.S. Environmental Protection Agency. This informative publication is available free of charge through the Alliance for Growth and Progress, 618 Wabash Street.

Thanks for your interest and attention, and please feel free to jot down your thoughts on the enclosed reply card. BASF wants to hear from you.

Jack M. Wehman
Venture Director
BASF Corporation

SOURCE: Personal letter received by the case author, December 7, 1988.

EXHIBIT 5

BASF Corporation   **BASF**
P.O. Box 234, Terre Haute, Indiana 47808

December 24, 1988

Dear Friend:

In recent letters I discussed the economic benefits and well-being of Vigo County should BASF select your industrial park as the home for its new Midwest manufacturing facility.

The response has been most impressive. The vast majority of the return cards and letters were positive and confirmed what I had already come to believe: Vigo County wants BASF.

Some excellent questions have also been raised about the type of employer BASF will make. In this third letter, we will answer those questions as well as address some additional pertinent issues. Here are the facts:

- The proposed economic redevelopment plan for the Vigo County Industrial Park is a tough but fair document. I support the adoption of the plan. The 500-employee automotive paint facility planned by BASF at the Midwest site would be only the first of many similar investments BASF is prepared to make in the Midwest.

- The $150 million commitment by BASF would represent the single largest investment ever made in Vigo County by an industrial employer. It would be accomplished *without* increasing taxes and, in fact, research shows that residents can expect a rollback in taxes.

- The tax base of Vigo County would increase significantly with the presence of BASF, benefiting all local public-supported institutions such as schools, libraries, hospitals and clinics. An expanded tax base also would mean more money for road systems and curbing, utilities and future building projects.

- Roughly 80 percent of our initial 500 employees would come immediately from the local work force. The jobs would be skilled, a vast percentage requiring at the minimum a high school diploma. Over the coming years employment is expected to increase with each new manufacturing plant, approaching 1,500 total employees, most of whom will come from the local region.

- BASF is prepared to work with the State of Indiana and the cities and counties in this region to share in the responsibility of training and developing such a skilled work force. That process likely would begin in 1989, two years before the plant is expected to be ready for production.

- BASF is known in the industry for its competitive wages, and although I am not at this time able to discuss salary scales, I can assure you that wages at the new Midwest facility will be more than competitive in the region.

- BASF is an equal employment opportunity firm. Our policy is to recruit, hire, train and promote based on a person's ability and without regard to his or her race, age, religion, national origin or physical handicap.

- BASF provides a comprehensive employee benefits program, including a medical plan for you and your family effective from the very first day you become an employee. A family dental plan is also available after the first six months of employment.

- Expanded life and accident insurance also are available to employees at extremely low rates. The minimum coverage is equivalent to one year's salary, and is provided at no cost to the employee.

EXHIBIT 5

Continued

- BASF also offers a 401(k) savings plan for all employees. Pension benefits are calculated from Day One. Normal retirement age is 65, but BASF allows you to continue to work if you so choose. If you do continue to work, service and earnings beyond age 65 also will be counted.

BASF is widely regarded as a quality employer, a leader in industry and a responsible company with vast experience in safety and environmental matters. Without doubt you would find BASF an economic asset to the Wabash Valley. But more importantly, I know you would find BASF a quality neighbor.

Jack M. Wehman
Venture Director
BASF Corporation

SOURCE: Personal letter received by the case author, December 28, 1988.

Union Carbide India Limited: The Bhopal Gas Incident

ARTHUR SHARPLIN, *McNeese State University*

I can say that I have seen chemical warfare. Everything so quiet. Goats, cats, whole families—father, mother, children—all lying silent and still. And every structure totally intact. I hope never again to see it.—MAYOR OF BHOPAL

In reality, there is but one entity, the monolithic multinational, which is responsible for the design, development and dissemination of information and technology worldwide.—INDIAN GOVERNMENT LAWYER

A corporation is not liable for the acts or omissions of another corporation by reason of ownership of stock.— UNION CARBIDE CORPORATION LAWYER

December 2, 1984, began as a typical day in the central Indian city of Bhopal. In the northern sector of town, shoppers moved about a bustling, open-air market. Here and there a customer haggled with a merchant. Beasts of burden, donkeys and oxen, pulled carts or carried ungainly bundles through the partly paved streets. Children played in the dirt. In the shadow of a Union Carbide India Limited (UCIL) pesticide factory, tens of thousands of India's poorest citizens milled about the shantytown they called home.

Inside the plant, several hundred Indian workers and managers went about their duties, maintaining and operating the systems that produced the mildly toxic pesticide Sevin. The plant was running far below capacity and most of it was shut down for maintenance. Poisonous methyl isocyanate (MIC) was used in making Sevin, but the system which produced MIC had been idle for six weeks. The Sevin unit was using MIC from a one-ton charge pot, which was periodically resupplied from either of two 15,000-gallon tanks (tanks 610 and 611). The tanks were half buried and covered with concrete. Tanks 610 and

Copyright Arthur Sharplin and the *Case Research Journal* (a publication of the North American Case Research Associaton).

Courtesy of Arthur Sharplin, McNeese State Univ.

The assistance and support of the Center for Business Ethics, at Bentley College, of which the author is a Fellow, is gratefully acknowledged. Union Carbide Corporation reviewed early drafts and suggested that certain factual errors be corrected, adding, "The fact that we have not commented on other statements [in the case] should not be construed as our affirming that they are correct." Finally, the author is grateful to certain anonymous Indian nationals without whose assistance this project would not have been possible.

611 respectively contained 41 and 20 metric tons of MIC at the time. A third storage tank (tank 619) was available for emergencies and for dumping off-specification MIC.

Sometime before midnight, several hundred gallons of water entered tank 610. News accounts would suggest the cause was improper maintenance procedures. But an Arthur D. Little consultant, hired by UCIL's U.S. Parent, Union Carbide Corporation (UCC), would conclude the water probably entered through a hose which a "disgruntled operator" connected to the tank during a 10:45 P.M. shift change.[1]

Whatever the source of the water, it reacted with the MIC, producing heat and gas. A relief valve soon lifted and MIC vapor began flowing through vent headers and out a discharge stack. Several of the workers noticed that their eyes started to water and sting, a signal they knew indicated an MIC leak. They reported this to the MIC supervisor and began to search for the leak. At about midnight, they found what they believed was the source, more than 200 feet from the tanks. They set up a fire hose to spray water on the suspected leak. It was 12:15 A.M. then, time for tea. The supervisors retired to the company canteen. A "tea boy" came to serve tea to the workers who remained on watch. The gas fumes were getting stronger, though, and the tea boy later said some refused to stop for tea. There were apparently other signals the reaction in the tank was growing more violent, such as increasing pressure gauge readings.

Within a few minutes, an operator called the supervisors back from the canteen. About a ton of MIC was transferred to the Sevin unit in an attempt to relieve the pressure. But the tank pressure gauge was soon pegged. A worker later said the concrete above tank 610 was moving and cracking. Someone sounded the alarm siren and summoned the fire brigade. As the futility of their efforts became apparent, many of the workers evacuated upwind, some scaling the chain-link and barbed-wire fence at the plant perimeter. At about 12:45 A.M., the vapor could be seen escaping from an atmospheric vent line 120 feet in the air.

The cloud of deadly white gas was carried by a northwest wind toward the Jai Prakash Nagar shanties, on the south side of the plant. In the cold December night, the MIC settled toward the ground (in the daytime, or in the summer, convection currents probably would have raised and diluted it).

As the gaseous tentacles reached into the huts, there was a panic and confusion. Many of the weak and elderly died where they lay. "It was like breathing fire," one survivor said. As word of the gas leak spread, many of Bhopal's affluent were able to flee in their cars. But most of the poor were left behind. When the gas reached the nearby railroad station, supervisors who were not immediately disabled sent out word along the tracks and incoming trains were diverted. This diversion cut off a possible means of escape but may have saved hundreds of lives. The whole station was soon filled with gas. Arriving trains would have been death traps for passengers and crews.

By 1:00 A.M., only a supervisor and the fire squad remained in the area of the MIC leak. The supervisor stayed upwind, donning his oxygen-breathing apparatus every few minutes to go check the various gauges and sensors. The fire squad sprayed water on the vent stack.

[1]Ashok S. Kalelkar (Arthur D. Little, Inc.), "Investigation of Large-Magnitude Incidents: Bhopal as a Case Study" (paper for presentation at The Institution of Chemical Engineers Conference on Preventing Major Chemical Accidents, London, May 1988), 26.

Of Bhopal's total population of about 700,000, tens of thousands fled that night, most on foot. An estimated 2,000 or more died and over 200,000 were injured.[2] An Indian appeals court later set the number of seriously injured at 30,000–40,000.[3] The surrounding towns were woefully unprepared to accept the gasping and dying masses. Confused crowds waited outside hospitals for medical care. There was no certainty about how to treat the gas victims, and general-purpose medical supplies were in hopelessly short supply. Inside the hospitals and out, screams and sobs filled the air. Food supplies were quickly exhausted. People were even afraid to drink the water, not knowing if it was contaminated.

The second day, relief measures were better organized. Several hundred doctors and nurses from nearby hospitals had been summoned to help medical personnel in Bhopal. Just disposing of the dead was a major problem. Mass cremation was necessary. Islamic victims, whose faith allows burial rather than cremation, were piled several deep in hurriedly dug graves. Bloating carcasses of cattle and dogs littered the city. There was fear of a cholera epidimic. Bhopal's mayor said later, "I can say that I have seen chemical warfare. Everything so quiet. Goats, cats, whole families—father, mother, children—all lying silent and still. And every structure totally intact. I hope never again to see it." A U.S. appeals court would later call Bhopal "the most devastating industrial disaster in history."[4]

By the third day, the city had begun to move toward stability, if not normalcy. The plant was closed and locked. A decision was made to consume the 20 tons of MIC in tank 611 by using it to make pesticide. Most of the dead bodies had been disposed of, however inappropriately. The injured were being treated as rapidly as the limited medical facilities would allow, although many people simply sat in silence, stricken by an enemy they had never known well enough to fear.[5]

COMPANY BACKGROUND

The Ever-Ready Company, Ltd. (of Great Britain) began manufacturing flashlight batteries in Calcutta in 1926. The division was incorporated as the Ever-Ready Company (India), Ltd. in 1934 and became a subsidiary of Union Carbide Corporation (UCC) of New York. The name of the Indian company was changed to National Carbon Company (India), Ltd. in 1941 and to Union Carbide India Limited in 1959. The 1926 capacity of 6 million dry-cell batteries per year had expanded to 767 million by the 1960s. In 1959, a factory was set up in India to manufacture flashlights.

By the 1980s, UCIL was involved in five product areas: batteries, carbon and metals, plastics, marine products, and agricultural chemicals. Exhibit 1 shows production statistics for UCIL products. Eventually, there were fifteen plants at eight locations, including the headquarters operation in Calcutta, and employed over 2,000. UCIL's petrochemical complex, established in Bombay in 1966, was India's first petrochemical plant.

[2]In Re Union Carbide Corp. Gas Plant Disaster, 809 F.2d 195 (2nd Cir. 1987).

[3]Union Carbide Corporation v. Union of India, Regular Civil Suit No. 1113 (High Court of Madhya Pradesh, Bhopal, India, 4 April 1988), 2.

[4]In Re Union Carbide Corp. Gas Plant Disaster, 809 F.2d 195 (2nd Cir. 1987).

[5]Except where noted, information in this section was obtained from anonymous sources in India and from dozens of news accounts which appeared in the months following the disaster.

EXHIBIT 1

Production Statistics

	1989 Cap.	1988–1989	1987	1986	1985	1984	1983	1982	1981	1980
Batteries (000,000)	917	718	536	572	528	510	510	512	411	459
Flashlights (000,000)	8	10	7	8	6	7	7	7	7	7
Arc carbons (000,000)	9	10	8	8	8	7	8	7	7	7
Carb. electrodes (000,000)	3	1	1	1	1	1	1	1	1	0
Printing plates (metric tons)	1200	450	358	416	393	376	412	478	431	399
Metal castings (metric tons)	150	31	22	18	19	17	18	13	16	15
Mn Dioxide (metric tons)	4500	4186	3620	4023	3670	3069	3335	3085	3000	2803
Chemicals (000 metric tons)	14	—	—	3	6	6	7	6	7	8
Polyethylene (000 metric tons)	20	—	1	7	19	17	18	17	20	19
Pesticides (metric tons)	—	—	—	—	18	1240	1647	2308	2704	1542
Marine prod. (metric tons)	—	—	—	—	—	272	424	649	642	601

The marine-products operation of UCIL was begun in 1971 with two shrimping ships. The business was completely export-oriented and employed fifteen deep-sea trawlers. Processing facilities were located off the east and west coasts of India. The trawlers harvested deep-sea lobsters in addition to shrimp. This division was closed in 1984 and the facilities were sold in 1986.

In 1979, UCIL initiated a letter of intent to manufacture dry-cell batteries in Nepal. A 77.5 percent-owned subsidiary was set up in Nepal in 1982, and construction of a Rs. 18 million plant was begun. The Nepal operation was solidly profitable by 1986.

The agricultural products division of UCIL was started in 1966 with only an office in Bombay. A letter of intent was issued by the Indian government that year to allow UCIL to set up a pesticide formulation plant at Bhopal. Land was rented to UCIL for about $40 per acre per year.

The initial investment was small, only $1 million, and the process was simple. Concentrated Sevin powder was imported from the United States, diluted with nontoxic powder, packaged, and sold. While UCC had no explicit technology-transfer agreement with the Indian government, there was continuing pressure under the Foreign Exchange Regulation Act to limit imports. This translated into demands by the government for UCIL to manufacture Sevin and its components, including MIC, in India. A UCC executive said later, "The last thing we or UCIL wanted to do was build a pesticide plant in India."

Another UCC executive later explained, "UCIL did not wish to incur the substantial capital investment of building a pesticide manufacturing plant in India because it was far less expensive to import finished pesticide from the U.S. and formulate it in India."[6] Eventually the investment at Bhopal exceeded $25 million, and the constituents of Sevin were made there. Another Union Carbide insecticide, called Temik, was made in small quantities at Bhopal. Exhibit 2 is a map of the Bhopal plant as it existed in 1984. Exhibit 3 is a flow diagram of the MIC production process.

The assets of UCIL grew from Rs. 558 million in 1974 to Rs. 1,234 million in 1983. (The conversion rate stayed near 9 rupees to the dollar during this period, moving to about 12 as the dollar strengthened worldwide in 1984 and 1985, then staying near 12 until 1989.) The *Economic Times* of India ranked UCIL number 21 in terms of sales among Indian companies in 1984.

Primarily as a condition attached to permission to construct the MIC project, UCIL had voluntarily diluted UCC's equity from 60 percent to 50.9 percent in 1977–78.[7] At the time of the Bhopal incident, UCC still held 50.9 percent, financial institutions owned by the Indian government held 25 percent, and the remaining 24 percent or so was in the hands of about 23,000 Indian citizens. The Indian Foreign Exchange Regulation Act (see Exhibit 4) generally

EXHIBIT 2   The UCIL Pesticide Factory at Bhopal

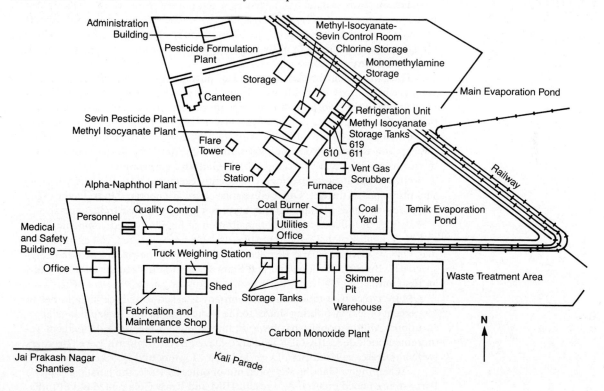

[6]Robert A. Butler to author, 17 July 1989, 5.

[7]"Amended Written Statement and Set Off and Counterclaim," Union of India v. Union Carbide Corporation and Union Carbide Corporation v. Union of India, Regular Civil Suit No. 1113 of 1986 (Court of the District Judge, Bhopal, India), 10.

EXHIBIT 3

The Methyl Isocyanate
Manufacturing Process

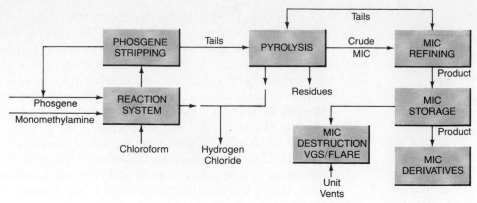

limited nonresident interest in multinational corporations operating in India to 49 percent. However, UCC was exempted from this provision based on its being a high-technology company.

Starting in 1967 an Indian served as chairman of the eleven-member UCIL board of directors. And foreign membership on the board was limited to four.

EXHIBIT 4

The Foreign Exchange
Regulation Act

The Act was originally enacted as a temporary measure in 1947. It was made permanent in 1957, then revised in 1973. The Act covers various aspects of foreign exchange transactions, including money changing, buying or selling foreign exchange in India or abroad, having an account in a bank outside India, and remitting money abroad.

The purpose of the Act is to restrict outflow of foreign exchange and to conserve hand-currency holdings in India. One provision requires that any company in which the nonresident interest is more than 40 percent "shall not carry on in India or establish in India any branch or office without the special permission of the Reserve Bank of India." But the Reserve Bank of India has authority to exempt a company from the provisions of the Act. The 40-percent requirement was changed to 49 percent by Rajiv Gandhi's government.

High-technology companies are frequently exempted from the equity-ownership provisions of the Act. Other companies that have operated in India for many years are sometimes exempted if they agree not to expand their Indian operations.

Policies in India regarding nationalization of foreign-owned companies have varied. A number of major oil companies have been nationalized. For example, Indian Oil Corporation, Bharat Petroleum, and Hindustan petroleum used to be, respectively, Burmah Shell, Mobil, and Stanvae (Standard Vacuum Oil Company, an Esso unit).

More typically, a multinational company is asked to reduce its holdings to 49 percent or less by offering shares to the Indian public and Indian financial institutions. Multinationals that have diluted equity to meet the 49 percent requirement include CIBA-GEIGY, Parke-Davis, Bayer (aspirin), Lever Brothers (which operates as Hindustan Lever in India), Lipton, and Brooke-Bond.

When Indira Gandhi was voted out of office in 1977, the Janata (Peoples') Party strengthened the Act. As a result, IBM and Coca-Cola pulled out of India. IBM's business in India was taken over by ICIM (International Computers Indian Manufacturers), a domestic firm. Another similar firm was set up to perform the maintenance services for the existing IBM computers.

In 1985, an expert on Indian industry affairs said, "Though the foreigners on the board are down to four from six in previous years, they continue to hold sway over the affairs of the company." However, UCC's chief litigation counsel, Robert A. Butler, wrote,

> None of Union Carbide Corporation's directors are on the Board of the Indian Company. All of the employees and officers of the Indian Company, including its Chairman and Managing Director, are Indian residents and citizens.

UCC said UCIL was not required to get its approval for even major capital investments, which were controlled by the UCIL board.[8] Monthly reports detailing operations and safety procedures were submitted by the Bhopal plant to UCIL headquarters in Bombay. UCC said these reports were not provided the U.S. parent, although certain periodic operating reports were submitted by UCIL to Union Carbide Eastern, a separate corporation charged with monitoring UCC investments in the Far East.[9]

UCC said it had conducted three safety audits at Bhopal at UCIL's request. The first two, in 1979 and 1980, were audits of personnel safety practices. The third was an evaluation of process safety in May of 1982. UCIL performed many safety audits itself.[10]

After the gas incident, UCC maintained it had never "had a presence in India"[11] and that UCIL was an essentially autonomous operation. A UCC executive said, "UCIL has been subject to less control by Union Carbide than any subsidiary I know of anywhere in the world."

OPERATIONS AT BHOPAL

On the surface, the UCIL insecticide factory was a typical process plant. A wide diversity of storage tanks, hoppers, and reactors were connected by pipes. There were many pumps and valves and a number of tall vent lines and ducts. Ponds and pits were used for waste treatment, and several railway spur lines ran through the plant.

Sevin is made through a controlled chemical reaction involving alpha-naphthol and MIC. Alpha-naphthol is a brownish granular material, and MIC is a highly reactive liquid that boils and becomes a gas well above usual daytime temperatures. In 1971, when plans were first made to make alpha-naphthol at Bhopal, a pilot plant was set up. A full-size alpha-naphthol plant (in fact, the world's largest) was finished in 1977.

In the meantime, work had begun on the ill-fated MIC plant. UCC provided the process design for part of the plant. Twenty senior Indian engineers went to UCC's Institute, West Virginia, pesticide facility in 1978 to study that plant's design and operation. An engineering company headquartered in Bombay, Humphreys and Glasgow, Pvt. Ltd., was retained by UCIL to produce the detail drawings for the plant and serve as general contractor. All the subcontractors were Indian firms. In 1979–80, five Americans were sent to assist the 1,000 or so Indian employees of UCIL in starting up the plant. All except

[8]Robert A. Butler to author, 17 July 1989, 5–6.
[9]Robert A. Butler to author, 19 July 1989, 6.
[10]Robert A. Butler to author, 19 July 1989, 6.
[11]Robert A. Butler to author, 26 May 1989, 9.

one of the Americans left in 1980. The other, with the title of "Works Manager," stayed on until December 1982, when he also left.

UCC was a world leader in MIC technology and provided much of the process design for the plant. But a UCC attorney later stated, "UCC was not involved with [the MIC plant's] construction and did not send engineers to supervise the construction."[12] A U.S. appeals court agreed, finding "The plant has been constructed and managed by Indians in India."[13] The attorney said UCC was uninvolved "both because UCIL was an autonomous company and because the Indian governmental regulations prohibited foreign involvement if Indians were capable of performing a given task."[14]

Even before 1980, when the MIC facility began operating, problems began to crop up with the alpha-naphthol unit. The latter system continued in various stages of shutdown and partial operation through 1984. V. P. Gokhale, managing director of UCIL, called the decision to make alpha-naphthol a "very large mistake." But he noted that the company was forced to do it to retain its operating license. The Bhopal factory was designed to produce 5,000 tons per year of Sevin but never operated near capacity; in the early eighties, UCIL was generally the third largest producer of pesticides in India, sometimes slipping to number four.

Annual profits of several million dollars from the Bhopal operation were originally predicted by 1984. But that was not to be, for several reasons. First, an economic recession made farmers more cost-conscious and caused them to search for less-expensive alternatives to Sevin. Second, a large number of small-scale producers were able to undersell the company, partly because they were exempt from excise and sales taxes. Seventeen of these firms bought MIC from UCIL and used it to make products virtually identical to Sevin and Temik. Finally, a new generation of low-cost pesticides was becoming available.

With sales collapsing, the Bhopal plant became a money loser in 1981. By late 1984, the yearly profit estimate had been adjusted downward to a $4 million *loss* based on 1,000 tons of output, one-fifth of capacity. To forestall what may have seemed inevitable economic failure, extensive cost-cutting was done. The staff at the MIC plant was cut from twelve operators on a shift to six. The maintenance team was reduced in size. In a number of instances, faulty safety devices remained unrepaired for weeks. Though instrumentation technology advanced at Union Carbide's other pesticide plants, the innovations were only partly adopted at Bhopal.

Upon reviewing the above paragraph, UCC's Chief Litigation Counsel, Robert A. Butler, wrote,

> This . . . suggests that the incident was due to cost-cutting, faulty maintenance, and understaffing. The facts do not support that claim. In fact, at the time of the incident the plant was well overstaffed.[15]

However, UCC Chief Executive Warren Anderson and Director of Safety and Health Ron Van Mynen had expressed a different view shortly after the incident. Anderson said, "I feel badly about it now, that we could have an operation within the Union Carbide complex that was running the way it [the

[12]Robert A. Butler to author, 26 May 1989, 6.

[13]In Re Union Carbide Corp. Gas Plant Disaster, 809 F.2d 195 (2nd Cir. 1987).

[14]Robert A. Butler to author, 17 July 1989, 7.

[15]Robert A. Butler to author, 26 May 1989, 6.

Bhopal facility] was running—in total disregard for operating procedures."
Van Mynen remarked,

> I had never been to Bhopal earlier, but some members of my team had been there.
> And I must admit that they were shocked at what they saw. When they had been
> there earlier the [safety] equipment was running according to s.o.p., and when we
> did get there in '84, after the event, it was not running, and it had not been run-
> ning. And it was a surprise to those gentlemen who had worked so hard in the
> startup of the plant.[16]

On the night of the disaster, several safety systems failed to work adequately
or were at least suspect. For example, the flare tower, used for burning carbon
monoxide, had been taken out of service to repair corroded piping a few days
earlier. UCC recommended maintaining MIC at temperatures below 5 degrees Celsius (41 degrees Fahrenheit) because it was an unstable liquid that
reacted unpredictably to changes in temperature. But the refrigeration unit
cooling the three MIC storage tanks had repeatedly malfunctioned and had
been shut down since June.

The UCIL directors, like the UCC parent, disclaimed fault for the incident.
The "Report of Directors," included in UCIL's 1984 annual report, stated:

> At no time had any significant fault been found with the working or safety precau-
> tions taken by your Company. Your Company had taken all safety precautions to
> avoid any accident in the Plant, which had been operated all along with trained and
> qualified operators.

In early 1985, the government of India cancelled the operating license of
the Bhopal plant, clearing the way for the plant's dismantlement. The likelihood that this would happen provoked a Bhopal political leader to remark,
"We've lost 2,000 lives; now must we lose 2,000 jobs?"

FINANCE

Exhibit 5 provides financial summaries for UCIL. Exhibit 6 gives selected
comparative financial statistics for the U.S. and India. During the months before the Bhopal disaster, UCIL's common shares, listed on the Bombay and
Calcutta stock exchanges, hovered around Rs. 30. They dropped to a low of Rs
15.8 on December 11, recovering only slightly in succeeding months. The
shares reached a high of Rs. 43 in January 1986 but then fell steadily to the
mid-teens by late 1987, rising again to the mid-twenties in July 1989. The exchange rate was Rs. 16.38 per U.S. dollar on July 16.

In 1975, the United States Export-Import bank, in cooperation with First
National Citibank of New York, approved loans of $2.5 million to UCIL for the
MIC project. Also, the Industrial Credit and Investment Corporation of India
(ICICI), a government agency, authorized a Rs. 21.5 million loan, part of
which was drawn in 1980. Finally, long-term loans were provided by several
other Indian financial institutions and insurance companies. Some of these
loans were guaranteed by the State Bank of India. UCC guaranteed none of
the loans of UCIL.

UCC stock was listed on the New York Stock Exchange. It traded near $50
in the months before December 1984, down from its historical high of $74,

[16]Kenneth Brooks, "Carbide's Report: How Bhopal Happened," *Chemical Week,* 27 March 1985, 9.

EXHIBIT 5

Financial Statements (Rs. 000,000 except as noted)[1]

Balance Sheet

	1984	1985	1986	1987	1988–89[2]
FUNDS EMPLOYED					
Fixed Assets	467	324	294	286	302
Investments	14	10	14	80	32
Net Current Assets	472	534	805	803	416
Deferred Revenue Expd			9	9	9
Bhopal Compn Deposit					690
	953	868	805	803	1448
FINANCED BY					
Share Capital & Reserves	686	687	698	706	776
Loan Funds	268	181	107	97	672
	953	868	805	803	1448

Summary of Operations

	1979	1980	1981	1982	1983	1984	1985	1986	1987	1988–1989[2]
Income	1465	1720	1881	2092	2122	2245	2444	2175	2010	2578
Materials Consumed	598	757	847	955	916	980	1057	874	803	971
Operating Exp Empl related	188	199	218	246	272	283	337	325	347	438
Other Operating Exp	228	265	315	364	395	391	382	385	315	390
Depreciation	32	37	41	42	48	50	56	39	22	24
Interest	20	32	28	53	58	47	31	24	19	33
Excise Duty	261	270	258	287	286	340	431	420	431	623
PBT	138	161	175	147	148	153	65	90	73	100
Income Tax	73	80	80	50	55	71	64	40	25	30
Net profit	65	81	95	97	93	82	13	50	48	70
Dividends	35	46	49	49	49	16	—	39	39	—

NOTE: Figures below in rupees

Sh. price: high 30.9 36.0 31.7 28.1 28.3 29.8 37.0 43.0

          low   25.5 22.0 24.9 23.3 21.5 18.5 17.1 20.0

[1]Column totals may not check and amounts less than 500,000 Rs. are shown as zero, due to rounding.

[2]Financial data are for the period 12/26/87 to 3/31/89.

reached in 1983. When news of Bhopal reached the U.S. the stock fell to near $30, to remain there until takeover rumors would propel it upward six months later. The rumors would soon subside, though, and the stock would trade near $30 throughout most of 1989.

THE GAF RAID

GAF Corporation increased its holdings of UCC stock in 1985 and announced a takeover effort. The two companies had markedly different corporate cul-

EXHIBIT 6

Comparative Financial Statistics for the U.S. and India

Year	U.S. Producer Price Index[1]	India Wholesale Price Index[2]	Conversion Rate[3]
1974	161.1	169.2	8.111
1975	175.1	175.8	8.914
1976	183.6	172.4	8.985
1977	195.8	185.4	8.703
1978	197.1	185.0	8.189
1979	215.8	206.5	8.108
1980	244.5	248.1	7.872
1981	269.8	278.4	8.728
1982	280.7	288.7	9.492
1983	285.2	316.0	10.129
1984	291.1	338.4	11.402
1985	293.7	357.8	12.352
1986	289.7	376.8	12.680

[1]Wholesale Price Index before 1978. Arithmetic average of monthly figures. Base year, 1967.

[2]Arithmetic average of April-March monthly figures. Base year, 1970 (April 1970-March 1971).

[3]Arithmetic average of monthly figures (rupees per dollar).

tures. GAF had a reputation for legal toughness, if not ruthlessness, having been successfully involved in massive toxic tort litigation (related to asbestos) for decades. GAF Chairman Samuel J. Heyman, an attorney, had muscled his way into control of the company in a bitter proxy fight in 1983. *The Wall Street Journal* reported a widespread belief that Heyman was likely to fire all the top managers of UCC if he ever gained control.

In contrast to what might have been expected from GAF, UCC Chairman Warren Anderson had expressed extreme sympathy for the victims of Bhopal and had even gone there to try to help. Though most of his attempts at providing financial and medical aid were rebuffed, he continued to assume major responsibility for the incident, saying it would be his main concern for the rest of his working life. Anderson also admitted the MIC plant should not have been operating in its condition at the time, one of several statements he made which later complicated his company's legal defenses. Anderson said, "Right from the beginning . . . we said that we'd accept moral responsibility," but from a legal standpoint, he noted, "It's their company, their plant, their people."[17]

Union Carbide managers rushed to erect takeover barriers and took actions to make the company less desirable as a merger candidate. Golden parachutes worth at least $8.8 million were adopted for forty two of the executives. Two operating divisions were set up, one for chemicals and plastics and the other for everything else. Various assets were written down by nearly $1 billion. The employee retirement plan was amended to free the $500 million "surplus" in the pension fund "for general corporate purposes." Union Carbide repurchased

[17]Kenneth Brooks, "Carbide's Report: How Bhopal Happened," *Chemical Week*, 27 March 1985, 10.

56 percent of its outstanding common stock, issuing $2.52 billion in high-interest (avg. 14.2 percent) debt in the transaction.

The Wall Street Journal later reported 3.2 million of the shares were purchased by UCC in a private deal with Ivan Boesky. Boesky's UCC machinations figured prominently in his subsequent conviction for various securities violations. GAF, too, was later charged with stock manipulation and other offenses growing out of its efforts to take over UCC and, having failed in that, to profit from the adventure. Boyd Jeffries, also later convicted of stock manipulation, was involved in the alleged GAF crimes. There was never any suggestion UCC was involved in these alleged offenses.

After the takeover attempt was thwarted, much of the UCC debt was repaid. Money for the repayment came from three major sources. First, the sale of Union Carbide's agricultural products and electrical carbon units and the sale of leaseback of the Danbury, Connecticut, headquarters building provided $875 million. Second, 30 million new common shares brought $651 million. Third, the divestiture of UCC's Consumer Products Division provided substantial funds. Within months, Union Carbide stock recovered to predisaster levels. After a three-for-one split in 1986 the shares continued to climb, reaching the low thirties (high eighties corrected for the split) by early 1989.

PERSONNEL

In 1984, all of UCIL's approximately 9,000 employees were Indians, according to UCC.[18] The Bhopal plant accounted for 10 percent of these. In general, the engineers at Bhopal were among India's elite—better educated, according to a UCC official, than the average American engineer. Most new engineers were recruited from the prestigious India Institutes of Technology and were paid wages comparable with the best offered in Indian industry. Successful applicants were given two years of training before being certified for unsupervised duty.

Until the late 1970s only first-class science graduates or persons with diplomas in engineering were hired as operators at Bhopal. New employees were given six months of theoretical instruction, followed by on-the-job training. As cost-cutting efforts proceeded in the 1980s, standards were lowered significantly. Some persons with only high school diplomas were hired, and training was said to be less rigorous than before. In addition, the number of operators on a shift was reduced, and many supervisory positions were eliminated. UCC officials have said that there is no evidence that lowered educational standards had any impact on the incident.[19]

The Indian managers at UCIL developed strong ties with the local political establishment. A former police chief became the plant's security contractor. A local political party boss, who was also president of the Bhopal Bar Association, got the job as company lawyer. *Newsweek* reported that a luxurious guest house was maintained by UCIL, and "lavish" parties were thrown there for local dignitaries.

In general, wages at the Bhopal factory were well above those in domestic

[18]"Amended Written Statement and Set Off and Counterclaim," Union of India v. Union Carbide Corporation and Union Carbide Corporation v. Union of India, Regular Civil Suit No. 1113 of 1986 Court of the District Judge, Bhopal, India), 11.

[19]Robert A. Butler to author, 19 July 1989, 9.

firms. Still, as prospects continued downward after 1981, a number of senior managers and junior executives began to abandon ship. The total work force at the plant dropped from a high of about 1,500 to about 900. This reduction was accomplished through voluntary departures rather than layoffs. An Indian familiar with operations at Bhopal said,

> The really competent and well-trained employees, especially managers and supervisors, got sick of the falling standards and indifferent management and many of them quit despite high salaries at UCIL. Replacements were made on an ad hoc basis. Even guys from the consumer-products division, who only knew how to make batteries, were drafted to run the pesticide plant.

A UCC attorney disputed this, writing,

> This is wholly inaccurate. Any individuals who left were replaced by competent, well-trained and experienced individuals. In addition, the reduction in the work force resulted primarily from the shut down of the alpha-naphthol unit rather than any alleged disillusionment on the part of the employees.[20]

In May 1982, a team from UCC headquarters audited the safety status of the MIC plant. The team listed as many as ten major deficiencies in the safety procedures that the plant followed. The high turnover in plant personnel was noted and commented upon. (A UCC official later commended, "The plant addressed all of these deficiencies well before the incident. None had anything to do with the incident."[21]) The team declared it had been impressed with the operating and maintenance procedures at Bhopal.

MARKETING AND DEMOGRAPHICS

The population of India was over 700 million persons in the 1980s, although its land area was only about one-third that of the United States. Three-fourths of India's people depended on agriculture for a livelihood. Only about one-third of the population was literate. Modern communications and transportation systems connected the major cities, but the hundreds of villages were largely untouched by twentieth-century technology.

English was at least a second tongue for most Indian professionals, but not for ordinary Indians. There were sixteen officially recognized languages in the country. The national language was Hindi, which was dominant in five of India's twenty-five states. The working classes spoke hundreds of dialects, often unintelligible to neighbors just miles away.

India's farmers offered at best a challenging target market. They generally eked out livings from small tracts of land. Most had little more than subsistence incomes and were reluctant to invest what they had in such modern innovations as pesticides. They were generally ignorant of the right methods of application and, given their linguistic diversity and technological isolation, were quite hard to educate. To advertise its pesticides, UCIL used billboards and wall posters as well as newspaper and radio advertisements.

Radio was the most widely used advertising medium in India. The state-owned radio system included broadcasts in local languages as well as in Hindi. Companies could buy advertising time on the stations, but it was costly to

[20]Robert A. Butler to author, 19 July 1989, 10.
[21]Robert A. Butler to author, 26 May 1989, 9.

produce commercials in so many dialects. Much of the state-sponsored programming, especially in rural areas, was devoted to promoting agriculture and instructing farmers about new techniques. Often the narrators mentioned products such as Sevin and Temik by name.

Movies provided another popular promotional tool. Most small towns had one or more cinema houses, and rural people often traveled to town to watch the shows. Advertisements appeared before and after main features and were usually produced in regional languages though not in local dialects.

Until the eighties, television was available only in the cities. During 1984, a government program spread TV relay stations at the rate of more than one each day, with the result that 80 percent of the population was within the range of a television transmitter by the end of the year. Still, few rural citizens had ready access to television receivers.

Pesticide sales were highly dependent on agricultural activity from year to year. In times of drought, like 1980 and 1982, UCIL's pesticide sales suffered severe setbacks. In 1981, abundant rains helped spur sales.

India had a very extensive network of railways; the total track mileage was second only to that of the U.S.S.R. The road and highway system crisscrossed the areas in between the railway lines. The railway system was especially significant to UCIL's pesticide operation because Bhopal lay near the junction of the main east-west and north-south tracks in India. An Indian familiar with the agricultural economy remarked, "Overall, physical distribution of pesticides is not too monumental a task. Getting farmers to use them and teaching them how are the real problems."

The marketing division for agricultural products was headquartered in Hyderabad, in southern India. Eight branch offices were scattered all over the country. Sales were made through a network of distributors, wholesalers, and retailers. Representatives from the branch offices booked orders from the distributors and wholesalers. Retailers got their requirements from wholesalers, who, in turn, were supplied by distributors. The distributors got their stocks from the branch offices. The branch office "godowns" (warehouses) were supplied directly from the Bhopal plant. The retailers' margin was 15 percent. Wholesalers and distributors each received about 5 percent. Most of the retailers were family or individually owned concerns, although some of UCIL's pesticides were sold at retail through government agricultural sales offices.

THE LEGAL BATTLE

After the Bhopal tragedy UCC and UCIL executives were charged with manslaughter and other crimes. UCC Chairman Anderson, along with the head of UCIL, was arrested and briefly detained by Indian officials when he went to India shortly after the incident. Seven UCIL employees were also arrested.[22] UCC investigators were barred from the plant at first, given only limited access to records and reports, and, for over a year, prohibited from interviewing employees.[23]

[22]Ashok S. Kalelkar (Arthur D. Little, Inc.), "Investigation of Large-Magnitude Incidents: Bhopal as a Case Study" (paper for presentation at The Institution of Chemical Engineers Conference on Preventing Major Chemical Accidents, London, May 1988), 7.

[23]Ashok S. Kalelkar (Arthur D. Little, Inc.), "Investigation of Large-Magnitude Incidents: Bhopal as a Case Study" (paper for presentation at The Institution of Chemical Engineers Conference on Preventing Major Chemical Accidents, London, May 1988), 3, 7.

Anderson said, "The name of the game is not to nail me to the wall but to provide for the victims of the disaster." He volunteered UCC to help provide funding for a hospital to treat the Bhopal victims. The company contributed $1 million to a victim's relief fund. It and UCIL set aside $20 million for relief payments. Though Anderson said the offer was unconditional, the Indian government spurned it.

UCIL offered to build a new plant, one that would use nontoxic inputs, on the Bhopal site. One proposal was for a nonhazardous formulation plant to be constructed by UCIL and operated by the state government. Alternatively, UCIL suggested a battery factory it would own and operate. Both ideas were turned down by the Indian government.

A number of U.S. and Indian lawyers rushed to sign up gas victims and their relatives as clients. On December 7, 1984, the first of some 145 "class action" lawsuits was filed in the U.S. on behalf of the victims of the disaster. For example, famed attorney Melvin Belli brought suit for $15 billion. In March 1985, India enacted the Bhopal Gas Leak Disaster Act, giving the Indian government the exclusive right to represent the victims. The Attorney General of India was authorized to sue Union Carbide in an American court. A Minneapolis law firm that specialized in product liability cases was retained to represent India. In February 1985, a judicial panel in the U.S. ordered all the lawsuits related to Bhopal consolidated in a single court—that of Judge John F. Keenan in Manhattan. The Attorney General of India asserted that compensation had to be in accordance with American standards and continued to press the lawsuit while engaging in out-of-court negotiations with Union Carbide.

In his statement before Judge Keenan, he argued,

Key management personnel of multinationals exercise a closely-held power which is neither restricted by national boundaries nor efficiently controlled by international law. The complex corporate structure of the multinational, with networks of subsidiaries and divisions, makes it exceedingly difficult or even impossible to pinpoint responsibility for the damage caused by the enterprise to discrete corporate units or individuals. Persons harmed by the acts of a multinational corporation are not in a position to isolate which unit of the enterprise caused the harm, yet it is evident that the multinational enterprise that caused the harm is liable for such harm.

A UCC attorney later remarked, "The government's multinational enterprise theory has never been sustained by any court in the world, and it lacks any legal basis."[24]

The primary focus of the U.S. case was UCC's plea of *forum non-conveniens*—that India, not the U.S., was the appropriate place for any trial because most of the documents, litigants, evidence, and witnesses were in India. UCC had reasons in addition to convenience and cost to prefer the Indian forum. Although both the Indian and the U.S. legal systems were based on English common law, punitive damages were almost unheard of in Indian courts and compensatory damage awards were generally much lower than in the U.S. For example, an appeals court in India was soon to estimate the following scale of compensation for Bhopal victims should the matter go to final judgment there:

[24]Robert A. Butler to author, 26 May 1989, 10.

Death or total permanent disability	Rs 200,000
Partial permanent disability	Rs 100,000
Temporary partial disability	Rs 50,000 [25]

As UCC struggled to recover from the disaster and restore its public image, two events thrust the company back to the forefront of international news coverage. First, in June 1985 hundreds of persons were affected by California watermelons grown on soil to which the Union Carbide pesticide Temik had been applied (improperly applied, according to the company). Second, in August a leak of the chemical intermediate aldecarb oxime at the company's Institute, West Virginia, plant, the only U.S. facility to make MIC, sent 135 people to hospitals. West Virginia governor Arch Moore publicly criticized Union Carbide's handling of the incident and Anderson admitted the company had waited too long to warn residents.

In May 1986 Judge Keenan ruled the case should be tried in India.[26] The decision would be affirmed by an appeals court in early 1987.[27] In September 1986 consideration of the suit resumed in the Court of the District Judge in Bhopal. UCC attorneys denounced the central and state governments in India for their alleged liability for the disaster. The company's answer denied every charge leveled against UCC. It claimed the factory was run by UCIL and pointed out that no U.S. citizen had been employed there for two years before the disaster. UCC also stated that sabotage was responsible for the disaster and alleged that there was a conspiracy among UCIL employees and a separate conspiracy among government investigators to conceal evidence after the incident.[28] The Indian government expressed outrage at Union Carbide's position and set its damage claim at $3.1 billion.

The hearings continued concurrently with out-of-court negotiations. As 1987 drew to an end, there were rumors of a settlement. Union Carbide offered $500 million in payments over time (then present value, about $350 million). Each dependent of the 2,600 people Union Carbide said were killed in the incident was to receive $2,000 a year for 10 years. The chronically ill would get $1,000 annually for the same period. And those slightly injured would be given a single payment of $500. The Indian government offered to settle for $615 million in cash. When news of a possible settlement leaked out, there was a furious public outcry in India. Former Indian Supreme Court Chief Justice P. N. Bhagwati demanded that any settlement include an admission of guilt by Union Carbide.

As the settlement talks appeared to break down in December 1987, Judge M. V. Deo ordered UCC to pay $270 million in interim compensation to the gas victims.[29] Union Carbide filed an appeal of the order, calling the idea of interim damages—before a defendant was found to owe anything at all—"unprecedented." The company continued to assert that it was confident of prov-

---

[25]Union Carbide Corporation v. Union of India, Order in Gas Claim No. 1113/86, Civil Revision 26/88 (High Court of Madhya Pradesh, April 4, 1989), 98.

[26]In Re Union Carbide Corp. Gas Plant Disaster, 634 F. Supp. 842 (S.D.N.Y. 1986, as amended June 10, 1986).

[27]In Re Union Carbide Corp. Gas Plant Disaster, 809 F.2d 195 (2nd Cir. 1987).

[28]Robert A. Butler to author, 19 July 1989, 10.

[29]Union of India v. Union Carbide Corporation, Gas Claim Case No. 1113 of 1986 (Court of the District Judge, Bhopal, India, 17 December 1987).

ing that the disaster was the result of sabotage and that it could not be held accountable in any case for the acts or omissions of UCIL, in which it claimed to only own stock. Judge Deo's decision was upheld by the High Court of Madhya Pradesh on 4 April 1988, although the interim award was reduced to about $190 million.[30] Both India and UCC appealed to the Supreme Court of India.

THE SETTLEMENT

On Tuesday, February 14, 1989, company lawyers were presenting arguments before the Supreme Court, when Chief Justice R. S. Pathak interrupted the proceeding. He then issued an order that UCC pay $470 million by March 31 "in full and final settlement of all claims, rights and liabilities related to and arising out of the Bhopal gas disaster." Acceptance of the order had reportedly been unanimously approved by the UCC directors in a telephone poll hours earlier. The order applied to all "criminal and civil proceedings" related to the Bhopal tragedy and thus purported to be a complete settlement of the case. UCC and UCIL paid their agreed-upon shares of the settlement—$425 million and $45 million, respectively—on February 14, 1989. The Indian Supreme Court was to oversee distribution of the funds.

UCC had previously set aside $250 million for damages and the company's insurance coverage was estimated at another $200 million. So paying the settlement would only result in an estimated $0.50 per share charge against 1988 earnings of $1.59 per share. UCC stock rose $2 a share on Tuesday and another $1.38 Wednesday, to close at $32.50, more than double the price (corrected for the three-for-one split) before the Bhopal tragedy. UCC was immediately touted as a prime takeover candidate, with an expected purchase price of about $50 a share, or $7 billion.

There was evidence some knew of the approaching settlement. A week before it was ordered, UCC stock jumped $2 a share on volume totaling over 8 percent of all outstanding shares. That was the highest volume of any NYSE stock in five months. UCC said it had no knowledge of any purported leak.

It was uncertain how and when the settlement money would be distributed to victims—or even how much of it would be. Bruce A. Finzen, one of the Indian government's U.S. lawyers, said, "Even at the rate of one hour per claim, you are talking about years of court time." The Indian government had already paid some survivors $800 or so for each immediate family member who perished. Medical care and certain other benefits had also been furnished by the government. But there were about 500,000 claims for relief, and only about 100,000 persons had been in the disaster area.[31]

There were immediate objections in India to the amount of damages and the nature of the settlement. But an editorial in *The Times of India* took a self-critical view:

> The government has been caught in a trap of its own making. It wanted as many applications for relief as possible to support its case for a bigger settlement. . . . I feel that many decent citizens were suddenly overcome by avarice. . . . It will be a very difficult task now to eliminate wrong claims. . . . In the first few days of the tragedy

[30]Union Carbide Corporation v. Union of India, Regular Civil Suit No. 1113 (High Court of Madhya Pradesh, Bhopal, India, 4 April 1988).

[31]K. F. Rustamji, "Coming to Terms with Bhopal," *The Times of India,* 8 March 1989.

the whole world sympathized with us. Carbide was prepared to do anything. . . . Aid was offered by several countries. . . . But at that time we thought it would hurt our national pride to take the help. (The Armenian earthquake has, however, set a new pattern of international help now). . . . We preferred to arrest the Carbide chairman. . . . The terrible suffering of the victims and their families has been subordinated, even made to appear irrelevant, by all the begging and brow-beating. All the bravery shown by those who struggled with the cloud's effect on the first day has been forgotten. . . . Now all that remains is to stand like vultures at the kill. The effect of all the propaganda war against the Union Carbide will be apparent in the coming years when we find that all foreigners, even the Russians, will look at any contract with India with suspicion, and press for safeguards so that liability of subsidiaries is not transferred to them.[32]

UCC chief Kennedy called the settlement "a fair resolution of all issues." And UCC attorney Bud Holman said the negotiations were like "walking up a winding staircase in total darkness," adding, "It's nice to be in the light." In its 1989 proxy statement, UCC reported it was continuing to spend $7–$8 million a year on "Bhopal-related litigation."

EXHIBIT 7
Excerpts from
Interviews

Gas victims and government officials in the Bhopal area were questioned in early 1987 concerning the gas incident. Upon reading excerpts from the questions and interviewee comments, a UCC attorney wrote they "are designed to inflame emotions, not inform the mind, and are of questionable value in an educational forum." He continued,

Such inflammatory rhetoric simply permit the participants to facilely blame companies such as Union Carbide without evidence and without a trial, rather than forcing the participants to confront the fundamental ethical issues facing host countries and companies which, of necessity, use toxic substances in their manufacturing processes.[33]

The abbreviated questions and responses are presented below.

Description of the incident?

A very thick layer of smoke caused uncontrollable tears, copious coughing, sneezing, vomiting. We ran to save our lives. We saw people in large numbers running here and there in great confusion, crushing each other, not bothering about anyone else.

I felt chilled and soon could not see.

I felt my eyes burning, like smoke coming from burning chilies. I was gasping for a breath of fresh air. I saw my neighbors in the same condition. A thin smoky layer was visible but its source was not known. Soon I was coughing and water was coming from my eyes and I fell unconscious.

At first I did not know what was happening because all my systems were affected. I was vomiting. My stomach was dislocated. My muscles were loose. Everyone was gasping for breath, running without any direction to find a safe place. Some of them demanded death as if was readily available at a grocery shop.

[32]K. F. Rustamji, "Coming to Terms with Bhopal," *The Times of India,* 8 March 1989.
[33]Robert A. Butler to author, 19 July 1989, 11.

EXHIBIT 7
Continued

Aftereffects?

I still do not know how bad it will get. It has become difficult to tolerate anything that is going wrong. I cannot remember like before.

I have become weak in body and mind. My memory has been affected badly. Carrying even small loads and fast walking has become a dream to me. I feel like an asthmatic patient.

The effect has subsided. But the resistance of the body is still down. My body has become allergic to muddy areas. The cough remains permanent and breathlessness occurs sometime.

Asthmatic, decreased vision, awfully unpredictable and irritable temper—future unknown, uncertain.

Loss in appetite, loss in weight, breathing trouble, uneasiness, poor eyesight, and weak memory power.

I cannot walk quickly and cannot run.

Assistance provided?

A mere Rs. 1500 has been provided as compensation and that is only to those whose income is below Rs. 500 a year. So we have not got any assistance so far from anyone.

Symptomatic treatment is being given without knowing the cause and the disease. This should stop.

None.

After three days I was treated at the hospital with antibiotics. But there was no definite diagnosis or treatment.

So far, nil. The policies made by the local government are unbelievable. They pay by economic and social status.

For us railway officers and our families nobody has done anything.

What should be done?

The M. P. [Madhya Pradesh, the state where Bhopal is located] government with the cooperation of the government of India and aided by Union Carbide or the American government should start a fully-equipped hospital basically concerned with lungs and eyes. Provision of work, housing, and education should be made.

Government should give proper treatment to the gas affected. They should rehabilitate those who lost their earner. They should stop a recurrence.

Next of kin of the deceased should be given sufficient money by UCIL. All affected people should be given suitable jobs by government. Proper treatment should be given by government out of fines imposed on Union Carbide because they have failed to give a safe design of the project and neglected all safety measures in the factory.

The affected people should be provided with good food to recoup their body. All over the world the Madhya Pradesh government has received donations for this so it must be utilized properly.

Nothing can be done now since everything is over.

Government should arrange to shift the factory to somewhere away from the town area.

EXHIBIT 7
Continued

The society at large, the government, and above all UCIL itself should have honorably taken to itself to soothe the sufferers. Their needs for the balance of their life span should be given gratis to them.

The government of India should pay compensation as applicable throughout the world. We are Indian nationals and all our interests are to be protected by the elected government.

What is likely to be done?

I am quite in the dark and disappointed.

I appears no one is serious to do much.

Considering the indifferent attitude of the Indian government, we are forced to compromise with our miserable lives. If anything concrete is done, it will be done only by UCIL.

Well, I wonder if anything is in store, the way it has fallen out.

Victims will be compensated and plants like this will be moved to remote places by government.

I am confident the government of India will pay compensation to all real sufferers.

Nothing.

Mostly non-affected persons and unemployed illiterate people, who chase the surveyors, get compensated.

Message for U.S. Business School Students?

Press your government not to allow multinationals like Union Carbide to operate anywhere in the world since they play with the life of people to enrich themselves.

More was expected and much better from the advanced elite in the community of nations. There is nothing but delay, tossing it from one door to another and from one country to another. It is a disgrace of the basest order to have left it to an indefinite body to compensate the sufferers, even if it was an additional burden. How can the most advanced society tolerate it?

The advanced nation like America while making any investment in developing countries should themselves ensure that all safety precautions are taken—before installing their factories. When they have already made this mistake at Bhopal, they should pressure their government and the management of Union Carbide to pay compensation without hesitation.

There is no question of talking to any other country. There is nothing to say but to blame the local administration for not arranging in a proper, methodic way in this modern world.

Multinational companies are playing with the lives of people and their property for the self interest of earning money at any cost and by any means.

NOTE: All statements excerpted in this exhibit were made by gas victims and government officials in the Bhopal area.

CASE PART IX

Total Quality Management

The Home Depot, Inc.

PAUL M. SWIERCZ, *The George Washington University*

It took a little more than a decade, but in this short period an Atlanta based retailer—The Home Depot, Inc. (Home Depot)—revolutionized the home improvement retailing market. By resolving the apparently contradictory goals of dedicated customer service and everyday low pricing, the company grew from four stores in Atlanta in 1979 to a chain of 147 massive (some over 100,000 square feet) warehouses offering more than 30,000 items. Sales volume in the decade from 1979–1989 increased from a modest $22 million to more than $2.7 billion.

Home Depot's meteoric rise has been well-documented in the business press, as have its innovative personnel policies. At Home Depot, people really do make a difference. The company pays above-average wages to its employees, approximately 90 percent of whom are full-time (an anomaly in the retail business). Salespeople have a reputation for being knowledgeable and prepared to answer even the most naive questions of would-be do-it-yourselfers (DIY's).

Corporate culture is promulgated through a variety of communications media and an intensive training program. For example, Bernard Marcus, Chairman, and Arthur Blank, President, personally have trained each of the company store managers, all of whom are promoted from within. Training is such an important issue at Home Depot that Marcus believes Home Depot employees become ill-suited to work anywhere else. He says, "Where do we find these people? Nowhere. We make them. We tell our people to make it here because they won't be able to make it at another organization. They'd be misfits."[1]

Individualism and entrepreneurialism are prized at Home Depot. "We teach from the top down," said Marcus. "We give employees the tools to do the job, then let them do it. At every level, they are not afraid to make decisions."[2]

The challenge for Home Depot in the 1990s and beyond, then, is to balance continued growth and retain its entrepreneurial spirit without sacrificing the values that have set it apart from other retailers. In 1979, Marcus predicted that

Paul M. Swiercz is Associate Professor, Department of Management Science, The George Washington University, Washington, D.C.

[1]*Fortune,* 12/29/88, p. 79.

[2]*St. Petersburg Times,* 12/24/90, p.11.

Home Depot would become "the Sears Roebuck of this industry."[3] Those who have witnessed the difficulties faced by Sears as it has attempted to adjust to changing business conditions will recognize the irony in Marcus' words.

HISTORY

In June of 1979, Home Depot opened its first stores in Atlanta, Georgia with 180 employees. Twelve years later the company had 147 stores in the Sunbelt (mainly Georgia, Florida, Texas, Arizona, and California) and the Northeast (see Exhibit 1), employing 22,000 employees with annual sales nearing $4 billion by the end of 1990.

Home Depot's CEO Bernard Marcus began his career in the retail industry in a small pharmacy in Milburn, New Jersey. He later joined Two Guys Discount Chain to manage its drug and cosmetic departments and eventually become the Vice President of Merchandising and Advertising for the parent company, Vornado, Inc. In 1972 he moved into the do-it-yourself home improvement sector as President and Chairman of the Board at Handy Dan/Handy City. The parent company, Daylin, Inc., was chaired by Sanford Sigoloff. He and Marcus had a strong difference of opinion over control, and one Friday at 5:00 p.m. in 1978, Marcus and two other Handy Dan top executives were discharged.

That weekend, Home Depot was born when the three men—Marcus, Arthur Blank (now President of Home Depot), and Ronald Brill (now Chief Financial Officer) laid out the plans for the do-it-yourself chain. Venture capital was provided by investment firms that included Invemed of New York as well as private investors. Two key investors were Joseph Flom, a takeover lawyer, and Frank Borman, then Chairman of Eastern Airlines.

When the first stores opened in Atlanta in 1979, the company leased space in three former Treasury Discount Stores with 60,000 square feet each. All three were suburban locations in the northern half of the city. Industry experts gave Home Depot 10–to–1 odds they would fail.

In 1980, a fourth Atlanta store opened, and the company had annual sales of $22.3 million. The following year Home Depot ventured beyond Atlanta to open four stores in South Florida and also had its first public stock offering at $12 a share. By early 1990 its stock had soared by 7,019 percent and split seven times.

The early eighties saw inflation rates rise over 13 percent with unemployment as high as 9.5 percent. These were tough times for most start-up companies, but Home Depot prospered as hard pressed shoppers sought out the best buy. The company was voted the Retailer of the Year in the home center industry in 1982 and had its first stock splits—January (three for two), April (five for four) and December (two for one).

By 1983, Marcus was a nationally recognized leader in the do-it-yourself industry. New Orleans was a strong market with many homeowners and young people, so Home Depot moved in with three stores. Other additions were in Arizona and Florida. Two stores opened in Orlando, in the backyard of the Winter Haven-based Scotty's, and one more in South Florida. Home Depot's strong drawing power became evident in stores as customers passively waited in long checkout counter lines.

[3]*Fortune*, 12/29/88, p. 79.

EXHIBIT 1 Store Locations

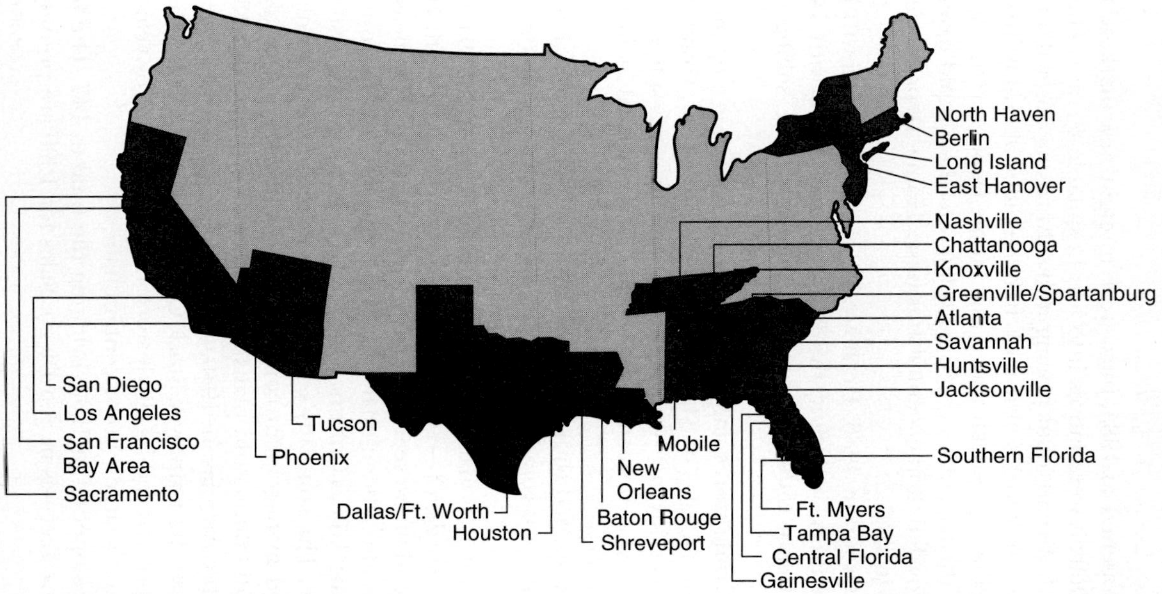

ALABAMA
- Mobile
- Huntsville

ARIZONA
- Phoenix
  - *Cave Creek*
  - *Mesa*
  - *Camelback*
  - *Thomas Road*
  - *Glendale*
  - *Scottsdale*
  - *Tempe*
- Tucson
  - *East Broadway*
  - *Oracle Road*

CALIFORNIA
- Los Angeles
  - *Huntington Beach*
  - *Fullerton*
  - *San Bernardino*
  - *Long Beach*
  - *Cerritos*
  - *City of Industry*
  - *La Mirada*
  - *Van Nuys*
  - *Pico Rivera*
  - *Covina*
  - *San Fernando*
  - *Upland*
  - *Corona*
  - *Monrovia*
  - *Tustin*
  - *Oxnard*
  - *Gardena*
- Sacramento
  - *Carmichael*

- San Francisco Bay Area
  - *Sunnyvale*
  - *San Jose*
  - *Fremont*
  - *San Leandro*
  - *Milpitas*
  - *Colma*
  - *San Carlos*
- San Diego
  - *Genesee*
  - *University Avenue*
  - *Oceanside*
  - *Chula Vista*
  - *El Cajon*
  - *Sports Arena*
  - *Escondido*
  - *Santee*

CONNECTICUT
- North Haven
- Berlin

FLORIDA
- Southern Florida
  - *Hollywood*
  - *Lauderdale Lakes*
  - *Dixie Highway*
  - *Hialeah*
  - *North Miami Beach*
  - *Palm Springs*
  - *Deerfield Beach*
  - *Flagler*
  - *Kendall*
  - *Lake Park*
  - *Margate*
  - *Davie*
  - *Jensen Beach*
- Jacksonville
  - *Atlantic*
  - *Blanding*
  - *Ramona*

- Central Florida
  - *Altamonte Springs*
  - *Colonial Drive*
  - *Southland Blvd.*
  - *Daytona*
  - *Melbourne*
  - *W. Colonial Drive*
- Tampa Bay
  - *Tampa*
  - *Clearwater*
  - *St. Petersburg*
  - *Brandon*
  - *Hillsborough*
  - *Port Richey*
  - *Largo*
  - *Sarasota*
- Ft. Myers
- Gainesville

GEORGIA
- Atlanta
  - *Decatur*
  - *Doraville*
  - *Marietta*
  - *Forest Park*
  - *Duluth*
  - *Kennesaw*
  - *Douglasville*
  - *Roswell*
  - *Buckhead*
- Savannah

LOUISIANA
- New Orleans
  - *Gretna*
  - *Harahan*
  - *East New Orleans*
- Shreveport
- Baton Rouge

NEW JERSEY
- East Hanover

NEW YORK
- Long Island
  - *East Meadow*
  - *Patchogue*

SOUTH CAROLINA
- Greenville
- Spartanburg

TENNESSEE
- Knoxville
- Chattanooga
- Nashville
  - *Madison*
  - *Antioch*

TEXAS
- Dallas/Ft. Worth
  - *North Richland Hills*
  - *Plano*
  - *Richardson*
  - *Arlington*
  - *Mesquite*
  - *Westmoreland*
  - *White Settlement*
  - *Carrollton*
  - *Northwest Highway*
  - *Forest Lane*
- Houston
  - *Bellerive*
  - *Lumpkin*
  - *Gulf Freeway*
  - *FM 1960*
  - *Stuebner*
  - *Market Street*

635

In 1984 Home Depot's common stock was listed on the New York Stock Exchange. Marcus believed about the only restraint Home Depot faced that year was its ability to recruit and train new staff fast enough. However, Home Depot was to soon face other problems. In December, things briefly turned sour when Home Depot bought the nine-store Bowater Warehouse chain with stores in Texas, Louisiana and Alabama. Bowater had a dismal reputation, its merchandise didn't match Home Depot's, and nearly all employees had to be dismissed because they were unable to fit the company's strong customer service orientation.

Of the 22 stores opened in 1985, most were in eight new markets. Going into Houston and Detroit were moves into less hospitable terrain. The company lost money with promotional pricing and advertising costs. This rapid growth into unknown territories also took management attention from the other stores. The media very quickly noted that Home Depot was having problems and suggested their troubles could be related to their rapid expansion into the already crowded home center business. Home Depot's earnings dropped 40 percent in 1985.

Marcus had to regroup in 1986. He slowed Home Depot's growth to ten stores in existing markets, including the first super-size store with 140,000 square feet. Home Depot withdrew from the Detroit market, selling its five new stores.

By 1987, six California stores and two Tennessee stores were opened and the company had annual sales of $1 billion. In that same year, Home Depot introduced an advanced inventory management system; as a result, inventory was turned 5.4 times a year instead of 4.5 times. It also awarded its first quarterly dividend.

In 1988, 21 stores opened with heavy emphasis in California. For the second time, Home Depot was voted the Retailer of the Year in the home center industry.

Home Depot expanded its market beyond the Sunbelt in early 1989 by opening two stores in the Northeast—East Hanover, New Jersey and North Haven, Connecticut. By the end of the year there were five stores in the Northeast.

The year 1989 was also a benchmark year for technological developments. All stores began using UPC (Universal Product Code) scanning systems to speed checkout time. The company's satellite data communications network installation improved management communications and training. Sales for the year totaled $2.76 billion, and plans were made to open a large 135,000 square foot store in Los Angeles. In 1989, the company made its initial contribution of $6 million to the Employee Stock Ownership Plan. On its tenth anniversary, Home Depot opened its 100th store (in Atlanta) and by year's end had become the nation's largest home center chain.

A total of 30 stores opened in 1990, bringing the total to 147. The largest store—140,000 square feet—is in San Diego. Sales for 1990 are predicted to be $3.8 billion.

Thirty-eight stores are planned for 1991 including further penetration in the Northeast—five stores are planned in Long Island, New York. A lumber distribution center will open near Chandler, Arizona, to serve the nine Home Depot stores in Arizona.

By 1995, the company projects a total of 350 stores with annual sales of $10 billion. The company will add 68 stores in the Northeast and on the west coast will expand from California to Washington state.

CORPORATE CULTURE

The culture at Home Depot is characterized by a strong emphasis on individuality, informality, nonconformity, growth, and pride. These traits reflect those of the founders of the company, who, within hours of being fired, were busily planning the Home Depot stores to go into competition with the company from which they had just been summarily dismissed. The culture is "really a reflection of Bernie and I [sic]," says Blank. "We're not formal, stuffy folks. We hang pretty loose. We've got a lot of young people. We want them to feel comfortable."[4]

The importance of the individual to the success of the whole venture is consistently emphasized at Home Depot. Marcus' statements bear this out: "We still are first-generation entrepreneurs . . . We are hands-on managers . . . We're individuals. People here think for themselves . . . Their dreams and desires can carry them wherever they want to go." While emphasizing the opportunities for advancement at Home Depot, Marcus decries the kind of "cradle to grave" job that used to be the ideal in America and is the norm in Japan. To him, this is "a kind of serfdom."[5]

Informality is always in order at Home Depot—"spitballs fly at board meetings" and there is always someone around to make sure that ties get properly trimmed. When executives visit stores, they go alone, not with an entourage. Most worked on the floors in the beginning and know the business from the ground up. They are approachable and employees frequently come forward with ideas and suggestions.

Nonconformity is evident in many different areas of the company, from the initial warehouse concept to the size and variety of merchandise to human resources practices. Both Marcus and Blank "flout conventional corporate rules that foil innovation." Training employees at all levels is one of the most powerful means of transmitting corporate culture and Home Depot uses it extensively. One analyst noted that Home Depot (in a reverse of the "top to bottom" training sequence in most organizations) trains the carry-out people first. "The logic is that the guy who helps you to your car is the last employee you come into contact with, and they want that contact to be positive."[6]

ORGANIZATIONAL STRUCTURE

The official organizational structure (see Exhibits 2, 3) of Home Depot is much like that of other retail organizations, but according to a human resources spokesperson, the environment is so relaxed and casual you feel like you can report to anyone. Marcus and Blank preside at the top of Home Depot's organization chart and are supported by five senior vice-presidents, including the Chief Financial Officer, the Senior Vice President of Corporate Development, and the Senior Vice President of Merchandising for the Eastern division. There are ten vice presidents, including Merchandising for the Northeast, Merchandising for the West, Human Resources, Legal, Finance, Advertising and Marketing, Distribution, three Vice Presidents of Store Operations, and the Controller.

[4]*St. Petersburg Times,* 12/24/90, p.11.
[5]*Business Atlanta,* 11/11/88.
[6]*Chain Store Executive,* 4/83, pp. 9–11.

EXHIBIT 2   The Home Depot Officers

From left to right:
Lawrence A. Smith, *Vice President–Legal;* Lynn Martineau, *Vice President–Store Operations;* E. Dennis Ross, *Sr. Vice President–Corporate Information Systems;* Bryant Scott, *Vice President–Store Operations;* Marshall L. Day, *Vice President–Finance;* Preston R. Kirby, *Controller;* Ronald M. Brill, *Sr. Vice President, Chief Financial Officer, Treasurer;* Larry Mercer, *Vice President–Store Operations;* Dick Hammill, *Vice President–Advertising & Marketing;* James Inglis, *Executive Vice President–Merchandising;* Donald P. McKenna, *Vice President–Human Resources;* Bill Hamlin, *Vice President–Merchandising/Western Division;* William E. Harris, *Sr. Vice President–Corporate Development;* Bruce Berg, *Sr. Vice President– Merchandising/ Eastern Division;* Dennis Ryan, *Vice President–Merchandising/Northeast Division;* Peter E. Cleaveland, *Vice President–Distribution.*

The three operational Vice Presidents are responsible for the Northeast, South, and West. Under each vice president is a group of regional managers. There are approximately 20 regional managers company-wide. Each regional manager is responsible for six to eight stores.

The stores and their merchandise are set up such that all the stores are very similar (see Exhibit 4). The company's corporate headquarters is responsible for this "look," but individual managers may change a display or order more or less of a product if they can justify the change. The managers within individual stores make decisions regarding their employees, such as firing and hiring, but they look to corporate in areas such as training. One manager of a store in Georgia said that if he did not like a particular display or promotion,

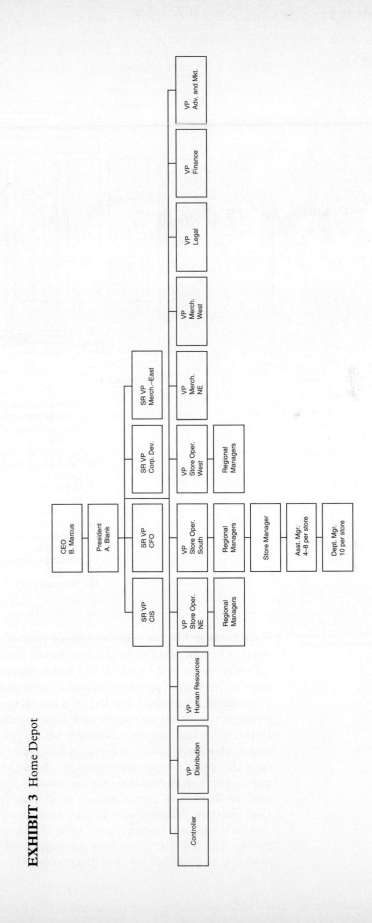

EXHIBIT 3 Home Depot

EXHIBIT 4

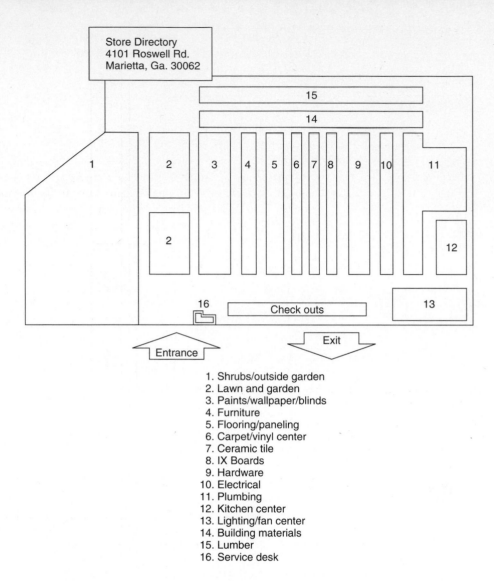

Store Directory
4101 Roswell Rd.
Marietta, Ga. 30062

1. Shrubs/outside garden
2. Lawn and garden
3. Paints/wallpaper/blinds
4. Furniture
5. Flooring/paneling
6. Carpet/vinyl center
7. Ceramic tile
8. IX Boards
9. Hardware
10. Electrical
11. Plumbing
12. Kitchen center
13. Lighting/fan center
14. Building materials
15. Lumber
16. Service desk

then it was at his discretion to change it or drop it. The manager went on to say that he and other store managers work hand in hand with corporate head-quarters and that if he wished to make "major" changes or had a significant store or personnel problem, he would deal with corporate.

At the store level, Home Depot is set up much as would be expected, with managers, assistant managers, and department managers. The average Home Depot store has one store manager whose primary responsibility is to be the master delegator. There are usually four to six assistant managers who preside over the store's ten departments. Each assistant manager is responsible for one to three departments. One assistant manager is responsible for receiving and the "back end" (stock storage area) in addition to his or her departments. One assistant manager acts as an administrative assistant in the "front end" (phones, customer service area, time clock) in addition to his or her depart-ments. The assistant managers are supported by department managers who are each responsible for one department. The department managers report directly to the assistant managers and have no firing/hiring capabilities. Assistant managers normally handle ordering and work schedules, etc. Department managers handle questions from employees and job assignments.

OPERATIONS

Operational efficiency has been a crucial part of achieving low prices while still offering a high level of customer service. From installing computerized check-out systems that eliminate item pricing to implementation of satellite communications systems in most of its stores, the company has shown that it has been and will continue to be innovative in its operating strategy.

By the end of 1989, every Home Depot store was using the Universal Product Code scanning systems which replaces most keying by the cashier and has resulted in faster customer check-out with greater accuracy. Home Depot's attitude of complete customer satisfaction has led the company to stock the shelves after hours in order to free clerks to help with customers during the day. In an effort to ease customer crowding new stores have been located very close to existing ones.

A money saving device has been an in-house, two-way TV network which allows Home Depot top executives to get instant feedback from local managers. This addition has increased employee motivation and saved many dollars due to timely information.[7] The network allows the company to communicate its operating philosophies and policies more effectively because information presented by top management can be targeted at large audiences.

Home Depot is firmly committed to energy conservation and has installed reflectors to lower the amount of lighting needed in a store. The reflectors darkened the ceiling but save thousands of dollars a year in energy bills. Further, it has purchased a computerized system to maintain comfortable temperatures, a challenge due to the stores' concrete floors, exposed ceilings, and open oversized doors for forklift deliveries. The system also has an automated feedback capability that can be used for equipment maintenance.

The adaption of the Point-of-Sale (POS) technology (computerized registers which record sales transactions and types, method of payment, etc.) has improved each store's ability to identify and adapt to trends quickly. The information provided by the POS technology is transferred to computer centers in Atlanta and Fullerton, CA where consumer buying trends are traced. This allows Home Depot to make adjustments to its merchandising mix and track both buying trends and inventory.

Home Depot and its employees continuously look for avenues to cut costs while maintaining quality. For example, the "Point of Sale" (POS) Coordinator discovered that leased phone/credit approval lines shared by many stores can be great money savers. Because the connection on the lines is continuous with no dialing required, authorizations can be obtained in far less time than with conventional dial-ups—4 to 8 seconds compared to 45 to 90 seconds.

In 1987 the company introduced an advanced inventory management system which has allowed it to increase inventory turns significantly over the past five years (from 4.2 in 1984 to 5.8 in 1989), allowing Home Depot to carry $40 million less in inventory, tying up less working capital to finance it. This efficiency permits a cost structure that is significantly lower than the competition.

---

[7]*Business Week,* 3/19/90.

Home Depot continuously experiments with new operating concepts. Its investment in new retail technology has paid off in areas such as inventory turnover, in-stock turnover, in-stock inventory positions, queuing problems, and information flow from the company's buyers to its store-level managers and employees.

FINANCE

Key indicators of financial success, net sales and net earnings, are shown below. (See Appendix A for a summary financial statement.)

While these indicators are useful, another indication of growth is earnings per share and comparison to the industry. Earnings per share (Figure 3) have grown 48.9 percent from 1985 through 1989, compared to 26.4 percent for the building materials industry as a whole, and 6.9 percent for the Standard and Poor's 500.[8]

One risk the company has faced as a result of its high growth strategy is liquidity and its ability to meet its debt service. Figure 4 tracks the company's debt burden. Figure 5 shows the debt to equity ratios.

Two additional but more subtle indicators of financial strength are:

- *Average sales per transaction.* Relatively steady until 1986, the average sales per transaction has risen steadily over the past three years and is currently at $32.65. (Figure 6)
- *Net sales per square foot.* Even with larger stores, Home Depot has increased net sales per square foot from $175 in 1985 to $265 in 1989 (Figure 7).

FIGURE 1
Net Sales

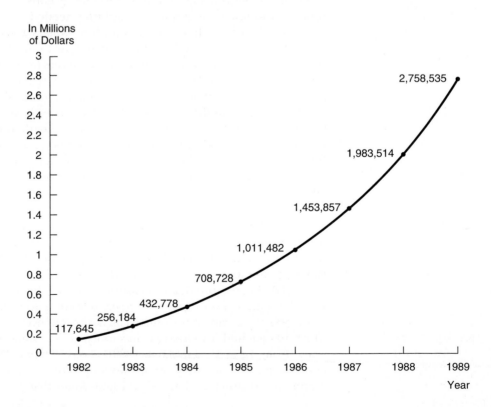

[8]Datext Information System, 1989.

FIGURE 2
Net Earnings

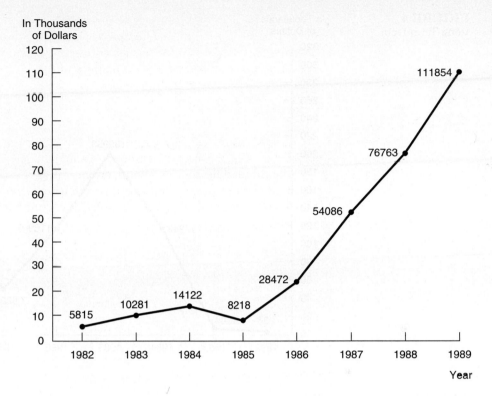

FIGURE 3
Earnings Per Share

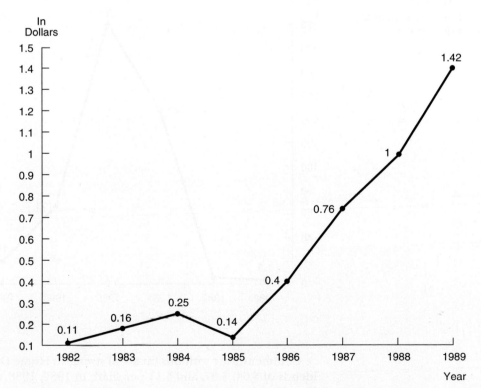

FIGURE 4
Long Term Debt

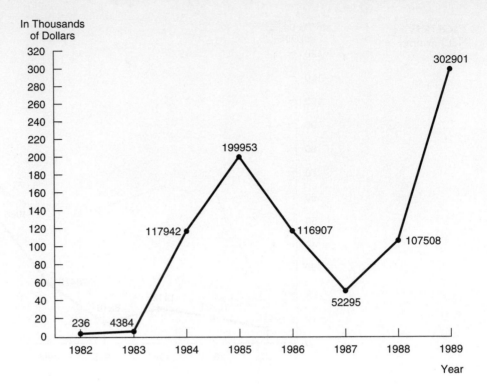

FIGURE 5
Long Term Debt to
Equity Ratio

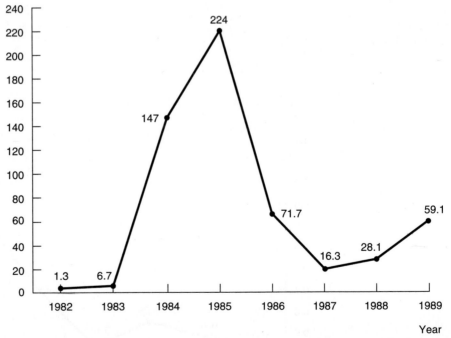

Commensurate with this financial strength, Home Depot has paid cash dividends of $.04, $.07, and $.11 per share in 1987, 1988, and 1989, respectively. Share holders have also been rewarded through a series of seven stock splits since the company went public in 1981, resulting in the current 79,000,000 shares outstanding.

FIGURE 6
Average Sales Per
Transaction

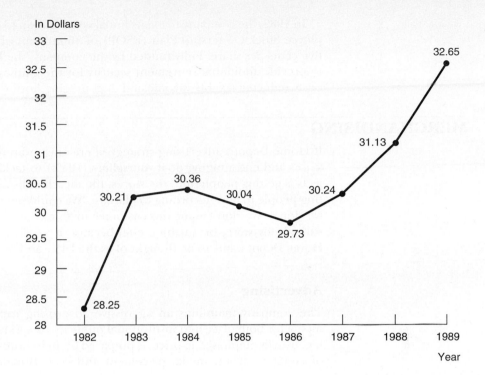

FIGURE 7
Net Sales Per Square
Footage

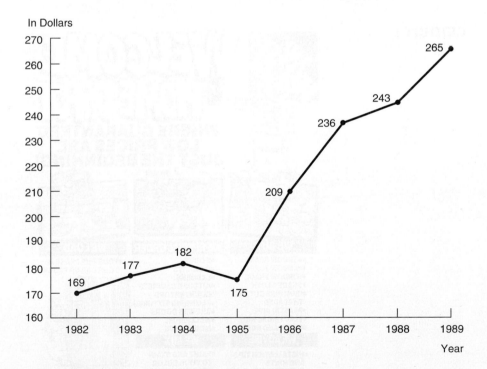

Home Depot has also encouraged employees to participate in and benefit from the company's success, as evidenced by the Employee Stock Purchase Plan, under which the company may grant eligible employees options to purchase up to 2,475,000 shares of common stock at a price equal to 85 percent of the stock's fair market value at the date of grant.

In 1989, the company made its initial contribution to the Home Depot Employee Stock Ownership Plan (ESOP) of $6 million, which represents about five cents per share. Fully funded by the company, the ESOP was established to provide additional retirement security for the employees, while simultaneously reducing taxable income and discouraging hostile takeover attempts.

MERCHANDISING

If Home Depot's advertising strategy of creating awareness of the company's stores and encouraging do-it-yourselfers (DIY's) to tackle more at-home projects is getting people into the stores, the merchandising mix is aimed at getting people to buy. According to Marcus, "We could sell them anything . . . but we don't. We don't want the customer to think we're a discounter, a food store, a toy store, or anything else, because it would confuse [them] . . . "[9] Home Depot wants to be thought of as the DIY warehouse, nothing less.

Advertising

The company maintains an aggressive advertising campaign using various media for both price and institutional publicity (see Exhibit 5). Print advertising, usually emphasizing price, is prepared by an in-house staff to keep control of context, layout, media placement and cost. Broadcast media advertise-

EXHIBIT 5

[9]Caminiti, p. 2.

ments are generally institutional and promote Home Depot the company, not just their pricing strategy. These advertisements focus on the "you'll feel right at home" ad slogan, name recognition, and increasing the perceived value of Home Depot's customer service.

Customer Target Market

The warehousing DIY market has gained impetus from the "baby boomers." The typical Do-It-Yourselfer is a married male homeowner, age 25–54, with a high school diploma or some college, and has an annual income of $20,000 to $40,000.[10] Projections through 1995 indicate that households headed by 25–35 year olds with earnings over $30,000 will increase by 34–38 percent. The 45–54 age group earnings over $30,000 will increase by 40 percent.[11]

Industry estimates show that DIY sales are growing at an average of 10 percent per year and project a 9 percent growth rate over the next five years.[12] These estimates are supported by the results of an independent survey[13] reporting that the self proclaimed do-it-yourselfer population has expanded by 6.7 percent since 1986.

Economics

The DIY industry exhibits a demand pattern that is largely recession proof. Since a mere 15 percent of Home Depots' business comes from contractors, a downturn in home construction has only a modest impact on Home Depot sales. In addition, analysts point out that during hard times, consumers cannot afford to buy new or bigger homes, and instead they maintain or upgrade their existing homes. Home improvement spending has declined in only one recession during the past twenty years.

Merchandising Strategy

The 1989 annual report states, "We are in the business of selling products, of investing to maximize sales, gross-margins and inventory turns." This statement captures the essence of merchandising, which is all those activities involved in the buying and selling of merchandise for a profit. More specifically, it involves long-range planning to insure that the right merchandise is available at the right place, at the right time, in the right quantity, and at the right price.[14] Success depends on the firm's ability to act and react with speed, spot changes and catch trends early.

The company's merchandizing unit is staffed with people who have prior experience in marketing products carried by Home Depot. Each merchandiser is assigned at least two product lines, and their responsibilities involve monitoring the samples volume, discontinuing lines which are trending downward, searching for new lines, negotiating with vendors, coordinating with store operations to resolve product problems, and training store employees on new products.

[10]*American Demographics,* March 1988, p. 21.

[11]*Population Bulletin,* February 1989, pp. 17–34.

[12]*Do-It-Yourself Retailing,* September 1989.

[13]*Hardware Age,* 1989.

[14]Ship, 1976, p. 3.

The merchandising strategy of Home Depot follows a three-pronged approach: 1) excellent customer service, 2) everyday low pricing, and 3) wide breadth of products.

Customer Service

Customer service helps differentiate Home Depot from its competitors. The provision of highly qualified, helpful employees, professional clinics and in-store displays has developed a customer service approach referred to as "customer cultivation." It gives DIY customers the support and confidence that no home pro-ject is beyond their capabilities with Home Depot personnel close at hand.

Home Depot employees go beyond simply recommending appropriate products, tools, and materials. Sales personnel cultivate the customer by demonstrating methods and techniques of performing a job safely and efficiently. This unique aspect of the company's service also serves as a feedback mechanism: employees helping the next customer learn form the problems and successes of the last one.

All of the stores offer hands-on workshops on projects such as kitchen remodeling, basic plumbing, ceramic tile installation, and other activities that customers in a particular locality have expressed an interest in. Offered mainly on weekends, they vary in length depending on complexity. Only the most experienced staff members, many of them former skilled craftsmen, teach at these workshops. Promotion of the workshops is done through direct mail advertising and in-store promotion.

Availability of sales personnel attending to customer needs is one clear objective of the Home Depot customer service strategy. Figure 8 shows overall staffing trends.

Pricing Strategy

Home Depot stresses its commitment to "Everyday Low Pricing." This concept means across-the-board lower prices and fewer deep-cutting sales. To ensure this, Home Depot employs professional shoppers to regularly check competitors' prices. The company's 1989 gross margin was 27.0 percent compared to the Home Center composite gross margin of 26.87 percent.[15]

One of the major reasons that Home Depot, Inc. is able to undercut the competition by as much as 25 percent is a dependable relationship with its suppliers. The company conducts business with approximately 1,900 vendors, the majority of which are manufacturers. A confidential survey of manufactures conducted by Shapiro and Associates found that Home Depot was "far and away the most demanding" of customers.[16] Shipping dates appeared as the main area where Home Depot was most vocal. However, manufacturers agreed that increased sales volumes have offset concessions made to Home Depot.

Products

A typical Home Depot store stocks approximately 30,000 products including variations in color and size. Each store carries a wide selection of quality and

[15]Jensen, Christopher, *DIY Retailing*, September, 1989.
[16]*National Home Center News,* 12/15/86.

FIGURE 8
Average Employees Per
Store

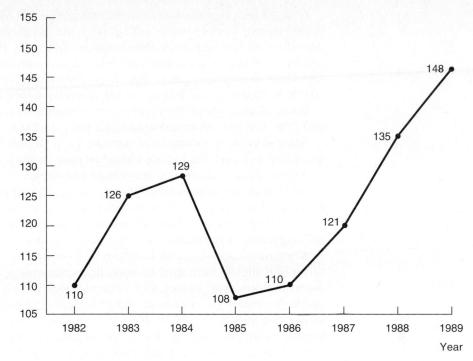

(SOURCE: Derived from 1989 financial report by calculating the ratio of employees to the number of open stores.)

nationally advertised brand name merchandise. The following depicts Home Depot's product grouping ranked by each grouping's contribution to total revenues for fiscal year 1990.

Product Group	% of Sales
Building materials, lumber, floor & wall coverings	31.0%
Plumbing, heating, & electrical supplies	29.0%
Seasonal & specialty items	14.6%
Paint & furniture	13.2%
Hardware & tools	12.2%
	100.0%

Average Store Profile

According to Bob Evans in the Store Planning Division of Home Depot, all of the stores are company-owned, not franchised, and most are "free standing, built to current Home Depot standards."

Home Depot owns close to 40 percent of its buildings, leasing the remainder, and Marcus plans to increase that percentage. While the company prefers locations surrounded by shopping centers, Marcus insists that the company is not interested in being attached to a shopping center or mall. Stores are placed in suburban areas populated by members of the Home Depot target market.

Construction time depends on site conditions, special local requirements and related factors. Depending on "if we have to move a mountain, fill a canyon, level a forest, or how many gopher turtles are in the ground that we have to relocate," building a store can take up to a year according to Evans.

Current building standards are 100,000 square feet for each store itself and 20,000 square feet of outside selling space for the garden department. Store sizes do vary, however, since the company "will make the store fit the land" and many of the original stores are located in leased strip-center space. Current store sizes range from 67,000 to 140,000 square feet, with an additional 10,000 to 15,000 square feet of outside (garden) selling space.

While Marcus would like to see stores averaging 120,000 square feet, Evans said that "the 100 (thousand square feet size) is what we're building most of."

Some stores have thousands of customers a week, and "just get too crowded," according to Evans. Marcus has estimated that "in some cases, we have 25,000 to 30,000 people walking through a store per week."

Because of the large number of customers, older stores are being gradually remodeled or replaced with new ones to add room for new merchandise, increase selling space for what is already there, and sometimes even to add more walking room on the inside and more parking spaces.

Since merchandising and inventory are centrally organized, product mix varies only slightly from store to store. Each, however, sports the Home Depot *look:* warehouse-style shelves, wide cement-floored aisles, end-displays pushing sale items, and the ever-present orange banners indicating the store's departments (see Exhibit 5). Most stores have banners on each aisle to help customers locate what they're looking for. Regional purchasing departments are used to keeping the stores well-stocked and are preferred to a single strong corporate department "since home improvement materials needed in the southwest would differ somewhat from those needed in the northeast" (Richards, p. 6–7).

HUMAN RESOURCES

Home Depot is noted for its progressive human resources policies, which emphasize the importance of the individual to the success of the whole company's operations.

Recruitment/Selection

Having the right number of people, in the right jobs, at the right time is recognized by management as critical. Employee population varies greatly among stores depending on store size, sales volume, and the season of the year. In the winter a store may have less than 75 employees but in the spring will add another 25–40 employees. Some of the larger northeastern stores have as many as 280 employees. Full-time employees fill approximately 90 percent of the positions.

When a store first opens, it attracts applicants through advertisements in local newspapers and trade journals such as *Home Center News.* A new store will usually receive several thousand applications. When seasonal workers and replacements are needed, help-wanted signs are displayed at store entrances. Walk-in candidates are another source—applications are available at the customer service desk at all times. There is no formal program to encourage employees to refer their friends for employment. At the assistant store manager level, direct recruitment contact is made with potential candidates who work for Home Depot's competitors.

Interviews are scheduled one day per week; however, if someone with trade experience applies, an on-the-spot interview may be conducted. "Trade" experience includes retail, construction, do-it-yourself, or hardware. The company tends to look for older people who bring a high level of knowledge and maturity to the position. In addition to related experience, they look for a person with a stable work history who has a positive attitude, is excited, outgoing, and a hard worker.

The selection process includes pre-employment tests (honesty, math, drugs). The stores display signs in the windows that anyone who uses drugs need not apply. Interviews are conducted with three or four people—an initial qualifier, the administrative assistant in operations, an assistant store manager, and the store manager. Reference checks are completed prior to a job offer. More in-depth background checks (financial, criminal) are conducted on management-level candidates.

Starting salaries typically range from $7-$11 per hour. In the Atlanta job market, salaries average about $8.60 per hour. A cashier with minimal experience may start at $5.50, and a highly-experienced tradesperson could be paid $15 or more. Managers do not hire anyone at minimum wage. Ronald Brill, CFO, explains: "People earning minimum wage don't have the commitment to the customer and the level of service we expect."[17]

Retention

Employee turnover varies from store to store. In the first year of operation, turnover may run 60–70 percent but can fall below 30 percent in future years. The company's goal is to reduce turnover to below 20 percent. The major causes of turnover are students who return to school, employees who are terminated for poor performance, and tradespeople who consider Home Depot an interim position (they often return to positions in their trades paying as much as $50,000 per year). Very few people leave the organization looking for "greener pastures" in the retail industry.

Rewards at Home Depot begin with above-average salaries followed by merit increases every six months; earnings can increase 10–11 percent per year. Store managers earn $45,000 base salary plus potentially lucrative stock options. Stock is also important to other employees in the organization—assistant managers earn stock options, and all employees can purchase Home Depot stock at a 15 percent discount through payroll deductions. One employee hired in 1979 invested $750 in stock; today that stock is valued at over $250,000. The ESOP provides full vesting within seven years.

Career development is formally addressed during semi-annual performance reviews with goals and development plans mutually set by employees and managers. The company is committed to promotions from within and has a formal job posting program. Vacancy lists are prepared at the regional level and distributed to the stores. Store managers are promoted from within. Affirmative action plans are used to increase female and minority representation.

Recognition programs emphasize good customer service, increased sales, safety, cost savings, and length of service. Badges, cash awards, and other prizes are distributed in monthly group meetings.

Communication is the key by which Home Depot perpetuates its culture and retains its people. That culture includes an environment in which employees can be happy and where they feel productive and secure. The company sells

[17] *New Jersey Star-Ledger*, 2/5/89.

employees on their role in Home Depot's success—they are giving the company a return on its assets. The environment avoids bureaucracy, is informal, intense, and encourages honesty and risk-taking. Each store maintains a strong open door policy, and a manager may spend two or three hours discussing a concern with an employee.

Top management is equally accessible to employees through frequent visits to the stores. An in-house TV broadcast, "Breakfast with Bernie and Arthur," is held quarterly. Impromptu questions are solicited from the employees. One recent broadcast addressed a 20 percent slip in Home Depot's stock when the Gulf crisis began and reassured employees of the chain's strength, predicting the stock market would rebound.[18] Department managers meet with employees weekly to provide new information and solicit feedback. Worker opinions also matter at the top. When the company planned to open on New Year's Day, the employees voted to close and prevailed. When the company wrote a checkout training manual, a store cashier from Jacksonville helped write it. Internal sales charts are posted on bulletin boards so employees will know how their store compares with others in the area.

Training

Home Depot believes that knowledgeable sales people are one of the keys to the company's success and spends a great deal of time training them to "bleed orange." Training, from the new employees' week-long orientation session to regularly scheduled training classes, is a priority for top management, usually costing around $400,000 for every new store.

Callers to the home office find that corporate executives spend most of their time in the stores, training employees. "We teach from the top down, and those who can't teach don't become executives," said Marcus, who, along with Blank, has personally taught every store manager and assistant manager to take care of the customer first, then stock the shelves.[19]

Regular employees go through both formal and on-the-job training. Classes are held on product knowledge, giving the employee "total product knowledge . . . including all the skills a trade person might have"; merchandising concepts and salesmanship, so that they can be sure that a customer has available, and will purchase, everything needed to complete their project; time management; personnel matters; safety and security; and how to interpret the company's various internally generated reports.

New employees average four (4) weeks of training before they are allowed to work on their own. Even then, when there are no other customers in the department, newer employees will watch more experienced employees interact with customers to learn more about products, sales, and customer service. Employees are cross-trained to work in various departments, and even the cashiers learn how to work the sales floor.

Recently, the company established the "Home Depot Television Network," allowing them, via satellite link-up, to make live Sunday morning broadcasts to every store. Topics include company policies and philosophies, product upgrades, etc. With the ability to target special or mass audiences, the training

[18]*Atlanta Journal-Constitution*, 9/8/90.
[19]*Business Month*, 9/89, p. 39.

possibilities are endless. The fact the programs are broadcast live, with telephone call-ins, enhances their immediacy and makes interaction possible.

Marcus believes his employees give 105 percent and they stay with Home Depot because "we train our people, listen to them, respond to them, acknowledge their efforts, and offer them opportunity."[20]

[20]*Business Atlanta,* 11/1/88.

References

Atlanta Journal-Constitution, 9/8/90.

Business Atlanta, 11/11/88.

Business Month, 9/89, p. 39.

Business Week, 3/19/90.

Caminiti, Susan. "The New Champs of Retailing," *Fortune,* 9/24/90.

Carter, Richard L., *et al.* "D-I-Y Activity, Hardlines Patronage on the Rise," *Hardware Age,* October 1989 (Chilton Company).

Chain Store Executive, 4/83, pp. 9–11.

Datext Information System, 1989. Georgia State University.

"Do It Yourself," *American Demographics,* v. 10, March 1988, p. 21.

Fortune, 2/29/88.

Hawkins, Chuck. "Will Home Depot Be The Wal-Mart of the '90s," *Business Week,* March 19, 1990, p. 124.

Jensen, Christopher. "Bar-Coding—A Status Report on Industry Standards," *Do-It-Yourself Retailing,* March, 1989, pp. 199–205.

Newark New Jersey Star-Ledger, 2/5/89.

Population Bulletin, v. 21, February 1989, pp. 17–34.

"Retail Do-It-Yourself Market Profile," *Do-It-Yourself Retailing,* September, 1989, pp. 53–65.

Saporito, Bill. "The Fix Is in at Home Depot," *Fortune,* February 29, 1988, pp. 74–79.

Shipp, Ralph D. *Retail Merchandising Principles and Applications.* Houghton Mifflin Company. Boston, 1976.

St. Petersburg Times, 12/24/90, p. 11.

"Study: Vendors Call Depot Toughest Negotiator," *National Home Center News,* December 15, 1986.

APPENDIX A Ten Year Selected Financial and Operating Highlights

The Home Depot, Inc. and Subsidiaries (Amounts in thousands, except where noted)

STATEMENT OF EARNINGS DATA

	1989	1988	1987	1986	1985	1984 [1]	1983	1982	1981	1980 [1]
Net sales	$2,758,535	$1,999,514	$1,453,657	$1,011,462	$700,729	$432,779	$256,184	$117,645	$51,542	$22,318
Gross margin	766,758	539,652	403,739	278,160	181,457	114,319	70,014	33,358	14,735	6,855
Earnings before taxes	182,015	125,833	95,586	47,073	11,619	26,252	18,986	9,870	1,963	856
Net earnings	111,954	76,753	54,086	23,873	8,219	14,122	10,261	5,315	1,211	453
Net earnings per share ($) [2]	1.42	1.00	.75	.40	.14	.25	.18	.11	.03	.01
Weighted average number of shares [2]	78,980	76,883	71,991	59,805	56,807	56,930	55,877	50,025	47,363	48,366
Gross margin—% to sales	27.8	27.0	27.8	27.5	25.9	26.4	27.3	28.4	28.6	30.7
Store selling and operating expenses—% to sales	18.3	17.8	18.1	18.7	19.2	17.2	17.0	16.5	19.0	20.6
Pre-opening expenses —% to sales	.3	.4	.3	.3	1.1	.4	.9	.4	1.5	.2
General and administrative expenses—% to sales	2.5	2.4	2.6	2.7	2.9	3.0	2.9	3.3	3.7	4.3
Net interest expense (income)—% to sales	.1	.1	.2	1.1	1.2	(.3)	(.9)	(.2)	.6	1.8
Earnings before taxes —% to sales	6.6	6.3	6.6	4.7	1.7	6.1	7.4	8.4	3.8	3.8
Net earnings—% to sales	4.1	3.8	3.7	2.4	1.2	3.3	4.0	4.5	2.3	2.0

BALANCE SHEET DATA AND FINANCIAL RATIOS

	1989	1988	1987	1986	1985	1984 [1]	1983	1982	1981	1980 [1]
Total assets	$1,117,534	$699,179	$528,270	$394,741	$380,193	$249,364	$105,230	$33,014	$16,906	$4,507
Working capital	273,851	142,806	110,621	91,076	106,451	100,110	49,318	12,901	5,502	1,399
Merchandise inventories	381,452	294,274	211,421	167,115	152,700	84,046	58,712	17,575	11,263	2,881
Net property and equipment	514,440	332,416	244,503	168,981	160,816	73,577	21,129	5,954	3,503	1,246
Long-term debt	302,901	107,508	52,298	116,907	199,943	117,942	4,384	236	3,738	1,013
Stockholders' equity	512,129	382,938	320,559	163,042	89,092	80,214	65,278	18,354	5,204	(285)
Book value per share ($) [2]	6.67	5.08	4.33	2.55	1.57	1.42	1.17	.72	.11	N/A
Long-term debt to equity—%	59.1	28.1	16.3	71.7	224.0	147.0	6.7	1.3	71.8	N/A
Current ratio	1.94:1	1.74:1	1.75:1	1.85:1	2.27:1	3.22:1	2.43:1	1.92:1	1.70:1	1.75:1
Inventory turnover	5.9x	5.8x	5.4x	4.6x	4.1x	4.2x	4.9x	5.8x	5.2x	6.2x
Return on average equity—%	25.2	21.6	21.1	20.3	9.7	19.3	24.5	45.1	58.7	N/A

STATEMENT OF CASH FLOWS DATA

Depreciation and amortization	$21,107	$14,673	$10,646	$8,697	$5,193	$2,368	$903	$389	$176	$126
Capital expenditures	204,972	105,123	89,235	52,363	99,767	50,769	16,081	2,883	2,488	186
Cash dividends per share ($) (2)	.11	.07	.04	—	—	—	—	—	—	—

CUSTOMER AND STORE DATA

Number of markets	30	24	19	17	15	11	7	3	2	1
Number of stores	118	96	75	60	50	31	19	10	8	4
Square footage at year-end	10,424	8,216	6,161	4,828	4,001	2,381	1,449	696	507	249
Change in square footage—%	26.9	33.4	27.6	20.6	68.0	64.3	108.2	37.3	103.6	36.1
Average square footage per store	88	86	82	80	80	77	76	70	63	62
Number of customer transactions	84,494	64,227	48,073	34,020	23,324	14,256	8,479	4,164	1,916	889
Average sale per transaction ($)	32.65	31.13	30.24	29.73	30.04	30.36	30.21	28.25	26.90	25.11
Number of employees	17,500	13,000	9,100	6,600	5,400	4,000	2,400	1,100	650	300

OTHER DATA

Net sales increase—%	38.0	37.6	43.7	44.3	61.9	68.9	117.8	128.3	130.9	217.7
Average total company weekly sales	$53,049	$38,452	$27,955	$19,451	$13,476	$8,166	$4,927	$2,262	$991	$421
Weighted average weekly sales per operating store	515	464	418	355	343	366	360	281	187	107
Comparable store sales increase—%	12.9	13.4	18.0	7.0	2.3	14.0	31.0	46.8	57.5	55.4
Weighted average sales per square foot ($)	303	282	265	230	223	247	245	210	153	89
Advertising expense—% to sales	1.1	1.5	2.0	2.4	3.2	2.5	2.9	2.6	3.4	3.2

(1) Fiscal years 1984 and 1980 consisted of 53 weeks, all other years reported consisted of 52 weeks.

N/A—Not applicable

(2) All periods have been adjusted for a three-for-two stock split-up declared in June, 1989 and effected in the form of a dividend.

APPENDIX B   *Top Ten Home Center Chains*

1. Home Depot
2. Payless Cashways
3. Builders Square (div. of K-Mart)
4. Hechingers
5. Lowes
6. Grossmans
7. Home Club (div. of Waban)
8. Channel Home Centers (pvt.)
9. Builders Emporium
10. Sutherland (pvt.)

SOURCE: John Caulfied, "Everything You Wanted to Know about Home Depot's History," National Home Center News (1986): 25–27.

The Lincoln Electric Company, 1989

ARTHUR SHARPLIN, *McNeese State University*

People are our most valuable asset. They must feel secure, important, challenged, in control of their destiny, confident in their leadership, be responsive to common goals, believe they are being treated fairly, have easy access to authority and open lines of communication in all possible directions. Perhaps the most important task Lincoln employees face today is that of establishing an example for others in the Lincoln organization in other parts of the world. We need to maximize the benefits of cooperation and teamwork, fusing high technology with human talent, so that we here in the USA and all of our subsidiary and joint venture operations will be in a position to realize our full potential.—GEORGE WILLIS, CEO, THE LINCOLN ELECTRIC COMPANY

The Lincoln Electric Company is the world's largest manufacturer of arc-welding products and a leading producer of industrial electric motors. The firm employs 2,400 workers in two U.S. factories near Cleveland and an equal number in eleven factories located in other countries. This does not include the field sales force of more than 200. The company's U.S. market share (for arc-welding products) is estimated at more than 40 percent.

The Lincoln incentive management plan has been well known for many years. Many college management texts make reference to the Lincoln plan as a model for achieving higher worker productivity. Certainly, the firm has been successful according to the usual measures.

James F. Lincoln died in 1965 and there was some concern, even among employees, that the management system would fall into disarray, that profits would decline, and that year-end bonuses might be discontinued. Quite the contrary—twenty-four years after Lincoln's death, the company appears as strong as ever. Each year, except the recession years 1982 and 1983, has seen high profits and bonuses. Employee morale and productivity remain very good. Employee turnover is almost nonexistent except for retirements. Lincoln's market share is stable. The historically high stock dividends continue.

A HISTORICAL SKETCH

In 1905, after being "frozen out" of the depression-ravaged Elliott-Lincoln Company, a maker of Lincoln-designed electric motors, John C. Lincoln took out his second patent and began to manufacture his improved motor. He opened his new business, unincorporated, with $200 he had earned redesigning a motor for young Herbert Henry Dow, who later founded the Dow Chemical Company.

Started during an economic depression and cursed by a major fire after only one year in business, the company grew, but hardly prospered, through its first quarter century. In 1906, John C. Lincoln incorporated the business and moved from his one-room, fourth-floor factory to a new three-story building he erected in east Cleveland. He expanded his work force to thirty and sales grew to over $50,000 a year. John preferred being an engineer and inventor rather than a manager, though, and it was to be left to another Lincoln to manage the company through its years of success.

In 1907, after a bout with typhoid fever forced him from Ohio State University in his senior year, James F. Lincoln, John's younger brother, joined the fledgling company. In 1914, he became active head of the firm, with the titles of general manager and vice president. John remained president of the company for some years but became more involved in other business ventures and in his work as an inventor.

One of James Lincoln's early actions was to ask the employees to elect representatives to a committee which would advise him on company operations. This advisory board has met with the chief executive officer every two weeks since that time. This was only the first of a series of innovative personnel policies which have, over the years, distinguished Lincoln Electric from its contemporaries.

The first year the Advisory Board was in existence, working hours were reduced from 55 per week, then standard, to 50 hours a week. In 1915, the company gave each employee a paid-up life insurance policy. A welding school, which continues today, was begun in 1917. In 1918, an employee bonus plan was attempted. It was not continued, but the idea was to resurface later.

The Lincoln Electric employees' association was formed in 1919 to provided health benefits and social activities. This organization continues today and has assumed several additional functions over the years. In 1923, a piecework pay system was in effect, employees got two-week paid vacations each year, and wages were adjusted for changes in the Consumer Price Index. Approximately 30 percent of the common stock was set aside for key employees in 1914. A stock purchase plan for all employees was begun in 1925.

The board of directors voted to start a suggestion system in 1929. The program is still in effect, but cash awards, a part of the early program, were discontinued several years ago. Now, suggestions are rewarded by additional "points," which affect year-end bonuses.

The legendary Lincoln bonus plan was proposed by the advisory board and accepted on a trial basis in 1934. The first annual bonus amounted to about 25 percent of wages. There has been a bonus every year since then. The bonus plan has been a cornerstone of the Lincoln management system and recent bonuses have approximated annual wages.

By 1944, Lincoln employees enjoyed a pension plan, a policy of promotion from within, and continuous employment. Base pay rates were determined by formal job evaluation and a merit rating system was in effect.

In the prologue of James F. Lincoln's last book, Charles G. Herbruck writes regarding the foregoing personnel innovations:

They were not to buy good behavior. They were not efforts to increase profits. They were not antidotes to labor difficulties. They did not constitute a "do-gooder" program. They were expressions of mutual respect for each person's importance to the job to be done. All of them reflect the leadership of James Lincoln, under whom they were nurtured and propagated.

During World War II, Lincoln prospered as never before. By the start of the war, the company was the world's largest manufacturer of arc-welding products. Sales of about $4 million in 1934 grew to $24 million by 1941. Productivity per employee more than doubled during the same period. The Navy's Price Review Board challenged the high profits. And the Internal Revenue Service questioned the tax deductibility of employee bonuses, arguing they were not "ordinary and necessary" costs of doing business. But the forceful and articulate James Lincoln was able to overcome the objections.

Certainly since 1935, and probably for several years before that, Lincoln productivity has been well above the average for similar companies. The company claims levels of productivity more than twice those for other manufacturers from 1945 onward. Information available from outside sources tends to support these claims.

COMPANY PHILOSOPHY

James F. Lincoln was the son of a Congregational minister, and Christian principles were at the center of his business philosophy. The confidence that he had in the efficacy of Christ's teachings is illustrated by the following remark taken from one of his books:

> The Christian ethic should control our acts. If it did control our acts, the savings in cost of distribution would be tremendous. Advertising would be a contact of the expert consultant with the customer, in order to give the customer the best product available when all of the customer's needs are considered. Competition then would be in improving the quality of products and increasing efficiency in producing and distributing them; not in deception, as is now too customary. Pricing would reflect efficiency of production; it would not be a selling dodge that the customer may well be sorry he accepted. It would be proper for all concerned and rewarding for the ability used in producing the product.

There is no indication that Lincoln attempted to evangelize his employees or customers—or the general public for that matter. Neither the chairman of the board and chief executive, George Willis, nor the president, Donald F. Hastings, mention the Christian gospel in their recent speeches and interviews. The company motto, "The actual is limited, the possible is immense," is prominently displayed, but there is no display of religious slogans, and there is no company chapel.

Attitude toward the Customer

James Lincoln saw the customer's needs as the *raison d'etre* for every company. "When any company has achieved success so that it is attractive as an investment," he wrote, "all money usually needed for expansion is supplied by the customer in retained earnings. It is obvious that the customer's interests, not the stockholder's, should come first." In 1947 he said, "Care should be taken . . . not to rivet attention on profit. Between 'How much do I get?' and 'How do I make this better, cheaper, more useful?' the difference is fundamental and decisive." Willis, too, ranks the customer as management's most important constituency. This is reflected in Lincoln's policy to "at all times price on the basis of cost and at times keep pressure on our cost . . ." Lincoln's goal, often stated, is "to build a better and better product at a lower and lower price." "It is obvious," James Lincoln said, "that the customer's interests should be the first goal of industry."

Attitude toward Stockholders

Stockholders are given last priority at Lincoln. This is a continuation of James Lincoln's philosophy: "The last group to be considered is the stockholders who own stock because they think it will be more profitable than investing money in any other way." Concerning division of the largess produced by incentive management, he wrote, "The absentee stockholder also will get his share, even if undeserved, out of the greatly increased profit that the efficiency produces."

Attitude toward Unionism

There has never been a serious effort to organize Lincoln employees. While James Lincoln criticized the labor movement for "selfishly attempting to better its position at the expense of the people it must serve," he still had kind words for union members. He excused abuses of union power as "the natural reactions of human beings to the abuses to which management has subjected them." Lincoln's idea of the correct relationship between workers and managers is shown by this comment: "Labor and management are properly not warring camps; they are parts of one organization in which they must and should cooperate fully and happily."

Beliefs and Assumptions about Employees

If fulfilling customer needs is the desired goal of business, then employee performance and productivity are the means by which this goal can best be achieved. It is the Lincoln attitude toward employees, reflected in the following comments by James Lincoln, which is credited by many with creating the success the company has experienced:

> The greatest fear of the worker, which is the same as the greatest fear of the industrialist in operating a company, is the lack of income. . . . The industrial manager is very conscious of his company's need of uninterrupted income. He is completely oblivious, evidently, of the fact that the worker has the same need.

> He is just as eager as any manager is to be part of a team that is properly organized and working for the advancement of our economy. . . . He has no desire to make profits for those who do not hold up their end in production, as is true of absentee stockholders and inactive people in the company.

> If money is to be used as an incentive, the program must provide that what is paid to the worker is what he has earned. The earnings of each must be in accordance with accomplishment.

> Status is of great importance in all human relationships. The greatest incentive that money has, usually, is that it is a symbol of success. . . . The resulting status is the real incentive. . . . Money alone can be an incentive to the miser only.

There must be complete honesty and understanding between the hourly worker and management if high efficiency is to be obtained.

LINCOLN'S BUSINESS

Arc-welding has been the standard joining method in shipbuilding for decades. It is the predominant way of connecting steel in the construction industry. Most industrial plants have their own welding shops for maintenance and construction. Manufacturers of tractors and all kinds of heavy equipment use arc-welding extensively in the manufacturing process. Many hobbyists have their own welding machines and use them for making metal items such as patio furniture and barbecue pits. The popularity of welded sculpture as an art form is growing.

While advances in welding technology have been frequent, arc-welding products, in the main, have hardly changed. Lincoln's Innershield process is a notable exception. This process, described later, lowers welding cost and improves quality and speed in many applications. The most widely-used Lincoln electrode, the Fleetweld 5P, has been virtually the same since the 1930s. The most popular engine-driven welder in the world, the Lincoln SA-200, has been a gray-colored assembly including a four-cylinder continental "Red Seal" engine and a 200 ampere direct-current generator with two current-control knobs for at least four decades. A 1989 model SA-200 even weighs almost the same as the 1950 model, and it certainly is little changed in appearance.

The company's share of the U.S. arc-welding products market appears to have been about 40 percent for many years. The welding products market has grown somewhat faster than the level of industry in general. The market is highly price-competitive, with variations in prices of standard items normally amounting to only a percent or two. Lincoln's products are sold directly by its engineering-oriented sales force and indirectly though its distributor organization. Advertising expenditures amount to less than three-fourths of a percent of sales. Research and development expenditures typically range from $10 million to $12 million, considerably more than competitors.

The other major welding process, flame-welding, has not been competitive with arc-welding since the 1930s. However, plasma-arc-welding, a relatively new process which uses a conducting stream of super heated gas (plasma) to confine the welding current to a small area, has made some inroads, especially in metal tubing manufacturing, in recent years. Major advances in technology which will produce an alternative superior to arc-welding within the next decade or so appear unlikely. Also, it seems likely that changes in the machines and techniques used in arc-welding will be evolutionary rather than revolutionary.

Products

The company is primarily engaged in the manufacture and sale of arc-welding products—electric welding machines and metal electrodes. Lincoln also produces electric motors ranging from one-half horsepower to 200 horsepower. Motors constitute about eight to ten percent of total sales. Several million dollars has recently been invested in automated equipment that will double Lincoln's manufacturing capacity for ½ to 20 horsepower electric motors.

The electric welding machines, some consisting of transformer or motor and generator arrangement powered by commercial electricity and others consisting of an internal combustion engine and generator, are designed to produce 30 to 1,500 amperes of electrical power. This electrical current is used to melt a consumable metal electrode with the molten metal being transferred in super hot spray to the metal joint being welded. Very high temperatures and hot sparks are produced, and operators usually must wear special eye and face protection and leather gloves, often along with leather aprons and sleeves.

Lincoln and its competitors now market a wide range of general purpose and specialty electrodes for welding mild steel, aluminum, cast iron, and stainless and special steels. Most of these electrodes are designed to meet the standards of the American Welding Society, a trade association. They are thus essentially the same as to size and composition from one manufacturer to another. Every electrode manufacturer has a limited number of unique products, but these typically constitute only a small percentage of total sales.

Welding electrodes are of two basic types: (1) Coated "stick" electrodes, usually 14 inches long and smaller than a pencil in diameter, which are held in a special insulated holder by the operator, who must manipulate the electrode in order to maintain a proper arc-width and pattern of deposition of the metal being transferred. Stick electrodes are packaged in 6- to 50-pound boxes. (2) Coiled wire, ranging in diameter from 0.035 to 0.219 inches, which is designed to be fed continuously to the welding arc through a "gun" held by the operator or positioned by automatic positioning equipment. The wire is packaged in coils, reels, and drums weighing from 14 to 1,000 pounds and may be solid or flux-cored.

Manufacturing Processes

The main plant is in Euclid, Ohio, a suburb on Cleveland's east side. The layout of this plant is shown in Exhibit 1. There are no warehouses. Materials flow from the half-mile long dock on the north side of the plant through the production lines to a very limited storage and loading area on the south side. Materials used on each work station are stored as close as possible to the work station. The administrative offices, near the center of the factory, are entirely functional. A corridor below the main level provides access to the factory floor

EXHIBIT 1   Main Factory Layout

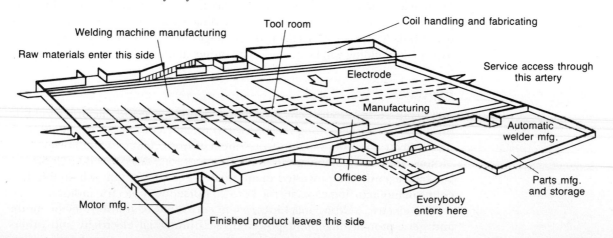

from the main entrance near the center of the plan. *Fortune* magazine recently declared the Euclid facility one of America's ten best-managed factories, and compared it with a General Electric plant also on the list:

> Stepping into GE's spanking new dishwasher plant, an awed supplier said, is like stepping "into the Hyatt Regency." By comparison, stepping into Lincoln Electric's 33-year-old, cavernous, dimly lit factory is like stumbling into a dingy big-city YMCA. It's only when one starts looking at how these factories do things that similarities become apparent. They have found ways to merge design with manufacturing, build in quality, make wise choices about automation, get close to customers, and handle theirs work forces.

A new Lincoln plant, in Mentor, Ohio, houses some of the electrode production operations, which were moved from the main plant.

Electrode manufacturing is highly capital intensive. Metal rods purchased from steel producers are drawn down to smaller diameters, cut to length and coated with pressed-powder "flux" for stick electrodes or plated with copper (for conductivity) and put into coils or spools for wire. Lincoln's Innershield wire is hollow and filled with a material similar to that used to coat stick electrodes. As mentioned earlier, this represented a major innovation in welding technology when it was introduced. The company is highly secretive about its electrode production processes, and outsiders are not given access to the details of those processes.

Lincoln welding machines and electric motors are made on a series of assembly lines. Gasoline and diesel engines are purchased partially assembled, but practically all other components are made from basic industrial products, e.g., steel bars and sheets and bar copper conductor wire.

Individual components, such as gasoline tanks for engine-driven welders and steel shafts for motors and generators, are made by numerous small "factories within a factory." The shaft for a certain generator, for example, is made from a raw steel bar by one operator who uses five large machines, all running continuously. A saw cuts the bar to length, a digital lathe machines different sections to varying diameters, a special milling machine cuts a slot for the keyway, and so forth, until a finished shaft is produced. The operator moves the shafts from machine to machine and makes necessary adjustments.

Another operator punches, shapes, and paints sheetmetal cowling parts. One assembles steel laminations onto a rotor shaft, then winds, insulates, and tests the rotors. Finished components are moved by crane operators to the nearby assembly lines.

Worker Performance and Attitudes

Exceptional worker performance at Lincoln is a matter of record. The typical Lincoln employee earns about twice as much as other factory workers in the Cleveland area. Yet the company's labor cost per sales dollar in 1989, 26 cents, is well below industry averages. Worker turnover is practically nonexistent except for retirements and departures by new employees.

Sales per Lincoln factory employee currently exceed $150,000. An observer at the factory quickly sees why this figure is so high. Each worker is proceeding busily and thoughtfully about the task at hand. There is no idle chatter. Most workers take no coffee breaks. Many operate several machines and make a substantial component unaided. The supervisors are busy with planning and record keeping duties and hardly glance at the people they "supervise." The manufacturing procedures appear efficient—no unnecessary steps, no wasted motions, no wasted materials.

The Appendix includes summaries of interviews with employees.

ORGANIZATION STRUCTURE

Lincoln has never allowed development of a formal organization chart. The objective of this policy is to insure maximum flexibility. An open-door policy is practiced throughout the company, and personnel are encouraged to take problems to the persons most capable of resolving them. Once, Harvard Business School researchers prepared an organization chart reflecting the implied relationships at Lincoln. The chart became available within the company, and present management feels that had a disruptive effect. Therefore, no organizational chart appears in this report.

Perhaps because of the quality and enthusiasm of the Lincoln work force, routine supervision is almost nonexistent. A typical production foreman, for example, supervises as many as 100 workers, a span of control which does not allow more than infrequent worker-supervisor interaction.

Position titles and traditional flows of authority do imply something of an organizational structure, however. For example, the vice-president of sales and the vice-president of the electrode division report to the president, as do various staff assistants such as the personnel director and the director of purchasing. Using such implied relationships, it has been determined that production workers have two or, at most, three levels of supervision between themselves and the president.

PERSONNEL POLICIES

As mentioned earlier, it is Lincoln's remarkable personnel practices which are credited by many with the company's success.

Recruitment and Selection

Every job opening is advertised internally on company bulletin boards and any employee can apply for any job so advertised. External hiring is permitted only for entry level positions. Selection for these jobs is done on the basis of personal interviews—there is no aptitude or psychological testing. Not even a high school diploma is required—except for engineering and sales positions, which are filled by graduate engineers. A committee consisting of vice presidents and supervisors interviews candidates initially cleared by the personnel department. Final selection is made by the supervisor who has a job opening. Out of over 3,500 applicants interviewed by the personnel department during a recent period, fewer than 300 were hired.

Job Security

In 1958 Lincoln formalized its guaranteed continuous employment policy, which had already been in effect for many years. There have been no layoffs since World War II. Since 1958, every worker with over two year's longevity has been guaranteed at least 30 hours per week, 49 weeks per year.

The policy has never been so severely tested as during the 1981–83 recession. As a manufacturer of capital goods, Lincoln's business is highly cyclical. In previous recessions the company was able to avoid major sales declines. However, sales plummeted 32 percent in 1982 and another 16 percent the next year. Few companies could withstand such a revenue collapse and remain profitable. Yet, Lincoln not only earned profits, but no employee was laid off and year-end incentive bonuses continued. To weather the storm, management cut most of the nonsalaried workers back to 30 hours a week for varying periods of time. Many employees were reassigned and the total workforce was slightly reduced through normal attrition and restricted hiring. Many employees grumbled at their unexpected misfortune, probably to the surprise and dismay of some Lincoln managers. However, sales and profits—and employee bonuses—soon rebounded and all was well again.

Performance Evaluations

Each supervisor formally evaluates subordinates twice a year using the cards shown in Exhibit 2. The employee performance criteria, "quality," "dependability," "ideas and cooperation," and "output," are considered to be independent of each other. Marks on the cards are converted to numerical scores which are forced to average 100 for each evaluating supervisor. Individual merit rating scores normally range from 80 to 110. Any score over 110 requires a special letter to top management. These scores (over 110) are not considered in computing the required 100 point average for each evaluating supervisor. Suggestions for improvements often result in recommendations for exceptionally high performance scores. Supervisors discuss individual performance marks with the employees concerned. Each warranty claim is traced to the individual employee whose work caused the defect. The employee's performance score may be reduced, or the worker may be required to repay the cost of servicing the warranty claim by working without pay.

Compensation

Basic wage levels for jobs at Lincoln are determined by a wage survey of similar jobs in the Cleveland area. These rates are adjusted quarterly in accordance with changes in the Cleveland area wage index. Insofar as possible, base wage rates are translated into piece rates. Practically all production workers and many other—for example, some forklift operators—are paid by piece rate. Once established, piece rates are never changed unless a substantive change in the way a job is done results from a source other than the worker doing the job.

In December of each year, a portion of annual profits is distributed to employees as bonuses. Incentive bonuses since 1934 have averaged about ninety percent of annual wages and somewhat more than after-tax profits. The average bonus for 1988 was $21,258. Even for the recession years 1982 and 1983, bonuses had averaged $13,998 and $8,557, respectively. Individual bonuses are proportional to merit-rating scores. For example, assume the amount set aside for bonuses is 80 percent of total wages paid to eligible employees. A person whose performance score is 95 will receive a bonus of 76 percent (0.80 X 0.95) of annual wages.

EXHIBIT 2   Merit Rating Cards

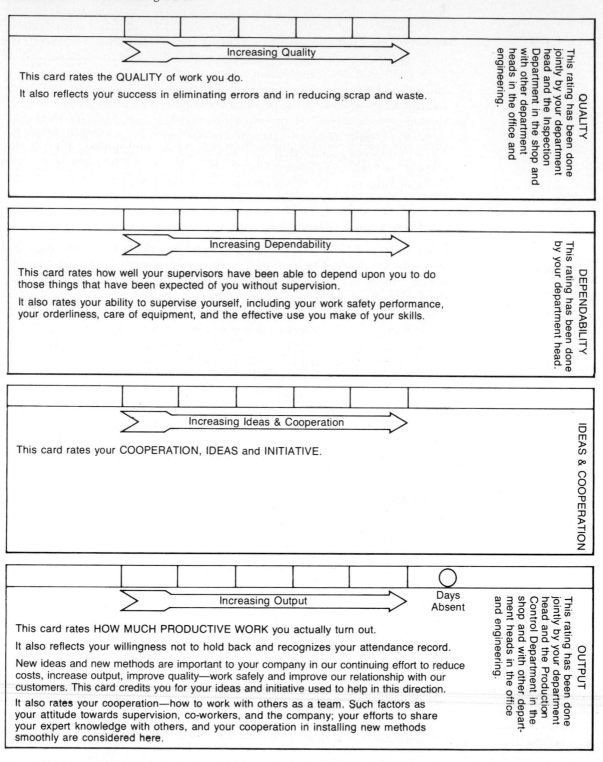

Increasing Quality

This card rates the QUALITY of work you do.

It also reflects your success in eliminating errors and in reducing scrap and waste.

QUALITY
This rating has been done jointly by your department head and the Inspection Department in the shop and with other department heads in the office and engineering.

Increasing Dependability

This card rates how well your supervisors have been able to depend upon you to do those things that have been expected of you without supervision.

It also rates your ability to supervise yourself, including your work safety performance, your orderliness, care of equipment, and the effective use you make of your skills.

DEPENDABILITY
This rating has been done by your department head.

Increasing Ideas & Cooperation

This card rates your COOPERATION, IDEAS and INITIATIVE.

IDEAS & COOPERATION

Increasing Output   Days Absent

This card rates HOW MUCH PRODUCTIVE WORK you actually turn out.

It also reflects your willingness not to hold back and recognizes your attendance record.

New ideas and new methods are important to your company in our continuing effort to reduce costs, increase output, improve quality—work safely and improve our relationship with our customers. This card credits you for your ideas and initiative used to help in this direction.

It also rates your cooperation—how to work with others as a team. Such factors as your attitude towards supervision, co-workers, and the company; your efforts to share your expert knowledge with others, and your cooperation in installing new methods smoothly are considered here.

OUTPUT
This rating has been done jointly by your department head and the Production Control Department in the shop and with other department heads in the office and engineering.

Vacations

The company is shut down for two weeks in August and two weeks during the Christmas season. Vacations are taken during these periods. For employees with over 25 years of service, a fifth week of vacation may be taken at a time acceptable to superiors.

Work Assignment

Management has authority to transfer workers and to switch between overtime and short time as required. Supervisors have undisputed authority to assign specific parts to individual workmen, who may have their own preferences due to variations in piece rates. During the 1982–1983 recession, fifty factory workers volunteered to join sales teams and fanned out across the country to sell a new welder designed for automobile body shops and small machine shops. The result—$10 million in sales and a hot new product.

Employee Participation in Decision Making

Thinking of participative management usually evokes a vision of a relaxed, nonauthoritarian atmosphere. This is not the case at Lincoln. Formal authority is quite strong. "We're very authoritarian around here," says Willis. James F. Lincoln placed a good deal of stress on protecting management's authority. "Management in all successful departments of Industry must have complete power," he said. "Management is the coach who must be obeyed. The men, however, are the players who alone can win the game." Despite this attitude, there are several ways in which employees participate in management at Lincoln.

Richard Sabo, assistant to the chief executive officer, relates job enlargement/enrichment to participation. He said, "The most important participative technique that we use is giving more responsibility to employees. We give a high school graduate more responsibility than other companies give their foremen." Management puts limits on the degree of participation which is allowed, however. In Sabo's words:

> When you use "participation," put quotes around it. Because we believe that each person should participate only in those decisions he is most knowledgeable about. I don't think production employees should control the decisions of the chairman. They don't know as much as he does about the decisions he is involved in.

The Advisory Board, elected by the workers, meets with the chairman and the president every two weeks to discuss ways of improving operations. As noted earlier, this board has been in existence since 1914 and has contributed to many innovations. The incentive bonuses, for example, were first recommended by this committee. Every employee has access to Advisory Board members, and answers to all Advisory Board suggestions are promised by the following meeting. Both Willis and Hastings are quick to point out, though, that the Advisory Board only recommends actions. "They do not have direct authority," Willis says, "and when they bring up something that management thinks is not to the benefit of the company, it will be rejected."

Under the early suggestion program, employees were awarded one-half of the first year's savings attributable to their suggestions. Now, however, the value of suggestions is reflected in performance evaluation scores, which determine individual incentive bonus amounts.

Training and Education

Production workers are given a short period of on-the-job training and then placed on a piecework pay system. Lincoln does not pay for off-site education, unless very specific company needs are identified. The idea behind this latter policy, according to Sabo, is that everyone cannot take advantage of such a program, and it is unfair to expend company funds for an advantage to which there is unequal access. Recruits for sales jobs, already college graduates, are given on-the-job training in the plant followed by a period of work and training at one of the regional sales offices.

Fringe Benefits and Executive Perquisites

A medical plan and a company-paid retirement program have been in effect for many years. A plant cafeteria, operated on a breakeven basis, serves meals at about 60 percent of usual costs. The employee association, to which the company does not contribute, provides disability insurance and social and athletic activities. The employee stock ownership program has resulted in employee ownership of about fifty percent of the common stock. Under this program, each employee with more than two years of service may purchase stock in the corporation. The price of these shares is established at book value. Stock purchased through this plan may be held by employees only. Dividends and voting rights are the same as for stock which is owned outside the plan. Approximately 75 percent of the employees own Lincoln stock.

As to executive perquisites, there are none—crowded, austere offices, no executive washrooms or lunchrooms, and no reserved parking spaces. Even the top executives pay for their own meals and eat in the employee cafeteria. On one recent day, Willis arrived at work late, due to a breakfast speaking engagement, and had to park far away from the factory entrance.

FINANCIAL POLICIES

James F. Lincoln felt strongly that financing for company growth should come from within the company—through initial cash investment by the founders, through retention of earnings, and through stock purchases by those who work in the business. He saw the following advantages of this approach:

1. Ownership of stock by employees strengthens team spirit. "If they are mutually anxious to make it succeed, the future of the company is bright."
2. Ownership of stock provides individual incentive because employees feel that they will benefit from company profitability.
3. "Ownership is educational." Owners-employees "will know how profits are made and lost; how success is won and lost. . . . There are few socialists in the list of stockholders of the nation's industries."
4. "Capital available from within controls expansion." Unwarranted expansion would not occur, Lincoln believed, under his financing plan.
5. "The greatest advantage would be the development of the individual worker. Under the incentive of ownership, he would become a greater man."

6. "Stock ownership is one of the steps that can be taken that will make the worker feel that there is less of a gulf between him and the boss . . . Stock ownership will help the worker to recognize his responsibility in the game and the importance of victory."

Until 1980, Lincoln Electric borrowed no money. Even now, the company's liabilities consist mainly of accounts payable and short-term accruals.

The unusual pricing policy at Lincoln is succinctly stated by Willis: "At all times price on the basis of cost and at all times keep pressure on our cost." This policy resulted in the price for the most popular welding electrode then in use going for 16 cents a pound in 1929 to 4.7 cents in 1938. More recently, the SA-200 Welder, Lincoln's largest selling portable machine, decreased in price from 1958 through 1965. According to Dr. C. Jackson Grayson of the American Productivity Center in Houston, Texas, Lincoln's prices increased only one-fifth as fast as the Consumer Price Index from 1934 to about 1970. This resulted in a welding products market in which Lincoln became the undisputed price leader for the products it manufactures. Not even the major Japanese manufacturers, such as Nippon Steel for welding electrodes and Osaka Transformer for welding machines, were able to penetrate this market.

Substantial cash balances are accumulated each year preparatory to paying the year-end bonuses. The bonuses totaled $54 million for 1988. The money is invested in short-term U.S. government securities and certificates of deposit until needed. Financial statements are shown in Exhibit 3. Exhibit 4 shows how company revenue was distributed in the late 1980s.

HOW WELL DOES LINCOLN SERVE ITS STAKEHOLDERS?

Lincoln Electric differs from most other companies in the importance it assigns to each of the groups it serves. Willis identifies these groups, in the order of priority ascribed to them, as (1) customers, (2) employees, and (3) stockholders.

Certainly the firm's customers have fared well over the years. Lincoln prices for welding machines and welding electrodes are acknowledged to be the lowest in the marketplace. Quality has consistently been high. The cost of field failures for Lincoln products was recently determined to be a remarkable 0.04 percent of revenues. The "Fleetweld" electrodes and SA-200 welders have been the standard in the pipeline and refinery construction industry, where price is hardly a criterion, for decades. A Lincoln distributor in Monroe, Louisiana, says that he has sold several hundred of the popular AC-225 welders, which are warranted for one year, but has never handled a warranty claim.

Perhaps best-served of all management constituencies have been the employees. Not the least of their benefits, of course, are the year-end bonuses, which effectively double an already average compensation level. The foregoing description of the personnel program and the comments in the Appendix A further illustrate the desirability of a Lincoln job.

While stockholders were relegated to an inferior status by James F. Lincoln, they have done very well indeed. Recent dividends have exceeded $11 a share and earnings per share have approached $30. In January 1980, the price of restricted stock, committed to employees, was $117 a share. By 1989, the stated value, at which the company will repurchase the stock if tendered, was $201. A check with the New York office of Merrill Lynch, Pierce, Fenner, and Smith at that time revealed an estimated price on Lincoln stock of $270 a share, with

EXHIBIT 3

Condensed Comparative Financial Statements ($000,000) [1]

Balance Sheets

	1979	1980	1981	1982	1983	1984	1985	1986	1987
ASSETS									
Cash	$2	$1	$4	$1	$2	$4	$2	$1	$7
Bonds & CDs	38	47	63	72	78	57	55	45	41
N/R & A/R	42	42	42	26	31	34	38	36	43
Inventories	38	36	46	38	31	37	34	26	40
Prepayments	1	3	4	5	5	5	7	8	7
Total CA	121	129	157	143	146	138	135	116	137
Other assets [2]	24	24	26	30	30	29	29	33	40
Land	1	1	1	1	1	1	1	1	1
Net buildings	22	23	25	23	22	21	20	18	17
Net M&E	21	25	27	27	27	28	27	29	33
Total FA	44	49	53	51	50	50	48	48	50
Total Assets	$189	$202	$236	$224	$227	$217	$213	$197	$227
CLAIMS									
A/P	$17	$16	$15	$12	$16	$15	$13	$11	$20
Accrued wages	1	2	5	4	3	4	5	5	4
Accrued taxes	10	6	15	5	7	4	6	5	9
Accrued dividends	6	6	7	7	7	6	7	6	7
Total CL	33	29	42	28	33	30	31	27	40
LT debt		4	5	6	8	10	11	8	8
Total debt	33	33	47	34	41	40	42	35	48
Common stock [1]	4	3	1	2	0	0	0	0	2
Ret. earnings	152	167	189	188	186	176	171	161	177
Total SH equity	156	170	190	190	186	176	171	161	179
Total claims	$189	$202	$236	$224	$227	$217	$213	$197	$227

Income Statements

	1979	1980	1981	1982	1983	1984	1985	1986	1987
Income	$385	$401	$469	$329	$277	$334	$344	$326	$377
CGS	244	261	293	213	180	223	221	216	239
Selling, G&A [3]	41	46	51	45	45	47	48	49	51
Incentive bonus	44	43	56	37	22	33	38	33	39
Income before taxes	56	51	69	35	30	31	36	27	48
Income taxes	26	23	31	16	13	14	16	12	21
Net income	$30	$28	$37	$19	$17	$17	$20	$15	$27

[1] Columns totals may not check and amounts less than $500,000 (0.5) are shown as zero, due to rounding.

[2] Incudes investment in foreign subsidiaries, $29 million in 1987.

[3] Includes pension expense and payroll taxes on incentive bonus.

EXHIBIT 4
Revenue Distribution

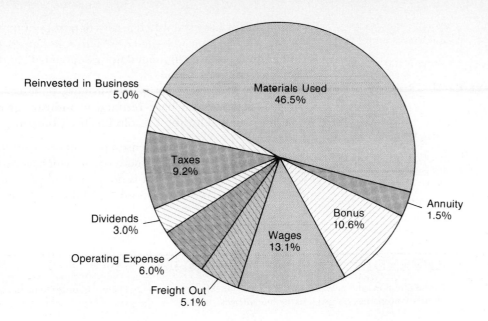

Reinvested in Business
5.0%

Materials Used
46.5%

Taxes
9.2%

Dividends
3.0%

Operating Expense
6.0%

Freight Out
5.1%

Wages
13.1%

Bonus
10.6%

Annuity
1.5%

none being offered for sale. Technically, this price applies only to the unrestricted stock owned by the Lincoln family, a few other major holders, and employees who have purchased it on the open market. Risk associated with Lincoln stock, a major determinant of stock value, is minimal because of the small amount of debt in the capital structure, because of an extremely stable earnings record, and because of Lincoln's practice of purchasing the restricted stock whenever employees offer it for sale.

A CONCLUDING COMMENT

It is easy to believe that the reason for Lincoln's success is the excellent attitude of the employees and their willingness to work harder, faster, and more intelligently than other industrial workers. However, Sabo suggests that appropriate credit be given to Lincoln executives, whom he credits with carrying out the following policies:

1. Management has limited research, development, and manufacturing to a standard product line designed to meet the major needs of the welding industry.
2. New products must be reviewed by manufacturing and all producing costs verified before being approved by management.
3. Purchasing is challenged not only to procure materials at the lowest cost, but also to work closely with engineering and manufacturing to assure that the latest innovations are implemented.
4. Manufacturing supervision and all personnel are held accountable for reduction of scrap, energy conservation, and maintenance of product quality.
5. Production control, material handling, and methods engineering are closely supervised by top management.
6. Management has made cost reduction a way of life at Lincoln, and definite programs are established in many areas, including traffic and shipping, where tremendous savings can result.

7. Management has established a sales department that is technically trained to reduce customer welding costs. This sales approach and other real customer services have eliminated nonessential frills and resulted in long-term benefits to all concerned.
8. Management has encouraged education, technical publishing, and long range programs that have resulted in industry growth, thereby assuring market potential for the Lincoln Electric Company.

Sabo writes, "It is in a very real sense a personal and group experience in faith—a belief that together we can achieve results which alone would not be possible. It is not a perfect system and it is not easy. It requires tremendous dedication and hard work. However, it does work and the results are worth the effort."

APPENDIX   *Employee Interviews*

Typical questions and answers from employee interviews are presented below. In order to maintain each employee's personal privacy, fictitious names are given to the interviewees.

Interview 1

Betty Stewart, a 52-year-old high school graduate who had been with Lincoln thirteen years and who was working as a cost accounting clerk at the time of the interview.

Q. What jobs have you held here besides the one you have now?
A. I worked in payroll for a while, and then this job came open and I took it.
Q. How much money did you make last year, including your bonus?
A. I would say roughly around $25,000 but I was off for back surgery for a while.
Q. You weren't paid while you were off for back surgery?
A. No.
Q. Did the employees association help out?
A. Yes. The company doesn't furnish that, though. We pay $8 a month into the employee association. I think my check from them was $130.00 a week.
Q. How was your performance rating last year?
A. It was around 100 points, but I lost some points for attendance for my back problem.
Q. How did you get your job at Lincoln?
A. I was bored silly where I was working, and I had heard that Lincoln kept their people busy. So I applied and got the job the next day.
Q. Do you think you make more money than similar workers in Cleveland?
A. I know I do.
Q. What have you done with your money?
A. We have purchased a better home. Also, my son is going to the University of Chicago, which costs $13,000 a year. I buy the Lincoln stock which is offered each year, and I have a little bit of gold.
Q. Have you ever visited with any of the senior executives, like Mr. Willis or Mr. Hastings?
A. I have known Mr. Willis for a long time.
Q. Does he call you by name?
A. Yes. In fact, he was very instrumental in my going to the doctor that I am going to now with my back. He knows the director of the clinic.

Q. Do you know Mr. Hastings?
A. I know him to speak to him, and he always speaks, always. But I have known Mr. Willis for a good many years. When I did Plant Two accounting I did not understand how the plant operated. Of course, you are not allowed in Plant Two, because that's the electrode division. I told my boss about the problem one day, and the next thing I knew Mr. Willis came by and said, "Come on, Betty, we're going to Plant Two." He spent an hour and a half showing me the plant.
Q. Do you think Lincoln employees produce more than those in other companies?
A. I think with the incentive program the way that it is, if you want to work and achieve, then you will do it. If you don't want to work and achieve, you will not do it no matter where you are. Just because you are merit rated and have a bonus, if you really don't want to work hard, then you're not going to. You will accept your ninety points or ninety-two or eighty-five because, even with that you make more money than people on the outside.
Q. Do you think Lincoln employees will ever join a union?
A. I don't know why they would.
Q. So you say that money is a very major advantage?
A. Money is a major advantage, but it's not just the money. It's the fact that having the incentive, you do wish to work a little harder. I'm sure that there are a lot of men here who, if they worked some other place, would not work as hard as they do here. Not that they are overworked—I don't mean that—but I'm sure they wouldn't push.
Q. Is there anything that you would like to add?
A. I do like working here. I am better off being pushed mentally. In another company if you pushed too hard you would feel a little bit of pressure, and someone might say, "Hey, slow down; don't try so hard." But here you are encouraged, not discouraged.

Interview 2

Ed Sanderson, a 23-year-old high school graduate who had been with Lincoln four years and who was a machine operator in the electrode division at the time of the interview.

Q. How did you happen to get this job?
A. My wife was pregnant, and I was making three bucks an hour and one day I came here and applied. That was it. I kept calling to let them know I was still interested.
Q. Roughly what were your earnings last year including your bonus?
A. $45,000
Q. What have you done with your money since you have been here?
A. Well, we've lived pretty well and we bought a condominium.
Q. Have you paid for the condominium?
A. No, but I could.
Q. Have you bought your Lincoln stock this year?
A. No, I haven't bought any Lincoln stock yet.
Q. Do you get the feeing that the executives here are pretty well thought of?
A. I think they are. To get where they are today, they had to really work.
Q. Wouldn't that be true anywhere?
A. I think more so here because seniority really doesn't mean anything. If you work with a guy who has twenty years here, and you have two months and you're doing a better job, you will get advanced before he will.
Q. Are you paid on a piece rate basis?
A. My gang does. There are nine of us who make the bare electrode, and the whole group gets paid based on how much electrode we make.

Q. Do you think you work harder than workers in other factories in the Cleveland area?
A. Yes, I would say I probably work harder.
Q. Do you think it hurts anybody?
A. No, a little hard work never hurts anybody.
Q. If you could choose, do you think you would be as happy earning a little less money and being able to slow down a little?
A. No, it doesn't bother me. If it bothered me, I wouldn't do it.
Q. Why do you think Lincoln employees produce more than workers in other plants?
A. That's the way the company is set up. The more you put out, the more you're going to make.
Q. Do you think it's the piece rate and bonus together?
A. I don't think people would work here if they didn't know that they would be rewarded at the end of the year.
Q. Do you think Lincoln employees will ever join a union?
A. No.
Q. What are the major advantages of working for Lincoln?
A. Money.
Q. Are there any other advantages?
A. Yes, we don't have a union shop. I don't think I could work in a union shop.
Q. Do you think you are a career man with Lincoln at this time?
A. Yes.

Interview 3

Roger Lewis, a 23-year-old Purdue graduate in mechanical engineering who had been in the Lincoln sales program for fifteen months and who was working in the Cleveland sales office at the time of the interview.

Q. How did you get your job at Lincoln?
A. I saw that Lincoln was interviewing on campus at Purdue, and I went by. I later came to Cleveland for a plant tour and was offered a job.
Q. Do you know any of the senior executives? Would they know you by name?
A. Yes, I know all of them—Mr. Hastings, Mr. Willis, Mr. Sabo.
Q. Do you think Lincoln salesmen work harder than those in other companies?
A. Yes. I don't think there are many salesmen for other companies who are putting in fifty to sixty-hour weeks. Everybody here works harder. You can go out in the plant, or you can go upstairs, and there's nobody sitting around.
Q. Do you see any real disadvantage of working at Lincoln?
A. I don't know if it's a disadvantage but Lincoln is a spar-

tan company, a very thrifty company. I like that. The sales offices are functional, not fancy.
Q. Why do you think Lincoln employees have such high productivity?
A. Piece work has a lot to do with it. Lincoln is smaller than many plants, too; you can stand in one place and see the materials come in one side and the product go out the other. You feel a part of the company. The chance to get ahead is important, too. They have a strict policy of promoting from within, so you know you have a chance. I think in a lot of other places you may not get as fair a shake as you do here. The sales offices are on a smaller scale, too. I like that. I tell someone that we have two people in the Baltimore office, and they say "You've got to be kidding." It's smaller and more personal. Pay is the most important thing. I have heard that this is the highest paying factory in the world.

Interview 4

Jimmy Roberts, a 47-year-old high school graduate, who had been with Lincoln 17 years and who was working as a multiple-drill press operator at the time of the interview.

Q. What jobs have you had at Lincoln?
A. I started out cleaning the men's locker room in 1967. After about a year I got a job in the flux department,

where we make the coating for welding rods. I worked there for seven or eight years and then got my present job.

Q.   Do you make one particular part?
A.   No, there are a variety of parts I make—at least twenty-five.
Q.   Each one has a different piece rate attached to it?
A.   Yes.
Q.   Are some piece rates better than others?
A.   Yes.
Q.   How do you determine which ones you are going to do?
A.   You don't. Your supervisor assigns them.
Q.   How much money did you make last year?
A. $53,000.
Q.   Have you ever received any kind of award or citation?
A.   No.
Q.   Was your rating ever over 110?
A.   Yes. For the past five years, probably, I made over 110 points.
Q.   Is there any attempt to let the others know?
A.   The kind of points I get? No.
Q.   Do you know what they are making?
A.   No. There are some who might not be too happy with their points and they might make it known. The majority, though, do not make it a point of telling other employees.
Q.   Would you be just as happy earning a little less money and working a little slower?
A.   I don't think I would—not at this point. I have done piece work all these years, and the fast pace doesn't really bother me.
Q.   Why do you think Lincoln productivity is so high?
A.   The incentive thing—the bonus distribution. I think that would be the main reason. The pay check you get every two weeks is important too.
Q.   Do you think Lincoln employees would ever join a union?
A.   I don't think so. I have never heard anyone mention it.
Q.   What is the most important advantage of working here?
A.   Amount of money you make. I don't think I could make this type of money anywhere else, especially with only a high school education.
Q.   As a black person, do you feel that Lincoln discriminates in any way against blacks?
A.   No. I don't think any more so than any other job. Naturally, there is a certain amount of discrimination, regardless of where you are.

Interview 5

Joe Trahan, a 58-year-old high school graduate who had been with Lincoln 39 years and who was employed as a working supervisor in the tool room at the time of the interview.

Q.   Roughly what was your pay last year?
A.   Over $56,000; salary, bonus, stock dividends.
Q.   How much was your bonus?
A.   About $26,000.
Q.   Have you ever gotten a special award of any kind?
A.   Not really.
Q.   What have you done with your money?
A.   My house is paid for—and my two cars. I also have some bonds and the Lincoln stock.
Q.   What do you think of the executives at Lincoln?
A.   They're really top notch.
Q.   What is the major disadvantage of working at Lincoln Electric?
A.   I don't know of any disadvantage at all.
Q.   Do you think you produce more than most people in similar jobs with other companies?
A.   I do believe that.
Q.   Why is that? Why do you believe that?
A.   We are on the incentive system. Everything we do, we try to improve to make a better product with a minimum of outlay. We try to improve the bonus.
Q.   Would you be just as happy making a little less money and not working quite so hard?
A.   I don't think so.
Q.   Do you think Lincoln employees would ever join a union?
A.   I don't think they would ever consider it.
Q.   What is the most important advantage of working at Lincoln?
A.   Compensation.
Q.   Tell me something about Mr. James Lincoln, who died in 1965.
A.   You are talking about Jimmy, Sr. He always strolled through the shop in his shirt sleeves. Big fellow. Always looked distinguished. Gray hair. Friendly sort of guy. I was a member of the Advisory Board, one year. He was there each time.
Q.   Did he strike you as really caring?
A.   I think he always cared for people.
Q.   Did you get any sensation of a religious nature from him?
A.   No, not really.
Q.   And religion is not part of the program now?
A.   No.
Q.   Do you think Mr. Lincoln was a very intelligent man, or was he just a nice guy?
A.   I would say he was pretty well educated. A great talker—always right off the top of his head. He knew what he was talking about all the time.
Q.   When were bonuses for beneficial suggestions done away with?
A.   About eighteen years ago.
Q.   Did that hurt very much?
A.   I don't think so, because suggestions are still rewarded through the merit rating system.
Q.   Is there anything you would like to add?
A.   It's a good place to work. The union kind of ties other places down. At other places, electricians only do electrical work, carpenters only do carpenter work. At Lincoln Electric, we all pitch in and do whatever needs to be done.
Q.   So a major advantage is not having a union?
A.   That's right.

C A S E

3

The Solid Shield Americas Project

PAUL J. SCHLACHTER, *Florida International University*

It was a late morning in early September, 1990. Thick gray clouds had settled over Costa Rica's central highlands where the airport headquarters of Aerocoop (Cooperativa de Servicios Aero Industriales, R. L.) was located. On the work floor of the Automotive Division, people's spirits were as unsettled and heavy as the atmosphere outside. Aerocoop's joint venture with Foremost Emergency Vehicles was barely 6 months old, and assembly work on the Solid Shield ambulance prototype had reached a crucial stage.

Tom Kearney, a technical consultant for Foremost, had arrived from Florida to review progress on the prototype. He didn't hear what he wanted to hear and didn't like what he saw. Even though the Costa Ricans had put in additional time beyond the hours they had budgeted for assembly work, the demonstration vehicle was far from ready. In addition, Aerocoop's engineers had not documented their work as they progressed. Kearney noted that some of the finishing did not measure up to Foremost's standards, and plywood pieces for the interior cabinets had not been cut to Foremost's specifications.

David Sastre was a veteran member of Aerocoop and served as the Solid Shield project coordinator for the Costa Ricans. He asked Kearney what he thought, as they walked across the floor to the plant office. Kearney voiced his concerns about where the project was headed: "The way it's going, I'm really not sure our truck will be finished in time for the dealers to see it." Foremost sales staff and distributors were scheduled to arrive from the United States in 2 weeks to see the vehicle, as everyone involved in the project was aware. Sastre

Copyright Paul Justin Schlachter and the *Case Research Journal* (a publication of the North American Case Research Association).

Originally presented at a meeting of the North American Case Research Association, November 1991. This case was written with the cooperation of management, solely for the purpose of stimulating student discussion. Data are based on field research in both organizations; all events are real, although the names of the organizations and the individual managers have been disguised.

Faculty members in nonprofit institutions are encouraged to reproduce this case for distribution to their own students, without charge or written permission. All other rights reserved jointly to the author and the North American Case Research Association (NACRA).

Paul J. Schlachter, Florida International University (at the time of the field research). Acknowledgments to officials of Frontline Emergency Vehicles, Inc. and Coopesa, R. L.

realized that the fortunes of the Automotive Division rested on the joint venture, and he asked Kearney what he thought should be done. Kearney said he was calling Ted Wise, Foremost's general manager of operations and head of logistics for the joint project, to fill him in on the situation.

Inside Sastre's office, Kearney expressed himself more frankly:

> There's no way it can be completed on time and to our specifications unless Wise comes down and supervises the rest of the work. I'll try to convince him. He doesn't like being away from our plant too long. But I'm telling you, that truck has to be ready for the salespeople. We won't accept any delay.

Kearney asked Sastre whether that opinion would be acceptable to Automotive's management. Sastre replied that he understood the urgency of the situation and would explain matters to the others. He began to ponder which approach he could use to convince the other Automotive managers to let the American take charge. He could imagine vividly their reactions, particularly those of his own boss Alfonso Cortés.

FOREMOST AND THE EMERGENCY VEHICLE INDUSTRY

Foremost Emergency Vehicles was located in an industrial-residential suburb in Florida, and had completed more than a decade of successful operations. It had always built custom vehicles for specific users. Its customers were private and public sector emergency services, located mostly in the middle Atlantic and northeastern states.

From his early days in emergency medical services as an owner of a fleet of ambulances, J. L. Burrows understood the user's point of view. In 1978 he began to build his own vehicles, becoming the founder and sole owner of Foremost. One of his first hires was the marketing manager: Bill Timms, an ambulance dealer who brought a firsthand knowledge of the product and valuable personal contacts. Ted Wise arrived in 1984; he had started as a production worker before becoming general manager of operations, and after 6 years he knew the various building processes in great detail. Although these 3 men were at different levels in the company's formal hierarchy, they interacted a great deal in practice because they contributed complementary skills to the management of Foremost.

The skilled work force of computer-aided designers, builders, and painters totaled 110. Turnover at beginning worker levels was moderate, but it was not considered a problem because the skilled individuals remained longer and they formed the backbone of the company's building expertise. Foremost had a lean administration and support staff of only ten persons, including secretaries, all of whom worked in small, functional offices on one end of the plant. A simplified diagram of the organization and lines of authority at Foremost is provided in Exhibit 1.

Foremost began in a garage with output of one vehicle a month, and grew gradually into a solid player in a very competitive and volatile industry. By 1990, output had reached fifteen to eighteen units per month, and annual sales were $10 million. Product knowledge was a given throughout the industry, because society expected and purchasers demanded durable and reliable vehicles. Timms felt very strongly that his company succeeded because it knew its product, relied on internal financing, and tracked its product costs carefully. Considering the small, decentralized, specialized market for ambulances

EXHIBIT 1

Foremost Emergency Vehicles, Inc., Simplified Organizational Diagram

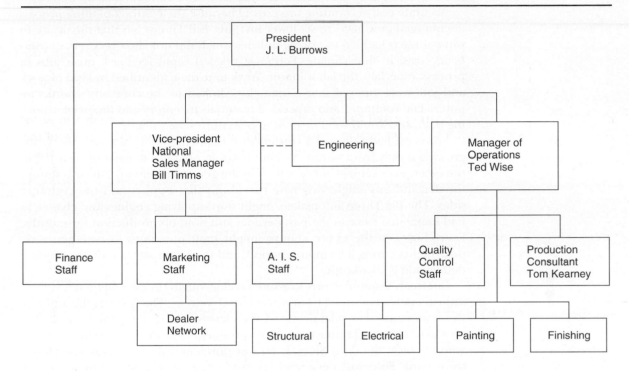

and rescue vehicles, an ambulance maker's accounting and cost control could be crucial to its success.

The emergency vehicle industry in the United States was comprised in 1990 of about forty manufacturers. Precise figures on the emergency vehicle industry were hard to come by, because companies were privately held and did not provide data to their industry association, the National Truck Equipment Association. Timms characterized the industry as cutthroat, full of competitors ready to underprice each other. Only a few of these businesses built standard-size ambulances and rescue vehicles for inventory and sale to dealers. For the most part companies built vehicles on order to customer specifications, providing a completed turnkey product with logo and all. These vehicles were built to last 15 years or more and so would not be replaced quickly. Customers included county and city governments as well as private emergency services, all of them located in the United States. Typical buyers had a small shopping list, normally buying only one unit at a time for $40,000 or higher; some acquired two to five. Total domestic orders in the entire industry varied between 3000 and 4200 units in a given year, and competition for these orders was unrelenting.

Custom work could be more profitable per unit than mass production of vehicles, but it could entail unforeseen additional engineering time and production hours, plus rework. It was not unusual for a customer who was visiting the plant just to see its vehicle in progress to ask for changes in the light bars or for additional accessories. External appearance counted for a lot in the emergency vehicle industry, and seeing the vehicle on the plant floor gave infrequent buyers a different perspective from what they saw at the blueprint stage. Despite the fact that the trucks would probably get scratched all over during the first few emergency calls, customers wanted them flawless at pick-up time.

Accurate cost accounting was crucial because the contract bidding process encouraged producers to set lower margins. Bill Timms felt that the desire to win contracts had led to pricing policies which did not allow recovery of overhead costs. In that climate, Foremost needed rapid feedback on it jobs in process, especially the labor inputs. Work time data, identified by kind of work and job, were entered into a time clock linked to the company's minicomputer. The computer also processed materials inventory and financial reporting data, and would soon be used to plan work schedules.

Foremost had followed a conservative financing policy through the years, growing mostly from within. As Timms saw it, greater financial risk existed in the emergency vehicle industry than in the general economy. Business slumps for that industry might originate from both the supplier and the customer sides. The Big Three automakers might stop supplying engines and chassis, as had happened twice in the past decade, and hold up production for months. Every buyer in the entire country might limit purchases to emergency replacements during a 24-month period, and then companies with outstanding debt would go bankrupt.

Internally inspired efforts to assure product quality in the emergency vehicle industry were reinforced from two external sources. The first was the automotive companies that manufactured the chassis. These companies conducted on-site training and inspections of the production processes used by the emergency vehicle builders. Since Foremost purchased its truck and van chassis from Ford, Foremost personnel received an annual training course on-site from Ford representatives, and annual inspections were carried out. Satisfying these two requirements led to membership in Ford's Qualified Vehicle Modifier (QVM) program, and Foremost was a charter member.

Second, all emergency vehicles in the United States must meet U.S. General Services Administration (GSA) certification, specifically the KKK-A-1822C standards. These set minimum performance standards, including acceleration speed, flashing light sequence, smoothness of ride, and quick access to emergency equipment. GSA inspectors visited the Foremost plant to inspect and test one of each general type. Foremost had five types of vehicles certified to the KKK-A-1822C standards.

Because these two external organizations were mostly concerned with patient safety and minimum performance levels, and conducted minimal sampling of product, they could not provide sufficient stimulus for Foremost to attain the kind of product quality that its customers wanted and needed. Foremost had to be concerned about the aluminum tube, sheet, and other materials, the thoroughness of the job (e.g., continuous rather than spot welding, properly wired harnesses, and perfectly fitting doors and molding), the appearance of the paint, logo, shine, and other finishing features, not to mention the performability of the lights and other equipment installed in the vehicles.

Although each worker was responsible for a particular phase of the building process, no worker operated in isolation. Foremost had no quality control department as such, and instead used teams of workers themselves to check work completed at certain intervals.

Timms said that Foremost was stimulated to maintain its level of quality product through ongoing feedback from customers. The company's low-volume, labor-intensive, job-order approach, as well as the small user market, implied close contact with customers:

> Our customers come here to pick up the trucks and look them over right on the floor. They stay for hours looking for any defect before they drive them away. This rubs off on all our people, because no one wants to have to answer for something they did wrong.

In this competitive environment, where everyone had to meet strict standards, companies could differentiate themselves by their service reputation. Timms placed a top priority on "customer loyalty," for reasons beyond a marketing manager's concern for customers:

> My customers compete with other government services for user and taxpayer dollars, and they have to justify their purchase to their constituencies. To this end they seek name recognition as well as a quality vehicle.

They also expected quick response when a part failed and needed replacement. J. L. said that he started Foremost after another company let him down:

> I bought an ambulance from them. Then one of the switches burned out, and I called them about it. They said they weren't responsible, even though it happened during the first week. Can you imagine! For a simple little switch, they not only lost my business, they gained a competitor!

BACKGROUND ON AEROCOOP

Aerocoop was begun in Costa Rica in 1963 by the employees of an aircraft repair company that had just gone bankrupt. From the beginning it was an employee-owned cooperative, constituted in accord with Costa Rican law. In the ensuing years, thanks to its prime location at Juan Santamaria International Airport, in a hangar leased from the government, and thanks also to protective legislation restricting other aircraft repair facilities from operating within a 40-kilometer radius, Aerocoop had grown into a multiservice organization. Recently, it had received further government support when its facilities at the airport were declared to be a duty-free zone. Historically, then, the cooperative had carried on business relatively free of domestic competition. A simplified chart of the organization and lines of authority at Aerocoop is provided in Exhibit 2.

Aerocoop's principal line of business was its traditional aircraft repair services, organized as the Aviation Division. Its large logo was clearly visible to all arriving air passengers. Its aircraft mechanics and other personnel performed routine repairs and overhauls in a work area large enough to handle four aircraft at a time, either full-sized jets (e.g., 727s) or older propeller craft. Aviation employed a total of 500 people, and generated about two-thirds of Aerocoop's revenues, all in hard currency.

In an adjacent shop area 120 skilled workers made up Aerocoop's Automotive Division. They built frames and equipped and painted full-size buses, minibuses, and vans, mostly for use in interurban transit inside Costa Rica. An administrative staff of more than twenty persons served Automotive, attending to quality control, cost reporting, planning, and design; they had just begun to install CAD equipment. David Sastre and the other operational support people had offices inside the plant itself, but most of the managers, including division general manager Alfonso Cortés, worked in a separate office building.

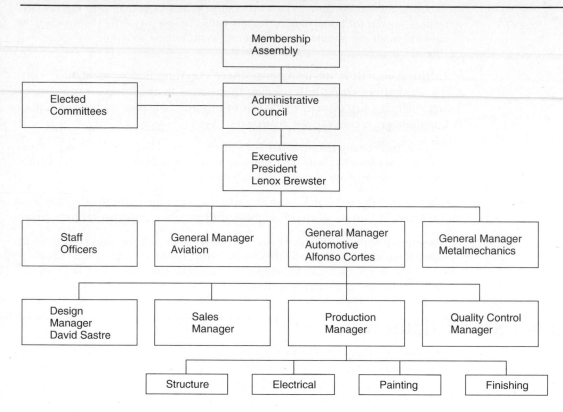

EXHIBIT 2

Aerocoop, R. L., Simplified Organizational Diagram

The Automotive Division, begun in the mid-1960s, had become the chief domestic producer of buses. It also built specialized vehicles in small batches, in response to requests from government agencies. For example, Automotive provided the *papamovil,* the enclosed booth attached to a pickup truck body which was used by Pope John Paul during his visit to Central America in 1983. The division's annual revenues, about a fourth of Aerocoop's total, were almost all in *colones,* Costa Rica's relatively weak national currency.

Automotive did not have the same external stimulus to achieve product quality as Foremost. Mandated performance standards were far less numerous and stringent for buses than for ambulances. In a country like Costa Rica, where secondhand and third-hand buses were widely used, brand-new vehicles had little trouble passing government inspections. Besides, high tariffs kept the number of imported new buses at a low level. As in the case of Foremost, consumers of Aerocoop products were very few in number, but the lack of viable alternative producers in Costa Rica took away much of their leverage. In such an environment, the workers' own abilities and pride were what most contributed to quality, both in individual work and group reviews. The Automotive Division had two quality-control supervisors, who played their part in "inspecting in" quality as work progressed inside the plant.

Including the small Metalmechanics Division and the newly centralized administrative departments, Aerocoop had a total of 800 employee-members.

EXHIBIT 3

Aerocoop, R. L., Common-Size Balance Sheets, 1989–1991

	Percent of total assets			Percent of change in absolute totals	
	9/30/89	9/30/90	3/31/91	'90/'89	'91/'90
ASSETS					
Cash	(0.1)	(1.3)	(1.0)	(961.5)	(1.4)
Short-term investments	2.8	4.5	0.1	69.2	(97.0)
Net receivables	31.9	32.8	20.5	8.6	(23.1)
Net inventories	27.3	21.8	35.8	(15.6)	101.5
Work-in-process	5.0	7.5	3.1	56.5	(49.3)
Other current	1.1	1.5	12.1	44.1	891.4
Total current assets	68.2	66.9	70.5	3.8	30.0
Net fixed assets	29.1	30.0	26.3	9.1	7.6
Other fixed assets	1.3	1.0	1.3	(18.7)	59.8
Long-term investments	1.3	1.8	1.5	50.7	0.0
Interdivisional accounts	0.1	0.2	0.4	111.4	145.8
Total assets	100.0	100.0	100.0	5.7	22.9
LIABILITIES AND STOCKHOLDERS' EQUITY					
Payables	23.6	30.3	43.4	35.6	76.0
Account payable	NA	NA	11.6	NA	11.4
Notes payable	NA	NA	31.8	NA	123.7
Other current	22.5	21.4	14.2	0.3	(18.6)
Total current liabilities	46.1	51.7	57.6	18.4	37.0
Long-term debt	19.7	8.6	12.9	(54.1)	85.4
Provisions	14.1	17.7	8.4	32.3	(41.6)
Total liabilities	80.0	78.0	78.9	3.0	24.4
Equity					
Social capital	14.6	10.6	8.8	(23.3)	1.8
Adjustments for					
quasi-reorganization	0.0	6.6	5.3	NA	0.0
Reserves	3.9	3.7	3.0	0.0	0.0
Prior period surplus	0.9	0.7	0.9	0.0	121.2
Current surplus	0.0	0.5	3.0	NA	703.9
Total equity	20.0	22.0	21.1	16.5	17.7
Total liabilities and stockholders' equity	100.0	100.0	100.0	5.7	22.9

Since 1988 it had maintained total assets equivalent to about US$10 million at a gradually depreciating exchange rate. Its total services in 1988 generated revenues equivalent at the time to $10 million. Revenues in 1989 and 1990 were in the vicinity of 200 million *colones,* representing an increase in dollars to $12 million. Exhibits 3 and 4 provide a common-size summary of consolidated balance sheets and earnings statements for Aerocoop for the years 1989 to 1991.

EXHIBIT 4

Aerocoop, R. L., Earning Performance 1989–1991

	1989	1990	1991 (6 months)
COMMON-SIZE EARNINGS (% OF TOTAL SALES)			
Sales	100.0	100.0	100.0
Less cost of sales	59.4	56.2	54.4
Less fixed expenses	19.4	16.1	16.9
Less selling expenses	2.5	4.3	4.5
Less administrative expenses	14.9	13.6	2.5
Operating income	3.7	9.8	21.7
Financial income	5.0	10.5	9.5
Other income	9.7	6.4	7.9
Less financial expenses	8.8	8.5	11.9
Less other expenses	8.6	17.8	4.9
Net income	1.0	0.4	22.3
Less central administrative expenses	NA	NA	16.1
Liquid income	NA	NA	6.2
EARNINGS PERFORMANCE BY DIVISION (PERCENT)			
Aviation Division			
Share of revenues	68.6	68.9	54.7
Return on sales	12.8	11.8	8.8
Return on assets	NA	18.7	6.8
Automotive Division			
Share of revenues	26.2	23.3	32.4
Return on sales	(25.1)	(13.5)	0.9
Return on assets	NA	NA	0.3
Metalmechanic Division			
Share of revenues	5.2	7.7	12.9
Return on sales	(23.0)	3.8	8.2
Return on assets	NA	NA	2.1

THE DEEPENING ECONOMIC CRISIS

Throughout its existence, Aerocoop had been a dependable source of hard currency for a Costa Rican economy impacted for decades by negative trade balances. Since the late 1970s the *colon* had suffered an annual devaluation against the dollar of 25 percent or more. Costa Rica's traditional sources of foreign exchange, among them coffee, bananas, and livestock, had declined gradually in price all during that time. In the face of the economic crisis, international lenders and consultants had recommended that the country lower its tariffs on imports, diversify its production, and seek to export competitively. Both the private and public sectors in Costa Rica encouraged a more diversified production, offering to potential exporters incentives such as marketing studies and tax exemption.

Historically a protected organization, Aerocoop was heavily challenged by the new economic environment. As airlines began to invest in newer, more fuel-efficient aircraft (Boeing 767s, Airbus 310s and 320s), Aerocoop's aviation mechanics needed to become certified to work on those planes or the cooperative would lose its most profitable business. If Automotive continued to build a single line of buses for all its customers, the division would face the same fate as Henry Ford's black Model T. The tourism and interurban bus lines were buying newer, sleeker models from countries like Brazil and Mexico, and paying less for them.

The costs of running the cooperative had also risen steadily over the years. A succession of socially conscious governments had authorized generous benefit packages for all employees in the country. Aerocoop's worker-members approved benefits for themselves during that time. But government contracts and other support gradually receded. The low-volume jobs that Automotive fulfilled for the government yielded lower margins as materials and labor costs increased. As its funds from operations turned negative, Aerocoop took on debt and became subject to domestic interest rates in excess of 35 percent.

Government meanwhile became smaller and leaner in response to IMF requirements. In 1990 the citizens voted into power a new administration that looked more favorably on privatization and showed less sympathy for the cooperative movement. It even promised tax breaks for interurban bus companies seeking to import new vehicles from Mexico.

A NEW, EXPORT-ORIENTED MANAGEMENT

In mid-1989 the cooperative's governing council (Consejo de Administración) chose CPA Lenox Brewster as its new executive president. Brewster was a native Costa Rican, with fluency in both Spanish and English, and he had held managerial positions with the wax giant S. C. Johnson. The choice of a person well-versed in financial matters reflected concern inside Aerocoop about its precarious financial situation. Brewster himself reminded everyone that the tax exemption and protected status that Aerocoop enjoyed should have translated into stable dollar revenues and comfortable margins on products and services. He felt that the cooperative could be a very profitable concern, rather than just breaking even, and he intended to convince the associate members that he was right.

From the start Brewster insisted to Automotive personnel that their division could not continue as it had in the past. He based his argument on the new economic order, in which imports would compete with Aerocoop for the limited domestic bus market. He emphasized that the rest of Aerocoop's membership would not accept an indefinite period of losses by the Automotive Division. Finally, he recommended that Automotive adopt a vigorous export strategy. In response, division personnel adopted a medium-range export goal of 75 percent of the divisions total output.

To help in finding export opportunities, Brewster approached CINDE (Costa Rican Investment and Development),[1] a quasi-private-sector promoter of Costa Rican exports in other countries. A market study commissioned by CINDE pointed to opportunities in the specialized vehicle markets. In August 1989 an official of CINDE in Miami helped to arrange a meeting of Automotive's general manager with Burrows and Timms at the Foremost headquarters.

WHY FOREMOST DECIDED TO GO TO CENTRAL AMERICA

For some time Foremost management had wanted to broaden its customer base beyond the customized market. Vice President Timms worked with his staff to create designs for a series of standardized vehicles with the trade name "Solid Shield." These designs formed the basis of bids that Timms had submitted on the larger-volume contracts. "I've never won one of those bids," Timms said, "because my competitors underbid me, but they don't include all their overhead in their estimates."

Timms knew the risks involved in tying up the company's working capital in unsold ambulances, especially because Foremost was relatively small and had always financed its growth internally. At the same time he saw advantages in having a finished goods inventory: "I can persuade my customers to purchase a truck on the spot if they see it parked in the lot, ready to drive away."

Foremost management realized that the company could only compete on the standardized vehicle bids by reducing product costs. Because the company purchased in relatively small quantities, it could do little about the cost of truck chassis and other building materials. Management did not feel that further efficiency in labor inputs could be achieved at their Florida facility. They had considered finding a low-cost source of skilled metal-working offshore that would match the company's quality standards as well as general industry standards. Because management was unaware that any such source existed, it put the project on temporary hold.

EARLY CONTACTS

About that time, the CINDE official and Aerocoop's Automotive Division manager came to Foremost. They told Burrows and Timms about the skilled workers at Aerocoop, their lowest wage levels, and their location only 6 shipping days away in an industrial duty-free zone. They also described the Costa Rican government's incentives for nontraditional exports, including facilitated movement of materials components into and out of the country. Burrows and Timms in turn described their own search for a low-cost source of skilled labor. Both sides decided to explore Automotive's potential role in assembling standardized modules for Foremost.

The following spring, as the political climate in Central America improved, Timms flew to Costa Rica. He was impressed by the caliber of mechanical skills of Aerocoop's member-workers. In addition, the Automotive plant facilities were more than double those at Foremost. Although the Automotive people had never built emergency vehicles for export or even worked with aluminum, their bus and cab experience was evident. Timms described the Solid Shield project to the management of Automotive and showed them his plans. Both sides agreed to build jointly a prototype of the simplest Type I model (see Figure 1). Foremost and Aerocoop workers would start work on the prototype in Florida, then Aerocoop would complete it in Costa Rica and return the finished product for sale in the United States.

The negotiators then discussed the terms of payment. Before going to Costa Rica, Timms had prepared cost and price estimates for the Type I vehicle. He knew that direct labor in Florida was costing Foremost $22 per hour, and that he would have to contract at a much lower price in order to make a profit. Foremost personnel had often worked on similar kinds of modules, and Ted

FIGURE 1
Solid Shield Ambulance
Series: the three basic
types of emergency
vehicle modules.

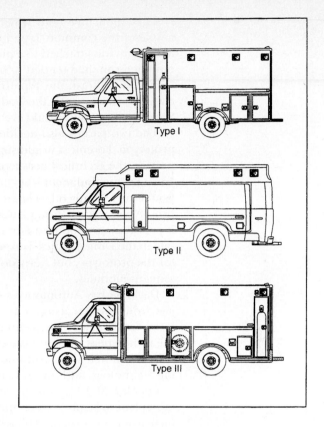

Wise gave him a reliable estimate of 500 labor hours, which they then inflated by 20 percent to allow for the extra learning time that Aerocoop workers would need for the prototype.

Aerocoop for its part had done its own calculation. Because Automotive workers had never built this kind of vehicle, division management made its work-time estimate at the higher end to lower the risk of loss. Although they held out for a time allowance of 800 to 850 hours per vehicle, Timms stuck firmly to his own number. As he recalled later,

> I saw that we weren't getting anywhere, so I told them that the deal was off and I started to leave the room to go back home. But they surrounded me to prevent me from leaving, and asked me not to break off the talks.

Eventually they accepted his offer of a labor standard of 600 work hours per Type I vehicle and a rate of $7 per hour. This more than covered a typical hourly rate for wages and benefits and other support costs, guaranteeing a substantial profit margin for Aerocoop if its workers met the standard.

VEHICLE CONSTRUCTION

The joint project, including the prototype and the units that would follow, required a sizable initial investment. Foremost management financed this from the company's own ongoing operations, just as they had done in other projects. Burrows and Timms expected to recover the funds (and other first-year investments) after 2 years of regular production and sales of the finished vehicles.

The ambulance body which Aerocoop workers began to build was an example of the common Type I vehicle, in which a module made of reinforced aluminum was attached to a pickup truck chassis (see Figure 1). The Type II, a modified van, had tended to be too small for its uses and was not in great demand. In contrast, the Type III was an aluminum module mounted on a cutaway van chassis with the body bolted permanently to the cutaway cab. The Solid Shield project would eventually include both Type I and Type III models.

The two parties also decided how to divide responsibilities for the Type I prototype. Foremost would supply the chassis and all other raw materials and provide the technical assistance necessary to build the module according to plan. Production would begin in Florida, where personnel from both firms would work jointly on welding and structure. Automotive would complete the prototype in Costa Rica, painting it and installing the plywood cabinets. Once it passed inspection by a Foremost agent, it would be returned to Florida for sale in the United States. Foremost personnel would build the electrical wiring for the prototype, but Aerocoop would assume responsibility for wiring of subsequent modules.

David Sastre, Automotive's director of design, agreed to supervise the project from the Aerocoop side, while at Foremost continuing oversight came from Ted Wise's office. Neither firm hired additional workers or managers at the prototype stage, but instead gave added responsibilities to their more reliable personnel. Six of Automotive's best welders learned the aluminum welding technology, and four others were trained in cabinetmaking.

On May 20, 1990, four project members from Aerocoop arrived at the Foremost plant to begin work on the prototype. They included Sastre and three foremen from the structure phase of the operation. They were accompanied by CINDE's consultant for the metalworking industry, who translated for both sides. The foremen had received training in aluminum welding in Costa Rica, and everyone on the team had studied the technical specifications for the module.

During their 2 weeks in Florida the Costa Ricans worked with Foremost personnel to build the frame, position the plates, then mount the unpainted module on a truck chassis. They observed and participated in the initial stages, including the building of structure, skin, and roof, and they helped to install aluminum compartments. They gradually learned to work with aluminum and make efficient welds on surfaces and edges.

The Foremost managers did not know Spanish, and few of the Aerocoop personnel closely involved in the project spoke English fluently. Although diagrams and technical terms were self-explanatory to some extent, communication on a basic level proved to be difficult. This did not affect the work in Florida, because the Costa Ricans observed and taped the process and relied on their interpreter. New communication problems emerged after they returned to Costa Rica, however, when they faced issues of product quality and finishing. Sastre resolved this temporarily by asking his nephew, Javier Laguna, to visit the plant and act as interpreter. Laguna also translated the Type I specifications into Spanish for them. His language ability and knowledge of vehicle assembly impressed Wise during a visit he made to Aerocoop in early August.

THE COSTA RICAN PHASE

When Foremost shipped the prototype module chassis, components, and raw materials to Costa Rica in mid-June, the body and plating work was completed and the module mounted on the truck chassis. The Foremost electricians had assembled the electrical harnesses in Florida and sent them along with the module. These were complex wiring networks designed for the emergency vehicle's electrical circuits. Seven harnesses with ten to fifteen wires each were used in the prototype, some of them six feet in length. More intricate work remained to be done. The Automotive workers had to smooth down the welds and the metal finish in general, build and insert additional metal storage compartments, assemble the plywood cabinets, spray-paint the module, apply the gloss, and do other required finishing work. Wise had detailed instructions prepared for all the work and he sent them down with the module. Included was a cut list specifying the number and size of pieces to be cut for the plywood cabinets.

The module was placed in a separate working area in the middle of the Automotive plant, dedicated to vehicles for export. The smoothing and compartment work and wiring installation took place there. No one was assigned full time to the prototype because the buses had priority; as a result crews were scheduled on the module at intervals. When the time came to install the cabinets and spray-paint the vehicle, it would be moved, in turn, to the required locations. The cabinet shop was located at one side of the plant; its personnel cut, sanded, and fitted the plywood pieces there. The painting area was located on the opposite side, and buses took up most of its schedule.

FINAL INSPECTION TIME

Back in Florida Bill Timms began the marketing phase of the project. Wanting to generate the maximum publicity from the one vehicle they were building, he considered alternative scenarios for his first public announcement. Because he was impressed by Costa Rica and the Aerocoop operation, and because offshore assembly of ambulances was untried and even unheard of in North America, he thought that Aerocoop itself would make an ideal showplace. For that reason, he decided to invite all of Foremost's United States dealers to Costa Rica on September 20, at the company's expense, to see the completed Type I prototype. Ted Wise told him it should be ready by then, based on his last visit and on reports he received.

Three weeks before the dealers were scheduled to go, Tom Kearney made a short inspection trip. Kearney was a technical consultant who worked part-time for Foremost, and he planned to help with the installation of the electrical harnesses. Sastre met him, described the project status, and accompanied him through the plant as interpreter. Sastre told him that Brewster and the governing council were putting pressure on Automotive to show some progress on its exporting strategy, to help Aerocoop weather its worsening liquidity crisis.

It only took an hour for Kearney to realize that the impression Wise had gotten from the fax reports was mistaken. The Solid Shield prototype still needed much finishing, cabinet installation, and painting work. Meanwhile, Automotive had reported 750 labor hours to that point, 25 percent above the time standard on which the cooperative would be paid. Kearney was very disappointed that no one from Automotive's staff had documented the work carefully. He also discovered that the cabinetmaking personnel were cutting the plywood pieces according to their subjective hunches rather than following the cut list Wise had sent them in June.

Kearney saw plenty that day to give him concern over the project. He expressed his concern to Sastre, and said he intended to call Ted Wise and suggest that he come right away. He thought Wise would have to supervise on-site the finishing work on the prototype. Sastre agreed that the project had reached a critical point, but he wondered to himself whether any of the options were satisfactory. For example, theoretically they *could* decide to abort the project, but that seemed unthinkable. As for more delays, Kearney had said that Foremost had ruled those out. And if Wise came down to take over, that would effectively leave him in control of several distinct activities in the plant in addition to the prototype. The other Automotive managers would not be thrilled at that prospect.

Sastre could remember one other time that an outsider had directly supervised a project at Aerocoop. Back in the 1960s, the United Nations Economic Commission for Latin America (CEPAL) had sent a Spanish management consultant to visit the cooperative and recommend ways to expand and diversify. That same visitor recommended starting a unit that eventually became the Automotive Division, and he served as its general manager for 15 years.

Sastre also commented that the Automotive workers knew Timms and Wise from their past visits to Costa Rica, and they respected the professionalism of the North Americans. Sastre thought there would be only token resistance to the arrangement Kearney suggested. However, he wanted to announce that proposal formally to the other Automotive managers, and would try to schedule a meeting that afternoon or the following morning. And he looked Kearney right in the eye when he said, "Tom, I hope you can stay for the meeting. You can persuade them better than I can about how important this is."

Note

1. CINDE began in the early 1980s as a means of introducing producers in Costa Rica to those in other countries, especially the United States. Its original source of funding, the United States Agency for International Development, has since been supplemented from several private sector organizations. From its offices in San Jose, Costa Rica, and Miami and other cities in the U.S. its technicians work as intermediates between businesspeople, sponsoring conferences as well as commissioning market studies for specific industries.